SOCIALIST ECONOMIES AND
THE TRANSITION TO THE MARKET

The rejection of central planning by so many countries in 1989 represents one of the truly extraordinary events in the history of economics. But the transition to the market also presents economists with formidable challenges because the path has never been trod before. The issues raised will remain at the top of the economic agenda for many years to come.

Socialist Economies and the Transition to the Market offers a unique combination of the general and the particular. The basic features of the command economy and trade between socialist economies are analysed together with the general issues involved in the transition to the market. There follow chapters on the original 14 socialist countries before 1989 and their individual experiences after 1989 (including the disintegration of the Soviet Union and Yugoslavia). They all provide the economic, political and historical detail necessary to understand their current problems. While most countries have opted for the marked economy and political democracy, North Korea and Cuba have retained the essential features of the traditional socialist economic and political system. China and Vietnam, in contrast, have gradually introduced partial, market-orientated reforms while still in the firm political grip of the communist party.

Ian Jeffries is a lecturer in the Centre of Russian and East European Studies, University of Wales. His publications include *The Industrial Enterprise in Eastern Europe* (editor, 1981), *The East German Economy* (joint editor with Manfred Melzer; advisory editor Eleanore Breuning, 1987), *A Guide to the Socialist Economies* (1990) and *Industrial Reform in the Socialist Economies* (editor, 1992).

SOCIALIST ECONOMIES AND THE TRANSITION TO THE MARKET

A Guide

Ian Jeffries

London and New York

First published 1993
by Routledge
11 New Fetter Lane, London EC4P 4EE

Simultaneously published in the USA and Canada
by Routledge
29 West 35th Street, New York, NY 10001

© 1993 Ian Jeffries

Typeset in Garamond by LaserScript, Mitcham, Surrey
Printed and bound in Great Britain by
Clays Ltd, St. Ives, PLC

British Library Cataloguing in Publication Data

A catalogue record for this book is available from the British Library.

ISBN 0–415–07579–3   ISBN 0 415–07580–7 (pbk)

Library of Congress Cataloging in Publication Data has been applied for.

ISBN 0–415–07579–3   ISBN 0–415–07580–7 (pbk)

CONTENTS

FIGURES

vii

TABLES

ACKNOWLEDGEMENTS

The intellectual capital of those studying recent developments in most of the socialist countries took a nose-dive in 1989 and presented analysts with a difficult choice of becoming essentially historians or making a massive investment in the entirely new topic of the transition from 'communism' to 'capitalism'.

I decided to take the plunge and a number of people have helped me along. I do not think it an exaggeration to say that the library staff at the University College of Swansea made the venture possible, since I rely totally on rapid and assured access to a vast range of material. The following deserve particular credit: Gwen Bailey, Merlyn Brown, Leslie Holland, David Painting, Hazel Pember, Ann Preece, Jane Richards, Clive Towse and Carole Williams. My thanks also go to Robert Bideleux, George Blazyca, Eleanore Breuning, Phillip Lawler and Lina Takler. Carolyn Stock did an excellent job of the typing up to the summer of 1991. Jeremy Collins of the Computer Centre spent a great deal of his valuable time patiently sorting out teething problems with my new word processor and printer and on other favours like transferring material to fresh disks. Neil Manning, David Blackaby and Lester Hunt were also very kind in helping to get the new system going, especially transferring the manuscript from the old system to the new. The college newsagent, Russell Davies, went out of his way to ensure an early and reliable supply of newspapers and magazines. I am very grateful once again to the porters in the Abbey, Fulton House and the Library; these are key personnel who are undervalued and underpaid.

Professor Norbert Walter kindly arranged the mailing of the Deutsche Bank research reports. I am also deeply indebted to the Hong Kong and Shanghai Bank for *China Briefing*, to the US embassy in London for *Problems of Communism*, and to the Vietnamese embassy in London for the *Vietnam Courier*. All these publications have been sent free of charge and are immensely valuable sources of information. The book was a particularly difficult one to get into print. I could not have asked for a greater degree of co-operation and flexibility from Alan Jarvis, Alison Walters, Alison Kirk, Ruth Jeavons, Sally Close and Louise Machin of Routledge. The copy-editor, Ray Offord, did a superb job.

Ian Jeffries
Centre of Russian and East European Studies
University of Wales

INTRODUCTION

The year 1989 was truly momentous in that it signified the failure of an entire system. 'Socialism' was to be replaced by some sort of 'Western-type' political and economic system in most of the fourteen countries studied in *A Guide to the Socialist Economies*. The Cold War, which had shaped and distorted post-Second World War history, was won by 'the West', it seems, but Boris Yeltsin more accurately describes it as a victory for both sides.[1] The abortive August 1991 coup in the Soviet Union ironically put the final nail in the coffin; towards the end of the year the Soviet Union ceased to exist. Yugoslavia, too, has disintegrated and Comecon and the Warsaw Pact no longer exist.

These momentous events mean that it is not possible simply to update *A Guide to the Socialist Economies*. Even so, it seems useful to retain a significant, albeit amended, part of the book in the shape of an analysis of events pre-1989 and then discuss what has happened since.

The original justification for writing a general textbook on the 'socialist' economies (as opposed to 'communist', since this final Marxian utopian stage had not been achieved) was not very difficult to find. The world population in mid-1988 was 5.1 billion and 1.6 billion resided in the fourteen socialist countries, 1.1 billion in China and 285 million in the Soviet Union alone. The Soviet Union was by far the largest country in terms of land area, covering a sixth of the world's land surface excluding Antarctica, and was then one of the two 'superpowers' in terms of military capacity.

Parts I and II give the reader some idea of the rich variety of economic systems found in this part of the world before 1989 and highlight some of the major problems that faced the countries. On the eve of their socialist development, they were basically agrarian in nature, with the exception of the German Democratic Republic (GDR) and Czechoslovakia. Since all the socialist countries, to varying degrees, either adopted or had imposed upon them the traditional Soviet-type system, it is useful to start by outlining that system and the problems it engendered. This provides a reference point for understanding the reasons for and nature of the various reform programmes.

Chapter 1 outlines the traditional Soviet economic system, a command economy with state ownership overwhelmingly dominant. While such a system enabled the Soviet Union rapidly to attain superpower status, the problems engendered ultimately proved fatal. Chapter 2 deals with foreign trade and the rise and fall of Comecon. Chapter 3 is devoted to economic reform before, during and after the Gorbachev era. The Soviet economy was not radically reformed, but the ex-Soviet republics are now generally aiming for a market economy, either individually or through various co-operative bodies such as the Commonwealth of Independent States. Chapter 4 analyses Mongolia's transformation from slavish copying of the Soviet Union to political democracy and the market. Chapter 5 emphasizes China's combination of tight political control and market-orientated economic reforms after 1978, particularly successful in agriculture in the shape of the 'household responsibility system'. Chapters 6 and 7 are devoted, respectively, to Cuba's and North Korea's essential adherence to a traditional Soviet-type political and economic system. Chapter 8 looks at Vietnam and its China-like combination of communist party control coupled with market-orientated economic reform.

Part II deals with pre-1989 Eastern Europe and devotes separate chapters to Albania, Bulgaria, Czechoslovakia, the GDR, Hungary, Poland, Romania and Yugoslavia. Two broad themes can be detected here, namely departures from the traditional system and the nature and origins of current problems. A typical arrangement is as follows: the political and economic background; reform of the planning mechanism (industry, manpower, the pricing and financial systems, agriculture, and foreign trade, capital and debt); and the private, non-agricultural sector.

Some general points may usefully be borne in mind while reading parts I and II:

1. The present is, of course, only understandable in the perspective of history. Albania and Cuba have a history of foreign domination, while it is surely no coincidence that North Korea and the GDR, poorer halves of divided nations, were reluctant reformers; radical change admits defeat in the race against 'capitalism'.

2. A successful call for increased individual initiative, responsibility and performance almost invariably requires material incentives in the form of improved supplies of consumer goods and services. China and Hungary had the answer in reforming agriculture first and in encouraging a healthy private sector.

3. Tinkering with a command economy gets one nowhere, but Chinese and Vietnamese agriculture, even in the absence of private land ownership, shows the value of partial reforms. This is particularly significant in the light of current debates on the transition to the market.

4. China especially also makes us think about whether political liberalization is a prerequisite for successful economic reform, at least in the short run.

A pre-1989 categorization of the fourteen countries

Albania and North Korea. These two countries kept closest to the Stalinist political and economic system. Albania practised a 'cult of personality' until the death of Enver Hoxha in April 1985 and North Korea still does towards its 'great leader' Kim Il Sung and its 'dear leader', son and heir Kim Jong Il. Communist Albania permitted neither private enterprise in industry nor direct foreign capital and even imposed a constitutional ban on foreign loans. North Korea has never allowed significant private enterprise, but is deeply indebted to foreigners.

Cuba. Cuba has always maintained strict political control and has never seriously departed from the traditional Soviet economic system. There has been flirtation with the sort of reforms associated with the Soviet Union after the mid-1960s, but the 1980s were generally considered to be a period of retrenchment and even retrogression in some respects. It would be unwise to ignore certain progression, however, in fields such as direct foreign investment.

The GDR and Romania. These were reluctant reformers. Tight political control was never relaxed, although it took a peculiarly personal form in Romania ('socialism in one family'). Radical economic reform was never attempted, although there were some interesting enough modifications. Thus the GDR experimented with the New Economic System in the 1960s and with combines/'perfecting' in the 1980s. More recently the private sector was encouraged. Living standards were the highest in the socialist world, although the backwardness compared to West Germany was even worse than generally realized when the countries were reunited.

Romania introduced a pale imitation of self-management and was actually the first to introduce joint equity legislation in 1971 (the Honecker regime in the GDR refused to allow in direct foreign investment). But the private sector was held back in Romania and completely paying off the foreign debt imposed a heavy burden on the people.

The economic foot-draggers: Czechoslovakia and Bulgaria. Had the 'Prague Spring' been allowed to blossom Czechoslovakia would have set a challenging political and economic pace, but after the 1968 invasion by Warsaw Pact forces a heavy mantle descended. Nevertheless, Czechoslovakia had the second highest living standards in the socialist world and avoided inflationary and serious foreign debt problems.

Socialist Bulgaria was always a loyal ally of the Soviet Union, stemming historically from Tsarist help in ending Ottoman rule in 1879. Bulgaria eschewed radical economic reform and the non-agricultural private sector was highly restricted, but note should be taken of its pioneering work in agro-industrial organization, a Hungarian-style symbiosis of collective and private agriculture, and its small enterprise programme.

China and Vietnam. The communist party has maintained strict control in both countries, but economic reform has been market-orientated. China set the economic reform ball rolling after 1978 by putting agricultural before industrial change, the 'household responsibility system' achieving considerable success on the whole. The main thrust of its reforms, including the 'open door' policy, survived the political clampdown following the June Tiananmen massacre of students calling for political democracy. Indeed, early 1992 saw the promotion of the economic reform process, although 'stability and unity' are still officially considered to be prerequisites for economic success.

Vietnam, in 1975, provided a laboratory experiment in a socialist country gobbling up a capitalist one (the opposite of today's situation in Germany). The stress of this helped promote market-orientated reforms and a more relaxed attitude towards the private sector. Its China-like agricultural reforms have been successful on the whole, but economic problems have been generally more severe than China's, e.g. there has been a continuous battle against high rates of inflation.

The economic 'paper tigers': Poland and the Soviet Union. Poland's industrial reforms of the 1980s were not in the main implemented, remaining Hungarian-like only on paper. Poland continuously struggled with severe inflationary and foreign debt problems, but agriculture was largely private, and a relatively relaxed attitude was taken towards the private non-agricultural sector (legal parity as of 1 January 1989). The Polish people were never resigned to communist party rule and the legalizing of the independent trade union and political organization Solidarity in August 1980, the Round Table agreement of April 1989 (when Solidarity was re-legalized after its banning in the martial law period) and the semi-free general election of June 1989 were remarkable events which predated the revolutions in Eastern Europe later in the year.

A bewildering number of economic changes were introduced in the Soviet Union, especially after the mid-1960s. But right to the end of the 1980s the economic system remained recognisably a command economy. In the early 1990s the economy collapsed as the old system disintegrated in the absence in a new one. The Gorbachev era (11 March 1985–25 December 1991) was remarkable, although mainly as regards domestic and international politics. *Glasnost* and *perestroika* became household terms. Radical economic reform was not implemented, although concessions to the private sector and direct foreign investment, for example, were important for their time. Gorbachev blew hot and cold as regards radical economic reform, hopping between the political poles in order to preserve the integrity of the country. He finally plumped for the market, but by then it was too late; the economic reform never left the paper and the country disappeared.

It may be worth placing obedient Mongolia in this category. The second people's republic (1924) followed the Soviet lead, but forged ahead politically and economically in the immediate aftermath of the 1989 revolutions in Eatern Europe.

Yugoslavia and Hungary. These countries were in the forefront of reform. Yugoslavia used its political independence to introduce a unique type of market socialism based on self-management by workers' councils of 'socially owned' enterprises. Agriculture was predominantly private and the private sector elsewhere was encouraged. But severe political and economic problems (such as inflation, foreign debt, unemployment and inefficiencies connected with the self-management system) ultimately proved too much when socialism collapsed in Eastern Europe.

Hungary's New Economic Mechanism of 1968 did not introduce market socialism, but its decentralized, largely indirectly steered economic system proved relatively successful and eased the transition to the market after 1989. Also rated positively was Hungary's relaxed attitude towards the private non-agricultural sector and the symbiosis between collectivized and private agriculture. Inflation and the highest *per capita* foreign debt in Eastern Europe counted among the problems of Hungary in the 1980s.

A post-1989 categorization of the fourteen countries

Cuba and North Korea. These two are still in the traditional mode, with the communist party in control and market-orientated economic reforms rejected. South Korea has grown more and more wary of reunification as the political and economic costs of German union have mounted.

China and Vietnam. The communist party is still in control, but market-orientated economic reforms have been introduced. Mass privatization on East European lines has been rejected,

although there are experiments with share ownership.

The Soviet Union and Yugoslavia. These countries have disintegrated and independent republics are in varying stages of democracy and transition to the market. The Soviet Union ceased to exist towards the end of 1991, this taking place remarkable peacefully. Major problems face the countries individually or in the embrace of voluntary organizations like the Commonwealth of Independent States, whose future is uncertain. The Yugoslav experience of parting has been extremely bloody and is a lesson for all. Czechoslovakia is to split in two, although peacefully.

East Germany. East Germany has been absorbed by West Germany at considerable political and economic cost.

The other countries of Eastern Europe. These are in the process of transition to Western-type political and economic systems and in varying degrees of turmoil in doing so. Hungary is the most successful and Albania the least. It is possible to subdivide these countries as regards policy in the transition. For example, Hungary has adopted a more gradualist, step-by-step approach, which contrasts in many ways with Poland's 'big bang'.

Part III deals with the transition from command to market economies in Eastern Europe. Chapter 17 discusses the general issues, specifically 'big bang' and sequencing, 'shock' therapy, privatization, Western aid and trade, coming together and growing apart, and the linkage between political and economic reform. The remaining chapters are devoted to what has actually happened in the individual countries, namely Albania, Bulgaria, Czechoslovakia, East Germany (German economic and monetary union), Hungary, Poland, Romania and Yugoslavia.

The speed of the collapse of socialism in Eastern Europe in and around late 1989 was astonishing, the communist regimes often folding like packs of cards. Of the many factors explaining this rapid demise, I would like to emphasize two. This is in no way meant to diminish the role of dissidents and dissident movements in the countries themselves, but the peoples of Hungary in 1956 and Czechoslovakia in 1968, for example, understandably failed to extricate themselves from Soviet control.

1. The role of Mikhail Gorbachev himself was crucial, especially his refusal to use Soviet troops to quell unrest in Eastern Europe. The 'inevitability school' try to play down Gorbachev's role, but if things were 'inevitable' why was everybody taken by surprise in 1989? Can one imagine a Brezhnev or an Andropov allowing events to move in the way they did? The importance of the individual in history should not be marginalized.

2. The second factor to be highlighted in explaining the rapid demise of many socialist regimes is the penchant of communist leaders to appoint 'yes men' and sycophants, people whose only ability in many cases was the ability to agree. Filtered information isolated the leaders from reality, the classic case being Ceausescu. The rotten edifice soon collapsed when power was lost and people lost their fear.

The collapse of 'communism' in Eastern Europe and the Soviet Union quite rightly brought much rejoicing, but the initial euphoria has been dampened. Historical comparisons have been drawn: for example, the break-up of the Austro-Hungarian and Ottoman empires in 1918 was followed by hyperinflation, depression and the rise of fascism, while the defeat of Hitler was followed by the Cold War. Historical lessons are being learned, however, including that of the Treaty of Versailles: the defeated should be helped, not crucified. There is increasing recognition of today's dangers:

1. The dashing of expectations is always a real danger. It can lead to a yearning for the past (whose pluses are always exaggerated and whose minuses are downplayed with time) or a temptation to yield to the dream peddlers (such as Stanislaw Tyminski, who pushed Tadeusz Mazowiecki into third place in the 1990 Polish presidential election). The most dangerous time

is when the old system is collapsing and a new one has not yet been put in place. The old system's perceived stability may seem to many preferable to the current chaos. One recalls Alexis de Tocqueville's perceptive observation that 'The perilous moment for a bad government is when the government tries to mend its ways'.

2. The worst aspects of nationalism have boiled to the surface after decades of suppression. The conflict in Yugoslavia is the worst case. Racist attacks have multiplied in post-reunification Germany. Bitter fighting has taken place in former Soviet republics such as Azerbaijan, Georgia and Moldova, while the potential for strife there is frightening (some 65 million of the former Soviet citizens lived outside their ethnic republics, of whom 25 million were Russians). Eastern Europe is still in large measure a veritable hotchpotch of ethnic groups.

3. The lack of 'civil society' was most dramatically demonstrated in Ceausescu's Romania. The term usually refers to widespread activities by individuals who voluntarily associate together in various forms outside the control of the state. Such 'life outside the state' was extinguished to the highest degree in Romania and this added to the horrendous legacy of the regime which represented 'socialism in one family'. But the problem exists in varying degrees everywhere, and free but inexperienced political parties are learning the hard way. Like nationalist parties everywhere, the hardest decisions often have to be made after the overriding goal (whether independence or the overthrow of a regime) has been achieved. It is not surprising that groupings like Solidarity in Poland and Civic Forum in Czechoslovakia have been torn asunder. The room for cynicism is enormous as the many who suffer during the harsh transitional period enviously observe the relatively few who benefit to high degree (frequently those who also did so under the previous regime).

4. There is the danger of new dogmas ruling the roost, stressing the virtues and not the

5

limitations of markets and privatization. The 'emerging' or more accurately 'new' democracies ('emerging market economies' or 'post-communist countries') are susceptible to visions at the very opposite economic pole to the past. In the West economics has grown worryingly apart from other academic disciplines and become increasingly specialized and abstract. Western economists need to be keenly aware of historical, political and social factors when offering solutions in the East European context. Some concern has also been expressed at the role of those who are essentially theoreticians in actual government. For example, the eminent and long-time radical economist Nikolai Shmelev commented as follows on the relatively young group of economists led by Yegor Gaidar for- mulating policy in Russia: 'These new smart guys are judging their policy mostly from economic textbooks rather than real life . . . they are much more brutal than we are. This is a highly painful surgical operation without any anaesthesia' (*IHT*, 5 February 1992, p. 9).

5. The problems of transforming socialist ('communist') systems to 'Western-type' ones have never been faced before. The roads to parliamentary democracy and market economics are strewn with obstacles.

As far as the economic transition to the market itself is concerned, the following major areas have been the subject of intense debate: the degree of 'shock' therapy (severe austerity measures), Poland being the guinea pig; a 'big bang' transition to the market and 'sequencing' of reform measures; the degree and type of privatization; the role of Western aid; the need for the West to practise what it preaches (such as free trade); and whether countries emerging from the rubble of 'empires' should 'go-it- alone' or form at least economic 'unions' between the previous 'bits'. Any political unions are likely to be of a very loose confederation type, built 'from the bottom up' and granting very few powers to the 'centre'. Realistically only 'commonwealths' and 'common markets' seem to be on offer.

The costs of the transition to the market are to varying degrees considerable in terms of loss of output, although factors such as the collapse of Comecon trade also play an important role. But it should be noted that the figures tend to overstate the contraction to some degree owing to factors such as the generally improving quality of products, greater reliability of statistics, and the inadequate account taken of the contribution of the expanding private sector.

Western observers were caught out by the events of 1989. Academics who had invested a lifetime in studying the socialist countries saw their intellectual capital mostly vanish overnight. I can only hope that the reader feels able to give a little credit to those who make the effort of trying to comprehend revolutionary changes.

Notes

1. 'The winners in this war were all those who opposed totalitarianism and defended democracy – in West and East. It is a common victory' (Yeltsin, in a speech in London on 10 November 1992).

Part I

THE SOCIALIST ECONOMIES OUTSIDE EASTERN EUROPE

1

THE TRADITIONAL SOVIET
ECONOMIC SYSTEM

On the eve of the First World War Russia was still a relatively backward, agrarian country. This was despite considerable industrial growth over the previous thirty years, the level of output doubling during the 1890s. The Soviet Union became one of the world's two 'superpowers' in terms of military capacity.

Various indicators may be used to assess the level of development of Russia in 1913. *Per capita* income was less than 40 per cent of France's, about 33 per cent of Germany's, 20 per cent of Britain's and 10 per cent of US *per capita* income (Gregory and Stuart, 1990: 36). In 1913 Russia accounted for only just over 4 per cent of world industrial output, compared with 10 per cent in 1941 and about 20 per cent in the mid-1980s. In 1917 Russia ranked as the fifth industrial power in the world and the fourth in Europe (Aganbegyan 1988b: 45–7). A high birth rate of around forty-four per thousand in 1913 was coupled with a relatively high death rate of around twenty-seven per thousand, the infant mortality rate being about 237 per thousand. Sixty per cent of the population over the age of ten was illiterate (Gregory and Stuart 1990: 39). The commodity structure of foreign trade was typical of a poor country, with exports of primary commodities, especially grain, paying for imports of manufactures, especially capital goods. Agriculture employed 72 per cent of the workforce (82 per cent of the population was rural) and contributed over 50 per cent of national product (Gregory and Stuart 1990:39); in 1928 agriculture contributed 60 per cent of

national income (Aganbegyan 1988b: 21). Serfdom had been abolished only in 1861, and the attempted switch to capitalist agriculture after 1906 came too late. This vast country, however, had enormous economic potential in the shape of a rich and varied natural resource endowment, despite climatic, transport and soil difficulties.[1]

The Bolsheviks, under Lenin, came to power in October 1917 with no detailed economic blueprint from the works of Marx and Engels.[2] Marx saw society inevitably progressing through various stages of development, namely primitive society, slavery, feudalism, capitalism, socialism and communism. Marx essentially provided a critique of capitalism, but socialism was only vaguely defined. There was to be the 'conscious social regulation of production' (as opposed to the 'anarchy' of the market), the 'common' ownership of the means of production, and distribution according to work (as opposed to need under communism).

The early years after the revolution saw state takeovers (without compensation) in banking, foreign trade and key industries like iron and steel. All land was nationalized, and the national debt, equivalent to 120 per cent of national income in 1917, was repudiated. The period of 'War Communism' lasted from 1918 to 1921. The overriding aim was to win the civil war against the Whites, who were aided by capitalist intervention from the spring of 1918 to September 1919 (e.g. Germany occupying the Ukraine). Nationalization was taken to extremes, with enterprises employing only one person in some cases. The market was replaced by a form of moneyless administration, local authorities mainly, with the central state practising campaign methods. Labour was directed and increasingly paid in kind, while agricultural products were compulsorily requisitioned (the *prodrazvyorstka*). Although allowing resources to be concentrated at the front, war communism was not sustainable as a peacetime mechanism, and gave way to the New Economic Policy (NEP; 1921–28), the study of which became topical in the Gorbachev era. Concessions were made to private enterprise, especially in retail trade, although the state still retained control of the commanding heights like metallurgy, armaments, fuels, and banking. The market mechanism was restored to a large extent. There were even (not very successful) attempts to attract foreign capital and enterprise. One of the world's classic hyperinflations was checked by output increases, an end to exclusive reliance on the printing press, and confidence inspired by a new currency. The pre-First World War output levels were broadly regained towards the end of the NEP period, planning institutions such as Gosplan were established, planning techniques were developed and the future was explored in the rigorous 'industrialization debate'.

It is useful to examine the traditional economic system in terms of goals, strategy, and the institutional framework.

GOALS

The Soviet Union being the only socialist country in what was perceived to be a hostile capitalist environment and thus in danger of an all-out invasion, the basic aim was to catch up with and surpass the leading capitalist countries, especially in terms of heavy industrial capacity and military power. This was encapsulated in a famous 1931 speech by Stalin: 'We are fifty or a hundred years behind the advanced countries. We must make good this distance in ten years.

Either we do it, or we shall go under' (for a fuller quotation see Ellman 1989a: 13). This goal was to be achieved by means of the chosen strategy and institutional framework. Stalin maintained that it was possible to build 'socialism in one country', socialism being, as shown above, the penultimate stage on the path to communism, where there is distribution according to need and no class conflict. There were other goals, of course, such as full employment and the absence of the extremes of income and wealth associated with capitalism. As is shown below, however, significant wage differentials are an important aspect of labour policy in the traditional system.

STRATEGY

During the 1930s the state used its allocative powers to devote the historically high figure of around a quarter of national output to investment (Bergson 1961: 237). Consumption was held down to a level judged adequate to maintain political stability and work incentives. Sectoral priority was awarded to industry, specifically about 40 per cent of total investment (Kaplan 1953: 52). The share in total industrial production of producer goods rose from 39.5 per cent in 1928 to 61.2 per cent in 1940 (Ellman 1989a: 139). The 'leading links' were iron and steel, heavy engineering, mining, electric power generation, and armaments. In a quantitative sense, foreign trade did not play a large strategic role; exports reached their lowest share as a proportion of national income of only 0.5 per cent in 1937. Nevertheless, the Soviet Union was able to import vital capital goods embodying the latest technology.

THE INSTITUTIONAL FRAMEWORK

Command planning

The economic problem, as conventionally defined – namely that of choosing which of an essentially infinite number of needs are to be met with the limited (scarce) resources available – is one that faces all societies. In a system of command planning the basic allocative decisions about what to produce and in what quantities are taken by the state, but in reality the whole economic hierarchy has to be involved in decision-making.[3] In highly simplified form the pyramid has the State Planning Commission (Gosplan) at its apex, branch ministries ('commissariats' before 1946) at the intermediate level and enterprises (production units) at its base (see Figure 1.1). Before embarking on this analysis it is important to understand the crucial role of the Communist Party in the traditional model in formulating and implementing policies, dominating economic, political and social life in a one-party state.

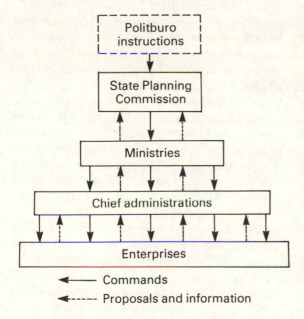

Commands
Proposals and information

Figure 1.1 The economic hierarchy

The State Planning Commission

The State Planning Commission received instructions about basic economic magnitudes from the party, especially the Politburo, relating to growth rates of national income and of its sub-categories of consumption, investment and defence, and to

vitally important goods. These instructions were relayed via the state apparatus, especially the Council of Ministers, and Gosplan combined these with the data/requests/proposals flowing upwards from the hierarchy to draw up plans of varying duration by means of 'material balances'. The annual, quarterly and monthly plans were operational; medium (five-year) plans and perspective plans of at least fifteen years' duration were much more highly aggregated and were operational only in relation to the investment plan. Many projects were spread over a number of years, and thus longer-term plans were needed for guidance. More recently annual plans were meant to be drawn up within the context of the allegedly more important five-year plan, but in reality changing targets and environmental and economic conditions ensured that the annual plan was still the operational one. The basic aim was to draw up a balanced plan that fulfilled the goals set by the Politburo.

Table 1.1 illustrates a material balance in simplified form. The major sources of supply and demand for a particular commodity were drawn up with the aim of attaining a rough balance. Deficits signalled the need for extra output. Production was typically by far the major source of supply, since 'taut' planning was exercised and imports were important only for certain commodities, such as capital goods during the 1930s. It is useful to distinguish between intermediate and final demand at this stage, since later on we shall be studying input-

Table 1.1 The Soviet Union: a material balance

Supply	Demand
1 Production	1 Intermediate use
2 Stocks at the beginning of the plan period	2 Final demand use (a) Consumption (b) Fixed investment
3 Imports	(c) Stocks at the end of the plan period (d) Exports

output analysis. Intermediate inputs are used up in the course of producing other goods.

The Soviet economy suffered endemic supply problems (see p. 17 for the effects) and one reason was the crudity of the material balance technique. Balances were heavily aggregated, the number of balances being far fewer than the number of 'commodities'. Even by 1981 the annual plan involved Gosplan drawing up material balances for only 2,044 products (though crucially important ones), Gossnab (the State Committee for Material and Technical Supply) 7,500, and ministries 25,000 (Shroeder 1982: 75). By way of contrast, Nikolai Shmelev (*Novy Mir*, 1987, no. 6, p. 136) put the number of items in industrial production alone at around 24 million. Then there was the 'iterative' problem. If, for example, the output of a particular good were increased, in the early years of planning usually only the first-order iteration (repetition) was carried out (i.e. estimates made of the effects on direct inputs). Further iterations (effects on the inputs needed to produce the increased inputs and so on) were ignored. For this reason excess demand was tackled as much as possible by, for example, reducing both the use of inputs per unit of output ('tightening of norms') and the consumption element of final demand (i.e. using the consumer sector as a buffer), as opposed to changing supply (i.e. increasing output).

The allocation of most non-labour inputs was handled by the 'materials allocation' system – the administrative distribution of raw materials, intermediate goods and capital goods. The supplying and using enterprises were matched centrally, and the all-important document was the *naryad* (allocation certificate), which specified the quantity of the product and the supplying organization.

Command planning is well named in the sense that the enterprise eventually received plan targets in the shape of a technical–industrial–financial plan (*tekhpromfinplan*). But since it is impossible for central planners to produce detailed, concrete plans in the abstract,

the economic hierarchy had to be involved, with the emphasis in the traditional system on vertical as opposed to horizontal (i.e. enterprise to enterprise) linkage. More specifically tentative, crudely balanced output targets ('control figures') were passed down the planning pyramid to be increasingly disaggregated (made more detailed) by ministries and enterprises. Suggestions/requests (the *zayavka* is an input indent, for example) were made at each echelon and passed back up the hierarchy. While the centre's major allocative decisions were preserved, this process of haggling and bargaining could be influential, as in suggested input substitution to meet a given output target. Annual plans were often late and were frequently changed; failure to fulfil by one enterprise had repercussions on others. It is worth noting at this point the importance of informal linkages that oiled the wheels of the economic mechanism in reality. Examples include, as is to be seen below, shady deals and downright illegal relationships between enterprises.

Before exploring the role of the enterprise, it is interesting to note that two areas of the economy have been left, in more normal times, largely to the market mechanism, namely the distribution of consumer goods and the allocation of manpower. These are interrelated in both a micro- and a macro-economic sense. Wages and salaries paid out in the production sector constitute the main means of payment for the consumer goods and services made available in the plan (which, in turn, provide the main incentive to work), while avoidance of inflation means matching the cash (rouble notes and coins) injected into the economy with the aggregate supply of consumer goods and services at established prices.

Distribution of consumer goods

There is essentially consumer choice (as opposed to sovereignty) in the command economy. This means that consumers can choose among the consumer goods and services made available in the plan, rather than being able to determine the allocation of resources, as in a competitive market economy.

Figure 1.2 shows how the distribution of a particular good may be handled. The supply curve is drawn parallel to the vertical axis, that is, perfectly inelastic with respect to price, to represent planned supply. A shift to the right of the schedule would indicate a decision to increase planned supply. The demand curve is estimated, and the market would be cleared at the equilibrium price of P_1.

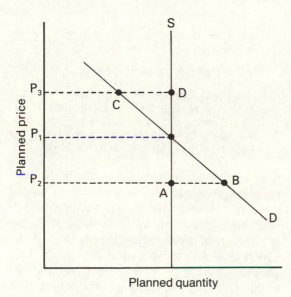

Figure 1.2 The distribution of a particular good

Although planners often attempt to set price at the market clearing level, this is typically not achieved, either because the demand curve is wrongly estimated in the first place or because it may have shifted over time; prices are often set for extended periods of time (see p. 20).[4] If the price is too low (P_2), then excess demand AB results and other forms of market clearing, such as queues, have to be employed. If the price is set too high (P_3), then excess supply CD causes stockpiles of commodities. The poor quality of many Soviet consumer goods, the reason for

which will be analysed later, may be seen to be reflected in this context as a demand curve well to the left of that estimated by planners (this latter estimated curve would go through point D), producing the above result. Note that in this case the turnover tax becomes a 'tax by difference', the difference between the wholesale and retail price less trade margins. In some cases, however, it is more like an excise tax.

It is important to note that the state deliberately underpriced some commodities and these were either formally rationed or distributed through queues, literally or in the form of long waiting lists. Foodstuffs (such as bread, dairy products and meat), transport fares and housing rents were typically heavily subsidized in socialist economies and remained constant for decades for political and income distribution reasons. For example, Soviet consumers received state subsidies amounting to over 50 billion roubles annually for basic foodstuffs and services (Shmelev, *Novy Mir*, no. 6, June 1987: 152), while in 1985 rents for state housing, fixed in 1928, took up only 3 per cent of an average family budget (Trehub 1987: 29). Queues were usually allowed to form for foodstuffs. There have been periods when rationing has been general, such as in the Soviet Union in the first half of the 1930s. Even in 1988, however, a coupon system for the sale of products such as meat, sugar and butter existed in eight of the fifteen republics of the Soviet Union (*Pravda*, 1 September 1988, p. 3). In December 1988 it was revealed that in the Russian Republic itself meat was rationed in one third of its regions, sugar in sixty-seven of its eighty-six territories and butter even in fertile areas such as the Volgograd and Rostov regions. As the economic situation deteriorated in 1990 rationing became more widespread, various republics and cities gave preference to their own residents, and some republics began limiting deliveries to other areas. In 1991 the economy went into free fall as the old system disintegrated before a new one could be introduced; towards the end of the year the Soviet Union itself ceased to exist as a political entity.

State housing has typically been rationed on

the basis of criteria such as need. The poor quality, non-availability and erratic supply of many consumer goods and services, coupled with the frequency of queues and rationing, provided a breeding ground for activities of varying degrees of legality. Katsenelinboigen (1977) paints a whole rainbow of coloured markets: red (official state stores), white (e.g. the free peasant market), grey (e.g. inter-enterprise bartering of inputs) and black (totally illegal activities).

Allocation of manpower

The fulfilment of plan output targets obviously requires the necessary labour and non-labour inputs, but there are contrasting ways of obtaining them. While the latter were essentially administratively allocated by means of the materials allocation system, the former mainly involved the use of the market mechanism, with administrative methods and moral suasion also employed.[5]

The command planning solution of labour direction, although used during the Second World War, was ruled out in more normal circumstances because of adverse effects on incentives (the War Communism period being informative in this respect). Market forces were heeded when the planners determined basic wage differentials, while the state controlled the education system, including the number of places available for particular courses of study. The state was able to use this combination, for example, to induce the increased supply of labour of the required skill needed to meet an altered production plan.

Figure 1.3 shows the demand and supply schedules for a particular type of skilled worker. The demand curve is shown as perfectly inelastic on the grounds that, with existing technology, the number of workers required is given by the planned level of output. Assume initially that supply equals demand, but that the new plan calls for increased output, which, with labour a derived demand, leads to a shift to the

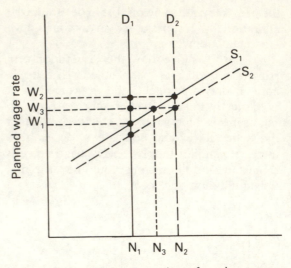

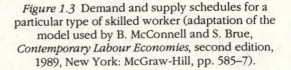

Figure 1.3 Demand and supply schedules for a particular type of skilled worker (adaptation of the model used by B. McConnell and S. Brue, *Contemporary Labour Economics*, second edition, 1989, New York: McGraw-Hill, pp. 585–7).

right of the demand curve to D_2. If the total supply of skilled labour were not increased, the wage rate would have to rise to W_2 to regain equilibrium, by attracting workers with the required skill from other sectors. But if the supply curve could be shifted to the right, by a combination of increasing the number of training places available and party propaganda, for example, as well as the inducement of higher wages to learn a new skill, the equilibrium wage rate becomes W_3 and the increased supply $N_1 N_2$ is the result of two sources, $N_1 N_3$ from other sectors and $N_3 N_2$ from the newly skilled.

The industrial worker's pay crudely consisted of two parts: (1) a state-guaranteed basic wage, which varied according to industrial branch, skill and region; and (2) the residual. This was affected by bonuses, related to such factors as plan fulfilment and the nature of the job (dangerous working conditions, for example). A basic rate (*stavka*) was set for a particular branch of industry, which determined the wage of the least skilled and therefore lowest paid worker. A tariff (scale) then established higher skill rates as a percentage of the basic rate, and there was also a set of regional coefficients to multiply the standard rate by. This formal system enabled the state to encourage labour to move to desired industries and regions and to adopt the desired skills. In addition, there was *de facto* room to manoeuvre for the enterprise manager, even within the constraints of an enforced wage fund, by manipulating norms and skill designations, for example. In the early period piece rates, as opposed to time rates, were dominant; a 100 per cent fulfilment of the norm, or output quota, would earn the *stavka* (Filtzer 1989: 90).

The non-market elements in manpower allocation have varied enormously over time. Forced labour camps were full as a result of the collectivization of agriculture and Stalin's purges. Although used for activities such as mining in inhospitable places, the camps served a mainly political function. High labour turnover during the 1930s, seen as a threat to plan fulfilment, was combated by means such as the 'work book'. This was introduced in 1938 and held by the enterprise manager; without it a worker could not, in principle, find another job. Increasingly harsh legislation eventually made even absenteeism and lateness criminal offences. Graduates of universities and technical schools were assigned to a place of work for two or three years. Moral suasion exercised by the party can be seen in operation, for example, when students and workers helped out at harvest time.

Trade unions were an arm of the state in the traditional model. They were organized along industrial lines with the result that worker and manager belonged to the same union. There was no collective bargaining between trade unions and management about basic wage and salary differentials, although the former exercised some marginal consultative roles. Strikes were considered to be counter-revolutionary and in any case unnecessary, although they were not actually outlawed in the constitution. This reduced the role of trade unions to the transmission of party policies, ensuring favourable conditions for plan fulfilment, protecting workers' interests (legal requirements as to health and safety, for example) and administering the social security system relating to sickness, work injury and pensions. Unemployment was officially declared to be eliminated by the end of 1930 (*CDSP*, 1988, vol. XL, no. 4, p. 4); work was regarded not only as a right but as a legal obligation. The Gorbachev era was far more frank about unemployment[6] and the need for unemployment pay.[7]

The industrial enterprise

Private enterprise was severely limited as regards:

1. *Area*. Handicrafts, agriculture and certain consumer services were acceptable, but selling goods made by other people was not allowed.

2. *Employment*. The employment of another person outside the immediate family in the production of goods for sale was illegal.

3. *Income*. Direct taxes were heavier than normal.

Thus the typical industrial enterprise was a state-owned plant, operating on the principle of one-man responsibility and control (*edinonachalie*) by a director appointed by the state or more strictly by the party: positions of any importance were to be found on its *nomenklatura* or list of key posts. Lower levels of management included the deputy director and chief engineer, complemented by the party cell and the trade union branch. The basic function of the industrial enterprise was to fulfil its 'technical, industrial and financial plan' (*tekhpromfinplan*). The operational plans (annual, quarterly and monthly) were expressed in terms of plan targets (success indicators), varying over time in terms of number and priority as particular problems arose. Output targets, however, were paramount. This is explicable in terms of the goals discussed earlier: the fact that a high proportion of production was used as inputs by other enterprises, the need to equate supply and demand via the use of material balances, and the difficulty of measuring quality. Gross output (*valovaya produktsiya*) measured the value of finished output plus net change in the value of goods in the process of production; output in physical terms involved units of measurement such as weight, numbers and length; and targets for more heterogeneous output were broken down into main assortment indicators. On the input side there was a plan for material technical supply and for labour utilization indicators, namely the wage fund (the total amount to be paid out in the plan period), productivity, average wage and number of workers by skill brackets. There were usually many other indicators, such as cost reduction, profit (as a percentage of cost rather than of capital), investment, innovation, delivery schedules and equipment utilization.

The industrial enterprise was a financially separate and accountable unit operating on a *khozraschyot* (economic accounting) basis, for the purpose of efficiently implementing the plan. Prices were fixed by the state and the enterprise account had to be kept in the local branch of the State Bank (Gosbank). The purpose of the latter was to help ensure plan compliance, the idea being that only payments in conformity with the plan should be permitted. Budgetary grants covered fixed capital needs and Gosbank had a monopoly over the granting of short-term credit, available at a nominal rate of interest which was fixed to cover only administrative costs. Management motivation involved negative consequences for non-fulfilment of the plan, such as loss of bonuses, expulsion from the party and its associated privileges, and possible imprisonment or even capital punishment for 'economic sabotage' during the darkest periods. Positive incentives were associated with fulfilment and overfulfilment. Bonus, socio-cultural and investment funds were linked to success indicators, especially output.

Enterprises producing goods for export or using imported commodities were shielded from the world market by the state monopoly of foreign trade and payments. The industrial enterprise was assigned to a foreign trade corporation. The FTC, in turn, was subject to the authority of the Ministry of Foreign Trade and the ministry to the State Planning Commission. The price paid to the enterprise producing the good for export was the domestic and not the world price; imports were paid for at the prices of comparable domestic commodities. This divorce of domestic and world market prices, coupled with arbitrarily determined exchange rates,[8] led to accounting 'profits' and 'losses' being made by the FTCs. Owing to a penchant for overvaluation of the rouble these were typically losses on exports and profits on imports. This was the mechanism by means of which exports and imports were involved in a sort of price equalization (*Preisausgleich*) with world and domestic prices, respectively. This separation of Soviet and foreign industrial firms greatly aggravated the problems already experienced with product quality. Although the traditional system played a crucial role in carrying out Stalin's goals, micro-economic problems of a severe kind arose.

Neglect of user need.

Output had only to be produced and not sold in the traditional Soviet economic system, while emphasis on one indicator led to neglect of others. The result was that quantity was stressed at the expense of quality. For example, physical indicators such as weight, number, or length resulted in too large, small or narrow objects respectively being produced, relative to user need. Gross output provides an incentive to use expensive inputs if these are reflected in product price and to orientate the product assortment towards those goods incorporating large amounts of these inputs. This neglect of the qualitative aspects of production was especially acute in low-priority sectors involved in heterogeneous output, such as textiles, and helps explain the seemingly paradoxical phenomenon of stockpiles of unsaleable products in a situation of general consumer goods scarcity. The problem persisted – only between 7.0 and 18 per cent of Soviet manufacturing output met world standards (Shmelev, *Novy Mir*, no. 6, June 1987, p. 148).

A tendency to understate productive capacity

The director had an incentive to provide such false information in the hope of achieving a 'slack' plan, one that called for less than feasible output,[9] since no bonuses were paid for anything less than 100 per cent fulfilment. Although extra bonuses were available for overfulfilment, the director was careful not to overfulfil by too much, since that would endanger fulfilment of subsequent plans. The 'ratchet effect', known in Eastern Europe as the 'base-year approach', means that this period's achievement is the starting point for next period's plan – 'planning from the achieved level', as it is also called (Birman 1978). The ratchet effect was a persistent problem because of its simplicity of use by data-deficient planners.

A tendency to over-indent for non-labour inputs and to hoard these as well as labour

Manpower was hoarded to meet unforeseen needs or the frequent changes in plans and to compensate for the erratic supply of inputs (catching up on production when they did arrive). These non-labour inputs too were hoarded, owing, for example, to the horrendous supply problems associated with the materials allocation system and to the fact that capital was a factor free to the enterprise. This led to such phenomena as *tolkachi* (expediters, unofficial supply agents, who bartered with each other, among other things) and a powerful inducement to self-sufficiency in the supply of inputs; parts of Soviet industry were notoriously non-specialized. Aganbegyan (1989: 43) valued the goods then hoarded by enterprises and departments at more than 460 billion roubles

(compared with a national income of 600 billion roubles), at least twice as high as it should have been.

Storming (shturmovshchina)

This is the mad rush to fulfil plans at the end of the planning period (such as the month), explained by such factors as the bonus system, delays in receiving inputs from other enterprises and the unwillingness of enterprises to show early eagerness in an environment where plans typically arrive late and are frequently changed (Bleaney 1988: 63).

Anti-innovation bias at the micro level

Innovation is the application of new ideas about products and techniques to the production process. While new priority large-scale technologies (in armaments, for example) are readily dealt with by command economies, vital, spontaneous, micro-level innovation was hindered by the traditional Soviet economic system:

1. There was no competitive pressure to stay in business as in market economies.
2. The incentive system meant jeopardizing short-term plan fulfilment and the prospect of 'ratchet effects'.
3. State-determined prices might mean adverse effects on value indicators.
4. There were the aforementioned problems of input supply.
5. R&D, traditionally taking place in specialized organizations within ministries, was separated from production (Berliner 1976).
6. There was frequent shifting around of managers to prevent 'familiness' (friendliness developing between the various individuals within an enterprise; coalitions could thwart the enterprises' superiors).

Thus it seems that the interests of enterprise, user and state often conflicted in the command economy, but it is important to note (Nove 1986) the impossibility of central planners generally knowing what is needed in precise, disaggregated detail. The price system (see p. 20) is denied this informational role and this is at the root of the reform problem.

The financial system

Any economy that wishes to reap the benefits of extensive specialization and exchange needs money to function as a medium of exchange, unit of account, store of value and standard for deferred payments. The command economy uses money (the experience of War Communism was influential here), but, given that resources were largely centrally allocated, it played an essentially passive role. This is best illustrated by repeating the point that an enterprise's non-labour inputs were distributed administratively; it was the *naryad* that was the vital piece of paper, money being automatically forthcoming. Price tags were attached to items of expenditure and revenue in order for it to be possible to draw up the account necessary for purposes of evaluation and control. Note, however, that since market elements were important in these areas, differential wage rates actively influenced manpower allocation, and consumers often exercised choice over the goods and services made available in the plan. Money was needed because it was impossible to plan physically the output of every single good and in order to monitor performance.

The concept of the total money supply in a command economy is not very meaningful because there are two payments circuits, 'household cash' and 'deposit transfer'. The latter circuit comprises the bookkeeping changes that cover practically all inter-enterprise transactions, while the former has implications for macro financial equilibrium. The state is concerned to keep a balance between the cash injected into the economy, largely via the paying out of wages and salaries, and the supply of consumer goods and services made available under the plan at established prices, in order to avoid inflationary pressures. This can be expressed with the aid of an equation: $PQ = Y + TP - S - T$, where P is the general retail price level (i.e. average retail price), Q is the quantity of consumer goods and services, Y is household income in the form of wages and salaries earned in the production of *all* goods and services, TP is transfer payments, such as pensions, paid out to households, S is household savings, and T is direct taxes levied on households.

In principle the Soviet Union was thus able to prevent open and repressed inflation. It is interesting and instructive, therefore, to examine why significant open inflation was a feature of the 1930s. While plans for the production of consumer goods were generally underfulfilled, there was a large leakage of cash into the system through the overdrawing of wage funds. This originated in (1) the high level of labour turnover, which itself was the result of a predominantly undisciplined labour force, recently arrived from the countryside, in search of higher earnings, and (2) the plight of enterprise directors desperate for labour to fulfil the all-important output targets. Managers indulged in all sorts of activities, such as artificial upgrading, to get round state-determined wage rates. The State Bank allowed wage fund transgressions for fear of jeopardizing output plans.[10]

There were attempts to correct the financial imbalance by encouraging household savings (S), including what were in effect forced bond sales, but the massive increases in direct taxes that would have been needed were ruled out by the necessity to preserve work incentives. What was left was P – retail prices were increased to move nearer to market clearing levels (thus causing turnover taxes, which were usually price-determined, to increase) and to soak up some of the excess purchasing power. It is worth noting that in the 1930s the Soviet Union experienced full employment and open inflation while the reverse situation existed in the capitalist West.

Y is worth exploring a little further because wages and salaries are paid out not only to people working in sectors producing consumer goods and services, but also to those who are not, namely in investment, social consumption and defence. These have to be absorbed by indirect taxes, direct taxes or savings (Ellman 1989: 233). If the latter two are ruled out, then indirect taxation must involve an average mark-up (m) over the costs of production of consumer goods and services given by the following equation:

$$m = \frac{Wsc + Wi + Wd}{Whc}$$

where W represents wages and salaries paid out in social consumption (sc), investment (i), defence (d) and household consumption (hc). The introduction of direct taxes and savings means that a lower mark-up will be needed. Note that the actual mark-up involves mainly the turnover tax and profit. If retail prices are not raised sufficiently to achieve financial equilibrium, the result is repressed inflation, which takes the form of queues, rationing and blocked purchasing power (i.e. forced savings or 'monetary overhang'). The extent to which repressed inflation existed in the Soviet Union in recent decades, however, has been a very controversial point. The sceptics point to the coexistence of stockpiles and queues, and consider rapidly rising savings accounts as normal consumer behaviour. By the late 1980s, however, the evidence was strongly in favour of repressed inflation. Shmelev (*CDSP*, 1989, vol. XLI, no. 44, p. 6), for example, estimates 150 billion to 200 billion roubles of 'hot money' (sometimes called 'mobile' money) that people would have spent immediately if goods were available. The Soviet government's estimate of the monetary overhang at the end of 1989 was 165 billion roubles, while Marrese (1990: 57) puts the figure at 233 billion roubles. Mounting budget deficits (120 billion roubles in 1989 or about 12 per cent of national income) were increasingly financed by printing money, while mounting difficulties were experienced on the production side (see note 13 for details).

The budget

Real resource flows were determined in the plan, but were also reflected in the consolidated budget at all levels of government. The major elements of expenditure were for the 'national economy', especially capital grants and subsidies, and for socio-cultural purposes, such as health and education. The budgetary category of defence significantly underestimated the real total, with elements such as weapons research tucked away under other headings. On the revenue side, the outstanding point to note was the overwhelming reliance on indirect rather than direct taxes. One important reason for this was to preserve the wage differentials needed for incentives in a market environment. The turnover tax was more important than profit payments in the early years. Since resource allocation was determined in the plan, the budget played a role in the quest for financial equilibrium.

The banking system

Banking was a state monopoly in the traditional economic system. The State Bank (Gosbank) was a *monobank*, that is, there was not the separation between the central bank and private commercial banks to be found in the West. Gosbank fulfilled the following functions in that it:

1. Issued cash.

2. Had a monopoly of gold and foreign exchange reserves (command economies typically have a specialized Foreign Trade Bank to deal with international payments).

3. Acted as the fiscal agent of government, collecting budgetary revenue and disbursing current expenditures (a separate Construction Bank handled the doling out of investment grants).

4. Had a monopoly of short-term credits for working capital purposes in line with the state plan.

5. Monitored plan fulfilment by enterprises by means of the obligatory account.

The Savings Bank serviced the needs of individuals. The overriding task then, reflecting the essentially passive role of money, was to aid plan fulfilment. Contrast this with the active exercise of monetary (and fiscal) policy in market economies.

Price determination

In the traditional system industrial prices were formally fixed by the state on the basis of planned branch *average* cost of production and a small profit mark-up on costs. Average cost was used in order to ensure overall branch profitability, while providing an incentive to lower costs. Costs included labour, raw materials, intermediate inputs, interest on short-term credits, and depreciation (though not allowing for technical obsolescence), but excluded a capital charge and a rental charge reflecting favourable location or plant modernity.[11] For consumer goods the difference between the wholesale price, including the mark-up of the wholesale organization where appropriate, and the retail price, less the retail mark-up, was the 'turnover tax'. Since the general rule was to try to set the retail price at market clearing levels, the turnover tax was generally price-determined (i.e. a residual). The tax was price-determining only when it was in effect an excise tax of a given amount. Retail prices reflected demand to varying extents, but wholesale prices ignored demand because of persistent shortages. Wholesale prices were based on average rather than marginal cost and were fixed for long periods of time, partly for administrative reasons and partly the better to assess enterprise performance over time. Wholesale prices were, therefore, not efficiency prices,[12] but they were not, of course, meant to play an important allocative role, factor substitution being one area where they were active. Instead, in line with the essential passivity of money, they served as a means of control and evaluation (*khozraschyot* and value indicators, for example). As already noted, domestic prices were separated from world prices by the state foreign trade monopoly. Radical price reform only becomes essential when a significant decentralization of decision-making is considered.

Agriculture

All land in the Soviet Union belonged to the state, although other bodies were allowed use of it. The main production unit in the early system was not the state farm (*sovkhoz*), but the collective farm (*kolkhoz*). Collectivization during the 1930s was forced, bloody and brutal. Only a nominally independent co-operative, the *kolkhoz* was subject to state plans and delivery quotas (the latter being concentrated upon after the mid-1950s) at state-determined prices which sometimes bordered on the confiscatory. In 1936 the compulsory procurement price for wheat, plus handling costs, was fifteen roubles a tonne; this wheat was sold to state milling enterprises at 107 roubles per tonne, the turnover tax thus amounting to ninety-two roubles (Nove 1961: 99). During the 1930s the compulsory procurement price for potatoes of 3.6 roubles a tonne contrasted with free market prices varying between thirty-seven and 200 roubles a tonne.

Peasant income for work on the collective farm was residual in nature, constituting that remaining from gross revenue after deduction of all other costs, including social security and equipment. The workday (*trudoden*) was not literally a calendar day, but each particular piece of work was valued at so many workdays. Its value was not known until the end of the year, the residual being divided by the total number of workdays earned. This uncertainty, the infrequency and low levels of remuneration (in kind as well as in money), the negligible impact of individual effort on total farm income, and the fact that the burden of a poor harvest was placed on the shoulders of the peasants (there was even a man-made famine in areas such as the Ukraine) had a disastrous effect on incentives. Collective farm peasants did not receive state pensions until 1964. Peasants devoted so much time to their private plots that a minimum number of days of collective work had to be introduced. Although severely restricted in terms of size and livestock holdings, these plots were a vital source of peasant cash income and of supply of such products as fruit and vegetables, dairy products and meat, which were either consumed in the household or sold on the free market.

There is still controversy about the role of agriculture as a source of forced savings, but collectivization provided food for the rapidly growing urban labour force, raw materials (like cotton) for industry and agricultural products for export (generally at relatively low cost to the state), and encouraged the movement of labour necessary for rapid industrialization. It was also hoped that collectivization would reap the benefits of industrial mechanization applied to large-scale farming units and secure party control in the countryside. Over time the average size of Soviet farm units increased. In 1937 the average collective farm comprised seventy-six households, but by the mid-1980s the number had increased to 484 (working 6,400 ha of agricultural land). Over the same period of time the state farm (which grew in importance at the expense of the collective farm, although the two in fact became more alike) employed, on average, 285 and 529 workers respectively (working 16,200 ha latterly).

The cost of collectivization was great. In the short term there was a reduction in agricultural output of around a fifth during 1928–32 and massive slaughter of livestock by unwilling peasants. The long-run health of the sector also suffered, agriculture often being described as the Achilles' heel of the economy. Apart from the income distribution system in collective farms (exacerbated by the large size of these multi-product farms, which made the link between effort and reward even more tenuous), the central planning of agriculture faces special problems, including the variety of constantly changing local conditions and difficulties of supervision, the vital importance of a timely supply of inputs in a sector dominated by seasonal factors (such as spare parts for repair and maintenance), and the fact that land and produce may be put to better use, as far as farmers are concerned.

Conclusion

Despite an industrial spurt in the late Tsarist era, the economy in 1917 and in 1928, after a recuperative period, was still basically agrarian. The traditional Soviet economic system adopted by Stalin after 1928 sought to achieve the main goal of rapidly matching the capitalist powers in terms of heavy industrial capacity and military strength. Implementation involved a strategy of investing a historically high proportion of national output and giving sectoral priority to heavy industry, with a limited role assigned to foreign trade. The institutional framework was that of a command economy, in which decision-making with regard to resource allocation was highly centralized. The distribution of consumer goods and the allocation of manpower, however, involved substantially market methods in more normal times. The prime function of the state industrial enterprise was to fulfil state plan targets, while the private sector was severely curtailed. Money plays an essentially passive role in a command economy, but the possibility of inflation is raised.

The traditional economic system enabled the Soviet Union rapidly to attain superpower status, albeit at the expense of serious economic problems. Chapter 1 has discussed the neglect of user need, understatement of productive capacity, hoarding of inputs, 'storming' and anti-innovation bias. The beginning of the chapter on the Soviet Union deals with other problems such as the scattering of investment resources and declining growth rates. Towards the end of 1991 the Soviet Union ceased to exist as a political entity. Today most of the countries that had at some time employed the traditional Soviet economic planning system have rejected it in favour of a market economy.

NOTES

1. The Soviet Union occupied a sixth of the earth's land surface, excluding Antarctica. In 1917 the population was 143 million (with a different land area), compared with 290.1 million in 1990.
2. According to the Julian calendar, which was used until February 1918, the start of the Bolshevik Revolution was 25 October 1917, but thereafter was celebrated on 7 November. The so-called 'bourgeois revolution' of February (March) 1917 actually overthrew Tsarism. The Treaty of Brest-Litovsk was signed on 3 March 1918 with Germany, Austria-Hungary, Turkey and Bulgaria, but was annulled on 13 November 1918.
3. The enterprise manager, for example, had some marginal decision-making autonomy with regard to input substitution and production choice within the aggregate plan target. Contracts drawn up between enterprises included things like delivery times and the detailed product mix. Kroll (1988: 360) views the main functions of contracts as to economise on information costs and to strengthen the customer's position, although a seller's market and the paramount importance of the production plan marginalize the role of contracts in the command economy.
4. Queues can also be due to other factors, such as a restricted number of poorly organized distribution outlets. Velikanova (*Literaturnaya Gazeta*, no. 16, 20 April 1988, p. 14) gives a figure of 65 billion man-hours a year spent shopping in the Soviet Union today. Plokker (1990: 404) quotes a 1988 Soviet source, which estimates that the average family may spend one month per year standing in queues. Shleifer and Vishny (1991: 347) cite another Soviet estimate that 30 million man-years are spent in queues annually, some 25 per cent of the waking time of every adult.
5. The *nomenklatura* system is one in which the party makes all important appointments, including those in the economy. The internal passport system, introduced in 1932, helped to control the geographical movement of people.
6. In 1987 a million people in Uzbekistan and a quarter of a million in Azerbaijan, for example, and an overall unemployment rate of 3 per cent, according to Nikolai Shmelev (*Novy Mir*, no. 6, June 1987, p. 148). More recent Soviet sources put the unemployment rate in Uzbekistan at 22.8 per cent and in Azerbaijan at 27.6 per cent (*CDSP*, 1989, vol. XLI, no. 44, p. 6), and the overall rate at 6 per cent of the able-bodied population, i.e. 8 million people are unemployed 'to all intents and purposes' (*CDSP*, 1990, vol. XLII, no. 14, p. 5). Nikolai Belov (deputy chairman of the State Statistical Committee) talked of some three million people unable to find work, but the total goes up to 13 million (out of a workforce of 164 million) if women, invalids and people temporarily between jobs are included (*The Independent*, 26 January 1990, p. 8). Western estimates are to be found in Gregory and Collier (1988). They calculate the one-month-or-more unemployment rate for 1974–79 from a survey of 2,793 Soviet émigrés to the United States to be 1.2 to 1.3 per cent; this compares with Wiles's estimate for 1962–63 of 1.1 to 1.8 per cent and Granick's for the late 1970s of 1.5 to 3.0 per cent (p. 625). At the end of 1990 the unemployment rate was in the range of 3 to 6 per cent (Oxenstierna 1992: 59). Adirim (1989: 460) proffers an overall figure of 6.2 per cent, including 'open' unemployment (people without a job), 'concealed' unemployment (people with a job providing insufficient work and earnings) and 'indirect' unemployment (people with a job, but with pay so inadequate that they are forced to search for additional work).
7. The first case involved those losing their jobs as a result of ministerial reorganization in 1985, being eligible for full pay for three months without affecting pension and other social security rights (normally pension rights were adversely affected if unemployment lasted more than a month).
8. The rouble was an inconvertible currency and was not, therefore, subject to supply and demand forces in world foreign exchange markets (see Chapter 2).
9. 'Taut' planning prevailed in general, with pressure to maximize output from given resources.
10. The leak associated with Y was later plugged by tighter regulations, which specified, for example, that overspending had to be made good within a matter of months.
11. In reality it was possibly the case that most prices of manufactured goods reflected individual enterprises' costs of production, owing to deals between the enterprise and the centre (Hewett 1988: 195–6); again, the reality was that the centre actually only set the prices of a few major products, such as raw materials, fuels, food, oil and grain. Most prices were actually set by ministries and enterprises on the basis of centrally given rules; only a few price proposals were seriously analysed by the overburdened centre (Hewett 1988: 192).

12. In market economies prices are determined by supply and demand, thus reflecting both costs and utility. Prices play crucial informational, incentive and allocative functions. Profit-orientated firms face changing supply and demand conditions, have an incentive to respond in an efficient manner and are able to reallocate scarce resources.

13. 'Monetary overhang' has been usefully defined as an excess of purchasing power over the total supply of goods and services at effective prices (Ellman 1989a: 244) and is seen in an unplanned accumulation of cash and savings accounts because of the lack of desired goods and services. Work incentives are severely adversely affected by the uncertainty of being able to translate money income into command over real goods and services. Converting repressed into open inflation by allowing prices to rise brings its own political dangers, while removing a given overhang by one-off measures provides no long-term cure; the root causes of the problem must be tackled by such measures as reducing the large budget deficits (or rather the part of the deficit financed by an increase in the money supply, the State Bank 'buying' state securities in exchange). Various proposals have been put forward for removing the monetary overhang. The most radical would be a comprehensive monetary reform involving the substitution of a new money; the problems here include panic buying if such a reform were even suspected and the fact that better-off citizens tend to hold much of their wealth in the form of real estate, valuables and hard currency. A partial monetary reform was implemented via the 22 January 1991 decree: 50 and 100 rouble notes were no longer legal tender (there were limits placed on the amount that could be converted), allegedly aimed at 'speculation, corruption, smuggling, forgery, unearned income, and normalizing the monetary situation and the consumer market'; limits were also placed on the amount of savings that could be withdrawn monthly in the form of cash for the first half of 1991. Partial measures to remove the overhang include such proposals as bond sales, the sale of housing and industrial assets, and the resale of more imports at high mark-up rates. One concrete measure, effective 1 January 1991 (though scrapped a year later), involved the imposition of a 5 per cent turnover tax on goods for production and technical purposes, consumer goods, jobs performed and paid services (the revenue being used for social and economic progress, to support the needy members of society and for stabilizing currency circulation), and the setting up of a stabilization fund (revenue raised from social security funds, depreciation funds, windfall profits resulting from excessive price rises, and the sale of shares) used to support enterprises adversely affected by circumstances beyond their control in the transition to the market, scientific research, the conversion of defence enterprises to civilian production and special republican subsidies. Amendments were made later on (see 'anti-crisis programme'). Indeed 1991 was the beginning of the end for the Soviet Union, financial chaos playing its part as output levels plummeted.

References

Some general references on the first three chapters include:

Aganbegyan, A. (1988b) *The Challenge: Economics of Perestroika*, London: Hutchinson.

Aganbegyan, A. (1989) *Moving the Mountain: Inside the Perestroika Revolution*, London: Bantam Press.

Bleaney, M. (1988) *Do Socialist Economies Work? The Soviet and East European Experience*, Oxford: Basil Blackwell.

Dyker, D. (1985) *The Future of the Soviet Planning System*, London: Croom Helm.

——(ed.) (1987) *The Soviet Union under Gorbachev: Prospects for Reform*, London: Croom Helm.

Gregory, P., and Stuart, R. (1990) *Soviet Economic Structure and Performance*, 4th edn, New York: Harper & Row.

Hare, P. (1987) 'Resource allocation without prices: the Soviet economy', *Economic Review*, 5, no. 2.

Hewett, E. (1988) *Reforming the Soviet Economy: Equality versus Efficiency*, Washington, D.C.: Brookings Institution.

Nove, A. (1986) *The Soviet Economic System*, 3rd edn, London: Allen & Unwin.

Ofer, G. (1987) 'Soviet economic growth: 1928–85', *Journal of Economic Literature*, XXV (December).

Schroeder, G. (1986) *The System versus Progress: Soviet Economic Problems*, London: Centre for Research into Communist Economies.

Smith, A. (1983) *The Planned Economies of Eastern Europe*, London: Croom Helm.

Zimbalist, A., Sherman, H., and Brown, S. (1989) *Comparing Economic Systems: A Political- Economic Approach*, 2nd edn, New York: Harcourt Brace Jovanovich, Part Three (pp. 93–316).

2

FOREIGN TRADE: THE RISE AND FALL OF COMECON

In the traditional Soviet economic system the state had a monopoly of foreign trade and payments, the purpose being to help carry out party policy and shield the domestic from the international economy. With direct control exercised over exports and imports, tariffs lose their conventional significance as protectors of home industry and sources of budgetary revenue. Two-tariff schedules have been used by command economies, however, as bargaining levers with the West in the quest for 'most favoured nation' treatment (the lowest tariff applying to all). Czechoslovakia, Hungary, Poland and Romania belonged to GATT before the 1989 upheavals and agreed to increase imports so as to simulate the effects of tariff reductions.

The institutional hierarchy ran from the State Planning Commission to the Ministry of Foreign Trade and on to the foreign trade corporations, which normally specialized in a particular product or group of products and which operated on a *khozraschyot* basis. The industrial enterprise that produced the good designated in its *tekhpromfinplan* as an export did not receive the world price but the domestic wholesale price, with appropriate adjustments in case of factors such as quality differences. The ultimate user of an import was charged the price of its nearest domestic substitute. There was a multiple exchange rate system (the term 'coefficients' is often used), with various rates for different products or groups of products. Exchange rates were arbitrarily determined,

with a tendency towards overvaluation. In consequence, the higher level of domestic prices for tradeable goods than the world price level typically resulted in accounting 'profits' on imports and 'losses' on exports made by the FTCs.

The separation of original producer and ultimate purchaser, except for perhaps contact over minor details such as precise delivery times, severely aggravated the problem of quality in production and marketing. Industrial enterprises in command economies produce according to plan and are unaffected by either competition in or, in any automatic sense, the movement of prices on the world market.

PLANNING AND FOREIGN TRADE

In textbook market economies, international trade is based on specialization according to comparative advantage, with firms equally interested in exports or imports in the search for maximum profits. In the traditional Soviet system exports were viewed as a means of paying for the import of goods either totally unavailable or in short supply at home, goods deemed essential to fulfil national plans; exports were not seen, for example, as a means of achieving full employment. As Winiecki puts it, imports were largely determined by drawing up material balances that showed the rough gaps between planned domestic demand and supply. These balances also showed exportable surpluses; if it was not possible to reduce imports,

24

it was the value of the imports needed to meet the planned growth rate that determined the value of exports (1988: 136). Abalkin talks of trade 'bridging gaps' in material balances (*CDSP*, 1989, vol. XLI, no. 46, p. 15). Inefficient domestic prices and arbitrarily determined exchange rates precluded a meaningful calculation of the gains from trade. The commodity structure of trade was determined by political factors (sales of armaments, for example), domestic resource endowment (the Soviet Union was the world's largest producer of oil) and the relative inefficiency of the economic system (the command economies had difficulties selling manufactured goods in Western markets).

In 1937 Soviet exports reached an all-time low of 0.5 per cent of national product, although this was due to a combination of deliberate isolation ('socialism in one country'), Western embargoes and deteriorating commodity terms of trade (i.e. the prices of primary products falling relative to imported manufactures). In 1913 the figure had been 10.4 per cent and in 1929 3.1 per cent (Gregory and Stuart 1990: 325). The 'trade aversion' to which command economies are susceptible was especially evident in the early years. Ellman (1989a: 289) summarizes the evidence for this: in 1955 the foreign trade of each Comecon member was below its potential (determined by the normal relationship between trade and factors such as population and *per capita* national income) by at least 50 per cent (Pryor); the situation was similar in 1958 and 1962 (Pryor) and 1970 (Hewett). In 1989 the East European Comecon countries (excluding the Soviet Union) plus Yugoslavia accounted for only 4 per cent of world trade (Institute of International Finance 1990: 1); total hard currency exports amounted to only 75 per cent of Hong Kong's and 80 per cent of South Korea's (p. 8).

Intra-Comecon prices

A fundamental feature was the use of some form of world prices, due to the lack of efficient domestic prices and meaningful exchange rates. The exact form varied over time, although world prices were allegedly cleansed of so-called business cycle and monopolistic and speculative influences, and adjustments were made to take account of such factors as differences in quality. The particular price formula was used to determine specific prices in the bilateral negotiations which also decided quantities. More specifically, current world market prices were used in 1949 and average prices of 1949–50 until 1956. Between 1958 and 1965 1957 prices were used, while average prices of 1960–64 were employed during the period 1966–70. Average 1965–69 prices were used over the period 1971–75, but 1975 saw a switch to a new system, namely an annually moving average of the previous five years (three in the case of some products). This system of price determination explains why the prices charged by the Soviet Union for oil deliveries to its Comecon partners lagged behind the upsurge in world prices after 1973–74 and 1979 and the decline after November 1985.

Another feature of more recent pricing policies pre-1989 was the policy of allowing, albeit still in a controlled fashion, domestic prices to reflect, to a varying extent, changes in world prices. Within Comecon this was taken to greatest lengths in Hungary. Since 1 January 1991 current world prices and hard currency transactions have been used. The forty-sixth and final meeting of Comecon was held in Budapest on 28 June 1991.

Determination of exchange rates

In market economies operating on a floating exchange rate regime, the price of one national currency in terms of another is determined by supply and demand forces operating in foreign exchange markets. In the long run such exchange rates approximate 'purchasing power parity', units of the different national currencies buying roughly equal amounts of internationally traded goods and services (i.e. the prices of similar goods on the world and domestic markets being approximately the same at the prevailing exchange rates). In command economies national currencies are not convertible into each other, into gold or into Western currencies, so they are not bought and sold on world foreign exchange markets (see Holzman's definitions in the glossary under 'convertibility'). The separation of domestic and world prices resulting from the state monopoly of foreign trade and payments thus ensures that exchange rates are arbitrarily determined. It should be noted, however, that tourist exchange rates differ from commercial ones in that the former have to take into account the effects of expenditure by tourists, who have the choice as to whether to buy the goods and services available or, indeed, whether to travel at all. Nevertheless, the frequency of black markets indicates some overvaluation of the domestic currency even here. The commercial exchange rates are thus units of account that are needed to draw up a balance of payments, with export and import statistics valued in *valuta* (foreign currency) roubles, say. The figures can be converted into domestic roubles by means of state-determined exchange rates (if given). As a half-way house to full convertibility, there is the possibility of partial convertibility, e.g. socialist Hungary's 'domestic' ('internal') convertibility, were domestic enterprises are able to buy and sell hard currencies at a unified exchange rate.

Reforms in foreign trade decision-making

In command economies foreign trade decisions are still largely the result of material balance planning and trade agreements, but more recent reforms increased the degree of decentralized decision-making to trade and production enterprises, and planners used a number of foreign trade indices. These indices were fundamentally flawed in that they relied on inefficient domestic prices and the absence of market-determined exchange rates which approximate purchasing power parity: hence they had only a marginal effect on decision-making, helping to eliminate grossly unprofitable transactions by crudely estimating foreign exchange earnings per unit of domestic resource expenditure and savings in domestic resources per unit of foreign exchange expended.

In helping to decide whether it is profitable to import a commodity, the following simplified import efficiency index (M_e) can be used:

$$M_e = \frac{P_d \cdot E}{P_f}$$

The inherent defects in this index can be seen in the inefficient domestic price (P_d) and the lack of a meaningful exchange rate (E) with which to compare P_d and P_f (the foreign price expressed in terms of foreign currency). A crude ranking of imports can be derived by comparing $\frac{P_d}{P_f}$ for each commodity. The same sort of ranking procedure can be followed for exports, comparing foreign exchange earnings per unit of domestic resource expenditure. Winiecki makes the point that these indices may have helped avoid gross errors at the level of a narrow product group at best, since even serious price distortions were at least of a similar type (1988: 147).

COUNCIL OF MUTUAL ECONOMIC ASSISTANCE

Comecon had ten full members at its peak: the Soviet Union, Bulgaria, Czechoslovakia, Hungary, Poland, Romania (these formed the original membership in January 1949), the GDR (joined 1950), Mongolia (1962), Cuba (1972) and Vietnam (1978). Albania joined in February 1949, but effectively ceased to be a member at the end of 1961 (membership was never formally revoked). Yugoslavia was the only 'limited participant' – after 1964 it had partial associate status, co-operating in most standing commissions, and was a member of other organs. The following had observer status: Afghanistan,

Angola, China, Ethiopia, Laos, Mozambique (Mozambique had made a number of unsuccessful applications for membership, the first in 1981), Nicaragua, North Korea (1957) and South Yemen. Co-operation agreements were signed with Finland, Iraq and Mexico.

Comecon was set up largely as a political response to the June 1947 Marshall Plan for the reconstruction of Europe and the 1948 split between the Soviet Union and Yugoslavia: Stalin feared possible imitators. Comecon was also the economic counterpart of the Organization for European Economic Co-operation (the OEEC subsequently became the OECD). Czechoslovakia, Hungary and Poland actually received invitations to participate in the Marshall Plan, but Stalin blocked any positive response. Western boycotts after the 1948 Berlin blockade helped push the socialist countries together, and the official aim was 'to develop economic collaboration between the socialist countries and to co-ordinate their economic progress on the basis of equality of rights of all member states'. Korbonski (1990b: 48) considers the real purpose was to solidify Soviet control over Eastern Europe by switching its trade from the West and helping to impose the Stalinist economic system.

Apart from occasional summits of leaders (General Secretaries), the main institutional bodies were as follows:

The *Council Session*. The chief body, although decisions (for example, aspects of economic co-operation) were not binding; usually, after 1984, a biannual meeting of prime ministers.

The *Executive Committee*. Deputy prime ministers, meeting quarterly; the chief executive organ of the Council Session, representing it between Session meetings. The committee elaborated on these policy recommendations and oversaw their implementation.

Council committees. For planning, material-technical supply, scientific and technological co-operation, and machine-building.

The *Permanent Secretariat*. Headed by Vyacheslav Sychov. Comecon's only permanent body, acting as a sort of civil service. The Secretariat, formed in 1954, drew up the agenda for the meetings of 1 and 2, undertook research, and prepared statistical reports.

Standing commissions. For the chemical industry, agriculture and construction, for example, dealing with detailed co-ordination in specific industries and areas. Increasing concern about damage to the environment caused by such factors as output indicators, heavy industry and nuclear accidents, led to the first meeting of the Commission on Environmental Protection on 28–31 March 1988.

COUNTER-TRADE

A wide variety of types of counter-trade are practised in the world at large (see *Financial Times* surveys). The simplest is barter, a straight swap in kind of goods or services of equivalent value. Others include: 'counter-purchase', which requires a varying proportion of payment in kind, with cash dominant as a rule; 'buy-back', where deliveries of plant and equipment are wholly or partly repaid in the form of output forthcoming from the project; and 'switch' trading, where trade imbalances between two socialist countries, for example, are cleared by involving a Western country. 'Offset' describes the situation where the seller takes in exchange goods from the purchaser's country that are used as inputs in the seller's products. Estimates of the present importance of counter-trade in total world trade varied between 5 and 10 per cent. Counter-trade accounted for at least 25 per cent of East–West trade (*The Economist*, 25 November 1989, p. 115). Major explanatory factors included: (1) the existence of command economies, with their currency and goods inconvertibility and difficulties experienced in exporting manufactures to the West; and (2) the debt crisis affecting many developing countries (as well as socialist countries) following the 1973–74 and 1979 oil price shocks. Rising interest rates on the massive credits granted by

Western banks in their early recycling of OPEC trade surpluses, declining exports to Western countries in recession, and severe credit restrictions in the 1980s all contributed. Given a desperate shortage of hard currency earnings and reserves, counter-trade helps maintain trade volume, even though it is relatively inefficient in comparison with multilateral trade under normal circumstances, where the full benefits of comparative advantage can be reaped. Even socialist countries themselves avoided counter-trade with Western partners if they were able to sell their products in other markets for convertible currencies which could then be used to buy in the cheapest markets.

Bilateral trade: the situation prior to 1 January 1991

Bilateral trade predominated in intra-Comecon trade. Here, trade is balanced between two countries over a period of time and is implemented via annual and longer-term, especially five-year, agreements. Multilateral trade, in contrast, involves surpluses and deficits with different partners which can be offset against one another through the use of convertible currencies. Bilateral trade still dominated despite its tendency to reduce the volume of trade (exchange limited to the country with the lesser export potential) and to force countries to accept goods of lesser value than could be otherwise obtained or bought at a lower price elsewhere. The situation within Comecon was complicated by the existence of so-called hard and soft commodities, stemming originally from the early stereotyped sectoral strategy of giving priority to heavy industry. A radial pattern of trade developed, with the Soviet Union as the major supplier of fuels and raw materials. 'Hard' goods were those particularly sought after within Comecon, because the internal price system undervalued them (relative to world prices) and they could be sold on and purchased from the world market for convertible (hard) currencies; examples include foodstuffs, fuels and raw materials. 'Soft' goods, such as low-quality, obsolete machinery and equipment, were the reverse. 'Structural' or 'commodity' bilateralism existed because partners had an incentive to balance trade in each of the two types of commodity taken separately.[1] Holzman mentions the extreme case where a product, classified as soft, contains inputs from the West paid for in hard currency. Here the cost of these inputs has to be reimbursed in hard currency (1987:100–1). Unplanned surpluses or deficits could be worked off by flows in subsequent periods, transfers of soft goods, or, more reluctantly on the deficit country's part, transfers of hard goods and payment in convertible currencies. The reluctance to use hard currencies was reflected in the very small percentage accounted for by multilateral trade (perhaps only 5 per cent of total trade: Gregory and Stuart 1990: 330).

The prevalence of bilateral trade could be explained by the following factors:

1. Such trade is administratively easier to handle by command economies. Five-year and annual plans take account of the implications of trade agreements, although the frequency with which output plans were changed is reflected in the flexibility characteristic of annual trade agreements (themselves more specific than the five-year trade protocols).

2. Minimization of the use of scarce hard currencies.

3. 'Currency inconvertibility'.

4. Currency inconvertibility is compounded by 'goods inconvertibility'. If one command economy has a trade surplus with another, this cannot be automatically converted into a claim on particular goods in the latter country (let alone in a Western country), because of the lack of direct and free exchange between ultimate purchaser and supplier. This claim can be met only by negotiations and provisions in central plans. Contrast this with the US dollar, for illustrative purposes. Dollars can be freely

converted into, say, French francs, which can be used by US buyers in free negotiations with French firms. Comecon countries, thus, had an incentive to avoid delivering hard goods to one another – these goods sold in the world market yielded currencies that could be used to buy the best-quality products at the lowest price. For multilateral trade to have become the norm within the CMEA would have required market-orientated economies using convertible currencies.[2]

The International Bank for Economic Co-operation (IBEC) was set up in 1964 to promote multilateral trade within the CMEA. The 'transferable rouble' (its predecessor was the 'clearing rouble', used after 1950 in bilateral trade between the Soviet Union and other Comecon members), was a unit of account used to transact intra-Comecon trade, with the backing of the capital provided by members in the form of domestic currencies and gold. Annual bilateral negotiations should not attempt bilateral trade balances, but should be followed by a multilateral trade session to cancel out most surpluses and deficits. Remaining imbalances were to be removed by deficit exporting to surplus countries, the latter paying in accumulated transferable roubles (see especially Holzman 1987: 100). The failure of the IBEC to overcome bilateralism was due to the unchanging fundamentals of trading relationships. The transferable rouble was simply a unit of account for drawing up members' trade balances with each other. Trade imbalances had to be negotiated away as before – the transferable rouble was not convertible, goods inconvertibility remained, and all countries strove, therefore, to avoid building up a surplus. The International Investment Bank was established in 1971 in order to encourage co-operation in major investment projects. However, its credits, with the exception of hard currency loans, of course, were mere reflections of negotiated transfers of capital goods, such as those used in Soviet energy projects.

Forms of Comecon co-operation prior to 1 January 1991

Stalin deliberately kept the Eastern European satellites separate. Thus until his death in 1953 Comecon played no effective role in co-ordinating trade, since it was restricted to such activities as registering bilateral agreements. After the mid-1950s, however, the theme became one of increasing plan co-ordination and economic integration, including investment, within Comecon. Critical events include the 1956 Twentieth Congress of the CPSU and the 1957 Treaty of Rome; Nello (1990: 6) notes how Comecon responded to events in the European Community in general, not least the 1992 single market. The problem was that the absence of markets left administrative (plan) methods as the chief way to achieve economic integration. This was complicated by the fact that Comecon was not a supranational planning agency. Khrushchev's 1962 suggestion to move towards such a system was thwarted by Romanian resistance especially. There existed an 'interested party principle' (declared in 1967), which allowed individual countries to opt out of any project. Individual countries still continued to draw up their own plans, although five-year trade agreements and five-year output plans coincided, and the former were reflected in the latter.[3] Nevertheless, the Soviet economist Ruslan Grinsberg described intra-Comecon trade as based on the 'left-over principle', where each country drew up its own five-year plan and then looked to partners for what it lacked (reported by Leslie Colitt in *FT*, 5 July 1988, p. 2). Holzman (1987: 21, 109) notes the antipathy to integration inherent in the command model, due to factors such as the unwillingness to close down large enterprises and whole industries and an aversion to migration and foreign ownership.

There were many cases and forms of co-operation, but they shared the common feature of being essentially the result of bureaucratic negotiations. The Stalinist years saw the adoption of stereotyped sectoral investment strategies that favoured heavy industry and involved reliance on mainly Soviet fuels and raw materials. In joint stock (mixed) companies between the Soviet Union and a country possessing ex-German assets, the Soviet Union usually contributed these assets and its partner an equivalent amount. They were a resented but effective means of exercising Soviet control over key areas of the economy, such as Romanian oil. They began to be dismantled after 1953, and compensation payments were waived after 1956.

Attempts to overcome these parallel industrial structures met with mixed results. In 1962 Romania flatly refused to specialize in primary products, for example, but there were many specialization agreements. These met with various degrees of success and focused mainly on finished goods, such as fork-lift trucks in Bulgaria, buses in Hungary and trams in Czechoslovakia. There was a relatively low degree of specialization in component manufacture. Administrative negotiations were undertaken by the standing commissions.

A common form of co-operation involved payment for plant and equipment, know-how and labour supplied by partner countries in the form of the output of the project. Thus the Soviet Union encouraged such activity in the construction of oil and gas pipelines and the mining of raw materials. The Druzhba (friendship) oil pipeline connects the Soviet Union with Poland, Czechoslovakia, Hungary and the GDR. The Soyuz (Union) gas pipeline, completed in 1978, runs from Orenburg in the Soviet Union to the Czech border, while the Yamburg pipeline from western Siberia to the Soviet Union's western border is the latest gas project. The Mir (Peace) is the united power grid. Many cases of joint R&D and standardization (including armaments) can be found. Comecon organizations such as Interchim indulged in the joint planning of particular sectors. Joint equity ventures went back as far as 1959, when the Haldex company

was formed by Poland and Hungary to extract coal and building materials from Polish slag heaps. It is interesting to note that all the Eastern European Comecon countries, except Honecker's GDR, permitted joint equity ventures with Western countries: Romania was the first in 1971 and the Soviet Union was the most recent, on 1 January 1987. Events such as the 1968 Warsaw Pact invasion of Czechoslovakia and the failure of economic reform in countries such as the Soviet Union in the 1960s led to a stress on economic co-ordination and integration.

The 1971 'Comprehensive (Complex) programme for the further extension and improvement of co-operation and development of socialist integration by CMEA member countries' to the year 1990 emphasized integration – increasing the division of labour, reducing differentials in development levels and widening markets – as opposed to trade co-ordination. Other aims included encouraging multilateral trade by increasing the use of hard currencies in settling trade imbalances. This blueprint for long-term co-operation covered a wide range of activities, including joint investment projects and the joint planning of individual branches of the economy by 'interested' members. Harmonization of individual economic plans was to be enhanced by the submission of draft medium- and long-term plans to other members and to Comecon bodies for discussion. In 1976 the stress was on sectoral integration, with joint planning for integration restricted to particular sectors. Administrative negotiation continued to be the mechanism of integration, however, and individual planning remained dominant.

The 1975 Agreed Plan for Multilateral Integration Measures, to apply to the 1976–80 plan era, related to ten major investment projects. These were to be integrated into the national plans of the countries involved in the form of 'special sections'. Eight were in the Soviet Union and mostly already begun, while most were related to Soviet energy, raw materials and transport (Wallace and Clarke 1986: 105). The second plan, adopted in 1981 for the period 1981–85, concerned the implementation of previously established target programmes in energy and raw materials, engineering, food supply, industrial consumer goods, and the Comecon transport network (Wallace and Clarke 1986: 105).

Comecon preoccupations and solutions

Eastern Europe generally followed a strategy of import-led (debt-led) growth during the 1970s, to stem the fall in growth rates experienced towards the end of the 1960s. Both investment and consumption growth targets were raised, the latter for incentives. Western credits were freely offered by banks, which were confident of Soviet backing and anxious to recycle OPEC surpluses, after the 1973–74 quadrupling of oil prices, to hitherto good repayers. These credits were sought in the hope of using imported capital goods, embodying the latest technology, to stimulate the hard currency exports needed to repay debt. Foreign technology was generally seen as a substitute for radical economic reform rather than the latter being a necessary accompaniment both for successful utilization and ongoing domestic innovation. Floating interest rates were the norm and they rose considerably during the second half of the 1970s. This factor, plus recession in the West, which restricted its importing and investment potential (the latter freeing OPEC funds), and unwarranted optimism about the prospects for exporting manufactured goods of sufficient quality to the West led to enormous repayment difficulties. The success in debt reduction in most countries in the early 1980s was due mainly to a contraction in imports. The Polish and Romanian debt rescheduling problems spilled over into the credit restrictions imposed on their CMEA partners. The Soviet Union was fortunate in having substantial gold reserves and hard currency earnings from oil and gas.

Comecon preoccupations were reflected in recent meetings, such as the 12–14 June 1984 summit of party leaders, the first time they had met since April 1969 on Comecon business. The Soviet grievance at being the major supplier of 'hard' goods lay behind the agreement that contained supplies of Soviet raw materials and energy at a given level (note that Soviet oil deliveries were reduced by about 10 per cent in 1982) were to be dependent on comparable products from its Eastern European partners. 'Comparable' meant world-quality machinery and equipment and industrial consumer goods, as well as food products and construction materials. The annual meeting of prime ministers in Havana on 29–31 October 1984 reiterated this agreement and witnessed a renewed Soviet call for East European investment in Soviet raw materials and fuels extraction, with the usual payment in output. Future developments should concentrate on co-ordination in electronics, automation, nuclear energy, raw materials and bio-technology. These choices reflected concern over a general technological lag behind the West and a general desire to encourage 'intensification', including the raising of labour productivity and the lowering of unit energy consumption.

The Warsaw meeting on 25–8 June 1985 to coincide with the start of the new five-year plans took an even longer general view, up to the year 2000. Themes included increased integration, reduction in energy and raw materials use, and the need to increase intra-Comecon innovation. The forty-first (special) session of the Comecon Council in Moscow on 17–18 December 1985 produced a 'comprehensive programme for scientific and technical progress', outlining a co-operative programme of co-ordinated R&D up to the year 2000. The chosen means included more co-ordinated investment plans and more joint ventures.

The emphasis on intensive growth was reflected in the goal of doubling labour productivity by means of a marked reduction in the input of energy and raw materials per unit of output and technological progress based largely on intra-Comecon efforts. Gorbachev stressed the need for 'technical independence from and invulnerability to pressure and blackmail by imperialism'. Soviet concern was enhanced by falling world oil prices after November 1985.

Five main areas were singled out for special attention: electronics, including the manufacture of super and personal computers and the use of optical fibres in communications systems; automation, including robots; nuclear energy, to reduce dependence on Soviet oil and gas; raw materials and components; and biotechnology. Three multilateral co-operation agreements were signed, namely computer-assisted production systems, optical fibre transmission systems and robot technology. The Complex Programme also stressed the need to develop 'direct links' between enterprises within Comecon.

The meeting of prime ministers on 3–4 November 1986 in Bucharest saw a repetition of the call for better-quality products to be supplied to the Soviet Union, increased direct links and closer co-operation in production and science and technology. The nuclear energy programme was to go ahead despite Chernobyl. Ryzhkov, the Soviet premier, complained that several members were still trying to deliver substandard commodities to the Soviet Union, called for increased direct links and joint enterprises, and criticized Comecon for being incapable in its present form of the effective co-ordination and integration needed to achieve intensification.[4]

This Comecon meeting was, without precedent, quickly followed by one involving the party leaders, the first since June 1984. A very secret affair, it ended with only a brief pledge to increase living standards through more intensive economic, scientific and technological co-operation. This was just one indication of the very real and continuing disagreements within the organization, not only Soviet complaints about quality, but other long-standing issues. These included the GDR's reluctance to integrate too closely with its less developed neighbours at the expense of its links with Western countries, especially the Federal Republic of Germany, and the pleas for preferential treatment and increased aid from Cuba, Vietnam and Mongolia.

The forty-third session of Comecon took place in Moscow on 13–14 October 1987. Particular attention was paid to the need to move in the direction of currency convertibility, itself seen as a way towards greater integration. While it was recognized that the transferable rouble was still to be used in most transactions in the foreseeable future, the plan was to try to make Comecon national currencies mutually convertible, especially through the medium of joint ventures. A common monetary unit that would be convertible into Western currencies was considered a long-term possibility.

At the meeting of Prime Ministers in Prague on 5–7 July 1988 the differing attitudes towards reform became very apparent, with Romania and the GDR taking a conservative position. The GDR stressed the need to co-ordinate five-year plans, while Romania actually failed to sign the final communiqué, which spoke of an 'understanding on gradually creating conditions for a mutual free movement of goods, services and other production factors, to create an integrated market'. The hope was for a gradual move towards a convertible rouble. Co-operation was to increase between the Soviet Union, Hungary, Poland and Czechoslovakia with Comecon reform in mind, while Cuba, Mongolia and Vietnam were promised increased technical assistance and credits. Nikolai Ryzhkov, the Soviet prime minister, informed the meeting that intra-Comecon trade had grown by only 4 per cent since 1985 and by 1.5 per cent in 1987.

Another more recent development was the stress on direct links between industrial enterprises, trading companies or research organizations in different Comecon countries for trade, joint production, component specialization or research and development. Experiments started in the early 1980s. This was seen as a move away from administrative methods of integration (more market-orientated co-operation, for instance, could help overcome the poor specialization in component supply, unreliable supply from abroad encouraging countries to be as self-sufficient as possible); a means of helping to avoid a repetition of the acute debt crisis of the early 1980s, by improving the supply of 'hard' goods; and a way of swapping surplus-deficit inputs. The problem with direct linkage was providing enterprises with sufficient independence in decision-making to make such co-operation meaningful. Ministries, in reality, often had a considerable influence in establishing links. The exchange of know-how seems to have been the dominant form of collaboration (Pekshev, *IHT*, 7 November 1988, p. 17). In March 1988, in a move towards overall convertibility, it was agreed that Czech and Soviet enterprises involved in such direct linkage (and joint ventures) could transact business in either the Soviet rouble or the Czech koruna (as opposed to the transferable rouble) at an exchange rate of 10.4 koruny to one rouble; particularly suitable transactions include one-off deliveries at agreed prices (Vetrovsky and Hrinda 1988: 13–14). Bulgarian and Soviet enterprises were also involved in a similar scheme. Joint equity ventures between socialist countries have a long history, but after 1 January 1987 these could be established on Soviet soil.

It is worth noting at this point that in recent years Czechoslovakia, the GDR, Poland and the Soviet Union imposed severe restrictions on the amount and types of consumer goods that were allowed to be taken out by visitors from socialist countries. This was due to domestic shortages as well as price distortions, and the lack of meaningful inconvertible currency exchange rates which led to the opportunity of resale profits for the individuals concerned, Polish citizens being particularly suspect.

No formal meeting of prime ministers took place in 1989, indicating disagreements. Meanwhile, Gorbachev's views were beginning to change, with increasing emphasis on the need to integrate with the world economy. In his speech to the UN General Assembly in December 1988 Gorbachev said that 'The world is becoming a single organism, and no country, regardless of its social system or economic status, is able to develop normally outside it'. In his speech in April 1989, during his visit to the UK, Gorbachev said that 'Our economic system presupposes the Soviet Union's closer integration with the world economy'. In December he said of Comecon that 'radical changes are needed in the mechanism of co-operation'. Without these changes 'it is inconceivable to accomplish one of the main tasks of the present day – to integrate gradually the economies of our countries into the all-European and world structures'.

A radical reform of Comecon was now in the air. The Soviet Prime Minister, Ryzhkov, proposed, on 13 December 1989, that Comecon trade 'starting in 1991, be based on current world prices and in convertible currency'. The communiqué of the annual meeting of prime ministers in Sofia, held 9–10 January 1990,

> underlined the absolute necessity of a decisive renewal of the whole system of mutual co-operation, of the mechanisms of multilateral co-operation within the Comecon framework, the fundamental renewal of the activities of the council, a verification of the functions and aims, and the preparations of a new statute that would reflect the current and future needs of co-operation for Comecon countries.

The speed of adjustment to a new system was, however, immediately the subject of disagreement, e.g. the Soviet Union suggested three years and Czechoslovakia five years.

A commission was established to review the whole organization of Comecon. At the Prague meeting on 27 March 1990 it was proposed to abolish multilateral co-operation, and plan co-ordination. Instead, bilateral trade and co-operation should be emphasized. The Secretariat should be reduced to the role of an 'information centre' (similar to the OECD), where research was carried out and statistical reports were drawn up. Disagreements centred on a number of points, e.g. countries like Poland and Czechoslovakia thought that individual members should be able to join other organizations like the EC or EFTA. The Soviet Union, on the other hand, disagreed and thought that Comecon itself should continue to have the right to make agreements with other bodies. Countries like Hungary, Czechoslovakia and Poland thought that preferential terms should not automatically be given to Cuba, Mongolia and Vietnam, but that aid should be on a bilateral basis (they also thought that those poorer countries should be excluded from any replacement body for Comecon).

One of the major problems of moving towards hard currency trading at current market prices is that the producers of 'hard' goods (e.g. Soviet oil) benefit disproportionately (it has been estimated that in 1990 Eastern European countries paid an average of only $6.50 per barrel of Soviet crude oil: Deutsche Bank, *Focus Eastern Europe,* September 1991, no. 22, p. 4). The producers of 'soft' goods (e.g. poor-quality manufactures) lose out (at least in the short run, because it takes time to adapt) because of the difficulty of selling not only in the West but also in Comecon countries under the new circumstances. This has led to another disagreement, with countries such as Czechoslovakia, Poland and Hungary demanding compensation, on the grounds that they were forced into the situation of being suppliers of manufactures to the Soviet Union.

The Executive Committee met in Moscow in early January 1991 and on the 5th approved proposals for the radical overhaul of the system of economic co-operation by member states. This included a draft charter for a new (transitional) body called the Organization for International Economic Co-operation to replace Comecon. A small secretariat and the two banks should remain, but the committees should go. Members are committed to 'market principles' and integration into the world economy and into regional economic groupings. Co-operation is to be on a market basis, between individual enterprises or within specific industries. Representatives of member governments are to be called whenever necessary. The drastically reduced functions include consultation and information, helping to solve regional infrastructural and environmental problems, supervising remaining trade agreements, and residual questions relating to trade restrictions. The forty-sixth and final meeting of Comecon was held in Budapest on 28 June 1991, Comecon being disbanded in a practical sense within ninety days (i.e. by 28 September; time was needed, for example, to discuss issues such as the disposal of property). The collapse of intra-Comecon trade, especially after the start of 1991, led to renewed interest in interim measures to help preserve trade and employment, e.g. barter trade (such as the July 1991 deal to swap Soviet oil for Polish medicines) and Western aid to finance East European exports to the Soviet Union. The following figures are provided by the United Nations Economic Commission for Europe (1992: 85, 87): in 1991 the Soviet Union reduced imports from its former CMEA partners by 62 per cent; intra-CMEA trade fell by 15 per cent in 1990. In 1990 trade between the Soviet Union and Eastern Europe fell by around 10 per cent and intra-East European trade by almost twice as much (Brada and King 1992: 41). In 1990 the volume of Soviet exports to and imports from Eastern Europe fell by 26.9 per cent and 12.1 per cent respectively, while the respective figures for 1991 were -31.9 per cent and -41.2 per cent (*FT,* 20 March 1992, p. 3). The OECD estimated a greater than 50 per cent decline in the volume of intra-Comecon trade in 1991 (*OECD Economic Outlook,* June 1992, no. 51, p. 43). As a very rough approximation two-thirds of the output decline in 1991 in the Central and Eastern European countries was attributable to the combined effect of the collapse in intra-Comecon trade and deteriorating terms of trade because of the much higher prices for imported energy. This is an average figure, ranging from less than one-third in Romania to almost all of the decline in Bulgaria (p. 43).

COMECON AND THE WEST

Comecon and the European Community

The socialist countries accounted for one-third of the world's national income (Comecon one-quarter), but only 12 per cent of world trade (Aganbegyan 1989: 196). In 1986 the European Comecon countries accounted for 8.8 per cent of world exports and 7.9 per cent of world imports (Szamuely 1989: 162). East–West trade accounted for just 4 per cent of world trade (*FT*, 22 June 1988, p.2). Comecon accounted for only about 7 per cent of the EC's foreign trade, while the reverse trade figure was at least a third (*The Economist*, 18–24 June 1988, p. 56). In 1987 trade between the EC and Comecon amounted to $52 billion (*FT*, 20 December 1988, p. 3). Over 60 per cent of the CMEA's exports to the EC were fuels and raw materials (including raw materials used in the production of foodstuffs and condiments), and only about 7 per cent constituted machinery and equipment. In contrast, machinery accounted for more than 35 per cent of imports from the EC (Sychov, *CDSP*, 1988, vol. XL, no. 25, p. 21).

Between 1957 (Treaty of Rome) and the mid-1970s, the EC was dismissed as the economic wing of Nato and a tool of Western imperialism and multinational corporations (Nello argues that Brezhnev recognized the reality of the EC in a 1972 speech and officials met from the summer of 1973 onwards: 1990: 7). While 1975 did not signify recognition, the signing of the Helsinki Accords saw Soviet and EC officials beginning to deal with particular problems, such as allegations of dumping. CMEA–EC talks began in 1977, but were broken off in 1981. The causes included the cooling post-Afghanistan atmosphere, conflicting interests – the Soviet Union wanted Comecon–EC trade negotiations, while the EC insisted on

negotiations with individual Comecon countries, with organization-to-organization talks confined to marginal issues like environmental protection (including nuclear safety), information exchange and industrial standards. Comecon was not a supranational body and, unlike the EC, ironically, had no common commercial policy that it could enforce.

On 14 June 1985 a letter was sent by Vyacheslav Sychov (Secretary General of Comecon) to Jacques Delors (President of the European Commission) calling for a recommencement of talks. Agreement was reached in September 1985 and talks resumed a year later. The 24 November 1986 letter received by Willy de Clercq (the EC Commissioner for External Relations) signified a major breakthrough in that Comecon conceded the EC argument that mutual diplomatic recognition should be coupled with EC negotiations with individual countries. Subsequent talks, starting in March 1987, however, ran into difficulties over the question of West Berlin. The Treaty of Rome explicitly included West Berlin as part of the EC, while the Soviet Union argued that the 1971 Quadripartite Agreement on Berlin precluded this. A joint declaration was eventually signed on 25 June 1988, the problem being solved by agreement to consider European Community territory as that defined by the Treaty of Rome and to state that the 1971 agreement was unaffected. In October Comecon listed eight main areas for negotiation, namely technical standards, environmental protection, transport, science and technology, energy, nuclear power, statistics, and economic forecasting.

The European Community signed a trade pact with Romania in 1980.[5] In April 1989, however, the EC formally suspended talks on a full trade and economic agreement because of Ceausescu's poor human rights record. In contrast, favourable treatment was promised countries like Poland (in the light of the Round Table Agreement). A ten-year trade (including agricultural products) and co-operation accord (including science but excluding technology) between Hungary and the EC was signed on 26 September 1988, with quotas on Hungarian imports into the EC being removed in three stages over the period up to the end of 1995. Dumping regulations still applied, however, while Hungary agreed to improve access to EC products and reduce the use of barter. The agreement did not apply to coal and steel or products covered by the multifibre agreement; mutual agricultural concessions were to be considered. On 19 December 1988 a four-year agreement on a number of industrial goods was signed by Czechoslovakia and the EC, involving increased imports and the supply of improved information by the former and quota concessions by the latter. Poland signed a five-year agreement in September 1989 and the Soviet Union a ten-year trade and co-operation accord in December. As a result of the upheavals in Eastern Europe in 1989, the EC has considerably improved on these concessions e.g. on 7 May 1990 a ten-year trade and economic agreement was signed with Czechoslovakia, while Hungary's and Poland's textile quotas have been increased (the date for the abolition of other quotas has also been brought forward). A trade and co-operation agreement with the GDR was initialled in March 1990, but this was quickly subsumed by German economic and monetary union on 1 July. On 3 April 1990 a trade and economic co-operation accord was signed with Bulgaria. On 1 August 1990 the EC announced a new type of association agreement intended to tie the free countries more closely to the EC, e.g. offering the prospect of a EFTA-type status. EC membership is seen as a distant but feasible goal.

On 30 September 1991 the EC granted increased quotas for beef, lamb and mutton from Czechoslovakia, Hungary and Poland, although sales to the Soviet Union financed by the EC would count as part of these quotas. On 22 November 1991 the EC and these three countries initialled an association accord, which was formally signed on 16 December. The accord not only envisaged the gradual dismantling of trade barriers after 1 March 1992 but also called for the freer movement of people and capital, and was seen as a necessary stage on the way to possible full membership of the EC (this was not guaranteed). The EC would reduce its trade barriers before the three. The Commerzbank (*The Economist*, 18 April 1992, p. 84) describes the accord in more detail: the abolition of tariffs on most manufactured goods, giving full and immediate access to EC markets; almost half Eastern Europe's current exports to the EC come from agriculture, textiles, steel and coal, but EC markets would only gradually be opened to these goods. Trade restrictions would be eliminated by the year 2000, with the exception of those relating to agricultural products. On 17 April 1992 the three formed the Central European Co-operation Committee as a mechanism to remove trade barriers between them and to help ultimate entry into the EC.

Dumping[6]

In trade between market economies, 'dumping' usually refers to a situation where a country exports a product at a price below its home price, or below its cost of production when there are no domestic sales, and undercuts a similar good produced in the importing country. The difficulties in proving allegations are normally great, but pale in comparison with cases involving market and command economies, given the way in which prices and exchange rates are determined in the latter. Western countries have used a number of additional criteria in their trading relations with command economies, including the prices of similar products in 'comparable' countries, estimated costs of production, and the trade weighted average prices of a number of exporting countries. Holzman (1976, 1987: Chapter 4, Chapter 6) suggests that, since foreign trade corporations in socialist economies are not interested in market disruption for its own sake and are simply forced to sell for what the Western market will bear, it is important to distinguish between short-run, crisis sales, justifying countervailing measures, and long-run supply at relatively low prices.

Co-ordinating Committee on Multilateral Export Controls

COCOM, a Paris-based organization, was set up in 1950 and includes all the Nato countries (except Iceland) plus Japan and Australia. The aim is to prevent the export of goods and know-how (computers and computer software, for instance), that could be used for military purposes. Exemption sales need unanimous approval. Until November 1985 listed items were updated every three years, but since then there has been a continuous review. This reflects the rapidity of technological change and the increasing overlap in the civilian and military use of technologies in fields such as telecommunications and computers. In October 1985 an advisory body called STEM (Security and Technology Experts' Meetings) was established, reflecting this increasing complexity. There have been changes in targets over time, in terms of products and countries. The rules governing the export of non-sophisticated personal computers (e.g. for educational use), have been relaxed, while separate, less strict lists were drawn up for China. The ending of the Cold War has naturally been reflected in a softening of COCOM restrictions. The 6–7 June 1990 meeting produced a new 'core list' of eight categories where strict controls apply (development and production of electronic systems; advanced materials; machine tools; telecommunications; sensor systems and lasers; navigation equipment and avionics; marine technology; computers and propulsion systems). The 23–4 May 1991 meeting finally decided on nine categories (ten were mooted at one time), the new list to come into effect on 1 September that year. The new system means that exports are not prevented unless the items are on the list: previously there was a general presumption that high technology items were banned unless permission was given. The collapse of the Warsaw Pact has meant that individual countries are treated differently, e.g. Poland, Hungary and Czechoslovakia were soon allowed to buy from the core list provided the items were deemed to be solely for civilian use.

CONCLUSION

The main aim in devoting a separate chapter to foreign trade is to avoid tedious repetition of the severe endemic difficulties experienced by command economies in conducting international trade between themselves and with the West. The traditional system is a state monopoly of foreign trade and payments, the purpose being to help carry out party policy and to shield the domestic economy from the world economy, thus isolating the domestic production unit. Inefficient domestic prices and arbitrarily determined exchange rates forced the use of (modified) world market prices. Comecon was analysed in the following ways: the reasons for the predominance of bilateral trade, such as currency and commodity inconvertibility; the forms of co-operation and integration; and preoccupations and solutions, such as Soviet complaints about the poor quality of partner manufactures in return for energy and raw materials, and the more recent stress on direct links between producing units in different countries.

The collapse of the socialist regimes in Eastern Europe brought about the demise of Comecon, an organization plagued with extreme difficulties in conducting trade between planning economies. Trading in hard currency and at current world prices took place after 1 October 1990.

NOTES

1. The Soviet Union was exceptional in that it frequently ran up long-term overall surpluses, while supplying hard goods in exchange for soft.
2. Western citizens, such as tourists, diplomats, exchange students and sales representatives, could either use their own currencies to buy scarce consumer goods in 'hard currency shops', or could exchange them for Comecon currencies to buy those goods and services available in ordinary sales outlets. This introduced an active element in the determination of tourist exchange rates, in contrast to commercial ones.
3. Annual trade plans were more detailed than the five-year protocols and had to exhibit flexibility because of the frequency with which annual output plans were changed.
4. This echoed Gorbachev's criticism at the 1986 Congress of the CPSU that Comecon had too many 'committees and commissions' and neglected 'economic levers, initiatives, socialist entrepreneurship and workers' collectives'.
5. The normal sequence was a trade agreement as a possible prelude to a full co-operation accord, which could include joint investment projects and technology transfer.
6. The following, as socialist countries, were, full members ('contracting parties') of GATT, with entry dates in brackets: Cuba (founding member in 1947); Czechoslovakia (founding member); Hungary (1973); Poland (1967); Romania (1971); Yugoslavia (1966). Bulgaria (observer status in 1967) and China (joined and left in 1950) applied in 1986, while on 15 August of that year the Soviet Union formally requested (in vain) observer status (see van Brabant 1988). The Soviet Union was granted observer status on 16 May 1990. Although there are obvious problems with planned economies being members, the relatively small size of the East European countries made compromise much easier than in the case of the Soviet Union and China. Concessions asked of planned economies include increases in imports. Hungary, Poland, Romania and Yugoslavia were members of both the IMF and the World Bank (Romania joined the World Bank in 1972 and its affiliate the International Finance Corporation on 23 March 1990). The Soviet Union applied for full membership of the IMF and World Bank in July 1991; special status in both organizations was recommended at the G7 conference held 15–17 July 1991 in London.

FURTHER READING

Comisso, D., and Tyson, L. (eds) (1986) *International Organisation*, 40, no. 2, (spring): 187–598, devoted to the response of the socialist economies to international disturbances.

The Economist Survey on Comecon, 20 April 1985.

Ellman, M. (1989a) *Socialist Planning*, 2nd edn, London: Cambridge University Press, Chapter 9.

The Financial Times Survey on East–West Trade, 13 December 1988.

Holzman, F. (1987) *The Economics of Soviet Bloc Trade and Finance*, Boulder CO and London: Westview Press. See especially the Introduction (pp. 1–29) and Chapter 4 (pp.91–112).

Korbonski, A. (1990a) 'CMEA, economic integration, and perestroika, 1949–1989', *Studies in Comparative Communism*, vol. XXIII, no. 1.

Smith, A. (1983) *The Planned Economies of Eastern Europe*, London: Croom Helm.

——(1987) 'Gorbachev and the world – the economic side', in D. Dyker (ed.) *The Soviet Union under Gorbachev: Prospects for Reform*, London: Croom Helm.

Van Brabant, J. (1980) *Socialist Economic Integration*, London: Cambridge University Press.

——(1988) 'Planned economies in the GATT framework: the Soviet case', *Soviet Economy*, 4 (January-March).

——(1989) *Economic Integration in Eastern Europe*, London: Harvester Wheatsheaf.

Wallace, W., and Clarke, R. (1986) *Comecon, Trade and the West*, London: Frances Pinter.

3

THE SOVIET UNION

ECONOMIC REFORM

Reasons for economic reform

The serious micro-economic problems associated with the neglect of user need, understatement of productive capacity, hoarding of inputs, storming, and an anti-innovation bias, have already been discussed at length in Chapter 1.[1] Mention should also be made of the 'scattering' (excessive spread) of resources (*raspilenie sredstv*), construction projects whose completion times were excessive relative both to plan norms and to those taken in the West. Various factors were responsible for this:

1. The greater ease involved in obtaining resources to complete projects (whose prospective benefits are typically exaggerated and whose initial cost estimates are understated), as opposed to starting them, encourages overbidding; supply difficulties make it necessary to keep options open.

2. The absence of a capital charge before the mid-1960s.

3. The tendency of output-orientated indicators to reward starting more than finishing.

4. The ambitions of self-interested departments.

5. The absence of the threat of bankruptcy in the event of investment failure.

6. New plants do not jeopardize short-term plan fulfilment, as does innovation (Winiecki 1988a: 18).

The serious environmental damage associated with the command planning system also deserves attention. It is ironic that pollution is considered to be an example of *market* failure, but it is not difficult to explain in the Soviet context. Reasons include the stress on output growth at all cost, the armaments race (especially nuclear weapons), the self-interest of the various groups in the economy, secrecy and the lack of any effective opposition groups, and the lack of suitable technology.

Obstacles to reform

Gorbachev himself listed a number of obstacles to reform. In a 17 May 1990 speech he mentioned the conservative nature of the Soviet people: 'The problem with the Soviet Union is the people's conservative way of thinking, their dogmatism . . . Changing people's mind is the most difficult thing. *Perestroika* depends on public opinion and it is conservative.' He frequently attacked the 'bureaucracy' in general and the branch ministries in particular. Gregory (1989a, b) draws an interesting distinction between *Khozyaistvenniki* (persons who actually allocate resources and are held responsible for the results, e.g. enterprise directors and ministers) and *Apparatchiki* (persons who issue instructions to or make rules for the resource allocators (e.g. the head of a finance department in the Ministry of Finance and persons in responsible positions in the planning department of Gosplan). Gregory argues that the *Apparatchiki* stand to lose more from reform,

Table 3.1 The Soviet Union: average annual rates of growth of NMP, GNP and GDP (%)

Measure	1951–55	1956–60	1961–65	1966–70	1971–75	1976–80	1981–85	1986	1987	1988	1989	1990	1991	1992
NMP	11.0	9.2	6.0	7.1	5.1	3.9	3.2	4.1	2.3	4.4	3.0	–4.0	–15.0	
GNP														
Joint Economic Committee of the US Congress	5.5	–	5.1	5.2	3.8	2.7	2.4	3.9	0.5	1.5	–	–	–	
CIA	–	–	–	5.1	3.0	2.3	1.9	3.8	1.3	1.5	1.4	–	–	
Ofer		5.7 (1950–60)	5.2 (1960–70)		3.7 (1970–75)	2.6 (1975–80)	2.0 (1980–85)							
UNECE (GDP)								–	2.9	5.5	3.0	–2.3	–17.0	
IMF (GDP)												–0.4	–9.0	–18.2 (forecast)

Sources: Schroeder (1986:20); Ofer (1987: 1778); D. Dyker *The Soviet Economy*, London: Crosby Lockwood, 1976, p. 18; Z. Fallenbuchl in *Canadian Slavonic Papers*, vol. XXX, no. 3, 1988 p. 306; *CDSP*, vol. XLII, no. 9, 1990, p. 17; vol. XLIV, no. 1, 1992 p. 5; Hanson P. (1990a:110); *Economic Affairs*, vol. 10, no. 6, p. 8;United Nations Economic Commission for Europe (1992:1, 105); IMF, *World Economic Outlook* (April 1992); *FT* (23 April 1992, p. 6;17 September 1992, p.6).

because they have fewer suitable skills than the *Khozyaistvenniki*; the latter have developed negotiating skills and personal connections in dealing with real-world problems, and are, therefore, more adaptable. Another interesting notion is that the Soviet Union's vast mineral wealth, especially oil, enabled the country to postpone serious economic reforms.

At the macro-economic level, the Soviet economy became more complex and experienced declining rates of growth of net material product (NMP),[2] as can be seen in Table 3.1. Official figures for the annual average rate of growth of NMP[3] show a falling trend. Aganbegyan (1988: 177) considers that, after taking account of factors such as hidden price increases, economic development came to a standstill at a point between the 1970s and 1980s. Western calculations, though lower and differing among themselves, also show this downward trend[4]. In the late 1980s the economy entered a state of crisis, with negative growth starting in 1990 according to official figures.

Soviet growth was of an 'extensive' type (largely due to increases in inputs, rather than to greater efficiency in the use of inputs, i.e. increasing factor productivity). Gregory and Stuart (1990: 488) estimate that only one-third of growth was accounted for by a rise in efficiency, compared with around two-thirds in the West. Ofer concludes that during the period 1928–85 the growth of factor productivity accounted for only 24 per cent of total GNP growth, falling to 20 per cent in the post-war period and to zero from 1970 on, when productivity growth stagnated or even became negative. Aganbegyan gives the following figures for the proportion of economic development arising from the growth of resources: 1971–85, two-thirds (thus only a third occurred because of an increase in efficiency); 1971–75, three-quarters; 1976–80, two-thirds; 1981–85, three-fifths (1988b: 10–11, 73). The drying up of the traditional sources of inputs[5] put massive pressure on the Soviet Union to adopt a more 'intensive' pattern of growth. The fall in the world price of oil at the end of 1985 reduced badly needed hard currency earnings (oil alone accounted for over 60 per cent of the total) and added to the pressure for reform.

Industrial reform

It is easy to be overwhelmed by the vast number of amendments that have taken place, but the system had not changed fundamentally by the end of the 1980s. Stalin's death in 1953 and Khrushchev's denunciation of the cult of personality at the famous Twentieth Party Congress in 1956 were landmark events, but debate about economic reform surged after the publication of Liberman's article in *Pravda* (9 September 1962). Liberman wanted to ensure that the interests of society and of the enterprise coincided. His proposals were often vague, but involved ending 'petty tutelage' over enterprises by allowing management greater decision-making powers over details (deliveries, main assortment and profit would remain as plan indicators), while profitability, subject to fulfilling the other indicators, was to determine the amount of retained profit feeding the incentive funds. Reform experiments started in 1964 with the Bolshevichka and Mayak clothing plants, for which sales (the result of directly negotiated contracts with retail outlets) and profitability were the main targets and which were allowed greater contact with customers and some limited scope for price alteration. The experiments were expanded in 1965. These preceded the 1965 Kosygin (then prime minister) reforms, which were originally to be applied to all industrial enterprises by 1968 and to the rest of the non-agricultural sectors of the economy by 1970.

Essential features of this reform included a restoration of Gosplan's powers; ministries and *glavki* beginning to operate on a *khozraschyot* basis; a reduction in the traditionally large number of success indicators to only eight, with the aim of decentralizing decision-making to a limited extent (for example, over assortment details); talk, hopelessly optimistic in the light of the retention of materials allocation more or less intact, of letting decentralized investment eventually amount to 20 per cent of the total; moving, without a timetable, towards wholesale trade. The indicators were value of sales (as opposed to gross output); profit (usually profitability, but sometimes profit increases); main assortment; wage fund; contributions to and receipts from the state budget; centralized investment and the introduction of new productive capacity; basic tasks for the introduction of new techniques; and material supply obligations. Profitability and the percentage increase in either sales or profits were to determine retained profits, although subject to fulfilment of the other indicators (note that profit was seen as a measure of the efficiency with which the other indicators were achieved). Three incentive funds were fed, namely the material incentive, socio-cultural and housing, and production development. Even these mild reform measures (a glance at the indicators show how all important areas of decision-making were still centrally controlled) had been whittled away by the end of the decade. Only the Ministry of Instrument-making, Automation Equipment and Control Systems and several glavki were on *khozraschyot* by 1970. Materials supply remained and 'sales' was not a significant improvement in conditions of acute supply scarcity. There was no radical price reform. It is worth noting Rubin's empirical study, however, which concludes that the 1965 reforms led to meaningful increases in managerial discretion over the wage fund and labour utilization (Rubin 1990: 490).

The old familiar problems remained unsolved, including plan changes and ratchet effects. The latter were supposed to be overcome by the use of more stable and uniform norms associated with the enhanced role of the five-year plan: in reality norms came to be reassessed on an annual basis and were differentiated for each enterprise (Aganbegyan 1988a: 59). Ministries continued to meddle. Hewett makes the important point that this is inevitable as long as ministries are held responsible for the performance of their enterprises (1988: 97); ministries still had to meet gross output targets, for instance (1988: 240). Aganbegyan points out that reform was only partially applied – for example, the attempt to transfer the new system to construction was not successful (1988a: 62). The reforms envisaged a movement towards long-term credits and away from capital grants. By 1974, however, bank credit accounted for less than 8.0 per cent of total industrial centralized investment finance (Dyker 1988: 92). Labour was still hoarded, although mention should be made of the 1967 Shchekino (chemical complex) experiment to help combat this problem. Here manpower reduction was reflected in increased bonus payments to the remaining workforce based on a given percentage of the wages saved (for a more detailed analysis see Arnot 1988). A more recent variation involved the railway system, beginning with the one in Byelorussia. Here the benefit accrued in the form of an increase in the tariff element of wage, supposedly less subject to ministerial interference (Trehub 1987: 10).

During the 1970s emphasis was given to improving (rather than decentralizing) management and planning by means of a movement towards an integrated, computerized information and control system. Extra success indicators were imposed on enterprises (such as labour productivity in 1973) owing to wage increases considerably exceeding productivity increases and, in 1971–72, the low percentage of output meeting world quality standards. Indicators such as main products in physical terms remained important. Decentralized investment was actually abandoned in 1976 because of supply problems. After the mid-1970s the material incentive fund was linked to contract fulfilment (still relatively ineffective in a sellers' market, it should be noted), with sales revenue reduced in the event of contract violations; the payment of managerial bonuses linked to other plan targets was also made conditional on contract fulfilment (Kroll 1988: 359).

The 1973 decree designated the 'production association' (*proizvodstvennoe obedineniye*) as the main production unit. These were mainly horizontal amalgamations of enterprises and were of three types, all on a *khozraschyot* basis: (1) production associations, subsequently comprising about four enterprises on average; (2) science–production associations, with integrated R&D institutes; and (3) industrial (administrative) associations, financed by profit deductions from enterprises and a replacement for the *glavki* (although the aim was for a more homogeneous enterprise membership). In 1984 the first two accounted for about half of both industrial output and employment (Nove 1986: 72); the remainder were taken care of by independent enterprises, mostly coming under industrial associations. The chief benefits were seen as the streamlining of the planning system by a reduction in the number of units to be centrally controlled, economies of scale, and encouragement given to technical progress. The average size of associations or enterprises was relatively large, at more than 800 workers (Aganbegyan 1988a: 168).

'Counter-plans' (*vstrechnye plany*), introduced in 1971, were a device to overcome managerial preference for 'slack plans', to induce enterprises to adopt more demanding targets than those set out in their five-year plans. Under this plan bonuses for fulfilment were higher than for overfulfilment of original targets. The problem was that managers now had a greater incentive to bargain for even lower initial targets, and ministries continued to alter plans in reality. In 1978 enterprises had to submit counter-plans when the regular plans were formulated in order to overcome supply problems; by 1981 only 7 per cent of industrial enterprises were offering counter-plans (Bleaney 1988: 60, quoting Bornstein).

There was a resurgence of interest in net output to combat the excessive use of components and materials. Experiments involving 'normative net output' (NNO) can be traced back to the 1960s. This is the sum of *required* (specified in centrally determined norms, as opposed to actual) wage costs, social insurance, and profit. The idea is that a reduction in non-labour inputs and less than norm expenditure on wages will increase profit and, therefore, incentive funds. Normative net output is a sort of 'shadow' price that can be used to determine the entire NNO for the enterprise by multiplying it by actual output. The 1979 decree used this concept both as an indicator and as a unit of measurement (for labour productivity and quality mix, for example). Three main indicators determined bonuses: labour productivity, quality mix, and fulfilment of delivery plans in terms of the volume of the most important products according to supply contracts. Other indicators, however, included volume of output in physical terms of the most important products, sales, profit, cost reduction, investment and the introduction of new techniques. Norms, used to identify inefficiencies, were tightened and greatly expanded in number to encourage greater efficiency in the use of inputs. Renewed emphasis was given to five-year plans. The idea here was that annual plans should be firmly based on the five-year plan. More stable norms should be fixed, for example for payments out of profit to the state budget, in order to overcome the 'free remainder' problem. This remains after the capital charge, rental charge and incentive fund retentions have been deducted from gross profit and renders fines for contract violation, for example, meaningless, since the sum would have gone to the state anyway. The decree saw the ultimate transfer to 'full' *khozraschyot*, covering investment as well as current expenditures and state obligations from own revenue.

There was an upgrading in the role of both counter-plans and of 'comprehensive' or 'programme goal' approaches to planning and management. These would deal with problems such as those relating to technological innovation and/or to the regions, and cross-sectoral boundaries. Pre-Gorbachev examples included the May 1982 Food Programme and the

November 1982 Energy Programme. On 26 August 1987 a programme was announced for the development of the area from Lake Baikal to the Pacific Ocean up to the end of the century (served by the Baikal–Amur railway). Another so-called 'territorial production complex' was based on the west Siberian oil and gas fields. A major problem was the lack of authority of the co-ordinating agencies, since production units were still subject to ministerial control (Nove 1986: 68).

There was increasing stress on worker brigades in enterprises after 1979, with the proportion of the industrial workforce affected increasing from 34 per cent to 71.7 per cent in 1984 (Slider 1987: 394–5) and 77 per cent in 1986 (Gregory and Stuart 1990: 270). In 1987 80 per cent of the workforce in industry and construction was affected, although the economic accountability form covered only a third of brigades in industry and around half in construction (*CDSP*, vol. XL, no. 10, 1988, p. 21); in 1989 the figure for industry was a little over a half (Schroeder 1992: 229). These groups of about twenty workers typically set their own work schedules according to assigned tasks and with supplied inputs. The aim was to increase incentives and discipline because of payment by results (such as completed houses) and powers to distribute collective bonuses among themselves, with workers disciplining themselves in effect through peer pressure. The experiment started in 1970 in the construction industry, where brigades benefited from a share in any savings achieved, but also bore any losses (Arnot 1988: 203).

The Andropov era

Andropov (November 1982–February 1984) succeeded Brezhnev (who, in turn, had succeeded Khrushchev in October 1964) as General Secretary of the CPSU. His short period of office, during which he was ill, was mainly significant for the impact he made on his protégé, Gorbachev. Andropov stressed order and discipline, running campaigns against absenteeism from work (even

involving a six-week police drive), drunkenness and corruption. He was a supporter of improved economic management. He also emphasized the need for a strong link between remuneration and both effort and skills. In the July 1983 decree, which began to be implemented on 1 January 1984 in two all-union (Heavy and Transport Engineering, and Electrotechnical Industry) and three republican ministries (Food Industry in the Ukraine, Light Industry in Byelorussia, and Local Industry in Lithuania), the main enterprise success indicators were contractual deliveries (in the sense that only sales that satisfied contracts were valid), labour productivity, cost reduction, the introduction of science and technology, profit, exports, and quality mix. At least 60 per cent of managerial bonuses depended on contractual deliveries (Taga 1989: 100). The Socio-cultural Fund was linked to the growth of labour productivity (measured by NNO). Stable norms were to be fixed for a five-year period, such as those relating the wage fund to the growth of NNO (thus linking pay and performance). Prices could be increased by up to 30 per cent for product improvements. Decentralized investment was reinstated and financed out of the development fund, depreciation reserves and credits, while preferential input supply was to be guaranteed. Wage fund economies accruing through job rationalization schemes were to be used to reward suitably skilled and productive workers. Efficient enterprises were not to be penalized as a means of supporting weaker brethren.

The Chernenko era

Chernenko (General Secretary February 1984–March 1985) cautiously echoed Andropov's call for greater efficiency, effort, organization, order and discipline. The Andropov reform was extended in 1985, with 12 per cent of industrial output affected by the start of the year. It was to be applied to all industry in January 1987. Dyker summarizes the Gorbachev July 1985 follow-on measures: the payment of managerial bonuses for other reasons should not be dependent on the fulfilment of contractual deliveries, as under the Andropov scheme; a system of price surcharges and discounts related to quality of products (including exportables); fines for delivering or the costs of correcting defective products to affect the bonus fund adversely (1987: 69–70). In June 1986 new measures were adopted in order to strengthen contract fulfilment. For example, if suppliers refused to sign contracts relating to the delivery of goods specified in planning orders, such goods would count as unfulfilled delivery obligations; and delivery obligations had to be totally met before any bonus was paid to managers who had fulfilled the total sales plan (Kroll 1988: 360).

The Gorbachev era

After he was appointed General Secretary on 11 March 1985 Mikhail Gorbachev profoundly altered the Soviet Union's domestic political situation and international relations. Terms familiar even to Western ears are: (1) *perestroika* or 'restructuring' of the whole of economic and social life, that is, all-around economic and social reforms; 'acceleration' (*uskorenie*) of growth was emphasized in the first few years, but attention then began to be focused on economic reform and its need for more stable conditions; (2) *glasnost* ('having a voice', openness); and (3) 'democratization'. The connection is that there has to be open admission of problems before reforms can be introduced to overcome them, with *glasnost* and democratization seen as the prerequisites for successful restructuring. Acknowledgement of past errors also helps ward off the threat of a return to the old system (Gregory and Stuart 1990: 466–9). Gorbachev highlighted the relative stagnation (*zastoi*) of the Brezhnev period; in June 1987 Gorbachev talked about it being a 'pre-crisis' period. The era became formally known as the 'period of stagnation'. Gorbachev (1987: 18–19) claimed a loss of momentum, especially in the latter half of the 1970s, and a fall in growth rates

to a level close to economic stagnation by the start of the 1980s.

One of the most significant features of the Gorbachev era was how political reforms leapt ahead of economic reform, although Gorbachev personally swung like a pendulum between the political poles in order to achieve his long-term goals (see Appendix 3.2 for a more detailed description of political events). Embryonic political parties (such as 'popular fronts') turned into openly independent parties. In a 13 January 1990 speech Gorbachev commented that 'I do not see any tragedy in a multi-party system . . .', and 7 February saw the formal end of one-party rule with the abolition of Article 6 of the 1977 Soviet Constitution; this defined the communist party as 'the leading and guiding force of Soviet society and the nucleus of its political system, of all state organizations and public organizations . . .' (the 1936 constitution referred to the party as the 'leading core'). The Supreme Soviet passed the necessary legislation allowing a multi-party system on 9 October 1990. Eastern Europe was set free by Gorbachev's refusal to use Soviet troops to suppress the demonstrations in late 1989. Serious economic reform had to wait until the 'Basic Directions for the Stabilization of the Economy and the Change-over to the Market' were adopted by the Supreme Soviet on 19 October 1990. With the very existence of the country under threat from some republics trying to secede in haste, economic reform took a back seat to preserving the union in the autumn of 1990. A greater degree of central control in general was seen as a prerequisite for further reforms:

the main thing right now is to strengthen state and public order and discipline and stabilize the situation so that people can live and work in peace, deal with the difficult problems facing us, and unfailingly push ahead with reforms, rather than turning back and looking for answers in the past. We shall not find them there.

(Gorbachev, Izvestia, 20 December 1990, p. 2).

A few months earlier (24 September 1990) the Supreme Soviet voted to allow Gorbachev to implement economic reform by presidential decree until 31 March 1992, although the decrees had to be in accordance with the constitution; they could be issued 'unless the USSR Supreme Soviet deems it necessary to establish different rules or recommends to the President of the USSR that a decision he has made should be changed or rescinded'. Ensuring that decrees are actually implemented, however, was a different matter. In April 1991 Gorbachev swung back to the centre ground of politics in order to promote economic reform.

GORBACHEV'S REMEDIES: A CHRONOLOGICAL ANALYSIS

The 1985 Party Programme (outline of party policy to the year 2000) contrasted strikingly with Khrushchev's utopian 1961 version: 'a communist society will, in the main, be built by 1980'. More realistic, though still ambitious, targets were set. For instance, aggregate output was to double by the year 2000 (achieved mainly by means of 'intensification') and individual housing was to be available for practically every family. (Note that a new party programme was to have been discussed at a special party congress, which Gorbachev proposed, on 25 July 1991, to be held towards the end of 1991 or in early 1992. The draft proposals included reference to the following: a federation of sovereign republics; a mixed market economy integrated into the world economy and with strong social protection; the party taking 'a positive attitude to the useful work of private entrepreneurs so long as it is within the law'; the abandonment of the focus on the working class; parliamentary democracy; and the inclusion '. . . in our ideological arsenal [of] the whole wealth of Soviet and world socialist and democratic thought'. The failure of the August 1991 coup, of course, led to the demise of the party and its programme. (See, for example, Gorbachev's speech in *CDSP*, 1991, vol. XLIII, no. 30.) Many of the proposals below were outlined in the 1985 programme and were subsequently extended and elaborated upon:

The need to create a new 'psychology of economic activity'

Gorbachev attacked what he called the peculiar psychology of the Brezhnev period ('how to improve things without changing anything') and the prevalence of inertia, bureaucracy, irresponsibility, bribery, theft and parasitism. What was needed was increased discipline, effort, responsibility and accountability. Practical steps taken included the anti-alcoholism campaign, which involved restrictions on hours and the number of sales outlets and rising prices. The policy was subsequently seen as a mistake as a result of problems such as loss of budgetary revenue, illegal distilling and the consequent sugar shortages. Enhanced importance was also given to cost accounting, which led to bankruptcies in a few cases (e.g. in March 1987 the Leningrad Building Association actually closed one of its enterprises for failing to meet its targets for costs, completion times and quality, and transferred its 2,000 workers to other jobs). Unemployment rose and unemployment benefit became payable: the terms of the January 1988 decree were subsequently improved and a new system began operating on 1 July 1991.

Economic management

Certain broad themes in Gorbachev's early reform strategy were discernible.

1. An increase in the decision-making powers exercised by the centre and by the production units at the expense of the obstructive ministries. This 'two-link' management system or 'double-thrust strategy' involved a concentration of and hence improved control over strategic decisions at the centre and delegation of operational matters to production units. The latter should face fewer obligatory targets and

have the ability to sell above-plan output to other enterprises or to the public. There should be greater financial accountability and a greater use of economic levers for indirect steering, inducing economic agents to perform in desired ways. The essence of *perestroika* lay in the transition from administrative to economic methods of management, with a greatly enhanced role for prices, finance, credit and work incentives (Aganbegyan 1988: 23). At the Nineteenth Party Conference in 1988 Gorbachev stressed the need for the party to refrain from interference in the day-to-day management of the economy, for the party to be freed from 'economic-administrative' functions and to shift to 'political methods of leadership' (*CDSP*, 1988, vol. XL, no. 30, p. 4). An important theme at the conference was that political reform was a prerequisite for successful economic reform. At a special plenum of the Central Committee held on 30 September 1988 six new 'commissions' were set up, for socio-economic, agricultural, personnel, ideological, foreign policy and legal affairs. These replaced or subsumed the twenty-two departments that supervised and tended to duplicate ministries. The commissions were headed by Central Committee Secretaries who were also Politburo members. They were involved in decision-making and reform implementation, but were, supposedly, to avoid the day-to-day interference associated with the departments.

2. Greater decision-making autonomy was to be allowed to production units involved in light industry, services and retail trade (fewer plan targets, greater ability to react to changes in demand) than to those in the heavy and defence industries.

3. There was to be greater regional decision-making autonomy, especially in the production of consumer goods, since local planning authorities are in a much better position to know local circumstances and needs, and in the provision of improved infrastructure to attract a larger and more stable labour force (to Siberia, for instance). In 1988, for example, the Estonian Republic was granted greater autonomy in a number of branches of industry (only 10 per cent of industry was then locally controlled) and in fuel and energy, transport, public services, education, culture, forestry, and the environment. Local authorities were to be allowed to receive a portion of the profits of enterprises within their areas plus a part of the turnover tax revenue derived from the sale of local goods, excluding wine, spirits and tobacco (Aganbegyan 1988b: 121). The three Baltic republics of Estonia, Latvia and Lithuania, Belorussia, the city of Moscow, Sverdlovsk province and the Tatar Autonomous Republic were to be the subject of experiments involving 'territorial self-financing'. Revenue sources were to be formed on the basis of long-term normatives, including receipts from all enterprises located in these areas (Gostev, *CDSP*, 1988, vol. XL, no. 45, p. 11). The 27 November 1989 law allowed the Baltic republics, as of 1 January 1990, greater control of natural resources, tax revenue (the federal budget would keep half the taxes paid by centrally administered enterprises), economic development plans, and monetary policy (*FT*, 28 November 1989, p. 3). At the Nineteenth Party Conference in 1988 it was decided that republics generally should be on a *khozraschyot* basis, which would enable them to determine net contributions to or receipts from the central budget. On 23 March 1990 the Supreme Soviet endorsed a bill (effective 1 January 1991) allowing republics generally increased authority as regards taxation, investment and resource management.

A stronger link between the performance of production units and workers and their remuneration

Gorbachev criticized the practice of wage and salary levels being maintained even when unsaleable goods were produced, the payment of automatic bonuses and equal pay for the conscientious and the negligent/incompetent, and the existence of inadequate differentials between skilled and unskilled. 'It is hardly a secret to anyone that many people even now receive wages for just showing up at work and hold their posts without having their actual labour contribution taken into account' (18 February 1988 speech, *CDSP*, 1988, vol. XL, no. 7, p. 7). Graduate engineers and technicians in construction receive slightly lower pay than manual workers, while in industry the pay of engineers and technicians is only 10 – 15 per cent higher than that of a labourer (Aganbegyan 1988a: 167). Thirty years ago scientists were the highest paid members of the workforce; they are now relegated to the fourth rank, behind workers in transport, construction and industry (Kostakov 1988: 96). Shcherbakov describes how bonuses were primarily linked to work norms rather than enterprise plans. Since work norms were infrequently revised, they were increasingly easy to overfulfil, despite problems with plan fulfilment (Shcherbakov 1987: 76). The incentive fund, on average, made up only a twelfth of the wage fund (in the best enterprises, such as Sumy, the fund reaching 15 per cent: Aganbegyan 1988b: 162).

Practical steps taken included basing the remuneration of scientists, technicians and industrial designers more (up to 50 per cent of pay) on their contribution to research and its application to industry, than on academic degree and length of service. Over the period 1986–90 pay scales for engineers, technicians and white-collar workers were to be increased by 30–35 per cent, while those of manual workers were to rise by only 20–25 per cent (Aganbegyan 1988b: 167). Teachers' salaries were to be raised by 30 per cent and those of doctors and medical workers by 40 per cent (Aganbegyan 1988:18–19). The September 1986 wage decree increased the proportion of total income accounted for by basic wage rates and widened the rates to take account of skills (Chapman 1988: 339, 1989: 24–7). Basic wage and salary rates were to account for 70–5 per cent of earnings generally, although for wage earners the share would be below 50 per cent in some sectors. Average basic wage and salary rates were to be raised as follows: wage earners 20–5 per cent; clerical workers and professionals such as management and engineers 30–5 per cent; leading professionals such as designers and technologists as much as 40–5 per cent. Management was to have a greater say about the amount of supplements to be added to basic rates and there was to be no maximum on individual bonuses (there were to be group ceilings). Output would have to meet quality standards and enterprises were to finance wage increases themselves. The targets for consumer goods and services set for the 1986–90 five-year plan were revised upwards in August 1988 for the sake of material incentives.

On 1 January 1989 a progressive wage tax was introduced (Hewett 1989: 63). Any increases in the wage fund above 3 per cent a year were to be taxed progressively: 50 per cent on increases in the range 3–5 per cent; 66.7 per cent for 5–7 per cent; and 75 per cent above 7 per cent. Exceptions were made, e.g. the system would not apply to consumer goods and services. Aganbegyan draws our attention to the labour tax; enterprises usually paid about 300 roubles per person per annum, although the sum was lower where labour was abundant (1989: 83). The problem of the increasing proportion of wages accounted for by benefits via 'social consumption funds' (such as education, health, housing, pensions, benefits and subsidies) and largely financed by the state budget is highlighted by Shcherbakov (1991: 230); in 1965 for every rouble of wages forty-six kopeks were received from the social consumption funds, while by 1984 sixty-nine kopeks were received. This weakened the link between effort and reward. Increasing amounts of goods and services were also distributed to workers at the workplace itself. Standing (1991) argues in favour of taxing enterprises not on money wage increases but on all *non-wage* payments beyond 25 per cent of total remuneration, for incentive purposes.

The more relaxed political atmosphere led to

a fragmentation of the trade union structure. In July 1989, for example, there were widespread strikes by coal miners whose 'strike committees' by-passed the official trade union in putting forward their demands for better wages, supplies, and living and working conditions. On 9 October 1989 the Supreme Soviet passed a law relating to labour disputes. Strikes (excluding politically inspired ones) were officially permitted (if a majority of the workforce voted in favour and after a conciliation process), except in key sectors such as transport, communications, fuel, energy and defence (this did not prevent a further, albeit not very successful, miners' strike in July 1990). Embryonic independent trade unions proliferated in such forms as 'strike committees' and 'workers' clubs'. The Donbas Union of [industrial] Workers was formed in September 1989. An umbrella organization called the Confederation of Labour was set up at a congress held at the end of April 1990, and on 26 October 1990 coal miners established the Independent Trade Union of Miners. At its 23–7 October congress the official All-Union Central Council of Trade Unions was transformed into a looser General Confederation of Trade Unions. The coal miners began a widespread strike on 1 March 1991 (at its peak daily coal output was down by more than a third: some other groups of workers followed, e.g. in Byelorussia) in which political demands featured strongly, including Gorbachev's resignation. It was not until May that agreement was reached, the terms including a possible doubling of miners' wages (linked to productivity increases); the transfer of control to republican authorities (though the federal government still levies a tax) and the retention of a large proportion of hard currency earnings. On 23 April the Supreme Soviet passed an 'anti-crisis' programme, which included a moratorium on strikes until the end of 1991 and 'emergency regimes' in key sectors such as power and transport.

A need to increase the quality of production

The continuing concern with quality led to the establishment of the State Quality Commission (Gospriomka), subordinate to the State Committee for Standards and operative since 1 January 1987. Initially applied to 1,500 enterprises covering 20 per cent of industrial production, the commission's scope was then extended. This method of tackling the problem was adapted from the defence sector, and was still bureaucratic and able to refer only to existing designs, however obsolete. Nevertheless, many enterprises subjected to its scrutiny failed to meet production targets, and workers lost bonuses. This led to strikes. Those in October 1987 at a bus assembly plant in Likino and at the Chekhov bus station illustrated the problems of apportioning blame – workers cited faulty equipment and lack of spares. Gospriomka was allowed to wither away; it was abolished in the Russian republic in 1990 and in the Ukraine in 1991.

The need for intensive growth

Intensive growth involves output increases due largely to greater efficiency of input use, especially by means of the application of modern science and technology. An improvement in quality is another aspect. A practical result of this policy was that increasing emphasis was placed on modernizing the existing capital stock rather than enlarging it. Specifically, the idea was to raise the proportion of capital investment devoted to technical reconstruction from little more than a third to more than half over the period 1986–90 (Aganbegyan 1988b: 14). This meant increased priority for sectors such as machine tools, instrument making, electronics and electrical engineering. As discussed earlier, the initial enthusiasm for accelerating growth faded; it was not conducive to economic reform.

Industrial reform

Co-ordinating Bureaus were set up in order to streamline planning and management (reduction of petty interference at lower levels, overlapping, duplication, and narrow departmental interests), to further scientific and technical progress, to raise quality, to encourage specialization and to improve materials supply. These bureaus, which were influenced by organizations in the defence sector, were the following: Gosagroprom, the State Agro-industrial Committee, formed out of the merger of four ministries and a supply committee in November 1985; the Bureau for Machine Building (October 1985); the Bureau for the Fuel and Energy Complex (March 1986); and the USSR State Committee for Construction (September 1986). The latter three were formed in order to co-ordinate the activities of the various ministries involved. In June 1989 Ryzhkov outlined a plan to reduce the number of ministries in the 'basic' branches from fifty-two to thirty-two e.g. a single ministry of metallurgy and only four in machine building. A prime task would be to promote scientific and technical progress (*CDSP*, 1989, vol. XLI, no. 33).

The 1985 experiments at the (Afto) Vaz (Volga car plant) at Togliatti and the Frunze machine tool enterprise at Sumy were extended to another 200 enterprises at the beginning of 1987. The Vaz plant, for example, has now been included in the foreign trade decentralization reforms, but, even before that, 40 per cent of hard currency earnings were allowed to be retained for imports (later 70 per cent; Aganbegyan 1988b: 151). Delivery, productivity and quality indicators were important, and the bonuses dependent on them were paid out to work brigades for distribution to individuals.[6] Norms were stable (for five years), such as those relating to the distribution of net profit between the state budget, the ministry and the enterprise (47.5 per cent, 5.0 per cent and 47.5 per cent, respectively, in the case of the Frunze association). Major problems included the lack of control over prices and supply difficulties. At the Sumy plant the incentive fund accounted for a third of total labour remuneration (double the average), while the development fund amounted to 5 per cent of the value of the capital stock (Aganbegyan 1988b: 164). Under the Vaz/Sumy system the enterprise or association was responsible for nearly all investment, except for entirely new plants (Dyker 1988: 101). Ministries were not allowed to redistribute funds between enterprises (Dyker 1987: 75).

From 1 January 1987 five industrial ministries and thirty-seven individual and amalgamated enterprises were placed on 'full economic accounting' (*polny khozraschyot*). In principle expenditures (including investment) had to be covered from revenue earned (or credits borrowed) and ministries were not allowed to transfer profits from profitable to loss-making enterprises. (Åslund makes the point that, in fact, the centre financed some of the investments in production; 1989: 94.) Stable norms dictated the share of profits going to the state budget and that retained by the enterprise. On 1 January 1988 the Lvov Conveyor Combine in the Ukraine became the first enterprise to grant its workers a share (3 per cent) of monthly profit unrelated to the fulfilment of plan targets. This overcame the problem that non-fulfilment of targets might be due to external problems such as non-delivery of inputs (*FT*, 11 December 1987, p. 3).

In June 1987 a new Law on the State Enterprise (Association) was adopted.[7] There was to be a transitional period during 1988–90, and 1991–95 was to be the first full five-year plan period when the entire system was operational. Gosplan was to become the nation's 'economic headquarters', focusing on strategic matters, the main national economic proportions, inter-sectoral co-operation, long-term science and technology programmes, structural investment policy, and balance in the national economy (note that in May 1991 Gosplan was retitled the Ministry of Economics and Forecasting). These ideas were to be embodied in perspective plans of fifteen years' duration and five-year plans that were also to take into account the needs of enterprises as expressed via ministries and republics. Increasing use was to be made of economic levers to steer the economy indirectly, including competitive state contracts, prices (new wholesale prices were planned to be introduced on 1 January 1990 and new retail prices on 1 January 1991) and monetary policy.

Monetary policy was to be carried out in the context of the 1988 reorganization of the banking system. Gosbank was to assume a role more akin to a Western central bank, with more independent banks comprising the Industry and Construction Bank (Promstroibank), the Agro-industrial Bank (Agroprombank), the Bank for Housing and Municipal Services and Social Development (Zhilsotsbank), and the Bank of Labour Savings and Credit Services to the Population (Sberbank). The Bank for Foreign Economic Activity (Vneshekonombank) replaced the Foreign Trade Bank. Interest rates were to be raised and stricter control was to be exercised over the repayment of credits, with most capital expenditures eventually being financed out of enterprise revenues or bank credit. All banks were expected to be run profitably and credit allocation was to be influenced by the expected profitability of projects (Panova 1988). A major problem was that customers were allocated a sectoral bank. Co-operative banks have been set up since March 1989 to offer customers a choice and to encourage innovation. One early estimate put the number of joint stock commercial banks at around 100 by August 1989, e.g. the USSR Bank for the Development of the Automobile Industry; there is an initial statutory fund, but these banks are on full economic accounting and self-financing; loans are financed from deposits attracted and profits are earned on banking operations (*CDSP*, 1989, vol. XLI, no. 35, p. 24). By June 1990 there were 310 commercial, co-operative and industry-affiliated banks (*CDSP*, 1990, vol. XLII, no. 25, p. 28). David Lascelles (*FT* Survey, 12 March 1990, p. XII) divides the independent banks into three

categories: branch banks created and owned by large enterprises, e.g. the car industry; co-operative banks; and innovation banks, e.g. the Innovation Bank of Leningrad. But commercial banks still only account for less than 2 per cent of total banking assets. In 1989 it was agreed to set up the Moscow International Bank, the first joint venture with Western banks. The new banking law, given its first reading in October 1990, foresaw a federal banking structure run along US or German lines.

Gorbachev (1987: 33) defined the restructuring of economic management as a shift in emphasis from primarily administrative to primarily economic management methods at every level. Ministries were not supposed to interfere in the day-to-day operation of the enterprises or to redistribute profits from efficient to less efficient enterprises. They were to move to a full *khozraschyot* basis and deal with aspects such as meeting the demand for the output of the branch as a whole, long-term R & D programmes, increasing exports, improving quality, and labour retraining. The administrative associations and *glavki* were destined to be replaced by 'state production enterprises', which would operate on a *khozraschyot* basis and supervise a number of large enterprises and production associations involved in R&D, production, transport, and marketing of related products; the related firms may be in the same area (Schroeder 1988b: 185). To be more precise, the June 1987 decree saw a future in which the industrial structure would be characterized by a few hundred giant vertically integrated enterprises operating in national-level markets, and thousands of republican and local enterprises handling regional and local markets and some of the needs of the national enterprises (Hewett 1988: 331, 352). The first inter-branch state associations were created in 1988: Energomash (Power Machinery) and Tekhnokhim (Chemical Equipment) are based in Leningrad, and Kvantemp (Quantum Electromechanical Production) is based in Moscow (*CDSP*, 1989, vol. XLI, no. 5, p. 13). Kvantemp,

Table 3.2 The Soviet Union: statistical survey

Measure	1971	1981	1982	1983	1984	1985	1986	1987	1988	1989	1990	1991	1992 (May)
Gross debt ($billion)		26.5	26.7	23.6	22.5	28.0	33.1	36.5	40.9	48.0	57.5	65.3	72.0
Net debt ($billion)	0.6	18.1	16.7	12.5	11.2	14.9	18.3	22.4	25.6	32.8	54.2	61.5	
Share of world trade, 1986 (%)	5.0												
Joint equity ventures, end 1989	1,274 registered; 184 operating												
Independent co-operatives, 1987	0.3% of consumer goods production; 0.37% of public catering; 0.67% of the volume of consumer services sold												
Agricultural output, 1985 (%)			Collective farms 35				State farms 40				Private plots 25		
Population, 1990	290.1 million												

Sources: Aganbegyan (1988b: 148); CDSP, vol XL, no 22, 1988, p. 13; Schroeder (1988b: 180); FT, 31 January 1990, p.20; 18 April 1990, p. 3; 9 July 1991, p. 16; 13 February 1992, p. 2; IHT, 4 March 1988, p. 17; 26 January 1991, p. 9; C. Jones in The Banker, May 1991, p. 23; IMF et al. (1990: 50); European Economy: the Path of Reform in Central and Eastern Europe, Commission of the European Communities, Brussels, 1991, p. 278; Deutsche Bank (Focus: Eastern Europe, no. 53, 1992, p.9). For figures on rates of growth of NMP, GNP and GDP see Table 3.1.

for example, involves twenty-four widely-spread enterprises from three ministries, and employs 50,000 (*CDSP*, 1989, vol. XLI, no. 6, p. 25). Others include Gazprom and Norilsk Nickel.

Schroeder (1992: 221) cites some figures to illustrate the monopolistic structure of Soviet industry. In the mid-1980s the average industrial enterprise employed 834 workers, compared with 186 in Hungary and eighty-six in a sample of capitalist countries; in 1987 1.4 per cent of enterprises accounted for 33.6 per cent of industrial output. In 1987–88 73.4 per cent of the industrial labour force worked in enterprises employing more than 1,000 workers (Kroll 1991: 147). The comparable figure for the USA in 1985 was only 25.8 per cent and for Poland in 1986 51 per cent (Fischer 1992: 95). An investigation carried out by the State Statistical Committee in 1989 found that, out of 340 industrial product groupings, 209 were each produced by an enterprise controlling half the Union market, while 109 were produced by an enterprise monopolizing at least 90 per cent of the market (*CDSP*, 1990, vol. XLII, no. 35, p. 32). The picture varies according to industrial branch, however, being relatively low in consumer-orientated industries; by contrast, 80 per cent of the volume of output in machine building was accounted for by monopolists (Kroll 1991: 144–5). When the aim became a more radical shift to a market economy, a resolution was adopted by the Council of Ministers in August 1990 to demonopolize the economy: 'highly monopolized' structures could be broken up; enterprises accounting for more than 70 per cent of the market could be subject to price and other controls; 'a differentiated approach' would be taken towards those enterprises within the 35–70 per cent range, while there would be no controls below 35 per cent. In this context, it is worth noting the June 1989 small enterprise decree, which allowed large state enterprises and associations to create small subsidiary enterprises from separable production units able to respond more flexibly to changes in consumer demand (Kroll 1991: 160). Kroll attributes this to the example of the small-business sector in Western countries, but the Bulgarian experience should also be noted.

In the 1987 Law on the State Enterprise the association was the basic production unit, operating on the following principles.

1. 'Self-management' (*samoupravlenie*). The idea was that workforces would take a more active part in enterprise plan formulation and in the election of management.

2. 'Full economic accounting' and 'self-financing' (*samofinansirovanie*). Both operating costs and capital expenditures were to be covered out of revenue earned. Investment was normally to be financed out of retained profit or from credits that would have to be repaid out of earned revenue. Centralized investment was to be restricted to things like the creation of new branches of production, major projects, transport infrastructure and urban reconstruction (Aganbegyan 1988b: 120). The lack of automatic subsidies to loss-makers opened the door to bankruptcies in theory.

3. *Samookupaemost*. This entailed at least a minimum rate of return on investment financed from whatever source (Hewett 1988: 326).

Enterprises were able to choose between two basic models of wage determination. (1) The wage fund is directly related to normative net output (more specifically the wage fund is based on the previous year's wage bill adjusted to take account of the growth of labour productivity: Kushnirsky 1989: 530) and the residual is left for (priority) taxes and interest payments and, after that, for the enterprise funds. (2) Wage payments are the final residual after payments for taxes, interest and the enterprise funds according to norms (Hewett 1988: 331). Both the wage fund and retained profit thus appear as the residual in the distribution of 'gross income', which is defined as the difference between sales revenue and non-labour production costs; 'net income' of the enterprise consists of the sum of the wage fund plus retained profits (Kushnirsky 1989: 530). Because of the extra risk involved, in

1989 the latter was used in enterprises that accounted for only 7.7 per cent of industrial output (Schroeder 1992: 228). By May 1988 51.5 per cent of workers in the material branches of production were covered by the new pay conditions (Chapman 1988: 354). By the start of 1990 75 per cent of industrial personnel were covered (Schroeder 1992: 228).

By 1990 managerial personnel were meant to be elected by the whole membership of the enterprise labour collective, including the director, although the elected director had to be confirmed by the 'superior organ' (nominations seem to be controlled by the regional party organization) and the heads of enterprise sub-divisions such as foremen and brigade leaders had to be approved by the enterprise director (Bova 1987: 82). Bova also notes the 1983 Law on Labour Collectives, which made biannual general meetings of the labour collective compulsory, and created the legal requirement for the election of 'production conferences' (to discuss and evaluate enterprise operations in an advisory capacity) in all economic institutions of more than 300 employees (1987: 78). A new, elected body called the 'labour collective council', open to all members of the collective, operated between general meetings, dealing with such matters as improving labour discipline and training, the use of the incentive funds, and increasing productivity (Bova 1987: 82). In December 1989, however, Ryzhkov announced the end of the system whereby workers elected management.

Under the 1987 law the enterprise was to draw up its own annual and five-year plans and to conclude contracts, based on:

1. Control figures. These are broad, allegedly non-mandatory targets, such as output, investment, wages, profits and scientific and technological progress, emanating from the central five-year plan.

2. State orders (*goszakazy*). In Makarov's opinion, the state order was intended to be 'a contractual agreement between Gosplan, the ministries or the republican authorities on the one hand, and the enterprise on the other, with mutual obligations – in other words an economic contract, freely entered into by both sides . . . the intention is that state orders will not encompass anywhere near all of national output; rather they will be limited to ensuring supplies for the most important projects in the social sphere, state investment projects, and defence' (1988: 458). Thus, as far as obligations are concerned, the state body ensures input supply, foreign currency allocations, capital investments, and profitable sales (Aganbegyan 1988b: 113). The idea was that contracts should be competed for when the new system is well established (Aganbegyan 1988b: 113). Abalkin, too, stressed that state orders should be limited to satisfying high priority strategic and social needs, should be the most profitable orders to the enterprise, and should be awarded, as a rule, on a competitive basis (*CDSP*, 1988, vol. XL, no. 8, pp.16–17). State orders were supposed to account, on average, for only 50–70 per cent of production value (Åslund 1989: 124). Note that there are also quotas (*limity*) for investment capital and materials centrally distributed (p. 123).

3. Direct orders from customers (at negotiated prices), which were to become increasingly important.

4. Stable, long-term normatives (*normativy*) were to be fixed for at least a five-year period after 1991 and were to be uniform over entire branches and sectors, rather than being applicable to individual enterprises, as was the case during the transitional period. These related to the size of the wage fund, which was linked to enterprise performance, budgetary payments, charges for working capital, the use of natural resources and so on (charges on capital assets could vary from 0 per cent to 12 per cent), and to profit flows to the state and ministries and into the enterprise bonus, socio-cultural and investment funds. In general normatives for the formation of economic incentive funds were tied to profits and gross income.[8] But other targets had to be fulfilled: product assortment

and delivery plans were among the most important (Gregory 1989b: 4; Gregory and Stuart 1990: 470–1). The ultimate aim was to replace normatives relating to the formation of the wage fund and the distribution of profits with taxes and state benefits (Gorbachev's speech of 29 July 1988; *CDSP*, 1988, vol. XL, no. 30, p. 8).

Some amendments to the Law on the State Enterprise (Association) were published in *Pravda* (11 August 1989, pp. 1–2):

1. Enterprises were independently able to form concerns, consortia, inter-branch state participation and other large-scale organizational structures, including the participation of co-operatives and joint ventures with foreign firms. Enterprises maintained their economic independence within the new structures.

2. Enterprises had the right to extricate themselves from the subordination of branch and territorial administrations.

3. State orders should not reach 100 per cent of productive capacity. Conflicts between enterprises and higher bodies over orders were subject to arbitration.

4. The use of enterprise net income for investment and remuneration purposes was regulated by the tax system.

5. Enterprises had the right, in the prescribed manner, independently to engage in foreign trade, including that with capitalist and developing countries. Trade could be transacted on a commission basis or by means of a newly created foreign trade organization acting on a *khozraschyot* basis.

Wholesale trade (i.e. a market in non-labour inputs, in which purchases are made from Gossnab wholesale stores) was gradually to become, within five to six years, the basic form of material-technical supply (in 1988 wholesale trade accounted for 15 per cent of the total volume of sales of 'production-and-technical output': *CDSP*, 1989, vol. XLI, no. 5, p. 13). It was to account for around two-thirds of the volume of resources sold through the supply system by 1992 (*CDSP*, 1988, vol. XXXIX, no. 52, p. 6). Note, however, that the sectors accounting

for about a quarter of the economy (defence, energy and communications etc.), would still be subject to direct state contracts. Aganbegyan (1988b: 137–8) put the timetable for wholesale trade at 60 per cent of all production by 1990 and 80–90 per cent by 1992. This would need to be phased in gradually because of the current excess money holdings of enterprises and the lack of price reform. State orders were to gradually decline in importance in favour of direct ties between producer and consumer.

One novel scheme was the opening on 16 October 1990 of the Moscow Commodity, Raw Materials and Stock Exchange, where a wide range of goods can be exchanged by enterprises. The number of commodity exchanges has increased rapidly; one source cites a figure of 370 registered (*Izvestiya*, 8 August 1991, p. 2) and another more than 500 (*Moscow News*, 15–22 December 1991, p. 10). An oil exchange started in Moscow on 18 December 1991. In Tyumen 10 per cent of all oil and gas as of 1 January 1992 was at the disposal of local authorities and a further 10 per cent was at the disposal of the gas-oil producers; both can export half of this and sell the other half at free prices on the home market (*Moscow News*, 15–20 December 1991, p. 10). By March 1992 some 40 per cent of Russian oil was being sold through the oil exchanges (John Lloyd, *FT*, 26 March 1992, p. 40). One estimate puts the turnover through commodity exchanges as a whole towards the end of 1991 at 2.5–3 per cent of total wholesale turnover (*CDSP*, 1992, vol. XLIV, no. 1, p. 6).

Enterprises accounting for around 60 per cent of Soviet industrial output were operating under the new system of self-financing as of 1 January 1988. The others were to have been included by the start of the next five-year plan, but this was brought forward to the start of 1989 as a result of the Nineteenth Party Conference. State orders, in reality, turned out to be no different from the old plan orders and there are cases where they have taken up more than 100 per cent of enterprise capacity. Directors often accepted such high orders because they represented the only way of ensuring inputs, while many managers prefer guaranteed sales. Another cause is the fact that ministries were still held responsible for providing the goods specified in their product lists. State orders were also used to ensure the production of goods which were unprofitable owing to the distorted price system, e.g. low-priced goods for pensioners and children. In 1989 and 1990 virtually all manufactured consumer goods were under state orders and all enterprises had to produce consumer goods and services of some kind (Schroeder 1992: 226). There were reports of enterprises refusing to accept state orders, however (see *The Economist*, 24–30 September 1988, p. 66; *FT*, 20 September 1988, p. 1; 16 January 1989, p. 12; 12 March 1990, p. xiv; Åslund 1989: 125). The July 1988 decree limited the percentage of an enterprise's output that could be taken up by state orders to 67 per cent and restricted the ordering to Gosplan alone. The actual share of state orders was about 90 per cent in 1988 and the intention was to reduce the overall share to 40 per cent in 1989; they accounted for well over half of total industrial production in 1989 and 1990 (Schroeder 1992: 226). Vid (deputy chairman of Gosplan) envisaged a declining share between 1988 and 1989 for the following sectors: engineering (from 86 to 25 per cent); fuel and power (from 95 to 59.4 per cent); metallurgy (86 to 42 per cent); chemical and timber (87 to 34 per cent); light industry (96 to 34 per cent); and building materials (66 to 51 per cent) (IHT, 7 November 1988, p. 14). Aganbegyan (1989) envisaged state orders accounting for less than 50 per cent of output in 1990 (p. 14), and 20–30 per cent by 1995 (p. 172); they would then be limited to defence, national construction projects such as atomic power, exports, and subsidized consumer goods such as children's clothing (p. 100).

The situation deteriorated badly as the command economy disintegrated and a new, more market-orientated system failed to take its place

(see Table 3.1). The economy entered a 'supply-side' recession, one due not to lack of demand but to disruption of supply links. As Shatalin put it,

> the main trouble for the past two years has been that, in taking leave of the plan-and-command methods in the economy (or, to be more precise, in attempting to take leave of them), we have failed to fill the vacuum with market methods of management . . .
> (*CDSP*, 1990, vol. XLII, no. 17, p. 1).

The power to enforce central decisions declined (as well as the Communist Party's 'trouble-shooting' role at the local level) and enterprises and various lower levels of government increasingly gave priority to 'their' enterprises and engaged in direct barter (black market activities in general increased). On 19 December 1990 Ryzhkov talked of the established structures being destroyed, but 'nothing effective has so far been created in exchange. This has directly affected the economy where there is neither plan nor market.' In his resignation speech on 25 December 1991 President Gorbachev remarked that 'The old system fell apart even before the new system began to work'.

A presidential decree of 27 September 1990 ordered enterprises, until the end of 1991, to maintain existing economic links and to fulfil contractual obligations for the delivery of raw and other materials and component parts. In reference to local authorities failing to meet delivery obligations, the actions of bodies of power and management leading to the disorganization of economic links between enterprises was considered impermissible. The government was also authorized to take 'extraordinary' steps to ensure the efficient functioning of the railways and other 'life-supporting systems'. On 14 December 1990 a decree 'to prevent disruption of production' was published. Republics and enterprises were forbidden from concluding deals with domestic and foreign entities that prejudiced existing planned economic links. A follow-up decree of 12 April demanded that republican and local authorities should cease withholding deliveries to other parts of the country. The problem, however, was actually to enforce decrees, especially when federal and republican legislation clashed. The situation was exacerbated by the decline of foreign trade in 1990 and especially in 1991. Soviet trade with Eastern Europe fell by 25 per cent in 1990 (Shleifer and Vishny 1991: 342), while in 1991 exports to and imports from this area fell by 31.6 per cent and 41.2 per cent respectively (*FT*, 20 March 1992, p. 3).

Foreign trade reform

Aganbegyan (1988a: 141–2) gives some interesting general figures relating to Soviet foreign trade. In 1986 exports consisted of fuels, mainly oil and gas, and electricity (53 per cent); other raw materials such as ores and timber (9 per cent); and machines, equipment and vehicles (14 per cent). Imports comprised foodstuffs and raw materials (over 20 per cent), metals and manufactures (over 8 per cent), industrial goods for mass consumption (around 12 per cent) and machines, equipment and vehicles (a little more than a third). Exports account for 6 per cent of national income (Aganbegyan 1989: 186). While the Soviet Union's share of world industrial output was about 20 per cent, its share of world trade was only 5 per cent (Aganbegyan 1988b: 148); the socialist countries accounted for 67 per cent of the Soviet Union's foreign trade in 1986, the CMEA 60 per cent (Aganbegyan 1988b: 153).

Under a decree published on 23 September 1986, the Council of Ministers' State Foreign Economic Commission (SFEC) was set up to co-ordinate the activities of all organizations having economic, financial, cultural, scientific or technical relations with foreign countries, the aim being to streamline and improve management. A licensing system for exports and imports was employed and control was also

exercised by foreign exchange controls. In January 1988 the Ministry of Foreign Economic Relations was formed out of the Ministry of Foreign Trade (which had previously lost a number of foreign trade enterprises) and the State Committee on Foreign Economic Relations (whose responsibilities included armaments and overseas aid). It had twenty-five FTCs and its functions included issuing licences for foreign borrowing.

The first day of January 1987 saw the start of an experiment to foster direct links between Soviet and foreign organizations. Twenty ministries and departments (such as Gosagroprom, the Ministry of the Chemical Industry, and Gossnab) and seventy-six major individual enterprises (such as the Vaz plant and Uralmash, a heavy engineering plant in Sverdlovsk) and amalgamated enterprises were granted the right of direct participation on their own behalf in export-import transactions in the world market and to retain a variable portion of foreign exchange earnings. Later figures were 65 and 105 respectively (Yuri Pekshev, deputy chairman of the SFEC of the Council of Ministers, *IHT*, 7 November 1988, p. 13). In a 20 July 1990 speech, Ryzhkov gave a figure of around 14,000 enterprises and organizations having the right to enter the foreign market (*CDSP*, 1990, vol. XLII, no. 30, p. 6). The oil industry was given the right to sell a portion of its output directly on the world market (Quentin Peel, *FT*, 30 March 1990, p. 2). A major extension of the scheme was announced in December 1988: as of 1 April 1989 any state or co-operative enterprise whose output is competitive on the foreign market may trade independently. (Aganbegyan states that in the socialist world market every business can export independently; 1988a: 184.) They had their own foreign trade enterprises operating on an economic accounting basis and were self-supporting with regard to hard currency dealings. Credits from the Bank for Foreign Economic Activity had to be repaid and responsibility had to be taken for any losses incurred. Imports of capital goods to modernize plants were encouraged, although as of 1989 10 per cent of enterprise hard currency earnings were allowed to be used for imported consumer goods.

The background to these changes was the dependence of the Soviet Union on primary commodities, especially oil, sold for US dollars when exported to the West. The hope was to improve the quality and saleability of its manufactures in order to widen its sources (and types) of convertible currencies. This was partly a response to the fall in the price of oil in late 1985. The Soviet Union's net hard currency debt was $0.6 billion in 1971 (Holzman 1987: 5); $9 billion in 1980 (*EIU Country Profile*, 1989–90, p. 41); $28.2 billion in 1988 (when the debt-service ratio was 20 per cent) (Hewett 1989: 56); and $36.5 billion in 1989 (*FT*, 18 April 1990, p. 3), with a debt-service ratio of 25 per cent (*FT*, 8 June 1989, p. 1). At the end of 1990 net debt was $54.1 billion (Colin Jones, *The Banker*, May 1991, p. 23). As of 1 November 1989, the Soviet was owed 85.8 billion roubles, 43.8 billion by other socialist countries and 42 billion by developing countries (*CDSP*, 1990, vol. XLII, no. 9, p. 9).

One result of the decentralization of foreign trade decision-making was a serious delay in payments by Soviet enterprises from October 1989. At its peak this may have affected up to 10 per cent of trade payments with Western suppliers (Quentin Peel, *FT*, 18 May 1990, p. 4). By October 1990 more then 2.5 billion roubles had been paid off, but 2 billion roubles was still owed (Quentin Peel, *FT*, 10 October 1990, p. 3). More recent estimates put the trade debt at some $5 billion (*The Economist*, 16 March 1991, p. 97) and $3 billion (*IHT*, 26 September 1991, p. 9).

On 1 November 1989 a new dual exchange rate system was introduced. The current rate for commercial transactions was maintained, but the one for 'non-commercial transactions' by Soviet and foreign citizens (e.g. travel) involved a substantial devaluation in order to check black market dealings: the rouble was devalued from 0.6065 to 6.26 roubles to the US dollar; as of 1 April 1991 Soviet citizens had to pay 27.6 roubles per US dollar for travel purposes, while the ceiling of $200 remained. Note, however, that these 'non-commercial transactions' only accounted for a fraction of 1 per cent of foreign trade turnover (*CDSP*, 1989, vol. XLI, no. 43, p. 27). On 1 November 1990 the commercial rate of the rouble (used in foreign trade transactions) was devalued from 0.56 to 1.79 to the US dollar (the tourist rate was devalued from 32 to 47 roubles to the US dollar on 4 November 1991). Four rates were established: the commercial rate; the official rate (used for statistical purposes and for calculating the debt payments by developing countries); the tourist rate; and the market rate (fixed in auctions).

The first hard currency auction took place in early November 1989, organized by Vneshekonombank, in which Soviet state enterprises with surpluses were eligible sellers (joint ventures and co-operatives were excluded). These auctions, at an annual rate, amounted to less than half a percentage point of the hard currency import bill (Philip Hanson, *The Independent*, 20 August 1990, p. 9). As of 1 January 1991, foreign exchange markets were to be set up in Moscow, other major cities and the capitals of the fifteen republics 'for deals in foreign currency to be concluded at the market exchange rate'. Eligible participants were those organizations with a legal status in the Soviet Union (including co-operatives and joint ventures, the latter being able to exchange roubles for hard currency at the market rate and thus repatriate rouble profits), working through 'inter-bank operations, operations at currency exchange auctions and other forms permitted by legislation'. Those excluded were private citizens and foreign firms with no registered legal presence in the Soviet Union. Gosbank, the Ministry of Finance, Vneshekonombank and government ministries 'will take measures to support the rouble's rate against the other foreign currencies . . . [and] will use the currency resources of the Soviet government and the governments of the main republics as well as funds drawn from foreign banks'. As a results of these changes, the rouble became partially internally convertible.

A presidential decree issued on 2 November 1990 centralized the management of foreign currency earnings through 1991, partly to ensure that foreign debt obligations were met. All enterprises (state, co-operative and private), except partially or wholly foreign owned ones, had to sell 40 per cent of hard currency earnings to Vneshekonombank at the new commercial rate of exchange. Of the remainder 90 per cent had to be sold to a new Union-Republics Foreign Currency Committee (comprising representatives of the federal External Economic Commission and the heads of government of all the republics) and 10 per cent to republican foreign exchange committees (also at the commercial rate). The same decree also reasserted central control over the export and import of goods 'of state importance' (e.g. oil, gas, gold, diamonds and high-technology goods).

After 1 August 1990 Soviet citizens were able to hold hard currency and to spend it in special shops (a network was to be set up for use by individuals and enterprises). Accounts could be opened without having to explain where the hard currency came from (until then these accounts were restricted to those who had worked abroad or who were in contact with foreign companies).

Direct foreign investment

Joint equity ventures with Western companies were first permitted as of 1 January 1987 (*CDSP*, vol. XXXIX, no. 6, pp. 15–16, 23).[9] The exact initial terms varied from deal to deal, but joint ventures were free to determine their own output and input plans. Western ownership was restricted to a maximum of 49 per cent and the managing director had to be a Soviet citizen. In December 1988 it was decided to end the 49 per cent ceiling and to allow foreigners to become chairman of the management board or director-general. On 26 October 1990 100 per cent

foreign ownership was decreed, although land could only be leased, not purchased.

Problems included the inconvertibility of the rouble. Originally all foreign exchange outlays, including repatriated profits, had to stem from export revenue; hard currency loans also had to be repaid out of export earnings. It then became possible for export earnings to be more indirect, as in the case of the enterprise set up by the US company Honeywell and the Soviet Ministry of Mineral Fertilizers. The venture provided process control systems for fertilizer plants to help export their products. Subsequent amendments enabled the remittance of profits to be in hard currency or in kind. In mid-1988 agreement was reached to allow the foreign exchange earned by one venture to be transferred to another producing for the domestic market. For example, in the American Trade Consortium the Chevron Oil Company's exports supplied hard currency to its fellow members, that is, only the group as a whole needed to be self-financing in convertible currency earnings. After 1 January 1991 joint ventures were able to exchange roubles for hard currency at the market rate in foreign exchange markets in order to repatriate rouble profits (see above).

The Foreign Investment Law was passed by the Supreme Soviet on 5 July 1991, with the following provisions: 100 per cent foreign ownership was permitted; nationalization of foreign property was allowed only when it was 'in the interest of society' and when there was full compensation in hard currency; repatriation of profits in hard currency; foreign concessions were possible in the 'prospecting, development and exploitation' of natural resources; excluded areas of activity were defence, medical, social and moral; land could only be leased and not sold to foreigners; provided foreigners took at least a 15 per cent stake in a joint venture, export and import licences and taxes were removed; the relationship between federal and republican laws was not finalized, but republican authorities were able to provide extra inducements such as tax concessions and federal law was to take precedence if republican legislation offered worse conditions over a ten-year period.

The first agreement to be signed was between Intourist (the Soviet travel agency) and Finnair to refurbish the Hotel Berlin in Moscow (a hard currency earner). According to Ivan Ivanov, vice-chairman of the State Committee on External Economic Relations, the Soviet Union registered seventy joint ventures; six of these were actually operating (*Kommunist*, August 1988, no. 12, p. 38); eleven socialist countries were involved, including Hungary and Yugoslavia (p. 45). According to Hanson (1989: 10), these had to date brought in less than 0.1 per cent of the annual flow of investment. Private foreign investment amounted to only $3.15 billion between 1987 and 1990 (*IHT*, 21 August 1991, p. 9, quoting the Vienna Institute of Comparative Economic Studies). By the end of 1989 1,274 joint ventures had been registered, but only 184 were operational (Quentin Peel and Mark Nicholson, *FT*, 31 January 1990, p. 20). Of the 1,274, about 90 per cent were with the West; almost one-third were in 'trade, tourism and light industry'; 30 per cent were in consultancy and R & D; only 5 per cent were in engineering; and 4.4 per cent were in agricultural and food processing (Quentin Peel, *FT*, 1 February 1990, p. 5). A more recent figure gives 2,905 registered joint ventures; 1,027 were actually operating and employing 103,700 (John Lloyd, *FT*, 27 April 1991, p. 2). Upwards of 4,200 joint ventures had been registered by 1 July 1991, although only a third were engaged in production; joint ventures account for only 0.4 per cent of total industrial output (*Moscow News*, 27 October-3 November 1991, p. 11). There were proposals to set up special economic zones, such as in Vyborg (Gulf of Finland), Novgorod, Nakhodka (Far East), and the Black Sea area. None actually materialized, however, in the Gorbachev era.

Non-state activity

Although May 1986 saw a crackdown on illegally earned 'non-labour' income (checks on large items of expenditure, increased fines), the following year brought a considerable relaxation in the laws governing private and (independent and voluntary) co-operative activity.[10] The aim was to improve rapidly the supply of scarce consumer goods and services (and thus provide an incentive to work hard), to tap underemployed manpower, and to provide the state with tax and licence revenue from previously black market sources.

Originally co-operatives (minimum membership, three) involved the following types of people: housewives, students over sixteen years of age, pensioners and, to a limited extent, state employees on a part-time basis. The last were eligible in order to protect the labour-short state sector. The 1 July 1988 decree on co-operatives relaxed state regulations by allowing broader rights in price formation, although centralized prices were to remain for state orders and products made with state-allocated inputs; the expansion of activities to include homes, roads and cultural clubs; the issuing of shares to both members and contracted employees; involvement in foreign trade, although formal permission was then still required; lawsuits; joint ventures with state enterprises and foreign companies; and the hiring of full-time workers laid off by state enterprises. Premier Ryzhkov reported that in 1987 they accounted for 0.3 per cent of consumer goods production, 0.3 per cent of public catering and 0.6 per cent of the volume of consumer services sold (*CDSP*, 1988, vol. XL, no. 22, p. 13). By 1 July 1989 there were 133,000 operating co-operatives employing 2,900,000 people; they produced 2–3 per cent of all goods and services with only 1.5 per cent of the labour force (Jones and Moskoff 1989: 29). Slider (1991: 798–9) provides the following figures: 3.5 per cent of all employees worked in co-operatives by the start of 1990; the contribution of co-operatives to national output (goods and services) was only around one per cent in 1988, but increased to 4.4 per cent in 1989 (over 15 per cent of services); the number of co-operatives in operation rose from 3,709 in July 1987 to 209,700 in July 1990, while the number of people employed increased from 39,100 to 5,219,500 respectively. At the start of 1990 co-operatives produced a little over 1 per cent of industrial production (Schroeder 1992: 223). Of the 6.1 million people employed in co-operatives at the end of 1990 about 4.2 million could be regarded as employed full-time (Oxenstierna 1992: 48). In the first half of 1991 there were 255,000 operating co-operatives employing 6.5 million people (Johnson and Kroll 1991: 287). It is important to note that the 1987 Law on the State Enterprise (Association) allowed state enterprises to set up co-operatives. These frequently operated under a lease agreement with the parent enterprise or branch ministry, but in some cases this led to employee buy-outs. A large percentage of the growth of the co-operative sector in the Soviet Union was accounted for by the reorganization of existing state enterprises and their sub-units rather than the formation of entirely fresh co-operatives. Co-operatives were a means by which state enterprises could enjoy greater autonomy. By the end of 1990 over 80 per cent of co-operatives were attached to state enterprises and they accounted for more than 80 per cent of the value of goods and sevices sold by co-operatives (Johnson and Kroll 1991: 287).

The October 1987 regulations specifically banned publishing and printing co-operatives. A 30 December 1988 decree listed the following banned areas: the making and selling of firearms, explosives, alcohol, religious artefacts, and most jewellery; the production of films and videos, the sale of which was authorized only under contract with a state enterprise (the buying and processing of secondary materials can be conducted only on these terms also); schools; and medical diagnostic work, obstetrics and the treatment of cancer and venereal disease. Shortly after it was announced that co-operatives fulfilling state orders and those charging prices no higher than those of the state would be given preference in terms of bank credit, input supply, and tax rates. In October 1989 further restrictions were placed upon co-operatives (CDSP, 1989, vol. XLI, no. 42, pp. 18–19): local authorities could fix maximum prices for basic consumer goods; state-determined prices applied where output was sold to enterprises under contract in fulfilment of a state order or made from materials supplied from state sources; state prices applied for goods purchased from state retail outlets and for goods imported.

'Individual labour activity' (under the law on which came into effect 1 May 1987) was permitted in certain defined fields (the local authorities decided precisely which might be allowed through the issue of licences). These included house, car and appliance repairs; public catering; tailoring; furniture making; private cars used as taxis; dressmaking; shoes; private tuition in subjects on official curricula; restaurants; pottery and ceramics; medical consultancy; nursing; and translation and secretarial work. Activities still banned included trade in goods produced by others, copying of video tapes, gambling, weapons repair, and discotheque management.

Individual labour activity was generally confined to 'jointly residing family members' over the age of sixteen, housewives, students, pensioners, the disabled and all citizens over the age of eighteen who have a state job (i.e. part-timers). Thus, there were restrictions in the shape of a general ban on the employment of non-family workers and on the use of sophisticated automated equipment. There was a system of progressive taxation: zero tax on income of less than 70 roubles a month; 13 per cent, the highest marginal rate on state sector wages and salaries, on income between 70 and 250 roubles a month, 20 to 50 per cent up to 500 roubles a month, and 65 per cent on income over 500 roubles a month. Note that a high licence fee could be substituted where income was difficult to check, such as in the case of taxi services. Resentment was caused by the high prices inevitably associated with deficient supply in the short run, while there was a problem with supplies, state enterprises being encouraged to provide recycled and waste materials.

In November 1986 only 97,000 private entrepreneurs were registered (Åslund 1989: 150); by the end of 1987 there were just over 300,000 (p. 167). A more recent official figure was less than half a million people (Hanson 1989: 4).

A property law was passed by the Supreme Soviet on 6 March and by the Congress of People's Deputies on 13 March 1990, and took effect on 1 July 1990 (*CDSP*, 1990, vol. XLII, no. 12, pp. 21–5). All forms of property were to be treated equally. Reference was made to 'individual' or 'citizens'' property (rather than 'private' property, since this was associated with exploitation, unemployment and social insecurity). Properties such as small enterprises, restaurants and hairdressers were affected, with the size of different types of property to be fixed by the republics or autonomous republics. The hiring of labour was allowed, provided pay and conditions were in accordance with Soviet law. Individuals were able to own buildings and machinery (e.g. houses, lorries, tractors and farm equipment), but land could only be leased (leases could be inherited, but not sold or sub-let). The bill also allowed the creation of 'subsidiary businesses' (allied to a state-owned enterprise).

A private enterprise regulation was adopted by the Council of Ministers on 9 August 1990 and passed by the Supreme Soviet the following February. There was need for registration, but the licence application had to receive an answer from the district council within two weeks; refusal could only be on the basis of excluded activities (medicines, weapons, pornography and jewellery) and recourse to the courts was possible to ensure that this requirement was met. Tax rebates were available for the first two years, and tax exemptions for business training or staff retraining. The ceilings on hired employees were as follows: industrial and construction enterprises 200; scientific and scientific

service enterprises 100; other enterprises in the production sphere 50; enterprises in the non-production sphere 25; retail trade enterprises 15 (*CDSP*, 1990, vol. XLII, no. 32, p. 21). The USSR State Property Fund (a state holding company) was set up to play a role in 'destatizing' federally controlled enterprises. Note that the decree provided for the formation of small enterprises from the structural units and subdivisions of existing state enterprises (Johnson and Kroll 1991: 288).

On 22 October 1990 the Supreme Soviet passed legislation imposing harsher penalties on various forms of black marketeering: speculation ('the purchasing of goods intended for the trade in the state sector and their resale for the purpose of profiteering'); the unauthorized sale of goods from depots and warehouses; the deliberate concealment of goods from customers; private price fixing by groups or individuals with access to scarce goods; and the selling of goods intended for the state sector at prices above the established limit (Mary Dejevsky, *The Times*, 23 October 1990, p. 13).

The measures being considered to promote 'destatization' or 'destatification' (*razgosudar-stvleniye*) and privatization prior to the abortive coup in August 1991 have now been overtaken, but it is worth noting the embryonic features. 'Destatization' is a broader concept than privatization: in the initial stages joint stock companies are formed, whose shares can be held by state holding companies; leasing, employee ownership and co-operative ownership could all follow, in addition to conventional privatization. The state was to retain direct control of defence industries, power plants connected to the national grid, railways, air-and seaports, communications and space research. About 50 per cent of the 'fixed production assets of enterprises of union subordination were to be removed from the sphere of direct state management' by the end of the first phase (end 1992) and 60–70 per cent by the end of the second phase (end 1995) (*CDSP*, 1991, vol. XLIII, no. 26, p. 13). Activities such as services were to be given priority in the first phase. The exact ownership of shares was not decided, but, in principle, the free distribution of shares was to be relatively small compared with sales (partly because of the need to absorb the monetary overhang). Preference was to be given to domestic citizens over foreigners as regards sales, to workers over other citizens as regards free distribution, and to co-operative ownership and to leasing over individual sales. The 12 August 1991 decree set up Soyuzgosfond to oversee the process. The republics were to be able to adapt the basic guidelines to some undetermined degree, e.g. the Russian republic was to give much greater priority to the free distribution of vouchers to workers and citizens (previous legislation had already allowed the sale of land to farmers).

In May 1990 the Kamaz vehicle enterprise was selected as the first large state enterprise to become a joint stock company. In March 1991 28 per cent of the shares were sold, mainly to customers such as transport enterprises and collective farms.

PRICES

Historically the infrequent wholesale price changes usually involved increases in order to reflect rising costs and to reduce subsidies, the aim being to allow most enterprises to operate profitably. Prices, however, were generally fixed on a cost-plus basis, although the profit mark-up was later on capital and was high enough to allow for the payment of a capital charge. This was introduced in 1965 and normally at 6 per cent of the undepreciated value of an enterprise's fixed and working capital. The charge was not formally counted as a cost, but was reflected in price indirectly through the higher mark-up. Rental charges were later paid by those industrial enterprises partic- ularly favourably situated and/or endowed with modern machinery.

Deviations from standard practice included a move towards marginal cost pricing in extrac-tive industries (oil, natural gas and iron ore). In 1967, for example, oil prices were based on the costs of average-sized enterprises working under worse-than-average conditions, with the more favourably situated fields making rental payments to the state.

In 1964 'analogue' pricing was introduced generally for new and improved products. This involved pricing in relation to improvements, in the form of higher quality, lower costs and so on, compared with the most analogous product. A lower limit (roughly the old cost-plus basis) and an upper limit (based on the improvements in use value) were fixed, with prices set nearer the upper limit the greater the shortage of the products, thus taking some account of demand. There also developed a system of producer price surcharges for above-standard quality and price reductions for below-standard goods.

In the 1987 proposals on wholesale prices it was envisaged that goods such as fuels, energy and basic raw materials would still be state-determined and raised substantially, relating them to world levels in order to encourage more efficient use (Aganbegyan put fuel prices and those of agricultural products at two or three times lower than world prices, and other raw materials at about half; 1989: 31). There would be scope, however, for prices between pur-chaser and supplier to be above the norm when quality was higher or innovation was involved. Thus a three-tier system of prices was in prospect: fixed (for basic goods), maximum (or range), and free (for luxury goods). For new machinery, equipment and instruments, greater use was made of negotiated 'contract prices', although these were still to be within state guidelines (Bornstein 1988: 329). At the 1986 congress Gorbachev suggested that prices should reflect not only outlays but also the consumer properties of goods, the degree to which they met the needs of society and con-sumer demand. He personally attacked the receipt of the same price for goods of very different quality and also criticized:

1. The high subsidies on basic foodstuffs at

the retail level. In 1989 total food subsidies amounted to 87.8 billion roubles or 17.8 per cent of total planned budgetary expenditure. These benefited higher-income families disproportionately because of their higher spending on these items and exacerbated shortages by diverting household expenditure. Hanson (1990a: 113) estimates that the elimination of food subsidies would increase food prices in state retail outlets by an average of 40 per cent; subsidies on food prices amount to over 10 per cent of NMP (p. 116). Valentin Pavlov (then chairman of the State Committee for Prices) revealed that subsidies were first introduced for food in 1965 (*FT*, 26 November 1987, p. 3). The average price of a kilo of meat in the late 1980s in a state shop was 1.8 roubles, which represented a subsidy of three roubles, the same applying to dairy products and bread. Although individual retail prices have changed, there had been no general revision since 1955 (Åslund 1989: 129).

2. The case of a pair of ladies' boots costing 120 to 130 roubles, or the same as the annual average consumption (62 kg) of meat;

3. Bread for being so cheap that children used loaves as footballs, a variation on the illegal feeding of bread instead of fodder to livestock because the former was cheaper than the latter (see report of the Murmansk speech in *CDSP*, 1987, vol. XXXIX, no. 40, p. 5).

New industrial wholesale prices were to be introduced on 1 January 1990 and new retail prices and agricultural procurement prices on 1 January 1991, but price reform was continually postponed.

Aganbegyan states that there were 24 million types of goods and services and that the prices of around 500,000 of them were set by the central government alone (1988b: 134). The aim originally was to confine centrally set prices to the most essential products, such as fuels, electricity, vital raw materials and some consumer goods (1988b: 119). Prices were to be reviewed at least every five years, or earlier if conditions altered sharply (1988b: 135).

Price reform was a real bone of contention in the debate over the future course of the Soviet economy. Central power slipped here too, e.g. in 1990 Moscow and Leningrad councils changed some prices against central wishes. A presidential decree of 4 October 1990 allowed enterprises to negotiate wholesale prices (albeit with state-determined maximum levels of profitability, with all excess profits going to federal and republican budgets in equal amounts), with exceptions such as oil, gas, electricity, rail charges, military products and farm supplies. As of 15 November the prices of 'luxury' goods such as gold, jewellery, furs, caviar, electrical goods and car parts were freed of controls. The Russian, Moldavian and Kazakh republics, however, immediately overruled this. On 1 January 1991 wholesale price increases were announced for many products, e.g. oil 133 per cent, gas 100 per cent, timber and timber products 100 per cent, metal 50 per cent, and engineering equipment 40 per cent. Wholesale prices increases without retail ones would lead to an increase in state expenditure on subsidies and so Premier Valentin Pavlov outlined a package of retail price changes to the Supreme Soviet on 18 February 1991 (further details being provided later). He also feared a 'price war' between republics if a federal reform was not implemented. On 2 April retail prices were to rise by about 60 per cent on average as a result of a two-thirds reduction in subsidies (to a point where the food sector as a whole would no longer make a loss, basic foodstuffs like milk, meat, bread and eggs still being subsidized). Some individual price increases were substantially higher, e.g. meat and meat products, milk and dairy products, bread and sugar. Other prices, in contrast, were frozen, e.g. petrol, coal, gas, electricity, medicines, synthetic clothes and shoes, plastic toys, coffee and vodka (to deter illegal brewing). Individual republics had some leeway to continue subsidizing some products at their own expense. A three-tier system of prices comprised the following categories:

1. 'Fixed'.

2. 'Maximum': these were to account for 15 per cent of products e.g. cars, timber products, washing machines, fridges, televisions and sewing machines.

3. 'Negotiated' (between suppliers and re-tailers): even here there were some restrictions (such as a maximum 20 per cent mark-up on the price paid to suppliers), while an auditing commission was empowered to remove prices from this category in the event of 'exploitation'. About 30 per cent of all products were supposed to be accounted for here.

Income compensation was to be partial, covering 85 per cent of the price rises. Pre-price-rise increases of sixty roubles on monthly wages, sixty-five roubles on pensions, sixty roubles for students and 40 roubles for children were granted. Compensation also took the form of a forty per cent increase in savings accounts (as they stood on 1 March 1991) and state savings bonds, although the extra sums in the savings accounts (gathering 7 per cent interest in addition) would be frozen for three years. The enterprise profit tax was reduced from 45 per cent to 35 per cent.

Bornstein (1988: 331) outlines the reform proposals for agricultural prices. Agricultural purchase prices were to cover the costs of farms operating under 'normal' conditions and to provide the profit needed for investment. From 1 January 1991 the number of geographical price zones for products (based on average zonal costs of production) were to be reduced, with explicit rental payments imposed on the more favourably situated farms. Subsidies on industrial inputs were to be eliminated and water charges imposed. State and collective farms were to start paying for land use as of January 1991 (Brooks 1990a: 41). The payment for land, in the form of a land tax or rental payment, was based on the quality and location of land (*CDSP*, 1990, vol. XLII, no. 13, p. 23).

AGRICULTURE

There is a dramatic difference between the agriculture of the Stalinist era and that of today. Although still very much a problem sector, it became highly subsidized. Investment was heavy, although often inefficiently used.[11] The state farm steadily increased in importance, although the differences between it and the collective farm lessened. In 1966, for instance, collective farmers were given monthly payments for work done based on state farm rates of pay. A noteworthy event was the growing importance of the 'autonomous (or normless) link' (*beznaryadnoye zveno*), in the sense of working without daily assignments. There were group variations in name or substance known as the contract brigade, team, small (typically around six) work group, group contract, small contract group, collective contract, and even family contract. This growth was at the expense of the 100–plus-strong brigades, where there was only a tenuous relationship between individual effort and reward.

Links vary, but can involve, for example, a small group of people, self-selected or even family members (there is also a tendency for these activities to overlap with work on the private plot), who are given responsibility for a piece of land or a livestock unit, supposedly allocated inputs, supposedly set broad output targets for up to five years and paid by results (Gagnon 1987). Work assignments are not set, however. Production in excess of target may be sold to the farm at a higher price or sold on the free market. Thus incentives to work are increased. Links have a history that can be traced back to the 1930s, but they had fallen into total disfavour by 1950. A revival began in the form of experiments in the late 1950s. Opposition then set in, a further revival took place in the late 1970s and Gorbachev, as the party secretary in charge of agriculture, gave his endorsement in March 1983 (Nove 1987: 21). Problems included input supply and a diminution in the authority of farm chairmen, whose responsibilities and remuneration remained unaffected (Johnson 1988b: 208). As a whole they accounted for about a half of the agricultural work force in

1985 and 76 per cent by the end of 1987 (Charles Hodgson, *FT*, 26 January 1988, p. 28). Wädekin provides the following information on 'normless links' and 'contract brigades': by 1984 19 per cent of the agricultural workforce was involved, with six and twenty four members respectively on average (1988: 208).

In his 23 March 1988 speech Gorbachev highlighted the 'family contract' and the 'rental or lease contract' (where both land and the means of production are leased; *CDSP*, 1988, vol. XL, no. 41, p. 4). He outlined farm policy as follows.

1. The lifting of restrictions on auxiliary activities such as processing, services and consumer goods.

2. The ability of collective farms to lease, both to other enterprises and to private citizens, part of the land assigned to them and also some of their fixed assets.

3. The ability to engage in foreign economic operations.

4. The possibility of revoking a co-operative's right to use land and even to liquidate the inefficient.

5. Further encouragement given to the private plot.

Gorbachev spoke favourably of experiments where a multi-layer structure was set up. Small groups were at the bottom ('primary co-operatives') and were on an economic accounting basis (including a separate bank account). Agro-industrial, inter-unit associations organized on a horizontal and vertical basis were in the middle and there was a similar organization at the provincial level. Note, however, that there would still be state guidance in forms such as tax and credit policy, state contracts and state orders (*CDSP*, 1988, vol. XL, no. 12, pp. 4–7).

The administrative mechanism of the 'agro-industrial complex', experiments dating from 1974, was basically established by 1982. This was part of the May Food Programme of that year. This involved a drive to increase food production and thus reduce food and foodstuffs imports, stemming in part from the US grain embargo of January 1980 to April 1981.[12] The aim of this complex of organizations was to co-ordinate farm production, input supply and other services, procurement, rural construction, transport, storage, food processing and sales. Previously individual production units were subordinated to different ministries (although the ministerial problem did not, in fact, entirely disappear). The ability existed to move sales and investment targets among the farms (Gregory and Stuart 1990: 313).

There developed a vertical hierarchy at the federal, republican, provincial and district level (Rapo). The hoped-for benefits included increased output and an amelioration of the problems of input supply and lack of farm specialization. In his 29 July 1988 speech Gorbachev, in fact, criticized the agro-industrial complex and recommended a changeover to the voluntary creation of joint management agencies by collective and state farms and to co-operative forms of service provision (*CDSP*, 1988, vol. XL, no. 30, p. 7). In November 1985 the State Agro-industrial Committee (Gosagroprom) was established, enveloping the previously separate bodies such as ministries (though a number of ministries survived as separate units) and service organizations, with the aim, among other things, of improving the co-ordination of input supplies. These bodies in fact survived, albeit under new names (Nove 1987: 22). *Gosagropromy* were also to be created at the republican and provincial levels, dovetailing with the existing Rapos at district level (Dyker 1987: 106).

In early 1988 attention began to be focused on the agricultural combine (*agrokombinat*), the agrofirm, and the agro-association (Butterfield 1990: 32–40). The agricultural combine was the first to appear, in the early 1980s, and involved a single management body controlling the whole process from purchasing to sale. The agrofirm involved only a few enterprises and activities, while the agro-association (started April 1987) had a more diverse management structure, each body concentrating on a particular activity. By early 1989 there were more than 330 agro-industrial combines and firms (p. 41).

The *private plot* accounted for about a quarter of total Soviet agricultural output[13] and only 3 per cent of sown area. Note that there were urban as well as rural plots. The average size of a private plot was 0.24 ha, but this varied from 0.32 ha in collective farms to 0.21 ha in state farms and 0.14 ha in other state enterprises and organizations (Hedlund 1990: 216). In 1984 they accounted for 58 per cent of potatoes, 30 per cent of vegetables, meat, eggs and milk, and 24 per cent of wool (*EEN*, 1988, vol.2, no. 1, p. 2). Their fortunes fluctuated considerably over time, depending on factors such as the political climate and the performance of the socialized sector, but the Gorbachev policy was one of encouragement through means such as increased credits and wider use of lease contracts by collective and state farms that provided additional plots of land on a long-term basis to sell produce under contract to farms and consumer co-operatives (*CDSP*, 1987, vol. XXXIX, no. 40, p. 16). After 1981 private individuals were able to obtain young animals and complementary inputs from farms under contracts that specified expected return sales of final products and at particular prices (Roucek 1988: 54). The limits on livestock were removed where the animals were being raised on contract and for ultimate transfer to the socialized sector (Gregory and Stuart 1990: 229).

At the Nineteenth Party Conference in 1988 Gorbachev stressed the need to promote *leasing arrangements* (*CDSP*, 1988, vol. XL, no. 26, p. 8) and elaborated upon this at the follow-up Central Committee plenum held on 29 July. A law on leasing was adopted on 23 November 1989. The experiments country-wide involved around a fifth of the 50,000 or so state and collective farms, typically with land leasing of around five years and inputs purchased from and sales made to the farm. (Rentals were used extensively until their abolition in the mid-1930s.) These experiments proved successful, it

was claimed, because leasing overcame the feeling that the means of production belonged to no one and forged a link between remuneration and performance, while socialism was preserved because state ownership remained: 'a person becomes the true master of the land and has a stake in seeing to it that the land and other means of production he rents are used with the maximum effectiveness and produce the highest returns' (Gorbachev, *CDSP*, 1988, vol. XL, no. 30, p. 6). He contrasted this with the situation where the average annual gross output of agriculture for 1986–87 grew by only 41 per cent over the average annual level for 1966–70, while over the same period capital investment increased by 140 per cent (*CDSP*, 1988, vol. XL, no. 41, p. 2). The period of the land lease should be up to fifty years (in December 1990 Gorbachev mentioned 100 years and the possibility of selling leases). The leasing applied to small groups or families (leases could be passed on to children), while Gorbachev also recommended an extension of the system of leasing of shops and plants in industry (*CDSP*, 1988, vol. XL, no. 30, p. 6).[14] The subsequent decree also approved the purchasing of machinery and the hiring of seasonal labour. 'Collective farms and state farms must be integrated with the individual sector through contracts' (Gorbachev, *CDSP*, 1988, vol. XL, no. 41, p. 8). There were variations. For example, on 5 July 1989 Lithuania (following Latvia) allowed families to use (but not sell or rent) up to 50 ha for an indefinite period (inheritance was permitted) (*CDSP*, 1989, vol. XLI, no. 27, p. 22).

The 'lease contracts' (*arendnye kontrakty* or *podriady*) were of two types, the 'targeted' ('share') and the 'free' ('fixed rent') leases (Brooks 1990a: 38–9 and 1990c: 88–9):

1. The 'targeted' lease was the more common of the two, usually involving a family, an individual or a self-selected small group. Part of the farm's assets are managed by the lessee, while the farm sells all the contracted inputs and markets all the contracted output. The 'rent' amounts to the difference between the price the

lessee receives for the contracted output and the price the farm receives for the marketed output.

2. The 'free' lease involves the lessees marketing their own output. This type is deemed appropriate in cases where the farm manager has little alternative use for the assets, e.g. labour-intensive orchard, vegetable and flower operations. Both types have a let-out clause if the lessee is adversely affected by circumstances beyond his control.

The response seemed to be poor. At the end of 1989 only 9 per cent of state and collective farms reported at least some leasing activities (Brooks 1990a: 39). Reasons included increased risk for the lessees, lack of goods to buy, lack of suitable implements, and loss of authority for the farm managers (p. 39). A Soviet source put the number of collective and state farms involved in some way at 4,911 at the end of 1989 (*CDSP*, 1990, vol. XLII, no. 9, p. 17).

The Gorbachev era saw farmers being paid a price bonus for major products (in 1986 50 per cent for meat and milk, for example, and up to 100 per cent for grain) on sales above the average level actually achieved in the period 1981–85, rather than income being tied to the fulfilment and over-fulfilment of delivery plans. Provincial authorities were given the power to set the prices of fruit and vegetables in their state outlets, while farms were now able to sell up to 30 per cent of their delivery quotas of fruit and vegetables (instead of just above-plan deliveries) on the free market or via co-operatives. Farm managers were able to earn bonuses of up to 25 per cent of normal pay. Designers of machinery applied by farms were now able to share up to half the extra profits forthcoming (*FT*, 14 August 1987, p. 20). In 1988 agricultural science and research and design centres began to move to a self-financing basis. After July 1987 urbanites were able to rent empty village houses and their adjacent plots, although an agreed quota of produce had to be delivered to the *kolkhoz*, which was also to be allowed to rent or sell equipment and buildings to individual members and to develop direct

trading links with agricultural co-operatives overseas (Hodgson, *FT*, 26 January 1988, p. 28). There were experiments with wholesale trade in the means of production, as in Lithuania, while *The Economist* survey (1988: 10) discusses the Estonian experiment. Here the state supported agriculture by means of higher product prices instead of input subsidies in order to favour those who produced more rather than those who make larger losses. Estonia was also the first republic to introduce land rent that varies with land quality.

The year 1989 saw further changes. In May grain prices were again increased, by over 50 per cent. In August it was announced that sales of wheat, peas, lupin and oilseeds above the average annual level (1981–85 for wheat and 1986–88 for oilseeds) would be paid for in hard currency (*CDSP*, 1989, vol. XLI, no. 33, p. 32). The experiment was to last through 1990 at least. Only 300,000 tonnes of grain were enticed by the end of 1989 (*CDSP*, 1990, vol. XLII, no. 27, p. 27), the total grain harvest for that year being 211.1 million tonnes. In September 1990 scarce goods like cars and videos were offered as a reward for increased deliveries of grain and vegetables. This followed the Russian republic's offer of 'harvest 90 cheques' in July, which guaranteed access to scarce consumer goods.

There were experiments in both state and collective farms involving 'shareholders' associations', whereby part of the workforce contributed funds and, in return, received dividends (dependent on profits) and regular reports from the director; the association board determined the use of funds (*CDSP*, 1988, vol. XL, no. 22, p. 22). Butterfield (1990: 45) reports cases of joint stock companies, e.g. a co-operative state farm jointly operated by a number of industrial, construction and agricultural enterprises, and a greenhouse state farm which sold shares to its own farmers and to industrial enterprises. The payment of the Provisyen hothouse vegetables farm was in kind and in cash dividends (Aganbegyan 1989: 50).

The Central Committee meeting on 15–16 March 1989 resolved to:

1. Abolish Gosagroprom on the grounds of interfering bureaucracy and overcentralization, replacing it with a commission of the Council of Ministers (USSR State Food and Procurements Commission). The Rapo was also abolished.

2. Encourage leasing in the general context of diversified forms of organization.

3. Raise procurement prices from January 1990, while holding state retail prices of basic foodstuffs such as bread, meat, milk and sugar steady for two to three years.

4. Increase the scope for contractual prices for early, perishable and seasonal products (e.g. fruit and vegetable prices to be set contractually between local authorities and farms; the former, however, had the ability to set ceiling prices).

The period 1988–89 was to see the changeover of all collective and state farms to full economic accountability and self-financing (*CDSP*, 1987, vol. XXXIX, no. 40, p. 16). As of 1988 more than 60 per cent of all farms had switched over to the new management methods (*CDSP*, 1988, vol. XI, no. 12, p. 5).

The possibility of private ownership of land was raised. Gorbachev himself was not in favour of the forcible break-up of state and collective farms. In his speech at the twenty-eighth Congress of the CPSU (2–13 July 1990), he said that 'The point of agrarian reform is to establish equal opportunities for all economic forms of farming. Let each of these forms prove its viability and effectiveness . . . those collective and state farms that are managing their operations skilfully . . . deserve every kind of support.' On 17 September 1990 Gorbachev expressed his opinion on the question of private land ownership: 'it is the sovereign right of the people to decide this question. It can be decided only through a referendum.' In a speech to artists and intellectuals on 28 November 1990, he stood resolutely against the idea: 'I cannot . . . accept the private ownership of land. Leasing, yes, even for 100 years and with the right to sell or bequeath leasing rights. But private ownership with the right to sell land? I cannot accept that (*CDSP*, 1990, vol. XLII, no.

48, p. 3). On 18 December he suggested that a referendum on private ownership should be held in each republic 'this winter', the CPD approving the idea in principle six days later.

On 3 December 1990 the Russian Federation's Congress of People's Deputies adopted legislation permitting private land ownership, although individuals were able to sell land only after ten years and even then only to the state. Some 40,000 'private farms' were created in the Russian republic in 1991, accounting for something less than 1 per cent of arable land (Yuri Chernichenko, *Moscow News*, 26 January–2 February 1992, p. 10). The total number had reached nearly 50,000 by the start of 1992 (Dimitry Kazutin, *Moscow News*, 8–15 March 1992, p.3). The United Nations Economic Commission for Europe (1992: 126) provides the following information: at the start of 1991 there were 4,432 family farms; at the start of 1992 there were 50,000, with an average size of 42 ha. (Note, however, that it is not clear to what extent 'private' involves ownership or leasing of land.)

In a 29 November 1990 speech to the Moscow City Communist Party Conference, Gorbachev promised to improve food supplies: 'We are guilty before the working class, I think, and me personally.' On 4 December he outlined various measures designed to improve food supplies: an extra 12 million acres for 'individual farming' for food production, and increased food processing and imports. There was also to be tighter control over distribution; the KGB was to set up a special 'economic sabotage unit' to combat such malpractices as the 'third shift' (during which employees sell goods illegally and at higher prices). In this context, it is also worth noting the 1 December 1990 decree ordering the establishment of worker control committees, elected at workplaces, to monitor 'all food and light industry enterprises, trade enterprises, public catering and communal services, food stores and co-operatives'. These committees had the authority, in cases of theft and speculation, to close 'guilty' enterprises temporarily and to propose the suspension or dismissal of personnel and the institution of criminal proceedings if necessary. On-site trials were envisaged for serious cases of embezzlement and profiteering.

The 5 January 1991 decree dealt with 'ineffectively used' agricultural land going to newly created peasant farms, leaseholders, agricultural co-operatives and individuals. By the spring of 1991 some 3–5 million ha were to be involved, although the total was to be higher once the republics and local authorities had carried out an inventory of such land by mid-1991. Lifetime leaseholds were envisaged and inheritance was permitted, but the land itself could not be bought or sold. A Land Bank was to be established for developing private plots. The decree 'envisaged the possibility' that state and collective farms could be voluntarily disbanded, but 'the compulsory break-up of collective farms, state farms and other agricultural enterprises is unacceptable'.

The background to these changes was the increasing use of rationing throughout the country. Even Moscow and Leningrad were forced to ration basic foodstuffs on 1 December 1990. It was not so much a case of an absolute shortage of foodstuffs (the 1990 grain harvest, for example, was 218 million tonnes, the second highest on record) as of shortages caused by losses due to factors such as inadequate storage and by the poor distribution network. Increased queueing and rationing also gave a somewhat misleading impression of shortage because there were substantial hoarding of goods at home, illegal sales (such as the 'third shift'), sales via work units and, of course, the alternative provided by the free market. Nevertheless, there was real hardship among groups such as pensioners unable to queue. The international community responded: for example, in December the USA agreed to provide agricultural credits on favourable terms, the European Community approved a combined grant–credit aid package for food purchases, Japan provided food credits, and Germany launched a 'Help Russia' campaign in the form of food parcels.

THE TRANSITION TO A MARKED-BASED ECONOMY

The 1987 Law on the State Enterprise (Association) was not designed to introduce a market economy and in important respects was not even implemented. Although Gorbachev oscillated in the political spectrum, he became convinced of the need for a bolder move towards the market. Some selected quotations from Gorbachev's speeches at the Twenty-eighth Congress of the CPSU (2–13 July 1990) give a flavour of his thoughts, especially his concern to introduce a 'regulated market economy' (an idea approved in principle by the Supreme Soviet on 13 June 1990) (see *CDSP*, 1990, vol. XLII, no. 27, pp. 1–13; 1990, vol. XLII, no. 29, pp. 8–18; vol. XLII, no. 34, pp. 15–18): 'The market functioned for a thousand years until the revolution.' 'In general, we see the market not as an end in itself, but as a means of raising the efficiency of the economy and people's living standards.' 'What we are talking about is the establishment of a . . . multi-sectoral model with diverse forms of ownership and management, and with a modern market infrastructure.' 'Has not our entire history not shown . . . the futility of attempts to get out of the plight . . . by patching up the command-and-administrative system? If we continue to act in this way . . . we shall bankrupt the country.' Indeed, his periodic shifts towards the hardliners can be interpreted as providing a more stable political atmosphere in which to push ahead with economic reform. It is nevertheless true that Gorbachev blew hot and cold over the more radical of the proposals, e.g., as is seen below, his enthusiasm for the Shatalin proposals quickly waned when it became clear that the role of the republics would be greatly enhanced. Subsequently Gorbachev became very much in favour of the more radical proposals to switch to the market.

A number of economic programmes were put forward in the late Gorbachev era. In November 1989 Abalkin suggested a diversity of ownership forms, macroeconomic stabilization and phased moves towards a competitive market-based economy (*CDSP*, 1989, vol. XLI, no. 46, pp. 11–15 and 39–40). The four phases are as follows:

1990. Legal preparations and macroeconomic stabilization measures.

1991–92. Implementation of the reform measures.

1993–95. 'Fine tuning' the economic mechanism. By 1995 80–90 per cent of ouput should be market-determined and the budget deficit reduced to 3–4 per cent of GNP. Abalkin ruled out Polish-style 'shock treatment', because he considered that the Soviet government did not enjoy the required level of trust by the population.

1996–2000. The firm establishment and development of the new economic mechanism.

In December 1989 the then prime minister Ryzhkov adopted on the whole a cautious attitude (*CDSP*, 1989, vol. XLI, no. 5, pp. 3–8). He emphasized the need to increase the production of consumer goods. The budget deficit should be decreased from 10 per cent to 2–2.5 per cent of GNP by 1993, but price reform should be delayed (for agricultural purchase prices from 1990 to 1991; new wholesale and purchase prices should be set in 1991 and retail price changes should be completed in 1992). Ryzhkov proposed the following transition to a market-based system:

1990–92. Because of the need to saturate the consumer goods market, state orders for consumer goods should be given in the first two years of the five-year plan. In sectors such as fuel, chemicals, timber, metallurgy and most building materials state orders should be reduced to 90 per cent of capacity.

From 1993 onwards. Economic methods were to go into force to the maximum extent. By 1995 the share of property relations should be: state enterprises 65 per cent, shareholding companies 15 per cent, and leased enterprises 20 per cent.

In May 1990 Ryzhkov spelt out his programme for the gradual move towards a 'regulated' market economy, with the aim of controlling inflation but preventing a sharp contraction of output (CDSP, 1990, vol. XLII, no. 21, pp. 8–13). The republics would be given more power, but the central authorities would decide how much. The stages were to be as follows:

1990. Laying the legal foundations of a market economy.

1991–92. Major steps to be taken towards the market, e.g. price reform.

1993–95. The further reduction of administrative restrictions. State orders (starting in 1991) should be gradually limited to defence needs, public education, scientific and technical programmes, market stocks for the population, and the creation of state reserves of materials and equipment. State orders will account for no more than 40 per cent of the total output of the means of production.

Some of Ryzhkov's proposals for price reform proved to be controversial and politically unacceptable. The proposal to triple the price of bread on 1 July 1990, for example, led to panic buying. Partial income compensation for price rises was envisaged. The more radical economists also claimed that administrative price increases without strict austerity measures were a recipe for high inflation.

In July 1990 came the so-called Yeltsin '500 day confidence mandate', so-called because the principal author was Grigori Yavlinsky (Yavlinsky resigned as deputy prime minister of the Russian Republic on 17 October 1990 in protest at the Soviet government's policies, which he felt stymied the 500 day programme). The emphasis was on privatization (partly as a means of achieving macroeconomic stabilization via sales proceeds) and the postponement of price liberalization. Yeltsin also favoured a genuinely free union of sovereign republics. The sequence ran as follows: first 100 days, legislation; next 150 days, stress on privatization and anti-monopoly laws; next 150 days, stress on market prices and competition; final 100 days, stress on 'aggressive stabilization'. The programme which actually emerged on 11

September 1990 was more on the lines of the Ryzhkov–Abalkin proposals than the expected compromise (CDSP, 1990, vol. XLII, no. 37). Macroeconomic stabilization would come first, including a series of state-controlled price increases; the budget deficit was to fall to 2.5–3 per cent of GNP in 1991. A market-based economy would be established by the end of 1995.

The Shatalin programme

Although Ryzhkov argued that the Shatalin programme would lead to a large rise in unemployment and inflation, Gorbachev seemed to sympathize largely with Shatalin at first ('I am more impressed by the Shatalin programme'), but then became concerned, especially with the power given to the republics. It has also been criticized for being too ambitious time-wise, especially with regard to destatization and privatization. There are a number of principles and a 500 day schedule (*CDSP*, 1990, vol. XLII, no. 35, pp. 4–12).

The principles

Austerity measures (stabilization) should come before price liberalization, otherwise inflation would result. The prices of up to 150 essential goods and services were to be frozen until the end of 1991, with wage indexation generally covering only essential goods and services. The republics would generally decide the balance of powers *vis-à-vis* the centre, in a voluntary economic union of sovereign republics (those opting out could take observer or associate status) although there should be a single currency, market, customs and banking system. A market economy was the aim and there should be equality in the treatment of ownership forms. A rapid process of 'destatization' and privatization was envisaged. Sectors such as defence, oil and gas, power, railways, the post office and long-distance communications, however, should remain in state hands.

The 500 day schedule

This can be described as a rapid sequential programme and runs as follows:

First 100 days, starting 1 October 1990. Stabilization measures, with the budget deficit reduced to 5 billion roubles by the end of 1990 and zero by the end of 1991 (spending to decrease, and revenue increased by some initial privatizations).

Days 100–250. The republican authorities would continue to issue state orders (although on a voluntary basis and at negotiated prices) in order to prevent a sharp fall in output. Further privatizations to take place.

Days 250–400. 'Stabilization of the market' phase, when the rouble would become internally convertible and privatization would progress (to account for 40 per cent of manufacturing, 50 per cent of construction and transport, and 60 per cent of retail trade and services by the end of the period). Between 70 per cent and 80 per cent of prices were to be deregulated, leaving fixed ones for essentials like oil, gas, steel, bread, meat, dairy products, sugar and basic medicines.

Days 400–500. The 'beginning of recovery' stage. Privatization to account for at least 70 per cent of industry and 80–90 per cent of construction, transport, retail trade and services.

Gorbachev's initial enthusiasm for the Shatalin scheme, however, declined as the political situation deteriorated. The powers given to the republics were one reason why the radical Shatalin programme was not adopted, but others included the failure of the West to grant large-scale aid (Jeffrey Sachs, IHT, 15 May 1991, p. 8).

Basic Directions for the Stabilization of the Economy and the Changeover to the Market

This programme was approved by the Supreme Soviet on 19 October 1990 (CDSP, 1990, vol.

XLII, no. 43, pp. 10–12; vol. XLII, no. 44, pp. 17–19; vol. XLII, no. 45, pp. 14–27). This involved greater concessions to Ryzhkov-Abalkin than expected. The term 'basic directions' suggests a vaguer scheme, e.g. the republics could interpret the directions and work out the details. The existing economic links and agreements between enterprises and the state were to remain in force until the end of 1991. The (unified) market (with a single currency) would eventually rule (except in sectors like defence, health, education, and science and technology), although the state would regulate the market to combat inflation, unemployment, and excessive wealth and regional differentials. Indexation linked to a minimum basket of consumer goods would vary: 100 per cent for pensions, stipends and subsidies, and up to 70 per cent for fixed-income groups like doctors and teachers (the range is 50–70 per cent, with the percentage declining as wages increase). All forms of ownership were to be treated equally. Destatization and privatization would take place 'over a long period'; initially the emphasis would be on sectors such as trade and services and on small enterprises in general. The centre would control defence, foreign policy, space research, and environmental standards.

Four stages were envisaged, although no firm timetable was attached. The movement from one stage to the next was conditional on achieving the goals set. One time scale mentioned related to the 'foundations' of a market being perhaps laid in eighteen months to two years.

Stage 1: emergency measures; stabilization, with the budget deficit reduced to 25 billion–30 billion roubles in 1991 (i.e. not exceeding 2.5–3 per cent of GNP). The state would retain control of the prices of products such as fuel, raw materials, construction materials and basic consumer goods. Price controls should generally last through 1992, by which time only the prices of bread, meat, dairy products, transport fares, medicines and a few other staples would remain fixed. A start was to be made to destatization and privatization.

Stage 2: severe financial restrictions and a flexible price system. Small businesses were to be privatized and a market infrastructure was to be established. The retail prices of many consumer goods would be gradually liberalized.

Stage 3: the formation of the market. The market infrastructure would continue to evolve, and destatization and privatization gather pace. A housing market would develop.

Stage 4: completion of stabilization. Stabilization of the market and the financial system, with the budget balanced and an ample supply of goods and services assured. Destatization and the establishment of a competitive market were to be pushed along, especially in the light and food industries, agriculture and services. The preconditions would be created for a move to the internal convertibility of the rouble (with enterprises in the Soviet Union allowed to buy and sell currencies at the market rate).

With the very existence of the country under threat, however, economic reform took a back seat to preserving the union in the autumn of 1990. Gorbachev saw a greater degree of central control in general as a prerequisite for a shift towards a market-based economy. In the referendum of 17 March 1991 (the Baltic republics, Armenia, Georgia and Moldavia did not take part) the total turn-out was 80 per cent and an overall 76 per cent 'yes' vote was given to preserving 'a renewed federation of equal sovereign republics . . .'.

The economic situation deteriorated further in 1991. Strikes escalated, led by the coal miners from 1 March. The miners' demands comprised political as well as economic ones (e.g. Gorbachev's resignation), but the May agreement included substantial wage increases and a transfer of control from federal to republican authorities (the former levying a tax).

On 23 April the Supreme Soviet approved Prime Minister Pavlov's 'anti-crisis' programme (*CDSP*, 1991, vol. XLIII, no. 16, pp. 1–7): a moratorium on strikes until the end of 1991; 'emergency regimes' in key sectors such as power and transport; an emergency system for the distribution of foodstuffs; the enforcement of planned contracts between enterprises and the end of restrictions on the flow of goods between republics; austerity measures, such as controls on investment spending; encouragement given to foreign investment and private agricultural activity; and the speeding up of both destatization/privatization (especially in small-scale service activities; one-third of all small enterprises by the end of 1991 and two-thirds by the end of 1992) and price liberalization (most prices affected by October 1992). On the same day, Gorbachev signalled a swing back to the centre ground of politics by signing the so-called 'nine plus one' agreement with nine republican leaders, including Russia's Boris Yeltsin (the Baltic republics, Georgia, Armenia and Moldavia did not take part; note, however, that Armenia accepted the anti-crisis programme later on). Essentially, the 'anti-crisis' programme was supported, although concessions were made: a new union treaty (of 'sovereign' states) was to be signed, which would involve a 'radical' increase in the role of the republics and allow them 'independently to decide on the question of accession to the union treaty' (those republics choosing not to sign the new treaty would have to pay world prices and in hard currency for energy and raw materials); there were to be fresh elections for 'organs of Soviet power' (a more broadly based federal government was likely in the meantime); and concessions were to be made on (already announced) price increases (e.g. rail and air fares) and sales tax increases (on goods in 'daily demand') and on wage indexation.

Decrees following the approval of the anti-crisis programme

The 16 May 1991 decree 'On urgent measures to ensure the stable operation of the basic branches of the national economy' (*CDSP*, 1991,

vol. XLIII, no. 20, p. 29): the basic branches refer to electric power generation, coal, oil, gas, chemicals, the metallurgical industries and railway transport; a ban on strikes; up to 10 per cent of output could be sold independently on the domestic market at contract prices or exported (provided above-export-plan deliveries were made); the bonus fund was increased in line with output above production levels achieved January-April 1991. On 19 May 1991 the USSR Cabinet of Ministers repealed the sales tax on socially significant goods that were in daily demand and on services for the population (*CDSP*, 1991, vol. XLIII, no. 21, p. 25). A Law on Restricting Monopolistic Activity was signed by Gorbachev on 10 July 1991 (*CDSP*, 1991, vol. XLIII, no. 30, p. 15). The presidential decree of 3 August 1991 'On urgent measures to increase the production of goods and services to the population' (*CDSP*, 1991, vol. XLIII, no. 32, p. 4): priority in terms of inputs and imports to sectors producing these goods, e.g. priority allocation of hard currency and reduced duties on scarce imported goods such as food and medicines, while luxury imports were restricted; recommendation that republican governments use barter in 1991 to ensure input supplies; republics encouraged to provide extra incentives to farmers and to enterprises producing consumer goods. On 13 August Agrosnab was set up to barter goods for grain. The USSR State Property Fund was set up by the 10 August 1991 decree. This fund was to oversee the destatization and privatization process and was to be accountable to the USSR president and Supreme Soviet.

The Union Treaty

The proposed signing of the Union Treaty was the immediate cause of the attempted coup of 19–21 August 1991. Although it was never signed, being surpassed in the following revolutionary circumstances, the main features are worth exploring.

The treaty was due to be signed on 20 August

1991 by Russia, Kazakhstan and Uzbekistan. The Baltic republics of Estonia, Latvia and Lithuania plus Armenia, Georgia and Moldavia did not intend to sign (secession from the union was, according to the treaty, to be on the basis of the Law on Secession), but the remaining six republics were expected to join the treaty by the end of 1991. The country was to be known as the Union of Soviet Sovereign Republics. Full details of the much debated treaty were not generally publicized and areas of disagreement remained. Nevertheless the basic format was available and federal powers and responsibilities were still significant despite the increasingly powerful role of the republics:

1. There was to be a USSR Supreme Soviet comprising the Council of the Republics (with members delegated by the individual republics: eleven from each union republic, four from each autonomous republic, two from each autonomous region and one from each autonomous area) and the Council of the Union (with members directly elected by the entire population on the basis of districts with equal numbers of voters). The federal cabinet was to include all the heads of government of the republics.

2. Federal (union) responsibilities were to include defence and foreign policy.

3. There was to be a common currency (with internal convertibility due, unrealistically, by 1 January 1991), financial system, customs regulations and market. A common monetary policy was blurred by the agreement that the money supply was to be agreed by all the participating republics. The federal authorities were to receive a fixed percentage of the tax revenue collected by the republics.

4. There were a number of key areas where the exact division of authority between the federal and republican authorities was still undecided, e.g. natural resources and property.

The picture was also complicated by separate inter-republican agreements, e.g. on 14 August 1991 the five Asiatic republics agreed to co-operate closely over economic matters (such as trade), while four days later Russia and Kazakhstan approved a 'single economic space'.

The 'Grand Bargain' ('window of opportunity')

In May–June 1991 a joint US–Soviet team met at the John F. Kennedy School of Government at Harvard University to devise a Western aid package to the Soviet Union of Marshall Plan proportions in return for implementing radical economic reforms. The leading figures were Grigori Yavlinsky (the former deputy prime minister of the Russian republic), Graham Allison and Robert Blackwill (see Allison and Blackwill 1991 and their summary article in *The Guardian*, 7 June 1991, p. 21). Other participants included Stanley Fischer of MIT.

The reasons for aid

Allison and Blackwill argue that events in the Soviet Union present an historic 'window of opportunity'. The Soviet people have concluded that their society has failed, while that of the West has succeeded. The violent disintegration of the Soviet Union would pose first-order threats to vital US interests. If internal retrenchment in the Soviet Union occurs, this could force the West to increase its military expenditure once again to a substantial extent (the US has already spent $5 trillion meeting the military challenge of the Soviet Union around the globe; 1991: 93–4).

Conditional aid

There should be a well designed (following basic IMF–World Bank principles), step-by-step, strictly conditional programme of assistance provided both to the federal authorities and to the republics to motivate and facilitate the rapid transition to a market economy. The key elements should include:

1. Special status with the IMF and World Bank: loans should eventually become available

from these institutions if the desired reforms are undertaken.

2. Massive technical assistance (e.g. training programmes for essential activities in the transition).

3. Financial assistance of $15 billion to $20 billion a year for each of the next *three* years in grants (not loans), the cost to be shared by the US, Europe and Japan. (The *Financial Times*, 11 July 1991, p. 2, estimated that $100 billion is equivalent to 0.6 per cent of one year's GNP from all the OECD countries over four years. (The *International Herald Tribune* 15 June 1991, p. 12) estimated that a $100 billion package, as a percentage of the donor nations' output, would be equivalent to an eighth of the burden of the Marshall Plan.)

Yavlinsky (*CDSP*, 1991, vol. XLIII, no. 20, p. 4) has talked of a 'joint programme of action designed to extend over three to five years, including stages with specific goals and reciprocal obligations'.

The conditions

1. Continuing political pluralism (including free elections and the signing of a Union Treaty, with the ability of republics to leave the union should they wish).

2. The main elements of the three-year transitional programme include stabilization (e.g. reducing the budget deficit by cutting defence expenditure and subsidies to state enterprises; the legalization of private enterprise; the gradual liberalization of prices; and demonopolization and privatization. Yavlinsky thinks it inappropriate to put precise figures on the privatization process, but thinks a 'sizeable portion' of GNP could be produced by private businesses by 1997 and that a privatization fund should provide every citizen with loans (and advice) to start businesses (Grigori Yavlinsky, *Moscow News*, 30 June–7 July 1991, p. 8).

A more detailed analysis is to be found in *CDSP* (1991, vol. XLIII, no. 25, pp. 11–14). There are two stages of the reform process:

1991–93. The creation of the legal and economic institutions of a market economy, and the beginning of privatization. This stage is divided as follows.

1. The preparatory phase 1991–early 1992: the conclusion of a union treaty and agreement on an economic union (with an Inter-republic Economic Committee implementing a uniform economic policy); the continuation of small-scale privatization and the forcing up of prices; the preparation of a detailed reform programme with the help of international economic organizations.

2. Stabilization and the formation of market relations (1992): full membership of inter-national financial organizations; balancing of the budget; price controls removed with the exception of vitally important goods; the independence of the central bank established; internal convertibility of the rouble for routine transactions; the foreign trade system liberalized; continuing privatization of small and medium enterprises and large enterprises transformed into joint stock companies; changeover of defence into civilian production to begin; liberalization of the market for agricultural out-put; social security measures, including food coupons for vitally important, subsidized goods and unemployment pay, and a tax-based incomes policy.

3. Consolidating stabilization, furthering privatization and implementing structural policy (1993). This phase would include the privatization of large enterprises, an anti-monopoly policy, land reform, and large-scale infrastructural investments in areas such as banking, transport and communications.

1994–97. The intensification of structural transformations. This includes: increasing the production of consumer goods; continuing privatization; the development of financial markets; increasing exports of industrial goods; development of the labour market; a decrease in foreign aid and an increase in private foreign capital. By the end of this period the Soviet economy would be closely integrated into the world economy.

The use of aid

Aid should be allocated 'appropriately' between centre and republics. Aid would go to general balance of payments support, project support for key items of infrastructure (e.g. transport and communications), and the maintenance of an adequate safety net.

Critique of the 'Grand Bargain'

There are two main arguments against large-scale Western aid: (1) it helps preserve the old system; (2) it allows the West to interfere in Soviet affairs.

Variations on a theme

Jeffrey Sachs (*IHT*, 15 May 1991, p. 8, and 16 May 1991, p. 6) also advocates a version of the 'Grand Bargain'.

Amount of aid. Aid should be of the order of $30 billion a year for five years. This figure is derived as an equivalent of current Polish aid of $4 billion a year (*The Independent*, 12 July 1991, p. 21) and of 5 per cent of Soviet GNP. The sum is also equal to something less than two-tenths of 1 per cent of the GNP of the industrial world. Half the sum would come from the international financial institutions such as the IMF and the World Bank and the other half direct from governments, of which the US share would be about $3 billion a year (the direct US contribution would be equivalent to 1 per cent of annual US defence spending).

The use of aid. Sachs thinks that the $30 billion should be divided into $10 billion packages, each used for the following: to support the convertibility of the rouble at a realistic exchange rate; to finance the import of consumer goods in order to stabilize markets during the phasing in of price liberalization; and for transport and communications and pollution control. By the third year the focus of aid would change from covering balance of payments deficits to project loans in those sorts of areas

which are unable to attract private investment. In more detail (*The Independent*, 12 July 1991, p. 21), Sachs envisages aid starting at the beginning of 1992, a few months before the scheduled national elections. This aid would help accelerate radical economic reforms and maintain living standards, in turn helping to create a more peaceful atmosphere for the elections. It would be necessary to sustain political support long enough for reforms to take hold. But the bulk of the aid would come after the elections, first in the form of a stabilization fund for the rouble and balance of payments support to ease the freeing of prices. Later on loans would be provided for the private sector and financial support for infrastructural investments. Aid would also be needed to convert defence to civilian output. The *International Herald Tribune* (4 January 1992, p. 7) cited Sach's suggested donor contributions: $5 billion a year from the IMF, $4 billion from the World Bank, $3 billion from the EBRD, and $10 billion from the Western countries ($3 billion each from the USA and Japan). For later revised estimates and more detail see Appendix 3.3.

The G7 London Conference, 15–17 July 1991

The Group of Seven leading industrial democracies (Canada, France, Germany, Italy, Japan, the UK and the USA) invited Gorbachev to attend the July 1991 conference. Gorbachev presented a package of reform ideas more along the lines of the 'anti-crisis programme' than the 'Grand Bargain', although during the conference Soviet representatives came up with some interesting proposals regarding aid, e.g. the conversion of some debt to equity, possibly some debt rescheduling and an emphasis on project aid; a stabilization fund to support rouble convertibility would need to be of the order of $10 billion to $12 billion.

Since the Soviet economic reform proposals were not deemed sufficiently radical and the G7 countries were not, as a group, convinced by the

'Grand Bargain' idea in any case, all that actually transpired was a six-point package.

1. Special status for the Soviet Union with the IMF and World Bank. No loans would be available, but technical assistance and expertise would be given on the design of economic policies. Special status with the IMF was granted on 4 October 1991. Under the terms of the agreement the IMF would conduct regular inspections and produce regular reports and policy recommendations. Technical assistance was available to implement agreed policies (such as in trade, fiscal and monetary policies; help was also available to set up statistical and social welfare systems). The Soviet Union was also able to attend IMF executive board meetings, but had to provide accurate statistics. The IMF would give 'favourable consideration' to requests from individual republics to be treated similarly. (Note that the IMF announced on 23 July 1991 that the Soviet Union had formally applied for membership of that organization and to the World Bank, although Gorbachev's letter was actually dated 15 July.)

2. All international institutions urged to work together and intensify efforts to give practical advice and expertise on how to create a market economy.

3. Institutions urged to help work for price decontrol and privatization.

4. Technical assistance, especially in energy, conversion of defence into civilian output, food distribution and nuclear safety.

5. Help for Soviet trade by improving access to Western markets and encouraging Soviet trade with Eastern Europe.

6. The (revolving) chairman of G7 to keep in close touch with the Soviet Union in order to monitor events; the chairman to visit the country once a year. The G7 finance ministers also to go to the Soviet Union.

THE ABORTIVE COUP OF 19–21 AUGUST 1991

On 19 August 1991 Gorbachev was ousted by the 'State Committee for the State of Emergency'. Known popularly as the 'Gang of Eight', they were Gennadi Yanayev (vice-president), Valentin Pavlov (prime minister), Boris Pugo (interior minister; he subsequently shot himself), Vladimir Kryuchkov (chairman, KGB), Dimitri Yazov (defence minister), Oleg Baklanov (first deputy chairman of the Defence Council), Vasily Starodubtsev (chairman of the Farmers' Union), and Alexei Tizyakov (president of the Association of State Enterprises). Others acting behind the scenes included Anatoly Lukyanov, the chairman of the Supreme Soviet, who was subsequently arrested and charged with treason. A veneer of legitimacy was attempted by claiming that Gorbachev (who had been on holiday in the Crimea since 4 August) was unable to carry out his duties as president 'owing to the state of his health'. In fact, Gorbachev was presented with the option of signing a decree proclaiming a state of emergency or resigning; he was placed under house arrest.

The coup caught most people by surprise, although there were many earlier signs and warnings of deep dissatisfaction among 'hard liners'. In his December 1990 resignation speech Shevardnadze had warned of a slide towards dictatorship, while on Friday 16 August 1991 Alexander Yakovlev (who had resigned as adviser to Gorbachev on 17 July) resigned from the communist party with the extraordinarily prescient comment that a 'Stalinist' core of the party was preparing a coup. Yakovlev resumed his role as adviser on 24 September, while Shevardnadze resumed his role as foreign minister on 19 November (albeit as head of the new Ministry of Foreign Relations; earlier in the month the Foreign Ministry and the Ministry of External Economic Relations had merged to form the new body). Shevardnadze replaced Boris Pankin, who became Soviet ambassador to the United Kingdom.

The immediate cause of the attempted coup was the proposed signing of the Union Treaty on 20 August by Russia, Kazakhstan and

Uzbekistan. The State Committee acted to stop, as they saw it, political and economic chaos, to prevent the disintegration of the country, and to preserve the power exercised by the federal institutions of the communist party, the KGB and the armed forces. The plotters have subsequently revealed that they feared increasing dependence on the USA. They relied on the assumed political passivity of most of the population, hopefully enhanced by economic dissatisfaction.

The statement released by the State Committee (*CDSP*, 1991, vol. XLIII, no. 33, pp. 1–4) referred to:

> the aim of overcoming the profound and comprehensive crisis, political, ethnic and civil strife, chaos and anarchy that threaten the lives and security of the Soviet Union's citizens and the sovereignty, territorial integrity, freedom and independence of our fatherland . . . to adopt the most decisive measures to prevent society from sliding into national catastrophe and ensure law and order, to declare a state of emergency in some parts of the Soviet Union for six months from 0400 Moscow time on 19 August 1991 . . . with a view to protecting the vital interests of the peoples and citizens of the Soviet Union and the country's independence and territorial integrity, restoring law and order, stabilizing the situation, overcoming the gravest crisis, and preventing chaos, anarchy and a fratricidal civil war.

Although the State Committee promised to adhere to the reform process, the radio appeal made much of the grave economic situation:

> The crisis of power has had a catastrophic effect on the economy. The chaotic and uncontrolled slide towards the market has aroused egoism [self-interest] – regional, departmental, group and individual.
> The war of laws [federal versus republic] and the encouragement of centrifugal trends has meant the destruction of the unified machinery of the national economy which has taken decades to evolve. The result has been a sharp decline in the standard of living of the great majority of the Soviet people and the flourishing of speculation and the black economy.

The decrees issued on the first day of the coup suspended political parties, social organizations and movements 'that prevent normalization'. Demonstrations and strikes were banned and censorship was imposed. Federal laws were given 'unconditional priority'. On the economic front administrative measures were decreed and populist measures taken: 'strict fulfilment of measures to preserve and restore vertical and horizontal economic ties between economic-management entities . . . and unfailing achievement of planned targets regarding production and supplies of raw materials and components'; 'a decisive struggle against the shadow economy'; laws against 'corruption, theft, profiteering, bungled management and other economic wrongdoing' to be enforced; 'moonlighting' by state employees to be eliminated; 'emergency measures' were to be employed to bring in the harvest, including drafting factory and office workers, students and soldiers; urban dwellers were to receive allotments (up to 0.15 ha each) to grow fruit and vegetables; control was to be exercised over food distribution, with priority for children and pensioners; there were to be price freezes or reductions for certain consumer goods and foodstuffs, and increases in some wages and pensions. A 20 August decree banned the purchase of foreign currency by private individuals for travel purposes (a decree issued by Yanayev on the same day overrode all of Yeltsin's decrees).

Nato stressed that Eastern Europe's security was 'inseparably linked' with that of Nato's. The West responded on the economic front by suspending much of its promised aid (EC humanitarian aid continued, for example). The

EC promised to speed up negotiations on associate status with Czechoslovakia, Hungary and Poland and to strengthen co-operation with Albania, Bulgaria and Romania. The suspension of aid was, of course, lifted once the coup had failed. But the USA in particular was still reluctant to agree large-scale financial aid. The 29 August meeting between President Bush and UK prime minister John Major produced a six-point plan: fulfil existing pledges of food credits; assess food aid needs for the winter; 'lifeline teams' from the state and private sectors to assess food production and distribution in the Soviet Union; accelerate technical assistance in e.g. energy and defence conversion; greater advice from the IMF and World Bank; and accelerate implementation of special associate status in the IMF with a view to full membership. Larger-scale financial aid would depend on a radical reform programme agreed with the West and with the republics (which are now to receive aid direct). Grigori Yavlinsky himself thought that there had to be inter-republic agreement on a reform programme and macroeconomic stability before the granting of large-scale financial aid.

The plotters were put on treason charges (note, however, that when most of them were formally charged on 14 January 1992 they were accused of attempting to seize power illegally; it was difficult to charge them with betraying a country which by then no longer existed and which they had tried to preserve). There was very little loss of life, e.g. three civilians were killed in Moscow. Although there was much talk of 'people's power', the bulk of the population (even in Moscow and Leningrad) remained passive: Tom Wicker (*IHT*, 9 September 1991, p. 4) cites an estimate by Yeltsin's aides of 1 per cent of the population of Moscow and some other cities taking part in demonstrations. Steve Crawshaw (*The Telegraph*, 28 October 1991, p. 10) suggests an upper figure of 100,000 taking an active part in resisting the coup. Yeltsin's call for a general strike was also not heeded, with very few actually striking (e.g. there was strong

support for Yeltsin among coal miners). There was sufficient *active* popular support, however, to swing the balance. Popular support as a whole was for Yeltsin personally and for constitutionality/legitimacy in general. Gorbachev had long been much more popular abroad than at home, largely because of the dire economic situation. In this context, the plotters relied on general economic discontent to ensure passivity (or even positive support from particularly disadvantaged sections of society); the West could and should have promised large-scale aid to the Soviet Union at the July 1991 G7 conference in London, since the plotters would have been less likely to assume passivity from a population at least perceiving the prospects of betterment. The odds against the plotters' chances of success would have lengthened. Gorbachev returned from the London conference largely 'empty-handed' and thus weakened politically after so many concessions to the West.

The consequences of the August coup

The consequences of the failure of the coup have been, without any exaggeration, of truly historical dimension. The Soviet Union is no more.

The demise of the communist party (CP)

The coup collapsed on 21 August and Gorbachev proclaimed he was back in control. He initially defended the party as a whole; the very next day he said that 'We shall do everything we can to undertake reform in the party in order to give it a sort of kiss of life'. But on 24 August Gorbachev resigned as General Secretary of the CP and recommended the Central Committee to dissolve itself and local bodies to form a new party of 'renewal'. CP property was to be taken over by local authorities, pending a final decision on the role of the CP in the coup. There was to be a ban on all political parties in the Interior Ministry and in all security agencies (including the armed forces and the KGB). On 29 August the Supreme Soviet suspended the operations of the CP, pending a judicial enquiry into its role in the coup; its bank accounts were frozen and financial operations halted. On 6 November 1991, the eve of the first anniversary of the revolution not to be celebrated, Yeltsin banned all communist party activities in the Russian federation and nationalized its property. (In May 1992 the legality of Yeltsin's decrees was formally challenged, but the tables were turned when the Russian Constitutional Court was asked to look into the charge that the communist party had acted illegally and unconstitutionally while in office, e.g. usurping state power, violating human rights, and supplying arms to international terrorist organizations. The hearing was set to start on 7 July.) The republics also took various actions against the CP. For example:

1. Russia: ban on CP cells in the army and nationalization of CP printing presses and publishing houses (23 August 1991); on the same day Yeltsin signed a decree suspending the CP 'pending a court determination of its involvement' in the coup (Gorbachev was present in the Russian parliament at the time and protested; it was seen as a personal humiliation for Gorbachev).

2. Latvia: ban on CP (24 August).

3. Lithuania: ban on CP (24 August).

4. Moldavia: ban on political activities in enterprises (23 August); ban on CP (24 August).

5. Ukraine: CP activities suspended and property seized pending investigation (26 August); immediate ban on CP (30 August).

6. Tajikistan; ban on political activities in enterprises (23 August); ban on CP cells in the Interior Ministry and law enforcement agencies (25 August); and ban on CP cells in workplaces (26 August).

The republics

The immediate reaction of other republics to the coup was extremely varied. For example, on Tuesday 20 August both the Ukraine and Kazakhstan proclaimed that the State Committee's orders did not extend to these republics. President Leonid Kravchuk of the Ukraine had prevaricated on the first day of the coup, however, and thought there should be no strikes. President Nursultan Nazarbayev of Kazakhstan was also against strikes, while the party later became known as the Socialist Party. Nazarbayev won the popular election for president on 1 December 1991 with an overwhelming 98 per cent of the vote, although he was unopposed. Kazakhstan did not declare independence until 16 December 1991. Kirghizia's president Askar Akayev opposed the coup. In contrast, Tajikistan and Uzbekistan did not condemn the coup. Even Armenia only called for 'staunchness and restraint' (20 August), while Georgia seemed to comply with the instructions of the coup leaders (e.g. President Zviad Gamsakhurdia promised that there would be no protests and that the National Guard would be transferred to the Interior Ministry and detailed to rural areas for military training). The country began to disintegrate, with many republics declaring independence.

The Baltic states. The Baltic states were incorporated into the Soviet Union in 1940, the result of the 1939 Molotov–Ribbentrop (Soviet–Nazi Germany) pact. Lithuania had already declared independence on 11 March 1990. Estonia and Latvia followed on 20 August 1991; Yeltsin recognised Lithuania in July 1991 and the other two on 24 August 1991. International recognition of the Baltic states quickly followed the collapse of the coup, starting with countries such as Norway and Denmark (25 August) and including the EC (27 August) and the USA (2 September). On 1 September Gorbachev's view of independence was that if this is the 'ultimate will and intention of the peoples of these republics, I believe we have to agree to it' (on 27 August he repeated that republics had the right to secede, but it had to be done constitutionally). Note that the USA waited for Gorbachev's announcement before committing itself, showing sensitivity towards and support for the Soviet president. The new State Council recognised the independence of the Baltic states on 6 September; there was unanimous agreement among Gorbachev and the ten republican leaders. Diplomatic relations were established between the Soviet Union and Estonia and Lithuania on 8 October and with Latvia on the 15th. Admission to the United Nations took place on 18 September 1991. The resolution approved by the Congress of People's Deputies on 5 September included the following general statement on secession:

> While respecting the declarations of sovereignty and acts of independence adopted by republics, the Congress stresses that the gaining of independence by republics that have chosen to refuse to join the new union necessitates negotiations with the USS to resolve the entire complex of problems relating to secession, as well as their immediate joining in the Nuclear Non-proliferation Treaty, the Final Act of the Conference on Security and Co-operation in Europe and other important international treaties and agreements, including those which guarantee the rights and freedoms of the individual.

The early years of independence proved to be difficult ones economically. The *Financial Times* (29 April 1992, p. 4) reported the respective growth and retail inflation figures for 1991 calculated by the IMF: Estonia -10.8 per cent (GDP) and 211.8 per cent; Latvia -7.9 (GDP) and 317 per cent; and Lithuania -12.8 per cent (NMP) and 224.7 per cent. The growth outlook for 1992 was even gloomier. All three countries set out to establish Western-type economies. Estonia replaced the rouble with the kroon on 20 June 1992, while Latvia and Lithuania also intend to introduce their own currencies.

Ukraine (24 August). Independence was overwhelmingly (90.85 per cent) supported in the referendum on 1 December. Independence was immediately recognised by Canada, Poland, Sweden and Hungary. Yeltsin, too, acknowledged Ukraine's decision. Leonid Kravchuk won the simultaneously run popular presidential election with 61.5 per cent of the vote. (Note that 'the' before Ukraine should now strictly be omitted; the name of the country means 'borderland' or 'outlying lands'). On 22 October it was announced that an independent army and a national guard were to be formed; the 12 December decree involved the Ukrainian president becoming commander-in-chief of the armed forces on Ukrainian territory except in the case of strategic nuclear weapons.

Belorussia (Belarus) (25 August).

Moldavia (Moldova) (27 August). Seen as a stage on the way to reunion with Romania, with diplomatic relations established on 29 August. Moldavia was incorporated into the Soviet Union in 1940, a result of the 1939 Nazi–Soviet pact. The population is two-thirds Moldavian. But one piece of the territory was given to the Ukraine and a piece of Ukrainian territory (the east bank of the Dniestre river) exchanged in return. On 2 September 1991 the Dniestre region of Russian-speaking people declared independence from Moldova, becoming the Dniestre Soviet Socialist Republic (41 per cent of the population are Moldavians, 28 per cent are Ukrainians and 23 per cent are Russians). A request was made to join Ukraine; this was turned down by Ukraine, which is against border changes. On 1 December 1991 the Gagauz and Dniestre areas ran (illegal, according to Moldova) referenda on independence. President Mircea Snegur stood unopposed in the popular election for that office in Moldova on 8 December 1991. The turn-out was 82.9 per cent and he won 98.17 per cent of the votes cast. Fighting broke out between Moldova and the Dniestre region.

Azerbaijan (30 August, confirmed by a referendum held 29 December 1991). On 2 September 1991 Nagorno-Karabakh (incorporated in 1923) declared independence from Azerbaijan, becoming the Nagorno-Karabakh Armenian Republic within the Soviet Union; it also took with it the neighbouring Shaumyan district (see below). On 2 January 1992, however, Azerbaijan declared direct presidential rule, Soviet troops having been removed from Nagorno-Karabakh. Ayaz Mutabilov (who welcomed the coup at first) was elected president by popular vote on 8 September 1991, although he was unopposed, since the opposition refused to put up candidates. He resigned on 6 March 1992, as discussed below. Turkey recognised Azerbaijan in November 1991, the first country to do so.

Uzbekistan (31 August, confirmed by a referendum held 29 December). President Islam Karimov kept silent until the coup had obviously failed. He then resigned from the Politburo (23 August) and banned the communist party from the armed forces, police and civil service. The communist party became the People's Democratic Party. Karimov won a popular election on 29 December 1991 with an overwhelming 85.9 per cent of the vote.

Kirghizia (Kyrgyzstan) (31 August). Askar Akayev thwarted a local army–KGB attempt to overthrow the government and later banned the communist party from government bodies and confiscated party property. He was unopposed in the 12 December 1991 popular presidential election. Akayev is in favour of political democracy and a market economy.

Tajikistan (9 September). President Kakhar Makhkamov was forced to resign in late August because of his failure to condemn the coup. There was, however, a communist party backlash (the party was renamed the Socialist Party, but reverted to its former name in January 1992). On 23 September parliament ousted acting president Kadredin Aslonov and replaced him with the former (dismissed in 1985) party chief Rakhman Nabiyev; the decree issued 22 September banning the communist party and taking over its property was revoked, and a state of emergency was declared in Dushanbe (but lifted 30 September). In another reversal communist party activities were suspended on 4 October and Nabiyev resigned on the 6th. A presidential election was held on 24 October; in a high turn-out (84.5 per cent) Rakhman Nabiyev won comfortably.

Turkmenistan (Turkmenia, but still usually referred to as Turkmenistan) (27 October 1991). A referendum on independence held the day before produced an over 94 per cent 'yes' vote. The president is Saparmuryad Niyazov. He remained silent during the coup, but subsequently nationalized communist party property.

The potential for border disputes is enormous. According to *Moscow News* (1–8 September 1991, p. 1), only 12 per cent of the borders between republics could be described as fixed. According to the 1989 census there were 102 separate nations and ethnic groups, while in the old Soviet Union some 65 million people lived outside their own ethnic republics (25.3 million of these were Russians, e.g. 11.4 million in Ukraine and 6.2 million in Kazakhstan; but there has been a considerable exodus from the Asiatic republics).

Note that Georgia had already declared independence on 9 April 1991 (the original intention was to implement this gradually). The political situation in Georgia, however, deteriorated rapidly. The opposition claimed increasingly authoritarian behaviour on the part of President Zviad Gamsakhurdia, complicity with the coup leaders and lack of economic reform. Clashes between government supporters and opponents occurred. A state of emergency was declared in Tbilisi from 25 September. On 22 December 1991 a mini civil war broke out in Tbilisi. The opposition formed a Military Council as a temporary government until a new election could take place. Gamsakhurdia, besieged in the parliament, eventually fled the country on 6 January 1992. Eduard Shevardnadze (who was communist party boss 1972–85) returned to Georgia on 7 March 1992 and three days later was made president of the State Council, set up to replace the Military Council. Fighting continued in South Ossetia over its desire to join North Ossetia in Russia, but Russia and Georgia agreed to send in a joint peacekeeping force in mid-July 1992.

Armenia had already planned a referendum on 21 September 1991 (Armenia's original intention was to use the Secession Law: see Appendix 3.2). The referendum produced a large turn-out of over 90 per cent and a 99.5 per cent 'yes' vote, and independence was proclaimed 23 September. Levon Ter-Petrosian was elected president by popular ballot on 16 October 1991; he had planned guerilla warfare had the coup succeeded. Yeltsin and Nazarbayev brokered an interim accord between Armenia and Azerbaijan over Nagorno-Karabakh (an enclave within the latter, but with a 76 per cent Armenian population), to be followed by detailed negotiations. The accord, signed on 24 September 1991, included a cease-fire and the principle of autonomy within Azerbaijan. Heavy fighting still broke out later in Nagorno Karabakh, however, and setbacks forced Azerbaijan's President Mutalibov to resign on 6 March 1992. He was replaced by Yakub Mamedov. But although Mutalibov was reinstated on 14 May as setbacks continued, he was ousted by the opposition the next day.

The new Union Treaty

A joint statement was presented to the emergency session of the Congress of People's Deputies (CPD) (held 2–5 September) on 2 September 1991 by President Nursultan Nazarbayev of Kazakhstan. All republics signed the statement except the Baltic states, Moldova and Georgia (although Georgia was an observer at the negotiations). It is popularly known as the 'ten-plus-one' agreement (ten republics plus Gorbachev). The measures outlined were meant to prevent a further collapse of the structures of power, pending the creation of a new political state system of relations between the republics and the formation of new inter-republican union structures. The temporary arrangements were as follows.

1. All the consenting republics should work out and sign a Treaty of the Union of Sovereign States (USS) in which each of them would be able to determine independently the form of its participation. This was popularly known as the 'à la carte' principle. The final resolution, passed on 5 September, said that the new union had to be based on the principles of inde- pendence and territorial integrity of states, the observance of the rights of the nations and of the individual, social justice and democracy.

2. An appeal was made to all republics, irrespective of the status they had declared, to conclude right away an economic agreement to co-operate within the framework of a free common economic space to secure the normal functioning of the economy, supply of the population and accelerated implementation of radical economic reform.

3. The creation, for the transitional period, of the following institutions: *Council of Representatives* of People's Deputies. Each republic to have equal representation (twenty deputies delegated by each republican Supreme Soviet). The council to decide upon matters of general principle.

State Council. This would comprise the Soviet president and top state officials from the republics. Its role was to co-ordinate foreign and domestic issues that concerned common republican interests. This was to be the most powerful body. In the finally agreed version, Gorbachev shared responsibility for the armed forces, KGB and Interior Ministry with the republican presidents. There was no vice-president. If Gorbachev fell ill, his powers were to revert to the Council.

Interim Inter-republican Economic Committee. This committee would comprise representatives of all the republics on a parity basis. Its role was to co-ordinate both the management of the economy and economic reform. It was to be accountable to the president, the State Council and the Supreme Soviet. It would replace Silayev's Committee for the Control of the National Economy.

The draft constitution, when ready, was to be considered and approved by republican parliaments and finally approved at a congress of plenipotentiary representatives of union republics. The status of all elected people's deputies of the Soviet Union was to be preserved during their elected term.

4. An agreement on defence, on the principle of collective security, to preserve united armed forces and military-strategic space, to carry out radical military reforms in the armed forces, KGB, Interior Ministry and prosecutor's office of the USSR. (The 5 September resolution referred to the principle of 'collective security and defence while preserving a single armed forces and single control of nuclear and other arsenals of the means of mass destruction'.)

5. Strict observation of all international agreements and obligations of the Soviet Union.

6. The rights and freedoms of citizens and the rights of national minorities.

7. Support for applications of the individual republics to the United Nations. Note that Ukraine and Belorussia already had UN status, although until then they had not had independent voices. The Baltic states, as mentioned previously, were admitted to the UN on 18 September 1991, while the others (with the exception of Georgia) became members on 28 February 1992.

On 3 September 1991, however, Gorbachev (with the agreement of the ten republics) decided to withdraw support for the Council of Representatives of People's Deputies. There had been adverse reaction to the proposals on various grounds (constitutional problems, the overwhelming shift of power to the republics at the expense of the centre, and the disproportionately low weight given to Russia). Instead, it was proposed to revamp the Supreme Soviet along the lines suggested in the previous Union Treaty. The Supreme Soviet was to comprise two bodies:

The Council of the Republics, with members nominated by the parliaments of the individual republics as an interim measure. The finally agreed distribution of the 332 seats was as follows, although each republic still only had one vote: each republic had twenty represen-tatives plus one for each of its autonomous republics or regions; Russia, for example, had fifty-two. This council had veto power over the decisions of the Council of the Union.

The Council of the Union, with representatives appointed by the republics on the basis of districts with an equal number of people (thus weighting republican representation according to population size). Members of the current Supreme Soviet were eligible for consideration.

The Supreme Soviet would deal with changes in the constitution, accept states into the new union, receive presidential reports on the most important domestic and foreign issues, confirm the union budget, declare war and conclude peace. But decisions still had to be ratified by republican parliaments.

The final vote by the Congress of People's Deputies was taken on 5 September 1991, with the new arrangements approved by 1,682 votes for to 43 against and 63 abstentions. These arrangements were, of course, temporary and no fixed time scale was announced for a more permanent Union of Sovereign States. The CPD did not vote itself out of existence in principle (its life extended to 1994), but there seemed no reason to call another emergency session.

On 26 September the names of the members of a new (federal) Presidential Consultative Council were announced; they included Eduard Shevardnadze, Alexander Yakovlev, Gavriil Popov and Anatoly Sobchak. Gorbachev himself temporarily found a new role as arbitrator between the republics, especially since the other republics feared a dominant Russia.

The role of Boris Yeltsin and the Russian republic

Boris Yeltsin, elected president of the Russian republic by popular vote, played a crucial role in defeating the coup. He epitomized legitimacy/ constitutionality and displayed immense personal courage. He provided leadership and focused resistance to the coup on the Russian parliament building (the 'White House'). Yeltsin and the Russian parliament also moved quickly once the coup began to founder to fill the power vacuum left by the crumbling of central authority. Some of Yeltsin's actions were of dubious legality, however, and aroused fears among some of the other republics of possible Russian domination (the republic accounted for over 51 per cent of the population and over 76 per cent of the land area of the Soviet Union). Yeltsin's actions included the following.

22 August. To transfer by 1 January 1992 control of Union-level enterprises and organizations on Russian territory apart from specified exceptions (Gorbachev subsequently described the early decrees as 'necessary at the time'). A 12 September decree specifically confirmed Russian control over oil, gas and coal.

23 August. Gorbachev and Yeltsin agreed to take over each others's presidency if one fell ill. Yeltsin suspended six newspapers, including *Pravda*, and dismissed the heads of the state media. (*Pravda* was set up by Lenin in 1912 and became the the communist party's official newspaper. It was not published on 24 August 1991 for the first time since the 1917 revolution and only reappeared on 31 August as an 'independent' paper. Publication was suspended for economic reasons on 14 February 1992, but it reappeared on 7 April although only three times a week.) The whole Soviet Cabinet of Ministers was forced to resign. Key appointments were Yeltsin nominees, e.g. defence: Yevgenny Shaposhnikov, KGB: Vadim Bakatin and interior: Viktor Barannikov (Russia's interior minister.)

24 August. It was announced that Russia was to take over the Soviet government, the Economy Ministry, the KGB and the Interior Ministry as far as its territory was concerned until a new Soviet government was formed. The Russian prime minister, Ivan Silayev, was named as head of a temporary four-man (subsequently expanded) Committee for Control of the National Economy. The others were Grigori Yavlinksky, Arkadi Volsky (head of the Scientific-Industrial League, an organization representing state and private employers) and

Yuri Luzhkov (chairman of the Moscow City Council). In effect, the committee took over the role of the Soviet Cabinet of Ministers (government).

26 August. Anxiety was caused by talk among Yeltsin's spokesmen of republics which left the union (except the Baltic states) having to discuss borders and the minorities question with Russia. By way of example, the Crimea was included in the Ukraine as recently as 1954.

28 August. Announcement that from 15 September onwards Russia would temporarily take over the institutions of the Soviet Ministry of Finance, Gosbank and Vneshekonombank on Russian territory. Russian control was claimed over foreign exchange and precious metals operations, but ceded back to the centre later the same day. Gorbachev warned Yeltsin not to act unconstitutionally (the previous day Gorbachev had announced he was against border changes). (Note that on 28 August the head of Gosbank, Viktor Geraschenko, and of Vneshekonombank, Yuri Moskovsky, were reinstated, partly to mollify Western anxiety.)

A Russian delegation went to Ukraine and agreed on an economic and military union. Borders were to remain. Other republics were invited to join without the involvement of the centre (temporary inter-state structures were deemed necessary).

30 August. A similar agreement was drawn up between Russia and Kazakhstan in order to prevent the 'uncontrolled disintegration' of the Soviet Union.

Note that of the sixteen autonomous republics within Russia, only ten had by then agreed that a new union treaty should be signed by Russia on their behalf. There are also five autonomous regions and ten autonomous areas. Around 20 per cent of the republic's population is non-Russian. On 25 December 1991 the name was formally changed from the Russian Soviet Federative Republic to the Russian Federation; on 17 April 1992 an alternative of simply Russia was added. Resistance to the Russian federal authorities was led by Tatarstan (which in

December 1991 was granted increased economic autonomy, over oil for example) and Chechen-Ingushetia (in November 1991 the former proclaimed its 'independence' as Chechenia). A Russian federation treaty was signed by most representatives on 31 March 1992 (for details see *CDSP*, 1992, vol. XLIV, no. 13, pp. 15–16). The autonomous republics of Tatarstan and Chechenia did not sign, preferring to deal bilaterally with the Russian federal authorities. Tatarstan (population 3.8 million, 48 per cent Tatar and 42 per cent Russian; an important oil producer) had held a referendum on 21 March 1991; the turn-out was 81.7 per cent, and 61.4 per cent said 'yes' to a 'sovereign state'. The federation treaty granted increased powers to the autonomous republics, but many crucial areas of decision-making were left vague, e.g. control over natural resources. The treaty was approved by the Russian Congress of People's Deputies on 10 April 1992.

There has, however, been political disarray in the Russian parliament over such matters as political drift, delays in implementing economic reform and Yeltsin's decree-making powers and authoritarian traits (e.g. the sending of interim unelected 'governor generals' to enforce policies in the regions). Vice-president Alexander Rutskoi became increasingly critical, talking of chaos (decrees were largely ignored, for example), a lack of democracy, the danger of Russia splitting up (into 'hundreds of banana republics' he said on 30 January 1992), and mistaken economic reforms (Rutskoi believes, for instance, that price increases should *follow* privatization, the relative saturation of markets, the introduction of competitive conditions, land reform and financial reform, and that there is a need for some planning). He deplored (30 January 1992) the 'impoverishment of the people', referring to the 'inept and often essentially experimental attempts' of the government, and talked (8 February 1992) of 'economic genocide', proposing a state of emergency for at least a year. Following the swingeing price increases on 2 January 1992, the chairman of the

Russian parliament, Ruslan Khasbulatov, argued that the government should resign and that Yeltsin ought to give up his second post as prime minister. Georgi Matyukin, chairman of the Russian central bank, attacked price rises before a competitive production and distribution environment was established. He also opposed the notion of a freely convertible rouble in prevailing conditions, since its value had been reduced to such an extent that property could be bought up too cheaply and Russian enterprises would be unable to import. On 28 October 1991 Yeltsin announced a radical economic reform package to the Russian Congress of People's Deputies (see below).

The control of the economy in the immediate aftermath of the coup attempt

Yeltsin's call for a general strike against the coup was not generally heeded. Although there was some response (e.g. from coal miners in Siberia, the Ukraine and Belarus) it was not widespread. As has already been discussed, Yeltsin and the Russian parliament stepped in to fill the power vacuum as central authority crumbled (sometimes on dubious grounds constitutionally).

The union Supreme Soviet met on 26–9 August 1991. Gorbachev, in his 26 August speech, stressed the need for the union treaty to be signed. Those republics unwilling to sign had to be given the right of 'independent choice', but all fifteen republics had vital economic ties and so work on an economic agreement had to begin right away. He said that gradual reform now had to be reconsidered and proposed the following measures:

1. The removal of all obstacles on the way to the market. There should be full freedom for entrepreneurship and the removal of monopoly, dictates from above and forcible methods. Market institutions should be created.

2. There should be a decisive shift of emphasis in the governing of the economy to the republics, with the union retaining legislative control for regulating a single economic space.

3. Macroeconomic stabilization.

4. The removal of all obstacles to putting land in the hands of those who wanted to work it.

5. The removal of 'economic populism', concentrating on basic issues of social protection during the transition to the market.

On 27 August Gorbachev threatened to resign if the union ceased to exist: 'The Soviet Union must be preserved as a union of sovereign states with a united army and a common economic treaty.' He announced agreement with Russia, Kazakhstan and Kyrgyzstan to begin negotiations on an economics accord, with the other republics eligible to join.

On 28 August the union Supreme Soviet ratified the dismissal of the Cabinet of Ministers. The allocation of duties was announced for the Committee for Control of the National Economy; this was expanded to include representatives from eleven other republics, besides Russia, with even the Baltic states sending 'active observers' (in mid-November the body was renamed the Inter-state Economic Committee). The individuals and their portfolios were as follows:

1 Ivan Silayev: defence, security, media, internal and external affairs, natural resources and the Ministry of Finance. On 18 September it was announced that Silayev was also to be chairman of the Inter-republican Economic Committee, but intended stepping down as prime minister of the Russian Federation (he did so in the first week of October).

2 Grigori Yavlinsky: overall economic strategy, drawing up the new reform programme.

3 Arkadi Volsky: industry, transport and communications.

4 Yuri Luzhkov: agro-industrial sector, trade (including urban food supplies during winter) and social affairs.

5 Ivan Saburov: overall economic questions.

6 A. Bektemisov: industrial supplies.

On 29 August 1991 the Supreme Soviet removed Gorbachev's powers to rule by decree. On Friday 30 August the deputy heads of Soviet ministries and economic experts from all the republics began a meeting in Moscow to work out an economic accord. On 1 September Gorbachev discussed economic measures (such as reductions in both wages and the money supply) with ten republics.

THE ECONOMIC COMMUNITY

The title 'economic union' was rejected in favour of 'economic community' or 'commonwealth'. The treaty was signed on 18 October 1991 by only eight of the remaining twelve republics (the Baltic states having been recognised as fully independent); Ukraine, Moldova, Georgia and Azerbaijan declined at that time (Ukraine and Moldova initialled the treaty on 6 November). The treaty was only in draft form, the details having to be worked out following detailed negotiations (hopefully only lasting until the end of the year) and ratified by the parliaments of the individual republics. An initial three-year duration was envisaged. Pressures to sign included the high degree of economic interdependence, aggravated by the highly monopolistic position of many suppliers (in 1989 the volume of inter-republic exchanges of Soviet-made output was more than 20 per cent of the USSR's GNP, the corresponding figure for the EC being only 16 per cent: *CDSP*, 1991, vol. XLIII, no. 41, p. 3) and pressure from Western countries concerned with issues like foreign debt. The main features of the draft treaty were as follows (*CDSP*, 1991, vol. XLIII, no. 42, pp. 4–9):

1. Free trade within a united market (a 'common economic space'). Co-ordinated policies in transport, energy, the monetary and banking system, finances, taxation and prices, customs rules and tariffs, and foreign economic relations.

2. It was recognised that 'concerted monetary and credit policies are of priority importance to find a way out of the crisis and controlling inflation'. There was also a need 'to preserve and strengthen the rouble as the common currency of a single monetary system', but this did not rule out national currencies, provided

they did not harm the community's monetary system. The immediate aim was an internally convertible rouble.

3. There was to be set up 'on the principles of a reserve system, a banking union including the central banks of member states' and an inter-state bank for issuing money, as well as a banking inspectorate with equal representation for republics to monitor the banking union's implementation of the charter. Pending the adoption of the charter, a provisional board of Gosbank USSR and republican central banks was to run the central banking system.

4. Limits were to be set on member states' budget deficits. Sums in excess would be considered a debt to other members. A community budget, to be formed by fixed payments from members, was not allowed to be in deficit.

5. 'Private ownership, free enterprise and competition form the basis of economic recovery.'

6. There was to be free movement of labour (coupled with a common social security system), the same legal conditions for business as for states' own nationals. Restrictions on the movement of goods and services were to be removed within an 'agreed period of time'. If contractual deliveries were not fulfilled, the offending republic had to compensate the others with the hard currency value of the goods.

7. The foreign economic commitments of the USSR would be honoured. The foreign debt burden was to be shared out (the remaining twelve republics actually agreed to do this 'jointly and severally' on 28 October 1991, after two days of talks with the G7 countries, i.e. others would assume the debts of defaulting republics). A bank was to be set up as a successor to Vneshekonombank to handle debt repayments; members recognised the need for a 'single procedure for accumulating hard currency receipts to service the foreign debt'. Assets, including gold and foreign currency reserves, were to be divided up. The G7 talks (19–21 November 1991) resulted in a memor-

andum of understanding on foreign debt, signed by eight republics there and then (i.e. excluding Ukraine, Azerbaijan, Georgia and Uzbekistan). A specific allocation of debt burden was to ensue, and the republics promised macroeconomic stabilization measures, price and exchange rate liberalization and free inter-republican trade (in agreement with the IMF). In return the G7 countries stood ready to support the following: a deferral of payments on the principal of medium and long-term official debt until the end of 1992 (worth about $3.6 billion); other creditors were to be urged to follow suit, bringing the total to $6 billion; G7 export agencies were to be asked to continue extending short-term lines and guarantees as an inducement for banks and suppliers to renew credit lines; and possible emergency financing of up to $1 billion, using gold as collateral. As of 5 December 1991 Vneshekonombank suspended payments on the principal of medium and long-term debt incurred before 1 January 1991 to commercial banks until 1 January 1993, in line with the G7 agreement. On 17 December the Western banks agreed to a postponement on the principal owed from 5 December 1991 to 30 March 1992 worth $5.4 billion; this was later extended to 30 June 1992 and then to 30 September.

The early debt-sharing arrangement gradually fell apart, however, and on 8 February 1992 it was formally agreed that each country should, if possible, pay its own debt. Ukraine had prior to this made it clear that it would itself pay 16.37 per cent of the debt and in mid-January had set up a foreign exchange organization to deal with this. (On 19 February 1992 Ukraine said it would take responsibility for some of the debt owed by the smaller republics, bringing its share up to a possible 21.13 per cent. On 13 March 1992 Russia and Ukraine agreed to pay for 61.34 per cent and 16.37 per cent of the debt respectively.) Moldova said it was unable to pay its share, but would forgo a claim on ex-Soviet assets if Russia paid on its behalf.

8. Customs policy towards third countries was to be co-ordinated, but member states were independently to regulate foreign economic activity and establish licences and quotas within the limits of overall quotas.

9. There was agreement on joint membership of the IMF, but individual membership was permitted.

Twenty-five detailed agreements were to be negotiated, including the following: the status and powers of community institutions (these were to include a council of heads of government, an executive inter-state economic committee, whose chairman was to be appointed by heads of government, and a court of arbitration); banking union regulations and monetary policy, and principles and mechanisms for servicing the foreign debt; the community budget; co-ordinated price reform and a list of those goods whose prices were to remain fixed at agreed levels during a transitional period.

The treaty provided for the possibility of new full or associate members, but the unanimous consent of existing ones was needed. Those republics not prepared to join the community would be penalized by, for example, having to pay world market prices and in hard currency for energy and raw materials.

YELTSIN'S RADICAL ECONOMIC PACKAGE FOR THE RUSSIAN REPUBLIC

In a speech to the Russian Congress of People's Deputies on 28 October 1991, Yeltsin outlined a programme of radical economic reform and 'shock' therapy for the Russian republic. This was a challenge to the other republics to follow suit or Russia would go it alone. Yeltsin stressed the urgency of action: 'The period for marking time is over. We are on the brink of collapse'; 'If we do not seize this new chance to break the unfavourable course of events, we shall condemn ourselves to beggary and our centuries-old state to disaster.' The proposals included the following.

1. Prices were to be freed 'in the current year' (exceptions, subsequently expanded in range, included basic consumer goods like bread, milk, salt, matches, vegetable oil and sugar, rents, baby food, railway and communications charges, oil, coal, gas and vodka). The 16 December 1991 was subsequently decided upon, but later postponed to 2 January 1992. Wages were also to be freed, but restraint was urged, as was regard to productivity. The real constraint on wages, however, was the threat of enterprise bankruptcy. A social safety net would include the raising of the minimum wage and pensions.

2. Austerity measures were to be introduced, including reductions in expenditure on defence and enterprise subsidies. The only central ministries and other bodies to be financed were those agreed in the Economic Community treaty, e.g. defence, transport and energy. (On 1 November the Soviet government decided to abolish most of these as of the 15th, especially branch ministries; the remaining ones included foreign affairs, defence, interior, culture, communications, railways, energy, nuclear energy and industry).

3. Privatization was to affect 50 per cent of small and medium enterprises (in industry, trade, transport and services) in the next three months. Rapid privatization here was possible through leasing to the workers and, if they were not interested, public auctions. The process would take longer for large enterprises; initially they were to become joint stock companies free of direct government supervision. Boards of directors could be rewarded by means of shares; workers could get 15–20 per cent of the shares. Foreigners would also be invited to invest. On 22 November, during a visit to Germany, Yeltsin talked about privatizing a third of large state enterprises in the Russian federation over the next three years.

4. Agriculture was to be subjected to land reform, and loss-making collective and state farms were to be closed down. A start was to be made by privatizing the property of grossly

unprofitable state and collective farms; land was to be transferred to individuals. The problem of land sales was to be dealt with.

5. A separate currency would be introduced if other republics insisted on having theirs. Yeltsin requested special powers (i.e. rule by decree) to implement these economic reforms. He proposed himself as prime minister. On 1 November 1991 parliament approved the following: a ban on all elections and referenda (aimed at declarations of independence by autonomous republics) until 1 December 1992; decrees to override legislation passed by federal, regional or local assemblies; the president to create or cancel executive bodies of power, with the ability to appoint administrators able to overrule local councils (the councils would be 'consulted' over the appointments); the Russian Supreme Soviet had the right to reject any draft presidential decree for up to a week before it was issued. Yeltsin optimistically thought in terms of real signs of recovery by the autumn of 1992.

Yegor Gaidar, formerly Director of the Institute of Economic Policy, was the main architect of the Yeltsin economic programme; he became deputy prime minister and minister of economics and finance in the Russian federation on 7 November 1991. (On 21 February 1992 he became simply minister of finance, with Andrei Nechaev appointed as minister of economics; in February he was made joint first deputy prime minister, retaining this position and responsibility for overall economic strategy when Vasily Barchuk became minister of finance on 2 April 1992; Yeltsin made Gaidar 'acting' prime minister on 15 June.). He said the Russian reforms were necessary because he had little faith in the economic treaty; strong links could still be maintained between republics, but mainly via bilateral agreements.

The November 1991 decrees

A statement issued by Russia, Ukraine, Belarus and Kazakhstan on 16 November declared that the Soviet Union was not authorized to represent their interests in international financial organizations like the IMF, World Bank and GATT. The republics would assume responsibility for existing financial obligations, but not for those 'taken on without their agreement by all-union and inter-republican organizations in the name of the USSR after the union has in fact ceased to exist as a single state'. On the same day Yeltsin issued a number of decrees which considerably enhanced the powers of the Russian republic at the expense of the centre:

1. 'On liberalizing foreign economic activities', effective as of 1 January 1992. The existing exchange rate regime was to be scrapped, including the general compulsory exchange of a portion of hard currency earnings by enterprises. (But a late December 1991 decree obliged the exporters of goods like oil, gas, timber and precious metals to sell 40 per cent of hard currency earnings to the Russian central bank at half the market rate; this was in order to help pay off the foreign debt and finance key imports. Exporters generally had to sell to the state at least 10 per cent of their foreign exchange earnings at the market price. New arrangements applied as of 1 July 1992; see postscript.) The rouble was initially to become internally convertible (e.g. importers would buy dollars through banks at the market rate of exchange) and ultimately fully convertible (provisionally at the end of 1992). (Note that the federal authorities had introduced a freely floating tourist rate of exchange as of 2 December 1991.) Controls would remain on the export of hard currency for investment purposes. Individuals were entitled to hard currency accounts, although strict limits were placed on the amounts that could be taken out of the country.

Enterprises were able to export and import without having to be specially registered. Note, however, that on 15 November 1991 Russia suspended oil export licences until 1 January 1992, including 'exports' to other republics, in order to ensure adequate domestic supplies. A

29 December 1991 decree came into force on 10 January 1992: Russia banned the 'export' of some sixty goods in short supply, such as food and alcohol, to those republics that had raised barriers to the 'export' of their goods to Russia. On 23 January, partly in response to the 22–3 January aid conference in Washington, Yeltsin suspended import tariffs retrospectively from 15 January until a new regime was established. This was introduced on 1 July 1992. It is worth noting here that in late March 1992 the USA announced the purchase of Russian space technology and nuclear fuel, while Russia was granted MFN treatment by the USA on 18 June 1992.

The gold and precious metals decree imposed Russian control over the whole process on its territory, from production to marketing. Mining enterprises were to be paid, in hard currency, 25 per cent of extracted gold and 25 per cent of precious metals sold on world markets. Producers of oil and gas were recently given permission to sell up to 40 per cent of their production on the free market, provided they fulfilled the state delivery quota (*Moscow News*, 29 March-5 April 1992, p. 11).

2. Russia was to take charge of the printing of money on its territory. On 22 November the Russian parliament resolved that 'By 15 December 1991 the Central Bank of Russia is to re-register the Vneshekonombank of the Soviet Union as a commercial bank servicing the foreign debt of the Soviet Union'. A resolution declared the State Bank of Russia to be 'the only body on Russian territory responsible for state monetary, credit and currency policy, the main aim of which is to strengthen the rouble' (from January 1992 until a new banking system was agreed with the other republics). The bank was to be responsible to the Russian parliament (not government, as Yeltsin proposed). Gosbank was only able to open an account with the Russian Central Bank to service the Soviet budget and internal debt.

3. Yeltsin proposed the following increases as of 1 December 1991: the minimum monthly wage should rise to 200 roubles and pay for nurses, doctors, teachers and other people working in 'budget-financed organizations' in science, culture and law enforcement by 90 per cent (as compensation for price rises). Restrictions on wages in 'off-budget' institutions were to be removed.

The December 1991 decrees

Russia's privatization programme of 26 December 1991

1. The privatization of shops, small and medium-sized enterprises in the construction and food sectors, light industry, and loss-making plants; trading companies; housing; local transport services. The targets for 1992 were as follows: 70 per cent of construction, light industry and automotive transport; 60 per cent of the food industry and retail shops; 50 per cent of the building materials industry and wholesale trade and public catering enterprises; and 20 per cent of unfinished construction projects. On 16 January 1992 Yeltsin talked of more than 70 per cent of shops, restaurants and 'trade centres' by the end of the year. The first phase of privatization was to be 2 January 1992–third quarter 1992, and the second phase was to begin in mid-1992.

Auctioning of the leases of small enterprises such as shops in Nizhny Novgorod (formerly Gorky) began on 4 April 1992, with a works collective given a 30 per cent discount if the bid for their own establishment was successful. Thirteen stores in Moscow had been privatized on 7 February 1992 (*CDSP*, 1992, vol. XLIV, no. 6, p. 27) (note that Moscow determines its own programme). Housing was to be freely apportioned to occupiers, although a tax was to be imposed on space above the norm. *Moscow News* (24–31 May 1992, p. 7) provides information on the percentage of enterprises accounted for by the private sector in Russia as of 1 April 1992: retail trade 0.7 per cent; public catering 0.7 per cent; and services 0.5 per cent.

2. In the short term at least the following, for example, would be excluded from privatization:

main transport services such as railways; water; forests; gold and platinum mining; the fuel and power complex; defence plants; the pharmaceutical industry; television and radio; banks; civil aviation; tobacco; alcohol; baby food production. Special government permission was needed, for example, in the case of oil and gas production and enterprises employing more than 10,000 workers or assets valued at over 200 million roubles on 1 January 1992.

3. Workers would be given non-voting shares for 25 per cent of the enterprise's stock. The workforce was also to have the opportunity to buy further shares (10 per cent was later specified) at a 30 per cent discount. Shares could be sold immediately. If the enterprise was sold outright to a foreigner, 10 per cent of the purchase price was to be distributed among the workers. Managers would have the option of purchasing 5 per cent of shares on preferential terms, with voting rights. It was later announced that vouchers would be issued to the public. Twenty per cent of the revenue raised through privatization was to be earmarked for 'social' expenditures generally.

In the April 1992 draft legislation two options were presented as regards workers. Workers in a particular enterprise could either receive 25 per cent of non-voting shares and buy 10 per cent of the voting shares at a substantial discount, or buy up to 51 per cent of the share capital of the enterprise without any restrictions on the sale of these shares. At least one-third of the collective must be willing to take the 51 per cent share. Each worker would be given a voucher worth no more than twenty months' average salary to purchase a stake in his or her enterprise. Some 85–90 per cent of property in total would be transferred to voucher holders, while the remainder would be sold. It was planned to end the requirement that buyers of state property are unable to resell for one year. It was hoped to start the mass privatization programme in autumn 1992. The actual approved legislation and the timetable are discussed in the postscript.

4. The situation as regards foreign investors was as follows: if enterprises were classified as 'strategic' there was to be a ceiling on the number of shares held; encouragement was given to invest in partly finished construction and loss-making enterprises; special permission was needed in the case of trading houses, insurance companies and banks, and if the enterprise employed 200 or more workers. In early March 1992 it was announced that a special rouble exchange rate would apply to foreigners to avoid cheap sell-offs, but this did not come about.

The draft of the new legislation on foreign investment was published in April 1992. Licences would be required from the Committee for Foreign Investments only in certain cases e.g. oil and gas, gold and diamonds, and the high-technology defence sector. Foreigners would be able to participate in auctions to purchase small enterprises employing less than 200 people and with assets of under 1 million roubles only with the permission of the local authorities.

The chairman of the State Property Committee, Anatoli Chubais, outlined the privatization programme on 7 February 1992. He expected a quarter of state enterprises in Russia to be sold off by the end of 1992, raising an estimated 92 billion roubles (350 billion roubles in 1993 and 500 billion roubles in 1994; in April these figures were revised to 72 billion, 350 billion and 470 billion roubles respectively). These figures compare with the 2 billion roubles raised in 1991 (*CDSP*, 1992, vol. XLIV, no. 6, p. 25). Chubais attacked the 'spontaneous privatization' which had taken place after the Russian parliament had adopted a law in July 1991, such as managers of state enterprises forming their own joint stock companies, leasing out premises and selling assets on commodity exchanges. He thought this process 'sublegal, even illegal, taking the form of outright theft' (*IHT*, 8 February 1992, p. 1). On 28 February 1992 he specifically attacked the Kolo company for buying up defence assets cheaply, while on 2

March Gaidar announced that the government's attention would henceforth be turned to this sort of corruption.

The Yeltsin decree on land of 28 December 1991

Russian collective and state farms were to reorganize themselves by 1 March 1992, the former into co-operatives and the latter into holding (share) companies. The chairman of any farm (who heads the privatization committee) was obliged to allow individual farmers to withdraw with a share of the land and property such as equipment. If a member's request for a plot of land was not satisfied within a month of submission, the farm chairman could be fined three months' salary. In the allocation of land 'Farm workers shall be given priority . . . Priority rights shall be granted to citizens who previously used plots of land under leases . . . The remaining undistributed land shall be transferred or sold . . . to citizens and juristic persons' (*CDSP*, 1992, vol. XLIV, no. 5, p. 28).

As of 1 January 1992 farmers would have the right to exchange or mortgage their land or pass it on to heirs. Land could also be sold, subject to the following conditions: if a crop grower were retiring on a pension, if the land were inherited, in the case of resettlement, or if the receipts were invested in the processing of farm produce, trade or construction in the countryside (Yuri Chernichenko, *Moscow News*, 26 January–2 February 1992, p. 10).

The Economist (11 April 1992, p. 93) provides the following information: by April 1992 around half of all farms, accounting for two-thirds of farm land, had opted either for family farms or for private associations in which land is privately owned but machinery shared. About 40 per cent of farms had chosen, at least for the time being, to form independent co-operatives. Only 10 per cent of farms had decided to stay as they were. The 80,000 private farms in Russia to date account for less than 1 per cent of gross agricultural output (*Moscow News*, 17–24 May 1992, p. 10). Private farms own only 2 per cent of land (*Moscow News*, 24–31 May 1992, p. 7). By the end of 1991 about 57 per cent of peasant farms in Russia were leased on a lifetime basis with the right of inheritance and 25 per cent were owned outright (Wegren 1992: 109).

Discrimination against the private sector in terms of supplies of inputs such as fertilizers and machinery was not allowed.

Note that an early January 1992 decree specified certain mandatory sales, albeit at market prices e.g. potatoes 25 per cent, grain 35 per cent, and meat and milk 45 per cent (the maximum for all produce in the case of private farms was 25 per cent) (*Moscow News*, 9–16 February 1992, p. 10).

Wegren (1992: 120) argues that collective and state farmers have overwhelmingly preferred to devote their energies to their private plots rather than venture into outright private faming. In 1990 output from private plots accounted for 65 per cent of the nation's potatoes (compared with 59 per cent in 1989), 33 per cent of vegetables (30 per cent in 1989), 30 per cent of meat (29 per cent in 1989), 28 per cent of milk (27 per cent in 1989) and 27 per cent of eggs (26 per cent in 1989).

The Yeltsin decree of 29 January 1992

With the aim of creating a competitive consumer market (including breaking the power of Mafia-like organizations), the decree specified the following (*CDSP*, 1992, vol. XLIV, no. 5, p. 29):

1. To grant enterprises, regardless of their form of ownership, as well as citizens, the right to engage in trade . . . without special authorization, with the exception of trade in weapons, ammunition, explosives, toxic and radioactive substances, narcotics, medicines and other goods whose sale is banned or restricted by existing legislation.
2. To establish that enterprises and citizens may engage in trade . . . in any place

convenient for them, with the exception of roadways, underground stations and areas adjacent to buildings housing state bodies of power and administration.

THE COMMONWEATH OF INDEPENDENT STATES

For some time it looked as though Gorbachev might be able to form a Union of Sovereign States (USS), but Ukraine's reluctance and ultimate refusal (after the 1 December 1991 referendum) in particular to join proved to be decisive in the end. The State Council met on 14 November 1991, but only seven republics agreed in principle to form a union (Russia, Belarus, Kazakhstan, Turkmenistan, Kyrgyzstan, Tajikistan and Azerbaijan). Uzbekistan had intended to join the talks, but the president was indisposed. The meeting on 25 November saw a somewhat different seven (Uzbekistan was represented, but not Azerbaijan) fail to initial the treaty, agreeing only to send a draft text to the individual republican parliaments.

The USS draft text was hazy on detail, but, although the centre would only have powers delegated by the republics, there were to be significant central authorities. The following were envisaged: a USS president, popularly elected for a five-year term; a Ministry of Foreign Relations, supervised by a Council of Foreign Ministers of the republics; a Ministry of Defence, co-ordinated by the republics; joint responsibility for fighting crime; a joint energy policy; and defence of human rights.

The presidents of Russia (Boris Yeltsin), Ukraine (Leonid Kravchuk) and Belarus (Stanislav Shushkevic: strictly, speaker of the parliament) met on 7–8 December 1991 in Minsk, the capital of Byelorussia (to avoid the impression of Russian dominance). Gorbachev was not invited. This historic meeting rejected the idea of the Union of Sovereign States and instead decided to form a Commonweath of Independent States (CIS). It was declared that

'The Union of Soviet Socialist Republics as a subject of international law and a geopolitical reality is ceasing its existence . . . activity of organs of the former USSR on the territory of the members of the commonwealth ceases'. The 'Minsk accords' pronounced the 1922 treaty founding the USSR dead. Minsk was declared the 'capital' ('headquarters' or 'co-ordinating centre') of the CIS, membership of which is open to former republics or indeed any other state meeting the requirements.

The details of the commonweath remained to be worked out, but certain broad concepts were agreed. For instance, there was to be joint control of nuclear weapons, and economic policy was to be co-ordinated within a single economic space. There were to be no central authorities as envisaged in the Union of Sovereign States, no federal president and no federal parliament. The 'co-ordinating bodies' were to play a minimal role, with members of the CIS regarded as subjects of international law.

Most of the remaining twelve republics expressed interest in joining, the five Asiatic republics, on 13 December, going so far as to 'declare their readiness to become equal co-founders of the Commonwealth of Independent States, taking into account the interests of all their subjects'.

Gorbachev's initial reaction was generally hostile, decribing certain aspects as 'illegal' and 'dangerous'. But he soon came round to accepting the idea and concentrated his concern on an orderly and constitutional transition. On 17 December Gorbachev and Yeltsin met and agreed that the Soviet Union would formally come to an end when the new year arrived. Decrees issued by Yeltsin on 19 December 1991 stated that 'All the buildings, including the Kremlin, as well as the property, assets and foreign currency of the Soviet president and the Inter-republican Economic Committee are transferred to the management of the Russian administration'. The foreign and interior ministries and the domestic intelligence wing of the KGB were taken over by Russia, with the intention of creating a new Russian Ministry of Security and Internal Affairs; the Foreign Intelligence Service of the KGB was taken over the following day (the idea of a new ministry was later scuppered by the constitutional court after unrest in the Russian parliament about the apparent re-emergence of a 'Stalinist' organization). The creation of a Russian Law and Order Ministry was also decreed. Only the Soviet Ministry of Defence and Ministry of Atomic Energy remained.

The CIS agreement was signed on 21 December 1991 in Alma-Ata, the capital of Kazakhstan, by eleven of the remaining twelve republics. Georgia only sent observers (although its president requested admittance on 26 December, amid serious fighting with the opposition that started four days earlier; the CIS would only consider entry when the conflict was resolved). The Soviet Union was declared dead: 'With the formation of the CIS, the USSR ceases to exist.' Gorbachev was not invited to attend and his suggestion of a final session of the Supreme Soviet to transfer power constitutionally was not taken up (the Supreme Soviet did vote for its own dissolution on 26 December, but there were so few deputies there that the end was farcical). The main features of the CIS were as follows.

1. The states were independent and disputes would be resolved peacefully. Existing borders were inviolable. There was to be no common citizenship (as Gorbachev suggested for a transitional period), but visa-free travel would be permitted.

2. 'Allegiance to co-operation in the formation and development of a common economic space, and all-European and Eurasian markets, is confirmed.' There would be no central budget, but the aim was to keep republican budget deficits to 3 per cent of national income at most. The more distant future of the rouble as a common currency was not decided upon. (Note that the question of intra-CIS trade prices was not decided upon, but the 8 February 1992 meeting talked of 'world prices', although at a rouble exchange rate of twenty to thirty to the US dollar; this was the rate which Russia then thought appropriate for defence of the rouble by a Western stabilization fund.) The 14–15 February 1992 meeting of the CIS in Minsk did not see much progress made, but the principle of free trade between republics was confirmed and there was agreement to allow the re-export of goods subject to licensing and quotas only with the consent of the republic which produced the goods. On 17 February Russia and Ukraine agreed on the terms for the issuing of a new currency, e.g. Ukraine would remit all roubles to the Russian central bank.

3. The supreme co-ordinating body of the CIS would be a Council of the Heads of State (the presidents). There would be a parallel Council of Heads of Government (prime ministers). These councils would 'co-ordinate the activities of the states of the new commonwealth in the sphere of common interests'. Meetings were to held at least twice a year and at least once every three months respectively. There were also to be ministerial committees on foreign affairs, economics and finance, transport and communications, social security and internal affairs; at least four meetings per year were envisaged.

4. The CIS was open to any other state which shared its goals and principles and provided all members agreed.

5. Russia would take over USSR membership of the UN, including the seat on the Security Council. Ukraine and Belarus (already UN members) and Russia would help the others to become members of the UN and other international organizations. (Note that Gorbachev had suggested common international representation and a CIS seat on the UN Security Council.)

6. The defence issue was far from resolved. The Soviet defence minister, Yevgeni Shaposhnikov, was named as temporary commander of the military (note that Gorbachev was formally commander-in-chief until his resignation.) Further discussions produced broad agreement: the Russian president and the

commander-in-chief were to control nuclear weapons, but Ukraine, Belarus and Kazakhstan would have to agree to their use, and the other CIS members would have to be consulted. Ukraine would remove or destroy tactical nuclear weapons by 1 July 1992 (actually achieved ahead of time after many objections) and destroy or dismantle strategic weapons by the end of 1994. Belarus's nuclear weapons would be removed or destroyed by mid-1992. At the 14 February 1992 Minsk meeting it was agreed that a council comprising the presidents of Russia, Ukraine, Belarus and Kazakhstan would command strategic nuclear weapons. Kazakhstan's attitude towards strategic nuclear weapons was very unclear for a long time. A protocol to the 1991 Start Treaty was signed by the USA, Russia, Ukraine, Belarus and Kazakhstan on 24 May 1992, pledging to implement it. The last three countries ageed to give up nuclear weapons by the end of the decade. On 16 June 1992, during Yeltsin's visit to the USA, further drastic reductions in strategic nuclear weapons were announced; the target numbers agreed in the 1991 Start Treaty were approximately halved.

As regards conventional defence, each republic could choose to have its own forces or join a single command structure. Subsequently, Ukraine, Azerbaijan, Armenia (announced 27 February 1992), Moldova, Belarus and Uzbekistan expressed interest in the former. Yeltsin announced plans to form a Russian National Guard. On 2 January 1992 Ukraine announced that, with the exception of strategic nuclear forces, it was assuming control of the armed forces on its territory (a ceiling of 220,000 was later fixed). Belarus assumed control on 12 January 1992 and Moldova of certain forces in March. The Black Sea Fleet became a real bone of contention between Russia and Ukraine. On 7 April 1992 Ukraine issued a decree assuming control over all forces on its territory, including the fleet. Yeltsin issued a counter-decree, but a potentially dangerous situation was calmed by the mutual suspension of the decrees and the

setting up of a joint commission. On 26 May it was announced that the fleet was to be divided up. Indeed the only area to be left to CIS joint military command was stategic nuclear weapons.

The 14 February 1992 meeting of the CIS in Minsk led to a clear assertion that Ukraine, Moldova and Azerbaijan would form their own armies and not join a unified command. The other eight republics (Georgia sent only an observer) agreed to a unified command for a transitional period of two years, although Belarus and Uzbekistan made clear their intention to opt out then. During the transitional period individual members were permitted to form their own armies, which 'may or may not join the unified force'. On 16 March 1992 Yeltsin announced the intention to form a separate Russian ministry of defence with himself as acting minister. A definite commitment to an army was made on 7 April 1992. A decree followed on 7 May, with Yeltsin as commander-in-chief; Russian personnel were estimated at 2.63 million out of the 3.7 million former Soviet armed forces, and the intention was to bring the former down to 1.5 million by 1996 (later put back to the year 2000). Pavel Grachev was appointed Russian defence minister on 19 May. On 16 March Kazakhstan proclaimed the setting up of a republican guard. A poorly attended CIS meeting in Tashkent produced a defence pact signed on 15 May 1992 by Russia, Armenia, Kazakhstan, Tajikistan, Turkmenistan and Uzbekistan. The signatories promised not to attack each other and to come to one another's asistance if a member were attacked by another country. On 4 June 1992 Russia announced that formal border controls would be established with Ukraine, the Baltic states and Azerbaijan. The meeting of the CIS on 6 July 1992 produced agreement on the setting up of a peacekeeping force to be employed in areas of ethnic strife; Moldova was mentioned as the probable first use.

International recognition of the CIS members was patchy. For example, China and Vietnam recognised all the republics, but the main Western countries discriminated. The USA recognized Russia, Ukraine, Belarus, Kazakhstan and Uzbekistan on 26 December, but, while the others were acknowledged to be independent states, diplomatic relations would be established with them only when it was confirmed that they followed 'responsible security policies and democratic principles' (President Bush). The upheaval in Georgia following allegations of undemocratic practices by President Gamsakhurdia gave rise to the gravest doubts (the EC and the USA did not recognise Georgia until 23 and 24 March 1992 respectively, after the return of Shevardnadze). The EC recognised Russia as the successor to the Soviet Union on 25 December and recognition was extended to Ukraine and Armenia the next day; eight republics were mentioned on 31 December 1991 as fulfilling EC conditions (Ukraine, Armenia, Azerbaijan, Belarus, Kazakhstan, Moldova, Turkmenistan and Uzbekistan).

Gorbachev's anticipated resignation came on 25 December 1991. He was the first leader of the Soviet Union to resign. The changeover was remarkably peaceful. His speech confirmed that he would have preferred a union of sovereign states, but he promised to help all he could:

> I firmly came out in favour of the independence of nations and sovereignty for the republics. At the same time I support the preservation of the union state and the integrity of the country . . . I shall do all I can to ensure that the agreements that were signed there lead towards real concord in society and facilitate a way out of the crisis.

His first new role was to become chairman of the International Foundation for Social, Economic and Political Research, a body set up soon after the abortive August coup.

Economic developments after the setting up of the CIS

Various agreements have been signed. For example, on 3 February 1992 Turkey, Bulgaria, Romania, Russia, Ukraine, Azerbaijan, Moldova, Armenia and Georgia formed the Black Sea Economic Co-operation Zone. At the summit meeting on 15 June a pact on economic and political co-operation was signed, with Albania and Greece also included. On 16 February 1992 Uzbekistan, Turkmenistan and Azerbaijan joined the Economic Co-operation Organization (ECO), a non-Arab Moslem body founded by Turkey, Pakistan and Iran; Tajikistan and Kyrgyzstan joined the next day. The Investment Development Bank funds joint projects. On 17 February 1992 the Caspian Council was formed by Iran, Russia, Azerbaijan, Turkmenistan and Kazakhstan. Russia joined Germany, Sweden, Finland, Norway, Denmark, Poland, Estonia, Latvia and Lithuania in the formation of the Council of the Baltic Sea States on 5 March 1992. The aims included aid to the poorer members of the group and strengthened ties with the EC.

Russia's drive to the market

Yeltsin took the controversial decision to start the transition to the market economy in Russia in earnest by liberalizing many prices on 2 January 1992. Some prices had already been freed, of course, as discussed earlier. According to Yeltsin (*CDSP*, 1992, vol. XLIV, no. 14, p. 5), 'By the middle of 1991 . . . 45 per cent of all output was being sold at unrestricted prices'. A number of prices remained controlled after 2 January, but even these were raised substantially, by 300 per cent on average in the case of basic consumer goods, according to the Russian minister of economics and finance, Yegor Gaidar (*FT*, 22 January 1992, p. 15). Approximately 90 per cent of consumer goods and 80 per cent of producer goods prices were freed from direct administrative regulation (*CDSP*, 1992, vol. XLIV, no. 9, p. 1). The guidelines for maximum increases in the case of controlled products were as follows: 200 per cent for rail fares; 300 per cent for bread, milk, butter, salt, vegetable oil, petrol, domestic electricity and central heating; 350 per cent for sugar; 400 per cent for vodka, medicines and matches; 500 per cent for coal and gas. Housing rents were frozen pending privatization. There were regional variations in price rises, however; some initial price rises exceeded expectations, and various adjustments took place over time (including falls). Note also that even 'contract' prices were subject to guidelines, such as a maximum 25 per cent trade mark-up on the producer's price for state trade enterprises not converted to 'commercial operations' (*CDSP*, 1992, vol. XLIV, no. 9, p. 3). Yeltsin set a 50 per cent maximum producer's margin on 16 January 1992 as a result of unexpectedly high price rises. In early February 1992 it was officially announced that, on average, prices had risen in January (compared to December 1991) by 300–50 per cent rather than the expected 250 per cent. Price stability was expected in February and a monthly inflation rate of around 10 per cent was predicted by the end of the year (see the section below on economic performance, pp. 104–5, for the actual figures). On 10 February 1992 train fares in Russia went up by 300 per cent and on 20 April the price of petrol rose fivefold. Petrol prices went up again on 20 May.

As regards wages and salaries the aim was that these should not be raised commensurately in most cases. 'One of the fundamental principles of the concept of social protection during the changeover to a market is that increases in income should not lag behind increases in prices by more than 30 per cent' (Deputy Prime Minister Aleksandr Shokin, *CDSP*, 1992, vol. XLIV, no. 14, p. 30). There was an approximate doubling of salaries in government-subsidized organizations (*Moscow News*, 5–12 January 1992, p. 5). In January, for example, teachers' pay went up 2.8 fold. On 1 January 1992 pensions, child benefit and the minimum wage were raised by 90 per cent to 342 roubles a month. On 5 February 1992 a further pension increase to 550 roubles was announced and yet again on 3 April to 800 roubles (and the minimum wage was to rise to 900 roubles on 1 May). The threat of strikes, however, was effective in

some cases, e.g. on 25 January Yeltsin announced a threefold increase in the tariff rate of coal miners and on 18 May 1992 doctors and teachers stopped their industrial action after large salary increases. The Russian State Statistical Committee reported that the cost of basic goods per person had increased from 340 to 1,300 roubles a month since price liberalization (Jonathan Steele, *The Guardian*, 4 February 1992, p. 8). In contrast *per capita* income was only 900 roubles a month (Jonathan Steele, *The Guardian*, 31 March 1992, p. 24). Official statistics for the first quarter of 1992 reveal that around one-third of the people in Russia had monthly incomes of 900 roubles or less, while the monthly subsistence level stood at 1,200 roubles (John Lloyd, *FT*, 24 April 1992, p. 2). In February 1992 the average monthly wage was 1,994 roubles, 2,567 roubles in industry (*Moscow News*, 31 May-7 June 1992, p. 10).

Apart from the fact that the price mechanism lies at the heart of resource allocation in a market economy, Gaidar rationalized the price reform as follows (see, for example, his article in *FT*, 22 January 1992, p. 15):

1. To reduce queues.

2. To restore confidence in the rouble (much of the trade between enterprises had become barter).

3. Once expected, price rises must take place right away because otherwise supplies would be withheld from the market in anticipation of future rises, while consumers would try to speed up purchases. The rapid liberalization of prices would increase supplies in the market as both dishoarding and increased production ensued. Prices would then start to fall.

Yeltsin hoped that by the autumn of 1992 Russia would have 'a more stable economy and a gradually improving quality of life'. In his new year's message Yeltsin again optimistically said that 'It will be hard, but the period will not be long. We are talking about six to eight months'. He claimed that prices would start to fall in the autumn of 1992. But this optimism began to fade, Yeltsin, in a coup anniversary speech of 21

August 1992, saying that 'The most important thing is to live through this year and in 1993 life will become easier for all of us'. Gaidar (13 January) talked of living standards falling for about eight months before levelling out; he predicted (16 January) that it would take at least a year and a half before prices and output stabilized: 'The first two years are the most difficult ones' (3 February 1992); towards the end of March 1992 he talked of the economy stabilizing by the end of the year.

4. To reduce the monetary overhang. To ensure that there was only a once-and-for-all price rise there was a need to reduce budgetary expenditure (e.g. defence) in addition to the subsidies saved through the price rises. The budget deficit, which was over 20 per cent of GDP in 1991 (Yegor Gaidar, *FT*, 4 March 1992, p. 17), could also be reduced by ensuring tax revenues through a 28 per cent VAT, a 37 per cent enterprise wage tax and a 32 per cent profits tax (operative as of 2 January 1992: note the lesson learned from the Polish experience, where the unprofitability of much of industry adversely affected budgetary revenue). The actual austerity budget for Russia for the first quarter of 1992, announced on 24 January, abandoned the original aim of balance and set the deficit at 11.5 billion roubles (1 per cent of GNP) and the expenditure total at 420 billion roubles. Construction and defence were particularly badly hit (defence was set to be reduced to 4.5 per cent of GNP; spending on weapons was to be only one-seventh of the previous level, but part of the savings was switched to pay for wage and welfare increases for the armed forces). Gaidar also stressed the need to curb the amount of credit issued (600 billion roubles in 1991 at an interest rate of only 6 per cent); much went to prop up inefficient enterprises (inter-enterprise debt rose from 39 billion roubles at the start of 1992 to 900 billion roubles by mid-April: John Lloyd and Martin Wolf, *FT*, 22 April 1992, p. 18). The chairman of the Russian central bank, Georgi Matyukin (who offered his resignation on 1 June 1992, although

it was not accepted until 16 July), estimates that cash in circulation doubled in 1991 (*IHT*, 14 January 1992, p. 2). In budget amendments announced on 5 February 1992, VAT on some food items was reduced to 15 per cent and abolished on canteen meals. The budget deficit for the first quarter of 1992 was raised to 25 billion roubles.

5. It was not possible to privatize and introduce anti-monopoly legislation before price liberalization. Gaidar has talked in terms of setting up a workable market mechanism within two years. There is also the argument that price liberalization focuses public anger on production and supply monopolies and thus helps dismantle them.

The critics of rapid price liberalization put forward the following arguments:

1. There was the danger of social unrest. There was inadequate protection for the most vulnerable groups in society in particular. Nikolai Petrakov argues that price liberalization meant that most income was spent on food, causing falling demand and output elsewhere in the economy; there was thus the danger of a social explosion. He believes that demonopolization and privatization should precede price liberalization (reported by Peter Pringle, *The Independent*, 27 March 1992, p. 10). He is also reported to support farming subsidies, adequate social security, price and wage regulation, and the commercialization of industry and services (*Moscow News*, 29 March-5 April 1992, p. 3). Petrakov recommends monetary reform, including an independent central bank and the introduction of a parallel, 'hard' rouble (*CDSP*, 1992, vol. XLIV, no. 7, pp. 9–10). In a March 1992 article Petrakov thought the then exchange rate for the rouble represented a 'several-fold' undervaluation and advocated a fixed and more realistic rate; other recommended measures included price and wage controls and improved domestic supplies by means of export controls and increased imports (*CDSP*, 1992, vol. XLIV, no. 11, pp. 1–4). He also thinks that corporate taxes should vary inversely with output in order

to stimulate production (*CDSP*, 1992, vol. XLIV, no. 12, p. 5). Oleg Bogomolov argues in favour of the more evolutionary path to the market adopted by Hungary and China (reported by Jonathan Steele, *The Guardian*, 21 April 1992, p. 21 and *CDSP*, 1992, vol. XLIV, no. 12, p. 5) and less stress on trying to balance the budget (*CDSP*, 1992, vol. XLIV, no. 10, p. 12).

No mass protests or labour unrest in fact followed the price rises, although there were some protests and at least two two students were killed by troops in Tashkent (capital of Uzbekistan) during 16–19 January 1992 (concessions followed in the form of increased grants and reduced food prices for students). Many point out that the privatization of sectors such as retail trade can be achieved quite rapidly.

2. The price increases would not bring forth the desired increase in production because of the dominance of state-owned monopolies in production and distribution. Matyukin, for example, stressed the prior need for competitive conditions. St Petersburg's mayor, Anatoli Sobchak, particularly stressed the prior need for land reform (*IHT*, 3 February 1992, p. 2). Some claimed that state managers maintained large inventories at high prices because they were unconvinced that the reforms would survive, while inflationary expectations were often mentioned as a cause of high prices. Grigori Yavlinsky (*CDSP*, 1992, vol. XLIV, no. 5, p. 3) feared hyperinflation would follow in the absence of demonopolization and privatization; he also stressed the need for real economic co-operation and co-ordination among the former Soviet republics.

The Russian government's economic policy was subjected to severe criticism in a report by the Centre for Economic and Political Investigation led by Yavlinsky (*Moscow News*, 24–31 May and 31 May–7 June 1992). The following points were made: a failed stabilization policy had left the economy on the verge of runaway inflation and a severe recession; and there was a need to keep a single economic space on the scale of the former Soviet Union, to accelerate privatization and land reform, to attack monopoly, and to liberalize foreign trade quickly. Vasily Selyunin (*CDSP*, 1992, vol. XLIV, no. 5, p. 5) worried that the maximum 25 per cent mark-up would encourage the purchase of the most expensive goods from wholesalers. Nikolai Shmelev (*Moscow News*, 5–12 July 1992, pp. 10–11) sympathizes with the government, which inherited 'an unbelievably bad situation'. Price liberalization resulted in the near elimination of money savings. This, Shmelev considers, was a risky and morally brutal act, but from a technical point of view was the most successful achievement of the government. A healthier currency and monetary system in general resulted. But any further decline in living standards would be very dangerous, since money savings and stocks of goods would not be available to cushion the blow. A more secure social security system is needed, especially with the prospects of rapidly rising unemployment. Russia can allow herself a modest budget deficit of say 3–4 per cent of GNP. Investment has been paralyzed and there has been a *de facto* flight of capital abroad, partly owing to government policy (e.g. enterprise taxation and compulsory hard currency exchange). Demonopolization and privatization (especially small and medium-sized enterprises) need to be speeded up. The common economic space within the limits of the former Soviet Union needs to be preserved.

Yeltsin himself actually attacked the 'Mafia-like structures striving to keep their dominance in [private] distribution'. Both Yeltsin and Gaidar (16 January) noted that production actually fell in some cases as prices were pitched too high by monopoly producers, who reduced output when goods were returned by the sales outlets. Yeltsin said that

The monopolists are ready to curtail production, shift to an expensive assortment of output, and even shut down production facilities. The customer remains totally defenceless. It is necessary to break up monopolism along the entire chain of the movement of goods, so that customers will finally be able to influence price setting.

3. The prices rises should have been synchronized with the start of large-scale Western humanitarian aid.

These criticisms did not go unanswered. In a speech to parliament on 13 February 1992 Yeltsin promised increased social protection for the most vulnerable. He also put Vice-president Rutskoi, a vociferous critic of the Russian government, in charge of agrarian reform.

On 27 February 1992 further measures were proposed, which Gaidar thought would help ensure 'a normally functioning market mechanism by the end of the year'. The number of controlled prices was to be further reduced to a bare minimum, namely medicines, baby food and local services such as housing and transport. The prices of basic consumer goods like bread, milk and sugar were to be freed by the end of March 1992 and those of oil and gas on 20 April. Anti-monopoly measures, backed up with penalties, were to be introduced and a balanced budget aimed for by the end of 1992. Gaidar hoped that monthly inflation would be down to 2–3 per cent by the end of the year. There was a reduction in the quantity of rouble notes issued during January compared with that in December, but the volume rose again in both February and March. Dyker points out that the average amount of cash in circulation had increased from 126.1 billion roubles in 1990 to 260 billion roubles in 1991 (Dyker 1992b: 31). Further measures announced on 27 February included the following (*CDSP*, 1992, vol. XLIV, no. 9, pp. 2–4): (1) all export quotas would be eliminated before 1 July 1992, with the exception of energy, whose deadline would be the end of 1993, and goods restricted for security reasons; there would be no return to quantitative limits on imports (note that import taxes, suspended January–June 1992 partly in order to increase the supply of goods while prices were being liberalized, were supposed to be fixed in the 5–10 per cent range

in August; in fact the new tariff regime came in on 1 July); and (2) obligatory state orders would be eliminated and all other elements of the centralized distribution of material resources would be eliminated by the end of 1992.

A more detailed programme of economic reform for 1992 was outlined on 2 March 1992, following IMF recommendations:

1. The removal of most of the remaining price controls by the end of March, the exceptions including local services such as housing rents and transport, and the domestic use of gas and electricity.

The freeing of the domestic price of oil on 20 April, reaching an estimated 2,000–2,600 roubles a tonne or about a quarter of the world price (the price of oil was raised from 70 to 350 roubles a tonne on 1 January 1992; Russia produces about 90 per cent of CIS oil). The internal price of oil would gradually rise to world levels over a period of eighteen months to two years, with an export tax accounting for the price difference. It was later announced that the oil price liberalization was to be postponed. On 18 May 1992 Yeltsin signed a resolution announcing the subsequent introduction of an initial range for oil prices of 1,800–2,200 roubles a tonne and a range for industrial users of gas of 1,100–1,600 roubles per thousand cubic metres (domestic users would still pay 260 roubles). Suppliers of oil would face a progressive tax of up to 90 per cent for a price in excess of 1,800 roubles, while profit confiscation and fines would apply after 2,200 roubles. A similar regime applied to gas (Russia accounts for 79 per cent of CIS gas). World prices would be charged those countries lacking special arrangements with Russia. Gaidar is quoted as saying that the impact was lessened by the fact that 40 per cent of Russian oil was at that time already traded in free markets (*IHT*, 19 May 1992, p. 13). On 30 May Yeltsin threatened to delay the freeing of energy prices, proposing that a committee should be set up to investigate the effects before a final decision was made. It was later announced (11 June) that oil prices would probably not be freed until the summer of 1993.

The decree permitting lower-level governmental authorities the discretion to free the prices of basic goods like bread, milk, sugar, cottage cheese, salt, cooking oil and matches was issued by Yeltsin on 7 March 1992, with the recommendation that the funds saved in subsidies should be used for the 'social protection of the population' (those especially badly affected, such as pensioners, children and large families). The prices of vodka and gold were freed on 7 May 1992; the state monopoly of vodka production was retained, but not that of beer and wine.

2. The budget deficit was to be reduced to 1 per cent of GNP by the end of 1992.

3. The restoration of VAT of 28 per cent on goods formerly excluded and its introduction on imports as of 1 July.

4. The introduction in midsummer of a temporary dual exchange rate system for the rouble, with an especially less advantageous rate for capital flows into Russia to avoid the situation where foreigners might buy up assets on too favourable terms. A single rate would untimately be achieved once the rouble had settled down. Gaidar wanted to stabilize the rouble at a realistic rate, stronger than fifty roubles to the US dollar (*FT*, 4 March 1992, p. 17); a rate of twenty-five to thirty was mooted (*FT*, 26 March 1992, p. 40), but forty to fifty was later thought more realistic (*FT*, 3 April 1992, p. 14). John Lloyd and Martin Wolf (*FT*, 21 April 1992, p. 1) reported that the aim then became a 'crawling peg' system starting at forty to fifty roubles to the US dollar, allowing gradual devaluations of the rouble in line with inflation rate differentials. The scheme finally chosen is discussed below.

5. A tightening of monetary policy, including an increase in reserve requirements for central banks to 20 per cent in April.

6. A tax-based incomes policy, with a progressive tax on pay increases exceeding the norm.

7. Improved social security arrangements for the most disadvantaged.

8. The scope of the programme would have to be reduced in the absence of substantial Western aid, including a stabilization fund of between $5 billion to $6 billion.

A crucial and acrimonious meeting of the Russian Congress of People's Deputies took place on 6–21 April 1992 (the 1,046 members were elected in March 1990 for five years). Yeltsin anticipated a number of problems. He had previously removed ministerial titles from individuals such as Gaidar while in fact preserving their roles. The economic reform programme was to be relaxed somewhat. An extra 200 billion roubles' worth of credit was to be provided. There were to be tax concessions. Industrialists were to be invited to join the government, i.e. people with practical experience. The energy price increases planned for June 1992 were to be delayed and introduced gradually. Gaidar (who emerged stronger from the congress) announced that the budget deficit for the first quarter of 1992 was 19.2 billion roubles or 1.5 per cent of GNP (compared with 18 per cent in 1991). But the deficit was expected to reach 5 per cent of GNP in the second quarter and the aim was to keep it within 5 per cent for the rest of the year. Note that the way the government calculates the deficit has been criticized. For example, Yavlinsky argues that foreign credits should not be included in revenues, while Russia's share of the internal debt of the former Soviet Union has been underestimated (*Moscow News*, 24–31 May 1992, p. 6). If calculated according to IMF methods the deficit in 1991 was 24 per cent; one alternative estimate of the deficit in the first quarter of 1992 was 4.8 per cent of GNP (*CDSP*, 1992, vol. XLIV, no. 15, p. 25).

Yeltsin wanted to retain his post as prime minister and his ability to appoint government ministers and issue decrees until 1 December 1992. At first the CPD only gave him until the end of July, but a compromise was reached after much wrangling; the government even offered to resign. Yeltsin offered to give up his premiership within three months and to appoint a second first deputy prime minister alongside Gaidar. Yeltsin announced that he intended to put the following proposal to the Russian Supreme Soviet (250 members elected by the Congress): 'If the Supreme Soviet does not approve the candidature for head of government, the president has the right to appoint within one month an acting head of government for up to one year or directly to be in charge of the work of government.' A resolution generally endorsed the government's economic programme. Although the government was to 'enact gradually' the recommendations of the CPD (such as 'the need to increase people's social protection', e.g. pensions, the indexation of savings, and pay rises for state employees like health workers and teachers), the measures were to take 'due account of present economic and social circumstances'. A constitutional amendment allowing the unrestricted buying and selling of land was not passed.

Russia and all the other former Soviet republics except Azerbaijan became members of the IMF on 27 April 1992. Gaidar hoped that an agreed reform programme could be decided upon by the end of June in order that Russia could take advantage of the conditional $24 billion Western aid package (including a $6 billion stabilization fund: see Appendix 3.3). Gaidar envisaged a full market economy by the end of the century. But negotiations with the IMF did not go smoothly. Yeltsin, who on 26 May vowed not to stand for a second term of the presidency in 1996, showed increasing anxiety about the effects of 'shock' therapy. A loosening of monetary policy was in the air, not least because of the shortage of rouble notes to pay workers. Georgi Matyukin, chairman of the Russian central bank, offered his resignation to parliament on 1 June, after criticisms of the lack of cash and growing inter-enterprise indebtedness and potential bankruptcy stemming from tighter and more expensive credits. Yeltsin appointed more interventionist-minded industrialists to the cabinet. Georgi Khizha, formerly a defence enterprise manager, privatization

adviser to St Petersburg and the head of the St Petersburg Enterprises' Association, became industry minister and a deputy prime minister on 21 May. On 30 May Viktor Chernomyrdin, the former head of the Soviet gas monopoly Gasprom, also became a deputy prime minister, replacing Vladimir Lopukhin as energy minister. The latter was a firm advocate of freeing energy prices. A second first deputy prime minister was appointed, Vladimir Shumeiko (a former enterprise manager in heavy industry, the former president of the Russian Confederation of Entrepreneurs' Unions, which represents state industry, and a former deputy speaker of parliament) being in charge of 'operations' as opposed to Gaidar being responsible for economic 'strategy'. Anatoli Chubais, already the privatization supremo and concerned about the delays to the privatization and bankruptcy laws, became a deputy prime minister.

On 15 June 1992 Yeltsin made Gaidar 'acting' prime minister to indicate his determination to push ahead with the reform programme. Yeltsin also issued a decree on bankruptcy. As from 1 July 1992 enterprises would have up to three months to pay off their debts or they would be declared bankrupt and subject to auctions open to foreigners. But on 22 June Gaidar announced that the extra credit to be made available over the next six months was to be raised from 200 billion to 500 billion roubles because of growing inter-enterprise debt.

The IMF and the Russian government's second stage of economic reform outlined on 30 June 1992 (see postscript)

The performance of the Russian economy

The United Nations Economic Commission for Europe (1992: 139–41) estimates that GDP in Russia fell by 9 per cent in 1991 (compared with a fall of 2 per cent in 1990), while industrial output fell by 8 per cent and agricultural output by 5 per cent. Output was expected to fall heavily in 1992 (see postscript). Official figures reveal that consumer prices rose by 245 per cent in January 1992 and a very high inflation rate was forecast for the whole year (see postscript).

The number of registered unemployed in Russia in early 1992 was very low, 70,000 at the start of the year and 118,400 by the beginning of April (*Moscow News*, 31 May–7 June 1992, p. 10). But a steep rise in unemployment was expected (see postscript). A new unemployment benefit scheme was to replace the previous complicated one in which benefit was a declining percentage of the previous wage. 'Augmented assistance' to those who lost their jobs as a result of the closing or major reorganiz- ation of enterprises would amount to no more than 90 per cent of their past average wages, while 'regular assistance' would not exceed 75 per cent of the minimum wage (*CDSP*, 1992, vol. XLIV, no. 9, pp. 1–2).

It may be appropriate here to point out the deep general concern at the degree of corruption and criminality characterizing the 'Wild West' (or perhaps more appropriately 'Wild East') stage of Russian marketization. In early April 1992 measures were taken to combat corruption in the civil service.

Policy in the other republics of the former Soviet Union

Table 3.3 shows the how much the republics of the former Soviet Union were dependent on one another as regards trade, especially the smaller ones.

Ukraine

Ukraine accounted for 17.9 per cent of the total Soviet population, while Ukrainians comprised 72 per cent of the republic's population. Ukraine is known for its agriculture, but it also has well developed industry. In 1990 Ukraine contributed 16 per cent of Soviet industrial production and 22.5 per cent of Soviet agricultural output (important products include grain, milk and meat; 26 per cent, 22.6 per cent, and 21.3 per cent respectively). The percentage shares for

Table 3.3 Population, NMP *per capita* and exports to other republics of the former Soviet Union

Republic	Population 1990	NMP *per capita* (% Soviet average)	Exports to other republics (% NMP) 1989
Russia	148.5	119.8	18.2
Ukraine	51.9	89.6	37.2
Uzbekistan	20.7	44.9	39.7
Kazakhstan	16.7	79.3	28.9
Byelorussia	10.3	113.4	64.8
Azerbaijan	7.1	58.9	58.1
Georgia	5.5	78.2	56.4
Tajikistan	5.4	39.0	46.0
Moldavia	4.4	88.6	60.6
Kirghizia	4.4	54.2	45.5
Lithuania	3.7	106.5	61.1
Turkmenistan	3.7	56.2	49.7
Armenia	3.4	82.0	52.2
Latvia	2.7	131.2	66.1
Estonia	1.6	137.0	66.4

Note. The *Financial Times* (23 April 1992, p.6) points out that only Azerbaijan, Russia and Turkmenistan have a positive balance in energy trade with the other republics.
Source. United Nations (1992) *World Economy Survey 1992*, New York, p. 29.

individual industrial products were as follows: coal 23.5; steel 34.1; iron ore 44.5; machine tools 23.6; television sets 35.8; and footwear 23.3. Ukraine imports 42 per cent of its energy needs e.g. the country produces only 8 per cent and 20 per cent of its consumption of oil and natural gas respectively (Karatnycky 1992: 98). Independent Ukraine soon began to diversify its sourcing of energy supplies, e.g. oil from Iran. The infamous Chernobyl nuclear plant was planned to be closed down by the end of 1993. A report published on 22 April 1992 put the number of deaths attributed to the 26 April 1986 accident in the range 6,000–8,000 rather than the official Soviet figure of thirty-one.

Ukraine unwillingly followed Russia on 2 January 1992 by itself raising prices, although not by precisely the same amounts. The fear, as in other republics, was that otherwise goods would flow to Russia in the absence of trade controls. The Ukrainian government doubled wages and salaries. Ukraine complained of an inadequate supply of roubles, receiving less than 4 billion rouble notes instead of the nearly 18 billion requested (Russia controlled all the printing presses). So, partly for this reason, on 10 January 1992 Ukraine introduced coupons. Coupons were reusable (unlike ration coupons) and could only be obtained at workplaces in order to increase work incentives, 25 per cent of pay or 200–400 coupons (depending on wage levels); the proportion was later raised to 50 per cent. State shops would accept only coupons for items costing less than 1,500 roubles. Roubles were still used for rents, payments for public facilities and taxi fares. The aim was to replace the rouble entirely by coupons from 1 March 1992 (later postponed) and introduce a new currency (the grivna) by August of that year (this too was postponed). Late 1992 was set as the target date for internal convertibility. The concern of other republics was that they could be flooded with unwanted roubles, but the meeting between Yeltsin and Kravchuk on 23 June 1992 produced an agreement to co-operate on a suitable mechanism for introducing the grivna as well as to shift to world prices in trade. Prior to this, however, on 12 June, Yeltsin had banned non-residents from hard currency auctions in Russia in order to prevent Ukrainians flooding the market with roubles in advance of the introduction of the new currency (*The Economist*, 27 June 1992, p. 120). As of 1 March 1992 75 per cent of wages was paid in coupons and the remaining 25 per cent was deposited in rouble bank accounts. All purchases in state shops valued at less than 4,000 roubles were henceforth to be made in coupons, while larger transactions were to be made via bank transfers, not cash. The wholesale sector, which previously used roubles, switched to coupons.

Various ambitious proposals were put forward to boost the status of the coupon before the (continually delayed) introduction of the grivna, but an over-supply of coupons led to a *de facto* depreciation of the coupon even against the rouble.

In April 1992 the budget deficit for the year was set at 2 per cent of national income. Wage indexation was to be limited to 70 per cent of price rises.

The IMF estimated that NMP fell by 3.4 per cent in 1990 and 9.6 per cent in 1991 (*FT*, 23 April 1992, p. 6). In June 1992 the IMF expressed concern about the budget and the slow pace of economic reform. Specific worries included heavy enterprise taxation, significant price controls, the prevalence of state orders, and delays in implementing the privatization programme. Kravchuk has expressed concern about the effects of 'shock' therapy, but it should also be remembered that Ukraine has had to build a new administration while still heavily dependent on Russia in particular. The dismissal on 11 July 1992 of the reform-minded deputy prime minister and economics minister Volodymyr Lanovoy and talk by the government in September of the possible reintroduction of a number of state controls added to the IMF's worries. Besides prices, the Ukrainian reforms to date include the following:

1. On 11 March 1992 a foreign investment law was passed by parliament. Incentives included the tax-free repatriation of profits for five years by existing joint ventures and exemption from taxes for the first three years of profitability in the case of new ventures (Karatnycky 1992: 98). Imported goods for own use were to be duty-free and exports were to be free of licences and duties. After the tax holiday joint ventures would pay only 50 per cent of local taxes, while repatriated profits would be subject to a 15 per cent tax. Nationalization was ruled out and existing foreign ventures were protected for 10 years from changes in legislation. Revenue earned within Ukraine could be used for buying domestic property in the privatization

programme. But a special exchange rate would be set for foreigners wishing to buy the local currency, in order to avoid too low a price for property. For the next two or three years at least foreigners would only be allowed to lease as opposed to own land. Foreign participation was to be limited in defined areas such as the defence industries.

2. The large privatization bill was approved on 6 March 1992. A scheme was chosen under which all Ukrainian citizens (including children) were entitled to free vouchers exchangeable for shares. Up to 40 per cent of assets would be accounted for this way. The remaining 60 per cent would be held by the state for subsequent sales to domestic and foreign investors. The target for 1992 was to privatize 250 large enterprises and 80 per cent of shops and small enterprises (by sale in the small privatization programme). Over a five-year period the aim was to privatize 65 per cent of large and medium-sized enterprises.

3. In February 1992 private land ownership was allowed (previously a maximum 50 ha land holding was permitted, which could be passed on to heirs). District councils were allowed to set aside farm land for private owners. Each owner would be given twenty acres free of charge; the land could be passed on to heirs but not sold.

On 5 March 1992 Kravchuk's powers were increased by the ability to appoint presidential plenipotentiaries ('prefects') to ensure local implementation of laws and decrees (an imitation of the situation in Russia). Concern has been expressed about Kravchuk's authoritarian traits and a weak political opposition, but minority problems have been minimized by the stress on a non-ethnic form of patriotism.

The Crimea was another bone of contention between Russia and Ukraine, to which the Black Sea peninsula was presented by Khrushchev in 1954. As early as 5 September 1991 the Crimea (65 per cent populated by Russians) announced that it was an autonomous and independent republic within Ukraine. On 5 May 1992 the Crimean parliament declared 'independence', announcing 'the creation of a sovereign state, the Republic of Crimea'. A referendum was set for 2 August 1992, asking the question 'Are you for an independent Republic of Crimea in union with other states?' On 6 May, however, the parliament confused matters by asserting that the Crimea was still part of Ukraine. Prior to the declaration Ukraine had granted the Crimea substantial autonomy (confirmed 30 June), but on 13 May the Ukrainian parliament annulled both the independence and the referendum declarations. The Crimea was given until 20 May to comply and its parliament did in fact do so. On 21 May, however, the Russian parliament declared the 1954 transfer of the Crimea to Ukraine to have been illegal. Discussion about the Crimea was avoided in the friendly meeting between Yeltsin and Kravchuk on 23 June 1992, but progress was made on the Black Sea Fleet and agreement reached to draw up a broad bilateral political treaty (in early August they agreed to postpone the division of the fleet until 1995, with joint command in the meantime).

The other republics

Price rises took place as follows: (1) Armenia 4 January 1992. (2) Azerbaijan 6 January 1992. On 18 January a 30 per cent reduction in the price of bread was ordered as of 1 February 1992, offset by an increase in the prices of goods like tobacco and alcohol. (3) Belarus 3 January 1992. (4) Kazakhstan 6 January 1992. (5) Kyrgyzstan 4 January 1992. (6) Turkmenistan 6 January 1992. On 19 January wage rises were linked to price increases for basic goods. (7) Uzbekistan 10 January 1992. Coupons were introduced on 16 January. (8) Moldova 2 January. Also introduced coupons on 1 February 1992.

Armenia. An economic blockade by Azerbaijan has been one result of the dispute over Nagorno-Karabakh.

The Law on Peasant and Collective Peasant Farms was passed in February 1991. A rapid privatization of land took place February–March

1991; plots were distributed by lotteries organized by region.

A general privatization programme was also outlined in February 1991, with priority to Armenian citizens.

Azerbaijan. Oil-endowed Azerbaijan is wrapped up in the dispute over Nagorno-Karabakh, but early economic policy was basically market-orientated. A privatization policy was in the process of being formulated. A parallel currency (the *manat*) was introduced on 15 August 1992.

Only one day after being reinstated as president and trying to impose a state of emergency, Mutalibov was ousted by the opposition Popular Front on 15 May 1992. A National Council was set up to govern the country in circumstances of setbacks in Nagorno-Karabakh and even in Azerbaijan itself as ethnic Armenian forces tried to establish a corridor between the enclave and Armenia itself. By the spring of 1992 an estimated 1,500 lives had been lost in the conflict over Nagorno-Karabakh. A successful counter-attack by Azerbaijan led to an agreement to effect a ceasefire in Nagorno-Karabakh on 1 September 1992 and with Armenia on 15 September. But it was not easy to be optimistic about the chances of success. Abulfez Elchibey of the Popular Front won the 7 June 1992 presidential election, dislike for the CIS being part of his programme (due in part to alleged Russian sympathy for Armenia). He argued that 'withdrawal' from the CIS was not strictly needed because parliament never actually ratified the various agreements.

Belarus. Policy in energy-deficient Belarus is basically market-orientated, but the reforms are being implemented more slowly than those of Russia. On 1 October 1991 the Supreme Soviet recognized the right of private land ownership. Foreigners, however, are only allowed to lease land. A general privatization programme is in the process of being drafted. The law on housing privatization came into effect on 1 July 1992. A parallel currency is to be introduced, on a par with the Russian rouble.

Georgia. Despite the political turmoil, decrees were issued in January 1992 dealing with the privatization of land (two or three hectares per family), housing, and small and medium-sized enterprises. The programme began to be implemented on 1 February 1992, but circumstances were difficult. The declaration of 'sovereignty' by Abkhazia on 26 July 1992 (actually the 27 July 1925 constitution was referred to) was followed by an invasion by Georgian troops in mid-August (though officially at first on the grounds of releasing kidnapped ministers). Yeltsin helped produce an agreement involving a ceasefire (effective 5 September 1992), a partial withdrawal and a peacekeeping force that would include Russian troops. But the fighting did not cease.

The entrepreneurial qualities displayed even in the socialist era augur well for the very long term. But in 1991 industrial output fell by 21 per cent, agricultural production by 5 per cent and retail trade turnover by 25 per cent (*CDSP*, 1992, vol. XLIV, no. 16, p. 17).

Kazakhstan. Resource-rich Kazakhstan's population comprises 40 per cent Kazakhs and 40 per cent Russians. President Nursultan Nazarbayev is pro-CIS and pro-market. Decrees issued in February 1992 concerned the privatization programme (*CDSP*, 1992, vol. XLIV, no. 6, p. 26). For instance, state agricultural enterprises were to be converted to collective enterprises, joint stock companies or other non-state forms of management by 1 March 1993. Another clause says that every employee of a privatized enterprise would be allotted a share of the property 'commensurate with his length of service and his labour contribution'. An early May decree specified that the workforce as a whole would be issued with free vouchers for the acquisition of up to 25 per cent of the shares of its enterprise (*CDSP*, 1992, vol. XLIV, no. 18, p. 23).

Private land ownership is policy, except for foreigners, who are only allowed to lease land.

A major joint venture exploration deal was signed in May 1992 with the Chevron oil company, quickly followed by another with British Gas-AGIP (Italian state oil company) on 1 July.

Kyrgyzstan. In resource-poor Kyrgyzstan reforms are market-orientated, following the Russian lead. The programme to privatize land (the fertile area is very limited) and small enterprises is complicated by the problem of allocation among ethnic groups (the population comprises 52.4 per cent Kyrgyz, 21.5 per cent Russians, 12.9 per cent Uzbeks, 2.5 per cent Ukrainians, and 2.4 per cent Germans). The August 1991 privatization programme included an element of free distribution by means of vouchers.

Moldova. Political conflicts have hindered economic reforms, but a market economy is the aim. The July 1991 privatization programme stressed vouchers. Land privatization is policy. Concern over events such the fighting in the Dniestre region and the consequences of price liberalization led to the resignation of the prime minister in June 1992. The 21 July 1992 agreement with Russia to send a joint peacekeeping force to the Dniestre region and to allow it self-determination in the event of Moldova uniting with Romania held out real hope.

Tajikistan. Tajikistan, where Persian (Farsi) is spoken, is unlike Azerbaijan, Kazakhstan, Kyrgyzstan, Turkmenia and Uzbekistan in that these countries speak Turkic languages and share a common cultural and religious tradition with Turkey. On the other hand Azerbaijan is the only one of the mostly Sunni-dominated countries in which the Shia Moslems are in the majority (Robert Mauthner, *FT Survey on Turkey*, 21 May 1992, p. iv). The president was elected, but the perpetuation of the old élite led to open unrest in April and May 1992. The Islamic/democratic opposition succeeded in securing the formation of a Revolutionary Coalition Council on 7 May to govern the country until parliamentary elections could be held on 6 December 1992. The allocation of seats between opposition and the administration in an uneasy coalition government was announced on 11 May. The potential for a civil war is there. Rakhman Nabiyev was forced to resign as president on 7 September 1992 after a further bout of unrest and fighting. But the situation continued to deteriorate.

Cotton is important. A privatization programme (excluding land) was outlined in February 1991, including an element of free distribution.

Turkmenistan. Gas, oil and cotton are important. A conservative, authoritarian regime still dominated by figures from the old one has been slow in introducing economic reforms. Steve Levine (*FT*, 19 June 1992, p. 4 and 8 July 1992, p. 32) reports that no dwelling can be sold for a decade, the state will relinquish no share of its enterprises, and the talk for now is only about joint ventures rather than wholly foreign-owned companies. Heavy social expenditures include free food for babies up to the age of one (part of an attempt to reduce the very high infant mortality rate) and subsidies to hold down the prices of basic foodstuffs. President Saparmuryad Niyazov was the only candidate standing in the election for that post on 21 June 1992. His Democratic Party is really a reincarnation of the old communist party.

Uzbekistan. Cotton and gold are particularly important, gas is produced, and a significant oil discovery was made in early March 1992. Economic policy is basically market-orientated and the Turkish political and economic model is favoured, an essentially secular state in which Moslems predominate. It is the only one of the Asiatic republics of the former Soviet Union where the Islamic Renaissance Party is banned.

CONCLUSION

The traditional Soviet economic system encountered severe economic problems, not only those outlined in Chapter 1, but also others such as the 'scattering' of investment resources, severe environmental problems and declining rates of growth of national income. These problems were in fact so severe as to help bring about the demise of the Soviet Union. An economic system had in essence failed. There were a bewildering number of economic reforms, but the Soviet system remained essentially a command one right to the end of the 1980s. In the Gorbachev era political reform swept ahead of the economic, and industrial preceded agricultural reform, which partly explains the Soviet crisis. Gorbachev had to struggle with the problems of political disintegration of the Soviet Union (something he desperately tried to avoid), democratization and economic reform all at the same time. He made the best of adverse circumstances and zigzagged politically to achieve his goals, an arguably necessary course of action, given the power of the party. The Yeltsins and the Kravchuks would not be where they are today without Gorbachev. Gorbachev did not seek the legitimacy of popular election and his firm commitment to a market economy came too late. In the late Gorbachev era command planning began to disintegrate without a market replacement, bartering between enterprises becoming more and more important. But some of the economic changes he introduced were remarkable in their historical context, such as the permitting of direct foreign investment, the erosion of the state monopoly of foreign trade and the expansion of the private and independent co-operative sectors. The proposal to introduce leasing on a grand scale in agriculture was also important.

The failure of the August 1991 coup proved to be the last nail in the coffin of the Soviet Union and the country disappeared towards the end of the year. Gorbachev resigned on 25 December 1991. The commanding figure became Russia's president, Boris Yeltsin, who set his country on a rapid and rocky road to the market. But strong, stable political parties have yet to emerge in Russia. The transformation was remarkably peaceful on the whole, although conflicts in Azerbaijan, Georgia and Moldova have been especially bitter and bloody. The now independent countries of the former Soviet Union face formidable tasks in changing over to

a different economic and political system. Most joined the Commonwealth of Independent States, but the prospects for this organization do not seem bright. Economic reform has so far been largely led by Russia rather than co-ordinated, while powerful Ukraine seems to see the CIS as a way of achieving a 'civilized divorce'. (Appendixes 3.1–4 here)

APPENDIX 3.1 PLANNING TECHNIQUES AND INVESTMENT DECISION-MAKING

Planning techniques

Material balancing was never supplanted as the core of command planning and was improved over time (by a greater number of iterations, for example). Nevertheless, input-output analysis and linear programming also played a subsidiary role.

Input–output analysis

This technique is associated with Leontief, who took part in the early work on drawing up balances of inter-sectoral flows before leaving the Soviet Union in 1925. Owing to Stalin's aversion to mathematical techniques, which he saw as a threat to political control, the first input–output table to be drawn up was for the year 1959.

An economy is characterized by inter-industry dependence. Thus coal is used as an input in other industries, while coal needs the output of other industries as inputs. Coal is also a final good, however, when used in the home for heating purposes, while primary inputs (e.g. labour) are also needed to produce coal. The question to be asked, then, is what the level of output of each industry should be in order to meet the total demand (intermediate and final) for that product.

Figure 3.1 shows a simplified input–output table for a closed economy (no foreign trade) with three sectors (industries). Reading across

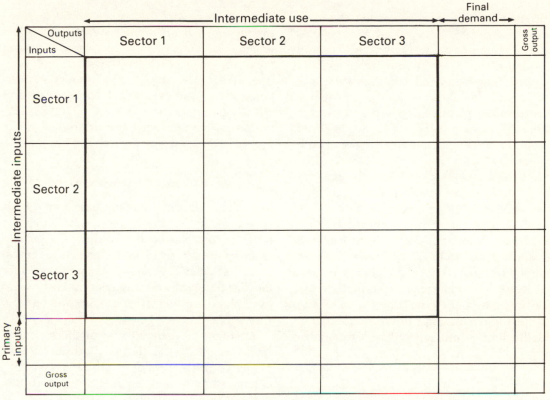

Figure 3.1 Input–output table

the rows, we see how the gross output of each sector is used as an input in the three sectors (i.e. including itself) and for final demand purposes (consumption and investment). Reading down the columns, it can be seen that each sector uses intermediate inputs from the three sectors and primary inputs, namely labour, land and capital.

The heavily outlined section, designated as Quadrant I in tables, captures the inter-sectoral relationships. From the information contained in each cell, an input coefficient can be worked out, specifying the amount of a particular input needed to produce a unit of output of a particular sector. Given targets for final demand, the process of matrix inversion enables mutually consistent gross output levels to be calculated, simultaneously meeting all the demands placed upon them. The effect of changes in final demand targets on the output levels of all sectors can be traced through. Treml (1989:

354–5) points out the usefulness of 'full' ('direct and indirect') coefficients per unit of final demand. These take account not only of direct material inputs into the production of a particular commodity, but also of indirect inputs (inputs themselves need inputs). An example from the 1988 table: a million rouble reduction in final deliveries of arms and weapons would release sixty-five workers directly but 119 in total.

When the technique was first worked on, great hopes were held out of input–output analysis. Yet it played only a peripheral role in planning: (1) variant analysis (e.g. the effects of higher percentage shares of investment during a five-year plan); and (2) in the final stages of planning for checking consistency. Its indirect effects on popularizing mathematical modelling and computer technology should not be forgotten, however. Major problems include:

1. The high degree of aggregation: the largest Soviet table so far is 600 x 600, while over 20,000 material balances are drawn up centrally (Gosplan alone 2,000). The number of sectors is, of course, tiny compared with the vast number of commodities. Treml (1989: 341–2) provides a more detailed picture: 1959 table, 83 sectors; 1966, 100 sectors; 1977, 1982 and 1987, 117 sectors. In 1966 republican and regional tables began to be drawn up.

2. The assumption of constant input co-efficients is unrealistic over longer periods of time, since technology changes.

3. The fact that Soviet industry is highly non-specialized. Input–output is conceived in terms of 'pure' sectors, on a 'commodity by commodity' basis. To be of operational value, in the sense of providing plan targets for individual enterprises, account would have to be taken of enterprise-specific input–output coefficients and the timely inter-enterprise distribution of inputs.

Linear programming

This was invented by Kantorovich in 1939, the first example illustrating how a plywood enterprise, with given plant and machinery, could maximize output subject to the fulfilment of an assortment plan. (Gardner notes that Kantorovich did not actually give linear programming its name, but he was the first in the area: 1990: 645.) Such constrained maximization problems can be looked at on two levels.

At the micro level, linear programming techniques have been used in: (1) production scheduling; (2) investment planning (this involves minimizing the cost of producing a given output, showing which plant should be closed or set up, where the new plants are to be located, and what their capacities should be); and (3) in optimal transport schemes (here their use, however, has been resisted by transport enterprises, whose main success indicator is the maximization of tonne-kilometres).

At the macro level, optimal planning involves the minimization of the cost of producing final output targets fixed by the state. Shadow prices emerge for all scarce factors, and, although these schemes are highly abstract and non-operational, optimal planning has helped overcome ideological aversion to concepts such as efficiency pricing and profit. Åslund (1989: 120) considers that the search for optimal planning had virtually ceased by the late 1980s.

Investment decision-making

Investment decision-making has been highly centralized in the Soviet Union; it is broadly the result of political decisions and inter-sectoral relationships. A programme to reduce armaments production would have implications for the metallurgical and engineering sectors, for example. Investment criteria, however, also play a role.

Although the general rule of thumb within branches was to use the most advanced techniques available, even during the 1930s informal criteria were developed in certain branches, such as electric power generation and the railways, to help choose between different ways of achieving a given output target. Suppose the possible variants to be Project 1 (a hydro scheme) and Project 2 (coal-fired power stations), with the former involving a higher initial capital outlay (I_1), but a lower annual operating cost C_1 (including depreciation, but excluding a charge on capital) than the latter. The more capital-intensive Project 1 will be chosen if the additional capital outlay can be recouped within a period of time equal to or smaller than the normative recoupment period fixed for that sector. More formally:

$$\frac{I_1 - I_2}{C_2 - C_1} = T \quad \text{(recoupment period: RP)}$$

If $T \leq T_n$ (normative recoupment period), then Project 1 is chosen; if $T > T_n$ then Project 2. The reciprocal of T is called the 'coefficient of relative effectiveness' (CRE). Project 1 is selected if $\frac{1}{T}$ (=E) $\geq \frac{1}{T_n}$ (=E$_n$), Project 2 if E<E$_n$. E represents the 'return' in the form of the savings on operating costs resulting from the additional capital outlay. For example, if RP = 8, then E = 0.125 (x 100 = 12.5 per cent). If RP$_n$ = 10, then E$_n$ = 0.1 (x 100 = 10 per cent), and Project 1 will be chosen.

Although a crude device (for example, there was no capital market in the Soviet Union, so the choice of E$_n$ is arbitrary), the CRE (a sort of interest rate) at least recognizes that capital has an opportunity cost. Over the period 1981–85 E$_n$ = 0.12, with exceptions (Ellman 1989: 159). It was formally accepted in the 1960 'Standard methodology for determining the economic effectiveness of capital investment and new technology', although other factors affected investment decisions, including political ones and physical indicators such as input utilization which may override CRE considerations. The 1969 amended version of the Standard Methodology also highlighted 'coefficients of absolute effectiveness', effectively incremental output–capital ratios [$\Delta Y/\Delta K$] and profit–capital ratios [$\Delta \Pi/\Delta K$], but these did not supersede conventional central allocative decisions and seemed to be more a check on efficiency. Ellman (1989a: 108) elaborates on these coefficients: ΔY refers to the income generated by a particular project, while ΔK is investment; $\Delta Y/\Delta K$ is compared to the normative coefficient of absolute effectiveness fixed for the particular sector for a five-year period, e.g. 1981–85 0.16 for industry, 0.07 for agriculture, and 0.05 for transport and communications. At the level of an individual industry Y refers to net output. Π refers to profit at the level of the individual enterprise.

APPENDIX 3.2 POLITICAL CHANGES

State bodies

Congress of People's Deputies (CPD) (2,250 members). Although the initial vote (first round March 1989) was only partially free (two-thirds of seats directly elected and one-third reserved for social organizations such as the communist party and trade unions – these reserved seats were to go next time), a surprising number of independent and radical deputies were elected. Sessions were lively and open.

The Supreme Soviet (542 members). This was the standing body of the Congress of People's Deputies, divided into the Soviet (Council) of Nationalities and the Soviet of the Union. Gorbachev was elected 'president' (Chairman of the Supreme Soviet) on 25 May 1989 (unopposed). Gorbachev's political strategy was to separate party and state and to increase the powers of state bodies at the expense of party ones. This process was taken a stage further under the new presidency, including the establishment of two presidential councils.

The new presidency as approved by the Supreme Soviet on 27 February and by the CPD on 13 March 1990

The new-style president was to be popularly elected for five years, with a two-term limit. The exception to the popular vote was the first election: Gorbachev (unopposed) was actually elected president (until March 1995) by the CPD on 15 March 1990. The president could propose both the appointment and the sacking of key people, such as the premier, to the Supreme Soviet and the CPD. After considerable debate it was decided that if the Supreme Soviet overrode a presidential veto on legislation by a two-thirds majority then the president would be unable to appeal to the CPD. The issuing of presidential decrees had to be done on the basis of existing laws and had to be consistent with the constitution. The president could introduce a state of emergency in specific localities, with immediate submission to the Supreme Soviet for approval. Note that on 24 September 1990 the Supreme Soviet granted Gorbachev powers to implement economic reform by presidential decree until 31 March 1992; he was able 'to give instructions on matters of property relations, organization of the management of the economy, the budget and financial system, pay and price formation, and the strengthening of law and order'. Two new councils were formed:

The Presidential Council. The Presidential Council played an advisory and policy presentational role, to the detriment of the party Politburo, in order to help implement Gorbachev's reform programme: its role was to 'work out measures to implement the cardinal planks of the domestic and foreign policy of the Soviet Union and to ensure the country's security'.

The Council of the Federation. The council comprised the presidents and prime ministers of the republics. The critical question here was the relationship between the republics and the federal state.

It is ironic that the swing to the right in the autumn of 1990 took place just as Gorbachev reached the pinnacle of international acclaim. On 15 October 1990 he was awarded the 1990 Nobel Peace Prize

> for his leading role in the peace process which today characterizes important parts of the international community. During the last few years dramatic changes have taken place in the relationship between East and West. Confrontation has been replaced by negotiations. Old European nation states have regained their freedom. The arms race is slowing down and we [the Nobel Committee] see a definite and active process in the direction of arms control and disarmament. Several regional conflicts have been solved or have at least come closer to a solution. The UN is beginning to play the role which was originally planned for it.

On the international level Gorbachev, by this time, had long become a household name. The urgent need to solve the country's domestic problems was an important explanation of his outstanding international achievements. The December 1987 INF treaty involved the scrapping of land-based, intermediate nuclear missiles, while the START treaty, signed at the Moscow summit 30–1 July 1991, *reduced* (for the first time) long-range nuclear weapons by some 30 per cent on average (35 per cent in the case of the Soviet Union and 25 per cent in that of the USA).[15] Nuclear disarmament was given a massive boost by Presidents Bush (27 September 1991) and Gorbachev (5 October) by proposals for further, large reductions in weapons; what was of historical importance was the inclusion of dramatic, competing *unilateral* gestures. For example, ground-launched theatre nuclear weapons were to be removed from Europe. Soviet troops were withdrawn from Alghanistan by 15 February 1989 as promised, while Soviet influence helped secure the withdrawal of Cuban troops from Angola and of Vietnamese troops from Cambodia. Gorbachev went to Beijing in May 1989. The countries of Eastern Europe were freed after Gorbachev's refusal to use Soviet troops in 1956 Hungarian or 1968 Czechoslovak style. At the Paris November 1990 meeting of the Conference on Security and Co-operation in Europe (CSCE) Nato and the Warsaw Pact declared that they were 'no longer adversaries'. The Warsaw Pact (formed 1955), already dead in reality, lost its formal military role on 1 April and its political role on 1 July 1991. Nato, formed in July 1948, is still a thriving organization; indeed the 7–8 November 1991 meeting decided to set up the North Atlantic Co-operation Council to consult more formally with the former members of the Warsaw Pact. Annual ministerial meetings and regular ones between ambassadors and military representatives were envisaged. Full membership of Nato is not ruled out in the long run, with Czechoslovakia, Hungary and Poland keen to join as soon as possible. The first meeting started on 20 December 1991; Russia (which replaced the old Soviet Union) astounded all by requesting that references in the final communiqué to the 'Soviet Union' be erased and by requesting membership of Nato in the long run. On 7 January 1992 it was announced that the post-Soviet Union states were formally to be admitted to the council. Ten more states joined on 10 March 1992 (Georgia was the one missing; admission was delayed until 15 April 1992). The 5 June 1992 meeting saw the signing of a protocol to the CFE treaty. (Note that Yeltsin continued the nuclear dismantling process. In visits to the USA, the UK and France in late January–early February 1992 Yeltsin announced that he no longer saw these countries as potential adversaries and that their cities would no longer be targeted. The USA and Russia made unilateral gestures and conditional proposals as regards nuclear reductions, Yeltsin proposing a reduction of long-range nuclear warheads to 2,000–2,500 each (there were then at least 27,000 in the ex-Soviet Union) and President Bush proposing 4,500. On 1 February 1992 Bush proposed the setting up of a joint centre to employ both US and ex-Soviet nuclear scientists.)

At home, however, the political climate in the later stages of the Gorbachev era continued to deteriorate. Economic reform took a back seat to trying to preserve the union, the very country itself. Although there was a formal procedure for secession, the impatience of republics such as Lithuania, Latvia and Estonia for early independence played a major role in the rightward swing; the line was finally drawn at the chaotic disintegration of the Soviet Union. One reason why Gorbachev finally opted for a less radical programme than the Shatalin scheme was to limit the powers of the republics. Personnel changes confirmed the drift, e.g. on 14 January 1991 Valentin Pavlov (appointed Finance Minister in 1989) became the new prime minister (Ryzhkov had a heart attack on 26 December 1990). Also in January Gorbachev lost the services of advisers of the stature of Nikolai Petrakov and Stanislav Shatalin. Petrakov's open letter of resignation said, among other things, that 'We are in trouble not because we are creating a market. We are not creating it, but destroying it.' Gorbachev began to rely increasingly on the army, the KGB and a resuscitated communist party.

The political situation took a very ugly turn when lives were lost in the Baltic republics. On the 11th Soviet troops took over the printing works and defence head quarters in Vilnius (the capital of Lithuania), and two days later the radio and television station (with loss of life). In Riga (the capital of Latvia) deaths also resulted from the 20 January attack on the Latvian Interior Ministry building by members of the Soviet Interior Ministry's special unit (OMON, more popularly called the 'black berets'). So-called 'National Salvation Committees' popped up, claiming readiness to take control away from the democratically elected parliaments.

On 25 January 1991 it was announced (although the order was actually signed by Pugo and Defence Minister Dmitri Yazov) that, as of 1 February, there would be joint police–army patrols in Moscow, all the republican capitals, and large industrial and military centres; they were formally to be used for 'certain demonstrations, major political events, or weekends and holidays if necessary'. The 26 January 1991 decree (rescinded 21 October) allowed KGB and Interior Ministry officials to enter any enterprise in the Soviet Union 'without hindrance' and demand documents, confidential commercial information and samples of goods. Full information could also be demanded of bank accounts (although the confidentiality of this and all other information was supposed to be respected once obtained). The alleged target was 'economic sabotage' and economic crime in general. The 29 January decree set up a committee to co-ordinate the activities of law enforcement bodies.

Gorbachev's new state structures

The CPD approved new state structures on 25 December 1990. But on 20 December Foreign Minister Eduard Shevardnadze stunned the audience by unexpectedly announcing his retirement (he had resigned from the communist party on 4 July 1991). He warned against the movement to dictatorship. The ambassador to the USA, Alexander Bessmertnykh, was appointed foreign minister on 15 January 1991.

The new bodies were answerable to the president and the new powers were meant to bring order to an increasingly chaotic situation before reforms were introduced:

Federation Council. This became the chief decision-making body, comprising the president, the vice-president and the presidents of the union (fifteen maximum) and autonomous republics (twenty). The main function was 'to co-ordinate the efforts of the centre and the republics'. The council was to meet every two months, and fundamental issues needed a two-thirds majority (there was no presidential veto). An inter-republican economic committee was to co-ordinate the economic relations between centre and republics.

The National Security Council. This replaced the Presidential Council and was headed by the vice-president. The council was in charge of 'implementing the country's all union policy in the field of defence . . . and guaranteeing stability, law and order'. In other words, the council co-ordinated the law-enforcement agencies within the framework of presidential rule. Membership included the heads of the military, the KGB, the Interior Ministry and the Foreign Ministry.

The Cabinet of Ministers. This replaced the Council of Ministers and was subordinate to the president, not the Supreme Soviet. Membership included the Soviet prime minister, deputy prime ministers, ministers, and republican prime ministers. The president could propose the appointment and dismissal of the prime minister and other ministries, but Supreme Soviet approval was needed (the Supreme Soviet could, in fact, pass a vote of no confidence in the president, but a two-thirds majority was needed).

The republics

Gorbachev introduced a Law on Secession (see below), but he was in favour of preserving the union. In an 8 October 1990 speech to the

Central Committee he warned of the danger of 'Lebanonization'; on 17 November he pronounced himself 'resolutely' opposed to dissolution, while on 23 November he said that the break-up of the union could lead to 'bloodshed and civil war'. On 12 December 1990 he said, 'We must beware of falling from one extreme to the other; instead of strong republics and a strong centre, instead of a strong central government, to have something that resembles an amoeba . . .'. In his new year message for 1991 Gorbachev said that 'For all of us Soviet people there is no more sacred cause than the preservation and renewal of the union in which all our peoples can live well and freely'. Ethnic clashes became numerous, such as those between Armenians and Azerbaizanis (especially over Nagorno-Karabakh), between Georgians and both Abkhazians and Ossetians, between Uzbeks and the Meskhetian minority (Meskhetian Turks transported from Georgia by Stalin), and between Uzbeks and Kirghizians. The brutal suppression of demonstrators in Georgia in April 1989, with loss of life, left an indelible mark.

By the end of 1990 all fifteen republics had declared their sovereignty or independence. But the Baltic republics of Estonia, Latvia and Lithuania, Armenia, Georgia and Moldavia expressed a wish to secede from the union; independence referenda were strongly supported (e.g. Estonia 77.8 per cent in March 1991; Latvia 73.6 per cent in March 1991; Lithuania 90.5 per cent in February 1991; Georgia 98.9 per cent in March 1991). Boris Yeltsin was elected president of the Russian Federation on 12 June 1991 with 57.3 per cent of the popular vote; on 29 May 1990 he had been elected chairman of the Russian CPD (the first session of which had begun on 16 May) and resigned from the communist party in July.

The Law on Secession

The draft bill presented on 21 March 1990 contained the following (*CDSP*, 1990, vol. XLII, no. 15, pp. 20–1):

The decision to hold a referendum was to be made by the republican Supreme Soviet at its own initiative or on the basis of a request signed by one-tenth of the citizens permanently residing in the republic and entitled to vote. The referendum was to be conducted by secret ballot no sooner than six months and no later than nine months after the adoption of the decision to raise the question of secession. A republican decision to secede from the USSR should be considered adopted by referendum if it wins the votes of at least two-thirds of the citizens who were residing permanently on the republic's territory at the time the question of secession was raised. The USSR Congress of People's Deputies was to establish a transitional period not to exceed five years, during which questions arising could be resolved. In the final year of the transitional period a repeat referendum could be held to confirm a decision to secede at the initiative of the republican Supreme Soviet or was obligatory if demanded by one-tenth of the citizens. If fewer than two-thirds of the resident citizens voted to confirm the decision to secede, the decision to secede should be considered rescinded. At the end of the transitional period the approval of the USSR Congress of People's Deputies was needed.

The Supreme Soviet passed emergency legislation on 24 October 1990 reasserting the supremacy of federal over republican law until the signing of a new union treaty. The 17 March 1991 referendum posed the question: 'Do you consider it necessary to preserve the Union of Soviet Socialist Republics as a renewed federation of equal sovereign republics, in which the rights and freedoms of all nationalities will be fully guaranteed?' The overall 'yes' vote was 76.4 per cent, but Estonia, Latvia, Lithuania, Moldavia, Georgia and Armenia did not take part. In April 1991 Gorbachev swung back to the centre ground of politics by signing an agreement with nine republican leaders (the Baltic Republics, Georgia, Armenia and Moldavia did not take part). Essentially the 'anti-crisis' programme was supported, although concessions included a 'radical' increase in the role of the republics and allowing them 'independently to decide on the question of accession to the union treaty'.

Events prior to the August 1991 attempted coup

Both Eduard Shevardnadze (in December 1990) and Alekander Yakovlev had warned of the dangers of a coup. Yakovlev resigned as adviser to Gorbachev on 27 July 1991. On 15 August the Central Control Commission of the party recommended that Yakovlev be expelled, but he announced his resignation the next day with the extraordinarily prescient comment that a 'Stalinist' core of the party was preparing a coup.

On a more democratic note, a statement announcing the setting up of the Movement for Democratic Reform was signed on 1 July 1991. A conference was later fixed for October. Leading figures included Shevardnadze, Yakovlev, Ivan Silayev (prime minister of the Russian republic), Gavril Popov (mayor of Moscow), Anatoly Sobchak (mayor of Leningrad), Aleksander Rutskoi (vice-president of the Russian republic), Nikolai Petrakov, Arkady Volsky (president of the Scientific and Industrial Association, which represented a number of important enterprises), and Stanislav Shatalin (who became chairman of the new Union of Democratic Parties on 17 July). On 20 July Boris Yeltsin signed a decree (operational from 4 August, although fully effective only by the end of 1991) allowing workplace political activity in the Russian republic only 'during non-working hours and outside the limits of state organs, institutions, organizations and enterprises'. Gorbachev disagreed and the Constitutional Review Commission was asked to examine the decree.

The issue that sparked the August coup was the Union Treaty. The coup and its aftermath are dealt with in the main text.

117

APPENDIX 3.3 WESTERN AID TO THE SOVIET UNION

Gennadi Burbulis (the first deputy prime minister of Russia, writing in the International Herald Tribune, 23 January 1992, p. 6) informs us that from December 1990 through December 1991 humanitarian goods valued at $1.4 billion were received by the former Soviet Union. This was the equivalent of only one day's nationwide consumption.

The 22–3 January 1992 international conference in Washington was held to co-ordinate humanitarian aid, although some extra aid was announced (see below) and further proposals included one from German Foreign Minister Genscher for the establishment of an international foundation to employ CIS nuclear scientists. It was announced that a second conference would be held in Lisbon in May 1992 and Japan offered to host the third.

A 20 January 1992 EC report (*IHT*, 22 January 1992, p. 2) calculated that of the total aid pledged since September 1990 ($79.8 billion or Ecu 62.4 billion), the EC had contributed 75 per cent (Ecu 47.4 billion). Germany alone had contributed 57 per cent of total aid (including Ecu 8.35 million for the removal and housing of Soviet troops). The USA had contributed 6 per cent and the UK 0.2 per cent.

At the May 1992 conference in Lisbon the figure of $86 billion was mentioned as the total amount of aid pledged by Western countries and international organizations to the former Soviet Union to date (most had not actually been disbursed). There was mutual agreement between donors and recipients that the emphasis should change from emergency to technical aid in order to increase the latter countries' absorptive capacity. The World Bank was expected to provide $1.5 billion in loans to the CIS in 1992 for industrial development, while the IMF was thinking in terms of $25 billion to $30 billion to the former Soviet Union over the next four to five years (Anthony Robinson and Patrick Blum, *FT*, 26 May 1992, p. 2). On 24 May

the USA, the EC, Japan and Russia initialled an agreement to set up the International Science and Technology Centre (see US aid below).

The United Nations Economic Commission for Europe (1992: 8) gives a figure of nearly $79 billion in aid commitments extended by the G24 countries between September 1990 and January 1992; gross disbursements in 1990–1991 were less than one-third of commitments.

The European Community (EC)

22 February 1991. Food aid worth Ecu 750 million approved.

23 May 1991. Terms finally agreed for Ecu 250 million in food aid.

7 October 1991. Ecu 2 billion ($2.4 billion) pledged out of a total of Ecu 6 billion (the rest should be supplied by the USA, Japan and Canada) credit facility to buy food and medicine. Of the EC portion, half was to be spent in the EC and half in Eastern Europe and the Baltic states. Not all was new, e.g. the EC included Ecu 250 million of the free food it was sending to the Soviet Union and an already agreed Ecu 500 million food credit guarantee. The new element was a Ecu 1.25 billion loan ($1.5 billion). The non-EC portion also included existing pledges, e.g. the US agriculture credit of over $1 billion already announced. Note that the aid was not unconditional; it depended, for example, on a demonstration of need and the ability of the Soviet Union to distribute food.

26 November 1991. Ecu 500 million credit guarantee for food aid (promised December 1990). One quarter to be spent in Eastern Europe and the Baltic States.

3 January 1992. Ecu 200 million ($240 million) worth of food aid to Moscow and St Petersburg to be distributed as follows: 5 per cent directly distributed to poorer sections of the population, but the remainder to be sold (with a maximum 20 per cent trade mark-up permitted) and the revenue raised to help the poor indirectly.

The *FT* (22 January 1992, p. 2) summed up EC

pledges to date as: agricultural credits Ecu 1.75 billion; food aid grants, Ecu 450 million; technical assistance for transport, energy, and food distribution and storage, Ecu 900 million.

Germany

The *Financial Times* (5 September 1991, p. 1) reported that German financial aid worth DM 60 billion (since 1989) constituted 56 per cent of Western aid to the Soviet Union. More than DM 30 billion had also been pledged to Eastern Europe, this constituting 32 per cent of Western aid. The German finance minister reported on 13 October 1991 that aid to the Soviet Union since 1989 amounted to 2.5 per cent of German GNP.

The German banks' share of the Soviet Union's foreign debt was $21.9 billion, but government guarantees covered 80 per cent (*IHT*, 24 December 1991, p. 11). In February 1992 Chancellor Kohl reported that Germany had committed itself to DM75 billion ($46.8 billion) in export credits and other forms of aid to the ex-Soviet republics, and a further DM30 billion to Eastern Europe (*IHT*, 7 February 1992, p. 2). On 5 February 1992 Kohl called for the equivalent of the OEEC to be set up (that organization had co-ordinated Marshall Plan aid).

The USA

11 June 1991. $1.5 billion agricultural credit guarantees.

1 October 1991. President Bush accelerates disbursement of $585 million in agricultural credits, part of the $2.5 billion credit to run to February 1992 (100 per cent of the principal guaranteed about a week earlier).

20 November 1991. $1.5 billion in credits, mainly for food. $1.25 billion for grain (especially for animal feedstuffs), to go to both central and republican authorities.

27 November 1991 The House of Represent-
atives (the Senate had already given approval) agreed to $400 million, to be used to store, dismantle and destroy Soviet nuclear weapons (also $100 million in food aid). On 1 February 1992 President Bush proposed the setting up of a joint centre to employ both US and top ex-Soviet nuclear scientists, the latter said to number 2,000–3,000. On 17 February it was announced that the US–Russia–Germany initiative would result in an International Science and Technology Centre in Russia, a clearing house to provide employment on non-military projects throughout the CIS. The USA provided $25 million and the EC $65 million.

12 December 1991. Secretary of State James Baker announced an international conference to co-ordinate humanitarian aid. As a result of the international aid conference in Washington (22–3 January 1992) President Bush pledged to ask Congress for an extra $645 million in grants for technical and humanitarian aid. It was also announced that the USA was to start air-lifting $61 million worth of food and medicine on 10 February 1992. 'Operation Provide Hope' was to involved fifty-four flights from Germany and Turkey over a two-week period to supply orphanages and hospitals throughout the CIS (except Georgia).

The UK

15 November. The 1990 UK 'know-how' fund was extended to the Soviet Union: £20 million over two years to provide, for example, skills and expertise in distribution, agriculture, energy, small businesses and financial services. It was announced on 17 July 1991 that this was to be increased to £50 million over three years.

30 January 1992. Extra £280 million in new medium-term export credits and investment insurance (as part of an IMF programme).

27 February 1992. Aid in the form of transporters and expertise to help the dismantling of nuclear weapons. Worth £10 million in the first year.

France

Yeltsin returned from his presidential visit to France of 5–7 February 1992 with a $370 million grain credit, $405 million under a barter agreement, and a new $22 million technical assistance credit.

The G7 meetings (Group of Seven: USA, UK, Germany, France, Italy, Japan and Canada)

On 13 October 1991 the G7 representatives met those from the Soviet Union. It was agreed that a G7 delegation should be sent to the Soviet Union, while the final communiqué spelled out the conditions for aid: 'the introduction of comprehensive economic reform programmes; the clear commitment by both the central and the republican authorities to the timely servicing of all financial obligations; the establishment of an operational framework for fulfilling the existing and future financial responsibilities of the centre and republics; and the full disclosure of Soviet economic and financial statistics'.

A secret contingency plan was drawn up to help the Soviet Union if it were unable to meet its repayments (especially debt repayments). It was estimated that there would be a cash shortage of more than $7 billion for the last few months of 1991. On 1 November 1991 Viktor Geraschenko estimated the Soviet Union to be $4 billion short in debt servicing in 1991.

The G7 meeting held in Munich on 6–8 July 1992 endorsed the $24 billion aid package discussed below, approved in principle $100 million to complement bilateral funding to improve the safety of nuclear power plants, and supported discussions on debt rescheduling via the Paris Club. Boris Yeltsin raised the possibility of debt for equity swaps.

Japan

On 8 October 1991 the following aid package was announced. Up to $2.5 billion in financial assistance. The new element was a $500 million loan for food and medical supplies and $200 million in other loans. Export credit insurance worth $1.8 billion (mainly a pledge to continue at the 1990 level). Tax breaks for private companies which donated in cash or kind. At the 22–3 January 1992 aid conference Japan pledged a further $50 million in emergency aid.

Japan is deliberately refraining from large-scale aid contributions owing to its policy of reclaiming the Kuril Islands, taken over by the Soviet Union at the end of the Second World War.

The World Bank and IMF

5 November 1991. $30 million for technical assistance. Peter Norman (*FT*, 8 October 1991, p. 20) makes the following points. If the current quota increase is ratified as planned, it has been estimated that $35–40 billion of IMF resources would be used for loans to the Soviet Union. The World Bank has at least $35 billion 'headroom' that could be used for lending to the Soviet Union.

31 March 1992. The IMF executive board agreed to recommend to the Board of Governors the formal admission of Russia with a quota of 3 per cent (the eighth largest), thus allowing borrowing of up to $4 billion a year. The former republics of the Soviet Union as a whole were allocated 4.76 per cent.

7 April 1992. A recommended IMF quota of 0.69 per cent for Ukraine, with borrowing of up to $1 billion a year.

April 1992. The World Bank's executive board recommended a quota of 5.25 per cent for the former republics of the Soviet Union, Russia alone 2.92 per cent. The World Bank envisaged the former Soviet republics receiving $1.5 billion in the financial year starting 1 July 1992 and in the range $4 billion to $5 billion by 1994.

15 April 1992. The IMF expected to channel $25 billion to $30 billion into the former Soviet republics over the next four years; the World Bank's contribution was estimated at $12 billion to $15 billion. The former republics of the Soviet Union excluding Russia might require $20 billion in 1992.

27 April 1992. All the former republics of the Soviet Union were admitted as members of the IMF and World Bank except Azerbaijan, which joined in May.

The International aid package of 1 April 1992

President Bush indicated his acceptance of the need for significant aid in a speech on 1 April 1992: 'If we do not do what we can to secure democracy in the lands of the Soviet Union, then the failure to act could carry a far higher price than this.' The announcement was timed to support Yeltsin in a forthcoming crucial meeting of the Russian parliament. The outline proposals for the $24 billion package for Russia financed by the G7 and other Western countries were as follows:

1. A $6 billion stabilization fund to support the rouble. It was later explained that this was to be financed by the G7 plus Belgium, the Netherlands, Sweden and Switzerland via the General Arrangements to Borrow; these countries, which formally gave their approval to the fund on 27 April, lend currency reserves to the IMF so that it can provide funds.

2. The provision of $18 billion in balance of payments support over the next three years. This was tentatively divided into: (a) $4.5 billion in loans from the IMF ($2.5 billion), the World Bank ($1.5 billion) and the EBRD ($0.5 billion), (b) $2.5 billion in debt restructuring, (c) $11 billion in loans and credit guarantees from the countries involved.

It was not clear precisely how much was new and what each country was to contribute. Bush admitted that there was 'not a lot of new money' (a figure of $3 billion for the USA was later suggested). The USA's contribution was estimated at 20–5 per cent of the $24 billion and up to 25 per cent of the stabilization fund. Bush was to propose to Congress that the USA should

finally pay the $12 billion to the IMF already tentatively agreed in previous negotiations. President Bush did propose an additional $1.1 billion in US grain credits ($600 million for Russia and the remainder to the other CIS states), however, and the USA would contribute up to $3 billion towards all the CIS stabilization funds.

The aid package was conditional and the main monitoring agency was to be the IMF. Jacques Attali thought the aid package to be only half the size needed (*FT*, 8 April 1992, p. 2). Peter Norman (*FT*, 13 July 1992, p. 13) cites one estimate that total G7 aid commitments to the former Soviet Union to date amount to only 0.2 per cent of the G7 countries' combined GNP (see Marshall Plan for comparison).

Estimates of aid required

1. Jeffrey Sachs (*The Economist*, 21 December 1991, pp. 111–14). Russia. In 1992 Russia needs $15–20 billion. This comprises: (1) Stabilization Fund of $5 billion. This is needed to pay a newly convertible rouble once a reasonable market rate is established. (2) Balance of payments support of $6 billion. This is needed for non-food imports and to support the rouble at the start of its float. (3) Food aid of $6 billion. The other republics. In 1992 these need about $10–15 billion, e.g. $5 billion for food aid. Similar sums needed for Russia and the other republics for three or four years of reforms, although there would be a switch to investment loans over time. There should also be an end to all debt repayments, both interest and principal, in 1992.

2. Boris Pankin (then Soviet foreign minister). He mentioned on 8 September 1991 the $100 billion mustered for the Gulf War. Gorbachev had mentioned this sum with the Gulf crisis in mind on 22 May 1991.

3. G7 meeting 15–17 July 1991: stabilization fund of $10 billion to $12 billion needed.

4. *CSCE conferences.* 10 September–3 October 1991: James Baker promised US direct

aid if there was merely a commitment (rather than active implementation) to reform, e.g. concrete plans for a market economy agreed with the republics. Soviet representatives initially requested $14.7 billion ($6.5 billion from the EC) in food aid for 1991–92 (in 1990 the Soviet Union imported $9.8 billion of food), but this was later reduced to $10.2 billion. A Soviet letter to Jacques Delors (President of the European Commission) talked of Ecu 5 billion to Ecu 6 billion ($6 billion to $7.25 billion) over the next nine months. Jacques Delors himself estimated that at least $2 billion in food aid was needed.

5. The US Department of Agriculture estimated in October 1991 that the Soviet Union required $10 billion to $11 billion to meet food and animal feed needs for the year.

6. Gennadi Burbulis (first deputy prime minister) (*IHT*, 23 January 1992, p. 6) contributes these points. Russia needs the following at a minimum: $6 billion for imports (which fell by more than a third in 1991); $7 billion for a stabilization fund to stabilize the exchange rate and support the process of currency convertibility; $6 billion for food and medicine; some deferral of interest payments on its debt in 1992.

Yegor Gaidar (*FT*, 22 January 1992, p. 15, and 4 March 1992, p. 17) makes the following points. There is an urgent need to stabilize the rouble. At present, the supply of foreign exchange is so small that the rouble is grossly undervalued, e.g. the prices of traded goods in Russia today are about twenty times below world prices calculated at the existing exchange rate. Tight money is the key to raising the external value of the rouble, but there is also need to peg the exchange rate in order to set a ceiling to inflation and to give enterprises the confidence to part with their dollars. A stabilization fund is thus needed to peg the rouble at a reasonable rate. Unless people can see that inflation is going to be capped, wages will increase again and a disastrous wage–price spiral will develop. There is need for a stabilization fund for Russia of some $5 billion, humanitarian aid in the form of

food and medicine in 1992 of about $6 billion for non-food imports (e.g. inputs to keep enterprises producing). Further debt relief is also needed for 1992.

7. In January 1992 the Russian government requested $17 billion in financial aid from the G7 countries, $12 billion for balance of payments support and $5 billion for a stabilization fund.

NOTES

1. Linz uses interviews with Soviet emigrants to examine these factors in the two decades prior to Gorbachev. This method has obvious limitations, but she concludes that there had been reduced scope for enterprise management autonomy, owing to the enhanced technical expertise of ministerial personnel and the huge documentation required of enterprises during annual plan negotiations. As a result, enterprise management was unable, to any significant extent, to over-indent for inputs, understate productive capacity, attain lower output targets or falsify data. During the 1970s light industry had to receive the trade organization's permission to change assortment plans, while the decade was characterized by government attempts to offset falling growth rates by increasing central controls rather than decentralizing decision-making (1988: 190–1). Linz has also published a complementary essay dealing with organizational change ('The impact of Soviet economic reform' in Linz and Moskoff 1988).

2. NMP differs from the United Nations 'system of national accounts', mainly because of the exclusion of so-called non-productive services, such as defence, general administration, education, finance and credit, and transport and communications serving households.

3. 'NMP produced' minus exports plus imports, measured in domestic prices, and minus losses due to abandoned construction and accidental damage, gives 'NMP utilized'.

4. In 1987 growth, officially defined on a Western GNP basis for the first time was calculated to be 2.9 per cent; 5.5 per cent in 1988, 3 per cent in 1989, and -2 per cent in 1990 (Åslund 1991a: 200). An explanation as to why growth estimates vary would involve factors such as data deficiencies, the exchange rate problem, the lack of efficiency prices, which years' prices are used in

time series, and the problem of new products. This is a complicated area and the interested reader is advised to consult the references cited.

5. Namely, influx of manpower from the countryside, increases in participation rates (especially among women) and increases in the proportion of national income devoted to investment. Aganbegyan places the decline in the potential of extensive growth via the growth of resources at the beginning of the 1970s (1988b: 23).

6. Brigades became increasingly important in Soviet industry in general, offering advantages like group pressure on individuals not to let the colleagues down.

7. See *CDSP*, 1987, vol. XXXIX, nos 24, 27, 30; EEN, 1987, vol. 1, no. 2; Gorbachev 1987; Kaser 1987a; Litvin 1987; Petrov in *The Guardian*, 6 November 1987, p. 18; Reut (Deputy Chairman of Gosplan) in *IHT*, 7–8 November 1987, p. 9; Tedstrom 1987; Aganbegyan 1988a, 1988b; *CDSP*, 1988, vol. XXXIX, no. 52; Hewett 1988; Makarov 1988.

8. Note that all enterprises were expected to manufacture consumer goods. After the start of 1988 it became possible for certain enterprises to issue non-equity shares to their own employees. The first was the Konveyer plant in Lvov; a variable dividend was payable and shares could be traded back to the plant bank at any time for their original value (David Remnick, *IHT*, 8 February 1989, p. 2; Quentin Peel, *FT*, 5 May 1989, p. 21 and 41). In his budget speech to the Supreme Soviet in October 1988 Finance Minister Boris Gostev outlined plans to extend share issues in order to mop up excess purchasing power, to improve attitudes towards state property and to provide alternative sources of enterprise finance. Shares would be differentiated according to an enterprise's own personnel and to other enterprises and organizations (*CDSP*, 1988, vol. XL, no. 45, p. 15). An individual worker's maximum would be 10,000 roubles' worth and shares would not involve any special voting rights. Shares in total could be up to 80 per cent of the value of an enterprise's fixed and working capital (a 30 per cent ceiling on own workers' shares and 50 per cent on other enterprises'). According to Aganbegyan (1989: 50), the dividends did not depend on profit and were more likely to be a fixed amount. The shares were thus more like bonds, and they could be sold to other workers in the enterprise or to outsiders. Some enterprises turned into joint stock companies selling shares to their employees, other enterprises or superior ministries;

a good example is the Kamaz automobile combine, converted in June 1990 (Filtzer 1991: 993).

9. Comecon enterprises were also included, such as the first Polish–Soviet joint venture (manufacturing cosmetics in Poland), announced at the end of 1987. The May 1983 decree, under Andropov, allowed joint ventures on Soviet soil with Comecon enterprises. The first was in October 1985 with Bulgaria (Åslund 1989: 140). For a detailed analysis see UN Economic Commission for Europe (1988) Economic, Business, Financial and Legal Aspects of East-West Joint Ventures, Geneva.

10. See *CDSP*, 1986, vol. XXXVIII, no. 42 and 1987, vol. XXXIX, no. 18; Roucek 1988; Plokker 1990. Grossman (1989: 79) defines the 'first economy' as the official, socialist one. The 'second economy' is defined as the aggregate of economic activities (production, trade and so on) which meet at least one of the following criteria: they are pursued directly for private gain, whether legally or illegally; they are pursued knowingly in contravention of the law in some significant respect(s), whether for private gain or for socialist benefit. Grossman also refers to 'crypto' private firms, state firms where a large part of the output is diverted to private gain (Harrogate World Congress of Soviet and East European Studies, July 1990). At the congress, Treml provided some estimates of the 'second economy' in 1989: official Soviet, 56 billion roubles; Koryagina, 100 billion roubles; others, up to 350 billion roubles. Treml reported his team's estimate for 1979: private economic activities constituted 14.1 per cent of actual state employment; 70 billion roubles' worth of materials were stolen. The official Soviet estimate of the 'second economy' in 1979 was 5 billion roubles.

11. Campaigns, like the Virgin Lands Campaign conceived by Khrushchev in 1954, tended to be overdone. The colossal scheme to divert water from north-flowing rivers to the Asiatic republics was scrapped in 1986. By 1985 the agricultural sector as a whole claimed a third of total investment and nearly 30 per cent of the labour force (Severin 1990: 121). In December 1989 it was announced that the debts of enterprises and organizations in the agro-industrial complex were to be reduced in proportion to the extent of leasing arrangements (*CDSP*, 1989, vol. XL, no. 49, p. 34), while in July 1990 all debts were completely written off (*CDSP*, 1990, vol. XLII, no. 28, p. 24).

12. The 1982 Food Programme up to 1990 mainly stressed the need to increase both infrastructural investment and farm prices (mushrooming subsidies cushioning retail prices), but also to decentralize decision-making to a greater extent to farms and within farms, and to encourage the private sector. Note that a perennial problem was the enormous loss of output during harvesting and afterwards. Gorbachev put the wheat loss in spoilage at 30 per cent of output (*CDSP*, 1989, vol. XLI, no. 4, p. 19); the grain loss due to harvesting, storage and processing was equal to the amount imported (*CDSP*, 1989, vol. XLI, no. 12, p. 12). In 1988 grain imports were 35 million tonnes. Anthony Robinson (*FT*, 9 January 1992, p. 2) cites an EBRD estimate that the average annual potato crop loss over the period 1986–90 was around a half, specifically 11 per cent in harvesting, 10 per cent during seed storage, 17 per cent during storage as food, 8 per cent in processing, 2 per cent during transport and 1 per cent at the retail level. Leyla Boulton (*FT*, 2 April 1992, p. 30) cites a World Bank report that the 1991–92 grain imports of 37 million tonnes would not have been necessary if grain losses could have been prevented. A third of food was lost through poor storage, waste, theft and inadequate transport.

13. Collective farms accounted for around 35 per cent of total agricultural output (Schroeder 1988a: 180). In terms of marketed output the shares in 1985 were as follows: state farms 49 per cent; collective farms 41 per cent; and the private sector 10 per cent (p. 180).

14. Leasing schemes involve enterprise subdivisions or even whole enterprises providing their parent organization (the enterprise and association respectively) with an agreed volume of output and a leasing fee. The lessee is able to dispose freely of production in excess of this amount (Filtzer 1991: 993). The lease lasts for seven years on average (*The Economist*, 14 January 1988, p. 47). Aganbegyan (1989: 84) says that the number of participants can vary from several to more than 100, and the lease can take a simple form (certain amount of output to be delivered) or a full form (where all expenses have to be covered by revenue earned). At the end of 1989, 1,332 industrial enterprises, 731 construction enterprises and 988 retail trade organizations were operating on the leasing principle (*CDSP*, 1990, vol. XLII, no. 9, p. 17). In the first half of 1989 leases accounted for less than 2 per cent of industrial output (Hanson 1989: 4); by the start of 1991 this figure had gone up to 5.2 per cent

(Filatotchev *et al.* 1992: 275). As of mid-1990 they accounted for 4.3 per cent of total industrial employment (Schroeder 1992: 225). In September 1991 leased enterprises employed 9 million people (6.6 per cent of the total number employed in the economy) (*CDSP*, 1991, vol. XLIII, no. 44, p. 24).

15. Policy is to switch resources increasingly from the military to the civilian sector of the economy. The prime minister Ryzhkov envisaged increasing the share of civilian output in the total produced by the defence sector from 41 per cent in 1989 to 49 per cent in 1990 and 60 per cent by 1995 (*FT*, 17 October 1989, p. 7). Enterprises in the defence complex supplied 100 per cent of the all-union output of television sets and household sewing machines, over 97 per cent of fridges and tape recorders, more than a half of motorcycles, and about 70 per cent of vacuum cleaners and washing machines (*CDSP*, 1989, vol. XLI, no. 35, p. 1). In 1989 25 per cent of the entire output of manufactured consumer goods was contributed by the defence industry (Quentin Peel, *FT* Survey, 17 January 1990, p. iii). Kushnirsky (1991: 23) points out, however, that (according to official figures) military procurement of hardware, weapons and systems only amounted to 3.6 per cent of total industrial output in 1989. The defence complex accounted for 15.3 per cent of total industrial output in 1985, 16.2 per cent in 1987, and 17.2 per cent in 1990 (Cooper 1991: 131). In 1988 42.6 per cent of the output produced by the military-industrial complex was non-military; by 1990 this figure had gone up to 50.2 per cent and by mid-October 1991 to 54 per cent (*CDSP*, 1991, vol. XLIII, no. 42, p. 30). The defence industries employ more than 5 million people (IMF *et al.* 1990) (the total labour force is around 170 million). Some stress that successful conversion requires control to be removed from the military command system (Jim Hoagland, *IHT*, 13 August 1991, p. 4). Taken to extremes, this argument could mean simple closure of defence establishments rather than conversion, with resources switched directly to the civilian sector. Gorbachev's plan was to reduce the armed forces to 3 million men by the year 2000. In a 3 July 1990 speech the then foreign minister Eduard Shevardnadze talked of a Soviet 'peace dividend' of 240–50 billion over the next five years, but warned that 'if we continue to spend a quarter of our budget on military expenditure . . . we will ruin the country once and for all. We simply won't need a defence.' At the G7 London

conference held 15–17 July 1991, the Soviet Union listed 400 plants to be totally converted and expressed the hope of eventually partially converting 80 per cent of the defence industry to civilian production; military procurements were to be reduced by 26 per cent 1988–91 and the intention was to accelerate this. The Deutsche Bank (*Focus Eastern Europe*, 13 December 1991, no. 33, p. 2) suggests that the conversion process may have been completed in less than a dozen out of a total of 5,000).

4

MONGOLIA: FROM PEOPLE'S REPUBLIC TO DEMOCRACY AND THE MARKET

POLITICAL BACKGROUND

A country of pastoral nomads,[1] Mongolia was ruled by China during the Qing dynasty (1644–1911), although Mongolia actually ruled China during the Yuan dynasty (1271–1368). Genghis Khan (1162–1227) was proclaimed ruler of 'All the Mongols' in 1206. Requesting Russian protection, Mongolia declared its independence from China on 1 December 1911.[2] Although China recognized Mongolia's autonomy under its suzerainty as a result of an agreement with Russia in November 1913 (Mongolia was finally induced to go along with this only in 1915), the latter reverted to a Chinese province 1919–21, after Chinese troops re-established control. On 11 July 1921 independence was once again declared after Soviet troops had arrived in Mongolia in pursuit of White Russian forces; a limited monarchy prevailed initially.

The Mongolian People's Republic formally came into being in November 1924, the second socialist country after the Soviet Union, with the latter's strong support. Only the Soviet Union recognized the new republic until after the end of the Second World War; the Chinese government formally recognized Mongolia's independence on 5 January 1946. Soviet troops stayed on until 1925; five divisions were stationed in Mongolia in 1966 and one was taken away in 1987. According to Milivojevic (1987: 562), Soviet forces were 'officially' stationed in Mongolia from 1921 to 1925, from 1936 to 1956 and after 1966, but unofficially at least some

Soviet forces were stationed there every year after 1921; also, uniquely, communist Mongolia had no domestic armaments industry (p. 564).[3]

Yumjaagiyn Tsedenbal became General Secretary of the Mongolian People's Revolutionary Party (MPRP, founded in March 1920 by Suhbaatar who died in February 1923) in 1940, prime minister in 1952 (replacing Horlogyn Choybalsan on his death), and (after removal 1954–58) president in 1974. In August 1984 Jambyn Batmonh (sometimes written Batmunkh) replaced Tsedenbal as party leader.[4] Other political events of note included the establishment of diplomatic relations with socialist China in 1949, membership of the United Nations in 1961 and the establishment of diplomatic relations with the United States on 27 January 1987. In 1985 border trade with China was resumed, but relations with China improved noticeably after Gorbachev's Vladivostok speech in July 1986, in which he said that Mongolia and the Soviet Union were discussing a partial withdrawal of Soviet troops.[5] In 1987 Mongolia renewed scientific and technical co-operation with China, after a span of two decades.

The year 1990 saw a profound change in Mongolia's political life. Opposition demonstrations started in December 1989 and these were officially condoned. On 21 January the MPRP decided to end party privileges (such as by the closure of special shops, rest homes and hospitals, and a decrease in the number of official cars). At the 12–14 Plenum the politburo resigned, it was decided to end the 'leading and guiding role' of the party, and Gombojaviyn Ochirbat was named as the new General Secretary of the MPRP (confirmed 13 April) instead of Batmonh. On 21 March Batmonh lost his presidency to Punsalmaagiyn Ochirbat, and Sharavyn Gungaadorj became prime minister (replacing Dumaagiyn Sodnom). The politburo is now known as the 'presidium' and the General Secretary as 'chairman', this being decided at the extraordinary party congress held 10–12 April (the first since 1921; delegates were also directly elected for the first time). Presidium members are not allowed to hold state posts, in order to separate party from state.

Article 82 of the constitution was formally abolished on 23 March 1990 (this described the MPRP as the 'guiding force' in society and the 'vanguard of the working people'). The extraordinary congress also ended party control over trade unions, cultural activities, the media, science and youth, although party cells were to remain in the police and army. Independent parties were formally legalized at the 10–11 May 1990 session of the National Assembly.

Free elections were held in July 1990, the first round on the 22nd and the second on the 29th. The MPRP competed against independent parties for the 430 seats in the Great Hural (National Assembly). The Little Hural (newly revived) has fifty-three seats, fifty directly elected; the chairman, deputy chairman and secretary of this standing legislature are elected by the Great Hural (this body meets only infrequently, only four times over its five-year term). The Little Hural appoints a cabinet of ministers e.g. Dashiyn Byambasuren was appointed prime minister on 10 September 1990.

The MPRP had a successful election, winning 345 out of the 430 seats in the Great Hural and over 60 per cent of the votes for the Little Hural. The turn-out was 92.4 per cent. The MPRP campaigned on a platform of 'humanitarian democratic socialism' and a 'state-controlled market economy' (more specific pledges included cancelling the debts of agricultural co-operatives). Other parties competing in the election included the Mongolian Democratic Party, the National Progress Party and the Social Democratic Party (these formed an electoral alliance and outperformed the other opposition parties), the Free Labour Party, the Greens and the Patriotic Front. The Mongolian Democratic Party was in favour of a more market-orientated economy, while the Free Labour Party was in favour of privately run shops and enterprises and market prices.

There was a coalition government. The Social Democrat leader (Radnaasumberelgiyn Gonchigdorf) became vice-president (the Little Hural elected him president of that body). The prime minister belonged to the MPRP, but he had deputies from the National Progress Party (in favour of a mixed, market economy) and the Mongolian Democratic Party.

On 28 November 1991 parliament decided to change the name of the country from the People's Republic to simply the Republic of Mongolia, this becoming law when the new constitution was introduced on 12 February 1992. The constitution stresses political democracy and the market economy.

In the 28 June 1992 general election, in which the turn-out was 91.6 per cent, the MPRP won seventy of the seventy-six seats in the new single chamber parliament. The Democratic Coalition won four seats, the Social Democratic Party one and an independent one.

ECONOMIC BACKGROUND

The population of this arid country reached 2,043,400 in January 1989 (compared to 649,300 in 1921), of whom 52 per cent are now urbanized. The population is growing rapidly, a cause of some concern because of factors such as rising youth unemployment (Sanders, *FEER*, 27 October 1988, p. 42). The population growth rate is 2.8 per cent and the infant mortality rate seventy-five per thousand (Sanders, *Asian Survey*, 1990, vol. XXX, no. 1, p. 66). Sanders (1987: 84–5) vividly describes the desperately poor state of the economy in 1921. (1) It was dominated by nomadic cattle-rearing. Ninety per cent of the population were nomadic herdsmen who owned no land. Fifty per cent of livestock was owned by feudal secular and church lords constituting just 7.8 per cent of the population (serfdom persisted until the revolution). Animal production accounted for over 90 per cent of national income (*Information Mongolia* 1990: 185); industry accounted for 8.5 per cent of national income in 1940 and 14.6 per cent in 1960 (p. 186.) (2) Foreigners dominated industry (e.g. coal mining, gold mining, power stations, leather, armouries, and the telegraph system); nationalization took place soon after the assumption of power. (3) There was heavy foreign indebtedness. (4) There was no national currency; mediums of exchange included sheep, foreign notes, and silver bullion and coins.[6] Resource endowment comprises mainly land suitable for livestock, timber, brown and coking coal, copper, molybdenum, gold, fluorspar, iron ore, wolfram, zinc, tin and lead. Approximately 60 per cent of the country has never been subjected to a proper geological survey (*EEN*, 1987, vol. 1, no. 8). See Table 4.1 for rates of growth of GNP.

The first attempt at a five-year plan was for the period 1931–35, but it was only after the Second World War that systematic planning took place. The first five-year plan ran from 1948 to 1952. Annual plans began in 1941 with the setting up of the Board of Planning, Accounting and Control. School leavers were directed to their place of work by the Directorate of the Mongolian Organized Work Force (Sanders 1987: 119). Enterprises and institutions were mainly responsible for housing their own workforces (p. 123).

ECONOMIC REFORM

Even when he first took over, Batmonh attacked waste, losses, and mismanagement, describing the system of economic management as the weakest link in economic work (Heaton, *Asian Survey*, 1986, vol. XXVI, no. 1, p. 86). At the Nineteenth Congress of the Mongolian People's Revolutionary Party in May 1986 he attacked bureaucracy, ill-discipline, irresponsibility, narrow thinking, and mere slogans (Heaton, *Asian Survey*, 1987, vol. XXVII, no. 1, p. 79). There started criticism of the 1960s and 1970s as an era of stagnation (*EEN*, 1988, vol. 2, no. 10, p. 4), obviously echoing Soviet sentiments. Tsedenbal was not explicitly named, however, until Batmonh's speech at the end of December

Table 4.1 Mongolia: average annual rates of growth of GNP, NMP, industrial output and prices (%)

1960–70	1970–75	1976–80	1980–85	1985–87	1987–88	1989	1990	1991
				GNP				
5.0	7.1	5.5	7.1	5.8	3.4	–	–	−20.0
				NMP				
								−13.0
				GDP				
				1987	1988	1989	1990	1991
				4.5	5.1	4.2	−2.1	−18.0
			Industrial output					−12.0
			Inflation					53.0

Sources: Faber (1990: 413); Kaser (1992:175); P. Hannam, *FEER*, 6 February 1992, p. 49; *The Economist*, 1 February 1992, p 62; FT (*World Economy Survey*, 21 September 1992, p. 14; uses Asian Development Bank data for GDP).

1988 (Sanders, *FEER*, 19 January 1989, p. 21). Sanders describes the December 1988 plenum of the Central Committee as a milestone for economic and political reform (*Asian Survey*, 1990, vol. XXX, no. 1, p. 59).

Ministerial reorganization took place in 1968. Ministerial amalgamations also included the 1986 decision to allow the Ministry of Agriculture to take over the Ministry of Water Supply in October and the establishment of one body in charge of construction (the State Construction Committee) in December (Sanders 1987: 62). In the early 1970s industrial production associations along Soviet lines began to be formed. A 'commission for perfecting management and the economic mechanism' was formed in 1986 (and reported to the Central Committee the following year) as well as a 'standing commission for agriculture and food supply' and two committees for increasing efficiency in the use of materials and for improving the repair of machinery and vehicles imported from the Soviet Union. The ministerial system was altered (see Sanders, *FEER*, 11 February 1988, p. 62, and *Asian Survey*, 1989, vol. XXIV, no. 1; *EEN*, 1988, vol. 2, no. 4, pp. 6–7), the changes being designed to streamline the planning process:

1. The State Construction Committee. This was formed in early 1987 out of the Ministry of Construction and two design institutes and placed under the control of Vice-Premier Sonomyn Luvsangomso.

2. In December 1987 the Ministry of Light Industry and Food and the Ministry of Agriculture were reorganized into the Ministry of Light Industry and the Ministry of Agriculture and Food Industry, the latter thus taking over food processing from the former. Robert Thompson (*FT*, 9 April 1990, p. 6) reports the dismantling of ten ministries. The Ministries of Agriculture and Light industry were merged.

3. The Ministry of Foreign Economic Relations and Supply assumed the functions of the Ministry of Foreign Trade, the State Committee for Material and Technical Supply, and the State Committee for Foreign Economic Relations.

4. The Ministry of Power, Mining and Geology was formed out of the Ministry of Fuel and Power Industry and the Ministry of Geology and Mining Industry.[7]

5. A new Ministry for Environmental Protection.

6. The State Committee for Planning and the Economy. This was formed at the end of January 1988 out of the State Planning Commission and the two committees for prices and labour and placed under the control of Vice-Premier Puntsagiyn Jasray.[8]

7. The State Committee for Science and Technology. This absorbed higher education in order to improve the link between university training and the research institutes.

Over 100 enterprises took part in a new 'economic experiment' in financial autonomy. The participating sectors included light industry, food production, fuel and power, public catering, and transport and communications. Construction, timber and services were included during 1987. Plan fulfilment had to cover all the relevant products (Sanders, *FEER*, 11 February 1988, p. 64). At the June 1987 Central Committee meeting Batmonh stressed the need for the restructuring of economic management, intensive growth and increased efficiency. In an earlier speech, in May of the same year, he listed a number of problems: the stress on fulfilling net plan indices, the continuing shortages of foodstuffs and consumer goods, the poor quality of many products, bureaucracy, lack of initiative and deficient housing (Jarret, *Asian Survey*, 1988, vol. XXVIII, no. 1, p. 84). Prime Minister Dumaagiyn Sodnom referred to over-centralization as the main problem of economic management and planning, and said that the remedy lay in the need to limit the role of the State Planning Commission to general capital investment policy and broad targets, with ministries and state committees making decisions on aspects such as the purchase of machinery and equipment. Provincial and town administrations and enterprise managers were to have greater autonomy and be financially accountable (as were work teams within the enterprise), while enterprise performance was to be judged by the fulfilment of export orders and sales contracts (Sanders, *FEER*, 10 December 1987, pp. 40–1). The 1988 plan avoided the subjection of every enterprise to highly detailed plan targets, enterprises being allowed, for the first time, to fill in the details of their own plans on the basis of a restricted number of central plan targets (Sanders, *FEER*, 11 February 1988, p. 62). Personal material incentives were also given increased attention (in 1988 pay scales dependent on enterprise revenue were introduced in light industry and food processing, internal trade, and supply: Sanders, *Asian Survey*, 1989, vol. XXIV, no. 1, p. 52). Considerably less than 5 per cent of prices were subject to negotiations between enterprises (Faber 1990: 416). There were also experiments in electing enterprise managers and team leaders. Local authorities[9] were given greater power over enterprises in their areas and were able to use a portion of the funds of enterprises for infrastructural purposes (*EEN*, 1988, vol. 2, no. 10, p. 5).

Kaser (1992: 167) uses the term 'Mongolian *perestroika*' to describe the 1984–9 period, indicating the continuing influence of Soviet ideas. Kaser (1987b) considers that the reform proposals did not amount to as far-reaching a reform as in the other socialist countries of Asia, and a growing labour force and available land and natural resources made the drive for intensive growth less urgent.[10]

The November 1988 Law on the State Enterprise came into operation on 1 January 1989, emphasizing the financial autonomy of the enterprise (Sanders, *Asian Survey*, 1990, vol. XXX, no. 1, p. 65). As in the Soviet Union, the principles of full cost accounting, self-financing and self-management were stressed, the last seeking greater involvement of the workforce in enterprise decision-making (including the election of the managers and a management council comprising at least 60 per cent workers) (*Information Mongolia* 1990: 188). 'State orders' were a feature, while enterprise indicators in-cluded 'realized production taking into account commercially negotiated contracts', net value added, profits and quality. Wholesale trade was expanded after late 1987, covering a wide range of producer goods (Kaser 1992: 169). Remuneration was to be based on performance; within the numbers employable and the wage fund, both set by the ministry, management had some discretion (e.g. whether to choose time or piece rates). World prices were taken into account in the pricing of exportables and import substitutes and some prices were deregulated (Kaser 1992: 170).

Mongolia predictably followed in the Soviet Union's footsteps, with Il Tod (*glasnost*) and Shinechiel ('renewal'; *perestroika*) emphasized. There was now talk of developing a 'state-controlled market economy' (Robert Thompson, *FT*, 11 April 1990, p. 22). State controls would remain in force only during the transition to a market economy (Sanders, *FEER*, 31 May 1990, p. 28). On 17 February 1990 the then prime minister, Sodnom, said that 'Our goal is to transform the central planning system . . . into a system based on democratic principles' (quoted in *The Times*, 19 February 1990, p. 11). In a 10 April 1990 speech at the 10–12 April extraordinary congress of the MPRP, General Secretary Ochirbat said of the economy, 'The situation is truly serious,' and quoted an unemployment figure of 27,000. In early November Deputy Prime Minister Dorligjav said 'We have no time to lose to transfer to a market economy.' State enterprises and some land would be parcelled into lots and distributed equally to all the people of Mongolia (*FT*, 3 November 1990, p. 3).

INDUSTRIAL DEVELOPMENT AND POLICY

Up to the start of the Second World War the limited amount of industrial activity largely concentrated on the processing of livestock products. The next two decades saw diversification into such activities as metalworking, timber-processing and consumer goods, followed by full-scale industrialization, with intra-branch diversification and modernization (Sanders 1987: 86–7). Soviet aid has been of substantial importance. In the five years to 1986 Soviet aid may have amounted to around $3 billion (*EEN*, 1987, vol. 1, no. 12, p. 6). Soviet aid was worth $800 million a year (*The Economist*, 17 March 1990, p. 69), while there were 50,000 Soviet technicians and experts in the country (Delfs and Sanders, *FEER*, 22 March 1990, p. 11). As of 1 November 1989, Mongolia owed the Soviet Union 9.5 billion roubles (*CDSP*, 1990, vol. XLII, no. 9, p. 9); a figure of $16 billion was quoted in January 1991, although in September 1990 it was agreed to postpone repayments until the year 2000 (there is no debt owed to Western banks) (Kaser 1992: 175). One source suggests that aid, largely from the Soviet Union and in the form of long-term, low-interest credit, financed about 50 per cent of investment during the late 1960s and the 1970s (Wallace and Clarke 1986: 98). The 1986–90 and 1985–2000 plans were to have focused on agriculture and improving food supplies (Heaton, *Asian Survey*, 1986, vol. XXVI, no. 1, p. 86).

AGRICULTURE

In 1919 over 90 per cent of national income originated in agriculture.[11] Land was nationalized in 1921 and this was followed by a redistribution of stock and property to poorer households. The first state farms were established in 1922–23 for controlling arable land and for cereal cultivation. Collectivization started in 1929. By the end of 1930 nearly 30 per cent of poor and middle peasant households had been forced into collectives, but unrest and the slaughtering of animals led to a retreat.[12] Among the policies implemented during the Second World War was the imposition of state procurements and obligatory wool deliveries upon individual households. Collectivization took place during the latter half of the 1950s, although some 'initial form' co-operatives, in most of

which only work was collective, were set up after 1935 (Jahne 1990: 71). By the end of 1959 collective farms accounted for 99.3 per cent of individual family holdings and 72.3 per cent of the total stock (*Information Mongolia* 1990: 190).

'Family links' or 'bases' (typically two or three families) were long the basic work units, with the two or three brigades per collective farm fulfilling functions such as supply and planning (Jahne 1990: 82). The bases were joined into teams, which were specialized by e.g. animal group (*Information Mongolia* 1990: 196). Some fodder was grown by the collective, but this was done mainly by state farms. In 1969 the livestock machine stations (set up in 1937) were transferred, without compensation, to the collectives. Herdsmen's families live in permanent settlements, and the herdsmen themselves drive the livestock to pasture according to season. From 1979 onwards collective members became entitled to state old-age pensions. Members had to work a minimum number of workdays for the collective (raised from 150 to 250 in 1967). There were controls on the number of livestock that could be held by individual members. In December 1987 co-operative members were permitted to own 100 head of stock per family living in the Gobi zone and seventy-five per family in the forest-steppe zone, compared with seventy-five and fifty per family respectively, before that date (Sanders, *FEER*, 11 February 1988, p. 62). Almost 25 per cent of livestock of a total of 22.6 million in 1987 was in private hands, either on townspeople's plots or in the herds of co-operative members (p. 62). *Individual holdings* of workers, employees and citizens after January 1986 were allowed eight to twenty-five livestock per household depending on areas. The same decree, as well as increasing the number of livestock allowed, permitted the sale of surplus produce through the co-operative trade network in addition to the state procurement system (the 1978 decree had fixed compulsory state procurements for some products).

A number of state farms developed into 'agro-industrial complexes', with their own processing plants (e.g. fruit and vegetables and flour)[13] and utilizing industrial techniques in farming. During the 1980s a number of 'Inter-cooperative Associations' were set up, providing co-operatives with feedstuffs, transport, and construction services (Jahne 1990: 77). After 1986 state farms and co-operatives benefited from higher state prices for procurements above the annual average rate of growth attained over the period of the last five-year plan.[14]

Less than 1 per cent of the country is arable and permanent crop land; more than 80 per cent is pasture and 10 per cent is forest and woodland (Jahne 1990: 69). The division of arable land was as follows: state farms, 69 per cent; herding collectives, 21 per cent; *personal holdings*, 10 per cent. The corresponding figures for livestock were: 6 per cent, 70 per cent and 22 per cent, respectively. Sanders reported several years of stagnant agricultural output, due to declining productivity in the livestock sector, with falls in average slaughter weight, *per capita* meat production trailing behind population growth, and meat exports declining. Livestock numbers totalled 22.6 million in 1986 and 1987, the same as in 1970 (*FEER*, 11 February 1988, p. 2). *Information Mongolia* (1990: 192–3) provides the following information for 1987. Animal products made up 69.7 per cent of gross agricultural output. State farms produced 31.9 per cent of total output (72.8 per cent of state output derived from crops); collective farms produced 47.2 per cent of total output (85.9 per cent of collective farm output derived from animal products); and the private sector accounted for 20.9 per cent of total agricultural output (26.4 per cent of total meat production, 40.8 per cent of total milk production and only 1.8 per cent of total potatoes and vegetables).

The 1985 Food Programme up to the year 2000 mimicked the 1982 Soviet programme of that name; an increase in food production, a decentralization of decision-making, an increase in private output, and improved incentives (Jahne 1990: 77).

FOREIGN TRADE

Comecon trade was overwhelmingly dominant. According to *Information Mongolia* (1990: 231), 1988 figures showed the division of Mongolian exports as: CMEA, 92.0 per cent; other socialist countries, 2.6 per cent; and capitalist countries, 5.2 per cent. The respective figures for imports were: 95.6 per cent, 2.3 per cent and 2.1 per cent. The percentage contribution to exports in 1988 was as follows: machinery, equipment and transport zero (there is no domestic engineering industry); fuel, mineral raw materials and metals 41.7; raw materials and products of non-food processing plus raw materials for making foods and foodstuffs themselves 39.2; chemical products, fertilizers and building materials 3.4; industrial consumer goods 15.7. The respective figures for imports were 30.2, 33.5, 10.5, 7.0 and 18.4.

Trade with the Soviet Union was dominant, although the exact proportion depended on Mongolia's relations with China. The Soviet Union was practically the country's only trading partner from the mid-1920s to 1953, when trade with China restarted. Eighty-five per cent of trade turnover was accounted for by the Soviet Union in 1956, 70 per cent in 1960 (when Mongolian trade with China reached 18 per cent), 60 per cent in 1966 (Sanders 1987: 100), and the figure then rose to around 80 per cent (Sanders, *FEER*, 10 December 1987, p. 42). In 1986 machinery and equipment constituted over 36 per cent of imports from the Soviet Union, the remainder being oil and petrol, textiles, consumer goods and foodstuffs (p. 42). The first five-year trade agreement was signed with China in 1986. The 1984 and 1985 agreements were short-term and concerned with border trade exchanges.

The state foreign trade monopoly was set up in December 1930. Foreign trade associations specialized by commodity. Mongolia became a member of Comecon in 1962. One factor inhibiting foreign trade was the dependence on Soviet railways. The road network was built with links to the Soviet rail network in mind. Air transport has increased in recent years (Ebon, *FEER*, 5 March 1987, p. 20). In 1987 total trade turnover was 5.4 billion togrog (£920 million). Western trade began to be encouraged. Japan is the leading 'Western' trading partner ($20 million turnover annually), others including Switzerland, West Germany and Britain (p. 8). The November 1988 Law on the State Enterprise allowed some enterprises to trade directly.

Currency auctions began in August 1990, made possible by the percentage of hard currency earnings allowed to be retained by exporters (Kaser 1992: 173). Customs duties were applied to all imports, rather than just private purchases, from 1 March 1991 (p. 173).

Joint equity ventures. The earlier Soviet–Mongolian joint stock companies (pre- and early post-Second World War), such as those in banking, trade, transport and mineral extraction were subsequently handed over into full Mongolian ownership. There are, however, a number of joint companies operating today (in transport, power supply and mineral extraction, for example), mainly in co-operation within the Soviet Union, but also with Bulgaria and Czechoslovakia. In 1981 the Mongolian–Soviet Erdenet copper-molybdenum enterprise came fully on stream. Two new joint ventures with the Soviet Union were to be set up, involving the production of sheepskin coats and felt footwear, and discussions are going on about projects in agriculture, building materials, the timber industry and energy (*EEN*, 1988, vol. 2, no. 10, p. 5). There is a Soviet uranium mine (Sanders, *FEER*, 30 November 1989, p. 73).

Joint ventures with Western companies were formally allowed under the March 1990 legislation (two had already begun, UK partnerships in wind energy and telecommunications). Wholly foreign owned companies were not allowed, but no ceiling was placed on foreign participation. They are especially encouraged in such sectors as high technology, mineral extraction and processing, and the processing of agricultural products. A February 1991 law

allowed foreign participation in oil exploration. A joint venture with Japan to produce television sets was planned to start operating in late 1990 (IHT, 27 February 1990, p. 13). Under the new constitution, which came into force on 12 February 1992, foreigners are able to lease land.

THE NON-STATE, NON-AGRICULTURAL SECTOR PRE-1990

By 1960 private trade no longer existed (*Information Mongolia* 1990: 226). From the start of the 1960s policy centred on the merging of workers and herdsmen and of state and co-operative property, with the possibilities of private property thought to be exhausted. Co-operatives produced nearly 20 per cent of gross industrial output in 1972; in that year most were nationalized, the few remaining producing less than 3 per cent of output (Kaser 1992: 170). More recent policy was to encourage co-operatives and private enterprises in the food industry and in services (*EEN*, 1988, vol. 2, no. 10, p. 5); Sanders reported a recent ordinance of the Council of Ministers encouraging the setting up of private co-operatives providing services, manufacturing and processing on a small scale (*FEER*, 30 June 1988, p. 27).

POST-ELECTION ECONOMIC DEVELOPMENTS: PRIVATIZATION AND THE TRANSITION TO THE MARKET

The transition to the market was scheduled to begin in January 1991. The November 1990 resolution of the Little Hural outlined a programme of privatization (Kaser 1992: 172). The state would still control key sectors (energy, mining, the railways, garment-making, meat processing and confectionery), but the remaining enterprises were to become joint stock corporations, whose shares would be distributed equally among Mongolian citizens of any age. Some arable land would be included, but grazing would revert to traditional common lands. *The Economist* (19 October 1991, p. 92) provides some further information. Each citizen of any age was to receive a voucher with a nominal value of 10,000 tugriks (arrived at by dividing the notional value of state assets by the population) for 200 tugriks (or nothing if very poor); vouchers could be used in both small and large privatizations. The programme involved 340 large and medium-sized enterprises and almost 3,000 small enterprises (IHT, 10 February 1992, p. 11). State-owned urban housing was to be sold off. By mid-1992 about 20 per cent of the vouchers had been turned in for stock and the process was expected to be completed by 1993 (Nicholas Kristof, IHT, 9 July 1992, p. 3).

The auction of shops started in Ulan Bator in May 1991; on 24 June 1991 a shop was sold with the land (the first time state land had been sold at auction). Simon Long (*The Guardian*, 8 June 1991, p. 8) reports the detailed programme announced 7 June 1991: the aim was to sell off 57 per cent of state-owned assets by the end of 1993 (this to include 2,200 of the 2,600 state factories and enterprises); livestock co-operatives were also to be privatized, but the farms themselves could decide how. *Euromoney* (supplement on Mongolia, July 1991, p. 13) presents a somewhat different programme: the intention was to transfer into private hands 100 per cent of the holding in small enterprises and 80 per cent of all state assets by September 1993. About 20 per cent of the shares in large enterprises was to be distributed to workers, while vouchers could be sold to domestic or foreign buyers rather than used in auctions. The first stock exchange was opened in Ulan Bator on 7 February 1992. According to a report in the IHT (10 February 1992, p. 11), foreign investors would be able to buy shares after the opening of a secondary market, possibly later in 1992, that would sell stock for cash rather than vouchers; foreigners would be restricted to owning a maximum of 49 per cent of any enterprise.

The powers of ministries have been reduced. Only four economic ministries now remain, namely National Economic Development, Trade and Industry, Energy, and Finance. In August 1990 the state bank monopoly came to an end and two commercial banks were set up in September (Kaser 1992: 172).

Macroeconomic stabilization measures have been taken (Kaser 1992: 172–3). On 1 January 1991 wholesale prices were adjusted closer to world levels (e.g. coal increased by 74 per cent and electricity 94 per cent). On 15 January 1991 fixed retail prices, wages and social security benefits were doubled (a limit was placed on the doubling of savings bank deposits, equivalent to eighteen months' average wage). Controls on other prices were changed to ceilings. The aim was to liberalize 80 per cent of retail prices by the end of 1991 (Kaser 1992: 173). Price controls were to remain, for example, on housing rents, telephones and some forms of energy. In September 1991, however, price controls were imposed (William Heaton, *Asian Survey*, 1992, vol. XXXII, no. 1, p. 52). Nevertheless, the budget deficit in 1991 was about 30 per cent of GDP (Peter Hannam, *FEER*, 6 February 1992, p. 50).

Mongolia has been badly affected by the disruption in Comecon trade relations, especially Soviet deliveries of energy, equipment and foodstuffs. Foreign trade fell 7 per cent in 1990 and even more sharply in 1991 (William Heaton, *Asian Survey*, 1992, vol. XXXII, no. 1, p. 53). Alexander Nicoll (*FT*, 27 March 1992, p. 6) reports that in 1991 foreign trade fell by about 50 per cent. Peter Hannam (*FEER*, 6 February 1992, p. 49) reports that trade with the Soviet Union fell by 60 per cent in 1991, with oil product deliveries at 70 per cent of the contracted amount. But the Soviet Union still accounted for three-quarters of foreign trade. Power cuts and rationing became more widespread (meat was put on ration in Ulan Bator on 16 May 1991). Efforts are being made to diversify trading links, such as with China and Japan. The tugrik was devalued from seven to forty to the US dollar on 14 June 1991. Mongolia became a member of the Asian Development Bank in February 1991.

At the end of January President Ochirbat visited the USA (reciprocating a visit to Mongolia by Secretary of State James Baker in August 1990); trade and scientific/technical agreements were signed and MFN status was granted. Japanese prime minister Kaifu visited Mongolia in August 1991 and pledged aid worth $7 million; a further $61 million was promised the following month (the Japanese Ministry of International Trade and Industry offered administrative guidance). At a meeting of international donors in Tokyo in September 1991 $150 million of aid was pledged (William Heaton, *Asian Survey*, 1992, vol. XXXII, no. 1, p. 54); in May 1992 the sum of $312 million was announced, albeit conditional on continued reform (*The Economist*, 4 July 1992, p. 65). Unemployment was 36,000 in April 1990 and was expected to reach 80,000 (about 16 per cent) by the end of 1991 (Kaser 1992: 175). The figure of 80,000 was reached by September 1991 (William Heaton, *Asian Survey*, 1992, vol. XXXII, no. 1, p. 53). This deteriorating situation makes the transition to a market economy especially difficult for a very poor country like Mongolia (see Table 4.1).

CONCLUSION

Mongolia, freed from Chinese control with Soviet help, formally became the second people's republic in 1924. This small country (in terms of population) of pastoral nomads gradually became more industrialized with Soviet aid and under effective Soviet control. Jambyn Batmonh began to criticize aspects of society and of the economy in the style of Gorbachev, although actual reform was limited (see especially the 1987–88 ministerial reorganization and the small-scale experiment in financial autonomy in the industrial sector). There were major changes in Mongolia's political climate after 1990, with free elections in July 1990 and June 1992 (the MPRP was the winner on both occasions). Mongolia had faithfully followed the Soviet Union's lead, but then bounded ahead in this regard. Mongolia has begun the transition to

a mixed market economy under very difficult circumstances.

NOTES

1. There are around 3 million Chahar Mongols in Inner Mongolia (an autonomous region of China) and Buryat Mongols in Siberia, mostly in the Buryat and Kalmyk autonomous republics. Jasper Becker (*The Guardian*, 6 April 1990, p. 12) quotes figures of 3.5 million in Inner Mongolia and Xinjiang Province in China, 350,000 Buryats and 156,000 Kalmyks.
2. It was formerly the Chinese province of Outer Mongolia.
3. One estimate puts defence spending at 6–8 per cent of GNP (Tai Ming Cheung, *FEER*, 25 July 1991, p. 16).
4. Batmonh became premier in 1974 and president in 1986. Tsendenbal was expelled from the MPRP on 15 March 1990 and stripped of all state titles on 20 April.
5. A Soviet motorized rifle division withdrew between April and June 1987, a 25 per cent cutback of the roughly 60,000 Soviet troops still left in Mongolia (Jarret, *Asian Survey*, 1988, vol. XXVIII, no.1, p. 81). In his famous speech to the United Nations (7 December 1988) Gorbachev promised that a 'large portion' of the troops would be withdrawn, subsequently quantified at three-quarters. The March 1990 agreement means that Soviet troops and their equipment will be withdrawn entirely by the end of 1992 (later fixed at September of that year).
6. The togrog or tugrik (=100 mongo) was issued in 1925 and became the only legal tender three years later. The official figure for *per capita* GNP is $660 (Sanders, *FEER*, 14 December 1989, p. 106). Kaser (1992: 175) estimates GNP *per capita* in 1991 at $580. In 1988 the percentage contributions to state budgetary revenue were as follows: turnover tax 64.0; profits tax 27.4; social insurance contributions 3.7; taxes and dues from the population 0.7; others 4.4 (Faber 1990: 415). The major sources of expenditure were as follows: national economic development 45.4 per cent and socio-cultural expenditures 38.7 per cent (*Information Mongolia* 1990: 229).
7. Note the importance of coal in power generation.
8. Membership of the Council of Ministers subsequently fell by about 25 per cent, and four vice-premiers were then largely in charge of economic planning and management.

9. Hurals are assemblies of deputies.

10. Sanders reported a labour surplus in urban areas and a shortage in rural areas, since migrants were attracted to the former by higher incomes (*FEER*, 30 June 1988, p. 27).

11. In 1985, by contrast, 25 per cent (Heaton, *Asian Survey*, 1987, vol. XXVII, no. 1, p. 80); industry 32.3 per cent (Heaton, *Asian Survey*, 1986, vol. XXVI, no. 1, p. 87). Sanders (1987: xvii-xviii) gives figures for agriculture of 18.3 per cent of GDP, industry 32.4 per cent, and trade and supply 31.6 per cent.

12. Milivojevic (1987: 565) argues that there was a nationwide revolt against both the regime and Soviet control, leading to the abandoning of collectivization and the reintroduction of large Soviet forces.

13. Sanders reported on the start of production of preserves at the Sharyn Gol Fruit and Vegetable Industry Association, a ten-year project built with aid from communist Bulgaria.

14. See Sanders (1987: 64).

5

THE PEOPLE'S REPUBLIC OF CHINA

China is the largest country in the world in terms of population (1.158 billion at the end of 1991). The 1989 birth rate was 2.08 per cent (1.968 per cent in 1991) and the death rate 0.65 per cent: 92 per cent of the population consists of Hans. In 1987 66.6 per cent of the labour force was employed in agriculture (Kueh 1989: 423) and 62 per cent of the population was rural (*FT Survey*, 12 December 1989, p. 38). China is third largest in terms of land area, after the Soviet Union and Canada. Approximately 22 per cent of the world's population is sustained on less than 8 per cent of the world's arable area. In 1979 only 11 per cent of the total land area of China was cultivated (50 per cent of India's land is arable), with just 0.12 ha *per capita* of the agricultural population, compared with India's 0.42 (World Bank 1984: 35). Table 5.1 shows rates of growth of NMP and agricultural output.

China is an ancient and continuous civilization. Notable dates include the foundation of the first centralized Chinese state during the Qin dynasty (221–206 BC) and the ending of the

Qing or Manchu dynasty (1644–1911) by Sun Yat-Sen. The Kuomintang Party (founded in 1924 by Sun Yat-Sen) and the Communist Party of China (founded in 1921) co-operated in the drive to break the power of warring landlords, but in 1927, following the earlier death of Sun Yat-Sen and under the new leader Chiang Kai-Shek, the former party turned on the latter. Mao emerged as leader of the CCP, now based on the peasantry (the famous 'Long March' to the north-west took place 1934–36). The Japanese annexed Manchuria in 1931 and waged general war in 1937. The two parties again collaborated in the fight against the invader (1937–45), but in the civil war that followed Japan's defeat (1946–49), Mao emerged victorious and Chiang Kai-Shek fled to Taiwan. Mao Tse-Tung (Mao Zedong) established the People's Republic on 1 October 1949 and died in 1976.

Although there were pockets of modern industry in the Treaty Ports and a commercial and monetary tradition, at the start of its socialist period China was, in other respects, a classically

Table 5.1 China: average annual rates of growth of NMP and agricultural output, 1952–90 (%)

	NMP				
1953–57	1957–65	1965–76	1976–85	1986–90	
6.6	2.1	5.1	8.8	7.5	

		Gross value of agricultural output *				
1952–57	1957–65	1965–75	1971–78	1980–82	1982–86	1986–90
4.7	1.2	4.0	4.3	7.5	13.0	4.6

Sources: Perkins, in R. Dernberger (ed.) *China's Development Experience in Comparative Perspective*, Cambridge, MA: Harvard University Press, 1980; Perkins (1988: 612, 628); Riskin (1987: 185); *China Briefing* (July 1991, p. 1).
* See note 9.

poor country. Eighty-nine per cent of the population was rural; average life expectancy was thirty-five years. The 1953 rate of population growth was 2.3 per cent, with a birth rate and death rate of 3.7 per cent and 1.4 per cent respectively. The literacy rate was 20 per cent. The commodity structure of foreign trade was characterized by mainly primary product exports and manufactured imports. In the period 1931–36, net investment was only about 3 per cent of net domestic product (Riskin 1987: 33), while the socialist regime also faced a hyperinflation on taking control.

In 1952, by which time the economy had largely recovered from decades of foreign and civil war, *per capita* GNP was only $50,[1] while agriculture employed 84 per cent of the workforce and contributed 60 per cent to net material product (Riskin 1987: 269). The 1953 census revealed a 1952 population of 575 million and shocked the party into a population control programme after 1956.[2] Previously, exclusive blame for poverty was based on capitalism and imperialism – Mao opposing birth control as a 'bourgeois Malthusian doctrine' (Fang Lizhi, *The Independent*, 18 January 1989: p. 19). By 1986 life expectancy had risen to a remarkable 66.9 years for men and 70.9 for women, while the 1981–2000 plan envisages a rise in real *per capita* income from $300 to $800. In 1988 *per capita* GDP in current prices was $340 (*EIU Country Profile*, 1989–90, p. 16), compared to $5,743 in Taiwan (FT, 17 May 1990, p. 38). The literacy rate in 1990 was 73 per cent (*The Economist*, 3 October 1992, p. 80).

Early socialist developmental aims put greater stress on equality in the distribution of income and saw international trade, even with other socialist countries, as a last resort to fill gaps between supply and demand (exports were seen simply as a means of financing unavoidable imports) and as a means of providing the capital goods needed to attain ultimate self-sufficiency. China has also made significant departures from the traditional Soviet economic system in a number of ways, even during the first five year plan (1953–57) when the greatest similarities can be found. For example, much more frequent use has been made of rationing (of basic commodities, such as grain, cotton cloth, edible oils, sugar and meat), not only for ideological reasons, but also as a means of controlling population movements. These departures provide a theme for the following sections on agriculture, central planning, manpower and industrial management.

AGRICULTURE

Agriculture has been subject to great policy swings. The land reform (1950–53) involved a massive redistribution of land and property to poorer peasants, while the subsequent strategy was geared to avoiding the calamity experienced in Soviet collectivization. There was a progression through varying degrees of co-operation, as 'mutual aid teams' and elementary and advanced agricultural producer co-operatives were formed before 1954, with the first accounting for some 60 per cent of peasant households in that year and the latter two rapidly increasing in number in 1955 (the elementary type accounting for 59 per cent of peasant households by the end of that year). The advanced type increased dramatically in 1956 (accounting for 88 per cent of households by the end of that year). According to Putterman (1988: 42), the elementary type recruited peasants on a substantially voluntary basis, but there was no real choice about joining the advanced co-operative.

Mutual aid teams

Involving five to fifteen households on average usually, these varied from simple labour exchange to the co-operative use of implements and draught animals. Compensation was in the form of proportionate rental payments for these two inputs.

Elementary agricultural producer co-operatives

Typically twenty to twenty-five households, these pooled land as well as draught animals and large implements, with remuneration based on a combination of rental payments for these contributions and remuneration for work performed.

Advanced agricultural producer co-operatives

These co-operatives involved 150 to 200 households (constituting a large village or a number of smaller villages). Land, draught animals and larger implements became co-operative property, with compensation payments spread over a period of up to five years. Private plots were allowed, though they were not to exceed 5 per cent of the average *per capita* cultivated area (Riskin 1987: 91). Collective remuneration, however, was entirely dependent on labour input – that is, the workday system. In November 1953 private trade in cotton cloth, grain and edible oil was declared illegal, and other commodities were included the following year.

The Great Leap Forward, 1958–60

This dramatic policy swing saw the ascent of politics and a decentralization of decision-making to the countryside (provinces and communes) in order to accelerate economic development and the transition to communism. Central government only retained control over inter-provincial transfers (Kane 1988: 55). In 1958 Mao vowed to overtake Britain in the production of iron and steel and other major industrial products within fifteen years. National output was to double in one year (Xu Dixin, quoted by Johnson 1988: 226). Extreme technological dualism ('walking on two legs') led to centrally controlled, large-scale, modern, capital-intensive enterprises accompanied by locally controlled, small-scale, technologically backward, labour-intensive plants such as the familiar 'backyard steel furnaces'. Local industrialization was meant to mobilize all unused resources (including surplus labour), supply consumer goods to the surrounding population and supply inputs to and process the output of agriculture. Surplus labour in agriculture (having a low or zero marginal product), it was assumed, could be redeployed at virtually zero opportunity cost, especially when accompanied by deep ploughing and close planting. The idea was that this could be used to operate the small enterprises needed to increase the degree of rural industrial independence and to build up the agricultural infrastructure, such as dams and irrigation schemes.

The 'people's commune', whose origins lay in large-scale water conservancy systems, was the key institution, with unified management of land and distribution of income. It was meant to release the huge human potential that Mao believed existed and to erode the differences between worker and peasant, town and countryside, and mental and physical labour. The commune was an administrative (covering education, health and public security, for example) as well as an economic unit, dealing with taxation, the assignment of production plans and procurement quotas, manpower allocation, and income distribution. It was divided into brigades and teams. Initially, the accounting unit was the commune or the brigade, while the team was the actual production unit (Johnson 1988: 226). The first commune was set up in April 1958, but by September 1958 90.4 per cent (99 per cent by the beginning of November) of peasant households were communized; the average size was 4,550 households. Rural markets were abolished in the autumn of 1958 (restored a year later). Private plots were reclaimed at the same time, only to be restored with a maximum of 5 per cent of local arable land in May 1959 (Skinner 1985: 400). Trees, large farm implements and draught animals were communized: a small number of other animals could be retained in theory. A varying proportion of income was distributed free in such forms as meals taken in communal (team) dining rooms, need ranked equally with work as a criterion for food distribution, and communal nurseries were intended to release women for work.

This pronounced move towards egalitarianism and distribution according to need as opposed to labour had a catastrophic effect on work incentives and effort. The quality of industrial products was generally very low. The demise of an objective statistical system led to hopelessly optimistic harvest forecasts (such as 1958 grain production doubling, which led to a subsequent reduction in both the total sown area and the percentage of this devoted to grain), blinding planners to the adverse effects of withdrawing labour from agriculture at peak periods when its opportunity cost was high and of too rapid consumption of grain in the early post-harvest months. Official figures subsequently showed the initial fall in agricultural output: the grain harvest totalled 170 million tonnes in 1959, 143.5 million tonnes in 1960, 147.5 million tonnes in 1961, and 160 million tonnes in 1962.[3] Famine stalked the countryside in 1960, optimistic reports caused the government to increase grain procurements, while output, in reality, was falling. State grain procurement as a percentage of output was as follows: 1959 45.4, 1960 39.1, 1962 29.1; in later years the figure did not exceed 25 (Kane 1988: 55). Despite a 15 per cent fall in grain output in 1959, the state compulsory grain procurement quota increased by 14.7 per cent (Lin 1990: 1238). The gross output of agriculture fell by 14 per cent in 1959, 12 per cent in 1960 and 2.5 per cent in 1961 (p. 1234). Lin argues that the main course of the catastrophic performance of 1959–61 was the change in the incentive structure due to the retraction of the right to withdraw from a collective in autumn 1958; he considers (and this is debatable) that previously membership was voluntary and that the threat that harder-working members might leave disciplines the potential shirkers. Lin thus downgrades other suggested causes of the crisis, e.g. poor weather, bad policies and management, and low incentives due to factors such as the sheer size of communes minimizing the link between effort and reward (pp. 1236–48). Official statistics show a rise in the death rate from 11.98 to 38 per thousand between 1957 and 1960. Using official demographic statistics, Penny Kane concludes that the minimum number of excess deaths in the officially designated 'three difficult years' between 1959 and 1961 was 14 million, with 26 million as the likely upper limit (Kane 1988). As regards total national income, official statistics show falls of 18 per cent in 1961 and 7 per cent in 1962 (Ellman 1989: 163), while it took six years to recoup the pre-GLF level (Mao and Hare 1989: 139).

The period between the GLF and the 'household responsibility system'

The GLF débâcle led to the reinstatement of centralized control and economic orthodoxy. At the end of 1959 the brigade (the pre-GLF advanced producer co-operative) became the basic unit of account and in 1961–62 the production team was re-established as the basic unit for production and income distribution. The government decreed that 90 per cent of the workforce was to be employed in agriculture proper (Riskin 1987: 128), and in 1962–65 the contracting out by the team of certain functions (such as fish and stock breeding, the tending of draught animals and the maintenance of farm equipment) and even land in some areas to individuals or small groups was permitted, foreshadowing the present household responsibility system (HRS) (Riskin 1987: 171). The number of communes was increased and the institution itself was retained as an administrative and planning body to transmit and carry out central decisions. In 1961 agriculture was termed the 'foundation' and industry the 'leading factor'. The following year sectoral priorities were ranked as agriculture, light industry, and heavy industry. The pre-responsibility system organization of agriculture was as follows.

1. The production team (twenty to fifty households, usually a small village or parts of a larger one) was the basic unit of production and income distribution and owner of land. It negotiated the fixing of compulsory state procurement quotas; the state set prices at levels below those needed to produce those sales on a voluntary basis (Perkins 1988: 609). Individual income distribution depended on a workday system – points were based on the quantity and quality of work contributed and advances were obtainable before the end-of-year reckoning. Lin (1988: 200) argues that, in general, peasants received fixed work points for a day's work regardless of work effort, with predictable effects on incentives. Putterman (1988: 431), too, argues that from 1964 to the late 1970s there were strong tendencies to use time-based work points, with little linkage to work effort in either a quantitative or a qualitative sense. The team itself owned enterprises, but points also accrued to the team (and to individuals in later years) as a result of work performed in brigade and commune industrial enterprises and collective infrastructure projects. Minimum food needs were met, however, regardless of work effort. This weakened incentives, especially in poorer areas where such minima took up a large proportion of output. Private plots provided income in kind and cash from the sale of products such as fruit and vegetables and meat (pork and poultry mainly) on free markets.

2. The production brigade, usually a large village or several smaller ones and consisting of seven to eight teams, was involved with the following: work needing the co-operation of a number of teams (power and irrigation schemes, for example, and their output distribution); the renting out of large machinery; primary education; health clinics; and the running of industrial and other enterprises, such as brickworks.

3. The commune (twelve to fifteen brigades) acted as a channel for the transmission of central plan orders and for materials allocation. It also provided secondary education and health services, disseminated political and techno-logical information, operated industrial and other enterprises (canneries, electronics, textiles and furniture, for example), collected taxes and procured farm quotas (at state-determined prices) on behalf of the state. The commune was the lowest level of state administration (also dealing with public security), and organized major irrigation and water conservancy schemes, using labour voluntarily donated by teams, which either directly benefited or were compensated in work points. A commune member required permission to leave.

State farms today play a relatively minor role overall, although they are not insignificant as a means of developing and reclaiming land in border regions (a role that was more important in the past). State farms occupy 5 per cent of nationalized land (Wädekin 1990a: 10).

The household responsibility system

Johnson (1988: 229) provides some very useful information on the situation in 1978: 294 million employed in agriculture; 52,780 communes, with an average of thirteen production brigades per commune and each brigade with seven to ten teams; 800 million total commune population, with an average of 15,000 per commune; each team had an average of sixty workers and thirty-five households.

In 1982 the commune lost its political and administrative functions to the resurrected county township (*xiang*). After that communes virtually disappeared, losing their enterprises and their powers to mobilize labour for capital construction projects (Riskin 1987: 299).[4] The brigade has now been replaced by the village. The rural enterprises owned by the teams and villages operate in a market environment and can be leased out to individuals. In 1987 rural industry produced more than 30 per cent of total gross industrial output (*EIU Country Report*,

1988, no. 1, p. 5). The share of non-agricultural output in the rural economy increased from 31 per cent in 1980 to 55 per cent in 1990 (*China Briefing*, July 1991, p. 3). There is some dispute about the year when the value of rural non-agricultural output overtook agricultural output; Tam (1988: 63; referring to rural industrial output only) gives 1985; Wong (1988: 3), 1986; and Dowdle (*FEER*, 24 March 1988, p. 76), 1987. The administrative restrictions on rural enterprise, except for cigarettes, were lifted in 1984, and by the end of that year private enterprise accounted for 14.2 per cent of the gross value of output in the rural enterprise sector (Wong 1988: 11, 26). Chen *et al.* (1992) provide the following information: by 1988 21 per cent of the rural labour force was engaged in non-agricultural activities (p. 206); in 1989 rural township–village enterprises accounted for nearly a quarter of China's total export volume (p. 207).

It is no coincidence that of the 'four modernizations' it is agriculture that comes first, since the population is still overwhelmingly rural. Perkins (1988: 613) makes the important point that reforms in agriculture were easier to implement than in urban areas because significant use was already made of markets. In 1964 and again in 1975 Zhou Enlai announced the aim of attaining the modernization of agriculture, industry, science and technology, and defence by the year 2000, but later more realistic goals were adopted, such as the quadrupling of gross agricultural output and industrial output between 1980 and the year 2000 (Lockett 1987).

The Third Plenum of the Eleventh Central Committee in December 1978 was the watershed as far as economic reform in general is concerned, but agriculture was given priority. China's success in reforming agriculture first proved to be of universal significance in the socialist world, helping to improve supplies of consumer goods and, therefore, incentives. Sicular's differentiation of two stages in policy regarding agricultural trade is useful:

1. *1977–82.* The old system of state procurement quotas was maintained, but quota prices were raised (by more than 20 per cent in 1979), premia on above-quota prices were increased (by between 30 per cent and 50 per cent for grain and oil-bearing crops), and a new 30 per cent price bonus for above-quota deliveries was introduced for cotton. Private markets (including urban) were encouraged, and by the early 1980s market trade was permitted in all products except cotton, which occurred later on. By 1984 18.1 per cent of all purchases of agricultural products took place at market prices, compared with 5.6 per cent in 1978. 'Negotiated' state trade was introduced for above-quota deliveries to the state, at negotiated prices which were in general not to exceed market prices (Sicular 1988: 286–8). Further encouragement was given to agriculture in the following forms: an increase in investment; a decrease in the amount of grain sold to the state, above local consumption needs, from 90 to 70 per cent (Johnson 1988: 231); a green light to private plots, which accounted for 5.7 per cent of arable area in 1978 and 7.1 per cent in 1980; and increases in product diversification and sideline production.

2. *The design of commercial policy.* This was subsequently modified, as we shall see, with the introduction of a single price for oil seeds (1983), cotton (1984) and grain (1985), and a contract system.

It is important to note that the HRS arose from below in the form of local experiments. These were endorsed centrally only later on (and only in poorer areas until late 1981), as a result of their obvious success. The official position in September 1978 was that the production team was to be the basic unit of production, distribution and accounting (Lin 1988: 201; Johnson 1988: 231–2), and that the important thing was to link effort and reward (Perkins 1988: 607). By July 1983 the HRS affected 93 per cent of production teams (Hartford 1987: 213). Initially, the reforms amounted to 'production responsibility systems', involving small groups and individuals, but the 'household responsibility system' had become overwhelmingly dominant by 1983–84 (Hartford 1987: 212). By December 1980 47.1 per cent of production teams operated reponsibility systems, and about 30 per cent of teams implemented household contracts (Ash 1988: 534, 538).

The HRS has a 'limited' and a 'comprehensive' form. Under the 'limited' form, the team devolves day-to-day management decisions to individual households, providing inputs, setting output targets and awarding work points to households for contract fulfilment (this determines household income). This type predominated in the first half of 1981, but thereafter the 'comprehensive' form rapidly became the norm (Hartford 1987: 213). Under the 'comprehensive system', the household is now typically leased land[5] and after meeting the sales quotas for specified basic products contracted with the team at state-determined prices (usually well below market prices: in 1988 the ratios of market prices to state prices were 1.94 for grain, 1.67 for edible oil, 1.17 for vegetables, and 1.22 for meat and eggs: *China Briefing*, March 1991, no. 38, p. 2), tax obligations, and payments for collective services provided by the team (irrigation, large machines, welfare, etc.), it is free to determine output, to consume output itself, and to sell to the state at the higher above-quota prices, at negotiated prices or in free markets.[6] The household also makes its own decisions regarding inputs and is able to apply directly for bank loans. There is a (legal) maximum placed on the number of 'helpers'.[7]

Households are now effectively allowed to sub-lease land among themselves, with the official stipulation that freely negotiated compensation can be given for improvements made to the land, although the village authority has to be informed of the whole arrangement. (Note that land is still publicly owned; one source cites the village as the owner of cultivated land and the state as the owner of urban land, major mountain areas, rivers and lakes: Kojima 1990: 372). It was during the September 1987 visit of World Bank officials that the intention was revealed of openly allowing leasing, on a general basis, of smaller plots to form larger units that are better able to employ modern machinery and technology, while allowing the lessor to concentrate on more specialized aspects of farming or leave the land altogether. The Thirteenth CP Congress in October 1987 referred to leases of up to twenty-five years and to the 'transfer of land use rights' (Long 1990: 17). Cheung notes that the transfer of responsibility contracts (in effect a form of land sale) arose in the grey market as early as 1982 and was formally permitted in 1983 (Cheung 1986: 66).[8] In 1984 contract duration, three to five years initially, was extended beyond fifteen years (perhaps effectively indefinitely) in order to encourage a long view among peasants towards the health of the land. Bornstein (1991: 29) notes that in some regions leases stretch up to fifty years. Land use can be passed on to children. The optimistic announcement in December 1984 gradually to end obligatory quotas and state-determined prices for all products except grain and cotton has been superseded by concern over the grain harvest and the generally more restrictive atmosphere from 1985 onwards.

There have been a number of changes in the grain procurement system, following the ending of price bonuses for above-quota deliveries of oil-seeds in 1983 and of cotton the year afterwards (Sicular 1988b: 471). After 1978 a compulsory grain quota was purchased by the state, which also promised to purchase further sales at a higher price (the farmer also had the option of the free market for above-quota sales). Delfs (*FEER*, 18 February 1988, p. 68) describes how this system broke down under the strains of subsidization, storage and transport imposed by the record 1984 grain harvest of 407 million tonnes, when the state effectively reneged on its promise to purchase all the surplus grain. The two-tier pricing system, in general, encouraged evasion of basic quotas in a situation where the state's ability to enforce deliveries had been weakened (Sicular 1988c: 691). Under the new 'contract purchase system', introduced in early 1985, farmers signed contracts. These were nevertheless still effectively obligatory, it seems – inducements were the uncertainty of future market prices, assured supplies of chemical fertilizers, credit priority (Ash 1988: 549), and the ultimate threat of loss of land (Prybyla 1987: 18). Contracts involved an agreement to supply agreed amounts of grain to the state at a price based on 30 per cent of the contracted amount at the old base price and 70 per cent at the old surplus price, and the state no longer promised to buy grain beyond the grain contract (Watson 1988: 7). Sicular (1988b: 694) notes, however, that if market prices of grain fell below the old quota prices, the state promised to purchase any amount at the old quota prices. It was announced on 10 November 1990, however, that, starting in 1991, there would be a return to the system of compulsory delivery quotas for grain at state-determined prices in order to enforce compliance (it was later announced that the retail price of rationed grain would gradually rise over the next five years).

The opening took place in September 1990 in Zhengzhou (Henan province) of the first wholesale cash and futures market for grain. Other markets for other crops were planned, e.g. one for rice was set up in Wuhan (Hubai province) in March 1991. Wholesale markets have been opened for rice in Wuhu (Anhui province) and for corn in Changchun (Jilin province) (Simon Holberton, *FT Survey*, 16 June 1992, p. vi). Colina MacDougall (*FT Survey*, 24 April 1991, p. iv) reports an experiment starting 1 April 1991 in Guanghan in Sichuan province: both the quantity and the price of grain are market-determined, with consumers given wage compensation. Tai Ming Cheung (*FEER*, 9 April 1992, p. 47) reports that all price restrictions on grain sold in Guangdong and Hainan were abolished in 1991.

Note that private plots remain and have been expanded, and the maximum proportion of cultivated area allocated increased from 7 per cent in 1978 to 15 per cent in March 1981 (Skinner 1985: 406). By 1981 private plots accounted for more than 40 per cent of peasant income (Ellman 1989a: 118).

Agricultural performance under the HRS has been impressive; the gross value of agricultural output (which included sideline production, such as fishing and forestry) increased at an average annual rate of 10.1 per cent in the period 1978–85.[9] Johnson estimates that the real income of farm people doubled during 1978–86 (1988: 234). Over the period 1978–88 the *per capita* real income of rural residents grew at an average annual rate of 9.6 per cent compared with a figure of 6.3 per cent for urban residents (Chen *et al.* 1992: 202). An empirical study by McMillan *et al.* (1989: 781–2) concludes that 78 per cent of the increase in agricultural productivity between 1978 and 1984 (when output rose by more than 61 per cent) can be attributed to the incentive effects of the HRS and 22 per cent to the incentive effects of higher prices. Lin (1992) divides the sources of output growth over the period 1978–84 into three categories and attributes the following percentages to them: increases in conventional inputs 45.79 per cent (especially the increase in the application of chemical fertilizers, 32.2 percentage points); productivity change due to the reforms 48.64 per cent; and the unexplained residual 5.57 per cent. Lin is critical of the McMillan *et al.* study and lists the causes of the increase in agricultural productivity as follows: the shift to the HRS (42.2 per cent); the increase in state procurement prices (15.98 per cent); the trend, e.g. technological change (29.74 per cent); and the residual (12.74 per cent). If one treats residuals as productivity change, as do McMillan *et al.*, then 89.73 per cent of the increase in total factor productivity can be attributed to the HRS. China changed from being a large food importer in 1978 to a net exporter by 1985 (The Economist, 11 April 1992, p. 93). Despite the general success of the HRS, however, a number of problems have arisen that have caused concern to the state.

1. The responsibility system and sideline activities have made labour a valuable asset and thus helped undermine the population control programme. Boys are especially favoured because they can carry on the family farm and provide for parents in their old age.

2. Land use has not always coincided with state preferences. The switch from grain to other more profitable crops and sideline activities contributed to a fall in the grain harvest from 407 million tonnes in 1984 (a then record) to 380 million tonnes in 1985 (390 million tonnes in 1986, 401 million tonnes in 1987, 394 million tonnes in 1988, 407.9 million tonnes in 1989, 435 million tonnes in 1990 and 435.24 million tonnes in 1991). In early 1987 the state took various measures to try to attain the 1987 plan target of 400 million tonnes (410 million tonnes in 1988, 450 million tonnes by 1990 and 480 million tonnes by the year 2000). These included increased state prices, reduced quotas to allow more free market sales, improved supply of subsidized inputs and levies on land used for other crops. The construction of houses and graves on farmland was banned in 1982. Concern about the cotton harvest led in December 1987 to incentives in the form of ensured supplies of low-cost fertilizer.

3. The responsibility system benefited from the existence of an extensive rural infrastructure, but there were signs that the concentration of activities on the household had led to deficiencies in the provision of collective works (such as drainage, flood control, and irrigation schemes) and the underutilization of the larger pieces of equipment such as tractors. In November 1987 village committees were given increased powers to try to overcome these problems, but not successfully, it seems, e.g. the severe floods of summer 1991 may have been partially caused by factors such as the failure to dredge rivers. Agricultural investment took only 3.4 per cent of the state budget in 1987, compared with 12 per cent in 1985 (*The Economist*, 26 March–1 April 1988, p. 48), while as a proportion of total investment there was a fall

from around 10 per cent in the 1970s to only 3 per cent in 1986 (Delfs, *FEER*, 18 February 1988, p. 66). A new body, called the China Agricultural Investment and Development Corporation, was set up in 1988 to reverse the fall in investment (*EIU Country Report*, 1988, no. 1, p. 14). Long (1990: 17) notes the use of the slogan 'scale farming' in 1989 to stress the advantages of collective efforts in irrigation and flood control. While the HRS is still a central feature of the overall reform programme in China, increasing attention has been paid to measures ensuring that such collective activities are not neglected.

4. Delfs (*FEER*, p. 67) describes the farming sector as consisting of 180 million household producers, each working small plots of land averaging 0.6 ha; Zhu Ling (1990) puts the average family farm at 0.5 ha of farm-land (p. 231); on average farms are dispersed into 9.7 plots (p. 234). The increasing fragmentation of land makes it increasingly unsuitable for crops such as grain or for the use of large machinery. In September 1987 experiments started in which local authorities leased out larger plots of land to private individuals for grain production on contract, the plots being formed out of the merger of smaller unused or underutilized plots. According to *The Daily Telegraph* (9 January 1988, p. ix) each family is allowed to rent up to seven acres of land from the township. There have been further reports of experiments in allocating more land to more efficient farmers, sometimes at the expense of the less efficient, and in encouraging amalgamation of the plots used by different families to form group units (Lynne Curry, *FT*, 5 October 1989, p. 40; Robin Pauley and Colina MacDougall, *FT*, 24 November 1989, p. 24; Colina MacDougall, *FT Survey*, 12 December 1989, p. 35).

5. There is concern about land being left idle as people move into subsidiary production, retaining it for family use in the event of a change in the political atmosphere (Colina MacDougall, *FT*, 30 September 1988, p. 6).

6. One result of the late 1980s austerity programme has been the use (e.g. in 1988) of

state promissory notes (IOUs) to pay peasants because of a cash shortage. These proved to be deeply unpopular.

CENTRAL PLANNING

There have been enormous policy swings in this as in other aspects of the Chinese economy, with seemingly self-sustaining cyclical movements revolving around 'economics versus politics' and 'centralization versus decentralization'. (Hsu notes that, until the recent reforms, the term 'decentralization' referred to lower-level government and not the enterprise: Hsu 1989: 502.) This phenomenon is caused by centrally induced rigidities and inertia and decentrally induced disorder. Some indication of the swings can be seen in the changing number of centrally determined material balances of Category I and II goods over time; these are widely used and specialized materials allocated by the State Planning Commission and the central branch ministries: 1952, 28; 1953, 96; 1957, 532; 1958, 132; 1963, 522; 1964, 592; 1966, 579; 1970s, low 200s; 1978, 210; 1981, 67 (Prybyla 1985: 569). The lack of effective medium-term (five years) and long-term planning during the period 1958–76 has been reflected in a number of problems facing China today. There are severe bottlenecks in the provision of infrastructure (especially energy, transport and communications), while the development of planning techniques, including input-output analysis, has been retarded.

The First Five Year Plan, 1953–57

During the First Five Year Plan familiar Soviet-type institutions were set up, material balancing was employed and economic calculation was dominant. The State Planning Commission was founded in 1952, although annual and even shorter-term planning was later taken over by the State Economic Commission, established in 1956. In 1954 the State Investment Commission was established and two years later the Materials Supply Office and the State Technology Commission. The plan was only approved midway through. Regional decision-making was more important than in the traditional Soviet model, but the economy was highly centralized. The centre controlled the output targets of the most important industrial and agricultural goods, total investment, sectoral allocation, and large projects; material balancing of the most important commodities and their inter-provincial flows; foreign trade turnover and commodity structure; total employment, total wages, labour allocation at national level, and allocation of scientific and technical workers (Donnithorne 1967: 462). The number of centrally allocated commodities increased from twenty-eight in 1952 to 235 in 1956, with the centre directing those enterprises producing these goods (the centre's share of industrial output rose to nearly 50 per cent by 1957; Riskin 1987: 101). The provinces and localities managed those enterprises under their direction, producing those commodities mainly used internally.

The Great Leap Forward, 1958–60

The GLF brought extreme administrative decentralization and politics in ascendancy over economics. There was disdain for the idea of economic efficiency. The 1958 reform concerned the following:

1. It considerably enhanced the decision-making powers of local government over investment and the supply of raw materials.

2. Most central enterprises were transferred to local control. The exceptions were large operations in strategically important sectors, although even these formally came under dual leadership.

3. The system of unified material balancing was changed into one based on regional planning and 'bottom-to-top' balancing.

4. The number of products controlled by the State Planning Commission was substantially reduced.

5. Local authorities were able to reallocate

centrally rationed materials held by all enterprises in their regions.

One result of all this was that sectors expanded without regard to inter-sectoral relationships. The statistical network collapsed and targets became unrealistic. Provinces gained increased revenue when they were allowed 20 per cent of the profits of the newly decentralized plants, and local authorities were also permitted to alter tax rates and to decide on credit policy. Enterprises in the state-owned sector were also given increased autonomy, with reduced plan targets. The system of unified retained earnings became enterprise-specific (Wu and Reynolds 1988: 461–2.) The centre still attempted to control key variables such as total investment, inter-regional allocation, and major projects, and the output of the most important commodities.

The period between the Great Leap Forward and the Cultural Revolution

This period saw the reinstatement of central command planning and the primacy of economic calculation. Central control over most of the enterprises and commodities that had been passed down was reinstated, although the power of local authorities continued to be relatively great compared with other socialist countries. Many decisions were taken by substantially self-sufficient provinces (and, later, even counties), with the centre concentrating on intra-provincial flows and the larger enterprises in strategic sectors (Perkins 1988: 607).

The Cultural Revolution

Prybyla (1985: 563) describes central planning during the 1961–65 period as being largely on an *ad hoc*, emergency basis, turning into a shambles by the late 1960s. The Cultural Revolution is normally dated 1966–76, but the most extreme aspects had ended by 1969. The reversion to more pragmatic policies and the attempts to diminish Mao's power, led by Liu

Shaoqi, resulted in a backlash. Following Mao's call for 'continuous revolution', Red Guards attacked 'old' ideas and 'capitalist roaders', research and higher educational programmes were decimated, professionals and critical party members (including Deng Xiaoping) were given menial jobs to perform and many intellectuals were persecuted. Mao used the army to restore control.

The decade was by no means homogeneous as regards the economic system, but, in general, there was a decentralization of decision-making, to local authorities in 1970 for example. Politics took command once again, and self-reliance and egalitarianism became the keynotes. Central command planning largely collapsed, to be replaced not by a market economy, but by a system whereby provinces, localities and enterprises were to be as self-reliant as possible in order to minimize the need for central co-ordination. The central bureaucracy, which Mao was averse to, could be reduced to a size commensurate with this restricted role. Centrally issued economic criteria were reduced to highly generalized forms such as the need for a high degree of local self-sufficiency in industry and agriculture. The number of centrally determined material balances was reduced, and central control concentrated on the modern, large-scale enterprises producing these goods. The notion of 'self-reliance' was also applied at the national level and found one of its reflections domestically in the 'grain first' slogan; this stressed provincial self-sufficiency in grain production.

Today China has what is officially described as a 'planned socialist commodity economy'; the term 'planned commodity economy based on public ownership' was introduced in 1984. Bergson (1985: 76–7) describes the reform as a greater emphasis on what the Chinese call 'guidance' planning as opposed to 'mandatory' planning, involving suggested state targets, increased decision-making autonomy for enterprises and provincial/local authorities, and greater emphasis on economic levers. What specifically these concepts and others such as 'socialism with Chinese characteristics' mean in reality will be explored in the following pages.

THE ALLOCATION OF MANPOWER

Do Rosario presents some basic statistics for 1987: 85 per cent of urban workers were employed by state-run enterprises; urban unemployment was officially given as 5.9 per cent in 1978 and 2 per cent in 1987 (*FEER*, 12 May 1988, pp. 72–3). Urban unemployment was 13.2 per cent in 1952, 5.9 per cent in 1957, and zero by 1971, it was claimed (Ellman 1989a: 180); by 1978 unemployment was once more recognized as a problem (p. 181). The figures were around 2 per cent on average in 1984–88, and 2.7 per cent in 1989 (4 million workers) (*China Briefing*, June 1990, no. 36, pp. 1–3). Urban unemployment was 2.6 per cent in 1990 (*EIU Country Report*, 1991, no. 1, p. 28). White (1988: 181) puts the state industrial and non-industrial workforce at 18.1 per cent of the total workforce and 70 per cent of the urban. In 1989 the number of migrant labourers reached 50 million, while in 1990 the number of sojourners (illegal, 'floating' residents) in major cities may have amounted to 80 million (Alan Liu, *Asian Survey*, 1991, vol. XXXI, no. 5, p. 393). (Note that there is 'surplus' or 'underemployed' labour in the countryside; Xue Mei in the October 1991 Newsletter of the Chinese Economic Association in the UK, p. 8, cites a figure of one-third of the total rural labour force.)

Manpower is an area where China made an early departure from the traditional Soviet economic system. Generally there was no labour market, on the grounds that labour is not a commodity and for purposes of state control over population movements. Manpower has typically been allocated to enterprises by institutions such as the school or area assignment office, and workers stay for their working lives. The 'iron rice bowl' mentality ensures a job and a wage (literally, everyone eats from the same pot regardless of work effort). Promotion and increased pay have been dependent more on factors such as seniority. Workers' housing [10] and medical insurance are also subsidized by the work unit (Hu *et al.* 1988: 77). Workers typically need permission to change jobs and are almost impossible to sack, however unsatisfactory. The enterprise 'congress' of workers and staff, which includes the party representative, has the final say. Since 1979, in Beijing and elsewhere, enterprises have been given a greater say in selecting individual workers within the manpower quota, while job seekers have been able to apply via the local labour bureaus to enterprises or through one of the new 'labour service companies'. These companies are sponsored by government bureaus or enterprises and are able to provide training and, in some cases, actual jobs in their own enterprises (White 1988: 194–5).

Wage and salary differentials have been small by Soviet and East European standards, and piecework payments were rare after 1956; then 42 per cent of industrial workers were so rewarded (Richman 1969: 314). Piecework payment barely survived during the Great Leap Forward and was actually banned during the Cultural Revolution; it was officially permitted once more by regulations enacted 1979–80 (Granick 1991: 283). Hussain and Stern (1991: 163) bring out the dramatic percentage change in the composition of nominal wages in the state sector between 1978 and 1988: time wages 85 to 49; piece wages 0.8 to 9.4; bonuses 2.3 to 17.2; and subsidies (cost-of-living payments) 6.5 to 21.4. Bonuses have been based more on factors such as tradition and seniority than on performance and skill and in any event are normally more equally dispersed. Hu *et al.* describe the present wage set-up as originating in the Soviet-type system introduced in 1956. Wages for workers in enterprises have three components: technical skill (determined by type and years of work experience), the wage grade level (determined by job requirements and responsibilities) and basic wages. There are eight grades of wages for workers, ranging from

Grade 1 for an inexperienced new worker to Grade 8 for a foreman. During the late 1970s and the 1980s bonuses were made available, but were seldom based on productivity. Wages for cadres and professional staff (in administration, schools, hospitals, etc.) have four components: basic wage, job responsibility, supplemental wage for years of work, and bonuses (Hu *et al.* 1988: 78). A small number of enterprises have recently been subjected to experiments where total wage bills have been determined by output or profit (p. 79). Their empirical findings are that wages are greatly influenced by the years of work experience, affiliation to a state-owned enterprise, and by occupation (especially for cadres). The wage system has not placed a great deal of emphasis on educational attainment or industrial affiliation; there is not much wage incentive for productive workers (p. 93). The 1988 wage reform tied the total wage fund of an enterprise to its performance (in that year around 30 per cent of all state enterprises were affected); in 1987 bonuses and wage supplements amounted to 45.7 per cent of basic wages, compared to 15 per cent in 1978 (Hsu 1992: 87).

Contract labour of some form has been around since the 1950s. During the GLF the percentage of non-permanent workers in the state economy rose to about 30 per cent, but declined during the Cultural Revolution to some 6 per cent (Korzec 1988:120–1). There have been experiments with contracts since 1979, especially in construction. Early experiments took place in Shanghai and the Special Economic Zones. In Shenzhen all workers are on contracts of limited duration (Korzec 1988: 121). In 1983, however, 96.8 per cent of state workers were still 'fixed' (White 1987b: 366, 1988: 183). In the year to October 1986 more than 80 per cent of all new state sector employees had signed labour contracts (White 1987b: 44). By the end of 1986 only 5.6 per cent of state workers were on contracts (White 1988: 196), 7.8 per cent of the workforce in state-owned industry by the end of March 1988 (*EIU Country Report*, 1988, no. 3, p. 16), 10 per cent (11 million workers) of the total workforce in state enterprises in 1989 (*China Briefing*, June 1990, no. 36, p. 3) and 13 per cent (13.5 million workers) at the end of 1990 (Hsu 1992: 87). From 1 October 1986 a more general contract system was introduced for new workers.[11] New prospective employees undergo tests and a trial period before negotiating the length of the fixed-term work contract with their employers.[12] There have also been recent moves to loosen the extraordinarily tight restrictions on sacking, such as in cases of gross violation of work rules and rudeness towards customers so persistent as to threaten the loss of sales. The right to strike was removed from the 1982 constitution, but strikes were not made illegal.

There have also been experimental relaxations of the rigid labour allocation system to provide a measure of choice for graduates and skilled workers on the one hand and employers on the other. Increasingly, enterprises are making specific requests to universities for graduates. Daniel Southerland (*IHT*, 20–1 February 1988, p. 14) reports that the state assigns jobs to 70 per cent of university graduates; the aim is to require most students to pay for their own tuition and to find their own jobs. In April 1989, however, it was announced (as part of the retrenchment process) that graduates would only be permitted to contact potential employers for information, and would not be allowed to find their own positions. Since the 1989 Tiananmen Square massacre, Beijing students have been sent for military training prior to university, and Beijing enterprises send new graduates to rural schools and enterprises for a year (Peter Ellingsen, *FT*, 11 August 1989, p. 3).

The year 1987 saw the start of a new pensions scheme. State enterprises would no longer be directly responsible for pensions, but would contribute instead 11.5 per cent of their wage bill (supplemented by contract workers paying 3 per cent of their monthly earnings) to a state insurance fund (do Rosario, *FEER*, 12 May 1988,

p. 74). On 28 February 1988 Beijing's first labour market was opened to help those registered (for a one yuan fee) to find another job.

Wage reforms involve a greater linkage between effort and reward, especially the increased use of piece rates and bonuses tied to performance. It is now also possible to send workers to the 'second front' (labour reserve team) of the enterprise on basic pay only. In 1985 government workers' salary increases began to be based mainly on performance and responsibility rather than length of service.

The tax system has also been employed to try to curb pay increases. The scheme introduced in 1986 involved the following penalty: if bonuses paid to employees exceeded the value of the wage bill for five months, the enterprise had to pay a 30 per cent tax, rising to 100 per cent for six months, and 300 per cent for over six months. On 1 January the following year the income tax system was revamped, the minimum taxable level was reduced to four times the average wage (half the previous level), and the maximum rate reached 60 per cent.

August 1986 was noteworthy since it marked the first state enterprise *bankruptcy* in China since 1949, after the enterprise had been warned in 1985 to return to profitability within a year. The assets of the Shenyang Explosion-proof Equipment plant were auctioned off; this was followed on 13 October 1988 by the opening of China's first labour exchange. Despite a number of other enterprises being placed under threat and the closure of the Nanchang Underground Department Store in November 1987, the proposed bankruptcy law was shelved. In the more conservative atmosphere prevailing, preference shifted towards merging failing enterprises with more efficient organizations. Inefficient army plants producing civilian goods can now be brought under civilian control, the first example occurring in January 1988 when CITIC took over a vehicle works (*EIU Country Report*, 1988, no. 1, p. 17). Approval of legislation to implement a bankruptcy law (for a trial one year period starting November 1988) was finally given at the Seventh National People's Congress (25 March– 13 April 1988), having awaited the passing of the law on the state industrial enterprise. An enterprise is declared bankrupt if 'because of a deficit caused by mismanagement, [it] cannot repay the debts which are due' (Solinger 1989b: 22). There still exists a preference for 'enterprise groups', in which solvent enterprises absorb their struggling brethren; this penalizing of the more efficient is referred to as 'whipping the fast ox' (David Dodwell, *FT Survey*, 24 April 1991, p. iv). *The Economist* Intelligence Unit (*Country Report*, 1991, no. 3, p. 23) reports some bankruptcies in July–August 1991, namely a Beijing collectively-owned foodstuff wholesale concern and a Dalien garments factory. The reluctance to bankrupt state enterprises has, of course, led to the usual problems associated with the 'soft budget constraint'.

Prior to 1978 it was claimed that urban unemployment was not a problem, but events such as the return of many school leavers and students sent to the countryside during the Cultural Revolution has brought about its open recognition. A form of unemployment pay has been available since 1986, however, for those workers who have been dismissed or lost their jobs through bankruptcy, or whose contracts have expired. Payments, financed by a 1 per cent levy on enterprise wage bills, will be available for up to two years for those employed for five years or more and for up to a year for less than five years. Seventy-five per cent of the previous wage is payable for the first six months and a fixed sum amounting to something less than a third of the average industrial wage for the remainder.

THE FINANCIAL SYSTEM

Pricing

Pre-1949 prices had a long-term influence because of the concern for stability in price determination, most industrial prices remaining stable for a quarter of a century after the mid-

1950s; there were only limited price changes during 1979–83 (Perkins 1988: 620). However, the subsequent basis used by the state (centre, province or county) of branch average planned cost plus a profit mark-up (large enough to permit most or all enterprises to operate profitably in each important production area) for industrial wholesale prices still largely applies today (see Prybyla 1987). New product prices have also long taken import prices into consideration to a lesser extent. China was slow to introduce a capital charge. Traditionally, enterprises have been provided with fixed and working capital in the shape of a grant, but the 1980s saw a change. In the early years of the decade experiments were begun, generally involving a small capital charge of 1–2 per cent, and in 1984 it was announced that there was to be a move away from grants to interest-bearing credits (3–6 per cent). In 1982 enterprises favourably located or favourably endowed were subject to a rental charge ('adjustment tax'). The October 1984 reform proposals included a charge on fixed and working capital and a rental charge for extractive industries.

Prices have tended to remain fixed for long periods of time and reform has been slow, despite the professed aim in October 1984 of restricting fixed prices to 'major' products and allowing considerably increased scope for range and freely negotiated prices. At the end of 1985 market prices accounted for more than 30 per cent of the value of industrial and agricultural output, while range prices covered 20–30 per cent (Chan 1986: 30). After some experiments in 1979 increasing use was made of range prices (plus or minus a percentage around the state price) and, to a lesser extent, market-determined prices ('negotiated' prices). According to do Rosario, 65 per cent of agricultural products, 55 per cent of industrial consumer goods and 40 per cent of industrial raw materials are no longer subject to fixed state prices (do Rosario, *FEER*, 16 July 1987, p. 70). She estimates that a third of the prices of all agricultural and retail goods are now freely

determined (*FEER*, 30 June 1988, p. 50). Ishihara (1987: 304–5) states that of the 47 per cent of total agricultural and sidelines production sold from rural to urban areas in 1985, 32.1 per cent involved purchases at state listed prices and 51.2 per cent involved 'negotiated' (which sometimes involves supervisory state organs in the negotiating process) or 'floating' (with upper, lower, or upper and lower limits) prices; the respective 1978 figures were 84.7 per cent, 1.8 per cent and 5.6 per cent. In 1984 there was offical acknowledgement that industrial enterprises could sell a percentage of their production on the market at range prices. In January of the following year they were permitted to charge a price a shade below local market prices; these new prices were termed 'market floating' prices (Chan 1986: 26–7). Thus a noticeable feature is multiple pricing for the same product. Ishihara (1990: 183) lists the respective percentage importance in terms of sales of state-determined prices, state-guided prices and market adjusted prices for the following categories in 1986 (1978 figures in brackets): peasants' agricultural products 37, 23 and 40 (92.4, and 7.6 for the last two categories combined); major capital goods 64, 23 and 13 (100 for the first category); and industrial consumer goods 45, 23 and 32 (97, and 3 for the last two categories combined). The multiple pricing system ('dual track' or 'double track') has led to many abuses, such as illegal reselling for a profit and an incentive on the part of managers to minimize the share of output handed over to the state. Post-Tiananmen there has been a gradual strengthening of the single (state-determined) price system. But there was also decontrol of the prices of a large number of producer goods on 1 September 1992 (see postscript).

In order to reduce the high level of subsidies paid out to stabilize the prices of staple consumer goods, attempts have been made since 1985 to raise retail prices. These were often been rescinded, however, in the face of public unrest and fears of inflation. Efforts with respect to luxury goods have been more successful. A general twelve month price freeze was introduced in January 1987. In August, owing to the ineffectiveness of the price freeze, retail prices of consumer goods under state control were to be unchanged for the remainder of the year, in view of the 6.3 per cent increase in the national retail price index in the first half of the year compared with the same period of 1986. In July 1988 a partial price freeze was implemented because of the inflation rate of 13 per cent in the first six months, with exceptions such as the better brands of alcohol and tobacco, which were to be sold at market prices. In September it was announced that further major price changes were to be shelved during a two year 'rectification' period. Yao Yilin (chairman of the State Planning Commission) said that price controls would remain for products such as grain, edible oils, cotton and steel, and that the multiple pricing system may last for two decades, officially until most goods are in excess supply. The following month price controls were actually reimposed on some basic commodities; for example, the prices of vegetables in northern cities were to be frozen for the winter period. A freeze was applied to state-controlled prices of essentials.

In December 1987 the city of Beijing extended rationing for grain and cooking oil to other products like pork (owing to factors such as a shortage of feed grain), eggs and sugar. Other cities are also affected, for example Shanghai and Tianjin in the case of pork. At the Seventh National People's Congress in 1988, it was announced that the World Bank (for the first time anywhere) was giving a policy-linked loan. Specifically, part of the $300 million is to be used for an experiment, to run in two areas (counties in Henan and Guangxi), to replace grain subsidies with income supplements. In fact this became a more general policy when, in the same year, urban residents began to be paid income supplements to compensate for food price increases, thus switching subsidies from products to incomes. Hangzhou became the first

city to introduce the new income subsidy scheme in mid-January 1988 (do Rosario, *FEER*, 26 May 1988, p. 72).

The year 1990 saw some significant price increases. On 1 November sugar prices were raised by 58 per cent; in the weeks previous to this salt, coal and petrol prices had been increased. Grain prices were to follow. On 1 May 1991 there were substantial increases in the prices of basic commodities, only partial wage compensation being paid, e.g. vegetable oil 158 per cent, flour 54 per cent, 55 per cent for wheat and 75 per cent for high-quality rice. On 1 April 1992 there were further rises in the prices of basic commodities, e.g. 40 per cent in the case of flour and rice, partially compensated for by wage increases. The government announced that as of 1 April urban residents would pay the same price for their rationed grain that the state pays farmers, although state subsidies still cover the cost of storage and distribution (*EIU Country Report*, 1992, no. 2, p. 26). Guangdong province experimented with the complete removal of grain price controls.

Banking

The banking system in China is now quite complex and includes joint ventures with and branches of foreign banks (in June 1992 it was announced that these branches, previously confined to the Special Economic Zones and Shanghai, could be set up in seven more coastal cities), and independent credit co-operatives (see the report on credit co-operatives by Edward Gargan, *IHT*, 8 August 1988, pp. 11, 13). At the apex of the domestic system is the People's Bank of China which, since 1984, has acted more like a Western central bank. The People's Bank is responsible for controlling the total volume of credit in line with the plan as well as that granted by individual banks. It fixes the discount rate at which the commercial banks are able to borrow from and the ratio of reserves to be deposited at the People's Bank and issues directives (e.g. to keep loss-making state enterprises solvent) and imposes credit rationing. Since 1984 the then newly established Industrial and Commercial Bank of China has provided short-and medium-term loans to urban industry and commerce and has taken over the function of accepting deposits from the general public from the People's Bank. The Agricultural Bank (re-established in 1979) mobilizes the savings of and provides credit to the rural economy as a whole; the People's Construction Bank deals in long-term funds for specific capital projects; the Investment Bank of China is concerned with investment credits and foreign capital; and the Bank of China handles foreign exchange transactions and dealings with foreign banks and governments. The People's Bank publishes credit targets and sectoral priorities, issues plan instructions, and allocates state funds to commercial banks to meet part of their planned expenditures (they are consulted during the drawing up of the credit plan). The remainder and above-plan loans are covered by attracting deposits.

A notable event took place in April 1987 with the opening of the Shanghai Bank of Communications. Fifty per cent of its shares are owned by the central government, 25 per cent by the Shanghai municipal government, about 20 per cent by other institutions and a maximum of 5 per cent by individuals. It has no state capital allocation and thus makes loans on the basis of the deposits it succeeds in attracting. The aim is to provide competition to totally state-owned banks in terms of both domestic and foreign business; it has overseas branches and branches in other cities in China. Domestic interest rates can be fixed within a range set by the People's Bank.

The banking reforms, which began in 1979, have three major goals (White and Bowles 1988: 28–36): (1) to encourage savings sufficient to match the investment rate of some 30 per cent; (2) to establish methods of monetary control; and (3) to increase the efficiency of credit allocation by enhancing the role of profitability – banks are able to retain 10 per cent of profits.

According to White and Bowles, the first aim has been met relatively successfully, the other two less so because banks are still ultimately subservient to the state plan. Thus, monetary targets have been continually exceeded, while the commercial banks have rarely used their theoretically draconian powers over loss-making enterprises to restrict credit to, restructure, reorganize management in, merge or even bankrupt enterprises. The situation as of 1987 was that credit constraints may even have become softer, the opposite to that planned (Bowles and White 1989: 487). Other interesting experiments include some local 'foreign exchange adjustment centres', which allow enterprises to trade their surpluses and deficits in foreign exchange, a number of bank branches to buy and sell promissory notes issued by enterprises short of funds, and local cases (such as in Shanghai) of direct interbank borrowing. Private citizens have been allowed to hold foreign exchange since 1985 (Baum, *Asian Survey*, 1986, vol. XXVI, no. 1, p. 46). Rural and urban credit co-operatives have also increased in importance.

The first experiments with stock issues took place in 1981, in the form of treasury bonds. Since 1986 the People's Bank has been authorized to approve the issuing of shares and bonds by companies to government, other enterprises, employees and outside individuals, which could, initially, be traded on a few rudimentary 'stock exchanges' in Shanghai, Shenyang, Tianjin and Beijing.[13] Shares normally consist of a basic fixed interest equal to that on bank deposits, or sometimes coupons giving the right to a scarce good or lottery ticket for such goods, plus a regulated element dependent on company profitability. In some cases the larger shareholders have a vote at a conference that elects the company board, which, in turn, elects the manager. The ownership rights associated with Western equities are absent, and Goldman and Goldman (1988: 558) point out that stocks are limited to a maximum of 30 per cent of the value of the capital stock of an enterprise. A

153

more recent source gives a figure of 50 per cent (Lynne Curry, *FT Survey*, 16 June 1992, p. iv). In March 1987 state enterprises were subject to greater restrictions. In general they were only able to issue bonds: exceptions included share-holding among enterprises for forging horizontal links (*China Briefing*, December 1988, no. 31, p. 9). In October 1988 a Shenjang bus and truck manufacturer began issuing freely tradeable shares in foreign exchange (Jasper Becker, *The Guardian*, 14 October 1988, p. 11). Progress towards large-scale stock issuing by state enterprises subsequently became another victim of the 'rectification process'. Later on progress was resumed.

Budgetary policy

The increasing activation of money is also reflected in budgetary policy. Adopting conventional Western practice and ignoring the curious Chinese one of counting borrowed funds (both foreign loans and treasury bond sales) in with revenue, China suffered a string of budget deficits over the period 1979 to 1991, with the exception of 1985. This has caused concern because of the printing of money to finance the deficit and the consequent implications for inflation.

The consolidated budget as a proportion of national income fell from 41.5 per cent in 1978 to 24.7 per cent in 1989 (Wong 1991: 692). A noticeable feature of budgetary revenue, in contrast to the Soviet Union, is the historically more important role played by enterprise profit deductions as opposed to turnover tax. In the late 1970s some 50 per cent of revenue derived from the former and a large proportion of the remainder from the latter, but between 1978 and 1980 the former had fallen by nearly 25 per cent (Ellman 1986: 434). Until 1990, recent years had witnessed a falling share of budgetary expenditure going to defence: in 1979, 20 per cent; in 1984, 15 per cent; in 1985, 12 per cent; in 1986, 10 per cent; and in 1987, 8.2 per cent. Over the period 1979–89 military expenditure was cut

by 25 per cent in real terms (Tai Ming Cheung, *FEER*, 27 February 1992, p. 15). Goldman and Goldman (1988: 566) estimate that the proportion of GNP devoted to defence declined from 13 per cent in 1973 to 8.6 per cent in 1983 and to 6–7 per cent to date. *The Economist* (20 June 1992, p. 90) cites a figure of 3.7 per cent in 1989. Post-Tiananmen China has witnessed a change: in 1990, 1991 and 1992 defence spending in real terms increased. Budgetary financing of investment in capital construction has also fallen from 80 per cent in 1979 to 54.4 per cent in 1984, the remainder financed from credits and plough-back profits (Kosta 1987: 153). A feature of the later 1980s austerity programme was the pressure exerted on workers to spend a portion of their wages on government bonds, up to 25 per cent according to the *IHT*, 18 July 1989, p. 6) and up to 30 per cent according to the *FT* (17 October 1989, p. 28). This policy was eased in 1991 and seemingly ended in 1992.

INDUSTRIAL MANAGEMENT

The Chinese state industrial enterprise (varying considerably in size) is still usually a plant, although there are also specialized integrated corporations and industrial associations with a nation-wide network of branches in existence. Enterprises are vertically integrating, as in the car industry, and horizontally integrating, as in textiles (Ling 1988: 522). Plant consolidation took place in and after the late 1970s to reap economies of scale and to increase efficiency in the use of inputs (Perkins 1988: 630). There are a number of sources indicating the size distribution of industrial enterprises. In 1982 small firms (five to thirty-three employees) accounted for 59.2 per cent of enterprises (compared to 6.6 per cent in Yugoslavia and 2.2 per cent in Hungary), while large firms (more than 243 employees) only accounted for 0.6 per cent of enterprises (compared to 33.5 per cent in Yugoslavia and 65.1 per cent in Hungary (Wong 1989: 38, Prybyla 1989: 12). In 1987 large and medium enterprises accounted for only 2.05 per cent of all industrial enterprises, but 33.1 per cent of the industrial labour force, 65.3 per cent of the fixed capital stock and 50 per cent of the gross value of industrial output (Kueh 1989: 431–2).

Even during the First Five Year Plan (1953–57), when the organization of the larger state industrial enterprises most resembled the traditional Soviet model, there were divergences: (1) the lack of control over manpower allocation; (2) virtually all profits and the depreciation fund were transferred to the state budget; (3) the *danwei* or workplace was an important provider of housing and the chief supplier of welfare services such as pensions and sickness and disability benefits; (4) management incentives were much less orientated towards bonuses and, instead, party praise or criticism, promotion or demotion, and measures of the general contribution to socialism and party goals were more important; plans were less taut and managers did not receive large bonuses linked to target fulfilment (Walder 1989: 242); and (5) income differentials between managers and workers were less prominent.

From 1958 to 1978 the departures from the Soviet model became much more pronounced, especially during the GLF and the Cultural Revolution. The principle of one-man responsibility and control was thrown out towards the end of the First Five Year Plan. During the GLF Mao's idea of involving management in labour and workers in management was implemented. Groups of workers became responsible for formerly specialized management functions such as quality control, repair and maintenance, and workers, administrative personnel and technicians formed work teams. Managerial bonuses were largely abolished and group bonuses replaced individual worker ones. Non-material incentives became more important, as did model workers, praise and criticism, and emulation campaigns. Between 1962 and 1965 'workers' congresses' were reintroduced, made up of elected representatives of workers and staff. In theory these were able to approve

leadership reports on enterprise affairs and to sack management, but in reality confined themselves to plan targets and welfare (Riskin 1987: 160). The number of obligatory indicators was reduced from twelve to four, namely quantities of important products, total employment, total wage bill, and total profit. During the Cultural Revolution workers took over many enterprises. In response, 'revolutionary committees' were established by the state, whose members were representatives of mass organizations, the party and the army (Riskin 1987: 186). These committees were, in effect, means of exercising party control over enterprise management.

The Cultural Revolution was followed by the reintroduction of a more traditional system of industrial organization. Industrial reform after 1978 aimed to change the relationship between state and enterprise, rather than just affecting the relative decision-making powers of centre and region. Reform experiments were first started in October 1978 in Sichuan province under Zhao Ziyang and widened after the following year. Halpern (1985) discusses the nature of the early experiments, including the ability of some of the experimental enterprises to determine above-plan production and sales and to increase decentralized investment. Hsu (1989: 512) describes the 1978–80 experiments in allowing enterprises to retain a portion of profits if they fulfilled their plan targets as leading to unwelcome budget deficits; this explains the introduction of the 'profit contract system' ('economic responsibility system') over 1981–82. Ellman (1986: 433) estimates that by the end of 1980 the experiment covered 60 per cent of the output of state industrial enterprises. The 1981 'profit contract system' involved a profit-sharing contract between state and enterprise – if the volume of profit exceeded target there was a division in fixed proportion between the two, and underfulfilment in principle meant a part of the sum had to be paid out of enterprise funds (p. 434). Hsu (1989: 512) notes that in reality, however, there was no penalty for failing to reach the profit base, and the system led to excessive control by local government. The result was the introduction of the 'tax for profit' system in 1983.

In 1983 there was a general switch to a system of defined taxes: the capital charge; the rental charge (called a 'resource tax' in extractive industries, and an 'adjustment tax' in industry, the purpose being to extract profit due to favourable external factors), a sales (so-called product) tax; and a profits tax. The share of profits retained by state enterprises increased from 3.7 per cent in 1978 to 42.4 per cent in 1986 (Prybyla 1987: 16). Other important changes in 1983–84 included the switch from gross to net value as the main output indicator, the ability of enterprises to sell most above-quota output direct to users, and the ending of working capital grants (Field 1984: 758).[14]

The May 1984 provisions and the Central Committee announcement of 20 October heralded a general extension of reforms to the state-owned industrial sector, to be introduced gradually over the following five years. In the May provisions state-owned enterprises were permitted to determine production plans after meeting state targets and to sell the resulting products at market prices. Unused assets could be sold; power was given to rearrange staff, to appoint middle-level administrative staff and to dispose of the bonus fund (Wu and Reynolds 1988: 463). The aim of the October 1984 measures (a 'planned commodity economy under public ownership') seemed to be: (1) to retain central control over key industrial and agricultural products, such as coal, oil, steel, armaments, heavy machinery, electrical equipment, cotton and cereals; (2) allowing sixty of the 120 industrial products and nineteen of the twenty-nine agricultural products currently assigned by the state, though representing a lower percentage of the value of output, to be produced within the context of general state guidelines or even the market (such as consumer goods, textiles, fruit and vegetables). Increasing stress was to be placed on indirect steering by means of economic levers such as prices, taxes, interest rates and credits. The key financial element involved a gradual end of state claims to a share of after-tax profit and, thus, a move towards a purely tax-based system. Gordon and Li (1991: 202) note that, in reality, investment decisions continued to be made primarily by state planning ministries or by local governments; proposed projects still needed to be approved at some level of government.

After meeting targets set by the state, which also guarantees the necessary inputs at state-determined prices, enterprises are now allowed to produce and sell (at negotiated prices, usually within a range, directly to buyers or at fairs, and via their own retail outlets in some cases) whatever they like and wherever they choose. This is the so-called self-disposal system. In 1989 industrial enterprises self-marketed about 30 per cent of output (Hsu 1992: 79). There is thus now some scope for purchase of non-labour inputs outside the materials allocation system. Citing Li Wenzhong (1985), Ishihara gave the following figures for the percentage of total production outside the central government distribution plan: coal, 50 per cent; steel materials, 40 per cent; lumber, 60 per cent; cement, 75 per cent; these were distributed at market prices. In 1985 the number of manufactured products subject to mandatory planning by the State Planning Commission was reduced from 123 to sixty (20 per cent of the value of all manufactured goods) (Hsu 1989: 512). According to Prybyla (*Asian Survey*, 1989, vol. XXIX, no. 11, p. 1028), the centre continued to draw up material balances for some sixty key commodity groups and to distribute about thirty key materials (e.g. 60 per cent of capital goods, 60 per cent of steel products and 45 per cent of coal).

In the immediate post-Tiananmen period, the state reverted to increased control over the pricing and distribution of key commodities such as coal, steel, cotton and grain. According to Dittmer (1989: 15), the number of commodities over which the centre resumed monopoly control rose from twelve or so to thirty-two. To provide an increased incentive to fulfil state output targets, a 'two-way (double) guarantee system' has been applied to 234 (initially) important enterprises (mostly in energy, raw materials, equipment and daily necessities); the state guarantees essential inputs in return for guaranteed deliveries of output, taxes and profits (Swaine 1990: 30).

The process of switching over to the 'contract responsibility system' ('management contract' or 'contracted managerial responsibility': see Hsu 1989, 1992; Blejer and Szapary 1990; Lee 1990) was begun in 1983. This system now dominates the state sector. Typically, contracts run for up to three years (sometimes up to five years) and stipulate the minimum amount of profit to be handed over to the state. Above-target profit is either fully retained by the enterprise or at least more lightly taxed, while failure to reach the contracted profit means, in principle, the payment of the minimum tax obligation (in reality the enterprise is usually able to renegotiate the contract, claiming circumstances beyond its control like input price increases). The result is that the whole tax liability of an enterprise is negotiated on a case-by-case basis (Blejer and Szapary 1990: 456). The contract can also involve e.g. cost reduction targets (in the case of loss-making enterprises). In early 1990 more than 90 per cent of state industrial enterprises were on the system (Hsu 1992: 83). In theory bidding is open, but in reality state officials typically select the former state directors (p. 84). An important reason for the switch over to the 'contract responsibility system' was the loss of revenue accruing to the government, due to tax evasion on the part of enterprises (Gordon and Li 1991: 203).

Chamberlain (1987) considers *party–management relations* in large and medium-sized enterprises. The Soviet-type principle of 'one-man management', adopted in the early 1950s, was replaced in 1956 by that of 'factory director responsibility under party committee leadership', in order to re-establish party control. In reality, however, the party committee secretary was in control (Chamberlain 1987: 632). In the late 1960s there were widespread experiments involving collective management by workers and cadres in 'revolutionary committees', but by the early 1970s the secretary had regained control. In 1976 the principle of 'factory director under party leadership' was formally reinstated (p. 633). Since May 1984 there has been a gradual application of the 'factory director responsibility system', which is not a return to the Soviet-type principle, but involves, in theory, the party committee and its secretary 'advising' the director and 'supervising' enterprise operations to ensure compliance with central party policies (pp. 645–6). The director is also meant to consult with the 'staff–workers congress', which disappeared during the Cultural Revolution and reappeared in 1975, and whose role is to 'deliberate' over policies, although it seems to have a decisive say over the use of funds for bonuses, welfare and safety. The 'management committee', chaired by the director and staffed by key individuals such as the chief engineer, accountant and economist, also plays a solely advisory role (p. 649). In reality, however, Chamberlain considers, the party secretary was still in charge, especially since the state enterprise law had been in circulation since late 1984 awaiting ratification, with reluctance being shown over the inclusion of a clause to direct party officials to support the director in the discharge of their managerial powers (p. 651).

A draft law on state-owned industrial enterprises was in fact published on 12 January 1988, and the so-called Industrial Enterprise Bill was subsequently approved at the Seventh National People's Congress in 1988. Under it the party's function is to 'guarantee and supervise the implementation of party principles and policies', leaving the director to assume responsibility for running the enterprise. The legislation was made effective in August 1988 and applies to state industrial enterprises accounting for 70 per cent of gross industrial production, but not to state commercial and financial enterprises.

Colina MacDougall expressed concern at a 10 December party circular, which emphasized that politics and ideology were an 'indispensable part' of management and proposed that the enterprise manager or his deputy could be the party secretary (*FT*, 31 December 1988, p. 3). Party control was tightened after the June 1989 Tiananmen Square massacre, but later relaxed when Deng firmly supported economic reform in January 1992.

As far as *regional decentralization* is concerned, after 1988 local governments contracted to remit a predetermined amount of revenue to higher levels and to retain all or part of the rest, e.g. Guangdong province over the period 1988–90 had to transfer the 1987 amount plus 9 per cent a year (Blejer and Szapary 1990: 466). The current trend is to reduce regional powers, especially on account of concern over inflation. The austerity programme, introduced in the autumn of 1988, led to regional protectionism. On 23 November 1990 the State Council issued a circular ordering local authorities to abolish local trade barriers, e.g. road blocks and local taxes and fines.

THE NON-STATE, NON-AGRICULTURAL SECTOR

The Chinese economy is mixed ('double tracked'). Do Rosario presents the following figures for 1987: 7.53 million industrial enterprises in total; around 98,000 state enterprises accounted for 60 per cent of total industrial output; 1.85 million collectives[16] (34.6 per cent of output, compared with 19.2 per cent in 1978); and 5.58 million individually operated enterprises (3.6 per cent of output); the remainder comprised mainly joint ventures with foreign companies (*FEER*, 8 September 1988, p. 130). In 1988 there were 6.2 million individually operated industrial enterprises accounting for 4.35 per cent of industrial output (do Rosario, *FEER*, 24 August 1989, p. 51). In 1989 the percentage distribution of industrial output was as follows: state 56.1; collective 35.7; and private

4.8 (Hsu 1992: 75).

At the Eleventh National People's Congress in 1988 the following figures were revealed for the end of 1987: there were 13.7 million private businesses, employing more than 21.6 million people and accounting for nearly 13 per cent of all retail sales; there were 115,000 private enterprises employing eight people or more and in total over 1.8[17] million. At the end of 1988 there were 14.5 million private businesses employing 23 million people, but by the end of June 1989 there were only 12.3 million respectively (*The Times*, 5 August 1989, p. 9). Private employment was 3.5 per cent of urban employment in 1985 (Johnson 1988a: 240). Private and co-operative rural non-agricultural employment now accounts for over 80 million jobs out of a total labour force of 370 million (Wu and Reynolds 1988: 463); 90 million jobs is a more recent figure (*IHT*, 19 March 1990, p. 9). The state sector *as a whole* now accounts for only around one-third of total GNP and 18 per cent of the total workforce, according to figures cited by Nicholas Kristof (*IHT*, 18 December 1991, p. 20).

The private and collective sector has been flourishing since 1979 in China, after experiencing a long-run downward trend. Gold (1989: 197) summarizes the history in terms of millions of individual enterprises and of their employees respectively: 1949–50, 4.14 and 8.26; 1956, 0.43 and 0.51; 1978, 0.30 and 0.33. This suppression was especially marked in 1956 and during the GLF and the Cultural Revolution, with only a mild respite in the first half of the 1960s. Under the new regulations, private businessmen are subject to a 35 per cent tax on net profit. There are also provisions for an adjustment tax on the individual income of the private investor (A. H. Hermann, *FT*, 4 August 1988, p. 18). Since 1986 it has been possible for local authorities to lease out failing enterprises to individuals (Goldman and Goldman 1988: 556 trace the leasing of industrial enterprises back to 1982). Some private enterprises and co-operatives today are descendants of the 'state capitalist' enterprises, in which owners became employees and between January 1956 and September 1966 were paid compensation in the form of interest payments normally equal to 5 per cent of the value of the shares (Goldman and Goldman 1988: 97). The first national law concerning the private sector went into operation on 1 September 1987, and at the Seventh National People's Congress in 1988 the constitution was amended thus: 'The state permits the private sector of the economy to exist and develop within the limits prescribed by law. The private sector is a complement to the socialist public economy.'

The post-Tiananmen atmosphere was frostier, adding to the problems caused by the austerity programme introduced in 1988. For example, state enterprises were increasingly sheltered from competition in terms of raw material and energy supply, while the 'six evils' campaign started in July 1989 to penalize private businesses involved in pornography, prostitution, the sale of women and children, narcotics, gambling, and profiting from superstition (*IHT*, 23 February 1990, p. 15). As unemployment has increased, however, there have been signs of a thaw. Currently the private sector is seen as playing a subsidiary but nevertheless useful role to the state sector. Prime Minister Li Peng talked of expanding the private sector in a 24 October 1990 speech.

THE 'OPEN DOOR' POLICY

In 1978 the policy was announced of opening up the economy to foreign trade, capital, technology and know-how in order to modernize and speed up the growth of the economy. An important event in the run-up to this announcement was President Nixon's visit to China in February 1972. On 23 January 1988 Zhao Ziyang gave a boost to the open door policy by stressing the need for all the coastal regions, especially Guangdong and Hainan, to establish closer links with overseas investors and with the world market, encouraging export-led growth

and a greater role for solely foreign-owned enterprises. Zhao seemed to wish to take advantage of the shift of labour-intensive industries away from economies like South Korea and Taiwan to countries like China, where wage levels are lower.

Foreign trade

In 1991 China accounted for 2 per cent of world trade (*China Briefing*, June 1992, no. 42, p. 8). Hussain and Stern (1991: 151) estimate that the weighted average of exports and imports to national income increased from 6 per cent in 1978 to 15.6 per cent in 1988.

The distribution of trade by country has changed dramatically over time, with the socialist countries' share falling from two-thirds in 1960 to 23 per cent in 1970, and to 15 per cent by the mid–1980s (with the developed capitalist countries taking more than 70 per cent). Note that this lack of dependence stood China in good stead with the collapse of trade between socialist countries in the wake of the events of 1989. The 1950s were a period of deep involvement with the Soviet Union in particular. The heart of the First Five Year Plan (1953–57) industrial programme was 156 Soviet aid projects, especially in heavy industry such as iron and steel, heavy engineering, vehicles, petroleum, mining and electric power. Soviet credits, know-how and technicians (only technical documents, licences and blueprints were provided free of charge) were involved, with interest rates of only 1–2 per cent, but short-to medium-term repayment periods. The Sino-Soviet quarrel, in addition to general aspects such as territorial disputes and leadership of the world socialist movement, involved Mao's objections to the denunciation of Stalin at the Twentieth Congress of the CPSU in 1956, the June 1959 Soviet abrogation of an agreement to pass on technology relating to the atomic bomb and Khrushchev's policy of peaceful coexistence with the United States. Khrushchev himself denounced the GLF and its premature attempt to hasten the attainment of communism. In 1960 the Soviet Union withdrew its aid personnel, and China paid off its debt within the next five years, earlier than planned. Sino-Soviet trade subsequently fell to virtually zero, and it was only in the mid-1980s that agreement was reached for Soviet experts to update seventeen of the old plants (including the Anshan Iron and Steel Works), collaborate on seven new projects, and provide much needed extra electrical generating capacity. In the late 1980s the Soviet Union accounted for only 3 per cent of China's foreign trade (Alexander Salitsky, FEER, 18 May 1989, p. 20) and in recent years has actually received Chinese credits ($333 million in 1990 to purchase clothing and light consumer goods, and $750 million in March 1991 to buy foodstuffs).

China has been treated more leniently by COCOM, has had observer status at GATT since November 1984[18] and is a member of the IMF, the World Bank (since May 1980) and the Asian Development Bank (since 1986). The USA granted the first MFN waiver in 1979 and extended the privilege for another year on 25 April 1990 despite Tiananmen.

There is now considerable diversity in the institutional structure of foreign trade in China, with the degree of decentralized decision-making dependent on broad economic circumstances. The Ministry of Foreign Economic Relations and Trade (MOFERT) acts as an umbrella organization. It was set up in March 1982 as a merger of the Ministry of Foreign Trade, the Import–Export Commission and the Foreign Investment Control Commission (established in 1979 to control the use of foreign exchange), with the aim of overcoming the considerable overlapping of decision-making authority among the old and new bodies.

The exact situation varies with circumstances, but the reforms laid greater emphasis on indirect steering of trade by the centre via the exchange rate, tariffs, taxes and subsidies, the cost and availability of credit, the amount of foreign exchange earnings allowed to be retained by local authorities and enterprises, and import licences. For example, balance of payments problems and declining foreign exchange reserves have at times led to a tightening of state controls on the use of retained foreign exchange earnings, export licences and foreign borrowing. Tariffs were raised throughout China on eighteen import categories in July 1985, e.g. cars and television sets. But in April 1992 these special 'adjustment taxes', designed to protect infant domestic industries, were removed (China Briefing, June 1992, no. 42, p. 7). According to China Briefing (February 1990, no. 35, p. 7), quotas and trade licences cover about one-half of foreign trade. Wang Jun (1989: 15–16) estimates that in 1986 command planning accounted for 50–60 per cent of exports and 40 per cent of imports, while guidance planning (control exercised indirectly) covered 20 per cent and 30 per cent respectively. In 1986 licensing was applied to at least 30 per cent of imports, while tariff rates were 27.2 per cent for imported intermediate goods, 31.1 per cent for capital goods and 62.6 per cent for consumer goods. The exchange rate is operational in the sense that in principle exporters receive and importers pay the world price, but a comprehensive subsidy system for exports still shields the domestic producer and trader from the full effect of international competition. There are, for example, subsidies for some imported raw materials to reduce the cost to users, and each producer of exported goods negotiates individually with the particular foreign trade corporation that bears the difference between the cost of production and the export price. Export subsidies were designed to overcome the strong inclination to deal in the easier domestic market, but these were scrapped 1 January 1991.

In 1979 enterprises were generally allowed to retain a percentage of export earnings (normally 7.8 per cent), in a credit account with the State Administration of Foreign Exchange Control (SAFEC), which controlled its use. The following year inter-enterprise sales were permitted, but the Bank of China set the rate of exchange and charged commission. In 1985 most provinces were allowed to retain 25 per cent of foreign exchange earnings, which was split equally with the exporting enterprise, but exceptions included the Special Economic Zones (100 per cent at first), Guangdong and Fujian (30 per cent), the electrical and machinery industry (50 per cent) and the tourist industry (30 per cent). After January 1988 the following applied: for light industry, arts and crafts, and garments, the province and raw materials suppliers retain 38.5 and enterprises 31.5 per cent, leaving only 30 per cent for the central government.

Sales of foreign exchange are organized via a number of local 'foreign exchange adjustment centres' ('swap centres'). These were first set up in Shenzhen in 1985 and there were more than ninety by the end of 1991 (*China Briefing*, January 1992, no. 41, p. 2). *China Briefing* (February 1990, no. 35, pp. 9–10) estimates that in 1988 these centres accounted for 34 per cent of the foreign exchange retained by enterprises and 6 per cent of the value of foreign trade. In 1989 15 per cent of export earnings were transacted through these centres (Hussain and Stern 1991: 152). For example, in Shenzhen rates are negotiated between buyers and sellers, although under the supervision of the SAFEC, while official rates are set in centres organized by local governments. Trading volume nationally increased by 37 per cent in 1989, by 54 per cent in 1990 (to $13.16 billion) and by 55 per cent in the first half of 1991. Some swap centres permit individuals to trade, although with tight restrictions on purchases of hard currency. There are also strict guidelines on how Chinese enterprises may spend hard currency purchases. (For details see *China Briefing*, no. 29, May 1988, pp. 6–7, no. 30, October 1988, p. 3, and no. 41, January 1992, pp. 2–3.) A National Foreign Exchange Swap Market was established on 8 August 1992.

On 1 January 1991 a nationally unified system of foreign exchange allocation was instituted (*EIU Country Report*, 1991, no. 1, p. 30): all foreign trade enterprises are obliged to sell 20 per cent of foreign exchange earnings to the central government at the official exchange rate; 10 per cent has to be sold to the local government and 10 per cent to the manufacturer of the exports. The central government can also choose to buy, at the 'swap market' rate, twelve percentage points of the sixty remaining with the foreign trade and one percentage point of the ten remaining with the manufacturer. In April 1991 a new policy was adopted of gradually devaluing the renminbi towards the swap market rate (*China Briefing*, January 1992, no. 41, p. 2).

The renminbi ('people's currency', or yuan) is still not a fully convertible currency, but the traditional system of the Ministry of Foreign Trade, operating through its foreign trade corporations, has been scrapped and replaced by a complicated set-up. The traditional central foreign trade corporations tend to specialize in standardized products such as grain and coal. There are now foreign trade corporations at the ministerial (industry), regional (including provincial and municipal levels, such as Guangdong, Fujian, and the three main municipalities), and even at the enterprise level. The China National Native Products and Animal By-products Import and Export Corporation is a state-owned, specialized foreign trade organization under the direct jurisdiction of MOFERT, with sixty-four branches in municipalities, provinces and autonomous regions. The China National Machinery and Equipment Import and Export Corporation operates under the Ministry of Machine Building (servicing the machinery and technology export and import needs of its industrial enterprises). Certain large enterprises have been allowed direct links with foreign companies – the National Chemical Fibres Corporation and the China National Petroleum Corporation, for example. However, after November 1989 decision-making was recentralized in the hands of MOFERT, with the power of approval over trade agreements. MOFERT itself was later obliged to gain clearance from the

Ministry of Materials and Equipment before issuing export or import licences because of domestic shortages and the lack of hard currency (*IHT*, 23 February 1990, p. 15).

Foreign capital

In addition to Western credits, the open door policy involves direct foreign investment. China borrowed in the 1950s (from the socialist countries, especially the Soviet Union), but borrowing (mainly from international organizations like the World Bank and from governments) did not restart until after 1978. When the law on joint equity ventures was promulgated on 14 July 1979, foreign ownership was limited to a maximum of 49 per cent and the life span to a maximum of thirty years, at which time there would be reversion back to full Chinese ownership. Subsequent amendments have allowed the following. (1) Up to 100 per cent foreign ownership. By the end of 1985 there were 120 solely foreign-owned enterprises (Kosta 1987: 158; *The Economist* gives a later figure of 225; 13–19 August 1988, p. 68). (2) A life span of fifty years and even more in certain cases. In May 1988 Shanghai Volkswagen became the first joint venture to receive permission to issue bonds to individuals and enterprises in China. Shen Xiaofang (1990: 63–9) attempts to measure the impact of direct foreign investment on capital, exports and employment. By the end of 1988 foreign private capital commitments amounted to $28.06 billion, $11.3 billion of which had already been utilized. Although direct foreign investment actually utilized only amounted to 2 per cent of total investment during the decade, in the first half of 1988 it accounted for 13–17 per cent of investment in the open coastal cities and 60–82 per cent in the five Special Economic Zones (depending on the exchange rate used). The share of foreign investment enterprises in total exports rose from less than 0.5 per cent in 1984 to 6 per cent in 1988, while they employed no more than 3 per cent of the total industrial labour force in 1988. Kwon's estimate (1989:

257) is that the SEZs and fourteen coastal cities together took 67 per cent of direct foreign investment in 1985 and 55.5 per cent in 1986. By the end of September 1990 26,500 foreign-invested enterprises had been approved (worth $37.8 billion in contracted investment), about 10,000 being operational: in 1990 they accounted for 12.6 per cent of total exports and an estimated 3 per cent of total industrial output (*China Briefing*, March 1991, no. 38 p. 8). In 1991 $11 billion of direct foreign investment was committed and $3.5 billion actually delivered (*The Economist*, 20 June 1992, p. 90).

The China International Trust and Investment Corporation (CITIC) was set up in July 1979 to 'introduce, absorb and apply foreign investment, advanced technology and equipment for China's construction'. It has become a vast 'socialist conglomerate' dealing in banking (including bond issues in Hong Kong, Japan and West Germany), trade (including arms), consulting and legal services, investment (including abroad, in order, among other things, to secure vital materials such as aluminium and timber), travel, property, and joint ventures with foreign partners at home and abroad. Its subsidiary, CITIC Industrial Bank (formally opened in September 1987, but actually operating since May of that year) deals in foreign exchange. It is a competitor, like the Shanghai Bank of Communications, of the Bank of China. Another subsidiary, a consultancy agency, was set up in November 1987 to provide assistance to joint ventures in trouble. At the same time CITIC Industrial Bank was given permission to set up retail branches throughout China and to collaborate with the Ka Wah Bank of Hong Kong. CITIC at present consists of sixteen separate enterprises, three of them abroad, and is to be renamed CI (Holdings) (*EIU Country Report*, 1988, no. 1, p. 12). In August 1989 CITIC was fined for tax evasion and illegal transactions.

There have been a number of problems associated with joint ventures, reflected in varying interest by Western companies and subsequent concessions by China. The causes lie in the conflicting interests of the host country and guest investors:

1. China is especially interested in foreign investment projects which embody the latest technology and which increase exports to hard currency markets. In contrast, Western companies are mainly interested in penetrating the domestic Chinese market.

2. The inadequate infrastructure (especially energy supplies, 72 per cent of which was generated by coal in 1987, and transport and communications) have caused perennial problems.

3. Manpower is mainly supplied by the Foreign Enterprises Service Corporation at wage rates above domestic levels. Since the Chinese workers and managers only receive approximately the prevailing domestic rate, the state imposes a sort of tax. There is also the argument that this is partly an attempt to encourage more capital-intensive techniques (Wall 1991: 21). Dismissals have been possible since 1981, but difficult to achieve in reality, needing the approval of the enterprise workers' committee or the relevant trade union. Other costs, such as housing and office rents for foreigners, are also very high.

4. Foreign companies are often not allowed to write detailed contracts and there is often Chinese insistence on signed contracts being renegotiated or new conditions are imposed by local government. The backward legal system relating to aspects such as patents or copyright is also a serious problem.

5. Wall (1991: 17) argues that a major deterrent is the *guanxi* effect (the need to cultivate connections with people who control the distribution of resources). For example, most multinational corporations are unable or unwilling to use the *guanxi* system as a substitute for the rule of law or the uncertainty of contracts (p. 18).

Concern over declining foreign interest led to concessions over time. In 1983–84 some were made that related to profit and other taxes and to tariffs, and other stimulatory factors such as the introduction of patent law and the possibility of marketing part of the output domestically; twenty-two further concessions were granted in October 1986. Foreign enterprises designated as 'export-orientated' (more than 70 per cent of production) or 'technically advanced' were provided with additional incentives: lower land rent and lower costs of raw materials and power; priorities in the supply of water, electricity, transport and communications, which were charged at the same rate as local state companies; easier hard currency loans; hard currency payments for designated import substitutes; tax concessions; and permission for ventures to swap foreign exchange surpluses and deficits among themselves – the same foreign investor involved in two or more ventures can be treated as a single unit for self-financing purposes. At the Seventh National People's Congress in 1988 it was confirmed that the foreign partner could provide the board chairman and that the remittance of profit and capital funds on termination of the project was assured. Disappointing off-shore oil exploration has also led to both extra concessions and permissions for on-shore drilling. Pearson (1991) argues that the liberalization of the foreign investment environment up to 1988 was due more to external pressures from foreign investors than internal pressures from reformist elements. Direct foreign investment was treated relatively favourably during the austerity programme introduced in late 1988. For example, in November 1989 more generous credit was allowed and governmental institutions were permitted to spend more on the purchase of products such as cars. Legislation introduced on 1 July 1991 standardized the tax rate, thus removing the disadvantages experienced by wholly foreign-owned enterprises (for details, see *China Briefing*, July 1991, pp. 5–6). On 25 June 1992 it was announced that service businesses such as retailing, transport and banking would be opened to foreign investors (*The Economist*, 4 July 1992, p. 64).

In May 1987 China raised its first loan in the United States since 1949. In June agreement was also reached with Britain on claims arising from pre-revolution debts, leaving the door open to bond issues in the London market, the first of which took place in September 1987.

The Special Economic Zones

Special Economic Zones (SEZs) were designated in order to isolate the rest of the country from Western influences until they were proved to be successful. Special foreign trade status was bestowed upon Guangdong and Fujian provinces in 1979, but SEZs were not formally designated until the following year. It is no coincidence that three of the SEZs (Shenzhen, Zhuhai and Shantou) are in Guangdong province, adjacent to Hong Kong and Macao, and Xiamen is in Fujian province, opposite Taiwan. Special status (e.g. permission to decide on foreign investment projects up to $30 million, and tax concessions) was also awarded to Hainan Island in April 1983 and it became both a separate province and a SEZ in 1988. That status was also given to fourteen coastal cities in April 1984 (thus spreading the concessions northwards).[19] In July 1985 attention was focused on only four coastal cities (Guangzhou, Shanghai, Tianjin and Dalian) with a better endowed infrastructure and a superior record in attracting foreign capital.

Shenzhen dominates, attracting nearly 70 per cent of the combined foreign capital investment of the original four zones by the mid–1980s. Shenzhen's population has grown from less than 100,000 in 1979 to more than 2 million today, with a GDP *per capita* of nearly $2,000 (*The Economist*, 5 October 1991, p. 21). (In 1989 Guangdong province accounted for 72 per cent of total foreign investment: Elizabeth Cheng, *FEER*, 15 March 1990, p. 39; nearly two-thirds of its output is now exported: *The Economist*, 5 October 1991, p. 22; in 1991 Guangdong accounted for 16 per cent of total exports, and state enterprises were responsible for only 23.1 per cent of the province's industrial output: *EIU Country Report*, 1992, no. 1, p. 22; the share of the province's industrial output contributed by state enterprises fell from 73 per cent in 1978 to 35 per cent in 1990, while that of foreign-invested and private enterprises combined rose from zero to 38 per cent – collectives were responsible for the remainder: Carl Goldstein, *FEER*, 23 April 1992, p. 21; in 1991 the province accounted for 8.5 per cent of total industrial output, 45 per cent of foreign investment and 19 per cent of exports: Simon Holberton, *FT*, 7 April 1992, p. 19.) The exact nature of the concessions granted to these areas has varied between themselves and over time. These include profits tax concessions, increased local decision-making powers over foreign trade decisions and the spending of convertible currency earnings (at the start of 1989 the SEZs' right to retain their foreign exchange earnings was reduced from 100 per cent to 80 per cent, while that of some inland provinces has been increased; Elizabeth Cheng, *FEER*, 12 January 1989, p. 45), reduction in or even elimination of tariffs, and greater control over the hiring and firing of workers. Market forces seem generally to operate in the SEZs.

Problems arose in the operation of the SEZ policy, so much so that in 1985 Deng described Shenzhen as 'an experiment that remains to be proved'. The SEZs as a whole were downgraded and greater attention was paid to cities like Shanghai and Tianjin, and there were general restrictions resulting from balance of payments and foreign exchange reserves problems. Particularly disappointing were factors such as: (1) the SEZs' initial failure to reach the roughly 60 per cent export–total output target set (only about 20 per cent was actually achieved in Shenzhen; foreign exchange earnings were less than foreign exchange expenditure even by the mid–1980s); and (2) the fact that foreign capital (mainly from Hong Kong) has favoured sectors such as tourism (hotels, etc.), retailing, construction (such as offices), and low-tech manufacturing rather than high-tech manufacturing and critical infrastructure projects in power and transport. About 60 per cent of Shenzhen's exports stem from subcontract processing (Elizabeth Cheng, *FEER*, 8 February 1990, p. 39). Wong (1987) points out the difficulties of achieving the aims of the SEZs, especially the development of new, remote isolated areas, with no industrial tradition and with their need for massive infrastructural investment.

Corruption, too, has caused alarm. For example, in 1985 officials on Hainan Island were revealed to have resold vast quantities of consumer durables (paid for, in part, by purchases of foreign currency on the black market), such as cars and television sets. These were imported tariff-free, supposedly for use on the island itself, but then resold on the mainland at substantial mark-ups. There was a subsequent ban on the diversion of imports from one province to another. Convicted officials, however, claimed that the resources were used to further development and social welfare rather than for personal gain. Black markets have inevitably sprung up for convertible currencies and 'foreign exchange certificates' (FECs, introduced in April 1980). FECs were meant to control the black market in convertible currencies, thus preventing unauthorized use by Chinese citizens. The aim is to phase out the FECs some time in the future. Increasing income differentials within the zones and between the zones and the non-favoured areas have also caused concern.

The SEZs and the open door policy in general weathered the austerity programme and the post-Tiananmen retrenchment (there was a sharp slow-down in the growth of contractual foreign investment in the year following June 1989, but then a rebound: *China Briefing*, January 1992, no. 41, p. 2). Indeed, the go-ahead has been given to develop the Pudong industrial, commercial and financial zone (not, so far at least, formally classified as a SEZ) in East Shanghai over the period 1991–95. Special concessions include a 15 per cent profit rate for foreign investors, land leases of up to seventy years, and tariff-free imports of raw materials and equipment; foreign participation in banking and services is encouraged (*China Briefing*, March 1991, no. 38, p. 4).

A number of 'bonded zones' either have been or are in the process of being set up, e.g. Shatoujiao in Shenzhen (the first, December 1987), Lianhuashan in Guangdong (March 1988) and Futian in Shenzhen (February 1990). Extra inducements are available, such as the importation of raw materials duty-free provided the finished product is exported (*China Briefing*, July 1991, pp. 7–8).

A later variation was announced in March 1991, with the setting up of twenty-seven 'special science and technology zones' within the SEZs; the normal tax rate for joint ventures is 15 per cent, but it can be reduced to 10 per cent for high-tech ventures and those exporting more than 70 per cent of output; tax exemption will apply for the first two profit-making years.

The SEZs' future seems assured. During a visit to Shenzhen and Zhuhai, starting 19 January 1992, Deng made the striking comment that 'Shenzhen's development and experience showed that our special economic zone policy is right. You must speed things up' (*IHT*, 29 January 1992, p. 3). At the end of March it was announced that Shenzhen was to expand in size more than sixfold. The idea was mooted of SEZs in Tibet and in areas along the borders with Russia, North Korea and Mongolia, and mention was made of the setting up of the Yangpu Economic Development Zone on Hainan Island. In Yangpu the focus was to be on high-technology export activities and partially/totally foreign-owned enterprises. In fact the use of land was to be determined by a Hong Kong consortium on a seventy-year lease. Extra inducements were to include the absence of restrictions on the repatriation of profits. Concessions in the treatment of foreign investment widened further, e.g. to Beijing. In the spring of 1992 Hunchun (in Jilin province in the north-east) became the sixth SEZ. Deng in fact gave the signal for a general speeding up of reforms.

The Economist (6 June 1992, p. 78) reports regional estimates of annual income per head in yuan: Shenzhen 4,205; Guangzhou (also in Guangdong province) 2,906; Xiamen 2,737; and Shanghai 2,334. By way of contrast the rural average was only 710, while Beijing's figure was 2,040.

PROBLEMS AND ECONOMIC REFORM

Developments pre-Tiananmen

The Chinese economy has become a fascinating field of study since Deng talked about 'socialism with Chinese characteristics' and quoted the old proverb, 'It does not matter whether a cat is black or white as long as it catches the mouse.' Restrictions were imposed in the mid–1980s, however, in response to a number of problems (see Table 5.2). The growth of national income was so rapid up to the late 1980s that infrastructural bottlenecks became exacerbated. Table 5.2 shows the picture as regards gross foreign debt. According to *The Economist* (19–25 March 1988, p. 92), foreign debt was negligible in 1981. Since 27 August 1987 companies have needed permission from the State Administration of Foreign Exchange Control (which now registers all foreign loans) to borrow abroad. Table 5.2 shows the record for inflation according to official figures. An austerity programme was begun in late 1988 to combat double-figure inflation.

The first two years of the Seventh Five Year Plan 1986–90 were to be years of consolidation. This involved: (1) reducing state expenditure, especially keeping fixed investment at the 1985 level in real terms to check over-plan capital expenditure; local authorities were required to keep within centrally determined limits; and (2) controlling consumption levels. The average annual rate of growth of national product was to be kept to 7.5 per cent. Note that over the period 1981–2000 it is still planned to quadruple industrial and agricultural output (raising *per capita* income from $300 to $800 in 1980

dollars), with priority sectors including energy, transport and communications, agriculture, light industry and tourism.

Deng (born in 1904, who made comebacks in 1975 and 1977) met increasing opposition from powerful figures like Peng Zhen (former chairman of the National People's Congress) and Li Xiannan (president 1983–88, who died on 22 June 1992 aged 83), who were disturbed at the ideological implications of reform and specific problems such as the decline in grain output. In 1983 there was a short-lived 'spiritual campaign' against Western ideas. Student demonstrations in December 1986 and January 1987, calling for greater democracy and freedom, led to a political clampdown and the dismissal of Hu Yaobang (General Secretary for seven years) in January 1987 for not doing enough to resist 'bourgeois liberalism'[21] and for other errors such as allowing consumption to increase too rapidly. The party was particularly disturbed at the threat to its control and to 'unity and stability'.

The death of Hu Yaobang on 15 April 1989 sparked off the student-led pro-democracy demonstrations in Tiananmen Square, Beijing (and in other cities), that were eventually brutally suppressed by the army in the early hours of 4 June. (Note that Gorbachev visited China on 15–18 May.) Zhao Ziyang, who opposed the use of force, lost his position as General Secretary on 24 June and was replaced by Jiang Zemin. At the end of July an anti-corruption and anti-privilege programme was announced (a concern that featured strongly in the students' demands). For example, 'high officials' (members of the Politburo, Party Secretariat and State Council) and their families were banned from business activities as of 1 September, and China's leaders were to be deprived of special allocations of food. Nevertheless, official statements have proclaimed continuity of economic policy, and major elements of the reform programme (such as the 'open door' policy and the HRS) have been adhered to on the whole. Important in this

Table 5.2 China: foreign debt, debt service ratio and average annual rates of growth of national income and retail prices (%)

Average annual rates of growth	1950–59	1959–62	1962–65	1965–79	1980	1981	1982	1983	1984	1985	1986	1987	1988	1989	1990	1991
National income									13.0	16.0	7.8	9.4	11.2	3.9	5.0	7.0
Retail prices	2.3	7.5	–4.1	0.2	6.0	2.4	1.9	1.5	2.8	8.8	6.0	7.3	18.5	17.8	2.1	3.4
Gross foreign debt ($ billion)										16.7	23.7	35.4	42.0	45.7	52.6	55.1
Debt service ratio										7.7	8.2	8.5	8.7	9.8	10.3	9.2

Sources: China Briefing, 1987 no. 27; July 1991, p. 4; Perkins (1988:623); Hussain and Stern (1991: 145); Economist Intelligence Unit, *Country Profile*, 1987–88; *Country Report*, 1990, no. 1, pp. 3, 8; 1992, no. 1, p. 3; *FT Survey*, 16 June 1992, p. vi; DIW, *Economic Bulletin*, 1992, vol. 29, no. 7, p. 8.

respect are the agreements reached with Britain and Portugal over Hong Kong (19 December 1984) and Macao (1987) respectively. The idea is to maintain their capitalist systems ('one country, two systems' – to become Special Administrative Regions) for fifty years after the handing over of power to China on 30 June 1997 and 20 December 1999 respectively. Deng has talked of a possible 100 years for Hong Kong, for example in January 1992. The big prize is Taiwan and the lure of peaceful reunification is an enormous incentive to rule out any lurch to the left. The survival of the economic reforms is also helped by the limited actual experience with traditional central planning, the discrediting of left utopian policies by the GLF and Cultural Revolution (and the consequent change in leadership and weakening of the bureaucracy), the relatively less pressing demands of the defence sector as a result of *détente* in foreign policy, and the intellectual theory of the 'initial stage of socialism'. This stresses the importance of current economic conditions rather than pure Marxist theory and the development of productive forces (see below).

It is worth tracing the events leading up to Tiananmen. During the September 1987 visit of World Bank officials, the intention was disclosed of furthering the reforms during the 1990s, including tendering for the management of state-owned enterprises, conventional share issues (although the state would hold a majority), the general sub-leasing of land in order to form larger units better able to employ modern technology, and less emphasis on domestic production of grain. On 1 October 1987 the *People's Daily* declared 'leftism' to be the main threat to progress.

At the Thirteenth Party Congress (25 October–1 November 1987) Zhao Ziyang was confirmed as General Secretary and made first vice-chairman of the party Central Military Commission; he became vice-chairman of the state counterpart at the Seventh National People's Congress the following year. In his opening address to the 1,936 delegates at the Party Congress (representing 46 million party members) he confirmed that the reform programme was to continue despite problems such as corruption, inflation and concern over the grain harvest. Zhao stated that the role of the state was not to exercise direct control over enterprises, but to determine macroeconomic policies, with the state regulating the market and the market guiding the enterprises. A high priority was attached to education to ease the skilled labour bottleneck. The ideological justification is to be found in the theory of the 'initial or primary stage of socialism', a process of gradually moving towards a modern industrial economy (which took place under capitalism in Western countries),[22] and a stage that started in the 1950s and which could last until beyond the mid-twenty-first century, by which time China would be a 'first-rank power'. During the 29 October 1987 conversation with the general director of GATT, Arthur Dunkel, Zhao Ziyang forecast that only 30 per cent of the economy would remain centrally planned in two or three years' time, compared with 100 per cent nine years ago and 50 per cent currently. Of course one must bear in mind that there is an incentive on China's part to stress market orientation, given the application to join GATT. This contrasts with the views of conservative leaders such as Chen Yun, who believes that change must be confined by the (albeit expanding) 'cage' of central planning. Specific measures included the confirmation that Hainan Island was to become China's thirtieth province and latest Special Economic Zone in April 1988. The scheme allowing even foreigners to lease land for up to seventy years was to apply to all SEZs and the main coastal cities initially and generally later on.[23]

Constitutional approval of the purchase and sale of land-use rights was given at the Seventh National People's Congress in 1988: 'The right to the use of land may be transferred according to law.' Major political events have included the stepping down of Deng Xiaoping from both the Standing Committee and the Politburo itself (the intention being to separate party and state) and the election of a new Central Committee from candidates whose numbers exceeded the (reduced) number of places available. There were sweeping reductions in the numbers of old guard members, and the intention was expressed of distinguishing between the categories of administrators, the 'political affairs' personnel (selected by the party for a fixed term of office to determine policies) and the 'professional work' personnel (on permanent tenure and selected through competitive examinations) to administer these policies. The new system was expected to be fully operational by 1992. As expected, Li Peng became acting prime minister on 24 November 1987.

At the Seventh National People's Congress (2,970 delegates met 25 March–13 April 1988) Li Peng was confirmed as premier. More cautious than Zhao Ziyang, he nevertheless supported the reform programme as a whole, adding, however, that he thought inflation to be 'the outstanding problem in our economic and social life' and to be caused by excessive use of currency, overinvestment (especially by provinces), the rapid growth of consumption funds, and aggregate demand exceeding aggregate supply. In early September it was announced that Zhao Ziyang had lost overall control of economic decision-making, thus strengthening Li Peng's conservative influence. This was closely followed by the announcement of a two year 'rectification' process, 'restoring control of the economic environment and rectifying economic order'. This included a shelving of further major price reforms, the reimposition of price controls on some basic goods, a slowing down of industrial growth and a reduction in public expenditure, and was due to inflation in particular. The party leadership was concerned about recent panic buying in shops and a rapid run-down of bank deposits.

The National People's Congress is formally described as the 'supreme organ of state power', although it is in reality more of a rubber stamp for party decisions already taken. In an attempt to alter this image, open debates were held, many resolutions were not passed unanimously and secret ballots for officials were held. Nevertheless, the Congress was used to approve both the legislative and constitutional basis of the reform programme (for example, the private sector, the transferral of use-of-land rights, joint ventures and bankruptcy) and the appointment of new officials. A number of specific aspects have already been discussed. Following the rural and urban reforms, plans were outlined for the streamlining of government administration. The purpose was to support the reform process in general and especially to tackle the problem sectors of energy, transport and raw materials supply (bottlenecks here hinder the growth of the other sectors). Specifically, there was to be a 20 per cent reduction in central government personnel and the creation of new bodies. A revamped State Planning Commission was set up (the State Economic Commission was scrapped and some staff were transferred); the aim was to strengthen the tendency away from direct control of enterprise management, which would be responsible for micro decision-making. New ministries were created for Energy (taking over the responsibilities of the Ministries of Coal, Petroleum, and Nuclear Power) and Materials. The aim was to improve the distribution of raw materials, particularly to end hoarding by ministries. The new ministry was to gradually reduce the number of production materials subject to restrictions from over 200 to about fifty (*China Briefing*, no. 29, May 1988, p. 2). The Labour and Personnel Ministry was split into the Labour Ministry (to oversee labour market reforms) and the Personnel Ministry (to oversee the new civil service system).

The National People's Congress held 20 March–4 April 1989 promised a few more years of austerity and reform retrenchment. Proposed measures included the use of the price and tax system to encourage agriculture at the expense of rural enterprises and grain at the expense of non-staple foodstuffs.

Developments post-Tiananmen

The austerity programme was a feature of the Fifth Plenary Session of the Thirteenth Central Committee held 6–9 November 1989. Restraint was to last at least through 1991 and a number of goals were set. Inflation was to fall below 10 per cent, annual growth rates were to be in the 5–6 per cent range over the next five year period 1991–95, and the budget and trade deficits were to be eliminated (Shambaugh 1989: 860). Even so there was some selective easing of credit constraints (e.g. as regards joint ventures and vital state enterprises) and within a few months Li Peng was quoted as saying that we must 'put an end to sluggish growth by the end of June' (*IHT*, 5 March 1990, p. 7). Interest rates were reduced in March and July 1990. In an August 1990 speech, however, Li Peng said, 'All important national projects must be included in the plan. We cannot develop blindly . . . We do not want to seek overly-rapid growth.' There seemed to be disagreement within the Chinese leadership about economic reform, but the balance seemed to swing towards the pro-reform group. Even the hard-line Li Peng informed a conference of foreign businessmen on 24 October 1990 that reforms would be implemented over the next ten years (including prices) and that the private sector would expand. The vested interest of the provinces in decentralization is an important consideration in maintaining the major planks of the reform process.

China's reaction to the events in Eastern Europe since late 1989 was perfectly predictable in an ideological sense. On 20 March 1990 Li Peng proclaimed that 'Socialist China will stand as firm as a rock in the East'; this quote comes from his speech at the National People's Congress held from this date to 4 April, the major theme of the Congress being 'stability and unity'. China has, however, recognized the new

regimes, and Li Peng visited the Soviet Union on 23–5 April (Chou Enlai visited in 1964).

The West's reaction to Tiananmen was to impose various sorts of diplomatic, military and economic sanctions, but there were soon signs of an easing. As early as July 1989 two senior US officials visited China (although this was not disclosed until December). The World Bank resumed lending for humanitarian reasons in February 1990 (e.g. earthquake damage). At the Group of Seven (G7) meeting in July 1990 Japan gained approval to activate its 1988 credit package (this actually began on 2 November) and the World Bank to lend for humanitarian, environmental and reform-enhancing reasons (the World Bank approved a non-humanitarian loan on 5 December 1990). The European Community lifted its non-military sanctions on 22 October 1990, partly as a reward for China's support of UN resolutions against Iraq in the aftermath of the 2 August invasion of Kuwait. President Bush met the Chinese foreign minister Quian Qichen on 30 November 1990 and Secretary of State James Baker visited China 15–17 November 1991. On 17 January 1992 the USA and China signed an agreement providing greater protection for US patents and copyrights, while on 21 February the USA lifted the high technology sanctions imposed in June of the previous year. Over the period 26 January – 7 February 1992 Li Peng visited Italy, Switzerland, Portugal and Spain and also (31 January) met President Bush at the United Nations.

The Central Committee meeting held 25–30 December 1990 discussed the Eighth Five Year Plan 1991–95 and the ten-year programme for the 1990s (the 'Ten-Year Development Strategy'). There was need for ratification by the National People's Congress (March–April 1991). The communiqué was sometimes vague and inconsistent, the result of behind-the-scenes disagreement. More specifically, however, there was reference to 'sustained, stable and co-ordinated growth'; the target for the average annual rate of growth of the economy during the

1990s was set at about 6 per cent. The economic structure was to be one which 'suits the growth of the socialist planned economy, based on public ownership'; this implies that the private sector would remain, but playing a subsidiary role. The major planks of the Chinese reform process were to remain: reference was made to the 'primary stage of socialism' and the need to 'firmly push forward reform and opening to the outside world'. 'The responsibility system with the household contract linking output to payment as the main form is in keeping with the present level of the productive forces in China's rural areas and must be maintained as the basic system for a long time to come.' 'Further efforts should be made to enhance the vitality of the enterprises, especially the large and medium-sized state-run enterprises.' 'It is necessary to handle properly the relations between the central and local authorities.' Some satisfaction seemed to be derived from what is seen as the chaos and growing unemployment in the former socialist countries in Eastern Europe.

Nothing unexpected happened at the National People's Congress held 25 March – 9 April 1991. Li Peng's opening address emphasised the themes of 'unity and stability', socialism ('Socialist China will stand as firm as a rock in the East') and adherence to the main aspects of economic reform ('Facts have shown that neither China nor any other country can do without reform and opening up'). Official policy remained a socialist planned commodity economy, with state ownership dominant. Concern was expressed at economic problems such as the large subsidies necessary to support state industry, but any 'shock' therapy was to be avoided (note that any substantial hardening of budget constraints on state enterprises risks large-scale unemployment, which, in turn, threatens the stability craved by the leadership; the dependence of most workers on the enterprise for social security and housing exacerbates the problem in China). (Note also that more general concern was shown in 1991 about inflationary pressures, stemming from the

previous relaxation of credit, but an official end to the austerity programme was proclaimed at the end of November of that year.) Li Peng also stressed the need to promote enterprise groups that transcend regional and industrial lines in order to combat regional trade barriers. Personnel changes included two new deputy prime ministers, the pragmatic reformist mayor of Shanghai, Zhu Rongji, and the more conservative head of the State Planning Commission, Zou Jiahua.

The failure of the August 1991 coup in the Soviet Union further isolated China. China's public reaction was to stress that what happened in other countries was an internal affair, that socialism would prevail, and that China had been proved right to emphasize political stability and economic prosperity. 'Secret' documents circulating in September 1991 among party members attacked Gorbachev and underlined the danger of multi-party democracy. Gorbachev's resignation on 25 December 1991 brought forth open condemnation, blaming him for 'political chaos, ethnic strife and economic chaos'. China recognized the new states diplomatically on 27 December 1991.

A crucial event took place when Deng paid a visit to Shenzhen and Zhuhai in Guangdong province, starting on 19 January 1992. Not only did he support the Special Economic Zones, but he commented positively on the economic reform process generally (*IHT*, 29 January 1992, p. 3): 'If capitalism has something good, then socialism should bring it over and use it. Reform is China's only way out. If you don't reform it's a dead-end street. Whoever refuses to reform will have to leave the stage.' Deng talked of Guangdong province becoming the fifth 'little dragon' (after Singapore, Taiwan, South Korea and Hong Kong) in twenty years and of the country needing to commit itself to economic reform for a century. Subsequently Deng regretted that Shanghai had not been made a SEZ. Also in January 1992 Li Peng told a gathering of provincial governors that the country had to 'quicken the pace of reform'; 'We must be able to fire people' (Sheryl WuDunn, *IHT*, 13 February 1992, p. 1).

The main division in the Chinese leadership is between those, led by Deng, who believe that economic reform is essential to maintain the communist party in power and keep China socialist, and those who believe that market-orientated reforms endanger both these aims (they argue that economic liberalization leads to political demands, as in Tiananmen). Reference is made to the 'one centre' (economic advance) and the 'two main points' (namely ideology/party control, commonly referred to as the 'four cardinal principles', and reforms/opening up to the outside world). Thus the promotion of economic advance is seen as the determining criterion when judging the value of other policies.

A clear indication of the ascendancy of Deng's policy of stressing economic reform came when Chinese newspapers, including the *People's Daily*, gave front-page treatment to a statement made by the normally highly secretive Politburo (which met 9–10 March 1992): 'firmly hold to the party's basic line and not waver for a century, grasp the opportunity to quicken reform and opening to promote the economy'; 'to judge whether a move is "socialist" or "capitalist" will depend mainly on whether it will benefit the development of the productive forces under socialism, the comprehensive national strength of our socialist country and the living standards of the people'. The greater threat was seen to come from 'leftism' rather than 'rightism'; vigilance should be maintained against 'right' deviation, but attention should mainly be focused on resisting 'left' deviation. In a circulated speech Deng maintained that if the economic reforms had been abandoned in June 1989 'there would have been chaos and a civil war would have occurred'.

The fundamental difference between socialism and capitalism is not whether there is more planning and market. A plan-ned economy is not equal to socialism, because capitalism also has planning; the market economy is not equal to capitalism, because socialism also has the market. Planning and market are economic means.

The National People's Congress met 20 March – 3 April 1992. In the opening speech Li Peng adopted a cautious approach, stressing the need for economic reform but avoiding an attack on 'leftism': 'To make China a powerful socialist country, standing firm as a rock in the East, we must concentrate on our domestic affairs, above all on more rapid economic development.' 'We must do two types of work at the same time, attaching equal importance to both. We should promote reform and opening to the outside world, and, at the same time, crack down on criminal activity of all kinds.' 'We must be on the watch for any ideological trend towards bourgeois liberalism, checking it the moment it appears and never allowing it to run rampant'; '. . . maintaining social and political stability is the prerequisite for reform'. Li Peng stressed the importance of the political education program-me, especially for university students. There was emphasis on the problem of loss-making state enterprises and a focus of economic reform would be making state enterprises more com-petitive and more responsive to the market. The experiment in stock markets was to be ex-panded. The growth target for 1992 was set at 6 per cent, as was that of the inflation rate. The Three Gorges Dam project was approved, but with considerable resistance; there were 1,767 'yes' votes, but 177 'no' votes and 664 absten-tions.

Although the rectification process had officially ended some time before the congress, concern was expressed at inflationary pressures. The then finance minister Wang Bing Quian (he resigned on 4 September 1992 and was replaced by Liu Zhongli) reported that the 1991 budget was 71 per cent above target. The 1992 defence budget was increased by 12 per cent, however, and the rate of income tax paid by state enterprises was to be cut from 55 per cent to 33 per cent over the following three years.

But even more surprising were the more than 150 amendments made by the Presidium (Secretariat) of the National People's Congress to Li Peng's Government Work Report, including references to the desirability of faster growth, more experiments with stock markets, greater encouragement to the private sector, markets for socialism, and of economic construction being the party's central task for 100 years. The most significant amendment politically was the following insertion: 'To accelerate the reform and opening to the outside, it is crucial for cadres at all levels to enhance further their consciousness of implementing the party's basic line and guard against "leftist deviations" while watching out for "rightist deviations".'

Dengist ideas looked set to dominate the crucial Fourteenth Party Congress in the autumn of 1992 (see postscript). A critical test for the economic reform programme would be whether a 'hard budget constraint' would be imposed on state enterprises, with all the consequences in terms of bankruptcies and unemployment.

CONCLUSION

A general introduction sketched the political and economic background to a country accounting for 22 per cent of the entire world population. Agriculture successfully headed the reform process in 1978 and this sequence, it could be argued, was an object lesson for countries like the Soviet Union. The reader should particularly note the dramatic policy swings over time, from the convulsions of the Great Leap Forward and Cultural Revolution to the present market orientation of the 'household responsibility system'. Another key point to grasp is the nature of the departures, from the beginning, from the traditional economic system. Until the current reforms there was virtually no labour market and rationing of consumer goods has been much more prev-

alent. Planning has been much less centralized, even during the First Five Year Plan 1953–57. The changes in the nature of planning and in the role of the industrial enterprise over time were analysed, ending with the application of the urban reforms first outlined in October 1984 and the passing of the state enterprise legislation in April 1988. The economy has gone a significant distance down the market road. Political reform has not followed suit, however, and multi-party democracy has been ruled out. This raises an interesting general question as to the extent to which political reform is a condition of successful economic reform. The Chinese leadership points to capitalist examples like Taiwan and South Korea, which developed rapidly under authoritarian regimes.

The non-state sector has rapidly expanded. The 'open door' policy was highlighted, with its implications for foreign trade and capital, and particularly emphasis was given to the 'Special Economic Zones' and the other coastal areas. The chapter discussed more recent preoccupations (such as inflation) and vital political events like the Thirteenth Party Congress in late 1987 and the Seventh National People's Congress in the spring of 1988, the latter giving constitutional backing to the reforms. The traumatic episodes in recent Chinese history have actually helped the reforms by discrediting ultra-leftism and ultra-leftists. The Tiananmen massacre on 4 June 1989 and the dramatic events in Eastern Europe after late 1989 led to a severe political clampdown ('stability and unity' is the theme). Communist party membership has held (48 million in August 1989). It is all the more noticeable then that major elements of the reform programme, such as the 'open door' policy and the HRS, have all along remained largely intact owing to their very success. The vested interest of the provinces in decentralization is also an important consideration in maintaining the major planks of the reform process. Deng strongly confirmed the value of the economic reform process in January 1992. China's economic reforms are of considerable interest in the context of the debate on the transition from a command to a market economy.

NOTES

1. Compared with $240 (in 1952 dollars) for the Soviet Union in 1928 (World Bank, 1984, vol. 1, p. 43).
2. It was not until the early 1970s, however, that the programme really took off, with the aim, set in 1980, of restricting the total population to 1.2 billion by the year 2000 (now 1.25 billion). A mixture of financial and non-pecuniary incentives and penalties have been applied especially to try to attain the goal of one child per family, formally adopted in 1979. This was relaxed somewhat in 1984–85 and tightened in 1987. After mid–1988 a surprising switch in policy took place, allowing families in rural areas to have a second child if the first was a girl, due to the difficulty of enforcing policy. But policy was maintained for urban areas and tightened up generally for larger families.
3. Poor weather was partly responsible. The 1958 grain harvest was actually somewhat larger than the previous record, attained the year before.
4. Currently, local bodies below the provinces (twenty-two, including Hainan Island: there are also five autonomous regions, including Inner Mongolia and Tibet, and the three municipalities of Beijing, Tianjin and Shanghai) are the prefecture, county, town and village.
5. Split up into plots of varying quality and distributed more or less equally among households, although the team may permit consolidation.
6. The quotas and the tax calculations are based on the land area and the average yield of the last three years, although there is now emphasis on stable quotas (Quaisser 1987: 178).
7. Cheung (1986: 67) placed this at seven, but this number has, in reality, been substantially exceeded at times.
8. All land in Hong Kong is 'owned' by the Crown.
9. Fourteen and a half per cent in 1984, 13 per cent in 1985, and 12 per cent in 1987. Excluding the output produced by rural industries, the figures are only 3.0 per cent for 1985, 3.5 per cent for 1986, 3.0 per cent for 1987, 3.2 per cent for 1988, 3.0 per cent for 1989, 6.9 per cent for 1990 and 3.0 per cent for 1991.
10. Monthly housing rental payments amount to only 3–5 per cent of a worker's money wage. By 1982 the value of urban subsidies exceeded the average wage paid (Johnson 1988a 235, quoting Lardy). The range of benefits provided by the traditional enterprise includes medical and labour insurance, child care facilities, pensions and guaranteed jobs for workers' children (White 1988: 184).
11. A notable exception is demobilized members of the armed forces. This is significant given the July 1986 plan to reduce the People's Liberation Army from 4 million to 3 million people. (It is worth noting here the 1987 decree that civilian goods must eventually be produced in all armaments establishments: *The Financial Times*, 1 May 1991, p. 4, reported that 42 per cent of military factories already produced civilian goods, while another 29 per cent were developing civilian business; in 1990 civilian goods accounted for 63.8 per cent of all products made by military factories. Tai Ming Cheung reports, in the *FEER*, 6 February 1992, p. 40, that the percentage of civilian goods increased from 8 per cent in 1979 to 65 per cent to date; the aim is 80 per cent by 1999.) Further exceptions are professionals, office workers and cadres. On 29 January 1992 Deng talked of reducing the armed forces from 3 to 2 million. Tai Ming Cheung (*FEER*, 27 February 1992, p. 15) reports a more modest intention to reduce the size of the army by 260,000 over the next few years from its current level of 3.2 million.
12. The contract system is often less effective than might be imagined, with cases of thirty to fifty-year contracts. Contracts are often routinely extended, and workers often fail to give notice before quitting (do Rosario, *FEER*, 12 May 1988, p. 74).
13. A computerized trading network connecting six cities (e.g. Beijing, Shanghai, Shenyang and the SEZ of Shenzhen) was opened for business in December 1990. The new Shanghai stock exchange opened on 18 December 1990 and the new one in Shenzhen on 3 July 1991. Plans were announced for exchanges in Zhuhai, in Guangzhou (capital of Guangdong province) and in northern China, but by mid–1992 early problems with the existing exchanges had led to delays. In December 1991 China Southern Glass (Shenzhen) became the first enterprise to sell shares to foreigners (so-called 'B' shares, bought for and yielding dividends in hard currency); these shares began to be traded in Shenzhen on 28 February 1992. The second enterprise was Shanghai Vacuum Electronic Device on 22 January 1992; its 'B' shares began to be traded on

the Shanghai exchange on 21 February 1992.

14. For a detailed analysis of the 1978–83 reforms see Lee (1986) and S. Jackson (1986).

15. Huang Yasheng (1990: 45) notes that in the mid-1980s output maximization was of minor concern to enterprise managers. His view is that managers are mainly interested in increasing the welfare of their own employees in the form of improved bonuses, housing and employment opportunities; plan target fulfilment is seen in this context. One reason for this is the fact that most managers rise from the ranks of employees. The role of the profit motive is debatable. For example, Jefferson and Xu (1991: 52–3) argue that the maximization of worker benefits, while prominent, is generally subordinate to the profit motive. Because the ability to dismiss workers is severely limited, managers view the profit fund as a critical source from which to reward labour for increased productivity.

16. Collectives can be owned by a group of individuals or by local governments. Collective ownership is officially defined as ownership in which 'the means of production are owned by the collective. It includes farming, forestry, animal husbandry, fishery and sideline occupations run by various rural economic entities, as well as enterprises and institutions run by townships and villages. Also included are the collective enterprises and institutions run by cities, counties and town neighbourhood committees' (*China Briefing*, 1991, no. 40, p. 1).

17. In April 1988 the National People's Congress voted to permit private businesses to take on more than seven employees outside the family (Gold 1989: 194). Wang Zhonghui (1990: 83) notes that the term 'private enterprise' refers strictly to those enterprises employing at least eight workers, the term 'individual enterprise' referring to those employing fewer. At the end of 1987 there were 225,000 private enterprises, employing more than 3.6 million workers (p. 86). An average of sixteen workers were hired in each enterprise, although some hired up to 100 people and there were boasts of up to 1,000 (p. 87). David Dodwell (*FT*, 22 March 1991, p. 7) reports a private shipping company employing 1,240).

18. China was a founder member in 1947, left in 1950 and applied to rejoin in July 1986. Since GATT encourages the use of GNP as a measure of national output, China subsequently adopted it as an important indicator.

19. Zhanjiang, Beihai, Guangzhou, Fuzhou, Wenzhou, Ningbo, Shanghai, Nantong, Lianyungang, Qingdao, Yantai, Tianjin, Qinhuangdao and Dalian. Note Sit's (*Asian Survey*, 1988, vol. XXIII, no. 6) use of the term 'Open Areas' to describe these, the SEZs, and other areas.

20. Over the period 1979–84 Hong Kong provided 60 per cent of total equity joint venture investment (Kamath 1990: 114); one reason is the unlimited access to the Chinese domestic market after reunification (p. 123). The figure was even higher for Shenzhen.

21. Western ideas such as free elections and freedom of assembly, speech and publication which threaten both socialism and the traditional view that, in reality, these merely cover up the bourgeoisie's domination of society.

22. At the Thirteenth Congress Zhao said, 'During this stage we shall accomplish industrialization and the commercialization, socialization and modernization which many other countries have achieved under capitalist conditions.' Schram (1988: 177–8) points out that the term 'underdeveloped socialism' was used in 1979 and 'primary stage' in June 1981, although the implications of the latter have only now been spelled out.

23. In September–December 1987 Shenzhen sold off fifty-year land leases to domestic companies (the first in China since 1949), followed in March 1988 by auctions open to foreigners as well. Shanghai, for example, has also held land lease auctions, the first to domestic enterprises in March and the first to foreigners in July 1988 (*China Briefing*, 1988, no. 30, p. 7). Guangdong province offered seven pieces of land in September 1989, with leases provisionally set at seventy years for residential properties and fifty years for industrial and commercial properties (*China Briefing*, October 1989, no. 34, pp. 7–8). Note that leasing refers to the use and not the ownership of land, although rights to the use of the land can be resold. Land in China is in 'socialist public ownership', which is of two types: (1) state ownership ('ownership of the whole people') or (2) collective ownership ('ownership by the working masses' or the peasantry at large, in practice the commune in the past or village and township organizations today). Urban land is state-owned, while suburban and rural land is collectively owned (Stephen Morgan, *FEER*, 14 July 1988, pp. 22–6).

6

CUBA

POLITICAL AND ECONOMIC BACKGROUND

Cuba was discovered by Christopher Columbus on 27 October 1492, but the conquest by Diego Velazquez did not take place until 1511. The first shipment of African slaves arrived in 1526, and a plantation-based economy subsequently developed. By the mid-1800s Cuba accounted for almost 40 per cent of world sugar production from sugar cane and 30 per cent of total sugar output (Perez-Lopez 1989: 1631). Slavery was not abolished until 1886. The third and final war of independence against Spain (1895–98; the others were in 1868–78 and 1879–80), in which the United States finally intervened, was followed by four years of US military government, until an independent republic was declared on 20 May 1902. Even after that date the United States exercised a dominant direct and indirect influence, respectively: (1) there were actual interventions in 1906–9, 1912 and 1917; the Platt Amendment was added to the 1901 constitution, allowing the United States to intervene 'for the preservation of life, property and individual liberty'; (2) economic links involved considerable investment and commercial treaties, such as the one in 1903, which provided preferential treatment for Cuban sugar imports into the United States and opened up the Cuban market to US imports. The new treaty in 1934 extended the range of products affected.

Fulgencio Batista led a military coup in 1934,

was elected president for a term in 1940, and led another coup on 10 March 1952. On 1 January 1959 the guerrillas of the 26 July Movement under Fidel Castro came to power, having overthrown Batista's dictatorship after a two year struggle. Full diplomatic relations were established with the Soviet Union in 1960, which led, together with the expropriation of US property, to the United States breaking off such relations with Cuba in January 1961. In that year (17 April) the Bay of Pigs invasion by 1,500 Cuban émigrés was defeated and socialism formally embraced. The Cuban Communist Party was founded in 1965. The 1962 Cuban missile crisis was defused when the Soviet Union agreed to remove the missiles and the USA promised never to invade Cuba. Cuba was a founding member of the Non-aligned Movement (see especially Azicri 1988).

Cuba tried to stay aloof from the recent Eastern European drama, 'socialism or death' ('socialismo o merte'), as Castro put it in a December 1989 speech. Cuba played a positive role in the Angola-South Africa peace accord of December 1988 (including the phased withdrawal of Cuban troops; the last left towards the end of May 1991, five weeks ahead of schedule), but was rocked by the December 1989 US overthrow of the Noriega regime in Panama (useful as a means of circumventing the US embargo) and the defeat of the Sandanista regime in the 25 February 1990 Nicaraguan general election. The end of the Cold War meant that Cuba was of less strategic importance for the Soviet Union even before the abortive coup in the Soviet Union in August 1991. The party daily *Granma* commented after the failure of the coup that 'whatever happens in the Soviet Union we will not move away from the path we have chosen. We shall continue with our independent, Cuban, socialist line' (reported in *IHT*, 31 August 1991, p. 5). On 11 September 1991 Gorbachev announced (without consulting Cuba) that a training brigade (representing 11,000 out of 14,000 Soviet military personnel) was to be withdrawn from Cuba and that henceforth relations between the two countries were to be based on 'mutually beneficial commercial exchanges'. Military and civilian aid was to be gradually reduced (Yeltsin ruled out future Russian aid). Cuba reacted pragmatically to the demise of the Soviet Union towards the end of 1991, extending diplomatic recognition to the emerging independent states.

At The Fourth Party Congress 10–14 October 1991, held in secret, Castro announced that 'Socialism or death does not apply because there will be socialism at any price'; 'we are going to defend ourselves alone, surrounded by an ocean of capitalism'. The congress resulted in only marginal political changes, e.g. the lifting of the ban on religious believers joining the party, the abolition of the Central Committee Secretariat (which tended to duplicate the work of ministries), direct elections to the National Assembly (rather than via the municipal assemblies), and some personnel changes in the politburo and central committee.

In 1959 the population of Cuba was nearly 7 million (10.5 million in 1989), of which an unusually high (for a developing country) percentage of 53 per cent was urbanized (70 per cent today).[1] Even so, agriculture dominated the economy, with industry, intimately linked to the former, only employing 17.4 per cent of the labour force in 1953, compared with agriculture's more than 40 per cent. (In 1970 industry still accounted for only 20 per cent: Eckstein

1981: 135; in 1986 industry contributed nearly 45 per cent of gross social product: *Abecor Country Report*, March 1988, p. 1.) The sugar industry alone accounted for 5 per cent of national product, 25 per cent of manufacturing industry, and 75–80 per cent of exports. In 1957–58 73.3 per cent of imports were consumer goods and only 17 per cent were machinery and industrial supplies (Azicri 1988: 121). In 1958 the sugar cane sector contributed 45 per cent of the value added in agriculture and livestock 20 per cent (Figueras 1991: 71). Large estates dominated the land area as well as sugar and cattle rearing, and crops like tobacco, food and coffee were mainly produced by small farmers (MacEwan 1981: 3–4). During the early 1950s Cuba was the main producer and exporter of sugar in the world (and is still the world's leading exporter of raw sugar). In 1960 the United States withdrew Cuba's sugar import quota and the following year imposed a trade embargo, later even including products from any third country that embodied Cuban inputs. Before the revolution the United States and Canada accounted for 70 per cent of Cuba's foreign trade, and Western Europe took a further 15 per cent (*EIU Country Report*, 1987–88, p. 23).

Mineral resources include nickel (the fourth largest reserves in the world), estimated at 19 million tonnes. Nickel and cobalt production was over 40,000 tonnes in 1981, 33,500 tonnes in 1985 and 35,800 tonnes in 1987 (*FT*, 18 May 1988, p. 34). Alumina, chromium, cobalt and iron ore are also significant. Domestic crude oil output was some 259,000 tonnes in 1981 and 868,000 tonnes in 1985 (Zimbalist 1988b: 25). Current output supplies 5 per cent of the country's needs of about 10 million tonnes a year; the Soviet Union supplied 12–13 million tonnes annually during the 1986–90 plan period, but began to reduce deliveries around early autumn 1990 (Tim Coone, *FT*, 8 March 1991, p. 30). The shortfall in Soviet oil imports has led to drastic energy saving measures. The country's first nuclear plant was due to begin operating in

1992–93, the aim being to reduce dependence on oil, but on 5 September 1992 it was announced that work was to be suspended because of unacceptable completion terms offered by Russia.

AGRICULTURE

In 1959 land ownership was very unequal, with 9.4 per cent of owners controlling 73.3 per cent of the land, and 66.1 per cent of owners holding only 7.4 per cent (Rodriguez 1987: 24). Wage labour, mainly seasonal, was common – this made up 60.6 per cent of the rural workforce in 1953 (Ghai *et al.* 1988: 6). A significant proportion of agricultural wage workers had access to a plot of land of between 0.25 and 1.0 ha (Kay 1988: 1240). The *17 May 1959 land reform* affected 70 per cent of agricultural land: a general ceiling of 402.6 ha per owner was fixed (1,342 ha in exceptional cases). Free tracts of 26.8 hectares were given to tenant farmers and squatters, with a possible maximum holding of 67.1 ha. Even the additional land was not usually paid for; expropriated landowners typically forfeited compensation by emigrating (Ghai *et al.* 1988: 9). As a result of the reform state farms occupied 51.5 per cent of total farm land (p. 11). Of the land affected, 60 per cent went to individual peasants. Sharecropping was abolished, as were rents in money terms and in kind for tenants. Large estates were at first given over to co-operatives, but from the middle of 1961 these were replaced by state farms (MacEwan 1981: 50).

The *second land reform* of 1963 saw the 67 ha limit made general for all private farms, with the result that the state held 76 per cent of all land and 63 per cent of cultivated land (MacEwan 1981: 73). According to Zimbalist (1988: 14), the private farmer today typically owns 20–60 ha of land. The state sector contributed 37 per cent of agricultural output in 1961 and 70 per cent within two years (MacEwan 1981: 70). At present state farms account for 83 per cent of land ownership (Table 6.1), 80 per cent of the agricultural labour force, 75 per cent of livestock, and 77.5 per cent of agricultural and livestock output (Kay 1988: 1246). In 1983 the *non-state farm sector* (collectives and individual peasant farms) accounted for 22.5 per cent of output (compared with 42.3 per cent in 1964 and 20.6 per cent in 1980) and owned 16.6 per cent of land (Kay 1988: 1260). The private sector's share of cultivated land continued to fall, from 37 per cent in 1963 to 30 per cent in 1975, when Castro declared that private farming, although destined

Table 6.1 Cuba: land tenure, foreign debt and average annual rate of growth of global social product

Average annual rate of growth of global social product (%)										
1962–65	1966–70	1971–75	1976–80	1981–85	1986	1987	1988	1989	1990	1991
3.7	0.4	7.5	4.0	7.3	1.4	–3.5	2.3	1.0	–5.0	

Debt owed to the West ($ billion)				
1974	1982	1986	1987	1989 (June)
0.66	2.86	3.87	5.7	6.78

Land tenure (Azicri) (%)		
Government property	Co-operative property	Individual private property
80.0	12.0	8.0

Source: Azicri (1988: xvi); Zimbalist (1987: 15–16); Zimbalist and Eckstein (1987: 8); *Abecor Country Report*, March 1988; July 1990; Economist Intelligence Unit, *Country Profile*, 1987–88, p. 7; 1989–90, p. 29; *The Economist*, 27 August 1988, p. 60; 17 December 1988, p. 65; *IHT*, 17 January 1989, p. 3; *FT*, 17 February 1989, p. 35; Perez-Lopez (1992: 114, 125).

for ultimate elimination, was indispensable for the foreseeable future (Zimbalist 1988: 197–8). Gey (1990: 97) gives the following percentage breakdown of land area by type of farm for 1974 and 1981 respectively: state farms 79.8 and 80.8; production co-operatives 0.1 and 4.0; private farms 17.9 and 12.7; plots of former farmers 0.3 and 0.3; plots of workers, etc., 1.9 and 2.2.

A 'revolutionary offensive' began in 1968 to increase state ownership, but the failure to achieve the 10 million tonnes sugar harvest brought about a change of mind in the early 1970s. In 1967 state farm workers lost their private household plots and the state began to interfere with the crop planting decisions of private farmers. The following year they were obliged to sell their produce to the National Agrarian Reform Institute at relatively low state-determined prices (Roca 1981: 86). Private plots were reintroduced in the 1970s, but at the start of the next decade the individual plots of state and co-operative farms were merged into collective plots for own consumption purposes (Gey 1987: 87) or for sales to the States. Small private plots were reintroduced in state farms in 1982 (Zimbalist et al. 1989: 374).

The early 1970s saw the start of a dual policy of amalgamating state farms and decentralizing administrative and work systems within each farm. By 1983 there were 422 state farms (a decade earlier there were about three times as many), with an average size of 14,255 ha and an average labour force of 1,390 (Kay 1988: 1246). While the revolutionary offensive of 1968 saw a switch from piece to time rates and a narrowing of earnings differentials, the SDPE (see below) involved the use of accounting methods and the calculation of indices such as cost per unit value of production (Kay 1988: 1247). Since 1981 'permanent production brigades' have been very gradually introduced into state farms. These brigades are on an economic accounting basis – they are assigned production targets and inputs, they are able to distribute a portion of profits to workers, they have a stable labour force and sometimes they are tied to a particular

land area (Kay 1988: 1251). By mid-1985 seventy-three of 406 state farms under the Ministry of Agriculture were affected (Ghai et al. 1988: 58). By 1986 120 were involved, with an average of seventy-five workers per brigade (Zimbalist 1989: 87).

State farms supply most domestically consumed foodstuffs (such as meat, eggs and milk) as well as exportables such as sugar and citrus fruits (Ghai et al. 1988: 71). Agro-industrial complexes now account for practically all the sugar cane state farms (only four in 1981); these are vertically merged with the mills (p. 34).

A state agricultural purchasing organization was set up in the early 1960s, and so too were various types of co-operatives; credit-service, mutual aid teams, and co-operatives in which land, livestock and equipment were collectively owned. The Credit and Service Co-operatives were the most successful – some 66 per cent of peasant farmers belonged to them by 1970 and 77 per cent a decade later.

Most early production co-operatives faded away (Kay 1988: 1255). *Collectivization*, put forward at the first congress of the party in 1975 on a voluntary basis, was slow until 1981–83 and then slowed again. The percentage of non-state sector land collectivized rose from 13 per cent in 1980 to nearly 58 per cent within three years and around 61 per cent at the start of 1986 (Gey 1987: 86), although in terms of the percentage of peasant farms belonging to production co-operatives, the figure was well below 50 per cent (Kay 1988: 1255). The average size of collective farm was 144 ha and twenty-three members in 1979 and 732 ha and fifty-one members six years later (pp. 1256–7). Peasants were encouraged to join co-operatives by factors such as the provision of old-age pensions, the lack of a private land market, the unwillingness of children to stay on farms and the inability to hire permanent as opposed to seasonal wage labour (p. 1255). Co-operatives are subject to negotiated procurement quotas and benefit from state supplies and the ability to hire labour at peak periods. All sugar, coffee, tobacco and beef production is subject to state procurement (Ghai *et al.* 1988: 47).

Co-operative and individual farms concentrate on specialized exportable crops, such as tobacco and coffee. In 1977 they accounted for 80 per cent of tobacco, 50 per cent of coffee, 50 per cent of fruit and vegetables, 16 per cent of sugar and 32 per cent of cattle (Ghai *et al.* 1988: 129, quoting Mesa-Lago). Only family members who directly cultivate farm land are permitted to inherit it, and the state has first refusal when land is sold. Private farmers have to sell a certain percentage of their crops to the state at official prices and, in return, have access to credit and inputs. The state uses subsidies and regulations to induce private farmers into state-owned projects (Azicri 1988: 113–4). Individual private farms are responsible for less than 10 per cent of both area and production.

In April 1980 a *free farmers' market* was introduced where, in addition to artisan products, above-procurement quota sales by individual farmers and co-operatives, if not sold to the state at above-quota prices, could be transacted. The free peasant markets accounted for 1 per cent of retail trade turnover in 1985 (Gey 1987: 90) and around 5 per cent of the value of food sales to the population (Zimbalist 1988: 13). This market was taken over by the state on 15 May 1986. Since then all farm produce, including that from private plots, has had to pass through the hands of the state. Reasons included the appearance of middlemen, excessive profits, tax evasion, and the illegal use of state resources such as lorries. Kay (1988: 1262) lists other factors, such as the reluctance of some farmers to sell to state marketing agencies and the idea that the co-operative movement was being hindered. A detailed analysis is provided by Deere and Meurs (1992) and Rosenberg (see Postscript). The National Association of Small Farmers (set up in May 1961) represents the interests of co-operative members and private farmers in negotiations with government bodies.

CENTRAL PLANNING AND THE INDUSTRIAL ENTERPRISE

In 1958 there were 2,000 enterprises in Cuban industry, mostly artisan workshops employing fewer than ten workers; the 162 sugar refineries and another 100 enterprises were the only ones with more than 100 workers; non-sugar industrial employment amounted to less than 10 per cent of the total workforce (Figueras 1991: 75).

The advice of Czechoslovak planners was particularly sought in the early 1960s. Mesa-Lago (1989: 98) describes the 1961–63 period as a failed attempt to introduce a traditional command economy. The period 1963–65 was one of debate on theoretical alternatives. Azicri (1988: 130–1) describes the 1964–6 stage of development as one in which new economic models were tested as well, with a centralized system used in industry (e.g. enterprises were financed through the state budget) and a more decentralized model used in agriculture. This was followed by the so-called 'moral economy' stage 1966–70. During this period certain departures from the traditional Soviet model were pronounced, such as the strong emphasis on moral incentives. These were inspired by the perceived need to stress independence. Then came the introduction of reformed Soviet-type measures during the 1970s.

The 1962–65 Four Year Plan was abandoned prematurely in 1964. Two years later the powers of the Central Planning Board (Juceplan: Junta Central de Planificación) were substantially reduced and those of the political leadership correspondingly enhanced. Annual plans were probably discontinued during 1965–70, and a number of special 'mini-plans' relating to particularly important regions or sectors were introduced, with the subsequent lack of national co-ordination associated with command planning. Note, however, that in 1968 a crude computerized input–output table of the industrial sector was compiled (Mesa-Lago 1981: 12). Annual plans were drawn up, starting in

1973, with five year plans and a perspective plan for 1980–2000 following. Zimbalist (1988: 77) points out that before 1976 Cuba did not have a five year plan or the basic institutions of planning. State enterprises (including those in agriculture) were tightly controlled and lost most of their financial independence by the imposition of budgetary finance and their inability to receive bank credits. Their plants were not the subject of close cost accounting. In 1967 personal taxes, including income and property taxes, were scrapped. In the late 1960s there were no individual bonuses or overtime pay.

The 1970s saw the implantation of reformed Soviet-type measures, the result of a disappointing economic performance during the 'moral economy' period (see Table 13.1), the subsequent greater reliance on Soviet aid and advice, and the greater integration with the rest of Comecon (1976–80), Cuba having become a member in 1972. The first Congress of the Cuban Communist Party took place in December 1975, at which the 'System of Economic Management and Planning' (Sistema de Dirección de la Economia, SDPE) was outlined, a system heavily influenced by the 1965 Soviet reforms and to be introduced in practice gradually from 1977 onwards. The SDPE was supposed to be fully operational by 1980 (Perez-Lopez 1990: 8).

The SDPE acknowledged the importance of economic levers such as interest rates, prices and taxes. Interest-bearing credits were available from the National Bank. Enterprises were put on an economic accounting basis, and management was given greater decision-making powers over matters such as manpower and investment. Profitability was given an enhanced role as an indicator, alongside output, quality, productivity and costs. A portion of profit, dependent on the fulfilment of plan indicators, could be retained for personal bonuses, investment and social projects. Zimbalist (1988a: 77) notes that until the SDPE material rewards to motivate management did

not exist, but afterwards managers received a share of the bonus funds roughly in line with the proportion of managerial salaries in the enterprise's total wage fund. Stimulation funds in enterprises were started in 1979 on an experimental basis (usually linked to indicators such as productivity, costs, output and exports) and by 1985 affected around 52 per cent of enterprises (Zimbalist 1988a: 77). Individual work norms applied to more than 50 per cent of the workforce (p. 77). In 1985, however, total bonuses (from the incentive funds and from meeting specific tasks such as savings on inputs) and overtime totalled only 10.6 per cent of basic wages on average (Zimbalist 1989: 80–1).

The State Price Committee (Comité Estatal de Precios) was established in 1976 and fixes the prices of over 1 million products. Local governments set the prices of locally produced and consumed goods such as those produced by artisans, and some prices are freely determined (e.g. perishable consumer goods towards the end of the marketing period) (Zimbalist 1988b: 38). Before the 1981 comprehensive price reform, prices in the material production sectors were either those of 1965 or, for new products, were based on the first-year-of-production price. The 1981 reform (in which new wholesale prices were introduced in January and retail in December) was based on 1978 prices, costs and structures, while the next comprehensive reform was meant to use those of the year 1985 (Zimbalist 1988b: 38). Wholesale prices are set on the principle of estimated branch average cost of production plus a profit mark-up sufficient for the typical enterprise to pay a profits tax and a social security tax and to finance the incentive fund. At present the mark-up varies according to plan priorities, but the intention was a uniform markup in 1989 (Zimbalist 1988b: 39). The Price Commission allows price surcharges for higher quality, new product designs and new styles (p. 39). The general rule is for retail prices to include a turnover tax aimed at balancing supply and demand (Mesa-Lago 1981: 18), and luxury or health-impairing goods such as tobacco, alcohol and cars to bear heavy rates (Zimbalist 1988b: 41). Import prices are either converted into domestic currency terms with the addition of the internal trade margins or based on an average converted price for the previous three years, with state subsidies or turnover taxes making up the difference with respect to the latter (Zimbalist 1988b: 47). According to Gey (1987: 92), the range of surplus products sold at market prices was increased during the 1970s and the number of rationed non-foodstuffs declined from 150 in 1980 to sixty-eight in 1985.

Production or service units of local importance were subjected to the dual subordination of elected Assemblies of People's Power. Set up in 1975, these could, for example, appoint and dismiss enterprise managers. The assemblies were also to 'take an interest in' the units still directly subordinate to the central bodies (Roca 1981: 99). The general increase in local participation and consultation in the processes of economic planning via these assemblies was complemented by attempts to enhance the role of workers and their organizations in the management of enterprises (White 1987a: 154). One-man management was replaced by a Management Council (comprising the director and other managerial personnel, and elected representatives of the party, the trade union and communist youth), there are monthly assemblies of workers in production sections, and elected workshop delegates attend a quarterly meeting with the Management Council (Zimbalist *et al.* 1989: 370). Fitzgerald (1989: 292–3) concludes that worker participation in basic production issues increased after 1970, but did not attain even the limited degree hoped for because of ill-prepared meetings, insufficient time made available, and lack of information. Meurs (1992: 235) concludes that limitations on administrative autonomy largely restrict worker participation to issues of plan implementation; workers have little decision-making power with respect to plan formulation.

Since 1980 some retrenchment has taken place. In February 1982 Castro criticized the SDPE, and the task of 'revitalizing' it went to a new body called the National Commission for the System of Economic Management, with the status of a ministry. Rather than destroy the SDPE Castro stressed the need to eliminate incipient capitalism and consumerism and to restore moral values (Perez-Lopez 1986: 32).

In December 1984 the role of the pro-SDPE Juceplan was reduced by the creation of a new 'Central Group', composed of the vice-presidents of the Council of Ministers, ministers with economic responsibility, and powerful party representatives. This group reviewed the 1985 and 1986–90 plans with the aim of promoting exports, economizing on imports and thus improving the balance of payments (Perez-Lopez 1990: 8). Zimbalist (1988a: 78) interprets this move as an attempt to reduce the powers of ministries, to facilitate lines of communication and command, to control investment spending and to deal with a deteriorating foreign exchange situation. In September 1988 the Central Group was replaced by a smaller body called the Executive Committee of the Council of Ministers.

As of 1983 about 600 products or product groups were centrally planned, amounting to 70–80 per cent of GSP (Zimbalist 1989: 74). White (1987a: 154–60) describes the economy in the mid-1980s as being highly centralized, administrative and directive. Only marginal use was made of economic levers, although repayable interest-bearing credits were increasingly used instead of budgetary grants to finance enterprise working capital and, after 1985, fixed capital needs. Only very limited independent decision-making was enjoyed by enterprises. For example, the horizontally or vertically integrated 'associations' or the greater number of medium to small enterprises were allowed only a small amount of retained profit to feed the stimulation, socio-cultural and investment funds. (Associations have been formed since 1977; by the end of 1985 there were forty-two associations in industry: Zimbalist 1992: 102.) In addition, only a marginal impact on planning decisions was made by the consulted Assemblies of Popular Power and enterprise workforces, although the degree of consultation was high by Eastern European standards. It is worth noting, however, the formation of work brigades in industrial enterprises since 1983, which are able to elect their own directors (although suggestions from above are not ruled out). These (1) form an accounting unit; (2) organize their own plans, although in conformity with the state plan via the contract made with the enterprise and constrained by allotted inputs; and (3) depend significantly on final result (Zimbalist and Eckstein 1987: 12; Jimenez 1987: 135). Gey (1987: 84, 95) estimates that in September 1985 only 5–6 per cent of workers in the productive sphere were in brigades, while the average number of workers per brigade was fifty-nine in 1985.

Zimbalist (1988: 12–13) views the 1986 measures to limit private activities and enhance the importance of moral incentives not as representing a reversal of direction or a repudiation of the SDPE and material incentives, but rather as a slow-down in the liberalization trend and a correction of excesses. His reasoning is that (1) while more activities have returned to the public sphere and there is greater control over foreign exchange, direct inter-enterprise contracting for inputs is being encouraged ('resource fairs', in operation since 1979, allow enterprises to trade unused inputs directly, and the 1980s have seen encouragement given to above-plan production: Zimbalist 1989: 74); (2) there is less reporting by enterprises to ministries; (3) there is pruning going on of administrative personnel involved in planning; (4) there is increased enterprise self-financing of investment; (5) the role of enterprise brigades is being extended; and (6) parallel markets are multiplying. Zimbalist (1992a: 102) also notes the following 1988 changes: there was to be a reduction in the number of commodities and commodity groups subject to central planning from 2,300 to 800; mandatory enterprise indicators were to be reduced from twenty-eight to eighteen; and the number of material balances drawn up by the materials allocations committee reduced by 31 per cent, these being passed down to the association or enterprise. Since 1988 experiments have been conducted with 'continuous planning', in which enterprises draw up their output and input plans (based on the previous plan and expectations of the next plan) before receiving their plan control figures; by mid-1990 about a third of productive enterprises had been affected. The post-1989 upheavals in Eastern Europe have led to an emphasis on sectoral as opposed to global planning because of the supply disruptions. Annual plans are now regarded as more hortatory than mandatory (p. 103). Zimbalist sees the 1989–early 1990s crisis leading to tighter government control over the economy, but controlled reforms have nevertheless continued and are designed to integrate the economy into the world market. Foreign trade is increasingly conducted by decentralized trading companies. Several big ones are largely handling their own foreign trade and are allowed to retain up to 70 per cent of their foreign exchange earnings to buy foreign inputs (Zimbalist 1992b: 415).

Mesa-Lago (1989), however, describes the general thrust of the 'rectification campaign' (see below) as being in the opposite direction to the contemporaneous reforms in Eastern Europe (p. 98), as being a middle point between the moral economy stage and the SDPE (p. 105); he quotes Castro's January 1987 speech, which described the campaign as 'not a 180 degree shift [from the SDPE], but an important change of direction' (p. 105). Perez-Lopez (1990: 3) agrees with Mesa-Lago, seeing the campaign as a process which emphasizes the dismantling of market-orientated mechanisms and enhances economic centralization. Prior to rectification, for example, Juceplan was responsible both for developing annual and five-year plans and for implementing the economic management system (i.e. the SDPE). In mid-1986 its economic management functions were transferred to a National Commission on the Economic Management System (p. 14). Other elements include the rejection of profit as a key indicator of managerial performance, the abolition of the farmers' free markets, restrictions on the private sector, the reintroduction of construction micro-brigades, and the emphasis on moral incentives (Perez-Lopez 1992: 115).

Castro's position seemed to be that while there was a need for strict cost accounting and economic calculation, there was to be no move towards the market mechanism, such as he perceived to be taking place in several other socialist countries at that time. At the Third Party Congress (4–8 February 1986) Castro stated that enterprise efficiency and profitability would not be meaningful if achieved simply by raising prices. While 'we still have a lot to learn in the field of efficiency, . . . becoming the sorcerer's apprentice [i.e. apprentice capitalists], is not the solution' (quoted in Dominguez 1986: 123). In an anniversary speech on 26 July 1988, his message was that effort should be concentrated on improving central planning; both capitalist methods and other countries' solutions were to be rejected. 'We must guard the ideological purity of our revolution. We will use nothing of any method that smells of capitalism' (quote taken from Julia Preston's report in IHT, 16 August 1988, p. 1). In a December interview Castro insisted that Cuba was undertaking its own changes and its own self-criticism. He much admired Gorbachev, but considered that the Soviet president had some political advisers who were enraptured with capitalism, and if they continued as they were they could do great harm to the Soviet people (reported by Geoffrey Matthews in The Times, 24 December 1988, p. 7).

Manpower and remuneration

In 1962 wages were made to vary with the degree of underfulfilment or overfulfilment of work norms. An eight-group wage scale (of approximately a three-to-one range) was set up, taking account of factors such as qualification and complexity. Time rates were dominant, with hourly tariffs taking into consideration other factors such as dangerous conditions. Wage differentials were meant to achieve goals such as incentives to improve qualifications, but in the first half of the 1960s political mobilization to achieve specific economic goals was also important (see Jimenez 1987: 128–30).

During the *'moral economy' stage 1966–70* emphasis was placed on moral incentives and collective (group) interests rather than individual material incentives, for ideological reasons and because of repressed inflation. Norming more or less came to an end, overtime payments were ended (overtime was expected to be donated free), and pay ceased to reflect the complexity of work. Wages were either frozen or reduced. For a while even time rates in many industrial workplaces were replaced by 'conscience time', with attendance depending on revolutionary consciousness (Ghai *et al.* 1988: 21). This policy was supplemented by appeals for voluntary labour, although some groups were paid. For example 'micro-brigades' were released by enterprises (the first in 1970), while remaining on the payroll, to work on housing and other social infrastructure projects. The brigades were meant to tackle under-employment and the housing shortage (Perez-Lopez 1990: 18). The remaining workforce was expected to work harder or donate overtime free, but Perez-Lopez (1990: 17) notes that the dwellings were allocated among all workers in the associated enterprises. The micro-brigades were phased out in the second half of the 1970s partly because of the adverse effects on enterprise payrolls at a time when financial accountability was given enhanced importance and partly because of concern over the allocation of housing, but were re-established in May 1986 (Perez-Lopez 1986: 34). Unlike in the 1970s, the state now reimburses enterprises for the wages paid out (Mesa-Lago 1989: 116).

The adverse effects on incentives led to serious problems such as increasing absenteeism in the late 1960s. In consequence, policy switched, in 1970, to greater emphasis on personal material incentives. From that date the Soviet-type worker norms, which were introduced in 1963–65 but poorly enforced after 1966, were gradually reintroduced (Mesa-Lago 1981: 19). In 1971 consumer durables such as cars and colour television sets and building materials were allocated to enterprises, with distribution mainly determined by work attitude and performance but also, to a lesser extent, by need. Similar criteria were applied to the allocation of housing, including that put up by the voluntary micro-brigades, and vacations (Mesa-Lago 1981: 27–8). In the same year it became compulsory for men to work, absenteeism leading to exclusion from vacations and benefits such as the works canteen and, in extreme cases, to periods in work camps (Zimbalist and Eckstein 1987: 11). The 1981 reform spread the wage range from 4.67:1 to 5.29:1. By the end of 1985 37.2 per cent of the labour force had pay tied to output (Zimbalist 1989: 75, 79). Over the period 1979–81 greater use was made of piece rates, by September 1979 affecting 36 per cent of the total working in production (Ghai *et al.* 1988: 37). Bonus schemes were introduced, linked to criteria such as the fulfilment of work norms, increased quality, input savings and repair and maintenance tasks (Kay 1988: 1248–9).

Since 1980 workers have been able to make direct contact with enterprises instead of having to go through the local labour office. The introduction of 'free, or direct, labour contracting' gave managers permission to hire and fire workers under certain defined conditions. In general workers are only sacked for misconduct (Ghai *et al.* 1988: 37). Enterprises still have to comply with their labour force plan,

however; this is the result of negotiations with the planning authorities, who have to be kept informed of hirings (Ghai *et al.* 1988: 35–6). Unemployment, according to official statistics, was 3.4 per cent in 1981 and nearly 6 per cent in 1988 (Mesa-Lago 1989: 112). Redundant workers are eligible for 70 per cent of their former wages while waiting to be re-employed and are allowed to work part time without affecting this benefit.

In 1986 major criticisms were levelled at many aspects of the existing economic system, and there was a sharp reversal of many policies. Bonus payments were to be related to the quantity and quality of performance and work norms revised upwards. Greater emphasis was to be placed on non-material incentives, while a new government commission was set up to monitor management techniques and suggest improvements. At the Third Congress of the Cuban Communist Party on 4–8 February 1986 and its December 1986 follow-up Castro catalogued a whole series of problems: bureaucracy, apathy, corruption, incompetence, irresponsibility, self-seeking, laziness, negligence, inefficiencies, profiteering, theft, absenteeism, waste, poor quality, unearned bonuses, low productivity, poor motivation and lack of accountability. He singled out people like high-earning artists, peasants charging high prices on the free market, and state managers who both overcharged and put the enterprise profit above the interests of the country as a whole. A 'rectification campaign' (*campana de rectificación*) and an austerity programme were set in motion. Perez-Lopez (1990: 9) traces the formal beginning of rectification to Castro's April 1986 speech commemorating the twenty-fifth anniversary of the Bay of Pigs invasion. Castro considered it more important to protect the moral sense of the workers by honest behaviour than merely to meet the enterprise plan at any cost. In Castro's view 'the first thing a socialist, a revolutionary, a communist cadre must ask himself is not if his firm is making more money, but how the country makes more'. He criticized managers 'who want their enterprises to be profitable by increasing prices and distributing bonuses by charging the earth for anything' (quoted in Dominguez 1986: 123). 'Although we recognize that there is room for bonuses under socialism, if there is too much talk of bonuses they will corrupt workers' (p. 124). 'Socialism must be built through political work. These market mechanisms only build capitalism.' The glories of the revolution were 'not based on money' (p. 124). 'Material incentives are necessary to a certain extent . . . But . . . socialism must be built with consciousness and moral incentives . . . In the search for economic efficiency we have created the breeding ground for a heap of vices and deformities and corruption' (quoted from Castro's June 1986 speech by Mesa-Lago 1989: 102). Specific measures included the more rigid application of work norms and the gradual introduction into enterprises of commissions (headed by party representatives) with power over hirings and firings (Fitzgerald 1989: 306). Meurs (1992: 238) sees increased emphasis on popular participation and political consciousness as important aspects of rectification.

The autumn of 1991 saw changes brought about by the deteriorating economic situation. Production schedules were generally reduced, with corresponding cuts in wages. But jobs were guaranteed, as was 70 per cent of the basic wage. Those on 100 pesos or less a month were to receive the full wage regardless.

The allocation of consumer goods and services

Rationing has been a more common and persistent feature of the Cuban economy than of the traditional Soviet system. On equity grounds and because of severe repressed inflation, the state introduced widespread rationing of staple foodstuffs and consumer goods in 1962 and made this general thereafter – in 1963 price controls were imposed on all goods and services. By 1968 there was free provision of

education, medical care, social security, and even services such as local telephone calls and water supply. Free meals at works canteens were made available to many workers and housing rent could not exceed 10 per cent of family income (Roca 1981: 86–7). Note that in 1960 the state took over houses and flats belonging to landlords and those who had left the country.

In line with the new overall economic policy in the 1970s, policy changes included: (1) the introduction of a water charge in 1971; (2) the December 1970 decision not to fulfil the promise made a decade earlier to scrap housing rents generally – only some low-income workers benefited (Roca 1981: 101); (3) some raised consumer prices – a dual pricing system was introduced in 1972 for certain commodities (this 'parallel market' was made more general in 1980), whereby extra-ration purchases in 'free shops' could be made at higher prices and some commodities were entirely derationed. In 1970 95 per cent of consumer spending was on rationed goods, but within ten years this had fallen to about 30 per cent (Turgeon 1990: 174). According to the *EIU Country Profile* (1987–88: 10), rationing accounted for 26 per cent of individual consumption, while the number of non-food lines subject to rationing fell from 150 to sixty-eight between 1980 and 1985 (p. 10).

From January 1985 onwards individuals were able to purchase their own homes outright from the state, or continue with rental (effectively mortgage) repayments, with past rent credited to the account. Individuals were also allowed to rent out accommodation at the full market price, provided ownership was limited to one home and they took responsibility for repairs and maintenance.

The year 1986 was generally one of reform retrenchment. The policy of individual home ownership was halted by the 'rectification' process and private sales were banned because of alleged profiteering (a state agency would henceforth deal with all housing sales). Restrictions were placed on the drinking of alcohol in bars. The austerity programme (the twenty-eight measures were dubbed Castro's 'commandments') put into operation at the beginning of 1987 involved sharp increases in electricity prices (38 per cent) and transport fares (urban transport 100 per cent) and reductions in canteen subsidies, television broadcasting hours, many ration allowances (e.g. kerosene, bottled milk and textiles), petrol allocation, and a limit on the number of cars available for state bodies. Note that many retail prices were revised in December 1981, including some staple foodstuffs, in order to reduce the high level of subsidies.

The situation deteriorated in 1990, owing to such factors as the disruption of Comecon trading links and reduced deliveries of Soviet oil. Delays in Soviet grain deliveries led to a reduction in the bread ration outside Havana (there were price increases in the capital) at the beginning of February; on 1 June 1991 the bread ration was standardized throughout the country, including the capital. The prices of products like eggs were increased. Later on rationing was extended more broadly to food, clothing and household goods. In the early months of 1990 preparations began to be made for a 'special period in a time of peace', e.g. experiments in using manual and animal power to save fuel, substituting wood for oil, tight restrictions on electricity consumption, the increasing use of bicycles, and the mobilization of office workers and redundant factory workers for spells in the countryside to boost agricultural output. Rationing became pervasive and in late 1990 the parallel market was abandoned. Perez-Lopez (1992: 124) places the beginning of the implementation of the special period at August 1990. Castro, in an interview in *The Guardian* (30 May 1992, p. 25),talked of the influence of long-standing plans for a 'special period in wartime' in the event of a naval blockade; priority programmes today are food first of all, but also tourism, biotechnology, pharmaceuticals, medical equipment and science. In 1991 announcements were made extending

rationing; liquid gas (the main cooking fuel) on 5 September and cigarettes and cigars four days later.

As the situation deteriorated in 1991 the people were being prepared for life with disrupted trade links and without subsidized Soviet trade and direct Soviet aid (see below). One report talks of a 25–30 per cent fall in GDP in 1991 (Damian Fraser, FT, 11 June 1992, p. 6). Cuba's 'zero option', mentioned by Castro in September 1991 (not surprisingly, following soon after the abortive coup in the Soviet Union the previous month), sees the possibility, for example, of the widespread use of soup kitchens, the absence of petrol for private use, and highly restricted supplies of electricity. The Fourth Party Congress (10–14 October 1991) stressed further belt tightening; priorities were to be health, education, a high degree of food self-sufficiency on the one hand and the quest for hard currency on the other (via exports, tourism and direct foreign investment). In late November a campaign started to persuade urban dwellers to raise chickens, while on 20 December 1991 further measures were introduced to save on oil, e.g. many workplaces were to close or at least to operate for shorter periods, while there were reductions in street lighting, television transmissions, public transport and air conditioning; floodlit sports were banned; priority was to be given to food production and hard currency earners like tourism and biotechnological pharmaceuticals. On 14 February 1992 the official prices of twenty-five agricultural products were raised. On 19 March the prices of non-rationed cigarettes were increased fivefold.

ECONOMIC STRATEGY

Sectoral strategy in the 1960s and 1970s

In the early years after the revolution there was a strong reaction to the dominance of sugar in the economy. Consequently, agricultural diversification became a key policy, although agriculture itself was allocated a declining share of state investment as industrialization received increased emphasis. Growth problems during 1962–64 and the willingness of the Soviet Union to enter into a long-term agreement in 1964 to purchase sugar at generous and stable prices (although payment was in the form of Soviet goods) led to a change in strategy. The price paid by the Soviet Union for Cuban sugar was approximately double the world market level during 1964–70 (MacEwan 1981: 97), while the former took over 40 per cent of the latter's sugar crop in some years during the 1960s (p. 217). Agriculture, especially sugar, was given priority, and industrialization was largely based on agriculture (refining, canning and shoe production, etc.), although it was also partly resource-based (nickel and cement production, for example). The ambitious 1970 sugar harvest target of 10 million tonnes was set in 1963; the actual crop-year harvest, however, was 8.5 million tonnes. The agriculture-based strategy in general (especially, in addition to sugar, cattle, tobacco, citrus fruits and coffee) was meant to save on imports and stimulate exports, thus increasing the foreign exchange available for imported capital goods. In the early 1970s sugar and its derivatives alone accounted for three-quarters of export earnings, reaching 86.4 per cent in 1974 (Hagelberg 1981: 141). In the period 1981–87 sugar accounted for 75 per cent of exports on average (Mesa-Lago 1989: 120). Even today the sugar industry accounts for 12 per cent of the workforce and 10 per cent of GSP (Azicri 1988: 169).

During the 1970s industrialization, similarly linked with agriculture (e.g. equipment such as mechanical cane cutters) and natural resource endowment, and with an emphasis on consumer goods, was given priority, attaining first priority in the late 1970s. After 1970 emphasis was placed on a gradually increasing, more efficient production of sugar (Perez-Lopez 1989: 1629); overall policies have had only a marginal effect on reducing sugar's role in the economy (p. 1627). Note, however, that there is considerable debate about whether Cuba has reduced its dependence on sugar exports (see, for example, Radell 1991).

'Debt-led growth' in the latter half of the 1970s

Cuba took advantage of the recycled OPEC funds to indulge in 'debt-led growth' (Turits's term, 1987: 163), hoping that the resulting increase in exports and decrease in imports would service the foreign debt. In the mid-1970s imports from the West came to around 40 per cent of total imports (Perez-Lopez 1990: 5). Initially Cuba had a good record of repaying its hard currency debt (see Table 6.1), but was forced to start rescheduling in March 1983. The debt–service ratio over the period 1981–85 was 58.7 per cent on average (Zimbalist 1988a: 152). Of the $4.68 billion hard currency debt at the end of September 1986, 57 per cent was owed to private credit institutions, while the debt to the Soviet Union amounted to 7.5 billion roubles (Zimbalist 1988c: 38). Cuba's hard currency debt as of June 1989 was $6.8 billion, with $2.1 billion owed to commercial banks and $50 million owed to multilateral agencies (*Abecor Country Report*, July 1990, p. 1). Debt repayments to the Soviet Union were suspended in 1972 and were to resume in 1986, but a further delay to 1990 at least was agreed upon (p. 39). A Soviet source puts Soviet aid per year at 3 billion roubles (Kortunov, *CDSP*, 1990, vol. XLII, no. 2, p. 15). The official Soviet debt estimate is that as of 1 November 1989 Cuba owed the Soviet Union 15.5 billion roubles (*CDSP*, 1990, vol. XLII no. 9, p. 9). Dominguez (1986: 135) estimates that Soviet bloc subsidies, excluding military aid, ran to at least a tenth of Cuba's gross national product after the mid-1970s. According to a report by Clyde Farnsworth (*IHT*, 17 March 1988, p. 3), Soviet subsidies, principally oil and sugar prices favourable to Cuba, ran at between $4 billion and $5 billion annually.[2] *The Economist* summarizes the picture as follows: most Western estimates put Soviet aid at around

$4 billion annually; a US estimate gives $6.8 billion for 1986, $4.7 billion in subsidies associated with purchases and sales, $1.5 billion for armaments and $600 million for aid projects (17 December 1988, p. 65). Purcell (1990: 114) quotes US estimates of Soviet civilian aid at $5 billion to $6 billion and military aid at $1.2 billion. The official US estimate of Soviet aid to Cuba in 1990 was $4.5 billion (*IHT*, 4 June 1991, p. 4). A more recent estimate of Soviet economic aid was $3.5 billion (*IHT*, 12 September 1991, p. 5). On 4 April 1992 Castro is reported to have estimated revenue loss in 1992 because of receiving only the world price of sugar at $2.5 billion (Colin Harding, *The Independent*, 21 April 1992, p. 11). In July 1986 Cuba suspended most principal and interest payments to the West. (Note that Cuba has had no dealings with the IMF since the early 1960s.)

In 1985 the value of exports plus imports constituted 50.1 per cent of net material product and 26 per cent of gross social product (Zimbalist 1988c: 21). In the mid-1980s the foreign trade of Cuba was dominated by the socialist countries (which took about 85 per cent), though Cuba's aim was to reduce this to about 80 per cent. This compares with an average of 65.2 per cent for 1971–75 and 73.3 per cent for 1976–80 (Fitzgerald 1988: 140). The Soviet Union alone accounted for around two-thirds, although imports from the Soviet Union fell during the first nine months of 1987 for the first time in nearly thirty years (Fitzgerald 1988: 3).[3] As a result of an agreement reached in 1976, following a similar nickel arrangement four years earlier, the Soviet Union paid above-world prices for sugar. For example, in 1982 the price paid by the Soviet Union was 29.9 centavos per pound, compared with 28.9 by the other Comecon countries and only 7.7 by the

Table 6.2 Cuba: statistical survey

Non-state farm sector, 1983: co-operatives and individual peasant farms (% contibution to agricultural output and land)

Output	Land
22.5	16.6

Sugar industry, 1988 (% of workforce and gross social product)

Workforce	GSP
12.0	10.0

Sugar harvest (million tonnes)

1970	1985	1986	1987	1988	1989	1990	1991
8.5 (target, 10)	8.1	7.4	7.1	8.1	8.04	7.6	6.0

Distribution of the labour force, 1985 (%)

State sector	Small farmers	Co-operative members	Self-employed	Private wage earners
93.2	3.2	2.1	1.2	0.4

Average annual rate of growth of gross agricultural output (%)

1970–75	1975–80	1980–85	1985–7
5.4	3.4	1.4	1.5

Source: Kay (1988: 1260); Azicri (1988: 169); Economist Intelligence Unit, *Country Profile*, 1989–90, p. 13; Mesa-Lago (1989: 105–7); D. Fraser, *FT*, 11 February 1992, p. 28; Meurs (1992: 236). For figures on rates of growth and Western debt see Table

capitalist countries (Perez-Lopez 1986: 20). In 1985 the price paid by the Soviet Union was 44.8 centavos per pound (50.6 cents per pound), compared to the world market price of 4.1 cents per pound; the respective figures for 1987 were 38.7 centavos per pound (38.7 cents per pound) and 6.8 cents per pound (Perez-Lopez 1990: 23). A Soviet source quotes a more recent figure of four times the world price (Kortunov, *CDSP*, 1990, vol. XLII, no. 2), while Purcell (1992: 132) mentions a Soviet price of 40 cents a pound in 1990. The 1991 agreement valued Cuban sugar at 24 cents a pound compared with a world price of 8 cents a pound (Damian Fraser, *FT*, 11 February 1992, p. 28).[4] Cuba also benefited from oil re-exports: these had been allowed by the Soviet Union after 1980 on the basis of consumption savings and aided by extensive substitution for oil of the waste product, *bagasse*, of the sugar industry. After 1983 these re-exports constituted the most important source of hard currency earnings (42 per cent in 1985, falling to 26 per cent in 1986). During the period 1983–85 oil re-exports accounted for 40 per cent of hard currency export earnings compared with 21 per cent for sugar (Perez-Lopez 1990: 5). Vergara (*IHT*, 14 September 1990, p. 7) notes that, although as recently as 1988 Cuba earned more in hard currency from oil re-exports than from sugar, shortfalls in Soviet oil deliveries have adversely affected this ability. In 1990, for example, there was a 20 per cent shortfall. The fall in oil prices after November 1985 had a devastating effect and this was aggravated by a depreciating US dollar, with imports mainly priced in other currencies because of the US embargo. The situation was made worse by a prolonged drought, which reduced the sugar harvest[5] (see Table 6.2) and by the fall in the value of the US dollar, in which its exports are mostly denominated.[6] The austerity programme since 1984 has involved a switch from domestic consumption and welfare spending to exports, in contrast to the earlier programme.

At the beginning of 1991 Cuban trade with the other and former socialist countries was scheduled to be in hard currency and based on current world market levels. A three-month transitional period was agreed with the Soviet Union, however (Perez-Lopez 1992: 123). As has already been discussed, Cuba has had to adjust to a world without Soviet aid, aid which began to be phased out after December 1990. In 1990 the Soviet Union refused to renew the five year trade agreement; henceforth trade relations were to be negotiated annually (Purcell 1992: 131). According to US estimates, subsidies from the CIS states in 1992 would amount to only $65 million; this represents just 2 per cent and 6 per cent of Soviet aid in 1990 and 1991 respectively (John Yang, *IHT*, 20 April 1992, p. 1).

Trade links within the former Comecon bloc have been badly disrupted since 1989. At the Fourth Party Congress (held 10–14 October 1991) Castro revealed that Soviet deliveries were only 38 per cent of those it had agreed to send by 30 September. One estimate puts Soviet oil deliveries in 1991 at less than a third of the expected level (Barbara Crossette, *IHT*, 6 December 1991, p. 3). In 1989 Cuban imports from the Soviet Union amounted to $5.52 billion; in 1991 the figure was only $1.74 billion at most (Zimbalist 1992b: 408). In a later interview (*The Guardian*, 30 May 1992, p. 25) Castro remarked that Cuba has to work with 40 per cent or less of the former volume of imports and with less than 50 per cent in the case of fuel imports. Indeed Cuba has been increasing trade with China and the countries of Latin America, for instance, ever since 1985. In a highly pragmatic way Cuba quickly started dealing with individual republics of the former Soviet Union, e.g. a three year trade agreement with Ukraine and exchanges of sugar for Russian and Kazakh oil.

The commodity structure of Cuba's exports in the mid-1980s was still dominated by primary products. (1) Food (overwhelmingly sugar, but also citrus fruits, fish products and live animals) – 80 per cent of total exports in all, with sugar alone making up some 75 per cent; in 1986 sugar provided 78 per cent of total exports (*Abecor Country Report*, 1988, p. 2). This compares with an average of 84.1 per cent for 1948–58 and 85.9 per cent in 1979 (Zimbalist 1988a: 6–7). (2) Other products like nickel and oil re-exports, which had risen sharply from only 0.1 per cent in 1975 to some 10 per cent. Note, however, that Cuba exports pharmaceutical products like vaccine against meningitis 'B' especially to Latin American countries. Cuba imports mainly fuels (around 30 per cent), machinery and transport equipment (roughly the same), and manufactured products (around 13 per cent) (Perez-Lopez 1986: 22).

Joint ventures

The February 1982 law allowed up to 49 per cent foreign equity (this can now be exceeded), with the aim of either exporting output or saving on imports. Production, pricing and manpower decisions are within the sphere of the venture. Priority projects in tourism, for example, pay a maximum net profit tax of only 30 per cent (Turits 1987: 172). Problems include the government's right to select the pool of domestic workers from which a joint venture may hire and even to transfer workers trained by a joint venture to another enterprise (Zimbalist 1992b: 412). There are agreements with Spain to recycle and export scrap metal (Perez-Lopez 1986: 20), with Japan in shipping, with Mexico in agricultural machine-building marketing, with Panama in finance and sugar refining (Zimbalist 1987: 17), and with Argentina in hotel construction (Turits 1987: 172). In September 1991 a joint venture with a Western mining company in nickel production was announced and one with a Venezuelan company in fertilizer production.

Cubanacan is a Cuban corporation, not subject to the planning system, involved in the promotion of joint ventures. By November 1990 it had created twelve, nine of them in tourism

(Zimbalist 1992a: 105). Other corporations largely independent of the central planning system have also been set up, and since 1990 there have been a number of projects in which foreign companies supply inputs in return for a share of the revenue generated. As of January 1992 there were around sixty joint venture or production-sharing deals functioning (Zimbalist 1992b: 412). A six-year contract was signed in December 1990 with a French consortium for offshore oil exploration.

THE PRIVATE, NON-AGRICULTURAL SECTOR

By 1961 the state sector accounted for 85 per cent of industrial output and 95 per cent two years later (MacEwan 1981: 70). During the 'revolutionary offensive' of 1968 the remaining rump of the private non-agricultural sector was eliminated, even the more important retail trade (Roca 1981: 85). In 1976 licensed private businesses were permitted in activities such as car, plumbing and appliance repairs, but the self-employed were not allowed to employ others or to resell products. The period 1976–85 was a relatively liberal one, but late 1988 saw arrests of 'speculators' (including those who sold their places in queues) and those producing consumer goods illegally. Those working in the private service sector must now be licensed and obtain a state certificate for all materials, the aim being to deter theft (Zimbalist 1992: 100). Mesa-Lago (1989: 105–9) provides some very useful information. The 1985 percentage distribution of the labour force was as follows: small farmers 3.2; co-operative members 2.1; state sector 93.2; self-employed 1.2 (0.9 in 1987); private wage earners 0.4 (0.3 in 1987). Private manufacturers and street vendors were banned as an element of the rectification process, while the 1986 restrictions included those on private housing construction and sales; at the end of 1988 the state became an obligatory partner in house purchases and sales.

The Fourth Party Cngress (10–14 October 1991) witnessed only marginal concessions, specifically to small tradesmen working 'on their own account', for 'individual gain', e.g. mechanics, carpenters and plumbers.

CONCLUSION

Cuba was a Spanish colony for some four centuries and remained under US influence for around sixty years. Fidel Castro came to power in 1959 and made Cuba the centre of world attention during the 1962 missile crisis. Despite industrialization, mainly linked with agriculture, the Cuban economy is still substantially agrarian in nature, with sugar remaining vitally important (Table 6.2). The country is heavily in debt despite past generous Soviet support. Particular points worth noting in this chapter are: (1) the early departures from the traditional system, such as the greater use of both consumer goods rationing and of moral incentives, the latter characterizing the so-called moral economy stage of development (1966–70); and (2) Cuba retrenching and even retrogressing in some respects. Thus, while the 1970s saw implementation of 1965–style Soviet reforms, in particular the 1975 System of Economic Management and Planning, the period after 1980 has been an era of retrenchment; there is considerable debate, however, about the interpretation of events after the mid-1980s, especially whether they amount to an actual reversal of the reform process. There is increasing stress, once again, on moral as opposed to material incentives, and some of the concessions made to private activity have been taken back. For example the 1980 free farmers' market for above-quota sales was monopolized by the state six years later. Cuba has become increasingly isolated as a result of the demise of the Soviet Union and socialist Eastern Europe. The economic backwash has further severely damaged an already rocky economy.

NOTES

1. In 1984 life expectancy was 73, compared with 61.8 in 1959 (Rodriguez 1988: 98); in 1965 infant mortality was 16.5 per thousand, compared with 34.7 in 1959 (Santana 1988:113).
2. The problems of calculating the value of aid include the relatively poor quality of many Soviet manufactured goods. Note that Cuba itself runs an extensive foreign aid programme (for details see Zimbalist 1988c: 37–8).
3. National product also declined by 3.5 per cent and investment by more than 20 per cent.
4. Note, however, the argument that the world price of sugar is not a good guide since only some 14 per cent of world sugar is sold at free market prices (Zimbalist 1988a: 7). The remainder is sold under preferential agreements at prices above the world market level, encouraging supply and discouraging demand and thus having a depressing effect on the world price (Zimbalist 1988c: 32). Perez-Lopez (1992: 123), however, says that the preferential price was out of line even with other preferential prices, such as the US import price and the EC import price from Lome countries.
5. Cuba has even had to buy in world markets in order to meet Comecon commitments.
6. Cuba's imports, on the other hand, are largely denominated in other Western currencies, owing to the US trade embargo, which was made fully operational in 1962 (the United States invoked the 1917 Trading with the Enemy Act). Since 1975, however, US companies have been able to trade legally with Cuba, although only indirectly via subsidiaries in third countries and only then with a licence obtained from the US Treasury (Jones and Rich: 1988). Trade between these US companies and Cuba reached $1.54 billion between 1982 and 1987 (Montero and Gonzalez 1989: 89) and amounted to $331 million in 1989 and $705 million in 1990 (Purcell 1992: 144). In early February 1992 the US company AT&T was given permission to improve telephone links with Cuba.
Licensing of subsidiaries has been tightened up, however, and on 18 April 1992, during the US election campaign, President Bush announced that ships which trade with Cuba would henceforth require licences to enter US ports.
In order to reduce the hard currency Cuba earns from the routeing of mailed packages via Mexico

Bush allowed the issuing of licenses for their direct shipment from Miami. In early May Bush proposed a further tightening of the trade embargo; aid and special trade benefits would be denied to countries providing Cuba with financial help or trading with Cuba at subsidized prices; US subsidiaries would not be allowed to engage in new trade deals with Cuba.

7

DEMOCRATIC PEOPLE'S REPUBLIC OF KOREA

POLITICAL BACKGROUND

A unified state from AD 668 to 1945, Korea was liberated (and divided at the 38th parallel) in 1945, having been part of the Japanese empire from 1910 to 1945. An isolated state, it was known as the 'hermit kingdom'. The North was occupied by Soviet forces in August 1945 and the United States occupied the South. At the 1943 Cairo conference the allies had envisaged an independent and unified Korea. In the Korean War (1950–53),[1] UN forces backed the South, the Soviet Union having absented itself from the Security Council, and China the North; the Soviet air force also took part (in October 1989 the Soviet Union formally acknowledged that its military personnel had participated). The Democratic People's Republic of Korea was proclaimed on 9 September 1948 and became a member of the Non-aligned Conference in 1975. Cumings (1988: 14) sees Korea as a civil war that started in 1945 with the Soviet and US occupations and then became enmeshed in the Cold War. The North suffered considerably more war damage than the South (Halliday 1987: 25); in 1953 power production was only 26 per cent of the 1949 level, fuel 11 per cent, chemicals 22 per cent, and metallurgy 10 per cent (p. 26).

The Korean Workers' Party has been led since 1948 by Kim Il Sung ('the great leader', who was born in April 1912 and became president in 1972), who has groomed his son Kim Jong Il ('the dear leader') as heir. There seems to have been an unsuccessful attempt within the party to thwart this succession in February 1991. Control over the armed forces was handed over to his son on 25 December 1991 (and the title of Marshal on 21 April 1992), although on 13 April 1992, two days before his eightieth birthday, Kim Il Sung was entitled 'Generalissimo'.

A neutral stance was generally taken in relations with China and the Soviet Union, although North Korea has warmed to post-Tiananmen China more than the Soviet Union, which exchanged embassies with South Korea on 1 January 1991 (President Roh Tae Woo of South Korea met Gorbachev in San Francisco on 4 June 1990 and visited Moscow in December; the decision to establish diplomatic relations was made on 30 September and Gorbachev visited South Korea 19– 20 April 1991). After the 9 October 1983 assassination, through bombing, of seventeen South Korean members of President Chun Doo Hwan's delegation (including three ministers) in Rangoon (Burma), North Korea performed the unlikely act the following year of providing aid relief (chiefly rice, clothing, cement and medicine) to the September flood victims in the South (in July 1990 North Korea accepted rice from a South Korean charity, albeit indirectly via Hong Kong and financed by Korean-Americans). In 1985 the first family exchange visits took place, specifically thirty North Koreans and thirty-five South Koreans; a second reunion was arranged for August 1992. The Democratic People's Republic did not participate in the Seoul Olympics, which opened 17 September 1988. The aim had been to co-host the games, but only five sports were offered. The only other non-participants were Albania, Cuba, Ethiopia, Nicaragua and the Seychelles. In 1972 the South Korean intelligence chief exchanged visits with the North Korean deputy prime minister, but this was topped by a series of meetings in 1990 between the two prime ministers (4–7 September in Seoul; 16–19 October in Pyongyang; and 11–14 December in Seoul). Little was actually achieved (some joint sports teams were agreed in February 1991 for international competitions), but the meetings themselves were significant. North Korea refused to attend the planned February 1991 talks in protest at military exercises in South Korea, but in late May North Korea decided to follow the South's example and apply for separate UN membership in time for the new session starting on 17 September 1991 (previously the North's policy was for a single, rotating seat). Talks resumed in October and the two sides agreed to draft a single comprehensive agreement (on 'reconciliation, non-agression, exchange and co-operation') and to meet again in December 1991). The agreement was ratified in February 1992. North Korea started talks with Japan in late September 1990. The success of the US-led allied forces in the 1991 Gulf War had a sobering effect on North Korea.

The autumn of 1991 saw considerable political movement internationally. On 28 October the USA agreed to pull all nuclear weapons out of South Korea by April 1992 (President Roh Tae Woo actually declared that this had been achieved in the South on 18 December 1991). The two Korean prime ministers met in South Korea 10–13 December and signed 'The Agreement on Reconciliation, Non-aggression and Exchanges, and Co-operation'. Among the aspects covered were direct economic exchanges and improved communications. The nuclear issue was to be discussed separately, South Korea making ratification of the accord dependent on the North accepting inspection of its nuclear facilities. On 31 December 1991 both countries initialled a draft agreement banning nuclear weapons from the peninsula. Both the December accords were signed in February by President Roh Tae Woo and President Kim Il Sung and went into effect on the 19th of the month after the 19–20 February 1992 meeting of the prime ministers. On 30 January 1992 North Korea signed an agreement to allow inspection of its nuclear installations by the International Atomic Energy Agency (which the North had joined in 1985). It was ratified on 9 April subject to a Korean peninsula free of nuclear weapons. The USA started talks with North Korea on 22 January 1992. The presidents of North and South were due to meet in March in the North.

North Korea was concerned at the expanding links between socialist countries and South Korea even before the freeing of Eastern Europe. South Korea's trade with China, initially indirect via Hong Kong and Japan especially, started in 1979 and there has been something of a history of joint ventures since 1985 (Jae Ho Chung, Asian Survey, 1988, vol. XXVIII, no. 10, pp. 1034, 1042). This trade has been estimated at $1.5 billion in 1987, compared with Sino-North Korean trade worth only $519.4 million (Delfs, FEER, 8 December 1988, pp. 21–2). In 1990 the respective figures were $3.85 billion ($5.8 billion in 1991) and $480 million (EIU Country Report, 1992, no. 1, p. 43). South Korea opened a trade office in Beijing in January 1991 and vice versa in Seoul in March; MFN treatment was mutually granted. The two countries even established diplomatic relations on 24 August 1992. Soviet–South Korean trade, which started informally in the late 1970s, increased from $48 million in 1983 to $889 million in 1990 (Byung-Joon Ahn, Asian Survey, 1991, vol. XXXI, no. 9, p. 819).

President Kim Il Sung practises a strong cult of personality and his policy of Chuch'e (Juche) or 'self-reliance' means that man is capable of mastering his own environment. According to Terry McCarthy (The Independent, 15 April 1992, p. 12), Chuch'e was first mentioned by the president in a 1955 speech. This policy made North Korea one of the most isolated of the socialist countries. Kim Il Sung has described *Chuch'e* as 'holding fast to the principle of solving for oneself all the problems of the revolution and construction in conformity with the actual conditions at home and mainly by one's own efforts. . . . man, a social being that is independent and creative, is master of everything and decides everything' (quoted in Rhee, Asian Survey, 1987, vol. XXXVII, no. 8, p. 890). This stresses the human factor in development and downgrades the importance of material incentives. Also downgraded is the importance of foreign trade and its accompanying specialization, owing to the fear of possible domination by larger powers. Originally the idea was that the superiority of socialism would be demonstrated and this would aid reunification (Gills 1992: 107); political independence requires economic independence (p. 111). Other aspects include the avoidance of imitating foreign models (Van Ree 1989: 52), immunity from world economic crises, and using available resources whenever possible, e.g. producing fertilizers from coal (Halliday 1987: 28). In recent years, however, there has been greater stress on foreign trade, capital and technology, especially with and from Western countries. The Third Seven Year Plan 1987–93 saw trade increasing almost twice as fast as national income (Mark Clifford and Sophie Quinn-Judge, *FEER*, 29 November 1990, p. 32). In January 1984 Kim Il Sung expressed an interest in expanding links with 'friendly' Western states (Rhee, Asian Survey, 1987, vol. XXXVII, no. 8, p. 888), a call repeated at the Democratic Republic's fortieth anniversary celebrations some four years later. Kim Jong Il called for stricter implementation of an 'independent accounting system of enterprises', a gradual increase in the managerial independence of state enterprises, greater use of economic criteria in decision-making and improved worker incentives, although there has been no notable decline in party influence (Koh, *Asian Survey*, 1988, vol. XXVIII, no. 1, p. 63).

North Korea has reacted predictably to the events in Eastern Europe since the end of 1989. Kim Il Sung, in a 14 March 1990 speech, said that 'We will hoist high the banner of the revolution, without any wavering, against imperialism and in favour of socialism' (quoted by Kie-Young Lee 1990: 8). On the occasion of his being made president for another four years on 24 May 1990, he said that socialism 'is the main trend of historical progress and this is the only road for mankind to take'.

Development strategy has been dominated by a stress on heavy industrialization (especially machinery), with light industry and agriculture developed together. During the 1954–56 Three Year Plan 81 per cent of industrial investment was devoted to heavy industry, while over the period 1961–76 the figure remained at about the same level (Van Ree 1989: 60–1). The Third Seven Year Plan was begun in April 1987 after a delay of two years,[2] with the following elements: (1) increases in gross industrial output by 1.9 times, gross agricultural output by 1.4 times, national income by 1.7 times and the value of foreign trade by 3.2 times, with grain output increasing by 50 per cent to 15 million tonnes by 1993, coal output rising from 70 million tonnes to 120 million tonnes and 300,000 ha of tideland to be reclaimed by 1993; (2) the basic task is to lay the material and technical foundation for the victory of socialism by following *Chuch'e*, modernization and science and technology; (3) the plan aims to solve the problems of clothing, feeding and housing the people (Koh, Asian Survey, 1988, vol. XXVIII, no. 1, pp. 62–3). In a report on the new Seven Year Plan, Prime Minister Yi Kun-mo warned against overemphasis on economic management and material incentives at the expense of political work (p. 64).

Selig Harrison (*IHT*, 27 November 1987, p. 4) concluded, on the basis of a visit to North Korea (23 September – 2 October 1987), that economic pressure seemed to be forcing North Korea into reducing military spending by means of an improvement in relations with South Korea and the United States and into allowing rapid importation of advanced industrial technology via a Chinese-style economic opening to the West.[3] In January 1988, however, the United States, accepting the evidence of North Korean involvement in the destruction of a South Korean airliner in November 1987, added North Korea to its list of countries that support terrorism (alongside Iran, Libya, Syria, Cuba and South Yemen), with adverse economic consequences for any future links (e.g. the USA voting against loans by international organizations).

ECONOMIC BACKGROUND

In the 1930s the area now constituting the North was more rapidly industrialized, especially in terms of heavy industry, than the South (Suh 1983: 199). In 1943 80 per cent of the North's gross industrial production was heavy (Van Ree 1989: 54). In 1945 the North's share of total Korean production was as follows: heavy industry 65 per cent; light industry 31 per cent; agriculture 37 per cent; commerce 18 per cent (Halliday 1987: 19). In 1946 agriculture contributed almost 60 per cent of national product (Yoon 1986: 61), while more than 90 per cent of industrial establishments were nationalized (Chung 1986: 189). The population was 21.7 million in 1990 (compared with 42.8 million for the South), nearly 70 per cent being urbanized. Energy needs are dominated by coal (75 per cent), backed up by hydro-electric power (15

per cent), with a deliberately low importance attached to oil (10 per cent), which the country lacks (figures quoted by Halliday 1987: 30). Minerals include coal, iron ore and non-ferrous metals such as gold, silver, zinc and lead.

The dearth of official statistics makes any real assessment difficult (see Table 7.1). *The Economist* (18 April 1992, p. 62) estimates that as recently as 1973 *per capita* GNP in North Korea may have been higher than in South Korea. In the mid-1980s the World Bank described North Korea as a lower middle-income economy, with a $900 *per capita* income, well above that of Vietnam ($150) and China ($300). The EIU *Country Report* (1988, no. 1, p. 38) estimates that *per capita* GNP was $2,296 in South Korea, compared with only $860 in North Korea, in 1986. The official North Korean figure for national income per head in 1986 was $2,400 (*EIU Country Report*, 1989, no. 1, p. 40) and in 1990 $2,530 (Rhee Sang-Woo, *Asian Survey*, 1992, vol. XXXII, no. 1, p. 58). A more recent estimate by *The Economist* (18 April 1992, p. 62) puts North Korea's *per capita* GNP in 1990 at $1,064, compared with South Korea's $5,569, while Robert Corzine (*FT Survey on Korea*, 27 May 1992, p. iv) cites an estimate for the North for that year of $27.3 billion for total GNP and $1,273 for GNP per head. In 1989 North Korea's GNP was $21.1 billion and *per capita* GNP $987, compared to South Korea's $210.1 billion and $4,968 respectively (Rhee Sang-Woo, *Asian Survey*, 1991, vol. XXXI, no. 1, p. 72). Rhee Sang-Woo (*Asian Survey*, 1992, vol. XXXII, no. 1, p. 58) cites Jeong Kap-young's estimate of $1,082–$1,620 for North Korea's *per capita* GDP

Table 7.1 North Korea: average annual rate of growth national income (%)

1954–56	1957–61	1961–70	1971–5	1976–80	1981–84	1986	1987	1988	1989	1990	1991
30.1	20.9	7.5	10.4	4.1	4.3	2.1	2.5	2.9	2.0	−3.7	−5.2

Source: Chung (1983: 172); Lee (1988: 1267); Economist Intelligence Unit, *Country Report* (19898, no. 4, p. 33); L. do Rosario, *FEER*, 10 October 1991, p. 75; R. Pauley, *FT*, 21 March 1989, p. 4; Rhee Sang-Woo, *Asian Survey*, 1991, vol. XXXI, no. 1; 1992, vol. XXXII, no. 1, p.58; Economist Intelligence Unit, *Country Report* (1992, no. 3, p. 5).

in 1989. One of the world's dramatically successful newly industrialized countries (NICs), South Korea vividly illustrates the relative inertia and technological lag experienced by socialist economies in general and their desperate need to attract foreign capital and technology. This is not to underestimate North Korea's achievement, especially its industrial development, compared with that of other socialist countries, after substantial destruction in the Korean War. In 1985 a 220 per cent increase in industrial ouput was reported for the period 1977–84. National income increased 1.8 times over the period 1978–84 (Suh, *Asian Survey*, 1986, vol. XXVI, no. 1, p. 84).

North Korea is believed to be spending about 22 per cent of GNP on defence, compared with close to 4 per cent in South Korea (Tong Whan Park, *Asian Survey*, 1992, vol. XXXII, no. 4, p. 363). A lower proportion (11.6 per cent) of the state budget was allocated to defence in 1992 than in the year before (12.1 per cent). North Korea has one of the world's largest standing armies.[4]

ECONOMIC PLANNING

North Korea has a rigid command economy, with economic plans containing very detailed output targets for each industrial enterprise (Pak 1983: 214). The 'unified and detailed planning' system introduced after 1964 increased central control. Rationing is, in fact, more common than in the traditional economic system in more normal times, with the workshop and residential areas used as means of distributing highly subsidized basic commodities (e.g. rice). As regards manpower, moral incentives are stressed, and school leavers are allocated in groups to particular jobs. Income tax was abolished in 1974. In 1958 a sort of Chinese-style Great Leap Forward was begun, involving a mass mobilization of people inspired by moral rather than material incentives. In February 1973 the 'Three Revolution Teams' (ideological, technological

and cultural) were initiated. Teams of young people were sent to enterprises to encourage workers to greater effort and to teach them new techniques (Rhee, *Asian Survey*, 1987, vol. XXXVII, no. 8, pp. 899–900). Campaigns and the accompanying exhortations are still a feature of economic decision-making. A campaign to save materials began in 1986 (*EIU Country Report*, 1989, no. 3, p. 34). In 1974 there was a 'seventy day battle', in 1980 a 'hundred day battle' and between 20 February and 9 September 1988 a 'two-hundred day battle', the last concentrating on major construction projects in energy, the metal industry and chemicals. Another 'two-hundred day battle' ran from September 1988 to April 1989. Electricity, coal and steel are seen as the key to the successful fulfilment of the Third Seven Year Plan (1987–93), and agricultural success involves increased irrigation, electrification, mechanization and chemicalization (the so-called four 'technical revolutions') (*EIU Country Report*, 1988, no.2, p.37; Koh, *Asian Survey*, 1989, vol. XXIX, no. 1, p. 40). Kim Il Sung's new year address for 1990 called for a new 'speed of the 1990s' (a 'work harder' campaign) in production, involving e.g. the speedy completion of large projects (*EIU Country Report*, 1990, no. 2, p. 35), and for emphasis on light industry (Kong Dan Oh, *Asian Survey*, 1990, vol. XXX, no. 1, p. 75). In 1990 electricity, coal, steel and foodstuffs were stressed (Rhee Sang-Woo, *Asian Survey*, 1991, vol. XXXI, no. 1, p. 73). A 'hundred and fifty day campaign' related to lead and zinc production started in August 1991 (*EIU Country Report*, 1991, no. 3, p. 38).

The First Five Year Plan actually ran from 1957 to 1960 and the First 'Seven Year Plan' from 1961 to 1970. The Six Year Plan covered the period 1971–76. Between the seven-year plans for 1978–84 and 1987–93 no annual economic plans were launched. The Third Seven Year Plan emphasizes light industry and agricultural modernization (Kie-Young Lee 1990: 4), and greater efficiency in general.

ECONOMIC MANAGEMENT

There have been periodic ministerial re-organizations. The late 1950s saw amalgamations, while in the latter half of the 1980s there was a reverse process. In January 1990 the Mining Industry Commission was divided into a Ministry of the Coal Industry and a Ministry of the Mining Industry, while the previous July saw a new Ministry of Local Industry established.

Since 1961 the 'Taean (Dae-an) Work System' has been in operation (Kang 1989: 204–5; *EIU Country Report*, 1988, no. 2, pp. 294–5). This was first applied to an electrical engineering enterprise. The industrial enterprise is run by a Factory Party Committee rather than an individual manager. The committee normally comprises twenty-five to thirty-five members, with managers, engineering staff and workers equally represented. Its executive board of six to nine people carries out day-to-day operations, and is dominated by the party secretary and managers. The party secretary's decision is final.

Some modest enterprise reforms were introduced in late 1984, with greater emphasis on economic accounting, some increased decision-making autonomy and an increased role for material incentives (Kang 1989: 206). Increased decision-making autonomy includes greater powers to fix bonus rates and other incentives; to decide the share of profits to reinvest; and to allocate manpower, equipment and materials. Material incentives are boosted by the power to devote up to 50 per cent of excess profits (compared with 20 per cent previously) to increasing output and welfare and other benefits (*EIU Country Report*, 1985, no. 3, p. 34, and 1986, no. 2, p. 39). The enterprise success indicators include physical production, exports, profits, costs and inputs, but physical indicators have top priority, followed by exports (Kang 1989: 206).

Labour compensation consists of the basic wage, bonuses and prizes (Kang 1989: 206–7; Kie-Young Lee 1990: 4). The basic wage takes account of factors such as job evaluation, length of service and technical ability. Bonuses, paid to work teams, depend on over-fulfilment of plan targets (e.g. cost reductions), while prizes can also be paid to individuals as well as used for collective incentives. The EIU *Country Report* (1985, no. 3, p. 34) notes that, within some enterprises, teams of four to six workers plan their own work schedules and determine their bonus rates.

Kang (1989: 202) reports some spread of the 'associated enterprise system', there having been experiments since 1975. The experiments involved linking geographically adjacent and related enterprises in order to save time and transport costs (Kie-Young Lee 1990: 4). The EIU *Country Report* (1986, no. 2, p. 39) describes the 1985 reforms as akin to the former GDR combines, in the sense that enterprises in related areas of activity (e.g. supplier–user) are encouraged to co-ordinate their operations in a formal manner, thus easing the materials supply system. The regionally based complex reports to the provincial party committee, while the vertically integrated complex has a central party committee to answer to (*EIU Country Report*, 1989, no. 4, p. 35).

Each enterprise pays a depreciation allowance and a capital charge (Kang 1989: 206). Some enterprises are allowed to export their own products and import the necessary materials with the foreign exchange so earned (Kie-Young Lee 1990: 6).

Rhee (*Asian Survey*, 1987, vol. XXXVII, no.8, p. 889) reports the August 1984 mass movement to increase basic consumer goods production by teams of part-time workers from locally available inputs such as waste and by-products. According to Lee (*Asian Survey*, 1988, vol. XXVIII, no. 12, p. 1268), small groups of workers in industrial enterprises, in co-operative farms and at home produce basic necessities for direct sale to consumers in markets. The EIU *Country Profile* for 1988–89 notes that provinces are responsible for consumer goods production, receiving no central investment but having to transfer tax revenue (p. 72).

AGRICULTURE

In the March 1946 agrarian reform land was redistributed to the tillers. Land was confiscated without payment from landlords who leased land to tenants (62.1 per cent of total arable land confiscated, itself 54 per cent of total arable land); landlords owning more than five hectares (23.8 per cent); Japanese (11.3 per cent); the church (1.5 per cent); and national traitors and expatriates (1.3 per cent). Those benefiting were landless peasants (61.5 per cent), small land-owning peasants (35.2 per cent), agricultural employees (2.3 per cent), and landlords who returned to farms (1.0 per cent). The land reform took less than a month to complete (Pak 1983: 216–17). Large landlords were allowed to own the same size of farm as the rest on condition that they moved to another district; most, however, went to the South (Halliday 1987: 22).

Collectivization spanned the period 1954–58, moving Chinese-style through three types of co-operatives. There were increasing degrees of co-operative activity, ranging from the pooling of labour and some collective use of implements and animals to the distribution of income based solely on work contribution. Co-operatives were designated 'collectives' in 1962, and each collective is broken down into work brigades (specializing in activities such as crops, livestock and machines) and these in turn into work teams ('specialized', 'mixed', or 'all-purpose') (Pak 1983: 217–19). According to the EIU (*Country Profile*, 1988–89, p. 66) there are now 'sub-work teams', where three or four families are allocated a piece of crop land and the necessary implements.

In 1970 land used by the collective farms accounted for 94 per cent of all arable land, while the state farm figure was 4 per cent. Note that all natural resources and forests were nationalized in 1947. There are still agricultural machine stations (Pak 1983: 222). Private plots are 0.02 of an acre (0.008 ha) at most (before 1977, 0.04 of an acre or 0.016 ha), but peasants were, until recently, only allowed to consume the produce themselves and not to sell it on markets (*EIU Country Profile*, 1987–88, p. 59). The EIU (*Country Report*, 1988, no. 1, p. 38), however, states that farmers' markets are now held two or three times a month, for an hour or so, for the sale of produce grown on the tiny plots (some 200 square metres each) and household goods manufactured by 'sideline work teams'. Urban workers help at harvest time. Koh (*Asian Survey*, 1988, vol. XXVIII, no. 1, p. 64) detects no measurable increase in the sphere of individual initiative, while official rhetoric still underlines the need to convert co-operatives into state farms. The increase in agricultural output is to be attained not through greater incentives but via an increase in cultivable land, mechanization and the use of chemical fertilizers.

Economic policy (Pak 1983) has, in general, given priority to heavy industry, but light industry and agriculture have been developed together. Industry provides support for agriculture in order to industralize it. Intensive farming is practised, especially involving the use of fertilizers and mechanization, and there are large infrastructural schemes – irrigation to protect against the effect of drought, and land reclamation, including land from the sea. Moral incentives have been stressed. The *Ch'ollima* ('flying horse') movement, which began in 1958, mimicked the Chinese Great Leap Forward in that it was designed to increase productivity by means of stress on ideological incentives to work hard. After the middle of the 1960s the work brigade was stressed (Pak 1983: 223–4). The *Ch'ongsalli* method of managing co-operative farms, started in 1960, stressed party direction of agriculture, strong one-man management, and ideological motivation, and established work brigades and teams (p. 224).

Harrison (*FEER*, 3 December 1987, p. 38) sees retrogression in policy. For example, he argues that there has been a recent decline in the autonomy enjoyed by co-operative farms: this has the aim of turning over control of co-operative property to the state in order to end the class differences between workers and farmers. Aidan Foster-Carter (*FEER*, 29 November 1990, p. 35) too sees a move to full state ownership during the next few years, with workers being paid a wage. The national agriculture conference held 10–13 January 1990 stressed the 'superiority of the socialist agricultural system', while calling for a more efficient use of resources (*IHT*, 16 January 1990, p. 15).

FOREIGN TRADE, DEBT AND INVESTMENT

Trade and foreign debt

Economic links with South Korea were largely severed and the commission set up in 1985 to deal with the re-establishment of commercial links became bogged down by intense rivalry. Nevertheless, the two countries have started to trade (albeit indirectly via third countries) on a small scale, with no duties on the North's imports into South Korea (Maggie Ford, *FT*, 17 January 1989, p. 6; Susan Chira, *IHT*, 2 February 1989, p. 1, and 3 February 1989, p. 2; *EIU Country Report*, 1989, no. 1, p. 31). The cumulative total of inter-Korean trade amounted to only $88.25 million in the two and a half years following its restart in October 1988; direct trading agreements began to be signed in December 1990 by enterprises from the North and South (*EIU Country Report*, 1991, no. 2, pp. 40–1). It was not until 27 July 1991 that North Korea actually officially recognised that direct trade had taken place (the first since 1948), specifically an exchange of southern rice for northern coal and cement (Shim Jae Hoon, *FEER*, 22 August 1991, p. 21); two-way trade volume was $23.34 million in 1989 and $25.61 million in 1990 (p. 24). In 1991 the volume of North-South trade was $192 billion, only 0.1 per cent of South Korea's total trade (*The Economist*, 4 July 1992, p. 75).

The policy of 'self-reliance' extended also to Comecon, where the country had only observer status, preferring industrialization and rejecting integration and specialization in minerals. It relied on the Soviet Union and China, however, for machinery, oil, coal and modern arms. The Soviet Union also built plants in exchange for a percentage of the output. In contrast, Vietnam changed strategy after the 1975 reunification and China after the Cultural Revolution.

In 1984 it was decided to pay greater attention to foreign trade, although three years later foreign trade totalled only $4 billion as compared with $88 billion for South Korea (Robin Pauley, *FT*, 21 March 1989, p. 4). Despite a policy of 'self-reliance', and in order to modernize its capital stock, North Korea purchased Western technology, machinery, equipment and even whole plants on a grand scale in the early 1970s. In the period 1970–82 80 per cent of imports and 48 per cent of exports were with capitalist countries (quoted in Rhee, *Asian Survey*, 1987, vol. XXXVII, no. 8, p. 901). A debt of about $2 billion with the West (about $3 billion in total) had been run up by 1982 (*EIU Country Profile*, 1987–88, p. 68).[5] Western banks' loans in the mid-1970s were used to finance infrastructural investments such as roads. By the end of 1987 $2.8 billion was owed to Western countries ($5.27 billion in total) (Kie-Young Lee 1990: 3). By the end of 1989 the gross foreign debt was $6.8 billion; $2.74 billion was owed to Western countries and $4 billion to communist countries ($3.1 billion to the Soviet Union alone) (*EIU Country Report*, 1991, no. 2, p. 40). The official Soviet figure for debt owed to the Soviet Union alone was 2.2 billion roubles as of 1 November 1989 (*CDSP*, 1990, vol. XLII, no. 9, p. 9). More recent estimates put North Korea's debt to the Soviet Union at some $4 billion (*EIU Country Report*, 1991, no. 3, p. 29) and 2.7 billion roubles (Louise do Rosario, *FEER*, 10 October 1991, p. 75).

North Korea defaulted in 1976,[6] the causes including the fall in mineral exports after 1974 and the difficulties in exporting manufactured products (Suh 1983: 209). Several debt reschedulings and delayed payments for imports have made North Korea a poor credit risk. Between March 1984 and June 1988 North Korea paid neither interest nor principal, but even before the former date interest payments were irregular (the last before that being in 1979) and principal repayments were nonexistent. In September 1986 Japan's Ministry of International Trade and Industry compensated domestic firms for their trade losses with North Korea (Koh, *Asian Survey*, 1988, vol. XXVIII, no. 1, p. 64), and in August of the following year Western commercial bank creditors declared a formal default. This allows the seizure, in that case by Swiss and British courts, of North Korean assets in the West such as gold and property. The debts were consolidated into two bank syndicates. North Korea was forced into a reopening of rescheduling talks in September 1988. A scheme suggested by one of the syndicates in June 1988 involves the following (a token initial repayment of $5 million was made on 1 July): a new loan of $900 million, with a formal North Korean government guarantee;[7] a separate schedule of payments on the so-called settlement loan (30 per cent of the $900 million), on which a fixed interest rate of 8 per cent is payable, with a final payment due on 15 December 1991. If this repayment schedule is maintained, the remaining 70 per cent will be written off; otherwise the whole $900 million will fall due. The scheme, however, led to disagreement between the bank syndicates (Fidler 1988: 25).

The Soviet Union's share of North Korea's foreign trade rose from around a quarter in the early 1980s to about 55 per cent in 1985. Non-ferrous metals, including gold, are important exports, especially for earning hard currencies. In 1987 work was being carried out on fourteen major Soviet-assisted industrial projects, including a plan to build a nuclear power station. Sixty-four major industrial projects have already been undertaken in the past forty years with Soviet aid (Koh, *Asian Survey*, 1988, vol. XXVIII, no. 1, p. 64). Van Ree (1989: 57) estimates that over the period 1957–76 the Soviet Union may have provided, on average, more than 10 per cent of total industrial investment in the form of grants and credits; aid from the socialist countries in total may have brought this figure up to 25 per cent. The long-term programme for economic and technical co-operation to the year 2000 sees North Korea providing labour in particular for construction and food production in the Soviet Far East (Quinn-Judge, *FEER*, 8 December 1988, p. 22). The 28 April 1991 trade agreement with the Soviet Union talked about a 'transition' to payments in convertible currency at world prices, which implied a Soviet concession regarding the 1 January Comecon rule (*EIU Country Report*, 1991, no. 2, p. 39). But trade with the Soviet Union fell dramatically in 1991. According to Rhee Sang-Woo (*Asian Survey*, 1992, vol. XXXII, no. 1, p. 59), imports from the Soviet Union in the period January-end July were only 1.2 per cent of the volume in the same period of 1990. China became the only country providing economic assistance to North Korea (p. 59).

The stress on self-reliance has been modified over time, with the foreign trade–income ratio 20 per cent in 1954–60, 19.2 per cent in 1961–70, 21.9 per cent 1971–77, and 21.4 per cent 1978–84 (Kie-Young Lee 1990: 12). There have also been marked changes in the importance of trade with the other socialist countries over time, falling from 99.6 per cent in 1955 to a low of 60.6 per cent for exports in 1975 and a low of 45.9 per cent for imports in 1974 (Chung 1986: 84). In terms of commodity structure exports during the 1950s consisted of more than 70 per cent mineral ores and during the 1960s and 1970s manufactured goods (mainly metals and pig iron), and inedible raw materials such as mineral ores and silk, more than 60 per cent. Among imports during 1970 machinery and transport equipment were the biggest items, followed by mineral fuels and food (Suh 1983: 208).

In 1986 North Korea opened up to tourists[8] in the drive to earn convertible currencies, and two years later (in October) South Korea lifted its trade embargo and allowed northern goods in duty-free. The United States followed with a slight easing of its trade embargo, imposed in 1950, allowing North Korean purchases of humanitarian items such as medicines.

Joint equity ventures

In September 1984 a joint venture law was promulgated in order to attract Western capital, technology and know-how, but with limited success to date. One hundred per cent foreign ownership is now permitted; the first three years constitute a tax holiday, with a possible extension; there is a 25 per cent net profit tax (Kie-Young Lee 1990: 6). Harrison (*FEER*, 3 December 1987, p. 38) estimates that fifty are under way (forty-four with Japanese-Koreans) (Table 7.2). Kie-Young Lee (1990: 7) thinks that the partners are mostly pro-North Korea businessmen in Japan (the Chongryun organization represents Korean residents in Japan; also known as Soren, the General Association of Korean Residents in Japan) and Korean residents in the USA; in the first half of 1985 there were almost seventy and by the end of 1987 100. The North Korean International Joint Venture General Company was founded in August 1986 in partnership with Japanese Koreans. This is a sort of holding company which both establishes and acquires other enterprises (Lee, *Asian Survey*, 1988, vol. XXVIII, no.12, p. 1264). There are now 100 joint ventures in North Korea (plus thirty overseas), over seventy of the 100 involving Chongryun entrepreneurs (*EIU Country Report*, 1991, no. 4, p. 40). From 1984 to the end of 1990 135 projects had been initiated, of which seventy-seven were with Korean-Japanese companies (Rhee Sang-Woo, *Asian Survey*, 1992, vol. XXXII, no. 1, p. 59).

Minerals and high technology are the areas favoured, but actual examples include hotel construction (France), clothing, food processing, car components, construction materials, chemical products, and department stores (Japan – mostly Japanese-Koreans) (Rhee, *Asian Survey*, 1987, vol. XXXVII, no. 8, p. 888). For example, the Rakwon (Paradise) department store is operated by Japanese-Koreans. Purchases, however, are restricted to hard

Table 7.2 North Korea: statistical survey

Average annual rate of growth of national income (%)											
1954–56	1957–61	1961–70	1971–75	1976–80	1981–84	1986	1987	1988	1989	1990	1991
30.1	20.9	7.5	10.4	4.1	4.3	2.1	2.5	2.9	2.0	−3.7	−5.2

Foreign debt ($ billion)		
	1982	1987	1989
Total:	3.0	5.27	7.87
West alone:	2.0	2.8	

Population (1990)
21.7 million (South Korea 42.8 million)

Sources: Chung (1983: 172); Suh, *Asian Survey*, 1986, vol. XXVI, no. 1, p. 84; S. Harrison, *FEER*, 3 December 1987, p. 38; L. do Rosario, *FEER*, 10 October 1991, p. 75; Shim Jae Hoon, *FEER*, 22 August 1991, p. 21, 24; Kie-Young Lee (1990: 3, 7); Rhee Sang-Woo, *Asian Survey*, 1991, vol. XXXI, no. 1, p. 72; Economist Intelligence Unit, *Country Profile* (1987–88: 68); *Country Report* (1989, no. 4, p. 33); *The Economist*, 18 April 1992, p. 62; Economist Intelligence Unit, *Country Report* (1992, no. 3, p. 5).

currency spenders such as foreign diplomats and privileged North Koreans who possess the 'red won' (a special form of currency with a red stamp), which can be converted into hard currency (Harrison, *FEER*, 3 December 1987, p. 37). There are also joint ventures with socialist countries, including a shipping enterprise with Poland, joint Soviet–North Korean timber projects in Siberia and four joint Chinese–North Korean power stations. A joint venture with the Soviet Union for the production of lathes in North Korea came into operation in 1989, while a sea-food joint venture with China was set up on North Korean soil in the same year. In early February 1989 it was announced that the first North–South Korean joint ventures, situated in North Korea, had been agreed upon in principle, involving the development of a tourist area, a ship repair yard and a railway rolling stock plant. The South Korean government vetoed the last two, however, on security grounds, while North Korea has frozen the other (kindly pointed out by Aidan Foster-Carter). In January 1992 North and South Korea agreed to set up the first joint business ventures to manufacture textiles and other consumer goods (*IHT*, 27 January 1992, p. 7). Joint ventures account for only around 1 per cent of exports (Sophie Quinn-Judge, *FEER*, 11 January 1990, p. 20).

In July 1991 the UN Development Programme formally took up the idea which had been floating around of a special cross-border economic zone in the Tumen river estuary bordering China and the Soviet Union. A management committee was set up in October at a conference attended by North Korea, China and the Soviet Union as well as the UNDP itself. The 27–8 February 1992 meeting was attended by the UNDP, North Korea, South Korea, China and Mongolia. Russia and Japan also sent observers. A final development plan was hoped for by July 1993. A 'zone of free economy and trade' was created near the end of December 1991 in the north-east, including the ports of Najin and Sonbong; the city of Chongjin was also to have 'free port' status (*EIU Country Report*, 1992, no. 1, p. 41).

THE PRIVATE NON-AGRICULTURAL SECTOR

In 1985 individuals were allowed to engage in small private handicraft production such as in knitting (*EIU Country Report*, 1985, no. 3, p. 34). There are also a few street food and drink vendors, for example. The dominance of state and collective enterprises in the economy can be seen in the figures given by Suh (1983: 199) for 1946 and 1956, respectively: national income, 14.6 per cent and 85.8 per cent; manufacturing, 72.4 per cent and 98.7 per cent; agriculture (1949), 3.2 per cent, and 1956, 73.9 per cent.

CONCLUSION

North Korea is one of the most isolated socialist countries, adopting, for instance, a policy of *Chuch'e* or self-reliance. A rigidly controlled society and economy are subjected to the cult of personality of 'the great leader' Kim Il Sung and 'the dear leader', Kim Jong Il (the son and heir). North Korea is in the same position as the former GDR in being the poorer half of a divided nation, and it may not be a coincidence that both are (were) reluctant reformers. North Korea was, however, much more isolated than the GDR. The high cost of the German experience has made South Korea extremely wary of rapid reunification (James Sterngold, *IHT*, 31 May 1991, pp. 11, 15). North Korea retains a highly centralized economic system, and moral incentives are high on the agenda. Few reforms have been applied in either the industrial or the agricultural sector. The country has run into debt repayment problems, the private sector remains severely constrained, and the September 1984 joint venture legislation has produced only a limited response, mainly from Japanese citizens of Korean descent. The demise of the Soviet Union and socialist Eastern

Europe and the uniting of the two Germanies has put considerable pressure on North Korea to soften its foreign policy and external economic relations. Nevertheless, to date, little has changed in the nature of North Korean society and economy. South Korea's enthusiasm for rapid unification has been dampened by the German experience. South Korean estimates put the cost range of reunification at $200 billion to more than $500 billion over five to ten years (Shim Jae Hoon, *FEER*, 26 March 1992, p. 54); in 1991 South Korea's GNP was $270 billion, by way of comparison (p. 56). Nevertheless, on 16 April 1992 South Korea's president Roh Tae Woo said that he continued to hope for reunification by the end of the decade (*IHT*, 17 April 1992, p. 2). Gills (1992: 107–8) argues that both countries now fear reunification, the North because it would imply the victory of capitalism and the South because of the cost; the South's policy is now to avoid a collapse in the North which would make immediate reunification a possibility. Andrew Mack (*IHT*, 13 May 1992, p. 6) quotes estimates of the economic cost of reunification over a ten-year period of $200 billion to $300 billion and suggests that many South Koreans now prefer a China-type combination of economic liberalization and political stability in North Korea to ease the transition to eventual reunification. John Burton (*FT Survey on Korea*, 27 May 1992, p. III) cites the following estimates of the cost of reunification: if it occurred soon, $30 billion to $50 billion annually during the first decade; even if reunification were postponed until 2001 the South would need to spend $240 billion during the following decade; while Bonn is spending 10 per cent of its budget on reunification, South Korea would have to spend more than half its budget.The South Korean government's favoured path to economic integration is a process of increasing trade while replacing indirect trade with direct trade, co-operating on projects in the Tumen area, and direct investment in light manufacturing ventures in the North, especially in export-orientated sectors such as textiles and footware. If sufficient economic progress is made in North Korea, the cost to the South of reunification in 2001 would still be about $90 billion by the year 2010. The question is whether rapid reunification will be forced upon the South, given the possibility of political and economic collapse when Kim Il Sung dies.

NOTES

1. North Korean troops crossed the 38th parallel on 25 June 1945. Since July 1953 the two Koreas have been separated by the Demilitarized Zone, which runs to the south of the 38th parallel in the west and to the north in the east. North Korea occupies 55 per cent of the whole. There are 43,000 US troops in South Korea.
2. The Second Seven Year Plan (1978–84) and the Six Year Plan (1971–76) were also extended by two years.
3. See also an extended article in *FEER*, 3 December 1987.
4. There are 995,000 troops in uniform in total; the army is 868,000 strong. This compares with the South Korean armed forces of 655,000; the army is 540,000 strong (Tong Whan Park, *Asian Survey*, 1992, vol. XXXII, no. 4, p. 363). Nicholas Eberstadt and Judith Banister (*Asian Survey*, 1991, vol. XXXI, no. 11, p. 1111) argue that the North Korean armed forces could be as high as 1,249,000 and cite a US estimate of 1,040,000.
5. At the end of 1986 $2.23 billion was owed to the West and $1.83 billion to the socialist countries, mainly to the Soviet Union. Officially the hard currency debt is estimated at only $1 billion (Harrison, FEER, 3 December 1987, p. 38). The United States imposes a ban on loans to North Korea.
6. The end-of-year hard currency debt was $1.4 billion, with a further $1 billion owed to the socialist countries.
7. The Foreign Trade Bank, which signed the previous loan agreements, has been eclipsed by the Korea Gold Star Bank, which now handles most of the external economic relations.
8. Except those from Japan (ban lifted July 1987, reimposed in 1989 and lifted again in 1991), the United States, Taiwan, Israel and South Africa.

8

THE SOCIALIST REPUBLIC OF VIETNAM

POLITICAL BACKGROUND

France began the colonial period for Vietnam in 1858 with the capture of present-day Da Nang, seized Saigon in 1861, and formed the protectorates of Annam and Tonkin by 1883. On 19 August 1945 a communist government was first proclaimed in North Vietnam, without the assistance of external forces. War with France began the next year, following the reimposition of colonial rule. Recognition of the Democratic Republic of Vietnam by the socialist countries took place in January 1950. France's defeat at Dien Bien Phu in 1954 was followed by the Geneva Accords in July of the same year that divided Vietnam along the 17th parallel and promised elections within two years in order to create a unified government and country. Saigon fell to North Vietnamese forces in April 1975 after a long struggle with the United States and thirty years of war in total. The United States had withdrawn its combat troops by March 1973, although formal reunification as the Socialist Republic of Vietnam did not occur until 2 July 1976. The reunification then represented the only example of a socialist country incorporating a relatively large capitalist area. UN membership followed on 20 September 1977. Over the period 1976–78 there came about a unified financial system (including one currency), banking system and budget (Spoor 1988a: 104–5). The constant official aim has been 'to build socialism and defend the Fatherland'. One theme is that the imposition of the northern model on the South resulted in such serious problems that reforms became necessary from 1979 onwards (see, for example, Beresford 1988).

Ho Chi Minh (born around 1890) founded the Vietnamese Communist Party on 3 February 1930, and this became the Vietnamese Workers' Party in February 1951 and the Communist Party of Vietnam in 1976. He left in 1911 and did not return until until thirty years later, although communist resistance dated from the 1920s. Ho died on 2 September 1969 and was succeeded by a collective leadership under Le Duan. Le Duan died in July 1986, to be followed by a stop-gap General Secretary of the Workers' Party, Truong Chinh, and his replacement on 11 December, Nguyen Van Linh (who himself retired on 26 June 1991 owing to ill health). The Sixth Congress of the party in December 1986 was a major event in both a political and an economic sense. Many of those who had led the country to triumph in war gave way: Truong Chinh (who was also president), Pham Van Dong (premier) and Le Duc Tho (chief negotiator with the United States at the Paris talks which ended January 1973, who died 13 October 1990) left the politburo, although they were named as 'comrade advisers' to the new politburo and the Central Committee in January 1987. In June Pham Hung and Vo Chi, both in their mid-70s, became premier and president, respectively. The former died in March 1988; his stand-in was First Vice-Premier Vo Van Kiet. A new, more technocratic, and provincially based leadership was left to deal with economic problems so serious that the 'renovators' ('renovation' is *doi moi*, also translatable as 'renewal', 'transformation' or 'radical change') coined the phrase, 'The North won the war, the South must manage the economy.' Do Muoi (seventy-one) became premier in June 1988 (and General Secretary of the Communist Party on 26 June 1991).

Relations with China deteriorated to the extent of a border war in February 1979 after the December 1978 invasion of Kampuchea (Cambodia), which overthrew the tyrannical Pol Pot regime. Further clashes took place later on. A treaty of friendship and co-operation was signed with the Soviet Union on 3 November 1978. Vietnam built up the world's fifth largest military organization.[1]

The reaction of the Vietnamese leadership to the dramatic events in Eastern Europe since the end of 1989 has been to draw a clear distinction between political and economic liberalization. Multi-party democracy has been rejected and political reform has followed the line of separating party and state (thus reducing the interference of the former in the running of the latter), ending abuses such as special privileges and corruption, and forging closer links with the people. As in China, stability is considered a prerequisite to successful economic reform (relations with China have warmed substantially, spurred on by the failure of the Soviet coup in August 1991; pragmatically, on 27 December 1991 Vietnam extended diplomatic recognition to the independent states which emerged from the break-up of the Soviet Union). Apart from the vague reference to 'imperialist and reactionary forces', the demise of socialism in Eastern Europe is put down to the failure to implement Vietnamese-type reforms. The Draft Platform for the Building of Socialism in the Transition Period, which emerged from the 17–26 November 1990 Central Committee session in preparation for the June 1991 Seventh Party Congress, reaffirmed the commitment to socialism:

In certain countries the communist parties have lost their leading role. Hostile forces are taking advantage of these errors and difficulties to launch a counter-offensive with a view to abolishing socialism. . . . Socialism will regain its vitality and, regardless of the tortuous path ahead, will prevail. Obviously the fundamental contradiction of capitalism has not dwindled away, but rather has grown more and more acute and is bound to lead capitalism to inevitable disintegration.

(*The Economist*, 8 December 1990, p. 73)

The Seventh Party Congress itself took place 24–7 June 1991. The retiring General Secretary, Nguyen Van Linh, proclaimed that 'We affirm once again our wish to follow socialism under the clear-sighted leadership of the party'. A multi-party system would lead to chaos; economic renovation was the priority and political stability was necessary for this. Seven members of the old twelve-strong politburo lost their positions, including Linh (ill health) and the foreign minister, Nguyen Co Thach (owing to his anti-China stance and his failure to improve relations with the USA substantially). The membership of the politburo was raised to thirteen, the average age reduced to sixty-four and southern representation increased. Do Muoi became General Secretary, indicating basic continuity of policy.

At home there has been evidence of a tightening of political control, e.g. increased control of the press, more people sent to political re-education camps, and the dismissal of the liberal Tran Xuan Bach from the politburo on 28 March 1990 for stressing the need for political reform to accompany economic reform (including thinking about the idea of a multi-party system). On the other hand, there have been some interesting political developments, e.g. in March 1990 the Club of Former Resistance Fighters was officially recognized as the Vietnam Veterans' Association. This association forms an embryonic loyal opposition in that it pushes for greater reform in such forms as more openness and a freely elected prime minister.

On the international scene there has been substantial movement. On 18 July 1990 the USA announced that it was to open talks with Vietnam on Cambodia and was withdrawing diplomatic recognition from the three-faction coalition (including the Khmer Rouge) that held the UN seat; the USA had belatedly realized the danger of the Khmer Rouge regaining control of Cambodia. US Secretary of State James Baker met foreign minister Nguyen Co Thach on 29 September (the latter visited the USA the following month). As a result of the signing of the UN-sponsored Cambodian peace settlement on 23 October 1991, the USA agreed to open talks with Vietnam on normalizing relations. During the first week of September Nguyen Van Linh visited China, accompanied by prime minister Do Muoi and former prime minister Pham Van Dong (the UN Cambodian peace formula followed soon afterwards). General Vo Nguyen Giap visited China on 19 September. Border trade between Vietnam and China had been flourishing well before these visits. The Vietnamese foreign minister, Nguyen Manh Cam, visited China 8–12 September 1991; even more significantly Vo Van Kiet and Do Muoi followed 5–10 November.

ECONOMIC BACKGROUND

Before 1945 more than 90 per cent of the population lived in the countryside (the figure is still 80 per cent today). In 1989 the percentage distribution of the workforce was as follows: agriculture 70.9; industry 11.7; and trade 6.5 (*Vietnam Courier*, 1990, no. 14, p. 6). The 311,620 square kilometres of Vietnam are poorly endowed in terms of soil and are periodically hit by typhoons. In the mid-1980s only about 21 per cent of the land area was usable for agriculture. There is only 0.094 ha of cultivated land *per capita* (*Vietnam Courier*, 1990, no. 10, p. 11). This is the third lowest in the world after Singapore and Japan (Esterline, *Asian Survey*,

1988, vol. XXVIII, no. 1, p. 88). Of the total agricultural land, 80–85 per cent is devoted to rice (Dellmo *et al.* 1990: 9). The forested area was at one time almost halved since the early 1940s, partly the result of enormous wartime damage caused by mass bombings, land clearances, and defoliation through the use of 'Agent Orange'. The forested area, however, increased from 23.6 per cent in 1973 to 28.16 per cent in 1983 (*Vietnam Courier*, 1990, no. 10, p. 9). More recent figures are as follows: land used for agriculture, 21.13 per cent of the total area of 'natural land' (38.5 per cent of the total 'land in use') and 'natural land' used in forestry, 28.33 per cent (*Vietnam Courier*, 1991, no. 24, p. 11). The country is not generously endowed with raw materials (coal being the principal energy resource, accounting for about 90 per cent of energy output), but self-sufficiency in oil was expected by 1992 (crude oil output increased from 2.7 million tonnes in 1990 to 3.8 million tonnes in 1991: *Vietnam Courier*, 1991, no. 26, p. 4).

Some basic demographic details are to be found in *Vietnam Courier* (1990, no. 10, pp. 10–11).[2] The April 1989 census put the population at 64,411,668, compared with 22,155,000 in 1943. The birth rate in 1989 was 31.3 per thousand, while life expectancy two years earlier was sixty-two for males and sixty-seven for females. Between October 1979 and April 1989 the average annual population growth rate was 2.13 per cent. In early 1991 the population reached approximately 67 million; in 1988 the death rate was seven to eight per thousand, while a population control programme has been vigorously pursued since the early 1960s (*Vietnam Courier*, 1991, no. 22, p. 10). The population growth target of 1.7 per cent a year on average for the periods 1981–85 and 1986–1900 was not attained (Nguyen Tuong Lai and Nguyen Thanh Bang 1991: 87). In 1987 the population was 80.3 per cent rural and agriculture employed 72.6 per cent of the workforce (Fforde and de Vylder 1988: 51). There are fifty-four ethnic groups, but the Kinh account for

84 per cent of the population (*Vietnam Courier*, 1990, no. 12, p. 13). One of the major tasks after reunification was to socialize the economy of the South. The literacy rate today is a high 88 per cent, compared with only 5 per cent in 1945 (*The Economist*, 28 March 1992, p. 73).

In 1954 the North's economy was overwhelmingly agrarian and technologically backward, with only 1.5 per cent of material product originating in modern industry (Beresford 1988: 129, quoting Chau). Beresford points out the contrast between this and the economy of the South in 1975, where a third of the population was urbanized and there was a large, market-orientated farm sector, with a fairly egalitarian distribution of land ownership in the Mekong delta, the main rice producing area, after the 1970–72 reforms. There was a flourishing tertiary sector and a small, import-dependent manufacturing sector accounting for 11 per cent of GDP in 1960 and 6.5 per cent in 1972. When US aid was suddenly cut off there was immense dislocation (Beresford 1988: 147–55). By 1975 industry and mining accounted for 11 per cent of the workforce in the North (p. 60), with the same percentage of the population urbanized (p. 156).

Table 8.1 shows official statistics for rates of growth of national income and total agricultural output and for 'paddy and paddy equivalent' (rice and rice equivalent, i.e. food production) in millions of tonnes. Agricultural production declined in 1979 and 1980 (*Vietnam Courier*, 1987, no. 1, p. 4) and in 1987 food production fell by 2 per cent, available grain *per capita* declining from 304 kg in 1985 to 280 kg in 1987 (Hiebert, *FEER*, 14 January 1988, p. 48). Vu Khoan, Assistant Minister of Economic Affairs in the Foreign Ministry, said on 6 April 1988 that annual food production *per capita* was 620 lb (280 kg), compared with 748 lb in 1985. Farms were being divided into smaller units because of the lack of mechanized farm machinery such as tractors; the situation was aggravated by a fuel shortage (reported by Barbara Crossette in *IHT*, 7 April 1988, p. 6). Rice and equivalent output

fell in 1977 and 1978 (*Vietnam Courier*, 1987, no. 2, p. 18) and in 1987. In May 1988 there was official recognition that more than 3 million people in twelve northern provinces were living 'at the edge of starvation', while nearly 8 million in the North would be 'seriously short of food' until the next harvest (Hiebert, *FEER*, 26 May 1988, p. 18). Hiebert lists the causes of the stagnation in food production over the previous three years as natural disasters, shortages of fertilizers and pesticides and poor farm prices. *The Daily Telegraph* (12 July 1988, p. 9) quotes a Vietnamese source as saying that about 10 million people faced hunger, 4 million faced serious hunger and twenty-one people had died of starvation in various northern provinces. Conditions eased in early June when the new harvest began. Up to 1989 grain production remained below 300 kg *per capita*, considered the minimum subsistence level, with periodic food deficiency resulting (Ronnas and Sjöberg 1991b: 4). More recent developments are analysed in the section on agriculture below. Kimura (*Asian Survey*, 1986, vol. XXVI, no. 10, pp. 1043–4) notes the incomplete and unreliable nature of Vietnam's statistics. He draws a clearer distinction between the average annual growth rate achieved during the Second Five Year Plan period (1976–80) of 1.5 per cent and the 5.9 per cent figure for the Third Five Year Plan period (1981–85). Vietnam is classified as one of the poorest countries in the world in terms of *per capita* income (Kimura presents a range of Western estimates, varying between $125 and $200 in 1983–84; p. 1040). Finkelstein (*Asian Survey*, 1987, vol. XXVII, no. 9, p. 982) quotes the US Department of State's 1984 figure of $160. The official figure for *per capita* income in 1983 was $101 (Fforde and de Vylder 1988: 48); in 1990 *per capita* GDP was $210 (*Vietnam Courier*, 1991, no. 18, p. 4). The party's aim is to double GDP per person by the year 2000 (*The Economist*, 28 March 1992, p. 73).

Unemployment is a considerable problem. *The Economist* (28 July 1990, p. 49) puts the urban unemployment rate at 20 per cent. In

Prime Minister Do Muoi's 1 July 1990 speech to the National Assembly, an unemployment figure of 6 million out of a workforce of 30 million was quoted (Douglas Pike, *Asian Survey*, 1991, vol. XXXI, no. 1, p. 82). Nguyen Tuong Lai and Nguyen Thanh Bang (1991: 85) cite a figure of 34 million being of working age. According to the April 1989 census, the urban unemployment rate was 9.1 per cent, while in the countryside 'useful working time' is now only 50 per cent; there is no unemployment pay (*Vietnam Courier*, 1991, no. 22, p. 5). The *Vietnam Courier* (1990, no. 10, p. 11) talks about a million more young people reaching working age every year without being able to find jobs. A later edition (1991, no. 24, p. 8) estimates that out of the 34 million people of working age 1.7 million are jobless while underemployment

amounts to the equivalent of an extra 6 million unemployed.

The situation is being aggravated by demobilization and by the return of Vietnamese workers from Eastern Europe as their contracts are amended. The first contracts were signed in the early 1980s, one reason being to help Vietnam pay off its foreign debt. At peak there were over 200,000 workers in the Soviet Union and Eastern Europe (e.g. 103,000 in the Soviet Union, 71,000 in the GDR, 37,000 in Czechoslovakia and 27,000 in Bulgaria: for details see *Vietnam Courier*, 1990, no. 10, p. 7). Over the last ten years more than 250,000 young people have been sent; the current contracts with the former GDR, Czechoslovakia and Bulgaria expired on 31 December 1990 (*Vietnam Courier*, 1990, no. 12, p. 4).

Table 8.1 Vietnam: foreign debt and average annual rates of growth of national income, agricultural output and prices

Average annual rate of growth of national income (%)									
1955–65	1966–75	1976–80	1981–85	1986	1987	1988	1989	1990	1991
6.5	6.0	0.4	6.4	4.6	–	6.0	2.3	2.4	2.4

Average annual rate of growth of agricultural output (%)					
1960–65	1965–75	1976–80	1980–85	1986	1987
4.2	0.6	2.0	6.2	4.4	1.6

Paddy and paddy equivalent (rice and equivalent) (million tonnes)											
1976–80 (average)	1975	1982	1983	1984	1985	1986	1987	1988	1989	1990	1991
11.5	11.6	16.6	17.0	17.3	18.2	18.5	17.6	–	–	21.4	21.7

Inflation (%)										
1980	1982	1983	1984	1985	1986	1987	1988	1989	1990	1991
25.2	80.0	55.0	50.0	160.0	700.0	400.0	310.0	33.0	60–70	67.5

Foreign debt, 1989 ($billion)	
Non-convertible area	Convertible area
6.5	2.2

Sources: *Vietnam Courier*, 1987, no. 1, p. 4, no. 2, p. 18; 1990, no. 11, p. 1, no. 13, p. 8, no. 14 p. 6; 1991, no. 18, p. 7, no. 26, p. 7; 1992, no. 27, p.1; *EIU Country Profile*, 1987–88, p. 14); Esterline (1988: 91); *IHT*, 23 April 1990, p. 7; 8 December 1990, p. 17; 11 October 1991, p. 17; 11 December 1991, p. 14; Fforde and de Vylder (1988: 28, 32, 50, 135); R. Cima (*Asian Survey*, 1990, vol. XXX, no. 1, p. 93); Porter (1990: 80); M. Hiebert, *FEER*, 4 April 1991, p. 52; Tran Duc Nguyen (1991: 8, 30); Dellmo *et al.* (1990: 9); *FT Survey*, 14 November 1991, p.18; *FEER*, 24–31 December 1992, p. 56.

There has been a dramatic improvement on the inflation front, for reasons which are discussed below in the section on financial reforms. From a figure of over 700 per cent in early 1987 (Ronnas and Sjöberg 1991a: 12), inflation was reduced to 34 per cent in 1989 (Porter 1990: 80).

By the end of 1987 non-convertible debt to the socialist countries, especially the Soviet Union, amounted to $6.5 billion, which is partly being repaid by sending workers to Eastern Europe (Esterline, *Asian Survey*, 1988, vol. XXVIII, no. 1, p. 91). Moreover, debts of $2.7 billion were owed to about thirty countries and international organizations (p. 105). In 1981 foreign debt was $3 billion, the debt–service ratio was 77 per cent of total exports and 218 per cent of exports to the convertible currency area (Spoor 1988a: 109). Cima (*Asian Survey*, 1990, vol. XXX, no. 1, p. 93) cites 1989 debt to the non-convertible area at over $6 billion and to the convertible area at $2.2 billion. As of 1 November 1989 the Soviet Union claimed that Vietnam owed it 9.1 billion roubles (*CDSP*, 1990, vol. XLII, no. 9, p. 9). The Soviet Union has agreed to write off at least a third of this (Douglas Pike, *Asian Survey*, 1991, vol. XXXI, no. 1, p. 84). During the period 1955–64 China and the Soviet Union were roughly equally important aid donors. China cut off aid altogether after the 1978 invasion of Cambodia, but between 1979 and the mid-1980s Soviet aid ran at an average of about $2 billion annually, roughly equally divided between economic and military aid. Ligachev (the Soviet representative at the December 1986 congress) promised to double economic aid, mostly loans repayable over thirty years, over the next five years. This was despite open admission by the Vietnamese that much had been squandered on poorly chosen projects, delayed commissioning of plant, and so on, and despite Western pressure to use aid as a lever for troop withdrawal from Kampuchea. In his 1 July 1990 report to the National Assembly, Prime Minister Do Muoi noted that over the past five years the Soviet Union had given Vietnam about 10 billion roubles in assistance, credits, commodity aid, technical assistance and written-off loans; he said that the Soviet Union had indicated that aid would no longer continue on this scale (Douglas Pike, *Asian Survey*, 1991, vol. XXXI, no. 1, p. 83). 'Foreign aid and debts' made up 22 per cent of GNP 1976–80 and 10 per cent 1981–88, but there was a substantial reduction after 1989 (*Vietnam Courier*, 1991, no. 26, p. 4). Annually Vietnam received from the Soviet Union some $2 billion in materials, equipment and goods from aid funds and loans; in 1990 these aids were reduced to negligible amounts (p. 7). Elliott (1992: 131) reports an official estimate that in the past Soviet loans had amounted to 25–30 per cent of budgetary revenue, but in 1991 this had fallen to 6–7 per cent. Aid dried up when the Soviet Union ceased to exist.

The IMF cut off loans in January 1985 because of Vietnam's inability to pay off its debts, which then amounted to $34 million (since January 1989 the $40 million owed to the IMF has been repaid: *The Economist*, 8 December 1990, p. 74). The United States has imposed a trade embargo since May 1975; the only exception permitted is deliveries of humanitarian aid. In 1987 the United States agreed to urge private charities to help the war disabled, e.g. with artificial limbs. In April 1991 the US agreed to provide $1 million in the form of artificial limbs through various humanitarian groups; a temporary US office was also set up in Hanoi to investigate servicemen still missing in action in South East Asia. The UN World Food Programme has contributed only modest amounts. By early 1987 gold and foreign exchange reserves had fallen to $15 million (about two weeks' imports) (Esterline, *Asian Survey*, 1988, vol. XXVIII, no. 1, p. 88).

ECONOMIC PLANNING AND INDUSTRIAL REFORM

After the July 1954 Geneva agreement, early

phases of reform involved the 1955–57 'reconstruction' and creation of the 'national economy' and the 1958–60 Three-year Plan. During the period 1958–59 Ho Chi Minh was attracted by Maoist thought. Increased emphasis was given to mass mobilization methods (socialist emulation and political activation, consciousness raising and exhortation), and in October 1958 a new system of management was introduced: 'Cadres take part in work, workers take part in management.' This followed Ho's September suggestions that leading officials do one day's manual labour a week and the others half of each day, while workers should be trained in administration (see Post 1988: 143–50). Doubts about the efficacy of mass mobilization techniques had set in by the end of 1959, and Post sees the September 1960 Third Congress of the Workers' Party as marking a decisive shift, in that Vietnam definitely became caught up in the Soviet pattern. The following five year plan laid emphasis on skills and firm managerial control as the means of increasing production (Post 1988: 150).

During the 1970s there was a general shift towards the co-ordination of plans at the provincial level, which, in 1979, allowed provinces to retain a certain percentage of foreign exchange earnings for their own use (White 1985: 101).

The Fifth Congress of March 1982 stressed the need to shift priorities away from heavy industry and towards agriculture and light industry (and their exports). The period 1982–85 saw criticism of 'bureaucratic centralism in economic policy' and the need for decentralization of decision-making to enterprises to free them from the day-to-day control of government agencies, to encourage more direct links between enterprises, to remove subsidies and introduce 'socialist accounting', and to tie pay to performance.

The Sixth Congress in December 1986 confirmed the new approach. The 1986–90 five year plan stressed the importance of agriculture, consumer goods and exports. The lack of progress in implementing the reforms led to their reaffirmation by the August 1987 Central Committee Plenum, which outlined the programme of implementation, starting with enterprises jointly operating with Soviet enterprises and with those producing consumer goods in 1988 and, finally, covering all enterprises by 1990 (Hiebert, *FEER*, 1 October 1987, p. 94). According to Porter (1990: 79), the starting enterprises were those dealing with other countries and those that received almost all their material supplies from the state; 1992 was later made the target year for shifting most enterprises to the new accounting system.

A number of ministerial mergers were undertaken in 1987 (e.g. a new Ministry of Agriculture and Food was set up), to reduce bureaucracy and overcome empire building, and many ministers were changed. At the beginning of April 1990 a dozen ministries and state institutions were merged into only three, the new ministries of trade, education and heavy industry. Financial control was emphasized: strict controls over investment spending, reduced employment in the state sector to combat excessive bureaucracy, and state organizations to move towards 'financial self-government and the acceptance of responsibility for profits and losses'.

As in the Soviet Union, during the 1980s in Vietnam there were attacks on corruption, abuses of power, complacency and obstruction, together with numerous personnel changes. There was a growing realization that winning wars is not at all the same as winning the peace. In July 1986 Truong Chin declared that 'we have held on too long to the system of centralism, bureaucratism and subsidization'. There would be no more target dates for socialist transformation. Since he became General Secretary in December 1986, Nguyen Van Linh has talked about the 'serious errors' of the previous ten years and the need for a 'complete and radical socio-economic *renovation*'.[3] This is needed in order to eliminate the managerial system characterized by a 'subsidy-based bureaucratic centralism mechanism' and replace it with a planning mechanism based on socialist cost accounting and business activities, consonant with the principle of democratic centralism. Nguyen Van Linh (1987: 15) says that state purchases of farm produce for sale at low prices involve subsidies equalling nearly a third of the budget. In June 1988 Linh said, 'The national economy has collapsed largely because the situation of faked profits and true losses has prevailed. We have been calculating the prices of equipment and materials too low for too long, compelling the state to make up for losses that were too big' (reported in *IHT*, 18–19 June 1988, p. 2). Renovation is needed in 'economic thinking' (economic laws have been ignored), production structure and economic management. While central planning should remain (there would be no return to chaotic capitalism), the plan must be worked out from the bottom upwards, although, it is stressed, under the guidance and regulation of the centre in order to ensure balance. More use should be made of economic levers, the operational decisions of production units should not be interfered with, and branch and territorial planning should be closely combined.

A notable event was the election, by secret ballot, of the manager of the Thanh Long Paper Mill by 133 representatives of cadres and workers, the provincial authorities subsequently officially confirming the appointment. Normally the provincial authorities or the competent ministry appoint managers on the basis of the local party committee and administration (*Vietnam Courier*, 1987, no. 8, p. 13).

Thayer (*IHT*, 15 April 1988, p. 4) sees the proponents of economic reform as a coalition of southerners (or officials with long experience in the South) and another group centred in the northern port of Haiphong. A municipal district in the port introduced an incentive-based contract system in agriculture in 1979 which was later adopted as a national model. The reformers are at present in the ascendancy despite the 1986 figures, which show that 73 per cent of the

1.8 million party members are in the North (p. 4). From an ideological point of view it is seen as possible to progress directly towards socialism by bypassing the capitalist stage, but not to miss out on the development of the market production stage.

The industrial enterprise

Between 1954 and 1960 state enterprises were not separate financial units, but came under the budget, with the state covering all investment and any losses and siphoning off any profits. The September 1979 reforms pointed in the direction of decentralization, under which enterprises were permitted to produce unplanned products and output above obligatory sales, which could be sold on the free market or to the state at negotiated prices. In order to widen wage differentials and thus increase incentives, a piece rate system of wage payment started to be introduced in 1980, but not very successfully; there were also bonuses for improving product quality and reducing the use of raw materials (Beresford 1988: 160–3 and 1992: 240). The enterprise production plan, as of January 1981, consisted of three parts: state-assigned output manufactured with state-supplied inputs; above-plan output resulting from inputs procured by the enterprise itself; and unplanned secondary output (including by-products). In this so-called 'three-plan' system, the respective percentage profit splits between the state budget and the enterprise were as follows: 50–50, 40–60 and 10–90 (Le Trang 1990: 159). By-products may be sold on the free market, if the state is not interested (Spoor 1988a: 107; 1988b: 119). According to the EIU, workers themselves are now able to use enterprise facilities on their own account to make goods for sale on the free market or to the state (*Country Profile*, 1987–88, p.190).

Under 'socialist cost accounting' state enterprises are allegedly self-financing and thus face the prospect of possible bankruptcy. It seems as though few enterprises have actually closed down, however, thanks to bank credits, although a bankruptcy law is supposed to be enforced. It is not clear exactly how much authority management has to dismiss workers or to determine wages, although it is clear that a minimum wage has to be paid; payment beyond this is according to work input and management has a choice of piece or time rates. Dellmo *et al.* (1990: 38–9) list the following constraints: enterprises have a social responsibility to keep unemployment low, e.g. they are not allowed to dismiss staff in order to increase profits and they are 'encouraged' to employ soldiers returning from Cambodia; managers have to 'consult' trade unions before dismissals. The intention is to switch gradually to a labour contract system, away from lifetime guarantees.

The resolution of the Sixth Party Congress went through an experimental phase until the end of 1988, when a set of reasonably comprehensive policies was implemented (Tran Duc Nguyen 1991: 31). The 'three-plan' system was formally abandoned in early 1989 (Dellmo *et al.* 1990: 28). According to Le Trang (1990: 167–9), most enterprises today are assigned only one target, namely 'contribution to the state budget'. Some enterprises producing important products have to fulfil two or three targets: 'value of output of products', 'output of principal products' and 'contribution to the state budget' (Fforde and de Vylder, 1988: 84, cite the thirty-five key enterprises referred to in the 1988 decree continuing to receive quantitative targets; these then represented about 50 per cent of total output). The intention was to shift to a tax-based system for state enterprises from 1991 onwards, as is already the case with non-state enterprises (Le Duc Thuy *et al.* 1991: 185). Input supply is largely the concern of the enterprise itself. Only especially important sectors (e.g. energy and railways) are able to buy fuel at controlled prices. Prices are mainly freed, the exceptions being vital materials such as iron and steel, cement, electric power, oil and petrol, timber, cotton and chemical fertilisers. An increasing number of enterprises are able to

trade direct with foreign companies, but the state still controls the issue of export and import licences. Import quotas also exist. Exporting enterprises are entitled to retain a portion of foreign exchange earnings.

These measures amount to a quite radical shift towards a market-based economy. Even so, there are many areas where decision-making authority is blurred, as in bankruptcy and dismissal of labour. The state still exercises considerable direct influence, as reflected e.g. in the right to establish and close down state enterprises. How much authority enterprise management has to alter the production profile is not clear; this can only be done 'within limits' (Dellmo *et al.* 1990: 30). Large enterprise investments seem to need some kind of state approval (p. 30). Indirectly, the state is able to lean on management in Hungarian NEM fashion: Ronnas and Sjöberg (1990: 150) note the interfering tendencies of district authorities in this respect.

The Draft Platform for the Building of Socialism in the Transition Period (Socio-economic Strategy for Vietnam up to the Year 2000) emerged from the Tenth Plenary Session of the Central Committee (Sixth Congress) held 17–26 November 1990 in preparation for the June 1991 Seventh Party Congress (*Vietnam Courier*, 1990, no. 14 (supplement), and 1991, no. 15, pp. 10–11). There was a renewed commitment to socialism. The regulated market-based economy was to be adhered to, policy being 'To build a planned commodity economy, to put into operation a market economy with state management'. The 'predominant role' would continue to be played by the socialized sector. The aim was to at least double *per capita* income over the period 1990–2000.

The Seventh Party Congress took place 24–7 June 1991. As has already been discussed there was a substantial change of personnel at the top (e.g. Do Muoi replacing Nguyen Van Linh as General Secretary; Do Muoi was himself replaced as prime minister by Vo Van Kiet on 9 August). As expected, the need for political stability as an essential prerequisite for economic renewal was emphasized. Reference was made to a 'socialist-orientated multi-sector commodity economy operating along a market mechanism under state management' (*Vietnam Courier*, 1991, no. 21, p. 4). The state sector plays the 'leading role', but the other sectors also have positive roles to play (p. 3).

The second plenum of the Central Committee (Seventh Congress) held 25 November – 4 December 1991 adopted the guidelines for socio-economic development 1992–95; the stress was on proceeding with economic reforms and curbing inflation (*Vietnam Courier*, 1992, no. 27, p. 5).

Financial reforms

The February 1959 reform involved a rate of exchange of one dong (the currency unit) for 1,000 old dong, with an upper limit of 2,000 new dong on the amount of money that could be exchanged (the remainder had to be held in accounts at the State Bank for a long period of time).

April 1985 saw a massive devaluation of the dong against the US dollar, from just below twelve to 100 dong to the dollar. In September a new dong replaced the old at a rate of one to ten, although immediate exchange was limited to 20,000 dong per family in order to penalize the free market traders. In fact, however, this penalized many state enterprises as well, since they used cash to purchase scarce inputs, this further increasing the goods shortage (and ultimately inflation, as the state later refinanced the enterprises in order to keep them going by increasing the money supply). Two weeks' advance warning, however, allowed black-marketeers to get rid of old dong and hoard hard currencies. Workers and cadres received extra cash to compensate for the loss of the coupon ration books (which were supplemented with some cash previously; Esterline, *Asian Survey*, 1987, vol. XXVII, no.1, p. 93). Wage and price reforms thus meant that employees' heavily

subsidized ration certificates were replaced by pay increases to compensate for the rise in retail prices. Subsequent wage increases were to be dependent on merit and productivity increases. The 'two price system' (free market and state ration prices) was to be replaced by the 'one price system' in order to eliminate black markets (this was largely achieved during 1989: Dellmo *et al.* 1990: 31). Subsidies to state enterprises, too, were to be replaced by a system of wholesale prices that was to reflect costs, while there was to be some further decentralization of decision-making. The following results ensued:

1. Soaring inflation (see Table 8.1).

2. Some reversal of policy (e.g. reintroduction of rationing for some basic necessities in January 1986 and of subsidies for some low-income earners).

3. The January 1986 sacking of Tran Phuong (Vice-Premier for Economic Affairs) and the June 1986 replacement of To Huu (a Vice-Premier of the Council of Ministers) by Vo Chi Cong.

4. A wholesale replacement of ministers (e.g. of Finance, Transport and Communications, Foreign Trade, Coal and Mining).

Anti-inflation policies were very successful at first, but inflation began to climb again after August 1990. The official figures for inflation were 700 per cent in 1986, 400 per cent in 1987, over 300 per cent in 1989, and 60–70 per cent in both 1990 and 1991 (*Vietnam Courier*, 1991, no. 26, p. 7). Curbing inflation once again became a key government aim in 1991 and 1992, the target for the latter year being 30 per cent (p. 7). Indeed, February 1989 saw the start of an austerity programme, monitored by the IMF:

1. In March the dong was devalued for the sixth time in four months, from 900 to the US dollar to close to the then free market rate of 4,500 (Cima, *Asian Survey*, 1990, vol. XXX, no. 1, p. 92).

2. A strict fiscal policy involved expenditure cuts in, e.g. subsidies (such as the end of the food subsidy system for state workers in 1989) and defence. Note that in 1988 the budget deficit

had been as high as 10 per cent of national income (Dellmo *et al.* 1990: 24). Wood (1989) notes that the decline of inflation was accompanied by the liberalizing of almost all prices, making the achievement all the more remarkable. Van Arkadie (1991: 44), however, notes that the resurgence of inflation (after August 1990) was partly due to the weakness of a tax system heavily dependent on enterprises. In 1990 the budget deficit amounted to one-third of government expenditure (Murray Hiebert, *FEER*, 19 September 1991, p. 68); in July 1991 premier Vo Van Kiet announced that foreign aid would only account for 6–7 per cent of the government's revenue in 1991, compared with 25–30 per cent the year before.

3. A strict monetary policy included high and positive real interest rates in order to encourage savings and discourage spending. Neil Wilson (*The Banker*, April 1990, p. 27) reports that in early 1989 interest rates were raised to 12 per cent a month on three-month time deposits in dong and to 9 per cent a month on demand deposits (local Vietnamese were also allowed to open foreign currency accounts). The ratio of the budget deficit to revenue was reduced from 33.7 per cent in 1988 to 19.1 per cent in the first half of 1989 (Tran Ngoc Vinh 1990:95). *The Economist* (24 February 1990, p. 68) reports a modest budget surplus for the whole of 1989.

The banking reform (the new law went into operation 1 October 1990) involves the division between the central bank (concentrating on credit regulation and the control of the money supply) and commercial banks (Agricultural Development Bank, Industry and Trade Bank, Bank for Investment and Development, and the Foreign Trade Bank), giving preference to profitable projects and those serving the priority sectors. Monetary control includes minimum reserve requirements. The participation of foreign banks was to be allowed. The first joint venture was Indovin, set up in January 1991 between the Industry and Trade Bank and the Suma Bank of Indonesia; its activities are restricted to foreign currency operations and the financing of foreign trade. The central bank has discretion whether to allow dealings in the domestic currency. The first foreign bank to be allowed to set up a branch was the French-owned Banque Indosuez; it was opened in Ho Chi Minh City on 14 July 1992 and is able to deal in dongs. Private and co-operative credit institutions have already been set up (these ran into trouble in the spring of 1990 as private enterprises went out of business and lax control was exercised by the authorities: *Vietnam Courier*, 1991, no. 16, p. 7). In December 1991 the first shareholder-owned (all the shareholders are business executives) commercial bank was established; it is the Saigon Commercial Shareholders Bank (*IHT*, 3 January 1992, p. 13).

An income tax system was introduced on 1 April 1991. Vietnamese citizens start paying tax on reaching 400,000 dong a month. The tax rate is between 10 per cent and 50 per cent on monthly income in the range 400,000 to 3 million dong, while a 30 per cent supplementary tax of 30 per cent is levied on incomes over 5 million dong a month. Foreigners have a higher tax-free limit of 800,000 a month, while tax in the range 10–50 per cent is imposed on monthly earnings between 800,000 and 16 million dong.

In July 1987 the Ho Chi Minh City Industrial and Commercial Bank was opened, the first commercial bank, with part (55 per cent) of the stock sold to private citizens for the first time. Keith Richburg reports the Haiphong Shipping Company's experiment in selling up to 49 per cent of its shares to private individuals and co-operatives, compensated by dividend checks; the purchase of five shares is accompanied by the entitlement to a company job (*IHT*, 13–14 August 1988, p. 14).

AGRICULTURE

Fforde and de Vylder (1988: 21–4) point out that Vietnam has a history in which almost all peasants belonged to a commune, although this system began to break down during the French colonial period. *Land reform* was implemented as early as 1953–54, involving land appropriation and redistribution, the colonial legacy having left most peasants as tenant farmers. *Collectivization* did not begin in the North until 1959, but by 1968 more than 90 per cent of peasants formally belonged to higher-level co-operatives. Beresford (1988: 130) points out Chinese influence in the staged process. 'Mutual aid' teams or 'production solidarity' groups were first set up, building on the existing wet rice practices of joint transplanting and harvesting and the lending of tools and draft animals. There next followed 'lower-level co-operatives' ('production collectives'), in which individual income depended on both labour and contributed land and means of production, and, finally, 'higher-level co-operatives', in which labour was the sole source of remuneration. The Chinese commune, however, was not emulated. Five per cent of the collective's land was devoted to *private plots* (this figure was sometimes exceeded), while agriculture was largely left alone during the war and a *de facto* reversion to family farming was permitted in many areas (Beresford 1988: 134). Co-operatives dominated agricultural output, state farms contributing only a small percentage (specifically 0.5 per cent of gross agricultural output in 1960 and 1.1 per cent in 1963; Spoor 1987: 347); state farms concentrated on export crops such as tea and coffee (today state farms occupy 16.5 per cent of the cultivated area: *Vietnam Courier*, 1990, no. 13, p. 6). In 1963 quotas were fixed for a given period, initially three years, on the basis of the average results for 1961–62, as an incentive to increase output. As far as the South is concerned, the decision to collectivize was taken in early 1977, the aim, stated the following year, being to complete the process by 1980 (by that year, however, only 50 per cent of agricultural households were in any form of collective: Beresford 1992: 246). By the start of 1986 87.2 per cent of peasants and 85.5 per cent of tilled land had been collectivized, according to Wädekin (1990a: 9), but there is

some dispute about the degree to which these were 'paper' as opposed to actual figures. Pryor (1991: 99) says that collectivization in the South was about 75 per cent complete by 1986, although most farms really resembled the Chinese mutual aid teams of the early 1950s.

In pre-1979 co-operatives there were compulsory procurement quotas for rice and pork, with a dual system of quotas and above-quota prices, while other products were subject to contract. During the 1970s the trend was towards locally negotiated procurements (White 1985: 100–1), and in June 1982 stress was laid on district and provincial self-provision of food (p. 101). From the late 1970s onwards the role of the district (between province and village) increased as regards transactions with the state, and integrating agricultural and industrial development at the local level (Werner 1988: 158). In 1976 the farm tax was based on the estimated gross output of the normal average crop, but this was changed nine years later to average yield per hectare in various geographical situations, tax rates being fixed for a three year period (Spoor 1988a: 111).

In January 1981, after experiments starting in Haiphong in 1978, a *'production contract' system* was introduced in the North, but this was not widespread in the South until the following year (note that land still belongs to the state). In this system individual peasant households, or sometimes work teams, lease land from the co-operative and take over most stages of production in exchange for contracted deliveries, keeping produce over the contracted amount (fixed on the basis of the average productivity of land over the preceding three years and set for a two to three year period) to be consumed by themselves or sold on the free market. Any shortfall in contracted deliveries must be made good the following year. (The remaining *private farms* sign contracts with the state.) Collectives provide inputs and communal services such as irrigation, pest control, and ploughing (White 1985: 97; Beresford 1988: 162; Vo Nhan Tri 1988: 80). Decrees issued April–November 1988 included the following amendments (Crosnier and Lhomel 1990: 3–4; Porter 1990: 80; Beresford 1990: 475–6): leases of up to twenty years were to be available (rather than the previous three years; up to fifty years in the case of some perennial crops); Tran Duc Nguyen (1991: 29) talks of a minimum fifteen years for leases: leases can be inherited or transferred (ceded) to other peasants, although renting land to others is not permitted; land allocations are to be in compact parcels rather than scattered strips; land allocation is to take account of efficiency and the fulfilment of commitments rather than simply family size or number of workers per family; supplies delivered to the state cannot exceed 60 per cent of output; a single tax was introduced, on average 10 per cent of the harvest, with the exact rate depending on land fertility; state purchase prices are negotiable (rather than fixed by the state); the hiring of seasonal labour is possible. Land is attributed to farming households on a long-term (fifteen year) contractual basis; the farmers can freely sell their produce after paying the agricultural taxes (*Vietnam Courier*, 1991, no. 25, p. 8). Ronnas and Sjöberg (1990: 150) note that, in reality, district authorities still often try to impose directives on co-operatives, although they are not formally entitled to do so. The formal position as regards ownership and use is that 'Land, resources and environment still belong to the entire people . . . But . . . the state hands over on a long-term basis the right to use them to the producers. This right of use may be bequeathed and transferred' (*Vietnam Courier*, 1991, no. 26, p. 15). The new system has been a major reason for the transformation in Vietnam's agricultural performance. In 1989, for example, 1.45 million tonnes of rice were exported (making Vietnam the third largest exporter after the USA and Thailand), in 1990 1.4 million tonnes (Murray Hiebert, FEER, 23 January 1992, p. 49) and in 1991 1 million tonnes (*Vietnam Courier*, 1992, no. 27, p. 1). According to official figures for 1989, the private and individual sectors accounted for more than 90 per cent of total agricultural production (*Vietnam Courier*, 1990, no. 14, p. 6). Pingali and Vo-Tong Xuan (1992: 715) point out that rice productivity is adversely affected by factors such as inadequate infrastructural investments in irrigation, water control, soil conservation, transport, and research.

In 1987 further measures were taken to combat problems with the supply and distribution of foodstuffs. In March the government removed checkpoints on roads, originally designed to prevent illegal private trading, and later formally authorized private individuals to form transport businesses in order to convey foodstuffs to market; thus controls on cross-provincial movement of goods were removed, especially facilitating the flow of rice from South to North.

Large-scale migration to the cities caused the *'redistribution' of the workforce* in 1986, which uprooted 1.3 million people in five years. Workers, mainly young people, were sent to the new economic zones (Esterline, *Asian Survey*, 1987, vol. XXVII, no. 1, pp. 93–4). Recently the aim has been to resettle up to 250,000 people annually, mostly from the North, in zones in central and southern Vietnam. Farmers are able to market that proportion of the crop remaining after the state extracts its share (Barbara Crossette, *IHT*, 28 April 1988, p. 6). Beresford (1988: 70, 151–2) sees the aims as increasing cultivated land area and transferring people from overcrowded cities and densely populated deltas in the the North. Between 1975 and 1985 around 2 million people had moved to the zones (p. 152). The *Vietnam Courier* (1991, no. 24, p. 8) traces the population movements back to 1961; over the past thirty years 4,820,000 have resettled in the new economic zones. Hiebert (*FEER*, 25 May 1989, p. 42) notes that pressure tactics were especially used 1975–80, but today propaganda and incentives are favoured.

An interesting innovation that sprang from the food problems of the late 1970s was the establishment in 1980 of a food supply organization, the Food Company of Ho Chi Minh City, under Madam Nguyen Thi Thi, outside the existing procurement and distribution system. Bank credits were used to purchase agricultural inputs and industrial consumer goods, which were then traded for food in the countryside. In 1983 the organization became an independent state enterprise, rather than a subdivision of the city's food department, and now processes foodstuffs and feedstuffs. It has a monopoly of the city's rice trade; it runs rice mills, noodle factories, bakeries and its own retail outlets; it has a small oil refinery, trading oil products for agricultural goods. It plans to build a solar power station to ensure electricity supply: piece rates provide an incentive to hard work. It now runs 7,000 retail stores. Plans are submitted to central authorities for incorporation into national economic plans.

FOREIGN TRADE AND INVESTMENT

Foreign trade

Comecon dominated Vietnam's foreign trade, the Soviet Union alone around 65 per cent in the early 1980s. Japan, however, which also offers long-term loans, was actually second to the Soviet Union as a partner. In 1989 the foreign trade commodity structure (per cent) was as follows: exports: raw and processed agricultural products (e.g. rice) 39.8; small-scale industry and handicrafts 27.5; products of heavy industry and mining (e.g. coal) 19.2; sea products (e.g. shrimps) 9.9; forest products 3.6; imports: raw materials and fuels 56.8; complete equipment and oil industry equipment 20.3; finished consumer goods 10.2; sundry equipment 7.4; spares and accessories 5.3. The socialist countries accounted for 46.4 per cent of exports and 73.6 per cent of imports (*Vietnam Courier*, 1990, no. 7, p. 10). Imports were 13 per cent of GNP in 1984 (Beresford 1988: xiv). Within Comecon during the 1980s there was a shift towards greater specialization in tropical products and light manufactures (p. 175). In February 1987 a commission for economic relations with foreign

countries was set up to develop links with Third World and Western nations. There are already assembly plants operating with licences from, for example, Japanese companies. A 70 per cent increase in exports was planned for 1986–90. There has been a US embargo since May 1975, 1964 in the case of North Vietnam. (Note that the US embargo has wider implications, deterring both foreign investment from other countries not wishing to offend the USA, for example Japan, and lending by international bodies. Nevertheless, December 1991 saw the first visit by a US trade mission since April 1975, while in mid-January 1992 a Japanese aid delegation paid an exploratory visit to Vietnam. Countries like Australia, Italy, Finland and the Netherlands offered aid in late 1991 and early 1992.) On 22 October 1990 Vietnam was granted diplomatic relations with the European Community (thus permitting EC aid) and is a member of the IMF, the World Bank and the Asian Development Bank (note that Vietnam failed to meet its repayments to the IMF in 1985 and became ineligible for further loans; Vietnam started to make interest payments in 1989, but one estimate puts the debt arrears at $140.6 million: *IHT*, 17 October 1991, p. 13). The upheaval in Eastern Europe has produced a number of broken contracts to import Vietnamese products. Current world prices and hard currency trading have generally been used since the start of 1991 (an agreement with the Soviet Union was reached on 31 January). Trade with the Soviet Union fell by 15 per cent in the first six months of 1991 (Murray Hiebert, *FEER*, 19 September 1991, p. 18).

The September 1979 reforms allowed exporting enterprises, with the approval of the Ministry of Foreign Trade, to sign contracts direct with foreign companies. Today producers not yet allowed to export direct are able to sell to any trade corporation (Fforde, *FEER*, 14 September 1989, p. 76). In 1981 Ho Chi Minh City, Hanoi, Haiphong and Da Nang were allowed to set up their own foreign trade corporations. The 1979 reforms allowed enterprises to use 10 per cent of planned and 50 per cent of above-plan foreign exchange earnings for the import of raw materials and spare parts, while in late 1981 all localities were permitted to export direct and to retain 70–90 per cent of foreign exchange earnings for the import of raw materials, machinery and consumer goods for their own use (Spoor 1988b: 121–2). Managers of state enterprises in Ho Chi Minh City were allowed, in 1987, to borrow funds from abroad in order to import modern equipment and technology, to enter into joint ventures with overseas companies and to employ 'overseas Vietnamese and technical advisers and managers'. Relatives of exiled Vietnamese were promised the facility of foreign currency accounts and a favourable rate of exchange, and the tourist door was opened to all foreigners and expatriates in 1986. Tighter import controls were introduced on 15 November 1991, foreign currency being made available only for 'essentials' until the end of the year. Hard currency can only be used for authorized imports; hoarding and speculation are illegal.

A foreign exchange centre was set up in Ho Chi Minh City on 30 August 1991 and a second one in Hanoi in November. The *International Herald Tribune* (29 November 1991, p. 14) reports intervention in the foreign exchanges to stabilize the dong; reserves are accumulated by requiring all commercial banks licensed to deal in foreign exchange to resell 30 per cent of the gold and dollars they buy to the central bank (Vietnamese enterprises earning hard currency must deposit their earnings in banks so that controls may be placed upon them).

Foreign investment

Vietnam is critically short of advanced technology and know-how. The 1977 law failed to attract very much foreign capital, because of the imposition of such restrictions as 49 per cent maximum foreign ownership and the necessity of local management. Power shortages still act as a deterrent. The last four Western companies exploring for oil left in 1981. Negotiations resumed in the mid-1980s and in 1988–89 offshore exploration agreements were signed with Shell and Petrofina, Total and BP (oil drilling ventures were also signed with Indian companies), with production sharing the basis. In 1990 oil agreements were signed with Canadian, Kuwaiti, Australian and Belgian companies. There has been little success to date. Exploration continued during the hiatus through Vietexopetro (founded November 1981), the Vietnamese–Soviet oil and gas company. A new law, which became operational on 1 January 1988, permits the setting up of solely foreign-owned companies and allows foreign companies to own up to 99 per cent of the equity of joint ventures; foreigners may be managing directors, but a Vietnamese must be at least deputy chief executive; profits and capital may be repatriated and nationalization is ruled out. Expatriates may be employed if local skills are lacking; profits tax is normally charged at 15–25 percent, but concessions are possible in remote areas or in special sectors such as timber. A two-year tax exemption from the first profit-making year is possible. Subject to Vietnamese law (including a minimum wage and hiring through local labour bureaus) and an arbitration process, foreign employers are able to hire and fire employees (Ungphakorn, *FT*, 19 January 1988, p. 4). Since June 1990 private Vietnamese enterprises have been able to set up joint ventures with foreign companies. Murray Hiebert (*FEER*, 20 February 1992, p. 52) noted only only three to date.

Examples of joint ventures are to be found in small-scale oil refining, tourism, telecommunications, coal and gemstone mining, edible oil refining, electronic telephone switchboards, television set assembly, and aluminium windows. During 1988–89 105 licences were granted and in seventy cases operations had begun (*Vietnam Courier*, 1990, no. 7, p. 10). By 31 May 1990 157 joint venture contracts had been signed (*Vietnam Courier*, 1990, no. 10, p. 10). By the end of May 1991 259 licences had

been granted with an aggregate capital investment of almost $2 billion: oil and natural gas
($520 million); manufacturing and food-
processing 166 ($783 million); hotels 54 ($463
million) (*Vietnam Courier*, 1991, no. 21, p. 8).
By November 1991 the number of licences had
gone up to 330 and capital investment to $2.5
billion (*IHT*, 27 November 1991, p. 19) and by
the end of January 1992 to 383 and $2.8 billion
(three-quarters to Ho Chi Minh City and its
hinterland) (*The Economist*, 4 April 1992, p. 70).
Some 80 per cent of non-oil foreign investment
has gone to the South (Teresa Poole, *The
Independent*, 5 February 1992, p. 23). The first
foreign investment forum was held in Ho Chi
Minh City 11–15 March 1991; there were 623
foreign guests from thirty-one countries
representing over 400 major companies.

On 18 October 1991 the Council of Ministers
promulgated the rules for 'export processing
zones' (*Vietnam Courier*, 1991, no. 26, p. 13 and
1992, no. 27, p. 11). For example, the profits tax
was to be 10 per cent for a manufacturer and 15
per cent for a supplier of services, with tax
holidays of four and two years after profits have
been made respectively. Both exports and the
imported inputs used in them were to be duty-
free. On 25 November the Council of Ministers
signed the order to set up the first zone on the
outskirts of Ho Chi Minh City. Work on the
six-year Tan Thuan project began on 6 February
1992 in collaboration with two firms from
Taiwan.

THE NON-STATE, NON-AGRICULTURAL SECTOR

Handicrafts began to be converted into co-
operatives in 1958. Twenty years later a 'socialist
transformation' campaign was launched against
large private traders in the South. This and the
attempt to transfer private businessmen to the
new economic zones led to the flight of the 'boat
people'. Particularly affected were the Hoa
people of Chinese descent (Finkelstein, *Asian
Survey*, 1987, vol. XXVII, no. 9, p. 980). Ungar

(1987–88: 609) lists a number of reasons, in
addition to the restrictions on private enterprise
and the impact of the new economic zones, to
explain the exodus of the Hoa people, including
fear of a war between China and the Soviet
Union and the prospect of military service.
There was a legal limit on private employment
of one to two people, although family labour
was largely unregulated (Fforde 1987: 25).

There is now a more relaxed attitude to the
private sector. By mid-1989, for example, the
employment limit on private enterprises had
been removed (Wood 1989: 565). In contrast, in
1978 private trade had been formally abolished
(although the black market survived), in 1983
taxes were increased on private establishments
such as restaurants, and a further attack was
made in 1985 via taxation and the occasional
forcing through of 'joint ventures' with the state.
In 1986 attitudes began to change and by the
following year licences were no longer required
for small businesses (such as bicycle repairs,
coffee shops and hairdressers), while workers
and civil servants (including teachers and
doctors) were openly encouraged to take a
second job during off-duty hours. Family
businesses and co-operatives were encouraged
by a whole series of measures. These included
tax holidays and exemptions for exporters;
availability of state credit and inputs on equal
terms with the state sector and even foreign
exchange; those producing exports allowed to
retain some of the foreign exchange for imports
of materials and equipment; freely set prices;
trademarks; sale of patents allowed; inventors to
be entitled to 15–20 per cent of the profits
resulting from applications of their ideas (see,
for example, *Vietnam Courier*, 1987, no. 7, p. 5).
In August 1987 private vehicles were allowed to
carry passengers and freight, with fares regulated for established routes, but free for special
services. In 1986 the Hanoi Party Committee
permitted registered individuals to have up to
five employees (Stern, *Asian Survey*, 1987, vol.
XXVII, no. 4, p. 480). There are, however, still
problems with credit allocation. Up to now only

5 per cent of lending by state governed banks has gone to the collective and private sectors, which account for two-thirds of gross domestic income (Phan Van Tiem 1991: 154).

By late 1985 the 'private and individual sector' (including craftsmen, peasants who had not yet joined co-operatives, small traders, individual suppliers of services, and self-employed people) produced one-third of the gross social product and accounted for 32.7 per cent of national income; the sector provided a living for about one-third of the population (*Vietnam Courier*, 1987, no. 4, p. 14). Tran Duc Nguyen (1991: 42) provides a percentage breakdown of gross domestic product by sector: state/joint state–private 1976 (35.9), 1986 (29.5) and 1989 (26.9); collective 1976 (19.5); and private 1976 (44.6). Because the leasehold system in agriculture makes it impossible to differentiate between the collective and private sectors, the combined figure for 1986 is 70.5 per cent and for 1989 is 73.1 per cent. The state and collective sectors have accounted for more than 80 per cent of total industrial output, while the private and individual sectors have accounted for more than 50 per cent of trade activity (*Vietnam Courier*, 1990, no. 14, p. 6). The non-state sector (private and co-operative) accounts for 50 per cent of industrial output (60 per cent of consumer goods) and 68 per cent of retail trade (*Vietnam Courier*, 1990, no. 10, p. 6). The private sector transacted 64 per cent of retail trade in 1990 and 70 per cent in the first half of 1991 (*Vietnam Courier*, 1991, no. 24, p. 7).

The private sector accounted for 17.6 per cent of industrial output in 1985 and 19.6 per cent in 1988 (Beresford 1992: 247). Since 1985 there have been joint state-private stores (Stern, *Asian Survey*, 1987, vol. XXVII, no. 4, p. 487). Hiebert reports on a Hanoi workshop with thirty employees, an example of the private firms stemming from the relaxation of controls there (*FEER*, 28 July 1988, p. 20). The Rising Sun Torch enterprise, producing battery-free torches, is a family firm that contracts out to some 1,000 people working in their own homes the inputs needed to produce the final product (reports by David Watts in *The Times*, 11 November 1987, p. 8, and Murray Hiebert, *FEER*, 17 March 1988, p. 20). Only a handful of private companies employ more than 1,000 workers (Murray Hiebert, *FEER*, 20 February 1992, p. 51).

A recent decree ensures that 'all commercial and service activities undertaken by economic institutions in the country are protected according to state law. . . . Individuals are entitled to pool their capital and set up their own business organizations or privately run corporations, which, however, must be registered.' All individuals and businesses are entitled to loans and accounts at the state bank, and all products produced by legitimate businesses can be distributed freely around the country (reported in *IHT*, 3 January 1989, p. 2).

The National Assembly passed a Law on Private Enterprise at the end of 1990, effective 15 April 1991 (*Vietnam Courier*, 1991, no. 16, p. 7). The state recognizes the long-term existence and development of private business and its equal rights before the law among other businesses. Those in state administration and army officers on active service, however, are debarred, to combat corruption. Managers and workers can be hired according to the owner's requirements and learning. Licences have to be granted within a period not exceeding thirty days from the day of application, but the chairman of the Council of Ministers must approve applications in the following sectors: explosives and toxic chemicals; the extraction of precious minerals; water and electricity on a large scale; broadcasting means; telecommunications, radio and television; publishing; sea and air transport; foreign trade; international travel. The private sector was spoken of positively at the Seventh Party Congress held 24–7 June 1991. The private sector is still seen as playing a subordinate role.

Vietnam's mini-privatization programme

Although no privatization along East European lines was envisaged, the National Assembly session held 10–26 December 1991 thought that 'It is urgent to turn a number of state enterprises into joint stock enterprises, a form of joint ownership between the state and individuals. This can be done with existing as well as newly built enterprises' (*Vietnam Courier*, 1992, no. 27, p. 7). The experiment seemed to involve the sale of shares in a number of enterprises at the provincial or local level in, for example, light manufacturing, meat processing and sea-food production. Employees have priority. The state would retain total control of strategic enterprises, such as steelworks, power plants and the railways, and majority control in other important areas. Crédit Lyonnais Securities (Asia) Ltd (a subsidiary of a French bank advising the government of Vietnam) has first refusal on up to 20 per cent of the shares in each of the enterprises to be affected. On 8 June 1992 seven enterprises to issue shares on an experimental basis were named.

The new constitution

The draft of a new constitution (to replace the 1980 one) was published on 30 December 1991 and ratified by the National Assembly on 15 April 1992. Politically there was to be no multi-party democracy, but the role of the communist party was to be reduced. The economic reforms were approved. The formal features of the constitution were as follows.

1. The communist party would continue to play a guiding role, to set the general political line. But the National Assembly's role was to increase: 'the National Assembly is the only body vested with constitutional and legislative powers'; it would convene three times a year instead of twice, appoint the prime minister, ratify the cabinet appointed by the prime minister, and elect the president as head of state (the president's powers were also increased).

2. The state ownership of land was retained, but plots could be allocated for long-term use and the rights to the use of the land could be inherited or sold.

The economic system was described as a 'socialist-orientated, multi-sectoral commodity economy driven by the state-regulated market system'. The status of the private sector was confirmed.

The formerly guaranteed rights to work, housing, and free health care and education were removed.

Foreigners had the right to own capital and assets and 'enterprises with foreign-invested capital shall not be nationalized'. The pledge on nationalization also applied to the Vietnamese private sector, but there is another article in the constitution which says that the state can requisition property at market prices on grounds of national security.

CONCLUSION

Vietnam was reunited in 1975 after decades of war against the Japanese, the French and the Americans. The country has made substantial progress in reducing inflation and introducing a market-based economy. There has been a Chinese-style reform of agriculture. The private non-agricultural sector has been given greater encouragement and there has been some share issuing (though there is no post-1989 Eastern European-type privatization programme). A big welcome is given to foreign capital. But reform has not followed suit, with multi-party democracy ruled out and stress laid on political stability.

NOTES

1. The standing army of some 1.1 million regular troops has been reduced to 500,000. Vietnamese troops had officially left Cambodia by midnight on 26 September 1989, although some 'advisers and technicians' may still be there (the troops entered Cambodia in December 1978 as a result of attacks by the Khmer Rouge regime).

2. The EIU (*Country Profile*, 1987–88, pp. 9–10), provides further demographic details: crude birth rate, forty-seven per thousand in 1960 and thirty-five per thousand in 1984; crude death rate, twenty-one and eight, respectively; infant

mortality, 157 and fifty, respectively; 1.5 million to 2 million deaths from military action, 1960–80, and 750,000 emigrants after 1975; life expectancy, forty-three years in 1960 and sixty-five in 1984; 85 per cent of the population literate. In October 1988 a tougher population control policy was announced (the previous one based on taxes and economic incentives was ineffective). Normally, a family with more than two children will be penalized by having to contribute towards education and medical care, do extra community work, accept a lower priority on housing waiting lists or building land allocation, and pay a higher rent for more living space. More than three children entails the inability to move into cities. Free contraceptives and abortion will be available and a 'com- mendation and award scheme' will encourage vasectomy and sterilization. Ethnic minorities in the northern mountains and central highlands are permitted three children (Hiebert, *FEER*, 8 December 1988, p. 32).

3. See *Vietnam Courier*, 1987, nos 1 and 2, and Nguyen Van Linh (1987) for his major speeches at the Sixth Congress of the CPV, 15–18 December 1986, and at the Second Plenum of the Central Committee, 1–9 April 1987. Linh was dropped from the politburo in 1982 for opposing the rapid socialization of South Vietnam after 1975, but he remained the party secretary for Ho Chi Minh City and his successful economic policies led to his reinstatement as a politburo member in June 1985.

Part II

EASTERN EUROPE TO 1989

9

THE PEOPLE'S REPUBLIC OF ALBANIA

POLITICAL BACKGROUND

Foreign domination has had a profound impact on political developments in the 'Land of the Eagle'. Roman and Byzantine rule was later followed by incorporation into the Ottoman Empire from 1466 to 1912. Independence was proclaimed on 18 November 1912. Zog was proclaimed king in 1928 and reigned until 1939 (he had made himself ruler in 1924). Pre-war economic dependence on Italy culminated in the invasion (and annexation) of April 1939, and the Nazi occupation lasted from 1943 to 1944. The country's independence was attained by November 1944, without the help of foreign forces, and a People's Republic was formally proclaimed in January 1946. Enver Hoxha and other partisans founded the Party of Labour of Albania in 1941 and he became General Secretary two years later. Until his death in April 1985 he maintained Stalin-like control of Albania. Stalinist orthodoxy led to the break with Yugoslavia in 1948. Yugoslav leaders were described as 'anti-communist renegades', as a result of Tito's quarrel with Stalin. In 1950 there was an unsuccessful attempt by Albanian exiles, backed by the UK and USA, to overthrow the government. Albania broke with the Soviet Union in 1961 after the Sino-Soviet split and after Khrushchev's denouncement of the cult of personality (1956), his acceptance of peaceful coexistence with the 'imperialist' United States (the Soviet Union became a 'social imperialist' power) and his moves of reconciliation towards

Yugoslavia in the late 1950s. Albania resisted Comecon plans for agricultural specialization and after 1961 trade with the Soviet Union fell from over 50 per cent to zero. Finally came the break with China in 1978. China had allegedly adopted 'social revisionism' after 'taking the capitalist path' in economic policy, and had become more friendly towards the United States after President Nixon's visit in 1972. Economic links with China were restored in 1983 and the Albanian foreign minister began a visit to China on 22 January 1991. In 1967 Albania banned all religious institutions and practices and became the first atheistic state in the world, an important reason being to stamp out any possible threat to national unity represented by the varying allegiances of Muslims and Christians.[1]

After Ramiz Alia assumed power as First Secretary in April 1985, something of a domestic and foreign relations thaw set in. For example, diplomatic relations were established with Spain in September 1986 and with Canada and West Germany in the same month of the following year.[2] The technical state of war with Greece, which had existed since the Italian invasion of Greece in 1940, was lifted in August 1987, and the following April the two countries signed an agreement to encourage border trade, having already agreed to set up a ferry link with Corfu. Two accords were signed with Turkey, one on economic, scientific and technological co-operation and the other on road transport. Albania took part in the Balkan Conference of Foreign Ministers on 24–6 February 1988.

Hosted by Yugoslavia and attended by Bulgaria, Romania, Greece and Turkey, it aimed at increasing regional stability and co-operation in the spheres of economic and cultural relations, tourism, the environment, and transport and communications. Albania's representative, Foreign Minister Reis Malile, stressed the need to respect the independence, national sovereignty and territorial integrity of neighbouring states. Policy on national minorities and their treatment is an internal question for each country, although other countries may have a legitimate interest and seek to transform the question into one that encourages stability and cohesion at home and good relations between states[3]. Malile said there was scope for improving economic (small-scale expansion of border trade, and removal of tariffs and licences for some goods, for example), transport, communications, and water management links[4]. The second conference took place in Tirana 24–5 October 1990. Diplomatic relations were resumed with the USA on 15 March 1991 (they were severed in June 1939 after the Italian invasion of Albania, while the informal US mission sent in 1945 to explore the possibility of resumption was withdrawn in November 1946). Those with the UK were restored on 29 May 1991 and with the EC the following month.

ECONOMIC BACKGROUND

Pre-war Albania was the most backward country in Europe. According to Schnytzer (1982: 1), in 1938 industry accounted for only 4.4 per cent of national income. Only 150 industrial enterprises existed, which were thinly scattered over the country, and nearly 50 per cent of them employed fewer than ten workers (p. 65). In 1927 *per capita* income was only $40 and 90 per cent of national income was derived from agriculture; in 1928 livestock products accounted for 65 per cent of exports (p. 14). In 1938 85 per cent of the population was rural (64 per cent in 1989) and average life expectancy was thirty-eight years (it was seventy-one by 1985).

Socialist Albania inherited an illiteracy rate of 85 per cent and no railway network.

On the other hand, Albania is relatively well endowed with natural resources. There are fertile soils, although 70 per cent of the country is classified as hilly or mountainous. There is extensive land reclamation and irrigation, but still only 0.2 ha of arable land *per capita* (Sjöberg 1989: 8). Fifty five per cent of arable land is currently under irrigation (Prescott 1986: 11). Resources also include energy (especially hydro-electric, but also coal, oil and gas), chrome (third only to the Soviet Union and South Africa in 1985 in terms of output; in recent years the second largest exporter after South Africa, *FT*, 20 February 1990, p. 7), nickel, copper, iron ore and manganese. Oil production (started in 1927) peaked at 2.5 million tonnes in 1974, but was only 1.2 million tonnes in 1990 (*IHT*, 16 August 1991, p. 14). Some 500,000 cubic metres of natural gas is produced annually (Kerin Hope, *FT*, 29 August 1991, p. 24).

Development strategy involved rapid rates of growth, especially industrial. The share of agriculture in net material product fell from 76.3 per cent in 1950 to 37.9 per cent in 1978 (Kaser 1986: 19) and achievements include allegedly stable prices (some prices actually fell). Transport and communication links with other countries have improved in recent years. For example, a freight ferry link with Italy was established in 1983 and a rail link with Yugoslavia in 1986; previous to this Albania was the only country in continental Europe inaccessible by train.

In 1989 the population of 3,182,417 was the fastest growing in Europe (2.1 per cent in 1986), but had the lowest *per capita* income. The following estimates for *per capita* GDP are available in Åslund and Sjöberg (1991:6): *The Economist* of 27 July 1991 $350; World Bank (for June 1991), $600; CIA (for 1990), $1,150; Åslund and Sjöberg, (for 1989 and 1990) $350–600. By comparison, the figure for Portugal (the poorest country in Western Europe) in 1989 was $4,250 and for Turkey $1,370 (p. 8). Two-thirds of the population are under thirty years of age, and 64 per cent of the population live in the country-side. In a July 1987 speech to the Central Committee Alia declared that Albania's development and foreign policy could not be separated from events in the rest of the world. He criticized the performance of some sectors of the economy, saying that export earnings were insufficient to purchase the new technology needed to develop industry.

Table 9.1 shows the performance of the Albanian economy. Sandström and Sjöberg (1991: 943) calculate that NMP *per capita* may have been more or less constant 1975–88.

CENTRAL PLANNING AND THE INDUSTRIAL ENTERPRISE

According to Schnytzer (1982: 18), the centralized economy was only introduced gradually, and the traditional plan indicators did not operate until 1959 because of a lack of qualified cadres.

In 1966 a decentralization of decision-making took place, but not so much to enterprises (the number of success indicators was decreased) as to ministries and district councils. The number of indicators approved by the Council of Ministers was reduced from 550 to seventy-seven for industry, 320 to forty-two for agriculture and 500 to 100 for investment and construction. Formerly all indicators for each enterprise were approved by the Council of Ministers, which approved plans quarterly (as opposed to only annually after 1966). Ministries were responsible for disaggregating the central plans, which were then passed to district councils (the latter became responsible for an increasing number of smaller enterprise from the mid-1960s onwards and especially after 1970), for co-ordination and for overseeing implementation (Schnytzer 1982: 33–4). Before 1966 the plan process was begun by passing down the draft annual plan from the centre for disaggregation; after that date the enterprise and district councils sent up plan drafts, based on the five year plan (Schnytzer 1982: 30). Ministries and district councils formally now controlled enterprise investment funds instead of the State Bank (p. 50).

In the mid-1980s the industrial enterprise had eight indicators to fulfil in its technical-industrial-financial plan (*plan tekniko-industrial financiar*): production; productive capacity; employment and payroll; material-technical supply and distribution of output; technical progress and scientific research work; cost plan; investment and basic construction; and financial plan; it operates on the principle of 'single management' (Kaser 1986: 9). Sjöberg (1990: 6–7) describes some experiments 1985–86 to reduce the number of success indicators in selected enterprises (and farms). By 1977 district councils had begun to lose their control over industry, but ten years later it was decided that districts were to be given a more active role in

Table 9.1 Albania: foreign debt and average annual rates of growth of NMP, industrial output and agricultural output (%)

	1961–70	1971–75	1976–80	1981–85	1986–8	1987	1988	1989
NMP	7.4	6.7	2.7	2.0	1.7	0.7	0.3	2.4
Net industrial output	–	–	–	–	–	1.8	1.7	2.5
Net agricultural output	–	–	–	–	–	0.6	–2.6	1.4
Gross Foreign debt (end 1989):		$400 million						

Source: Sandström and Sjöberg (1991: 937–43) Åslund and Sjöberg (1991: 6–20); United Nations Economic Commission for Europe (1992: 86).

planning (Sjöberg 1990: 6–7). Sjöberg (1991: 117) notes that in 1978, just before the break with China, planning was made more centralized; he argues that the 'reform' waves during the 1980s were only minor modifications intended merely to redress difficulties as they arose. By 1983 more than 200 material balances were drawn up by the State Planning Commission and notified by the Council of Ministers. The centre also drew up an 'urgent list' of imports for the Ministry of Foreign Trade (Kaser 1986: 9). After November 1986 there was some recognition of the need for economic reform. For example, in his 3 November 1986 report to the Ninth Party Congress Ramiz Alia acknowledged that

> The lack of experience needed to know foreign markets with the international complications increased the difficulties for the development of the economy . . . the targets of the plan were not fully accomplished in particular branches of the economy, such as the oil industry, in some agricultural and livestock products, in financial income and in exports. As a consequence, some imbalance was created in the economy. There were shortcomings, also, in supplying goods for the people as the plan envisaged.
>
> (Quoted in Costa 1988: 235)

Mild measures already taken included the introduction in the late 1970s of bonuses of 2–30 per cent of wages for increased production, but in December 1987 Ramiz Alia formally ruled out the introduction of Soviet-type reforms. Even at the Ninth Congress he said, 'The main way for the increase of productive capacities is that of reconstructions or expansions of the existing ones' (Costa 1988: 235). A leading article in *Zeri i Popullit* (The People's Voice) gives a flavour of Albanian attitudes towards *perestroika*:

> It was Khrushchev who, at the Twentieth Congress of the CPSU, began the great counter-revolutionary transformation, that process of 'reforms' which destroyed socialism, paved the way for the restoration of capitalism . . . *Perestroika* is broader in extent than all the 'reforms' undertaken by Gorbachev's predecessors . . . [and] aims to eliminate everything that hinders the complete transition to unfettered capitalism.
>
> (*Albanian Life*, 43, no. 3, 1988, pp. 37–40)

In an 11 January 1990 editorial the paper declared that 'The prescriptions of the capitalist road, of *perestroika* and bourgeois reformism are unacceptable to our people and party (quoted in *The Guardian*, 12 January 1990, p. 10). This followed Alia's new year's message of 1 January in which he blamed the events in Eastern Europe on the absence of truly socialist policies. He did recognize that Albania faced some economic problems, such as the need for more food and consumer goods.

Until the split in 1978 Albania tended to mimic Chinese policy to some extent; the introduction of a form of workers' control in 1966 was a pale imitation of the Cultural Revolution. In order to pressurize managers into disclosing hidden reserves and to appease workers disappointed with consumption growth, workers' control involved the ability to give advice to management in the drawing up of the enterprise plan (Schnytzer 1982: 27). In 1968, however, after considerable criticism, workers' committees could be elected only on an *ad hoc* basis as specific problems cropped up and membership was confined to production workers only (p. 42). In 1970 the role of the mass meeting in enterprise annual plan formulation was reduced to submission of a draft plan to the State Planning Commission via the ministry (for centrally controlled enterprises) or the district council (for locally controlled enterprises) (Kaser 1986: 9). Kaser (1986: 3, 9) describes the post-1966 measures as a reversion to the traditional Soviet system. The trade union branch became able to recommend the sacking of a manager.

There was no legal *private sector* in industry until 1990.

At the Ninth Congress in November 1986 it was reported that over the period of the Seventh Five Year Plan (1980–85) national income had increased by 16 per cent, while 45 per cent of investment had been devoted to industry (especially heavy industry) and 30 per cent to agriculture. The aim of the Eighth Five-year Plan (1986–90) was to devote 83 per cent of investment to industry and agriculture, with the latter receiving thirty-two percentage points (*Albanian Life*, December 1986, pp. 6–7). During the 1980s engineering, as an aspect of import substitution, and chemicals, as a support for agriculture, were given increased priority.

Manpower

Until the mid-1960s the sort of wage and salary differentials associated with the traditional Soviet model were typical. In 1966, however, a policy of far greater egalitarianism was followed, with actual reductions of salaries in the higher ranges implemented in 1967 and 1976. In 1976 the maximum 'vertical' pay scale differential was fixed at 1:2.5, and the maximum 'horizontal' range for laborious work or special locations at 1:1.66 to 1.233 (Kaser 1986: 13). Sjöberg (1989: 6) considers that these egalitarian moves were motivated by the desire to reduce urban–rural differentials and hence the attractiveness of jobs in the towns. Greater stress was laid on moral incentives; managers, however, continued to receive certain perquisites, such as the use of a company car (no private cars were allowed) and party members had special access to scarce commodities. The benefits of productivity increases were given in the form of periodic price reductions (in 1950–69 and 1982–83, for example) rather than higher nominal wages.

Negative effects on work incentives, however, led to complaints of absenteeism and declining work discipline and labour productivity. In 1980, as a consequence, a stronger link was forged between pay and performance in both state enterprises and agricultural co-operatives via the payment of bonuses and other benefits such as holidays for plan fulfilment. The 1986–90 Five Year Plan included the increased use of such bonus payments.

After 1958 there were attempts to involve administrative employees (including management after 1968) in production on a paid basis. This, together with the encouragement given to young people to offer their services voluntarily, was inspired by a desire to reduce the gap between town and countryside and between mental and physical labour (Schnytzer 1982: 36). Beginning in the early 1970s there was a programme to reduce the number of administrative personnel in the productive enterprises, while many office workers 'volunteered' to work on an assembly line (Bowers 1989: 452). By 1975 the party's rotation effort had been extended to include even former deputy ministers and enterprise directors (p. 453).

The financial system

The budgetary system was progressively centralized after 1971 (Sjöberg 1990: 5). As was typical in the socialist world, taxes on state enterprises and co-operatives provided the bulk of budgetary revenue, there being no income tax after 1967. In 1984 96 per cent of revenue came from turnover tax and profit deductions (Kaser 1986: 15). On average, about a fifth of national income was devoted to defence during 1981–84 (*EEN*, 1988, vol. 2, no. 12, p. 5). There was extensive rationing of highly subsidized basic commodities and state housing (private housing existed and was especially common in the countryside). 'Luxury' consumer goods bore a heavy tax; the *EEN* reported the appearance of twenty foodstuffs for 'special' occasions at very high prices (1988, vol. 2, no. 21, p. 8).

AGRICULTURE

In pre-socialist Albania 85 per cent of the population lived in the countryside, where 3 per cent of the rural population owned 40 per cent of arable land and 14 per cent owned no land at all (Prescott 1986: 5). In 1989 64 per cent of the population was rural and just over 50 per cent of the workforce was employed in agriculture (Åslund and Sjöberg 1991: 15). In 1944–45 land above what was considered to be a family's needs was confiscated and redistribution took place. Private peasants, however, were subjected to compulsory delivery quotas. Collectivization began in November 1946, was accelerated in the late 1950s and completed in 1966, by which time all land was either collectively or state-owned.

Sjöberg (1989: 1–15; 1990: 7) describes trends in economic policy. After June 1963 a policy of self-sufficiency in bread grains was followed, probably being achieved by 1976. This was partly due to greater emphasis on incentives in the form of increased procurement prices, reduced taxes, and the granting of social security payments, including old-age pensions, to farmers. A policy of district self-sufficiency in food production was also followed. An intensification programme was launched in 1981 in order to increase yields via increased mechanization, irrigation, melioration, fertilizers and insecticides.

Private markets were banned in 1981, although impromptu peasant markets sprang up in many places in the mid-1980s (Sjöberg 1991: 118–9). Private plots were eliminated on state farms in the latter half of the 1960s, and although they were allowed in co-operatives (albeit with a maximum of 500 square metres) they decreased in size over time. Surplus private output had to be sold to the co-operative at state-determined prices. In 1971 monthly advances for the co-operative peasants were introduced, with an end-of-year residual paid according to plan fulfilment. The 1975 experiment of combining family-owned livestock into joint herds subsequently spread, the pressure to transfer livestock to co-operatives eventually leading to slaughtering and meat shortages. In late 1981 the remaining private livestock in lowland districts and all sheep and goats in mountainous areas were collectivized (Sjöberg 1989: 6). In 1983 co-operatives specializing in animal husbandry were set up (Sjöberg 1991a: 119). In 1985 'brigade herds' were introduced into state and collective farms. The livestock previously collectivized were allocated to the brigades, which decided on manpower use and distributed the resulting output to member families. They were soon followed by brigade plots. In late 1988 some co-operatives were allowed to sell produce direct to the towns at market prices, and the practice widened (Sjöberg 1990: 6–9). In late December 1989 it was decided to improve meat supplies by giving co-operative families and private plot holders young livestock, and to allow co-operatives nation-wide to sell their surplus output in local markets (*EEN*, 1990, vol. 4, no. 1, p. 5). A 1986 concession involved acreage being turned over to collective farms for private tillage, provided that the crop was shared among brigade members. The ultimate aim was to eliminate private farming by means of the gradual transformation of co-operatives into state farms where all property was state-owned and where the loss of plots was allegedly compensated for by wage security.

Although about twenty co-operatives a year were being converted, co-operative farms still dominated Albanian agriculture. In the mid-1980s state farms only accounted for some 25 per cent of agricultural output. In 1971 'higher-type agricultural co-operatives' were introduced as transitional institutions towards full state farms. These 'higher types' differ from traditional co-operatives in a number of ways, in that they: (1) receive state budgetary grants instead of repayable long-term bank credits; (2) have exclusive use of a single Machine Tractor Station instead of having to share (the MTS is used to ensure state rather than co-operative ownership of large machinery and as a means of party propaganda); and (3) pay guaranteed piece-rate wages every fortnight amounting to 90 per cent of the planned payroll, the remaining 10 per cent being paid after the end-of-year accounting on successful fulfilment of plan targets. A number of co-operatives were transformed into full state farms, which own their own machinery and equipment and act as stockbreeding and seed distribution centres. Kerin Hope (*FT*, 9 October 1991, p. 30) provides the following information: co-operatives employed more than 40 per cent of the workforce, while the state farms employed 15 per cent; while co-operatives supplied local towns, state farms also exported products like meat, fruit and vegetables.

Although uniform retail prices prevail, procurement prices are lower for co-operative farms operating in more favourable circumstances (Prescott 1986: 9). Thus a form of rent extraction is in operation. The present overall strategy for agriculture revolves around 'intensification', especially through the greater use of pesticides and fertilizers.

Communist Albania claimed to be 95 per cent self-sufficient in food, with agriculture accounting for around a quarter of exports (*EIU Country Profile*, 1987–88: 32). A prolonged drought 1987–90 (there was also one 1983–85) adversely affected not only agricultural output but also the production of hydro-electric power. Independent experts estimate that the average annual rate of growth of agricultural output in the 1980s was less than 3 per cent (Kerin Hope, *FT*, 9 October 1991, p. 30). Sandström and Sjöberg (1991: 938) give the following figures for the average annual rate of growth of agricultural output in per cent: 1981–85, 3.0; 1981, 3.7; 1982, 4.0; 1983, 9.4; 1984, –3.5; 1985, 1.6; 1986, 4.2; 1987, 0.4; 1988, –6.4.

FOREIGN TRADE

Soviet aid and trade were important until 1961. According to Kaser (1986: 3), Albania started to open up trade with the West in the early 1970s, but after the mid-1970s import substitution was followed to extreme lengths. The desire for self-reliance and self-sufficiency increased after the split with China in 1978. Åslund and Sjöberg (1991: 3) put foreign trade dependence at around 6 per cent of GDP in the second half of the 1980s. Chinese aid ended in July 1978, but the rift started with China's invitation to President Nixon in 1971. About 45 per cent of foreign trade was with Comecon and 25 per cent with the EC (*FT*, 20 February 1990, p. 7). The 1976 constitution actually incorporated a ban on loans or direct investment from capitalist countries, although *EEN* reports the acceptance in October 1987 of a DM 6 million grant from the FRG for 'technical assistance' as part of the process of establishing diplomatic relations (1987, vol. 1, no. 15, p. 8). The FRG provided at least DM 15 million over a two-year period (Kerin Hope, *FT*, 6 March 1990, p. 2). The Soviet Union said that as of 1 November 1989 Albania owed it 127.8 million roubles (*CDSP*, 1990, vol. XLII, no. 9, p. 9). Recent strategy stressed the need to reduce imports, but recognized the need to increase exports of foodstuffs, raw materials (such as chrome, copper and nickel) and energy (such as electricity) in order to finance absolutely vital imports of the capital goods required to update the outmoded capital stock. Otherwise, domestic production of equipment was stressed: this was a change from the 1962 role of domestic production of spare parts for imported machinery (Kaser 1986: 8). Exports constitute 10 per cent of gross social product (Pashko 1991: 137). Trade links with China were formally restored in 1983, and Western companies are helping to develop chromite and ferro-nickel processing. This strategy was preferred to joint equity ventures or any radical reform of the economy. In 1988 the following were signed: an agreement on economic co-operation with the FRG (June); an agreement on economic, scientific, and cultural co-operation with Algeria (June); a protocol on economic co-operation and an agreement on international road transport with Turkey (August) (*Albanian Life*, 43, no. 3, 1988, p. 45). In August a ten-year barter deal with the Philips company was signed, involving the exchange of Albanian cement and tobacco for electronic components, measuring equipment and, at a later stage, colour television assembly kits and television lighting and studio equipment (*FT*, 18 August 1988, p. 2). Formal economic relations with the Soviet Union, including direct trade, were resumed on 31 August 1990; a trade, economic and technical agreement was signed on 13 January 1991.

In 1988 exports in percentage terms comprised: mineral and metals (e.g. chrome, copper and nickel) 39.8; fuels 7.9; electricity 7.3; agricultural products (e.g. vegetables) 16.1; processed foodstuffs 8.7; unprocessed foodstuffs 8.2; consumer goods 9.7; building materials 1.5; chemicals 0.8. Imports comprised: capital goods 31.5; spare parts 4.8; fuels, minerals and metals 23.1; chemicals 12.7; building materials 0.1; non-food agricultural products 13.5; foodstuffs 8.1; and consumer goods 6.2 (Pashko 1991: 137).

CONCLUSION

A history of foreign domination helps explain communist Albania's economic and political isolation, its quarrels in turn with its one-time major allies the Soviet Union and China. Despite some relaxation after the death of Enver Hoxha in 1985, the economy remained relatively isolated (although trade links were expanding),

and the poorest country in Europe was still tightly controlled in every sense. The following points are worth highlighting: Albania banned all religious institutions and practices in 1967; there was no legal private sector in industry and there was a state monopoly of domestic as well as foreign trade; the country was in the process of converting agricultural co-operatives into state farms, where all property belonged to the state and where there were no private plots; and the constitution allowed no loans or direct investment from capitalist countries. Until the upheavals in Eastern Europe in 1989 there seemed to be no prospect of real economic reform.

NOTES

1. The 70 per cent who were Muslims (making Albania the only 'Islamic' country in Europe) looked towards Turkey, while 20 per cent were Greek Orthodox. There were also Catholics, some 10 per cent.
2. The FRG's Foreign Minister Genscher visited Albania in October 1987, the first Western minister to do so.
3. Observers took this to be a positive reference to Serbia's autonomous province of Kosovo (largely populated by ethnic Albanians), which has now lost its autonomy. Ethnic Albanians now constitute 90 per cent of Kosovo's population.
4. See Malile's speech reproduced in *Albanian Life* (1988, 41, no. 1).

10

BULGARIA

BACKGROUND

In 1878, with the help of Tsar Alexander II, Bulgaria was liberated from nearly 500 years of Ottoman rule, and Russia continued to safeguard the country's interests against British and French efforts to bolster Turkey. Bulgaria sided with Germany in the First World War. There was a fascist military–royalist coup in 1923 against the elected but violent Agrarian Party government, which carried out a land redistribution even more egalitarian than that of 1878–80. Bulgaria joined the Axis pact in the Second World War. It did not declare war on the Soviet Union, however. In fact, the Soviet Union declared war on Bulgaria on 5 September 1944, although three days later the latter did the same against Germany. Todor Zhivkov, who became first secretary in March 1954 and president in 1971, was always a loyal supporter of the Soviet Union. Zhivkov resigned as party secretary on 10 November 1989 and was expelled from the

party on 13 December. On 18 January 1990 a warrant was issued for his arrest on the grounds of 'incitement to ethnic hostility and hatred, unwarranted receiving of excessive amounts of public property and gross malfeasance'. The communist party became the Bulgarian Socialist Party and won 211 of the 400 seats in the Grand National Assembly in the free election of June 1990.

Bulgaria's 9 million inhabitants live in a country that is relatively well endowed with fertile soils, although the rainfall is not dependable, and is relatively poor in energy and minerals. Some low-grade coal and copper, bauxite and lead are to be found. The plan was to let nuclear energy contribute almost half of electricity by 1995 (*EEN*, 1989, vol. 3, no. 3, p. 7).[1] In pre-socialist Bulgaria 75 per cent of the population was classified as rural (28 per cent today), and agriculture contributed 65 per cent of national output. McIntyre (1988: 69, 97) makes the interesting point that the transition to

Table 10.1 Bulgaria: average annual rates of growth of NMP and GNP (%)

	1949–52	1953–57	1958–60	1961–65	1966–70	1971–75	1976-80	1981–85	1986	1987	1988	1989
NMP	8.4	7.8	11.6	6.7	8.8	7.8	6.1	3.7	5.3	4.7	2.4	−0.3
GNP (CIA)	–	–	–	–	–	7.5	1.0	0.9	4.8	−1.0	0.9	−0.1

Sources: Lampe (1986: 144); McIntyre (1988a: xvi); *Bulgaria*, January–March 1988, p. 8; Institute of International Finance (1990: 14); *International Currency Review*, 1990, vol. 20, nos 4 and 5, pp. 75, 77; CIA (1990: tables 1 and C-3); United Nations Economic Commission for Europe (1992: 293).

a Soviet-type system in the post-war period was aided by a number of factors, such as active state intervention in the inter-war economy, a relatively even distribution of land and general poverty in the countryside, and a co-operative tradition in agriculture. Table 10.1 shows the official figures for average annual rates of growth of NMP and GNP.

INDUSTRIAL REFORM

Communist Bulgaria undertook a continuous stream of reforms (Kaser 1981; Dellin 1970; Feiwell 1979; Lampe 1986; Jackson 1986a; McIntyre 1988a). In May 1963 a decree authorized the establishment of a horizontally integrated DSO (*durzhavenski stopanski obedineniya*, state economic organization), later to become the basic production unit. In July of that year some 2,000 industrial enterprises were merged into 120 DSOs. The December 1965 'Theses' provided a blueprint of the New System of Management (Nov Sistem na Rukovodstvo). Although the economy was to remain highly centralized, organization was to become more efficient by means of a reduction in the number of production units, which also allowed the centre to exert firm control over strategic decision-making, and by means of an increase in the amount of detail decided below. (The industrial structure became more concentrated over time: in 1965 9.6 per cent of enterprises employed more than 5,000 workers, but by 1987 the figure had risen to 41.4 per cent; Jones and Meurs 1991a: 316). The number of compulsory indicators for the Five Year Plan was reduced to four, though these were very broad and readily open to further subdivision: physical output, ceiling on investment, ceiling on inputs and foreign trade targets. There was talk (only) of a tiered system of prices, fixed (on the basis of average cost plus a 2 per cent mark-up), range and a very restricted 'free' category. Profitability was to become a more important determinant of incentive funds (up to 70 per cent of profits could be retained) and

there was to be a move away from investments financed by budgetary grants towards retained profits and interest-bearing credits, although investment decisions remained tightly controlled from above. A capital charge averaging 6 per cent of the value of enterprise fixed and working capital was introduced. The wage fund indicator was abandoned and replaced by a progressive income tax.

Even though pre-1968 rhetoric outstripped practice (a not uncommon feature in Eastern Europe), that year still marked a clear change of course, due mainly to a fear of loss of party control should reforms remotely approaching those of pre-invasion Czechoslovakia be introduced. A labour shortage also became apparent at the start of the 1970s. The number of plan indicators was increased to include, for instance, a wage fund limit and deliveries in volume terms. The idea of tiered prices was abandoned. Lampe (1986: 204) points out that it was the DSOs and not the ministries that supervised the new system of supply contracts between enterprises, with prices determined by enterprise bargaining. In November 1970 the number of DSOs was reduced from 120 to sixty-four (thirty-five in industry) and the following month enterprises were shorn of their legal autonomy; larger ones became 'subsidiaries' (still allowed to sign contracts and hold bank accounts) and smaller ones became 'subdivisions' which were fully absorbed. The DSO became the basic production unit, dominating its constituent parts, distributing inputs, allocating plan tasks, determining investment, and relegating the subsidiary to the role of executing plan targets, especially for volume, assortment and quality of output, input utilization and technical levels. Counter-planning was introduced in 1972. Apart from the DSOs, a number of co-ordinating agencies and alternative 'economic organizations' were set up after 1974, such as vertically integrated combines. The main aim was to streamline the command planning system.

The term 'New Economic Mechanism' was

used throughout the 1970s and beyond, but any resemblance to Hungary was in name only. Bulgaria continued to be a command economy, although the *1979 proposals*, first applied to agriculture, are worth noting (see Kaser 1981 in particular). The main objective in these and the 1982–83 measures was to achieve financial accountability and greater self-financing (including investment financed internally or from credit, both needing servicing out of revenue earned, and payments to the budget). In these 1979 proposals the ministry could officially impose only five broad indicators on the DSO or equivalent economic organization (instead of the previous twenty-five), namely (1) 'realized production' (production in saleable form disposed of to recipients) in physical terms, subdivided into exports, co-operative deliveries and spare parts and deliveries to the domestic market; (2) net output in value terms; (3) foreign exchange earnings on exports and/or maximum foreign exchange expenditure; (4) limits on supplies of raw materials, intermediate inputs, energy and 'certain deficitary materials and equipment'; and (5) payments to the state budget. In turn, the DSO or equivalent imposed four indicators on its 'subdivisions', namely (1) production in physical units by type and quality; (2) 'normed cost of production per unit of output'; (3) tasks for the application of new techniques; and (4) maximum number of personnel. There was to be full self-accounting for all enterprises, and the wage fund was linked to productivity and allowed a share in profit increases. Management was to benefit from plan overfulfilment but suffer salary reductions for failure to fulfil norms. The DSO or other economic organization was able to sell above-plan output once its planned production targets had been fulfilled. Above-plan output could be sold in own shops, abroad (on commission or through a foreign trade corporation) or to a local government authority. A number of wholesalers were permitted to establish production plants. Economic organizations could apply for long-term (up to ten years) credit, although invest-

ment remained highly centralized. Decentralized investment was steered by the availability and cost of credit, and successful enterprises paid less interest than unsuccessful ones. There were also interest rate rebates for overfulfilling export targets, especially in hard currency markets. According to M. Jackson (1986a: 49), branch ministries reverted to state budget financing after being placed on an economic accounting basis in 1976. Within the enterprise, brigades became increasingly placed on an economic accounting basis (M. Jackson 1986a: 50). Increasing emphasis was placed on worker brigades (as is common in other socialist countries); these averaged around sixteen per enterprise in Bulgaria. They were provided with output targets and inputs, arranged their own work schedules, and were paid by results. In December 1986 the first direct elections were held by workers of their factory managers. In March of the previous year workers at enterprises failing to fulfil output targets were required to increase their working week from five to six days until the deficit had been eliminated (Miskiewicz 1987: 80). There were some interesting changes after 1979 (Lampe 1986:217–8; McIntyre 1988: 119–22, 1988a: 602–4 and 1992: 65–9).

1. The 'initiation of small enterprises' programme began in 1980–81. These were state-owned, semi-autonomous, small and medium-sized units within DSOs, with some flexibility to respond to changing market needs (the room to manoeuvre included product design, production methods, marketing and pricing).[2] The Bulgarian Industrial Association (BIA) was set up in 1982 as a 'voluntary membership organization', providing managerial and consultancy services and playing an entrepreneurial role in the setting up of new enterprises where there are gaps in the market, initially in areas like clothing, small appliances and speciality foodstuffs, but more recently also in research and technical applications and computer services. It also helped existing enterprises to develop new projects.

2. There were strong links between the BIA and the Mineral Bank-Bank for Economic Initiatives (MB) set up in 1986 and jointly owned by the Bulgarian National Bank (a half) and about 200 large economic organizations (the other half). The MB provided credit for above-plan investments in large enterprises that help achieve the plan more effectively (rewards involved lower interest rates, while penalties included both higher interest rates and salary reductions), and for the small enterprise programme, based on criteria such as the pay-back period, energy savings and potential for foreign exchange earnings.

3. Measures were taken during 1982–83, mainly concerning financial incentives and prices. 'Final economic performance' (net income) was the major plan indicator, but there were also targets for tax payments, limits on input use and minimum export levels. The minimum wage was abolished. Experiments tested managerial performance in relation to net income over a five year period with demotion possible, while ministers' salaries depended to some extent on the performance of their organizations. The Bulgarian National Bank was allowed to hold regional competitions for investment credits.

The New Economic Mechanism was thus gradually modified after 1979. The general aim was to increase the importance of indirect steering and allow the centre to concentrate on strategic matters, with production units (able to sign legally binding contracts) having greater decision-making authority, free from the petty tutelage typically exercised by ministries. Ministries were amalgamated into fewer bodies in order to streamline the planning process, and to prevent both empire building and meddling in day-to-day enterprise management. For example, the new Ministry of Trade and Material Resources fused the ministries of construction, foreign trade, internal trade and material resources.

The financial system

A basic idea of the New Economic Mechanism was that bank credits should be increasingly based on the criterion of economic effectiveness. Capital investment credits required at least a 35 per cent contribution by an investor from own resources (Jackson 1986a: 52). In June 1987 a Hungarian-type two-tier *banking system* was established, with the Bulgarian National Bank (as a central bank) supervising eight commercial banks, which were owned by the National Bank and economic organizations, which elected bank directors and take part in shareholders' meetings. They were sector-orientated (such as electronics and transport), competed for customers and faced the threat of bankruptcy. The state still had to finance desired projects that did not meet commercial criteria; the commercial banks did not have to make loans to unprofitable companies, which had to resort to state subsidies or price support (Lev Kokushin, *Bulgaria*, November–December 1987, p. 34).

There was a tiered system of prices (Jackson 1986a: 53; Lampe 1986: 219): fixed prices for basic consumer goods, communal services, fuels, energy and raw materials; ceiling; range; and contract prices. Wyzan (1989: 650) makes the point that food prices were generally not subsidized, so that official retail and collective farm market prices were closer than normal in Eastern Europe. Foreign trade organizations were able to contract freely with enterprises for above-plan output, and wholesalers and retailers were able to negotiate over the prices of non-essential products. Increasing regard was taken of changes in world prices.

The Thirteenth Party Congress in April 1986 saw an attack on the defects of the current system: corruption, bureaucracy, incompetence, inertia, irresponsibility, inefficiency, alcoholism and absenteeism. Sweeping personnel changes took place (younger and more technocratic people were installed) and order, discipline and responsibility were stressed. Subsequent changes included the establishment of new state councils for agriculture and forestry, intellectual development, social affairs and economic affairs. McIntyre (1988a: 115, 118) suggests, however, that the closure of six major industrial ministries may have been more apparent than real, especially in light of the creation, in May 1986, of five 'voluntary associations' in construction, trade, light industry, electronics and food and tobacco; these may possibly have been mere sub-sections of the councils. In August of the following year, however, it was announced that these were to be scrapped along with three ministries (finance, trade and education) and five committees (research and technology, state planning, labour and social affairs, prices, and science) and replaced by four new ministries: economics and planning; foreign economic relations; agriculture and forestry; and culture, science and education. Within the enterprise, brigades were emphasized. D. Jones (1991: 222–3) is of the opinion that although the extent of workers' influence on decision-making was strictly limited, the 1986 Labour Code was a turning point in industrial relations; formally at least some power was shifted from the enterprise and its union-based structures to the work brigade and its non-union-based structures (for a fuller account of worker participation and worker self-management in Bulgaria see Jones and Meurs 1991b).

The 1987 reform proposals

The June 1987 plenum of the Central Committee approved the introduction of the 'Principles of the Concept of the Further Construction of Socialism in Bulgaria', to be phased in after 1 January 1988 (see especially Hristov 1987: 10–18). The basic idea was to leave 'strategic' matters to the centre, with planning to remain the principal instrument through which the state managed the economy, e.g. via 'state orders' (these were supposed to cover e.g. major products for the domestic markets, the main investment projects, and international obliga-

tions; the necessary inputs and foreign exchange were assured). Current and executive affairs (including joint ventures with foreign companies) were to be left to self-managing economic organizations, the aim being to keep each function to the lowest level where it could be independently performed. There was a three-tier system of enterprise, corporation, and association. The last was the co-ordinator of general policy (in electronics, for example), while leaving, on the whole, a substantial measure of autonomy to constituent organizations, although in sectors such as power generation there was a highly centralized structure. Managerial decision-making at the corporation level was undertaken by a collective body called the 'economic council' and comprising enterprise directors. The same applies to the association, although day-to-day affairs were left to a chairman and a deputy chairman, both elected by the board of directors, plus a limited number of executives. Note that enterprise directors were elected after late 1986, although the list of candidates was drawn up by 'public organizations'. During plan formulation representatives of the Ministry of Economics and Planning and the banks had 'dialogues' with corporations and, where necessary, with enterprises (Aroio 1989: 90).

The state still controlled the prices of 120 basic commodities, subsidizing them if necessary, but, as a rule, domestic prices had to match those that could be obtained for the commodities on the world market. This applied to users of raw materials, although those producers operating under very unfavourable natural conditions were subsidized. Interest rates, allegedly, also matched world levels. Bankruptcy was a possibility. The reforms allowed a higher proportion of profits to be retained; at that time up to 80 per cent was taxed away, excluding local rates and taxes. As of 1 January 1988 a unified system of tax rates was introduced: profit, 40 per cent; fixed capital charge, 3 per cent; municipality profits tax, 5 per cent; a value-added tax was to have been introduced by 1991 (Angelov 1989: 15). Pay was tied to performance (specifically value added), with only a minimum wage remaining. The salaries of the techno-scientific intelligentsia and university graduates were to have been increased, those of managerial personnel linked to indices such as profit margins and profit size, while heads of R&D units were to be paid in accordance with the increased profits made by production units using their ideas. These were meant to overcome problems associated with the relatively low pay of administrative–managerial personnel.

Grandiose schemes for top government included increasing the role of the state *vis-à-vis* the party, with the National Assembly (parliament) turned into a 'collective working body of self-management'. There was the vague idea of somehow making the enterprise collective the formal owner of property. The January 1989 decree called for the transformation of enterprises into 'firms', with provision made for the distribution of shares to a firm's employees (these shares could only be resold to other employees); possible forms included joint stock companies and limited liability companies owned by partners, while bonds could be issued for specific investment purposes (Wyzan 1990c: 5–7). Multi-candidate elections took place, such as the February 1988 local elections. The Council of Ministers and the State Council were to have been abolished and replaced by a 'new headquarters of state power'. The Council of Ministers would be replaced by a 'national co-ordinating body'. In January 1988 the proposal was accepted of limiting all top party officials to two five year terms, while after the first of that month municipal authorities were financed directly from the central government rather than indirectly through regional councils.

AGRICULTURE

Land belonged to the state, except that around detached homes and weekend houses (McIntyre 1988a: xix). The *collectivization process* came to an end by 1958, when collective farms accounted for 92 per cent of total arable land. Collective farmers were granted old-age pensions in 1957. Until 1959 members were compensated for loss of their land through a rental payment. The next two years witnessed an amalgamation of collectives into 957 large farms with an average of 4,500 ha (Lampe 1986: 148–9). A decade later another merger programme was undertaken. In 1967 co-operative farmers were formed into fixed brigades specializing in one task as near to their own village as possible, and they were the first in Eastern Europe to receive state pensions and health benefits (Lampe 1986: 203); Bulgaria was the first country, in the early 1960s, to introduce a minimum income for collective farmers. In the late 1980s agriculture still employed a fifth of the workforce.

Agro-industrialization

During the 1970s a 'process of industrialization' of agriculture took place (after experiments in 1968–69) based on the 'agro-industrial complex' (*agrarno-promishlen komplex*: APK), normally a horizontal integration of co-operative farms, state farms and their servicing centres (some vertical integration took place, as with agriculture, fertilizer production and final sales); and the 'industro-agrarian complex' (PAK), which vertically merged farms with industrial enterprises processing and selling agricultural products such as sugar (e.g. the DSO Rodopa; see Kaser 1981 and Wiedemann 1980). In the period 1970–72 the existing fifty-six state and 744 collective farms were grouped into 170 APKs, the former two types of farm eventually losing their juridical autonomy and becoming mere operating sections of the latter (McIntyre 1988: 100). In 1977 there were 143 APKs with an average size of 24,500 ha of tilled land and 5,552 members; by 1980 the respective numbers were 283, 10,421 and 2,823 (Wyzan 1990b: 220). By 1982 the average APK covered 16,000 ha, while the PAK and NPK were roughly twice that size (Lampe 1986: 207). Although still subject to the central plan when executing the most important targets, there was still considerable scope for independent decision-making with regard to details. Cochrane (1990b: 236) notes, however, that, as of 1985, as much as 80 per cent of production was said to have been still mandated by state plans. Boyd (1990: 71–2), too, notes that, despite greater decentralization, agriculture was still subjected to the overall framework of state-directed production; in addition the reforms of the 1970s and 1980s failed to stimulate productivity growth (p. 82).

The 'scientific–productive complex' (NPK) was particularly important for the incorporation of scientific institutes. Capital-intensive modern industrial farming methods were designed to reap economies of scale, to save on scarce labour and to increase processed agricultural product exports (Lampe 1986: 207). In 1976 the National Agro-industrial Union was formed, absorbing the Ministry of Agriculture and Food three years later, whose purpose was to control the entire food sector, from farm production, to processing, and right through to marketing (Cook 1986a: 61). In March 1986 the union was subordinated to a new Ministry of Agriculture and Forestry (Wyzan 1990a: 296).

The APK was divided into brigades. Each brigade was assigned a particular land area or production line and each was on an economic accounting basis, with a wage fund linked to net income (Cook 1986a: 65). Under the New Economic Mechanism, which was first applied to agriculture in 1979, the number of central plan targets was reduced from twenty-four to four: delivery quotas; minimum hard currency earnings coupled with import ceilings; payments to the state budget; and ceilings on domestic input use (Cook 1986a: 64). Rent on agricultural land was differentiated according to fertility (Aroio 1989: 90).

According to the *EEN* (1988, vol. 2, no. 8, p. 6), a November 1987 resolution divided the agro-industrial complexes into some 2,500 self-managing work teams designed to function as financially independent economic enterprises, although implementation was delayed owing to administrative bottlenecks. In September 1988 Zhivkov re-emphasized the importance of the brigade and the transformation of the APK into a purely administrative body; he also echoed Gorbachev's call for leases of up to fifty years. But, as Wyzan (1989: 649) points out, Zhivkov was fond of repeated and ill-considered organizational change.

Private plots

There were always a few individual farms in mountainous areas. Private plots were first allowed in 1957; plot sizes ranged from 0.2 to one ha; a further 0.1 ha was granted for each head of cattle raised (McIntyre 1988b: 611). Active encouragement was given during the 1970s, such as the removal in the early 1970s of restrictions on the number of livestock. In 1977 abandoned APK land was provided for housewives, pensioners and agricultural workers to use in their spare time; the APK assisted in such ways as inputs and contracts to raise livestock (Wyzan 1990a: 288–9, 1990b: 226). As as result they accounted for 14 per cent of cultivated land by 1980 (Lampe 1986: 210). In 1985 the private sector accounted for 13 per cent of arable land and a quarter of gross farm output; it was especially important (figures for 1986) in meat (42 per cent of total output), fruit (42 per cent), vegetables (37 per cent) and eggs (50 per cent) (Cochrane 1988: 50). Products could be sold on the free market, to the state or to agro-industrial complexes, with which contracts could be signed, bringing benefits in the form of seed and fodder at favourable prices. As in Hungary, the state sector and private plots were mutually supportive (this has been the case especially since 1974); the former provided the latter with inputs and services in return for contractual sales of much of the output, which was then sold through the state distribution system

(McIntyre 1988a: 102, 1988b: 610). There were also auxiliary farms run by industrial and other non-agricultural enterprises, especially for works canteens but possibly also for sale of the produce to their workers (McIntyre 1988b: 610). Direct leasing of plots to urban residents began in 1977 (McIntyre 1988b: 103). In 1981 further encouragement came in the following forms: socialized bodies were permitted to include output purchased from the private sector in their obligatory sales to the state, while the income derived from sales by private producers was rendered tax-free (Cochrane 1988: 49). The series of harsh winters and summer droughts in the mid-1980s resulted in further incentives being offered to private production and rises in the prices of many consumer goods. The hiring of labour outside the immediate family was not allowed.

FOREIGN TRADE, DEBT AND INVESTMENT

Foreign trade and debt

Although actually starting the decade with a relatively high level of debt, Bulgaria was not tempted into borrowing Western credits during the 1970s on such a large scale as its then allies, although engineering was expanded and modernized and by 1976 the hard currency debt–service ratio of 44 per cent was actually the highest in Eastern Europe. Both the ratio and the net debt itself ($3.7 billion at the end of 1979) were reduced, by a programme that especially concentrated on reducing imports and re-exporting Soviet oil (after the late 1970s), to 20 per cent and $1.8 billion respectively by the end of 1982 and $0.9 billion by the end of 1984. Bulgaria resumed borrowing in 1985, after the December 1979 cessation, and net debt climbed as shown in Table 10.2. The debt–service ratio was 30 per cent in 1987 (IHT, 4 March 1988, p. 17). As of 1 November 1989 Bulgaria owed the Soviet Union 433.6 million roubles (CDSP, 1990, vol. XLII, no. 9, p. 9).

Exports accounted for 23 per cent of GDP in 1988 (*FT*, 29 June 1990, p. 2). Comecon always dominated Bulgaria's foreign trade, but by 1986 its share had risen to 79.2 per cent, the Soviet share alone to 59.2 per cent. The composition of exports changed substantially over time. There was a decline in the importance of foodstuffs, from around 49 per cent in the mid-1960s to 22 per cent two decades later. On the other hand the importance of manufactured products rose (machinery not far short of 50 per cent), reflecting the overall strategy of development; this involves, in particular, capital goods (including hi-tech items like robots and computers), and chemicals (including petrochemicals). Bulgaria was one of the most enthusiastic supporters of intra-Comecon trade and technology collaboration, and benefited from specialization agreements, fork-lift trucks being the best known example (mechanical engineering, biotechnology and electronics were broad areas of specialization in the late Zhivkov era). Imports were dominated by Soviet raw materials and oil (reduced by 10 per cent in early 1983, partly to encourage more efficient use by Bulgaria, but still adequate to allow exports of oil and petrochemicals). Machinery, however, accounted for around a third. Bulgaria did not escape Soviet complaints about the quality of products exchanged for ensured supplies of Soviet energy and raw materials. The organization of foreign trade was modified. Some enterprises such as Balkancar had their own trading organizations, while Machinoexport, for example, represented seventeen industrial companies.

Joint equity ventures

Access to Western hi-tech and know-how was gained mainly through industrial co-operation agreements, but after March 1980 joint ventures with Western companies with majority foreign ownership of equity were allowed. There was not much success. This was because of the restrictions then imposed: the chairman of the management board had to be Bulgarian and all

Table 10.2 Bulgaria: statistical survey

Average annual rate of growth of NMP (%)

1949–52	1953–57	1958–60	1961–65	1966–70	1971–75	1976–80	1981–85	1986	1987	1988	1989
8.4	7.8	11.6	6.7	8.8	7.8	6.1	3.7	5.3	4.7	2.4	–0.3

Net hard currency debt ($ billion)

1979	1984	1985	1986	1987	1988	1989
3.7	0.9	1.6	3.7	5.1	6.2	8.3

Registered joint equity ventures, mid-October 1989: 35

Private agriculture (including private farms) (%)

1985 Arable land	1985 Agricultural output
13	25

Population (1988): 9 million

Sources: Lampe (1986: 144); McIntyre (1988a: xvi); Cochrane (1988: 50); Institute of International Finance (1990: 14); European Economy: the Path of Reform in Central and Eastern Europe, Commission of the European Communities, Brussels, 1991, p. 161; United Nations Economic Commission for Europe (1992: 293).

decisions had to be unanimous; the foreign tax rose from 20 per cent for profits retained in Bulgaria to 30 per cent for repatriated profits. Machinery and equipment imported by the foreign partner were subsequently made free of tariffs. The January 1989 decree allowed wholly foreign-owned subsidiaries (Wyzan 1990c: 9). Fifteen joint ventures were in operation at the end of 1987 (FT, 14 April 1988, p. 3). By mid-October 1989 thirty-five were registered (FT, 19 January 1990, p. 6). Actual examples included industrial robots, machine parts, hotels, chemicals and biotechnology.

THE PRIVATE NON-AGRICULTURAL SECTOR

This was not a flourishing sector of the economy. In the early 1980s private restaurants were allowed to operate for a short time only in Black Sea resorts, while there were some unpublicized experiments in Sofia, the capital, in 1985. Co-operatives especially benefited. For example, co-operative taxis competed with state taxi services, but had to charge the same price as the latter and could only operate up to four hours a day on a part-time basis. According to the June 1987 'private labour decree' individuals or groups were allowed to set up, on a part-time basis, small workshops within state enterprises, and also retail shops, bakeries, laundries, repair shops, cafes and restaurants, tailoring and transport and building services; tourists could be accommodated by families. The ban on employing outside labour applied here too, but in January 1989 an employment ceiling was fixed of ten on a permanent basis; an unlimited amount of seasonal labour could be employed, however (Wyzan 1990b: 6). According to OECD figures, private enterprise as a whole accounted for 8.9 per cent of GDP in 1988 (FT, 29 June 1990, p. 2). Panusheff and Smatrakalev (1990: 66) divide GNP in 1988 into the following contributing sectors: state, 92 per cent; co-operative, 3.2 per cent; and private, 4.8 per cent.

CONCLUSION

A loyal ally of the Soviet Union, Bulgaria undertook a continuous stream of reforms that did not, however, radically alter the nature of its command economy. Even the 'Principles of the Concept of the Further Construction of Socialism in Bulgaria', gradually phased in after 1 January 1988, were not as in Hungary; they promised only that 'strategic matters' would be left to the centre and detailed decision-making to the enterprises. Interesting aspects included pioneering work in agro-industrial organization, the Hungarian-style symbiosis of socialized and private agriculture, the small enterprise scheme, progress in high technology and a manageable foreign debt. Joint equity legislation did not prove to be highly successful in attracting foreign capital, and the private, non-agricultural sector was not flourishing. Bulgaria was caught up in the dramatic events of late 1989, although the Bulgarian Socialist Party won a majority of seats in the Grand National Assembly as a result of the free election of June 1990. The party came second to the Union of Democratic Forces, however, in the election of 13 October 1991.

NOTES

1. Serious concern has been expressed about the safety of Bulgaria's nuclear power plants, but the country relies a great deal on them, e.g. the Kozluduy plant supplies 40 per cent of electricity production. Two of the five reactors were closed for modernization in July 1991.
2. Winiecki is highly critical of the programme. The managers of these enterprises were former deputy ministers and heads of various bureaus, etc., whose managerial qualities were at best suspect but who had the right connections to input supplies; they subcontracted as much as possible and earned significantly more than previously. 'The only thing that has happened is that the shortages have been rearranged among enterprises and part of the ruling stratum gets more than before' (Winiecki 1988b: 33).

11

CZECHOSLOVAKIA

BACKGROUND

The First World War resulted in the disintegration of the Habsburg Empire and Czechoslovakia emerged in 1918 (28 October) as a separate state under President Tomas Garrigue Masaryk. The new country combined two very different economies, namely the industrialized Czech lands of Bohemia and Moravia and the more backward agrarian Slovakia (23 per cent of the total population, but only 8 per cent of total industrial output) (*Czechoslovak Economic Digest*, 1991, no. 4, p. 5); Slovakia's share of industrial output increased to 13.5 per cent in 1948 and 29.5 per cent in 1989 (p. 6). A firm democratic tradition was established in the inter-war period. The Munich agreement (signed by Britain, France, Italy, and Germany on 30 September 1938), however, did away with Czech independence and left Nazi Germany in increasing control. Germany annexed the Sudetenland (the German-speaking area); in March 1939 the protectorate of Bohemia and Moravia and the puppet state of Slovakia were set up. The communist party assumed complete power in February 1948, having actually done quite well in the circumscribed but otherwise relatively free elections to the Constitutional National Assembly of 26 May 1946 (partly because of the Munich agreement), which left it the strongest party, with 38 per cent of the vote. The country became a federated socialist republic comprising the Czech and Slovak Socialist Republics.

Czechoslovakia was already an advanced industrialized country, although not particularly well endowed with raw materials, at the start of the socialist era. By 1930 nearly 35 per cent of the working population was employed in industry (36.3 per cent in 1950) and in 1938 it was the only surviving democracy in central and south-east Europe (Teichova 1988: 33, 80). Myant (1989: 1) puts the proportion of the 'active population' employed in mining and manufacturing in 1930 at 45 per cent, compared with 18 per cent in Poland and 22 per cent in Hungary. Czechoslovakia ranked in the top ten industrial producers, in the top seven suppliers of arms and, among European countries, in the top echelons for export dependence (Teichova 1988: 20). Winiecki (1988a: 207) considers that here, at the turn of the twentieth century, was to be found one of the world's top five centres of heavy industry. In 1938 *per capita* national income was 75 per cent of that of France (Myant 1989: 2). Vladimir Dloughy (the then head of the State Planning Commission) puts *per capita* national income in 1938 10 per cent higher than Austria's, whereas now it is 35 per cent lower (*IHT*, 5 December 1989, p. 11).

The 'Prague Spring' was ended by the Warsaw Pact (excluding Romania) invasion of 1968.[1] Gustav Husak became First Secretary in April 1969, replacing Alexander Dubcek. Dubcek had replaced Antonin Novotny on 5 January 1968 (Novotny had become General Secretary in 1953 and president four years later). Dubcek was expelled from the party in June

1970. On 17 December 1987 Husak himself lost his general secretaryship to Milos Jakes, although retaining the presidency which he had gained in 1975.

The 15.7 million population had the second highest standard of living in the socialist world, but it was only with the advent of Gorbachev that meaningful political and economic reform became a post-1968 possibility. The Seventeenth Party Congress in March 1986 saw an attack on problems such as corruption, inertia, inefficiency and bureaucracy, similar to that at the Soviet Congress. The harsh suppression of the 17 November 1989 students' demonstration was a key catalyst in the 'velvet revolution'. On 24 November the politburo resigned. Jakes was replaced as a General Secretary, expelled from the party on 7 December, and arrested on 6 June 1990 for abuse of power and violating the law over the 1968 invasion. Husak lost the presidency on 10 December 1989 and was expelled from the party on 17 February 1990. Dubcek was elected speaker of the Federal Assembly on 28 December 1989 and Vaclav Havel elected president the day afterwards. The free election of June 1990 was won by Civic Forum (and its Slovak counterpart Public against Violence).

Socialist Czechoslovakia depended heavily on imports of fuel and energy, especially from the Soviet Union. The economy is endowed with only limited raw materials – for example, low-grade coal is the sole energy resource of note, providing around 55 per cent of total energy. Despite Chernobyl, a major nuclear programme is under way. Nuclear energy was planned to account for 25 per cent of electricity by 1990 and over half by the year 2000 (*EEN*, 1988, vol. 2, no. 10, p. 7), compared to 6 per cent in 1980. This is still the policy. Currently, lignite accounts for 70 per cent and hydro-electricity 5.0 per cent (*Abecor Country Report*, June 1988, p. 2). Table 11.1 shows the rates of growth of national income.

INDUSTRIAL REFORM

The fact that Czechoslovakia was a relatively industrialized country before the Second World War accounts, in part, for an early attempt to modify command planning. In the late 1950s enterprises were amalgamated into associations, emphasis was placed on financial planning, and some small measure of decentralization of decision-making was allowed. The deep-seated ills were not cured, and a negative growth rate in 1962 added to the list; the Five Year Plan was abandoned in August of that year. Batt (1988: 171) considers that the main reason for the introduction of economic reforms in the mid-1960s was the need to preserve political stability – poor economic performance was a threat to party legitimacy.

The most radical reform measures outside Yugoslavia were taken in 1966–67 (Feiwell 1968; Holesovsky 1968, 1973; Kyn 1970; Staller 1968; Teichova, 1988). The 1966–67 measures largely abandoned directive planning and generally allowed enterprises to determine their own output and input mix in the light of maximizing net value-added. The industrial associations (VHJs; created in 1958) were amal-

Table 11.1 Czechoslovakia: average annual rates of growth of NMP and GNP (%)

	1951–55	1956–60	1961–65	1966–70	1971–75	1976–80	1981–85	1986	1987	1988	1989
NMP	8.2	6.9	2.0	6.9	5.7	3.6	1.8	2.6	2.1	2.3	0.7
GNP (CIA)					4.7	2.2	1.2	2.1	1.1	1.8	1.0

Sources: Abecor Country Report, June 1988, June 1989; EIU, *Country Profile*, 1987–88, p. 12; Smith (1983: 40); Institute of International Finance (1990: 15); CIA (1990: tables 1 and C-6); United Nations Economic Commission for Europe (1992: 293).

gamated into trusts (Teichova 1988: 152). Workers' councils began to be set up in 1968. These included representatives of workers, management, banks and state bodies, and were to have determined the main enterprise decisions and to have appointed managers. Batt (1988: 224–5) makes the point, however, that although there was a certain element of spontaneity in the establishment of workers' councils, started by CKD Praha and Skoda Plzen, the process was rather slow, and popular interest only became keen after the Warsaw Pact invasion, when councils took on a patriotic aspect. The state exercised indirect control via instruments such as credit policy, capital charges (6.0 per cent on 'basic means' and 2.0 per cent on 'assets'; Teichova 1988: 153), a tax on value added, payroll surcharges (30 per cent on wage growth), and varying taxes on other uses of retained profit. The state intended to retain control of the overall share of investment and consumption in national income, but decentralized investment was to constitute as much as 40 per cent of total investment. Banks took account of commercial criteria as well as state guidelines and foreign trade considerations in allocating investment credits. A tiered system of prices was introduced. The first stage (1 January 1967) saw the introduction of fixed prices (15 per cent of important producer goods, such as raw materials, fuels and energy, and more than 75 per cent of consumer goods, mainly basic foodstuffs), limit prices (80 per cent of producer goods), and free prices (5 per cent of producer goods and 20 per cent of consumer goods). The second stage, which began in the summer of the same year, increased the importance of the limit category, introduced a standard sales tax, and envisaged the prices of around 50 per cent of all products being freed by 1969. It was also planned to narrow the gap between domestic and world prices (Teichova 1988: 154–5). The relationship between enterprise and association gave rise to difficulties, such as association influence over investment and financial transfers between enterprises, but

it was intended eventually to make membership voluntary. Enterprises and foreign trade corporations were to be allowed to trade direct with foreign partners.

The August 1968 Warsaw Pact invasion (Soviet troops had been withdrawn in November 1945) quickly halted the whole liberalization process and by mid-1970 most of the economic reform had been abandoned. Batt traces the events. In October 1968 the government forbade the further extension of the 'experiment' in enterprise councils, and in May the following year the concept of self-managing councils was formally rejected. In June and July 1969 it became apparent that enterprise autonomy and non-command planning were not acceptable; industrial associations were required to deliver specified goods to the state, while the 1970 plan targets, published in July, were to be mandatory. Central wage controls were reintroduced in the latter half of 1969, while a price freeze introduced in 1970 lasted for virtually a decade. Brezhnev and rest of the Soviet leadership disliked the continuation of 'spontaneous' post-invasion developments, such as the voluntary establishment of new associations (which started in December 1968 in engineering) and the work of the Federal Planning Ministry on a new law of planning, which continued up to mid-1969 (Batt 1988: 226–7).

Some 1967 elements remained, such as the stress on credits as opposed to budgetary grants in the financing of state-determined investments, and some enterprises being allowed to continue trading direct with foreign partners. Enterprises were still meant to cover most of their expenditure from revenue, and the success indicators included deliveries of goods to the domestic market (rather than gross output), exports, fixed investment, and profit. A capital charge was still imposed, and the wage fund was linked to the volume of sales.

In 1977 prices were based on average cost plus mark-ups on capital and wage costs. Prices of raw materials, fuels and electricity were raised in order to economize on their use and investment goods' prices lowered to stimulate factor substitution and thus savings on scarce labour. Rising world prices of raw materials and fuels led to the 1978 'complex experiment', which involved twelve associations, covering 150 industrial enterprises, nine foreign trade corporations and twenty-one research institutes. This provided the basis for the gradual introduction of the March 1980 'Set of Measures to Improve the System of Planned Management of the National Economy after 1980' (Rychetnik 1981).

The industrial association (VHJ) became the basic production unit. It usually involved a horizontal integration of enterprises, either a *koncern* (a large enterprise alone or one linked with smaller ones) or a trust (where enterprises of comparable size are merged), but there was also the vertically integrated *kombinat*. The economy remained tightly controlled, with familiar plan indicators, such as production, sales, technical development, fixed investment, material inputs, labour, wages and financial tasks, still to be found. There were, however, several interesting features echoing those in other Comecon countries. Norms and plans were supposed to be fixed for a five-year period and value-added was to play an important role in wage bill determination, although basic wage rates were to remain centrally controlled. The 'wage bill limit' consisted of two parts: a 'basic wage bill limit' linked to value added and an 'incentive component' related to profitability. Material incentives were also affected by: (1) a 'rewards fund' (a share of profits was dependent on meeting targets for product quality and technical level and on labour economies); and (2) the 'cultural and social needs fund' (this was linked to the wage bill, profit, labour productivity, product assortment, exports, product quality and fixed asset utilization). Exports were encouraged by an 'export stimulation fund'. Payments to the state, such as payments out of profit, a capital charge and social security contribution, had priority over material incentive

funds. Decentralized investment was abandoned and budgetary grants, as opposed to retained profits and credits, were supposed to be the exception rather than the rule. There was no radical price reform, though there were attempts to take greater account of movements in world prices; raw material and fuel prices were increased and quality surcharges (and discounts) introduced. Bank credit policy, including hard currency, was geared to import saving, export promotion, and restructuring.

The 1980 set of measures was formally destined to be replaced by a programme for the '*comprehensive restructuring (prestavba) of the economic mechanism*' when thirty-seven 'principles for the restructuring of the economic mechanism' were laid down in January 1987 and adopted at the Central Committee session in December 1987.[2] The State Enterprise Act was passed on 14 June 1988. The programme was not designed to come fully into effect until the start of the 1991–95 Five Year Plan. Experiments began in 1987, with twenty-two enterprises taking almost 8 per cent of the output of centrally controlled industry, mostly in the export-orientated consumer goods branches; a further thirty-eight enterprises accounting for over 19 per cent of industrial output were placed on the new system in January 1988 (Janeba 1988: 46–7). The old VJHs were dissolved and 'state enterprises' established. In 1988, on average, a centrally controlled industrial enterprise employed 2,064 (Rychetnik 1992: 113).

The centre was to concentrate on 'strategic' decisions, the planning of overall social and economic development. An intensive type of development was of paramount importance, making full use of scientific and technological progress and a deepening of the international division of labour. The old-style directive aspects of the state plan were to be significantly curtailed, with a transition to a new mechanism primarily orientated towards indirect steering of the economy via the use of economic levers ('economic methods'), such as deductions into the state budget, prices, credit and wages. The prevailing stress on the annual plan was gradually to give way to the primary role of the Five Year Plan. Broadly speaking, economic and technical questions were to be decided at the particular management level having responsibility and access to the necessary information. Ministries were to be confined to such aspects as investment projects affecting the branch of industry as a whole (i.e. structural change and Comecon integration) and were to refrain from behaviour like redistributing profits from successful to less successful enterprises. There were some ministerial amalgamations, such as Metallurgy, Engineering and Technology. The state plan (e.g. 'state orders': in effect mandatory plan targets, with the state ensuring input supplies) formed the basis of the enterprise plan, but the latter was also to take account of the economic contracts concluded, thus expanding the role of horizontal relationships. Within its area of business, and after fulfilling state tasks, the enterprise had greater room for independent decision-making (including investment). There were to be only a limited number of key indicators, especially net output and profit, while enterprises were able to determine the total number of workers, the qualifications structure, and payment over the wage tariffs laid down. The state could impose limits for scarce raw materials and for foreign currency, however.

A significant part of pay was to be dependent on the final results of the enterprise – specifically, 'disposable profit'. By 1990 the incentive portion of wages paid from disposable profit was to have increased from the then average of 3 per cent to between 7 per cent and 10 per cent at minimum, this figure gradually increasing over the course of the next Five Year Plan; this proportion was to vary between categories of workers in order to widen differentials (Resolution, *Czechoslovak Economic Digest*, 1988, no. 1, p. 25). Enterprises were to be placed on the basis of 'full cost accounting' and 'self-financing': 'An enterprise shall defray its needs and costs from takings obtained primarily from

its entrepreurial activities as well as from other sources' ('Law on state enterprise' in *Czechoslovak Economic Digest*, 1988, no. 6, p. 11, henceforth 'Law'). This implied a reduction in subsidies and the possibility of liquidation, although the founding organ should first attempt a gradual programme of consolidation, direct administration for up to three years and merger or division ('Law', p. 14). In January 1989 thirty-eight enterprises, including Skoda Plzen, were declared insolvent and were thus subject to restructuring and stricter quality control.

Enterprises had to give at least six months' notice of changes in the labour force. They had to try to redeploy affected workers in other jobs but, failing that, to secure positions in other places in collaboration with relevant bodies. Greater use was to be made of the brigade system, a common trend, as we have already seen. The norms imposed upon enterprises (such as for profit deductions into the obligatory rewards, development, socio-cultural, reserve, and foreign exchange funds; tax rates, e.g. profits tax; and payments into the state budget, e.g. wage fund charge) were to be uniform and stable. Encouragement was given to the establishment of direct links with enterprises in other Comecon countries, while a portion of any hard currency earnings could be retained by the enterprise.

Enterprise managers were to be elected. Normally the founding body (e.g. the central or local government body) was to organize a competition from which a list of applicants would be drawn up. The workers' collective would elect the manager, although the founding organ had to confirm the decision. The 'self-management' bodies were the 'assembly' and the 'council', the former being the highest authority of the workers' collective and which had to meet at least twice a year. At first glance their functions appeared significant. They could, for example, approve the enterprise plan submitted by the manager. There were, however, constraints on this. For instance resolutions relating to deliveries concerned with defence, state security and the fulfilment of international obligations could not be passed without the consent of the representative of the enterprise founder, while the manager could take a dispute with the council or assembly to the founder for a final decision (Resolution 1988: 76).

While the law on state enterprises was meant to come into effect gradually over the period 1 July 1988 to 1991, a reform of wholesale (but not retail) prices was to be implemented by 1 January 1989, taking account of socially necessary costs, demand and world prices. The wholesale prices of fuels and raw materials were to include a 50 per cent mark-up on total wages paid out and a 4.5 per cent profit mark-up on capital (Resolution 1988: 21). In certain cases, and under specified conditions, 'contract prices' could be negotiated between enterprise and customer ('Law', p. 32). Credit policy was to pay greater attention to efficiency (thus not being used to cover up inefficiency), while a change in the banking law in December 1989 involved the creation of a central bank and independent commercial banks.[3]

An extreme view of the reality of planning is expressed by Vaclav Klaus and Tomas Jezek (*FT*, 13 December 1989, p. 17). They consider that for more than two decades there was mere 'playing at planning'; large, monopolistic enterprises used their superior information to 'dictate' plans to the central authorities.

The reform measures arose, to a large extent, from the impact of Gorbachev on Czechoslovakia. There was disagreement within the country, with Lubomir Strougal (Premier 1970 until October 1988, replaced by Ladislav Adamec) more enthusiastic than Central Committee secretary in charge of ideology Jan Fojtik. Jaromir Matejka was secretary of the committee on economic reform. Husak himself, in early 1986, warned against any mechanical imitation of other countries' experience and pronounced himself in favour of a creative use of those experiences in a search for answers best suited to Czechoslovakia's special needs and circumstances. Nevertheless, he criticised

overcentralization and, while rejecting market-orientated reforms, accepted the need for greater decentralization of decision-making. After Gorbachev's visit in April 1987 a more positive attitude became discernible. Even conservative Central Committee member Vasil Bilak, who resigned from the politburo in December 1988, supported the current proposals, this following a February 1987 attack on reform that he considered merely a convenient cover for anti-socialist tendencies. Milos Jakes, who was chairman of the National Economic Commission before he became General Secretary on 17 December 1987, seemed likely to undertake a cautious implementation of the reform programme, warning against 'hurried' attempts at economic reform. He rejected any analogy between the 1968 reforms and the present ones, stressing that the latter would preserve the leading role of the party, social ownership of the means of production and the planned economy. The October 1988 change of government indicated a conservative approach to reform, Fojtik warning against weakening the role of the party and strengthening the private sector. At the end of 1988 both the GDR and Czechoslovakia decided to bring the next party congress forward a year to May 1990, arousing speculation about possible top leadership changes.

AGRICULTURE

When Czechoslovakia emerged as an independent state after the First World War nearly a third of agricultural holdings accounted for only 3 per cent of arable land, while 0.5 per cent of holdings farmed almost 20 per cent (Teichova 1988: 27). As a result of the land reforms of the 1920s 64 per cent of all agricultural land was taken up by holdings of 5 ha to 20 ha (amounting to 95 per cent of all holdings), and only 1 per cent of all agricultural enterprises farmed more than 50 ha each (accounting for around 20 per cent of agricultural land in total) (Teichova 1988: 12). Schimmerling (1991: 188)

Table 11.2 Czechoslovakia: statistical survey

Average annual rate of growth of NMP (%)

1951–55	1956–60	1961–65	1966–70	1971–75	1976–80	1981–85	1986	1987	1988	1989
8.2	6.9	2.0	6.9	5.7	3.6	1.8	2.6	2.1	2.3	0.7

Private sector in agriculture in 1985 (including private farms) (%)

Arable land	*Output*
3.0	10.0

Net hard currency debt ($ billion)

1974	1980	1986	1987	1988	1989
3.1	3.6	2.8[a]	3.7	4.4	5.4[b]

Population, 1991: 15.7 million (62.8 per cent Czechs and 31.9 per cent Slovaks)

Sources: See Table 11.1. Cochrane (1988: 48); EIU, *Country Profile*, 1987–88, p. 37, and 1989–90, p. 39); *European Economy: the Path of Reform in Central and Eastern Europe*, Commission of the European Communities, Brussels, 1991 pp. 43, 278.
Notes: a Debt–service ratio 20 per cent.
b Debt–service ratio 16 per cent.

cites the following figures: 70 per cent of farms were smaller than 5 ha and accounted for only 23.1 per cent of agricultural land; the respective figures for farms of 5–20 ha were 25 per cent and 41.3 per cent, and for farms above 20 ha 5 per cent and 35 per cent.

The *1945–51 land reforms* took place in three stages, the final one fixing a 50 ha ceiling for private ownership (p. 104). Collectivization followed. From the mid-1970s onwards emphasis was given to the establishment of agro-industrial enterprises combining farms and processing. Only four obligatory and 31 non-binding orientation indicators were set, although lower levels often added more (Cummings 1986: 112). In January 1982, as part of the New System of Planned Management of the National economy, decision-making in agriculture was decentralized to some extent, especially as regards day-to-day operations. The federal level issued only two obligatory targets, procurement of grain and the slaughter of animals, although up to three extra targets could be added by local officials (Cummings 1986: 113). Agriculture employed 12 per cent of the labour force in 1988.

The figures for occupation of total farm land

in 1986 were co-operatives, 64.5 per cent, and the state sector, 30.5 per cent (Matousek 1988: 47). An interesting variation was to be found in the Slusovice co-operative in south Moravia, a model imitated elsewhere in Czechoslovakia. This farm of 8,000 ha and 3,500 employees produced, in addition to products such as cereals, milk and potatoes, computers for agricultural and school use, biochemical products, agricultural machinery and micro-electronics (*EEN*, 1987, vol. 1, no. 9, pp.4–5). The co-operative was split into financially autonomous units called 'microstructures' (e.g. transport and milking) and managers were assessed at regular intervals in terms of criteria such as innovation and working conditions. After the 'velvet revolution' the co-operative was split up into different shareholding companies (*EEN*, 1990, vol. 4, no. 16, p. 8).

The September 1987 draft law on co-operative farming was to have been implemented by 1989. Important aspects involved full cost accounting, implying the phasing out of subsidies, and increased scope for decentralized decision-making after fulfilling state plan obligations (Matousek 1988: 47–58). For the agro-food complex as a whole, as of 1 January

1989, payments into the state budget were 50 per cent each from wages and bonuses and from profits (Cerny 1988: 52). The 1980s saw encouragement given to non-agricultural activities; on average more than 20 per cent of co-operative members became engaged thus (Myant 1989: 201).

The private sector

The private sector, in 1985, accounted for only 3 per cent of arable land and 10 per cent of gross farm output, while the percentage figures for individual products were as follows: potatoes 14; vegetables 40; fruit 60; meat 15; eggs 40 (Cochrane 1988: 48). In addition to private plots there were still private farms, largely in hilly areas. The maximum size of private farm was set at 1 ha (the average size is 0.4 ha according to *EEN*, 1987, vol. 1, no. 9, p. 3), but grazing rights were allowed on some state lands. In 1980 they accounted for less than 2 per cent of the agricultural labour force (Cummings 1986: 113). The 1980s saw encouragement given to the private sector. In 1982, for example, revenue from the sale of food produced by part-time individuals became tax-free (Cummings 1986: 114).

FOREIGN TRADE, DEBT AND INVESTMENT

Foreign trade and debt

Foreign trade accounted for a third of national income and was heavily orientated towards the socialist countries (78.6 per cent in 1986; around 75 per cent with Comecon), with the European Community taking 9.7 per cent and developing countries 5.3 per cent. Over the following year the socialist countries' share had risen to four-fifths, the Soviet Union and GDR accounting for 43 per cent and 7.0 per cent respectively of total foreign trade, while the developing countries' share had slipped to 3.5 per cent. The FRG and Austria were the most important Western trading partners (*Abecor Country Report*, June 1988, p. 2). Comecon trade increased in importance during the 1980s (1960, 64 per cent; 1986, 74.6 per cent), the Soviet Union alone accounting for 44.4 per cent in 1986 (see *EIU Country Profile*, 1987–88, p. 31). Comecon specialization agreements assigned, for example, trams to Czechoslovakia (although the Soviet Union and Poland make them for domestic use only) in return for relinquishing railway passenger rolling stock. Engineering goods accounted for over half total exports; the range of engineering output was so broad, however, that it covered 70 per cent of the world assortment (Voracek 1988: 495–6).

Myant (1989: 192–3) describes Czechoslovakia as being a cautious borrower during the 1970s; even though foreign debt was not insignificant by the end of the decade, a relatively large amount had been spent on machinery. Czechoslovakia has the lowest *per capita* net hard currency debt in Eastern Europe. A string of hard currency trade surpluses (1983, $1 billion; 1984, $850 million; 1985, $700 million), one of the results of an austerity programme aimed at reducing investment and imports, helped reduce the size of the net hard currency debt.

Although the planning and management of foreign trade remained highly centralized, there were various experiments after 1981. Some individual enterprises were given direct trading rights, retention of part of convertible currency earnings was allowed, and a number of producers (for example the Skoda and CKD engineering enterprises) were merged with their competent foreign trade corporations. The experiments, which began in 1983, also permitted enterprises to employ foreign trade organizations on a commission basis (Lodahl 1989: 226). After 1987 enterprises were able to keep all the proceeds from the sale of export licences (*EEN*, 1988, vol. 2, no. 8, p. 5). On 1 January 1989 a uniform commercial exchange rate for trade with non-socialist countries was introduced, adjusted weekly against a weighted basket of five currencies (*EIU Country Profile*, 1989–90, p.9). The law of December 1989 obliged enterprises to sell the foreign exchange targeted in the state plan to the State Bank, while foreign exchange auctions began in July 1989.

Joint equity ventures

Czechoslovakia published a decree in August 1985. Foreign ownership was originally limited to a ceiling of 49 per cent and the manager had to be a Czech national. The profits tax rate was 50 per cent (compared with 75 per cent for a native company); there was a social security tax of 25 per cent of the total salary bill and a 25 per cent tax on all dividends (*EEN*, 1987, vol. 1, no. 12, p. 2). Practical examples were few; there were ventures set up in electronics, biotechnology, video production and hotels, for instance. By April 1988 there were only nine joint ventures with Western firms (Valenta 1989: 27); as of 31 December 1989 there were fifty-five joint ventures (Kupka 1992: 298). After 1 January 1989 there was no minimum start-up capital and no upper limit on the Western share in the joint venture; a foreign corporate body or person could hold shares and a Westerner could be director of a company or chairman of the board. The only excluded sectors were those 'important for defence and security' (Margie Lindsay, *FT Survey*, 13 December 1988, p. 39). Examples of joint ventures with the Soviet Union include the Robotics enterprise and the Elisa biotechnology company (*EEN*, 1988, vol. 2, no. 20, p. 4, and no. 23, p. 6).

THE PRIVATE NON-AGRICULTURAL SECTOR

This sector was severely repressed, even by East European standards. A savage economic elimination of self-employed craftsmen and industrial producers took place during 1948–53. Of the 383,000 small companies in 1948, only 47,000 remained by 1956, and sixteen years later only 2,000 self-employed craftsmen still functioned (Teichova 1988: 104).

Valenta (1989: 27) dates a greater degree of encouragement to 1982, e.g. part-time, non-family employees were allowed. In 1986 the sector was further encouraged by things like tax reductions. From January 1988 onwards small shops and restaurants could be leased from the state, although subject to strict controls on profit margins and to the condition that non-family members were not employed. In 1988 the private sector accounted for less than 0.5 per cent of non-agricultural output (Grosfeld and Hare 1991: 136). According to OECD figures, private enterprise as a whole contributed 3.1 per cent of GDP in 1988 (*FT*, 29 June 1990, p. 2). In the 1980s only 7.5 per cent of the means of production was privately owned (Kupka 1992: 297).

CONCLUSION

Czechoslovakia was, untypically, an industrialized country on the eve of its socialist period, while the reforms associated with the Prague Spring would have transformed the economy and society. The 1968 Warsaw Pact invasion led to a heavy mantle descending on the country. Milos Jakes replaced Gustav Husak as General Secretary in December 1987, but the former only held out the promise of a cautious implementation of modest reforms. Nevertheless, Czechoslovakia had one of the highest living standards in the socialist world and the lowest *per capita* net hard currency debt in Eastern Europe. The 'velvet revolution' restored Czechoslovakia's democratic tradition.

NOTES

1. Justified by the 'Brezhnev doctrine', which saw the suppression of counter-revolution as the joint responsibility of all socialist countries (i.e. once a socialist country always a socialist country). *Pravda*, 25 September 1968, provided an explanation for the invasion: 'The peoples of the socialist countries and the communist parties have and must have freedom. . . . However, every decision of theirs must harm neither socialism in their own country, nor the

fundamental interests of other socialist countries, nor the worldwide workers' movement. . . . Every communist party is responsible not only to its own people but also to all the socialist countries and the entire communist movement. . . . A socialist state that is in a system of other states constituting a socialist commonwealth cannot be free of the common interests of that commonwealth.' In March 1989 Gorbachev told Karoly Grosz (the then Hungarian General Secretary) that no external force should interfere in the domestic affairs of a socialist country. In his address to the Council of Europe in Strasbourg in July 1989, Gorbachev recognized 'the sovereign right of each people to choose their social system at their own discretion . . . Any interference in internal affairs, any attempts to limit the sovereignty of states . . . are inadmissible . . . The philosophy of the concept of a "common European home" rules out the probability of an armed clash and the very possibility of the use or threat of force, and above all military force, by an alliance against another alliance, inside alliances or whatever it may be.' A Warsaw Pact communiqué of 8 July 1989 said that 'There are no universal models of socialism; nobody is the holder of truth . . . Relations should develop on the basis of equality, independence and each nation's right to make its own political line, strategy and tactics, without outside interference.' During his visit to Italy in early December 1989, Gorbachev said that 'the Prague Spring was right then and it is right now. It was democratization'; it was a time of acute East–West confrontation and there had been 'interference by both sides', but since 'political and other methods were available to the authorities at the time, the military action was not quite appropriate'. On the same day (1 December) the Czech communist party leadership condemned the 1968 invasion and an apology was offered at the party congress held 20–1 December. On 4 December 1989 the Soviet Union, Bulgaria, the GDR, Hungary and Poland (Romania did not partake in the invasion and was therefore omitted) signed a joint statement which said that the invasion constituted 'interference in the internal affairs of a sovereign Czechoslovakia and must be condemned'.

2. See the Central Committee resolution adopted at the Seventh Session, 17–18 December 1987, *Czechoslovak Economic Digest*, no. 1, (1988); Cervinka (1987); Rohlicek (1987); Kerner (1988); *FT Survey*, 9 October 1987.

3. The main sources of budgetary revenue were, as usual, profit transfers from economic organizations (43 per cent) and turnover tax (24 per cent) (*Abecor Country Report*, June 1988, p. 2). On 15 November 1987 individuals were allowed hard currency bank accounts up to a certain limit for overseas travel, withdrawable without permission from the Ministry of Finance. Relatives and friends in the West were then allowed to pay for the necessary travel documents for Czech citizens. Enterprises had to sell a specified proportion of foreign exchange earnings to the State Bank. Experimental hard currency auctions began in July 1989.

12

THE GERMAN DEMOCRATIC REPUBLIC (EAST GERMANY)

INTRODUCTION

The German Democratic Republic (GDR) had the highest standard of living among the socialist countries and, along with Czechoslovakia, was an advanced industrialized country before the socialist era. Economic policy was shaped by Soviet domination, especially in view of the country's position on the front line between East and West, and by the continual comparisons it suffered with the Federal Republic of Germany (FRG) rather than its poorer socialist neighbours. One estimate put the GDR's *per capita* GNP, in the mid-1980s and calculated according to Western methods, at two-thirds that of the FRG (Marer 1986c: 611). According to OECD figures, GDP *per capita* in 1988 was $9,361, compared with the OECD countries' average of $14,637; Czechoslovakia was given $7,603, Hungary $6,491, Bulgaria $5,633, the Soviet Union $5,552, Poland $5,453 and Romania $4,117 (*FT*, 29 June 1990, p. 2). The comparisons with the FRG, enhanced by the access of GDR citizens to West German TV and radio, made demonstrating the superiority of socialism and the quest for party legitimacy uphill work, even among those born after the Second World War and even though there was a general perception of progress having been made in the fields of economic and social policy. Legitimacy was largely sought in rising living standards, rather than liberal reforms or appeal to nationalism, although there was latterly increasing evocation of the past to invoke patriotism. Since socialism was the *raison d'être* of the regime, this put close restraints on reform. Particular resentment was felt because of the inability of GDR citizens normally to travel to the West (the major exceptions being pensioners; this relaxation occurred after 1964), even though the late Honecker years saw a significant increase in permissions given for 'urgent family visits'.

What was particularly fascinating was the impact of Gorbachev's ideas for economic and political reform on the GDR. Talk of *glasnost*, 'democratization' and *perestroika* and sweeping personnel changes, especially at the top, were naturally unsettling to a conservative leadership long used to proclaiming the virtues of its socialist system in the battle against capitalism and fearful of the possible consequences of political relaxation at home and of being exposed should events in the Soviet Union reverse course again.

The Soviet Union had a natural interest in the economic diversification to be found within Comecon and the GDR's relative economic success attracted attention. In May 1985 Gorbachev praised the GDR's endeavours to reach international standards in production and the following June what he called 'inter-industry associations'. Aganbegyan (1988a: 94) thought positively about the incorporation of design and research organizations into large production enterprises, as has happened with the combine, and said that the Soviet Union was making use of the GDR's experience; many formerly independent institutes and construction departments were being turned into large productive concerns. The penchant for mergers and super-ministries, the nature of the Soviet foreign trade reforms, the idea of quality control, and the concessions to private and co-operative activity also suggested GDR influence. Gorbachev personally attended (as with the Polish, but in contrast to the Hungarian, Czechoslovak and Bulgarian congresses) the Eleventh Congress of the SED (Sozialistische Einheitspartei Deutsch-lands, Socialist Unity Party of Germany) on 17–21 April 1986. That made him the first Soviet General Secretary to do so since 1971. The generally self-congratulatory tone of the conference contrasted markedly with that of the CPSU. Gorbachev again praised the GDR's success, describing the economic system as dynamic and flexible and its performance as high and smooth. He also complimented the work ethos of its citizens, although he did not specifically mention the combine. (Åslund 1989: 182–3 argues that the 1987 Soviet reforms, however, appeared to be inspired more by the Hungarian experience; later on the Soviet Union showed marked disinterest in the GDR.) Honecker, General Secretary of the SED, indulged in some mild criticism – the need to improve service in shops, for instance – but listed the GDR's economic achievements, in robotics for example. He stressed the importance of continued 'perfecting' of planning and management: 'We may not yet have reached a state of perfection, but we have made good headway.'

Speaking at the Free German Trade Union Federation Congress in April 1987, Honecker again listed the GDR's successes since 1971, such as rising living standards and technical progress: 'We wish to continue this path with further success . . . the GDR has an efficiently functioning system of economic and social planning.' He spoke of the considerable changes that had taken place since he came to office and the open discussion that already allegedly existed in the party and trade unions. Since 1971 the SED had adapted Marxism-Leninism to fit

the conditions prevailing in the GDR and had made use of the 'valuable experience' of other socialist countries. In an interview in *Stern* (9 April 1987) Kurt Hager (Central Committee secretary in charge of ideology) said there would be no election of company directors, while in October he confirmed that the GDR would carry on with existing policies because it was on the sensitive dividing line between East and West. The overriding aims seemed to be the maintenance of political control and the 'perfecting' of the present system.

The speed at which the Honecker regime disintegrated in 1989 astonished everyone. Gorbachev's vision was an essential pre-requisite; he had warned the Honecker regime of the need to adapt and that Soviet troops would not be used to maintain it. One of the other decisive elements was the flood of people to West Germany (343,854 in 1989 alone), sparked off by Hungary's decision to dismantle its border fence with Austria in May. On 9 November the borders between the two Germanies, including the Berlin Wall, were opened. Honecker was replaced as General Secretary of the SED (renamed the Party of Democratic Socialism on 16 December) by Egon Krenz. The whole politburo and central committee resigned on 3 December, and those two bodies were replaced by a new executive chaired by Gregor Gysi. Hans Modrow had already been confirmed as prime minister on 13 November.

In the 18 March 1990 free election there was a surprise win for the Alliance for Germany, comprising the Christian Democratic Union, the German Social Union and Democratic Awakening. Lothar de Maizière became prime minister. German economic and monetary union took place on 1 July, political union took place on 3 October, and an all-German general election was held 2 December (won comfortably by Chancellor Kohl's CDU/CSU–DSU/FDP coalition).

Table 12.1 shows official figures for rates of growth of produced national income.

Table 12.1 GDR: official statistics for rates of growth of produced national income and CIA figures for rates of growth of GNP (%)

Produced national income

1950	22.0	1963	3.5	1976	3.5
1951	21.1	1964	4.9	1977	5.1
1952	13.7	1965	4.6	1977	3.7
1953	5.5	1966	4.9	1979	4.0
1954	8.7	1967	5.4	1980	4.4
1955	8.6	1968	5.1	1981	4.8
1956	4.4	1969	5.2	1982	2.6
1957	7.3	1970	5.6	1983	4.4
1958	10.7	1971	4.4	1984	5.5
1959	8.8	1972	5.7	1985	4.8
1960	4.5	1973	5.6	1986	4.3
1961	1.6	1974	6.5	1987	3.5
1962	2.7	1975	4.9	1988	3.0
				1989	2.0

GNP (CIA)

1971–75	1976–80	1981–5	1986	1987	1988	1989
3.1	2.3	1.9	1.5	1.7	1.1	1.2

Sources: Statistical Yearbooks of the GDR; CIA (1990: tables 1 and C-9).

Political background

Major early political events include the following: the split of Germany after the defeat of Hitler; the June 1948 monetary reform (introduction of the Deutschmark) in the Western zones led to the Berlin Blockade and Airlift (June 1948 to May 1949), and to the creation of Nato in July 1948; the foundation of the GDR on 7 October 1949; Walter Ulbricht became General Secretary of the SED in July 1950, to be replaced by Erich Honecker in May 1971; the 17–18 June 1953 uprising; the building of the Berlin Wall in 1961; the June 1972 Quadripartite agreement (the United States, Britain and France on the one side and the Soviet Union on the other) on transit rights between West Berlin and the FRG and the accompanying agreement signed by the West Berlin senate and the GDR on travel between West and East Berlin. The December 1972 treaty between the GDR and the Federal Republic guaranteed the current border.

Economic background

The end of the Second World War

Hitler's defeat led to the division of Germany and left the two parts at the front line between socialism and capitalism. The GDR started off in generally worse shape than the Federal Republic, even though what is now the Federal Republic suffered greater wartime destruction. The GDR's industrial production was only 10–15 per cent of its pre-war level. There was a loss of over 40 per cent of industrial capacity (Dennis 1988: 128). The Soviet Union demanded heavy reparations. The dismantling of industrial fixed capital assets amounted to 26 per cent of the 1939 level (compared to 12 per cent in the Western zones) and there were also payments from current production (none was imposed in the Western zones). Reparations and occupation costs accounted for an estimated 25 per cent of social product between 1946 and 1948 (DIW 1989: 6). More than a quarter of industrial capital assets were dismantled by the Soviet Union (Dennis 1988: 128). In contrast, the Federal Republic fared much better in this respect and actually became a recipient of Marshall aid after 1948.[1]

The economic structure of the GDR was unbalanced, in contrast to that of the Federal Republic. The GDR's industrial structure was relatively strong with respect to machine tools, office machines, textile machinery, optical equipment, electrical engineering, motor vehicles, light industry, textiles and aircraft. On the other hand, chemicals, iron and steel, heavy engineering and shipbuilding were weakly developed, the present area of the GDR producing only 1.3 per cent of the pre-war total of pig iron. In 1938 the share of iron ore was only 1.3 per cent and of hard coal 1.9 per cent (Strassburger 1985: 114). In 1939 *per capita* industrial output was slightly higher than that of the present-day Federal Republic. In terms of total industrial output and population, the GDR territory accounted for 29 and 25 per cent respectively in 1944 (Childs 1987: 4). In the mid-1930s about 83 per cent of foreign trade was with the West. The GDR, like Czechoslovakia, was thus in the unusual position of being an advanced, industrialized (albeit unbalanced) country before the start of its socialist era.

Resource endowment

East Germany is generally poorly endowed with raw materials, with important exceptions such as brown coal and potash.[2] These two, however, are heavy polluters (potash, for example, exacerbates an already acute water supply problem), and brown coal extraction reduces the amount of already scarce land available for agricultural purposes (in 1985 only 0.37 ha *per capita*, compared with 0.45 in Czechoslovakia, 0.53 in Poland, 0.62 in Hungary, 0.67 in Romania, 0.70 in Bulgaria and 2.15 in the Soviet Union (Merkel 1987: 213).[3] This poor resource endowment meant that the GDR was heavily dependent on imports of fuels and raw materials, especially from the Soviet Union (the GDR imported some 60 per cent of its raw materials). Whenever the commodity terms of trade deteriorate, such as during the period following the 1973–74 oil shock, albeit with a lag, given the Comecon pricing system, particular attention was paid to increasing both domestic production to substitute for imports (although characterized by rising marginal costs) and the efficiency of resource utilization (reflected in economic reform measures).

Labour was also an acutely scarce factor of production in the GDR and this was reflected in economic policies such as the drive for 'intensification' (*Intensivierung*). The total population was 16.7 million in 1939 and reached a post-war peak of 19.1 million in 1947 (swollen by refugees). The population was only 16,639,877 at the end of 1986.

Between 1949 and the building of the Berlin Wall (12–13 August 1961) almost 2.7 million migrants from the GDR were registered by the federal and West Berlin authorities. They were mainly young (just below half less than twenty-five years of age), skilled workers, professionals and entrepreneurs.

GDR policy promoted both an increase in the birth rate (1974 saw an all-time low of 10.6 per thousand) and in the participation of women in the workforce by measures such as the generous provision of creches and kindergartens, maternity grants and reduced working hours. As a result, the figure of 88 per cent of women of working age either at work or in training was the highest in the world (Edwards 1985: 10). In 1982 28 per cent of women in employment were in part-time work (p. 82). In 1983 females accounted for 49.5 per cent of persons employed, excluding apprentices (1950, 40.0 per cent; 1980, 49.9 per cent; *Statistical Pocket Book of the GDR*, 1984, p. 28).

The scarcity of labour as a factor of production had a profound impact on both political (severe restrictions on movement to the West) and economic policy in the GDR. Incentives were needed to encourage a high level of commitment and productivity. Compensations for the acute shortage of labour included attempts to increase the amount of shift work and to maintain the tradition of a highly skilled workforce by a system of education having a strong vocational bent. East Germans were seen as relatively hard-working, efficient, disciplined and honest by their socialist partners, although German reunification came as a great shock. But the German tradition did encourage a greater willingness to work with and within the rules and regulations of a command economy. In recent years there were some 85,000 foreign workers in the GDR, including 54,000 Vietnamese and 5,000 Cubans (see e.g. *IHT*, 9 October 1990, p. 4).

PLANNING

The GDR up to and including the Honecker era

258

always maintained a command economy. Real political power was exercised by the Politburo (Politbüro der SED) and the Secretariat of the Central Committee of the SED, whose members belonged to the Politburo. After 1976 the Order of Planning (*Planungsordnung*) was the most important aspect of plan methodology, regulating the planning of the national economy and of its economic units, sectors and regions for both five year and annual planning (Tröder 1987: Chapter 6). It contained a list of plan indicators for the economic units and was designed to enhance the role of the Five Year Plan as the chief form of state direction of the economy. Long-term planning was described as the preparatory stage of five year planning, the latter being the 'main steering instrument' from which are derived 'annual slices'. The planning order realistically had to take account of deviations of annual plans from the guidelines, to allow for factors such as changes in demand, new technologies and altered world market circumstances, but the Five Year Plan itself was no longer redrawn. Note that five year and annual plans applied to all combines, but the former applied only to selected enterprises. Combines disaggregated the plan tasks received from ministries down to enterprises whose managements drew up detailed plan drafts and concluded preliminary inter-enterprise contracts. This was an important co-ordinating instrument of sub-plans because through them enterprise outputs could be legally guaranteed and bottlenecks identified at an early stage.

THE HISTORY OF ECONOMIC REFORM IN THE GDR [4]

The New Economic System, 1963–71

The NES was the result of: (1) the 'growth crisis' (*Wachstumskrise*) – produced national income increased by only 1.6 per cent in 1961 and 2.7 per cent in 1962 and investment stagnated; (2) the particularly serious microeconomic problems of command planning in such a relatively advanced economy; and, arguably, (3) the Soviet need for a laboratory to observe the effects of reform. The ambitious Second Five Year Plan (1956–60) was first revised downwards and then replaced by a Seven Year Plan (1959–65), following the Soviet lead. The 'main economic task', adopted at the Fifth SED Congress in July 1958, was to catch up with and overtake the Federal Republic in *per capita* production of major foodstuffs and consumer goods by 1961 and in labour productivity by 1965. The reason was to staunch migration to the Federal Republic by holding out the promise of a much higher standard of living. By 1960 it was clear that this strategy was not going to be successful. The attempt to increase consumption rapidly, while maintaining the other items of expenditure, led to inconsistencies, stresses and strains. The Seven Year Plan, which collapsed in reality in 1961, was formally annulled at the Sixth Congress of the SED in January 1963 with the announcement of a new plan for the period 1963 to 1970. This was the background to the building of the Berlin Wall in August 1961. When it was realized that the production of foodstuffs and consumer goods could not be increased fast enough to induce people to stay voluntarily, direct action was needed to staunch the labour haemorrhage. This meant that the aims of the 'main economic task' were, in a way, given up because they were unrealistic. The period 1961–63 was one of consolidation. 'Guidelines for the new economic system of planning and management of the national economy' followed the formal announcement at the Congress of the NES: this was renamed the 'Economic System of Socialism' in April 1967 – ironically, to indicate permanence.

The NES did not represent a reform along Yugoslav, pre-1968 Czechoslovak or post-1968 Hungarian lines, but an attempt to achieve state goals more effectively by means of a combination of traditional command planning (with its use of directives) and the greatest use in pre-1989 East Germany of indirect steering of enterprises by means of mainly monetary instruments ('economic levers'). These included net profit deductions, taxes, prices, fund formation, and the cost and availability of credit. These levers were designed to influence enterprise behaviour in line with the state plan. The NES was the first comprehensive, post-Liberman reform and the most radical among Comecon countries in the early 1960s. Note, however, that the NES was only gradually introduced from 1964 onwards, the whole panoply of instruments only really operating by 1969–70. By this time the system was already amended by the introduction of 'structure determining tasks'. The hope was to bring about a scientific and technical revolution, a highly efficient, dynamic, innovative economy, which would prove the superiority of socialism and, at the same time, maintain effective party control.[5]

The VVB (*Vereinigung Volkseigener Betriebe*: Association of Nationally-Owned Enterprises) was an essentially administrative (in contrast to operational production) intermediate body between ministry and enterprise. The VVB declined in importance during the 1970s and finally disappeared during the 1980s.

The number of compulsory plan indicators imposed on enterprises was reduced, although still covering the main areas of activity: for example, gross output, product groups, sales (home and abroad), fixed capital, science and technology and the wage fund (formerly there were also indicators for number of employees, average wage levels and labour productivity). Incentive funds were linked to net profit (*Nettogewinn*: gross profit minus the capital charge) and the other indicators – the bonus fund was reduced when the wage fund was overdrawn, for example. There was thus room for increased micro decision-making in areas such as investment, product and input mix, the composition and organization of the labour force, contracts, and foreign trade. Enterprises were able, for example, to conclude short-term foreign trade contracts not anticipated in the plan, provided they were approved by the foreign trade organ and did not adversely affect other planned export obligations and other plan targets. Enterprises received the right to employ convertible currencies for imports on overfulfilling export plans or underusing planned allowances by means of import substitution or cheaper purchasing. Hard currency credits were available for imports if future export sales were made possible. The decentralization of decision-making is particularly stressed by Granick, who describes the situation in mid-1970 as profit 'satisficing' (Granick 1975: 212). Keren also talks of lower bodies deciding on the more routine, operational matters, while major, strategic decisions remained with the state (Keren 1973: 557).

Indirect steering of decentralized activity was to be achieved via economic levers (*ökonomische Hebel*): thus, for example, decentralized investment was to be influenced by differentiated net profit deductions, the capital charge, and the availability and cost of credit. Parsons (1986: 36) notes that the NES saw an increase in negotiated credit conditions, while branch and district offices of the State Bank had the power to choose which projects to finance and each office was evaluated on the basis of its earnings in line with the self-financing principle – in and after the NES credit was granted to the enterprise as a whole, rather than for a particular product, as previously (p. 37). The 'principle of earning one's own resources' (*das Prinzip der Eigenerwirtschaftung der Mittel*) meant not only that enterprises and VVBs should cover current expenditure from their own revenue, but that investment was no longer to be financed exclusively from budgetary grants (as previously), but out of profit, depreciation allowances and interest-bearing credits. The 'unitary enterprise result' (*das einheitliche Betriebsergebnis*) for exporting enterprises involved the direct influence of foreign as opposed to domestic prices. The enterprise contract system was improved, violations involving price discounts and reimbursements for losses incurred.

The capital charge (*Produktionsfondsabgabe*, production fund levy) on the gross value of the fixed and working capital of an enterprise, to encourage greater efficiency, was introduced into industry from the beginning of 1967, with differentiated rates of 1 per cent, 4 per cent and 6 per cent. With the exception of agriculture, it was made a uniform 6 per cent after 1971.

The period 1964–67 saw a three-stage price reform, moving timewise from raw materials and materials, from semi-finished products to finished products, with prices rising by 70 per cent, 40 per cent and 4 per cent for each group respectively on average. These prices replaced the old system, largely based on 1944 prices. Figure 12.1 (relating to the late 1970s, strictly) shows the main price elements involved with producer and consumer goods, with wholesale price (still) based on an average cost plus mark-up basis.

In 1968 the 'capital-related price' (*fonds-bezogener Preistyp*) was introduced. This in-volved a percentage profit mark-up (maximum 18 per cent) on the *necessary* (as opposed to actual) capital input (based on the experience of the most efficient enterprise in a product group).[6] This price type covered about a third of industrial production by the end of 1970. 'Price dynamization' measures, introduced in 1968 and scrapped at the end of 1970, were intended to bring about price reductions by two methods. The first expected price reductions down to a floor of permissible profit per 1,000 marks of necessary fixed and working capital once a ceiling had been exceeded.[7] The second method foresaw the gradual lowering of the prices of what were then new and improved products, in order to encourage enterprises to develop products of a technically higher standard later on. Maximum prices, allowing room to manoeuvre below these levels, were introduced for consumer goods and products

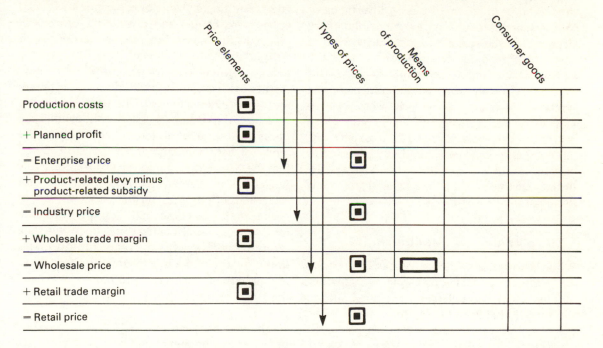

Figure 12.1 GDR: the price structure of producer and consumer goods (from *Lexicon der Wirtschaft-Preise*, East Berlin, 1979, cited by Melzer in Jeffries *et al.* 1987: 145)

subject to rapid technical development. 'Contractually agreed' prices were subject to calculation guidelines, but allowed for lower or
higher rates of profit than planned; these could
be fixed by producer and purchaser, and were
prominent in spare parts, one-off products and
special machines. A general price freeze for
existing products was introduced in 1971.
Pricing problems were an important factor in the
demise of the NES since prices were based on
average costs, they neglected demand and
lacked flexibility. (See Melzer 1983, 1987a, b.)

The state was unable to implement its
structural goals by means of indirect steering.
Decentralized investment departed markedly
from the lines of development desired by the
state, owing to inefficient prices, among other
things. This led to the introduction of 'structure-
determining tasks' (*strukturbestimmende
Aufgaben*) for the period 1968 to 1970. These
concerned production, processes, investment or
basic research projects that exert a revolutionary
influence on the scientific and technical level of
development of the economy and ensure the
achievement of the highest world standards (for
example, automation, semiconductors and
synthetic materials). These tasks were planned
in precise detail from the centre and given
priority in materials supply. Not unexpectedly,
the relative neglect of non-priority tasks led to
bottlenecks and shortages, rebounded on the
priority sectors, and thus aggravated an already
acute supply problem.

The period of recentralization 1971–79

While lacking a new theoretical basis, the period
saw a distinct shift back to the pre-NES situation,
although significant elements remained, such as
the capital charge, parts of fund formation and
the principle of earning one's own resources.
There was an increase in the degree of centralized decision-making – in the realm of product
assortment and investment, for example - and in
the number of plan indicators – number of
employees as well as the wage fund, for ex-

ample. The main role of profit was simply to
satisfy the financial requirements of the plan.

On 3 May 1971 Erich Honecker replaced
Walter Ulbricht as First Secretary of the SED and
at the Eighth Congress of the SED (15–19 June
1971) three leading tasks were set:

1. The 'chief task' (*Hauptaufgabe*) was a
quantitative and qualitative improvement in the
supply of consumer goods.

2. The need for all-round 'intensification'
(output increased mainly by means of the more
efficient utilization of existing factors of production, especially through technical progress;
the term was first used in the early 1960s).

3. An active social policy, which included a
massive housing programme (1976–90), and
numerous individual measures, such as
increased pensions and reductions in working
hours for shift workers.

There was a close linkage between these
goals. The slogan 'Unity of economic and social
policy' was coined and awarded a prominent
place in the party programme at the Ninth
Congress of the SED in May 1976. This linkage
helped compensate for the lack of a new
theoretical basis and provided a central theme
for the new Honecker era. The party leadership
was careful to make the 'chief task' conditional
upon the success of intensification, but the
'unity of economic and social policy' showed
that the time had come to reward the relatively
neglected consumer, provide incentives for
increased effort and illustrate the virtues of
socialism. Baylis (1986: 388) describes this idea
as a sort of 'social contract' in which the state
offers material benefits and other improvements
in the quality of life in exchange for hard work
and political loyalty. The disturbances in Poland
in 1970 reinforced the importance of the
present.

The raw material-poor GDR was battered by
the increases in energy and raw material prices
after the 1973–74 oil shock, though they were
delayed by the Comecon pricing system. The
GDR's response was to avoid any fundamental
revision of the recentralized economic system.

Domestic prices were increased in stages from 1976 onwards to reflect rising import prices, lower priority was given to consumption and slightly higher priority to exports (although the 'chief task' was not formally abandoned). Resort was had to heavy borrowing from the West; the main imports from the West were not capital goods but raw materials and intermediate goods (DIW 1989: 8). The 1970s economic system did not overcome the fundamental problems afflicting the GDR economy and proved unable to provide the necessary 'intensification' of the economy.

THE 1980S

The 1980s saw the GDR coping with severe foreign trade and payments problems, with the enhanced need for 'intensification' pursued by means of the combine (*Kombinat*) and the 'perfecting' of the economic mechanism.

The 1973–74 oil price shock was followed by that of 1979. The accumulated trade deficit for the years 1976–80 amounted to just under VM 29 billion, VM 25 billion with Western countries and VM 9 billion with the Soviet Union; there were surpluses with some East European countries. (The valuta mark, foreign currency mark, was used in the presentation of the GDR's foreign trade results; more recently VM 1 = DM 0.74.) It took from the mid-1970s to 1984 for the GDR to restore an annual trade surplus with the Soviet Union, while indebtedness to the West rose from $6.76 billion in 1977 to a peak of $11.67 billion in 1981 (when the debt–service ratio was 35 per cent) and then fell to $6.83 billion in 1985 (Cornelsen 1987: 52).[8] In the early 1980s the GDR was also caught in the backwash of Poland's and Romania's international debt problems, which led to Western banks' restrictions on credit, and suffered a 10 per cent fall in Soviet oil deliveries (down from around 19 million to 17 million tonnes in 1982) coupled with lagged price rises. In 1984 the price of Soviet oil was 183 transferable roubles a tonne, compared with an average of 52 transferable roubles over the period 1976–80 (Klein 1987: 274). These foreign trade and payments problems enhanced the need for all-around intensification, in order to make more efficient use of factor inputs ('improving the relationship between expenditure and result'), for increased domestic output of energy and raw materials and a reduction in imports. Note that although producer prices of energy were raised after 1976, the GDR was the only Comecon country not to change its prices and rates for energy consumption to private households (Bethken-hagen 1987: 61).

The 1981–85 Five Year Plan targets were set surprisingly high.[9] Furthermore, growth was to be achieved with no increase in inputs (i.e. achieved by means of intensification). Given the unwillingness to demote consumption seriously (note the rise of Solidarity in Poland) and to sacrifice defence spending, it was investment that suffered; 1982, 1983 and 1984 were years of negative growth. This stored up trouble for the future, hampering structural change and technical innovation; it was to prove devastating when the economy was subjected to the intense competition consequent upon German economic and monetary union.

In view of these ambitious targets, an 'economic strategy for the 1980s' was developed and expounded by Honecker at the party congress in April 1981, essentially revolving around intensification. The limited investment for expansion purposes was to be concentrated on a small number of priority projects in sectors involving key modern technologies: by 'key' technologies were meant micro-electronics, CAD/CAM (computer-aided design and manufacturing), modern computer technology, automated production systems, industrial robots, biotechnology, laser technology, and new processes and materials. The emphasis, however, was to be on the renovation and modernization of the existing capital stock. Along with the acceleration of scientific–technical progress (broad application of micro-electronics and robots, for example), stress was to be increasingly placed on the quality of and value added to products.

Given the deficiencies of the 1970s recentralized system and an unwillingness to return to an NES-type system (decentralization of decision-making without radical price reform would lead to serious divergences between the lines of development preferred by the state and those by the production units, for example), intensification was sought in a substitute model that eschewed radical price reform and decentralization worth talking about, but which would hopefully raise productivity. The answer was seen in making the combine the main production unit and in the 'perfecting' (*Vervollkommnung*) of the economic mechanism.

The combine

Combines[10] were not around in significant numbers until 1968–69; existing combines were used to help implement 'structure-determining tasks'. Acceleration during the third wave of combine formation (1978–80), however, saw it established as the basic production unit (combine decree of 1979). By 1981 combine formation was essentially completed, with 133 *Kombinate* in centrally directed industry and construction. They varied in size from 2,000 to 80,000 employees, with an average of 25,000, and constituted twenty to forty enterprises (Bryson and Melzer 1987: 52). According to Stahnke (1987: 29), the average in industry was 25,000 to 30,000 employees and twenty to thirty enterprises (in construction 10,000 and fifteen, respectively). By 1986 the number had fallen to 127; there were also ninety-four combines in regionally directed industry, with an average of some 2,000 employees and producing mainly consumer goods. In 1987 only 4.4 per cent of manufacturing firms employed fewer than 100 people, compared with 35.9 per cent in the FRG (Collier and Siebert 1991: 198).

The combine was a horizontal and vertical amalgamation of enterprises, under the unified control of a director-general. The 'parent enterprise' (*Stammbetrieb*: enterprises under the direction of a dominant parent enterprise) was increasingly the most important organizational type and was destined to be the sole one. Other types included enterprises under the direction of an independent management body; management carried out by a group of the leading enterprises in various product groups; and a single large enterprise.

The activities of a combine spanned the whole range from R&D, in order to encourage innovation, to marketing, so as to improve quality. The vertical element involved the incorporation of the most important supplier enterprises, with the aim of improving the acute supply problems that afflict command economies. The combine was seen as a means of streamlining the command economy, rather than replacing it, by, for example, reducing the number of production units to be centrally directed and allowing central bodies and ministries to concentrate on 'strategic' matters. For example, the director-general had to report each investment of more than 5 million marks, without a maximum value in the case of certain projects, to the SPC, which also specified the contractors (Tröder 1987: 88). According to Cornelsen (1987: 46), the combines' share of total investment in equipment increased from 14 per cent in 1980 to 34 per cent in 1985. Note that major investment projects of national importance were in large measure centrally planned and major percentages of their finances were covered by budgetary grants (Parsons 1986: 33). Further advantages were seen in the following:

1. Improving information relating to actual production processes, the combines having to submit their plan drafts not only to the competent minister but also to the State Planning Commission, the Ministry of Finance and the State Bank.

2. The reaping of economies of scale.

3. Concentrating production.

4. Making more rational use of materials.

5. Encouraging innovation and the modernization of assets by the in-house manufacture of rationalization equipment and parts.

6. Improving the supply of consumer goods by the combines ultimately having to devote at least 5 per cent of output to consumer goods.

7. Improving foreign trade decision-making.

8. Aiding labour redeployment and retraining.

The broad targets passed down by ministries allowed room for manoeuvre, but monitoring bodies kept a close and frequent check on plan fulfilment. Stahnke (1987: 31) lists the sort of limitations placed upon combines: no unilateral increases in investment or other inputs; requirements to increase the production of consumer goods, achieve product and process change-overs of the order of 30 per cent a year, reduce stocks, reduce transport costs and increase shift work. There were ten industrial ministries, Coal and Energy having the most (twenty-two) combines and Machine Tools and Processing Equipment having the fewest (six) (Stahnke 1987: 29).

In 1981–82, in order to encourage exports and to improve knowledge about international markets, twenty-four foreign trade enterprises were placed under the joint jurisdiction of the Ministry of Foreign Trade (MFT) and the particular combine whose production profile matched that of the exports. Twenty with export ranges dissimilar to those of any combine were subject to the joint jurisdiction of the MFT and an appropriate industrial ministry. The situation in 1986 was that sixty-four foreign trade enterprises were divided into five groupings: twenty-three subject to the dual authority of the MFT and the particular combine; twelve subject to the dual authority of the MFT and the appropriate industrial ministry; twelve also subject to the dual authority of the MFT and the industrial ministry, but whose enterprises were reorganized into sixty-one foreign trade units, without legal rights of their own, which were supposed to co-operate with combines; seven enterprises and combines empowered to engage directly in foreign trade transactions; and ten still subject to the direct and sole authority of the MFT. Note that although this arrangement eroded the strict separation of production and foreign trade, which was a feature of the traditional Soviet model, all foreign trade enterprises were still ultimately supervised by the MFT (Jacobsen 1987; Klein 1987).

The director-general of the combine was responsible for disaggregating the plan tasks received via the ministry to its own enterprises. The decision-making rights of the combine increased with respect to both the latter organizations. Although the enterprise remained a legally independent unit and was able to draw up contracts with other enterprises both within and without the combine, the director-general of the combine was authorized to transfer tasks, functions and plant from one enterprise to another, to hire and fire enterprise managers, and to create new enterprise divisions.

Disadvantages of combine formation were: (1) the adverse effects on innovation of monopolies and the diminution of cross-branch co-operation; and (2) related to enterprise decision-making rights: the division of authority between enterprise and combine was not always clear, but the former certainly lost out significantly; there was always the danger of a parent enterprise appropriating advantageous portions of a programme to itself.

A more recent experiment involved sixteen major combines, which were granted increased decision-making authority (including the use of export earnings). The aim was to include all combines by 1991.

Perfecting of the economic mechanism (direct and indirect steering)

Direct steering

The system of material balancing was further refined with the aim of increasing consistency and flexibility (Melzer: 1987b, c). In 1982–83 roughly 76 per cent of production (and 87 per cent of foreign trade) was centrally determined in 2,136 balances, while a further 2,400 balances (some 24 per cent of production) were drawn up by the authorized combines and confirmed by the competent director-general. By 1986 the respective totals were 1,135 (451 state plan balances, dealing with goods described as of national economic importance, and 684 drawn up by ministries) and 3,400. Input–output tables (625 × 625), accounting for 75 per cent of total production, were mainly used for the elaboration of plan tasks in the annual and five year plans (Kohler 1989: 179).

In 1982 the system of norms and normatives (upper limits for the use of specific materials in the shape of obligatory state targets), designed to reduce materials use, was reviewed, tightened and extended. The success indicator system was also amended (see Table 12.2).

On 1 January 1979 the 'final product' (*Endprodukt*) indicator was introduced for combines, equal to commodity production less deliveries of intermediate inputs between enterprises within a combine. This was done in order to reduce materials use and prevent commodity production being inflated by intra-combine transactions. But the problem of inefficient subcontracting outside the combine led to its replacement by a new indicator called 'net

Table 12.2 GDR: indicators of performance evaluation in industrial combines and enterprises

Regulation of June 1980	Regulation of April 1981	Regulation of March 1983
Basic indicators of performance evaluation		
Industrial commodity production	Industrial commodity production	
Net production[a]	Net production[a]	Net production[a]
Basic materials costs per 100 marks of commodity production[b]	Basic materials costs per 100 marks of commodity production[b]	Net profit[c]
		Products and services for the population
		Exports
Further qualitative indicators		
Net profit[c]	Enterprise result	Labour productivity on the basis of net production
Increase in labour productivity	Increase in labour productivity	
Reduction in the cost of production	Reduction in the cost of production	Costs per 100 marks of commodity production
Proportion of products with quality labels	Proportion of products with quality labels	Production of products important in national economic terms, especially newly developed products and products with quality labels.
Production meeting contractual obligations for domestic use and exports	Production meeting contractual obligations for domestic use and exports	
	Completion of investment projects/objects on time and meeting quality requirements	Materials costs per 100 marks of commodity production[b]

Sources: A. Scherzinger, 'Weiterentwicklung des Wirtschaftsmechanismus in der DDR', *Wochenbericht des DIW* 1983, no. 41, p. 510; cited by Meizer, in Jeffries *et al.* (1987: 104).
Notes:
[a] 'Net production' (simplified) = commodity production *minus* consumption of materials (basic materials, energy, other materials), *minus* consumption of productive services (bought-in services, repairs, transport and warehousing costs, other productive services), *minus* rents and leases, *minus* depreciation.
[b] In the GDR the concept of 'basic materials' (*Grundmaterial*) comprises all the man-made objects that form the material substance of the product. It is thus only part of the wider concept of 'materials', which comprise basic materials, energy, water, fuel, lubricants and other materials.
[c] 'Net profit' (simplified): unitary enterprise results of the enterprise or combine (i.e. including foreign trade profits and losses), *plus* subventions in accordance with statutory provisions, *minus* capital charge, *minus* profits not earned by own economic performance, *minus* profits from exceeding the manpower plan, *minus* fines, transferred to state budget.

production' (commodity production minus all deliveries of intermediate inputs, including those from outside the combine: see Table 12.2 for details). At the same time another new indicator called 'basic materials costs per 100 marks of commodity production' was introduced. After 1983 the following, designed to improve materials use and the relationship between expenditure and use, were regarded as the main indicators: 'net production' (*Nettoproduktion*); 'net profit' (*Nettogewinn*: see Table 12.2); 'products and services for the population' (*Erzeugnisse und Leistungen für die Bevölkerung*) and 'exports' (*Export*). These replaced the former main indicators, 'industrial commodity production' (*industrielle Warenproduktion*) a measure of gross output that tended to encourage production regardless of costs and sales) and 'basic materials costs per 100 marks of commodity production' (*Grundmaterialkosten je 100 Mark Warenproduktion*). Of late there were about 100 indicators in centrally directed industry. Table 12.2 shows the other important indicators then in operation, including the somewhat relegated cost indicators.

Indirect steering

If planned profit (note that impermissible profit, stemming from violations of price or quality regulations, is confiscated) was not achieved, there not only arose financing problems and adverse effects on fund formation, but access to funds such as those relating to performance and investment could be blocked altogether. In the event of overfulfilling profit targets, especially if connected with exports, a higher proportion than in the past could flow into incentive funds. Planned 'net profit deductions' had now to be met in full even in the event of a profit shortfall, previously a part being remitted. Enterprises were, consequently, now obliged to draw on their funds or to turn to credits, although the quantity of credit was conditional upon proof of remedial action. If the net profit deductions were not realized promptly, and in full, the competent bank was authorized to deduct the sum due from the relevant account of the offending combine or enterprise. Incentive funds, linked to the success indicators, were designated for specific purposes and closely monitored.[11]

The capital charge was designed to encourage early completion of projects and to deter delays. With early commissioning of new plant, the charge had only to be paid from the date of the planned start, while an extra 6 per cent penalty was imposed in the event of not meeting plan deadlines, of excess stocks and of idle plant. After 1986 the capital charge was based on the net as opposed to gross value of fixed and working capital, to encourage the retention in use of older capital assets. This was accomplished by imposing a lower capital charge on older equipment. The capital charge was not considered to be part of the enterprise's costs and had to be paid out of earnings.

Credit policy was also employed to achieve the desired state goals. The standard rate of interest was 5 per cent, but penalty rates of up to 12 per cent could be charged on overdue repayments, while the rate could be as low as 1.8 per cent, for credits used for the introduction of new key technologies for example (Buck 1987: 190).

An important innovation was the 'contribution for social funds' (*Beitrag für gesellschaftliche Fonds*), which was introduced in industry at the start of 1984, in construction, foodstuffs and water supply at the beginning of 1985 and in transport and forestry the following year. This was essentially a payroll tax of 70 per cent of the wage fund, designed to promote more efficient use of labour by raising its cost and to contribute to the financing of social services such as education, housing and health. For new products this contribution was included in the fixing of their prices (not reduced if manpower was decreased, thus providing the incentive), but for existing products the previous prices continued to apply until subject to a general revision. In the meantime, a revenue supplement was allowed, but it covered only part of the levy in order to retain some pressure for increased efficiency. There was also an additional charge of 5,000 marks for every employee above the planned limit (Haustein 1989: 103).

The increase in the number of regulations and in the power of combines led to a corresponding enhancement of the role of monitoring bodies, in order to prevent departures from state goals. [12]

Price determination

After 1976 there were annual, staged price revisions, reflecting increases in the cost of energy and raw materials (Melzer: 1983, 1987a, b). The pricing of new and improved products in accordance with the 'price–performance relationship' (*Preis-Leistungs-Verhältnis*), introduced in 1976, was abandoned in late 1983. This was a form of analogue pricing, relating to the improvement in use value characteristics compared with the most analogous existing product. Manufacturers were allowed to reflect 70 per cent of the improvement in price and consumers benefited to the tune of 30 per cent, while additional profit to manufacturers was only allowed for two years and removed over the following three. It was abandoned because of the lack of objective criteria for measuring use value, and, above all, the strong tendency of enterprises to overstate improvements. The prices of new products of late were determined on the basis of calculable costs, including the contribution for social funds, taking into account the price limit set in the development stage and the prevailing norms for input use (part of the cost reductions during the first two years had to benefit the use; afterwards prices could not exceed the given level of costs plus normal profit).

After 1986 extra profits were allowed for two years in order to stimulate innovation (previously it was three years), depending on efficiency criteria such as the level of export profitability and savings in materials. For commodities already in production, the position from 1976 onwards was that cost reductions achieved by manufacturers (via reductions in materials usage, for example) within a five year plan period did not result in lower prices. After 1984 prices remained unchanged until a general, planned price revision. Goods with quality labels were allowed a 2 per cent markup. For goods sold in *exquisit* and *delikat* shops (special shops where quality GDR and Western goods were sold for GDR marks at relatively high prices) much higher profit supplements were allowed, and spare parts were also permitted higher supplements. On the other hand, price discounts penalized below-standard goods. During 1988 new regulations were introduced that were designed to encourage consumer goods production: combines that agreed to manufacture goods in short supply were allowed a 20 per cent mark-up on the normal wholesale price; an extra 10 per cent was added if the goods were delivered before the contract date, but failure to deliver seasonal goods on time resulted in a lower price; retail prices were unaffected (reported by Leslie Colitt in *FT*, 4 August 1988, p. 2; see also Jan Vanous in *Soviet Economy*, 1988, vol. 4, no. 3, p. 188). According to the 1985 regulations for new products, a portion of the cost reductions achieved during the first two years had to benefit users in the form of a price reduction. After that time extra profit had to be given up and prices could no longer exceed the price limit. After two years the price was to be fixed as the level of expenditure accepted by state bodies, including normal profit (Melzer 1987b: 15–16).

The GDR policy of preventing increases in retail prices was amended substantially in 1979. Basic foodstuffs (such as bread, potatoes, fish, meat and bakery products), children's clothing, housing rents and transport fares, remained immune from increases for political and distributional reasons. For example, bus and train fares had not changed since 1949, while rent took only about 3 per cent of urban household income. But the prices of high-quality industrial consumer goods, such as televisions, cars, refrigerators, washing machines and cameras, which were already heavily taxed, now had to cover costs and allow for a normal profit.

It is worth noting that on 1 January 1965 compensation became payable to owners and agricultural producers when land was used for non-agricultural purposes. This was followed in 1968 by the introduction of a charge for the use of land removed from agriculture and forestry, differentiated according to the quality of land and the subsequent use, and reflected in an increased capital charge. A charge for the use of water was also introduced in 1971. All these measures were aimed at increasing efficiency in resource utilization. In the event of emission norms being exceeded, charges for water and air pollution were introduced in 1971 and 1973 respectively. While payments for the use of land and water were included in the planned costs of production (unless norms were exceeded), the payments for excessive pollution were not, thereby reducing enterprise profit and incentive funds (Debardeleben 1985: 159).

Summary of the reforms

The 'perfecting' strategy was clearly not based on any new theoretical blueprint, but judgements on its results were varied. Hamel and Leipold (1987, Chapter 14), following Höhmann, succinctly laid out the opposing 'Popperian' and 'Krylov' theses. The Popperian thesis, following Karl Popper's reform strategy of piecemeal social engineering, holds that step-by-step improvements are possible in command economies (see, for example, Cornelsen, Melzer and Scherzinger). The Krylov thesis is based on the Russian poet's fable of four animal musicians who kept swapping seats but in vain as far as musical harmony was concerned. This doubts the possibility of an economically efficient amendment of a command economy, rather like Gertrude Schroeder's view of Soviet economic changes. She described them as a 'treadmill' of

reform, unable to solve basic problems because the system itself remained basically unchanged (Schroeder 1986).

AGRICULTURE

Agriculture employed less than 11 per cent of the labour force.[13] Co-operative farmers dominated GDR agriculture, in 1985 accounting for about 87 per cent of total LN (*Landwirtschaftliche Nutzfläche*, land used for agricultural purposes), 89 per cent of livestock and 80 per cent of the capital stock in agriculture (Merkel 1987: 218–19). Co-operatives employed 84 per cent of the agricultural workforce, compared to 15 per cent in the case of state farms (Deutsche Bank, *Unification Issue*, 1991, no. 64, p. 2). Thus, the state farm (*Volkseigenes Gut*) played a much smaller role in the GDR than in the Soviet Union, many state farms being involved in research and breeding. One estimate puts the state farms' contributions in 1988 as follows: agricultural land, 7 per cent; livestock, 12 per cent; seed and plant production, 20 per cent; breeding and productive livestock, 18 per cent (European Parliament 1990: 20).

The dominant production unit was the agricultural producer co-operative (*Landwirtschaftliche Produktionsgenossenschaft*). This was a large unit, in 1985 accounting for 1,369 ha of LN on average (4,608 in crop production). In 1988 the average crop unit employed some 240 workers and was composed of about 500 farms previously privately run; the average livestock production unit employed 110 persons and had 1,500 head of livestock (European Commission 1990: 20). The co-operative was modelled on the Soviet collective farm and was subject to state plans and procurement quotas. But there were differences. For example, while all land was owned by the state in the Soviet Union, the figure was only 30 per cent in the GDR. Land ownership in the GDR co-operative was a mixture of co-operative and private. Although the right to the use of land (with the exception of the private plot) belonged to the co-operative, individuals were compensated when land was used for industrial purposes and when land shares were paid off. As far as individual contributions in the form of machines, livestock and buildings were concerned, these became co-operative property, although there could be partial compensation if minimum levels were exceeded.

The basic form of labour organization was the brigade, subdivided into divisions and these, in turn, into 'work groups'. Remuneration was mainly based on the 'work unit'. The individual work unit was influenced by factors such as the degrees of responsibility and difficulty of the particular type of work. Its final value was not known until the year-end accounts had been done, and the total number of work units was divided into net income. This residual form of income was ameliorated by the fact that advances were allowed to co-operative members. There were also experiments to compensate members along state sector lines.

As far as pricing policy was concerned, in order to increase efficiency of resource use, the government adopted a policy of increasing producer prices and reducing subsidies on agricultural inputs (this was also part of the general policy of achieving a high degree of self-sufficiency in the production of foodstuffs). This culminated in the 1 January 1984 price reform, which led to an average price increase of 60 per cent in product prices and the ending, more or less, of subsidies on factor inputs such as feedstuffs, machinery, fuels, mineral fertilizers and construction materials. The crop producing co-operative was now also subject to a fixed levy per hectare of LN, differentiated according to land quality, poor-quality land being exempt and some farms even receiving a grant. Co-operatives also paid a progressive profits tax.

History

The *land reform* of 1945–52 confiscated about two-thirds of the land from those possessing more than 100 ha, excluding the church, distributed in the shape of small farms, while a number of landed estates became state farms. There was also confiscation of the land owned by those described as Nazi activists and war criminals.

Collectivization took place from 1952 until the spring of 1960. By that time the privately farmed agricultural area had been reduced to less than 8 per cent (Brezinski 1990: 535). Co-operatives accounted for 37 per cent of agricultural land at the end of 1958 and 84.2 per cent at the end of 1960 (Childs 1987: 7). Originally there were three types of agricultural co-operative (I, II and III), but Type III gradually replaced the others (it was almost completely dominant by the mid-1970s). In Type I members

Table 12.3 GDR: statistical survey

Net hard currency debt ($ billion)	1977	1981	1985	1986	1988	1989
	6.8	12.5	6.5	7.9	10.4	18.5

Private enterprise, including private farms, 1985 (% national income): 2.8

Independent private farms, i.e. excluding private plots, 1985 (% of net output of agriculture): 3.7

Private sector in agriculture, 1987 (% of agriculture area): 9.2

Population, end 1986: 16.6 million

Sources: Brezinski (1987: 86–7; 1990: 536–9); Cochrane (1988: 48); Cornelsen (1987: 52); EIU, *Country Profile*, 1987–88, P. 35, and *Country Report*, 1989, no. 4, p. 17.
Notes: For rates of growth of produced national income and GNP see Tabel 12.1.

only contributed land, with livestock and the means of production remaining individually controlled. In Type II livestock, except draught animals, remained privately owned. The two-tier system of producer pricing (above-plan deliveries commanded a higher price) came to an end for crops in 1964 and for animal products in 1969 (DIW 1989: 102; Schinke 1988: 200).

Reorganization began in the early 1970s, with the aim of applying industrial methods to agriculture. Large, specialized (in crop production or animal husbandry) entities came to dominate. There were, however, experiments with 'co-operation councils' (*Kooperationsräte*) to try to overcome the problems of such a division. These councils comprised representatives of the crop and animal husbandry entities and sought to co-ordinate their activities, such as feedstuff supply. There were around 1,200 councils, each comprising between two and four livestock production plants and one crop production unit (European Parliament 1990: 20). After 1984 they acted as a channel for the plans passed on by the district council. These entities evolved out of non-specialized production units. Inter-enterprise (co-operative and state) co-operation in various forms arose, e.g. the Co-operative Division for Crop Production: these were mainly transformed into specialized agricultural co-operatives during the latter half of the 1970s. There gradually emerged out of this the independent, specialized units of today. Inter-enterprise co-operation latterly took the form of organizations like the agro-chemical centres. These supplied and applied chemical fertilizers and plant pest control agents, and were also increasingly involved in seeding. In addition there were inter-enterprise organizations involved in livestock. The 'co-operative association' (*Kooperationsverband*), originally created in 1967, was a vertically integrated organization spanning production, processing and even retail sales. Only large efficient producers were eligible and membership was voluntary (Schinke 1990: 259).

There were also other organizations of note.

The district enterprises for rural technology maintained and repaired agricultural machinery. The Machine Tractor Stations were abolished in 1963 and their machinery and equipment transferred to co-operatives. In addition there were factory farming combines under county control. These were mostly concerned with poultry and eggs, but some with pork and beef. After the Ninth Congress of the SED in 1976, eleven agro-industrial associations were set up (involving, for example, crop production, fodder plants, agro-chemical centres and land improvement enterprises) as a step on the way towards the formation of an agro-industrial complex. There were only fourteen at peak (Schinke 1990: 259).

Private production

An official distinction was made between 'private' agriculture and 'individual' ('personal') agriculture (Brezinski 1990: 536). 'Private' agriculture comprised private farmers and church-owned farms; the state did not directly regulate their activities, agriculture was the main occupation and occasionally even non-family labour was employed. 'Individual' agriculture was only a supplement to the regular job and most production was consumed by the persons involved. The state only supported 'individual' farming, because the state was able to integrate and control it, e.g. private plots but not private farms were entitled to a tax-free income of 7,000 marks (Brezinski 1987: 97). In 1985 there were 5,900 private farms and some farms owned by the church (Brezinski 1987: 87). In 1987 private use as a whole accounted for 9.2 per cent of the total agricultural area (compared with 19.3 per cent in 1960 and 8.8 per cent in 1983); this was broken down into the household plots of members of agricultural co-operatives (3.9 per cent, 11.2 per cent and 3.3 per cent respectively); private farms, plots of the members of the Association of Small Gardeners, Settlers and Small Animal Breeders (founded 1959, with a membership comprising workers and employees, co-operative farmers, retired people and young adults aged eighteen to twenty-five) and others (5.3 per cent, 8.1 per cent and 5.5 per cent respectively)(Brezinski 1990: 538). Independent private farms accounted for 23.7 per cent of net agricultural production in 1960 (note that the official figure excluded production from private plots from 1970 onwards), 3.7 per cent in 1985 and 4.1 per cent in 1988 (p. 539). Wädekin (1990c: 249) puts the private sector's share of total agricultural output at 10 per cent in the early 1980s.

During the 1960s (which was a decade of discouragement as regards private agriculture) it was decided that only co-operative members had the right to a plot. The private plot of co-operative members was fixed at 0.25 ha (with a family maximum of 0.5 ha) and central restrictions were lifted on the number of livestock (the co-operative could still impose them). Private production was important for certain commodities such as meat (more than 20 per cent of total output in 1985) and eggs and fruit (more than 50 per cent) (p. 88). According to the *DIW Handbuch* (1985: 188), private holdings accounted for approximately 5 per cent of total livestock: horses, 33 per cent; sheep, 15 per cent; pigs, 10 per cent; poultry, 25 per cent; and rabbits almost 100 per cent. About 30 per cent of fruit, 11 per cent of vegetables and 100 per cent of honey were privately produced.

INTERNATIONAL TRADE

GDR data were given in Valuta Marks and for total turnover only. Neither the rate of exchange between the VM and the domestic mark nor the (fixed) one between the VM and the transferable rouble was made known officially. In 1986 VM 1 = $0.304 or DM 0.661 (DIW 1989: 166).

In 1980 around 30 per cent of produced national income was exported (*DIW Handbuch* 1985: 294). In 1988 the GDR accounted for little more than 1 per cent of world trade, compared to West Germany's 10 per cent (European Parliament 1990: 100). Comecon accounted for about 63 per cent of GDR trade (the GDR some 16 per cent of intra-Comecon trade, second to the Soviet Union) and the Soviet Union alone about 39 per cent.[14] The GDR was a major supplier of relatively high-quality, high-technology capital goods (e.g. machine tools,[15] industrial robots and computers) to Comecon and was heavily dependent on imports of fuels and raw materials, especially from the Soviet Union. Of the approximately 23 million tonnes of GDR oil imports, 17 million tonnes came from the Soviet Union. Since domestic consumption was only about 10 million tonnes, GDR exports of oil and oil products to the West constituted an important source of hard currency earnings, especially given the difficulty of selling manufactured goods in Western markets. The exact amount of oil re-exported was the subject of controversy; it was significantly affected by the world price of oil and the value of the US dollar. Specialization agreements within Comecon affected the GDR. In 1971, for example, the GDR agreed to cease production of trams in exchange for passenger cars. In 1987 the percentage commodity structure of the GDR's total foreign trade was as follows: exports ('machinery and transport equipment' 48; 'fuels, minerals and metals' 16.6; 'industrial consumer goods' 16; imports 34.1, 38 and 5.6 respectively (*EIU Country Report*, 1989, no. 4, p. 2).

The GDR was granted valuable special concessions in its trade with the Federal Republic. Note that the latter referred to its exports to the GDR as 'deliveries' and its imports from the GDR as 'purchases'. Apart from the obvious ties of nationality, the FRG considered close economic links and increasing GDR living standards as important for Western security, while the GDR was a reluctant participant in Soviet plans to increase intra-Comecon links, providing the Soviet Union with top-quality manufactures in return for stable supplies of energy and raw materials. Note, however, that the relative impact of inner-German trade varied, the GDR only accounting for 1.6 per cent of the FRG's foreign trade in 1986, while the FRG accounted for around 14 per cent of the GDR's foreign trade (Schäuble 1988: 213). West Germany ranked second in the GDR's foreign trade, whereas the latter was only thirteenth in the former's (Leptin 1989: 280). GDR exports to the FRG were allowed in free of tariffs and levies and the GDR enjoyed value added tax concessions, the West German importer being able to obtain a tax refund for the VAT on imports. West Germany did, however, impose quotas on certain items (e.g. about 80 per cent of agricultural imports were so affected, but manufactures such as steel and textiles were also subject to quotas in order to prevent dumping). There was a bilateral clearing system organized by the two central banks. The *Verrechnungseinheit* (VE: settlement unit) was the clearing unit of account used in trade between the two countries. Its value corresponded to that of the DM, but the VEs earned by the GDR could only be used for purchases in West Germany. The 'swing' provided an interest-free overdraft facility up to a certain limit, raised from DM 600 million to DM 800 million in July 1985, which thus allowed a delay in repaying the deficit until the annual settlement. The cumulative surplus for the FRG on the bilateral clearing account stabilized at between DM 3.5 billion and DM 4 billion after 1978 (Lisiecki 1990: 524). The government of the FRG guaranteed West German bank credits to the GDR, while GDR exports of foodstuffs even escaped the post-Chernobyl restrictions. As Baylis points out, West German credits during the Western squeeze helped re-establish East German creditworthiness, while the FRG supplied vital producer goods, emergency materials and spare parts to help overcome shortages and bottlenecks (Baylis 1986: 418).

The GDR also had valuable sources of hard currency earnings in the following: transit and road facilities to and services provided for West Berlin; the Genex-Geschenkdienst (handling gifts paid for in DMs from the West to GDR citizens of goods and services produced in the GDR, Comecon or the West); Intertank (convertible currency service stations); 'intershops' (convertible currency shops); and the 'sale' of prisoners, which began in 1963 and had cost the FRG more than DM 1 billion by autumn 1987 (David Marsh, *FT Supplement*, 16 April 1988, p. i, and FT, 26 February 1990, p. 18). Another estimate puts the bill for 33,750 political detainees 'purchased' by West Germany at DM 3.5 billion over the period 1963–89 (*IHT*, 24 December 1991, p. 2). It has been estimated that in the mid-1980s the total value of fees, concessions, gifts and so on from the FRG amounted to around 1.5 per cent of the GDR's GNP calculated on a Western basis (Marer 1986c: 613). Leptin (1989: 285) puts the average annual sum during the first half of the 1980s (excluding parcels and prisoners) at DM 2.5 billion. According to Lisiecki (1990: 527), the GDR and its citizens together received annual subsidies totalling around DM 5 billion from West Germany; if the gains from inner-German trade and the so-called 'non-recorded activities' are included the sum increases to DM 6 billion to DM 7 billion.

The GDR was reluctant to increase its involvement in direct links between enterprises within Comecon. In 1987 such an agreement was reached, for example, between a Soviet and an East German enterprise to develop a micro-electronic sewing machine, but the GDR's enthusiasm waned owing to the failure of a joint project to develop a programmable washing machine (see Leslie Colitt, FT, 22 July 1987, p. 2).

The GDR was isolated among the East European Comecon states in not allowing joint equity ventures with Western companies. This was possibly due to apprehension about the prospect of a sizeable influx of West German capital, technology and know-how, which could have been seen as an admission of domestic economic failure.

THE NON-STATE, NON-AGRICULTURAL SECTOR

Åslund (1985) has analysed the non-agricultural sector. He estimates that in 1979 the private sector contributed 3 per cent of net material product outside agriculture and employed 5.2 per cent of the non-agricultural labour force. Following the early nationalization measures there was a falling trend with cycles: a socialist offensive (1952–53), relatively late because of the uncertainty surrounding reunification; a liberal interlude (1953–57); a second socialist offensive (1958–60); a period of successful competition between the state and private sectors during the period of the New Economic System; a third socialist offensive (1971–75), in which the first half of 1972 was especially prominent. The period after 1976 saw the granting of tax and credit concessions and many new licences for handicrafts, trade and catering. Excluding apprentices, employment in the private trades sector increased by 11,844 to 258,100 between 1980 and 1984. In 1985, 15,000 new licences were granted. The 1986–90 plan foresaw further growth of the sector, encouraged by a tax-free two years and low-interest credit.

Brezinski (1987: 86) provides percentage figures for the share of private enterprises in national income: 1950, 43.2; 1960, 12.5; 1970, 5.5; 1975, 3.4; 1980, 2.9; 1982, 2.8; 1983, 2.8; 1984, 2.8; 1985, 2.8. A sectoral breakdown of the 1985 net output figures shows (per cent): industry (including manufacturing handicrafts, but excluding construction), 2.3; construction, 5.9; agriculture and forestry (excluding household plots), 3.7; domestic trade, 2.7; and transport, posts and telegraphs, 0.8. In 1985 private production accounted for 58.9 per cent of handicrafts (manufacturing trades and the services were allowed to employ up to ten people, although the actual average number of employees was only three: DIW 1989; 87); retail trade, 5.1 per cent; restaurants, 3.1 per cent; and new houses, 15.1 per cent. Note that private construction enterprises accounted for around 6 per cent of construction output, but were mainly engaged in repair and renovation, since new private houses are mainly built by individual house owners (Brezinski 1987: 90). 'Groups of supply' were to be found in trades and services, in which a socialized enterprise guided a group of private enterprises with the aim of planning supply and allocating tasks. Chambers of commerce and of trade (directed by district councils since 1985) were concerned with input supplies to the private sector, price control, quality, wages and the promotion of vocational training (Brezinski 1987: 99). 'After-work brigades' began operating in the 1970s and comprised employees of nationalized enterprises. Wages were legally determined and were exempt from income tax and social security contributions (p. 89). There were also 'DIY organizations' (training centres).

Mention should also be made of the existence of (1) production and trade co-operatives; and (2) semi-state enterprises: these were first set up in 1956, accounted for 10 per cent of industrial production in 1971, and were nationalized the following year (Childs 1987: 9).

CONCLUSION

The socialist, poorer half of a divided Germany, the GDR nevertheless had the highest standard of living in the socialist world. Like Czechoslovakia, the GDR was an industrialized country from the beginning, and the latter continued to benefit from substantial economic concessions granted by the FRG, such as the FRG allowing in East German goods free from tariffs or levies. Particularly important aspects to notice are the 1960s New Economic System (the first systematic attempt at overall reform in Comecon) and the more recent stress on improving economic performance by means of the combine and the 'perfecting' of the economic mechanism. The Honecker regime rejected any radical reform of the economy, shared with communist Albania the distinction of having no prospective joint equity legislation, but was relatively successful in reducing the country's foreign debt in the first half of the 1980s. The Honecker regime collapsed like a pack of cards in late 1989.

NOTES

1. It should be noted, however, that the Federal Republic took in many refugees from the eastern provinces of the Third Reich and paid substantial compensation to Israel.

2. Primary energy consumption in 1984 was as follows: raw lignite, 71 per cent; oil, 11 per cent; natural gas, 10 per cent; and nuclear power, 3 per cent (Bethkenhagen 1987: 65). In 1988 lignite accounted for 85 per cent of electricity and nuclear 10 per cent (European Parliament 1990: 91).

3. The GDR and Czechoslovakia became the chief suppliers of uranium to the Soviet Union after the Second World War. The joint uranium mining enterprise Wismut became totally German-owned on 16 May 1991; the Soviet Union received no compensation but Germany had to pay the clean-up costs. Until 1954 Soviet officials ran it alone (John Tagliabue, *IHT*, 21 March 1991, p. 9).

4. See Leptin and Melzer (1978); Jeffries *et al.* (1987: Chapter 3); Hamel and Leipold (1987).

5. In political terms, Ulbricht envisaged a special path for the GDR, involving a 'socialist human community', which would harness the technical revolution and help harmonize social classes and strata (Dennis 1988: 42).

6. Note that the capital charge was levied on the actual value of fixed and working capital.

7. According to the 1969–70 regulations, enterprises were initially allowed to deduct the full amount of profit loss from net payments due to the state, as an incentive to reduce costs.

8. The EIU (*Country Profile*, 1987–88, p.35) estimates the GDR's net hard currency debt at $12.5 billion in 1981, $6.5 billion in 1985 and $7.9 billion in 1986. It was $10.4 billion at the end of 1988 (*EIU Country Report*, 1989, no. 4, p. 17). The figure of $18.5 billion at the end of 1989 was officially given. It is worth noting Childs's point that by the second half of the 1970s priorities revolved around savings in energy and raw materials and boosting exports, a far more prudent investment policy than Poland's (1987: 63).

9. An annual average rate of growth of produced national income of 5.1–5.4 per cent, for example, compared with a planned figure of 5 per cent and an actual figure of 4.1 per cent over the period 1976–80.

10. See Melzer (1981); Bryson and Melzer (1987); and Stahnke (1987).

11. Combines and selected enterprises were able to finance specific imports from a hard currency fund financed from overfulfilment of export targets.

12. Some new, like the Inspectorate of Quality.

13. See Merkel (1987); *DIW Handbuch* (1985: Chapter 4.4); Thalheim (1981: Chapter 5).

14. See Jacobsen (1987); Klein (1987); Baylis (1986). These official figures were revised after Honecker's fall to show a much lower share of the GDR's foreign trade for the Soviet Union and a much higher share for West Germany. Osmond (1992: 82, 254, see Postscript) shows how the revised figures for 1988 have the Soviet Union's share falling from, 37.5 per cent to 24.5 per cent (22.9 per cent in 1989) and West Germany's rising from 7.0 per cent to 19.7 per cent (20.6 per cent in 1989).

15. Jost Prescher (head of the GDR's export–import agency) gives the following information relating to machine tools. In 1987 the GDR ranked seventh in the world in terms of machine tool output and fourth in terms of exports. Sixty to seventy per cent of output was exported, although only 10–15 per cent of exports went to the West (reported by Nick Garnett in *FT*, 15 November 1988, p. 25).

13

HUNGARY

POLITICAL AND ECONOMIC BACKGROUND

Hungary became an independent country in November 1918 as a result of the disintegration of the Austro-Hungarian Empire. A short-lived 'national Bolshevik' regime ('Soviet republic') was established by Bela Kun 21 March – 4 August 1919. Its suppression was followed in 1920 by the regency of Miklos Horthy (awaiting the return of the Habsburg monarchy), a right-wing regime which sided with Germany in the Second World War. This country of 10.6 million people is endowed with good climate and soils (about 70 per cent of the land is cultivated), but is mainly poor in raw materials. There are important exceptions, such as bauxite and coal, uranium and manganese. Oil production reached 2 million tonnes in 1986, about a fifth of the country's needs. In 1941 25 per cent of the labour force was employed in industry or mining; in 1938 nearly 50 per cent of those employed in industry were in handicrafts (Batt 1988: 51).

Imre Nagy, who was prime minister in 1956 until the Soviet invasion, was executed two years later. The trauma of the October–November 1956 revolution (until February 1989 officially described as a 'counter-revolution') and economic factors such as Hungary's heavy dependence on foreign trade led to the introduction of a unique economic mechanism. Immediate political repression was followed by economic reform to provide the material basis

for mollifying the population and by a process of relative political relaxation.[1]

At the Thirteenth Party Congress,[2] 25–8 March 1985, Janos Kadar, who became General Secretary of the Hungarian Socialist Workers' Party in 1956, stressed the need to continue with cautious fine-tuning of the economic reforms despite severe economic difficulties. The latter are illustrated in Table 13.1, which shows falling rates of economic growth,[3] rising inflation and an increasing net hard currency debt (the highest *per capita* in Eastern Europe). Kadar's view was that 'Those who are not against us are for us'. Kadar looked back on five years of hardship and worries since the last congress, during which the living standards of a third of the workers had fallen and those of the remaining two-thirds had stagnated, owing to the need to repay the debt. A further round of austerity measures was adopted in September 1987.

Kadar successfully warded off threats to his position (such as in late 1986), but he was finally ousted as General Secretary at the end of the special party conference held 20–2 May 1988 – special in the sense that it was the first to be held between the normal four year conferences. Just short of his seventy-sixth birthday, he was nominally compensated with the new honorary post of Party President (losing even this in May 1989). Karoly Grosz (fifty-seven) was appointed General Secretary, having been made prime minister only in June 1987. He remained as the latter until November 1988 when he was replaced by Miklos Nemeth. Rezso Nyers became Minister of State for Economic Affairs. In

Table 13.1 Hungary: foreign debt and average annual rates of growth of produced Net Material Product and prices (%)

Net Material Product

1951–55	1956–60	1961–65	1966–70	1971–75	1976	1977	1978	1979	1980	1981	1982	1983	1984	1985	1986	1987	1988	1989
13.2	7.6	7.5	6.2	6.4	3.0	7.1	4.0	1.2	–0.9	2.5	2.7	0.3	2.5	–1.4	0.9	4.1	–0.5	–1.1

Inflation (average annual)

1961	1962	1963	1964	1965	1966	1967	1968	1969	1970	1971	1972	1973	1974–80	1981–85	1986	1987	1988	1989
1.0	0.5	–0.7	0.5	1.1	1.8	0.6	0.0	1.3	1.3	2.2	2.8	3.4	7.5	6.8	5.3	8.6	15.7	17.0

Net foreign debt ($ billion)

1970	1981	1982	1983	1984	1985	1986	1987	1988	1989
1.0	7.8	7.2	6.9	7.3	9.5	12.9	16.2	15.9	19.4

Sources Smith (1983: 40); *EIU, Country Profile*, 1987–88, pp. 11, 35; 1989–90, p. 18; M. Marrese, in *Economic Reforms in Eastern Europe*, Brussels: NATO, 1980, p. 187; Kerpel and Young (1988: 96); *Abecor Country Reports*, May 1989, p.1); Hare (1990a: 4); Institute of International Finance (1990: 15); CIA (1990: tables 1 and C-12); *European Economy: the Path of Reform in Central and Eastern Europe*, Commission of the European Communities, Brussels, 1991, p. 278; *FT Survey*, 30 October 1991, p. iii; United Nations Economic Commission for Europe (1992: 293).

the new eleven-strong politburo were liberals such as Imre Pozsgay (president of the People's Patriotic Front) and Rezso Nyers, architect of the original economic reform, who became the Central Committee secretary in charge of economic affairs in 1962. Sweeping changes in the main party bodies meant substantial losses for the old guard.[4] Two bills were passed by Parliament on 11 January 1989 concerning the rights of association and assembly. The former permitted the establishment of independent organizations, including trade unions, provided they were not contrary to the constitution. This was followed by the bill dealing with the conditions enabling independent political parties to be set up, the formal acceptance of the principle of a multi-party system occurring in February. On 24 June 1989 the powers of Grosz as General Secretary were diluted by the setting up of a four-strong party presidium headed by Nyers and including Pozsgay and Nemeth, one of its tasks being to prepare a party programme for the forthcoming free election. At the Fourteenth Party Congress, held 6–9 October 1989, the party was renamed the Hungarian Socialist Party (with Reszo Nyers as president), committed to a multi-party, democratic system and a market economy along Scandinavian lines (with mixed ownership and a welfare state). On 18 October 1989 the 'People's Republic' became simply the 'Republic' of Hungary. The 1990 free election (the two rounds were on 25 March and 8 April) resulted in a victory for the Hungarian Democratic Forum, which campaigned on a social market economy ticket, but one cautious in terms of privatization and foreign capital. A coalition government was formed with the Independent Smallholders' Party and the Christian Democratic People's Party.

THE NEW ECONOMIC MECHANISM

The main features of the New Economic Mechanism

Although the New Economic Mechanism (NEM) was introduced *en bloc* on 1 January 1968, there were earlier changes of note. During the first half of the 1960s the number of state industrial enterprises was further reduced from the 1950 level, from 1,368 to 840, in order to maintain central control as directive planning was relaxed (Marer 1986a: 244). In the late 1950s and early 1960s the (relatively modest) changes included employee profit-sharing schemes, a reduction in the number of enterprise indicators (especially in light industry) and improvements in the determination of prices, to reflect costs and world levels better. In 1964 a 5 per cent charge on the value of fixed and working capital was introduced and treated as a component of costs – this was abolished in 1980.

The NEM did not transform Hungary into a model of market socialism, where state-owned enterprises operate in a market environment. Although traditional command planning was abandoned, the state still set macro targets. Five year plans guided investment, for example. There were no longer specific enterprise targets in the annual plan, which included aggregate targets for magnitudes such as the growth of total output and investment. State enterprises drew up their own output and input plans on the basis of negotiated contracts, but the state employed a 'visible hand' to steer them mainly indirectly via informal pressures and economic levers such as prices, taxes, the cost and availability of credit, tariffs and import licences. Kornai (1986) describes the system as a combination of certain elements of market coordination and, more important, indirect bureaucratic control. 'Regulator bargaining' took the place of plan bargaining in the sense that the enterprise was vertically dependent on a bureaucracy that made innumerable micro interventions in areas such as investment, managerial appointments, firms' entry into and exit from industries, subsidies, prices, taxes and credits.

Direct methods included large investment projects in sectors such as energy, mining and the infrastructure. The state also reserved the right to issue orders to enterprises as a last resort. Marer describes direct planning in the micro sphere as limited to infrastructural investment, large investments in priority sectors, central allocation of a few inputs, administrative regulation of the defence industries and the fulfilment of Comecon obligations. Taxes and subsidies were adjusted to ensure that the enterprise did not lose out financially (Marer 1986a: 240).

Until the mid-1980s state industrial enterprises worked within the constraint of their basic production profiles, although they were permitted to expand and modernize their plants to some degree,[5] to hold (after 1977) a share of the equity of small joint venture subsidiaries and (after 1982) to set up their own subsidiaries, although they were still legally responsible for them. Thus the state set up large new enterprises and still effectively decided on the closing down of enterprises, control of investment in general being considered necessary to avoid 'capitalist business cycles' and to maintain full employment.[6]

The typical state industrial enterprise was always relatively large, even though most state enterprises were freed from compulsory membership of trusts or associations in 1968 (Bauer 1988: 453). In 1968 there were only 840 industrial enterprises (Comisso and Marer 1986: 426). Kornai (citing Roman) states that in 1975 the three largest producers accounted for more than two-thirds of production in 508 of 637 industrial product aggregates (Kornai 1986: 1699). In a 1985 unpublished manuscript Kornai (quoted by Bechtold and Helfer 1987: 19) says that only 715 state-owned firms controlled 93 per cent of industrial output, with 37 per cent of them employing more than 500. In 1987 there were over seven establishments per industrial enterprise, with an average of 329 workers per establishment in heavy industry and 273 in light industry (Hare 1990b: 584). Within socialist industry (quoting Szalai) there were 259 'large enterprises' (employing more than 1,000) out of 1,157 in 1980, and 372 out of 1,225 in 1987; in the period 1983–87 large enterprises accounted for 83.5 per cent of sales (p. 589). In 1988 there were only two enterprises producing domestic

chemicals and barely twelve in many branches of light industry and food processing (Hare 1992: 148); in 1987 state enterprises, employing 1,206 on average, accounted for 90.44 per cent of gross industrial output (p. 147). After 1980 many effective monopolies were split up in order to encourage competition.[7] In the period 1980–85 the number of trusts fell from twenty-four to nine and more than 400 new and independent organizations were created out of this process and out of the division of enterprises (von Czege 1987: 133).

In 1980 the three industrial ministries were merged into a single Ministry of Industry in order to reduce ministerial interference and resistance to reform. In December 1987 a ministerial change was announced, including the merger of the Ministry of Trade and the Ministry of Foreign Trade into a new Ministry of Commerce (under Jozsef Marjai), the setting up of the first Environment Ministry, the establishment of the Planning and Economic Commission under Peter Medgessy (combining the functions of the Ministry of Finance and the planning, prices and wages and labour commissions) and the setting up of a new Ministry of Health and Social Affairs under Judit Csehak.

There is some dispute about how important a role *profit* played in industrial enterprise decision-making, this generally being considered much stronger in agriculture and in the co-operative and private sectors. The introduction of a profits tax in 1968 gave an incentive to increase profits, since the enterprise would gain a share (rather than all exceeding incentive funds being transferred to the state budget). Kornai (1986: 1726), however, considers the profit incentive to have been weakened by the 'soft budget constraint' and the importance of vertical dependence on the bureaucracy.[8] Crane, on the other hand, has assessed the results of interviews conducted in mid-1982. Rewards for managers were based on the formula

$$\frac{P}{(W+K)}$$

(where P is profits, W is the total wage bill, and K is the enterprise's fixed assets); this determined between a half and three-quarters of bonus income (which itself equalled a third to half of base salary). On the other hand, superiors' recognition affected career and salary, while a 'complex evaluation' by superiors, involving factors such as plant safety, increasing hard currency exports and decreasing energy use, was also important (Crane 1986: 440). The main aim was to avoid a loss, with its adverse effects on bonuses and possible dismissal (Crane 1986: 442). It is also worth noting that the tax regime that existed before 1 January 1988 meant a sharp difference between gross and net profit, the lack of value-added tax and of a personal income tax placing a large budgetary burden on enterprise profit.

The trend over time was towards greater refinement of the NEM despite some setbacks. *The period 1972–78*, for example, was one of retrenchment, due to a deteriorating trade and payments situation and the superior performance of small and medium enterprises relative to larger ones. In November 1972 fifty of the largest enterprises (accounting for 50 per cent of industrial output) were subjected to special ministerial supervision and benefited from special concessions. These large enterprises were not happy with smaller ones adversely affecting their supplies of labour and materials. The activities of smaller enterprises were more tightly controlled and some were even merged into the larger ones. 'Plan juries' (interministerial, functional and sectoral advisory committees on enterprise plans) were introduced, and emphasis was placed on 'complex evaluation'. This involved such criteria as technological progress and other aspects of long-term development. Other measures included a greater isolation of domestic from world prices and increased use of quantitative regulations such as purchase quotas and central allocations. Macro policy following the 1973–74 oil shock involved increased investment and growth and a switch to Comecon trade, which was to lead to the severe trade and debt problems afflicting Hungary today (Marer 1986a: 246). On the other hand, some individual measures were taken that enriched the reforms. In 1976, for example, the obligatory division of net profit into the enterprise reserve, development, bonus and housing funds was abandoned and replaced by tax regulation (Marer 1986a: 263).

Despite growing external economic problems and others involving inflation, declining growth rates and living standards for much of the population, and the considerable income and wealth differentials attributable to the operation of the extensive 'second economy',[9] the period after 1979 saw a return to the path of reform (such as the splitting up of large enterprises and encouragement given to the private sector) as well as the introduction of austerity measures.

January 1985 marked the start of a two-year *managerial reform*. The largest enterprises, such as those in electric power generation, oil, aluminium, armaments and transport, were unaffected. These accounted for about a third of all employees (Ellman 1989a: 84). Here managers and management staff were still hired or fired by the minister. In medium and certain large enterprises (employing more than 500 workers), however, 'enterprise councils' were formed, comprising representatives of workers and management (employees formed at least half the membership) and the secretaries of the party, the trade union and the Communist Youth League. The council elected the managers and staff, but the ministry or local authority (the founding body, in other words) had the right to veto the candidacy of aspiring directors and to dismiss any elected director. Formally, the manager was in charge of day-to-day operations, while the council made 'strategic' decisions. The new management structure was able to decide on such factors as the issue of bonds, asset transfer and mergers with other enterprises (Adam 1987: 612). In enterprises with a workforce of less than 500, the employees themselves (the general assembly or delegated representatives) hired and fired the manager and staff without ministerial interference (these accounted for only 2–3 per cent of all employees: Ellman 1989: 84). In reality, of course, the usual party and state pressures made themselves felt, but it is still worth noting that one of the motivating forces of this reform was to enhance enterprises' independence from ministries.

After January 1982 '*private work partnerships*' ('enterprise contract work associations' or 'work teams') were allowed in state enterprises; groups of workers were able to hire equipment at negotiated rates for work after normal hours to fulfil contracts with their own enterprise or, with permission, outside enterprises. A maximum limit of thirty was placed on the membership (fifteen is usual), who were able to undertake extra production or provide services such as cleaning and maintenance (Noti 1987: 72). Among the reasons for setting up these bodies were labour shortages and the wish to lessen worker dissatisfaction with declining real wages in their normal jobs; thus workers could be retained (Adam 1989b: 50). In 1986 14.3 per cent of all employees in state industry were involved (p. 56). Problems encountered included resentment of higher earnings felt by the other workers and a temptation by those involved to slack during regular working hours.

As in all other socialist countries there was general reluctance to close down 'uneconomic' enterprises (despite the associated problems of the 'soft budget constraint'), not only to avoid unemployment ('temporary restructuring of manpower'), but also to avoid having to import substitute commodities. On 1 September 1986, however, a *bankruptcy law* (the Liquidation Act) was introduced, the first in Eastern Europe. Courts were able to declare an enterprise bankrupt and company managements or creditors, including banks, could take proceedings. Until 1 January 1989 there were only specific examples of 'job-finding support' for workers, but still not a general system of unemployment benefit. There were retraining schemes and early

retirement programmes, and 'relocation benefits' (especially to help with the severe housing difficulties), usually paid for six months in lieu of notice, have been available since 1986 for workers made redundant in groups of at least ten (Susan Greenberg, *FT*, 5 January 1988, p. 2). A form of (progressively decreasing) unemployment benefit was available for up to a year, but enterprise managers could avoid the bureaucratic procedures involved in shedding labour this way by e.g. not declaring ten workers redundant all at once (Sziraczki 1990: 717–8). This first unemployment compensation was introduced in 1986, but the ten-or-more lay-off eligibility condition was lifted in 1988 (although a worker still had to be formally dismissed by an employer) (Hars *et al.* 1991: 172). Other eligibility conditions included employment at some time during the past year and eighteen months' service during the previous three years; unemployment compensation was in the range 50–70 per cent of the individual's average wage, depending on the cause of dismissal and length of receipt of benefit. The January 1989 scheme involved the following (Micklewright 1992: 6); eligibility for unemployment benefit demanded eighteen months' employment in the three years prior to a claim, the duration of unemployment benefit was twelve months in a three year period, and benefits declined over time within a range of 70–50 per cent. In the event of expired entitlement a further year's benefit equal to 75 per cent of previous benefit was available.

The first half of 1987 saw only three companies liquidated and in September of that year Karoly Grosz, who had held the premiership since June, stated that in 1986 30 per cent of budgetary expenditure went in support of unprofitable enterprises. In 1979 about 800 workers were made redundant at the Raba works, the first case on a mass scale. Between September 1986 and December 1987 the Ozd steelworks reduced its workforce by 17.7 per cent or 2,400 employees; the total number of redundancies attributable to enterprise reorganization, employment reduction and plant closure did not exceed 15,000 – 20,000 cases a year, or 0.3 per cent of the labour force (Sziraczki 1990: 715).

Manpower allocation and wage determination and taxation

Under the NEM there was a labour market in Hungary and 'full employment'.[10] This led to problems such as high labour turnover and the frequency of second and more jobs, with adverse effects on the state sector.[11] Ranges of basic wage and salary rates were set centrally (the ranges tending to increase over time), dependent on factors such as the level of skill, the degree of responsibility and working conditions. Total pay was the sum of these plus profit share. Until 1 January 1988, however, wage control was mainly exercised by subjecting above-norm pay increases to highly progressive taxation. In 1968 the tax base was average pay increases, designed to avoid unemployment among unskilled and low-skilled workers as productivity rose. In 1983–84, however, there was a switch to increases in total wage bills in order to avoid distortions in manpower allocation. In more extreme circumstances wage freezes were introduced.[12]

In 1980 an average of 63.9 per cent of the gross profit of enterprises was taxed away (Heinrich 1986: 157), and by 1985 this had risen to 80 per cent (Adam 1987: 614, quoting Gado). In 1989 a single corporate income tax was introduced, with a top rate of 50 per cent on profits. *The tax reforms introduced on 1 January 1988* were designed to help shift part of the burden from successful enterprises to consumers in the shape of a value-added tax ('general turnover tax') on all but basic goods and services. The maximum rate was 35 per cent on, for example, luxury durable consumer goods; the basic rate was 25 per cent. The other advantage was that the tax system was uniform, in contrast to the previous individual bargaining between enterprise and state. The other element of the new system was a progressive income tax: 20 per cent up to 60 per cent at first, then 17 per cent up to 56 per cent; there was to be no tax deduction for the first two children. The tax was paid by employers or the self-employed, partly in an attempt to trap more second economy earnings and thus moderate growing income disparities. Take-home pay allegedly remained the same because of increases in pre-tax basic money wage rates. Local councils captured a share of personal income tax. Various criticisms led to concessions to modify the effects on certain low-income groups. In September 1987 approval was given to pension increases and increased family, child and maternity allowances.

THE FINANCIAL SYSTEM

The banking system and monetary policy

The NEM system originally involved the state, which determined credit tranches for designated sectors. Enterprises were allowed to compete within those totals, and greater use was made of interest rates and forecast rates of return.

On 1 January 1987 the banking system was reorganized, with the National Bank of Hungary becoming more like a conventional central bank, exercising indirect control over five commercial banks (Colin Jones, *The Banker*, February 1988, pp. 19–20). Of the five, three were new, namely the Hungarian Credit Bank, the Commercial and Credit Bank and the Budapest Bank,[13] and two, established in the 1950s, changed their status, namely the Hungarian Foreign Trade Bank and the General Banking and Trust Company.[14] The commercial banks were joint stock companies. The state had majority share ownership in all but the Hungarian Credit Bank, and state and co-operative enterprises the remainder (individuals were debarred). The National Bank of Hungary retained its monopoly of foreign exchange, foreign borrowing and the issue of forints. The commercial banks were able to compete for customers after July 1987 (during the first six months they were assigned) and to develop according to commercial success (starting-up capital was provided by the state). The main aim was to improve the efficiency of credit allocation (credit was mainly allocated on a commercial basis) and to increase financial responsibility. Commercial criteria were allegedly employed, the banks as creditors were able to instigate bankruptcy proceedings in court against defaulting enterprises, and each bank's revenue was dependent on the profitability of its transactions.

But the banking reforms were handicapped from the beginning: enterprises that were the banks' clients were allowed to buy shares, while the banks were saddled with a large volume of bad debts. Commercial banks were able to issue shares for the purpose of capital raising for enterprises. Further developments followed (Colin Jones, *The Banker*, July 1990, pp. 29–30). In January 1989 commercial banks were allowed to offer personal banking services to individuals. The National Savings Bank gained a commercial banking licence that included corporate clients. The post office savings bank was hived off and called Post Bank, with full commercial banking authority. The savings co-operatives were permitted to establish their own joint commercial banks. In January 1990 the Bank of Hungary delegated all trade-related foreign currency transactions to six more banks, bringing the total to eleven. It retained only capital transactions, including hard currency borrowing and debt management.

There developed rudimentary interbank and inter-enterprise markets in short-term credit. After the idea was first mooted in 1982, subsequent legislation made it possible for foreigners to open convertible currency accounts, encouraged by competitive interest rates and Swiss-style secrecy rules.

The first bonds were issued in 1981 by the National Savings Bank on behalf of local authorities. After 1 January 1983 not only scrutinized local authorities (for public utilities and so on) but also enterprises (including co-operatives and, after 1987, the new commercial banks) were able to sell bonds to other enterprises or individuals.[15] The bonds were fixed-term, with some offering a variable element in the interest rate linked with profitability. Until 1 January 1988 bonds sold by enterprises to individuals had to be guaranteed by the Ministry of Finance; after that date the commercial bank handling the issue took over responsibility. From 1988 onwards enterprises were able to issue bonds without permission and to fix the interest rate, and there was a 20 per cent tax on bond earnings (*EEN*, 1987, vol. 1, no. 12, p. 5).

In October 1987 the first joint stock company was set up since 1948, the Gallakarbon transport company (a joint venture between the Budapest Bank and Tatabanya Coal Mines), with freely marketable shares. Private citizens were allowed to hold a maximum of only a quarter of the share capital and to trade shares within the enterprise.

A new company law was introduced from the start of 1989, allowing the general establishment of joint stock companies whose shares could be offered to the general public and to foreigners (*EEN*, 1988, vol. 2, no. 3, p. 3). Among the small number of previous such companies was the Tungsram light bulb manufacturer, whose shareholding was restricted to company employees (the 14 October 1987 decree legalized employee shareholding). The enterprise decided the size of dividends. Employees were able to cash in their shares and sell shares to fellow employees, although this applied only to shares purchased – those given by the company were not transferable (*EEN*, 1987, vol. 1, no. 12, p. 5). The aim was to create a competitive capital market, encouraging enterprises and individuals (individuals were to be able to have a majority holding in state enterprises) to utilize their spare funds more productively. Share ownership was to be available to all, including foreigners (up to 100 per cent) and there were six types of companies: (1) 'joint incomes' company, formed by at least two individuals, who have unlimited liability; (2) 'deposit' company, formed by at least two individuals, but with differing sorts of partners, internal with unlimited and external with limited liability; (3) 'joint stock' company: liability is proportional to shareholding; (4) 'limited liability' company: the same, but intended primarily for subsidiaries of existing companies; (5) 'joint venture': involves foreigners, liability being in proportion to shareholding; and (6) 'association', formed only by institutional shareholders, who have unlimited liability. There was no requirement for worker representation in a company's management, but it was not ruled out, and employees could retain up to a third of total voting power. The one-person business was originally meant to be unaffected by these changes, but was, in fact, covered by the limited liability legislation. Co-operatives would be allowed to buy shares in other companies (see *EEN*, 1988, vol. 2, no. 11, pp. 3–4, and vol. 2, no. 20, p. 7). Firms of lesser importance were allowed a majority of privately owned shares; this majority permitted them to employ up to 500 people (Leslie Colitt, *FT*, 7 October 1988, p. 2). In large state enterprises a 30 per cent ceiling was imposed (William Underhill, *The Daily Telegraph*, 5 October 1988, p. 12). Problems arose in the form of compulsory minimum amounts of starting capital and the stipulation that a government institution owning a third of the shares automatically controlled 51 per cent of the company (*The Economist*, 15–21 October 1988, p. 61).

The Budapest stock exchange opened on 1 January 1989, although it was restricted to members only, under the new regulations. Note that a stock market had been operating since July of the previous year, dealing with the stocks of forty state enterprises and clients in the shape of state enterprises and co-operatives (*The Economist*, 5–11 November 1988, p. 130). It was not until 21 June 1990, however, that the stock exchange opened on a full-time basis (three days a week previously).

Prices

One of the major problems that arose over time was the narrowing of the levels of producer and consumer prices. This was due to the increase in producer prices and, via subsidization, the holding down of consumer prices. This effect was so pronounced that the two were roughly equal by the mid-1970s and the latter, for a short time afterwards, were actually higher than the former. The absence of a two-tier price system meant low taxation of consumption. Subsequent price increases at the retail level and the new taxation systems beginning on 1 January 1988 were designed to remedy this. The aim was to make the consumer price level, with specific exceptions, higher than the producer level, in order to reflect costs of production.

The 1968 reform introduced a four-tier pricing system of fixed, ceiling, range and free categories. After 1980 most prices were not state-determined in a formal sense. 'Competitive pricing' (abandoned by the end of the 1980s) was designed to act as a substitute for the lack of competitive pressures in the domestic economy. This meant that the prices of, for example, important raw materials and energy approximated world levels. Various other rules affected other commodities, such as regard for world price changes, similar profit margins to those on hard currency exports (to lessen the attractiveness of domestic sales and thus stimulate exports), hypothetical hard currency import prices and 'fair' profit margins.[16] Marer estimates that the set of competitive rules for determining industrial producer prices introduced on 1 January 1980 accounted for 70 per cent of industrial output, while about 20 per cent was determined purely by domestic market forces (Marer 1986a: 258; about 10–20 per cent of combined agricultural and industrial output, p. 260). Free prices accounted for 58 per cent of consumer purchases in 1987 (Adam 1989a: 141).[17] In non-competitive branches, agricultural product and construction producer prices were set on the basis of average cost plus profit mark-up (Adam 1987: 618). The prices of basic foodstuffs such as bread were still controlled, while fruit and vegetable prices were market-determined. The 1985 reform stressed the principle of supply and demand, provided that costs were 'justifiable' (Swain 1987: 24). In that year provision was made for the profit margin in hard currency markets and later on there were only two categories in manufacturing industry, one concerning the price ruling in hard currency markets and the other concerning the 'price club', where proof of competitive conditions allowed free prices (Adam 1987: 619). Enterprises that were members of a 'price and wage club' undertook to attain increases in, for example, profitability and exports; if successful they are allowed to indulge in exceptional price and wage increases (Voszka 1989: 114). After 1 April 1988 the aim was to decontrol consumer prices, with the exception of staple commodities and a number of public services.

AGRICULTURE

The socialized sector

The December 1921 land reform served to redistribute only 10 per cent of estate land to 400,000 landless or near-landless rural house-holds; each received less than 1 ha on average and was burdened with compensation pay-ments (kindly pointed out by Robert Bideleux). The 1935 census revealed that 0.8 per cent of landowners owned 46.4 per cent of agricultural land, while 76.1 per cent owned 12.0 per cent (Batt 1988: 51). *The 1945 land reform* involved the confiscation and redistribution of all holdings of more than 57 ha (Heinrich 1986: 159). Forced *collectivization* took place during 1949–56. The 1956 revolution led to two-thirds of members leaving the collective farms, but recollectivization took place in 1958–62, although this mainly relied on persuasion and incentives (e.g. land and other assets contri-buted being compensated and the chairman directly elected by members; Marer 1986a: 237).

In 1957 compulsory delivery targets were abandoned and replaced by voluntary contracts at (more generous) state-determined prices.[18] Economic reforms were generally introduced in agriculture before industry; mandatory plans were scrapped for the former in 1966. In 1967 co-operatives were permitted to pay a guar-anteed annual wage, with the residual 10–15 per cent constituting a dividend dependent on net profit (Marer 1986a: 135). The following year non-agricultural activities were allowed, such as food processing, electronic products, construction, component parts and repair shops (diversification out of agricultural production entirely if desired; Swain 1987: 28), and two years later the limits on small-scale livestock holdings were deemed to be the prerogative of co-operatives themselves (Batt 1988: 265). The market mechanism was most effective in agri-culture (and in retail trade), although the state had considerable monopsony power in the case of many products.

According to Vankai (1986: 343), collective and state farms had to draw up a five year plan in accordance with the broad national economic objectives relayed by the Ministry of Agriculture. The plan had to be approved by the Ministry, which had the task of summing all the individual plans. If national objectives did not seem likely to be met, changes in economic levers were used indirectly to steer farms in the desired direction.

After the late 1950s most farm prices were set annually on the basis of national average pro-duction costs, with account being taken of production incentives and the aim of raising farm incomes (Marer 1986a: 260). Purchase prices were determined so that a farm on average land would be able to cover average costs plus a small (normal) profit margin, with rent being taxed away from farms occupying above-average quality land (Marrese 1986a: 335). In 1981 state-determined prices affected nearly 40 per cent of agricultural output, covering such products as maize, wheat and beef. The producer prices of those products that heavily employed hard currency imports were used for hard currency exports, or were hard currency import substitutes, were based on world market prices (Hartford 1985: 131). The income of co-operative members depended not only on work performed but also on rental payments for land ceded by individuals.

Agricultural co-operatives dominated the scene, although they only owned half the land they farmed, the remainder belonging to the state and individuals, mainly their own members (Hartford 1985: 124). In the mid-1980s they accounted for just over 50 per cent of the gross output of agriculture and some 75 per cent of the agricultural workforce, and occupied 82 per cent of arable land and 4,000 ha on average. The respective approximate figures for state farms (involved in a great deal of experimental work) were 15 per cent, 16 per cent, 15 per cent and 7,700 ha. In 1988 18.4 per cent of the labour force was employed in agriculture.

The private sector

The private sector in 1985 contributed 34 per cent of gross farm output (crop 26 per cent and livestock 42 per cent) from 13 per cent of arable land (Cochrane 1988: 48–9), over half of this from farm household plots and under half from private farms (which only accounted for about 1 per cent of agricultural land) and the auxiliary holdings of the non-agricultural population. In the same year personal plots accounted for 5.99 per cent and auxiliary holdings 5.7 per cent of the area farmed, while the private farms (average size 3.6 ha) covered 1.3 per cent of cultivated land (Lang, Csete, and Harnos 1988: 232). The private sector (figures for 1985) was especially important in products such as meat (51 per cent), fruit (60 per cent), vegetables (65 per cent) and eggs (61 per cent) (Cochrane 1988: 48–9). In addition to private plots of 0.30–0.60 ha per member (where the restrictions on keeping animals or owning machinery were removed), co-operatives were permitted to rent land to individuals and to provide them with inputs, advice and marketing channels. Policy during the 1970s and 1980s was geared to integrating private agriculture into the socialist economy, with co-operatives providing services for household plots and loaning out funds to construct buildings housing animals raised under contract to the co-operatives (Swain 1987: 28). In 1980 permission was given to purchase tractors of up to 30 h.p. (Cochrane 1988: 49). Experiments were begun involving the fixed-term hiring out of land, equipment and/or buildings by co-operatives to individuals for

Table 13.2 Hungary: statistical survey

Joint equity ventures, 1 July 1989: 628

Private sector in agriculture, including private farms (%)

1985 *Agricultural output*	1985 *Arable land*
34	13

Contributions to NMP, 1984 (%)

State sector	*Co-operatives*	*Household farming*	*Auxiliary production of employees*	*Formal private sector*
65.2	20.6	2.8	5.9	5.5

Population, January 1992: 10.3 million (peak 10.7 million in 1982)

Sources: Cochrane (1988: 48–9); Kornai (1986: 1692); *IHT*, 19 January 1990, p. 9.
Note: For figures on growth rates, inflation and net hard currency debt see Table 13.1.

activities such as grazing or workshops (*EIU Country Profile*, 1989–90, p. 19).

In 1985 state farms followed the practice, already instituted in co-operatives, of employee election of the farm director and management committee. 'Agrocomplexes' were joint undertakings providing a range of inputs such as feedstuffs, or stock and construction services, or involved in processing agricultural commodities. 'Technically operated production systems' came in two forms, namely 'proprietory' and 'technological transfer'. The former was owned by co-operative and state farms and leased out automated technology packages to participating farms, while the latter provided member farms with technical training, introduction to new technology, and assistance in obtaining the credit needed to purchase their own equipment (Hartford 1987: 198–200).

In the early 1980s there was a resurgence in some state and co-operative farms of decentralized work groups, which acted as subcontractors to the farm, which provided administrative services (Swain 1987: 30).

In the 1985 reform farms were given the choice of three methods of wage regulation, the growth in gross income (value-added) per worker, the growth of the average wage or a tax on each individual employee's income.

FOREIGN TRADE, DEBT AND INVESTMENT

Foreign trade and debt

Hungary is highly dependent on foreign trade, exporting about 50 per cent of net material product (*EIU Country Profile*, 1987–88, p. 29). As a proportion of GDP in 1988 exports were 37.6 per cent and imports 34.8 per cent (Hare 1992: 163). In the mid-1980s about 53 per cent of trade was conducted with Comecon (the share showed a falling trend after 1968), with the Soviet Union alone accounting for 32 per cent of total trade. The Soviet Union supplied Hungary with energy and raw materials and took delivery of Hungarian foodstuffs and manufactures such as computers and buses. The OECD countries accounted for 35 per cent of trade and developing countries 12 per cent. The 1987 figures for Hungarian exports were Comecon 51 per cent and the Soviet Union 32 per cent, and for imports 47.5 per cent and 28.5 per cent respectively (Emma Klein, *Guardian Survey*, 5 May 1988, p. 12).

Hungary had the most liberal foreign trade system within Comecon. Industrial enterprises either had their own trading rights (270 by the start of 1986; von Czege 1987: 134) or were allowed to choose a foreign trade corporation to act on their behalf, on commission or on a risk-taking partnership basis (most trade is carried out by trade corporations). A few foreign trade corporations were able to trade in any commodity, while in other cases the product lines assigned to the corporations overlapped in order to increase competition (Marer 1986a: 253). After 1 January 1988 any state-owned enterprise or co-operative was able to trade with the West on condition that, for example, it had qualified staff and registered with the Ministry of Trade (Kerpel and Young 1988: 69). There were two import licensing schemes, the first where enterprises had hard currency quotas and the second where the centre relocated discretionary licences (Winiecki 1989: 378). Until 1976 exchange rates were called 'foreign trade multipliers'. Five years later a uniform exchange rate for hard currencies was introduced; formerly there had been one for foreign trade and a second for other transactions. The value of the exchange rate was based on the average producer-price-based cost of producing a unit of convertible foreign exchange in exports; the rate changed with the fluctuations in the exchange rate of a basket of (ten) hard currencies (Adam 1987: 622). The forint became 'internally' convertible, Hungarian enterprises being able to buy and sell hard currencies for current account purposes at a unified exchange rate (see glossary). In the first eight months of 1989 import liberalization accounted for 39 per cent of hard currency imports, compared with 32 per cent in 1988 (Hare 1990b: 585). The target was 85–90 per cent in 1991. Within Comecon Hungary was the most persistent advocate of the reforms needed to make currency and goods convertibility possible and thus stimulate multilateral trade, while the country played an important role in Comecon's plans for science and technology in areas such as computers, software and biotechnology. Two-thirds of Comecon trade was based on contracts drawn up by Hungarian enterprises (Hare 1990b: 585).

Table 13.1 traces Hungary's net hard currency debt position (gross debt less foreign assets). The debt-service ratio (interest and repayment of principal as a proportion of hard currency exports) was 65 per cent in 1986, compared to 20 per cent in 1975 and 45 per cent in 1989. The National Bank of Hungary provided the following figures for the end of September 1988: net debt $10.4 billion (gross $17.3 billion minus foreign assets of $6.9 billion); but if non-interest-bearing foreign assets are excluded (mostly trade credits and soft loans to developing countries), the net figure rises to $13.4 billion (reported in *IHT*, 26–7 November 1988, p. 14). This situation was the result partly of policies adopted in the 1970s and partly of the parallel retrenchment in the reform process.

The 1973–74 oil price shock produced increased energy and raw material prices and recession in the industrialized West. The Hungarian response up to 1979 was to accelerate the growth of total output, investment and consumption (the last for incentives), financed by foreign credits, which were supposed to lead to the increase in exports needed for repayment. The domestic economy was increasingly isolated from world markets and Comecon trade became more important (Marer 1986b).

In 1979 policy changed on both fronts, with an austerity drive to reduce imports, investment and consumption, and to boost exports, and a return to the path of economic reform. Batt (1988: 277) sees late 1978 as marking a major shift in long-term economic strategy, from import substitution to export promotion, the whole policy signalling a resuscitation of the reform. In 1982, however, Hungary came close to debt rescheduling as it was caught in the backwash of the Polish and Romanian crises, having already been subjected to rising interest rates and facing declining markets after 1980 because of the restrictive monetary policies adopted by the advanced Western countries. It was avoided by a combination of intensified austerity measures, especially severe constraints on imports (there was a licensing system for imports and exports), and credits provided by the IMF and the World Bank, which Hungary joined in May 1982.[19] The 'consolidation programme' agreed upon in 1987 combined new reform measures with an austerity programme for 1988–90. The July 1988 extraordinary Central Committee meeting passed the more severe of two austerity programmes for further discussion and for approval at the October Central Committee meeting. It was envisaged that unemployment would rise from around 30,000 to 100,000, inflation would increase to more than 15 per cent as subsidies on consumer goods were reduced, and the forint would be further devalued.

It is of interest to note that the first hard currency state lottery draw took place on 2 October 1988 (the prizes were luxury consumer goods), and four days later it was announced that the first free-trade zone in Eastern Europe was to be set up around Sopron, with a special economic zone a more distant possibility.

Joint equity ventures

In 1972 a decree on 'economic associations with foreign participation' was published, with several amendments thereafter, such as occurred at the beginning of 1986. It became possible for foreign ownership to exceed 50 per cent,[20] and the concessions became more generous over time, especially for reinvestment.[21] On 1 January 1989 100 per cent foreign ownership was permitted, while no licence was needed for joint ventures with minority foreign ownership; only registration was required. By the end of 1985 fewer than sixty ventures were operating and by mid-1988 about 140 were operating (Kerpel and Young 1988: 69). By 1 July 1989 628 joint ventures with Western companies were registered (John Holusha, *IHT*, 19 January 1990, p. 9). An early example of privatization came in May 1989, when 49.65 per cent of the Tungsram light bulb Company was sold to a consortium of Western banks; the US General Electric company then took over these shares plus enough to attain a 51 per cent majority (GE's stake increased to over 75 per cent in June 1991).

Joint ventures were extended to banking. The Central European International Bank (CIB), founded in 1979, had its headquarters in Budapest, but it was the only 'offshore' organization – the National Bank of Hungary owned 34 per cent, with each of two banks from Japan and one each from France, West Germany, Austria and Italy owning 11 per cent. It transacted business only in convertible currencies, providing credits to and accepting deposits from foreign as well as Hungarian firms, although it set up a subsidiary dealing in domestic currency transactions. In 1986 the CIB also began to lease Western equipment to Hungarian enterprises. It was not subject to Hungarian foreign exchange laws or regulations issued by the Hungarian National Bank. The Citibank-Budapest Bank, which began operations in January 1986, was a joint venture between Citibank of New York (which had an 80 per cent share) and the Central Exchange and Credit Bank. It did not deal with individuals, but provided investment and trade credits to Hungarian and Western enterprises and accepted deposits in forints and convertible currencies. Interest rates were fixed independently of the National Bank.

In January 1987 the Unicbank was established. It was a venture bank jointly owned by the World Bank's International Finance Corporation and two Western banks (with 15 per cent each) and six Hungarian institutions (owning 55 per cent). Later in 1987 the International Investment Agency (involving the Hungarian Foreign Trade Bank and two Austrian banks) was set up to provide financial services for joint ventures, while in March of that year the Hungarian Foreign Trade Bank formed a joint venture brokerage firm with a Liechtenstein holding company and an Austrian bank.

THE NON-AGRICULTURAL PRIVATE AND CO-OPERATIVE SECTOR.

The 'first economy' consisted of state enterprises, co-operatives, government agencies and officially registered non-profit-making institutions, while the 'second economy' comprised the formal (officially licensed) and informal private sectors.[22] In 1984 the following contributed to net material product: the state sector, 65.2 per cent; the non-state sector, 34.8 per cent (co-operatives, 20.6 per cent; household farming, 2.8 per cent; auxiliary production of employees, 5.9 per cent; and the formal private sector, 5.5 per cent) (Kornai 1986: 1692). The private sector accounted for 20 per cent of total investment (*Abecor Country Report*, May 1988, p. 1), 10 per cent of retail sales (*The Economist*, 7 April 1990, p. 112) and less than 5 per cent of industrial output (Hare 1992: 149). At the July 1988 extraordinary Central Committee meeting, Miklos Nemeth (Central Committee secretary responsible for the economy) stated that there should be no fear of the idea of the private sector eventually accounting for 25–30 per cent of national output.

Bauer (1988: 455) makes the interesting point that concessions to the private sector encountered less resistance from vested interests than those made to the state sector. Socialist Hungary had a flourishing private sector, and the private, co-operative and state sectors were put on an equal footing. An already relatively generous limit of seven non-family members and twelve inclusive of family members in private firms was raised to thirty on 1 January 1988 (*EEN*, 1988, vol. 2, no. 3, p. 3).[23] After 1981 it was possible to lease state property to individuals, e.g. shops and restaurants. Private guest houses were permitted to have up to thirty guests. (See section on the new company law for later changes.)

The health of the co-operative sector was indicated by the production of 6 per cent of total industrial output (*Abecor Country Report*, May 1988, p. 2). According to Magas (1990: 100), industrial co-operatives were subject to a 100 persons or members maximum. The Skala-Coop was the largest retail organization. It was formed in 1973 by 200 consumer co-operatives to compete with the state retail organizations, but then expanded into wholesale trade, industrial production and international trade. It had its own import–export organization and undertook joint ventures with Western companies (Table 13.2). It has also issued bonds to individuals and other enterprises.

The first private insurance company was set up in 1986.

CONCLUSION

Hungary overcame the trauma of the 1956 revolution to introduce overnight on 1 January 1968 the most radical reform in Eastern Europe outside Yugoslavia. While the New Economic Mechanism did not turn Hungary into a model of market socialism, the state achieved its aggregate plan targets overwhelmingly indirectly, via the use of economic levers, leaving the enterprise typically free from the need to fulfil the success indicators associated with the traditional Soviet economic system. Informal pressures were also important. There was pioneering work in elected management, while the 'second economy' was large and flourishing. Although socialist Hungary faced problems of considerable magnitude (especially a severe foreign debt problem and worries about inflation), the flirtation with market mechanisms was to help considerably in easing the transition to a Western-type economic system after 1989.

NOTES

1. Legislation in 1983 allowed multi-candidate elections, including non-party candidates. The independent Democratic Union of Scientific Workers was set up on 14 May 1988, followed by the Motion Picture Democratic Trade Union and (in February 1989) by the first blue-collar union (the Solidarity Workers' Trade Union Federation). The situation in 1990 was as follows (*EEN*, 1990, vol. 4, no. 24, p. 7): the trade union movement is dominated by the National Association of Hungarian Trade Unions (NAHTU), which inherited 3 million members from its predecessor (the official body); in September 1991 the union claimed 2,680,000 members, i.e. two-thirds of organized workers (*EEN*, 1991, vol. 5, no. 19, p. 8). The Democratic League of Independent Trade Unions (DLITU, formed in 1988) had eighty-four member bodies and a membership in total of 130,000. The National Union of Workers' Councils (NUWC) has 106,000 members and the Autonomous Trade Unions Group is also worth mentioning. There is also now an Arbitration Council dealing with employer–union matters. Since August 1991 the direct deduction of union membership fees from wages has needed the approval of individuals; 1.2 million workers agreed to subscribe to NAHTU, but DLITU (which now claims more than 250,000 members) and NUWC declined to use the 'contracting in' system (*EEN*, 1991, vol. 5, no. 20, p. 4). The property of NAHTU was to be redistributed among all the trade unions.

2. Important political changes at the congress included limiting the tenure of a future General Secretary to two terms of office totalling ten years.

3. Using the growth-accounting methodology developed by Edward Denison, Robert Jerome evaluates the economic growth of Hungary in the period 1950–85, with estimated post-reform average annual rates of growth of 3.5 per cent for 1970–75, 2.0 per cent for 1975–80 and 1.1 per cent for 1980–85. Jerome found a marked decline in productivity growth, with increases in factors (mostly capital, specifically plant and equipment) accounting for nearly all of total growth in the post-reform period. He concludes that this is similar to other socialist countries like Bulgaria and that the reforms did little to improve the performance of the Hungarian economy over what it likely would have been (Jerome 1988: 112–13).

4. Eight of thirteen of the previous politburo and

not far short of a third of the Central Committee lost their positions.

5. At the start of the 1980s enterprises were allowed to determine up to 30 per cent of turnover without special permission (von Czege 1987: 134). After 1985 they were able to change their sphere of economic activity, provided they informed their founding organ and the appropriate branch ministry (Swain 1987: 34).

6. According to Schüller (1988: 32), about 50 per cent of investment was directly determined by the centre, while decisions regarding the remainder (excluding self-financed maintenance, rationalization and small expansion investment) were influenced by credit policy. According to Kornai, only about 20 per cent of investment in state enterprises was decided at the level of the enterprise during the 1980s (*The Economist Survey*, 28 April 1990, p. 15).

7. Technical economies of scale were sacrificed, since plant size was generally small. Where these economies were significant some trusts remained, such as in aluminium. On 1 January 1988 the Ganz Mavag engineering concern was divided into seven enterprises.

8. State financial support in the form of subsidies, price increases or tax reductions was forthcoming to cover any losses. This ensured the survival of inefficient enterprises, but did not encourage financial discipline.

9. Essentially the non-regulated sector, involving both legal and illegal private activity, which expanded rapidly during the 1970s because of the restrictions placed upon the small and medium-sized enterprises.

10. In mid-1987 10,000 were officially estimated to be 'seeking work'; some 400 unemployment offices were set up.

11. Causing wide income disparities; those working full-time in the 'first economy' were especially disadvantaged. By the late 1980s 70 per cent of men had more than one job and between 1976 and 1986 the average working day increased from eight and a half to fourteen and a half hours (Celestine Bohlen, *IHT*, 28 February 1990, p. 2).

12. In the first quarter of 1986 and the four months to March 1987, for instance.

13. In 1987 the Budapest Bank absorbed the State Development Bank, which operated the secondary bond market after 1984. This market became largely concentrated in the new bank. Budapest's first stockbroking house, Co-Nexus, opened on 20 January 1988 (*EEN*, 1988, vol. 2, no. 3, p. 3).

14. The three new banks were not allowed to handle foreign exchange transactions, while the former of the two previously existing banks, for example, dealt with the financing of foreign trade in both forints and hard currencies.

15. Note that it was the National Savings Bank that handled the accounts of individuals and that banks themselves were only able to issue bonds to enterprises. Individuals were allowed to trade bonds freely after 1984.

16. 'Financial bridges' were the taxes and subsidies that spaned the divide between domestic and world prices.

17. The so-called 'free' category of prices could still be subject to delays and profit margin restrictions.

18. Although until 1968 local government procurement recommendations, reflecting the state plan, tended to carry the force of orders (Hartford 1987: 130). Quotas for bread grains were imposed until 1969 (Bleaney 1988: 103).

19. Hungary has been a member of GATT since 1973 and has benefited from MFN concessions in its trade with the United States since 1978. In the autumn of 1989 these MFN concessions were made permanent.

20. First conceded to the financial and service sector and, after 1985, to manufacturing; up to 99 per cent generally and in cases like hotels even 100 per cent.

21. There was a maximum corporate tax on profits of 40 per cent for the foreign partner and 20 per cent during the first five years in areas like electronics, hotel construction and packaging technology. It was possible for individual firms to be awarded a five year tax holiday; tax concessions depended on factors such as the degree of foreign involvement.

22. Second jobs were attractive because of the possibility of pilfering materials from the state sector.

23. In addition, limited liability was given to private individuals when in partnership with state enterprises or co-operatives (*EEN*, 1988, vol. 2, no. 3, p. 3).

14

POLAND

POLITICAL AND ECONOMIC BACKGROUND

Poland is the largest country in Eastern Europe in terms of population (37.9 million in mid-1989) and area, with good agricultural land (about 60 per cent of land is used for agricultural purposes) and minerals such as coal,[1] copper, silver, natural gas, lead, zinc and sulphur. Poland lies in a vulnerable geographical position on the north European plain and has a history of dismemberment.[2] In 1772 Russia, Prussia and Austria devoured a third of the country, and by 1795 Poland had ceased to exist. Re-emerging as an independent country only in 1918, Poland in the inter-war years was caught up in war against the Soviet Union in 1919–20 and a military coup in 1926. Marshal Pilsudski was in control 1926–35 in his capacity as 'supreme commander' and defence minister, although he maintained the trappings of parliament. The period 1935–39 saw rule by 'the colonels'. Pre-war Poland was basically agrarian, only around 20 per cent of the working population being employed in industry in 1930 (28.2 per cent of the labour force was still employed in agriculture in 1988). The Nazi–Soviet pact of 1939 included a secret agreement to partition Poland. Twenty per cent of the population died during the Second World War amid massive destruction.

Wladyslaw Gomulka was restored to power in 1956 (he was prime minister from 1945 to 1948) and replaced by Edward Gierek after the 1970 disturbances. Gierek was removed in September 1980 and replaced by Stanislaw Kania. General Wojciech Jaruzelski (defence secretary since 1968) became General Secretary of the United Workers' Party in October 1981, later became president (Chairman of the Council of State), but resigned his post of prime minister, assumed in February 1981, in favour of Zbigniew Messner (November 1985). There were riots in Poznan in 1956 against depressed living standards and anti-price-increase protests in 1970, 1976 and 1980.

Solidarity was born August 1980 (the legalizing agreement was signed on the 31st), suspended December 1981, formally banned the following October and relegalized in April 1989 (as a result of the so-called Round Table Agreement between Solidarity and the government). The fact that Solidarity was a working class movement confronting the alleged representatives of that class ultimately undermined the regime. In the partially free election of 4 June 1989 and the run-off of the 18th, Solidarity won all the allotted opposition seats in the Sejm and ninety-nine out of the hundred Senate seats (one going to an independent). Jaruzelsky was elected president on 19 July by a margin of only one vote. Tadeusz Mazowiecki (formerly editor of Solidarity's weekly newspaper) was confirmed as prime minister on 24 August and the new government took office on 12 September. The Solidarity-led government included members of the Polish United Workers' Party, the United Peasants' Party and the Democratic

Party. Under Leszek Balcerowicz, the minister of finance, Poland entered into a severe austerity programme ('shock therapy') to control inflation and a rapid transfer to a market economy.

ECONOMIC STRATEGY IN THE 1970S

Poland was a key player in import-led growth during the 1970s (see Chapter 2).[3] Edward Gierek replaced Wladyslaw Gomulka as First Secretary in December 1970, following rioting over increases in the price of food. These were the climax of a switch in emphasis away from consumption and towards investment, which itself was the result of an attempt to reverse the slowdown in growth rates that had occurred by the mid-1960s (see Table 14.1). Gierek's remedy involved increasing consumption to provide incentives for increased output while borrowing massively from the West in order not only to import capital, technology and know-how (to boost the convertible currency exports needed to pay off the debt by the end of the 1970s) but also to import consumer goods, raw materials (including grain to feed livestock), semi-fabricates, components and spare parts. Thus investment and consumption rose in tandem. This import-led strategy of the first half of the 1970s was seen as a substitute for radical economic reform, but the reforms actually undertaken were meant to improve management and to encourage innovation in order to take advantage of and to further the new techniques and know-how.

Although the period 1971–75 witnessed an annual average rate of growth of 9.4 per cent, the economy soon ran into trouble (see Table 14.1). In 1979 produced national income fell by 2.3 per cent and there were chronic balance of payments and foreign debt problems. By the end of 1981, Poland's net hard currency debt had reached $25.5 billion, mainly short and medium term. The debt–service ratio rose to 101 per cent in 1980 (see Blazyca 1986: 19, 76–7). In March 1981 Poland suspended repayments on the principal of the debt, which led to a drying up of fresh Western credits.

There was also severe macro disequilibrium, with money wages increasing faster than planned,[4] 40 per cent over the 1971–75 period, compared to Gierek's target range of 17–18 per cent. Open and repressed inflation were also at significant levels. Investment climbed to 35.7 per cent of national income by 1975, compared with some 25 per cent on average during the 1960s. Investment plans were exceeded, owing to such factors as pressure both (1) from enterprises: the lack of penalty for failure encouraged irresponsibility, while 'hooking on to the plan' implied that it was easier to obtain resources to finish projects already under way; and (2) from Western banks anxious to recycle OPEC surpluses. The absorptive capacity of the economy was exceeded, the system was still incapable of making use of and developing the new technologies, and a broad spread of projects was adopted, which meant exaggeration of the normal problems of the 'scattering of resources' (ever longer gestation periods often resulted in product obsolescence). Priority was given to enlarging the capital stock rather than modernizing it and to sectors such as ferrous metallurgy, petrochemicals and engineering (shipbuilding and cars, for instance) which were import-intensive and badly hit by the world recession. Infrastructural investments, such as energy and transport, as well as agriculture and consumer goods were relatively neglected; the result was bottlenecks. There were large cost overruns in projects like the giant steelworks at Huty Katowice, and foreign machinery and technologies were often unable to be utilized effectively. There was often a lack of complementary inputs and skilled personnel. Other problems included the following: (1) many investment projects that were import-substituting rather than export-promoting; (2) the poor project decision-making process, ignorance of export potential, and future dependence on imported inputs; (3) insufficient awareness of the need to meet world market demands in terms of price, quality and delivery times; and (4) the attempt to insulate the economy from world inflation (Fallenbuchl 1986: 363–9). Blazyca (1986: 31)

Table 14.1 Poland: foreign debt and average annual rates of growth of produced national income, GNP and prices

Produced national income (%)

1951–55	1956–60	1961–65	1966–70	1971–75	1976	1977	1978	1979	1980	1981	1982	1983	1984	1985	1986	1987	1988	1989
8.6	6.6	6.2	6.0	9.4	6.8	5.3	2.8	–2.3	–6.0	–12.0	–5.5	6.0	5.6	3.4	4.9	1.9	4.9	–0.2

GNP (CIA) (%)

1971–75	1976–80	1981–85	1986	1987	1988	1989
6.5	0.7	0.7	2.3	–2.0	1.6	–1.6

Inflation (%)

1980	1981	1982	1983	1984	1985	1986	1987	1988	1989
8.5	18.4	109.4	21.9	15.0	15.1	17.7	26.0	60.0	244.0

Gross hard currency debt ($ billion)

1981	1986	1987	1988	1989
25.9	33.6	38.8	39.2	41.0

Net hard currency debt ($ billion)

1971	1981	1985	1986	1987	1988	1989
0.8	25.1	28.2	31.9	35.8	35.6	37.5

Sources Blazyca (1986: 19, 26, 76–77; 1991: 23); EIU, *Country Profile*, 1987–88, pp. 17, 21; 1989–90, p. 13; *Country Report*, 1989, no. 3, p. 2; 1990, no. 1, p. 4; 1991, no. 4, p. 3; Kolankiewicz and Lewis (1988: xiv): *Polish Perspectives*, 1990, vol. XXXII, no. 3, p. 56; Institute of International Finance (1990: 15); CIP (1990; tables I and C–15); *International Currency Review*, 1990, vol. 20, nos. 4 and 5, p. 75; *European Economy: the Path of Reform in Central and Eastern Europe*, Commission of the European Communities, Brussels, 1991, p. 278.

describes the leadership as losing control of the economy amid the wage push of the workers and the investment push of the powerful ministries. Kolankiewicz and Lewis (1988: 104) talk about investment policy responding to various lobbies and pressure groups.

The mounting difficulties resulted in a sharp reversal in the latter half of the 1970s. The mid-1970s *economic manoeuvre* involved re-centralization of decision-making in 1976, an attempt to link wage increases with produc-tivity, a drastic decline in both imports and investment,[5] and an increase in exports (with the aim of achieving a hard currency trade surplus by 1979). The attempt to divert food-stuffs to exports and the associated rise in domestic prices led to the strikes of summer 1980 and the rise of Solidarity.

Table 9.1 shows the negative growth rates associated with the period 1979–82. In 1981 exports to non-socialist countries fell by 22.1 per cent, and imports from them decreased by 31.5 per cent (Kolankiewicz and Lewis 1988: 23). Over the period 1978–82 national output fell by nearly a quarter, investment halved and con-sumption declined by about 15 per cent (*World Bank Report* 1988: 29). According to official figures, the 1978 production and consumption levels were not restored until a decade later; it is likely that living standards have not yet been restored (Lipton and Sachs 1990a: 104). Martial law was imposed on 13 December 1981 (ended 21 July 1983) with the aim of stabilizing the economic and political situation, and Solidarity was banned, despite the 31 August 1980 Gdansk agreement. Consumer goods shortages became severe, rationing was widespread, and the state felt secure enough to impose food price in-creases without the disturbances that had char-acterized the previous attempts in 1970, 1976 and 1980. Vital industries were militarized and 'operational programmes' instituted. Positive growth resumed in 1983 (see Table 14.1).

Financial policy has been aimed at restoring macroeconomic equilibrium. Wage and salary increases during the 1980s were far in excess of plan and of productivity increases (partly de-liberately in order to avoid industrial unrest), but regular increases in retail prices were achieved, without political disturbances, in order to re-duce both subsidies and the extent of rationing. Meat was partially rationed, and petrol was rationed from the beginning of 1982 to that of 1989. Table 14.1 provides the record for inflation. In 1985, in order to combat the black market, individuals were allowed to put hard currency into interest-bearing accounts with no questions asked. After 1 April 'undocumented' earnings (those not earned or presented as gifts from abroad) were placed in a non-interest-bearing account for a year.[6]

Socialist Poland's net hard currency debt mounted steadily, as Table 14.1 illustrates.[7] The debt–service ratio of 67 per cent in 1986 was the highest in Eastern Europe. There were regular reschedulings, and austerity policies were heavily orientated towards increasing exports. Convertible currency trade surpluses were attained in 1983–86 despite obstacles such as US retaliation for the imposition of martial law and the banning of Solidarity.[8] Poland rejoined the IMF in June 1986, having withdrawn in 1950 even though a founding member, and joined the World Bank in the same year. In November 1988 the World Bank made its first loan to Poland.

INDUSTRIAL REFORM

Significant economic reforms were implemented as early as 1956–57; enterprise decision-making powers were increased (the number of compulsory indicators was reduced to eight), and workers' councils formed spon-taneously and were legalized. The director was supposedly subject to the dual authority of the workers' council and the ministry. But recentral-ization soon began in 1958. The number of plan indicators was increased, the powers of workers' councils were curtailed (in December 1958 they were incorporated into state-run 'workers' self-management conferences'; party and trade union appointees outnumbered workers' council representatives and meetings were chaired by the party secretary), and 'associations' were established. These associations behaved essentially as administrative links between enterprise and ministry, allocating disaggregated plan tasks in traditional fashion, and were endowed with research, marketing and project design functions.

The period between 1958 and 1972 was one in which a command economy was subjected to relatively insignificant administrative changes and experiments, such as the use of 'leading enterprises', involving a loose form of association, 'patron enterprises', where a technological leader benefits whole groups, and the setting up of vertically integrated *kombinats* in 1969 (Blazyca 1980b).

The 1972 blueprint led to the 1973–75 experiment involving the use of WOGs (*wielkie organizacje gospodarcze*, large economic organizations).[9] These operated on a *khozraschyot* basis and were given enhanced powers of decision-making at the expense of both enterprise and ministry. WOGs were able to decide for themselves how to manage their internal affairs and enjoyed varying degrees of independent decision-making as regards product mix, depending on product scarcity. These powers extended to employment, wage policy, price fixing (especially for new products), investment and output assortment. Obligatory indicators still remained, however, and included sales, exports, in some cases the level of production in physical or value terms, investment, inputs and financial norms. These indicators were conditional with respect to incentives, but the basic incentive scheme involved value added and profit. The traditional wage fund limit was abandoned and replaced by a link between the wage fund and value added and by a 20 per cent tax on the wage fund. Basic managerial salaries were tied to the growth of wage and salary scales, but depended on the growth of value added being greater than that of employment. Managerial bonuses were related to the level of or increase in net profit and were conditional

both on fulfilment of the other plan indicators and on wage payments not exceeding the disposable wage fund. A link was to be forged between domestic and international prices by means of various 'multipliers' (exchange rates, effectively) and exports were to be encouraged by WOGs, which would be allowed a share of foreign currency earnings and greater involvement in export promotion and price regulations, with the foreign trade corporation acting as an agent.

By mid-1974 approximately 100 pilot units accounted for nearly 50 per cent of socialized industry, but the latter half of the decade witnessed a recentralization process, due to deteriorating world and domestic conditions and to the excess demand caused by an ambitious growth strategy. *Recentralization after 1976* involved controls on employment, wages linked to productivity increases, the imposition of investment limits, the strengthening of ministerial powers, an increase in the number of enterprise indicators, an excess profits tax on windfall profits from exports, and a progressive tax on unplanned growth of the wage fund.

The industrial reform of 1 January 1982

On paper this was a Hungarian-type reform that was intended to be applied only gradually over a period of three to five years. In reality so little of the reform was actually carried out that it was only at the Tenth Party Congress of 29 June – 3 July 1986 that a firm resolution was adopted to implement it.

The reform, in principle, laid stress on indirect steering of the economy via the use of economic levers. The state would still be responsible for infrastructual investment and large investments in key sectors. The enterprise was to be: (1) free of most state-imposed targets: there were exceptions related to goods of national importance such as armaments, basic consumer goods and exports needed to meet trade agreements; (2) 'self-financing', that is, normally operating without subsidies, bankruptcy thus becoming a possibility; pay was to be tied to enterprise performance (enterprises were to be free to set wage scales, subject to central guidelines on relative rates) and controlled indirectly via taxes on average pay increases before 1983 and total pay increases afterwards; and (3) 'self-managed': workers, either directly or via workers' councils, were to be given significantly enhanced decision-making powers, including consultation about management decisions relating to output, employment, and prices and to have the final say in the spending of social welfare funds.

Gomulka and Rostowski (1984: 389) consider that the main aim of the enterprise under such a scheme would seem to be the maximization of after-tax wages and bonuses, including retained profits, per employee, similar to the system in Yugoslavia. Brodzka (1987: 30) summarizes the purpose of the reform as: (1) the introduction of an economic system based primarily on economic, financial and market mechanisms rather than central administrative regulation, with a decisive increase in the autonomy of enterprises and the general application of profit as the criterion of choice of output in place of quantitatively determined targets (enterprises freely determine the distribution of most of their profits); (2) the state would be able to influence the economy through policy and financial instruments; (3) a decline in the role of ministries and an enhanced role for banks; and (4) the eventual emergence of a capital market. Blazyca sees the essence of the reform as the abandonment of short-term central planning, with enterprises drawing up their own plans on the basis of negotiated contracts at (eventually) free prices.

There was a *three tier system of prices*: state-determined ('administered') prices for energy, for example); 'regulated', mostly based on a cost-plus formula; and 'contractual' or freely negotiated. Balcerowicz (1989: 45) gives figures to estimate their respective relative importance. In terms of the percentage of total sales of consumer goods in 1982 (1987 figures in

brackets): 35 (45), 15 (2), and 50 (53); in terms of basic and raw materials: 20 (29), 5 (3), and 75 (68). Prices were to be more closely linked with world levels (especially for raw materials) and were increasingly to reflect domestic supply and demand forces.[10] According to Kaczurba (1988: 25), until the early 1980s the domestic price system was largely isolated from world prices. After that 'transaction prices' were introduced, accounting for about 85 per cent of trade turnover by the end of 1987. These were effectively export and import prices converted through the current exchange rate, set by comparing domestic and foreign production costs in foreign trade prices.

Some enterprises were to be given *direct trading rights* (349 at the end of 1985; Blazyca 1986: 100) and others were to have the option of entering into commission contracts with foreign trade corporations. At the end of 1989 nearly 2,000 organizations were directly engaged in foreign trade, of which forty were traditional foreign trade organizations, with a few retaining trade monopolies in products such as coal and copper (Institute of International Finance 1990: 37). Enterprises producing goods for export were allowed to retain a percentage of hard currency earnings, hard currency bank credits were to be available and there were to be foreign exchange auctions. Enterprises were later permitted to export independently if exports constituted at least 5 per cent of the value of their production (rather than 25 per cent as previously) (*Abecor Country Report*, April 1988, p. 2). A single exchange rate was introduced on 1 January 1982, with convertibility as the ultimate aim. The exchange rate was set against the dollar to make most enterprises profit from exporting to the West, but subsidies still protected domestic industry (*EIU Country Profile*, 1987–88, p. 16).[11]

The ministries were reduced in number from twelve to six and were supposed to be endowed with reduced powers. The 'associations' of enterprises (*zjednoczenia*), channels for relaying detailed central plan targets and exercising close supervision, were scrapped in mid-1982, but ministries (responsible for structural change and technological progress) then began to encourage enterprises to join together in new 'amalgamations' (*zrzeszenia*) by means of improved input and foreign exchange supply. There were 616 'amalgamations', of which only thirty-one were compulsory, and they embraced almost all the 6,065 state enterprises; there were also *kombinats* (Kolankiewicz and Lewis 1988: 111).

In the event, many aspects of the reform were not carried out. *Martial law* was in operation from 13 December 1981 to 21 July 1983. (Jaruzelsky claims that Andropov and Suslov warned him that Soviet intervention via the Warsaw Pact was the alternative; Jaruzelsky also claims that such intervention would have delayed the appearance of Gorbachev and the end of the Cold War.) Military commissars were made superior to enterprise managers in large enterprises, coal miners were enlisted and general labour direction was introduced. Unjustified absenteeism became a criminal offence. The forty-two hour week agreed upon in December 1981 for most workers (i.e. three of every four Saturdays were work-free) was rescinded in February 1986. Crucial workers like coal miners were affected by the introduction of martial law. Solidarity was outlawed in October 1982 and replaced with new official trade unions.[12] Workers' councils were introduced in 1981, while workers' self-management did not begin to operate until two years later. Formally workers' councils were endowed with substantial powers, e.g. the formation of plans and investment decisions. But although the plant-based workers' councils were elected by the workforce, they were not very influential in reality (they did resist enterprise amalgamations). After the martial law period, self-management was allowed to operate in 5,230 enterprises (out of 6,580), although in 1,371 of the former figure the power to nominate and dismiss the director was not allowed (they still had a veto over the government's choice: these 1,371 were described as being of 'fundamental significance for the economy' and employed 80 per cent of the workforce). Their number was reduced to 400 in 1987–88 (Kolankiewicz and Lewis 1988: 114). The law did not, to varying degrees, apply in certain cases, such as banks, railways and defence establishments (Kolankiewicz 1987: 61–2). Apart from the usual bureaucratic resistance to reform, supply difficulties emanating from negative rates of growth and crippling foreign debt (see Table 14.1) left the materials allocation system essentially intact; here the ministries were the chief channel. Central allocation applied to half of fuels and major materials, especially imports (for which a licensing system exists) and government contracts confer privileged access to supplies (*World Bank Report* 1988: 30).

Even after the enactment of the 1983 bankruptcy law, only eleven state enterprises were closed down; in 1988 140 enterprises were put on a hit list, but liquidation procedures were only started in thirty-three cases (Lipton and Sachs 1990: 108). Subsidization was still on a massive scale and a selective basis.[13] Former deputy premier Zdzislaw Sadowski (who had chief responsibility for the reform programme until he lost his position in the government in September 1988) emphasized the alternatives to bankruptcy in the form of reorganization, such as changes in the product mix and the splitting up of big enterprises into smaller units (*Polish Perspectives*, 1988, vol. XXXI, no. 1, pp. 10–11). Nevertheless, in June 1988 it was decided to close twenty-one medium and small enterprises, and 140 in total faced liquidation.

Severe restrictions were placed on enterprises' use of hard currency earnings; 80–85 per cent of foreign exchange remained centrally allocated in 1986 (Blazyca 1986: 42). According to the EIU (*Country Profile*, 1987–88, p. 39), in 1985 the share of hard currency imports financed through enterprise foreign exchange accounts was 14.9 per cent, falling to 13.9 per cent in 1986. In 1987 ROD balances (convertible currency retention quotas) were held by 2,500 enterprises, and about a quarter of hard currency expenditure was financed in this way. By the early 1990s at least half of all export earnings was to be accounted for in this fashion (Kaczurba 1988: 26). After the first half of 1987 there were fortnightly auctions of US dollars by the Export Development Bank,[14] where enterprises were able to sell surplus foreign currency to other enterprises needing to buy.

On 15 March 1989 a free market in foreign exchange for private individuals was introduced. Individuals could also apply for a licence to operate retail exchange bureaus. In March 1985 two types of hard currency accounts for individuals were opened, one for approved earnings yielding interest and the other only able to be converted into the former after one year (*EIU Country Profile*, 1987–88, p. 16). In July 1987 this was changed into a system whereby the central bank issued savings certificates for fixed terms of one, two or three years at interest rates of 3 per cent, 8 per cent and 9 per cent respectively, with a premium after three years if the interest was allowed to accumulate (*Polish Perspectives*, 1988, vol. XXXI, no. 1, p. 54). In the following November the National Savings Bank was turned into an independent commercial bank, which, from 1 June of the following year, entered the market for the purchase and sale of dollar-denominated coupons for use in hard currency shops.

Tax reliefs and subsidies have, in reality, been granted on a discretionary basis, showing the influence of relative bargaining strengths. Blazyca (1987: 49) provides a splendid example of how vested interests could undermine reform. In 1982 a tax was placed on increases in average wages over a certain percentage; firms' complaints of rigidity brought about a tax linked to wage growth exceeding 0.5 times the growth in the volume of enterprise output. This shifted firms' attention to output volume, while special pleading arose from those firms whose favourable output record in the previous year now penalized them. There followed discriminatory degrees of tax relief. A great obstacle to reform,

however, was provided by the powerful ministries. Direct intervention took the form, for example, of 'operational programmes', the command planning of particular areas. In 1983 'government contracts' were introduced, and enterprises were induced by input and foreign exchange supplies to fulfil orders for goods. The former was to be phased out and the latter increased. In the same year employment offices began to assign people to enterprises (Kurakowski 1988: 17). The state budget later claimed most enterprise depreciation allowances, and enterprises forfeited the required percentage of any sum invested, which they have to deposit in banks, owing to the failure to fulfil criteria such as deadlines and pay-back (Kurakowski 1988: 28).

The Tenth Congress in 1986 was attended by Gorbachev personally. Jaruzelski was critical of many aspects of the Polish economy, such as bureaucracy, the reluctance of managers to accept responsibility and low levels of productivity. He promised, however, a better implementation of the reform, designated as the 'second stage' of the reform. The 1986–90 Five Year Plan revolved around energy and materials savings, increased exports to the West and restoring domestic equilibrium.

The October 1987 'second stage' of the reform

Aspects of the 'second stage' included the following:

1. *A three-year programme to restore macro equilibrium*, reducing inflation to 9 per cent by 1990, eliminating balance of payments deficits by 1991 and achieving zloty convertibility by the mid-1990s. Reducing subsidies implied steep rises in the prices of fuel and energy to bring them into line with world levels and a 40 per cent increase in the prices of consumer goods and services (matched by income rises). Full employment was to be seen as the right to 'effective' work.[15]

2. *A streamlining of the institutional*

framework. This involved not only a reduction in the number of central administrators, but also an integration of the enterprises in sectors such as coal, steel, petrochemicals, paper and electronics in order to centralize sales and purchasing programmes at home and abroad.[16] At the ministerial level it was envisaged that 'super-ministries' would be created in industry, energy and transport. The new ministries included the Ministry of Industry (superseding the ministries of energy and power, chemical and light industry, metallurgy and engineering, and materials and fuel management); the Ministry of Development and Construction; the Ministry of Transport, Shipping and Communications; and the Ministry of External Economic Relations (Chelstowski 1988: 13–14). There was also to be an increase in the powers of regional and local government bodies, including the transfer to them of a number of enterprises (p. 15).

3. Even so, an *anti-monopoly law* was planned and became operational on 1 January 1988. According to Brodzka (1987: 32), the rule whereby it was necessary to get prior permission for any business undertaking was to be abandoned and from then on a statement of intent was to suffice. A list of 'large monopolist structures' was to be drawn up that should be divided into smaller autonomous units, making it possible for enterprises to split if justified on efficiency grounds (Chelstowski 1988: 17). A competitive banking system, comprising nine state-owned 'credit' banks, was to be created by 1 January 1989. Enterprises were free to choose a bank, while banks were allowed to set differential charges and interest rates. The state monopoly of the procurement and wholesale distribution of food was to be ended, while the private and co-operative sectors of the economy were to be treated on a par with the state sector (e.g. given access to hard currency loans). State enterprises were to be permitted to sell bonds and shares,[17] to invest their earnings in partnerships or joint ventures, and to choose their own banks (Brodzka 1987: 32). There was talk of possible joint state–(domestic) private

ventures (the terms of joint ventures with foreign companies were to be improved). There was also talk of 'benefits for persons temporarily without employment' (Brodzka 1987: 32).

In the *29 November 1987 referendum*, however, the government failed to get the required 51 per cent of eligible voters necessary to secure approval for its economic and political programme. Of the 67 per cent of the electorate who voted, 66 per cent approved the economic aspect and 69 per cent the political aspect, but they only constituted 44 per cent and 46 per cent respectively of the total potential electorate. As a result, the government planned to implement parts of the economic programme more slowly. Specifically, food price increases planned for 1988 would take place over a three year period; prices would increase by an average of 40 per cent in 1988 instead of 110 per cent and retail prices as a whole would go up by 27 per cent on average as opposed to 40 per cent. On 1 February 1988 there was an average increase in prices of 27 per cent, with food prices rising by 40 per cent, accompanied by some protest marches and a 20 per cent increase in average pay, and on 1 March 1988 there were increases in the cost of bus and tram fares (66 per cent), and newspapers and nursery school charges. On 1 April 1988 coal prices were raised by 200 per cent and gas, heating fuel and electricity by 100 per cent. There would be no further price increases for the remainder of the year, meat rationing would remain during 1988, and there would be a lessening in enterprise profit tax reductions planned for that year, budget deficit reductions, and the rate of decentralization of raw materials distribution. On 1 October 1989 domestic electricity prices rose by 150 per cent, gas by 100 per cent, postal changes by 130 per cent, and private telephone charges by more than 100 per cent.

The end of April 1988 saw the start of over two weeks of isolated but significant labour unrest, the first since the introduction of martial law. The economic causes included the high inflation rate,[18] and political factors included the quest to relegalize Solidarity and protests against the detaining of its supporters. The government's response was a mixture of force, concessions and the taking of special powers. There were wage concessions, accompanied by adjustments to the enterprise tax system. Special powers legislation (first mentioned in March) was passed, valid to the end of the year, which provided the government with the following powers: (1) labour disputes were only to be sanctioned if supported by the official National Trade Union Alliance (an outright ban was mooted at first); (2) to delay or reverse wage and price increases or even to impose freezes; to impose new taxes on individuals and enterprises; (3) to control spending decisions, including investment; (4) to liquidate and merge/divide enterprises more quickly; (5) to order redundancies; and (6) to dismiss management (see *Polish Perspectives*, 1988, vol. XXXI, no. 3, p. 56). This interference with the rights of enterprises and labour was deemed necessary to ensure the success of the economic reforms (ironically) and to combat inflation.

Despite these special measures, further strikes broke out in mid-August 1988 in which the demand for Solidarity's recognition figured much more prominently. Lech Walesa met Interior Minister General Czeslaw Kiszczak on a number of occasions, the first on the last day of the month, and the government agreed to broad talks, beginning in mid-October. After a critical report from a parliamentary commission, which claimed, among other things, that actual economic reforms had been minimal, Prime Minister Messner and his government resigned on 19 September. He was replaced shortly afterwards by Mieczyslaw Rakowski. October saw the new Industry Minister, Mieczyslaw Wilczek (a successful private businessman), preparing to draw up a 'hit list' of 140 unprofitable enterprises, followed by the announcement of the 'progressive liquidation', over the period up to the end of 1990, of the Gdansk shipyard (over 10,000 workers; the government stressed the losses incurred by the shipyard, with one

eye on the international lenders, while the opposition attributed political reasons, since Gdansk was the birthplace of Solidarity).

The October 1988 talks failed to materialize, but the following January the Polish leadership accepted the principle of trade union pluralism, subject to conditions such as abiding by the constitution, working within the law and supporting economic reform. Solidarity agreed to enter into discussions, these beginning on 6 February 1989. The Round Table Agreement was reached on 5 April. Solidarity was relegalized. In the June 1989 election, the lower house, the Sejm, was to have 65 per cent of its seats reserved for the Polish United Workers' Party and its allies, with the remaining 35 per cent contested by the opposition alone. All the seats in the new upper house (Senate) were to be freely contested. Both houses were to elect a new executive president. Solidarity and the government agreed on 80 per cent indexation of wages. There were also promises to decontrol farm prices and land sales. (See the introductory section on the political background.)

AGRICULTURE

Poland did not undertake a radical land reform after the First World War; only 10 per cent of total arable land (25 per cent of estate land) was redistributed from landed estates to landless (or nearly so) peasants between 1919 and 1939 (kindly pointed out by Robert Bideleux). After the 1944 land reforms the average size of land holding was still only 6.4 ha (Kolankiewicz and Lewis 1988: 33). Compulsory delivery quotas were imposed on peasant farmers in 1951. The collectivization process, which had begun in 1949, was reversed in 1956. At the end of 1986 land tenure as a percentage of arable land was as follows: individual land holdings, 72.0; state farms, 18.5; collective farms and agricultural circles, 3.9; others (e.g. State Land Fund: the fund took land from private farmers, in exchange for compensation in such forms as old-age pensions, and then sold or leased it to socialized or private farms), 5.6 (p. xv). The private sector is also dominant in respect of agricultural output, contributing 78 per cent in 1985. In 1970 the figure for output was 85 per cent, and for agricultural land 81 per cent.[19] In the early 1950s the maximum private holding was set at 15 ha, but this was increased during the 1970s, to reach 50 ha by the end of the decade (CIA Analyst 1986: 454). The 50 ha maximum applied in south and central Poland, but 100 ha in the north (*The Economist*, 21 October 1989, p. 70). The average private farm, sometimes not even in one piece, however, is very small. In 1982 it was only 6.6 ha, excluding farms of under 2 ha, and 5 ha including them (Cook 1986b:474). In 1986 the farm structure, in hectares, was as follows: 0.51–2, 29.6 per cent; 2–5, 28.09 per cent; 5–7, 12.2 per cent; 7–10, 12.9 per cent; 10–15, 10.6 per cent; and over 15, 6.7 per cent (Cochrane 1988: 53). Technology was typically backward (horses were more common than tractors), while farmers relied mainly on inputs from the state sector (e.g. the state exercised monopoly power over the supply of machines, chemicals and building materials, and monopsony power over the purchase of the product). By contrast, in 1984 the average state farm was 3,169 ha in size (Blazyca 1986: 5).[20] In 1988 28.9 per cent of the workforce was still employed in agriculture.

Even after the reversal of collectivization in 1956, however, private farmers were still required to meet state obligatory delivery quotas for products such as grain, potatoes, meat and milk. In January 1972, however, this system was replaced by for one of voluntary contracts, although, of course, the state could still use its considerable monopoly and monopsony powers: prices and input supplies were also improved. On 1 January 1989 the state monopoly in the purchasing of many agricultural products came to an end (with exceptions such as tobacco, poppy seed and hemp). The monopoly in respect of fruit and vegetables had been ended some years earlier (*Polish Perspectives*, 1989, vol. XXXII, no. 1, p. 57). Pouliquen (1989: 70) thinks that the official 1987 figure of 13 per cent of sales accounted for by family farms is possibly an underestimate.

State farms were given priority during the 1960s.

Cook (1984, 1986b, 1988) describes agricultural policy during the 1970s as guided by a belief that the socialized sector could be strengthened by bureaucratic intervention without injuring the private sector. Thus, for example, agricultural circles (co-operative bodies providing services; the circles were initially intended by the Gomulka regime after 1956 to encourage the private sector to mechanize:

Table 14.2 Poland: statistical survey

Arable land, 1986 (%)			
Individual holdings	*State farms*	*Collective farms and agricultural circles*	*Others*
72	18.5	3.9	5.6

Private Sector's contribution to total agricultural output, 1985 (%): 78.0

Private non-agricultural sector's share of national income, 1987 (%): 7.0

Joint equity ventures, December 1989: 800

Population, mid-1989: 37.9 million

Sources: Kolankiewicz and Lewis (1988: xv, 127); *Polish Perspectives*, 1988, vol. XXXI, no. 1, p. 51; EIU, *Country Report*, 1990, no. 1, p. 17.
For figures on growth, inflation and debt, see Table 14.1.

Korbonski 1990a: 272) were taken into state control in 1973; crop and cultivation schedules were also imposed by local administrators during the 1970s (Kurakowski 1988: 23). Land sales were prohibited if the result would have been farms of less than 8 ha (Cochrane 1988: 50).

The Solidarity era[21] saw the start of a period of encouragement given to private agriculture, with promises of permanent status and improved input supplies, credit, prices and opportunities to purchase land from the State Land Fund.

The impact of free market prices varied between commodities. While only 5–8 per cent of grain was so priced, the figure for the marketed output of fruit, vegetables, flowers and eggs was over 60 per cent (Quaisser 1986: 566). Government price determination was affected by factors such as the state of the consumer goods market and the cost of farm inputs. After 1983–84 there was an annual adjustment in purchase prices to take account of rising input prices; previously, purchase prices had been based on factors such as the average cost of production (Quaisser 1986: 276). Herer (1988: 174) makes the point that the prices of products such as wheat, milk and sugar beet were fixed by the state, but had to take account of the free market price. April 1989 saw the abolition of state controls over producer prices, the state thereafter only setting guaranteed (minimum) prices (Cochrane 1990a: 68).

The 1 August 1989 decree abolished both meat rationing and retail price controls on most foodstuffs (*EIU Country Profile*, 1989–90, p.6 and Cochrane 1990a: 64–8). This 'marketization of the food economy' led to a 180 per cent increase in food prices in August and helped cause near hyperinflation overall. The only retail price controls to remain were those on low-fat milk and cottage cheese, infant formula and plain bread.

The Polish Roman Catholic church's 1982 plan to aid private agriculture with Western funds has had a chequered history. The plan mainly involves sales of Western commodities such as machines to private farmers to provide the zlotys to finance schemes such as water supply, storage and repair facilities, and the equipping of farming colleges. The original sum was envisaged as $2 billion to $3 billion, but this was drastically reduced to $25 million. Cardinal Jozef Glemp abandoned the scheme altogether in September 1986 on the grounds of the state's desire to exercise control. In July of the following year the Polish government approved a $10 million US government scheme, and on 18 September the Church Agricultural Committee was formally set up, which was exempt from taxes and customs duties and free from state control.

The Foundation for the Development of Polish Agriculture was set up, with government approval, on 20 February 1988. This is a non-profit-making organization backed by the Rockefeller Foundation and managed by a council including agronomists and businessmen from the United States and Western European countries and a minority of experts from Poland itself, although permission was originally needed from the Polish Ministry of Agriculture for specific activities. The aim is to promote agricultural exports in particular and to improve agriculture in general. For example, the first loan from Western banks, of $2.4 million over three years, was used to import high-protein pig feed in order to stimulate exports of ham to the United States, the proceeds going to improve educational, technical and commercial projects in agriculture.

JOINT EQUITY VENTURES

From 1985 onwards Poland allowed joint equity ventures with Western companies, originally on the following conditions: a normal maximum 49 per cent foreign ownership (exceptions being possible); the head had to be a Polish citizen; repatriated hard currency profits had to be earned by exports (the other possibility was for foreign partners to buy Polish goods with zloty earnings for resale in the West); a proportion of foreign exchange earnings had to be sold to the state; and the profits tax was to be reduced as the proportion of output exported rose. Few ventures were actually set up. In 1986 the Polish national airline entered into one with an Austrian construction company and a US hotel chain to refurbish a terminal–hotel complex. By the end of 1987 there were sixteen ventures in operation (*Polish Perspectives*, 1988, vol. XXXI, no. 1, p. 51). A new law, operational after 1 January 1989, allowed the following: wholly foreign-owned enterprises; joint foreign–private Polish ventures; top management to be foreign; an extension of the normal tax holiday from two to three years (up to six years for priority sectors); a reduction in the basic profits tax from 50 per cent to 40 per cent (lower rates, in proportion to output exported, apply, down to 10 per cent for 100 per cent exports); and only 15 per cent (instead of 25 per cent) of hard currency earnings was to be sold to the state at the official rate (Peter Montagnon, *FT*, 17 November 1988, p. 9). Repatriated hard currency dividends were taxed at a rate of 30 per cent, while foreign partner dividends retained in Poland avoided this (Margie Lindsay, *FT* Survey, 13 December 1988, p. 39). By December 1989 there were about 800 joint ventures (*EIU Country Report*, 1990, no. 1, p. 17). By the end of March 1990 there were 1,231 (Blazyca 1992: 193). The 'Polonia' companies are discussed in the following section.

THE PRIVATE NON-AGRICULTURAL SECTOR OF THE ECONOMY

According to Åslund (1984, 1985), the sector reached its nadir in 1955, and from that point onwards the state recognized the value of the private sector, albeit restricted, to complement the state sector. A process of cyclical recovery after 1956 resulted in a 1982 private sector figure of 5.9 per cent of the non-agricultural labour force (Åslund 1984: 428). A more favourable attitude was usually taken during periods of

political thaw and deteriorating economic conditions (Mroz 1991: 678). The employment maximum for a handicraft enterprise was raised from one employee in 1955 to six (eight in construction) in March 1966, and then fifteen (excluding members of the family, pensioners and apprentices). On average handicraft firms employed only about two people and the figure was lower for other private firms (Åslund 1984: 429). In 1986 private industrial establishments employed two people on average, while co-operatives employed thirty (Lipton and Sachs 1990a: 84). The limit was subsequently raised to fifty (*FT*, 24 December 1988, p. 2). According to Kurakowski (1988: 15), the non-nationalized, non-agricultural sector of the economy employed nearly 10 per cent of the non-agricultural labour force, and Dobija (*The Independent*, 26 November 1987, p. 11) reports that private enterprise accounted for seven per cent of industrial output and that in the Lomianki district just outside Warsaw private firms employed between two and ten people on average (several employed up to 100). In 1989 the state sector accounted for 92.6 per cent of industrial sales (at current prices, compared to 96.2 per cent in 1985), while the private sector share was 7.4 per cent (compared to 3.8 per cent in 1985) (Blazyca 1992: 186–7). At the Thirteenth Congress of the Democratic Party in 1986 there was a call for an increase in the private sector's share of national income from the current 7 per cent to perhaps 25 per cent (Kolankiewicz and Lewis 1988: 127). The leasing of state property was allowed in 1964. Twelve years later it was made possible for foreigners who were once Polish citizens (and later on others) to set up sizeable private companies in Poland – the 'Polonia' companies, which are owned by former Polish citizens, pay no tax for three years and can repatriate 50 per cent of hard currency earnings; Kolankiewicz and Lewis (1988: 127) give a figure of 683 firms. Bobinski (*FT*, 16 December 1987, p. 5) states that their association, called Interpolcom, represented only 660 Western-owned companies (compared with 695 at the end of 1986), owing to stricter hard currency regulations and tax increases. In 1986 there were 670 Polonia companies, employing 61,619 people (on average ninety, with the largest 800) (Rostowski 1989: 203).

During 1987 and 1988 further encouragement was given to the private sector as part of the new round of reforms. As of 1 January 1989, the private sector was, theoretically, treated on a par with the state and co-operative sectors as regards taxation, number of employees, access to credit and input supply. Instead of needing authorization as before, private enterprises were able to register without licences, except in certain defined activities such as explosives and drugs. In September 1987 the first meeting took place of the independent Economic Society of Warsaw, even though it took some time afterwards to actually get registered. The aims of this organization and the Industrial Society of Krakow, comprising private businessmen and economists, were to encourage the private sector and the market economy in general. The advice given to start-up private enterprises was expected to bring in revenue in the form of a fee and a share of future profits.

Rostowski (1989: 194–5) estimates that in 1986 the private sector as a whole (including agriculture) accounted for almost one-third of the total labour force, and between 38 per cent and 45.2 per cent of personal money incomes (compared with an official figure of 24.5 per cent). He considers the official figure of 18.2 per cent (of which agriculture 10.2 per cent) of produced national income to be a considerable underestimation, although the true share is probably considerably smaller than the share in personal money incomes.

CONCLUSION

Poland has a history of political dismemberment. World attention was focused on the country during the 'Solidarity era'. A whole series of industrial reforms was undertaken, the January 1982 version being largely thwarted by factors such as severe supply bottlenecks. Its 'second stage' version was announced in October 1987. This reform was along Hungarian lines, but largely remained on paper too. According to legislation operative as of 1 January 1989, the private sector was, in theory, treated on a par with the state and co-operative sectors. Socialist Poland had, like Yugoslavia, a largely private agriculture and shared problems such as high foreign indebtedness and inflationary tendencies. Poland showed quite clearly the need for political reforms to accompany the economic, involving society more in decision-making in return for shouldering the burden of austerity.

NOTES

1. Coal accounted for nearly 70 per cent of primary energy consumption in 1980. Hard coal output in 1987 was 193 million tonnes, of which 31 million tonnes was exported, making Poland the world's fourth largest producer. In 1988 coal output was 193 million tonnes (28.8 million tonnes exported) and in 1989 178 million tonnes. Coal provided 8 per cent of export earnings (*FT*, 26 May 1990, p. 3). The first nuclear reactor was not due to be operational until 1991.
2. See especially Kolankiewicz and Lewis (1988: Chapter 1).
3. See Blazyca (1980b); Nuti (1981a, b); and Brus (1982).
4. One reason for this was the linkage of wages to value-added, the latter being boosted by price increases resulting from the manipulation of 'new' products.
5. Investment fell to 26 per cent of national income in 1979. Blazyca (1986: 17) shows that the annual average rates of growth of investment and import volume respectively were 17.8 per cent and 27.3 per cent for 1971–75; 1.0 per cent and 11.4 per cent for 1976; and -0.9 per cent and -5.8 per cent in 1977–79. Investment fell by 12.3 per cent in 1980, 22.3 per cent in 1981 and 12.1 per cent in 1982 (p. 25): this extended completion times and enlarged bottlenecks.
6. Note that Pewex stores supplied scarce goods for convertible currencies. Since 1 July 1990 Pewex has been obliged to price goods in zloties as well as in hard currencies; since 1 January

1991 zloties only can be used (*EIU Country Report*, 1990, no. 1, p. 18).

7. Poland also owed 6.5 billion roubles, mainly to the Soviet Union (Kolankiewicz and Lewis 1988: 98). As of 1 November 1989 Poland owed the Soviet Union 4.96 billion roubles (*CDSP*, 1990, vol. XLII, no. 9, p. 9).

8. In 1984 fishing and aircraft landing rights were restored, but it was not until February 1987 that US credits and MFN treatment were reinstated.

9. See Nuti (1977, 1981a); Wanless (1980); Brus (1982); and Blazyca (1980b).

10. The EIU (*Country Profile*, 1987–88, p. 16) suggests that in the setting of the prices of such products as cigarettes, vodka and cars, black market prices were used.

11. Kurakowski (1988: 36) describes the exchange rate as fixed to cover the domestic cost of 80 per cent of all exports.

12. A membership figure of around 7 million is usually given for 1987–88. Membership was a little over half the eligible workforce at the start of 1987, compared with a peak of over 80 per cent for Solidarity.

13. In 1985 subsidies in total, including those for final consumption, amounted to 39.2 per cent of total state expenditure (*EIU Country Profile*, 1987–88, p. 33). *EEN* (1988, vol. 2, no. 6, p. 5) estimates that subsidies have amounted to around half of state expenditure in recent years. Subsidies paid to agriculture and food processing amounted to 19 per cent of total budgetary expenditure in 1987 (Cochrane 1990a: 66–7).

14. Set up in January 1987 to encourage exports, with shares owned by the state, banks and other state and co-operative enterprises.

15. Note that the restoration of living standards was now not envisaged to take place until 1995 at the earliest (Kolankiewicz and Lewis 1988: 100).

16. Enterprises were encouraged to join by funding, tax concessions and increases in retained foreign exchange earnings.

17. In 1987 an experiment was begun in a textile factory in Lodz to sell stocks to its employees. In October 1989 Treasury bonds were issued for the first time since the 1930s.

18. Forty-five per cent in the first quarter of 1988, compared with the same period in the previous year.

19. Until 1981 socialized agriculture had priority purchase rights from the State Land Fund. Retiring private farmers only received a pension if their land holdings were handed over to this organization.

20. For an analysis of the performance of private and state agriculture see Boyd (1988).

21. The organizations banned in 1982 were Rural Solidarity, Solidarity of Individual Farmers, and Farmers' Solidarity. Rural Solidarity was legalized in May 1981 and outlawed in October 1982.

15

ROMANIA

BACKGROUND

Wallachia in the late fourteenth century and Moldavia in 1455 were absorbed into the Ottoman Empire. Russia annexed Bessarabia (south-east Moldavia) 1812–1918 and subjected the remaining two areas to a sort of protectorate status 1829–53. Under the terms of the Treaty of Paris of 1856, following Russia's defeat in the Crimean War, the principalities of Wallachia and Moldavia were placed under the joint protection of the European Great Powers, Turkey retaining only formal sovereignty. In 1859 a single prince was elected who, two years later, gained international recognition for his administrative unification. This *de facto* statehood was internationally recognized by the 1878 Treaty of Berlin. During the First World War Romania fought against the Austro-Hungarian Empire and annexed Transylvania (whose ethnic Hungarians had opted for union with Hungary in 1867), Bukovina and Bessarabia; these annexations were confirmed by the 1920 Treaty of Trianon. A royal dictatorship was established in 1938, the monarch forming his own fascist organization (the Front of National Rebirth), and increasingly closer economic links helped lead to alliance with Germany during the Second World War, until 1945, when Romania switched sides. (See Crowther 1988: Chapter 2.)

President Nicolae Ceausescu, who became First Secretary of the Romanian Communist Party in 1965 after the death of Gheorghe Gheorghiu-Dej (party leader since 1944) and who effectively introduced a form of family rule in Romania, exercised a relatively high degree of foreign policy and economic independence from the Soviet Union. Severe debt problems moderated this stance in the 1980s, however, and there is the argument that the impression of independence was deliberately exaggerated in order to gain access to Western capital and technology. Soviet troops were withdrawn in 1958, and 1962 saw both the last Warsaw Pact troop exercise on Romanian soil and the rejection of Khrushchev's plans to make Comecon a supranational planning agency and Romania mainly a primary producer. Romania boycotted Warsaw Pact troop manoeuvres in other countries after August 1967 (staff still participated), did not break off diplomatic relations with Israel after the 1967 Arab–Israeli War, sent an ambassador back to Albania as early as January 1963, was the first Comecon country to recognize the European Community, and spoke out against the invasion of Czechoslovakia in 1968 (although on the grounds of political sovereignty and not of support for liberal reforms). With the arrival of Gorbachev, Romania no longer served a useful function as an 'independent'. Late 1989 saw the demise of Ceausescu. On 21 December he was booed by elements of what was meant to be a supportive rally and the next day the National Salvation Front led by Ion Iliescu took over the running of the country. Ceausescu and his wife Elena were executed on Christmas Day. The National Salvation Front won the free election of May 1990.

Before the Second World War Romania was one of the poorest of the European nations, a mainly agricultural country, with 75 per cent of the population classified as rural and a similar proportion of the labour force working in agriculture (in 1988 28.5 per cent of the labour force). *Per capita* national income in 1937 was less than half that of Czechoslovakia (Crowther 1988: 55, 175, based on Berend and Ranki). Agriculture provided a subsistence living to most of the agricultural population and export crops to Western Europe. Only 8 per cent of the labour force was employed in industry in 1938. Industry was overwhelmingly orientated towards consumer goods and the processing of raw materials; only oil production was large-scale and modern (see Tsantis and Pepper 1979: 1; Gilberg 1975: 9). Agricultural products accounted for 65 per cent of exports, and manufactures only 2 per cent (Crowther 1988: 55, quoting Spulber). Even by 1950 agriculture employed about three-quarters of the workforce and contributed nearly 40 per cent to the national product (Shafir 1985: 139 and 109). The population in 1988 was 23.1 million[1] and the country is well endowed with agricultural land, energy and raw materials.

Table 15.1 shows net hard currency debt and official figures for rates of growth of NMP. Note that there was particular concern about the meaningfulness of official Romanian statistics.

INDUSTRIAL REFORM

The pre-1967 Romanian economy seems to have been even more highly centralized than its pre-1965 counterpart in the Soviet Union; targets were imposed on industrial enterprises with little consultation. After a series of experiments, *the blueprint of industrial reform ('Directives')* appeared in December 1967, although the first stage of implementation actually ran from 1969 to about 1972 (Granick 1975; Smith 1980, 1981; Spigler 1973).

The basic production unit was to be the 'central' *(centrala)*, usually the result of a country-wide horizontal integration of one large enterprise with smaller ones, with location of headquarters at the site of the former. The first central was not set up until 1969, due mainly to ministerial resistance to loss of power. Plan targets were of the traditional type, such as output and assortment, sales, exports, imports, cost reduction, material inputs and financial aspects: these remained obligatory, but the degree of consultation was stepped up. According to Granick, there was little real decision-making below the level of the ministry. The role of the enterprise involved little more than enhancing technical efficiency. For example, while ministries could reallocate individual enterprise tasks within aggregate central targets, enterprises could administer only the details of previously concluded contracts. Managerial behaviour could not in any sense be explained by bonus maximization, since bonuses were easily obtained – the targets were not only slack but were frequently changed, partly to fit in with ministerial assessment of managers. This was more important in determining managerial rewards than plan fulfilment. Romanian industry remained even more tightly controlled than its Soviet counterpart (Granick 1975). The central was responsible for imposing disaggregated plan targets on constituent enterprises, including gross output, assortment of key products in physical terms, material supplies, labour productivity, wage fund, investment, and payments to the state budget.

The directives stressed financial discipline, showing greater concern for cost and profit and the need to increase the role played by interest-bearing credits in the financing of state-determined investments. There were some limited concessions to decentralized investment, and credit policy in general included the use of penal interest rates if credit conditions were not met. The incentive system involved reducing the impact of bonuses by integrating most of them into basic wage and salary scales and introducing penalties for non-fulfilment of plan targets. A distinction was made between above-

Table 15.1 Romania: foreign debt and average annual rates of growth of NMP and GNP (%)

NMP

1951–55	1956–60	1961–65	1966–70	1971–75	1976–80	1981	1982	1983	1984	1985	1986	1987	1988	1989
14.2	6.6	9.0	7.8	11.3	7.3	2.2	2.6	3.4	7.7	5.9	7.3	4.8	3.2	1.7

GNP (CIA)

1971–75	1976–80	1981–85	1986	1987	1988	1989
6.8	1.3	1.0	3.5	-0.8	1.7	-1.5

Net hard currency debt ($ billion)

1981	1986	1988	March 1989
9.8	5.8	3.0	Zero (official claim)

Sources Shafir (1985: 110); Smith (1983: 40); EIU, *Country Profile*, 1987–88, pp. 13, 34; 1989–90, p.36; *Abecor Country Report*, October 1988, p. 1; Institute of International Finance (1990: 15); CIA (1990: tables 1 and C–18).

plan profit due to the enterprise's 'own activities' (a part of which was to finance bonuses and socio-cultural activities, with the rest going into the state budget) and that due to external circumstances, which was to be surrendered to the state budget.

A novel innovation was the replacement of 'one-man management' by 'collective management', involving a board of management at the enterprise level (called a 'workers' committee' after 1971) and an 'administrative council' at the level of the central, later called a 'council of the working people'. Until 1971 the *de facto* powers of management boards were not great and enterprise autonomy between 1971 and 1978 was negligible.

During *the second stage of implementation* (1973–78) the number of centrals was approximately halved, each constituting about fifteen enterprises and 32,000 employees. The declared aim was to reduce ministerial power and move management closer to production. Consequently, centrals were to deal with intra-central material balancing and materials and labour transfer between constitutent enterprises. The number of centrally allocated products, however, actually increased from 180 to 720 in 1974. Centrals were to co-ordinate their plans with functional ministries (such as Labour and Finance) and with local authorities, while substantial numbers of engineering personnel were transferred to enterprises to concentrate on technical matters. The desirability of enhancing the importance of credits as opposed to grants was confirmed, although from 1973 onwards state approval was needed for all investment. In 1971 the profit mark-up on average cost was shifted from costs to capital employed.

A wholesale price revision in the period 1974–76 aimed at reducing subsidies and the considerable differences in profitability between branches. Capital and rental (land tax) charges were introduced in 1971, although in 1977 the former was replaced by a progressive tax on planned profit in excess of 15 per cent: turnover tax was reduced in part compensation.

Personal income tax on public sector earnings was replaced by a tax on the wage fund.

The third stage of the Romanian reform was announced in March 1978 and put into operation from the start of 1979. The *'New Economic–Financial Mechanism'* was theoretically based on the principle of workers' self-management and had as its main aim financial discipline, i.e. increased financial accountability for decisions still largely made by the centre. Economic and financial self-management involved the covering of most costs, including socio-cultural services and investment, out of revenue (the latter is also to be financed by credits rather than grants). A prime stimulus was the damage caused by rising world prices of raw materials and energy, and this pressure to economize on raw materials and other inputs also caused net output to be the replacement for gross output as the main enterprise indicator and increased emphasis to be given to cost reduction and export indicators. Other remaining indicators included gross output, investment and labour productivity. Compulsory payments to the state budget (such as taxes on profits, net output and the wage fund) and repayment of bank credit had priority over the enterprise's own funds in the distribution of planned profits, but over-plan profits were divided up according to set rules. Monthly wages and salaries were affected by bonuses and penalties for over- and under-fulfilment of gross output, labour productivity, exports or material consumption targets, while funds for personal bonuses and socio-cultural activities were fed by over-plan profits caused by overfulfilling targets such as cost reduction, physical output and exports. Bonuses from planned profits were reduced if the net production indicator and delivery contracts for physical output were not fulfilled. Despite the complexity of the scheme, bonuses accounted for only about 5 per cent of earnings. A single rate of exchange between the leu and the dollar and the transferable rouble was established with respect to enterprise accounting. This forging of a direct link between domestic and world prices helped to identify profitable and loss-making enterprises. The 1988 regulations based price on planned average branch costs of production plus an average profit mark-up of 6–8 per cent (up to 10 per cent for exports). If profit increases were the result of cost reductions they could be retained in full for the first year and 50 per cent thereafter. Retail prices were to remain unchanged (Dijmarescu 1989: 54).

'*Self-management*' in Romanian industry was not equivalent to its Yugoslav counterpart (see especially Smith 1980, 1981). Workers were actually in a minority on 'workers' committees', compared with managerial–technical staff and representatives of the party and the trade unions. Although there appeared to be a degree of real consultation in plan setting, the committees seemed to be mainly a means of achieving centrally determined goals by going over the head of management in questions such as the search for hidden reserves. It is also worth noting that large production units also performed social functions such as the provision of housing and education.

The New Economic–Financial Mechanism (NEFM) underwent changes, but communist Romania always retained a command economy. In 1981 the minimum wage was abolished, while pay was subsequently tied to enterprise performance, especially in export and mining activities. On 1 September 1983 a new piece rate system was introduced, which meant the end of the former guarantee of a monthly income equal to 80 per cent of an employee's regular pay and of the 20 per cent limit on extra income dependent on plan fulfilment (Shafir 1985: 124). Thus wages were related to output without upper or lower limits as an incentive to increase production (Turnock 1986: 275). A new employee had to sign a contract with an enterprise to work there for at least five years. During that time the employee was given only half of profit share entitlement, with the remainder placed in a bank account. Premature quitting of the job resulted in forfeiture of both this sum and the years counting towards pension rights (Shafir

1985: 124–5). Iancu (1989: 134–5) refers to the 'global contract system', in which working collectives (brigades of workers, technicians and engineers) undertook to meet plan commitments; there was no floor or ceiling to income and there were penalties for non-fulfilment. Holders of 'social shares' were entitled to interest at an annual rate of 5 per cent (up to 8 per cent in the case of above-plan profits); these shares could be inherited, but only sold back at face value to the issuing enterprise. In addition to the practice of schoolchildren, students, teachers and clerical workers donating a number of days of free labour at harvest time, the September 1985 draft law required everyone over eighteen years of age to contribute an unpaid six days each year in public work or an equivalent monetary compensation. A new poll tax was introduced and the proceeds were paid over to local and regional councils. The normal 1–2 May holiday was rescinded in 1987 for those working in enterprises not fulfilling their output plans. In August 1987 workers were granted bonuses for overfulfilling export targets.

Harsh winters aggravated power shortages to such an extent that in October 1985 the military took control of coal-fired and hydro-electric power plants,[2] with the civilian director subordinated to an army officer and workers subjected to army regulations. Absenteeism was treated as absence without leave or desertion. In 1987 there were rumours of possible military takeovers of larger industrial enterprises and mines, in response to worker unrest and strikes due to the austerity measures. In October a state of emergency was declared in energy before the onset of winter, thus militarizing the sector. Several ministers for mining and energy were also dismissed in that month. Sweeping personnel changes in general may perhaps be seen as a substitute for economic and political reform. In a January 1987 speech Ceausescu called for a more effective application of the NEFM and the system of 'self-management' and 'self-financing', rejecting moves towards market socialism and private enterprise as incompatible with socialism. On 5 May he stated that no one could speak about the reform of socialism through the so-called development of small private property; capitalist property, small or large, was capitalist property. Ceausescu thought it inconceivable that production units and sectors of the economy should become 'independent'. This demonstrated the conservative way in which 'self-management' and 'self-financing' were interpreted in Romania.

In June 1987 Ceausescu, as chairman, announced that the Supreme Council on Socio-economic Development (SCSD) was to be placed in 'supreme command' of the economy, the State Planning Commission functioning as secretariat of the Supreme Council. The SCSD was to be responsible for both drafting and implementing economic policy and was to play a more important role in drawing up plans. Departments in charge of economic and social policy were to be represented on the SCSD's new standing board. This move, together with others (such as the merging of the ministries of chemicals and petrochemicals and the creation of new ministries of mining and oil) could be seen as an assertion of party control over a more streamlined planning system, in an attempt to avoid radical economic reforms. Ronnas (1990: 52) makes the interesting point that plan targets, both at the macro and at the enterprise level, were increasingly based on Ceausescu's personal directives. By any standards the Romanian economy remained highly centralized.

In 1988 there were 2,091 industrial enterprises, 1,532 owned by the state (employing 1,724 on average) and 559 co-operatives; about 91 per cent of employees worked in the former and 9 per cent in the latter (Lucian Croitoru, *Romanian Economic Observer*, November–December 1990, pp. 61–3. In 1985 enterprises employing over 5,000 workers accounted for 36.8 per cent of industrial output (Smith 1992: 204). In that year 22.7 per cent of all state-wide enterprises employed more than 5,000 workers; thus monopoly producers are quite common (Montias 1991: 190).

AGRICULTURE

The socialized sector

The land reform of 1920–23 redistributed over 6 million ha (amounting to 66 per cent of estate owners' arable land) to peasants with little or no land (kindly pointed out by Robert Bideleux). In 1945 another *land reform* took place. The decision to *collectivize agriculture* was taken four years later and the process was completed by 1962. Note, however, that some independent private farms still existed in mountainous regions, although no person outside the family was allowed to be employed and a progressive tax was levied. In 1985 co-operatives accounted for 61 per cent of the cultivated area, state farms and other state institutions 30 per cent and private agriculture 9 per cent (*EIU Country Profile*, 1987–88, p. 17). In 1971 co-operative farmers were allowed minimum monthly advances, although two years later these became dependent on the fulfilment of plan targets (state farms were also affected). After 1982 peasants had to work at least 300 days for the co-operative or at other specified places. Compulsory livestock quotas were introduced in 1984, and it was also decreed that every farmstead that did not meet the (raised) obligatory procurement deliveries could be deprived of the use of *private plots* or, as far as individuals are concerned, the plots could be transferred to the co-operative or into state ownership. Only those peasants meeting the quotas could sell any surplus on the open market, where maximum prices were actually state-determined (Shafir 1985: 117). Compulsory delivery quotas of food products were also imposed on private farms. In 1986 both the private plots of collective farmers and independent private farms became subject to central planning (Ronnas 1989: 553–4). According to Turnock (1986: 185), in 1983 local authority certificates were needed for individuals who wished to sell their own fruit and vegetables on the open market at maximum prices set by the state. Individual and co-operative farmers had to register all their animals and had to breed animals under contract to the state.

As a result of the 1970s measures, individuals or groups were able to sign contracts with co-operative farms to work at piece-rate pay or in sharecropping arrangements, while more land was made available for family use if plans were fulfilled (Shafir 1985: 109). After 1979 there were experiments with agro-industrial associations, concerned with processing agricultural products (Turnock 1986: 185).

At the end of March 1988 an actual timetable was announced for a highly controversial scheme of so-called 'systematization' (sistematizare). The origins can be traced back to a July 1972 conference, but it was made law in 1978. The idea was to destroy 7,000 to 8,000 of the 13,000 villages (villages of less than 3,000 residents were the ones affected), creating instead 550 'agro-industrial centres' by the year 2000. This deadline was extended a short while later. The aims were as follows: originally to increase cultivable land by up to 300,000 ha, but Ceausescu conceded, in November 1988, that this was not feasible (*EEN*, 1988, vol. 2, no. 25, p. 5); reduce the costs of providing rural infrastructure and 'improve' services and housing (in the form of blocks of flats); enhance police surveillance (*EEN*, 1988, vol. 2, no. 7, p. 7; no. 10, p. 5; no. 22, p. 3); remove the remaining differences between urban and rural life, including living standards; take account of the replacement of people by machines in agriculture; and reduce ethnic differences (the Hungarian government was openly concerned that this last point was a way of further suppressing the Hungarian minority in Romania). As Ceausescu put it in a 2 June 1988 speech, the programme 'would eliminate essential differences between villages and towns, increasingly draw working, living and cultural conditions in villages and towns closer to each other and create the necessary prerequisites for a homogeneous society' (reported in *FT*, 21 June 1988, p. 2).[3] As Ronnas (1990: 19) puts it,

Table 15.2 Romania: statistical survey

Agricultural area 1985 (%)		
	State farms and other	
Co-operatives	*state institutions*	*Private sector*
60.8	29.7	9.5

Joint ventures, end 1987: 5

Population, 1988: 23.1 million

Sources: EIU, *Country Profile*, 1987–88, p. 17; Iancu (1989: 125); *FT*, 14 April 1988, p. 3.
For rates of growth of NMP and GNP, and for net hard currency debt, see Table 15.1.

'systematization' was aimed at integrating the rural population into the socialist economy and was viewed officially as a means of creating 'one unified population of workers'. In a 28 November speech Ceausescu hinted at some possible policy amelioration in saying that a considerable number of villages could already be rated as 'genuine agro-industrial towns'. Ceausescu stressed the gradual and long-term nature of the programme, and no deadline was set (Ronnas 1989: 547). Each family with a farming background was initially deemed to be entitled to a private plot of up to 250 square metres; this was reduced to eighty for others (*EEN*, 1988, vol. 2, no. 22, p. 3). In November 1988, however, a general figure of 300 square metres was announced (*EEN*, 1988, vol. 2, no. 25, p. 5). The process did not get far. Between 1970 and 1980 the number of villages fell by twenty (Ronnas 1989: 557). Only ten were completely destroyed (Victoria Clark, *The Independent*, 5 January 1990, p. 12).

The private sector

Individual farms were mostly in mountainous regions and were subjected to a 5 ha maximum (Bethkenhagen in DIW 1989: 250). In 1980, as a percentage of agricultural land, individual farms accounted for 9.4 per cent, the private plots of co-operative farmers 6.2 per cent, co-operatives 54.4 per cent, state farms 13.6 per cent and other state lands 16.4 per cent (Turnock 1986: 184). In

1985 the percentage division of the agricultural area by sector was as follows: private 9.5; co-operatives 60.8; and state 29.7 (Iancu 1989: 125). In 1981 the private sector as a whole accounted for nearly 14 per cent of cereal output, more than 22 per cent of maize, over 60 per cent of potatoes, more than 40 per cent of vegetables, 93.9 per cent of fruit, nearly 44 per cent of meat, almost 60 per cent of milk and eggs, and over 46 per cent of wool (Shafir 1985: 45). In 1985 the private sector occupied 14 per cent of arable land and was responsible for 59 per cent of potatoes, 40 per cent of vegetables, 63 per cent of fruit, 48 per cent of meat, 59 per cent of milk, and 57 per cent of eggs (Cochrane 1988: 48). According to Wädekin (1990c: 249), in the early 1980s 40 per cent of total agricultural output was contributed by the private sector. A more recent estimate puts the contribution of 'peasant holdings' at 30 per cent of agricultural output (Bridget Bloom, *FT,* 26 January 1990, p. 42). Obligatory elements persisted. For example, there were mandatory quotas for products such as potatoes, milk and eggs, and from 1986 plotholders were required to devote 500 square metres to wheat. This was to be delivered to the collective farm in return for the lower yield from an equivalent area on the collective farm (Cochrane 1988: 49). There was a theoretical maximum limit of 0.15 ha for private plots, but in practice this was often restricted to 250 square metres (*EEN*, 1988, vol. 2, no. 15, p. 4). Montias (1991: 188) refers to private plots generally being limited to a quarter of a hectare and subject to confiscation by the management if an insufficient amount of time was worked on the collective farm.

FOREIGN TRADE, DEBT AND INVESTMENT

Foreign trade and debt

According to OECD figures, Romania exported 11.2 per cent of its GDP in 1988 (FT, 29 June 1990, p. 2). Romania's more independent role in foreign policy cost it dear in terms of the lack of access to cheap Soviet oil (due to the Moscow price formula) following the 1973–74 and 1979 OPEC price hikes. The cost was especially high in view of the massive expansion of the petrochemical industry and of oil refining capacity with exports to the West in mind. This capacity increased from 16 million tonnes in 1970 to 34 million tonnes in 1987. Romania became a net oil importer in 1977. Domestic production fell from 14.7 million tonnes in 1976 to 11.5 million tonnes in 1984, when 9 million tonnes was re-exported in the form of refined and processed products; 10.5 million tonnes was re-exported in 1986. In 1988 9.4 million tonnes of oil was produced, while in 1989 9.17 million tonnes was produced and 21.8 million tonnes imported. It was not until December 1985 that agreement was reached with the Soviet Union to increase oil deliveries by 250 per cent over the following five years, up to 5 million tonnes annually from 2 million tonnes in 1985; in 1986 6.3 million tonnes were actually delivered. World oil prices started to fall in November 1985.

Romania continued to stress all-around, rapid industrialization, especially heavy industry, despite Khrushchev's plea for Comecon specialization. Crowther (1988: 132) traces the origins of the desire for autonomous industrialization back to a pre-socialist history of economic subordination to powerful neighbours. Ferrous and non-ferrous metallurgy, petrochemicals (even though domestic oil production was declining) and engineering were priority sectors during the 1970s, since they were badly hit by the world recession. The energy-intensive strategy of expanding the petrochemical industry, oil refining capacity and engineering was based on the expectation that exports of machinery and equipment would pay for oil imports and for other raw materials, and that these would be processed with the aid of Western capital goods bought with borrowed funds to provide hard currency exports.

In late 1981, following Poland, Romania asked to reschedule its hard currency debt, by which time the debt–service ratio was 35 per cent. Service payments were suspended in early 1982 and rescheduling took place in 1982, 1983 and 1986, the last partly due to the effects of Chernobyl on exports of foodstuffs. Romania's response was a severe, IMF-inspired austerity programme, mainly affecting imports, defence and domestic consumption, in order to try to repay the debt by 1990.[4] The idea was to avoid such overdependence again. Hard currency trade surpluses were achieved in 1983, 1984, 1985 and 1986 as a result of a drastic reduction in imports and a fall in domestic consumption, and the net hard currency debt fell to $5.8 billion by the end of 1986 from a peak of $9.8 billion in 1981, as shown in Table 15.1. Borrowing, however, was to resume in the mid-1980s. In April Ceausescu announced that Romania had fully paid off its foreign debt by the end of March 1989 and did not intend to borrow again.

In November 1987 there were serious protests against economic conditions in Brasov and other places, especially pay reductions linked to the non-fulfilment of performance targets, redundancies, price increases, serious food shortages and fuel restrictions. These constituted the most serious disturbances since the three-day Jiu Valley miners' strike in August 1977 (the strike focused on the attempt to reduce wages and pensions when state production targets were not met), although unrest and strikes punctuated the 1980s. Forced labour direction was also rumoured to be a factor elsewhere. State reaction included promises of short-term bonus payments, pay increases from mid-1988 onwards and increased food supplies, but the general strategy of rapid debt repayment and aversion to market reforms was confirmed. There was to be a change to a district-based production and distribution system, with each district allowed to retain output in excess of planned quotas. The harsh winters of 1984–85 and 1985–86 greatly aggravated supply problems, and drastic measures were taken to restrict power use by households. Rationing of basic commodities, especially foodstuffs such as bread, sugar and cooking oil, increased after 1981, when bread rationing was introduced after a gap of twenty-seven years.[5]

Romania joined GATT in 1971 and the IMF and the World Bank the following year. MFN treatment was given to Romania in 1975 on the basis of a relatively independent foreign policy and a liberal stance on Jewish emigration. Human rights abuses, however, caused second thoughts in the United States, and on 26 June 1987 the US Senate voted to suspend MFN status for six months while a review was carried out. The Reagan administration actually extended MFN for another year on 2 June 1987. But before the renewal date Romania 'renounced' MFN status and other trade benefits, such as US government-supported credits, because of unwillingness to make concessions in this regard. The share of foreign trade turnover with Comecon varied with the political climate. Between 1960 and 1980, for example, Comecon's share fell from 66.8 per cent to 33.7 per cent, and that of the Western countries rose from 22.1 per cent to 32.8 per cent. After that it increased once more (Shafir 1985: 49).

Joint equity ventures

Romania was actually the first Comecon country to introduce a joint equity venture law relating to Western companies in 1971, the Western contribution not to exceed 49 per cent. Profits were taxed at 30 per cent, with a surcharge on repatriated profits and a discount of 20 per cent on profits reinvested for five years (*EIU Country Profile*, 1989–90, p. 38). Ventures were few after early successes in areas such as textiles, electronics and engineering; prior to the December 1989 revolution only six were in operation (Montias 1991: 191). In May 1987 approval was given to direct links between Soviet and Romanian enterprises.

CONCLUSION

Ceausescu's Romania distinguished itself

politically by adopting a relatively independent foreign policy and stood out more recently because of draconian domestic economic policies established to eliminate its large foreign debt (fully paid off by the end of March 1989, according to Ceausescu). These caused civil disturbances even under one of the most tightly controlled political regimes, where power was mainly in the hands of the Ceausescu extended family. The 'systematization' programme aroused general condemnation. The economy remained highly centralized. Nevertheless, Romania introduced some novel ideas, such as a pale imitation of a self-management system, and was actually the first Comecon country to pass joint venture legislation as far back as 1971. December 1989 saw the demise of Ceausescu and a free election was held in May 1990.

NOTES

1. The goal was a population of 30 million by the year 2000. A draconian anti-abortion law was introduced in 1966, and the tax system was used to encourage larger families. Unemployment increased rapidly in the late 1980s; one reason was the large increase in new entrants to the labour force due to the increased birth rate following the 1966 law (Teodorescu 1991: 75).

2. In normal circumstances coal accounted for about 40 per cent of electricity, hydro-electric power 20 per cent, and oil and gas 40 per cent. The long-delayed nuclear programme was estimated not to contribute until the early 1990s.

3. According to Janet Heller, owners of private homes in general which were appropriated by the state were compensated by no more than 25 per cent of their real value. The aim in converting owners into tenants was to create a collective rather than an individual mentality (*EEN*, 13 December 1988, p. 4).

4. The strategy of very broad industrialization and constructing grandiose infrastructural projects, such as the Danube–Black Sea Canal, continued. The sharp reduction in imports was a major factor in the increasing obsolescence of the industrial capital stock.

5. Teodorescu (1991: 75–8) provides a useful account of the effects of debt repayment on living standards.

16

YUGOSLAVIA

BACKGROUND

Yugoslavia became an independent state in December 1918 (although the name only emerged in 1929, at first it was known as the Kingdom of Serbs, Croats and Slovenes), following the defeat of Austria-Hungary and Turkey in the First World War. The new state centred on Serbia, which had achieved its independence from Turkey in 1878. The assassination by the Bosnian nationalist Gavrilo Princip of Archduke Franz Ferdinand, heir to the Habsburg throne, at Sarajevo on 28 June 1914 sparked off the First World War. During the inter-war period a parliamentary democracy quickly degenerated and finally turned into a monarchical dictatorship; parliament was closed down by King Alexander in 1929. Maintaining the unity of this quarrelsome region remained a perennial problem.

The Socialist Federal Republic of Yugoslavia was proclaimed in 1945 under Josip Broz Tito, who led the partisans to victory, both against the Axis Powers and in the civil war. McFarlane (1988: 6) notes that in September 1944 an agreement was signed with the Soviet command before Soviet troops actually crossed into Yugoslav territory. Tito died in May 1980 and bequeathed an annually rotating presidency; the collective presidency consisted of nine members, eight from the republics and autonomous provinces plus the president of the presidium (President of the Central Committee of the League of Communists[1]). The major features of Yugoslav politics were:

1. The country's non-aligned status (the ending of the Cold War marginalized the importance of this). Tito broke with Stalin in July 1948 over the question of sovereignty and Yugoslavia was expelled from the Cominform.[2] The Comecon blockade (1949–53) helped push Yugoslavia into increased trade with the West and into a different economic system.

2. Its regional diversity and decentralization of decision-making.[3] Yugoslavia was composed of the republics of Slovenia, Croatia, Bosnia and Hercegovina, Montenegro, Macedonia and Serbia. Within Serbia there were the autonomous provinces of Vojvodina (with a substantial number of people of Magyar stock) and Kosovo (of mostly Albanian stock): their autonomy was substantially reduced in March 1989 and ended more or less altogether by September 1990. Slovenia and Croatia began to push for a much looser confederation, with independence in mind if this was not achieved. In free elections (April 1990 in Slovenia and April–May 1990 in Croatia) nationalists won in the shape of the Democratic United Opposition of Slovenia (DEMOS) and the Croatian Democratic Alliance. Serbia, on the other hand, was in favour of a Serbian-dominated, strong federation. The situation deteriorated drastically in 1991, as explained in Chapter 25.

Besides linguistic, religious, cultural and ethnic differences, there were economic gulfs in terms of *per capita* income and levels of unemployment, despite regional aid, with wealthy Slovenia at one end of the spectrum and poor

Kosovo at the other. McFarlane (1988: 60) gives some illuminating statistics for 1981, comparing the respective figures for the unemployment rate (the Yugoslav average was 12.6 per cent) and for social product per inhabitant (the Yugoslav average being equal to 100): 1.3 per cent and 205.8 for Slovenia, and 27.3 per cent and 26.8 for Kosovo. In 1985 Slovenia scored 201 and Macedonia only 65 in relation to the average Yugoslav *per capita* social product equal to 100 (Artesien 1989: 14). Anthony Robinson (*FT*, 5 July 1991, p. 2) cites some 1990 figures in dinars for average monthly salaries: Yugoslavia (average) 4,122; Slovenia (the highest) 5,528; and Kosovo (the lowest) 2,244. Samuel Brittan (*FT*, 9 September 1991, p. 15) cites the following figures for 1990: the unemployment rate was 20 per cent for Yugoslavia on average, 5 per cent for Slovenia and 65 per cent for Kosovo, while GNP *per capita* was $5,434, $12,618 and $1,302 respectively.

Federal decision-making in this country of over 23 million was often delayed or thwarted altogether by the veto power exercised by self-interested republics, with economic consequences in the form of wasteful duplication of capacities and the lack of national product and capital markets. Inter-republican relationships deteriorated in the late 1980s. For example, Serbia began a boycott of Slovenian goods in late November 1989. During Gorbachev's March 1988 visit to Yugoslavia, the joint declaration went beyond the 1955 and 1956 Khrushchev–Tito agreements, recognizing that no one had a monopoly of truth and that the Soviet Union could benefit from the experience of the Yugoslav system of self-management. Countries had a right to choose their own ways of social development and the threat or use of force to interfere in the internal affairs of other states should be ruled out. Gorbachev conceded Soviet blame for the 1948 split and viewed non-alignment in a positive light. On 22 January 1990, at its congress, the League of Communists decided to abolish the leading role of the party (although some independent parties already

existed in reality). On 29 July 1990 Prime Minister Ante Markovic (he assumed that role in January 1989) announced that he was to form a new all-Yugoslav party, the League of Reform Forces.

The Yugoslav Communist Party inherited a country in which three-quarters of the population was rural and the same proportion of the labour force was employed in agriculture. Land reforms in the 1920s redistributed land from large estates to small peasant farmers. By 1931 91 per cent of agrarian households were landholders. In 1931 68 per cent of peasant families owned only 30 per cent of the land, however, and there were many landless labourers (McFarlane 1988: 5). In the 1930s almost 70 per cent of farms were less than 5 ha (Dyker 1990: 5). Primary commodities accounted for more than 80 per cent of exports before the Second World War. There was good arable land for crops like grain and a variety of raw materials such as copper and bauxite.[4] The former Habsburg territories in the north (Croatia, Slovenia and Vojvodina) were relatively industrialized, in contrast to the subsistence agriculture that characterized the south. Table 16.1 summarizes the principal statistics for growth, inflation, and debt.

MARKET SOCIALISM IN YUGOSLAVIA

'Self-management'

A traditional planning system was voluntarily adopted initially. Yugoslavia, after the proclamation of the Basic Law in June 1950, however, developed a unique system of market socialism based on the principle of 'self-management' of the socially owned[5] industrial enterprise via an elected workers' council. An enterprise could be set up by the state, by existing enterprises, by a bank, or by a group of individuals. The principle of self-management arose from a desire to achieve Yugoslavia's own brand of socialism through decentralization, to further mass participation, to stress independence (neither

Soviet-type nor capitalist), to defend the country, to overcome the nationalities problem (and reduce regional disparities), and to avoid class distinctions between workers, managers and owners. The essential feature was that enterprises did not have state targets imposed upon them, but the state steered the economy both indirectly via economic levers and directly through measures such as temporary wage and price freezes. It was also possible for temporary management boards ('enforced management', which overrode the principle of self-management) to be set up to restructure heavy loss-making enterprises (e.g. the MKS steelworks in Serbia; reported in the article by Judy Dempsey in *FT*, 28 October, 1987, p. 6).

The basic organization of associated labour

The market structure was highly imperfectly competitive. According to Estrin (1983: 103), the bottom 20 per cent of enterprises produced some 1 per cent of industrial net output in 1966 and the bottom 30 per cent only 2 per cent in 1972, while the top 5 per cent of enterprises accounted for 41.2 per cent of industrial net output in 1966 and the top 1.7 per cent accounted for over 30 per cent in 1972. By 1973 only 4 per cent of industrial enterprises in the social sector employed fewer than 125 workers, while 57 per cent employed more than 1,000 (Estrin and Takla 1992: 263). In 1970 the largest ten companies produced 22.8 per cent of industrial output. Sacks (1983: 30, 33) maintains that in 1969 the fifty largest industrial enterprises were responsible for 26 per cent of total industrial sales and in 1981 for 53 per cent, the year when the 130 largest accounted for three-quarters of sales.

The large size of many industrial enterprises gave rise to concern that the notion of self-management would be compromised by the power of management and state administration. In consequence, the 1971 constitutional amendments, which were later incorporated into the

Table 16.1 Yugoslavia: foreign debt and average annual rates of growth of gross social product, GNP and prices (%)

1946–52	1952–62	1957–61	1961–65	1966–70	1971–75	1976–80	1981–85	1986	1987	1988	1989
					GSP						
2.3	8.3	10.4	6.8	5.7	5.9	5.2	1.1	3.5	–1.1	–2.0	0.8
					GNP (CIA)						
					4.6	5.5	1.3	3.5	–0.6	0.1	–1.0

				Inflation				
1952–62	1963–73	1974–79	1980–85	1985	1986	1987	1988	1989
3.6	13.0	33.3	48.7	72.4	89.8	120.8	194.1	1,256

	Gross hard currency debt ($ billion)			
1981	1986	1987	1988	1989
18.3	19.4	20.2	18.7	17.3

	Debt–service ratio		
21.0	45.0 (peak)		28.0

Sources: Mencinger (1987: 107–10); EIU, *Country Profile*, 1987–88, p. 34; 1989–90, pp. 10, 35; CIA (1990: tables 1 and C-20); Institute of International Finance (1990: 5, 20); *FT Survey*, 29 June 1989, p. 1; 6 July 1990, p. 37; 17 December 1990, p. 15; 27 June 1991, p.14; Estrin and Takla (1992: 265).

1974 constitution, meant that the Basic Organization of Associated Labour (BOAL) replaced the enterprise as the basic legal and economic unit (the enterprise now being a 'working organization of associated labour'; in some cases working organizations are grouped into 'complex organizations of associated labour'; Lydall 1989: 13) as the basic legal and economic unit. Each BOAL represented a stage in the production process, the smallest unit producing a marketed or marketable product. An enterprise constituted a BOAL or a group of BOALs in voluntary association. Each BOAL might become independent or join another enterprise, provided no contract was broken, and was represented on the enterprise workers' council and management board (Prout 1985: 65; Marer 1986c: 625). If there were more than thirty workers the BOAL elected the workers' council.

The manager was elected by the workers' council from a list drawn up by a nominating committee. More recently half of the members of the committee (compared to two-thirds at first in 1953) were politically appointed, including representatives of local government. The workers' council supplied one-third of the representatives, the rest being accounted for by the commune (local authority) and the trade union (Lydall 1989: 105). A majority of two-thirds of all members was needed for decisions. There is controversy about the distribution of the decision-taking powers between the workers' council and the manager and the danger, too, of over-generalizing. In theory managers were responsible for 'day to day' operations, but, in reality, their role was larger, owing to the greater technical expertise and information at their disposal and the ability to present ensuing alternative policies, and the fact that they also often exercised greater political influence.[6] Workers, on the other hand, tend to be more interested in matters of immediate personal concern such as remuneration and the allocation of tasks, and socio-cultural benefits such as housing. It is also difficult to pinpoint an enterprise maximand, since managers are influenced by such factors as growth, prestige, and political favour, but most observers point to 'net income' (wages and profits, i.e. gross income minus the cost of non-labour inputs, depreciation, capital charges and taxes) and perhaps 'net income per employee' (this would help explain the relative aversion to employing extra workers). If managers did indeed take the lion's share of decisions, this would tip the balance towards profit. Åslund (1989: 190) stresses the interest in maximizing state capital per worker; there was a tendency to level wages within the enterprise and maximize the wage level relative to other enterprises. Grosfeld (1990: 12) raises the problem of social ownership: the absence of transferably property rights is a powerful disincentive to be concerned about the net worth of assets. In this connection, for example, Lydall (1989: 76) notes that enterprises were not allowed to sell physical assets, at least not until they were fully depreciated. (See the section on investment planning below for further discussion of these points.)

PLANNING

In 1951 the Federal Planning Commission was scrapped, as was command planning. More recently the federal government did have the right to intervene directly, by imposing a wage freeze for example, but only temporarily and only to preserve the unity of the market. Of the economic levers, fiscal policy was weakened by the 1965 measures, which confined federal responsibility to areas like defence, foreign debt management, pensions, and the regional fund (only about 25 per cent of total government expenditure was then controlled by the federal government: Lydall 1989: 65), and the 1971 measures, which deprived the federal government of most of its revenues. The turnover tax, the main previous source of federal revenue, went to the republics, leaving such items as customs duties. Even monetary policy was weakened by negative interest rates (monetary control was exercised via credit directives and changes in reserve requirements); the unwillingness to see large-scale bankruptcy; and the avoidance of credit restrictions by enterprises that provided credit to each other. Foreign trade was steered by means of tariffs, quotas, licences and foreign exchange regulations. The intention over time was generally to move towards the market and the 1982–83 Kraigher Commission report suggested the creation of a more unified market economy and further reforms to increase efficiency.

Scholars have tended to identify sub-periods. Estrin (1983), for example, describes 1952–65 as the 'visible hand' period (involving, for instance, tight state control over investment and foreign trade) and 1965–74 as the 'market self-management' period (involving, for example, a significant liberalization of prices, trade and investment). Mencinger (1987: 102) sees 1974–82 as a distinct move away from market socialism, a period characterized by 'social compacts' and 'self-management agreements'. Estrin's term is 'social planning', while Ben-Ner and Neuberger (1990) use 'negotiated planning' (they see it introduced in the wake of strife between regions and groups and as a compromise between centralizers and decentralizers: p. 788). Contractual planning, which acted with the market, involved information exchange and agreements between government authorities ('socio-political communities'), trade unions and economic chambers (representing enterprises), which eventually led to a plan. Social compacts were not legally binding and mainly covered broad policy objectives such as prices and pay (principles determining the proportional division of enterprise net income between personal income, fringe benefits and accumulation: Lydall 1989: 60) at a republic or inter-republic level. Social 'contracts', as Schüller (1988: 41) calls them, were concluded between territorial authorities, economic chambers, trade unions, and the party. Self-management agreements, on the other hand, were legally binding contracts, dealing with investment and the delivery of goods and so on, between

economic agents such as enterprises and BOALs (see Estrin 1983: 72–7; Prout 1985: 71–2). Ben-Ner and Neuberger (1990: 786–7) blame the effective abandonment of the negotiated planning system in 1983 on widespread dissatisfaction with its performance, weaknesses including its collusive rather than competitive nature, and the difficulties of enforcing contracts.

Prices

Prices were mainly centrally determined in the earlier periods. It was the intention of the 1965 reforms largely to replace price controls with market-determined prices, but since fiscal and monetary policies were inadequate to deal with inflation, administered prices were retained (including temporary price freezes, e.g. 1 October 1987 until June 1988). Control was tightened after 1965 and by the end of the decade covered 70 per cent of products (Estrin 1983: 70). Until 1973 the prices of basic products such as electricity, sugar and oil were set at the federal level, and a number of other basic services and food set by communes. Wholesale trade margins were worked out by republics and retail margins by communes. Federally fixed maxima were set for important products such as steel and coal, while others were subject to notification and delays when seeking increases (Prout 1985: 165). Price controls did not cease after 1973. In October 1980 federal and republic 'communities of price' were established. These contained sectoral representatives of both producers and consumers and set prices after consulting the particular socio-political communities, 'economic chambers' and trade unions, using criteria such as market conditions and world market prices (Prout 1985: 168). According to the EIU (*Country Profile*, 1987–88, p. 14), by November 1986, 39 per cent of goods prices were freely determined. As a result of liberalization this figure had risen to 70 per cent by August 1988 (Aleksandar Lebl, *FT*, 12 August 1988, p. 2).

Remuneration

Yugoslavia is prone to inflationary pressures. One element in this situation is the strong proclivity of workers' councils to favour wages (the term 'personal incomes' is used: Lydall 1989: 76) at the expense of reinvestment when allocating net revenue. This is due to such factors as the workers' time horizon being limited to their span of employment, itself due to such factors as the lack of property rights. Pay policy has, therefore, reflected such problems (Prout 1985).[7]

By the end of 1957 wages had ceased to be a contractual element in cost. Until 1965 strict legal controls were placed on the distribution of enterprise net revenue (after non-labour costs and taxes) for remuneration, investment, socio-cultural expenditures and reserves. An important reason for this was to limit the growth of personal incomes, in order to generate the savings needed for the higher rates of growth of investment and national product. In that year, however, all such legal restrictions on the allocation of net revenue were lifted. Before 1955 taxes were levied on the size of the wage bill, but then, because of the increasing degree of monopoly, there was a change to net revenue: specifically, if net revenue was 25–40 per cent of the total wage bill, a tax from zero to 9.4 per cent was payable, while a 60 per cent proportion meant a rate of 37.3 per cent (McFarlane 1988: 152). In 1965 the net revenue tax was scrapped and taxes were thus imposed solely on personal income funds. (At the same time the capital charge on fixed assets was reduced; it was scrapped altogether in 1971 and replaced by a compulsory payment into the Federal Fund for the Less Developed Regions; the Union was to increase the proportion of investment financed by the enterprise: Dyker 1990: 64.) In 1972 pay control switched to the social compact system, while there have also been periodic temporary wage freezes, for example in 1983 and 1987. The constant concern about money wage rises greatly exceeding productivity increases culminated in the 'intervention law' (operative 1 March 1987), which reduced wages to the average level of the final quarter of 1986, froze them until June 1987 and linked future increases to the growth of productivity. Adverse reaction included strikes: official figures show 851 strikes involving 88,000 workers in 1986, and 1,570 and 365,000 respectively in 1987. This led to qualifying measures: the prices of products increasing more than 20 per cent were to be pegged at the 31 December 1986 level (20 March 1987), and wage regulations were not to apply to tourism, construction, education and health or industries with 'long-run production cycles'.

The role of trade unions has been reduced to what McFarlane (1988: 197) describes as something little different from that of advisory bodies or social welfare agencies. Specific functions after 1952 included ensuring that legal minimum wages were paid and fulfilling an educational–cultural role, while the 1974 constitutional changes left each republic's government to deal with its own union movement (p. 53). Trade unions are officially responsible for nominating the members of the workers' council (Lydall 1989: 20).

Although actual bankruptcies have been few, unemployment is a serious problem: this despite the fact that more than 500,000 Yugoslavs work abroad. The average unemployment rate was 14.8 per cent in 1989 (Prasnikar and Pregl 1991: 192), but there were large regional variations. According to Laura Silber (FT Survey, 6 July 1990, p. 38), the mid-1990 unemployment rate in Kosovo was nearly double the national average of 18 per cent. Lay-offs are few, but the enterprise had to find alternative jobs for those workers made redundant for economic reasons. There was no federal or uniform system of unemployment benefit; only 3 per cent of the jobless were given financial compensation while unemployed (FT Survey, 22 June 1988, p.iv). A new law operative since 1 January 1987 gave loss-making enterprises six months to recoup the previous year's losses, during which wages were reduced to the minimum level.

Failure to respond allegedly resulted in bankruptcy.

Estrin *et al.* (1988: 465–77) point out that the widening of inter-firm and inter-industry income differentials since the late 1950s was a major problem. Their conclusion is that the main reasons are to be found in labour allocation factors (such as immobility) and monopoly power rather than in capital market imperfections which permitted capital rents to be appropriated as workers' income. Estrin (1991: 192) notes that the entry of new enterprises was very limited even in the period of maximum reliance on the market (1965–73) and non-existent thereafter. Because all new enterprises of any size had to be socially owned, only the political authorities had an incentive to establish new ones and these authorities concentrated on existing enterprises; these existing ones were averse to employing new workers.

Investment planning

The social investment system was in operation until the end of 1963 (Prout 1985). Essentially this involved the centre deciding upon aggregate investment and its sectoral allocation. The banking system supposedly granted branch credits to enterprises on the basis of such criteria as expected rate of return, the degree of self-financing and foreign trade implications. Estrin (1983: 65), however, considers that, in reality, political and regional factors predominated. After that date the Federal Investment Fund was scrapped and its assets were distributed to three banks (for investment, foreign trade and agriculture). A new investment fund involving concessionary loans to aid the less developed areas was established in 1966, however, financed from enterprise contributions. Under the contractual agreement system, social compacts included investment targets, which firms competed for and ultimately incorporated into self-management agreements (Prout 1985: 74; see also Marer 1986c: 627). Under this 'self-management planning system', planning agents were meant to harmonize their programmes with other relevant parties (Bendekovic and Teodorovic 1988: 257). By the end of the 1960s investment was financed in the following ways: approximately 10 per cent budgetary, 45 per cent bank credit, and 45 per cent enterprises (Bleaney 1988: 136).

Major problems in the field of investment included substantial duplication between republics (typically plants are too small to reap all the economies of scale), general over-investment due to this duplication, the growth motivation of managers and local leaders, and the existence of negative interest rates (which themselves enhanced the desire to use funds locally; note also that eventually no capital charge was imposed by the state on an enterprise's capital stock). Lydall (1989: 89) argues that local or regional authorities were disinclined to set up enterprises which would compete with existing ones in their own areas. There was also a strong incentive to invest using bank credits, because failure was unlikely given the state's unwillingness to allow bankruptcies. In any case, it was difficult to attach blame. All this encouraged irresponsibility. The unwillingness of banks and government authorities to bankrupt enterprises was an important cause of the growth of credit, which fuelled increases in the money supply and hence inflation; this reached 290 per cent by January 1989 (see Table 16.1). Lydall (1989: 3) cites a report by Bajt which found that the productivity of Yugoslav fixed investment was only 70–75 per cent of the average of that of Portugal, Spain, Greece and Turkey over the period 1960–80.

One enterprise could eventually invest in another at an agreed rate of return or for a share in profits, but the former was not entitled to management rights and was unable to sell its holding (Bleaney 1988: 142).

Banking

The process of consolidation that began in 1946 ended with two banks, the National Bank and the Investment Bank, the latter exercising control over investments and foreign borrowing. By the 1950s six regional state banks, mainly serving agriculture, and ninety communal banks had been established, although the latter were scrapped in 1952. A Foreign Trade Bank and an Agricultural Bank were also set up (McFarlane 1988: 89–90). In 1961 the National Bank renounced its commercial functions, while communal banks were reintroduced: two-thirds of their management boards were to be nominated by workers' councils located in the territory (p. 90). 'Basic' banks were controlled by their 'founders' (usually local enterprises but also local authorities) and most belonged to an 'associated' bank whose principal role was to arrange finance for large projects and to undertake foreign exchange transactions (Lydall 1989: 155).

The slackness of monetary control was highlighted by the 1987 Agrokomerc scandal (*EEN*, 1987, vol. 1, no. 8, pp. 4–5). Agrokomerc is a multi-product company in Bosnia-Hercegovina (originally employing more than 13,000 people), which was ultimately unable to honour the vast number of promissory notes it had issued to cover its grandiose, partly politically driven investment programme. These notes were automatically underwritten by the Bihac Bank in the same republic (the bank's chairman was Agrokomerc's deputy chairman) and purchased by other banks, which subsequently ran into financial losses. This was only the tip of the iceberg. (The promissory note system was introduced in 1975 to facilitate inter-enterprise transactions.) Agrokomerc's issue of uncovered notes (i.e. not backed by sufficient assets) began in late 1986 when the firm's subsidiaries started to issue notes to themselves and to cash them at banks. Bankruptcy was avoided by creditors agreeing to write off nearly 50 per cent of the debt, with repayments of the rest spread over five years.

More recent banking policy involved the phasing out of the present commercial banks and the setting up of new ones, in which at least ten enterprises contributed to the start-up capital. The boards of directors were to be composed of bankers, not enterprise directors. The bank assembly would nominate the executive board, but would be unable to authorize credits or be involved in business discussions. At the beginning of 1990 banks were allowed to transform themselves into private, limited liability joint stock companies and they had emerged as such by the end of March. Joint ventures with foreign banks were not allowed until 1989 (Uvalic 1991b: 202).

Some novel financial innovations in 1987 include the sale of negotiable debentures by the electric power industry of Serbia, and investment funds provided by Investbanka of Belgrade on a risk-sharing basis (rather than charging fixed interest). On 28 February 1990 the Belgrade stock exchange resumed trading, and Ljublyana and Zagreb followed soon afterwards.

AGRICULTURE

In the 1945 land reform an upper limit of 25–45 ha was placed on the private ownership of land (Dyker 1990: 10). The drive to collectivization started in 1949, but was made voluntary the following year, by which time a fifth of the arable area was affected. The compulsory sale of foodstuffs to the state at fixed prices was suspended and the Machine Tractor Stations were abolished. In 1952 the peasants were given the option of liquidating work co-operatives (McFarlane 1988: 99).

The private sector dominated Yugoslav agriculture, owning, in 1985, 80 per cent of arable land and accounting for 69 per cent of gross farm output (Cochrane 1988: 48) and 85 per cent of livestock. The 10 ha limit to private farm size was fixed in May 1953 (with a 15 ha ceiling in less fertile areas), but this was modified in two respects: (1) in hilly and mountainous regions republic authorities had the right to exceed this maximum or to reduce it in fertile regions (in Croatia, for example, the lowland maximum was 20 ha and the hill maximum 40 ha); and (2) in practice, land could be rented from other individuals. The average holding, however, was only 3.2 ha and can be fragmented into as many as nine separate plots (Cochrane 1988: 50). Only 6 per cent of farms had more than 10 ha of ploughland (Miller 1988: 235). In November 1988 it was agreed to raise the maximum from 10 ha to 30 ha (*The Economist*, 29 October–4 November 1988, p. 60). Private farmers were encouraged to join co-operatives, but this policy was not very successful in production, although it was rather more so in marketing (Cochrane 1988: 50). The socialized sector included agro-industrial combines (usually spanning the range from primary activity to sales of processed products), state farms and co-operatives (Cochrane 1988: 577). Socialized organizations accounted for most of input supply and of the purchasing, processing and distribution of agricultural products (p. 584). Dyker (1990: 109) notes that in 1967 the agricultural procurement monopoly of the general co-operatives was broken.

Although the 1965 and later decrees stressed the prime role of the market in price determination, in reality the state exercised control over the prices of major agricultural products such as wheat, meat and rice. (See Loncarevic 1987: 631, 1988: 250–8.) Prior to 1978 there were support prices: (1) 'guarantee' prices – intervention prices at which purchasing organizations or local authorities were obliged to buy if prices fell below the fixed level; and (2) 'minimum' prices – applying mainly to industrial crops; the purchasing organizations, mainly manufacturing enterprises, were not allowed to pay less than these. In 1978 'producer guide' prices were set at the federal level as guidelines for the price determination of major products; these applied to sales by social sector farms and to state purchases from private farms, and were meant to be relatively stable. Support prices, for example, could fall below the guide only to certain (varying) extents. The prices of other products, such as fruit and vegetables, were

Table 16.2 Yugoslavia: statistical survey

Private sector in agriculture, 1985 (%)	
Arable land	*Output*
80	69

Joint equity ventures, October 1987: 275

Private non-agricultural sector, 1986 (% total production): 5.7

Population, 1989: 23.69 million

Sources: see Table 16.1; Cochrane (1988: 48); *FT*, 22 December 1987, p. 12; *FT Survey*, 17 December 1990, p. 15. For growth, inflation, and debt figures see Table 16.1.

largely market-determined, but even here the republic authorities were able to set and guarantee prices. From 1 January 1985 onwards only guarantee prices were set centrally for 'products of particular social interest', as the major products were called.

From 1 September 1984 55 per cent of prices were market-determined, 33 per cent were set by agreements between self-management units and only 7.5 per cent were subject to direct government fixing (Loncarevic 1988: 250). But about 80 per cent of the total value of farm production was subject to official price control (Loncarevic 1988: 253). The prices of certain products processed by the food industry (e.g. flour and sugar) were set at the federal level, while others came under republican or autonomous region control. The regional authorities also set price limits for the wholesale and retail prices of basic products such as bread, sugar, oils, meat and milk. Important agricultural inputs such as machinery and fertilizers had their prices controlled at the federal level (Loncarevic 1988: 252). The following criteria were used in price determination: the production pattern; changes in labour productivity and in income; world market prices; and market forces (pp. 254–8). An event worthy of note was the creation, in May 1988, of the Slovene Farmers' Union, an independent organization, albeit under the umbrella of the Socialist

Alliance. Non-political, its aim was to further agricultural reform.

FOREIGN TRADE, DEBT AND INVESTMENT

Foreign trade

In 1985 exports accounted for 26 per cent of gross social product (Artsien 1989: 42). Until 1961 export and import price coefficients were used to steer foreign trade, but served to shield the domestic economy. In that year these coefficients were scrapped and tariffs were gradually to replace quantitative restrictions (Prout 1985: 21, 26). Trade liberalization ensued.

1. Zero protection for agriculture and timber; 10–40 per cent tariff rates for consumer goods and 17–60 per cent rates for industrial goods; in 1965 nominal tariffs were reduced from an average of 23.3 per cent to 10.5 per cent.

2. A single exchange rate was introduced. Several devaluations in the early 1980s were followed in 1983 by the introduction of an exchange rate which was adjusted daily to a basket of foreign currencies (Uvalic 1991b: 208).

3. National Bank foreign exchange allocations and import quotas determined the flow of imports: the aim was integration into the world economy and ultimate full convertibility of the dinar, but subsequent balance of payments problems put an end to this hope (McFarlane 1988: 121–2).

The allocation of foreign exchange

By the end of 1955 exporters had to sell all their foreign exchange earnings to the National Bank, while in 1967 a share of foreign exchange earnings could be retained by exporters. Six years later an interbank foreign exchange market was introduced, and the central bank bought and sold to influence the exchange rate (Prout 1985). On 1 January 1986 a new scheme relating to foreign exchange was introduced. This replaced the system introduced in July 1984 whereby enterprises transferred 54 per cent of hard currency export earnings to the federal government (allowed a share of enterprise foreign exchange earnings in 1963) and local authorities, with that part of the remainder not needed for their own use supposedly sold on the interbank foreign exchange market. In reality, however, very little found its way on to this official market, since more profitable transactions could be negotiated privately. The new scheme required all foreign exchange to be sold within sixty days to banks, which then resold. Enterprises no longer had foreign currency accounts, although individuals still did. The aim was to restore the foreign exchange market (and ultimately full convertibility of the dinar) and to reduce imports – the continual devaluation of the dinar made repurchase increasingly expensive. The scheme provided the federal government with a means of influencing the use to which the scarce foreign exchange was put.

The IMF and the path to indebtedness

Yugoslavia was a member of the IMF since its foundation and a full member of GATT since 1966. Stand-by agreements with the IMF meant that conditions had to be laid down in the period 1981 to 16 May 1986, when these agreements were replaced by 'enhanced monitoring'. This involved twice yearly checks on performance for the benefit of creditors, conceded after Western banks agreed to multi-year rescheduling. There was friction over some of the policy measures, the IMF consistently favouring positive real interest rates, the relaxation of price controls, free trade, a depreciating dinar, financial discipline, wages strictly linked to productivity and free markets for goods and factors of production.

Fresh stand-by financing was agreed with the IMF in April 1988 and in the middle of May a programme was put into operation that involved deflationary reductions in the money supply and in public expenditure, the lessening of price controls, wage moderation, import liberation and measures to increase exports.

The path of Yugoslavia towards serious foreign payments and debt problems is a familiar one (Babic and Primorac 1986). The basic strategy after the Second World War was to industrialize as quickly as possible, with relative neglect of traditional exports. Rapid rates of growth of gross material product were achieved (see Table 16.1). During the 1970s more rapid rates of growth of consumption, investment and imports (also induced by overvaluation of the dinar) than total output led to rising trade deficits. Institutional changes encouraged external borrowing. Specifically, from 1967 onwards large enterprises and authorized commercial banks were able to borrow abroad directly, while this concession was made general in 1972.

Heavy borrowing from the West during the 1970s as well as the recessionary effects following the 1973–74 and 1979 oil price shocks brought about severe foreign trade and payments difficulties for Yugoslavia. Table 16.1 shows Yugoslavia's foreign debt position over the 1980s. As of 1 November 1989 Yugoslavia owed the Soviet Union 394 million roubles (*CDSP*, 1990, vol. XLII, no. 9, p. 9). Deflationary measures were taken from 1978 onwards and debt reschedulings from 1983. Particular emphasis was placed on reducing imports at first, but increasing exports was later given more attention.

Joint equity ventures

There have been many changes since joint equity ventures were first allowed in 1967, relaxing the conditions of operation in the urgent search for high technology, capital and know-how. In November 1984, for example, majority ownership was allowed (up to 99 per cent), excluded fields were narrowed down to insurance, retail trade and social services (other than in health recreation), and on completion the foreign partner would be able to repatriate the full value of the original investment. It was announced in October 1987 that conditions were to be further relaxed, allowing equal rights for both partners, extending the scheme to all sectors except social services, education and insurance (although in the small number of customs-free zones insurance and reinsurance would be allowed), promoting small and medium-sized enterprises and allowing individuals in Yugoslavia to buy stocks. Further concessions announced the following year included joint power to choose management and to hire and fire workers, although the foreign partner must contribute at least a 30 per cent share of the equity. One hundred per cent foreign ownership was allowed from 1 January 1989 (except in sectors such as insurance and airlines) and private Yugoslav enterprises could latterly form joint ventures with Western companies.

THE PRIVATE NON-AGRICULTURAL SECTOR

In 1946 a maximum of five workers, including family members, could be employed in handicrafts, and in hotels three employees outside the family could be taken on. The maximum later varied between republics. Ten were allowed in Slovenia up to 1987, when the ceiling was raised to twenty. The republic also dealt with licence applications far more speedily than others. Misha Glenny gave a figure of 7.5 per cent of Slovenian GNP accounted for by private businesses and discussed further legislation meant to open up all manufacturing and service enterprises, including parts of the health service, and raise the employment ceiling to a possible 125 (*Guardian Survey*, 16 May 1988, p. 13). Treatment of the sector has varied over time, depending on the political situation, but it was encouraged in recent years. In 1986, according to Judy Dempsey (*FT*, 22 December 1987, p. 12), the sector accounted for 5.7 per cent of total production. The Markovic programme involves a fundamental transformation of the ownership situation.

THE 1988 NATIONAL PARTY CONFERENCE

The national party conference (29–31 May 1988)

saw much criticism of the failure to implement reforms and of unacceptable aspects of party life such as corruption. Short-term remedies included price increases (petrol, 32.2 per cent; rail fares, 38.5 per cent; coal, 30.3 per cent; electricity, 31 per cent; postal services, 28 per cent), while longer-term remedies revolved around deregulating the goods, money and labour markets. In November greater substance was given to reform ideas. The 'enterprise' was to replace the BOAL as the basic unit, with profit as the main objective; socially owned enterprises were to be permitted to issue shares and bonds, partly in order to tap the hard currency deposits owned by Yugoslav citizens at home or abroad,[8] estimated at some $10 billion and $10 billion to $20 billion respectively (Cavoski 1988: 47); 100 per cent foreign ownership was to become possible; banks were to become independent financial units and the National Bank was to act more like a central bank in a Western economy; price controls were to be exceptional (controls were to remain over certain basic foodstuffs; policy included raising the relative price of capital to labour); the private sector was to be encouraged and new forms of ownership were to include mixed state–private and state–co-operative.

CONCLUSION

Socialist Yugoslavia did not owe its existence to the Red Army, and soon after the Tito–Stalin quarrel of 1948 Yugoslavia launched itself into developing a unique system of market socialism based on 'self-management' by workers' councils of 'socially owned' enterprises. Private agriculture was dominant and the private non-agricultural sector was treated in a relatively relaxed fashion in more recent years (Table 16.2). The country disintegrated, however, under intense political and economic strains.

NOTES

1. The Yugoslav Communist Party was renamed the League of Communists of Yugoslavia in November 1952.
2. The Communist International Bureau, set up in September 1947 to promote international communism and Soviet control over the movement, was dissolved in 1956. Its predecessor, the Comintern, was dissolved in 1943.
3. There were two chambers at the federal level. The first was elected directly by communes in each republic or province, while the second (the Chamber of Republics and Provinces) was elected by a joint session of the chambers of the particular republic or province. This delegate system plus the unanimity practice of the latter chamber (which decided major economic issues) helps explain the difficulty of reaching federal decisions (Bleaney 1988: 139). Thomas Foran de Saint-Bar (*IHT*, 24 July 1991, p. 4) notes some unifying factors; more than 75 per cent of the population speak Serbo-Croat and 88 per cent are Southern Slavs.
4. Energy resources were not well exploited, however. It is also worth noting that in 1987 Yugoslavia decided not to build any more nuclear power stations, there being one already in operation.
5. The industrial enterprise is owned by society and not by the state; thus the workers' co-operative is able to use but not sell the enterprise's capital stock (Mirkovic 1987).
6. McFarlane (1988: xiii) cites workers' complaints that managers resubmitted proposals until they were accepted. On the other hand, note should be taken of managers' complaints that the decision-making process under self-management was extremely slow. Nora Beloff (*FT*, 5 August 1991, p. 13) cites Neca Jovanov's argument that decisions were, in reality, taken by 'communist-sponsored bosses'; the director and his aides, the representatives of the party and trade union, and the chairman of the workers' council (who had the task of getting the workforce to stamp its approval).
7. Inflationary pressure was also caused by the following: the operation of the soft-budget constraint; envy of earnings in profitable concerns; and the existence of several factors that encourage investment, namely the difficulty of pinpointing responsibility, regional

duplication and negative interest rates. Bleaney (1988: 150) attaches importance to the devolution of price controls to the 'communities of price' as an inflationary spur because of local pressure to gain resources at the expense of others. Enterprises' control over banks and growing inter-enterprise credit helped to undermine monetary control.

8. A novel scheme to attract the hard currency capital of Yugoslavs abroad was proposed in 1985. Three year loans to Yugoslav companies would secure a job for the person concerned (or a nominated alternative) as well as interest. Latterly restrictions were placed on hard currency withdrawals by individuals because of the deteriorating economic situation.

Part 3

THE TRANSITION FROM COMMAND TO MARKET ECONOMIES IN EASTERN EUROPE

17

GENERAL ISSUES IN THE TRANSITION FROM COMMAND TO MARKET ECONOMIES

THE TRANSITION TO THE MARKET: 'BIG BANG' AND 'SEQUENCING'

'Big bang'

Some of the leading proponents of this approach

Sachs and Lipton. A programme of rapid and comprehensive market transformation, comprising the following inter-dependent elements:

1. Prices to find their equilibrium levels in the context of an open, market economy with a convertible currency.

2. Elimination of restrictions on private economic activity. As regards privatization Sachs has changed his mind somewhat. In an article in *The Economist* (13 January 1990, pp. 23–8) he viewed 'large' privatization (see below) as a process which would take some considerable time. But he now advocates a much speedier programme in order to reap the economic benefits and to prevent political considerations bringing the whole process to a halt, e.g. the largest 500 industrial enterprises in Poland should be privatized within four years (Lipton and Sachs, 1990b: 327).

3. Discipline to be imposed on remaining state enterprises through the ending of soft budget constraints, demonopolization and exposure to competition.

4. The establishment of price stability in countries where there is severe macroeconomic disequilibrium. Where there is a serious problem with inflation, there is need for 'shock' treatment or therapy involving strong austerity measures (see separate section below).

It should be noted here, however, that there is as yet no generally agreed terminology. 'Shock' therapy is sometimes seen as a component part of 'big bang', while on other occasions the reverse is true. The terms are also often used interchangeably, e.g. the two overlap when price liberalization involves a reduction in expenditure on subsidies. The author's predilection is to keep the two terms separate as much as possible, using 'big bang' to refer to the switch to the market.

The following reasons are put forward by Sachs and Lipton and the others listed below for such a rapid and comprehensive programme:

1. Piecemeal changes cannot work because of the interdependence of every part of the overall reform.

2. The bureaucracy must be bypassed by market forces.

3. To avoid the problem of vested interests in shrinking sectors delaying reform. Changes have to be fast enough and fundamental enough to create vested interests in favour of the new system which are more powerful than those interested in the old one (*The Economist*, Survey entitled *Business in Eastern Europe*, 21 September 1991, p. 30).

4. Inflation must be brought under control in order, among other things, to generate confidence in the currency.

5. Partial reforms can hinder the remaining elements of the old system while they persist at least.

6. The new 'rules of the game' must be laid

out quickly and clearly to avoid turmoil, un- certainty and inconsistency (Sachs 1992: 7).

7. New governments should make use of the brief 'honeymoon period' allowed by electorates.

The Institute of International Finance (1990). If the transformation to a market-based economy is to succeed, it will have to be pursued 'more or less simultaneously' (p. 30). The reforms needed to lay the basis of successful liberalization are: market prices, a competitive economy with the dominant role played by the private sector; a Western-style banking system; a liberal foreign trade system; and a convertible currency. These economic reforms need to be accompanied by attitudinal and institutional changes (e.g. an end to inter- ventionist attitudes, the introduction of political reform, and the defining and enforcement of property rights). These reforms must be sup- ported by firm fiscal and monetary policies.

The Bank for International Settlements (Annual Report, published 11 June 1990, as reported in *IHT* 12 June 1990, p. 9: and *FT* 12 June 1990, p. 4):

> Partial reforms are likely to be met with only partial success. A step-by-step approach tends to disregard the close interaction between price liberalization, decentraliza- tion of decision-making, financial discipline and indirect economic management. It would seem more advisable to pursue a strategy under which the move to a market economy is based on a comprehensive plan with all principal reform steps preferably being taken as soon as possible. Rather than trying to mitigate unavoidable friction during the transition by suppressing and thereby slowing down the pace of reform, adjustment shocks should be alleviated by social policies which are compatible with the institution of a market economy.

The IMF (*FT*, 23 April 1992, p. 6). There is need for 'bold and comprehensive reform so as to put in place all the main elements of a free-market system from the outset'.[1]

Janos Kornai (1990a, b). Kornai argues that 'the shift in property relations towards privat- ization, the package of measures needed for stabilization, liberalization, and macroadjust- ment, and the strengthening of political support for these changes are inseparably intertwined. None of these tasks can be accomplished with- out completing the others . . . the various parts of the programme add up to an organic whole and offer a *comprehensive* plan for trans- formation'. Timewise, Kornai thinks in terms of completing a package of stabilization measures within a year of a new government's inaugur- ation (1990a: 103), but a set of market-clearing prices would take longer than a year to emerge (p. 152). But stabilization and comprehensive price reform (partial price changes fuel inflation as cost, price and subsidy increases impact on other sectors: 1990b: 140) must run together, e.g. to reduce subsidies, prices must signal the loss-makers (1990a: 159).

Henning Christopherson (EC Commissioner: introducing the European Commission report *Economic Transformation in Hungary and Poland* on 14 May 1990). The commissioner's remarks are of interest because a specific time scale is mentioned. 'I am not suggesting that they [the Eastern European countries] should attempt reforms by the big bang method over- night, but I am talking about rapid adjustments, perhaps over six to twelve months.' There is need to take a series of quick, logical steps to create market economies; reforms must be credible and pursued systematically, thoroughly and not too slowly if the behaviour of people and companies is to change. A stabilization plan is the first priority.

Anders Åslund. The transition has to be achieved rapidly. It must also involve a comprehensive switch to a fully fledged market economy with a strict macroeconomic stabili- zation policy, together with a comprehensive domestic and external liberalization (1992b: 168). Åslund notes, however, that the transition will last for 'years'.

Critique of the 'big bang' approach [2]

1. The oft-quoted idea that 'you don't try to cross a chasm in two jumps' (see e.g. Sachs, *The Economist*, 13 January 1990, p. 23) is a curious one to use as an argument in favour of the 'big bang'. Apart from the danger of not making it in one leap and disappearing into the abyss, it ignores the possibility of (gradually) building a bridge. Coupled with 'shock' treatment, a rapid change of system could put intolerable strains on society. Much of the economy inherited from the communist regions would simply not be able to survive in open competition with the rest of the world. East Germany is a first class example; even in the embrace of a wealthy 'twin' the overnight exposure of the relatively inefficient East German economy consequent upon economic and monetary union with West Germany proved dire in the short run (although, of course, East Germany is unable to devalue its currency). Attitudinal and structural rigidities are enormous, e.g. attitudes to work and labour immobility. Jonathan Steele (*The Guardian*, 21 April 1992, p. 21) is critical of those Western governments counselling rapid marketization and shock therapy in the belief that this is the way to prevent a revival of the old system; Steele considers that there is no danger of such a revival (in Russia), while the potential social and political consequences of shock therapy are unpredictable. There is also the danger that promises of a rapid changeover raise expectations of better times ahead to a degree which can only end in tears. The wholesale destruction of industry means loss of markets at home and abroad; it is much more difficult to re-enter them once links have been severed.

Estimates by the IMF for Eastern Europe on average (Bulgaria, Czechoslovakia, Hungary, Poland, Romania and Yugoslavia) indicate the dimensions of the problem: declines in GDP of 7.1 per cent in 1990, 13.7 per cent in 1991 and 9.7 per cent in 1992 (forecast); this was coupled with consumer inflation of 142.2 per cent, 134.9 per cent and 796.4 per cent respectively (*FT*, 17

September 1992, p. 6). Figures provided by the United Nations Economic Commission for Europe (1992: 57) show average falls in output of 10 per cent in 1990 and 14 per cent in 1991: 'The declines in output are so large that the recession which started in the fall of 1989 could now be described as a depression . . . whose depth is comparable with the economic depression of the 1930s'. It should be noted here that these falls in output are the result of a number of factors, including deflationary policies, the switch to a new system and the demise of Comecon. The precise apportionment of blame on these and other factors is the subject of a growing literature in itself (see, for example, *Economic Policy*, no. 14, 1992; Charemza (1992), who analyses the information gap; and Brada and King (1992), who dispute the existence of a 'J

Table 17.1 GDP per head among European countries, 1990 (US$)

Country	GDP per head
Switzerland	32,790
Finland	26,070
Sweden	23,680
France	19,480
Austria	19,240
Germany	18,970
Italy	16,850
UK	16,070
Spain	10,920
Greece	6,000
Portugal	4,980
Russia	4,610
Ukraine	3,680
Czechoslovakia	3,140
Hungary	2,780
Bulgaria	2,210
Poland	1,700
Romania	1,640
Turkey	1,630

Sources: The Economist Survey of the European Community, 11 July 1992, p. 26.

curve' phenomenon, an initial worsening of economic performance due to the switch to a new system).

2. The feasible speed of transformation is a source of debate. Of course proponents of the 'big bang' do not say that economies can be transformed 'overnight'. Kornai, for example, talks about 'step-by-step' changes (1990a: 54) and increasing the proportion of the private sector as fast as possible to a point where it constitutes the greater share of GDP (p. 80), while maintaining strict financial discipline over the declining state sector (p. 101). In an article on Poland (1992: 6) Sachs argues that the reforms can and should be introduced in three to five years, while restructuring may take a decade or so. Nevertheless, the 'big bang' critics point out how long it took the Western countries to lay the vital foundations of an efficient market economy, such as institutions, attitudes and laws to enforce contracts.[3] Jacques Attali, president of the European Bank for Reconstruction and Development, said shortly before its inauguration in April 1991 that something like two decades would be needed to bring a Western-type political and economic system to Eastern Europe: 'These countries need 2,000 billion Ecus over twenty years to organize their economies to the level of the rest of the world, but the main point is that the money will come from the reorganization of their own economies and their own savings' (quoted by Deborah Wise, *The Guardian*, 12 April 1991, p. 11). The Czech Valtr Komarek (*IHT*, 7 January 1992, p. 6) criticizes the idea of achieving a transition to a market economy in two or three years when at least a decade is needed.

3. There is the argument that giving initial priority to one element of the reform induces intense pressure to tackle the next one, e.g. price liberalization leading to urgent reform of the near state monopoly of production and distribution.

Sequencing ('sequential' or 'staged' programming)

The idea of sequencing springs from the doubts cast upon the wisdom and feasibility of recommending a rapid, comprehensive transformation of a command into a market economy. But terminological problems abound, with a real danger of fruitless semantic arguments. No one has ever suggested that *everything* can be done 'at once', so the argument revolves around the question of how much can or should be attempted at the 'same' time. 'Big bang' advocates do support actual major sequences, such as Russia's freeing of many prices (see below). The author's inclination is to view sequencing as a more realistic and productive approach than 'big bang', exploring the merits and demerits of various *sequences* or *orders* in which reforms may be introduced. There is, however, more agreement than may be apparent at first glance.

The debate is young, but macroeconomic stabilization where needed is generally seen as a priority. Measures such as lifting restrictions on the private sector can be rapidly accomplished. Structural changes, on the other hand, take time (compare the running down of a huge heavy industry/defence complex with the time it took the UK government to prepare just British Steel for privatization) and the speed of privatization depends on the methods employed (see below). Blanchard *et al.* (1991: xiv) argue that controlled privatization must precede restructuring on the grounds that *de facto* privatization would in any case take place in such a way that there would be a political backlash and failure of the reform programme. There is a general dispute about whether restucturing should precede privatization or whether the private sector would do the job more efficiently.

There is debate about, for example, whether price liberalization should precede or follow demonopolization (excess profits stemming from the lack of competitive pricing would be made in the case of the former, for example, while the benefits of improved price signals are initially lost in the case of the latter). The freeing of most prices on 2 January 1992 by Russia illustrates the problems. The advocates say that the benefits include reductions in queues and the monetary overhang, restoration of confidence in a currency, and dishoarding and increased production (the argument here is that, with staged price increases, supplies will be withheld from the market in anticipation of future rises, while consumers try to speed up their purchases). The sceptics point out that such a move not only risks a price–wage spiral and social unrest, but relies heavily on a pronounced supply response (both dishoarding and increased production) to increase the supply of goods (especially in the absence of large-scale aid and/or imports). The existing state monopolies are not conducive to such a response; indeed it is possible for output to fall in some cases, at least in the short run, as high prices result in a return of goods from trading to producing enterprises and, in consequence, a cut in production. Participants in the debate include Boycko (1991), who favours rapid and comprehensive decontrol of prices on the grounds of efficiency, credibility, the reduction of queues and the decrease in the power of bureaucrats over the allocation of goods. Blanchard *et al.* (1991: chapter 1) argue in favour of stabilization and price liberalization proceeding together. Rybczynski (1991), on the other hand, favours priority for demonopolization and privatization, to improve the supply response. (Note that 'demonopolization' in a structural sense involves the breaking up of large enterprises, but relatively low tariffs and state regulation via 'anti-trust' legislation are also aspects.)

Whether reform of the financial sector should come before or after reform of the goods and labour markets is also controversial. Lawrence Brainard (*The Guardian*, 12 November 1990, p. 15) suggests the vital necessity of reforming the banking system in order to make capital allocation efficient, especially the need to write off the vast amount of bad debt and to inject new capital. This could be done, for example, by the government replacing these troubled loans with long-term bonds that pay a positive rate of interest or by allowing in Western banks. One problem with the Brainard scheme, however, is that it is seen as part of a wider reform, in which 'Enterprise restructuring, privatization and banking reform must go forward together', which begs the question of sequencing. Calvo and Frenkel (1991b) also stress the importance of well functioning capital markets; they argue that reform of financial markets should be given high priority in the sequence of transformation measures. McKinnon (1992) argues that a step-by-step transition to a market economy needs to be supported by a proper sequence of fiscal, monetary and foreign exchange measures. He suggests how domestic tax and monetary arrangements might be better managed in order to avoid inflation and how, in moving towards free trade, explicit policies governing tariffs and foreign exchange convertibility can best parallel and complement the evolving constraints on money and credit in domestic commerce.

When to liberalize foreign trade is not clear. Portes (1990: 14) notes the experience of developing countries, on the basis of which it is recommended that liberalization of the current account of the balance of payments should normally precede liberalization of the capital account (in order to avoid capital inflows unduly appreciating the exchange rate) and liberalization of the goods markets should come before factor markets. *The Economist* (5 January 1991, p. 61) also notes experience in the Third World, where the order is usually stabilization and then opening up the economy to foreign trade, usually accompanied by devaluation. But *The Economist* cites the doubts expressed by Ronald McKinnon about the efficacy of devaluation in Eastern Europe, where many enterprises cannot even cover the cost of material inputs; labour costs measured in foreign currency will fall, but materials costs will be at world levels. Early exposure to world competition could devastate the domestic economy. On the other hand, say the free-traders, price distortions are eased and competition is introduced (especially important when there is a highly monopolistic structure of industry).

Murrell (1990: 224–7) makes some interesting points along Schumpeterian lines, focusing on institutional factors rather than static resource allocation. He disagrees with the idea that price reforms must come first, arguing that price irrationalities may not have a profound effect on economic performance and that price reform endangers job security. It may be better to delay such reform until the process of institutional reform is well under way. On a broader front, he argues against comprehensive reform, emphasizing the search for sectors in which the process of free entry is least likely to harm vested interests and in which the process of selection of the most productive organizations is least likely to be impeded (the Chinese 'household responsibility system' is cited as a successful example). Murrell (1992) favours an 'evolutionary' policy, one combining the gradual phasing out of the old institutional framework (the sudden demise of Comecon is used as an example of what can go wrong), active promotion of new private sector activity, and gradual privatization. He comments favourably on Hungary's handling of the transition.

Other points are worth making:

1. The sequences cannot be neatly ordered in time, one following on precisely when the previous policy finishes; the real world is a muddle. Indeed each sequence is a matter of degree, e.g. how many prices to free at once.

2. Sequencing varies between sectors, e.g. privatization can be achieved much more quickly in small-scale activites such as retail trade.

3. Sequencing also depends on circumstances. For example, Jude Wanniski (*IHT*, 2 September 1991, p. 6) points out that in countries such as the (former) Soviet Union where individual wealth is largely in the form of bank deposits, early price liberalization would wipe out this wealth and further reduce confidence in the currency and thus incentives. Wanniski recommends reaffirming the value of deposits with a gold guarantee in order to boost confidence and incentives. In a later article (1992: 23) he talks of government bonds indexed to gold or foreign exchange at a high rate. Calvo and Frenkel (1991a: 296–7, 1991b: 147) also make the point that the optimal pace and sequence of reform measures depend on the particular circumstances in different countries; these circumstances reflect varying historical backgrounds, institutions, entrepreneurial traditions, and attitudes towards the market.

4. It is commonly pointed out (e.g. Calvo and Frenkel 1991a, 1991 b) that the economic programme must be credible, that the government intends to stick to it.

5. Klaus (1992b: 75) calls for rationality and pragmatism:

We know that just as an economy cannot be centrally planned, so an economic transition cannot be centrally planned and administered. The economic transition is a process with many forces, many constraints, many policies. We have to react, and react rationally … So the sequencing issue very often discussed in economic literature is partly artificial, a rationalistic illusion of the intellectuals.

6. There is also the obvious problem, of course, of knowing exactly what sort of market economy is aimed for; the West, after all, offers a huge variety of regimes. It is worth noting, too, the section in Chapter 23 on the experience of the 'Pacific tigers', which provide alternative models of development ('A survey of Asia's emerging economies', *The Economist*, 16 November 1991).

7. The degree of consensus has increased over time as aspects like the time dimension and feasible packages are analysed more deeply.

There is agreement that the speed of transition depends on factors such as the particular political circumstances (such as the degree of popular support and the availability of Western aid). There is agreement that terms need to be defined more precisely. For example, Nordhaus (1990) is of the opinion that what may be referred to as a 'big bang' is, in fact, simultaneous *partial* liberalization of, say, prices and international trade (as in Poland).

The idea that a certain 'critical mass' (minimum scale) is needed before transformation can really get going is a worthwhile avenue to explore. Simultaneous action in as many areas as possible is needed; which ones, of course, is another interesting subject of debate. Fischer and Gelb (1991: 101) talk of the sequential introduction of groups of complementary policy reforms; they suggest the need for a large initial bundle, including macroeconomic stabilization (where necessary), price reform, trade reform, small-scale privatization and emergency unemployment insurance.

The G7 (Group of Seven major industrial democracies)-commissioned report on the Soviet economy (page references below refer to IMF *et al.* 1990; see also a summary in *OECD Observer*, April–May 1991, no. 169, pp. 11–16) may possibly be described as a 'modified' big bang programme. 'The transformation of the Soviet economy is bound to be extraordinarily complex and will take may years to complete' (p. 16). 'Time will be needed to complete this process but the initial changes have to be sufficiently deep and wide that they are seen to mark an irrevocable break with the past and to establish a climate in which private economic activities are encouraged and protected' (p. 47). These initial changes must comprise three closely related elements:

1. *Macroeconomic stabilization*. This should be a strong programme, designed to reduce the budget deficit rapidly to or below the level of 2–3 per cent of GDP (p. 18).

2. *Immediate decontrol of most prices* (p. 18). There is a need for a significant and broad-based liberalization of prices in an environment of increased domestic and external competition (p. 47). A few prices for key industrial inputs (especially energy) might be adjusted progressively to world levels, perhaps over three years after an initial sharp adjustment. There should also be controls on housing rents (temporarily) and on the prices charged by public utilities. A social safety net (including unemployment compensation) will be needed to protect the most vulnerable from the short-term adverse consequences of the reform process (until a comprehensive system can be set up) and in the early stages of the transition an incomes policy should be used to put a ceiling and a floor on wage increases. It may also be necessary to shield a few sectors from intense international competition for a short period (e.g. by tariffs, but not quotas).

3. *Ownership reform*. Initially, the development of the private sector should be fostered by the rapid privatization of small enterprises, especially in transport, storage and distribution services (p. 27). The privatization of larger enterprises will necessarily take longer, but the 'commercialization' of large state-owned enterprises (making them financially and managerially autonomous) should be proceeded with in order to subject them to a hard budget constraint (exceptions could include temporary assistance to viable enterprises in the course of restructuring).

There is also general agreement that the sort of 'tinkering' with the economic system typical of the Soviet Union and most countries of Eastern Europe for most of the post- war period proved to be largely a dead-end. Schroeder's evocative phrase 'treadmill of reform' comes to mind, while Kornai (1992a: xxv) goes so far as to argue that the socialist system

is incapable of stepping away from its own shadow. No partial alteration of the system can produce a lasting breakthrough . . . reform is doomed to fail: the socialist system is unable to renew itself internally so as to prove viable in the long run. So the time for really revolutionary change does come in the end . . . leading society toward a capitalist market economy.

But certain radical partial reforms have been very successful on the whole, for example Chinese and Vietnamese agriculture. China's overall economic reform programme in particular is a major challenge to the 'big bang' arguments. For example, Chen *et al.* (1992: 222) argue that 'To a significant degree, China's reform demonstrates that gradual and partial reform can be successful'. They see as one key lesson the idea of a leading sector as an element in the sequencing problem. China's agricultural reforms provided the impetus to rural industry through rising incomes, savings and surplus labour, rural industry in turn becoming a leading sector. Even the partial reforms in urban industry produced some positive results, spurred on by competition from non-state enterprises. The authors are aware, however, of the limitations of the leading sector argument for the smaller countries of Eastern Europe. Fischer and Frenkel (1992: 38) argue that, while gradual reform can be more successful in China, the countries of the former Soviet bloc have to move as fast as possible to transform their economies because of the collapse of the non-market system. Also China is a one-party state.

'Shock' therapy ('cold turkey' treatment)

This is the cure suggested for economies in severe macro-disequilibrium. This includes the situation where a large 'monetary overhang' exists or there is open inflation (e.g. Poland and especially Yugoslavia suffered hyperinflationary conditions in late 1989). Reasonable financial stability is seen as an essential prerequisite for introducing an efficient market-based economic system. For example, enterprise managers have no incentive to operate efficiently if they are always sure of being bailed out by the state (the 'soft budget constraint'). An interesting point is

made by Waldemar Kuczinski, adviser to the ex-Polish prime minister Mazowiecski: the Polish economic programme causes 'people to spend their hours trying to increase their income to get what they need, instead of spending hours waiting in line to get what they need' (*IHT*, 2–3 December 1989, p. 15). There is also the argument that the freely elected governments should use the 'honeymoon' period to gain popular backing for painful 'short term' measures.

Characteristics of macro-disequilibrium include large budget deficits (due to factors such as heavily subsidized basic consumer goods and 'soft-budgeted' enterprises), financed largely by increasing the money supply. The cure involves severe austerity measures in forms such as tight fiscal and monetary policies and strict controls over wage increases. The effects include 'short-run' declines in output, bankruptcies, growing unemployment and falling real wages (although simply looking at what happens to nominal wages and prices can exaggerate the fall in real wages in any actual sense because of former rationing, black market purchases and the decline in the value of money balances due to inflation).

The following points may be made about shock treatment:

1. The level of shock should depend on the degree of macro-disequilibrium. There is the danger of seeing deprivation and hardship as being almost an end in themselves or at least an automatic passport to future happiness.

2. The long-run prospects for reform may be excellent, but there is the great danger of a social backlash in the short run, a yearning for the perceived security of the old days. Political democracy and markets could become associated with intolerable hardship for too long a period of time. President Walesa's authoritarian tendencies may be as much a product of circumstances as of personality. Nikolai Petrakov, Gorbachev's ex-economic adviser, warned that 'The political aspects of shock therapy must be soberly considered and take precedence over

the economic' (quoted by John Lloyd, *FT*, 25 April 1990, p. 2).

It is essential to set up as generous a system of social security as possible (e.g. unemployment benefit, combined with labour retraining), backed up by substantial Western economic aid. This is not only to prevent any popular backlash, but also to help the government free the price system and allow hopelessly inefficient enterprises to fail. It is also worth reminding ourselves that the now much-admired Western economies have, to varying degrees, highly developed social welfare systems. It is not surprising to see that advocates of the 'big bang', like Sachs and Kornai, advocate generous Western financial support, such as for labour retraining, stabilization funds (to stabilize exchange rates and help make currencies convertible), cancellation of most foreign debt, and grants for infrastructural and environmental purposes. Kornai (1990a: 168) describes the stabilization operation as the best occasion for aid. It is not clear to what extent advocates of shock therapy and rapid market transition would modify their views were Western aid to be ruled out.

Blanchard *et al.* (1991: 90) make the specific point that there should be generous unemployment pay for a limited period, say six months, then a phasing out. Workers should then be required to take a job, enter a training programme or take part in a programme of public works.

PRIVATIZATION

The major defects of state or 'social' ownership (as in Yugoslavia) are those of potential property abuse ('everybody's property is nobody's property') and soft budget constraints (to use Kornai's (1992b: 7) famous term, where inefficiency is financed by governments unwilling to see unemployment and enterprise closures on a large scale. 'No state-run enterprises could ever go bankrupt. The result of that situation was the bankruptcy of the whole [Soviet] system'

(Alexander Yakovlev, *Moscow News*, 19–26 January 1992, p. 11).

The speed at which privatization proceeds depends very much on factors such as the method employed. For example, the free distribution of shares is considerably faster than a British-style sell-off via public share offerings. Jeffrey Sachs for one has altered his views, being originally rather gloomy about the prospects for rapid privatization. Circumstances differ, too, with some countries lacking sufficient individual savings because of open inflation (e.g. Hungary and Poland); in other countries, such as the Soviet Union, the sale of shares is seen as a means of reducing the monetary overhang. Other important considerations are:

1. Concern for 'fairness', e.g. the perceived need to avoid extremes of wealth distribution and to avoid the *nomenklatura* benefiting disproportionately (such as the early abuses by management in Hungary and Poland). There is general agreement now that the state must control the privatization process rather than allow individuals to feather their own nests. 'Spontaneous' privatization essentially means that 'those entrusted with state assets take possession of them in one way or another or initiate arrangements for their disposal to private agents'; earlier forms of uncontrolled or 'wild' spontaneous privatization in Eastern Europe involved 'a more or less sophisticated theft from the state or society as a whole', such as state managers obtaining shares or guaranteed jobs in the new companies (United Nations Economic Commission for Europe 1992: 231).

2. Concern to avoid any sort of 'cheap sell-out' to foreigners taking advantage of ignorance and lack of experience (especially in the early stages) while enjoying the benefits of foreign investment (apart from the package of scarce factors of production, foreigners provide a useful alternative to the domestic *nomenklatura*).

3. The question of whether to restructure the usually monopolistic industries before or after privatization.

4. How to avoid massive unemployment.

5. How much of the economy the state should still own or at least control via regulatory bodies. This is an age-old problem, of course, e.g. 'natural' monopolies where massive economies of scale prevail (see the section below on market socialism).

6. Whether to restore property to its former owners. Such restitution may be considered 'fair', but can constitute a serious obstacle to investment, e.g. in East Germany the slowness in dealing with claims so adversely affected the situation that the legislation was substantially amended. Cepl (1991: 367–75) draws a distinction between property returned in its original form ('natural' restitution), financial restitution, and restitution in the shape of vouchers exchangeable for shares in enterprises to be privatized. Cepl is dubious about 'natural' restitution because people entitled to receive property often have no experience of running businesses; delays involved in selling or even renting the property would reduce economic activity. Those who receive housing in physical form may find rent controls and tenant protection still in operation, while there are commitments to maintain the property.

It is not surprising, then, to find considerable disagreement about how, how fast and to what extent privatization should be carried out. The following schemes have been suggested.

British-style sell-off of individual companies via public share offerings

Some of the problems here are:

1. It is difficult enough to value individual companies in advanced market economies. In the Eastern European countries the problem is magnified many times and would mean a very slow process of privatization. Any need to restructure a company slows the process even more (e.g. British Steel and the UK electricity industry). Susan Viets (*The Guardian*, 28 May 1990, p. 9) estimates that in the UK only 5 per cent of business assets had been privatized in ten years. Two dozen companies have been privatized over a twelve year period (*The Economist*, 11 May 1991, p. 83). In 1979 the nationalized industries in the UK accounted for around 10 per cent of GDP and employed 1.5 million people; over the course of a decade or so some 50 per cent of the nationalized sector was privatized (Mullineux 1992b: 4).

2. Competition has often been neglected in the UK, with examples of state monopolies being transformed into private ones, e.g. British Telecom, British Gas. Doubts have been expressed about the effectiveness of the regulatory bodies.

3. It is not clear that public utilities (such as water supply) are good candidates for privatization. Indeed, there are many examples of successful state ownership in directly-productive activities, e.g. the French motor car industry and British Steel in the run-up to privatization. Even Kornai, for example, accepts state ownership in areas like roads and would tolerate 'small islands' of state ownership in directly productive activities (Kornai 1990a: 93, 59). There is the danger of going overboard in generally disparaging the state sector and seeing the private sector as a panacea. State indirect control via regulatory bodies over natural monopolies, like water supply, would still be needed even if they were privatized.

There is still some disagreement among Western economists about the issue of shareholder control. Galbraith (*The Guardian*, 26 January 1990, p. 23) draws attention to the distinction between ownership and control in Western economies: he argues that since ownership normally resides in shareholders, unknown to management and often exercising ineffective control, it would make no decisive difference were it state ownership (as in notable cases it is). Grosfeld (1990a: 12), on the other hand, makes the standard case that the shares of private firms are marketable, the share price reflecting a firm's prospects (including management performance); as a last resort a takeover is possible. The soft-budget constraint is also likely to be more of a problem with state enterprises.

It is important to note that small enterprises, especially those in the service sector, can be more easily privatized. The problems involved in selling off a restaurant, say, are insignificant compared to the case of a steel complex and it is no coincidence that small-scale privatization has been quick off the mark in Eastern Europe.

4. The UK and US model of relatively powerful stock markets with relatively widely dispersed ownership has been criticized on grounds such as lack of effective management control and short-termism. Corbett and Mayer (1991), for example, argue in favour of the German–Japanese model, where banks are more heavily involved in ownership and management and thus have a longer-term commitment to enterprises. Sceptics include Blanchard *et al.* (1991: 54) on such grounds as the banks' lack of experience.

5. In Eastern European countries there is the problem that some (perhaps substantial) portion of the funds available for share purchase arose from activities considered to be socially unacceptable, e.g. well paid jobs obtained through the influence of the communist party, corruption and black market dealings. This exacerbates the general problem of share sales accruing to the wealthier members of society (an especially acute problem in the case of auctions). The counter-arguments are that it is extremely difficult to distinguish ill-gotten gains and that it is better to employ 'dirty' money in productive activities today.

Holding companies

Blanchard and Layard (1990) recommend a speedy move to private ownership, in order to provide the right incentives to enterprises, ideally by giving the nation's capital to the people. Enterprises should be grouped into (say five) holding companies and each individual (including children, although they would not be allowed to sell while they remain as such) would be given so many shares in each company in order to diversify portfolios. During

their lifetime (perhaps ten years) the holding companies would reorganize (even close) and sell enterprises. Adult citizens would be allowed to trade their shares (for cash or enterprise shares) in a phased process (perhaps 20 per cent in the first year, rising to 100 per cent by the fourth). Blanchard *et al.* (1991: Chapter 2) also see holding companies playing an important though preferably not exclusive role (they see merit in the government holding some shares as a source of revenue, workers being given some shares in their own enterprises, and pension funds being given some shares as a way of partly funding the retirement scheme). Holding companies are supported for reasons of speed, fairness and control (which necessitates the existence of owners with a substantial stake in enterprises).

Various criticisms have been levelled at schemes. Christopher Bobinski and Martin Wolf (*FT*, 2 August 1990, p. 16) list the following:

1. A small number of holding companies aggravates the problem of monopoly.

2. The political difficulty of not being able to allow the collapse of such large bodies could mean a soft budget constraint.

Borensztein and Kumar (1991: 321), on the other hand, argue that the limited time span helps overcome the potential problem of financial intermediaries becoming new government agencies with questionable incentives to respond to enterprise mismanagement and susceptible to bureaucracy or worker pressure against restructuring. A soft budget constraint could operate in order to prevent large-scale unemployment.

Mutual funds

Unlike holding companies, which have sole control over their enterprises, mutual funds hold enough shares in each enterprise to exercise influence. Andrzej Repaczynski and Roman Frydman (reported by Christopher Bobinski and Martin Wolf, *FT*, 2 August 1990, p. 16, and Borensztein and Kumar 1991) suggest the following scheme. Vouchers should be issued free to the population. These could be transferred to mutual funds in return for fund shares (some direct purchases of shares in enterprises by individuals is not ruled out). The funds would use vouchers to 'buy' shares in different state enterprises in a series of auctions. This scheme ensures both speed and 'fairness'. The other advantage is that control can be exercized over management: numerous individual owners cannot do this. The spontaneously emerging mutual funds may have to be mainly run by Western financial institutions, at least at first.

Mutual funds, however, may offer unrealistic capital gains to attract the vouchers distributed to individuals. Liquidity problems stemming from this include the possibility of a 'short term' attitude to profits at a time when the opposite is needed and even an early mass sale of shares when stock markets are in their infancy.

Enterprises owned by their own workers

Although a certain percentage of the shares of any particular enterprise being distributed to its own workers is a common feature of many actual schemes (to help cultivate an interest in the overall financial viability of the firm and make any austerity programme and indeed the whole privatization process more acceptable), 100 per cent transfer raises a number of problems.

1. It seems unfair that workers, who represent only a part of society, should receive all shares. In Poland, for example, the industrial workforce only constitutes one-third of the total workforce (Sachs and Lipton 1990: 61). There is the particular problem of retired workers.

2. The profitability of enterprises varies enormously – some may go bankrupt, while workforces in highly profitable sectors would benefit disproportionately at the other extreme.

3. Sachs and Lipton think that it would not be sensible for workers to keep their financial capital and their labour earning power in the same enterprise; the shares of other enterprises

should be held, via a pensions fund, for example (1990: 61). The Yugoslav experience of 'self-management' is often seen as not setting a happy precedent on the whole, with, for example, a propensity to favour wages rather than reinvestment when net revenue is allocated. But it should be stressed that Yugoslav enterprises are 'socially owned'; there are no equity shares for workers to sell. There are examples of true, successful co-operatives, as in Spain (Mondragon); here the workers are also the owners. Nevertheless some critics fear that workers would actively resist production and employment reductions, thus hindering the flexibility necessary for restructuring.

4. It is likely that foreign investment would be deterred.

The sale of enterprises is possible, of course. With management buy-outs the incumbent managers acquire a controlling interest in the enterprise that employed them, while in the case of employee buy-outs a controlling interest is aquired by employees outside the management (Filatotchev et al. 1992: 265). Unlike a labour co-operative all buy-outs retain an element of vertical control by a management team (p. 265). While there is direct control and there are no 'absentee' shareholders, there are problems, e.g. the danger of assets being sold by the state too cheaply owing to the 'insider' knowledge of existing management (p. 268). On a lesser scale there is support for management having a shareholding sufficient to provide an incentive to take a long-run view of the welfare of the enterprise, while varying degrees of profit-related pay for workers have been suggested to help tackle inflation and unemployment.

The free issue of vouchers to the populace

The idea here is that the vouchers are used to bid either directly or indirectly (via holding companies or mutual funds) for enterprises due for privatization, overcoming the initial enterprise valuation problem and appealing from the equity point of view. The privatization process is relatively rapid, encourages public support, and is not dependent on adequate savings being available. The problems with this scheme include the lack of revenue raised for the state and/or for companies, and the wide spread of ownership in direct voucher allocation, at least at first, which could lead to difficulties in appointing and ensuring efficient managers.[4] The threat of a takeover, as a means of disciplining management, is not very effective with broadly dispersed shareholdings (Borensztein and Kumar 1991: 310). Vouchers are particularly popular where there is a lack of private savings. But there is a strong possibility that the poorer sections of society will rapidly sell their shares. This, in turn, leads to increasing concentration of ownership and the danger of an inflationary spending spree (Medvedev, *CDSP*, 1991, vol. XLII, no. 22, p. 10). A collapse in stock market prices as a result of a mass sale of shares would be a poor start to a new market system. Another problem is deficient information about enterprises available to ordinary citizens if the coupons are used to purchase shares directly and the related danger of 'insider trading' where individuals with special access to information make unwarranted profits. An alternative would be to sell to keen investors and distribute any proceeds to the public via temporary tax reductions (Mullineux 1992b: 19).

Frantisek Nepil (*FT*, 16 August 1989, p. 15, and letter to *The Economist*, 7 December 1991, p. 6) is concerned about pension contributions. He argues that, since the state invested these over the years in enterprises, a free distribution of shares would amount to giving away the pensioners' assets. Because pensions still need to be paid, the government will need to replace a part of its income (equivalent to dividends) by taxes. The people will, therefore, not receive the shares free but on credit. The costs and benefits of a free distribution of shares will affect various age groups differently, and there is likely to be an increase in consumer spending and a takeover by foreign investors as shares are sold.

Nepil argues in favour of a scheme whereby each person receives his or her due share of the state pension fund and then arranges his or her own private pension. Private pension funds and insurance companies would use the funds to buy shares in privatized enterprises. There is also the advantage that the money is not 'dirty', illegally or unfairly earned in the socialist era. (For a discussion of partial privatization via the capitalization of pension funds using the Treasury's shares, see Sachs 1992: 11.)

Market socialism

There are many variations of 'market socialism', but essentially it involves a market economy in which social ownership predominates. Nuti (1989: 85–105) presents a novel theoretical scheme which preserves the essence of market socialism, while simulating a capitalist stock market in order to gain the associated benefits (liquidity of equity shares; a meaningful current valuation of enterprises as an indication of past and future performance; and a mechanism for reallocating productive assets through mergers or takeovers). There are three stages:

1. Enterprise managers are asked to assess the current value of their productive assets. Other enterprises can bid for these assets, and the challenged enterprise must either release or revalue them. Tax and bonus provisions would encourage truthful reporting of asset values.

2. A stock exchange is set up. Each enterprise's founders (branch ministries, say) are issued with a number of shares equal to the enterprise's net worth, and these must be sold to any state agency (such as enterprises, banks, pension funds and insurance companies). Shares carry voting rights, including the appointment and dismissal of managers.

3. Individuals are excluded from ownership and control of enterprises, but are still able to risk making losses and gains on fluctuating share values via schemes such as bets, and loans or deposits indexed to share performance.

Nuti (1990: 13) himself is aware that market

socialism cannot be regarded as a blueprint in central Eastern Europe today, but thinks of it as a model that might have been, better than the alternatives experimented with in the past. Competitive leasing of state assets and significant state shareholdings in private companies are worthy of greater consideration (p. 15). To many, private ownership is essential. For example, for Winiecki (1989) there is no substitute for the risk of the losses and gains associated with the private ownership of capital assets; state ownership means nobody's ownership. Grosfeld (1990a: 143) notes that directors cannot be expected to behave as though they were the owners and would be subject to political pressure from all sorts of vested interests. Kornai believes that the problem is that 'state property belongs to everyone and to no one' (1990a: 51), and refers to the Hungarian experience, where direct bureaucratic regulation of the state sector was merely replaced by indirect bureaucratic regulation (p. 59). There still remains, of course, the problem of the degree of private versus co-operative/state ownership.

THE WESTERN RESPONSE: AID AND TRADE

Western Aid

There is considerable controversy about both the extent and the timing of Western governmental aid to the countries of Eastern Europe. Both problems have already been illustrated by the 'Grand Bargain' debate in the Soviet Union, where the advocates of such a programme stress the need for large scale aid to *accompany* the reform process. There is more general agreement as to the virtues of humanitarian aid (such as emergency foodstuffs and medicines) and technical assistance in such forms as expert advice in the design of economic policies, the establishment of market institutions, management training, and the setting up of legal, statistical and accounting systems and institutions.

The major arguments against *substantial* Western governmental aid are as follows.

1. The economies are unable to absorb such aid.

2. Large-scale aid reduces the incentive to make the often unpleasant changes needed to move towards market-based systems. Large-scale aid helps preserve the existing system. Indeed, domestic production may be adversely affected by inflows of aid in kind driving down prices. The country may become aid-dependent, a permanent 'basket case'. The extreme argument is that the illusory benefits of large-scale aid would simply raise expectations of economic improvement, the dashing of which would be dangerous; in addition the West would be blamed. In turn nationalists in recipient countries see a danger in Western interference; in April 1992 the Russian vice-president Alexander Rutskoi described Western aid as 'free cheese in the mousetrap'.

3. The problem of financing.

Those in favour of large-scale aid, of perhaps Marshall Plan dimensions (as is the author), respond as follows.

1. The absorption argument may well be exaggerated, but, in any case, aid can be used to *increase* the absorptive capacity of these economies, especially when aid is conditional on the implementation of market reforms. Technical aid on a *large scale* can be used to set up market institutions, but there is also vast scope for retraining labour and management and for improving the infrastructure (such as modern transport and communications systems), state administration, and the environment. These are essential inducements to private foreign direct investment, which packages capital, modern technology and know-how. Chapter 21 (East Germany) shows the potential for aid absorption.

2. The counter to the incentive-reduction argument is not only that this is not necessarily the case, but also that it is essential to avoid a social backlash against shock treatment and precipitous economic transformation, which could discredit democracy and marketization.

The most dangerous time is the period when the old system is collapsing and the new system is not in place; emergency aid on a large scale is vital to help counteract rapid declines in output. Too much 'shock' could be counter- productive and actually lead to a backlash against the market reform process, particularly as the 'pain' is largely here and now while the benefits are mostly longer-term and dependent on the success of the reforms. The United Nations Economic Commission for Europe (*Economic Bulletin for Europe*, 2 December 1991, vol.43, pp. 7–9) said that 'The declines in output in Eastern Europe and the Soviet Union are now so large that it would be appropriate to speak of a depression'; 'It seems likely that social unrest will increase in 1992 and that in some countries there will be increasing pressure to dilute or abandon the reform process.' The commission recommended a new 'Marshall Plan' of co-ordinated Western aid, albeit with emphasis on technical assistance in setting up market structures. The commission is critical of the idea of a 'big bang' market transformation and repeated the call for a 'Second European Recovery Programme' in its Economic Survey of Europe in 1991–1992 (1992: 9): 'Many of the people in these countries must now be wondering whether the invisible hand of the market is really an iron fist' (p. 4); 'A growing fear is that the increasing economic strains will lead to disillusion and impatience with both the idea of the market and the democratic process' (p. 1).

The author believes that there is a truly historic opportunity to demonstrate the best aspects of Western society and to help secure the world-wide shift to democracy stimulated by events in the former Soviet bloc. The West could and should have promised large-scale aid at the July 1991 G7 conference in London. The plotters of the August attempted coup in the Soviet Union would have been less likely to assume passivity from a population at least perceiving the prospects of betterment and Gorbachev's status would not have been weakened. As it turned out the failure of the coup precipitated the final demise of the Soviet Union, but it could easily have turned out very differently. Aid is now essential to consolidate the Yeltsin regime in Russia and other progressive administrations. Aid could also temper the growth of nationalism, which thrives under dismal economic circumstances. Aid helps sustain political support for reforms long enough for them to take hold (Jeffrey Sachs, *IHT*, 16 May 1991, p. 6). Aid would also help prevent a massive migration of people from Eastern Europe to the West by stimulating the domestic economies. In the case of the Soviet Union aid in maintaining oil production would help ensure stable world oil prices. Aid to ensure the safety of nuclear power stations in the former socialist countries would be of universal benefit too, as would aid to reduce environmental damage in general (perhaps in the form of corresponding debt reduction). Flourishing markets would be created in the longer run as a result of helping the new democracies to get on their feet.

There is general support for the idea of *conditional* aid, i.e. aid (excluding emergency donations of such items as food and medicines) linked to political and economic reform. But there is the argument that economic conditions, such as those laid down by the IMF, should not be overly demanding and that aid should *accompany* rather than follow reforms (or at least be disbursed quickly in tranches as each defined reform target is achieved).

3. The problem of financing can be approached in a number of ways:

The 'peace dividend'. Despite the not inconsiderable short-run adjustment problems, the end of the Cold War provides enormous scope for transferring resources from armaments to civilian production. After spending trillions of dollars during the Cold War, it seems extraordinary to say that billions cannot be found to aid the 'defeated' crying out for assistance. The 'pay-off' is immeasurable in terms of future security, and helping prevent future coups and the appearance of extreme right-wing regimes.

The USA alone spent annual sums in the region of $300 billion in the late 1980s. In 1990 the G7 countries spent $500 billion on defence (*FT*, 9 July 1992, p. 20).

The Gulf Crisis also showed that funds can be found if the case is strong enough, particularly if the reciprocal benefits are great. The Marshall Plan (European Recovery Programme) provides some perspective on what is affordable, even though it was literally a post-Second World War 'recovery' programme for essentially market economies rather than one to help the transition to a market. There have been various estimates of the size of Marshall Plan aid, an important benchmark by which to compare current efforts. During the three-and-a-half-year authorization period of the Marshall Plan, the USA granted 1.3 per cent of GNP; the EC could, on this basis, consider a total of $200 billion to Eastern Europe and the Soviet Union (*FT*, 28 December 1989, p. 10). The Marshall Plan represented 5 per cent of one year's US GNP over five years (*FT*, 24 June 1991, p. 16). In today's terms this represents the equivalent of $1,000 billion for all the OECD countries (Anatole Kaletsky, *The Times*, 9 July 1991, p. 23). Between 1946 and 1955 the USA (with a GNP one third of today's) contributed a total (in 1989 dollars), i.e. including the Marshall Plan, of $171 billion to Western Europe's recovery, i.e. $17 billion annually (Zbigniew Brzezinski, *IHT*, 8 March 1990, p. 4). Marshall Plan aid, in current dollars, amounted to more than $125 billion (Henry Kaufman, *IHT*, 11 July 1990, p. 4). The Marshall Plan pledged 2 per cent of US GNP, the equivalent of $100 billion today (Charles Krauthammer, *IHT*, 30 November 1991, p. 8). Susan Strange (*IHT*, 25 January 1990, p. 4) suggests that one of the clever ideas of the Marshall Plan was to offer aid ($17 billion in 1947 dollars, or about ten times that in today's money), but to insist that the recipients, not the donors must decide who was to get how much. *The Economist* (15 June 1991, p. 51) estimates that Marshall Plan aid delivered by 1950 amounted to $12.5 billion, $70 billion in today's terms. In 1950 this was equivalent to 4.4 per cent

of US GDP; $70 billion today is only 1.5 per cent of GDP. In current dollars the Marshall Plan cost the USA $75 billion (Georges de Menil, *IHT*, 17 February 1992, p. 6). Susan Collins (1991: 221) notes that the Marshall Plan transferred to sixteen West European economies an average of 2 per cent of their GNP per annum during 1948–51. The United Nations Economic Commission for Europe (1992: 8) talks of a Marshall Plan equivalent today of $16.7 billion a year. Edward Balls (*FT*, 21 April 1992, p. 6) notes the following: the resource flow was $13 billion between 1948 and 1951, the equivalent of more than $70 billion in today's prices and averaging 2.5 per cent of GNP; the aid was conditional on stabilization policies, price decontrol, reduced trade barriers and co-operation to revive intra-European trade. Eichengreen and Uzan (1992: 14–15) point out that the $13 billion transferred between 1948 and 1951 averaged only 2.5 per cent of the combined national incomes of the recipient countries over the period and that the aid could have financed no more than 20 per cent of their capital formation even at its height. They argue that the crucial role of the Marshall Plan was in laying down conditions, such as the liberalization of trade, production and prices.

In answer to the argument that countries could provide much of the funds themselves by reducing defence spending, it could be said that arms reductions are properly dealt with in separate arms negotiations and that foreign know-how and technology are still needed. But Western aid is also needed to help the conversion of defence production to civilian use (this would also curb arms exports by countries desperate for foreign exchange), the retraining of army personnel, the employment of nuclear personnel to prevent proliferation, and the destruction of Soviet nuclear and chemical weapons.

Note that 'counterpart funds' formed part of Marshall Plan aid in that an individual country had to establish a fund which was the equivalent of US aid in local currency, its use being the result of bilateral discussions. In current circumstances an Eastern European country could, for example, be made to spend local currency funds on pollution control (Susan Strange, *IHT*, 25 January 1990, p. 4).

A variation on this theme was put forward by the Czechoslovak Foreign Minister Jiri Dienstbier (see Anthony Lewis, *IHT*, 23 May 1990, p. 8; and Anthony Solomon and John Mroz, *IHT* 12 July 1990, p. 6). The idea was to establish a special fund in the EBRD (see below) (worth $16 billion spread over three years) to finance exports from Czechoslovakia, Hungary and Poland to the then Soviet Union in order to maintain trade and employment. Under supervision, the three exporters would be required to use the proceeds earned to modernize their economies, while the Soviet Union would 'repay' the credit by investing an equivalent sum in roubles. The major criticism against using Western credits to encourage the Soviet Union to purchase goods from Eastern Europe was that the old patterns of trade would be preserved for longer (there was also the allied criticism that US agricultural credits to the Soviet Union would discourage the purchase of products from Eastern Europe).

The European Bank for Reconstruction and Development (EBRD)

Based on an idea of President Mitterrand in October 1989, the bank's charter was signed on 29 May 1990 and the EBRD was inaugurated on 15 April 1991. Situated in London, its twenty-three-strong board of directors is headed by Jacques Attali (Attali thinks it significant that the bank is the first institution of a united Europe and of the post-Cold War era). Originally there were thirty-nine participating countries and two institutions. Shareholding was as follows: EC countries, the EC Commission and the European Investment Bank 53.7 per cent – West Germany, France, Italy and the UK hold 8.5 per cent each; the seven (former) Warsaw Pact members plus Yugoslavia 13.5 per cent (the Soviet Union had a 6 per cent shareholding, but its eligibility for loans was limited to the stipulated one-third paid-in capital for at least a three year period); USA 10 per cent; Japan 8.5 per cent; the EFTA countries 10.7 per cent; the other members are Malta, Cyprus, Mexico, Egypt, Morocco, Lichtenstein and Israel.

The bank was capitalized at Ecu 10 billion, one-third of the capital being paid in, with the remainder on call (although the bank can also raise 'special funds' to finance technical assistance and training). There is simple majority voting, although an 80 per cent majority weighted by voting power is required to alter the statutes. Funds can be used for loans at market rates of interest, investment in equity capital, joint ventures, underwriting guarantees, and technical assistance grants. Sixty per cent of funding (as a whole and for individual countries) is to be devoted to the development of the private sector (although state enterprises in the process of being privatized are eligible), with 40 per cent used for infrastructure investments such as transport and communications. (This split was the subject of considerable debate.) The aim is 'to promote private and entrepreneurial initiative in the central and Eastern European countries committed to and applying the principles of multi-party democracy, pluralism and market economics'. Priorities are to encourage the private sector, reform of the financial sector, and the environment and the infrastructure (especially energy and telecommunications). Attali also views the bank as a catalyst for private and public money to join projects. In the publication *Operational Challenges and Priorities: Initial Orientations* (released 5 May 1991), the bank saw its major role in the short term including a heavy emphasis on technical expertise, consulting and training.

The EBRD has not been without controversy. While the arguments in its favour finally won the day (a further means of helping introduce and strengthen market economies and political democracy in Eastern Europe at a time of uncertainty which limits private initiatives), considerable reservations have been raised. Foremost among these is that it duplicates the work of much larger existing organizations like the World Bank (with a tenfold lending capacity compared to the EBRD). *The Economist* (Survey 12 October 1991, p. 52) goes so far as to argue that the whole idea is counterproductive in that the EBRD attracts staff better employed elsewhere and leads to unco-ordinated advice. There has been considerable resistance to Attali's plea for extra resources to create a soft-loan facility to help especially with the conversion of defence to civilian production and with the restructuring of sectors such as nuclear power.

It is also worth noting that in September 1991 the new chairman of the World Bank, Lewis Preston, created a new regional office for Europe and the Soviet Union.

In February 1992 it was decided that 60 per cent of loans should go to Eastern Europe and the Baltic states and the remaining 40 per cent to eleven of the remaining ex-Soviet republics (the one missing was Georgia). The ex-Soviet Union's 60,000 shares (6 per cent of the total) would be reallocated, e.g. 40,000 to Russia and 100 to Turkmenistan. The eleven were formally admitted as members on 30 March 1992.

The EBRD's first report was published on 30 March 1992. Since its inception the bank had been involved in twenty projects worth Ecu 621 million ($765.3 million): in 1991 eleven loans and three equity (co-financing) investments worth Ecu 427 million and in the first quarter of 1992 four loans and two equity investments worth Ecu 194 million. Commitments were forecast to be Ecu 1 billion for the whole of 1992 and Ecu 2 billion in 1993.

The forms which aid can take

Debt forgiveness. It is notable that some 'big bang' advocates like Sachs put in a strong plea. Sachs argues (*The Economist*, 13 January 1990, p. 28) that any attempt by the West to collect more than a small amount of debt would, as he puts it, subject Eastern Europe to 'financial servitude' for the next generation, especially galling since it was the previous communist regimes which were responsible. Western banks should be pressed to accept debt reduction, and debt–equity swaps should, he believes, be avoided, since the new governments in Eastern Europe need the money. It is worth mentioning the arguments put forward by Leszek Balcerowicz (the former Polish Finance Minister) that a reduction in debt servicing is needed to convince people that their sacrifices are not solely for the benefit of foreigners and to attract foreign investment.

Grants versus credits. The argued emphasis on the former is because of the need to avoid further future debt repayment, at least as long as the level of foreign debt remains high. The counter-argument is that credits are more likely to be used efficiently.

A variation on a theme is to be found, for example, in some of the EC food aid being sold to Russian consumers rather than distributed free. The major benefits are to encourage dis-hoarding of goods, to reduce prices at a time of high inflation, and to use the revenue raised to protect the poorer sections of society.

Capital goods versus consumer goods. The case for the latter revolves around the need to provide incentives for people to work hard (especially in the painful transitional period), with such incentives lacking when shortages of consumer goods are severe. But both can be useful. Agriculture, for example, could benefit enormously if farmers were induced to increase deliveries in return for imported consumer and capital goods.

Trade versus aid

The two are not, of course, mutually incompatible, but the anti-aid lobby often speak in favour of improved access to Western markets for Eastern European imports, e.g. EC agriculture, steel and textiles. At the G7 London conference held 15–17 July 1991 support was given to opening up Western markets (including these areas) and it is of some interest to note that Western advice to Eastern Europe to switch to free-market mechanisms is, in turn, putting pressure on Western governments to practise what they preach (e.g. in relation to the EC's CAP and Japanese protectionism). Opening up Western markets is not only of direct benefit, but also helps the emerging market economies indirectly, e.g. direct foreign investment is stimulated.

The liberalization of foreign trade often features strongly in 'big bang' programmes, using arguments such as the need to expose the domestic economy to international competition and to improve prices. A switch from quantitative controls to primary reliance on tariffs and the exchange rate is recommended. But the main danger is that too rapid exposure to intense world competition would have a devastating effect on the generally relatively inefficient production units, as can clearly be seen in the case of East Germany. Merely allowing the exchange rate to depreciate (something which East Germany is unable to do) is not an adequate response. There may be arguments about the exact sort of protection offered to domestic enterprises (subsidies versus tariffs, etc.), but there is a powerful case for substantial protection, at least for the 'transitional' period. Otherwise the domestic economy could be devastated. There are likely to be severe balance of payments constraints as import demand is high and export potential often limited in the short run (due e.g. to the relatively poor quality of manufactured goods).

The European Payments Union (EPU)

There are a number of proponents of setting up a scheme similar to the EPU for Western Europe (1950–58), including Susan Strange (*IHT*, 24 January 1990, p. 4, and 25 January 1990, p. 4), Robert Hormats (*IHT*, 12 January 1990, p. 4); Gunther Schleiminger (*IHT*, 18 June 1990, p. 2); Anthony Solomon and John Mroz (*IHT*, 12 July

1990, p. 6); *The Financial Times* (21 November 1991, p. 24); and the United Nations Economic Commission for Europe (1992).

As Strange puts it, the USA used the leverage of Marshall Plan aid to force European countries to liberalize and expand trade among themselves but simultaneously allowed them to use exchange controls to discriminate against dollar imports during the transitional period to 1958 (otherwise the attractiveness of US imports would have quickly used up the dollars). Aid money was used to establish a multilateral payments scheme at the expense of bilateral barter. What by 1950 became the European Payments Union employed the scheme whereby once a month deficits and surpluses were offset and only the net differences had to be settled. Payments were initially in members' currencies, but EPU credit was available for a surplus and most of any deficit had to be settled in gold or dollars.

The idea that some such scheme may be applied to Eastern Europe derives from concern about trade between (former) Comecon members decreasing faster than trade with the West increases and that Western goods could prove overwhelmingly attractive. The suggestion here is that there should be a central credit fund and discrimination against Western imports. Van Brabant (1991: 161–3) sees merit in regional economic co-operation among the countries of Eastern Europe to buy the time necessary to restructure their economies while maintaining trade volume; this would prepare them for an orderly accession to the EC in the more distant future. There is also the suggestion that the members of the Commonwealth of Independent States could make use of a similar arrangement in the transitional period to a market (see, for example, *The Economist*, 1 February 1992, p. 100).

The scheme has not been without its critics, however. For example, Vaclav Klaus, the Czechoslovak finance minister, thinks that this would create 'a poor man's Europe'. The scheme would help preserve the old trade pattern and deter integration into the world economy. Kenen (1991: 236–7) argued that a payments union without the USSR would have meant far less scope for trade expansion than there was in Western Europe after the Second World War, while one with the USSR would not have worked well because the Soviet Union would have been a 'structural creditor' in the years ahead. Kenen also pointed out that a payments union would have involved the re-centralization of transactions with the other members and might have been at the expense of trade with the rest of the world (p. 264). Blanchard *et al.* (1991: 87–9) were similarly sceptical. The Soviet Union's dominance would have been a political problem, while the Soviet Union would have had very little economic interest in the scheme because of its perpetual surpluses. Time for adjustment would have best be gained by export credits and subsidies to exporters. Rosati (1992: 77–81) pointed out that circumstances are very different today, particularly the need for a comprehensive restructuring of East European economies coupled with a major reallocation of resources among sectors and branches. Rosati saw merit instead in replacing Comecon with an OEEC-type organization with close links with and support from the OECD and the EC.

COMING TOGETHER AND GROWING APART

Both processes can be seen at work in the 'socialist world'. Vietnam became a united country in 1975, when the socialist North enveloped the 'capitalist' South. The lesson here is that the central planning system failed to cope with the absorption of the South to such an extent that market-type mechanisms had to be introduced. The reunification of Germany involved the opposite scenario, the 'capitalist' West taking over the socialist East. The process has been far from smooth, however, with the economy of East Germany getting into serious difficulties in the short run. The German

experience has made South Korea extremely wary of rapid economic union with North Korea. The Soviet Union and Yugoslavia have disintegrated and the Czechs and Slovaks are to go their own ways. There are a number of general points to be made here:

1. There are always problems when changes are made, either divergence or convergence.

2. The political factor is supreme – if the will is there the problems can be overcome.

3. Whether countries form a federation or confederation (i.e. a looser form of association) the key to success is that they freely choose to do so. Independence is not incompatible with a successful economic union.

4. The international political aspects may be helped by the CSCE.

The Conference on Security and Cooperation in Europe (CSCE)

The Helsinki Conference lasted from 3 July 1973 to 1 August 1975, when the Helsinki Final Act (Helsinki Accord) was signed by thirty-five countries. All the European nations were represented, with the exception of Albania (observer status was granted on 10 July 1990), plus Canada and the USA. The Final Act was a sort of substitute for the general peace conference which never took place after World War II. There were three so-called 'baskets': security in Europe (confirmation of existing boundaries in particular); co-operation in economics, science and technology, and the environment; and human rights (although this 'basket' was widely ignored by the Soviet and East European regimes, it proved crucial in the long term by giving legitimacy and power to the dissident movements).

There were follow-up conferences in Belgrade (1977), Madrid (1979), Stockholm 1984–85, and Vienna 1986. The first economic conference was held in Bonn in April 1990. This recognized 'that democratic institutions and economic freedom foster economic and social progress'; 'multi-party democracy based on free, periodic elections'; 'that the performance of market-based economies relies primarily on the freedom of individual enterprise'; and 'that economic freedom for the individual includes the right to own, buy, sell and otherwise utilize property'.

The Paris CSCE Conference was held in Paris 19–21 November 1990, signifying the formal end of the Cold War. The number of signatories was reduced to thirty-four with the unification of Germany (and raised again to thirty-five on 19 June 1991 with the admission of Albania as a full member). The Baltic states of Estonia, Latvia and Lithuania became members on 10 September 1991, following the abortive Soviet coup, appropriately during the Moscow CSCE Conference on human rights. Russia replaced the Soviet Union, and the remaining ex-Soviet republics (with the exception of Georgia, which did not apply) were admitted on 30 January 1992. Slovenia and Croatia were only granted observer status at that time. Georgia, Slovenia and Croatia were admitted on 24 March 1992 and Bosnia-Hercegovina was on 30 April 1992.

The Moscow conference, which ended 4 October 1991, announced the 'Moscow mechanism' for intrusive monitoring of human rights: if a country refuses to co-operate in an investigation, any six states can send a team; in serious cases nine states are able to send a fact-finding mission to the country right away. On 19 November the sixteen Nato and six Warsaw Pact members signed the following:

The Conventional Forces in Europe (CFE) Treaty. This restricted (by 1994) each alliance to 20,000 tanks, 30,000 armoured combat vehicles, 20,000 artillery pieces, 6,800 combat aircraft, and 2,000 attack helicopters in the area between the Atlantic and the Urals. This was to be followed by negotiations leading to a chemical weapon ban and manpower reductions. Mention was also made of the 'prospect' of negotiations on reducing short- range nuclear weapons (note that the 1987 Intermediate Nuclear Weapons Agreement between the USA and the Soviet Union had abolished that category).

A Joint Declaration. The twenty-two countries declared that 'in the era of European relations, which is beginning, they are no longer adversaries, will build new partnerships and extend to each other the hand of friendship'. 'None of their weapons will ever be used except in self-defence or otherwise in accordance with the Charter of the United Nations.' Each state can choose to be a member of an alliance or not.

All thirty-four signed the Charter of Paris on 21 November. This ended the era of confrontation and division of Europe, and supported the peaceful settlement of disputes, the principle of self-determination, democracy, human rights and the market economy.

New institutions were to be set up: a Permanent Secretariat (Prague); an Election Observation Office (Warsaw); a Conflict Prevention Centre in Vienna (to monitor unusual military activities and to exchange military information; an emergency meeting of the CSCE can be called if a member complains of unusual military activity near its borders); and an Assembly of Europe. A human rights charter was to be drawn up, heads of state or government were to meet every two years; and foreign ministers were to meet at least once a year.

The first full meeting was in Berlin on 19–20 June 1991. A new emergency mechanism was set up to deal with 'major disruptions endangering peace, security or stability' or violations of the Helsinki principles (e.g. human rights). Any member could initially seek clarification from the state(s) involved and the relevant information had to be submitted within forty-eight hours. If the situation was still not resolved, any member could request an emergency meeting, provided that support was given by at least twelve other members. There were considerable restrictions imposed, however. The principle of 'non-interference in internal affairs applies', while no decisions or solutions could be imposed, since the unanimity rule that covers all CSCE proceedings still applied. A modification of the consensus rule, however, was allowed at the 30–1 January 1992 meeting in Prague: in the case of 'clear, gross and uncorrected violations of CSCE commitments' a majority of member states could take 'appropriate action . . . if necessary in the absence of the state concerned'. This is known as the 'consensus minus one' rule.

On 21 May 1992 Nato agreed in principle to play a peacekeeping role in Europe outside its member states. At the 6 June meeting a formal statement said that, on request, Nato was 'prepared to support, on a case-by-case basis . . . activities under the responsibility of the CSCE'. At its 9–10 July 1992 meeting the CSCE formally accepted the possibility of requesting Nato (or Western European Union) forces for peacekeeping purposes and also established the new post of Commissioner for National Minorities.

THE LINKAGE BETWEEN POLITICAL AND ECONOMIC REFORM

The specific question here is whether political liberalization is a condition of successful economic reform. There is no easy answer to this, as with other questions. It is almost certainly true in the long run, but within a shorter time span a number of cases make one think, e.g. China and the 'Pacific tigers' such as Taiwan and South Korea. The arguments in favour of democratization and market-orientated reforms proceeding together include the gaining of popular support, overcoming the bureaucracy and other powerful vested interests, and hindering any reform reversal, while the counter-arguments include the need for a strong, unaccountable central authority able to take tough decisions, ensure law and order and control trade unions. In the transitional period to full democracy there is the argument that the political system could have problems even functioning, thus hindering the switch to the market. (Political democracy and a regard for human rights are, of course, worthy goals in themselves.) There is also the related question of whether market-orientated economic reforms lead to pressure to liberalize politically or whether they are needed to keep

such changes at bay. This issue lies at the heart of the debate among the Chinese leadership.

APPENDIX 17.1 AID TO EASTERN EUROPE

G24 aid

Roger Boyes (*The Times*, 24 September 1991, p. 8) reports that since the 1989 revolutions the G24 countries have pledged $31 billion to Eastern and Central Europe, excluding the Soviet Union. (In addition there were credits from the IMF and the World Bank worth $9.4 billion, and the Club of Paris debt forgiveness of $18.3 billion.) But only a third of G24 aid can be counted as joint assistance and only a fraction of that has actually been paid out. For example, G24 credit guarantees are aimed at encouraging Western exports. By the end of May 1991 only 13.1 per cent of the promised aid had actually been passed on, and only 9.7 per cent of the promised credit lines had been taken up.

Anthony Robinson (FT, 2 June 1992, p. 6) cites an IEWS report which shows that although the G24 countries have pledged $27 billion to Central Europe, the amounts actually disbursed in 1990 were as follows: Czechoslovakia 2 per cent; Hungary 17 per cent; and Poland 27 per cent.

The United Nations Economic Commission for Europe (1992: 8) estimates that between January 1990 and June 1991 the total of aid committed by the G24 countries to Eastern Europe amounted to $32 billion, but only about a fifth consists of grant aid.

The European Community

The EC co-ordinates G24 aid under the Phare programme (Polish and Hungarian Aid for the Reconstruction of the Economy). Western governments plus the IMF and the World Bank have pledged $27 billion in aid to Hungary, Poland and Czechoslovakia, but only 14 per cent is in grant form (*The Economist*, 16 May 1992, p. 44).

17 October 1991. EC allows EBRD to use Ecu 40 million of EC funds for technical assistance to Eastern Europe and the Soviet Union.

16 December 1991. EC speeds up disbursement of Ecu 200 million in food aid and releases Ecu 500 million tranche of loan guarantees.

The IMF and the World Bank

Peter Norman (*FT*, 8 October 1991, p. 20) reports that if the current quota increase is ratified as planned, the IMF's capital resources will increase by 50 per cent to 135 billion SDRs or $185 billion. During the World Bank's fiscal year (started 1 July) lending to Eastern Europe was to increase by just over $1 billion to $2.9 billion.

Nato

19 December 1991. Nato offered to help distribute aid (transport, etc.).

The foreign capital needs of Eastern Europe

Jacques Delors, president of the European Commission (17 January 1990) 'If we were to confine ourselves to extending our own internal arrangements for helping regions lagging behind . . . to the six countries on the road to democracy we would need an extra Ecu 14 billion a year. If we were to add European Investment Bank intervention in these same regions, another Ecu 15 billion would be required . . . over a period of five to ten years.'

Gianni de Michelis (Italian foreign minister, 19 March 1990). The EC allocates $15 billion a year in aid to Eastern Europe; 0.25 per cent of EC GDP should be set aside for such aid, roughly ten times what is currently being proposed.

IHT (4 October 1991, p. 13). The World Bank and IMF estimate that the fledgling democracies of Eastern Europe (excluding the Soviet Union) need at least $20 billion a year of foreign capital until the end of the decade for substantial economic gains to be made, if the economies are to grow at all.

IHT (4 January 1992, p. 7). One estimate for the Soviet Union and Eastern Europe combined says that for the capital stock to reach the level of Western industrial countries there is need for $180 billion a year for ten years. The external requirements would amount to over $100 billion a year for a decade.

NOTES

1. 'As for the former centrally planned economies engaged in transformation to market-based systems, the experience with reform in Eastern Europe has highlighted the need for a comprehensive approach to structural reform together with a decisive effort at macroeconomic stabilization. It is important to create, at the outset, the legal and institutional framework to encourage entrepreneurship, private enterprise, and competition. These lessons have important implications for the economic transformation of the states of the former USSR' (*IMF Annual Report*, 1992, p. 13).
2. The term 'big bang' is sometimes used in a partial sense, e.g. a 'big bang' approach to price liberalization means freeing all prices at once.
3. Rey Koslowski ('Market institutions, East European reform, and economic theory', *Journal of Economic Issues*, 1992, vol. XXVI, no. 3, p. 697) considers that 'The importance of institutions for the establishment of market exchange in Eastern Europe demonstrates the poverty of the neoclassical approach of assuming functioning institutions. This approach fails adequately to take into account the underlying legal structure provided by the state in establishing property rights, as well as the ubiquitous state regulation that has become constitutive of twentieth century capitalism. In presuming that economic behaviour can be universally abstracted from the peculiarities of societies, neoclassical economics all too easily succumbs to explanatory misconceptualizations of the post-totalitarian situation, which lead to unfounded optimism regarding economic reform and naiveté regarding privatization.'
4. See also Bolton and Roland in Postscript.

18

ALBANIA

POLITICAL BACKGROUND

The dramatic events in Eastern Europe soon began to have their effect even in Albania; the overthrow of Ceausescu was particularly influential. There were rumours of demonstrations in December 1989–January 1990 (e.g. in Skhoder). The speech of Ramiz Alia (First Secretary of the Party of Labour) to the Ninth Plenum of the Central Committee on 22 January 1990 is of considerable interest, because he blamed the events in Eastern Europe not on the failure of socialism as such but on 'revisionism' (*Albanian Life*, 1990, no. 47, no. 1, pp. 1–7).

How could it happen that the working class could become supporters of the restoration of capitalism? The deplorable fact is that the peoples of these countries saw the revisionist regime, its bureaucracy, its violence, its economic stagnation, its technological backwardness, etc., as products of the socialist system, of Marxism–Leninism, which they now reject. It was the reality in the countries of the East which alienated the masses from the state power. Our party was correct then, in its titanic struggle against revisionism . . . In the field of foreign policy, our line is not and has never been that of isolation in a besieged fortress. Our policy is one of peaceful, friendly cooperation – political, economic and cultural – with foreign countries.' Pluralism of parties ' . . . would not be an expression of democracy, but a means to weaken national unity and create the conditions for the destruction of socialism.

Alia proposed the following changes:

1. 'Meetings of the grass-roots organizations of the party should be open, that is, the agenda and place of meetings should be published and any worker who wishes to attend should be welcomed.'

2. 'Decisions on the selection and appointment of specialists and cadres should be further improved so that the most skilful and devoted people are in the party and state organs.'

3. 'The terms of office of members of the District Party Committees, District People's Councils and the Party Central Committee, together with Deputies to the People's Assembly, should be limited to four or five years.' One-third of the members of all state and party bodies should be replaced every election.

4. (People's Assembly) 'two or three candidates for a constituency should go forward on the ballot-paper.' (Note that candidates were then chosen by the Democratic Front, an umbrella organization dominated by the party.)

On 8 November 1990 Alia's recent speech to the Central Committee appeared in the press. He made the following proposals.

1. The 10 February 1991 elections should be multi-candidate although not multi-party. Individuals could run as independents or as candidates for recognized social organizations

like trade unions and the Writers' League; their platforms should 'conform with the interests of the nation'. There should be inner-party debate and democracy. 'The article that has to do with the party as the "only leading political force of the state" should be redefined more precisely in the constitution.' 'The party should not give orders or commands, it should not concentrate in its hands the prerogatives belonging to other organizations.' 'It should not and cannot exercise state power directly.'

2. Religious freedom should include the re-opening of churches and mosques.

The road to democracy and international acceptance

Foreign affairs. In a 20 April 1990 speech at a Central Committee Plenum Alia talked about the restoration of diplomatic relations with the USA and USSR being 'on the agenda', while those with the EC might be in the country's interest. On 30 July diplomatic relations were actually restored with the Soviet Union. On 5 June Albania was accepted as an observer at the CSCE (Conference on Security and Co-operation in Europe) meeting in Copenhagen. The next day Albania asked to join the organization, while on 9 August Albania was granted observer status at Vienna-based talks on security and confidence-building measures (which are part of the CSCE process). Albania was accepted as a full member of the CSCE on 19 June 1991, becoming the thirty-fifth member. The decision to join the Nuclear Non-proliferation Treaty was made on 16 August 1990 (Albania is to build its first nuclear research reactor, with UN development funding).

Domestic affairs. On 22 February 1990 Albania admitted for the first time that it was holding political prisoners, convicted 'for activity to overthrow the people's power through violence'. Releases followed. On 8 May it was decided to liberalize the criminal code. The Justice Ministry, abolished in 1965, was restored. The number of capital offences was reduced from thirty-four to eleven and the death penalty for women was abolished. 'Economic crime' remained a capital offence, including theft of state property and economic sabotage, as well as treason, espionage, terrorism, geno-cide and murder; but 'anti-state agitation and propaganda' was now punishable by five to twenty-five years' imprisonment rather than the death penalty. Attempting to leave the country illegally was previously a treasonable offence (ten to fifteen years imprisonment), but the penalty was reduced to a maximum of five years. In fact any adult was now able to apply for a passport, although there were considerable obstacles (such as the lack of hard currency).

Albania also relaxed its formal position as an officially atheistic state. On 9 May Deputy Prime Minister Manush Myftiu announced that 'the question of religious belief is a matter of cons-cience for every individual', while the then UN Secretary General, Perez de Cuellar, said on 13 May, during a visit to the country, that the churches might be reopened (Alia is reported to have said later, however, that 'Religion is wholly free in Albania ... but its open, formal practice is banned. No churches are allowed': C. L. Sulzberger, *IHT*, 29 June 1990, p. 6). There was a report of the reopening of a church and a mosque in Skhoder on 11 November 1990. 'Religious propaganda' was no longer a crime.

The July 1990 'invasion' of various embassies in Tirana was resolved by allowing the 6,000 or so would-be emigrants to leave the country. On 22 August work was begun building a wall around the embassy quarter, but a flood of people would later seek to leave the country.

Alia addressed the UN on 28 September 1990. The writer Ismail Kadare defected on 25 October, because he was convinced that the regime would not introduce post-1989 Eastern European-type reforms. This proved to be a poor prediction, but he did not return until 11 May 1992. Domestic events escalated when student pro-democracy protests in Tirana began on 9 December 1990. These spread to other towns and other groups such as workers (e.g.

the steel centre of Elbasan). The government adopted a two-pronged strategy of concessions on the one hand and penalties on the other in order to keep control of the situation.

On 11 December 1990 five full politburo members and two candidate members were dismissed, while a Central Committee meeting 'expressed the opinion that it is to the benefit of the further democratization of the country's life and of pluralism to create political organizations in accordance with the laws in force'. The next day the Democratic Party was founded by students and intellectuals such as Gramoz Pashko and Sali Berisha (who later became president of the party), the first independent party since 1944. Others followed, such as the Albanian Ecology Party, the Christian Democratic Party, the Republican Party of Albania, and the (Greek ethnic minority) Concord Party. Also formed was the Forum for the Defence of Human Rights. The decree legalizing independent parties was issued on 17 (and approved 19) December, specifying that they cannot be 'fascist, racist or anti-national', cannot be founded from abroad, and cannot aim 'to overthrow the constitution of the Socialist Republic of Albania'. The Democratic Party's newspaper, *Democratic Renaissance*, was first published on 5 January 1991, formal authorization of opposition newspapers taking place on 28 December 1990. The date of the first free election was originally fixed for 10 February 1991, one which the opposition successfully tried to postpone in order to have more time to organize. The new date was 31 March (second round 15 April), the opposition promising in return to support the call for an end to both strikes (until 1 May) and high wage demands. In the first week of 1991 it was declared that 202 political prisoners were to be released (191 others had been pardoned since the previous June). Further releases followed and on 12 March 1991 the government announced that those remaining were to be released.

Violent protests, however, were contained by the policy and army; 157 people were arrested and put on trial. Prison sentences ranged from five to twenty years. A mass exodus started in December 1990, especially members of the Greek minority at first, and there was some loss of life. By mid-April 1991 all Albanian Jews (something over 300) had left for Israel. As is usual, minorities feared they might be discriminated against in the new nationalistic circumstances. Some Albanians, mainly non-Greeks, returned, but a mass general exodus started again at the end of February 1991. One estimate puts the number leaving between June 1990 and mid-March 1991 at around 80,000 (David Binder, *IHT*, 26 March 1991, p. 3). There were further disturbances in the early months of 1991, e.g. in the port of Durres over dashed expectations of being able to take the ferry to Italy; there were student hunger strikes and class boycotts (Enver Hoxha's name was subsequently removed from that of Tirana University); a number of Hoxha statues were pulled down; and several days of rioting and a shoot-out at a military academy led to further loss of life. On 20 February 1991 Alia appointed a new, eight-member government and took direct presidential control of it; a new presidential council was also set up. Fatos Nano became the new prime minister. On 7 March 1991 the port of Durres was placed under military control as a result of a mass exodus and a ban was imposed on mass gatherings in Tirana, Durres, Vlore and Shengjin. There were further riots by would-be emigrants in April, while another mass exodus started in August owing to the dire economic conditions.

The general election of 31 March 1991 and 7 April 1991

The first free election in the post-war period produced a 95 per cent turn-out and was judged to be on the whole acceptable by the international observers. The Party of Labour of Albania (PLA) won the election fairly comfortably, although relying on the countryside (where there was a fear of large private landowners returning) and the south; the Democratic Party did well in the cities and larger towns. In the first round of voting, the distribution of seats in the 250 member People's Assembly was as follows: PLA 162; Democratic Party 65; Omonia (ethnic Greek party) 3; and the National Veterans' Organization 1. The nineteen remaining seats were decided in the second round of voting on 7 April (including that of the prime minister Fatos Nano). The PLA won another seven seats to take it over the crucial 167 seats needed for a two-thirds majority (necessary to alter the constitution). The Democratic Party won another ten seats (it won 30 per cent of the popular vote in total) and Omonia another two.

Although Alia failed to win his Tirana constituency, he remained president; he was re-elected president by parliament 4–5 May 1991, although he had to resign his position as party secretary and as a member of the politburo and Central Committee. The party hard-liners tended to do better than the 'liberal' PLA candidates. The party programmes were as follows:

The Party of Labour of Albania (PLA). The PLA held a special conference on 26 December 1990 in order to draw up an election manifesto. The political programme included the following: 'non-stop' democratic reform; separation of party and state; Marxism, not Stalinism; 'freedom of conscience and faith'; and human rights 'according to contemporary European norms'.

The economic programme included the following: 'replacing the system of rigid centralized direction and administration with the mechanisms of a market economy'; 'a balance between the state sector and free initiative', while 'The great state sector will vie and co-ordinate action with the co-operative and private sector'; state enterprises to be broken up into smaller units in order to increase competition; 'The fiscal system associated with the economic reforms will ensure an equal distribution of income'; invest-

ment priorities to be shifted away from heavy industry towards tourism, services and consumer goods; foreign credits to be sought and the lek to be made gradually convertible; agricultural co-operatives to remain, but to be 'independent' and provisions made for 'other forms of ownership', including private.

Note that at the post-election congress held 10–13 June 1991 the PLA changed its name to the Socialist Party (12 June) and Fatos Nano was elected president (13 June). Its new programme, published 3 July, identified itself with the principles advocated by European social democratic parties; it supports the creation of a market economy, but reforms should be introduced gradually; privatization has support, but the party favours preservation of the agricultural co-operatives and of state control of vital industrial sectors (Biberaj 1991: 11); planning still has an indispensable role to play (p. 16).

The Democratic Party. The manifesto pledged a Western-style political democracy, coupled with the rapid introduction of a market economy based on private property. There should be a free distribution of land to farmers and the industry privatization programme should include the discounted or even free distribution of shares to workers. In the state sector there should be a five-day, forty-hour week. The Democratic Party claimed that the PLA used scare tactics against it, saying that the DP would bring back large landowners and sell the country out.

The Republican Party. The aim was a gradual transition to a market economy and adherence to UN, Helsinki and CSCE principles.

Post-election events

The Democratic Party boycotted the opening of the new parliament in protest at the loss of life during the anti-PLA demonstrations. Its call for a one-day strike on 4 April, however, met a mixed and rather muted response.

A new draft constitution was published 10

April 1991 (Remzi Lani, *The Guardian*, 10 April 1991, p. 6). Albania was to become simply 'The Republic of Albania' rather than 'The People's Socialist Republic'. The future state was defined as 'democratic and juridical, based on social equality, on the defence of freedom and the rights of man and on political pluralism'. Private property was endorsed and reference was made to the fundamental rights and duties of citizens, the right to strike, demonstrate and emigrate.

A general strike started on 16 May 1991, the demands of the Independent Trade Union Federation (as the most important grouping) including a 50 per cent increase in pay, a reduction in the working week from forty-eight to thirty-six hours, and a ban on women working night shifts. About half the urban work-force may have been involved at the peak. On 4 June the prime minister, Fatos Nano, resigned and was replaced by Ylli Bufi the next day (the then Minister of Food). There was a return to work on 8 June; a 50 per cent pay increase was conceded as part of a no-strike deal until the new election. A government of 'national stability' was set up on 12 June; six political parties were represented, but the individual members of the coalition government were detached from their parties during its temporary period of office. There were twenty-two cabinet members: ten were members of the Party of Labour of Albania (now the Socialist Party), including interior and foreign affairs (Muhamet Kapllan); Fatos Nano became the Minister of Foreign Economic Relations. The Democratic Party was given defence and most economic portfolios (Gramoz Pashko became the deputy prime minister and economics minister with overall responsibility for the economy; Genc Ruli became finance minister). The opposition agreed to participate in order to prevent chaos, which, in turn, could have led to a state of emergency or even a military coup.

In his speech outlining the new programme, Ylli Bufi stressed political rehabilitation (political prisoners were declared innocent on 30 September 1991), the restoration of order and stability, austerity measures, a return to work, further democratization and marketization, the privatization of small enterprises and some land, price reforms, and the need for foreign aid. In July he talked of privatizing agriculture and liberalizing prices by the autumn of 1991. The government's plans also included foreign trade liberalization, limited convertibility of the lek, and the creation of a social safety net. The new government's Economic Programme of June 1991 is dealt with later on in the chapter.

James Baker, the US Secretary of State, received a warm welcome from the people of Tirana on his 22 June 1991 visit. He promised a small amount of aid ($6 million in the form of powdered milk, medical equipment and medicine). After a visit to Albania by its representatives, the EC voted (24 July 1991) to supply emergency food and medicines amounting to Ecu 500,000 ($590,000); an extra Ecu 2 million was added on 12 August.

As 1991 wore on the economic situation turned increasingly desperate, with looting, rioting and general lawlessness. Chaos would not be an over-dramatic description. On 4 December Sali Berisha pulled the seven Democratic Party members out of the coalition government on the grounds that the socialists were hindering economic and political reforms, that there was a need to bring forward the date of the next general election to 23 February 1992 at the latest instead of May, that the socialists were destabilizing society in the hope of discrediting democracy, and that more should be done to bring former communist officials to book. (Note that the Democratic Party itself started to split, with Gramoz Pashko at loggerheads with Berisha over the wisdom of leaving the coalition and over economic reform. Berisha is more inclined towards 'big bang' and 'shock' therapy than Pashko, who was actually expelled from the Democratic Party on 29 June 1992 after the election.) On 11 December 1991 a new prime minister was appointed; Vilson Ahmeti was a non-partisan technocrat, an engineer and former food minister. A new election was fixed for 1 March 1992. No party was allowed to represent an ethnic minority so Omonia, for example, could not stand; the Union for Human Rights in Albania was formed to contest the election (in which it won two seats).

The general election of 22 and 29 March 1992

The Democratic Party won convincingly. The Democratic Party and its parliamentary allies, the Social Democrats and Republicans, secured between them the two-thirds of seats necessary to change the constitution. In the first round the Democratic Party won 62 per cent of the vote and ninety-two out of the 140 seats (compared with 25 per cent and thirty-eight seats respectively for the Socialist Party) and won an additional eleven seats in the second round. Alia resigned as president on 3 April 1992 and was replaced by Sali Berisha on 9 April. Presidential powers were increased, e.g. the ability to give direct orders to members of the government. The new prime minister was Alexander Meksi (14 April), head of a coalition government including the Social Democrats and Republicans. The new chairman of the Democratic Party was Eduard Selami (17 April).

The new prime minister outlined an economic programme of marketization and privatization on 18 April 1992. Meksi said that 'The Albanian economy is going through its worst crisis since the war and there is only one way out – the application of radical reforms in the economy as shown by the experience of former Eastern bloc countries'. The reform programme is discussed in the postscript.

ECONOMIC POLICY PRIOR TO THE 1991 GENERAL ELECTION

Ramiz Alia's proposals for economic reform

In a number of speeches over recent years Ramiz Alia laid the foundations for modest but nevertheless significant reforms in the Albanian context.

In his speech to the Eighth Central Committee Plenum in September 1989, Alia accepted that 'sluggards, the careless and the irresponsible . . . can be left without work' (Schnytzer 1992: 48). In an October 1989 speech he stated that indirect rather than direct steering would characterize the new economic system (p. 48).

In his address to the ninth Plenum of the Central Committee of the Albanian Workers' Party on 22 January 1990 he made the following points (*Albanian Life*, 1990, no. 47, no. 1, pp. 1–7):

Another important task is to fulfil our tasks in the economic field, in the field of the people's nutrition and clothing.

Enterprise directors, heads of clinics, of university departments and institutes, should be appointed only after broad discussion and approval by the workers of the centre concerned, and should be subject to removal by these workers should they fail to live up to their responsibilities.

Enterprises were to be divided into small units (brigades or departments).

In every workplace stimuli should be given for increasing productivity and reducing production costs. While we should maintain democratic centralism and socialist planning, we should transfer from the centre to the grass roots many competences in the field of planning. Decisive steps should be taken to enable the enterprises to enjoy that independence recognized by the laws of the political economy of socialism.

District Committees were to have their own sources of revenue and be free to engage in investment.

In the field of remuneration, wages in the state sector should depend not only on the realization of the norm in the concrete workplace, as it is today, but also on the final results of the enterprise. Wages should be made a more powerful incentive, by way of remuneration for overfulfilment of the plan, in order to stimulate those sectors in which we are more interested, such as oil, chrome, exports, etc.

Products of the first necessity should continue to be sold at fixed prices, but for some other goods, not of first necessity, prices may be allowed to fluctuate, so that the supply–demand factor becomes a stimulus to an increase in the productivity of labour.

An increase in the supply of industrial goods and foodstuffs for the market is one of the main priorities of the 1990 plan. A few days ago we adopted the decision that every co-operative family in the countryside should be provided with livestock to meet its needs for meat.

Citizens could undertake private building for their own use. Individuals and groups could contract among themselves and/or with the state for building purposes.

In his Central Committee speech of 17 April 1990, Alia said (*Albanian Life*, 1990, no. 48, no. 2, pp. 1–2):

> This plenum is concerned mainly with improving the economic mechanism – with the self-financing of enterprises [long-term bank credits would be the rule and grants the exception], with the distribution of the profit resulting from overfulfilment of the plan, with the enhancing of the role of the market, etc. In future, enterprises which overfulfil the plan may pay the workers concerned up to 25 per cent extra annually.

> In future the co-operative peasants themselves will decide to preserve collectivized herds or to sell them off to the individual co-operative peasants. If the peasantry considers that the keeping of a cow or some sheep or goats in their personal plot

is more effective . . . livestock from the small herds could be given to the co-operativists in return for payment.

On 7 July 1990, at a Central Committee meeting, Alia announced 'confined and controlled' concessions to the private sector. Specifically, encouragement should be given to services and crafts; there should be more cobblers, tailors, saddlers, watchmakers, nut sellers and confectioners. Alia also mentioned the need to increase the wages of the lowest paid workers.

The enterprise

On 7 May 1990 the then prime minister, Adil Carcani, gained the approval of the People's Assembly for a number of changes (*Albanian Life*, 1990, no. 48, no. 2, p. 47). The law was to come into effect on 1 January 1991 (Pashko 1991: 139). Enterprises were to be divided into three categories (Schnytzer 1992: 51–2).

1. Enterprises producing important goods (such as oil, chrome, copper, coal, electrical energy, textiles, sugar, flour and edible oils) were to remain subject to the physical planning of output.

2. Enterprises producing consumer goods made of 'metal, wood, ceramics and terra cotta, etc.' would be free to determine their own levels of output and prices.

3. All other enterprises were to receive from the central authorities a global sales target and output targets for exports and commodities to be delivered outside their own districts. For goods to be sold within the enterprise's own district, planned output would be determined by the enterprise in conjunction with the Executive Committee of the local People's Council.

The principle applies that when output is centrally planned inputs should also be provided centrally.

As regards wholesale prices, instead of being based on branch-average costs of production they were to be based on the highest-cost producer in the branch (there were earlier experiments in mineral extraction and agriculture).

This shift towards marginal cost pricing was aimed at reducing planned losses and, therefore, subsidies. After the March–April 1991 election the PLA appears to have planned a price reform, adjusting prices first to 'value' and then to world market levels; wage compensation and indexation were envisaged (Åslund and Sjöberg 1991: 18).

Certain enterprises were thus to be able to determine production plans of their own accounting for up to 20 per cent (in some factories and all co-operative farms up to 100 per cent) of their productive capacity (Pashko sees this aspect of the reform applying to small and medium-sized enterprises, those subordinated at the district level as well as co-operatives; Pashko 1991: 141). Enterprises were to be free to sell this above-plan portion on the domestic market at supply and demand prices. In the case of exports, foreign trade was to continue to be conducted through state foreign trade enterprises. The foreign exchange earned for above-plan exports could be used too for imports such as equipment. It was recommended that the foreign currency fund should be used for technological and raw material imports (Pashko 1991: 142).

Enterprises were to be allowed to retain 90 per cent of their planned profit (previously all went to the state budget); they were to be responsible for their own financing and to have access to bank credit (for working capital needs or for unplanned investment where retained profits are inadequate: at least 85 per cent of profit must be re-invested, with 5 per cent left for the incentive fund). A subsidy would only be provided to enterprises making losses due to circumstances beyond their control: in other cases various sanctions could be imposed, e.g. credits at higher rates of interest, the sacking of management, the transfer of capacity or even closure of the enterprise. Budgetary financing was reserved for investment in schemes of national importance, such as transport and power supply (Pashko 1991:141).

On 9 July 1990 the ministers of light industry, the food industry, public services and internal trade were replaced.

Wage determination

The then prime minister, Adil Carcani, tackled this problem on 7 May 1990, gaining the approval of the People's Assembly (*Albanian Life*, 1990, no. 48, no. 2, p. 47). If an enterprise (or department within an enterprise) planned an above-plan increase in net income and succeeded, half the extra profit would go to investment and half to bonuses. Workers could receive bonuses of up to 25 per cent of their pay. On the other hand, unplanned losses would mean a reduction in wages of up to 10 per cent.

Only the total wage bill was to be decided centrally, with the enterprise able to determine the distribution among workers. The wage bill could continue to be exceeded if the production plan were overfulfilled. Management would have discretion over how much new labour to hire (and would not be obliged to create jobs for new entrants), but would have to find new jobs (in co-operation with district authorities) for those it wished to sack; persistently loss-making enterprises would be closed, provided that new jobs could be found.

As its July 1990 plenum, the Central Committee resolved to increase the wages of the 250,000 lowest-paid workers (one-third of the workforce, according to Alia) by 10–20 per cent. Workers laid off through circumstances beyond their control (e.g. shortages of energy or raw materials) would receive 80 per cent of their normal wages. Those responsible for the shortages would receive only half their normal wages (*EEN*, 1990, vol. 4, no. 15, p. 4).

January 1991 saw an increasing number of strikes. The coal miners succeeded in gaining pay increases of between 30 per cent and 50 per cent depending on length of service. The retirement age of miners was reduced to fifty. Further strikes led the government to seek and gain approval for a new law requiring fifteen days notice of a strike and enabling parliament to suspend a strike if it threatened the national interest. Independent trade unions (e.g. the miners) were formally legalized on 18 February 1991. As explained above, the May–June 1991 general strike was an important reason why a coalition government of 'national salvation' was set up.

The private sector

It was announced on 12 July 1990 that craftsmen and others (e.g. traders) wanting to start their own small businesses would be 'allowed to carry out services individually in private, at home, in the streets, in the shops and ambulatory point'. These licensed private businesses were only allowed to employ family members, not 'day labourers' (this restriction was subsequently removed). They were to set their own prices, but had to pay income tax and make their own provision for pensions and sickness benefits.

One estimate put the number of private entrepreneurs at 1,500, while 7,000 service units had already been privatized, e.g. craftsmen, fruit and vegetable traders, butchers and restaurants (Disa Haastad, *The Guardian*, 14 December 1990, p. 25). In November 1990 the figure of 1,251 private enterprises was given (*Albanian Life*, 1991, no. 49, p. 18).

As far as co-operatives are concerned, all new small co-operatives had to follow the practice of selling their products through state shops (prices received being fixed by the state) (*EEN*, 1990, vol. 4, no. 15, p. 4).

The 28 February 1991 decree 'on the use by citizens of cars, motor cycles, small trucks and tricycles' allowed individual car ownership; state enterprises were allowed to sell their official cars and motorcycles through retail outlets supplying spare parts. Enterprises attached to the Transport Ministry were able to sell their cars to their drivers for use as taxis. In early 1990 occupants were able to buy their flats and set up urban housing co-operatives, but progress was slow during the course of the year (Åslund and Sjöberg 1991: 16).

THE ECONOMIC PROGRAMME OF JUNE 1991

The coalition government's programme consisted of the following elements (Åslund and Sjöberg 1991: 13–20):

Agriculture (this is dealt with below).

Privatization. There was a call for 'rapid and far-reaching privatization of the economy'. Privatization of industry was to proceed in 1992 by means of free distribution via financial intermediaries (mutual funds or holding companies). Free distribution of housing to current occupants was also planned. There was to be a rapid auctioning off of 25,000 small enterprises (e.g. shops and restaurants; September was mentioned initially), although the first round was to be reserved for Albanian citizens. In cases such as oil and vital infrastructure projects discretionary involvement by the government was called for. Foreign investment was to be encouraged.

On 14 October 1991 it was announced that church land and property confiscated in 1967 were to be returned. (On the other hand, following the March 1992 general election, an announcement was made, on 19 May 1992, that all buildings belonging to the Socialist Party were to be seized.)

Macroeconomic stabilization. This was to be achieved at the 'earliest possible date'. The three key elements were stated to be price liberalization, currency convertibility and a balanced budget, and they were to be introduced simultaneously. The plan was to liberalize nearly all prices by 1 October 1991 (exceptions included basics such as bread, sugar and cooking oil). Devaluation of the lek was to precede its linking to the Ecu. A free-trade regime was envisaged, with a unified 10 per cent tariff. The intention was to balance the budget (there was a deficit equal to 30 per cent of the budget in 1990) by means of, for example, shutting down enterprises deemed to be hopeless and a 20 per cent reduction in defence spending.

Economic performance

In 1990 the economy started to decline, but this was nothing compared to the collapse in 1991. Table 18.1 shows the record. Åslund and Sjöberg (1991: 19–20) suggest that by May 1990 inflation was more than 30 per cent on an annual basis and rising, while unemployment exceeded 50,000 (another 40,000 state employees were temporarily dismissed at 80 per cent of their pay); perhaps only a quarter of the previous production capacity was utilized in the summer of 1991. In the first half of 1991, compared to the same period of 1990, industrial output plunged 69 per cent and exports 56 per cent (pp. 9, 12); agricultural output fell by 55 per cent (official statistics cited by Kerin Hope, *FT*, 9 October 1991, p. 30). Unemployment is now more than 50 per cent of the urban workforce and inflation 500 per cent (Kerin Hope, *FT*, 7 May 1992, p. 2). *The Economist* (7 September 1991, p. 60) talks of the unemployment rate being close to 40 per cent and GDP per person being $350 (27 July 1991, p.43). National income fell by 55 per cent in the first half of 1991 (Supplement to *Euromoney*, February 1992, p. 2), while in the second half of 1991 industrial production fell by more than 50 per cent (Judy Dempsey, *FT*, 3 March 1992, p. 3). Bread became the only unrationed basic food (*Albanian Life*, spring 1992, issue 52, no. 1, p. 5); infant mortality was 30.8 per thousand (p.6).

FOREIGN AID

As Albania has moved towards political democracy and a market economy, Western aid has followed. The flood of refugees to Italy has increased the urgency of improving conditions in Albania itself. The EBRD voted to admit Albania as a member on 8 October 1991, and

Table 18.1 Albania: foreign debt and rates of growth of GDP, industrial output, agricultural output and prices (%)

GDP	
1990	1991
−10.0	−29.9

Net industrial output	
1990	1991
−11.1	−60.0

Net agricultural output	
1990	1991
−0.7	−60.0

Net foreign debt ($ billion)	
end 1990	end 1991
0.254	0.6

Sources: Åslund and Sjöberg (1991: 6–20); *Economic Bulletin for Europe*, 1991, vol. 43, p. 26; Kerin Hope, *FT*, 7 May 1992, p. 2; United Nations Economic Commission for Europe (1992: 64, 86); *The Banker*, September 1992, p.23.

formal membership was expected before the end of the year. Recent Italian aid includes the following: on 13 August 1991 an extra $85 million; during the visit by the Italian president, the first since 1943, a promise was made to meet basic food needs until November 1991 (much of this food has actually been sold rather than given away by the Albanian government); on 13 September Italy promised a further 120 billion lire (£60 million) over three years to finance imports of machinery for food processing and infrastructural projects in particular. On 3 September the EC announced that it would finance the delivery of Hungarian wheat to Albania. Greece promised $20 million, as did Turkey. On 17 September 1991 the G24 countries agreed to provide more than $150 million in emergency aid (*Albanian Life*, 1992, issue 52, no. 1, p. 27), while a July 1992 G24 visit promised food and longer-term aid. At the end of May 1992 the USA and Turkey promised food aid worth $10 million and $50 million respectively.

Gramoz Pashko has talked of the communists leaving a foreign debt of $400 million (cited by Kerin Hope, *FT*, 24 August 1991, p. 3). In May 1991 a moratorium on around 25 per cent of total foreign currency obligations was negotiated with foreign banks (Åslund and Sjöberg 1991: 22).

A ten-year trade and co-operation accord was signed with the EC on 11 May 1992. The EC was to scrap all discriminatory quotas on imports from Albania, while Albania was beholden not to use licensing and foreign exchange controls against EC exports.

Foreign investment

In February 1990 Fatos Nano, then of the Institute of Economic Studies, made the following interesting remarks (*FT*, 20 February 1990, p. 7): 'We can develop all kinds of joint economic activities except classical credit arrangements. We are not yet open to classic joint ventures.' Foreign technology investment was welcome, 'while we invest our labour and materials, and we will share the profit and risk. We can repay foreign investors through the product.' Pilot projects, such as in clothing and shoes, could be set up, but 'we will not share ownership. That must remain Albanian.' Two decrees were finally issued on 31 July 1990 (John Lloyd, *FT*, 2 August 1990, p. 2):

The protection of foreign investments allowed investment by foreign companies on the same terms as domestic enterprises. Investments would not be 'nationalized, expropriated, and would not be subject to any similar measures except specific cases for public purposes, and then always with compensation'.

The economic activities of enterprises with the participation of foreign capital. Authorization could come from the competent ministry, or, in the case of banking, from the Bank of Albania.

Treatment was to be the same as for domestic enterprises. In January 1991 the People's Assembly approved a decree 'On the creation of banks with the participation of foreign capital and the opening of foreign banks in Albania'.

Joint ventures could only be formed with an Albanian state enterprise, but the foreign share could be as high as 99 per cent. Government priorities for foreign investment include raw materials extraction, agriculture and foodstuffs, light industry such as textiles, tourism, exports, and import substitutes.

There now exists a French–Albanian venture selling domestic handicrafts and imported foodstuffs for hard currency. A group of Greek construction companies signed a protocol to construct a motorway from the Greek border to the Albanian port of Durres; Albania was to supply labour and building materials, and Greece equipment, technical assistance and overall management of the project (*FT*, 16 August 1990, p. 5). Albania is now interested in help from Western oil companies (possibly with land sold for exploration). An agreement with Germany's Denemex to extract oil has already been signed (Disa Haastad, *The Guardian*, 14 December 1990, p. 25). By the end of August 1991 contracts for offshore oil and natural gas exploration had been signed with four Western oil companies and two more were expected the following month (Kerin Hope, *FT*, 29 August 1991, p. 24). At the end of January 1991 a joint venture with an Italian shoe manufacturer was announced; one with a French company to form the first airline was announced in mid-August.

On 26 December 1990 the formation of a joint venture bank (Iliria Bank) was announced (opened 5 April 1991), the partners being the Albanian State Bank for Relations with Foreign Countries (established in December 1990) and the Swiss Iliria Holdings. An important function was to encourage foreign investment. Iliria Holdings has also set up another joint venture (Iliria Tourist), with the Albanian state tourist company (Albturist: this Albanian company only holds 20 per cent of the capital).

The idea of special economic zones was mooted in July 1991.

The Law on Land Rental of 5 October 1991 barred foreigners from purchasing land, but permitted them to lease it (Supplement to *Euromoney*, February 1992, p. 2). Joint ventures are granted a reduced tax rate of 5 per cent for two years and tax holidays are possible (p. 2).

In June 1990 negotiations were started with both the IMF and the World Bank for prospective entry. Formal applications came in January 1991. Gramoz Pashko puts Albania's foreign debt at $400 million (reported by David Binder, *1HT*, 9 October 1991, p. 2).

AGRICULTURE

The prices of minerals and agricultural produce were to be based on the costs of production in low-quality mining areas and on poor farm land. There were to be four zones (lowland, upland, mountainous and the north-east), each receiving progressively higher prices as production costs rise (*EEN*, 1990, vol. 4, no. 10, p. 2). Agricultural co-operatives were encouraged to open shops in the towns to sell their own produce at prices set by themselves. Alternatively, above-plan food production could be sold to the state at prices 50 per cent above those paid for planned levels, only a 10 per cent bonus being paid until then (EEN, p. 2).

Families might keep an unlimited number of livestock. Private plots were enlarged, starting in July 1990; generally this amounted to 0.2 ha for state farm labourers and 0.4 ha for collective farmers (Äslund and Sjöberg 1991: 10). In the general breakdown, however, the common land more or less ceased to be worked; in important agricultural areas perhaps as little as 25 per cent of agricultural land has been tilled; as of 25 April 1991 the sown area amounted to only 60 per cent of that of a year earlier (p. 10).

There were several reports in 1990 of increasing trading activity in urban areas, where farmers sell their produce on the free markets (e.g. Peter Humphrey, *The Independent*, 24 February 1990, p. 10; and David Binder, *IHT*, 16 May 1990, p. 7).

On 3 March 1991 the government announced a ban on food exports because of domestic shortages and a stepping up of food imports.

The Land Bill was passed 22 July 1991 (*EEN*, 1991, vol. 5, no. 17, p. 7, and no.18, p.7; Åslund and Sjöberg 1991: 14–15). The June economic programme talked about completing the privatization of agricultural land before the end of 1991. In the July Land Bill all local co-operative land was to be redistributed by local committees to co-operative farming families free of charge on the basis of 0.1 ha per family member (state farms were to remain intact for the time being). Land could be inherited and the intention was to allow land sales after five years. The aim was to have all co-operative land distributed before the end of September (this amounted to about 80 per cent of arable land). Theft of crops on co-operatives became so widespread that unofficial land distribution took place in many districts; the official distribution will take account of the unofficial one, but not the boundaries of pre-communist days; those who have emigrated are still eligible for their share (Kerin Hope, *FT*, 9 October 1991, p. 30). Only 40 per cent of state farm land is to be shared out among farm workers (p. 30). There have been reports that production has been disrupted in places by an unwillingness to work until the land allocation has been settled (Helena Smith, *The Guardian*, 24 September 1991, p. 20) and a switching away from grain production to work on private plots (Kerin Hope, *FT*, 5 September 1991, p. 3).

The *EEN* (1991, vol. 5, no. 25, pp. 1–2) reports that by December 1991 around 50 per cent of the 532,000 ha of land earmarked for private distribution (out of a total of 680,000 ha of agricultural land) had been allocated; the process would be largely completed within three or four months. Family holdings range from 0.8 ha to 2.8 ha. About 320,000 ha of land has now been distributed, amounting to over 60 per cent of total agricultural land (*EEN*, 6

January 1992, vol. 6, no. 1, p. 7); this figure went up to 380,000 (*EEN*, 16 March 1992, vol. 6, no. 6, p. 6). About 75 per cent of former co-operative and state land has been privatized, with an average of 1.2 ha of land for highland families and 1.4 ha for lowland families; new laws allowing the unrestricted purchase and sale of land are expected soon; the ruling Democratic Party has proposed that former owners of land should be compensated in cash up to a maximum of 5 ha per claim (*EEN*, 13 April 1992, vol. 6, no. 8, p. 5). Some 400,000 ha have now been officially privatized. The 150,000 ha remaining under state farm management have been divided into 280 farms with an average 550 ha (compared with about forty-five farms in the socialist era). A proportion, if not all, of this land, would eventually be sold. Privatization of co-operative land has been smoothest in remote highland regions, unaffected by the settling of newcomers; here co-operative lands have simply been returned to the pre-1946 heirs (*EEN*, 22 June 1992, vol. 6, no. 13, p. 5). But one unfortunate result of the privatization process has been the rekindling of old family disputes over land ownership (*Albanian Life*, 1992, no. 53, p. 13).

19

BULGARIA

POLITICAL BACKGROUND

Political developments

Todor Zhivkov resigned as party secretary on 10 November 1989, being replaced by Petar Mladenov (who had been foreign minister since 1971). Zhivkov was expelled from the party on 13 December, and on 18 January 1990 a warrant was issued for his arrest on the grounds of 'incitement to ethnic hostility and hatred, unwarranted receiving of excessive amounts of public property and gross malfeasance' (his trial started on 25 February 1991; on 26 June 1992 he was charged with the creation of prison camps; he was given seven years imprisonment on 4 September 1992 for misappropriation of state property and funds). (Note that the ethnic hostility charge refers to the programme to assimilate the Turkish minority: in 1989 350,000 Turks left the country, but half have since returned: *The Economist*, 19 October 1991, p. 79.) Petar Mladenov also became president on 17 November 1989, while losing his party secretary role to Alexander Lilov on 2 February 1990 (he in turn was replaced by Zhan Videnov in December 1991, although as leader of the Bulgarian Socialist Party by then). Mladenov resigned as president on 6 July 1990, however, having said that 'The tanks had better move in' during a demonstration on 14 December 1989.

On 29 December 1989 the rights of the Turkish minority were restored, being able to reclaim their jobs and property. On 15 January 1990 parliament approved the deletion of the clause describing the communist party as 'the guiding force in society and the state'. Georgi Atanasov, who had become prime minister in March 1986, resigned on 1 February 1990 and was replaced three days later by Andrei Lukanov, who had been Minister of Foreign Economic Relations since August 1987; Lukanov himself stepped down on 7 July, to make way for the new post-election government; he was reappointed on 30 August 1990 and finally named his team on 20 September, having failed to form a coalition government with the opposition parties (of the sixteen ministers, thirteen were from the Bulgarian Socialist Party and three were independents). (Lukanov was arrested on 9 July 1992 on charges which included misappropriating state funds in the communist era, specifically providing aid to left-wing regimes in the Third World.) While the party's name was changed to the Bulgarian Socialist Party, a new Bulgarian Communist Party was launched on 21 June 1990. Although new parties had already been formed, the National Assembly formally allowed the setting up of new parties on 3 April. After much wrangling Zhelu Zhelev of the Union of Democratic Forces was elected president on 1 August 1990 and popularly elected on 19 January 1992 with 53.3 per cent of the vote (he did not get over 50 per cent of the vote in the first round on 12 January).

The general election

The two rounds of the election for the Grand National Assembly (Sobranie) took place on 10 and 17 June 1990. Table 19.1 shows the result. It can be argued that the Bulgarian Socialist Party benefited from the tradition of conformity and submission during Ottoman Empire and communist party rule. The economic aspects of the party manifestoes were as follows:

Bulgarian Socialist Party. The manifesto talked of a 'mixed and socially-orientated economy, functioning on market principles'. There should be equal competition between different forms of ownership. There should be a gradual change to a market economy, with a pronounced social security system (e.g. unemployment pay; an increase in family allowances and an increase in paid maternity leave). Mladenov's comment on 30 January 1990 about the idea of replacing the communist ideal with a capitalist one is of interest in this context: 'It is obvious that if one accepts such ideas, we will embark on social cataclysm, mass unemployment, and political and social anarchy.' A cautious approach should also be adopted towards privatization, although in the services sector

Table 19.1 Bulgarian general election, June 1990

Party	Seats	% vote
Bulgarian Socialist Party	211	47.15
Union of Democratic Forces	144	36.20
Movements for Rights and Freedoms	23	6.03
Bulgarian Agrarian Party	16	8.03
Fatherland Union	2	
Independents	2	
Fatherland Party of Labour	1	2.50
Social Democratic Party (non-Marxist)	1	
Total	400	100

things could be speeded up. As regards agriculture (Judy Dempsey, *FT*, 7 June 1990, p. 38), land can belong to anyone 'who wishes to cultivate and use it efficiently'. The 'untapped potentialities of co-operative farming must be preserved and developed', but membership must be voluntary. 'Everyone who wants to farm must have the opportunity to obtain land with or without paying for the land tenure and enjoy the right to inherit it . . . we want a new land Act which will restore the ownership of land to the tillers'. The impression was given that the Union of Democratic Forces would privatize the land and sell it to foreigners (Judy Dempsey, *FT Survey*, 17 May 1991, p. 18).

The new manifesto was issued 1 February 1990 at an emergency party congress. There was a commitment to multi-party democracy. 'We are founding a new type of modern Marxist party, inspired by the everlasting ideals and values of Marx, Engels and Lenin'. The aim was to create 'a humane and democratic socialism'.

Union of Democratic Forces. This was composed of nineteen political movements. The manifesto spoke in favour of a rapid transfer to a market economy with a strong private sector. There should be a return of land to the original owners. But if records could not be traced those who wished to farm land should be allowed to own it, although only after a three to five year period during which they would have to 'show their commitment to the land'.

Bulgarian Agrarian Party. The party was in favour of an 'open, socially orientated market economy' with equality in all forms of ownership. About half of existing fixed assets should be 'destatized' in the foreseeable future (Pishev 1991: 102). All land taken over during collectivization should be returned to the former owners or their descendants, on condition that they farm it. There should be no return to large landowners or capitalists, so 'speculators' would not to be allowed to purchase large amounts of land (Judy Dempsey, *FT*, 6 June 1990, p. 2).

A strike led by the trade union Podkrepa,

starting on 26 November 1990, culminated in the resignation of Prime Minister Lukanov three days later. On 7 December Dimitar Popov (a judge, chairman of Sofia's municipal court, with no party affiliation) was appointed caretaker prime minister until a new general election could be held. The National Assembly approved a new eighteen-member coalition government on 20 December 1990. The three main parties were represented, the Bulgarian Socialist Party, the Union of Democratic Forces and the Bulgarian Agrarian Party: there were eight representatives from the Socialist Party and five were independents. Ivan Kostov was named as finance minister. On 12 July 1991 a new constitution was approved, with a democratic society at its heart; shortly afterward 29 September was fixed as the new date for parliamentary and local elections (although a postponement was announced in August).

The second free election was actually held on 13 October 1991 for the 240 seats in the Grand National Assembly. The turn-out was 83.9 per cent. Table 19.2 shows the result.

In the summer the UDF Liberals, the UDF Centre and the 'Nikola Petkov' Agrarian Union split off from the UDF as an umbrella body and each failed to reach the 4 per cent of the vote required to gain parliamentary seats. A new alliance called the United Agarian Party (led by Tsanko Barev) also failed to win any seats. The UDF National Movement (led by Filip Dimitrov) formed a minority government, with parliamentary support from the MRF (led by Ahmed

Dogan). The MRF was not given posts in the government, owing to national sensitivity about the Turkish minority, which is represented by the MRF (soon after the election there was a restoration of the right to teach the Turkish language in school for two hours a week). The economic reform programme was continued. In the municipal elections the BSP did better, being able to appoint more than half of all town mayors.

THE GOVERNMENT'S ECONOMIC PROGRAMME

Austerity measures

As the economic situation deteriorated shortages and rationing increased. On 16 August 1990 it was announced that sugar would be rationed from 1 September. Since then sugar, cooking oil, flour, eggs, cheese and detergents have been rationed in most areas. Petrol rationing was introduced on 15 October 1990 (forty litres a month per motorist) and on 1 January 1991 ordinary petrol sales were suspended for about two weeks (exceptions included food delivery vans, ambulances and other 'vehicles for social needs' such as buses; a shorter, one-week ban occurred in the previous month).

Attempts have been made to gain greater control over the monetary system. The banking system consists of the National Bank of Bulgaria (a new central bank Act came into force on 29 June 1991), the Bulgarian Foreign Trade Bank, the State Savings Bank and commercial banks (seventy-seven of them, according to *Bulgarian Quarterly*, 1991, vol. 1, no. 3, p. 118). The first private bank was formed on 28 April 1990. Also in April 1990, the NBB introduced a non-remunerated minimum reserve requirement of 5 per cent on deposits. Commercial banks are now required to maintain a minimum equity to assets ratio of 4 per cent (Judy Dempsey, *FT Survey*, 17 May 1991, p. 18). On 1 April 1991 the lev became the only legal tender.

Table 19.2 Bulgarian general election, October 1991

Party	Seats	% vote
Union of Democratic Forces (UDF National Movement)	110	34.36
Bulgarian Socialist Party	106	33.14
Movements for Rights and Freedom	24	7.55

The Popov economic package

An IMF-inspired programme was eventually drawn up. Agreement was reached in February 1991, with IMF credits totalling more than $500 million to be phased in until early 1992 ($85 million was released in February, $110 million in March and a further $50 million over each of four stages). Some parts of the programme still need parliamentary approval, but there are two main elements: the further liberalization of the economic mechanism is dealt with below, but the other part was an austerity package.

The budget deficit was to be reduced from 13 per cent of GDP in 1990 to 3.5 per cent of GDP in 1991 (Judy Dempsey, *FT Survey*, 17 May 1991, p. 16, and Gordon Hughes 1991: 168) (it actually turned out to be 5.8 per cent of GDP; United Nations Economic Commission for Europe 1992: 94). This was partly to be achieved by expenditure reductions on, e.g. defence (reduced to 3 per cent of the budget), state administration and subsidies. On 1 February 1991 subsidies were withdrawn on all goods except heating, petrol and children's clothes (Judy Dempsey, *FT Survey*, 17 May 1991, p. 16). The resulting price rises averaged nearly 700 per cent e.g. bread 611 per cent, milk 500 per cent, meat 500 per cent, cheese 477 per cent, heating 1,650 per cent, electricity 713 per cent, coal 1,375 per cent, public transport 1,100 per cent. The intention was to liberalize 80 per cent of prices; exceptions as regards producer prices included some fuels and electric power. Official estimates put the rise in consumer prices at 150 per cent in February 1991 alone and at 411 per cent between October 1990 and the start of March 1991 (D. Jones 1991: 214). The prices of consumer goods at the end of March 1991 were 3.8 times higher compared with December 1990 and 5.7 times higher compared with May 1990 (Karabashev 1991: 80). In 1990 the fall in the real after-tax wage may have been as much as 10 per cent (D. Jones 1991: 219). The January 1991 legislation provided for a maximum increase in wages, pensions or unemployment benefits, expected to compensate on average for only 70 per cent of anticipated inflation; workers on the minimum wage would be fully compensated (p. 219). There was an 80 per cent tax on the growth of wages above 3 per cent (*Bulgarian Quarterly*, 1991, vol. 1, no. 3, p. 96). The 200 day 'social pact' (the Agreement on Social Peace) between the government, trade unions and employers (constituting the so-called Tripartite Committee) also included a ban on strikes until July 1991. Tripartite corporatist structures have thus emerged (D. Jones 1992: 460–3). These include the following: the March 1990 General Agreement; the May 1990 national labour agreement; the August 1990 agreement to halt further price rises until the indexation system became effective; the December 1990 Agreement on Social Peace; and the June 1991 agreement (which, for example, gave complete indexation for forthcoming energy price increases).

The interest rate (the refinancing rate for commercial banks) was raised from 5 per cent to 45 per cent and to 52 per cent on 10 June 1991, but was reduced to 47 per cent in July and increased again to 54 per cent at the end of August.

The minority UDF government's proposals were put forward on 24 March 1992; the 1992 budget deficit was to be 4.3 per cent of GDP.

Economic performance

Table 19.4 indicates that inflation was a serious problem in 1991. The monthly consumer inflation rate in 1991 was 13.6 per cent in January, 122.9 per cent in February, 50.5 per cent in March, 2.5 per cent in April, 0.8 per cent in May, 5.9 per cent in June, 8.4 per cent in July and 7.5 per cent in August (*Bulgarian Quarterly*, 1991, vol. 1, no. 3, p. 117). Tables 19.3 and 19.4 show that unemployment has increased rapidly, while output has fallen.

Marketization

No state economic plan was drawn up in 1990

Table 19.3 Bulgaria: unemployment

		Numbers unemployed	Unemployment rate (%)
1990	June	22,400	0.5
	December	65,100	1.6
1991	January	74,000	
	February		
	March	124,100	3.0
	April		
	May		
	June	223,000	5.1
	July		6.8
	August	302,000	6.9
	September	342,000	7.8
	October		
	November		
	December	425,000	11.0
1992	January		
	February		
	March		14.0
	April		
	May		
	June		
	July		
	August		
	September		17.0
	October		
	November		
	December		

Sources: OECD Employment Outlook, July 1991, p. 21; OECD Economic Outlook, December 1991, p. 56; Deutsche Bank, Focus: Eastern Europe, 1991, no. 26, p. 2; Economic Bulletin for Europe, 1991, vol. 43, p. 28; R. Boyes, The Times, 21 January 1992, p. 9; IHT, 6 April 1992, p. 9; Commission of the European Communities, Employment Observatory, 1992, no. 2, p. 9, no. 3, p. 9.

Table 19.4 Bulgaria: foreign debt and rates of growth of GDP, industrial output, agricultural output and prices (%)

GDP	
1990	1991
−12.0	−23.0
Industrial output	
1990	1991
−12.6	−27.0
Agricultural output	
1990	1991
−8.6	−6.4
Inflation	
1990	1991
26.3	334.0
Net debt ($ billion)	
End 1990	End 1991
11.2	10.9

Sources: Kaser and Allsopp (1992: 2); DIW Economic Bulletin, 1992, vol. 29, no. 4, p. 5; OECD Economic Outlook, December 1991, p. 56, June 1992, pp. 41–2, December 1992, pp. 123–6; United Nations Economic Commission for Europe (1992: 45, 65, 86, 93, 302, 304); The Banker, September 1992, pp. 23, 33.

(Karabashev 1991: 76). In November 1990 demonopolization legislation was passed. For example, the construction and wine enterprises were broken up (four wine enterprises were split into thirty-three new ones). Enterprises established informal contracts with one another and inter-enterprise credits increased rapidly.

The government programme of April 1990 envisaged that the proportion of prices set contractually by buyers and sellers should rise from 12 per cent in 1989, to 40 per cent in 1990 and 60 per cent in 1991 (Wyzan 1990c: 13). The deputy finance minister, Yevgeni Vzunov, was later reported to have said that 80 per cent of prices were to be freed from controls by the end of 1990 (Laura Colby, IHT, 5 September 1990, p. 2).

As regards labour, independent trade unions have been set up. Most belong to federations. The Podkrepa (Support) Independent Federation of Labour was actually founded in February 1989; the president is Konstantin Trenchev. The socialist organization Bulgarian Trade Unions became independent and changed its name to CITUB (Confederation of Independent Bulgarian Trade Unions) in February 1990. Krastyo Petkov was elected president. The

Edinstvo (Unity) federation was formed in early 1991. Establishing membership is not easy (D. Jones 1992: 459–66). The CITUB membership figure of 3.7 million in early 1990 (about 87 per cent of the workforce) seems an exaggeration, but in any case it fell. By February 1991 the figure may have been closer to 2 million. At that time Podkrepa claimed 317,600 compared with less than 300,000 in September 1990. Edinstvo claims 230,000, but this has been severely questioned. Strikes were legalized in early March 1990.

Unemployment compensation was introduced in late 1989 (D. Jones 1991: 224–5). Benefit in the first month is the same as the gross wage of the previous month, but then falls by ten percentage points each month to 50 per cent in the sixth month. After that, for a maximum of three months, benefit is equal to the minimum wage. Eligibility conditions relate to dismissal and working for a certain period.

Privatization

The 23rd of March 1990 saw the end of the ceiling placed on the number of people (which was ten) that a private enterprise could employ. Ivan Pushkarov became the minister of industry, trade and services; he was in favour of rapid privatization, but against a Polish-type voucher system. His goal was to privatize 20–30 per cent of state industry over three years (Judy Dempsey, *FT Survey*, 17 May 1991, p. 18).

The Popov programme included proposals for speedier privatization; privatization and property rights legislation was expected to be in place by the autumn of 1991. A number of 'small' privatizations (retail trade, tourism, crafts and transport) were launched after some delay in June 1991 with the auctioning off of some petrol stations. But 'large' privatization is still at the parliamentary committee stage (*EEN*, 20 January 1992, vol. 6, no. 2, p. 7). Most of state industry has been transformed into joint stock companies, but privatization legislation has been held up; government proposals emphasize the use of auctions and rule out the use of voucher schemes, although there is provision for preferential non-voting shares to be allocated to workers in the enterprise at a substantial discount (Alan Smith, *Business Europa*, May-June 1992, pp. 14–15). Anthony Robinson (*FT Survey*, 3 July 1992, p. vi) provides the following information. A privatization law was approved by parliament on 8 May 1992, but still needs further implementary legislation to come fully into effect. At least 20 per cent of the shares of privatized enterprises will be retained by the government and used to finance social security funds and limited compensation for former owners. Up to 20 per cent of a company's equity can be offered at a preferential price, while a successful staff purchase at an auction permits a 30 per cent discount on the sale price (Deutsche Bank, *Focus: Eastern Europe*, 1992, no. 51, p. 7).

EEN (6 July 1992, vol. 6, no. 14, p. 7) talks of economic reform legislation slowly advancing, notably with a 'restitution' bill which hands back property expropriated in the late 1940s.

Credit Bank was the first private bank.

D. Jones (1992: 463–4) cites the following estimates: by September 1990 private employment stood at 100,000 in about 40,000 small enterprises; the private sector still accounts for only about 5 per cent of GDP.

FOREIGN TRADE, AID AND CAPITAL

Foreign trade

Bulgaria became a member of both the IMF and the World Bank on 26 September 1990.

The state monopoly was abolished in 1990 and all enterprises henceforth had the right to engage in foreign trade (Karabashev 1991: 83). A 20 per cent export tax was imposed on a wide range of products in February 1991 (Judy Dempsey, *FT Survey*, 17 May 1991, p. 16). The first half of 1991 saw a gradual dismantling of trade restrictions and barriers (Deutsche Bank, *Focus Eastern Europe*, 1991, no. 26, p. 3).

On 2 April 1990 there was a massive devaluation of the lev (Wyzan 1990c: 2); in February 1991 the lev was devalued further (from ten to thirty to the US dollar). A complex exchange rate regime was set up. After 1 August 1990 enterprises were allowed to retain 50 per cent of hard currency export earnings, but the other 50 per cent had to be sold to the state at a rate of 2.93 leva to the US dollar. Approved enterprises were allowed to purchase hard currency at this rate (Pishev 1991: 109). With the setting up of the interbank foreign exchange market in February 1991 enterprises have not had to sell hard currency to the state. In that month the first foreign exchange transactions were launched on the Bulgarian interbank market, while the new floating, unified exchange rate subsequently recovered from its initial weakness (Deutsche Bank, *Focus Eastern Europe*, 1991, no. 26, p. 3).

Bulgaria's relatively heavy dependence on Comecon trade, especially with the Soviet Union, has meant a particularly hard transition. Soviet oil supplies have been less than contracted for and this led, for example, to the price of petrol nearly doubling on 23 July 1990. Until 1989 Soviet oil deliveries were around 11 million tonnes, but in 1990 this fell to 7.8 million tonnes; the 1991 agreement specified 5 million tonnes (Judy Dempsey, *FT*, 2 May 1991, p. 3).

The USA granted MFN status in November 1991.

Bulgaria's convertible currency current account was in deficit in both 1990 and 1991, at $1.2 billion and an estimated $0.9 billion respectively (*OECD Economic Outlook*, June 1992, p. 43).

Foreign aid

Bulgaria has been relatively neglected as regards Western aid. On 18 February 1991 the UK government extended its 'know-how fund' to Bulgaria. This fund already applied to Poland, Hungary and Czechoslovakia and is designed to provide technological, economic and educa-tional assistance. In Bulgaria the particular emphasis was to be on advising small businesses, banking, public administration, retraining and management; the initial sum was likely to be only £1 million for the year.

In February 1991 the European Community agreed to give food aid (Ecu 100 million) and to extend European Investment Bank loans to Bulgaria. The EC confirmed a $400 million loan on 11 November. The World Bank has provided a loan of $250 million and the G24 countries have promised a further $800 million (*FT*, 10 October, 1991, p. 3). According to *The Economist* (Survey, 12 October 1991, p. 49), aid approved since June 1989 included the IMF $0.5 billion and G24 $1.4 billion. The Deutsche Bank (*Focus Eastern Europe*, 1991, no. 26, 24 October, p. 3) provides the following information. In July 1991 the EC ratified (conditional) balance of payments aid of around $350 million, while other OECD countries have irrevocably pledged some $200 million; an official estimate puts total foreign lending in 1991 at $620 million.

Bulgaria has been experiencing difficulties in repaying foreign debt. On 30 March 1990 the Foreign Trade Bank (responsible for about 85 per cent of the gross debt) announced that it was postponing payment on the principal owed to banks (but even most interest payments were unpaid after June). Subsequently, Bulgaria has sought the rescheduling of its entire debt. On 18 April 1991 the Paris Club of creditor governments agreed to reschedule the debt owed to them by the Bulgarian government and the Bulgarian Foreign Trade Bank over ten years with a six year grace period. But on 11 March 1992 the IMF announced a delay in the extension of the one year stand-by agreement, due to such factors as the lack of progress on privatization legislation.

Foreign capital

The profits of foreign companies and joint ventures (where foreign investment exceeds $100,000 and 49 per cent) are taxed at 30 per cent (40 per cent otherwise) (Supplement to *Euromoney*, February 1992, p. 12). The Popov programme included a promise of legislation more conducive to foreign investment. The new law was passed in February 1992 (Judy Dempsey, *FT*, 10 February 1992, p. 2; Alan Smith, *Business Europa*, May–June 1992, p. 14): restrictions on the repatriation of profits were abolished; Western companies were permitted to own Bulgarian enterprises; foreign investors were able to set up their own enterprises; the National Bank was able to authorize foreign companies to acquire a share in Bulgarian banks or to set up their own banks; foreigners were allowed to acquire ownership rights in buildings, presumably for business purposes, and residential property by applying to build that property; but land ownership was still ruled out (leases for up to 101 years were available); permission from the Council of Ministers would be needed for foreign investment in, for example, 'sensitive geographical regions' and 'particular areas of activity'.

By October 1991 there were 800 joint ventures, with $300 million of foreign capital committed (Scott 1992: 56).

AGRICULTURE

The 16 February 1990 reform (*EEN*, 1990, vol. 4, no. 4, p. 5). Restrictions were lifted on the size of privately owned farms; indefinite leasing of farming land was allowed, as was the right of children to inherit land; farmers were allowed to sell their produce direct to local markets rather than to co-operative farms; an Agricultural Bank was established to provide cheap credit for purchasing new equipment from domestic or foreign suppliers. Nevertheless there was still some resistance to private land ownership, partly out of fear of large Turkish land purchases.

On 1 February 1991 the retail prices of most vegetables, fruit and flowers were decontrolled (Wyzan 1991: 91).

The 22 March 1990 decree (*IHT*, 24–5 March 1990, p. 13). There were to be free-market prices, except for bread, milk, meat, sugar, vegetable oil and baby foods (ceilings were set for these products at the retail level, but their wholesale prices were also raised at the expense of the state budget; Wyzan 1991: 91). Taxes were to be reduced from 20 per cent to 10 per cent and were to apply equally to co-operatives and private farms. Farmers were to be allowed to retain half the foreign currency earned from exports. The agricultural sector's debt to the state was to be written off.

The government abolished state orders for agricultural products at the beginning of 1990 (Wyzan 1991: 90).

On 15 May 1990 the government proposed that the original owners or their heirs should be allowed to reclaim up to 20 ha (200 da) of land in the plains and up to 30 ha (300 da) in hilly areas (note that 'owners' do not include those whose land was expropriated under the 1946 law, which limited land ownership to these amounts). The conditions were that land could not be bought or sold for three years and that the land had to be farmed (otherwise the land had to be leased to working tenants); it was hoped that most land plots would be in private hands by the end of 1991 (Ariane Genillard, *FT Survey*, 17 May 1991, p. 17); in 1990 private farmers produced 45 per cent of total meat production (p. 17). An unlimited amount of land could be farmed privately if leased (Wyzan 1990c: 12). Some additional information about the draft law passed by the parliamentary committee on agricultural policy and reform in November 1990 is given by Davidova (1991: 201). Those who had ownership claims but were not farming must leave their land collectivized (receiving rent in exchange) or transfer it (with compensation in the form of state bonds) to the State Land Fund, with the same conditions applying to members of co-operatives who ceased to be members and did not intend to cultivate the land themselves; for a five-year period from the date of ownership recognition (limited to 20 ha or 30 ha) private owners would not be allowed to grant land or lease or to sell it to individuals (it was not then decided what was to happen after five years); individuals were not allowed to lease their land to others. Farmers were to be free to form co-operatives. The main source of credit is the Bank of Agricultural Credit, founded in March 1990. The Land Law was adopted in late January 1991, but implementation was to be delayed until the autumn (Karabashev 1991: 82).

According to the Deutsche Bank (*Focus Eastern Europe*, 24 October 1991, no. 26, p. 2), the distribution of arable land had hardly begun to date.

On 18 September 1990 food exports were banned until the end of March 1991 in order to alleviate domestic shortages. Bans on agricultural exports persist; 1991 export taxes reached 30 per cent on meat products, cereals and cheese (Ariane Genillard, *FT Survey*, 17 May 1991, p. 17).

20

CZECHOSLOVAKIA

POLITICAL BACKGROUND

The relatively peaceful run of events gave rise to the term 'velvet revolution'. President Havel acknowledged Gorbachev's role in making the events possible and urged the West to provide greater assistance to the Soviet Union. It could be argued that internal political factors ranked higher than economic ones, since living standards in socialist Czechoslovakia were second only to the GDR and Czechoslovakia, unlike the GDR, did not have a Western 'half' to compare with.

On 24 November 1989 the politburo and secretariat of the communist party resigned. Milos Jakes (who was expelled from the party on 7 December 1989 and arrested on 6 June 1990 for abuse of power and violating the law over the 1968 Warsaw Pact invasion) was replaced as General Secretary by Karel Urbanek. Urbanek, in turn, was replaced by Vasil Mohorita on 21 December (though as *First* Secretary; on 4 November 1990 he, in turn, was replaced by Pavol Kanis). The prime minister, Ladislav Adamec, resigned on 7 December (though he became party chairman on the 21st, and remained in that position until 2 August 1990, when he was replaced by Vasil Mohorita); Marian Calfa (who resigned from the party on 18 January 1990) was his successor. Gustav Husak lost the presidency on 10 December 1989. On 17 February 1990 he was expelled from the party, along with Vasil Bilak (who was arrested on 6 June with Jakes) and Lubomir Strougal, among others. Husak died on 19 November 1991. A new government was sworn in on 10 December 1989, with communists in a minority even then (their numbers subsequently shrinking even more as members left the party, e.g. Valtr Komarek, first deputy prime minister in charge of economic affairs, and Vladimir Dlouhy, deputy prime minister put in charge of the State Planning Commission).

Alexander Dubcek was elected speaker of the Federal Assembly on 28 December 1989 and Vaclav Havel was elected as (the 'philosopher') president the day afterwards. After the general election, on 5 July 1990, Havel was re-elected president (unopposed) by the Federal Assembly for a two year term. The dissident playwright Havel was one of the founding members (along with others such as Jiri Nemec, Pavel Kohout, Zdenek Mlynar, Jan Potocka and Jiri Hajek) of Charter 77, which was founded in January 1977 as a civil and human rights group arising in response to the 1975 Helsinki Final Act. Charter 77, in turn, gave rise to Civic Forum (and its Slovak counterpart Public against Violence), formed two days after the 17 November students' demonstration which was harshly handled by the authorities.

At the end of November 1989 the Federal Assembly approved the abolition of Article 4 of the constitution, which referred to the party's 'leading role' in society. This was an important part of the process leading to a free election the following year. The agreement to pull out Soviet troops by 1 July 1991 was formally signed on 26

February 1990, a process spread over three phases; the last troops actually left a short while before the deadline. On 20 April 1990, after some dispute, the country became known as 'The Czech and Slovak Federative Republic'.

A major problem was the degree of Slovak autonomy to be allowed, with even Slovak independence mooted. From an economic point of view, Slovakia is disproportionately saddled with the defence industries (80 per cent, according to Ariane Genillard, *FT Survey*, 8 November 1991, p. v); Slovakia's strategic location close to the Soviet Union influenced the bias towards heavy industry and armaments, with many industries highly dependent on imports of Soviet oil and raw materials (*Czechoslovak Economic Digest*, 1991, no. 4, p. 9). After much wrangling the devolution bill was passed on 12 December 1990, dealing with the division of powers between the federal and republican governments (the Czech National Council has 200 deputies and the Slovak National Council has 150 deputies). The federal authorities were to retain control over the military, foreign policy and trade, oil and gas supplies (the Czech–Slovak joint stock company manages the oil pipeline, but the federal government had the right to control energy distribution as a whole in emergencies), policy over national minorities, and broad economic strategy. The federal government had the right to raise its own revenue and would not have to rely on republican transfers. But many details remained unresolved, e.g. transport and the ownership of natural resources (other assets belong to the republics). The presidency of the central bank would rotate annually between the Czech and Slovak republics. In March 1991 Havel expressed his preference for a referendum to determine whether the Czech and Slovak republics should become independent. In February 1992 the Slovak National Council rejected the Czech and Slovak parliamentary commissions' accord.

The 17 June 1991 meeting at the castle of Kromeriz made further progress. For example, it was agreed that the treaty should have legal rather than purely symbolic status, although not international legal status, as the Slovaks would have liked.

The June 1990 general election

This took place 8–9 June 1990, with a turn-out of 96 per cent. The Federal Assembly has two assemblies (houses): (1) Assembly of the People, 150 seats representing all electoral districts in the federation, comprising ninety-nine Czech and fifty-one Slovak. (2) Assembly of the Nations, 150 seats divided equally between the Czech and Slovak halves. Table 20.1 shows the result. The economic aspects of the party programmes were as follows.

Civic Forum–Public against Violence. The party programme was announced 10 April 1990. While it was broadly in favour of a mixed, competitive market economy, there was an air of caution. A comprehensive social welfare system was needed and foreign capital should not be allowed to become too dominant.

The Communist Party. Unusually for Eastern Europe these days, the party kept its name. At the congress held 20–1 December 1989 support was given to the idea of a 'socialist market mechanism'. The state should retain its dominance in heavy industry, but the private sector should be allowed to flourish in sectors like services. Land should not be sold to foreigners.

Christian Democratic Union. Extensive privatization was favoured.

A coalition government was formed, with Civic Forum–Public against Violence inviting six independents and two representatives of the Christian Democratic Union.

In the local elections, held 23–4 November 1990, Civic Forum–Public against Violence saw a fall in support, although nationalist parties did poorly. The percentage distribution of seats was as follows in the Czech republic: Civic Forum 31.7; independents 27.7; Communist Party 14.4; Czech People's Party 12.1; Moravian Autonomy Movement 2.6; Social Democrats 1.6. In the

Table 20.1 The Czech and Slovak general election of June 1990

Assembly of the People

	Seats	% vote
Civic Forum–Public against violence	87	46.6
Communist Party	23	13.6
Christian Democratic Union	20	12.0
Moravian–Silesian Society	9	5.4
Slovak Nationalist Party	6	3.5
Coexistence	5	2.8
Total	150	*

Assembly of the Nations

	Seats			% vote (total)
	Total	Czech	Slovak	
Civic Forum	83	50		45.9
Public against Violence			33	
Communist Party	24	12	12	13.7
Christian Democratic Union	20	6	14	11.3
Moravian–Silesian Society	7	7		6.2
Slovak Nationalist Party	9		9	3.6
Coexistence	7		7	2.7
Total	150			

* Five per cent of vote necessary to gain seats.

Slovak republic the results were as follows: Christian Democrats 27.4; Public against Violence 20.4; Communist Party 13.6; independents 12.8; Co-existence (Hungarian party) 6.3; Slovak Nationalist Party 3.2. The turn-outs were 75 per cent and 64 per cent respectively.

Civic Forum saw its divisions increase. The Civic Forum conference held 12–13 January 1991 voted to turn it into a right of centre party along Klaus lines. But on 8 February 1991 it was decided that it should become an umbrella organization for separate groupings, the right (centred on Vaclav Klaus and the Democratic Right parliamentary club; later on, the Civic Democratic Party was formed) and the liberal (centred on Deputy Premier Pavel Rychetsky and Foreign Minister Jiri Dienstbier and the Liberal Club, which emphasizes 'human values and the rights of the individual' during the process of economic reform). The two groupings planned to act as coalition partners until the 5–6 June 1992 general election.

Slovakia's Public against Violence, which became known as the Civic Democratic Union, also split. In March 1991 the Slovak prime minister, Vladimir Meciar, formed the Movement for a Democratic Slovakia, which adopted a more nationalistic stance, stressing much greater Slovak autonomy (e.g. the need for a Slovak president and national bank) and more interventionist, less harsh economic reform (the Slovak economy suffers disproportionately in terms of unemployment since, as already noted, it is much more dependent on heavy industry and armaments). At first Meciar hedged his bets, but later devised a strategy should his party win the election in Slovakia: a declaration of sovereignty, a separate constitution, and a referendum on whether to maintain the federation. On 23 April 1991 Meciar was replaced as prime minister by his deputy, Jan Carnogursky of the Christian Democrats. Carnogursky was very ambivalent at first, having a vision of a separate seat for an independent Slovakia within Europe, with maximum aid and independence from Czech regions in the meantime; he favoured a separate constitution, which could be implemented if insufficient concessions were granted in the federation. He later became more positive towards the federation. Alexander Dubcek was elected chairman of the Slovak Social Democratic Party on 29 March 1992; the party advocates greater state intervention in the economy, but firmly supports the federation. Public opinion in Slovakia was certainly largely in favour of greater autonomy, but a majority of people still supported the federation. Some anxiety was expressed at the prospects for minorities in an independent Slovakia (the Hungarians, for example, constitute 10.8 per cent of the republic's population).

The June 1992 general election

This took place 5–6 June 1992, with a turn-out of over 85 per cent. Table 20.2 shows the result. The differences were pronounced, with Klaus's Civic Democratic Party victorious in the Czech republic and Meciar's Movement for a Democratic Slovakia in the Slovak republic. Klaus deemed a federation worth while only if the economic reform programme were continued and strong federal powers preserved. Klaus was asked to try to form a government, but the negotiations failed. He totally rejected Meciar's offer of a mere economic and defence union of two states with separate UN membership. The 20 June accord allowed the Czech and Slovak parliaments to decide the framework for dissolution of the country by 30 September 1992; ratification would be needed by the federal parliament. A transitional administration of only five ministries (economics, finance, defence, foreign affairs and the interior) was formed, charged with carrying out a 'velvet divorce'. Jan Strasky became interim federal prime minister, while Klaus headed the administration in the Czech lands and Meciar that in Slovakia. The accord did not mention a referendum, but President Havel felt strongly

that there should be one. Havel, although unopposed, failed to gain re-election by parliament on 3 July, due mainly to Slovak opposition. He resigned on 20 July 1992. Later developments are discussed in the postscript.

THE JUNE 1990 GOVERNMENT'S ECONOMIC PROGRAMME

The government was slow in formulating the details of many policies even after the June 1990 election. Hence, it is of interest first to examine the views of individuals, disagreements being one of the reasons for the sluggishness.

Valtr Komarek became first deputy prime minister with overall responsibility for economic policy on 10 December 1989, although by May of the following year he had been replaced by Vaclav Vales. Subsequently he returned to the Institute of Economic Forecasting, from whence he had come. He resigned from the Communist Party on 8 January 1990 and in April 1991 joined the Social Democratic Party. Komarek stressed caution; a rapid move to the market would lead to economic ruin. Demonopolization should precede price reform and privatization; restructuring and improved management were more important than ownership.

Vaclav Klaus, who was at the Economic Forecasting Unit, became finance minister on 10 December 1989, although he narrowly escaped demotion the following June when he was offered (and declined) the governorship of the central bank. Unexpectedly, he was elected chairman of Civic Forum on 13 October. He does not believe in a 'third way', either market socialism or *perestroika*; the aim is to create a 'normally functioning market economy', so there is no desire to undertake new social experiments (Klaus 1992b: 73). Klaus (1992: 115) argues that for all East Europeans 'the only practical and realistic way to improve their living standards is the total abolition of central planning, the dismantling of price and wage, exchange rate and foreign trade controls, and the radical transformation of existing property

Table 20.2 The Czech and Slovak general election of June 1992

Assembly of the People
150 seats, 99 representing Czech electoral districts and 51 Slovak

Czech	No. of seats	Slovak	No. of seats
Civic Democratic Party	48	Movement for a Democratic Slovakia	24
Left Bloc	19	Party of the Democratic Left	10
Social Democrats	10	Christian Democrats	6
Republican Party	8	Slovak National Party	6
Liberal Union	7	Hungarian People's Party	5
Christain Democrats	7		
Total	99	Total	51

Assembly of the Nation
150 seats divided equally between the Czech and Slovak halves

Czech	No. of seats	Slovak	No. of seats
Civic Democratric Party	37	Movement for a Democratic Slovakia	33
Left Bloc	15	Party of the Democratic Left	13
Social Democrats	6	Christian Democrats	8
Republican Party	6	Slovak National Party	9
Liberal Union	5	Hungarian People's Party	7
Christian Democrats	6	Social Democratic Party	5
Total	75	Total	75

rights'. He is an outspoken advocate of the market economy and of monetarism: 'A market economy without adjectives' (quoted in *The Economist*, 10 February 1990, p. 93); 'We are the monetarists of Eastern Europe' (quoted in *The Times*, 5 February 1990, p. 27). With easy money no real changes in the economic behaviour of any agents can be achieved. Klaus believes in a rapid but nevertheless phased introduction of the market, what he terms the 'nurturing of the market' (John Lloyd, FT, 5 March 1990, p. 2). There should be a 'gradual, but at the same time relatively quick and organized, transition to a market economy' (quoted by Gerard Davies, *The Guardian*, 28 March 1990, p. 24). Klaus (1992b: 75), however, believes in a 'pragmatic' reform process, with the need to react to events pragmatically and rationally during the complicated transition period. Earlier he said that with the money supply under control there should be rapid removal of price controls, by the end of 1990 preferably rather than the two to three years suggested by some of his opponents. Klaus did not foresee a large increase in unemployment, e.g. the service sector could be expanded to absorb those leaving industry, but thought there would be no 'dramatic improvement' resulting from the reforms for two years (Stephen Fidler, *FT*, 22 September 1990, p. 2).

Klaus also has strong views on privatization. In March 1990 he said that the first businesses to be privatized would be small shops, services and workshops. All forms of ownership needed to be put on an equal footing. Not all sectors need to be affected: 'No one would want to privatize railways or water distribution.'

The Klaus scheme for privatization was as follows. State enterprises should be turned into joint stock companies in which the state holds the shares at first. Everyone would be distributed with non-tradeable vouchers exchangeable for company shares at a token price (because of the lack of savings, the relatively favourable budgetary situation and in order to avoid excessive dependence on foreign capital). The vouchers would have a fixed value; the greater the demand for the shares of any particular enterprise the more vouchers needed to buy them. The shares could then be traded on a stock exchange. The European Bank of Reconstruction and Development should help finance the voucher scheme.

Richard Wagner was president Havel's personal adviser on the economy and the environment. He takes a cautious approach, being opposed e.g. to rapid, wholesale privatization.

Vladimir Dlouhy, another member of the Economic Forecasting Unit, became deputy prime minister and head of the State Planning Commission on 10 December 1989. He resigned from the communist party on 29 December 1989. In July 1990 he became head of the new Ministry of the Economy. As head of the State Planning Commission he saw to its dissolution in April 1990. He favoured the creation of a single Ministry of Economics as a replacement for the industrial branch ministries, and the turning of the Prices Board into an anti-monopoly office (Leslie Colitt, *FT*, 29 March 1990). The Prices Board subsequently did, in fact, disappear. Dlouhy was sceptical about the Klaus privatization plan: there is need to settle the financial situation of enterprises, including debt, while it is not clear how the voucher system would generate the necessary capital. Dlouhy emphasizes foreign investment. (Wolfgang Münchau, *The Times*, 6 August 1990, p. 23.)

Vaclav Havel. The former president was cautious at first, but later swung behind a speedier economic programme (e.g. in his 17 February 1991 speech). He favours a welfare state. Havel felt the need for increased presidential powers, but parliament was not persuaded (e.g. to call a referendum with 20 per cent public support, to dissolve the federal assembly and to rule by decree until the second general election on 5–6 June 1992).

The austerity programme

Czechoslovakia did not face the severe inflationary problems experienced in Poland, for example, and so 'shock' therapy was not necessary. During 1985–89 the average budget deficit was 0.9 per cent of national income (Begg 1991: 269). Czechoslovakia rejoined the IMF on 21 September 1990 (and the International Finance Corporation the day afterwards). The 1990 budget was outlined on 27 March 1990. The aim was to transform the 1989 budget deficit (1.6 per cent of national income) into a surplus (5.4 billion crowns or 0.9 per cent of national income in 1990). There were to be reductions in expenditure on areas like defence and internal security (12.5 per cent) and subsidies to industry, agriculture and food processing (10.7 per cent), while health care, social welfare, housing, education and the environment actually benefited from an increase in spending. The actual surplus in 1990 was 2.4 billion crowns (Begg 1991: 269). The aim as regards the 1991 budget was for a surplus of 8 billion crowns (1 per cent of national income), but the actual outcome was a deficit of 18.6 billion crowns (*Czechoslovak Economic Digest*, 1992, no. 1, p. 18); this amounted to 1.9 per cent of GDP (United Nations Economic Commission for Europe 1992: 94). Total subsidies were reduced from 16 per cent of GDP in 1989 to only 4.6 per cent in 1991 (Val Koromzay, *OECD Observer*, February–March 1992, no. 174, p. 35). Credit policy was relaxed at the start of May 1991 because of the large fall in output. For example, on 1 May enterprise turnover tax rates were lowered (in percentage terms, from 32 to 29, 22 to 20 and 12 to 11). A balanced budget was the aim for 1992.

A wage inflation tax policy is in operation. There is a 200 per cent tax when wage costs are exceeded by 3–5 per cent and 750 per cent when they are exceeded by more than 5 per cent (*Czechoslovak Economic Digest*, 1991, no. 4, supplement, p. 9). According to Tomes (1991:

197), the ceiling above which the special wage tax is imposed is based on the previous year's average wage in the same enterprise (1991 Maximum Wages Legislation); employment policy in general (including wages) is discussed in the Council for Economic and Social Agreement (active since November 1990), which brings together the government, trade unions and employers. Preserving competitiveness is a key consideration (Deutsche Bank, *Focus: Eastern Europe*, 1992, no. 40, p. 2). Existing exemptions from the wage tax include foreign companies, joint ventures and the bonus element in profit-related pay (Samuel Brittan, *FT*, 30 May 1991, p. 23). There is a minimum wage. The council agreement for 1991 aimed to limit the fall in real wages during the year to less than 10 per cent (Begg 1991: 270). The January 1991 General Agreement between the federal, Czech and Slovak governments and the trade unions included a moratorium on industrial action throughout the year, provided commitments on employment, wages and social security were adhered to; the 10 per cent figure for real wages was one of them (*EEN*, 1991, vol. 5, no. 24, p. 8).

Towards the end of April 1992 new tax laws, based on EC practice, were passed for implementation as of 1 January 1993 (Ariane Genillard and Anthony Robinson, *FT*, 30 April 1992, p. 2). Value-added tax was set at a normal rate of 23 per cent and at a 5 per cent rate on essential goods. The corporate income tax was fixed at 45 per cent and the maximum rate of personal income tax at 47 per cent.

As regards prices, there have been some notable changes as a result of the reduction in subsidies. On 9 July 1990 the average price of 30,000 food items increased by 24.6 per cent (there being income support by way of compensation). The reduction in Soviet oil supplies led to a petrol price increase of about 50 per cent on 19 July 1990, while transport fares doubled as of September 1990. Petrol rationing was introduced in October 1990: above the 25 litres per motorist per month the price rose by a third. In early December 1990 wholesale energy

prices rose by up to 75 per cent. The prices of goods and services accounting for 85 per cent of national income were liberalized on 1 January 1991; price controls remained, however, on e.g. basic foodstuffs, water, coal, oil, electricity, telecommunications, rents and transport. In the energy sector the following percentage price rises were imposed: coal 246; brown coal 246; natural gas 117; domestic heating 390. On average the price of electricity remained unchanged in order to encourage a switch from brown coal to electricity, but in March 1991 it was announced that electricity rates for industry were to go up by 80 per cent on 1 April and for households by the same amount later on. Housing rents were raised in the summer of 1991. In May 1991 gas prices rose by 134 per cent and coal prices by 324 per cent. According to an OECD report (*FT*, 8 January 1992, p. 2), between 1990 and October 1991 the percentage of GDP under regulated prices fell from roughly 85 per cent to 5 per cent. According to *Euromoney* (supplement, February 1992, p. 18), the autumn of 1991 saw price controls removed on bread, milk and meat, leaving granulated sugar as the only major food product still subject to price control.

On 1 January 1990 a new banking law came into operation, introducing a two-tier banking system as part of the process of exercising firm monetary control. The State Bank became an independent central bank (Komercni Bank), with commercial banking in the hands of commercial and savings banks. The Investment Bank's role is to provide long-term credits to both state and private enterprises. Foreign banks are allowed (the Tatra Bank, the first with foreign shareholders, began operating on 18 September); licences to open foreign banks will be reserved for those involved in lending to Czechoslovakia. The Consolidated Bank was set up in March 1991 to take over part of the inherited bad debts. In October 1991 a recapitalization fund was formed; commercial banks were to be issued with bonds by the National Assets Funds against future receipts, to be used as a hedge against losses from bank-ruptcies and bad debt write-offs. The 50 billion crowns in these convertible bonds compares with the total debt of the 'entrepreneurial sphere' of 500 billion crowns (*Czechoslovak Economic Digest*, 1991, no. 6, p. 7). Commercial banks are then allowed to swap debt for equity in enterprises being privatized. The onus of choosing which enterprises to recapitalize (i.e. to save) is thus placed on the banks.

Economic performance

Table 20.3 shows how unemployment has risen sharply. The unemployment rate is much higher in the Czech republic than in Slovakia; in December 1991 the respective figures were 4.1 per cent and 11.8 per cent. The *OECD Employment Outlook* (July 1991, p. 22) notes that while employment in the state sector fell by 215,000 over the year to the third quarter of 1990, for 1990 as a whole employment in the private sector rose by some 200,000.

The rules for the closure of enterprises have been laid down (EEN, 1991, vol. 5, no. 8, p. 2): management can decide in the case of enterprises employing up to 500 people; the government must be informed before closure in the case of enterprises employing between 500 and 3,000; and the state decides on larger enterprises.

Table 20.4 shows how total output and industrial output have fallen. In the first half of 1991 national income had fallen by 13.8 per cent and industrial output by 14.3 per cent compared to the same period in 1990 (*Czechoslovak Economic Digest*, 1991, no. 4, pp. 14, 17). An OECD report (*FT*, 8 January 1992, p.2) provides the following information for the first half of 1991: there were falls of 27 per cent in real wages, 37 per cent in personal consumption, 9.2 per cent in GDP and 13.8 per cent in NMP.

Table 20.4 shows the record as regards in-flation. In January 1991 the monthly rate was 25.8 per cent, but it was only 1.8 per cent in June and 0.1 per cent in July and August

Table 20.3 Czechoslovakia: unemployment

		No. unemployed	Rate of unemployment (%)
1990	June	12,600	0.2
	December	77,000	1.0
1991	January	119,478	1.5
	February	152,323	1.9
	March	184,720	2.3
	April	223,208	2.8
	May	255,635	3.2
	June	300,767	3.8
	July	363,000	4.6
	August	400,000	5.1
	September		5.6
	October		5.1
	November	500,000	6.3
	December	524,000	6.6
1992	January	550,000	7.1
	February		6.9
	March		6.5
	April		6.0
	May		5.6
	June		5.5
	July		5.4
	August		
	September		
	October		
	November		
	December		

Sources: Czechoslovak Economic Digest, 1991, no. 3, p. 28; no. 5, p. 16; 1992, no. 1, p. 62; Deutsche Bank, *Focus: Eastern Europe*, 1991, no. 31, p. 2; 1992, no. 40, p. 2; 1992, no. 53, p. 8, no. 58, p. 11; *OECD Employment Outlook*, July 1991, p. 21; *Economic Bulletin for Europe*, 1991, vol. 43, p. 28; J. Mladek, *IHT*, 8 January 1992, p. 13; Commission of the European Communities, *Employment Observatory*, 1992, no. 2, p. 9; DIW, *Economic Bulletin*, 1992, vol. 29, no. 7, p. 3.

(*Czechoslovak Economic Digest*, 1991, no. 4, p. 15 and no. 5, p. 15). The figure for September was 0.3 per cent, for October 0.0 per cent, for November 1.6 per cent and for December 1.2 per cent (United Nations Economic Commission for Europe 1992: 93). The monthly inflation rate was only 0.4 per cent and 0.3 per cent respec-tively in January and February 1992 (Deutsche Bank, *Focus: Eastern Europe*, 1992, no. 49, p. 6).

Table 20.4 Czechoslovakia: foreign debt and rates of growth of GDP, industrial output, agricultural output and prices (%)

GDP	
1990	*1991*
−1.7	−16.0

Industrial output	
1990	*1991*
−3.5	−23.4

Agricultural output	
1991	*1990*
−3.5	−8.8

Inflation	
1990	*1991*
10.0	58.0

Net debt ($ billion)	
End 1990	*End 1991*
7.0	6.5

Sources: Kaser and Allsopp (1992: 2); DIW *Economic Bulletin*, 1992, vol. 29, no. 4, p. 5; 1992, vol. 29, no. 7, p. 2; *Czechoslovak Economic Digest*, 1991, no. 3, p. 11; 1992, no. 1, p. 18; 1992, no.3, p. 2; Deutsche Bank, *Focus: Eastern Europe*, 1991, no. 31, p. 1; 1992, no. 40, pp. 2–3; 1992, no. 53, p. 8; 1992, no. 3, p. 2; *European Economy: the Path of Reform in Central and Eastern Europe*, Commission of the European Communities, Brussels, 1991, p. 24; V. Komarek, *IHT*, 7 January 1992, p. 6; J. Mladek, *IHT*, 8 January 1992, p. 13; United Nations Economic Commission for Europe (1992: 45, 65, 86, 93, 298, 302, 304); OECD, *Economic Outlook*, June 1992, p. 41); *The Banker*, September 1992, pp. 23, 33.

Marketization

Central planning was phased out during 1990 and a start made on setting up new legal forms. The State Planning Commission and the State Price Board were abolished. The 1988 enterprise law was amended in April 1990. The employees' self-management bodies were dissolved. A new two-tier structure was set up, comprising a supervisory board (half of whose members are elected by full-time employees and half by the founder) and a director (appointed and dismissed by the founder, although in consultation with the supervisory board). The autonomy of the enterprise is emphasized. For example, any registered enterprise is now free to engage in foreign trade. Note that in the case of pubic utilities there is no supervisory board.

There has been noticeable progress in demonopolizing industry. For example, Peter Marsh (*FT*, 7 April 1990, p. 2) reports that Slovchemia recently split up into twenty-two separate units specializing in various types of chemicals; these units operate independently and many were to be privatized. Under the Law on Protection of the Economic Competition, passed in January 1991 and effective 1 March 1991, there was to be close monitoring of cartel and merger deals as well as of enterprises accounting for 30 per cent or more of the market. Permission is needed if a cartel agreement means a market share greater than 5 per cent of the national market or 30 per cent of the local one (Rychetnik 1992: 122). Michael Reynolds (*FT*, 26 September 1991, p. 12) provides further information. There is a Federal Office of Competition and there are two anti-monopoly offices (one Czech and one Slovak); the federal body has jurisdiction where the entrepreneurs concerned account for over 40 per cent of the relevant market in the whole country.

As regards labour, the state-controlled official trade union body (ROH) disbanded itself on 2 March 1990. Strike committees, formed in November 1989, became independent trade unions. Most joined the Czechoslovak Confederation of Trade Unions (CSKOS), established in March 1990 and led by Igor Pleskot.

Tomes (1991: 196–7) describes how the February 1991 Employment Act set employment compensation at 60 per cent of an individual's net wage for the first six months and at 50 per cent for the next half year, for a maximum period of twelve months following job loss. To be eligible a person must have been employed for a minimum of a year during the previous three years and a suitable job could not be offered within a week. The social security steps in after this. Benefit equal to the minimum old-age pension is paid out if a person is unemployed and is a first-time job seeker, or has not been employed in the previous three years. An amendment involved raising the benefit applicable when unemployment is due to restructuring to 65 per cent and 60 per cent respectively, while retraining brings 75 per cent of previous take-home pay for the duration. In January 1992, apart from graduates, eligibility was restricted to those who had genuinely lost their jobs and were actively seeking work, and the period of entitlement to benefit was halved (Commission of the European Communities, *Employment Observatory*, 1992, no. 2, p. 14).

As of 1 January 1992 former communist party officials or those people linked with the old secret police are barred for five years from public office, including managerial positions in enterprises where the state has 51 per cent or more of the equity. This is the controversial *lustrace* (purification or screening) law.

Privatization

It is worth mentioning at the start of this section the attempt by Hughes and Hare (1991) to rank branches in terms of their long-run viability and competitiveness, measuring value added at world market prices. If the comparative advantage index is negative it means that the value of inputs used is greater than the value of output; in 1987 19 per cent of manufacturing output was so characterized. If the index is between 0 and 1, value-added is positive but it would be more efficient to import (58.6 per cent). If the index exceeds 1 the product should be exported (only 22.4 per cent) (p. 91). The respective percentage figures for Hungary and Poland were as follows: 24.2, 68.9 and 6.9 (for the period 1986–88) and 23.6, 65.5 and 10.9 (in 1988). In a later article (1992: 84) Hughes and Hare suggest that the calculation of 'domestic resource cost' in each branch of the economy (the ratio of value-added in domestic prices to value added in world prices) may help in the formulation of an industrial policy.

The private enterprise law of April 1990 relaxed controls considerably. Private enterprise was allowed in all spheres of activity except those designated as state monopolies and no limits were placed on the number of employees or on the amount of capital invested. Public companies were allowed to issue shares to individuals, groups and companies, and 'reasonable' participation of foreign capital in the economy was permitted. Full constitutional recognition was given to private property and foreigners were allowed to acquire property rights.

There seems to be general agreement that the state should have a major say in 'strategic' enterprises and public utilities. Klaus himself at first envisaged selling 70 per cent of the economy initially and retaining 30 per cent (*IHT*, 24 September 1990, p. 11). The government intends to privatize about 70 per cent of state enterprises (*Czechoslovak Economic Digest*, 1991, no. 6, p. 4).

On 2 October 1990 both houses of the federal assembly voted to repeal the 1959 Act that dealt with the forcible taking over of property between 1955 and 1959 (housing, restaurants, shops and small businesses, but not agricultural land incorporated into co-operative farms).

The Restitution Law

(See Daniel Arbess, *FT*, 7 March 1991, p. 33, Cepl 1991, Kupka 1992, and *Czechoslovak Economic Digest*, 1991, no. 4, supplement, p. 12).

This Law was passed by parliament on 21 February 1991 and was to apply from 1 April. It deals with the physical restitution of or compensation for non-agricultural property arbitrarily expropriated after 25 February 1948 (the date of the communist seizure of power) and not covered by the October 1990 law. Individual Czechoslovak citizens permanently residing in the country (or their heirs, if they were resident citizens) were able to make claims by 30 September 1991. As regards the 'obliged person' holding the property being claimed, the following apply: there is an obligation to maintain the condition of the property and hand over possession no later than 31 October 1991; generally a refund of any purchase price paid for property is claimable; and the former owner has to pay compensation for 'substantial' increases in the value of property (if the former owner is unwilling to pay for any increase in value, only financial compensation is available). The following are exempt from physical restitution: property held by certain joint ventures and domestic companies and by other countries; substantially reconstructed buildings, and land on which one or more buildings have been constructed since expropriation. Former owners eligible for only financial compensation are subject to a cash limit of 30,000 crowns, plus shares in privatized enterprises up to a value of a further 30,000 crowns. Kupka (1992: 304) notes, however, that by 1948 no more than 13.7 per cent of the means of production was left in the private sector (although contributing 33.4 per cent of NMP).

The Small Privatization Law

Most non-restitutable properties and businesses of a local, 'non-public' character (e.g. shops, restaurants, small workshops and service enterprises) are being auctioned under the Small Privatization Law (effective 1 December 1990). Only citizen residents are allowed to bid in the first round of any auctions. New owners cannot sell to foreigners for two years. Credits to cover up to 50 per cent of the cost are available. The first auctions actually started on 26 January 1991 and the second round on 16 June 1991. Local industries (e.g. construction) were to be restructured as joint stock companies and the shares sold to investors, with preference given to employees (*Czechoslovak Economic Digest*, 1991, no. 1, p. 16). Concern has since been expressed about small enterprises being bought with wealth accumulated before 1989 and about the *de facto* backing of many bids by foreign funds. Some 15,000 shops, restaurants and small businesses have been auctioned off since

January 1991 (Deutsche Bank, *Focus: Eastern Europe*, 27 November 1991, no. 31, p. 3). Some 10 per cent of shops and restaurants were in private ownership by the end of 1991 (*The Economist*, 4 April 1992, p. 87).

The Major Privatization Law

This was passed on 26 February 1991, taking effect on 1 April. Excluded property includes natural resources, public transport facilities, church property and assets which may be subject to the restitution laws or small privatization (*Czechoslovak Economic Digest*, 1991, no. 6, p. 5). Each larger-scale enterprise had to develop a 'privatization project'; the target date deadline of 30 November 1991 for those in the first wave was later extended. The shares were to be initially owned by a federal or republican National Property Fund. The first wave of privatization was to involve 2,285 large enterprises (twenty-nine by the federal authorities, 1,630 by the Czech government and 626 by the Slovak government), while the second wave was to involve 1,842 (twenty-one, 1,248 and 573 respectively) (*Czechoslovak Economic Digest*, 1991, no. 6, p. 29). A mixture of a number of share-issuing devices was outlined:

1. Domestic and foreign flotation (note that a 100 per cent takeover by a foreign company requires the approval of the government; in all other cases the sponsoring ministry is involved, usually the industry ministry).

2. Controlled auction to foreign investors.

3. 'Investment points': this has been influenced by the Klaus scheme, partly arising because of the lack of sufficient savings. Every adult Czechoslovak citizen (aged eighteen or over and currently residing in the country) would be issued with a fixed number of 'investment points' (1,000) exchangeable for shares in bidding rounds, where the 'price' of shares in terms of points in individual enterprises would eventually settle down to equate supply and demand. The price of the points was 1,035 crowns (something over the average weekly

wage), thirty-five crowns to buy a voucher booklet and 1,000 for the voucher stamps. The coupons began to be distributed on 1 October 1991 and by the end of January 1992 nearly 8 million people had registered (the final number was put at 8.5 million; about 11 million were eligible). A late surge of interest was brought about by the appearance of well over 400 investment funds by that date, many promising large capital gains if individuals took shares in the funds in exchange for their points. These have the advantage of helping individuals lacking information to invest their points directly in enterprises, but the chances of financial fraud are considerable and there is the danger of a 'short term' attitude towards profits and even a large-scale sale of shares to overcome liquidity problems stemming from the promised returns. To help prevent overpowerful funds each fund is only able to hold a maximum 20 per cent stake in any one company and must have stakes in at least ten different enterprises. If in the bidding process an enterprise is up to 25 per cent oversubscribed, individual claims are met in full before those of funds are considered (Summers 1992: 34). The funds attracted nearly three-quarters of the voucher points issued (*The Economist*, 12 September 1992, p. 97); 72 per cent of voucher holders, according to Ariane Genillard (*FT Survey*, 3 July 1992, p. iii); some 5 million voucher holders have entrusted some or all of their points to investment funds (DIW, Economic Bulletin, 1992, vol. 29, no. 7, p. 5). The lack of information about the financial viability of enterprises available to ordinary citizens was a serious criticism of the whole programme and 'insider trading' became a real problem. The minimum amount of points able to be invested in any one enterprise was fixed at 100 and the maximum at 1,000. Three per cent of the stock of a company had to be set aside for the restitution fund to meet the claims of former owners (Kupka 1992: 308). The Slovak republic mandates that 35 per cent of companies' assets must be issued in vouchers, while the Czech republic insists that a minimum of 20 per cent of corporate assets should be set aside for voucher privatization (*Czechoslovak Economic Digest*, 1991, no. 6, p. 6). If all the shares in an enterprise are to be sold to voucher holders, half the shares have to be offered to its employees (Deutsche Bank, *Focus: Eastern Europe*, 1992, no. 40, p. 4). *The Economist* (16 May 1992, p. 102) estimated an average 50 per cent stake to have been sold in the voucher programme in the first wave. The average enterprise was expected to offer about 60 per cent of its equity to the voucher programme (Arianne Genillard, FT, 22 May 1992, p. 2). Registration of bids for shares in 1,446 enterprises started on 18 May 1992. The planned five bidding rounds for the entire first wave were due to finish in the autumn.

Stock exchanges were to be set up in Prague and Bratislava.

The number of registered private entrepreneurs on 31 March 1991 was 655,000 (*Czechoslovak Economic Digest*, 1991, no. 3, p. 29). According to an OECD report (FT, 8 January 1992, p. 2), the number of private entrepreneurs rose from 86,000 in 1989 to 921,000 in August 1991; in that month the private sector accounted for 1.2 per cent of industrial production, 13 per cent of domestic trade and 5–6 per cent of construction.

FOREIGN TRADE, AID AND CAPITAL

Foreign trade

Czechoslovakia faced a number of early problems. Comecon shifted to hard currency trading at current world market prices on 1 January 1991, which meant at least a short-run deterioration in the terms of trade as imported energy prices increased and the prices of the relatively uncompetitive manufactured exports fell. Soviet oil deliveries were 13.2 million tonnes in 1990, but only half of this amount was expected in 1991. German economic and monetary union at the beginning of July led to the cancellation of many contracts by East

Germany (communist Czechslovakia's second largest trading partner after the Soviet Union). Trade with the Soviet Union fell steeply. In the first eight months of 1991 the dollar value of exports to the Soviet Union fell by 38 per cent and that of exports to the rest of Eastern Europe by 11 per cent, compared with the same period of 1990 (*FT Survey*, 8 November 1991, p. ii). Czechoslovakia has reacted, for example, by signing a payments agreement with Russia (involving barter and cash settlements in both hard currency and national currencies). In 1991 the former Comecon countries accounted for less than 30 per cent of foreign trade (32.2 per cent of imports), while the EC accounted for 40.7 per cent of exports (compared with 24 per cent in 1988) and a third of imports; the EFTA countries were responsible for 10 per cent of foreign trade (Ariane Genillard and Anthony Robinson, *FT*, 15 May 1992, p. 4).

On 24 January 1990 the foreign minister, Jiri Dienstbier, announced a gradual phasing out of arms exports; in 1991 it was envisaged that arms exports would be around an eighth of their level in recent years. But the effects on unemployment (especially in Slovakia, where the sector is concentrated) have brought about a less idealistic stance.

As far as exchange rate policy is concerned, 8 January 1990 saw a devaluation of the koruna against hard currencies (further devaluations followed during the year on 15 October and 29 December, bringing the commercial and tourist rates closer together) and a revaluation against the transferable rouble and other Comecon currencies. In March 1990 Czechoslovakia was the first to announce withdrawal from the Comecon exchange rate system. The koruna became 'internally' convertible on 1 January 1991 (on current account: a single exchange rate applied, thus unifying the tourist and commercial rates), enterprises in Czechoslovakia being able to buy and sell hard currencies from and to the state bank (access to hard currency by individuals was severely restricted) (see glossary). Generally 30 per cent of foreign exchange earnings had to be sold to the state bank (100 per cent in the case of enterprises which bought hard currency with crowns in order to export).

The old foreign trade system was gradually dismantled. The former foreign trade corporations lost their monopoly status, and since 1 February 1991 permits to conduct foreign trade have not generally been needed (Jaroslav Krsyl, *Czechoslovak Economic Digest*, 1991, no. 2, pp. 7–10). There is, however, a licensing system for imports and for exports of goods in limited supply domestically. The average tariff rate is 4.5 per cent, but the range is from 0 per cent to 70 per cent (*Czechoslovak Economic Digest*, 1991, no. 6, p. 8). All quantitative restrictions were lifted (*Czechoslovak Economic Digest*, 1991, no. 5, p. 7), but in the second half of 1991 import quotas were introduced for some agricultural products, e.g. meat and butter (*Czechoslovak Economic Digest*, 1992, no. 1, p. 5).

A 20 per cent import surcharge was imposed on certain consumer good and food imports, in agreement with GATT. This was reduced to 18 per cent in April 1991, 15 per cent in June 1991 and 10 per cent in January 1992.

A trade agreement with EFTA was signed on 20 March 1992, effective as of 1 July 1992.

In 1991 the current account of the balance of payments in convertible currencies was slightly in surplus, to the tune of $400 million (*Czechoslovak Economic Digest*, 1992, no. 3, p. 3). This was much better than the forecast deficit of $2.5 billion. The corresponding figure for 1989 was a surplus of $400 million and for 1990 a deficit of $1.1 billion (Val Koromzay, *OECD Observer*, February–March 1992, no. 174, p. 35). In 1991 95.4 per cent of payments were settled in convertible currencies, compared with 49.6 per cent in 1990 (*Czechoslovak Economic Digest*, 1992, no. 3, p. 32).

Western aid

The attitude of the Czechslovak leadership was cool. Former president Havel did say that 'we don't want money: we want advice, we want opinions, we want to learn to work hard' (reported in *FT*, 19 March 1991, p. 34). Havel softened his stance somewhat, however. In an article in the *IHT* (15 July 1991), he thought that the West could help in vital restructuring when unemployment was likely to rise substantially; he highlighted the opening up of Western markets and Western aid to the Soviet Union for the purchase of East European goods. Klaus has described Western financial aid as inflationary; what he prefers is direct private investment. Prime Minister Marian Calfa stressed improved access to hard currency export markets and technical aid in improving financial services. Deputy Foreign Minister Zdenko Pirek emphasized help to run and modernize a market economy with training and education. The president of the central bank, Josef Tosovsky, thought help would be welcome in setting up a stabilization fund to support the forthcoming internal convertibility of the koruna (reported by Stephen Fidler, *FT*, 23 June 1990, p. 2).

Aid approved since June 1989 includes IMF $1.7 billion, World Bank $0.5 billion, and G24 $2.1 billion (*The Economist*, Survey, 12 October 1991, p. 49).

Foreign capital

The initial profits tax regime on direct foreign investment was as follows. If the percentage foreign involvement was less than 30 per cent there was a flat rate tax of 55 per cent, but if it was more than 30 per cent the rate fell to 40 per cent. Joint ventures were to be subject to the already discussed new tax regime operating as of 1 January 1993, unless they had already negotiated the then available two year tax holiday (Ariane Genillard and Anthony Robinson, *FT*, 30 April 1992, p. 2). Under the law on major privatization foreign nationals are not excluded from ownership of land, but under another law they cannot own agricultural land (*Czechoslovak Economic Digest*, 1992, no. 1, p. 28). On 9 December 1990 the government of the Czech republic decided to allow Volkswagen to take

an initial 31 per cent stake in Skoda (perhaps rising to 70 per cent by 1995), in preference to the rival bid from Renault–Volvo; as of 15 April 1991 the new company was called Skoda Automobilova. Other German companies involved include Siemens (railway locomotives and power engineering, for example) and Mercedes-Benz (trucks). As of October 1991 Germany accounted for 31.9 per cent of foreign investment in Czechoslovakia and Austria for 30.5 per cent (*Czechoslovak Economic Digest*, 1991, no. 6, p. 27). President Havel put foreign investment in 1991 at around $700 million; 80 per cent of this was German, with the VW–Skoda deal alone accounting for half the German investment (*IHT*, 9 February 1992, p. 11). According to figures cited by Tom Redburn (*IHT*, 1 April 1992, p.8), as of December 1991 German investment amounted to $532 million, compared with $350 million in Hungary, $187.7 million in Poland, $30.5 million in Romania, and $5.4 million in Bulgaria; the figure for the CIS was $500 million. In the past two years the Czech lands of Bohemia and Moravia have attracted 96 per cent of the $800 million invested in Czechoslovakia (*The Economist*, 30 May 1992, p. 42).

Foreign investment in the six major banks (including Komercni Banka) is limited to 25 per cent, with individual foreign investors even lower at 10 per cent (*IHT*, 20 September 1991, p. 13).

By October 1991 there were 4,000 joint ventures, with $500 million of foreign capital committed (Scott 1992: 56).

AGRICULTURE

On 13 December 1990 the government outlined its land bill. Former owners could claim back their land. Where there was no claim the land would be rented out or sold, although sales to foreign individuals or companies were ruled out. Burton Bollag (*IHT*, 6 June 1991, p. 4) and Kupka (1992: 304–5) give the following information: the parliament passed a land bill on 21 May 1991; physical restitution of the same property is not possible in cases such as built-on land; the original landowners or their heirs can each reclaim the equivalent of about 370 acres (149.74 ha) of farm land, provided they live in Czechoslovakia; co-operatives have to start paying rent for the land if farmers remain in the co-operatives (most are, at least initially, expected to do so); another law was expected in 1991 governing the distribution among farm members of the property left after their land has been returned (this includes land taken from churches, much of which will not be returned). The original owners were given until 31 December 1992 to make their claims (maximum 150 ha); the federal government is drafting legislation aimed at dismembering the large state and collective farms (Judy Dempsey, *FT Survey*, 8 November 1991, p. v). Ash (1992: 24), however, argues that there is a desire to prevent the break-up of state farms into smaller units; state farms are to be transformed into joint stock companies prior to privatization and then Czechoslovak citizens will be able to exchange vouchers for shares, with a certain proportion retained for farm workers.

There was a demonstration on 12 March 1991 by farmers protesting against the break-up of collective farms. Schimmerling (1991: 190) cites evidence to suggest that there is limited interest in family farms, owing to factors such as the security associated with co-operative farming. Brooks *et al.* (1991) make the general point that throughout Eastern Europe many producers are choosing to delay their emergence into full private individual production until conditions improve. Factors such as the removal of food subsidies and a monopolistic processing sector cause problems for agriculture in the transitional period.

There are minimum prices established for some agricultural products, with intervention purchases and sales (*Czechoslovak Economic Digest*, 1992, no. 1, p. 13). Products include wheat, rye and beef. Judy Dempsey (*FT Survey*, 8 November 1991, pp. v–vi) reports falling prices, growing surpluses, decreasing state subsidies and the collapse of the Soviet market. The resulting discontent led to the unveiling in October 1991 of the Federal Fund for the Regulation of the Agricultural and Food Market, a supposedly temporary institution. The fund does not directly subsidize farms, but resources are available to subsidize exports and for intervention buying. There are also import quotas, e.g. for potatoes and wine (Ash 1992: 18).

21

EAST GERMANY: GERMAN ECONOMIC AND MONETARY UNION

POLITICAL BACKGROUND

The pace of political events in late 1989 was simply breathtaking. The vision shown by Soviet president Gorbachev was an essential prerequisite, but other decisive elements included the movement of East Germans to the Federal Republic (West Germany). In 1989 there were 343,854 Übersiedler compared to 39,832 the previous year, mostly young and skilled, and 190,674 in the period 1 January – 1 July 1990 (in addition 1989 saw 377,055 ethnic Germans or *Aussiedler* migrate to West Germany from other countries in Eastern Europe; 397,000 in 1990 and 221,995 in 1991). Some 360,000 moved from East (or perhaps more aptly now Eastern) Germany to West Germany in the year following economic and monetary union on 1 July 1990 (DIW, *Economic Bulletin*, 1991, vol. 28, no. 9, p. 2); over 200,000 moved in 1991. Note that a large number of asylum seekers represents a considerable problem in itself; in 1991 alone there were 256,000.

In March 1989 Hungary signed the UN convention on refugees and two months later began to dismantle its border fence with Austria. On 10 September Hungary 'suspended' the 1969 agreement with the GDR regulating travel to third countries, while refugees from the West German embassies in Prague and Warsaw added to the flood. The world turned upside down on 9 November 1989 when the borders between East Germany and West Germany, including the Berlin Wall, were opened. Erich Honecker was replaced as General Secretary of the SED (the Socialist Unity Party was renamed the Party of Democratic Socialism on 16 December) by Egon Krenz. The whole politburo and Central Committee resigned on 3 December, and these two bodies were replaced by a new executive chaired by Gregor Gysi (re-elected 27 January 1991) (Hans Modrow having been confirmed as prime minister on 13 November).

In the 18 March 1990 free election there was a surprise win for the Alliance for Germany (comprising the Christian Democratic Union, the German Social Union and Democratic Awakening), with 48.14 per cent of the vote and 193 seats in the 400 member Volkskammer (People's Chamber). This victory reflected a general desire for rapid unification and the greater assurance of West German aid and favourable terms for economic union (including the conversion ratio between the East Mark and the Deutschmark). A five-party coalition government was formed, with Lothar de Maizière as prime minister, which included the main opposition party, the Social Democratic Party (which won 21.84 per cent of the vote and eighty-seven seats). The Social Democratic Party pulled out of the East German coalition government on 19 August 1990; four days earlier the prime minister had sacked the finance minister, Walter Romberg, and the agriculture, Minister Peter Pollack, and had accepted the resignation of the economics minister, Gerhard Pohl.

On 23 August 1990 the Volkskammer chose 3 October as the date of unification (with the name of the country remaining the Federal Republic of Germany). In the period from then to the all-German general election on 2 December, the number of seats in the West German Bundestag was increased from 519 to 663 in order to accommodate the 144 East German representatives. Five East German ministers joined the West German government. The treaty to harmonize the legal and political systems was signed by both governments on 31 August 1990 and was ratified by both parliaments in September. Berlin was to be the capital, but Bonn was to remain the seat of government until the Bundestag had put the issue to the vote (this was done on 20 June 1991 and rather surprisingly it was decided, albeit by a narrow vote of 338 to 320, that government and parliament should be gradually transferred to Berlin; they should be fully operational by 2003–05; the Bundestag is to move in 1995, but the Bundestag decided, on 5 July, to stay in Bonn for the time being).

The elections to the (five) reconstituted Länder (abolished in 1952; the term 'new federal states' is now an alternative to East Germany) took place on 14 October 1990 and proved to be another triumph for the now united CDU (43.6 per cent of the total vote, an absolute majority of the seats in Saxony, the largest single party in Mecklenburg, Saxony-Anhalt and Thuringia, and the second largest party in Brandenburg, excluding East Berlin). The SPD won 25.2 per cent of the total vote and took the largest number of seats in Brandenburg. The CDU was seen as the party most likely to cure East Germany's economic ills.

In the 2 December 1990 all-German general election (the first since 1932) the government coalition, as expected, won comfortably. The seats in the 662 seat (519 West German and 143 East German) Bundestag were distributed as follows: CDU/CSU–DSU/FDP coalition 398 (the FDP gained considerably, with seventy-nine seats); SPD 239; PDS seventeen; and Alliance 90, Greens eight. Helmut Kohl was formally re-elected Chancellor on 17 January 1991. Noticeable personal changes included the resignation of economics minister Helmut Haussmann, who was replaced by Jurgen Möllemann on 15 January 1991. De Maizière temporarily resigned all his party and government posts (including vice-chairman of the Christian Democratic Party and his role as minister without portfolio) over allegations of Stasi links in the past. He retained his seat in the Bundestag all the time and in February 1991 the inquiry found that, although he might once have been an informant, he never sold information or incriminated anyone. This verdict did not quell the controversy, however, and de Maizière resigned from the party and its vice-chairmanship on 6 September after a dispute about its decline in East Germany.

The speeding up of the unification process surprised even seasoned observers. Chancellor Kohl's ten-point programme outlined (without consultation) on 28 November 1989 and the idea of the 'treaty-based (contractual) community' (Vertragsgemeinschaft) soon became obsolete (this idea, mooted by Modrow before Kohl, involved the forging of closer links by jointly tackling economic and social problems of common concern in the framework of 'confederative structures'). Gorbachev, on 30 January 1990, said of German unity that 'In principle, no one has any doubt about it'; Kohl decided on 7 February to press for German economic and monetary union (GEMU) and it actually took place on 1 July 1990. On 16 July 1990 Gorbachev agreed to allow a united Germany the choice of being in Nato, albeit on certain conditions (such as a 370,000 limit on a united German army and no Nato forces in East Germany during the three to four year transitional period while Soviet troops remain).

The 'two-plus-four' negotiations between the two Germanies and the USA, the Soviet Union, France and the UK, which only began in March, were concluded by the 12 September 1990 Moscow 'Treaty on the Final Settlement with

Respect to Germany'. Although the treaty needed to be ratified by the governments of the wartime Allied Powers (it was ratified by the all-German parliament on 5 October and by the USSR Supreme Soviet on 4 March 1991), the four decided to sign an agreement on 1 October 1990 to suspend their rights and responsibilities relating to Berlin and Germany as a whole in the meantime. Apart from these rights and responsibilities, the treaty included the following agreements: existing borders to remain; no manufacture and possession of and control over nuclear, biological and chemical weapons by the new Germany; German armed forces to be limited to 370,000 within three to four years; until Soviet troops were totally withdrawn, only German territorial defence units which were not integrated into Nato would be stationed in East Germany – after withdrawal only units of the German armed forces assigned to Nato might be stationed in East Germany; US, French and UK armed forces would, upon German request, remain in Berlin until the Soviet withdrawal. One result of the failure of the coup in the Soviet Union in August 1991 was a Soviet offer to withdraw troops before the deadline of the end of 1994.

On 13 September 1990 a 'Treaty on Good Neighbourliness, Partnership and Co-operation' between West Germany and the Soviet Union was initialled by Hans-Dietrich Genscher (foreign minister 17 May 1974–17 May 1992) and Eduard Shevardnadze and signed by Chancellor Kohl and President Gorbachev on 9 November. Of twenty-year duration, the treaty included agreement on: the immutability of present borders; a non-aggression clause; a mutual quest for arms reductions and an increase in economic, scientific, technical, ecological and cultural links; and West German help to defray the cost of the Soviet troop withdrawal (DM 12 billion plus a DM 3 billion interest-free credit spread over four years). A treaty on 'good neighbourliness and friendly co-operation' was also signed by Germany and Poland on 17 June

1991. It included agreements on the inviolability of borders, non-aggression and the guarantee of minority rights. The Bundestag and the Sejm (Polish parliament) ratified the border agreement on 17 and 18 October 1991 respectively.

German unification is to be welcomed wholeheartedly. It is worth noting, however, that there was nothing inevitable about the extremely rapid pace. Even GEMU could have been slowed by the granting of substantial aid to the Modrow regime (on 4 February 1990 Chancellor Kohl stated that substantial aid to East Germany was necessary before the East German election, but this was not forthcoming) and the earlier ending of the special financial inducements granted to migrants. It just so happened that 2 December 1990 was the date of the next general election in West Germany, thus subjecting events to short-term political expediency. East Germany's economic distress became a dominant consideration, but the extent of the collapse after GEMU gave further weight to the argument that a slower process of reunification would have been desirable. Karl Otto Pöhl, the then president of the Bundesbank, was forced to accept the rapid speed of monetary union by political pressure. Seen from a wider perspective, there were also strong arguments for a slower pace of unification in order to draw up an entirely new constitution that could have taken full account of East German interests and identity. Kohl used the announcement of the Soviet attempted coup on 19 October 1991 as justification of speedy reunification, but fell silent when it failed. Racist attacks increased in both parts of Germany after reunification and extreme right parties gained ground in West German state elections, also profiting from concern over the large number of asylum seekers. The serious outbreak of strikes over wages in West Germany in the spring of 1992 was directly related to the question of the distribution of the burden of financing reunification.

THE ECONOMIC POLICIES OF THE MODROW REGIME

Planning and the market

The East German government after November 1989 was in a dilemma. On the one hand, the more radical economic reform was, the more similar would be the two economic systems and, therefore, the greater the pressure for unification (this would be aggravated by the increased flow of people westwards as unemployment rose in East Germany). On the other hand, the less radical economic reform was, the greater the impulse to migrate.

The government certainly intended moving towards a more market-orientated system – Prime Minister Hans Modrow talked about a 'market-orientated planned economy'. In his November speech to the Volkskammer he thought that there should be 'no planning without the market, but no unplanned market economy . . . This does not mean that central planning will be abolished, but a real socialist planned economy needs the market'.[1] He spoke against party interference and the 'arbitrary ordering around of the economy to its detriment'. Prices should reflect costs, and prices of basic commodities should reflect 'economic reality'. 'Idiotic' subsidies should be abolished. In a December speech to managers, he talked about the need for decentralization of decision-making, a new management training institution and an independent central bank.

On 21 November 1989 came the announcement that more than half the state-decreed plans for individual branches of the economy and also ten-day and monthly targets for enterprises were to be abolished. Local authorities were to have greater independence as regards spending.

Gregor Gysi (the then SED chairman), in a 17 December speech, attacked wasteful subsidies and rigid plan targets and spoke in favour of expanding the private sector and greater devolved decision-making authority in agriculture.

On 3 January 1990 Christa Luft (the then minister for the economy) suggested that East Germany must begin 'The transition to an efficient market economy, although account had to be taken of social and environmental concerns'. On 11 January it was announced that the State Planning Commission was to be replaced by an Economic Committee, comprising directors, economists and political groups. The combines were to be split up and a trust body (Treuhandanstalt) was set up on 1 March 1990 to deal with restructuring, liquidation, credit guarantees and privatization. Privatization was not a priority at this time, but the Modrow directive envisaged transforming the combines into joint stock companies, affixing the suffix AG (*Aktiengesellschaft*) to their corporate names and setting up East German citizens as their shareholders (THA report, *IHT*, 18 March 1992, pp. 11–13). In Vincentz's opinion (1991: 2), the aim was to rescue parts of the old economic system rather than to transform the economy.

At the Free German Trade Union Federation congress held 1–2 January 1990, the FDGB's independence was proclaimed from party and state. There was to be increased devolution of authority to the constituent unions, e.g. the FDGB's share of income derived from members' contributions fell from about 60 per cent to 15 per cent. The right to strike was demanded and increased worker participation in enterprise decision-making proposed.

The private sector

The Modrow government believed that, while the state sector should be dominant in sectors such as energy, heavy industry and transport, the private sector should be encouraged. Hans Modrow himself, as early as 18 November 1989, talked about the possibility of it taking over small firms (especially those producing consumer goods). Christa Luft mentioned the possibility of widespread privatization, while Christian Meyer (the then deputy minister for foreign trade) envisaged a 'tidal wave' of small and medium-size enterprises. A 300 employment ceiling was mooted. The smaller enterprises nationalized in 1972 would be offered back to the original owners. The Association of Small and Medium-sized Firms was set up in December 1989 and this was followed the next month by the Private Employers' Federation.

Financial policies

Prices and subsidies. On 25 January 1990 it was announced that price controls were to be removed in stages by 1992. As regards subsidies, the plan was to reduce the huge annual sum spent (around EM 51 billion) in three stages. As a first step, it was announced on, 15 January 1990, that the subsidies on items like children's clothes and shoes would be reduced by EM 1.2 billion. The corresponding price rises would be compensated for by an additional monthly allowance of EM 45 for each child up to twelve years of age and EM 65 for each child aged thirteen and over.

On 19 February 1990 the Round Table (comprising government and opposition, which gained Volkskammer approval on 29 January 1990) voted to abolish EM 30 billion of food subsidies before the election (with a compensatory payment of EM 150 per person), but this was revoked three days later because of the consequent panic buying in the shops.

The government proposed to the Round Table that the price of household electricity should be tripled and that there should be a drastic reduction in the output of brown coal (lignite) in order to reduce both energy consumption and pollution (there had already been an increase in the prices of electricity and brown coal on 3 January 1990, the aim being to avoid power cuts). The government envisaged a doubling in nuclear energy's share of electricity from the current 10 per cent or so, with the help of Western technology.

Banking. On 1 April 1990 the Staatsbank became an independent central bank, losing its commercial operations to Deutsche Kreditbank, which was formerly part of the state bank and which now provides finance for industry and banking services for the population. The Foreign Trade Bank (Aussenhandelsbank) lost its monopoly of foreign exchange and credit activity. Both East German enterprises and foreign companies were to be able to buy shares in East German commercial banks, while these banks, in turn, were to be able to buy shares in enterprises.

Taxation. On 7 February a draft of the tax bill was put forward. The top rate of income tax was to be reduced from 90 per cent to 60 per cent. Although the top rate of corporation tax remained 50 per cent, a progressive rate was meant to encourage smaller enterprises.

Foreign trade, aid and capital

Foreign trade

An immediate problem in this respect concerned the availability of many low-priced and heavily subsidized goods and services in East Germany together with open borders. A number of measures were taken to deal with the situation: on 22 November 1989 the export of antiques was banned; two days later it was decreed that only East German citizens and authorized foreigners working in the GDR were allowed to buy a whole range of goods, including children's clothing, car parts and cameras; on 4 January 1990 West Germans were not allowed to place 'bulk' orders for services such as dry cleaning, shoe repairs and tailoring.

Foreign aid

On 24 January 1990 West Germany announced a DM 6 billion low-interest credit to modernize the East German economy. On 4 February Chancellor Kohl said that substantial economic aid was necessary before the election, but this did not materialize. The then West German foreign minister Hans-Dietrich Genscher, speaking at the founding congress of the Free

Democratic Party, thought that instant and comprehensive aid to East Germany was needed (e.g. to improve health and the environment). On 5 February Christa Luft called for DM 10 billion to DM 15 billion to compensate East Germany for the difficult post-war conditions; it was needed to boost economic growth and to facilitate the move towards partial convertibility of the EM. This was rejected by West Germany, but the Federal Republic promised to start releasing credits for small and medium-sized enterprises, and to provide DM 20 million for urban restoration.

At the start of January 1990 the DM 100 per annum (DM 30 until 1987) 'welcome money' given to East German visitors was replaced by a DM 2.9 billion 'foreign currency fund' (West Germany providing DM 2.15 billion). East German citizens were allowed to exchange up to EM 200 a year on favourable terms, namely EM 100 at parity with the DM and the other EM 100 at 5:1. The proceeds of the funds were to be used for infrastructural and tourism projects in East Germany.

(Note that, as of 24 December 1989, West German visitors to East Germany no longer needed visas and were not forced to exchange DM 25 a day at parity.)

Foreign capital

In a 17 November 1989 speech to the Volkskammer, Hans Modrow made the ideological breakthrough: 'The GDR is open to suggestions by our capitalist partners that were earlier treated cautiously or ignored . . . Joint ventures, direct investment, profit transfers, pilot projects to preserve the environment are no longer foreign words to us.' A 49 per cent maximum stake in a joint venture by a 'foreign' (including West German) partner was suggested at first, but on 12 January 1990 the Volkskammer agreed to a higher percentage when this was 'in the interests of the economy' (e.g. new technology). The draft law presented two weeks later stipulated this condition when the enterprises involved

were small. Christa Luft was reported as saying that small West German companies could start up fully-owned subsidiaries in East Germany (David Marsh, *FT*, 18 January 1990, p. 2).

GERMAN ECONOMIC AND MONETARY UNION (GEMU)

The West German government estimated that the GDR economy was about one-tenth the size of West Germany's, while in the second half of 1990, according to the Federal Statistics Office, East Germany's GNP was 8.3 per cent of West Germany's. Monetary 'union' is not a very apt term because the East mark (EM) was simply replaced by the Deutschmark (DM), with the Bundesbank in control of monetary policy. Monetary union in general is usually seen as the final stage of countries coming together, exchange rate adjustments being used to ease the transitional stage of uniting two unequal economies. Speedy union, it was argued, would bring benefits in such forms as the assurance of a sound, convertible currency. Although there are obvious differences in circumstances (e.g. the early post-war economy was not a command one), the June 1948 currency reform, coupled with the abolition of most price controls and rationing, was the prelude to the West German 'economic miracle' (*Wirtschaftswunder*). This experience seemed initially to set a happy precedent.

Economic 'union' essentially involves the adoption of – or, perhaps more accurately, incorporation into – West Germany's 'social market economy'. Even here, however, some phasing in was inevitable. Certain prices (eg. housing rents and property leases, public transport and energy tariffs) were to continue to receive temporary subsidies. (Rents for state-owned houses were to rise by up to 360 per cent on 1 August 1991.) West German income and corporate taxes were introduced in January 1991. The general achievement of West German environmental standards was set for the year 2000 (although this varies: for example, emission standards for new investment projects applied from the beginning of July 1990, while existing lignite power stations have to adapt by 1996). Privatization was seen as needing time.

The terms of monetary union

The final conversion ratios between the EM and the DM were more generous than generally anticipated. The previous black market rate had fluctuated in the range 5–10:1. Holger Schmiedling argues that, based on the admittedly imperfect yardstick of the measured competitiveness of East German exports to the West, the EM was worth only DM 0.23; in 1989 the foreign currency coefficient, which gives the EM value of domestic inputs necessary to earn one DM of exports, was 4.4 (*FT*, 25 February 1991, p. 17). The nominal wage ratio pre-GEMU, however, was not greatly out of line with the productivity ratio (a typical East German industrial worker, in terms of EM at a conversion ratio of 1:1, earned about one-third the DM wage of his West German counterpart). Estimates of the ratio of East German labour productivity to that of West German pre-GEMU varied. There was a general impression pre-GEMU that the ratio was 50 per cent, but this was quickly seen to be far too high. One at the lower end of the range was given by the West German finance minister Theo Waigel, namely 30 per cent (the Deutsche Bank, *Focus: Germany*, 20 January 1992, no. 70, p. 1, gives the same figure for 1991). Note that there were considerable sectoral variations. According to the Federal Statistics Office, the average gross monthly wage in East Germany in the second half of 1990 was DM 1,357 (37 per cent of the West German level); productivity, however, was only 28.5 per cent of the West German level. Some argue that the initial conversion ratio is not important, since East German wages would have to rise sufficiently in any case in order to staunch labour migration to West Germany (e.g. Portes in *European Economy: the Path of Reform in Central and Eastern Europe*, 1991, p. 5).

The Bundesbank had recommended 1:1 for personal savings up to EM 2,000 and 2:1 for everything else (although its president, Karl Otto Pöhl, later conceded that the actual overall 1.8:1 came close to his proposal). Political pressure forced something of a change of mind, for Pöhl had warned against rapid monetary union, stressing the need for prior structural change, the prior phasing in of a competitive market economy and a conventional monetary policy. Pöhl was not even consulted when the then West German economics minister, Helmut Haussman, unexpectedly announced, on 6 February 1990, that GEMU was to take place. On 19 March 1991 Pöhl restoked the controversy when he said that 'We introduced the DM with practically no preparation or possibility of adjustment, and, I would add, at the wrong exchange rate . . . So the result is a disaster, as you can see. I am not surprised I predicted it'. East Germany had been rendered 'completely uncompetitive'. Pöhl accepts that monetary union was inevitable: 'I am not criticizing the decision. But the outcome was predictable.' On 16 May 1991 Pöhl announced his resignation as of October 1991, although personal factors were stressed. In fact his successor (Helmut Schlesinger) took over on 1 August, the term running until 30 September 1993 (Hans Tietmeyer then taking over). The actual terms of monetary union between the EM and the DM were as follows:

Individual savings. One to one for individuals aged sixty and over for savings up to EM 6,000; aged fifteen to fifty-nine up to EM 4,000; aged below fifteen, up to EM 2,000. These figures applied to savings held 31 December 1989; for deposits legally accrued during the first half of 1990 the conversion ratio was 3:1. Two to one was the rate for remaining savings and cash in circulation. Non-residents were allowed to exchange EM into DM at 3:1 only to the extent that these were issued by GDR banks after 31 December 1989.

Wages and pensions. One to one. (Pensions were fixed at 70 per cent of most recent net earnings after forty-five years of work.)

Corporate debt. Two to one. At the end of 1989 such debt was estimated to be EM 260 billion. The term 'debt' is a little odd, however, since it is owed internally, the result of enterprises having formerly to transfer most net revenue to the state budget and, therefore, being forced to borrow from the banks. Thus there is no clear relationship between the debt owed by and the viability of individual enterprises; one powerful argument for writing off the debt is that viable enterprises could be needlessly bankrupted. Although across-the-board debt relief has been ruled out, the German government considers it on a case-by-case basis (*The Times*, 4 May 1991, p. 23).

The effects of German economic and monetary union

Output and employment

There is some dispute about the long-run prospects of East Germany. They are generally seen as excellent, but the most pessimistic observers fear a south Italy (Mezzogiorno) scenario where the area remains permanently less developed, experiencing relatively high unemployment and sustained migration of younger people. There is, however, general agreement that the short to medium term is and will be extremely, difficult given the relatively obsolete capital stock and uncompetitive enterprises in many sectors of the economy.

Unemployment. Unemployment increased substantially, while output fell dramatically (see Tables 12.1, 12.2 and 12.3). Honecker's GDR was a fully employed economy (in 1989 there were 8.7 million employees and apprentices plus a further 1 million self-employed and co-operative members). Table 12.1 gives the figures for unemployment and 'short time' working in East Germany since GEMU. Note that the first (temporary) peak in unemployment was in July 1991, while there was a surge in January 1992 due to the end of government support for short time working and the use of the figure 7.9

Table 21.1 East Germany: unemployment and 'short time' working

Month	Unemployment No.	Unemployment Rate (%)	'Short time' working Numbers
1990 January	7,000	0.1	
June	142,096	1.6	229,975
July	272,017	3.1	656,277
August	361,286	4.0	1,440,000
September	444,825	5.0	1,720,000
October	537,799	6.1	1,770,000
November	590,199	6.7	1,770,000
December	642,182	7.3	1,800,000
1991 January	757,200	8.6	1,855,524
February	786,992	8.9	1,903,614
March	808,389	9.2	2,000,000
April	836,900	9.5	2,000,000
May	842,000	9.5	1,960,000
June	843,000	9.5	1,910,000
July	1,068,600	12.1	1,620,000
August	1,063,200	12.1	1,451,000
September	1,030,000	11.7	1,300,000
October	1,048,000	12.0	1,200,000
November		11.7	
December	1,037,709	11.8	1,030,000
1992 January	1,340,000	16.5	520,000
February	1,290,000	15.9	
March	1,200,000	15.5	
April		15.2	
May	1,115,000	14.6	
June	1,123,000	13.8	
July	1,188,200	14.6	
August	1,168,700	14.4	285,000
September	1,110,000	14.1	
October	1,097,500	13.9	
November			
December	1,100,000	13.9	

Sources: various issues of Deutsche Bank, DIW, *Financial Times* and *International Herald Tribune*.

million instead of 8.8 million for those considered capable of gaining employment. The Deutsche Bank (*Focus: Germany*, 14 January 1992, no. 69, pp. 1–5) provides the following interesting information for December 1991. Between the fall of the Berlin Wall and 1991

Table 21.2 East Germany: unemployment predictions

The five institutes

1 *Autumn 1990 report.* Unemployment to average 1.4 million in 1991, peaking at 1.7 million. Short time working to average 1.75 million in 1991, peaking at 2 million.

2 *Autumn 1991 report.* Unemployment to average 1.4 million in 1992, peaking at 1.5 million in the summer.

The German government

1 *Autumn 1990 (FT Survey,*29 October 1990, p. 1). Unemployment to peak at 2 million in 1991.

2 *8 March 1991.* Unemployment to average 1.1 million–1.4 million in 1991 and to peak at 1.6 million–1.9 million by the end of the year.

Norbert Walter (Deutsche Bank)

FT, 3 January 1991, p. 12. Unemployment may peak at 2 million (more than 20 per cent).

David Goodhart

FT, 16 January 1991, p. 19. Unemployment may peak at 3 million.

German Council of Economic Advisers

1 Unemployment will peak at 1.7 million by the end of the year, with short time working peaking at 2 million (*FT,* 16 April 1991, p. 2).

2 November 1991: unemployment will average 1.35 million in 1992 and short time working 915,000.

Deutsche Bank

Focus: Germany, 14 January 1992, no. 69, p. 1. Unemployment to rise to 1.4 million on average in 1992 and short time working to fall to 700,000.

DIW

1 *Economic Bulletin,* January 1992, vol. 28, no. 11, p. 8. Unemployment may peak at almost 1.5 million by summer 1992.

2 *Economic Bulletin,* June 1992, vol. 29, no. 4, p. 10. Unemployment may peak at 1.4 million by the end of 1992.

Sources: DIW *Economic Bulletin,* 1990, vol. 27, no. 10; Deutsche Bank, *Unification Issue,* 1991, nos. 61, 63.

Table 21.3 East Germany: rates of growth of GNP and GDP (%)

Measure	1990	1991	1992[a]
DIW			
GNP	−13.3	−30.3	6.0
GDP	−14.0	−33.9	2.5
Deutsche Bank			
GNP	−14.0	−29.5	7.5
GDP		−32.8	4.0
Five institutes (Berlin, Essen, Hamberg, Kiel and Munich)			
Autumn 1990 (GNP):	−15.0	−10.0	
Autumn 1991 (GNP):		−20.0	10.0–15.0
Spring 1992 (GNP):	−14.4	−30.3	10.5
Spring 1992 (GNP):	−14.7	−33.9	7.0
Autumn 1992 (GNP):		−28.4	5.5
(GDP):		−31.4	3.5

Sources: DIW, *Economic Bulletin,* August 1992, vol. 29, no. 6; Deutsche Bank, *Unification Issue,* 28 October 1991, no. 61; 19 November 1991, no. 63; Deutsche Bank, *Focus: Germany,* 20 January 1992, no. 70; 2 April 1992, no. 77, 5 October 1992, no. 93; *FT,* 22 October 1991; 24 December 1991; 14 April 1992; 28 October 1992, p. 2; DIW *Economic Bulletin,* June 1992, vol. 29, no. 4.

[a] Estimates.

employment in East Germany fell by about 2.5 million (in 1989 there were 9,861,000 employed, 8,916,000 in 1990 and only 7,250,000 in 1991); 450,000 East Germans were employed in West Germany, i.e. commuted daily; 600,000 were in early retirement; just under 400,000 were involved in job creation schemes; nearly 450,000 were taking part in training and retraining schemes (excluding 'short time' workers); about 175,000 constituted 'hidden reserves', mainly married women. Some of these figures were later revised: employment fell by 3 million; there were 750,000 in early retirement and 540,000 commuters (Deutsche Bank, *Focus: Germany,* 2 April 1992, no. 77, p. 4).

For some, 'short time' (*Kurzarbeit*) meant no time; on average, short time workers were employed for only half their normal working time (DIW, *Economic Bulletin,* 1990, vol. 27, no. 10, p. 5); nearly half were effectively idle (Deutsche Bank, *Unification Issue* no. 37, 30 January 1991, p. 2), while in June 1991 on average these people worked only 40 per cent of scheduled hours (*Deutsche Bank Bulletin*, July 1991, p. 17). A large increase in open unemployment was forecast after 30 June 1991 as employment protection schemes came to an end (e.g. in the metal and electrical engineering industries and for civil servants); the actual increase was less than anticipated. Note, however, that other forms of aid were available, such as retraining and early retirement (in April 1991 retirement at fifty-five on two-thirds final pay was announced). As the unemployment situation deteriorated, further measures were taken, e.g. on 4 February 1991 Chancellor Kohl announced that job creation schemes and apprenticeships were to be made available to all East German school leavers. West German regulations allow unemployed or temporarily laid off people to be paid about two-thirds of their previous wage (specifically, 68 per cent for one year if married and 63 per cent if single; the percentage then fell to 58 and 52 per cent respectively). A short time working arrangement was introduced in East Germany, the state paying 68 per cent of the previous wage (plus an additional 22 per cent paid by the enterprise, bringing the total to 90 per cent); this scheme was scheduled to be phased out at the end of 1991 (Siebert 1991b: 314). Regional unemployment is an acute problem, given frequent local dependence in the GDR on large-scale plants. Buechtemann and Schupp (1992: 103) argue that the 'losers' in the reunification process are clearly to be found among the unemployed 'outsiders', whereas the employed 'insiders', and especially those who have gained employment in West Germany, are the clear 'winners'. Among the 'winners' in terms of employment are overrepresented those who used to be the 'winners' under the old socialist regime – broadly senior executives in GDR state industry.

It can be argued that the East German–West German wage differential constitutes an important determinant of capital inflows into as well as future labour flows from East Germany

(the Bundesbank estimated that an earnings ratio of at least 60 per cent of the West German level was required to stop the flow: Samuel Brittan, *FT*, 3 September 1990, p. 15). But Akerlof *et al.* (1991: 3) argue, on the basis of survey data, that few workers wish to migrate for higher West German wages, most preferring to work in East Germany or wait for new jobs there if unemployed. The real cause of most migration is the lack of employment in East Germany, not the East German–West German wage differential: 'Higher wages will cause more migration by increasing unemployment than they will deter by closing the wage gap.' The narrowing of the differential has been very rapid and substantially helped contribute to more gloomy forecasts about output and employment in East Germany. Early on there was considerable industrial unrest among many groups of workers (e.g. in the metal goods industry, insurance, local government, textiles, footwear, the postal service, shipbuilding, the railways, retail trade and agriculture). Large demonstrations against unemployment began on 18 March 1991. Mergers have taken place between West German and East German trade unions (e.g. IG Metall, Gesamtmetall and IG Chemie). The merger process is now complete and, surprisingly, union membership (about 50 per cent of the workforce) is higher than in West Germany (David Goodhart, FT, 10 April 1991, p. 3). IG Metall's aim is pay parity by April 1994 and working hours parity by 1998. Public service workers' pay will equalize by 1995. A fifth of workers in East Germany are on contracts calling for wage equality by 1994 (*The Economist Survey*, 23 May 1992, p. 10). Strong trade unions have generally faced demoralized and demotivated enterprise management, who also lacked a secure future, and organized employers' associations. The THA has no role in pay negotiations.

Nominal wages rose by more than a third in 1990 (Holger Schmiedling, *FT*, 25 February 1991, p. 17); between the last quarters of 1989 and 1990 wages rose by 40 per cent, and most observers think the gap will close in at most three to four years (Lutz Hoffman, *FT*, 25 February 1991, p. 17). The summer and autumn of 1990 saw East German wage rises in the range 20–50 per cent (Norbert Walter, *FT*, 3 January 1991, p. 12). In 1991 wages increased by over 60 per cent, while productivity growth was almost zero (DIW, *Economic Bulletin*, 1992, vol. 29, no. 6, p. 7). David Goodhart (*FT*, 27 November 1990, p. 3) reported that East German wage levels were already 40–45 per cent of those of West German levels; public service workers were to receive 60 per cent of their West German counterparts' salaries as of 1 July 1991 (*FT*, 18 March 1991, p. 6). By the end of 1990 the average wage per East German employee was 50 per cent of the West German counterpart (Siebert 1991a: 34). The ratio of wages per employee in East Germany to those of West Germany rose from 32 per cent in the second half of 1989 to about half in the first half of 1991; labour costs per hour worked in East Germany rose by 73 per cent between the second and fourth quarters of 1990, while East Germany's wages were already two-thirds of the UK's and more than five times those of Poland (Martin Wolf, *FT*, 1 July 1991, p. 14). The Deutsche Bank (*Focus: Germany*, 10 March 1992, no. 75, pp. 3–4) quotes a Halle Institute of Economic Research estimate that in 1991 unit wage costs in East German industry were about 70 per cent higher than in West German industry. East German pay is now 60 per cent of the West German level (Karl Otto Pöhl, *IHT*, 3 July 1991, p. 13); more precisely, average union rates are now 60 per cent of the West German level (*Deutsche Bank Bulletin*, July 1991, p. 19). David Goodhart (*FT Survey of Germany*, 28 October 1991, p. xi) makes the point, however, that these figures need to be adjusted for longer hours, shorter holidays and fewer fringe benefits in East Germany; looking at total labour costs, the average East German earns about 45 per cent of the West German level. In an 11 May 1992 speech Chancellor Kohl talked of East German wages and salaries reaching 44 per cent of West German levels in 1991, while productivity was only 29 per cent.

East Germany is unable to devalue its currency in order to remain competitive because of monetary union and this has had a depressing effect on output and employment. Temporary wage subsidization is one solution recommended, e.g. Akerlof *et al.* (1991), *The Financial Times* (21 March 1991, leader, p. 22) and *The Economist*, 6 April 1991, p. 77). Akerlof *et al.* (1991: 80–1) argue in favour of a 'self-eliminating flexible employment bonus programme', the value of the bonus falling to zero as wages in East Germany approach those in West Germany. Advantages of the programme include speeding up privatization, increased investment, lower unemployment and reduced migration. The budgetary cost would allegedly be low, perhaps even negative, because of the savings in unemployment benefit and the tax revenue raised. The *Financial Times* (26 July 1991, leader, p. 12) advocates a uniform employment subsidy set at a fixed proportion of the difference between East German and West German wages to discourage further wage convergence. In a later leader (*FT*, 20 May 1992, p. 11) subsidies for the *private* sector were mentioned. The real wage to employers would be lowered, while migration to West Germany would be deterred (Richard Portes, *FT*, 25 March 1991, p. 21). David Begg and Richard Portes (*IHT*, 19 June 1991, p. 4) argue that since the basic conflict is between the need to raise Eastern living standards and the need to make industry competitive by lowering real wages, assistance should take the form of an employment subsidy. A uniform employment subsidy should be available to every enterprise in East Germany but should decline to zero within four years; the subsidy would initially be 75 per cent of current East German wages and would be reduced by one-third in each of the next three years. Begg and Portes argue that the panoply of current subsidies should be scrapped and replaced with this uniform employment subsidy and a full, immediate writing off of enterprise debt. Paul O'Brien and Niels Westerlund (*OECD Observer*, August–September 1991, no. 171, p. 31) think there is a case for replacing current subsidies with a direct employment bonus that would vary according to the difference between the wage actually paid by an East German enterprise and the basic wage in that industry in West Germany. This, it is argued, would provide enterprises and their managers with an incentive to resist wage increases and would enhance competition between East German enterprises. In the longer term, however, they see the creation of new enterprises as the surest way to restructure and to reduce unemployment.

Those critical of wage subsidies include the IMF[2] and Samuel Brittan (*FT*, 30 May 1991, p. 23). He argues that there is the danger of subsidies becoming permanent and that a tax-based incomes policy is preferable. The Bundesbank argues that broad wage subsidy programmes ultimately slow the creation of viable jobs because they preserve overstaffing and hinder the relocation of workers into profitable sectors; the bank also argues that the real wage differential is not so wide when consideration is given to things like lower housing rents, while qualified workers are often motivated more by lack of suitable work in East Germany than the prospect of higher wages in West Germany (Richard Smith, *IHT*, 19 July 1991, p. 11). The Deutsche Bank (*Unification Issue* no. 47, 22 May 1991, pp. 1–3) argues similarly: existing structures would be preserved and the adjustment process hindered; the main obstacles to competitiveness are not prices or wages but narrow product ranges, outdated technologies and excessive vertical integration; across-the-board industrial employment subsidies benefit those companies which have already been privatized, leading to windfall profits; targeted support programmes are preferable. Siebert (1991b: 314) puts the greater danger at wage subsidies quickly finding their

way into higher wages. David Goodhart (*FT Survey*, 28 October 1991, p. xi) argues that lower wages might hinder the renewal process by making the wrong products artificially economic; he supports the government policy of subsidizing new investment.

Private households in East Germany are better off in real terms than before reunification. The DIW (*Economic Bulletin*, January 1992, vol. 28, no. 11, p. 15) calculates that real income per head rose by 11.5 per cent in 1990. The real disposable income of East German households increased by 10 per cent in 1991, with a forecast rise of 6 per cent in 1992 (DIW, *Economic Bulletin*, 1992, vol. 29, no. 6, p. 13). It is worth noting that these figures underestimate the actual increase in living standards, because of factors such as improvements in the quality and availability of goods. The Deutsche Bank (*Focus: Germany*, 20 January 1992, no. 70, p.3) points out that gross wages and salaries per East German worker were 44.6 per cent of the West German level and private consumption was as much as 56.9 per cent.

The forecasts for unemployment have always been difficult to make, but the early ones gave way to gloomier predictions for a while. The real Cassandras put the peak at 4 million, but these dire predictions soon faded away, as Table 21.2 shows. Although not as bad as some earlier predictions, the figures nevertheless paint a grim picture.

Output. The drastic falls in output in 1990 and 1991 are shown in Table 21.3. Estimates vary because of immense statistical difficulties in translating East German performance into conventional terms and also because of varying definitions (e.g. gross *national* product includes the income earned by East Germans working in West Germany, whereas gross *domestic* product does not). The same organization understandably revises its own figures over time, with the figure for 1991 changing from around –20 per cent to around –30 per cent, e.g. Deutsche Bank and the five institutes. The early consensus that the turning point would be mid-1991 changed for a while to autumn 1991 – spring 1992 or even later (the end of the Gulf War was difficult to predict at first). The DIW (*Economic Bulletin*, 1991, vol. 28, no. 10, pp. 1–2) now says that total output did not decline during the second quarter of 1991; the East German economy seemed to bottom out some time during the summer of that year. Construction and services (especially retail trade, banking and insurance) were actually expanding and leading the way to recovery. The growth in construction started in the spring of 1991 (DIW, *Economic Bulletin*, 1992, vol. 28, no. 11, p. 7). The December 1991 Bundesbank report (Richard Smith, *IHT*, 19 December 1991, p. 9) notes that even industrial production was beginning to recover slowly: 'The eastern German economy has probably passed its low point even if the recovery is not yet broad-based or self-sustaining.' The five German economic research institutes' autumn report published in October 1991 (Deutsche Bank, *Unification Issue*, 1991, no. 61; the 22 October issues of the *FT, IHT* and *Guardian*) was also cautious. It pointed out the danger of rapid wage rises and a burgeoning budget deficit and saw no signs of a sustained recovery: 'Above all, the forces for self-sustaining economic growth are lacking', i.e. government inflows from West Germany are largely driving the East German economy. Nevertheless, strong gains were forecast for 1992, albeit from a depressed base. In his 11 May 1992 speech Chancellor Kohl pointed out that *per capita* private sector investment in East Germany was only two-thirds that in West Germany. According to Christopher Parkes (*FT*, 12 May 1992, p. 2), East Germany provided less than 3 per cent of all German exports.

In the six months after the 1948 currency reform in West Germany industrial production rose by more than 50 per cent, whereas in East Germany July–December 1990 it fell by more than 50 per cent despite substantial subsidization (Holger Schmiedling, *FT*, 25 February 1991, p. 17). Industrial production in 1990 fell by almost 30 per cent (*Deutsche Bank Bulletin*, July

1991, p. 9). The DIW (*Economic Bulletin*, 1991, vol. 28, no. 4, pp. 1–2) puts the decline in East German industrial output at 28 per cent and that of manufacturing output at 30 per cent. In the first year after GEMU (i.e. the year to July 1991) East German industrial production fell by 43 per cent. A few sectors actually increased (e.g. printing by 21 per cent), but most fell by varying percentages, e.g. precision engineering, office equipment and steel foundries by more than 75, mechanical engineering 56.9, chemicals 40.2, oil refining 4.3, and food processing 4.3 (Quentin Peel, *FT*, 16 October, 1991, p. 3). The DIW (*Economic Bulletin*, 1991, vol. 28, no. 9, p. 10) estimates that in the year following GEMU industrial output (excluding construction) fell by 53 per cent. The Deutsche Bank (*Unification Issue*, 13 December 1991, no. 67, p. 4) puts the fall in industrial manufacturing output in 1991 at 55 per cent (a predicted 20 per cent increase in 1992). The percentage falls in the output of individual sectors in 1991 were as follows (with estimates for positive growth in 1992 in brackets): precision engineering, optics –81 (+1); office equipment, data processing –74 (+2); electrical engineering –68 (+21); non-ferrous minerals – 65 (+61); mechanical engineering –63 (+11); foundries –61 (+9); wood processing –59 (+13); chemicals –51 (+8); food, beverages and tobacco –49 (+30); textiles –48 (+6); iron and steel –38 (+9); motor vehicle construction –34 (+12); steel construction –30 (+31); oil processing –14 (+6); and printing –12 (+32). In a later publication the Deutsche Bank (Focus: Germany, 2 April 1992, no. 77, p. 2) puts the fall in total industrial output in 1991 at 22 per cent.

The Deutsche Bank (*Focus:Germany*, 20 January 1992, no. 70, pp. 1–3) provides the following statistics for 1991: East Germany's GNP amounted to only 7.4 per cent of the West German level (8.3 per cent in the second half of 1990) and 6.9 per cent of all-German GNP; *per capita* GNP was 29.3 per cent of the West German level; the productivity of East German workers was only a shade less than 30 per cent of their West German counterparts; manufacturing industry as a percentage of East German gross value-added fell from 65 per cent in 1988 to 44 per cent in the second half of 1990, and to only 34 per cent in 1991, while the respective figures for services show increases from 7 per cent to 17 per cent and to 23.8 per cent.

It is worth noting that job creation has been rapid. An early prediction of both the East German and West German government was 500,000 new jobs to be created in 1990. Mary Brasier (*The Guardian*, 28 September 1990, p. 28) reported the birth of 100,000 new businesses since the March election and the death of 3,000. In the first ten months of 1990 226,000 new private businesses were registered in East Germany, about half in the hotel and catering trade and the retail sector, 33,000 in handicrafts and 2,000 in tourism (Norbert Walter, *FT*, 3 January 1991, p. 12); the registrations amounted to 281,000 for the year as a whole. According to *The Economist* (6 April 1991, p. 10), some 1 million new jobs and 300,000 new enterprises had been created to date since the start of 1990. The DIW (*Economic Bulletin*, 1991, vol. 28, no. 6, p. 13), however, points out that while 360,098 enterprises were registered and 46,390 deregistered between the start of January 1990 and the end of March 1991, these figures include, for example, businesses reconstituted or split off from larger ones; net new business creation probably amounted to at most 100,000 units. By the end of August 1991 only about 175,000 of the 435,000 net registrations could be considered to be new businesses (DIW, *Economic Bulletin*, 1992, vol. 28, no. 11, p. 6). The March 1992 THA report mentioned that 500,000 companies had been founded since November 1989 (*IHT*, 18 March 1992, pp.11–13).

Inflation

Karl Otto Pöhl, the then President of the Bundesbank, was less optimistic than the West German government originally was that taxes would not have to be raised to finance unification; he stressed the need to control public spending. The government's attitude to tax increases gradually changed: first came talk of raising taxes only as a last resort, with blame attached to the Gulf crisis; on 9 November 1990 Chancellor Kohl talked of new 'duties' being necessary, including environmental ones such as those on leaded petrol, carbon dioxide emissions and motorway use; on 23 November the proposed corporate tax cuts were shelved until the 1995 parliamentary session; on 11 January 1991 it was announced that social insurance contributions were to go up from April 1991. On 12 February 1991 the new Economics Minister Jurgen Möllemann announced a new ten-point three-year plan to help East Germany; this involves an extra DM 10 billion per year, including extra expenditure on retraining (only 30,000 short-time workers are currently receiving job retraining; if a retraining programme were turned down without good cause, the person would have to wait eight weeks before becoming eligible for unemployment benefit (*IHT*, 9 March 1991, p. 9) and the infrastructure and a one-year extension to the 12 per cent of investment grants for investors in East Germany (Möllemann estimates that a company investing DM 100 million would recoup DM 49 million in grants and tax write-offs: *IHT*, 9 March 1991, p. 9). The finance was to come from spending reductions, but also tax increases, although other factors like the Gulf crisis and aid to the Soviet Union and Eastern Europe were also blamed. As regards East Germany, particular blame was placed on the extent to which Comecon trade collapsed. Theo Waigel admitted on 21 February that these three factors were the causes of prospective tax increases; the latter included a one year 7.5 per cent personal and corporate income tax surcharge, an increase in the insurance tax from 7 per cent to 10 per cent and an increase in petrol tax from 1 July (these were agreed in talks with the opposition on 14 June). In February 1992 it was agreed that VAT would increase from 14 per cent to 15 per cent in January 1993 and that the extra revenue raised would go into the Unity Fund (discussed below) to finance East Germany. In its March 1992 report the Bundesbank urged the government either to restrain spending or face the possibility of having to raise taxes again. On 8 March 1991 the government agreed an extra DM 12 billion for both 1991 and 1992, focusing on help for local authority spending on social infrastructure, job creation schemes, and investment in housing, shipyards and the environment. The government initially earmarked DM 50 billion for East Germany in its 1991 budget, having spent DM 45 billion in 1990 (*IHT*, 9 March 1991, p. 9).

Karl Otto Pöhl was basically optimistic as to the effects of GEMU on inflation. The 1990 West German inflation rate was 2.7 per cent, lower than that of 1989 (2.8 per cent). The initial impact of monetary union on the West German money supply (M3) was of the order of a 15 per cent increase, matched by an increase in capacity of somewhat less. The DIW gave figures showing a 13.5–14 per cent increase in M3 and an increase in productive potential of 11 per cent (*Economic Bulletin*, September 1990, vol. 27, no. 7, pp. 10–11). Most forecast only modest upward pressure on interest rates. In October 1989 there was a rise of 1 per cent in West German interest rates, the discount rate (the rate at which banks receive limited loans from the Bundesbank collateralized with short term bills) increasing from 5 per cent to 6 per cent and the Lombard rate (the rate at which banks receive unlimited emergency short-term loans from the Bundesbank) from 7 per cent to 8 per cent. On 1 November 1990 the Lombard rate was raised to 8.5 per cent and on 31 January 1991 to 9 per cent, when the discount rate went up to 6.5 per cent). On 15 August 1991 the discount rate was raised to 7.5 per cent and the Lombard rate to 9.25 per cent, the Bundesbank expressing concern at wage increases and the West German inflation rate in the year to July of 4.4 per cent (the highest since November 1982; the previous peak was 7 per cent in 1974, while the annual rate reached 4.8 per cent in March

1992 before falling). Interest rates were raised once again on 19 December, to 8 per cent and 9.75 per cent respectively, while West Germany's average inflation for 1991 was 3.5 per cent (the highest since the 4.6 per cent of 1981). The discount rate was raised to 8.75 per cent on 16 July 1992, signalling continuing concern about inflation.

In East Germany consumer prices rose 9.8 per cent in the second half of 1990 and an estimated 18 per cent in 1991 (Deutsche Bank, *Unification Issue*, 1991, no. 57, p. 13). The Deutsche Bank *Bulletin* (July 1991, p. 8) put the inflation rate at -4 per cent for the whole of 1990; inflation was an estimated 18 per cent in 1991 and 15 per cent in 1992, compared to the five German economic research institutes' estimates of 12 per cent for both years (*Unification Issue*, 1991, no. 61, p. 3). Later on the Deutsche Bank put the figures at 14.2 per cent in 1991 and 12 per cent in 1992 (*Focus: Germany*, 2 April 1992, no. 77, p. 4) and the five institutes at 13.6 per cent and 12 per cent respectively (with 0.2 per cent for 1990) (*IHT*, 13 April 1992, p. 7, and *FT*, 14 April 1992, p. 3). The German Council of Economic Advisers predicted a 1992 inflation rate of 8.5 per cent (Deutsche Bank, *Unification Issue*, 1991, no. 63, p. 4). The DIW figures (*Economic Bulletin*, 1992, vol. 28, no. 11, p. 2) were −2.7 per cent for 1990, 12 per cent for 1991 and 12 per cent for 1992. Important factors affecting inflation include:

The effect on consumption and savings of the conversion of East German savings and wages into Deutschmarks (in 1987 East German savings deposits amounted to EM 141.9 billion and cash in circulation EM 15 billion). There was no inflationary spending spree, partly owing to the uncertainties associated with unemployment, the attraction of Deutschmark interest rates and the lack of other forms of wealth such as shares. The interesting aspect was the massive switch in spending towards West German and foreign goods. This moderated somewhat in 1991, but even so in that year West German deliveries to East Germany amounted to DM 207 billion, while the reverse flow was only DM 38 billion (Deutsche Bank, *Focus: Germany*, 2 April 1992, no. 77, p. 2). The effects of GEMU on individual East German prices were very diverse, with the formerly heavily taxed consumer durables like cars and TV sets coming down and the formerly heavily subsidized commodities like basic foodstuffs going up.

The supply response of both the East German and West German economies. The West German economy, while operating at a high rate of capacity utilization, benefited from the inflow of young, skilled and highly mobile workers, as well as the switch in demand. The West German economy was in excellent overall shape to shoulder the cost burden of unification. The West German government originally estimated that the extra tax revenue from higher growth would be as follows: DM 8.2 billion in 1990, DM 28.4 billion in 1991, DM 34.7 billion in 1992, and DM 43.7 billion in 1993. Actual West German growth in 1990 was 4.5 per cent (1.5 percentage points due to reunification, according to the Federal Statistical Office), compared to 3.9 per cent in 1989. An early official 1991 estimate was 2.5–3 per cent (0.5 percentage points due to reunification); the actual growth of GNP was 3.1 per cent. The DIW (*Economic Bulletin*, 1991, vol. 28, no. 9, p. 4) estimates that in the year following GEMU the West German economy grew by over 4 per cent, with 2.3 percentage points due to reunification. In 1989 West German household savings were of the order of DM 190 billion and capital exports DM 100 billion. The surplus on the current account of the balance of payments was DM 107.6 billion in 1989 (reduced to DM 77.4 billion in 1990, the figure including East Germany for the second half of the year), thus providing scope for increasing imports (which dampens inflationary pressures), easing the West German capacity problem and avoiding a balance of payments constraint on East German growth. In 1991 a deficit of DM 34.2 billion was recorded.

Only modest West German growth was forecast for 1992, perhaps of the order of 1 per cent. In the spring of 1992 the serious outbreak of strikes over wages in West Germany was directly related to the question of the distribution of the burden of financing reunification.

The financial cost to West Germany of unification

It is impossible to be in anyway precise. As Theo Waigel said (26 June 1990): 'Only a soothsayer or a swindler can estimate the costs of German unity.' Early forecasts were too optimistic. It is, nevertheless, useful to mention some of the elements:

1. Spending on East German pensions (70 per cent of average net wages after forty-five years of contributions), unemployment pay, infrastructure and environmental protection; here there are benefits to other countries, including West Germany itself. The Munich-based IFO economic institute estimates that DM 210 billion would be needed up to the year 2000 to produce the same quality of environment as in West Germany; sewage disposal needs more than DM 100 billion; and more than DM 200 billion is needed for the modernization of the road and rail network (Deutsche Bank, *Unification Issue*, 1991, no. 60, p. 1). Blanchard *et al.* (1991: 92) cite Siebert's estimation that the total amount of capital required for restructuring in East Germany amounts to some 25 per cent of West Germany's GNP. David Gow (*The Guardian*, 13 February 1992, p. 10) reports an estimate by the Institute for Economy and Society (IWG) that investment of DM1,850 billion would be needed over fifteen to twenty years to equalize employment rates in East Germany and West Germany. On 16 January 1991 a number of tax incentives to promote investment in East Germany were announced: a 50 per cent write off of the investment undertaken during one year, spread over a period of between one and five years; additional tax-free earnings allowances of DM 600 for a single person and DM 1,200 for a married person; and the assurance that the West German system of local taxes on property and capital paid by firms (to be phased out in West

Germany itself) will not be imposed on East Germany.

2. A reduction in defence spending as the Cold War melted away completely.

3. Control of the flow westwards would reduce spending on migrants in West Germany itself, while there are savings to be gained from reducing subsidies to West Berlin and the West German regions bordering East Germany (to be eliminated by the end of 1994).

4. The East German Staatsbank estimated that East Germany's net foreign debt was $18.5 billion at the end of 1989. It is worth noting the German Unity Fund (Deutsche Einheit), amounting to DM 115 billion over the period 1990–94; DM 20 billion of this was to come from West German budgetary savings and DM 95 billion from borrowings on capital markets. The idea was to finance unification without a rise in taxes, but this, as has been seen, was an aim not achieved. In August 1991 it was announced that a further DM 6 billion a year was to be added to the fund for 1992, 1993 and 1994. The extra revenue raised from the increase in VAT from 14 per cent to 15 per cent as of January 1993, agreed in February 1992, would also go to the fund, amounting to an extra DM 33.6 billion in 1992–94.

On 27 June 1991 Pöhl estimated that DM 150 billion would be transferred from West Germany to East Germany in 1991. The DIW (*Economic Bulletin*, 1991, vol. 28, no. 5, p. 13) puts public financial aid to East Germany at DM 45 billion in 1990 and DM 97.5 billion in 1991; the latter represents about half of East Germany's national product (p.8). In the year following GEMU DM 110 billion in public funds was transferred from West Germany to East Germany (DIW, *Economic Bulletin*, 1991 vol. 28, no. 9, p. 2). The net transfer of public funds (taking account of the increased tax receipts resulting from the rise in demand from East Germany) was DM 105 billion in 1991, rising to an estimated DM 125 billion in 1992 (DIW, *Economic Bulletin*, vol. 28, no. 11, p. 6). The Commerzbank (see its report in The Economist,

16 November 1991, p. 116) estimates that transfer payments from West Germany make up two-thirds of East Germany's GNP; this is the figure for 1991 (DM140 billion) also mentioned by the new Bundesbank president Helmut Schlesinger (*FT*, 18 November 1991, p. 2). In its March 1992 report the Bundesbank provided the following figures (*IHT*, 19 March 1992, p. 11, and *FT*, 19 March 1992, p. 24): in 1991 net transfers from West Germany to East Germany amounted to over DM 139 billion (5.5 per cent of West Germany's national product) and were likely to rise to DM 180 billion in 1992 (6.5 per cent of West Germany's national product); DM 60 billion in 1991 went to private households, meaning that West Germany financed one-third of consumption in East Germany (in 1992 the forecast was a rise to DM 85 billion and 40 per cent respectively); East Germany contributed only 3.5 per cent of total German tax revenue, compared with a figure of 20 per cent as regards population. The gross transfer of public funds to East Germany in 1992 was estimated to be DM 215 billion, DM 180 billion net after the payment of DM 35 billion in eastern taxes; only a quarter was destined to go for investment purposes (*The Economist Survey*, 23 May 1992, p. 9). The volume of transfers would be of the order of 60 per cent of East German output in 1992 (DIW, *Economic Bulletin*, 1992, vol. 29, no. 4, p. 15).

The overall German budget deficit was given as 3 per cent of GNP in 1990 and 3.3 per cent in 1991, but the figures exclude the borrowing of organizations such as the THA.

THE PRIVATIZATION PROGRAMME

A trust body (agency) or holding company (Treuhandanstalt, THA) was set up in March 1990: this deals not only with privatization, but also restructuring, liquidation and credit guarantees (to provide temporary protection to enterprises). The East German parliament passed a law reconstituting the THA on 17 June 1990, entrusting it with the combines and enterprises, but also the property belonging to organizations such as the Stasi and the army. On 13 July 1990 the new management board was convened for the first time and in October the THA was given its first legislative mandate to privatize the East German economy. All told, 40 per cent of East Germany's surface area and 50 per cent of its workforce became the THA's responsibility, with a mandate to build a private sector and secure the livelihoods of 4 million people. Its first task was to keep the 8,000 large companies in business. The THA, for example, assumed responsibility for the debt owed to East German banks. (See THA report, *IHT*, 18 March 1992, pp.11–13.)

The management has changed. Detlev Rohwedder (head of the West German company Hoescht) was originally chairman of the supervisory board, until he was replaced by Jens Odewald (chairman of the West German Kaufhof department store chain); on 21 August 1990 Rohwedder was named as replacement for Reiner Gohlke (former chairman of the Bundesbahn) as chairman of the executive board, Gohlke having resigned the previous day. But Rohwedder was assassinated by the Red Army Faction on 1 April 1991. He was replaced by Birgit Breuel, who was formerly in charge of the fifteen regional offices; she became a member of the executive board in October 1990 and president on 13 April 1991. Hero Brahms was appointed vice-president (a new post). The Federal Finance Ministry is now responsible for the THA.

The THA was endowed with the ownership rights of around 8,000 'large' enterprises (those with more than 250 employees) employing around 4 million people, with the combines being split up.[3] In October 1990 Rohwedder estimated them to be worth nearly DM 200 billion. By February 1991 the number of enterprises had risen to 9,200 because of continuing subdivision (Lutz Hoffman, *FT*, 25 February 1991, p. 17). The number of enterprises subsequently increased to 10,500 (Siebert 1991b: 295). Originally enterprises were obliged to draw up Deutschmark balance sheets by 31 October

1990 in readiness for privatization. The date was subsequently extended to the end of June 1991 for bigger enterprises and the end of September for smaller ones. There was a further extension to the end of 1991. Four thousand companies had produced Deutschmark balance sheets to date (David Goodhart, *FT*, 1 July 1991, p. 6).

The THA also administers two-thirds of the forested area and almost 30 per cent of agricultural land (*IFO-Digest*, 1991, vol. 14, no. 2, p. 8). On top of this there is non-agricultural land accounting for almost a quarter of the surface area of East Germany; only a tiny fraction has been privatized to date (DIW *Economic Bulletin*, 1991, vol. 28, no. 5, July, p. 6). The THA is responsible for state farms and forests and the agricultural and forestry land used by co-operatives and individuals (Siebert 1991a: 16–17). The DIW (*Economic Bulletin*, 1991, vol. 28, no. 6, p. 3) summarizes the legal situation: agricultural producer co-operatives had to perform a division of net assets and reconstitute themselves in corporate form by the end of 1991; the land itself belongs either to private individuals, only some of whom are actually co-operative farmers, or is currently being administered by the THA (in the case of land expropriated 1945–49); 22 per cent of the land belongs to co-operative members, 47 per cent to non-members and 24 per cent to the THA (p. 18). The Deutsche Bank (*Unification Issue*, 1991, no. 64, pp. 1–4) provides useful additional information. Before the 1989 revolution GDR agricultural productivity was about 40 per cent of the West German level and a narrow range of low-quality standard products were produced (p. 1). The sector has suffered, owing to such factors as the initial switch in demand to West German and foreign foods, but the medium and long-term prospects are quite favourable (pp. 1, 3). As of autumn 1991 one-third of co-operatives were still structured as before, another third had drawn up private enterprise solutions, 17 per cent were working on such a strategy, and 15 per cent had declared bankruptcy (p. 2). Interest in reclaiming property and starting private businesses has been limited; perhaps 10 per cent at most of co-operative farmers were then attracted by the idea because of uncertainty, lack of business skills, poor qualifications and a shortage of capital; many farmers favour continuing collective operations under a new legal guise, registered co-operatives or limited liability companies (p. 2). The Deutsche Bank considers that a policy based on the ideal of the 'family farm' would be misguided, although the average co-operative is too large at present (p. 3) (note that the average farm in West Germany has only 18 ha under cultivation: p. 1). The DIW (*Economic Bulletin*, 1991, vol. 28, no. 5, p. 18) is also critical of agricultural policy attempting to establish the family-run farm as the dominant model; while not recommending the continuance of the present production co-operatives, the DIW argues that there are competitive advantages in larger production units. Leslie Colitt (*FT*, 19 June 1992, p. 2) reports the following changes in leasing arrangements: state farms (not co-operatives) were to be leased to farmers for twelve years rather than for only one year in order to facilitate planning; sales could then take place. At the end of October 1991 only about 2 per cent of the THA's land had been sold or leased to private investors (United Nations Economic Commission for Europe 1992: 245).

Siebert (1991a: 16, 1991b: 297) notes that enterprises controlled by municipalities and counties (plus the land belonging to them) have come into the trustee ownership of the federal government (not of the THA); municipalities are able to apply for these enterprises. Public buildings are the property of the relevant political authorities, while publicly owned housing has been awarded to municipalities. The railways and the postal service are deemed special property.

Actual sales speeded up after a slow start. On 14 January 1991 the THA said that more than 450 large enterprises had been privatized, raising DM 2.5 billion in sales revenue (*IHT*, 15 January 1991, p. 11). The THA reported on 18 April that 1,261 industrial enterprises had been privatized,

403 in the last quarter of 1990 and 858 in the first quarter of 1991; West German companies purchased 90 per cent of them, foreigners 5 per cent and the remaining 5 per cent were management buy-outs. An 'especially generous' attitude would henceforth be taken towards management buy-outs, preference being given in the event of equal bids; the aim was to sell at least one-third of the 6,400 small to medium enterprises controlled by the fifteen regional offices to existing management, checks being made to ensure the support of the workforce (*IHT*, 22 April 1991, p. 7). The percentage sectoral breakdown of the sales was as follows: capital goods and motors 40; food and drink 30; electronics and scientific instruments 17; and chemicals and rubber 12 (David Goodhart, *FT*, 19 April 1991, p. 3, and David Gow, *The Guardian*, 19 April 1991, p. 15.) David Goodhart reports (*FT*, 1 July 1991, p. 6) that 2,200 had been sold, 544 in May alone; foreigners accounted for only eighty-one (France eighteen, Switzerland fourteen, Sweden nine and the USA eight). By the end of July 1991, 2,986 had been sold, raising DM 11.6 billion, but 7,200 remain; only 115 enterprises had been sold abroad (David Goodhart, *FT*, 9 September, 1991, p. 11). By August 1991 nearly 3,400 enterprises has been privatized, reducing the number still under the control of the THA to about 7,000; DM 12.5 billion had been raised from these sales (DM 21 billion by the end of February 1992); foreigners had bought 156 of the enterprises (Deutsche Bank, *Unification Issue*, 1991, no. 58, p. 2). A greater effort was made after April–May 1991 to involve foreigners. By the end of September the number of enterprises privatized had gone up to 3,788, by the end of October to 4,237, and by the end of 1991 to 5,200 (France forty-four, Switzerland forty-two and the UK twenty-six). The March 1992 THA report revealed the following (*IHT*, 18 March 1992, pp. 11–13): in the previous twenty-one months the THA had privatized around 5,500 manufacturing and service companies (leaving the THA still administering 5,800) and

nearly 15,000 retail outlets, securing over DM 100 billion in investment in East Germany and over 1 million jobs (the proportion of the workforce employed by THA companies had fallen from 50 per cent to 22 per cent). Some 250 non-German companies (these exclude foreign-owned companies in West Germany) had invested more than DM 10.5 billion (DM 8.5 billion in 1991). Of the 900 management buy-outs more than 50 per cent had fewer than twenty employees.

A later report put the total privatization at almost 7,000, with 4,800 enterprises remaining; the THA hopes to complete the privatization part of its programme by the end of 1993, a year earlier than expected (Frederick Studemann, *The Guardian*, 9 May 1992, p. 35). The number of people working in remaining THA enterprises fell to 2.9 million at the start of 1991 and 1.4 million at the start of 1992 (DIW, *Economic Bulletin*, 1992, vol. 29, no. 4, p. 7). The July 1992 THA report made the following points (*IHT*, 7 July 1992, pp. 15–16): as of 1 June 1992 7,613 enterprises had been privatized, resulting in DM 29.3 billion in payments, DM 138.5 billion in investment guarantees, and 1.16 million jobs secured; 807 companies had been returned to their former owners; 4,637 companies (mostly employing under than 250 employees) remained unsold, the aim being to reduce this figure to 2,500 by the end of 1992; since the beginning of the THA 390 non-German companies had invested DM 11.6 billion ($7.4 billion) in THA enterprises (excluding an estimated DM 4 billion in the pipeline or purchases made by German subsidiaries of multinational companies and also excluding foreigners' 'greenfield' ventures in East Germany) and guaranteed 106,000 jobs.

The smaller enterprises nationalized in 1972 quickly started being returned to their former owners. A subsidary was set up to deal with the so-called 'small privatizations'. Service establishments such as restaurants and cafes began to be sold off or leased. More than 70 per cent of shops had been privatized by early 1991 (David Goodhart and Andrew Fisher, *FT*, 7 February 1991, p. 4); the THA had privatized 25,000 shops and other service enterprises by spring 1991 (David Goodhart, *FT*, 5 April 1991, p. 18). Siebert (1991b: 298) reports that by 30 April 1991 the larger retail stores and smaller hotels had all been privatized, while figures of 76 per cent and 62 per cent applied to small stores and pharmacies and restaurants respectively. In March 1992 the THA reported that it had privatized nearly 15,000 retail outlets.

The 15 June 1990 agreement between the East German and West German governments provided a basis for property claims. The period 1945–49 is unaffected because of the reunification treaties agreed with the Soviet Union; the German constitutional court confirmed on 23 April 1991 that land and property seized between 1945 and 1949 could not be reclaimed by the former owners, although some partial compensation was recommended. Those who left after 1949 or their heirs had the right in principle to reclaim assets left behind. Property was to be returned 'as far as this is possible, taking into account the social and economic realities that have developed over the last forty years'. This meant that domestic tenants would be able to see their present contracts through. Buildings which had been converted for 'general or commercial use' or for community use or firms which became part of larger units would not be affected. Siebert (1991b: 297) notes that compensation is used when pieces of land of different owners have been combined into new units and cannot be easily separated, e.g. land used for housing, roads and industrial buildings. It was estimated that perhaps as much as one-fifth of property would still have been the potential subject of property claims (David Goodhart and Leslie Colitt, *FT*, 12 September 1990, p. 4). The same applied to farms which became part of larger production units or co-operatives (working farmers have the right to reclaim their land from co-operative or state farms). If the present occupants and former owners could not reach agreement, state compensation would be paid. Most larger West German companies (e.g. Daimler-Benz) quickly renounced their claims. Considerable confusion surrounded the competing claims of various levels of local government to property. A revised property claims agreement followed (David Goodhart and Leslie Colitt, *FT*, 12 September 1990, p. 4):

1. Claims on small businesses had to be submitted before 16 September and all other claims before 13 October 1990.

2. The vast majority of claimants would not be able to reclaim the land or property itself. Article 41 of the unity treaty stated that property needed for urgent business reasons (such as employment-creating investment) could be sold. Claimants' monetary compensation was based on what the property was worth when it was taken over, plus 1 per cent annual interest payments on that sum. David Goodhart (*FT*, 30 November 1990, p. 18) reports that as much as 40 per cent of the East German land area was the subject of claims from former owners.

New rules were issued on 6 February 1991 because of the deterrent effect on investment of the huge number of claims. It became easier for new investors to take over East German property, the claimants, when identified, being compensated financially later on. Any claimants would have four weeks to take over the contract; the entire enterprise had to be taken over, with payments made by the claimant for any improvements to the property. Before any legal decision was finally made a claimant might be able to take over an enterprise, but if the claim was rejected the original investor only would only have to pay the agreed contract price. (*The Financial Times*, 31 March 1992, p. 2, reports that only 3.2 per cent of the 2.4 million property claims had been processed to date. But it was the intention to resolve all of them by 1994 instead of the year 2000 owing to the imposition of strict time limits on individual claims. The Deutsche Bank, *Focus: Germany*, 2 April 1992, no. 77, p. 4, reports that, of the roughly 2 million restitution claims submitted,

less than 5 per cent had been clarified in a legally binding manner.)

On 7 March 1991 the THA announced that it was to sign deals with more than fifty international banks and management consultancies to arrange sales: each would be offered a package of around ten enterprises and be paid both a daily allowance to cover costs and a fee for every sale.

On 15 March 1991 the Bundestag agreed to a further relaxation of the legislation. The THA now has the authority, until the end of 1992, to give priority to any investor judged to provide the best job-sustaining and creating programme (Richard Smith, International Herald Tribune, 13 March 1991, pp. 11–13); the key determinant is now speedy construction (Deutsche Bank, *Unification Issue*, no. 44, 2 April 1991, p. 1). Vincentz (1991: 10) says the aim of getting the highest price was supplemented or even replaced by the size of the investment pledged and the number of jobs secured.

> A Treuhand-type sale does involve a buyer, but what that buyer bids with, in addition to cash up front, is the size and sophistication of investment and, most important, the number of jobs to be guaranteed . . . By committing themselves to holding on to their investments for two to three years at the stipulated levels of activity and employment, and consenting to pay stiff penalties for failing to do so, purchasers temporarily cede their freedom of action.
>
> (THA report, *IHT*, 7 July 1992, p. 16).

A former owner would at least have to match any other offer. Investors are generally compelled to retain their new company's assets for five to seven years as a rule (THA report, *IHT*, 18 March 1992, pp. 11–13). The new policy covers the Nazi property seizures of 1933–45 as well as the post-1949 socialist ones.

The July 1991 OECD report recommended that a variety of ownership forms should be more strongly encouraged, including management buy-outs, greater use of auctions and share offerings to the public; enterprises should try to restructure themselves and sell off component parts of their operations (Richard Smith, *IHT*, 26 July 1991, p. 11). The March 1992 THA report mentioned 900 management buy-outs, although over half of them had fewer than twenty employees. During a trip to London on 26 November 1991 Birgit Breuel talked about greater contracting-out to independent investment banks, flotation on stock markets, and large-scale public tender for groups of small enterprises (tender sales were introduced in January 1992: THA report, *IHT*, 7 July 1992, p. 15). To speed up the privatization programme the THA now encourages industrialists to invest in 'holding companies', limited liability partnerships handling up to ten struggling enterprises. In return for buying shares and helping to oversee management the industrialists receive salaries. The parnerships would run for three years, after which the still unprofitable enterprises would be bankrupted (Frederick Studemann, *The Guardian*, 9 May 1992, p. 35). On 7 January 1992 the Sachsenmilch dairy company of Dresden became the first East German company to be listed on German stock exchanges; after the share flotation 49 per cent would be traded, the remaining 51 per cent held by a subsidiary jointly owned by a Stuttgart company and Saxon enterprises.

In mid-March 1991 the THA agreed to undertake a 'socially acceptable regional policy' and to form special cabinets with the five East German state governments in order to enhance the integration of structural and regional policies. Restructuring was to be given greater priority (critics argue that this should have been left to the private sector). The Finance Ministry has estimated that the THA would need DM 400 billion up to the year 2000 (less when allowance is made for proceeds from privatization) if it were to give priority to restructuring rather than liquidating weaker enterprises (David Goodhart, *FT*, 5 April 1991, p. 18). The THA would no longer be able to close large plants without agreement with the local authority (David Goodhart, *FT*, 22 March 1991, p. 2). The closing down of enterprises which dominate entire regions (such as those in mining, steel, chemicals and shipbuilding) would be devastating in terms of unemployment. It is thus policy to retain the industrial core of a particular area, the core acting as a foundation for growth (Breuel 1991: 30).

In April 1991 the THA and the trade unions agreed that the former would compensate dismissed employees even if the partially or completely shut down firm was unable to pay out of its own assets (Vincentz 1991: 10). On 17 July 1991 the government, employers and trade unions agreed to set up job-creation enterprises. The THA's role is to provide start-up help, premises, machines and managerial personnel for these enterprises, which are to be involved in urban renewal projects, public works, cleaning up the environment and retraining workers. The sceptics point to problems such as the possible adverse effects on competing firms in the private sector (Deutsche Bank, *Unification Issue*, 1991, no. 59, p. 3). By the end of 1991 there were more than 300 'employment and training companies' (DIW, *Economic Bulletin*, 1992, vol. 29, no. 5, p. 16).

As regards bankruptcies, it is interesting to note that at the time of GEMU the directors of the former combines estimated that one-third of industrial production was up to international standards, one-third had to be scrapped, and the remaining one-third needed restructuring with international help to survive. In September 1990 the then chairman of the THA, Detlev Rohwedder, estimated that at least 1,000 of the 8,000 large enterprises would have to be liquidated. Adrian Bridge (*The Independent*, 25 March 1991, p. 21) reported that 150 enterprises had been closed to date; 333 enterprises either had been or were in the process of being liquidated, involving 87,292 jobs (David Gow, *The Guardian*, 19 April 1991, p. 15) (some 500 businesses were in these two categories, according to Deutsche Bank, *Unification Issue*, no. 44, 2 April 1991, p. 1). The number of enterprises liquidated to date was 525 (David Goodhart, *FT*, 8 August 1991, p. 12); *The Economist* (14 September 1991, p. 22) cites a figure of more than 600. Breuel (1991: 28) reports a figure of 700 by late 1991, albeit mostly small enterprises, while the DIW (*Economic Bulletin*, 1992, vol. 29, no. 4, p. 7) reports 983 by the end of the year. In April 1991 the THA was given permission to sell off separate parts of an enterprise (David Goodhart, *FT*, 9 April 1991, p. 25). The THA is reported as saying that at least 70 per cent of the 7,000 enterprises could be rescued from bankruptcy (*IHT*, 27 September, 1991, p. 13). Some voice criticism of the relatively small number of enterprises closed; they argue that the resources used subsidizing inefficient enterprises would be better employed setting up new ones.

The THA pays interest on the inherited debt and provides credit to keep enterprises operating. The old debts total DM 100 billion and DM 7 billion is paid in interest (Siebert 1991b: 303). The THA has taken over 85 per cent of the old debts of the 2,600 enterprises sold to date and the ecological liabilities have also generally been assumed too (David Goodhart, FT, 8 August 1991, p. 12). Investors are required to take on up to 20 per cent of pollution liabilities (Ian Gaunt, FT, 29 August, 1991, p. 20). The interest on the DM 100 billion was to be paid by the THA until the end of 1991 (Vincentz 1991: 4).

On 27 March 1991 the THA announced that the DM 19 billion government-backed bank loan made to enterprises, due to be repaid by 31 March, was to be postponed indefinitely (*IHT*, 28 March 1991, p. 11). (Note that East German enterprises had to discard the considerable social security role they formerly played, e.g. the provision of child and health care facilities.) The THA had a deficit of DM 21 billion in 1991; a forecast was made of DM 31.5 billion for 1992.

The THA, in conjunction with the Federal Ministry of Finance, has decided to set up the Treuhand-Ostberatungsgesellschaft, an independent private sector consulting company dealing with questions concerning privatization in Eastern Europe (*IHT*, 7 July 1992, p. 16).

FOREIGN TRADE AND CAPITAL

East Germany and the European Community (EC)

The salient features of the GDR's trade with the EC in 1988 were as follows (DIW *Economic Bulletin*, 1990, vol. 27, no. 3, pp. 1–4): the EC (excluding West Germany) accounted for only 5 per cent of East Germany's foreign trade; about 90 per cent of East German exports to the EC were manufactured goods (consumer and producer goods), the rest being mining and agricultural products; EC exports to East Germany were primarily manufactures (especially investment goods). A noticeable feature was the domination of GDR trade by inter-industry trade, while EC economies are characterized by a high degree of intra-industry trade (European Commission 1990: 32). On 13 March 1990 the EC and East Germany initialled a ten-year trade and economic co-operation agreement. The EC had an embargo on new members before 1993, but East Germany was an obvious exception. As early as 17 January Jacques Delors described East Germany as a 'special case', saying that 'There is a place for East Germany in the community should it so wish'. One estimate put a united Germany's GNP at 27.8 per cent of the EC's total GNP (25 per cent for West Germany alone) (David Marsh and David Goodhart, *FT*, 10 December 1990, p. 9). The share of EC population goes up from 19 per cent for West Germany alone to 23 per cent for a united Germany. Theo Sommer (editor of *Die Zeit*), writing in *The Independent* (3 October 1990, p. 17) and in *European Affairs* (February–March 1991, p. 41), reported West Germany alone accounting for 26.7 per cent of EC GDP and a united Germany 31 per cent.

With political unification East Germany became a full member of the EC, with all the costs and benefits that entails. An early estimate by the European Parliament (1990: 147–8) put the net burden on the EC budget of East German entry into the EC at around Ecu 1 billion for a transitional period of a few years (additional expenditure of Ecu 2 billion and additional revenue of Ecu 1 billion). Ecu 1 billion represents only about 2.1 per cent of the 1990 Community budget. A later estimate (21 August 1990) put the net figure at Ecu 500 million, the extra budgetary expenditure of Ecu 2 billion (Ecu 1 billion for regional and social spending; Ecu 880 million to Ecu 900 million for agriculture; Ecu 150 million for other purposes) partially offset by extra revenue of Ecu 1.5 billion. (Note that West Germany is the largest net contributor to EC funds; Ecu 6.2 billion in 1988.) Thus West Germany would shoulder the lion's share of the burden of supporting East Germany during the difficult transition period (only about 20 per cent being borne by the EC as a whole, according to Martin Bangemann, vice-president of the European Commission). The European Commission estimated that German reunification would add half a percentage point to the EC's growth rate in 1991 (David Goodhart, *FT*, 16 March 1991, p. 3). East Germany is protected for a while from the full rigours of competition, e.g. subsidies and cheap credit to industry, agricultural support and the phasing in of environmental standards. On 13 September 1990 the European Parliament gave the European Commission permission to negotiate special provisions with East Germany until the end of 1990. There is to be a phasing in of safety, quality and environmental standards (those relating to air and water by 1996, for example). EC nuclear safety rules, however, applied immediately (the last nuclear reactor, at Greifswald, was closed on 15 December 1990; two new nuclear power plants are to be built). In its March 1992 report the Bundesbank calculated that that in 1991 East Germany received DM 3.5 billion from the EC, but because of Germany's increased overall contribution the EC's net contribution was only DM 1 billion (*IHT*, 19 March 1992, p. 11).

As far as agriculture is concerned, the situation is summed up in European Commission (1990: 80–1): although initially, from 1 July 1990 onwards, East Germany introduced a system of quantitative import controls and restrictions in order to protect its domestic agriculture, these proved to be unworkable and had been given up by 1 August. As regards the maximum guaranteed quantities EC-wide for different products, most were to be reviewed in the near future. Thus, with the sole exception of intervention quantities for beef and processed tomatoes, the maximum guaranteed quantities currently in force were not to be changed for a while. On the other hand, East German production would be discounted when output against these quantities was measured. A significant reduction in milk production had to be achieved by 1 April 1991, however, so from that day on the quota regime for milk would apply in East Germany. Since East Germany has to abide by existing EC quotas set for individual products like milk and sugar, in some cases drastic reductions in output are necessary, e.g. milk production will have to be scaled back by 30 per cent compared to 1989 (Deutsche Bank, *Unification Issue*, 1991, no. 64, p. 2). The degree of affection afforded by the CAP has shielded East German agriculture far more than industry.

East Germany and Comecon

East Germany also faced the problem of Comecon agreements, most of these originally being renewable in 1991. The EC allowed the existing arrangements to continue until the end of 1991 as far as the East German area alone was concerned, renewable for a year. EC normal tariffs or quotas agreed earlier in bilateral deals were temporarily waived, but Comecon goods (especially agriculture products, steel and energy) would have to be confined to East Germany (GATT agreed to this waiver on 13 December 1990). East German industrial exports to the Soviet Union and Eastern Europe were encouraged in order to preserve jobs. The

Soviet Union agreed to purchase surplus East German agricultural products. But East German exports in general fared badly, despite East German enterprises being able to get ten-year credits (repayable after three years) for 100 per cent of their Soviet orders. The exchange rate of DM 2.34 per transferable rouble was fixed on 1 July 1990. Repayment of the Soviet Union's accumulated transferable rouble deficit of some DM 15 billion was deferred for several years, with the funds being regarded as an interest-free loan during this moratorium; DM 9 billion is being provided by the German government to ensure delivery of goods to the Soviet Union (Commerzbank Report, *The Economist*, 20 April 1991, p. 76). In general the German government provided credit guarantees for Comecon contracts which survived the transition to hard currency trading, at least for those enterprises considered survival candidates (David Goodhart, *FT*, 16 January 1991, p. 19). In January 1992 credit guarantees for exports to the ex-Soviet republics were restricted.

Both Hungary and Czechoslovakia have complained about the cancellation of a number of contracts by East German companies, which had earlier been designated to purchase Hungarian and Czech products. For example, Czechoslovakia cited 230 million transferable roubles' worth of cancelled contracts, while Hungary sought DM 500 million in compensation. Substantial fraud has been exposed, involving the export of non-existent or other countries' goods; the transferable roubles earned in 1990 were exchanged for Deutschmarks at a favourable rate. The fraud amounted to DM 1.5 billion (FT, 12 February 1991, p. 4). The German government calculated that the Soviet Union and the East European countries owed 10 billion transferable roubles as a result of Comecon arrangements (DM 2 3.4 billion at the exchange rate used by the government), e.g. Soviet Union 6.4 billion roubles and Poland 800 million roubles (David Marsh, FT, 13 March 1991, p. 4).

Comecon shifted to hard currency trading at current world prices on 1 January 1991. Not only were oil prices thus raised, but East Germany had difficulties selling its relatively poor-quality manufactures. The European Parliament (1990: 113) reported estimates that at world market prices the GDR would have obtained 15–20 per cent less for its machinery and equipment on the Soviet market. The Soviet connection especially was very important in the short run. The East Berlin Institute of Applied Economic Research has estimated that in 1988 260,000 workers were directly employed in industrial exports to the Soviet Union and 220,000 indirectly; the 480,000 total accounted for 15 per cent of total employment in East German industry (DIW *Economic Bulletin*, 1990, vol. 27, no. 6, pp. 14–15). The federal government estimated that in 1989 around 850,000 jobs in the commercial sector were directly dependent on intra-Comecon trade as a whole and a further 500,000–600,000 jobs in ancillary industries and other producing sectors were at least partly dependent (Deutsche Bank, *Focus: Germany*, 10 March 1992, no. 75, p. 2).

In 1991 East German exports to Comecon countries as a whole fell by 60 per cent, with exports to individual countries as follows: the Soviet Union -45 per cent; Bulgaria -91 per cent; Hungary -86 per cent; Romania -85 per cent; Czechoslovakia -81 per cent; Poland -66 per cent (Deutsche Bank, *Focus: Germany*, 10 March 1992, no. 75, p. 2). Total East German exports fell by 7 per cent in 1990 and by 53 per cent in 1991 (p. 2). But owing to factors such as generous export guarantees, the Soviet Union's share of East German exports (excluding intra-German trade) actually increased: 40.3 per cent in 1989, 46.7 per cent in 1990 and 54.7 per cent in 1991 (when the total share of all the former Comecon countries was over two-thirds) (p. 2).

East Germany was owed DM23.4 billion ($12.8 billion) by its former Comecon partners, the Soviet Union alone DM15 billion (*IHT*, 11 July 1991, p. 13).

Foreign capital

As regards direct foreign investment, East Germany has an enormous advantage over its Eastern European neighbours of now having a sound, fully convertible currency; thus profit repatriation is no problem. Investment inducements included a 12 per cent investment grant; originally this was to be applicable from 1 July 1990 to 30 June 1991, when the rate was to be reduced to 8 per cent for another year. On 12 February 1991, however, the 12 per cent rate was given a one year extension. The then Foreign Minister Hans-Dietrich Genscher said that an investor putting DM 100 million into East Germany would receive up to DM 57.3 million in such forms as grants, subsidies, tax write-offs and special depreciation rates (*IHT*, 4 May 1991, p. 11). Nevertheless, some disappointment has been expressed at the results, especially at first. The following problems have emerged.

1. The overall capital inflow was disappointing at first. In the first six months of 1990, 2,800 joint ventures were signed or approved, with a combined start-up capital of DM 1 billion; 95 per cent were with West German companies (*IHT*, 9 August 1990, p. 11 and *FT*, 9 August 1990, p. 6). One early estimate put the private investment flow into East Germany in 1990 at DM 5 billion (David Marsh, *FT*, 13 November 1990, p. 22). Blaine Harden (*IHT*, 24 January 1991, p. 2) put West German investment in East Germany in 1990 at $35 billion. Only 10 per cent of new businesses in East Germany stem from 'foreign' companies (David Goodhart and Andrew Fisher, *FT*, 7 February 1991, p. 4). Only 5 per cent of all investment in East Germany has come from outside Germany as a whole (Hans-Dietrich Genscher, *The Times*, 4 May 1991, p. 23). A more recent figure puts this at 12.5 per cent (*IHT*, 22 February 1992, p. 9). The section on privatization has already provided some up-to-date statistics.

2. The European Commission is unhappy at the monopolistic implications of some of the mergers (in July 1990 East Germany promised to abide by EC competition rules, even though political unification had not then been achieved). Leon Brittan, the European competition commissioner) wrote to the East German government on 28 June 1990 expressing concern. The following proposals or deals have been especially highlighted: banking (Deutsche Bank and Deutsche Kreditbank; gas (Ruhrgas and Verbundnetzgas; the remaining 55 per cent stake was sold off to other German and foreign companies in September 1991); electricity (on 22 August 1990 West Germany's 3 power utilities were allowed to take control of 60 per cent of East Germany's electricity distribution network): airlines (Lufthansa and Interflug); and insurance (Allianz and Staatliche Versicherung). There is a potential dilemma in weighing competition against survival, and the Lufthansa–Interflug saga illustrates this. An initial Lufthansa 26 per cent stake bid for Interflug was withdrawn and replaced by an outright takeover offer. Other airlines, such as British Airways, expressed interest too. The Gulf crisis and recession in most of the Western countries, however, had a crippling effect on air travel and on 8 February 1991 it was announced that a timetable for the closure of Interflug was to be worked out because of unsustainable losses. Two days later Lufthansa announced that it was no longer interested in taking over the former East German airline. Interflug was closed down by the end of April 1991. The German cartel office is also concerned about oil refining and distribution.

It is also worth noting that the EC has queried West German subsidies paid to West German firms investing in East German sectors such as motor vehicles.

3. The restitution claims of former owners have been a major obstacle to inward investment. Although this is now less of a problem, the changing nature of the regulations in itself creates uncertainty.

4. Corporate debt: policy is to consider relief on a case-by-case basis (decree of 29 August 1991, p. 2).

5. Environmental clean-up costs. The

Bitterfeld region, for example, is extraordinarily polluted by lignite and chemicals.

6. A poor infrastructure.

ECONOMIC PROSPECTS

The long-run prospects for East Germany within a united Germany are generally considered to be excellent, although some see the danger of a permanently relatively disadvantaged and depressed region (like Italy's Mezzogiorno). For example, Michael Burda (in *European Economy: the Path of Reform in Central and Eastern Europe*, 1991, p. 126) argues that under current circumstances such a syndrome seems increasingly likely, since migrants with the best alternative options leave and take their human capital with them. As we have seen, however, the short and medium term is and will be very difficult ones for East Germany. The official government forecast was that it would take five years for East Germany to attain economic and social parity with West Germany (David Goodhart, *FT*, 18 March 1991, p. 6). During a visit to East Germany on 7 April 1991 Chancellor Kohl said 'I am convinced that in four to five years East Germany will be transformed into a flourishing landscape.' On 10 April he said that 'For me it is quite clear we shall solve the economic problems and we shall need five years . . . but I fear that after forty-five years' experience it will take longer than three, four, five years before we are able to celebrate full unification'. But the DIW predicted that it would take twenty years for East German living standards to match those in West Germany (reported in the *IHT*, 11 February 1992, p. 21), while Quentin Peel (*FT*, 14 February 1992, p. 2) refers to the Prognos (Basle) Institute's estimate that East German *per capita* GNP will be 87 per cent of West Germany's by the year 2010. Economics Minister Möllemann, in a 15 September 1992 speech, confessed that 'We face the total collapse of the social and economic system in eastern Germany. It is impossible to overcome this in two or even five years. We need a whole decade.' Indeed, Chancellor Kohl himself, in an anniversary speech on 3 October 1992 admitted that 'the economic cure of the new federal states will last longer and cost more than we thought . . . Two years of German unity have been a learning process for all of us, including me.'

East Germany and West Germany are natural partners, sharing a common language, history, culture and industrial tradition. The industrial structures are similar, e.g. both are strong in engineering. West German capital, technology and know-how can be combined with relatively cheap (at least initially, although the speed at which the East German–West German wage differential is closing is causing alarm) and skilled labour and management. East Germany provides a significant market (for consumer durables, for instance), a trained labour force, good trade connections with Eastern Europe and a services network. However, East Germany has limited natural resources (lignite and potash are especially important), its infrastructure (e.g. telephone system) is relatively poor (though rapidly improving), and there are severe pollution problems (especially due to its heavy reliance on lignite as a primary energy source: 71 per cent in 1984).

The picture varies across the board, of course. The more favourable prospects are to be found in sectors such as textile machinery, printing presses, petrochemicals, machine tools, measuring and control equipment, optical instruments (although the market for precision and optical machinery has been depressed), computers and software, glass, services (including retail trade) and tourism. The construction industry was initially depressed because local authorities were starved of funds but recovery began in early 1991 (construction output only fell by 5 per cent in 1990: Deutsche Bank, *Unification Issue*, no. 51, 24 June 1991, p. 2). Services and construction together led the recovery. A less rosy outlook characterizes such sectors as lignite and lignite-based chemicals, mining equipment, plastics, consumer electronics, shipbuilding, heavy engineering and transport equipment (although railway wagons are better placed), textiles and clothing, foot-wear, confectionery, coffee, consumer electronics and agriculture (there were signs of recovery in food production in early 1991 as consumer demand switched back to local products to some extent). But an injection of foreign capital, technology and know-how can often work wonders, as can be seen in the motor car industry (e.g. the Trabant has been phased out and replaced by VW models).

The German government was forced to take a more interventionist attitude towards the East German economy as the situation deteriorated. The 1948 experience proved to be not so appropriate as hoped, since it did not deal with the problems of the transition from command to market economy. The old *Ordnungspolitik* was geared to creating the right environment for the private sector to flourish, such as the provision of a basic infrastructure, a sound currency and a competitive environment (Richard Smith, *IHT*, 4 March 1991, p. 9). But merely setting up a framework for the operation of market forces is insufficient. Kenneth Parris goes as far as to recommend an updated version of Roosevelt's New Deal, with large retraining programmes and infrastructural job creation schemes (*IHT*, 12 April 1991, p. 4). On 12 April 1991 the government decided to set up two joint committees with the opposition Social Democrats (plus representatives from Neues Forum), one dealing with property rights and administration and the other with employment and retraining.

NOTES

1. In his 17 November 1989 speech, Modrow talked of 'an economic reform which must raise the autonomy of the economic units, in order to increase their performance significantly, to reduce central direction and planning to a required reasonable level.'
2. Wage subsidies would impede the restructuring of labour markets by preserving employment in non-viable enterprises and by reducing incentives to develop human capital or launch new businesses (IMF, Annual Report, 1992, p. 19).
3. There are 'supervisory boards' for enterprises under the control of THA (Wendy Carlin and Colin Mayer, 'Restructuring enterprises in Eastern Europe', *Economic Policy*, 1992, no.15, pp. 327–8). They comprise representatives of other companies (from West and East Germany), banks, local authorities and employees. Their functions include the monitoring of management, the development of restructuring plans and the promotion of privatization. The board chairman is almost always a West German. While oversight of day-to-day management is devolved to supervisory boards, the THA keeps control of management through access to THA-guaranteed liquidity and investment credits.

22

HUNGARY

POLITICAL BACKGROUND

In the general election there were two rounds, 25 March and 8 April 1990. The result is shown in Table 22.1. The economic aspects of the main party programmes were as follows (there being general support for a market economy):

Hungarian Democratic Forum (leader Jozsef Antall). Its origins go back to September 1987, although initially it was only a 'non-political movement'. The HDF advocated a social market economy and gradual agrarian reform. There was a cautious attitude to privatization, which

Table 22.1 The Hungarian general election of March–April 1990

Party	Seats	% vote
Hungarian Democratic Forum	164	42.49
Alliance of Free Democrats	92	23.83
Independent Smallholders' Party	44	11.40
Hungarian Socialist Party	33	8.55
Federation of Young Democrats	21	5.44
Christian Democratic People's Party	21	5.44
Independents	6	1.55
Joint candidates (backed by several parties)	4	1.04
Agrarian Alliance	1	0.26
Total	386	100.0

needed 'adequate supervision' by government. Demonopolization should come first in the case of large enterprises and not all sectors should be privatized. There should be a sale of shares at a discount to local communities, hospitals, universities, social foundations and state enterprise employees. Care had to be taken as regards foreign investment because of a possible popular backlash. The IMF programme was supported, but attempts should be made to keep the 'inevitable' unemployment to a minimum by means of retraining schemes. A gradual rather than 'shock' approach was preferred. Foreign debt should be repaid, although improved terms should be negotiated, but there should be no debt-for-equity swaps.

Alliance of Free Democrats (leader Janos Kis until his replacement as party chairman by Peter Tolgyessy in autumn 1991). The origins of the party lie in the umbrella organization Network of Free Initiatives, formed in early 1988. Support for the market and privatization and for the IMF austerity programme. The emphasis should be on voluntary associations rather than the state in the solution of social problems. Support was expressed for debt-for-equity swaps.

Independent Smallholders Party (leader Istvan Prepeliczay). The manifesto stressed the primacy of private property. The distinctive feature was the proposal, as far as possible, to restore land to those who owned it in 1947. Compensation should be made where this was not possible. Co-operatives were still likely to be dominant in reality, but they should be voluntary and profit-seeking.

Hungarian Socialist Party. The party advocated a mixed market economy with sound protection of the less fortunate members of society.

Federation of Young Democrats. The party's roots can be traced to early 1988. Its youthful leadership (all in their twenties; there was a party membership age limit of thirty-five) advocated a rapid move towards a competitive market economy based on private ownership.

Christian Democratic People's Party. Individual freedom was stressed, but there should be care for the poor. Voluntary co-operatives and small private farms were espoused.

Arpad Goncz of the Alliance of Free Democrats became interim president on 2 May 1990 and president on 3 August 1990 (elected by the National Assembly after the failure of the 29 July referendum to produce anywhere near the more than 50 per cent turn-out required to decide whether to elect the president by popular vote). In return, the Free Democrats agreed to constitutional changes which limited the required two-thirds parliamentary majority to only twenty pieces of legislation; for the others a simple majority would suffice.

The Hungarian Democratic Forum, whose leader, Jozsef Antall, became prime minister, formed a coalition government with the Independent Smallholders' Party and the Christian Democratic People's Party. Antall outlined government policy on 22 May 1990. He talked about full membership of the EC 'within the coming decade' (he specified 1995 on 17 July, with associate status by 1992) and the need for a 'social market economy', the poorer sections of society being protected by a comprehensive welfare system. The government would 'launch an attack on the hopelessly conducted' parts of the economy, with rapid action taken against the thirty to forty habitually loss-making enterprises. Wholesale privatization would begin in the retail and service sectors, and by the end of

1993 the share of foreign capital in the economy 'may multiply'. Antall ruled out any wholesale return of property to former owners. There would be two years of hardship before an economic upturn; during that period there would be a 'significant rise' in unemployment, double-digit inflation and declining output and living standards. There would be a 100 day package to curb inflation. The exchange rate would be made partially convertible at first and fully later. (On 16 June 1990 the finance minister Ferenc Rabar proposed a convertibility target for the forint of some time between the end of 1991 and the middle of 1992.) As far as agriculture was concerned, land redistribution would take account of 1947 ownership. Anyone could state a claim, but priority was to go to those who now farmed the land. State farms would remain, while family farms and voluntary co-operatives were to be encouraged.

The government's actions were for some time generally rather indecisive and in the 14 October 1990 local elections government parties did poorly. In April 1991 the HDF agreed to the proposal of the Federation of Young Democrats for an all-party parliamentary round table on issues of national importance. One factor helping the economic reform programme to go ahead was the fact that the Hungarian people were relatively experienced in the field of market economics.

On 3 March 1992 the Constitutional Court rejected the November 1991 bill to put on trial those accused of 'crimes committed in the name of communism' (such as high treason, premeditated murder and causing fatal injury). The court refused to lift the statute of limitations, in effect saying that people could not be convicted for activities carried out under a different legal system.

On the international front, the 11 March 1990 agreement with the Soviet Union set a 30 June deadline for the withdrawal of Soviet troops. They actually withdrew about two weeks before the deadline.

THE GOVERNMENT'S ECONOMIC PROGRAMME

The austerity programme

This was IMF-inspired. The budget deficit in 1989 was 54.2 billion forints (2.84 per cent of GDP). On 22 November 1989 parliament rejected the three year programme, but the budget was approved on 21 December. The main aim was to reduce inflation to 15 per cent in 1990. There was to be a reduction in the projected budget deficit from 21 billion forints to 10 billion forints (0.5 per cent of GDP in 1990), with annual subsidies being reduced from 210 billion forints to 170 billion forints. Prices and interest rates were raised (e.g. in early February 1990 food prices were increased on average by 25 per cent and public transport fares by 30 per cent).

On 29 June 1990 the government unveiled an emergency package of measures to satisfy the IMF. The aim was to achieve a net saving of 25 billion forints in order to meet the 10 billion forint target for the budget deficit. Two-thirds of the savings were to be met by reducing spending (such as reducing subsidies on agricultural exports) and the remaining third by price increases. On 9 July there were price increases of 20 per cent on petrol and 25 per cent on cigarettes and alcohol, followed on 1 August by 45 per cent on coal, 10 per cent on heating gas and 44 per cent on electricity in the big cities. Petrol prices rose a further 65 per cent on 26 October, which led to protests by taxi and lorry drivers. As a result the government promised to halve the increase, consult more regularly with trade unions and employers via the 'interest co-ordination council', and introduce a free market in oil. The actual 1990 budget deficit turned out to be 1.4 per cent of GDP (*Economic Bulletin for Europe*, 1991, vol. 43, p. 31). At the start of 1991 electricity prices were raised by 50 per cent and the price of heating fuel by 80 per cent; in April coal prices were to go up 130 per cent and central heating by 150 per cent.

At the beginning of November 1990 Gyorgy Matolcsy (chief economic adviser to the prime minister) caused controversy by outlining a radical six month programme. The proposals included more severe austerity measures (e.g. heavy reductions in subsidies on items like food, household energy, transport and mortgages), further price, wage and import liberalization (90 per cent of prices are now deregulated: Clifford Stevens, *IHT*, 4 March 1991, p. 12), income tax reform (a 10 per cent reduction in the personal income tax rate coupled with abolition of the tax allowance), and speedier privatization. On 28 November Finance Minister Ferenc Rabar announced his intention to resign on account of the programme; he was subsequently replaced by Mihaly Kupa. The 1991 budget was eventually approved on 31 December 1990: the budget deficit was targeted at 78 billion forints (2.3 per cent of GDP) and the current account deficit at $1.2 billion. A stand-by IMF loan of $1.6 billion was agreed 21 February 1991. The actual 1991 budget deficit was 4.7 per cent of GDP (United Nations Economic Commission for Europe 1992: 94).

The IMF agreement of 27 November 1991 contained the following: the budget deficit for 1992 would be 70 billion forints (1.9 per cent of GDP). Consumer inflation was projected to fall from 30 per cent to 15 per cent by December 1992. IMF credits would be $435 million in 1992 ($970 million in 1991). But a considerable budget deficit overshoot seemed likely.

Economic performance

Tables 22.2 and 22.3 give the picture as regards unemployment, output, inflation and foreign debt. Unemployment increased rapidly after mid-1989, the number of unemployed more than tripling by the end of 1990 (Hars *et al.* 1991: 166). On average real wages declined by about 6 per cent in 1990 (Cukor and Kovari 1991: 179). Output fell in both 1990 and 1991, and inflation remained a problem. Modest but positive growth was the government's hope for 1992, but a further decline in output seemed increasingly likely as the year went on.

Marketization

Hungary's long experience with the NEM has helped the transition to a market-based economy.

Table 22.2 Hungary: unemployment

		No. unemployed	Unemployment rate (%)
1990	January	23,426	
	June	41,800	0.8
	December	79,500	1.7
1991	January	103,000	2.0
	February	128,386	
	March	144,800	3.0
	April	164,000	3.5
	May	165,022	
	June	185,600	3.9
	July	218,000	4.6
	August	251,000	5.2
	September	294,100	6.1
	October	317,700	
	November	351,300	7.3
	December	406,100	8.3
1992	January*	440,000	
	February		
	March		
	April		9.3
	May	522,000	10.0
	June		
	July		
	August		
	September		11.4
	October		11.6
	November		
	December		

Sources: OECD Employment Outlook, July 1991, p. 21; Economic Bulletin for Europe, 1991, vol. 43, p. 28; Deutsche Bank, Focus: Eastern Europe, 1 July 1992, no. 50, p. 4; 10 August 1992, no. 53, p. 8; 30 September 1992, no. 58, p. 11; United Nations Economic Commission for Europe (1992: 68); Kornai (1992b: 9); Commission of the European Communities, Employment Observatory, 1992, no. 2, p. 5, no. 3, p. 9.
* A new basis of calculation was introduced in January 1992.

Table 22.3 Hungary: foreign debt and rates of growth of GDP, industrial output, agricultural output and prices (%)

GDP	
1990	1991
−4.0	−10.0

Industrial output	
1990	1991
−8.3	−13.5

Agricultural output	
1990	1991
−3.8	−3.0

Inflation	
1990	1991
28.9	35.0

Net foreign debt ($ billion)	
End 1990	End 1991
15.94	14.55

Sources: Deutsche Bank, Focus: Eastern Europe, 1991, no. 32, pp. 1–2; 1992, no. 39, p. 2; 9 April 1992, no. 43, p. 2; 10 August 1992, no. 53, p. 8; OECD Economic Outlook, December 1991, p. 55; June 1992, pp. 41–2; OECD Employment Outlook, July 1991, p. 21; FT Survey, 30 October 1991, p. III; European Economy: the Path of Reform in Central and Eastern Europe Commission of the European Communities, Brussels, 1991, p. 278; The Economist Survey, 21 September 1991, p. 5; Kaser and Allsopp (1992: 2); DIW, Economic Bulletin, 1992, vol;. 29, no. 4, p. 5; Lorine (1992: 1,002, see Postscript).

But problems remain, such as the highly monopolistic structure of industry. In this regard the 1990 Deregulation Act allows enterprise sub-units wishing to become independent to appeal to the Ministry of Industry if enterprise councils refuse permission. The Office of Economic Competition administers the Act on the Prohibition of Unfair Market Practices, passed 20 September 1990 (Michael Reynolds, FT, 26 September, 1991, p. 12). Agreements restricting competition are prohibited whether they are concluded in Hungary or not. Exemptions are possible but increasingly difficult to obtain when the joint market share of the parties exceeds 30 per cent. Activities resulting in abuse of 'economic superiority' (defined as 30 per cent market share) are banned. Notification is needed in the case of mergers where the joint market share of the merging parties exceeds 30 per cent or joint turnover is more than 10 billion forints. Fines can be imposed.

A new unemployment benefit scheme came into effect in March 1991 (Micklewright 1992: 7), modifying the one discussed in Chapter 13. For those previously unemployed eligibility requires a year's insured employment over the previous four years. The period of benefit ranges from six months to two years, depending on the period of insured employment over the previous four years. For the first half of the benefit entitlement period 70 per cent of the previous gross earnings is paid and 50 per cent for the second half. At the beginning of 1992 the period of entitlement was reduced by 25 per cent (Commission of the European Communities, *Employment Observatory*, 1992, no. 2, p. 14).

The new Central Bank Act entered into force on 1 December 1991, giving the National Bank independent status along German lines. Enterprises and commercial banks would be permitted to write off up to 150 billion forints of bad debt (Anthony Robinson, *FT Survey*, 30 October 1991, p. i). The regulations limited any single non-bank shareholder in a bank to 25 per cent.

Hare and Revesz (1992: 254) argue that Hungary's more gradualist, step-by-step approach has suited it better than a 'big bang', which would have disrupted established market relationships and expectations. Ironically, Hungary may be close to its maximum realistic speed of transition.

Privatization

The draft conversion (transformation) law (as discussed by the National Assembly on 30 May 1989) allowed enterprise councils or the general assemblies of employees to decide for themselves whether to convert to share ownership. The privatization programme was changed in the light of the early abuses of so-called 'spon-taneous privatization', with managers benefiting in the form of shares or well paid positions in the new private firms as the assets were sold off cheap; assets were also leased cheap to managers. It was, in any case, difficult to value assets, and the December 1989 deal involving the Swedish–Dutch hotel group Quintus taking a 51.6 per cent stake in Hungar Hotels was actually stopped because of the low price paid. Even later on, the June 1990 sale of 40 per cent of the share capital of the travel agency Ibusz was criticized by a parliamentary committee for, among other things, being underpriced (the offer was twenty-three times oversubscribed in total and even more so in the case of the foreign tranche, but the share price later fell heavily).

A new scheme was introduced on 1 April 1990, whereby all but very small privatizations had to have the approval of the State Property Agency (SPA, which was under parliamentary control; in July the agency came under the direct control of the government and Istvan Tompe was replaced as director by Lajos Csepi). The only occasion when the SPA had no right to intervene was when the enterprise chose open bidding (Mizsei 1992: 293). Mizsei argues that controlled spontaneous privatization remained the main form of private enterprise expansion, besides the establishment of new businesses (p. 293). Schwartz (1991: 1733) outlines later amendments: until mid-1990 the SPA only had veto power over privatization proposals, but subsequently had the authority to initiate or conduct programmes; in September 1990 a two-thirds majority of the enterprise council was needed for privatization; in early 1991 investors were allowed to ask the SPA direct to privatize an enterprise, thus bypassing any unco-operative management committee. The three principal forms of privatization were to be the public offering of shares, competitive bidding, and employee share ownership (eventually this was limited to 10 per cent of the shares of the particular enterprise, sold at a discount). The avoidance of a large 'giv e-away' of shares is due to the need for budgetary revenue and to improve management. It is possible that 10–15 per cent of shares may be assigned to pension funds and insurance companies to help develop the private sector (Hare 1991: 13). Tenders were to be put out for advisers on privatization.

The Compensation Law was passed in April 1991 (Marrese 1991: 170). Since the law only applies to property nationalized after 8 June 1949, it deals primarily with the land and assets of former peasants and owners of small businesses; most larger concerns were nationalized prior to that date. Only partial compensation is available and will not necessarily involve restitution of the original property. Each claimant may receive up to 5 million forints in financial compensation in any combination of three forms: vouchers to purchase small businesses, flats, land or company shares; annuities that provide an annual flow of income for life; and land on condition that it is cultivated by the claimant for at least five years. Land compensation may not exceed 1 million forints. The constitutional court blocked the compensation bill on 29 May on the grounds that it discriminated in favour of peasants, but the bill was finally approved in early August. Towards the end of April 1992 options were broadened to include, for example, swapping the interest-bearing coupons for shares in a real estate mutual fund to be set up to manage commercial office space owned by the SPA (*IHT*, 30 April 1992, p. 13).

The pace of privatization has been the subject of much debate. On 16 May 1990 Prime Minister Jozsef Antall talked about reducing the state sector's share of output from 90 per cent to 25–30 per cent 'within a few years' (five years had been mentioned earlier: Ian Traynor, *The Guardian*, 10 April 1990, p. 8); pinned down the following month, he thought fifteen large companies could be privatized in 1990 (reported by Wolfgang Münchau, *The Times*, 25 June 1990, p. 27) and up to 150 over the next eighteen months (*The Economist*, 15 September 1990, p. 63). Peter Bod (the Trade and Industry Minister), on

26 June 1990, said that 'two-thirds of the economy will be privatized in the next four years', although privatization of enterprises employing fifteen or fewer people (such as shops, restaurants and petrol stations) could go ahead quickly (reported by John Lloyd, *FT*, 27 June 1990, p. 3); when small enterprises are sold their employees are given priority (Colin Jones, *The Banker*, September 1990, p. 18). By the end of 1991 only 10 per cent of shops and restaurants were in private ownership (*The Economist*, 4 April 1992, p. 87). Foreign investors are not allowed in small retail trade. Lajos Csepi has said that the government wanted to reduce state ownership from 80–90 per cent of the economy to 40–50 per cent within three years (*IHT*, 17 September 1990, p. 11). Giles Merritt (*IHT*, 26 November 1991, p. 4) argues that the key to creating an 'entrepreneurial revolution' is a substantial increase in 'micro-lending', i.e. small loans of $10,000 or less; banks tend to avoid these risky credits.

On 15 September 1990 the State Property Agency announced a list of the first twenty enterprises to be fully privatized, including Ibusz (travel), Hungarhotels, the Centrum department store chain, and Richter Gideon (drugs). There was some delay and the first sale was finally set for June 1991 (Pannoplast, a plastics company). Nicholas Denton (FT, 29 October 1991, p. 26, and *FT Survey*, 30 October 1991, p. vii), however, reported difficulties with the programme: not one of the twenty companies was then out of state ownership; the planned autumn 1991 privatization of the Danubius hotel chain was postponed for six months (subsequently postponed yet again), while it was unlikely that the twenty-company programme would go to the stock market in the foreseeable future; problems with the Danubius privatization included tax relief and land claims. Denton later reported that only two significant transactions had been concluded (*FT*, 6 May 1992, p. 3).

Great hope is now attached to 'self-privatization' in which companies choose from a list of consultants (paid 5 per cent of proceeds) approved by the State Property Agency and are then expected to find private investors; 'self-privatization' began in October 1991 with 348 small and medium-sized enterprises. There is a promise to sell an enterprise within 100 days of anyone making an offer, whether Hungarian or foreign; an offer would automatically induce an audit and an open auction. In January 1992 the State Property Agency proposed making privatization more attractive by using revenue raised to feed three funds; these would aid restructuring and unemployment and provide guarantees against hidden liabilities such as environmental damage (Nicholas Denton, *FT*, 14 January 1992, p. 2). On 5 May 1992 the 'self-privatization' or 'simplified privatization' programme was extended to 278 medium-size enterprises (Nicholas Denton, *FT*, 6 May 1992, p. 3). Liquidation is an increasingly significant method of privatization (Denton, *FT Survey*, 3 July 1992, p. iv). Thus far around 10 per cent of the equity of all nationally owned companies has been placed in private hands, mostly foreigners; in 1991 80 per cent of all privatization proceeds came from foreign investors (Deutsche Bank, *Focus: Eastern Europe*, 21 July 1992, no. 51, pp. 3–4).

At the end of September 1990 a three year privatization programme was announced; this saw around half the state sector being privatized over that period, including all small businesses (Hare 1992: 161); another target set earlier was 70 per cent of industry within five years (p.161). At the end of the three year privatization period, private ownership is expected to account for 30–35 per cent of all business capital, and the share of the state to fall below half (Jaroslav Fingerland, *Czechoslovak Economic Digest*, 1991, no. 2, p. 16). The private sector should account for 30–35 per cent of GDP within three years (Nicholas Denton, *FT*, 28 September 1990, p. 6). By 1993 it is hoped to privatize 500–600 firms; by 1996 50–60 per cent of state-owned assets are supposed to be privatized (*The Economist*, 11 May 1991, p. 84).

There has been debate about how much state involvement there should be in sectors such as energy, utilities and key manufacturing industries like vehicles, engineering and pharmaceuticals. The state takes a dominant role in sectors such as aviation, railways, telecommunications, energy and steel (Giles Merritt, *IHT*, 26 November 1991, p. 4). The state seems likely to retain a majority stake in insurance and mining. For industries deemed to be of central strategic importance (such as the electricity supply industry, oil production, trading and refining, and natural gas production, import and transmission, though not regional gas distribution or coal mining) a minimum 51 per cent share would be preserved for central government ownership (Stephen Perkins, *OECD Observer*, April–May 1992, no. 175, p. 28). In November 1991 the first coal mine in the whole of Eastern Europe was privatized (pp. 24, 27). In a small number of cases, such as vehicle manufacturing and the national airline, Malev, a minimum 51 per cent share would be retained for Hungarian nationals (p. 28).

Nicholas Denton (*FT*, 29 May 1992, p. 2) reports a shift towards domestic over foreign investors: the former would be preferred in the case of similar bids (previously price was all-important); domestic investors unable to afford to buy a state enterprise outright would be helped by concessional leasing, payment by instalment or option arrangements; and institutions such as universities would be given state assets.

Kornai (1992b: 11) noted, in a lecture delivered in early January 1992, the impossibility for the time being of accurately measuring the rapid growth of the private sector. Most estimates of its contribution were in the range 25–35 per cent of GDP (adjusted to take account of officially unrecorded activities).

FOREIGN TRADE, AID AND CAPITAL

Foreign trade

About 90 per cent of imports are now licence-free, compared with 70 per cent in 1990; the figure may rise to 92 per cent during 1991 (Nicholas Denton, *FT*, 10 April 1991, p. 4). The average tariff rate was reduced from 16 per cent to 13 per cent in February 1991 (William Dullforce, *FT*, 19 April 1991, p. 6), but some tariffs were later raised, e.g. to 25 per cent for colour TV sets (Nicholas Denton, *FT*, 11 October 1991, p. 3). Export subsidies have been maintained for agricultural products. There were substantial devaluations of the forint in December 1989 (11 per cent), in January 1991 (15 per cent) and in November 1991 (5.8 per cent). The November devaluation was to be the last abrupt change, 'step-by-step' changes to be the rule henceforth. Since 1 January 1991 Hungarian enterprises have been able to pay for imports with forints provided suppliers will accept them; the suppliers themselves are able to exchange the forints for hard currency, invest them or put them into forint accounts in Hungary. The aim was to make the forint fully convertible in 1993–94. The forint had become 'internally' convertible for current account transactions in the late socialist era (see chapter 13 and the glossary); Hungarian households have only limited access to foreign currencies at the official exchange rate (*OECD Observer*, 1992, no. 178, p. 22).

Hungary has made a relatively successful switch to trade with the West. The share of exports going to former Comecon partners fell from 41 per cent in 1989 to 32 per cent in 1990 (*The Economist*, 7 September 1991, p. 137). The respective figures for total trade with Comecon were 40 per cent and 29 per cent (Clifford Stevens, *IHT*, 4 March 1991, p. 12). In 1991 the former Comecon countries accounted for only 19 per cent of Hungary's exports; hard currency export earnings amounted to $10.2 billion, compared with $6.3 billion in 1990 (Nicholas Denton and Anthony Robinson, *FT*, 20 May 1992, p. 6). Currently a good 70 per cent of exports goes to OECD countries (Deutsche Bank, *Focus Eastern Europe*, 4 December 1991, no. 32, p. 1). Hungary's convertible currency current account in $ billion was as follows (*OECD Economic Outlook*, June 1992, p. 43): 1988 –0.8; 1989 –1.4; 1990 0.1; and 1991 0.5 (estimated; 0.267 was the figure generally given later on).

On 18 January 1990 Hungary suspended old licences for exports denominated in transferable roubles. The Ministry of Foreign Trade was to review all export licences and contracts for trade in transferable roubles on a case-by-case basis, the aim being to switch more to Western trade and thus reduce its rouble trade surplus. In 1989 the surplus was 762 million transferable roubles with the Soviet Union alone; at the end of March 1990 an agreement was reached to convert this to $720 million (*EEN*, 1990, vol. 4, no. 9, p. 2).

Agricultural export subsidies remain.

Foreign aid

On 5 December 1990 the G24 countries agreed in principle to provide $700 million in the form of a stabilization fund in order to support the forint's move towards convertibility.

Hungary's debt–service ratio was 59.2 per cent in 1990, but fell to 41.3 per cent (Lorine 1992: 1001).[1] Hungary has continued to service its foreign debt and has not had any of it written off.

Foreign capital

Since the beginning of 1991 even a majority foreign stake in a joint venture has not needed licensing approval (Mizsei 1992: 288). By the end of March 1991 some 7,000 joint ventures had been registered (*IHT*, 5 August 1991, p. 9). Nearly a quarter of exports is now accounted for by joint ventures (*The Economist*, 16 February 1991, p. 82). On 7 June 1991 a new banking law was approved: government approval is only needed if the foreign share exceeds 10 per cent, but a 25 per cent limit applies.

In 1989 and 1990 $2 billion of foreign capital flowed into Hungary, equal to two-thirds of all foreign investment in Eastern Europe and the Soviet Union combined (Deutsche Bank, *Focus: Eastern Europe*, 1991, no. 32, p. 2). Between the end of 1989 and late 1991 around $2.5 billion in foreign investment was attracted, a sum exceeding the combined total for the Eastern European countries excluding East Germany (Blaine Harden, *IHT*, 17 December 1991, p. 2). In 1991 an estimated Ecu 3 billion in investment was expected to flow into Eastern Europe and the Soviet Union, half to Hungary (Jacques Attali, *IHT*, 20 December 1991, p. 12). In 1991 direct foreign investment amounted to $1.46 billion (Deutsche Bank, *Focus: Eastern Europe*, 26 February 1992, no. 39, p. 2). Nicholas Denton (*FT*, 21 April 1992, p. 33) provided the following information: in 1991 over $1.7 billion of foreign capital flowed into Hungary (over 5 per cent of GDP); the cumulative amount since 1988 was more than $3 billion, about 60 per cent of the total for all of Eastern Europe. By the end of April 1992 the total had risen to $3.5 billion (Nicholas Denton and Anthony Robinson, *FT*, 20 May 1992, p. 6).

AGRICULTURE

In January 1990 the government initiated an almost full liberalization of agricultural prices (Marrese 1991: 166). Farm subsidies were reduced from 100 billion forints in 1988 to 40 billion forints in 1991, with a ceiling of 29 billion forints on export subsidies (Anthony Robinson, *FT Survey*, 30 October 1991, p. vi). In 1991 Hungary cut its agricultural export subsidies by 50 per cent, having already reduced them sharply the previous year (*The Economist Survey of the European Community*, 11 July 1992, p. 25). Support for agriculture also includes intervention buying – in the case of grain, for example – and tariffs (Ash 1992: 15).

Laszlo Sarossy (State Secretary for Agriculture) outlined government policy in autumn 1990 (Judy Dempsey, *FT Survey*, 17 September 1990, p. viii). The co-operatives would not be demolished overnight. Large state farms would be reduced in number, but some would be retained for research purposes. Private ownership would be based on the following principles: former, living owners of agricultural land were entitled to up to 116 ha (where possible land they had farmed prior to 1947); descendants of deceased landowners were to be allowed to share a maximum of 100 ha, on condition that the land was farmed; co-operative farmers were eligible for 1.5 ha per person, with easy credit available; co-operatives were allowed to keep the remaining land; former forest owners would be compensated with agricultural land worth twice as much; foreigners were not allowed to buy agricultural or forest land.

On 2 October 1990, however, the constitutional court rejected a proposal to return land to former owners; this was because the bill gave preference to land over other nationalized assets (Mizsei 1992: 295). There was a proposal to pay compensation for land (not animals or equipment) in the form of bonds exchangeable for land up to a maximum of 50 ha. It is proposed that churches should be able reclaim buildings owned before 1947, but not landed estates.

In April 1991 parliament passed the Compensation Law (Marrese 1991: 170–4), the details of which have already been discussed. As of the spring of 1991 the transformation of agricultural co-operatives had been very slow (at that time they controlled 70 per cent of agricultural land and produced 73.2 per cent of agricultural output; of the land used by co-operatives 60 per cent is owned by the co-operatives, 35 per cent by members and 5 per cent by the state, but ownership rights are complicated by the previous trading of land for rationalization purposes). The government has decided that the process should not force all co-operatives to be dismantled. It may not be possible to provide the exact parcel of land formerly or at present owned in restitution. Former owners who decide to be compensated in the form of land must continue to cultivate that land for at least five years. State farms that specialize in research, product development and training agricultural specialists will continue in their present form. Marrese argues that the slow transformation of agriculture is due to factors such as the confusion over property rights, the general unprofitability of production and claims for environmental damage. By the end of 1991 the control of land was as follows (Ash 1992: 21): co-operatives 65 per cent; state farms 20 per cent; and private farms 15 per cent. The private sector's share was supposed to increase to 50 per cent by the end of 1992 and to 80 per cent within three years.

Some further information is provided by Anthony Robinson (*FT Survey*, 30 October 1991, p. vi): in theory the Compensation Law could return up to 10 per cent of the land to former owners; the claims can go back to May 1939; small landholders are entitled to full compensation up to a limit of 200,000 forints, but those who agree to farm their own land for at least five years are entitled to a grant of 800,000 forints; co-operatives are expected to remain the basis of agriculture.

Ash (1992: 22–9) adds the following points: members wishing to leave are entitled to payment for their share in the co-operatives in the form of land or equipment; anyone who has been a member of a co-operative over the past five years or their heirs can claim a share in co-operative assets. In the case of claims on land currently occupied by state farms or owned by the state a certain percentage is to be put up for auction. The government has decided to retain twelve large state farms, mainly producing corn, and privatize the rest.

NOTES

1. Lorine, H. (1992) 'Foreign debt, debt management policy and implications for Hungary's development', *Soviet Studies*, vol. 44, no. 6.

23

POLAND

POLITICAL BACKGROUND

In the partially free election of 4 June 1989 and the run-off of the 18th, with turn-outs of 62 per cent and 25 per cent respectively, Solidarity won all the allotted opposition seats in the Sejm and ninety-nine out of the 100 senate seats (one going to an independent). Only two of the thirty-five (unopposed) candidates on the government's National List gained the necessary majority of votes in the first round (299 out of the 460 seats in the Sejm were reserved for the communist party and its allies). Wojciech Jaruzelsky was elected president on 19 July 1989 by a margin of only one vote. Mieczyslaw Rakowski replaced Jaruzelsky as General Secretary of the Polish United Workers' Party (PUWP) on 29 July. Czeslaw Kiszczak became prime minister on 2 August, but resigned only fifteen days later unable to form a government. Tadeusz Mazowiecki (formerly editor of Solidarity's weekly newspaper) became the new premier, confirmed on 24 August, and the new government took office on 12 September 1989 for a maximum four year term. Mazowiecki did not present a detailed economic programme during his acceptance speech, but made several proposals: 'Those institutions which have been blocked, such as the market, must be set free. The role of the state should be similar to that in Western countries.' More specifically, he promised an anti-inflation policy, and requested more generous debt rescheduling and Western aid: 'He who helps early helps twice.'

Solidarity (winning all the contested 161 seats) came to an agreement with the United Peasants' Party (UPP) (allocated seventy-six seats in the 460 member Sejm) and the Democratic Party (DP) (twenty-seven seats), both formerly subservient to the PUWP (173 seats: another twenty-three seats were occupied by its Catholic allies). In the new government the positions were allocated as follows: Solidarity (eleven, including finance, industry, construction, labour and social policy, Central Planning Office and Economic Council), the PUWP (four, namely defence, interior, transport, and foreign trade), the UPP (four, including agriculture), the DP (three, namely scientific development, domestic trade, and communications), and one independent (foreign ministry).

In the local elections of 28 May 1990 there was a poor turn-out of only 42.1 per cent. The percentage distribution of seats was as follows: Solidarity 41.4 per cent; independent and citizens' candidates 38 per cent; Polish Peasants' Party 6.5 per cent; Social Democracy of the Republic of Poland 0.28 per cent.

There was a government reshuffle on 6 July 1990. Among the notable changes were General Czeslaw Kiszczak of the SDRP at the Interior Ministry (replaced by Krzysztof Kozlowski) and Defence Minister General Florian Siwicki of the SDRP (replaced by Piotr Kolodziejczyk).

At the end of December 1989 the PUWP agreed to change the country's name from the Polish People's Republic to the Republic of

Poland. At the end of January 1990 the PUWP was renamed Social Democracy of the Republic of Poland (SDRP), with Leszar Miller as general secretary and Alexander Kwasniewski as chairman of the general council. Its platform was opposed to 'attempts to change the system to introduce capitalism', but saw the need for a 'social market economy'.

Solidarity later split, notably into the Citizens' Movement for Democratic Action or ROAD (which was formed on 16 July 1990 to support Mazowiecki's campaign for presidency) and the Centre Alliance (which was formed on 12 May 1990 to support Lech Walesa). Membership of Solidarity has fallen from 10 million at its peak to something over 2 million today (the former official trade union, now called OPZZ, has about 5 million). On 23 February 1991 Marian Krzaklewski, a Silesian worker, was elected leader of Solidarity to replace Lech Walesa (Walesa's own choice was Bogdan Boruszewicz). On 3 March 1991 the Centre Agreement party emerged, a centre right party of Christian Democratic hue and led by Jaroslaw Kaczynski; he advocates Catholic social teaching and a Western-type economy.

The Polish presidential election was held before the new powers had been defined by parliament, the result of pressure from Lech Walesa. Six candidates contested the first round on 26 November 1990, in which the turn-out was 69.6 per cent. Walesa took 39.96 per cent of the vote, but Mazowiecki only came third with 18.08 per cent. He was beaten into second place by a little known émigré Polish-Canadian-Peruvian businessman Stanislaw Tyminski, who attracted 23.1 per cent of the votes on dreams of individual economic success in a 'democracy of money', sheltered by a social welfare net; the road to prosperity was to be relatively painless and fast. (On 13 March 1991 he registered his own 'Party X'; the platform included abolition of the tax on wage increases, but a 50 per cent income tax. It was announced on 17 September that, because of forged support signatures, the party would only be able to compete in four constituencies out of thirty-seven, a maximum forty-four candidates for the 260 seats in the Sejm and eleven for the 100 senate seats.) Mazowiecki's defeat was attributed to popular adverse reaction to the economic programme and the lingering influence of the *nomenklatura*. Mazowiecki immediately offered his resignation as prime minister, but parliament insisted that he should prepare a report on his term of office for debate, in order to ensure that he stayed on until a replacement could be found. His resignation was formally accepted on 14 December, but he did agree to stay on temporarily. Mazowiecki set about establishing a new party called Democratic Union. In an acrimonious run-off against Tyminski on 9 December, Walesa took around three-quarters of the vote. The turn-out, however, was only 53.4 per cent. Walesa was sworn into office on 22 December 1990, promising to speed up privatization to make Poland 'a nation of owners' and to adopt the Balcerowicz programme 'with modifications'.

On 14 November 1990 the Polish and German foreign ministers signed a treaty confirming the present boundaries. The first Soviet troops started to leave in April 1991 and all were due to do so by 1993. On 27 October 1991 it was agreed that combat troops should withdraw by November 1992 and all troops by the end of 1993. It was later agreed that most troops would leave by 15 November 1992.

Walesa had considerable difficulty in forming a new government. Jan Olszewski tried, but gave up, claiming 'important differences' with Walesa (allegedly over the proposed members of the administration). Walesa suggested that Mazowiecki should stay on until spring 1991, but he declined. Eventually, Jan Kryzystof Bielecki (a businessman and leader of the Liberal Democratic Congress Party) agreed to be prime minister until the next general election (Walesa suggested 26 May, but the Sejm decided on an election by 30 October 1991; the actual date was later set for 27 October after much wrangling between Walesa and parliament).

Bielecki was confirmed in office on 4 January 1991. He offered a degree of policy 'correction', e.g. more rapid privatization, with greater emphasis on the distribution of free shares to the public; and farmers to be protected from the 'unfair' competition of cheap foreign food.

The general election of 27 October 1991

This was the first entirely free election in the post-war period. The turn-out was a low 43.2 per cent, a figure which seemed to be an ominous statement on Poland's experiment with 'shock' therapy. A multitude of parties competed for the 460 seats in the Sejm and the 100 seats in the senate (some 120 parties and groups), with no minimum threshold. Consequently there are twenty-nine parties in the Sejm, and twenty-two groups and six independents in the senate. The result of the election is shown in Table 23.1.

Democratic Union. The leaders are Tadeusz Mazowiecki, Jacek Kuron and Bronislaw Geremek. It was formed in autumn 1990 by three groups, including ROAD.

Alliance of the Democratic Left. This is made up of three ex-communist groupings, namely the Polish Social Democratic Party (leader Alexander Kwasniewski), the OPZZ trade union, and independents like Wlodzimierz Cimoszewicz. The Alliance favours a slower pace of economic reform and higher social security benefits.

Catholic Electoral Action. The grouping was right of centre and strongly pro-Catholic Church. The main component party was the Christian National Union.

People's Peasant Party. Favours greater protection of and support for farmers.

Confederation for an Independent Poland (KPN). A strongly anti-communist, nationalistic right-wing party led by Leszek Moczulski. Penalties should be imposed on ex-communists.

Table 23.1 The Polish general election of October 1991

Party	% vote	Seats in Sejm	Seats in the senate
Democratic Union	12.31	62	21
Alliance of the Democratic Left	11.98	60	4
Catholic Electoral Action	8.73	49	9
People's Peasant Party	8.67	48	8
Confederation for an Independent Poland (KPN)	7.50	46	4
Citizens' Centre Alliance	8.71	44	9
Liberal Democratic Congress	7.48	37	6
Farmers' Solidarity	5.46	28	7
Solidarity Trade Union	5.05	27	12
Polish Beer Lovers' Party	3.27	16	
German Minority	1.17	7	
Christian Democrats	2.36	5	1
Polish Western Union	0.23	4	
Labour Solidarity	2.05	4	
Party of Christian Democracy	1.11	4	3
Union for Political Realism	2.25	3	
Party X	0.47	3	
Movement for Silesian Autonomy	0.35	2	
Democratic Party	1.41	1	

(There were ten other parties with one seat each)

Citizens' Centre Alliance. A Catholic party originally supportive of and supported by Lech Walesa (a rift later developed) and led by Jaroslaw Kalzynski. Favours reflating the economy and removing Balcerowicz and his ideas; it considers recession to be more of a problem than inflation. Its candidate for prime minister was Jan Olszewski.

Liberal Democratic Congress. The party of the prime minister at the time of the election. Bielecki strongly favours continuing with the economic reform programme.

Post-election developments

The immediate comment on the economic reform programme was interesting. Bielecki declared the election 'A vote against the market economy'. Walesa put forward a number of alternative political scenarios, including one involving himself as prime minister. He thought there a need to carry on broadly with the economic reforms, but there should be a 're-orientation' towards greater protection for those victimized by the economic upheaval and a greater effort to limit the recession and create jobs: 'we should continue the construction of an economic order which meets the aspirations of the nation' (29 November speech).

There was no clear-cut winner, indeed no clear-cut political grouping able to form a government. A series of bargaining sessions started between Walesa and various coalitions seeking to form a government. The Sejm met on 25 November and Wieslaw Chrzanowski of the Christian National Union was elected speaker by a surprisingly large majority. Bielecki offered his government's resignation, but the Sejm did not accept it until 5 December 1991. On 5 December the president reluctantly (partly because he wished the economic reforms to continue in essence) asked Jan Olszewski of Citizens' Centre Alliance to form a government and the Sejm approved this decision the following day. The other four parties in the coalition were the Christian National Union, the People's Peasant Party, KPN and the Liberal Democratic Congress (LDC). But the LDC pulled out on 12 December, because of a proposed softening of 'shock' therapy (Olszewski's main aim was to do something about the recession; he thought the pain should be 'equally shared'), and the KPN did so three days later over seat allocations in the cabinet. On 17 December Olszewski offered his resignation, claiming lack of support from Walesa, but the next day the Sejm refused to accept it.

In fact, the new government was approved on 23 December 1991, containing six from the Centre Alliance, three from the Christian National Union, two from the Peasant Party, and ten independents. Balcerowicz was removed. His position as head of economic policy in the cabinet was taken by Jerzy Eysymontt (the former head of the Central Planning Office, whose main aim was to reverse the recession), while Karol Lutkowski became finance minister. The new government said that 'further economic sacrifices' were needed, but the pain should be spread more evenly, e.g. there would be increased spending on social and job-creating projects. In a communiqué published 5 February 1992 the government expressed the view that 'the gains from the market reform strategy launched in 1989–90 have been more modest than originally predicted, while the social costs and burdens have proved to be greater than expected'. Taxation on state enterprises would fall. The IMF agreement was expected to be renegotiated. The budget would be allowed to rise from 3 per cent to as much as 4.5 per cent of GNP if necessary. Privatization was to continue, albeit with modifications.

THE ECONOMIC PROGRAMME

The name of Leszek Balcerowicz, the (former) minister of finance, has become synonymous with 'big bang' and 'shock' remedies. From the beginning he was in no doubt about the reasons and remedies for Poland's situation. When he outlined the government's economic programme in October 1989 (quoted by Martin Wolf, *FT*, 18 December 1989, p. 20) he outlined the dismal economic position Poland was in:

> We are embarking on the reshaping effort under extremely adverse conditions. The economy is in ever more tenuous disequilibrium . . . The ecological disaster, the housing crisis, the foreign debt problem, emigration by the most active part of the young generation – these have been swelling for years. In recent months additional crisis symptoms surfaced or mounted in force: a rapid price climb linked with a wage explosion, the flight from the zloty, the growing deficit of the state budget and also a fall in output.

His remedy was as follows (quoted by John Duffy, *IHT*, 11 June 1990, p. 11):

1. A stabilization or severe austerity programme, more commonly known as 'shock' treatment (therapy). Balcerowicz made the point that it was necessary to take advantage of the 'honeymoon' period, when the new government could not be blamed for taking harsh measures.

2. 'A set of measures which will focus on the supply side and, we hope, reactivate the economy in a non-inflationary way.'

The Western economy is the only model 'verified in practical experience'. What Poland needs is a 'normal Western market economy'. The 'objective is to set up a market system akin to the one found in the industrially developed countries. This will have to be achieved quickly, through radical actions' (quoted by Martin Wolf, *FT*, 18 December 1989, p. 20). At the end of December 1989 Balcerowicz stated that 'Our proposal is an economy based on a market mechanism, with a structure of ownership like that in developed countries, open to the world, its rules clear'.

The actual economic programme began 1 January 1990 and constituted the following elements (exchange rate policy is dealt with later):

'Shock' therapy

This refers to strict fiscal, monetary and incomes policies, deemed essential elements in the battle against near hyperinflation.

Inflation

Poland faced near hyperinflation in late 1989. The average rate of inflation for 1989 was 244 per cent, but the annual rate for the year to December 1989 was 640 per cent (*EIU Country Report*, 1990, no. 1, p. 4). The aim was to reduce the average monthly rate of inflation to 4–5 per cent by June 1990 and 2–3 per cent for the rest of the year. The actual monthly record (compared to the previous month) is as follows: December 1989, 17.7 per cent; January 1990, 78.6 per cent; February 23.9 per cent; March 4.7 per cent; April 8 per cent; May 4 per cent; June 3.4 per cent; August 1.8 per cent; September 4.8 per cent; October 5.7 per cent; November 4.9 per cent; and December 5.9 per cent. The rise in the inflation rate was at first due to what Balcerowicz calls 'corrective inflation', the result of the sudden reduction in subsidies (inflation in the early months was higher than expected nevertheless). In May 1991 Balcerowicz declared the aim of a 30 per cent inflation rate for 1991.

Note that inflation had eroded the value of real money balances and hence monetary overhang was not a problem.

The budget deficit

According to *The Economist* (survey entitled 'Perestroika', 28 April 1990, p.16) the average fiscal deficit in the period 1980–88 was less than 2 per cent of GDP; in 1988 it was 0.3 per cent. In 1989, however, it was 8.1 per cent of GDP (Gomulka 1990: 134). The aim was to approach a balanced budget in 1990, to help control the money supply and hence inflation. There was a budget surplus of 0.5 per cent of GDP in 1990. The April 1991 agreement with the IMF fixed a budget deficit target of 0.5 per cent of GDP.

On the expenditure side of the budget, subsidies were to be reduced from 38.5 per cent of total expenditure to 14 per cent, a reduction equal to 7 per cent of GDP (DIW, *Economic Bulletin*, 1990, vol. 27, no. 3, p. 14). Balcerowicz estimated that subsidies had been reduced from 15 per cent of GDP in 1989 to 5–6 per cent (*FT Survey*, 2 May 1991, p. vii). The turnover tax was replaced by a uniform value-added tax on 1 January 1991. A Western-type income tax regime was to be introduced in 1992.

The reduction in subsidies resulted in some spectacular price increases. On 1 August 1989 meat rationing and price controls on most food-stuffs were ended, giving a big boost to inflation (food prices increased 180 per cent in August). On 1 January 1990 most prices were freed. At the end of 1990 only 17 per cent of consumer prices and 12 per cent of industrial producer prices remained subject to control (Adam Gwiazda, *European Affairs*, 1991, no. 4, p. 32). Around 95 per cent are now market-determined. The prices still remaining under state control included household rents in the state sector, postal services, public transport fares, electricity, coal and gas. There resulted some extraordinary individual price increases, e.g. 1 January 1990 coal 600–700 per cent; gas 400 per cent; electricity 400 per cent; rail and road transport 250 per cent. The price of electricity went up another 80 per cent on 1 July, when price controls were lifted on coal and skimmed milk and cheese. There was a 50 per cent increase in petrol prices on 5 October. On 1 January 1991 electricity went up in price by 20 per cent and gas by 80 per cent. Shops that previously sold consumer goods for hard currency must now sell for zloties.

The budgetary situation deteriorated in 1991. The March budget had foreseen a deficit of 4,306 billion zloties, but by August this figure had been revised upwards to 24,000 billion zloties. Anticipated revenue was down by 21.5 per cent (revenue from state enterprises was only a third of the expected figure because of the recession, while the private sector was the beneficiary of substantial concessions). The

Bielecki government responded by trying to persuade the Sejm to approve a 14.5 per cent reduction in government expenditure on the March figure (although spending on social welfare, health and education was to increase). Parliamentary resistance led to an offer to resign by Bielecki on 30 August 1991. It was not accepted, but the Sejm refused to grant limited emergency powers to the government to push through legislation up to and beyond the October elections (specifically to the end of January 1992). The IMF decided to delay negotiations until the new post-election government was in place. A new budget was finally agreed on 27 September, with a planned deficit of 26,000 billion zloties and spending reductions of some 15 per cent. The actual budget deficit in 1991 was 3.4 per cent of GDP (United Nations Economic Commission for Europe 1992: 94).

Pay policy

In Poland there has been a persistent tendency for wage increases to exceed both productivity and prices. Control over wage rises has taken the form of a wage inflation tax (*popiwek*) in the state sector (the private sector is exempt). Money wage increases above a centrally determined norm were subject to a high and sharply progressive tax on wages. The norm was based on the previous month's consumer price increase multiplied by an indexation coefficient (Gora 1991: 162). There was a clear relaxation after June 1990 following an acknowledgement of dampening inflation and the high social costs of the policy (Blazyca 1991: 27). A number of enterprises were allowed to increase their wage bill without punitive taxation; these were those that did not enjoy a monopoly position and had been converted to joint stock companies, even if state-owned, or private sector firms (Milanovic 1992: 526).

Monetary policy

An important aspect of 'shock' therapy was

control over the money supply. The National Bank of Poland was not allowed to give credit to the government to support any spending over-shoot (*EIU Country Report*, 1990, no. 1, p. 8). On the demand side the aim was to set real positive interest rates. The basic money interest rates, for example, were set as follows: January 1990, 36 per cent; February 20 per cent; and March 10 per cent.

The Olszewski government's programme

The Olszewski government (approved 23 December 1991) allowed the steep price rises programmed for early January 1992 to proceed, e.g. an approximate doubling of home central heating, gas 70 per cent, electricity 20 per cent and alcoholic drinks 20 per cent. The pro-grammed budget for the first quarter of 1992 was also taken over. There were warning strikes in the period 8–16 January. On 15 March the prices of petrol and other fuels increased between 20 per cent and 31.5 per cent.

The new programme was outlined in mid-February 1992 and envisaged a fiscal and monetary relaxation. The budget deficit for the whole of 1992 was to be allowed to rise to within 5 per cent of national income. A balanced budget was to be achieved by 1994. There was to be an increase in the turnover (sales) tax as of 1 April 1992. The money supply was to rise at a rate greater than inflation, but a tough wages policy was designed to reduce real incomes in 1992 by 5 per cent (after a 2 per cent rise in 1991). There would be no increase in consumption over the next three years. On the other hand, encouragement was to be given to investment (e.g. to restructure state enterprises), and exports were to be boosted (and imports discouraged) by zloty devaluation and a more favourable treatment of wage rises in enterprises with a good export performance. Extra price guarantees for agriculture were envisaged. The inflation target for 1992 was set at 40 per cent with single-digit inflation by 1994 (Balcerowicz originally had this in mind for 1991).

Unemployment was meant to stabilize in 1993. This general softening of the fiscal and monetary stance of the government led to the resignation of the finance minister, Karol Lutkowski (offered 17 February 1992 and accepted two days later). He was replaced by Andrzej Olechowski, a former vice-president of the central bank and deputy foreign trade minister; the Sejm gave its approval on 28 February 1992.

But on 6 March the Olszewski government's budget proposals were rejected by the Sejm. A new set of proposals, including reduced social spending, was proposed, one more in line with previous policies. The IMF-approved target was to keep the budget deficit in 1992 to 5 per cent of GDP, i.e. a deficit of 65,500 billion zloties. An attempt in April to form a ten-party coalition, including Democratic Forum and the Liberal Democratic Congress, failed. The political and economic turmoil increased when on 6 May the government failed to get the necessary two-thirds majority in the Sejm to overturn a consti-tutional tribunal's ruling that 1991 indexed-linked pension and pay increases for state employees had to be paid. Since this would add over 28,000 billion zloties to the budget deficit, Finance Minister Olechowski resigned, although he agreed to stay on until the budget debate in parliament.

In a speech delivered on 8 May 1992 Walesa reiterated the case for a more powerful presidency, specifically long French lines. For example, Walesa thought the president should be able to appoint and dismiss the prime minister and cabinet (instead of simply being able to nominate the premier).

The Olszewski government fell to a vote of no confidence on 5 June 1992. Relations with Walesa had always been poor, culminating in the president's statement on 26 May that he had 'lost trust in the present government'. Waldemar Pawlak of the People's Peasant Party (and former member of the United Peasants' Party in the socialist era) was appointed prime minister. The budget holding the deficit to 5 per cent of GDP was passed. But Pawlak failed to form an administration and offered to resign on 2 July. On 10 July 1992 the Sejm accepted his resignation and replaced him with Hanna Suchocka of Democratic Union. She headed a seven-party coalition government (see postscript).

The effects of 'shock' therapy

Unemployment has risen rapidly and output has fallen quite dramatically.

Unemployment

The government originally based its estimates for the funds available for unemployment compensation on an unemployment level of 400,000 in 1990. But already at the end of December 1989 Balcerowicz thought the figure could rise to 890,000.

Table 23.2 gives the actual monthly unemployment figures. Note that a proportion were previously unemployed to all intents and purposes, while there is some debate as to how high the actual level of unemployment is today, e.g. some work is done in the black economy. The Ministry of Labour calculated that, of the then 1.2 million registered unemployed, only 14 per cent lost their jobs because of the closure of enterprises; more than 40 per cent were school or college leavers, most of whom probably work in the unregistered retail sector (*The Economist*, 4 May 1991, p. 54). The *OECD Employment Outlook* (July 1991, p. 22) notes that, while employment fell by more than 1.6 million in the state sector over the year to the end of December 1990, employment in the private sector rose by over half a million. In the eighteen months to July 1991 the private sector created 1 million jobs (*The Economist*, 22 February 1992, p. 45). Fallenbuchl (1991: 62) quotes one estimate that 600,000 to 800,000 of the then total of 1,125,000 registered unemployed had additional income from unreported activities.

Note that only a small number of enterprises have actually been bankrupted to date. No large

Table 23.2 Poland: unemployment

		No. unemployed	Unemployment rate (%)
1990	January		0.3
	February		0.8
	March		1.5
	April		1.9
	May		2.4
	June		3.1
	July		3.8
	August		4.5
	September		5.0
	October		5.5
	November		5.9
	December	1,126,100	6.1
1991	January		
	February		
	March	1,322,100	7.1
	April	1,370,000	7.4
	May	1,435,500	7.7
	June	1,574,100	8.4
	July	1,749,900	9.4
	August		9.8
	September	1,970,900	10.4
	October		
	November		
	December	2,155,600	11.4
1992	January	2,230,100	11.9
	February		
	March		12.0
	April	2,238,400	12.2
	May		
	June		12.6
	July	2,400,00	13.1
	August		
	September		
	October		13.5
	November		
	December		

Sources: Gora (1991: 157); Deutsche Bank, *Focus: Eastern Europe*, 1992, no. 41, p.1; 1992, no. 53, p. 9; 1992, no. 55, p. 4, no. 58, p. 10; *Economic Bulletin for Europe*, 1991, vol. 43, p. 28; Commision of the European Communities, *Employment Observatory*, 1992, no. 2, p. 9; United Nations Economic Commission for Europe (1992: 68); Ash (1992: 14).

state enterprise was subject to bankruptcy in 1990 (Gora 1991: 148). Inter-enterprise credit has increased substantially, thus preserving the soft budget constraint to some extent. Other explanatory factors include the laying off of workers, lower real wages and the help given by Comecon links before the shift to hard currency trading on 1 January 1991. Signs of trouble, however, have multiplied. For example, in July it was reported that the giant Ursus tractor manufacturer was in deep financial trouble and mass lay-offs ensued the following month.

The Employment Act was amended on 27 July 1990 (see, for example, Gora 1991: 149). Individuals are normally eligible for unemployment benefit if they are actively seeking work and have been employed for at least 180 days during the year prior to registration. The benefit was calculated as follows: 70 per cent of previous wages for the first three months; 50 per cent for the next six months, and 40 per cent for nine months following that. Those who have never worked are paid the minimum wage and school leavers receive twice this. But unemployment pay is never to be higher than the average wage or lower than 95 per cent of the minimum wage. Anyone who rejects two suitable jobs or retraining offers within thirty days or who does not attend the employment office daily will cease to be eligible. Redundant workers are entitled to a month's wages. Christopher Bobinski (*FT*, 14 June 1991, p. 2) argued that generous redundancy provisions and the wage control system moderated the increase in unemployment; more often than not it was cheaper to keep staff on on half or even quarter pay. Under the new Employment Act of December 1991 there is normally a twelve month limit on a person's entitlement to unemployment benefit (Commission of the European Communities, *Employment Observatory*, 1992, no. 1, p. 20). A uniform rate of cash benefit, equal to around 36 per cent of average earnings, was introduced in March 1992 (Commission of the European Communities, *Employment Observatory*, 1992, no. 2, p. 14).

The question as to how far 'real wages' had fallen during 1990 is difficult to answer. Merely looking at nominal wages and prices saw a 30.4 per cent fall (Gora 1991: 162). But this is an exaggeration because of the increasing availability of goods (queues were prevalent in the past) and the eroding effects of inflation on money balances. Berg and Sachs (1992: 139–41) dispute the official figure of a fall in real private consumption of 15.3 per cent in 1990; they suggest a fall of 4.8 per cent at most.

The question as to how far the population can be pushed without rebelling is a central one in the whole experiment. There was initial majority support for the government, but it fell away rapidly. Batt (1991: 84–5) provides evidence from opinion polls: Mazowiecki's support was in the range 93–85 per cent between November 1989 and March 1990; public support for the Balcerowicz programme peaked at 35 per cent in January 1990 at the time of its implementation, but this had fallen to only 9 per cent by April. There are examples of industrial unrest. In January 1990 there were some unsuccessful strikes among coal miners demanding higher pay increases; there was a subsequent agreement, however, to compensate the loss of Saturday working by means of a 40 per cent increase in weekday earnings (Christopher Bobinski, *FT*, 8 March 1990, p. 3). Railway workers began to strike on 20 May 1990, demanding a 20 per cent pay increase (promised before the implementation of the shock treatment) and the dismissal of management. A national strike was averted by the intervention of Lech Walesa, who arranged a suspension of action. Coal miners staged short strikes in November 1990. The defeat of Mazowiecki in the presidential election suggested a substantial loss of public support for the economic programme. In May 1991 there were strikes by copper ore miners, urban transport workers and dustmen. There was a day of protest by Solidarity on the 22nd. June saw an easing of the wage restraint policy, e.g. the tax-free earnings threshold was increased. Enterprises which laid off surplus workers were to be allowed to retain (tax-free) half the savings in wage costs, provided they had paid their taxes.

Output

Table 23.3 shows the relevant figures, with output falling and unemployment increasing substantially. Note that whereas the output of the state and co-operative sector declined by 21 per cent, the private sector as a whole increased by 17 per cent and the non-agricultural private sector by 26 per cent (Fallenbuchl 1991: 66). The private sector now accounts for 22 per cent of total industrial output (*FT*, 24 December 1991, p. 2). In 1990 more than 500,000 new businesses were registered, mostly in retail trade, wholesale trade and warehousing, road transport and related services, and construction (p. viii); around 300,000 of the 516,000 were trade enterprises (p. vi). In an interview with Martin Wolf (*FT*, 16 July 1990, p. 36), Balcerowicz thought the main reason for the larger than expected fall in output to be the reaction of enterprise managers, who passed on the rise in input costs in product price increases, behaving as though they did not believe that the tough macroeconomic policies would hold and allowing output to adapt to falling demand. There was relatively little effort to increase efficiency or search for new products and markets. The monopolistic structure of industry was also a factor (see below). Heavy industry has been less affected than light industry because of the greater political pull exercised by the former.

The official output figures have been questioned. For example, Berg and Sachs (1992: 147) argue that the fall in GDP in 1990 may have been as small as 4.9 rather than 12 per cent.

Some particular criticisms of the Balcerowicz programme

Marek Gruchelski (Central School of Planning and Statistics, Warsaw) (see Seumas Milne, *The Guardian*, 30 November 1990, p. 26). Gruch-

Table 23.3 Poland: foreign debt and rates of growth of GDP, industrial ouput, agricultural output and prices (%)

GDP	
1990	1991
−12.0	−7.0
Industrial output	
1990	1991
−24.2	−12.0
Agricultural output	
1990	1991
−2.2	−2.0
Inflation	
1990	1991
586.0	70.0
Net foreign debt ($ billion)	
End 1990	End 1991
43.7	42.9

Sources: Deutsche Bank, *Focus: Eastern Europe*, 1992, no. 41, p. 1; 1992, no. 53, p. 9; A. Robinson, *FT*, 18 February 1992, p. 20; *FT Survey*, 2 May 1991, p. ii; *The Economist*, Survey, 21 September, p. 5; C. Jones, *The Banker*, May 1991, p. 23; Economist Intelligence Unit, *Country Report*, 1991, no. 4, pp. 6,20; Kaser and Allsopp (1992: 2); DIW, *Economic Bulletin*, 1992, vol. 29, no. 4, p. 5, vol. 29, no. 10, p. 3; OECD, *Economic Outlook*, June 1992, pp. 41–2; United Nations Economic Commission for Europe (1992: 45, 65, 302, 304); *The Banker*, September 1992, pp. 23, 33.

elski argues that the Balcerowicz programme is unsuited to a monopolistic economy where inflation is driven by endemic shortages and inefficiencies in the use of capital. The depressed state of the economy has hindered the restructuring of the economy, while the exchange rate was defended far too long. The wage inflation tax should be removed, but price controls introduced. Output should be boosted by stepping up capacity utilization and concentrating production in the most efficient plants; round-the-clock shift working should be introduced in many enterprises for five to seven years.

Melvin Fagen (*IHT*, 5 December 1990, p. 4); Stanley Katz (*FT*, 24 April 1991, p. 19). Japan and the 'Pacific tigers' – South Korea, Taiwan and

Singapore – provide an alternative model. The state took an active role, using e.g. export incentives, subsidies, tariffs and low-interest rate credits to protect the economy until it was able to compete freely on the world market. Foreign knowledge and technology rather than equity investment were sought.

Towards a more interventionist policy

The deep recession affecting the state sector prompted the Bielecki government to take a more active role in restructuring polish industry. A new commissioner, Henryka Bochniarz, was appointed in July 1991. Although there was to be no financial bail-out, 'crisis teams' would advise enterprises on restructuring, debt relief and asset sales. The tax and credit system would be used to encourage enterprises to respond as part of an emerging 'industrial policy'.

The remedy offered by Sachs and Lipton

Sachs and Lipton (1990: 48) described Poland as aiming to create the legal, economic, financial and administrative conditions necessary for a market economy during the course of 1990. There was a rapid liberalization of prices and international trade. They recognize that certain things take longer to accomplish, such as a shift of emphasis from heavy to light industry. Sachs was cautious on privatization at first, but both he and Lipton now favour as rapid a process as possible; specifically, the largest 500 industrial enterprises should be privatized within four years (Lipton and Sachs 1990b: 327). Not only would the economic efficiency gains be reaped, but this would avoid political considerations bringing the whole process to a halt. International competition would substantially mitigate the monopoly problem. Lipton and Sachs advocated the following strategy: the largest enterprises should be converted into joint stock companies owned by the Treasury; a few could simply be sold off, but most shares would be rapidly distributed in tranches – at a zero or discounted price to workers and management for political and incentive reasons; free to financial institutions such as mutual funds, pension funds and commercial banks (for management control purposes) whose shares would in turn be distributed or sold to households; finally the government should retain a portion of the shares and gradually sell them off, especially to 'core investors' to enhance the monitoring of enterprise management.

Marketization

The traditional central one year plan was abolished at the start of 1990, indirect economic control being exercised via fiscal, monetary, incomes and exchange rate policies (DIW, *Economic Bulletin*, 1990, vol. 27, no. 3, p. 15). Enterprises were free to make most decisions related to output, prices and foreign trade. Workers' councils have assumed an increased practical role, such as changing managers and in output decisions; in March 1990 workers' councils were given the right to dismiss managers without having to consult the Industry Ministry. Brada reports some administrative allocation of producer goods because of the large differences between domestic and world prices (*Journal of Comparative Economics*, 1990, vol. 14, no. 4, p. 58).

Privatization

At the end of 1989 the economically active population was 18,371,000. The state sector employed 63 per cent and the private sector 31.8 per cent (22.2 per cent in agriculture and 9.6 per cent in non-agricultural activities) (Gora 1991: 154).

Waldemar Kuczynski became minister of privatization on 14 September 1990, replacing Kristof Lis. The body responsible for the implementation of policy is called the Ministry of Property Transformation.

Before looking at the privatization it is useful to look at the industrial structure in Poland

(Sachs and Lipton 1990; figures for 1986). Monopoly is a real problem (at least domestically, international competition mitigating the effects). There were only 982 enterprises in the state sector with 100 or fewer employees. The average number of employees per state-owned enterprise (excluding co-operatives) was 1,132 and per individual plant was 378. By contrast there were on average sixty-six workers per plant in a 1986 survey of Western economies (p. 49). There were 7,800 industrial enterprises in the state sector (p. 53). The 115 largest industrial enterprises (more than 5,000 employees each) accounted for more than one-fifth of employment and output; enterprises employing 50–100, so important in the growth of Western economies, were virtually absent (Lipton and Sachs 1990: 82–4). In Eastern Europe generally there is a lack of small independent firms servicing large enterprises (p. 85). According to Christopher Bobinski and Martin Wolf (*FT*, 2 August 1990, p. 16) there were more than 7,000 'significant' state enterprises, accounting for 90 per cent of industrial output. Blazyca (1992: 185–6) provides some further useful information: at the end of 1989 there were 6,008 state industrial enterprises, each employing 695 on average. In 1988 the largest 113 enterprises (employing more than 5,000) accounted for 23 per cent of state industrial sales and 25.2 per cent of employment. The top 428 state enterprises accounted for 47.8 per cent of total industrial sales and 52 per cent of employment.

The measures

An Anti-monopoly Law was adopted on 24 February 1990 and the Anti-monopoly Office was set up in April the same year (Michael Reynolds, *FT*, 26 September 1991, p. 12). Sanctions are stringent, e.g. managers of defaulting companies can be fined personally and fines on companies can be up to 15 per cent of turnover. The office has the power to divide and liquidate companies which permanently limit competition.

The early experience of privatization was not an entirely happy one. One of the problems was the so-called 'emancipation of the *nomenklatura*', where managers converted state enterprises into companies in which they held a controlling interest and where the shares were undervalued (*Polish Perspectives*, 1989, vol. XXXII, no. 4, p. 72). Managers of state enterprises also awarded profitable contracts to newly privatized enterprises in which they held shares, and also sold shares to one another at a discount. Since the spring of 1990 managers of state enterprises have not been allowed to hold posts in competing private enterprises. It is also worth noting here that an investigation into the banking system began in June 1991, with allegations of mismanagement and corruption, e.g. over credit guarantees and the earning of interest on the same funds switched between different accounts to take advantage of the slow processing of transfers. A new banking law was approved by the Sejm on 22 September; banks are restricted to lending a maximum 15 per cent of their capital to any one client.

The privatization bill, after much debate, finally passed the Sejm on 13 July 1990, by 328 votes to two, with thirty-eight abstentions. The senate approved the bill on 26 July, by sixty votes to seven, with two abstentions. The individual features of the programme were as follows:

1. As regards the larger companies, there was to be a 20 per cent limit on the discounted shares purchased by the workers belonging to any particular enterprise (the value of preferences not exceeding the annual wage bill). These shares were to be sold at half price, with low-interest credits or deferred payments used because of the lack of savings. Farmers were also to get priority consideration in firms with which their products were linked.

2. All Poles were to get free certificates (privatization bonds) with which they would be able to buy shares (20 per cent of the value of shares was the figure initially fixed, but an increase was a possibility). The certificates

could be sold, used to bid for shares in particular enterprises, or invested in mutual funds.

3. Enterprises were to be transformed into joint stock companies. The Treasury would sell shares on the open market within two years. The process was still to be under state control, although one-third of the board of directors were to be elected by employees (two-thirds appointed by the Treasury) as long as at least half the shares belonged to the state. As soon as the state relinquished its majority share the board was to be elected by the shareholders. The veto powers of workers' councils, management and founder bodies over privatization could be overridden.

4. The normal limit on foreign ownership of capital was 10 per cent, but exceptions were seen as possible and likely.

5. Privatized enterprises could possibly be freed from wage controls.

6. Bankrupt enterprises were to be sold at auction, either in one piece or in parts.

7. Small and medium-size enterprises were already being sold off or leased', e.g. shops and restaurants (*Abecor Country Report*, June 1990, p. 2: the private sector labour force had increased by 27 per cent to 1.5 million). Ten per cent of urban shops were privatized in the first six months of 1990. Some preference was given to employees in the sale or leasing of small firms (Colin Jones, *The Banker*, September 1990, p. 17). Around 75 per cent of retail trade is in private hands (Christopher Bobinski, *FT*, 22 November 1991, p. 2). By the autumn of 1991 this figure had risen to 80 per cent (compared to 30 per cent in 1989). In September 1991 the private sector accounted for 75 per cent of trade, 45 per cent of construction and 80 per cent of road transport (Grant Kirkpatrick and Val Koromzay, *OECD Observer*, 1992, no. 177, p. 36).

Public utilities are to be retained by the state (Mroz 1991: 686)

The privatization timetable

Balcerowicz said, 'We must transform owner-ship faster than any nation has done before.' Earlier on he had remarked that 'Our programme is the first in history to attempt to move from a state monopoly economy to a market economy as it exists in Western countries.' The Mazowiecki government planned to privatize 50 per cent of state assets in three years, but in January 1991 the Bielecki government spoke of this being achieved in two years (Blazyca 1991: 15).

The strategy was to privatize the most efficient enterprises first. In May 1990 Universal, a foreign trade company, was privatized. Polish investors took up 60 per cent of their allocation, but foreigners only one-sixth of their allocation of 30 per cent of the public subscription. The company had been made into a joint stock company in 1984 (with 51 per cent of shares held by the state and the remainder by state producers and retailers). The issue was handled by Big Bank, which, in February 1990, became the first state financial institution to start privatizing itself through a public share subscription offer (state enterprise shareholdings were reduced to 41 per cent).

Eight large enterprises were planned to be privatized by the end of September 1990 and forty within the next year. On 1 October 1990 seven enterprises were transformed into joint stock companies; the shares of five started to be floated at the end of November: Exbud (building renovation), Slaska (cables); Tonsil (consumer electronics); Krosno (glass) and Prochnik (textiles). Although the offers were oversubscribed, problems later emerged: for example, Krosna shares were temporarily suspended owing to heavy selling. The Swarzedz furniture enterprise was privatized in June 1991. The famous Wedel confectionery enterprise followed in October, being distinctive for PepsiCo already having bought a 40 per cent stake.

In July 1991 it was announced that five Polish banks were to be paired with five Western ones to provide technical assistance; in the autumn a privatization process was to be set in motion.

Foreigners were to be offered a 20 per cent stake in each and Polish individuals and institutions 40–50 per cent, with the state retaining 20–30 per cent. Also in June 1991 parliament approved the sale of 49 per cent of the shares in the Polish airline LOT.

In the presidential election campaign, Mazowiecki stood for privatizing half of state enterprises over three years. Walesa called for 70 per cent and the distribution of vouchers to enable people to buy shares (each voucher worth 100 million zloties). Later on, in an interview for *Moscow News* (24–31 May 1992, p. 5), Walesa talked of the need to speed up the privatization process by making loans, repayable in ten to fifteen years, available to any Pole prepared to buy shares. He also suggested that mass unemployment and plant closures could be avoided by reconstructing and modernizing enterprises.

Jan Krzystof Bielecki was confirmed as prime minister on 4 January 1991. He chose Janusz Lewandowski as his privatization minister. Bielecki aimed to privatize half the state sector within three years and to achieve the ownership structure of Western Europe within five years (Fallenbuchl 1991: 55–6). There was to be increased emphasis on the distribution of free shares to the population (to overcome the lack of private savings), shares awarded to managers involved in a successful sell-off, and direct sales aimed particularly at strategic investors or employees rather than scattered owners. The proposals for the percentage distribution of shares in the largest enterprises was as follows: workers 10; pension funds 20; commercial banks 10; state 30; and the public 30. Almost all shares would be held, at first, in mutual funds in order to discipline enterprise managers. Balcerowicz advocated a greater role for management buy-outs.

The Bielecki privatization programme was unveiled on 27 June 1991 by the privatization minister, Lewandowski. Some 400 large industrial enterprises were listed, accounting for around a quarter of industrial sales and employing 1.6 million people (12 per cent of the industrial workforce). (Another 600 was expected for 1992.)

Between five and twenty National Wealth Management Funds (NWMFs: joint stock investment companies working like Western-style mutual funds) were to be set up. They would be endowed with 60 per cent of the shares in each of the 400 enterprises, 10 per cent of the shares being given free to the workers in their own enterprises and 30 per cent being retained by the state (the treasury). Each adult Polish citizen (over eighteen years of age) was to receive vouchers worth one share in each of these NWMFs rather than receiving shares directly; the value of the vouchers would not be known until 1992 and trading would probably not begin until spring or summer 1993. Out of the 60 per cent, 33 per cent of each enterprise would be concentrated in just one investment fund, to encourage close supervision of enterprise management (although there is the danger of the NWMFs forming cartels). The remaining 27 per cent (out of the 60 per cent) would be distributed equally among the other NWMFs.

Each NWMF was to have a Polish chairman and some board members, but day-to-day management would be by Western banks and fund management firms. The NWMFs were to be allowed to sell shares in their companies to local and foreign investors, issue new shares, raise new loans, and enter into joint ventures and management contracts.

The Bielecki programme began taking a sectoral approach to privatization, asking Western advisory companies to look at whole industries and their prospects. In mid-October 1991, however, the competent minister, Janusz Lewandowski, announced a drastic scaling back of the privatization programme, due to the prospective social consequences in terms of unemployment and bankruptcies. The number of enterprises listed was reduced from 400 to 204 (representing only 7 per cent of industrial sales). Public shareholdings in the NWMFs were not likely to be issued until May 1993. In 1991 12 per cent of the 8,500 state enterprises were privatized, the larger ones by public share offers; eight enterprises were sold to foreigners (Mullineux 1992a: 5). To date fewer than thirty large enterprises had been privatized (Deutsche Bank, *Focus: Eastern Europe*, 18 March 1992, no. 41, p. 3). The vast majority of liquidated enterprises have been sold to management and workers. Since 1990 some 540 state enterprises employing 180,000 people have been privatized via liquidation, but most are small (Christopher Bobinski, *FT Survey*, 3 July 1992, p. iv). According to Poznanski (1992: 646) the picture is somewhat different. In the liquidation procedure enterprises, whether financially solvent or not, are dissolved and their assets are offered for sale to managers and workers. These buyouts reached a total of 650 enterprises in 1991, with the majority small (under 200 workers) and typically in transport, construction and services.

Tomasz Gruszecki became privatization minister in the Olszewski government (approved 23 December 1991). Gruszecki stated that 'Privatization policy must be subordinated to industrial policy' (*The Guardian*, 7 January 1992, p. 8). In his early pronouncements he favoured mass domestic privatization over foreign investment and stressed the need to clarify the ownership problem. The aim was to privatize half of Polish industry within two years. The Olszewski programme for 1992 listed 200 enterprises for mass privatization in the first round, set to begin in the second half of 1992 (another 200 were to be listed for the second round). There would be a nominal charge for, instead of a free distribution of, 'participation certificates' (vouchers) to citizens, in order to induce a more positive attitude to ownership. The vouchers would be exchangeable in 1993 for a bundle of shares in the new NWMFs. The shares of the enterprises themselves would be held by the mutual funds, for purposes of management control; the funds would eventually be liquidated (probably after a decade). Any enterprise attracting the attention of a foreign investor would be removed from the mass privatization list. In addition there were to be ten public share offerings and thirty to forty enterprises sold to foreign investors in 1992.

President Walesa has proclaimed himself in favour of the return of property to former owners as far as it possible, with financial compensation for the rest. But on grounds of cost among other things this has been ruled out. Former owners are only able to make claims if they return to Poland and if their property was seized in violation of communist laws. In most cases even here only partial compensation is available and in the form of bonds entitling them to buy shares in newly privatized enterprises.

The Warsaw stock exchange was reopened on 16 April 1991. During the year only six enterprises were listed, but eighteen others were sold to foreign investors (*The Guardian*, 7 January 1992, p. 8).

Fallenbuchl (1991: 66) provides some information on the increasing importance (in percentages of the total) of the private sector in 1989 and in 1990 respectively: non-agricultural employment 12 and 15.7 and industrial sales 7.4 and 13.4. Blaine Harden (*IHT*, 3 January 1991, p. 2) cites a World Bank estimate that the private sector accounts for more than 30 per cent of total industrial production. Official Polish figures for the non-agricultural sector show the following percentages of employment accounted for by the three sectors (*FT*, 3 February 1992, p. 3): state 62; private 25; and co-operative 13.

The *FT Survey* (28 April 1992, p. iv) provides a summary of official figures for the respective percentage shares of the private sector in 1989, 1990 and 1991 (projected): GDP 28.4, 34.7 and 40.0; employment, including private agriculture, 47.2, 49.9 and 50.0; employment, excluding private agriculture, 31.1, 33.6 and 33.2; industrial output 16.2, 17.4 and 19.4; and trade 59.5, 63.7 and 75.0. The respective percentage figures in 1990 and 1991 (projected) were as follows: foreign trade 8.6 and 28.4; exports 4.8 and 14.4; and imports 14.4 and 42.2.

FOREIGN TRADE, AID AND CAPITAL

Foreign trade

The exchange rate regime as of 1 January 1990

Confidence in the zloty is a key aim of the government. The zloty became 'internally' convertible, citizens and enterprises being able to exchange it for hard currency for current account transactions (see glossary). Enterprises have to sell all their foreign exchange earnings to the National Bank, but are allowed to buy foreign exchange when needed. A single exchange rate was set at 9,500 zloties to the US dollar for all current transactions, bringing it in line with the free-market rate (previously there had been three rates: the official commercial rate of 6,000 zloties to the dollar as of 22 December 1989; the rate prevailing in the enterprise auctions; and the free-market rate). The exchange rate was 'managed' by the National Bank, keeping an eye on the free market rate (more than 10 per cent deviation from the market rate signals the need for exchange rate or interest rate adjustments) and with the aid from the West of a $1 billion stabilization fund (not called upon). For a long time the rate held up against the dollar, people running down their dollar hoards as the recession took hold. The rate, in fact, held until 17 May 1991, when there was a 14.4 per cent devaluation against the US dollar (from 9,500 to 11,100 zloties) in order to make exports more competitive. After this the exchange rate for the zloty was to move against a trade-weighted basket of five major currencies (the US dollar, the Deutschemark, the pound sterling, the French franc and the Swiss franc). In October 1991 it was decided that the zloty should be gradually devalued, on a monthly basis, i.e. a crawling peg system was adopted. Towards the end of February 1992 there was, however, a 12 per cent devaluation.

The foreign trade regime as of 1 January 1990

Quantitative restrictions on imports from the West have mostly gone, and have been replaced by tariffs. In January 1990 a new tariff regime was introduced, with an average *ad valorem* rate of 12 per cent. Manufactured imports faced an average rate of 21 per cent, 40 per cent in the case of cars and other luxury goods. In mid-1990 most duties were set at the zero or 5 per cent level; tariffs on 57.9 per cent of the tariff lines are now zero, while tariffs on only 36.5 per cent of tariff lines are more than 10 per cent (Martin Wolf, *FT Survey*, 2 May 1991, p. v). Note that exports only constituted 15 per cent of GNP in 1990 (p. v). On 1 August 1991, however, customs duties were increased to 14 per cent on average, e.g. 20 per cent on electrical equipment, 25–35 per cent on food and textiles, and 45 per cent on luxury goods.

On the export side, quotas apply to fifty primary goods (e.g. coal and meat) during the transitional period to a market economy; these are designed to prevent the re-export of primary goods from Comecon countries and thus ensure supplies to the domestic market (DIW, *Economic Bulletin*, 1990, vol. 27, no. 3, p. 13). Export quotas also apply to steel, textiles and shoes, products which face restrictions imposed by other countries (Peter Montagnon, *FT Survey*, 20 November 1990, p. vi).

There was a sharp increase in the importance of foreign trade in the early post-reform period. Imports as a proportion of GDP rose from 13.6 per cent in 1989 to 22.8 per cent in 1991; the respective figures for exports were 9.2 per cent and 15.3 per cent (Christopher Bobinski and Anthony Robinson, FT, 22 May 1992, p. 3).

Current trade problems

There was a shift to hard currency pricing at current world market prices after 1 January 1991. In anticipation of this, Poland and the Soviet Union decided (on 17 May 1990) to conduct 10–15 per cent of their 1990 trade in hard currency. As with the other former Comecon countries, Poland has been badly hit by the decline in this trade since the start of 1991. In 1989 over a third of Poland's trade was with the former Comecon countries, but in 1991 this fell to only 17 per cent (Christopher Bobinski and Anthony Robinson, *FT*, 22 May 1992, p. 3). In 1988 the EC accounted for 28 per cent of Poland's total exports and imports, but in 1991 the EC took 54 per cent of exports and 48 per cent of imports (David Marsh, *FT*, 11 May 1992, p. 4). Poland's convertible currency current account in $billion was as follows (*OECD Economic Outlook*, June 1992, p. 43): 1988, –0.3; 1989, –1.2; 1990, 0.7; and 1991, –2.1 (estimated). In 1990 Poland achieved a surplus of $1.2 billion on its trade balance with the OECD countries, but this turned into a deficit of $2.7 billion in 1991 (David Marsh, *FT*, 11 May 1992, p. 4).

Trade agreements with the ex-Soviet republics have not all gone smoothly, e.g. the December 1991 agreement with Russia to supply gas (among other things like oil) had to be re-negotiated in January 1992 when gas supplies were deficient.

Foreign aid

Poland's pleas for substantial debt forgiveness and other forms of generous Western aid fell on deaf ears for a long time. 'He who helps quickly helps twice,' said (former) Prime Minister Mazowiecki on entering office. Foreign financial aid has been running at about 3–5 per cent of GNP since Solidarity came to power (Jeffrey Sachs, *IHT*, 16 May 1991, p. 6). The Western aid to date includes the following:

1. $1 billion stabilization fund from twenty-two Western countries ($300,000 grant plus $700,000 credit).

2. IMF stand-by loan of $725 million (February 1990). IMF credit of $1.6 billion over three years (19 April 1991). In the summer of 1991 the IMF suspended a tranche of $104 million because most of the conditions had not been met.

3. EC-co-ordinated food and agricultural aid programme of July 1989 worth $302 million. 'Counterpart funds' involved the domestic sale of Western agricultural products for zloties which were then used e.g. to improve food processing. The EC co-ordinated G24 (Group of Twenty-four) aid programme is called Phare. In 1990 Poland and Hungary were to benefit to the tune of $370 million.

4. USA (18 November 1989): $852 million over three years.

5. UK: £50 million 'know-how' fund, e.g. advice in financial and privatization programmes, training of managers. An extra £7.7 million was granted on 26 May 1992 to promote the development of small businesses.

6. World Bank: $781 million for five projects since January 1990, e.g. $360 million to improve the export sector (possible $2.5 billion over the next three years).

7. Debt rescheduling: on 16 February 1990 the 'Paris Club' (Western government creditors – the 'London Club' involves banks), which was owed about $27.7 billion at the end of 1989, granted an eight year grace period before repaying the $9.4 billion interest and principal in arrears or due before March 1991.

8. On 14 March 1991 Western governments agreed to forgive about half the $33 billion owed to them because of Poland's example of rapidly converting to a market economy; the high percentage of debt owed to governments (total debt was $48.5 billion and $11 billion was owed to banks) is the result of Poland ceasing repayments to governments only in the early 1980s (Steven Greenhouse, *IHT*, 16 March 1991, p. 9). The net present value of the government debt would be reduced by 50 per cent over two stages, 30 per cent over the first stage, lasting three years (amounting to an 80 per cent reduction in interest payments, the annual interest payments being reduced from $3.3 billion to $660 million) and 20 per cent over the second stage. The first stage of debt forgiveness was dependent on signing an IMF agreement and the second on fulfilment of its terms. Creditor

governments were able to choose from three options: forgiving principal, offering below-market interest rates, or transforming interest payments into principal and then offering low interest rates. Germany was the largest creditor nation, with $10 billion (DM 4.5 billion is to be written off); France was owed $5.2. Individual countries might offer a further 10 per cent debt concession. On 20 March the USA announced that it would write off 70 per cent in total (of the $2.9 billion debt; an extra 10 per cent would be unilaterally reduced and the other 10 per cent would be converted into zloties and spent on the environment), while France announced on 7 April that 60 per cent in total had been offered.

It should be noted that considerable concern has been expressed internationally about the illegal buying of Polish debt by Polish officials for down to 20 per cent of its nominal value (the 1988 agreement with lenders forbade this). Fozz (Foreign Debt Servicing Fund), set up in early 1989, was closed down at the end of 1990. Janusz Sawicki, the deputy finance minister and chief debt negotiator, was dismissed on 23 August 1991. He was followed eight days later by Grzegorz Wojtowicz, the head of the National Bank. The debt–service ratio in 1990 was 71 per cent (*The Economist*, 2 March 1991, p. 120.).

9. Aid amounts to about $4 billion a year, $2.5 billion from the IMF, the World Bank and Western governments and $1.5 billion from the annual reduction of the debt service burden (Jeffrey Sachs, *The Independent*, 12 July 1991, p. 21). Aid approved since June 1989 includes: IMF $3 billion, World Bank $2.2 billion and G24 $8.1 billion (*The Economist*, Survey, 12 October 1991, p. 49).

Foreign capital

Amendments were introduced to existing legislation early on. There were to be no constraints on repatriating hard currency profits, but only 15 per cent of domestically generated profits could be repatriated; unsuccessful ventures could only be liquidated after ten years; there was to be a three year tax holiday; the foreign partner had to contribute at least $50,000 and at least 20 per cent of the shares.

On 14 June 1991 the Sejm approved a draft foreign investment law (it also needed the approval of senate and the president). The following apply:

1. Foreigners are able to buy more than 10 per cent of the shares in privatization issues on condition that they obtain a licence from the Privatization Ministry.

2. The areas of the economy where licences are needed to operate are limited to the management of ports and airports, armaments production, real estate dealing, wholesale trade in imported consumer goods, and the provision of legal services.

3. The minimum contribution is ended.

4. There are no limits to the repatriation of profits for those investing more than the equivalent of Ecu 2 million (tax relief on profits is also available in this case, although it should not exceed the capital invested in the joint venture). On the other hand, the automatic tax holiday was ended.

5. Interior Ministry permission is needed for land sales to foreigners.

The Central Statistical Office estimate that $198 million of foreign capital had been invested by the end of 1990 (Christopher Bobinski, *FT*, 15 June 1991, p. 2); so far nearly 4,000 foreign investment licences have been issued (p. 2). By the end of March 1991 3,750 joint ventures had been registered (*IHT*, 5 August 1991, p. 9). Foreign investment amounts to less than $1 billion (*The Guardian*, 22 January 1992, p. 11). Since 1989 6,000 joint ventures have been registered; foreign investment amounted to around $1 billion (Blaine Harden, *IHT*, 11 February 1992, p. 21). Official figures show that 5,000 joint ventures and foreign-owned projects were in place by the end of 1991, with a declared investment value of $690 million (Anthony Robinson and Christopher Bobinski, *FT Survey*, 28 April 1992, p. vii).

AGRICULTURE

Farmers have been badly affected by the 'shock' treatment and have been demanding minimum guaranteed prices, lower interest rates on credit and high tariffs on imported food. The minister for agriculture Czeslaw Janicki resigned on 5 July 1990 over his failure to persuade the government to do more to help the sector. The OECD estimates that farms were barely subsidized at all in 1991 and there was a 36 per cent fall in farm incomes between the last half of 1990 and the first half of 1991 (*The Economist Survey of the European Community*, 11 July 1992, p. 25).

The government, however, has provided some assistance. There was the promise to provide guaranteed prices above market levels for the 1990 grain harvest (a record 28 million tonnes, up 1.5 million tonnes on 1989: *FT Survey*, 2 May 1991, p. x), while there had already been some intervention purchasing in the case of pigs and wheat. Price support for sugar producers was introduced. Subsidies were extended to whole milk as well as skimmed, because the latter encouraged excess production of butter, while extra funds were made available to modernize the dairy sector as a whole. On 26 July 1990 the government introduced a two month ban on the sale of the grain supplied as food aid by the West in order to support prices. The EC expressed some unhappiness at keeping on supplying grain when Poland became able to export. In April 1991 food tariffs were increased by 10 per cent on average and there were further increases in August. Towards the end of February 1992 guaranteed minimum prices were introduced for milk, wheat and rye by the Olszewski government.

The more radical free-marketeers hope that the pressure on the sector will encourage the growth of larger farms (Christopher Bobinski, *FT*, 21 March 1990, p. 3).

Existing state farms are likely to be converted into genuine co-operatives; the World Bank pinpoints great efficiency gains in the privatization of state marketing and processing (*FT Survey*, 2 May 1991, p. x). Fallenbuchl (1991: 65) considers that state farms are expected to be privatized as complete units, perhaps becoming limited stock companies, partnerships or state experimental farms; it appears that the legality of the agrarian reform of the late 1940s has been accepted and that any illegal expropriations would be compensated in the form of government securities or capital vouchers. Mizsei (1992: 295) points out that the economic significance of restitution is very modest, partly because of the structure of land ownership and partly because the pre-war capitalist class consisted mainly of Jews and Germans whose ownership cannot be re-established for the most part. Ash (1992: 24) makes the following points about state farms: their break-up is not envisaged and instead they will either be sold, rented or kept in state hands; purchasers must have a viable commercial strategy; state farm workers are to have priority in privatization and are to be permitted to buy their houses or apartments. In 1991 the state grain processing and trading agency was broken up (p. 34).

24

ROMANIA

POLITICAL BACKGROUND

The collapse of the Ceausescu regime was dramatic. At the congress held 20–4 November 1989 Nicolae Ceausescu was unanimously re-elected leader and president. But on 21 December he was booed by elements of what was meant to be a supportive rally; the next day the National Salvation Front (NSF) took over running the country, formally being sworn in as the government four days later. It was not a bloodless revolution, over a thousand people losing their lives. There is dispute about the extent to which the revolution was spontaneous, with allegations of an organized coup playing a significant role. The cowing of the population by the Ceausescu regime, including most intellectuals, certainly left a political vacuum filled by the NSF. Smith (1992) argues that the destruction of 'civil society', plus the exceptionally broad industrial structure with its obsolete capital stock (partly a result of manic debt repayment), make for a particularly rough ride for Romania in its transition to a new society and economy.

On 26 December Ion Iliescu became president of the Council for National Salvation and Petre Roman prime minister (he retained the premiership after the May 1990 election). Ceausescu and his wife Elena were executed on Christmas Day. On 29 December 1989 the 'Socialist Republic' became simply 'Romania' and one-party rule was formally abolished. Freedom to travel abroad was announced on 3 January 1990. On 2 February 1990 the Provisional Council of National Unity was set up, with representatives of other parties and groups; the council, however, was not able to veto government decisions.

The general election

The Romanian general election took place on 20 May 1990 for the Assembly of Deputies and the Senate (119 seats). The results for the Assembly of Deputies are shown in Table 24.1. The NSF won ninety-two of the 119 seats in the Senate. On the same day Ion Iliescu was elected president with a massive percentage of the vote (85.07), Radu Campeanu of the liberals coming second with 11 per cent.

The main economic elements of the party programmes were as follows:

Table 24.1 The Romanian general election of May 1990

	Seats	*% vote*
National Salvation Front	263	66
Hungarian Democratic Union	29	7
National Liberal Party	29	6
Ecology movement	12	3
National Peasants' Party	12	3
Other	51	15
Total	396	100

The National Salvation Front. While generally in favour of a mixed and regulated market economy, the NSF adopted a very cautious approach. The state sector was to remain dominant, although an expansion of private enterprise (for example, services) was to be encouraged. Rapid marketization and privatization would lead to large-scale unemployment. A minimum wage and a forty-hour week were offered. A cautious attitude was also needed towards both foreign investment (the slogan was 'We shall not sell off the country') and price reforms. While collective farms were to remain the mainstay of agriculture, peasants should be able to obtain land which they would be free to manage themselves (though not to sell).

National Liberal Party. The leader is Radu Campeanu. The platform offered rapid privatization, transfer to a market economy, debureaucratization and removal of communist managers.

National Peasants' Party. The leader is Corneliu Coposu. The party adopted a much less cautious approach to the market and to privatization than the NSF, but a more cautious one than the liberals towards foreign capital (an attitude fostered by the power of German capital in the inter-war period). As regards agriculture, a radical platform was adopted: the collective farm system should be abolished and land tenure given to the working farmers. Long leases would ultimately progress to full ownership of the land.

Geza Domokos leads the Hungarian Democratic Union.

Extreme nationalist parties have also emerged such as the Romanian National Unity Party (which incorporates the Romanian Unity Alliance and elements of Vatra Romaneasca and the Republican Party).

Although the campaign and the election itself were flawed, international observers were broadly satisfied; the large margin of victory was an indication of clear majority public support for the NSF and for Iliescu. However, anti-government demonstrations continued (especially against ex-communist activists holding power) and international disapproval was expressed verbally and concretely when miners brutally cleared Bucharest of the demonstrators 14–15 June 1990 (e.g. the decision of the EC not to sign a trade and co-operation agreement until 22 October 1990, and denial of most Western aid; G24 aid was not extended to Romania until 30 January 1991). There did seem to be an anti-socialist prejudice in the Western response, however. There was certainly the danger that indebtedness to groups like the miners could prove inhibiting to economic reform.

The Roman and Stolojan governments

At the NSF's first national convention, Petre Roman was re-elected party leader (17 March 1991) and gained approval for the reshaping of the NSF into a social democratic party committed to a market-based economy. A new 'steering college' was also established. On 29 April there was a substantial cabinet change. Three ministers from outside the NSF were recommended by Roman: Mihnea Marmeliuc (Labour and Social Protection: but disowned by the National Liberal Party); Dinu Patriciu (Public Works: member of the youth wing of the National Liberal Party); Valeriu Pascaru (minister of agriculture and food in charge of land reform and privatization; he is a member of the Agrarian Party). Viktor Stanculescu was moved from defence to industry. The Finance Ministry was merged with the Economics Ministry (still headed by Eugen Dijmarescu); thus Theodor Stolojan was dropped. Patriciu and the recommended sports minister Radu Berceanu, however, were not approved by parliament.

On 22 March 1991 a treaty on 'co-operation, good neighbourliness and friendship' was signed by Romania and the Soviet Union. They pledged that neither would participate in any alliance directed against the other and that neither would allow the use of its territory by a third party to commit an act of aggression against the other. Romania considers that the treaty does not rule out future membership of Nato, however, because it is a 'defensive' rather than a 'hostile' defence organization.

The Roman government fell in September 1991, the result of violent demonstrations from the 25th to the 28th in Bucharest by miners (joined by some ordinary citizens) demanding improved pay and working conditions, a price freeze and political changes (including Iliescu's and Roman's resignations). Economic concessions and the use of force by the police restored order. Theodor Stolojan became prime minister on 1 October 1991. He is a staunch, pro-market reformer, a technocrat who vowed not to stand in the forthcoming election. A coalition government was approved on the 18th, the twenty-one-member cabinet including six from the NSF and four representatives from the Liberal Party. Nine were independents, but there was one each from the Democratic Agarian Party and from the Romanian Ecology Movement. The finance minister was George Danielescu and the director of the National Privatization Agency was Adrian Severin, who had also resigned from the Roman government because of the slow pace of reforms. A new election was to be held (later fixed for 27 September 1992; see postscript for result). The new prime minister said that the previously announced Roman freeze on the prices of fuel, energy, basic foodstuffs, rents on state properties and state services would continue (only a limited amount of petrol per individual would continue to be subsidized). The subsidies on these products would be gradually reduced over the next two years. Wages were to be index-linked, with miners allowed to keep the rises already granted. The reform programme was also set to continue. Indeed Stolojan promised to accelerate the transition to the market while persevering with macroeconomic stabilization. The reform measures, outlined on 6 November 1991, are dealt with later in the chapter.

The new constitution was approved in a referendum held 8 December 1991; there was a 67 per cent turn-out and 77 per cent of those who voted approved.

In local elections held 9 and 23 February 1992 fourteen opposition parties (including the Liberal Party, the Peasants' Party, the Hungarian Democratic Union and Civic Alliance), combining to form the Convention for Democracy, did especially well in the major cities. But the National Liberal Party later left the Convention.

At the NSF convention held 27–9 March 1992 Petre Roman was re-elected party leader, with majority support for his vision of a Western-style social democracy. The vote for the presidential candidate was delayed; thus there was no automatic selection of Ion Iliescu, who would have to accept the Roman line if he were to be chosen. In fact Iliescu decided to stand on behalf of 'Democratic NSF', which split off in April 1992.

THE ROMAN GOVERNMENT'S ECONOMIC PROGRAMME

The austerity programme

On 1 January 1990 Iliescu announced the cancellation of 'megalomaniac' construction projects such as the Danube–Bucharest Canal and the House of the Republic in the capital, the money saved to be spent on repairs to buildings damaged during the revolution. Banking reforms were declared a priority, a Western-style division into a central bank and commercial banks being the aim. Some early price rises were imposed, e.g. on 11 July there were substantial increases in the price of petrol, water, newspapers and luxury goods.

As part of the 'leap towards the market', on 1 November the leu was devalued from twenty-one to thirty-five to the US dollar (having been reduced from sixteen to twenty-one in January 1990; on 1 April 1991 there was a further devaluation, from thirty-five to sixty to the US dollar). The aim was to make the leu internally convertible by early 1992. Export subsidies were to be eliminated and most price controls were to be lifted. Roman foresaw price rises in the 100–20 per cent range, although controls would be retained for twelve products, such as domestic energy, bread, meat, sugar, butter and rents (subsidies for rents and household heating were to remain until early 1992); partial indexation of monthly earnings (some 70 per cent) and pensions (750 lei and 400 lei respectively) would be coupled with a minimum wage. Energy subsidies for industry were to be reduced to bring prices into line with those paid by households. An increase in inflation and unemployment was foreseen. Public protests during December, including trade unions, however, led to a six-month postponement of the January price reforms until 1 June 1991 (later shifted forward to 1 April; a maximum price increase of 125 per cent was laid down for the most basic commodities). The 1st April 1991 also saw the introduction of a progressive personal income tax system, with rates between 6 per cent and 45 per cent. The finance minister (Teodor Stolojan) and the minister of state for industry and trade (Anton Vatasescu) submitted their resignations on 20 March 1991 because the economic reform programme was not radical enough and because of the extent of wage compensation for price increases (the resignations, however, were subsequently withdrawn), e.g. the 1 April price liberalization still left some price ceilings and cash compensations. Petrol prices were doubled on 1 September 1991. The political disturbances of 1991 led to a partial price freeze on 8 October; the goods and services affected were bread, milk, edible oils, sugar, meat, public transport and state housing rents, with prices frozen until April or perhaps even July 1992. On 5 May 1992 the remaining 25 per cent subsidies on basic consumer goods were removed.

In its submission to the IMF Romania planned a budget deficit of 25 billion lei (1.5 per cent of GNP) in 1991 (Ariane Genillard, *FT*, 28 March 1991, p. 3). But the actual budget deficit in 1991 was 3.1 per cent of GDP (United Nations Economic Commission for Europe 1992: 94).

Table 24.2 Romania: unemployment

		No. unemployed	Unemployment rate (%)
1991	March	79,200	0.7
	May	138,900	1.2
	June	169,900	1.6
	July	217,100	2.0
	August	237,800	2.2
	September	260,500	2.4
	October		
	November		
	December	337,500	3.1
1992	January		
	February		
	March		4.9
	April		
	May		
	June		
	July	700,000	6.0
	August		
	September		8.0
	October		
	November		
	December		

Sources: Economic Bulletin for Europe, 1991, vol. 43, p. 28; United Nations Economic Commission for Europe (1992: 68); Commission of the European Communities, *Employment Observatory*, 1992, no. 2, p. 9, no. 3, p. 9; Deutsche Bank, *Focus: Eastern Europe*, 1992, no. 58, p. 5.

Tables 24.2 and 24.3 show the record as regards unemployment, output and prices.

Marketization

After the downfall of Ceausescu there was a decentralization of decision-making in the economy. For example, the then minister of the national economy, Victor Stanculescu, suggested that the state would control the production and distribution of 400 basic materials, compared with 2,000 previously (reported by Victor Mallet, *FT*, 22 January 1990, p. 16). Rigid

Table 24.3 Romania: foreign debt and rates of growth of GDP, industrial output, agricultural output and prices (%)

GDP	
1990	1991
−8.2	−14.0

Industrial output	
1990	1991
−19.8	19.0

Agricultural output	
1990	1991
−2.9	

Inflation	
1990	1991
4.2	161.0

Net debt ($ billion)	
End 1990	End 1991
0.7	2.8

Sources: Economic Bulletin for Europe, 1991, vol. 43, p. 28; EEN, 1992, vol. 6, no. 4, p. 5; C. Jones, The Banker, May 1991, p. 3; The Economist, Survey, September 1991, p. 5; Euromoney, Supplement on Romania, Sept–Oct 1991, p. 2; Fry and Nuti (1992: 29); DIW, Economic Bulletin, 1992, vol. 29, no. 4, p. 5; OECD, Economic Outlook, June 1992, pp. 41–2, December 1992, pp. 125–6; United Nations Economic Commission for Europe (1992: 45, 65, 86, 93, 298, 302, 304); UN, World Economic Survey, 1992, p. 194.

plan targets were relaxed, but state guidelines given to enterprises which were able to make independent sales and purchases (including abroad). Emphasis was to be placed on indirect steering via economic levers, but these were inadequate at first. The *centrala* were to be abolished by March 1991 (*EEN*, 1990, vol. 4, no. 21, p. 6). Montias (1991) describes the system in the first ten months of post-Ceausescu rule in the following terms: a very loosely co-ordinated system with limited market elements (p. 185); the old planning system was weakened without being dismantled; according to official figures the number of material balances was reduced from 2,200 in 1989 to around 600; conditions were chaotic, e.g. enterprises did not know what materials allocation they would receive (p. 187).

The economy quickly became a shambles, caught between two stools; an official statement maintained that 'The old command structures persist, but they cannot operate. The bold option has been taken for a market economy, but it cannot operate because there are no structures to make it work' (quoted by Michael Simmons, *The Guardian*, 15 March 1991, p. 21). In the autumn of 1990 parliament passed a law giving state enterprises financial autonomy; this meant they could draw up contracts with private businesses (Ariane Genillard, *FT*, 4 June 1991, p. 11).

On 28 June 1990 Prime Minister Petre Roman gave an enthusiastic outline of policy regarding marketization (note that there were differences of opinion within the government). 'Our foremost mission is to make a historic transition of unprecedented scope, namely from a super-centralized economy to a market economy. The state must abandon to the greatest possible extent its role as proprietor and manager.' Many enterprises had performed badly, with production falling and wages increasing: 'such a course can lead to an uncontrollable explosion of the economic mechanism'. In mining, engineering, construction and light industry there was an 'unjustified and intolerable' fall in productivity. (On 9 April Roman had cited an 18 per cent fall in production during the first quarter of 1990, compared to the same period in 1989, and a 16 per cent increase in wages). 'The present state of the economy can only be overcome by radical reform, carried out in quick steps. Plastic surgery and artificial adjustments of the old structures cannot but deepen our crisis.' Roman's shift in attitude towards the market was influence by a rapidly deteriorating economic performance and the collapse of central planning. In an 18 October 1990 speech to parliament, he announced a 'leap towards a market economy', to run until June 1992.

In July 1991 the government wrote off up to half the internal debt accumulated by state enterprises (*EEN*, 'General Briefing on Romania', 20 August 1991, p. 5).

A new constitution was adopted by parliament on 21 November 1991; it defines Romania as a market economy and guarantees private property rights.

Labour

Legislation was quickly introduced to improve pay and working conditions. At the end of December 1989 a number of Ceausescu provisions were abolished, e.g. the requirement that six days of 'patriotic labour' a year had to be donated or a tax paid instead (students also no longer had to work two days a month in enterprises) and the fining of workers and managers for not fulfilling plan norms. Seventy-five per cent of wages would still be paid if production were halted because of input shortages. A general five day working week has been in operation since March 1990 (previously three Saturdays in a month had to be worked). Miners have been particularly favoured: from 1 February 1990 a five day rather than a six day working week (a reduction in weekly hours from forty-two to thirty); a generous productivity scheme; double pay for shifts worked on national holidays; full pay during hospitalization due to work; pensions for widows of miners killed underground; and a safety programme.

The relaxation of labour controls has had inflationary consequences. On 28 June 1990 Petre Roman called for a six month moratorium on wage claims due to pay increasing much faster than (the actually falling) productivity. During this period the state would maintain the real value of pay. A wage inflation tax is designed to dampen wage increases; an 80 per cent tax rate applies above a certain ceiling (*EEN*, 'General Briefing on Romania', 20 August 1991, p. 4).

A new unemployment compensation scheme was approved on 4 December 1990, with 80 per cent of wages being received during the first six months. After this some workers would be retrained and others offered credits to start up their own businesses. Workers would contribute 1 per cent of their pay and employers 4 per cent into the scheme. (Note that many farmers and those with private incomes above a certain limit are not eligible.) At present the typical situation is that the unemployed receive between 50 per cent and 60 per cent of their last monthly net wage for six months, depending on length of service (Commission of the European Communities, *Employment Observatory*, 1992, no. 1, p. 20).

Independent trade unions are now allowed. The largest federation of free trade union is Fratia (Fraternity). The trade union situation is as follows (*EEN*, 1990, vol. 4, no. 24): the National Provisional Committee for Organizing Free Trade Unions (successor to the official trade union body) has a membership of about 3 million; Inter-syndical Union 1.3 million membership; Alpha 1.3 million (Alpha's policy is to distribute all the nation's assets by means of share vouchers, individual distribution being dependent on length of service). According to Jacques Neher (*IHT*, 15 January 1992, p. 11), more than 50 per cent of the 11 million workforce now belong to trade unions.

Privatization

The NSF has allowed tenants to buy some of the state housing stock, partly to reduce the monetary overhang. By mid-1991 50 per cent of state housing had been sold to the public (*Euromoney*, Supplement on Romania, September–October 1991, p. 8).

Under Ceausescu the private non-agricultural sector was practically non-existent. In October 1990 there were 70,000 private enterprises, only 5 per cent of which made material goods (Lucian Croitoru, *Romanian Economic Observer*, November–December 1990, p. 62). By mid-May 1991 the number had increased to 142,713, of which 48,300 were in the 'productive sphere' (*PlanEcon Business Report*, 1991, vol.1, no.13, p. 11). In March 1990 four categories of private economic activity were authorized (*IHT*, 8 February 1990, p. 11; *EEN*, 1990, vol. 4, no. 8,

p. 2): (1) small enterprises employing up to 20 people, (2) profit-making local 'associations' (co-operatives), with a maximum of ten individuals (e.g. lawyers), (3) family businesses, (4) self-employment.

The regulatory body is the National Commission for Small Industries and Services, directed by Virgil Pasu. Armaments, alcohol and drug production, petroleum and mineral extraction, and the printing of books are not permitted. Finance can come from individuals, bank credits or, with the authorization of the Foreign Trade Bank, from foreigners. Small enterprises can set their own prices and either trade direct with foreign companies or via the existing foreign trade organizations. All foreign currency earnings are to be held in the Foreign Trade Bank and 50 per cent have to be compulsorily converted into lei. Small enterprises can associate and work together, with the approval of the new commission. There is a progressive tax system, with a maximum profits tax rate of 50 per cent.

In May 1990 Prime Minister Petre Roman, a more radical reformer by nature than Iliescu (Iliescu believes in an active role for the state in furthering technical progress and industrial modernization, for example), announced that privatization should be rapid in certain sectors of the economy like tourism, foreign and domestic trade, and construction. There followed two pieces of legislation.

1. On 31 July 1990 the privatization bill passed through the Assembly of Deputies and the Senate (Smith 1992: 215–16; *EEN*, 1990, vol. 4, no. 16, p. 3). The state would retain complete control of 20 per cent of enterprises (including mines, post, telecommunications, airlines, steel, railways, armaments and energy). Eighty per cent of state enterprises were to be converted into joint stock 'commercial companies' before privatization. The National Agency for Privatization, supposedly starting in the first quarter of 1991, would distribute free to adult residents (except criminals convicted on 'moral and financial' grounds) 30 per cent of the value of the capital of these joint stock companies in the form of vouchers exchangeable for shares. Shares could be sold only on condition that both seller and buyer had resided in Romania for a year after the period of distribution. A possible 30 per cent of the shares of a particular enterprise was to be offered to employees over eighteen years of age, who had worked at that enterprise for at least five years. Payment could be in the form of cash (special credit facilities were to be made available) or vouchers. A block of shares was to be reserved for foreigners. The sale of shares to the public was expected to start in the last quarter of 1991.

After considerable debate the privatization law was finally passed by both the Assembly of Deputies and the Senate, and promulgated by the president on 12 August 1991. Five Private Ownership Funds (in effect mutual funds) were to be set up and to receive 30 per cent of the shares of the commercialized enterprises (in mixed bags of the more and less efficient enterprises) for free distribution, in turn, to adult Romanian citizens (they lack savings). Each citizen was to receive a certificate of ownership in each of the funds and the fund shares would be tradeable. The remaining 70 per cent of the shares of commercialized enterprises were to be held in a State Ownership Fund; the privatization process was to proceed via a number of channels, including auctions, direct sell-offs and sales to foreigners. Of the 70 per cent, 10 per cent of shares was to be sold to employees of the enterprises at a 10 per cent discount and the remaining 60 per cent was to be sold off eventually to Romanian and foreign private investors (*Euromoney*, Supplement on Romania, September–October 1991, p. 6). The board of governors of each Private Ownership Fund would initially be chosen by the government and approved by parliament (p. 7). The certificates in the funds would be tradeable with other Romanian nationals after one year, but could not be transferred to foreigners for five years (p. 7). Initially the certificates carry no voting rights, but within five years each fund board must determine a procedure for the owners to elect a new board. The State Ownership Fund was obliged to reduce its holdings by 10 per cent annually (p. 7).

A more rapid privatization of small industrial and service enterprises was to be carried out, including leasing and sales (credits will be available). The former restrictions have been removed. But by the end of March 1992 only around 180 out of several thousand smaller units had been sold by auction (Deutsche Bank, *Focus: Eastern Europe*, 1992, no. 51, p. 7).

2. On 8 August 1990 a new law was announced controlling private retailing, specifically the *biznitari* (profiteers and black-marketeers). It became illegal to add a retail margin of more than 10 per cent on unprocessed goods bought from state or co-operative enterprises, or 20 per cent on goods which had been repackaged or stored.

On 18 October 1990 Prime Minister Roman foresaw the privatization of half the value of the capital stock within three years (Montias 1991: 192). Some 6,000 commercial enterprises (53 per cent of the equity value of industry) were to be privatized over the next seven years, starting in June 1992 (*Euromoney*, Supplement on Romania, September–October 1991, p. 7); the remaining 340 enterprises would stay under the control of the state (p. 7). In the meantime as many as thirty large enterprises were to be sold, starting in January 1992 (p. 7). In fact the schedule for privatizing these thirty enterprises was not set out until 5 May 1992 (*EEN*, 1992, vol. 6, no. 10, p. 5).

The first private bank was opened on 15 April 1991. As regards bank loans that were used to cover past losses by enterprises, these were due to be replaced by the end of September 1991 with non-negotiable government instruments held by the National Bank of Romania (*Euromoney*, Supplement on Romania, September–October 1991, p. 8).

FOREIGN TRADE, AID AND CAPITAL

Foreign trade

In February 1990 the tourist and commercial exchange rates were combined (twenty-one lei to the US dollar).

On 11 September 1990 it was announced that enterprises could retain 30 per cent of the hard currency earned from exporting for their own use (50 per cent from February 1991). (The remainder of earnings has to be sold to the state at the official rate of sixty lei to the dollar: Ariane Genillard, *FT*, 4 June 1991, p. 11.) Since 1 October 1990 auctions have enabled enterprises with spare foreign exchange to sell to other enterprises. Romanian banks started trading foreign exchange on 18 February 1991. Since 3 May 1991, as part of the drive towards convertibility, the leu has been the only legal tender (except that hard currency can be used in duty-free shops, free zones, payments made by diplomats and at airports and ports). The new Stolojan government declared 'residents'' convertibility (for current account transactions; see glossary) on 6 November 1991, unifying the official rate (sixty lei to the US dollar) and the (fluctuating) interbank rate (the Roman government had planned this move on 1 October). On 5 May 1992 Romanian enterprises were freed from the obligation to sell a percentage of their hard currency earnings to the state; the state would intervene in the foreign exchange market to try to stabilize the leu, albeit at a depreciated rate against the US dollar (*EEN*, 11 May 1992, p. 5).

For seven months from 1 October 1990 individual Romanians or foreign tourists were only able to take out of the country goods of very limited total value. In May 1991 limits were placed on the amount Romanians could take out of the country.

Quantitative restrictions on imports were removed at the start of 1991 (*Euromoney*, Supplement on Romania, September–October 1991, p. 4).

Romania's convertible currency current account was in deficit to the tune of $1.7 billion in 1990 and an estimated $1.0 billion in 1991 (*OECD Economic Outlook*, June 1992, p. 43).

Foreign aid

On 3 January 1990 foreign borrowing was permitted once again, Ceausescu having vowed not to borrow any more after claiming that the foreign debt had been paid off by the end of March 1989.

In February 1991 the EC granted food aid worth Ecu 500 million and agreed to extend the European Investment Bank's remit to Romania. The EC confirmed a $500 million loan on 11 November. The aid approved since June 1989 includes that granted by the IMF, $0.8 billion, the World Bank, $0.2 billion, and the G24, $1.5 billion (*The Economist*, Survey 12 October 1991, p. 49). A $300 million World Bank loan, due in November, was postponed at the end of September 1991. In June 1992 the World Bank announced a loan of $100 million for credits to private farmers (Virginia Marsh, FT, 10 July 1992, p. 28).

On 10 April 1991 a $748 million IMF credit was agreed. On 9 May 1991 the UK extended its 'know-how' fund to Romania.

Since December 1989 the USA has provided more than $100 million in humanitarian aid, mainly food and medicine, and $20 million in technical assistance; the USA also recently pledged $10 million to improve farming as part of a G24 package (*IHT*, 29 May 1992, p. 15).

Foreign capital

Judy Dempsey reports (*FT*, 18 October 1990, p. 3) that a draft law would allow foreign companies to buy up to 100 per cent of a Romanian enterprise. According to the *Romanian Economic Observer* (November–December 1990, pp. 20–1), the March 1990 legislation stipulated the following: a 30 per cent profits tax; a two-year tax holiday plus a

possible 50 per cent reduction in profits tax for another three years; a 50 per cent reduction to apply if profits were reinvested in Romania. The November 1990 law stipulates that, of the lei profits due to the foreign partner, a quota of 8–15 per cent of the foreign partner's capital contribution can be repatriated in hard currency obtainable from currency exchanges run by authorized banks. Under the April 1991 legislation profits in lei of up to 15 per cent of the investor's paid-in contribution to the capital of the commercial enterprises can be repatriated at the official exchange rate (sixty lei=one US dollar) and the remainder at the current auction rate (Judy Dempsey, *FT*, 10 August 1991, p. 2). Foreign investors are not allowed to own land or buy residential buildings unrelated to business investment (Judy Dempsey, *FT*, 16 April 1991, p. 18).

On 28 May 1992 Romania and the USA signed an investment treaty which pledged to 'encourage and protect investment'.

By October 1991 there were 4,800 joint ventures, with $210 million of foreign capital committed (Scott 1992: 56). Between January 1990 and the end of June 1992 direct foreign investment amounted to $387 million (Virginia Marsh, *FT*, 8 July 1992, p. 3).

AGRICULTURE

The 26th of December 1989 marked the end of the 'systematization' programme, the aim of which was to destroy 7,000 to 8,000 of the 13,000 villages and replace them with 550 'agro-industrial centres'. Food exports were suspended until mid-1990 (the Soviet Union agreed to suspend food imports from Romania the next month) in order to increase domestic supplies (neglected under Ceausescu in order to pay off the foreign debt) and food rationing was abolished. The following month it was decided to increase imports of animal feedstuffs to stimulate meat production. Even a 1992 source (Virginia Marsh, FT, 10 July 1992, p. 28) reports that the government banned the export of most staple food items because of poor prospects for that year's harvest. Early measures included increasing the size of private plots to half a hectare per member of the collective farm (Montias 1991: 188); compulsory deliveries from private peasants were abolished in January 1990 (p. 182).

Some indication of the extent of former statistical exaggeration can be seen in the figure for the 1989 grain harvest. In the autumn of 1989 Ceausescu announced a record harvest of over 60 million tonnes, but the actual figure turned out to be only 18.4 million tonnes (Judy Dempsey, *FT*, 17 May 1990, p. 42).

On 1 January 1990 Ion Iliescu announced a major change (decrees followed at the end of the month). Individual farmers could own up to 5,000 square metres of land each and sell the produce on free markets. Those belonging to co-operatives would have priority and had to work the land, this going 'to those who will cultivate the land themselves without engaging other people on subcontracts'. Those peasants forced to migrate to the towns would have the right to return to the countryside and receive 2,500 square metres if they promised to cultivate the land and pay a special tax. The land surrounding co-operative peasants' homes was to become private property and could be bequeathed to children. Gardens and courtyards in the towns confiscated by the party were to be returned to their former owners. After finishing work for the collective, farmers were also able to rent land on condition that at least 70 per cent of output was sold to the collective. Individuals were able voluntarily to form co-operatives with their private land if they wished, while those in existing collectives or state farms were entitled to elect a 'general assembly' (which decides production quotes and agrees delivery contracts with the state). Draft legislation foresaw an initial limit of 100 ha on individual land ownership and a five year ban on its resale; state farms were excluded from the proposals (*IHT*, 8–9 September 1990, p. 2). In an October 1990

speech the prime minister promised that peasants would be allowed to withdraw from the collective farm with land equivalent to that with which they entered, but monetary compensation would not be available in lieu (Montias 1991: 188).

On 18 January 1990 it was decreed that land (50,000 ha) and (forty-five) agro-industrial production units belonging to the communist party should be turned over to the state (all other property and sixty industrial enterprises were also affected).

A land law was passed in February 1991 (*EEN*, 'General Briefing on Romania', 20 August 1991, p. 4). Some 80 per cent of arable land was to be returned to its former owners. The land received from the state was limited to a maximum of 10 ha, although up to 100 ha was allowed through purchase or inheritance. Land received through restitution could be sold immediately; family members and neighbours had the right of first refusal on farm land for sale to deter fragmentation (Brooks *et al.* 1991: 158). Co-operative farmers were allowed, if a majority was in favour, to become shareholders.

By May 1990 the percentage distribution of agricultural land ownership was as follows: co-operatives 45.7; state 29.8; and peasant households 24.5 (compared with 61, 30 and 9 respectively in 1988) (Lucian Croitoru, *Romanian Economic Observer*, November–December 1990, p. 62). A later source puts the private sector's share of farm land at 36.7 per cent (Ash 1992: 20). Virginia Marsh (*FT*, 10 July 1992, p. 28) quotes the Ministry of Agriculture as saying that more than 70 per cent of agricultural land was now in private hands, but fewer than 120,000 out of 5.1 million new landowners had received title to their property. The lack of title means that private farmers cannot raise capital using land as collateral and that there are difficulties in buying and selling land. A later report gives a figure of 82 per cent of agricultural land in private hands (*FT*, 4 August 1992, p. 24).

25

YUGOSLAVIA

POLITICAL BACKGROUND

On 22 January 1990 the League of Communists of Yugoslavia decided, at its congress, to abolish the leading role of the party. This formally allowed the formation of independent parties, but some already existed in reality. On 29 July Prime Minister Ante Markovic announced that he was to form a new all-Yugoslav party, the League of Reform Forces.

The republican problem

The old Yugoslavia had disintegrated. The question was whether the country could hold together in some looser form and how many republics would decide to join. The past dogs the present. It is thought, for example, that of the 1.7 million Yugoslavs who were killed in 1941–45, about 1 million died in ethnic fighting, much of it Croat versus Serb (Blaine Harden, *IHT*, 24 June 1991, p. 4). A Croatian fascist (Ustasha, meaning 'uprising') puppet regime (the 'Independent State of Croatia') was set up by Nazi Germany in April 1941, led by Ante Pavelic (who had set up the Ustasha or Croatian Revolutionary Organization in 1929). The regime was responsible for the deaths of over 500,000 Serbs and 70,000 Jews in 1941–45 (Thomas Foran de Saint-Bar, *IHT*, 24 July 1991, p. 4).

Slovenia

The Deutsche Bank (*Focus: Eastern Europe*, 1991, no. 25, pp. 15–16) provides the following information: 2 million population (8 per cent of the Yugoslav total); 91 per cent are Slovenes;19 per cent share of Yugoslav GNP; indexed *per capita* income 210 (Yugoslav average: 100); industrial output 20 per cent of the Yugoslav total; exports 28.8 per cent of the Yugoslav total and imports 25 per cent; unemployment now over 10 per cent. In the late 1980s Slovenia generated 18 per cent of Yugoslav GNP, 21 per cent of total industrial production and 23 per cent of total exports (Ferfila 1991: 23); Slovenia owed 9.9 per cent of Yugslavia's hard currency foreign debt (p. 28). Thus Slovenia was the wealthiest republic in the old Yugoslavia. Independent Yugoslav parties made their first appearance in Slovenia, specifically after January 1989. In September 1989 Slovenia claimed the right to secede. On 22 January 1990 the Slovene delegates walked out of the congress of the League of Communists of Yugoslavia when its view of the need for relatively autonomous parties in the six republics and two provinces (a 'League of Leagues') did not gain general support. On 4 February the League of Communists of Slovenia (LCS) became known as the LCS–Democratic Renewal Party, formally becoming autonomous.

A free election took place on 8 April 1990, with the following results for the eighty-seat assembly. DEMOS (Democratic United Opposition of Slovenia, comprising six parties) won 55 per cent of the vote (forty-seven of the eighty seats in the assembly); Democratic Renewal Party 17 per cent; ZSMS (former Youth League)

460

14.5 per cent; and the Farmers' Party 12.8 per cent. DEMOS favoured secession as a last resort, if a very loose federation could not be achieved; it is pro-market and privatization (with nationalization as a first step), and supports a separate currency. There have been disputes, however, e.g. Joze Mencinger resigned his vice-presidency in April 1991 because he considered the marketization programme of the Slovene government to be too rapid and disagreed with the idea of issuing vouchers to the population, exchangeable for shares, in order to speed up the privatization programme. The privatization bill had not been passed to date and other economic legislation had also been delayed (Judy Dempsey, *FT* Survey, 30 March 1992, p. v). A new (convertible) currency, the tolar, was introduced on 8 October 1991. Domestic politics have not been plain sailing. Demos was formally dissolved at the end of 1991, the independence of Slovenia having been achieved. On 23 April 1992 Janez Drnovsek replaced Lojze Peterle as prime minister.

On 22 April Milan Kucan (Democratic Renewal) was elected president.

On 2 July 1990 Slovenia declared its 'independence' – Slovenian laws could override federal ones, the latter only applying when they do not conflict with the former. The Slovenian constitution was amended to this effect on 28 September; another amendment dealt with republican control over (civilian) territorial defence forces (on 2 October the federal presidency instructed Slovenia to overturn this). On 14 January 1991 Yugoslavia's constitutional court annulled Slovenia's declaration of sovereignty.

The 23 December 1990 referendum ('Do you want Slovenia to become an autonomous state?') produced an overwhelming 88.5 per cent positive response from a 94 per cent turnout. Six months of negotiations were allowed to see whether a sufficiently loose confederation could be arranged; otherwise Slovenia was to become independent. On 20 December the federal authorities threatened economic sanc-

tions if the referendum went ahead. On 20 February 1991 constitutional amendments were approved by the Slovenian parliament which specified the precedence of Slovenian over Yugoslav laws: 'All sovereign rights of the republic of Slovenia transferred to the Socialist Federal Republic of Yugoslavia are invalidated.' The federal presidency declared these amendments to be unconstitutional on 28 February. On 7 March 1991 the Slovenian parliament adopted a law which said that 'Slovene men will complete military service only in the republic's territorial defence units and police force unless they wish to serve in the Yugoslav People's Army'.

Croatia

The Deutsche Bank (*Focus: Eastern Europe*, 1991, no. 25, p. 10) provides the following information: population 4.7 million (20 per cent of the Yugoslav total); 75 per cent Croats and 12 per cent Serbs); 26 per cent of Yugoslav GNP; indexed *per capita* income 130 (Yugoslav average: 100). The second free election in Yugoslavia took place in Croatia, the first round on 22 April and the second on 6 May 1990. There is a tricameral parliament, with 116, 80 and 160 seats contested. The election was won by the Croatian Democratic Union, with sixty-seven, fifty-four and seventy-nine seats respectively (43 per cent, 54 per cent and 27 per cent of the votes). The SKH–SDP alliance (Party of Democratic Renewal – the former communist party – and the Socialist Party) did well, with 37.5 per cent, 34 per cent and 35 per cent respectively of the votes. The Croatian Democratic Union, like DEMOS in Slovenia, saw secession as a last resort if a very loose federation could not be realized; both republics supported 'an organization of sovereign states based on mutual agreement'.

The leader of the Croatian Democratic Union, Franjo Tudjman, became president. He was re-elected on 2 August 1992, and on the same day his party won the general election.

Unlike Slovenia, Croatia has a difficult minority problem. On 1 October 1990 the Serbian minority declared itself autonomous; the 'Serbian autonomous region of Krajina' was declared on 1 March 1991 (Kraijina means 'frontierland'). The declaration was repeated on 22 December after the Croatian constitutional changes. On 12 May 1991 a referendum in Krajina (declared illegal by Croatia) produced a turn-out of 95 per cent and a more than 90 per cent 'yes' vote to join Serbia and thus stay in Yugoslavia. On 19 December the three Serb areas of East Slavonia (Baranja and Western Srem), West Slavonia and Krajina (Banija, Kordun and Lika) declared an independent Serbian Republic of Krajina.

On 21 December 1990 the Croatian constitution was altered to declare sovereignty, the armed forces, diplomatic relations and international agreements all being affected. On 19 May 1991 Croatia held a referendum on whether to remain in the Yugoslav federation or to become independent with the option of joining other republics in a new alliance of sovereign states. The turn-out was 86 per cent and more than 94 per cent said 'yes' to an 'independent sovereign state'.

On 9 January 1991 the federal presidency ordered the army to disarm all 'illegally armed groups' by 19 January (later extended by two days). Both Slovenia and Croatia refused to comply at first, but the situation was defused by the 25 January agreement; Croatia agreed to demobilize (but not disband or disarm) its defence forces, while the Yugoslav army would 'lower the level of combat readiness'. On 30 January the Yugoslav army ordered the arrest of Martin Spegelj, the Croatian defence minister, on the grounds of plotting an armed rebellion; Croatia refused to comply. On 8 April 1991 the Yugoslav military court in Zagreb postponed his trial indefinitely after demonstrations.

Slovenia and Croatia agreed on 13 February 1991 that there should be a joint declaration of independence if either republic were attacked by the Yugoslav army. On 21 February 1991 Croatia, following Slovenia's lead the previous day, proclaimed the supremacy of Croatian laws over federal ones: all federal laws were invalidated which 'threaten Croatia's interests and sovereignty, territorial integrity or place the republic in an unequal position'. Four months were allowed before 'dissociation' began. The federal presidency ruled this Croatian supremacy to be unconstitutional on 28 February 1991.

Note that next to nothing has been done about economic reform. Indeed in February 1991 parliament decided to transform 'social' into state property in order to increase state control of the economy, although this was seen as an 'interim' measure before privatization. A market economy is policy. A new currency was introduced on 23 December 1991.

Serbia

The Deutsche Bank (*Focus: Eastern Europe*, 1991, no. 25, p. 12) provides the following information: population 10 million (41 per cent of the Yugoslav total); 67 per cent Serbs, 13 per cent Albanians and 4 per cent Hungarians; 35 per cent share of Yugoslav GNP; indexed *per capita* income 85 (Yugoslav average: 100). Serbian control over the autonomous province of Kosovo continued to tighten (Kosovo's population is around 2 million and some 90 per cent may now be Albanians). On 24 March 1990 Serbia took control of the police and on 5 July dissolved Kosovo's government and parliament; this was in response to the 114 Albanian parliamentary deputies declaring 'an independent and equal union within the Yugoslav federation with the same contractual status as the other republics' three days earlier. (Note that Albanians had formed the Democratic Forum on 1 July, the aim being to gain full republican status within the Yugoslav federation by peaceful means.) On 28 September Serbia promulgated a new republican constitution: Kosovo and Vojvodina came under even greater direct control, their status under the 1974 constitution being annulled (note that the federal constitution was not altered). Vojvodina's 2 million population largely comprises, in percentage terms, 54.4 Serbs, 18.9 Hungarians and 5.4 Croats. The powers of the Serbian president were increased, e.g. the ability to propose the Serbian prime minister and to dissolve parliament. On 24 May 1992 the Albanians in Kosovo managed to run their own unofficial presidential and parliamentary elections. Ibrahim Rugova was the successful (and only) candidate for president and the Democratic League of Kosovo was the successful party. Owing to discrimination and sackings Albanians have set up their own structures, such as in education and health.

Serbia threatened to reopen the republican border question if Slovenia and Croatia got their way. On 30 May 1991 Milosevic said that 'those who want to constitute their own national states must realise they cannot take with them compact parts of other nations who want to stay in Yugoslavia'. Something like 30 per cent of Serbs live outside Serbia.

In an all-Serbian referendum (boycotted by the Albanians of Kosovo) the vote was in favour of deferring multi-party elections until a new constitution was drawn up.

On 16 July 1990 the Serbian League of Communists and the Socialist Alliance merged to form the Serbian Socialist Party (SSP), Slobodan Milosevic being elected chairman the next day. The SSP programme is conservative, stressing an importance role for the state: 'full and unconditional privatization of social property has a transparent ideological motivation and sees it as an advocacy of general plunder and theft. . . ' (Laura Silber, *FT*, 19 July 1990, p. 2).

Relationships with Slovenia deteriorated. On 30 November 1989, 130 Serbian enterprises vowed to break off all economic links with Slovenia in retaliation for its ban on a Serbian rally in Ljublyana. After that there was a boycott of Slovenian goods by Serbia. On 23 October 1990 duties were imposed on Slovenian and Croatian 'imports' (on 14 January 1991 Yugoslavia's constitutional court ordered Serbia to lift these duties; they were replaced by, for example, compulsory deposits on 'imports' and higher rents for Croatian and Slovenian enterprises on Serbian soil). Slovenia retaliated and Croatia removed tariffs on imported foreign cars, thus depressing demand for Yugoslav cars (all made in Serbia), and imposed high taxes on holiday homes owned by Serbs. The federal government did get national agreement for all these trade restrictions to cease as of 1 June 1991, but implementation was uncertain even before the political situation deteriorated drastically.

Milosevic convincingly won the 9 December 1990 presidential election with 65 per cent of the vote, Vuk Draskovic (Party of Serbian Renewal) coming an unexpectedly poor second with only 16 per cent. The Serbian Socialist Party fought the parliamentary election campaign on a platform of Serbian nationalism, a strong Yugoslav federation, and promises of economic security. In the December 1990 election (rounds on the 9th and 23rd) the Serbian Socialist Party had a sweeping victory, winning 194 out of 250 seats (48 per cent of the vote); the opposition parties won only forty-eight seats (nineteen went to the Party of Serbian Renewal, Draskovich not being elected, and two to the League of Reform Forces) and the remainder to independents. On 24 May 1992 opposition parties and prominent intellectuals formed the Democratic Movement of Serbia (DEPOS).

Draft legislation seeks to create 'state capitalism' rather than a free enterprise system, by converting socially owned enterprises into state-owned entities (Laura Silber, *FT Survey*, 27 June 1991, p. 15). The Deutsche Bank (*Focus: Eastern Europe*, 1991, no. 25, p. 13) argues that although the new Serbian constitution, ratified in September 1990, calls for a market economy, government policy seems to favour a market-orientated fine tuning of the worker self-administration currently in place.

Bosnia-Hercegovina

The Deutsche Bank (*Focus: Eastern Europe*, 1991, no. 25, p. 9) provides the following information: population 4.6 million (19 per cent of the Yugoslav total); 40 per cent Moslems, 32 per cent Serbs and 18 per cent Croats); 12 per cent share of Yugoslav GNP; indexed *per capita* income 66 (Yugoslav average: 100). The ethnic mix has been estimated at 43.7 per cent, 31.3 per cent and 17.3 per cent repectively (*The Guardian*, 27 March 1992, p. 25). The Moslems were first counted as a separate nationality in the 1971 census. A free, multi-party election was held on 18 and 25 November 1990. The parties split along ethnic and religious lines mainly, namely the Croatian Democratic Union, the Serbian Democratic Union and the Moslem Union for Democratic Action. The League of Reform Forces also campaigned. The new president is the Moslem leader Alija Izetbegovic. He at first suggested a compromise 'asymmetrical community' in which Serbia, Bosnia-Hercegovina, Macedonia and Montenegro would form a Yugoslav union in loose association with Croatia and Slovenia. The Bosnia-Hercegovina and Macedonia plan envisaged a loose confederation, a 'community' of separate, sovereign states: there would be a federal police force and army, but each republic would also have its own security force (including an army) and foreign policy; federal offices and institutions would be spread all over the country; there would be a single currency.

Montenegro

The Deutsche Bank (*Focus: Eastern Europe*, 1991, no. 25, p. 12) provides the following information: population 0.7 million (3 per cent of the Yugoslav population), 69 per cent Montenegrins, 13 per cent Moslems and 6 per cent Albanians; 2 per cent share of Yugoslav GNP; indexed *per capita* income 73 (Yugoslav average: 100). The communist party polled well in the December 1990 election, as in Serbia, winning eighty-three of the 125 seats in parliament. The party changed its name to the Democratic Party of Socialists in June 1991. A close federation was policy. The president is Momir Bulatovic.

Macedonia

The Deutsche Bank (*Focus: Eastern Europe*, 1991, no. 25, p. 11) provides the following information: population 2.2 million (9 per cent of the Yugoslav total); 67 per cent Macedonians, 20 per cent Albanians and 4 per cent Turks); 6 per cent share of Yugoslav GNP; indexed *per capita* income 61 (Yugoslav average: 100). The first round of voting in the general election took place on 11 November 1990. The contesting parties included the League of Communists of Macedonia–Party of Democratic Change (thirty-one seats), the Albanian Party for Democratic Prosperity (in alliance with the People's Democratic Party) (twenty-five seats), the Macedonian National Front (a coalition of the Internal Revolutionary Macedonian Organization and the Movement for Macedonian Action) (thirty-seven seats) and the League of Reform Forces (nineteen seats). Non-communist parties won a majority of the 120 parliamentary seats; a tri-partite coalition government was formed between the first three parties listed. President Kiro Gligorov supported market liberalization and a decentralized federal government. The question asked in the 8 September 1991 referendum was whether to approve a sovereign and independent Macedonia which retained the option of joining a suitable union of sovereign Yugoslav states (including Slovenia and Croatia). The turn-out was over 75 per cent despite a boycott by Albanians and Serbs and the 'yes' vote was 99 per cent (i.e., some 74 per cent of registered voters). Parliament declared Macedonia a sovereign and independent state on 18 September 1991.

General political developments from 1991 onwards

Yugoslavia came close to civil war in the first half of 1991. On 2 March Serbs in the Croatian town of Pakrac clashed with Croatian police and the army helped restore order (on 29 March rebel Serbian police units occupied the Plitvice national park; there followed a clash with the Croatian police on the 31st and the army once more intervened; the army ordered out special Croatian police units). Serbia displayed its own lack of internal unity when anti-communist, mostly student-inspired demonstrations took place in Belgrade 9–14 March (and again a year later). Vuk Draskovic (leader of the Party of Serbian Renewal) was arrested for a few days; he demanded the resignation of the Serbian government. The immediate cause of the demonstrations was control of the media, especially television, by the Serbian Socialist Party led by Slobodan Milosevic. But severe economic problems were in the picture too, many workers not having been paid for months, for example. Concessions quickly followed, e.g. the head of television and four of the management team were sacked, detainees began to be released, and the interior minister, Radmilo Bogdanovic, offered to resign (the offer was accepted by the Serbian parliament on 10 April).

Federal authority declined even more. On 12 March the eight-member federal presidency met at the behest of the military and declared itself 'paralysed'. The president, Borisan Jovic (a Serb), stepped down on the 15th when the collective presidency (which is commander-in-chief of the Yugoslav armed forces) refused to heed the army request for 'adequate measures' to be taken (in effect declaring a state of emergency). The stepping down seemed to be part of a ploy to involve the army (on the 20th the Serbian parliament rejected Jovic's resignation when it became clear that the ploy had not worked). Vice-president Stipe Mesic (a Croat, who was due to take over the top position

in any case on 15 May) became acting president. Milosevic reacted on the 16th by not recognizing the presidency: 'I want to declare that the republic of Serbia will not recognize a single decision of the federal presidency, because in the existing circumstances any such decision would be illegitimate.' The Serbian withdrawal was supported by the representatives of Montenegro (Nenad Bucin) and Vojvodina (Jugoslav Kostic). Milosevic ordered the mobilization of reservists and the urgent formation of 'additional Serbian militia units'. The Serbian minority in Krajina (25 per cent of Croatian territory) declared independence from Croatia (on 1 April 1991 it was announced that Krajina was joining Serbia). Thus, in an ironic switch, Milosevic's policy was destroying the Yugoslav state which he had pledged to preserve as a tight federation.

But five members of the collective presidency still met (and were thus just quorate) and declared that it had 'opted for the path of democratic dialogue between the republics as the only real way to overcome the crisis'. The presidency refused to accept the resignation of the Kosovo representative, Riza Sapunzhia (which had been ordered by the Serbian parliament), on the grounds that he was responsible to the Kosovo parliament (suspended by Serbia). A meeting was called for the 21st. The army remained silent for a while but on 19 March issued a statement:

> The Yugoslav People's Army, as in the past, will not interfere in the political negotiations about the country's future. [But] . . . will under no circumstances allow armed inter-ethnic armed conflicts and civil war in Yugoslavia . . . will confidently secure the borders of Yugoslavia from all threats and will not allow any changes until agreement is reached about these borders in accordance with the country's constitution.

Milosevic, in a change of mind, attended the 21 March meeting of republican and federal leaders, which itself decided on future meetings of the republican leaderships to solve matters

465

peacefully. At the 21 March meeting the idea of a Yugoslav 'common market' was presented by the federal government, with a single currency and (independent) central bank. Milosevic and Tudjman met on 25 March and decided to try to settle the issue within two months. They agreed on removing Prime Minister Markovic from office and dividing parts of Bosnia-Hercegovina between them, leaving a separate Moslem republic.

On 12 April 1991 the collective presidency agreed to hold a referendum on the future status of Yugoslavia in each republic by the end of May. Slovenia, however, stressed that it had already held such a referendum (on 23 December 1990), which had committed it to become independent by 23 June, while Croatia would dissociate itself from the federation if an agreement was not reached by 30 June.

Early May 1991 saw further ethnic clashes in Croatia, with loss of life. On 5 May the collective presidency (in the absence of the Croatian president Tudjman) talked of the country being on the brink of civil war and authorized the Yugoslav army to intervene in ethnic conflicts. A soldier was killed in Split on 6 May. A three day emergency meeting of the collective presidency, the prime minister and the heads of the republics agreed the following on 9 May: (1) the army and the federal police would be given powers for one month to intervene in ethnic trouble spots in Croatia, but the army's request for a state of emergency was denied; (2) civilian armed units and police reservists would be disarmed; (3) Croatia's borders were inviolable; (4) a commission would investigate the problem. Implementation of the agreement, however, was another matter, e.g. Tudjman said that police reservists would only be demobilized in areas where there was tension, Croatian police would accompany the army and federal police, and he would only talk to lawfully elected Serbs in Croatia.

On 15 May 1991 the Croat Stipe Mesic was due to become president, but failed to get the minimum five (out of eight) votes necessary (Serbia, Kosovo and Vojvodina voted against and Montenegro abstained). On 19 May Prime Minister Markovic announced the members of a seven-member 'co-ordinating committee' (including the defence minister, Veljko Kadijevic, and the interior minister, Petar Gracanin). It became known that as of 6 May the USA had withdrawn aid (worth some $5 million a year) and also US support in international financial organizations (such as the IMF, which had already frozen a $1 billion stand-by loan, and the World Bank) for credits to Yugoslavia. The US Export–Import Bank was also expected to declare Yugoslavia uncreditworthy. The USA was especially concerned at the situation in Kosovo, but also at other things like the Mesic affair (the USA promised to renew aid if Mesic were to be elected). On 24 May the USA explained that the withdrawal of aid would be selective. On 19 June 1991 the CSCE conference expressed 'friendly concern and support for the democratic development, unity and territorial integrity of Yugoslavia'; the sides were urged to 'resolve their dispute peacefully', since it was recognized that it was up to the people of Yugoslavia to decide their own future.

The crunch came when Croatia and Slovenia (in that order) both unilaterally declared independence on 25 June 1991, a day earlier than anticipated. When the Yugoslav army moved to secure Slovenia's external borders, fighting broke out (in Croatia it took the form of ethnic Serb–Croat clashes). The European Community moved in quickly with a three-point plan, but it took three attempts to produce the Brioni agreement (7 July).

The initial three-point plan stipulated that: Stipe Mesic had to be confirmed as president (this was done on 30 June); there was to be no further movement towards independence for three months; negotiations were to start by 1 August at the latest; and the army was to withdraw to barracks. The Brioni agreement added the following: the federal army, under the control of the collective presidency, was allowed to patrol Slovenia's external borders with Austria, Italy and Hungary for the interval of the truce; the Slovene territorial forces were to be deactivated and had to return all equipment and weapons seized from the army; the Slovenian police could man the customs posts, but only 'acting in conformity with federal regulations'; thirty to fifty EC observers were to be sent to monitor the situation in Slovenia.

EC aid was suspended (followed by US aid on 7 July) and an arms embargo imposed. The EC had promised an Ecu 807 million loan over five years; in addition Ecu 35 million in 1991 and Ecu 100 million in 1992 as part of the G24 programme).

The crisis in Slovenia seemed to be resolved in favour of the republic when the collective presidency (with the exception of Mesic himself, apprehensive of the effects on Croatia) announced, on 18 July, that the Yugoslav army would leave Slovenia within three months: 'The command, units and institutions of the people's army should no longer be stationed on the territory of the republic of Slovenia until there is final agreement over the future of Yugoslavia.'

The situation in Croatia deteriorated rapidly, however, with heavy fighting and loss of life in the areas dominated by Serbs. The Yugoslav army was no longer under federal political control and sided more and more with the increasingly successful Serbs. A Croatian blockade of federal army barracks led to a large-scale attack by the army on 20 September 1991. President Mesic called for officers and soldiers to desert, saying that the generals were out of control, and Prime Minister Markovic called, unsuccessfully, for the resignation of Defence Minister General Veljko Kadijevic (note that he did resign on 8 January 1992, allegedly on health grounds, although the previous day the air force had shot down a helicopter carrying EC monitors; his 'temporary' replacement was chief-of-staff Blagoje Adzic). Various ceasefire agreements failed to stick, despite the involvement of the EC, CSCE and the Soviet Union. The Serbian strategy was to control the Serbian-dominated areas of Croatia (as part of 'Greater Serbia') and only allow the remainder of Croatia to secede.

On 8 October 1991 Croatia and Slovenia reactivated their 25 June declarations of independence, the three-month moratorium having expired. On 15 October Bosnia-Hercegovina issued a 'memorandum on sovereignty' (ethnic Serbian members of parliament walked out), being only willing to accept a loose confederation which included Croatia and Slovenia as an alternative to independence.

The federal government collapsed and Serbia (in league with Montenegro) assumed control of the federal presidency and government on 3 October 1991. Stipe Mesic formally resigned as president on 5 December 1991, saying that 'Yugoslavia does not exist any more', while Ante Markovic resigned on 20 December, protesting against what he called a 'war budget' for 1992 (81 per cent of expenditure on the armed forces). The economic reform programme was, of course, not implemented; indeed the economy has been badly affected (see Table 25.1). Property has been destroyed. Inter-republican trade has declined drastically; there has been heavy recourse to printing money, while barter and hard currency deals have increasingly replaced dinar ones; and there have been mutual confiscations of property and imposition of discriminatory taxation. Tourism has, of course, been decimated, especially in Croatia, while individuals have been denied access to hard currency accounts. Debt repayment has been adversely affected (e.g. suspended as regards payments to lender governments in the Paris Club in the summer of 1991). An official federal estimate suggested that *per capita* GNP in 1991 would fall back to the 1965 level (Donald Allan, *IHT*, 29 November 1991, p. 4). Even Slovenian output fell by an estimated 15 per cent in 1991 (Deutsche Bank, *Focus: Eastern Europe*, 1992, no. 48, p. 4). There were 600,000 registered refugees by the end of 1991 (by mid-May 1992 the UN estimated over 1.2 million for the whole of the former Yugoslavia). On 23 December 1991 Croatia introduced its own currency, while three days later Serbia replaced old dinars with new ones to prevent a flood of currency from Croatia (a new substitution took place on 1 July 1992). Hyperinflation in Serbia reached extraordinary levels (in May 1992 the monthly rate was 102.3 per cent). Serbia applied the same tariffs on Croatian and Slovenian 'imports' as on all other foreign goods. Serbia introduced wage and price controls on 1 July 1992 and an emergency economic programme on 9 July (e.g. sweeping powers to control the sale of goods).

The West's initial reaction was to try to preserve Yugoslavia, albeit in a looser form and with minority rights fully protected. But this soon proved to be unrealistic. In October 1991 the EC put forward the idea of a 'free association of sovereign and independent republics', with current borders (or only changed peacefully, by negotiations) and a high degree of antonomy and protection for the areas dominated by ethnic minorities. The EC (supported by the USA and Soviet Union) threatened sanctions to ensure compliance with its peace proposals. The EC actually imposed trade and aid sanctions on 8 November 1991, including the following: immediate suspension of the 1980 trade and co-operation agreement; the reintroduction of import quotas on Yugoslav textiles; inadmissibility in the General System of Preferences; and formal suspension of the benefits in terms of agricultural assistance under the EC-administered Phare programme. Although these penalties were aimed at Yugoslavia as a whole, 'positive compensatory measures' would be available for 'parties which do co-operate in a peaceful way towards a comprehensive political solution on the basis of the EC proposals'. Recognition of independence for individual states would only come about in the framework of an overall peace settlement that included guarantees of the rights of national and ethnic groups. The day after the EC imposed sanctions the USA said it would follow suit and the G24 countries as a whole suspended aid on the 11th. The EC lifted its sanctions on Bosnia-Hercegovina, Croatia, Macedonia and Slovenia

on 2 December 1991, but the USA formally approved sanctions on the whole of Yugoslavia on the 6th (the USA accounts for some 5 per cent of Yugoslav trade). On 10 January 1992 the EC offered to lift sanctions on Montenegro, provided its forces were withdrawn from the Dubrovnik area; this was done on 3 February 1992. It was not until 6 April that it was announced that EC sanctions on Serbia would be gradually lifted if certain conditions were met.

A United Nations ceasefire (the fourteenth in total) was negotiated on 23 November 1991 and both sides requested a UN peacekeeping force.

Under pressure from Germany, the EC announced, on 17 December 1991, that it would recognize the independence of Slovenia and Croatia and of any other republic on 15 January 1992 provided it met defined conditions regarding human rights, guarantees of the rights of ethnic and other minorities, democracy, peaceful negotiations on border and other issues, and participation in the EC and UN peace process (Germany actually recognized Slovenia and Croatia on 23 December 1991, but diplomatic relations were only to start on 15 January 1992). Bosnia-Hercegovina applied for recognition on 20 December, three days before the deadline, but the Serbs in the republic announced that they would form a 'Serbian republic' on 14 January 1992 if the EC went ahead. Macedonia also applied. The fifteenth ceasefire started on 3 January 1992 (organized by the UN), Serbia and Croatia having two days earlier agreed to a UN peacekeeping force. Because of the relative success of the ceasefire, the UN sent fifty military observers on 13 January 1992.

The EC recognized Slovenia and Croatia on 15 January 1992, an action described by Serbia to be in violation of international law (the USA waited until 7 April). Doubts were expressed about Croatia's policy on minority rights (specifically the lack of constitutional guarantees), especially by France and the UK, but Germany immediately established full diplomatic relations with both. The Badinter Commission reported favourably on Macedonia, but a referendum was required and Greece objected to the name (which allegedly implies territorial claims; a 'no territorial claim' condition was attached to recognition). Note that on 12 January the Albanians in Macedonia declared autonomy and on 9 February the Serbian minority announced that a referendum on local autonomy would be held. Bosnia-Hercegovina is a problem because of its ethnic mix (on 9 January the Serbs threatened to set up a 'Republic of the Serbian People of Bosnia-Hercegovina' if the EC recognized the republic). On 23 January the EC offered recognition of Bosnia-Hercegovina on the basis of an affirmative referendum, later fixed for 22 February. The referendum was actually held 29 February–1 March 1992, the turn-out being 63.4 per cent (there was a Serbian boycott) and the 'yes' vote was 99.43 per cent. Turkey recognized both Macedonia and Bosnia-Hercegovina on 6 February 1992. Bulgaria also quickly recognized Macedonia, while on 4 August 1992 Yeltsin said that Russia would do so. Montenegro held its own referendum on 1 March 1992; the turn-out was 66 per cent, and 96 per cent voted to remain part of Yugoslavia.

The UN ceasefire held sufficiently well for Secretary General Boutros Boutros Ghali to recommend (13 February 1992) that a peace-keeping force be sent (and raised from 10,000 to 14,000); on 21 February the Security Council agreed to send the UN Protection Force. War weariness had set in, with perhaps more than 6,000 killed since June 1991 (some put the figure at 10,000 by April 1992). Nevertheless, considerable initial resistance to the UN plan came from the Serbian leader in the Krajina area of Croatia, Milan Babic (later replaced), and President Tudjman of Croatia had to be leaned on by Germany to stop raising questions.

The UN Protection Force sent in an advance contingent in March 1992, but most personnel arrived 4–25 April. The main areas of deployment were the Serb areas of Croatia (there were also observers in Bosnia-Hercegovina, while UN headquarters were in the capital, Sarajevo). Its roles included supervising the withdrawal of the federal army from Croatia, the disarming of militias on both sides, and safeguarding Serbian rights in Croatia. The Serbian areas in Croatia were to be self-administered territories pending a final settlement.

The situation in Bosnia-Hercegovina turned ugly, despite a history of ethnic tolerance and respect. The 18 March 1992 agreement between Moslems, Croats and Serbs seemed to hold out some hope; a sort of 'cantonization' was outlined in which three autonomous areas would be demarcated within existing republican boundaries One problem was the lack of easily divisible areas because of ethnic intermingling, and the Bosnian government totally rejected the notion in June, after fighting had broken out in early April between the Serbs (backed by the Yugoslav army) and the Moslems/Croats (the Bosnian government was supported by some Bosnian Serbs it should be noted). The government saw it as a means of dismembering the country. There remained the suspicion that the Serbs and Croats intended to carve up Bosnia between them. But there was also a rumour that Croatia and Bosnia planned a confederation, while the two countries actually formed a military alliance on 15 June 1992 (the military co-operation pact of 21 July provided for joint military operations 'in the event that the efforts of the international community continue to yield no results'). On 20 June 1992 Croats unilaterally declared the Croat canton of Bosnia-Hercegovina and on 5 July the autonomous 'Croatian Community of Herceg-Bosna'.

When the EC and USA recognized Bosnia-Hercegovina on 7 April 1992, the Serbs proclaimed the independence of the 'Serbian Republic of Bosnia' in order to remain within the truncated Yugoslavia (note that 60 per cent of total arms production was situated in Bosnia before Yugoslavia disintegrated). The Bosnian capital, Sarajevo, came under siege (after lengthy negotiations the UN opened the airport for humanitarian aid purposes on 29 June, the day after French President Mitterrand's dramatic visit to the city). The Bosnian state presidency proclaimed a state of emergency on 8 April, adopting special powers to rule by decree; two days later the foundation of a Bosnian army was declared. On 4 May the Bosnian president appealed for foreign military intervention and for UN intervention six days later. On 20 June he declared that a state of war existed with Serbia, thus allowing a general mobilization. A Bosnian government report of 10 May 1992 gave the figure for those killed in the conflict at 1,320 and put the number of homeless at 670,000. Later government reports were as follows: the number killed 2,225 (20 May); 5,190 killed or missing and 1.2 million homeless (27 May); 5,700 dead (2 June); 7,000 dead (19 June); 40,000 dead, including unconfirmed deaths (20 June).

On 27 April 1992 Serbia and Montenegro declared a new Federal Republic of Yugoslavia. The declared successor state comprised 44 per cent of the area and 39 per cent of the population of the old one. On 5 May the new Yugoslavia declared that it would renounce control of the army in Bosnia-Hercegovina within fifteen days, but an estimated 80 per cent of personnel were ethnic Serbs (the 'Serbian Republic of Bosnia' took control over these on 13 May). A major purge of top Yugoslav army personnel took place on 8 May, including the acting defence minister, Adzic, and the commander of the army in Bosnia. Increasing outside pressure was put on Yugoslavia. On 11 May the EC called for the withdrawal of the army from Bosnia or its disbandment there. At the same time the EC announced the recall of the ambassadors of all member countries from Belgrade and its support for suspension of Yugoslav membership of the CSCE. On 12 May the USA recalled its ambassador and the CSCE suspended Yugoslavia from discussions about Bosnia-Hercegovina until at least 30 June. On 15 May a UN Security Council resolution called for the withdrawal of Yugoslav army and Croatian

forces and for the disbanding and disarming of all irregular forces. The phenomenon of 'ethnic cleansing', committed mainly but not entirely by Serbs, caused considerable concern; mixed areas are 'cleansed' by forcibly driving other ethnic groups out. Croatia, Slovenia and Bosnia-Hercegovina were formally admitted as members of the UN on 22 May 1992. The 31 May 1992 general election in the new Yugoslavia was formally boycotted by the Serbian opposition parties and by the Albanians of Kosovo. The turn-out was 55 per cent in Serbia and 57 per cent in Montenegro. The Serbian Socialist Party won seventy-three out of the 138 seats in the House of Deputies. The other seats were allocated as follows: the ultra-nationalist Serbian Radical Party, thirty-three; the Montenegrin Socialist Democratic Party, twenty-three; the Democratic Community of Hungarians of Vojvodina, two; the League of Communists Movement, two; and independents, three. Dobrica Cosic became president and the émigré Milan Panic (a successful businessman in the USA) was appointed prime minister on 2 July and sworn in on 14 July. Internal opposition began to grow, however. Anti-war demonstrations took place, the opposition parties formed DEPOS, and the Serbian Orthodox Church issued a critical statement.

International sanctions on the new Yugoslavia were stepped up. The degree of control exercised by Serbia over Serb irregulars fighting in Bosnia was the subject of considerable dispute. Nevertheless, on 27 May 1992 the EC proposed trade sanctions, including export credits but excluding specified foodstuffs and medicines, and an end to scientific and technological co-operation. It was decided, however, that an oil embargo would not be feasible without UN backing (Serbian production amounts to about a fifth of its oil reqirements, while the oil suppliers are non-EC countries). In 1991 more than half of Serbia's and Montenegro's exports went to the EC, but the volume of trade had already plummeted prior to sanctions. The UN agreed to impose even wider sanctions on 30 May: a trade ban, including oil but excluding foodstuffs and medicines; the cutting of air links; the freezing of assets abroad; a reduction in the size of diplomatic missions; and the end of cultural, scientific and sporting contacts. On 10 July the WEU (Western European Union) in conjunction with Nato decided on an air and sea operation to monitor shipping in the Adriatic as a means of helping enforce sanctions. GATT suspended Yugoslavia on 19 June 1992 and so did the CSCE at its 9–10 July 1992 meeting (at least until 14 October). Later developments are discussed in the postscript.

THE MARKOVIC ECONOMIC PROGRAMME

This was in two phases:

An IMF-inspired austerity programme

This was introduced in December 1989, the main aim being to reduce inflation drastically (in 1989 the average inflation rate was 1,252 per cent and it reached up to a peak of 2,700 per cent: *FT Survey*, 6 July 1990, pp. 37, 35). The following elements were involved:

The measures

Restrictive monetary and fiscal policies. Control was to be gained over both the money supply and budgetary spending. Interest rate controls were to be lifted.

Wage control. Wages were pegged to the Deutschmark level, to which the dinar itself was fixed, i.e. wages were to be effectively frozen from 15 December for six months. According to the August 1990 law on personal incomes, enterprises that paid more than the average wage increase in their republic had to do so in the form of shares.

Prices. Prices were largely liberalized. Only 20 per cent of all retail prices and 24 per cent of industrial goods prices remain controlled (*Abecor Country Report*, February 1990, p. 1);

these included electricity, petrol, rail transport, rents, post, medicines, mineral oil derivatives, iron and steel and essential raw materials, whose prices were held down. According to Estrin and Takla (1992: 270), 75 per cent of prices were freely determined in 1989, and in December 1989 all indirectly controlled prices (those needing approval by the Federal Price Office) were abolished.

Foreign trade. As of 1 January 1990 the new dinar (= 10,000 old dinars) was originally fixed at seven to the Deutschmark until 30 June, but it actually remained at this rate until the end of the year. One reason was to introduce an element of competition into the economy (import liberalization had this in mind too). The original plan was to go over to a floating exchange rate regime on 30 June, but this was not put into operation (Dyker 1992a: 15). On 1 January 1991 the dinar was devalued to nine to the Deutschmark; further devaluations took place on 19 April 1991, to thirteen to the DM, and on 15 August 1991 to twenty-two to the Deutschmark. In 1992 the dinar was again devalued on a number of occasions: on 26 January 1992 to sixty-five to the Deutschmark; by 26 per cent in March; by 57.5 per cent in April; and by 85 per cent on 1 July. There was only current account convertibility of the dinar, i.e. for current transactions in goods and services. By the end of September 1989 only 13 per cent of imports were subject to licensing (compared to 48 per cent in 1987) (Estrin and Takla 1992: 270). Customs duties decreased significantly (*Abecor Country Report*, February 1990, p. 2).

Economic performance

Inflation. Table 25.1 shows the record. Markovic was successful in the first half of 1990, with the monthly inflation rate falling from 42 per cent in January to –0.6 per cent in June, but the second half brought nothing but disappointments (Dyker 1992: 17–18). The Serbian government upset federal monetary policy at the end of December 1990, for example, when it authorized the Serbian National Bank to make it an illegal loan of 18.3 billion dinars (a sum equivalent to half the planned money supply increase in 1991). The Yugoslav National Bank attempted to recoup the money, which Serbia needed to cover the costs of increasing pensions, wages and subsidies. The federal authorities imposed monetary restrictions on all banks and republics. But Croatia, Macedonia and Montenegro also printed money in January 1991 without federal authorization (Judy Dempsey and Laura Silber, *FT Survey*, 27 June 1991, p. 16). Thus several republican national banks, primarily the Serbian National Bank, violated monetary regulations by spending part of obligatory reserves (Uvalic 1991b: 209).

Output. Table 25.1 shows the record for output and unemployment. Whereas in 1989 only five enterprises had bankruptcy proceedings taken against them, 350 were declared bankrupt in the first half of 1990 (Estrin and Takla 1992: 272). According to Uvalic (1991a: 46), 141 enterprises went bankrupt in the 1986–89 period. The new bankruptcy law (incorporated in the December 1988 Enterprise Law) involves theoretical insolvency if debt is not paid within sixty days, but enterprises borrow short-term in order to delay the threat for another sixty days. The federal social accounting agency reported in February 1991 that a third of all Yugoslav companies, employing 2 million people, were insolvent (Judy Dempsey and Laura Silber, *FT Survey*, 27 June 1991, p. 16).

The second phase

This was unveiled on 29 June 1990. The main emphasis was to be on the introduction of a more Western-style market economy. One problem, as explained by Estrin and Takla (1992: 276), was that there was no general agreement on the precise sort of reform that was required, either within the central government or between republics. The other was that the political disintegration of the country was

Table 25.1 Yugoslavia: foreign debt, unemployment and rates of growth of GDP, industrial output, agricultural output and prices (%)

GDP	
1990	1991
–7.5	–15.0

Industrial Output	
1990	1991
–10.5	–21.0

Agricutural output	
1990	1991
–4.8	7.6

Inflation	
1990	1991
121.0	164.0

Net foreign debt ($ billion)	
End 1990	End 1991
11.0[a]	11.2

Unemployment			
December 1990	May 1991	June 1991	December 1991
1,386,500 (13.6%)	1,489,000 (14.6%)	1,498,800 (14.7%)	200,000 (19.6%)

Sources: Deutsche Bank, *Focus: Eastern Europe*, 1991, no. 25, p. 4; *Economic Bulletin for Europe*, 1991, vol. 43, p. 28 ; *FT Survey*, 27 June 1991, p. 14; United Nations Economic Commission for Europe (1992: 86).
Note. [a] Debt–service ration 19.2 per cent.

scarcely conducive to the implementation of a federal economic programme, whose main elements were as follows:

Fiscal policy

The aim here was to increase the importance of the federal level at the expense of the republics. VAT was to be introduced by 1994 and there was to be a personal income tax system. The federal authorities were to become increasingly less reliant on customs duties and indirect taxes.

The annual total budget amounted to 40 per cent of GNP in 1990; the federal government intended to reduce total expenditure to 34 per cent of GNP in line with IMF requirements (Judy Dempsey, *FT*, 21 March 1991, p. 3). The actual budget deficit in 1991 was 17.5 per cent of GDP (United Nations Economic Commission for Europe 1992: 94).

Wages

Wages were to be increased only on condition that enterprises were operating soundly and that a portion of profits would be set aside for reinvestment; loss-makers were not to be allowed to raise wages (*FT Survey*, 6 July 1990, p. 37). A federal-republican agreement hoped to hold wages to the September–November 1990 average for the whole of 1991 (Estrin and Takla 1992: 274).

At the enterprise level a clear distinction was to be drawn between labour and other costs, and wages were to be composed of two parts, a basic wage (forming a minimum wage) and a profits-related bonus (John Lloyd, *FT Survey*, 29 June 1989, p. vi). Workers were to have an influence on management similar to that exercised by their West German counterparts (John Lloyd, *FT Survey*, 5 December 1989, p. 31).

Banking

Judy Dempsey (*FT Survey*, 29 June 1990, p. v) explains the reforms. Internal banks were to be phased out. New banks were to be set up, provided that the minimum capital formation was 20 billion dinars ($150 million) and that at least ten enterprises contributed to the start-up capital. The boards of directors of banks were to be composed of bankers, not enterprise directors. The bank assembly would nominate the executive board, but would be unable to authorize credits or be involved in business discussions. Markovic thought private banks were a possibility.

At the beginning of 1990 banks were allowed to transform themselves into private joint stock companies; by the end of March they had emerged as limited liability joint stock companies. They were thus able to expand their equity base. In July Yugoslavs were permitted to invest in bank stock. (Rosamund McDougall, *The Banker*, September 1990, p. 13).

By mid-1991 Yugoslav citizens with hard currency accounts could withdraw no more than $585 a month.

Stock exchanges

On 28 February 1990 the Belgrade stock exchange resumed trading, although trade was restricted to Serbian government treasury bonds. The exchange in Ljublyana opened on 29 March, followed by the one in Zagreb.

The market and privatization

The December 1988 Enterprise Law replaced the 1976 Law on Associated Labour. The 'enterprise' replaced the BOAL as the basic production unit and there was to be freedom to establish any type of enterprise. Competition among diverse forms of ownership and legal forms was the key. The decision-making authority of managers was increased *vis-à-vis* self-management bodies, these becoming advisory in principle (Estrin and Takla 1992: 270). Markovic was aware of the need for property rights legislation: 'We have to clearly identify the owners of capital and begin the process of recapitalization and privatization' (Laura Silber, *FT*, 30 June 1990, p. 2). 'We shall see the start to the process of changing anonymous capital into social capital' (John Lloyd, *FT Survey*, 29 June 1989, p. iii). The August 1990 Law on Social Capital set out to define property rights.

Markovic proposed the transformation of socially-owned enterprises into shareholding companies within the next two years (*EEN*, 1990, vol. 4, no. 15, p. 6). A core element of the reform programme was privatization, as set out in the federal law on social property of August 1990 (Uvalic 1991b: 203). If a socially owned enterprise had not been partially privatized within two years, a newly formed restructuring body would take over the process (Laura Silber, *FT*, 31 July 1990, p. 2). The forms were to include, for example, nationalized firms and employee share allocation. The federal emphasis was on worker ownership. In the case of the latter, existing and former workers would be able to buy shares (or be given them in place of pay increases) in their particular enterprise at a discount proportionate to years of service. These shares could ultimately be traded on stock exchanges (*Euromoney*, supplement on Yugoslavia, September 1990, p. 16). Employees were entitled to a 30 per cent discount plus an additional 1 per cent for every year of employment up to a maximum of 70 per cent of the nominal value of the shares ('internal' shares are issued to workers and pension funds, but not the general public: Estrin and Takla 1992: 269; Uvalic argues that internal shares are offered for sale to citizens as well and notes that internal shares are not immediately tradeable: Uvalic 1991b: 203). Payment could be spread over ten years. Workers made redundant because of privatization would receive a lump sum compensation equivalent to six months' wages. The 30 per cent discount also applied to Yugoslav citizens and pension funds. There were various limits placed on the issue of internal shares, and other shares could be offered for sale to domestic and foreign enterprises or individuals through public auctions (Uvalic 1991a: 41, 1991b: 203).

There was republican disagreement on this issue. There was resistance from the Socialist Party in Serbia, while Slovenia and Croatia wished to transform 'social ownership' into state ownership in the first place before privatization was undertaken. Slovenia was planning to sell nearly all its enterprises. There were also variations on the details of the federal scheme (see Uvalic 1991b: 205).

POSTSCRIPT

FOREIGN TRADE

In February 1991 Czechoslovakia, Hungary and Poland agreed to co-ordinate their approach to the European Community at a meeting in Visegrad (Hungary) to further the aim of eventual full membership. The three agreed, for example, to form a free trade zone as a way of gaining entry into the EC. On 23 September 1992, however, Hungary and Poland decided to form a free trade zone on their own by the start of 1993, while attempting separate arrangements with the two halves of Czechoslovakia at a later stage (Nicholas Denton, *FT*, 24 September 1992, p. 6). The first in the series of meetings between the Visegrad three and the EC took place on 28 October 1992. One result was an attempt to specify the entry criteria before December 1992. Just before Christmas 1992 Hungary, Poland and representatives of the soon-to-be independent Czech and Slovak republics signed a free trade agreement linking the Visegrad four (Anthony Robinson, *FT*, 30 December 1992, p. 8).

Concern has been expressed at the EC's use of anti-dumping regulations against exports such as steel products from these countries. The findings of some research on the EC association agreements with Czechoslovakia, Hungary and Poland by Jim Rollo and Alasdair Smith are discussed by Edward Balls (*FT*, 19 October 1992, p. 6). Agricultural products and the 'import-sensitive' industrial products (such as iron and steel, chemicals and textiles) account for 33 per cent of Czechoslovak exports to the EC. The respective figures for Poland and Hungary are 42 per cent and 51 per cent. Excluding food and food products, these sensitive products account for 5.4 per cent of total EC employment and the share is much higher in exposed regions in France, Germany and southern Italy. But imports of sensitive manufactures from Eastern Europe are, in all cases, equivalent to less than 1 per cent of total EC gross production. Even on the worst-case scenario for EC producers (a 400 per cent rise in Eastern European exports of sensitive products) the result would be only modest falls in EC production in each sector, ranging from 4.6 per cent in textiles to 1.3 per cent in food products.

Since July 1992 free trade agreements between EFTA and Czechoslovakia, Hungary and Poland have been implemented (*OECD Economic Outlook*, December 1992, p. 125). 23–4 November 1992: The first meeting of the COCOM Co-operative Forum took place. It was decided that the former Warsaw Pact countries would be permitted to import sensitive technologies for civilian purposes and when adequate export controls were in place. Hungary had been removed from the list of proscribed destinations earlier in the year.

RUSSIA

The Russian government's second stage of economic reform

This was outlined on 30 June 1992:

1. *The exchange rate regime.* The schedule was originally outlined on 5 May 1992 by Konstantin Kagalovsky, who was chief official in charge of negotiations with the IMF. On 1 July 1992 a single (unified) exchange rate for the rouble was to be established and the rouble was then to float for a month in order to find a defendable level of perhaps 80 to the US dollar. The rouble was to become internally convertible as regards current account transactions on 1 August 1992 at a rate fixed against the US dollar, with the rouble allowed to move 7.5 per cent either side of par. The stabilization fund would be available to defend the rouble if necessary. Devaluation was not ruled out altogether, however. Instead of the special exchange rate mentioned earlier for foreigners wishing to participate in the privatization process, the government would multiply the book value of a property by some coefficient or possibly organize special auctions for foreigners (Martin Wolf, *FT Survey*, 13 May 1992, p. iv).

On 1 July 1992, however, the unified rate for the rouble was actually set at 125.26 to the US dollar. This was based on the average market rate over the previous month and compared with a market rate of 144 on that particular day on the Moscow Interbank Currency Exchange. But the rate quickly became that established on the exchange at its twice-weekly auctions (the rouble soon plummeted against the US dollar). All exporters were subject to mandatory sales of half their foreign exchange earnings at the unified ('market') rate, 30 per cent to the central bank and 20 per cent to commercial banks to be sold on the domestic hard currency market (*Russian Economic Trends*, 1992, vol. 1, no. 2, p. 33). *Russian Economic Trends* (p. 33) describes the rouble as now 'internally' convertible in principle. Importers are free to buy dollars on

production of a certificate of import. Private citizens are free to buy dollars for any purpose, but they are not allowed to take more than $500 outside the country except to pay for authorized travel. Foreigners still have limited rights to take out dollars (though they can repatriate profits) and enterprises can only buy dollars for purposes of import. Note that the exchange rate was not actually fully unified on 1 July, since organizations buying centralized imports continued to receive their foreign exchange at a price below the market rate (p. 33).

2. *The tariff regime as of 1 July 1992* (*Russian Economic Trends*, 1992, vol. 1, no. 2, p. 31). In order to maintain budget revenues, export taxes doubled to an average rate of 40 per cent for raw material exporters. Previously exporters of raw materials paid export taxes at an average rate of 20 per cent and had to surrender 40 per cent of their foreign exchange earnings at approximately half the market rate. This surrender represented an additional 20 per cent tax, so that the effective tax rate has remained unchanged. An import tax was introduced at a rate of 5 per cent (medicine and food were both zero rated and luxury goods such as cars were rated 10 per cent). The tariff was increased to an average rate of 15 per cent on 1 September 1991.

3. *The privatization programme.* The legislation was passed by the Russian parliament on 11 June 1992 and on 19 August Yeltsin outlined the voucher plan (note that 'check' is typically used in official circles in Russia in order to avoid too westernized a term). All citizens of Russia (including children born before 1 September 1992) would be eligible and vouchers could be used to buy shares in privatized enterprises or private investment funds, or sold (even to foreigners). On 6 October Yeltsin decreed that vouchers could also be used to buy land, housing and municipal property such as shops and small businesses (note that land refers to 'parcels of land that go with enterprises being privatized or land that is connected with entrepreneurial activity': *CDSP*, 1992, vol. XLIV, no. 41, p. 31). Citizens were to obtain their vouchers

1 October–31 December 1992 for a small registration fee of 25 roubles for vouchers worth 10,000 roubles (many authorities later extended the period by one month). These vouchers would be exchangeable for shares 1 January–31 December 1993. Although in nominal terms the vouchers were worth only around two months' average salary (earned in mid-1992), they would be used 'to acquire property at the old prices on the last balance-sheet appraisals of enterprises' (*CDSP*, 1992, vol. XLIV, no. 34, p. 7). The vouchers would be redeemed by the central government and cash raised would go to regional and local governments.

Large enterprises are defined as those that either employ more than 1,000 people or had a book value of fixed assets as of 1 January 1992 of over 50 million roubles. Approximately 4,500 large state enterprises are subject to compulsory privatization. Medium-sized enterprises either employ more than 200 people or had a book value of 10 million to 50 million roubles; these may be privatized if their work collective so wishes (*CDSP*, 1992, vol. XLIV, no. 40, p. 7). Except for utilities and a few defence enterprises, large enterprises were obliged to transform themselves into joint stock companies and to submit plans for privatization (the 1 July decree envisaged converting enterprises into joint stock companies by 1 November and enterprises submitting privatization plans by 1 October 1992: *CDSP*, 1992, vol. XLIV, no. 27, p. 28). A board of directors was to be set up, including managers, workers, a representative of a local privatization agency and officials from the level of government which owns the enterprise. Enterprises were encouraged to restructure themselves prior to privatization and subdivisions of an enterprise could become independent.

The employees of large enterprises could choose from among the schemes on offer (*Russian Economic Trends*, 1992, vol. 1, no. 2, p. 37; *CDSP*, 1992, vol. XLIV, no. 40, pp. 7–9):

1. The workers would be given 25 per cent of (non-voting) shares, with the option to purchase 10 per cent of (voting) shares at a 30 per cent discount on 1991 book value. A three-year instalment plan is available and vouchers can be used. Managers have the option to buy 5 per cent of the voting shares at 1991 book value.

2. Subject to a two-thirds majority vote, employees have the right to purchase up to 51 per cent of the enterprise's capital at 1.7 times 1991 book value. Up to 50 per cent of the value of the stock may be paid for with vouchers. Shares not given or sold to employees are to be sold by closed bid auction to the general public. Thirty-five per cent of shares will be sold in exchange for vouchers. The remainder will be sold for cash. Employees and managers are free to use their vouchers and cash to buy these shares too. (By late September 1992 about one-third of the enterprises subject to mandatory privatization were leaning towards option 1, about half to option 2, and the rest were vacillating.)

3. A group of employees (not necessarily the entire work collective) may agree to reorganize an enterprise. The agreement must be approved by at least two-thirds of the work collective and it will be in effect for one year. Under the agreement, the group has to reorganize the enterprise within one year, investing the employees' personal money in it in an amount at least 200 times the minimum wage established in the Russian Federation for each member of the group. If the terms of the agreement are met, the members of the group will receive the right to acquire 20 per cent of the ordinary shares at face value. In addition, all enterprise employees, including members of this group, may acquire an additional 20 per cent of the shares on the same terms as option 2.

The first large entity to be privatized under the voucher scheme was the Bolshevik cake and biscuit enterprise in Moscow. The tender was scheduled for 9–24 December 1992 and 44 per cent of shares were available by voucher (employees had opted for 56 per cent).

Other aspects are as follows (*CDSP*, 1992, vol. XLIV, no. 26, pp. 33–4) Privatization is prohibited in certain areas (e.g. mineral and water resources, military property, the central bank, and television and radio centres); permission for privatization would be needed in areas such as weapons, machinery for the nuclear power industry, the fuel and energy complex, commercial banks, news agencies, enterprises in any sector that occupy dominant positions in the federal or local markets, major enterprises with more than 10,000 employees, rail, air and water transport enterprises, and the producers of alcoholic beverages. Enterprises were divided into three groups, 'small' (with 200 or fewer employees and a book value which does not exceed 1 million roubles; these can be sold at auction or by closed bid), 'large' (these were to be converted into joint stock companies), and the remaining enterprises (able to be privatized by any of the methods established by the programme). A decree relating to the oil industry was signed by Yeltsin on 27 November 1992 (*IHT*, 28 November 1992, p. 17). All organizations involved in extracting, refining and transporting oil products would be converted into joint stock companies. The state would hold 38–49 per cent of shares in the companies for a period of three years. Foreign investors would be offered no more than 15 per cent of the shares and the pipeline network would remain under state control.

Larisa Piyasheva, who was dismissed from her position as adviser on privatization to the mayor of Moscow, is critical of the amount of state property to be divided up: 'We are dealing with only a small percentage of all property that . . . Russia's citizens have coming to them . . . On average, 60 per cent of all national property will remain in the hands of the state . . . The state will want to sell some things on the open market and it will keep other things for itself' (*CDSP*, 1992, vol. XLIV, no. 36, p. 30).

According to a 14 June 1992 decree, owners of a joint stock enterprise that has been purchased by means of sale through a competitive procedure or auction have the right to sell the enterprise's land (and to buy extra land for expansion). (Note that the 25 March 1992 decree had ruled that land sites could be sold during the process of privatization, i.e. the land sites on which the privatized enterprises are located can be not only leased but also privatized: *Russian Economic Trends*, 1992, vol. 1, no. 2, p. 41.)

The privatization programme presented to parliament on 2 July 1992 envisaged all small industrial enterprises, foreign trade and consumer services, and a 'considerable part' of housing being privatized within fifteen months. A third of medium-sized and large enterprises were to be privatized over this time period and a half by 1995.

On 2 October 1992 Yeltsin decreed the pilot sale of land by auction (near Moscow). *Moscow News* (15–22 November 1992, p. 2) reported that the first land auction had taken place (in Ramenskoye in the Moscow region). On 1 November 1992 there was an auction of lorries in Nizhny Novgorod; vouchers could amount to half the value of each bid. The privatization programme as a whole in Nizhny Novgorod is aided by the International Finance Corporation (this offshoot of the World Bank concentrates on the private sector). Grigory Yavlinski advised the Nizhny Novgorod authorities on economic policy in general.

The Economist (7 November 1992, p. 52) provides the following figures on the respective percentages of shops, restaurants and other services privatized as of 1 July 1992: St Petersburg (47.7 per cent, 30.5 per cent and 34.3 per cent); Moscow (41.9 per cent, 25.2 per cent and 35.5 per cent); Nizhny Novgorod (39.5 per cent, 84.0 per cent and 38.0 per cent). Over 14,000 small businesses have been privatized in Russia as a whole (11 per cent of the total); one official estimate puts the number of people working in the private sector at 30 million (*The Economist*, 28 November 1992, p. 94). By September 1992 22,300 small enterprises had been privatized (*Russian Economic Trends*, 1992, vol. 1, no. 2, update table 13). On 14 January it was unexpectedly announced that some 500 large- and medium-sized enterprises were to be privatized by April 1993. Fourteen out of Russia's forty-nine regions were to be involved, starting with Volgograd (known for a time as Stalingrad). Advice was being given by the International Finance Corporation and Western accounting firms. The regional authorities were to prepare the list of candidates after conducting 'survivability tests' on enterprises.

The IMF and the economic programme

The $24 billion international aid package was conditional on an agreed IMF programme. This was laid out in three stages:

1. *The period 8 July–October 1992*. The release of $1 billion, Russia pledging the following: to reduce the budget deficit from 17 per cent to 5 per cent of GDP and monthly inflation from 15 per cent to no more than 10 per cent by the end of 1992; to tighten monetary policy and co-ordinate policy with the other countries in the rouble zone; and to continue with structural reforms, such as enterprise bankruptcy and privatization.

2. *The period October 1992–mid-1993*. The release of a further $3 billion, conditional on further macroeconomic stabilization and market-orientated reforms.

3. *The period following the completion of stage two*. The activation of the $6 billion stabilization fund. Budget in near balance, inflation in line with that in the West, and rouble convertibility.

On 5 August 1992 the IMF agreed to release the $1 billion (to boost Russia's foreign exchange reserves), and this was followed by a World Bank loan of $600 million (for imports). This was in spite of considerable concern about the prospects for the reform programme:

1. Inter-enterprise debt had mounted at a rapid rate, rising from 34 billion at the end of December 1991 to 3,004 billion roubles by the end of June 1992 (*Russian Economic Trends*, 1992, vol. 1, no. 2, p. 15). On 1 July 1992 a programme of clearing the debt by 5 October began (the debt subsequently fell to 1,200 billion by the end of August). Commercial banks were authorized to extend special loans to debtors to allow them to pay their debts. These payments, when received, were to be credited to special accounts of creditors. But these accounts could not be spent by the creditor enterprises before 5 October 1992, when a decision was to be taken about the future liquidity of these assets. The *Financial Times* (21 January 1993, p.2) reported a resurgence of inter-enterprise debt to around 3,500 billion roubles.

Viktor Geraschenko, the former chairman of the Russian central bank, became its acting head on 17 July, the day after Georgi Matyukin's resignation was accepted (Yeltsin made Geraschenko a member of the government on 17 November).

Sachs and Lipton (*FT*, 16 October 1992, p. 23) stressed the need to staunch the flow of credits to enterprises and the budget. 'The money supply has approximately doubled since 1 July, when the floodgates of credit were opened . . . There can be no illusions: Russia's transformation to a democratic market-based society will require years of change . . . the process could soon turn from orderly change to dangerous chaos if there is hyperinflation.'

2. Parliament agreed a budget of 950 billion roubles on 17 July 1992, 100 billion roubles more than originally conceived (62 billion roubles of this was for food subsidies). Gaidar had argued for a total budget of 800 billion roubles. The day before, on 16 July, it was announced that VAT was to be reduced on most goods from 28 per cent to 20 per cent on 1 January 1993 (the reduced rate was to apply immediately to 'socially necessary' goods, mainly basic foodstuffs). In the first quarter of 1992 there was a slight budget surplus, but in the second quarter this turned into a deficit equal to 10.6 per cent of GDP (*Russian Economic Trends*, 1992, vol. 1, no. 2, p. 8). The budget deficit for the first half of 1992 was equal to 7.5 per cent of GDP and there was a serious deterioration in July and August (Gaidar, *CDSP*, 1992, vol. XLIV, no. 38, p. 2).

On 24 July 1992 Yeltsin talked of energy prices not being completely free until the end of 1993. In mid-September the limits on oil prices were again raised. Sales up to 4,000 roubles are free of tax and for prices above this there is a tax rising to 50 per cent. There are also limits on profit margins (*Russian Economic Trends*, 1992, vol. 1, no. 2, p. 16). As regards consumer prices, note that in March 1992 the federal government abolished all federal controls and federal subsidies. Local authorities retain the right to impose maximum prices on consumer goods, but subsidies have to be met from local budgets (p. 16). On 8 May 1992 legislation was introduced which stated that if an enterprise has a market share larger than 35 per cent for one of its products, then it must report any change in price to regional authorities for consumer goods and to federal authorites for industrial goods. Further legislation was introduced in early August which set explicit profit limits for monopoly enterprises (p. 17).

Events leading up to the seventh session of the Russian Congress of People's Deputies in December 1992

Arkady Volsky and Civic Union

Arkady Volsky is president of the Union of Industrialists and Entrepreneurs, whose prime role is to defend the interests of state enterprises. Volsky, Rutskoi and Nikolai Travkin are the leaders of Civic Union, an organization founded in August 1992 as an alliance of the All-Russia Renewal League, the People's Party of Free Russia and the Democratic Party of Russia. Volsky outlined the main points of disagreement with the government in an interview given and a speech delivered in September 1992 (*CDSP*, 1992, vol. XLIV, no. 36, p. 12, and no. 39, pp. 9–10):

1. The immediate task should be to prevent the disintegration of the economy and plummeting production. The social costs of the reform should be minimized.

2. The creation of a market and a class of private owners are not ends in themselves. The goal should be an efficient, socially orientated market economy and a normal standard of living for the population. There should be a sensible combination of state regulation and decentralization. (Note that Yeltsin has praised the Chinese economic system; see, for example, the article by Andrew Higgins in *The Independent*, 30 November 1992, p. 17.)

3. The pace of the reforms, including privatization, is too rapid. More time is needed for adjustment and the collapse of manufacturing industry should be prevented. The question of converting major enterprises to joint stock companies in a very short time should be taken off the agenda and the percentage of state ownership in the economy should not be determined in advance. It is necessary to encourage collective ownership by workers, and employees themselves should make the decision as to whether to create an open or closed joint stock company. The process of 'voucherization' should be spread over two or three years and the use of vouchers should be broadened to include things like the payment of major medical services. Jonathan Steele (*The Guardian*, 10 October 1992, p.24) outlines Volsky's alternative restructuring–privatization programme in greater detail. Small-scale private enterprise should be encouraged as well as the private sector in agriculture. Most industrial enterprises, however, would remain in state hands while they are being modernized. These would be required to restructure themselves and draw up plans for future growth. State credits would encourage those with viable new profiles of conversion, while the rest would be closed down over a three-year period.

4. Bankruptcy should take account not only of financial but also social factors; a bankruptcy decision should be taken only in court and not by a government bureaucrat.

5. The creation of a single economic space with appropriate inter-state structures is an indispensable condition for the Russian

economy's survival. But the economy should not be too open to other economies, since only 16 per cent of enterprises could withstand international competition (reported by Jonathan Steele, *The Guardian*, 16 November 1992, p. 10). Volsky is dismissive of the value of Western aid, citing the situation in East Germany: 'no one but we ourselves can raise Russia from its knees' (*CDSP*, 1992, vol. XLIV, no. 36, p. 12). (Note that a 'tight' Russian federation is advocated: *CDSP*, 1992, vol. XLIV, no. 42, p. 23.)

6. In order to stave off hyperinflation, the prices of energy, transport services and basic foodstuffs should be frozen for six months. A progressive tax should be imposed on unwarranted increases in the wage fund during the transitional period.

A chronology of events leading up to the congress

Yeltsin tried to mollify the state industrialists, but at the same time sought new powers to push the main elements of the reforms along. On 29 July 1992 he expressed a wish that in 1993 he should have powers to rule by decree and to appoint top executives for a transitional period. He also thought that the Congress of People's Deputies should be scrapped. Earlier, in a 7 July 1992 decree, Yeltsin had given wide powers to the 'security council' to help determine and implement policy; the four permanent members were Yeltsin, Rutskoi, Gaidar and Yuri Skokov. Yeltsin also set up a Council of the Leaders of the Republics of the Russian Federation, which first met on 15 October 1992. Skokov was appointed secretary of the former council and head of the latter council. In a 6 October 1992 speech to parliament Yeltsin talked of the need to modify the economic reform programme to some extent. On the same day Gaidar stressed the need to tighten fiscal and monetary policy and ruled out the Chinese economic model on the grounds that China was not a democracy with political opposition: 'Russia is not China . . . China has retained a powerful structure of

authoritarian management; all attempts by the opposition to destabilize the situation have been cruelly suppressed . . . in order to follow the Chinese path it would have been necessary to work out a political strategy different from the one that the Russian parliament voted for in 1990.' (Note that on 18 December 1992 Yeltsin, during a visit to China, commented on that country's economic system. China began its economic reform fourteen years ago, while Russia only started in January 1992. 'The Chinese tactics of reform are not to hurry, not to force, without revolutions, without cataclysms, which is very important, and I think that for us has a certain significance. Russia does not need revolutions or cataclysms either': *IHT*, 19 December 1992, p. 5.)

October 1992 produced claims of a possible 'constitutional coup', to be carried out by those opposed to the government's reform process. On 21 October Yeltsin tried, unsuccessfully, to persuade parliament to postpone the opening of the new session of the Congress of People's Deputies from 1 December 1992 (when his power to issue decrees without legislative approval would come to an end) to March 1993. On 28 October 1992 Yeltsin banned the National Salvation Front (established only three days earlier by communists and nationalists opposed to Yeltsin and the government) for calling for 'the overthrow of the legally constituted authorities' and for 'destabilizing society'. Yeltsin also banned the 5,000–strong parliamentary guard, which had been formed in October 1991 and which had become directly answerable to the speaker of parliament, Ruslan Khasbulatov.

On 29 October 1992 Yeltsin announced that he would halt the troop withdrawal from the Baltic states (although it seems as though the process continued). He claimed the need to protect Russian civilians and to come to an agreement about the social rights of Russian soldiers and their families. Yeltsin sent extra troops to the Russian autonomous republic of North Ossetia on 1 November 1992 to intervene in the fighting between Ossetian and Ingush forces. The Ingush claim the right to land in North Ossetia taken from them in 1944. On 2 November 1992 Yeltsin declared a state of emergency in North Ossetia and Ingushetia to last until 2 December 1992. (Chechenia and Ingushetia were joined in 1934, but in June 1992 Russia declared Ingushetia a semi-autonomous republic; Chechenia had declared its 'independence' in November 1991.)

14 November 1992. Yeltsin attended a congress of the Union of Industrialists and Entrepreneurs. The union and the government were to try to reach agreement before the start of the next and crucial session of the Congress of People's Deputies on 1 December 1992. Yeltsin, however, ruled out 1 trillion roubles in fresh credits, the restoration of state orders and price and wage freezes.

25 November 1992. Deputy prime minister and information minister, Mikhail Poltoranin, resigns. This was seen as a concession to Civic Union, as was the abolition the next day of the post of State Secretary, which was created for Gennadi Burbulis. (Note that Burbulis was immediately reappointed as head of a presidential advisory council. On 26 December 1992 Poltoranin was put in charge of the Federal Information Centre, a newly created body designed 'to increase the role of the press, news agencies, television and radio in elucidating state policy . . . to secure, through print and the mass media, the distribution of timely and wide information about the progress of reforms in Russia and to clarify government policy'.)

26 November 1992. In a speech to parliament Gaidar committed the government to the main principles of the reform programme; there could be 'no retreat from the strategic course of changes . . . we are not ready to combine incompatible approaches'. Specifically, Gaidar ruled out a return to a centralized distribution of resources, a price and wage freeze, a 'limitless' money supply and intervention to support the rouble at an artificial rate. The acting prime minister was prepared, however, to provide extra support during the transition period for those enterprises with a long-term future.

29 November 1992. Yeltsin declared that 'Radical reforms need a strong social base and an appropriate structure, maybe a party, maybe a political movement.'

30 November 1992. The Russian Constitutional Court decides that Yeltsin was correct in banning the CPSU and the Russian Communist Party at the national level (the court avoided a ruling on the question of whether the party had acted unconstitutionally or in criminal fashion; the court simply said that by the time of the ban the former had effectively ceased to exist and the latter had not been officially registered). But the court also decided that Yeltsin had been wrong to ban the local branches of the communist party (the primary organizations), since their members had been elected and had paid for local property, out of dues. The court drew a distinction between state property, which should not be returned, and party property, which should (local property should be returned, for example, but the vagueness of the distinction meant that disputes would have to be resolved on a case-by-case basis).

The Congress of People's Deputies 1–14 December 1992

In his speech to the 1,041 deputies on the opening day of the congress, Yeltsin stressed the need for a breathing space of between a year and eighteen months to consolidate the reforms: 'We favour a strict and coherent state and industrial policy that would lead us along the golden path between the freedoms of the market and a regulatory role for the state . . . In the period of building a market economy, we need a well-considered protectionism'. Yeltsin proposed the indexing of savings. Ruslan Khasbulatov pleaded for a 'Scandinavian' rather than an 'American' type of economic system.

Gaidar, in his speech delivered on 2 December, argued that there was little room to manoeuvre as regards economic reform. He criticized the alternatives put forward by

Khasbulatov: 'At the moment the choice is more crucial. It is between pursuing reforms or giving in to criminal delays which are pulling our country down . . . the real dilemma facing our society is far more dramatic than a choice between these two models.' If the reforms are not pursued 'then we will develop not according to the American or Swedish pattern, but according to African or Latin American patterns . . . [leading to] the chronic poverty and political instability, the populist politicians and dictatorships so common in Third World states'. Arms sales would continue to 'reliable' partners, but not to zones of conflict (recent deals included the export of arms to China, India, Iran and Syria). On 1 January 1993 proper border posts would be set up, for export control for example. On the following day of the congress, however, Gaidar made a more conciliatory speech: 'Our friends and colleagues from the centrist factions underestimate the opportunities for compromise and flexibility in co-operation to build a normal, civilized economy'. A slower rise in the price of oil to the world level was promised.

On 4 December congress voted 668 to 210 (with thirty-four abstentions) in favour of a resolution expressing dissatisfaction with a government economic reform programme deemed 'contrary to the interests of the majority of citizens'. The following day a resolution giving the Supreme Soviet and the CPD the right to approve all top government posts failed to achieve the required two-thirds majority (694), but the shortfall was only four votes. (Note that the Supreme Soviet already had the power to approve a 'full-time' prime minister, Gaidar being only an 'acting' premier; Yeltsin could keep Gaidar in that role for three months before submitting a name for approval.) On 5 December congress approved an amendment to the constitution allowing land sales subject to restrictions (albeit reduced, e.g. sales would sometimes be allowed after five rather than ten years). Deputy prime minister Chubais revealed that the government would like a voucher scheme to apply to land privatization.

On 8 December 1992 Yeltsin offered to allow the Supreme Soviet the right of veto over the defence, security, interior and foreign ministers in return for approving Gaidar as prime minister. The CPD accepted this offer the next day, but still rejected Gaidar as prime minister by 486 to 467 (a simple majority of 521 had been needed for approval).

Yeltsin savagely attacked the congress on 10 December: 'Congress is a bulwark of conservative forces and reaction. The reforms which have been carried out for a year in Russia are in serious jeopardy. A high-powered offensive has been launched at the congress against the course pursued by the president and the government, against those real changes that have kept the country from economic disaster throughout the past months. What they failed to do in August 1991 they have decided to repeat now by means of a creeping coup. We are being pushed towards a dangerous brink beyond which there is nothing but destabilization and economic chaos. We are being pushed towards civil war. I see only one way out of the most profound crisis of power, a nationwide referendum . . . I am proposing that the congress schedule a referendum for January 1993 with the following wording: "Who should be given the task of taking the country out of the economic and political crisis, of reviving the Russian Federation? The President of the Russian Federation or the presently constituted Congress of People's Deputies and Supreme Soviet?"' Yeltsin said he would resign if he lost the referendum to be held on 24 January 1993 and a fresh presidential election would follow. If Yeltsin won, parliamentary elections would be held on 27 March 1993. Yeltsin asked his supporters to start collecting the million signatures needed for a referendum in the absence of support from one-third of the deputies in the CPD. He also called upon reformist deputies to follow him out of the congress hall, but only around 150 did so. The CPD reacted by adopting a resolution which would ask people whether they supported early elections for the presidency (whose mandate expires in June 1996) and for the CPD (elected for the period March 1990–March 1995). The congress also adopted a constitutional amendment providing for the impeachment of the president if he tried to introduce a state of emergency without its consent. The chairman of the constitutional court, Valery Zorkin, called on Yeltsin and Khasbulatov to meet under his auspices to seek a compromise.

On 11 December congress voted to amend the law to preclude a referendum that would result in the dissolution of any high state body before the end of its term. The opposing camps met only briefly and issued a statement agreeing to settle problems by 'constitutional means'. The following day a compromise was reached. Gennadi Burbulis was dismissed as Yeltsin's adviser and a nine-point accord was agreed. The accord included the following elements: (1) Yeltsin would present to congress a list of candidates for prime minister; the president would be able to choose one of the three candidates receiving the highest congressional votes; if Yeltsin's choice was not endorsed by congress, he could appoint an acting premier until the next session of congress in April 1993; (2) a referendum was to be held on 11 April 1993 on the basic principles of a new constitution; (3) before the referendum, congress would abstain from considering any laws changing the balance of power between the executive, the legislature and the judiciary; (4) congress would have the right of veto over the defence, security, interior and foreign ministers.

The final day of the December session of the congress produced a shock result. Yeltsin (reluctantly) chose Viktor Chernomyrdin as prime minister and congress (enthusiastically) endorsed him by 721 votes to 172. Yeltsin had produced a list of five candidates for congress to consider, but Gaidar only came a poor third with 400 votes, behind Yuri Skokov (637) and Chernomyrdin (621). Gaidar resigned as acting premier and announced that he would not join the new government. Nevertheless, he was convinced that the changes 'have a great momentum of their own and it is very difficult to reverse them'; 'the main lines [of the reforms] have been set down and they will continue' (although he later expressed concern that the privatization programme might be amended to increase the proportion of shares going to workers and managers). On 17 December 1992 Yeltsin announced that Gaidar was to become his personal adviser on economic policy (Gaidar had just taken up the post of director of the Institute for Economic Problems in the Transitional Period).

Chernomyrdin (see p. 104) had been made energy minister and a deputy prime minister on 30 May 1992, one of a number of more interventionist-minded industrialists appointed around that time as a concession to the industrial lobby (he had become gas industry minister in February 1985 and head of Gazprom in 1989). He broadly thinks along Civic Union lines. A flavour of his ideas can be detected in some of Chernomyrdin's comments after his appointment: 'I am for reforms, in favour of deepening reforms, but without impoverishing the people'; 'the reforms should now take a somewhat different tone . . . First of all, the decline of production must be stopped. No reform can proceed if industry is in ruins . . . We are going to give priority to basic industries . . . A country like ours, with its great wealth and powerful infrastructure, should not turn into a nation of shopkeepers'; 'I am for a market economy, but not for a bazaar. I am for a real market.' The following day he remarked that 'I have never given anyone reason to say that the course of reform would be changed under my leadership. I am for deepening reforms. There is no way back.' Chernomyrdin repeated, however, that the priority was to stop the fall in industrial production. He also saw the need for controls on energy prices (he quickly increased credits to the energy sector; note also that a programme to double Russia's nuclear energy capacity by the year 2010 was approved on 28 December 1992: *IHT*, 14 January 1993, p. 1) and said that, while he supported privatization, he did not favour 'landslide privatization'. On 5 January 1993 he issued a government decree restricting the profits of enterprises producing basic goods to between 10 and 25 per cent of the value of sales (e.g. bread, milk, butter, meat, sugar, salt, tea, children's food and some raw materials).

Yeltsin visited China 17–19 December 1992 (a number of political, military and economic agreements were signed and the two countries pledged 'to regard each other as friends'). He returned to Russia earlier than planned, saying that 'they have begun to fight for portfolios too early, to pull apart the cabinet, so the master must return and restore order there'. On 20 December it was announced that the 'core' of the reform team was to be retained, that the 'basic current team' was to be preserved. This proved to be the case when the actual list of cabinet ministers was revealed on 23 December. The reformist casualty was Pyotr Aven, the minister of foreign economic relations (he was in charge of negotiations with the West about debt rescheduling), who had resigned the previous day in anticipation. He was replaced by his deputy, Sergei Glazyev. Boris Fyodorov was appointed as a deputy prime minister with the role of co-ordinating overall financial and economic policy. (He had resigned as Russian finance minister in 1990 over the slow pace of reform in the then republic of the former Soviet Union; he subsequently took up positions in the EBRD and the World Bank.) The other new deputy prime minister to be appointed was Yuri Yarov, the deputy speaker of the Supreme Soviet. (Note that on 22 December the Supreme Soviet confirmed that the president had the power to dismiss the prime minister.)

As head of economic policy Fyodorov quickly pitched a pro-reform tone. He put control of inflation as the number one priority and vowed to continue the reform programme (he had attacked Gaidar's record on inflation: 'The Gaidar government was repeatedly accused of having a rigid monetary policy, but it did not. Billions of roubles of worthless money were poured into the economy': *IHT*, 19 January 1993, p. 14; *FT*, 19 January 1993, p. 2). Although reform needed to take the 'social factor' into account, 'market-orientated relations will ultimately help our country out of a difficult situation. These envisage that the state will no longer support enterprises which cannot withstand competition.' Enterprises should be reorganized and less able managers dismissed. Fyodorov's criticism of the 5 January 1993 decree on price controls (see above) led to a major climbdown by Chernomyrdin. On 18 January 1993 the controls were lifted on all prices except those charged by monopoly suppliers. Fyodorov outlined the government's stabilization proposals on 20 January, with the aim of reducing inflation to 5 per cent a month by the end of 1993 and reducing the budget deficit to 5 per cent of GNP.

The MITI report (the Japanese Ministry of International Trade and Industry)

Anthony Rowley (*FEER*, 13 August 1992, pp. 59–60) summarizes the MITI report, which was presented to the Russian government in May 1992. The advice should be compared with that offered by the IMF. What is needed 'is for the government to take emergency measures to halt the output decline. Japan provides a useful example as it experienced a drastic plunge in production from 1945–49.' The thrust of Japanese policy after the war was to encourage competition, initially among domestic suppliers. Russia's priority should be to divide its state monopolies into competing companies, supplied by chains of smaller companies. Given the shortage of investment capital in key industries, MITI suggested that Russia could learn from the Japanese post-war experience of channelling funds through government institutions and private banks. Capital accumulation could be encouraged through preferential taxation schemes. Russia should also establish Japanese-style 'priority production programmes' to ensure the supply of essential goods.

Agriculture

Some additional information is to be found in *CDSP* (1992, vol. XLIV, no. 33, p. 28) and in *Russian Economic Trends* (1992, vol. 1, no. 2, pp. 37–8). By 1 August 1992 there were 132,903 peasant (private) farms in Russia, compared with 49,770 on 1 January 1992 (the number increased to 173,000: *FT*, 6 January 1993, p. 2). The average size of farm was 41 ha. From 1 January 1992 all collective and state farms were required to re-register as private farm holdings, private farm co-operatives or joint stock companies which could subsequently be broken up into smaller holdings. State farms retained the right to stay in their current form, but only after a vote taken by the workforce. Individual members of the collective and state farms had the right to take individual ownership of 'their share' of the land upon request to the authorities (about half of private farms have arisen in this way). By 1 July 1992 only 33 per cent of collective and state farms in Russia had re-registered and 44 per cent of those decided to retain their previous status. Denis Shaw ('Further progress with land reform' *Post-Soviet Geography*, 1992, vol. XXXIII, no. 8, p. 554) points out that as of 1 August 1992 private farms accounted for only 2.4 per cent of all agricultural land in Russia.

Western aid

September 1992. The EC's Tacis programme of technical assistance to the CIS and Georgia involves mainly advice, expertise, know-how and practical experience to help establish market economies and democratic societies. Ecu 850 million was to be made available over two years. On 9 December the European Commission approved Ecu 450 million of this aid, including Ecu 100 million to improve nuclear safety. Ukraine was to receive Ecu 48 million and Ecu 57.4 million was to go to Georgia, Armenia, Azerbaijan and the central Asian states combined. In 1991 the EC committed Ecu 400 million to the region (Lionel Barber, *FT*, 10 December 1992, p. 4).

The third international Conference on Assistance to the New Independent States (to co-ordinate aid for twelve states of the former Soviet Union, i.e. excluding the Baltic states) took place in Tokyo 29–30 October 1992. The IMF estimated that Russia would need at least $22 billion in official aid in 1993. The United States pledged new aid worth $412 million, e.g. $260 million for food and $14 million in medical aid. Japan pledged $100 million, mainly in the form of medical and food aid. A more permanent structure was envisaged in which the World Bank would be responsible for co-ordinating long-term technical aid.

9 November 1992. The UK doubles its 'know-how' fund to £100 million and extends the period beyond three years. Some £280 million in export credit guarantees was ready for disbursement.

The IMF. At present as much as a third of the IMF's worldwide technical assistance effort is being devoted to Russia and other countries of the former Soviet Union (John Odling-Smee, *FT*, 10 December 1992, p. 18).

Germany. On 16 December 1992, during the visit of Chancellor Kohl, agreement was reached to withdraw ex-Soviet troops from Germany by 31 August 1994 instead of by the end of that year. In return, Germany promised an extra DM 550 million to help house returning troops and an extra DM 1 billion for 'victims of Nazi persecution'. Germany also agreed to defer for eight years repayment of the DM 17.6 billion owed in transferable roubles to the former GDR. The DM 17.6 billion accounts for almost half the DM 36 billion owed by Russia to Germany (*IHT*, 17 December 1992, p. 2).

The $24 billion aid package of 1 April 1992. There is some dispute about how much of this aid was actually dispensed in 1992. Jeffrey Sachs (*IHT*, 23 December 1992, p. 8) contends that Russia received only about $10 billion and even this was overwhelmingly in the form of short-term commercial credits of less than three years.

The second Strategic Arms Reduction Treaty (Start 2)

On 29 December 1992 the US Secretary of State, Lawrence Eagleburger, and the Russian Foreign Minister, Andrei Kozyrev, announced that an agreement on Start 2 had been reached and that a treaty would be presented to their presidents for signing (the treaty was signed by Bush and Yeltsin on 3 January 1993). Whereas Start 1 aims finally to reduce strategic (long-range) nuclear warheads by approximately a third, Start 2 aims to reduce them by two-thirds. By the year 2003 the United States is to have some 3,500 warheads left (about the level of the early 1960s) and Russia is to have around 3,000 (roughly the level of the mid-1970s; the deadline could be reached three years earlier if sufficient US help is given for dismantling). Long-range, land-based missiles with multiple warheads are to be eliminated. Belarus, Kazakhstan and Ukraine had earlier agreed to become non-nuclear states, but implementation was another matter. Start 1 needs to be fully ratified before Start 2 can come into effect. Ukraine, for example, had not even ratified Start 1, although President Kravchuk expressed confidence that parliament would do so.

The Times (4 January 1993, p.1) provides detailed figures. In 1990 the United States had 12,646 strategic nuclear warheads and the Soviet Union had 11,012. Start 1 would reduce the totals to 8,556 and 6,163 respectively, while Start 2 would reduce them further to 3,500 and 3,000 respectively.

The performance of the Russian economy

Output. The rates of growth of Net Material Product (NMP) and industrial output (in brackets) since the mid-1980s are as follows (*Russian Economic Trends*, 1992, vol. 1, no. 2, p. 48): 1985, 2.0 per cent (3.4 per cent); 1986, 2.4 per cent (4.5 per cent); 1987, 0.7 per cent (3.5 per cent); 1988, 4.5 per cent (3.8 per cent); 1989, 1.9 per cent (1.4 per cent); 1990, −4.0 per cent (−0.1 per cent); 1991, −11.0 per cent (−2.2 per cent). Compared with the same period of 1991, in the first quarter of 1992 NMP fell by 14 per cent and industrial output by 13 per cent. In the second quarter of 1992 NMP fell by 22 per cent and industrial production by 14 per cent (in July by 21.5 per cent, in August by 27.2 per cent and in September by 24.8 per cent) (p. 48 and update table 11). Until the second quarter, the decline in output was due largely to supply factors (the collapse of the command economy and of both 'inter-republican' and Comecon trade; in 1991 Russian imports from the other republics of the then Soviet Union fell by 46 per cent and the decline steepened the following year: *The Economist*, A Survey of Russia, 5 December 1992, p. 10). But in the second quarter demand-side factors became important. Demand conditions tightened, partly owing to cuts in budgetary purchases, especially defence goods, but also owing to a steep fall (in real terms) in both consumer expenditure (after price liberalization) and investment. In the first quarter there was a large build-up of stocks as enterprises continued to produce at previous levels. In the second quarter, however, enterprises acted to prevent further stockbuilding by substantial cuts in production (p. 5 and p. 28).

The Russian government forecast that national output would decline by some 25 per cent in 1992 and by 5–8 per cent in 1993. The respective predicted falls in industrial production were 18–20 per cent and 8–10 per cent (Tony Barber, *The Independent*, 16 October 1992, p. 11).

The president of Kazakhstan, Nursultan Nazarbayev, claimed, in a 19 August 1992 speech, that 65 per cent of the fall in production on the whole territory of the former Soviet Union was due to the breaking of economic ties and that another 20 per cent could be attributed to the loss of ties with the former Comecon countries of Eastern Europe (*CDSP*, 1992, vol. XLIV, no. 33, p. 23).

One bright spot was the 1992 grain harvest in Russia. At 100 million tonnes it was 20 per cent higher than the year before (*The Economist*, 26 December 1992, p. 139).

Unemployment. Information on the monthly totals of people 'out of employment' (i.e. not in work, but seeking and available for a job) are provided by *Russian Economic Trends* (1992, vol.1, no. 2, p. 34 and update table 12). The registered unemployed numbers are in brackets, lower figures because those people still being paid by former employers are not counted (a worker is eligible for pay for up to three months after redundancy). The figures are as follows: January, 484,400 (64,000); February, 552,580 (93,100); March, 617,660 (118,400); April, 695,400 (151,000); May, 742,350 (176,500); June, 779,860 (202,900); July, 842,690 (248,000); August, 888,210 (1.3 per cent of the labour force) (303,000 or 0.4 per cent); September, 921,260 (367,470). Only 1.7 million working days were lost between January and June 1992 because of strikes lasting more than one day, mainly in 'budget' sectors such as education and health (p. 20). An unemployed worker receives full pay for three months and then a declining percentage of the most recent two months' pay during the following year. Unemployment benefit can never be less than the minimum wage, while those who have never had a job receive the minimum wage. Benefits end after a year, after which the intention is to provide income support through public works or training programmes (p. 22).

Inflation. The monthly rate of increase in consumer prices in 1992 (compared to the previous month) was as follows (*Russian Economic Trends*, 1992, vol. 1, no. 2, p. 58 and update table 1): January, 244.97 per cent; February, 38.28 per cent; March, 29.76 per cent; April, 21.65 per cent; May, 11.96 per cent; June, 18.62 per cent; July, 10.00 per cent; August, 9.00 per cent; September, 12.00 per cent; October, 23.86 per cent. John Lloyd (*FT*, 6 January 1993, p. 2) reports 33 per cent in November and 25 per cent in December.

The Soviet inflation rate was 5.6 per cent in 1990 and 86 per cent in 1991 (*FT*, 23 April 1992,

p. 6). The World Bank predicted a Russian inflation rate of 2,200 per cent in 1992 (*FT*, 25 September 1992, p. 4).

Foreign trade and debt. In the first six months of 1992 imports continued to collapse, while Russian exports were 35 per cent less in dollar terms than a year earlier; crude oil exports were 16 per cent less (*Russian Economic Trends*, 1992, vol. 1, no. 2, pp. 31–2). The foreign debt now amounts to $80 billion (*Moscow News*, 22–9 November 1992, p. 3). On 28 August 1992 Gaidar stated that Russia was unable to pay more than $2 billion of its external debt in 1992 even though Russia and the CIS countries were due to repay $9.8 billion. As of 27 July 1992 Russia had paid about $1 billion (*Russian Economic Trends*, 1992, vol. 1, no. 2, p. 45). As of 1 January 1992 the Soviet Union had bequeathed a foreign debt of $68 billion ($50 billion of which was owed to other governments and $18 billion to commercial banks); by mid-1992 the figure was $75.4 billion and has since climbed to $86 billion (*IHT*, 17 December 1992, pp. 9, 11). Fifty-two per cent of the debt is due to be repaid 1993–95, while there was $7 billion of debt relief in 1992. By the end of November 1992 four republics of the former Soviet Union had arranged for Russia to pay their share of the debt and seven others were still negotiating.

Pay and living standards. The average monthly wage in roubles (that for industry in brackets) was as follows: January 1992, 1,438 (1,801); July 1992, 5,452 (6,256) (*Russian Economic Trends*, 1992, vol. 1, no. 2, p. 59). The minimum wage and the minimum pension were raised to 900 roubles a month in May 1992 and to 1,350 roubles in September (p. 22). In November 1992 the minimum pension went up to 2,250 roubles a month (this compared with the officially estimated cost of a minimum food basket of nearly 2,500 roubles in October); the average wage was 7,500 roubles a month (*Moscow News*, 22–9 November 1992, p. 10). For the population as a whole, food consumption in 1992 has been roughly the same as in the early 1970s (*Russian Economic Trends*, 1992, vol. 1, no. 2, p. 25). On 22 September 1992 Gaidar reported that in the year to August 1992 consumer prices had increased by 1,460 per cent as against only a 960 per cent increase in the pay of workers and office employees (*CDSP*, 1992, vol. XLIV, no. 38, p. 1). By the end of June 1992 the number of people with incomes below the poverty threshold (1,200 roubles a month) was around 13 million (p. 2). Jonathan Steele (*The Guardian*, 3 December 1992, p. 21) reports the findings of the International Institute of Economic and Social Reforms headed by Stanislav Shatalin. Average incomes had barely kept up with half of the rise in prices, at least 80 per cent of the population had suffered 'a sharp worsening in their standard of living' and some 17 per cent of the population were on the verge of survival; 'If current economic policy is not changed, Russia may lose half its industrial production.' John Lloyd (*FT*, 5 January 1993, p. 15) says that 'end-of-year figures show wages have risen twelve-fold over the past year in nominal terms, but there has been a twenty-fold rise in the consumer price index'.

THE CIS AND THE OTHER REPUBLICS

Brief histories of the former republics of the Soviet Union

Armenia. Yerevan and Nakhichevan became part of the Russian Empire in 1828 and further territory was annexed after the 1877–78 war with the Ottoman Empire. Independence was achieved in May 1918, for the first time since the Middle Ages, but Bolshevik control was established by the end of 1920.

Azerbaijan. Incorporated into the Russian Empire in the early nineteenth century. Independence was achieved in May 1918, but Bolshevik control was established in 1920. Nagorno-Karabakh was granted to Azerbaijan in 1923.

Belarus (Belorussia). Incorporated into the Russian Empire in the late eighteenth century. Independence was declared on 25 March 1918, but it became a Soviet republic on 1 January 1919.

Estonia. Incorporated into the Russian Empire in 1710, after Peter the Great defeated Sweden at the Battle of Poltava in 1709. Declared independence in 1918, but was incorporated into the Soviet Union 1940–41 and 1945–91.

Georgia. Incorporated into the Russian Empire in the early nineteenth century. Independence was declared after the Russian Revolution, but the Bolsheviks took control in 1921. Stalin was a Georgian.

Kazakhstan. Gradually incorporated into the Russian Empire during the eighteenth and nineteenth centuries.

Kyrgyzstan (Kirghizia). Incorporated into the Russian Empire during the nineteenth century. A Soviet autonomous Turkestan republic was formed in 1918, but in 1924 this was divided into the republics of Kighizia, Tajikistan and Uzbekistan.

Latvia. Incorporated into the Russian Empire in 1710, after Peter the Great defeated Sweden at the Battle of Poltava in 1709. Declared independence in November 1918, but incorporated into the Soviet Union 1940–41 and 1945–91.

Lithuania. Incorporated into the Russian Empire in 1795. Independence was declared in February 1918, although in 1919 Vilnius (Wilno) was captured by Poland. Incorporated into the Soviet Union 1940–41 and 1945–91.

Moldova (Moldavia). Most of Bessarabia (south-east Moldavia) was gained by Russia in 1812. In 1918, however, Bessarabia became part of Romania. The Moldavian Soviet Socialist Republic was incorporated into the Soviet Union 1940–41 and 1945–91.

Russia. Russia's origins are to be found in the Ukraine (Kiev Rus) in the ninth century. Vladimir, Grand Prince of Kiev (980–1015), adopted the Christian faith in its Eastern Orthodox (Byzantine) form as the state religion. The Muscovite Principality emerged pre-eminent out of the Mongol (Tatar) domination of the thirteenth and fourteenth centuries and subsequently evolved into the Russian Empire (it expanded eastwards, but not into other continents, with the exception of Alaska which was sold to the United States in 1867). Ivan IV (Ivan the Terrible) was crowned Tsar (or Czar; Emperor, from the Roman Caesar) of 'all the Russias' (including the Ukraine and Belorussia) in 1547. The Romanov dynasty, inaugurated in 1613, came to an end when Nicholas II abdicated following the February (March according to the new calendar) 1917 Russian Revolution. The Bolsheviks under Lenin took control after the October (November) 1917 Revolution. They pulled Russia out of the First World War in December 1917, signed a separate peace with Germany in March 1918 (Brest-Litovsk) and won the civil war of 1918–21. After Lenin died in January 1924 Stalin ruthlessly fought and won a succession struggle with his main rivals Nikolai Bukharin (executed in 1938) and Leon Trotsky (exiled and then murdered, at Stalin's behest, in 1940). Stalin (literally 'man of steel') died in 1953. The Soviet Union ceased to exist towards the end of 1991.

Tajikistan. Incorporated into the Russian Empire during the nineteenth century. Bolshevik control was established in 1921.

Turkmenistan. Incorporated into the Russian Empire during the nineteenth century. The Red Army took control in 1920.

Ukraine. The Ukraine, then known as 'Little Russia' (Malorussia), was united with the Russian Empire in 1654–86. A Ukrainian republic was proclaimed on 25 December 1917, but the Ukraine was incorporated into the Soviet Union on 30 December 1922.

Uzbekistan. Incorporated into the Russian Empire during the nineteenth century.

Recent developments in the former republics of the Soviet Union

According to the 1989 census 25.3 million Russians lived in the other republics. *The Independent* (16 November 1992, p. 10) published figures showing the proportion of Russians in the population of each of the various republics, in descending order: Russia (81.3 per cent), Kazakhstan (36.5 per cent), Latvia (34 per cent), Estonia (30.2 per cent), Ukraine (21.8 per cent), Kyrgyzstan (21.5 per cent), Belarus (13.2 per cent), Moldova (13 per cent), Turkmenistan (9.5 per cent), Lithuania (9.4 per cent), Uzbekistan (8.3 per cent), Tajikistan (7.5 per cent), Georgia (6.2 per cent), Azerbaijan (5.6 per cent) and Armenia (1.5 per cent). Many Russians moved after the break-up of the Soviet Union, especially from the Asiatic republics and war zones. On 24 September 1992 Gaidar mentioned the problems Russia was experiencing in having to cope with 460,000 refugees from the former republics.

9 October 1992 meeting of the CIS. It was decided to set up an inter-governmental clearing bank. Tajikistan was offered a CIS peacekeeping force (actually troops from Kyrgyzstan, although Kyrgyzstan later withdrew the offer).

4 January 1993, Kazakhstan, Kyrgyzstan, Tajikistan, Turkmenistan and Uzbekistan declare the aim of a common market.

Ukraine

18 September 1992. Russia froze financial transactions with Ukraine, refusing to accept any more payments from the Ukrainian central bank (owing to its large-scale granting of credit to Ukrainian enterprises). A series of short-term, one-off trade arrangements followed. Trade between Russia and Ukraine constituted 72 per cent of total trade within the former Soviet Union (Chrystia Freeland, *FT*, 23 July 1992, p. 4).

30 September 1992. Prime Minister Vitold Fokin resigned (he was appointed in October 1990).

1 October 1992. The whole government resigned after a vote in parliament.

2 October 1992. Valentyn Simonenko became acting prime minister.

13 October 1992. Leonid Kuchma was appointed prime minister, the former director of the largest nuclear missile enterprise in Ukraine. He talked of an 'evolutionary' transition to a market economy and of the economy being guided by 'a combination of administrative and market methods'. In contrast to Gaidar, he had spoken positively about the Chinese economic model.

12 November 1992. Ukraine announced that as of midnight the rouble would cease to be legal tender. It would be replaced by a new coupon (karbovanets). Roubles could be exchanged on a one-to-one basis within three days. The introduction of the grivna would have to await economic reform and the establishment of a stabilization fund.

18 November 1992. Prime Minister Kuchma surprised parliament with a speech advocating stabilization and market-orientated reforms in order to combat the dire economic situation. He cited an 18 per cent fall in GNP and a 2,200 per cent increase in wholesale prices since the start of 1992. There should be a stricter monetary and fiscal policy. Monthly inflation should be reduced from 30 per cent to 2–3 per cent within a year and the budget deficit from 44 per cent to 5–6 per cent of GDP. Privatization and market reforms in agriculture should be speeded up. Kuchma recommended certain controls, such as on wages in state enterprises, foreign currency controls and export restrictions (with tariffs on imports). Minimum living standards should be preserved for those most adversely affected by the changes. Parliament granted Kuchma wide powers to take economic decisions until at least 1 May 1993. Kuchma ordered (on 2 December 1992) preparations to be made to privatize a quarter of all small businesses and retail outlets within four months (*EEN*, 1992, vol. 6, no. 25, p. 3). He launched an anti-corruption drive and thought that 'there are no alternatives to the market and even if someone were to try to recreate the old system it would lead to a complete catastrophe' (reported by Chrystia Freeland, *FT*, 21 December 1992, p. 34). Restructuring and privatization should be speeded up, while Kuchma was lobbying for a 'social compact' that would place a moratorium on strikes and political demonstrations (Chrystia Freeland, *IHT*, 2 January 1993, p. 8).

23 December 1992. It was announced that

from the beginning of 1993 the number of goods and services subject to price controls would rise by 25 per cent (*IHT*, 24 December 1992, p. 13). The measures would remove price controls on some basic foodstuffs (including milk, butter and some types of bread), but would tighten controls on goods such as metals, chemicals, oil, sugar, meat and eggs as well as goods produced by monopolies. The government also published a list of enterprises and organizations approved to export most natural resources and issued a decree allowing people to apply to own the land they used as allotments.

5 January 1993. Ukraine announced that it would pay its own share of the foreign debt of the former Soviet Union, thus overturning the November 1992 deal with Russia. On 16 January the two countries signed an agreement on their respective shares of both the debts and assets.

Privatization (*Moscow News*, 11–18 October 1992, p.10). The privatization programme should be completed within four to five years. By the end of 1995 46 per cent of all property should be in private hands, compared with 4 per cent at present. Each citizen was to receive vouchers worth 30,000 coupons/roubles. It would be possible to purchase with vouchers 70 per cent of property being privatized, but the vouchers themselves would not be able to be sold for cash (shares, of course, could be sold later on).

Agriculture (*CDSP*, 1992, vol. XLIV, no. 33, p. 28). As of 1 July 1992 9,600 private farms had been registered, with an average size of 19 ha.

Economic performance In 1992 inflation was 2,500 per cent and the budget deficit was 36 per cent of GDP (note that by giving plots of land to private citizens Ukraine has created 13 million private smallholders; these garden plots are the main source of food for the cities) (Edward Balls and Chrystia Freeland, *FT*, 18 January 1993, p. 2).

Armenia

Agriculture (*CDSP*, 1992, vol. XLIV, no. 33, p. 28). As of 1 July 1992 a large proportion of farms had been converted to peasant farms, of which there were 229,000 (with an average size of a little more than 1 ha). Intends to introduce its own currency (the dram).

Azerbaijan

Agriculture (*CDSP*, 1992, vol. XLIV, no. 33, p. 28). As of 1 July 1992 230 private farms had been registered, with an average size of 44 ha.

September 1992. Oil deal with BP–Statoil.

7 October 1992. Parliament rejects CIS membership.

Belarus

Agriculture (*CDSP*, 1992, vol. XLIV, no. 33, p. 28). As of 1 July 1992 1,800 private farms had been registered, with an average size of 19 ha.

Economic performance. The DIW (*Economic Bulletin*, 1992, vol. 29, no. 10, p. 3) forecast a fall in GDP in 1992 of 17 per cent and an inflation rate of 1,200 per cent.

Estonia

23 June 1992. Became a member of the World Bank. In the autumn of 1992 the IMF approved a stand-by loan of $41 million for the following year, while the World Bank earmarked $30 million. In 1992 Estonia received Ecu 10 million under the EC's Phare programme (*FT Survey*, 16 December 1992, p. 14).

7 September 1992. Free trade agreement with Russia.

20 September 1992. Parliamentary and presidential elections, but up to 40 per cent of the adult population was unable to vote because of the relatively strict citizenship law (about 62 per cent of the total population is Estonian). The election produced a right-of-centre, nationalist coalition, but no presidential candidate had 50 per cent of the vote, so parliament had to decide.

One forecast put the fall in GNP in 1992 at 16.5 per cent (*Euromoney*, September 1992, p. 72).

Georgia

During August 1992 vicious fighting broke out in Abkhazia. The Abkhazians constitute only 17–18 per cent of the population of Abkhazia, but scored significant military successes against Georgia with the aid of volunteers from the Confederation of Caucasian Mountain People. This organization was formed in 1991 with the ultimate aim of forming a confederation of Moslem peoples from the Caucasian areas of Russia, Georgia and Azerbaijan. Georgia also suspected that the Abkhazians were obtaining weapons from Russian troops in the location. On 3 October Georgia threatened to take over all Russian military hardware on Georgian soil, which led to a deterioration of relations with Russia.

11 October 1992. Eduard Shevardnadze was elected speaker of parliament, with 95 per cent popular support on a high turn-out (the title 'president' was deemed unsuitable after the ousting of the previous incumbent).

National income fell by 5 per cent in 1989, by 12 per cent in 1990 and by 25 per cent in 1991 (Steve Levine, *FT*, 24 August 1992, p. 10).

Kazakhstan

Privatization. Ten per cent of state industry claimed to be privatized (*EEN*, 24 August 1992, vol. 6, no. 17, p. 5).

Agriculture. As of 1 July 1992 7,800 private farms had been registered, with an average size of 274 ha (*CDSP*, 1992, vol. XLIV, no. 33, p. 28). Land sales are forbidden (Ahmed Rashid, *FEER*, 3 December 1992, p. 20). Land has not been privatized, but is being leased to farmers and others with the right of inheritance (Denis Shaw, 'Further progress with land reform', *Post-Soviet Geography*, 1992, vol. XXXIII, no. 8, p. 556).

President Nazarbayev favours a CIS economic council to co-ordinate policy, a CIS banking union for those remaining in the rouble zone, and making the rouble a supranational currency (*CDSP*, 1992, vol. XLIV, no. 33, p. 23).

Economic performance. While there was an overall fall in GDP in 1992, agricultural output actually increased by around 30 per cent; industrial output fell by some 20 per cent (Deutsche Bank, *Focus: Eastern Europe*, 10 December 1992, no. 63, p. 3) (note that the same source reports that the liberalization of prices for staple goods was rapidly abandoned in January 1992: p. 3).

Kyrgyzstan

Agriculture. As of 1 July 1992, 7,300 private farms had been registered, with an average size of 55 ha (*CDSP*, 1992, vol. XLIV, no. 33, p. 28). Land sales are forbidden (Ahmed Rashid, *FEER*, 3 December 1992, p. 20).

September 1992. Joins the IMF. The IMF, World Bank and donor countries have promised credits worth $300 million to $400 million (*Moscow News*, 15–22 November 1992, p. 10). Intended to introduce own currency by 1995.

Latvia

The United Nations Economic Commission for Europe estimated that in the first half of 1992 GDP fell by almost a third compared with the same period of 1991, 'the largest decline in any transition economy not racked by civil law or armed conflict' (reported by Frances Williams, *FT*, 7 December 1992, p. 2). Latvia now has a relatively strict citizenship law. Only around 52 per cent of the population is Latvian. Only citizens are able to receive land as property to be owned by them and people who were citizens before 1940 (or their descendants) are eligible for 'a little more' by way of privatization vouchers (*Moscow News*, 8–15 November 1992, p. 7).

Towards the end of July 1992 the rublis was introduced, with the eventual aim of introducing the country's own currency (the lat). In the autumn of 1992 the IMF approved a stand-by loan of $82 million for the following year, while the World Bank earmarked $45 million (*FT Survey*, 16 December 1992, p. 14).

Lithuania

Lithuania has not followed Estonia and Latvia as regards its citizenship law. About 80 per cent of the population is Lithuanian.

Privatization. Deutsche Bank (*Focus: Eastern Europe*, 23 October 1992, no. 59, pp. 3–4) provided the following information. Privatization was said to be making good progress. Around 15 per cent of state enterprises had been privatized, including some large ones. Small-enterprise privatization was some 80 per cent complete. Privatization is by auction (small enterprises), purchase of shares (large enterprises) or vouchers. There were some 300 investment funds. There is a list of enterprises which can only be purchased with hard currencies. To date foreigners are still not permitted to buy land. Lithuania claims to have privatized more than 50 per cent of state-owned dwellings (John Lloyd, *FT*, 19 November 1992, p. 22).

Finance. Deutsche Bank (*Focus: Eastern Europe*, 23 October 1992, pp. 2–3) reported that preparations were being made for the introduction of the country's own currency (the litas). Since 1 October 1992 the 'talonas' (coupon) had served as an interim currency (officially convertible within Lithuania), after circulating for roughly one year as a parallel currency. But even since 1 October the rouble and convertible currencies such as the dollar had been accepted as means of payment in the private sector. In the autumn of 1992 the IMF approved a stand-by loan of $82 million, while the World Bank earmarked $60 million (*FT Survey*, 16 December 1992, p. 14).

8 September 1992. Agreement in principle with Russia to withdraw its troops by the end of August 1993.

The general election. The two rounds were held on 25 October and 17 November 1992 and produced an extremely disappointing result for Vytautas Landsbergis, speaker of parliament and leader of Sajudis (the nationalist grouping, meaning 'the movement'). The Democratic Labour Party, led by Algirdas Brazauskas, won an absolute majority of seats in the Seimas (parliament), specifically seventy-three out of 141 seats (Sajudis won only thirty). He had taken the Lithuanian Communist Party out of the CPSU in December 1989. Brazuaskas benefited from the deteriorating economic conditions, including deficient fuel supplies from Russia. (Industrial output fell by 50 per cent in the first ten months of 1992: *The Economist*, 21 November 1992, p. 59; *Euromoney*, September 1992, p. 72, forecast a fall in GNP of 19 per cent in 1992.) He campaigned on a platform of a more gradual and less harsh transition to the market and of improved relations with Russia.

Moldova

Agriculture (*CDSP*, 1992, vol. XLIV, no. 33, p. 28). As of 1 July 1992 284 private farms had been registered, with an average size of 3 ha.

7 October 1992. Romania–Moldova committee to co-ordinate the two parliaments. An investment fund for joint ventures was to be considered.

Tajikistan

Agriculture (*CDSP*, 1992, vol. XLIV, no. 33, p. 28). As of 1 July 1992 four private farms had been registered, with an average size of 16 ha.

Akbarshah Iskandarov, speaker of parliament, became acting president after Nabiyev was forced to resign on 7 September 1992. Iskandarov ruled out the creation of an Islamic republic. The situation deteriorated during the summer of 1992, with the level of fighting approaching that of a civil war. Nabiyev sup- porters actually took over government buildings in Dushanbe 24–5 October, but the attempt to topple the government failed. With the approval of the government, Russian troops secured the main roads leading into the capital, the airport, the railway station and the television centre. In fact the government appealed for more Russian troops.

12 October 1992. It was announced that Tajikistan intend to retain the rouble.

19 October 1992. Imamali Rakhmanov replaced Iskandarov as acting president.

10 December 1992. Moslem and liberal democratic forces were overcome and Rakhmanov took over in Dushanbe the following day. One report talked of one in ten of the population being displaced by the civil war (*IHT*, 24 December 1992, p. 2).

Turkmenistan

Agriculture (*CDSP*, 1992, vol. XLIV, no. 33, p. 28). As of 1 July 1992 100 private farms had been registered, with an average size of 10 ha.

Uzbekistan

Agriculture (*CDSP*, 1992, vol. XLIV, no. 33, p. 28). As of 1 July 1992 4,400 private farms had been registered, with an average size of 8 ha.

2 November 1992. Uzbekistan gave up any claim on the assets of the former Soviet Union in return for Russia assuming responsibility for Uzbekistan's share of the debt.

The IMF

April 1992. The Board of Governors agreed to admit fourteen of the states of the former Soviet Union; membership of the fifteenth (Azerbaijan) was agreed on 4 May 1992 (IMF, *Annual Report*, 1992, p. 29). By the end of July 1992 Armenia (0.05 per cent), Belarus (0.20 per cent), Estonia (0.03 per cent), Georgia (0.08 per cent), Kazakhstan (0.17 per cent), Kyrgyzstan (0.04 per cent), Latvia (0.06 per cent), Lithuania (0.07 per cent) and Russia (3.00 per cent) had actually become members (pp. 70–1, IMF quotas at the end of April 1992 in brackets). The total quota was 4.76 per cent, with the remaining individual quotas as follows: Azerbaijan (0.08 per cent), Moldova (0.06 per cent), Tajikistan (0.04 per cent), Turkmenistan (0.03 per cent), Ukraine (0.69 per cent) and Uzbekistan (0.14 per cent). (A CIS meeting was held on 22 January 1993, at which Azerbaijan was only an observer. Seven members signed a charter on closer political and economic integration. Ukraine, Moldova and Turkmenistan only signed the memorandum, allowing them time to reflect.)

MONGOLIA

The reforms, designed to move the economy to a market-based system over three and a half years, were supported by an IMF stand-by arrangement for SDR 22.5 million approved on 4 October 1991 (IMF, *Annual Report*, 1992, p. 61). In August 1992, however, the IMF froze two parts of the stand-by facility totalling SDR 8.8 billion ($12.6 billion) until the specified conditions were met, especially monetary targets (Peter Hannam, *FEER*, 29 October 1992, p. 71). This triggered a halt in $25 million of loans from the World Bank and the Asian Development Bank. Puntsagiyn Jasray was appointed prime minister on 21 July 1992 and took some time to choose a cabinet and formulate an economic programme. Even so, at the start of October most state-controlled prices were increased sharply (e.g. some grades of flour fivefold) and interest rates were also raised. In the first nine months of 1992 industrial output declined by 17.9 per cent from a year earlier (p. 72).

Hugh Fraser (*FT*, 27 November 1992, p. 6) provides the following information on privatization. Each citizen receives a voucher worth 10,000 tugriks, of which 7,000 tugriks can be used for larger privatizations and 3,000 tugriks can be used to buy livestock or small businesses. Between February and October 1992 121 enterprises were floated on the Mongolian stock exchange and the target was set at 500 by the end of the year. The enterprises excluded from privatization are bankrupt ones or those considered too important (e.g. significant hard currency earners such as the Gobi cashmere enterprise). Around 90 per cent of small shops and 60 per cent of livestock are now in private hands. As regards economic performance, inflation was 120 per cent in 1991 and averaged 14 per cent a month in the first seven months of 1992 (partly because of the liberalization of prices). A fall in GDP of around 5 per cent was expected in 1992, compared with a fall of 9.2 per cent the previous year.

CHINA

A special issue of *The China Quarterly* (1992, no. 131) is entitled 'The Chinese economy in the 1990s'. J. Chai ('Consumption and living standards in China') concludes that 'Since 1978 real *per capita* consumption in China has risen at an average annual rate of 7 per cent … As a result, the standard of living of the average Chinese citizen in 1990 was more than double that of 1978' (p. 721). Y. Kueh ('Foreign investment and economic change in China') provides estimates of the impact of foreign investment on the Chinese economy. In 1985 direct foreign investment accounted for 2.26 per cent of total 'fixed assets investment' (16.01 per cent of fixed investment in the Special Economic Zones). In 1990 the figures were 4.03 per cent and 33.72 per cent respectively. If capital borrowing from abroad is added to direct foreign investment, the respective percentages go up to 5.14 per cent (25.79 per cent) in 1985 and 11.04 per cent (49.30 per cent) in 1990 (p. 656). In 1991 foreign-invested enterprises accounted for 16.8 per cent of total exports and 45.8 per cent of the exports of the SEZs (p. 668).

The EIU (*Country Report*, 1992, no. 3, p. 19) reported the following. The 1992 'three irons' campaign seemed to be petering out in the face of worker unrest. The 'three irons' are the iron ricebowl of lifetime guaranteed employment, the iron post of job security for enterprise officials, and the iron wage of pay unrelated to performance. A new enterprise law was adopted on 30 June 1992, but as yet only applied experimentally in a few enterprises and only to be implemented 'over a period of time'. The idea is that enterprises should be free to import, export, invest, negotiate with foreign partners, hire and fire workers, set their own prices and even declare themselves bankrupt.

A survey on China (*The Economist*, 28 November 1992) provides some updated information. The official figures given for GNP *per capita* (e.g. the World Bank's estimate of $370 for 1990) are a considerable underestimate (p.

1). Whereas in 1978 around 700 kinds of producer goods were allocated by the plan, by 1991 the number was below twenty. Even in the case of state enterprises, according to one estimate, in 1989 around 56 per cent of inputs were purchased outside the plan and almost 40 per cent of output was sold outside the plan. Today the market distributes almost 60 per cent of coal, 55 per cent of steel and 90 per cent of cement (p. 7). The state sector now accounts for only just over 50 per cent of industrial output, compared with 78 per cent in 1978 (p. 8). The respective shares of non-agricultural employment are 40 per cent and 60 per cent (p. 16). If agriculture and services are included, the state's share of output is now no more than 25 per cent (p. 8). In 1978 farming accounted for 70 per cent of rural output and industry for only 20 per cent. Today the former's share is around 45 per cent and the latter's only a percentage point or two less (p. 16). By the early 1990s rural industries accounted for almost 40 per cent of industrial employment, more than a quarter of industrial output and nearly a quarter of exports (p. 15). Around $20 billion was traded in swap centres in 1991 (p. 18). By 1991 there were roughly 20,000 foreign ventures, with a cumulative investment of $22 billion. Some $3.5 billion was invested in 1991 alone (the *FEER*, 24–31 December 1992, p. 72, puts the figure at $4.2 billion) and $6.6 billion was invested in the first nine months of 1992 (p. 18). Today foreign-financed ventures account for a quarter of the exports of manufactures (p. 18). One estimate puts the share of direct foreign investment provided by overseas Chinese from Hong Kong and Taiwan at almost three-quarters (p. 19). Foreigners are for the first time being allowed to set up service businesses (p. 18).

G. Feder, L. Lau, J. Lin, and X. Luo (1992), 'The determinants of farm investment and residential construction in post-reform China', *Economic Development and Cultural Change*, vol. 41, no. 1 report as follows. The average family farm is 0.55 ha and there are, on average, nine plots per farm (p. 6). There were several incidents in different parts of China during the second half of 1988 in which local authorities forced the consolidation of small farms (p. 7).

9 August 1992. The start of the distribution (by queue, with very large numbers physically standing in line) of application forms for shares at the Shenzhen stock exchange led to serious disturbances over allegations that corrupt officials had given themselves preferential access. Note that the stock exchanges mentioned in the text refer to the officially sanctioned ones. It seems that unofficial ones have sprung up and some may even have continued to operate after being ordered to close (e.g. the one in Hainan, it is claimed). A watchdog securities commission was announced in late October 1992. Until the start of 1993 only Fujian, Guangdong and Hainan were allowed to list enterprises on the Shanghai and Shenzhen stock exchanges. But other provinces are now permitted to list some of their top enterprises (*FEER*, 14 January 1993, p. 55; *IHT*, 4 January 1993, p. 7).

1 September 1992. Central price control was ended on 593 materials and industrial products, including, for example, soda ash, high-quality steels, glass and electrical machinery. This reduced the number directly priced by the government to eighty-nine, from 737 at the end of 1991. The reform was not expected to have too great an impact on the prices of consumer goods. On 28 November 1992 the government announced the removal of price controls on rice and other basic grain products in Sichuan province (this had been accomplished in the autumn in Anhui and a number of other provinces). The intention was to do the same throughout the country in one to three years. On 1 December 1992 the prices of meat and eggs in Beijing were decontrolled (the only ration coupons remaining were for grain and cooking oil). Income compensation was to be given in all cases (Sheryll WuDunn, *IHT*, 30 November 1992, p. 2).

9 October 1992. Confirmation that Zhao Ziyang, during the events of Tiananmen Square, made the serious mistake of 'supporting the turmoil and splitting the party'.

China Brilliance Automotive Holdings became the first state enterprise in mainland China to sell shares abroad (in the United States).

China Briefing (October 1992, no. 42, pp. 1–3) reports the decision in late June 1992 to open up the retail trade sector to joint ventures with foreign companies on an experimental basis. Until then foreign investment had been confined to food services (e.g. McDonald's) and small supermarkets (mostly attached to foreign-invested hotels). In early September it was announced that foreign companies would be able to establish joint venture travel agencies, albeit with operations restricted to holiday resorts catering for overseas tourists (p. 5). In addition, five northern cities (four in March 1992 and one in August) were granted the equivalent of 'open coastal city' status in order to encourage border trade (one city is Hunchun, clearly related to North Korea's Tumen river development) (pp. 7–8).

Carl Goldstein (*FEER*, 24–31 December 1992, pp. 72–3) adds some further information about foreign investment. In June 1992 twenty-one more cities were authorized to offer extra incentives. About 90 per cent of the cumulative foreign investments have gone into the coastal provinces, 40 per cent in Guangdong alone. In 1991 a Japanese retailer became the first foreign company to win permission to open a joint venture department store. From 1979 to 1991, according to government figures, actual investment amounted to around 59 per cent of contracted investment.

By November 1992 225 representative offices of foreign banks had been set up in fourteen cities, while in thirteen cities sixty-seven foreign financial institutions had been allowed to open branches (*IHT*, 14 December 1992, p. 18).

11 October 1992. Trade agreement with the United States. The United States withdrew its threat to raise tariffs on a wide range of Chinese goods in return for a lowering of trade barriers to US goods and for the publicizing of China's trade rules.

15 December 1992. It was announced that, as of 1 January 1993, there would be a 7.3 per cent reduction in general tariffs; the tariff rates on 3,371 items would be reduced. Other measures that were to be taken included reducing the need for licences on two-thirds of imports within two years, while a promise was also given to cut the overall tariff rate to 15 per cent (*IHT*, 16 December 1992, p. 21).

The Fourteenth Party Congress (12–18 October 1992)

12 October 1992. General Secretary Jiang Zemin's speech to almost 2,000 delegates lauded Deng's ideas: 'we must hold high the great banner of socialism with Chinese characteristics'; 'if we fail to develop our economy rapidly, it will be very difficult for us to consolidate the socialist system and maintain long-term social stability'; 'the goal is to build a socialist democracy suited to Chinese conditions and absolutely not a Western, multi-party, parliamentary system'; the development of a 'socialist market economy' was the only way forward: 'we are convinced that a market economy established under the socialist system can and should operate better than one under the capitalist system'; macroeconomic levers should be the main means of control ('macro-regulation' became a catchword); the plan should, for example, set 'strategic targets', include growth forecasts and deal with investment in the infrastructure; there should be an integrated national market with no regional protectionism, markets embracing 'bonds, stocks ... technology, labour, information ... real estate, so as to form an integrated national market system open to all'; shareholding will 'help promote the separation of the functions of government from those of enterprises'; 'we must change the way in which state-owned enterprises operate and push them on to the market'; China should allow 'efficient enterprises [to] prosper . . . inefficient ones will be eliminated'; to help any unemployment problem the service sector should expand and the social security system should be reformed; the public sector (which includes collective enterprises) would remain dominant, but should compete 'in the market on an equal footing' – the private sector would act as 'a supplement' and some small state enterprises should be leased or sold to collectives or individuals; most prices were eventually to be market-determined; the growth target was to be raised from 6 per cent to 8–9 per cent a year during the 1991–95 Five Year Plan; it was necessary to tackle corruption, bureaucracy and incompetence.

On the final day of the congress the delegates gave unanimous approval to Deng's reforms (although he himself only made a brief appearance on the day after the formal end of the congress, which he had been asked to attend as a 'specially invited guest'). The new Central Committee was also chosen. The number of full members was increased from 175 to 189 (46.7 per cent were new members, compared with a third in 1987). The number of alternate members was fixed at 130. It was claimed that relative youth was an important consideration; it was said that 61 per cent were below the age of 55 and that the average age was 56.3. Also noticeable was the higher representation of the army, the educated and the provinces. The charge of nepotism was avoided by not favouring the leaders' children.

The new politburo and its standing committee were announced on 19 October 1992, another triumph for Deng. The politburo was increased from fourteen to twenty-two, with an average age of 62.4 (there were fifteen new members, including Zou Jiahua, head of the State Planning Commission). The standing committee, the politburo's inner core of leaders, was increased from six to seven. There were three new members, Zhu Rongji, General Liu Huaqing (the army's representation in the party as a whole was boosted to help ensure political stability, including the suppression of any

worker unrest over unemployment as enterprises are closed) and Hu Jintao (the former party secretary for Tibet). The crucial appointment from an economic point of view in particular was that of Zhu Rongji (aged 63), who was previously only an alternate member of the Central Committee. He was mayor of Shanghai 1987–92, restoring order there in 1989 without resort to the military. Staunchly in favour of economic reform, in June 1992 he was made head of the Economic and Trade Office (some observers see this as an embryonic MITI, the Japanese Ministry of International Trade and Industry). The Central Advisory Commission was abolished during the congress. This 'retirement home' for veteran party members had tended to become a source of resistance to economic reform.

Post-congress developments

18 December 1992. At a national conference on the economy, Jiang Zemin says that China 'must prevent the economy from overheating. The growth rate must be in harmony with the economic structure and capacity of our economy.' Li Peng warns that China 'must consider how much the economy can bear' and that the economy should grow 'at a proper speed'. National income was expected to increase by 12 per cent in 1992 and 10 per cent in 1993, while inflation was 6.2 per cent in 1992 (*IHT*, 21 December 1992, p. 10; 31 December 1992, p. 13). The *FEER* (24–31 December 1992, p. 58) provides performance estimates for 1992 and 1993 by a panel of economists from fourteen countries. In China GDP was expected to grow by 11–12 per cent and 8–9 per cent respectively (the Asian Development Bank's figures were 12 per cent and 11 per cent: p. 52), while inflation was put at 6–7 per cent and 10 per cent respectively.

28 December 1992. It was announced that 100,000 redundancies had taken place in the coal industry (most workers had found other jobs) and that massive lay-offs were to follow.

Each laid-off coal worker was eligible for an interest-free loan to help start a business or find work elsewhere. In September 1992 a state knitting enterprise in Chongqing had been declared bankrupt. Some 3,000 workers had lost their jobs (most were given early retirement), the biggest single bankruptcy in China up to that time (*IHT*, 29 December 1992, pp. 11, 13).

3 January 1992. It is announced that in 1993 around 57 per cent of coal output will be sold at market prices, compared with about 20 per cent in 1992 (*FT*, 4 January 1993, p. 13).

CUBA

Jonathan Rosenberg ('Cuba's free-market experiment: los mercados libres campesinos, 1980–1986', *Latin American Research Review*, 1992, vol. 27, no. 3) provides the following information. By May 1980 the free farmers' markets were ready to start opening. The permitted sellers were private farmers, members of co-operatives, state farmers and owners of agricultural backyards, patios or small rural plots. Sellers could only handle their own produce, i.e. they were not allowed to act as intermediaries for other producers. Products deemed valuable in foreign exchange terms (such as cocoa, sugar, tobacco and coffee) could not be sold. Nor could beef, because the aim was to increase the size of herds (p. 60). Reasons for the closure of the markets in May 1986 included the appearance of illegal intermediaries and the sale of banned products. Rosenberg also provides some additional information on the restrictions imposed on private farmers in general. Private farmers are prohibited by law from buying land and they can legally hire labour only during periods of peak need, such as harvest time (p. 71).

In November 1992 a trade agreement was signed with Russia.

24 November 1992. The UN General Assembly supports a Cuban resolution condemning the Cuban Democracy Act (passed in the United States in October 1992). This non-binding vote in the UN disapproved of the Act, which widened the ban on unlicensed trading with Cuba to foreign-based subsidiaries of US companies. Any ship used in trade with Cuba would be barred from visiting US ports for six months after departing from Cuba.

Economic performance. Euromoney (September 1992, p. 72) forecast a fall in GNP of 20 per cent in 1992. Zimbalist is quoted as saying that the Cuban economy shrank by 45 per cent in the period 1989–92 (*IHT*, 28 December 1992, p. 2).

NORTH KOREA

15 July 1992 currency decree. Existing won notes were to be replaced by new notes at par within five days. One possible aim was the curbing of black market activities generated by food shortages in the official network. An exchange limit was set of 500 won per family, but this apparently led to riots in several cities. The government then reportedly promised to raise the ceiling to 900 won, exchanges taking place on three occasions over a period of months (i.e., 300 won on each occasion).

15 August 1992. The scheduled family reunions were cancelled.

20 October 1992. A foreign investment law was announced, although it had actually been adopted on 5 October (*IHT*, 21 October 1992, p. 20; John Burton, *FT*, 21 October 1992, p. 6). 'The state encourages investments, above all, in sectors that require high and modern technologies, those which produce internationally competitive goods, sectors of natural resource development and infrastructure construction, and scientific research and new technology development sectors.' During the first five years of operation foreign-funded enterprises in these sectors will receive preferential treatment as regards, for example, tax and bank loans. Wholly foreign-owned enterprises are allowed in what are in effect special economic zones, where the corporate tax rate is 14 per cent, foreign companies are allowed to lease land for up to fifty years and tariff exemption generally applies. Compensation is to be given in the event of 'unavoidable' nationalization. The total capitalization of joint ventures to date is some $100 million.

20 November 1992. During his visit to South Korea Yeltsin announces that Russia will be ending military aid for North Korea.

11 December 1992. Kang Song San becomes prime minister. An economic reformer, he had been premier from 1984 to 1986.

29 December 1992. China announces that as of 1 January 1993 trade with North Korea will be conducted in hard currency cash transactions rather than barter (*IHT*, 30 December 1992, p. 2).

Economic performance. Euromoney (September 1992, p. 72) forecast a GNP growth rate of 0.8 per cent in 1992.

VIETNAM

22 July 1992. Vietnam accedes to the 1976 Treaty of Friendship and Co-operation in South-east Asia, the first step towards possible full membership of ASEAN (Association of South-east Asian Nations, comprising Brunai, Indonesia, Malaysia, the Philippines, Thailand and Singapore).

23 September 1992. General Le Duc Anh becomes president.

23 October 1992. The United States announces that Vietnam has agreed to provide 'all information' about POWs and MIAs in the Vietnam War. This was considered an important step on the path to the possible normalization of relations. The United States promised some modest but speedy aid for flood victims and military veterans. This was followed up on 14 December 1992 by an announcement that US companies would be allowed to sign contracts, open offices in Vietnam, hire staff and carry out feasibility studies and technical surveys. But fulfilment of contracts still depended on the lifting of the trade embargo.

30 November–4 December 1992. Li Peng visits Vietnam, the first visit by a Chinese prime minister for twenty-one years (Zhou Enlai was the last one).

22 December 1992. Diplomatic relations are established with South Korea.

The mini-privatization programme. Four of the original seven enterprises selected to issue shares on an experimental basis were dropped, but a further nine were added to the list in late July 1992. The number now on the list is thus twelve. The experiment includes the sale of some of the shares to employees and to foreigners. The government is to retain 30 per cent control of 'corporatized' enterprises (Murray Hiebert, *FEER*, 20 August 1992, pp. 50–1).

Foreign trade. The number of enterprises allowed to engage in direct foreign trade has increased from around 300 in 1991 to nearly 500, including six private firms (Murray Hiebert, *FEER*, 14 May 1992, p. 56). In 1991 exports of crude oil accounted for nearly one-third of total exports. Rice exports fell to about 1 million tonnes. Singapore, Japan and Hong Kong together accounted for half of Vietnam's foreign trade and the former Soviet Union for 13 per cent (p. 56).

Foreign aid. On 6 November 1992 Japan approved a thirty-year 45.5 billion yen ($370 million) commodity loan (1 per cent interest and a ten-year grace period). Japanese commercial banks had to provide bridging finance worth an extra 23.5 billion yen in order that Vietnam could pay off debt arrears to Japan. The commodity loan was to be used to import goods for resale on the domestic market in order to finance mainly public works projects. Since 1978 Japan had only provided some small amounts of humanitarian and cultural aid.

Foreign investment. On 23 December 1992 the National Assembly approved a new investment law (*IHT*, 23 December 1992, p. 15). The duration of joint ventures was extended from twenty to fifty years (up to seventy years in 'necessary cases'). In 'special cases' joint ventures would be allowed to open overseas bank accounts. Tax breaks already given to joint ventures would be extended to selected wholly foreign-owned investment projects. Joint ventures in priority sectors are exempt from paying a 15 to 25 per cent tax on profits for the first two years and are eligible for a 50 per cent tax reduction for another two years. Earlier in December the prime minister had revealed that foreign investment approvals increased by 73 per cent in 1992 to about $2.1 billion. Over the past five years Taiwan had headed the list of licensed projects with over $800 million, followed by Hong Kong with $600 million and France with $475 million.

Anthony McDermott (*FT*, 11 September 1992, p. 4) reports the following. There were 416 joint ventures in operation at the end of August 1992, involving capital investment of $3.35 billion (of which $1.69 billion had been raised). Of the 416 projects, 233 (with a capital investment of $1.11 billion) were in industry, eighteen ($900 million) in oil and gas, forty-one ($660 million) in hotels and tourism, and fifty-five ($166 million) in services. Official statistics released on 1 January 1993 revealed that Vietnam had licensed 555 projects over the previous five years with a registered capital of more than $4.5 billion; in 1992 nearly 200 projects involving $2 billion had been licensed (*IHT*, 2 January 1993, p. 9).

Population. In October 1992 it was announced that the population was 70.7 million. In 1989 the tax system was amended to penalize families with more than two children (*IHT*, 28 October 1992, p. 2).

Economic performance. Government estimates for 1992 were announced on 9 December 1992 (*IHT*, 10 December 1992, p. 17): growth of national income 5.3 per cent; industrial production 14.5–15.0 per cent; agricultural output 4.4 per cent; and inflation 15 per cent. The *FEER* (24–31 December 1992, pp. 56–8) provides forecasts for 1993, made by a Vietnamese government minister and by a panel of economists respectively: GDP, 8 per cent and 7.3 per cent; inflation, 14–15 per cent and 20 per cent. The total rice harvest in 1992 was 21.5 million tonnes and rice exports amounted to 1.4 million tonnes (*FT*, 13 January 1993, p. 26).

GENERAL ISSUES

Privatization. Patrick Bolton and Gerard Roland ('Privatization policies in Central and Eastern Europe', *Economic Policy*, October 1992, no. 15) reject mass give-away schemes for two main reasons: (1) governments have major problems in raising sufficient revenue through taxes and (2) incumbent management is left in place at the moment of privatization and no satisfactory procedure is set up to remove inefficient management or to replace existing managers (as regards the possibility of holding companies, it is unclear how effective these would be or how they, in turn, would be monitored). But straightforward auctions benefit those with wealth acquired during the socialist era. Potentially good managers may not have access to this wealth and may not be able to borrow against future income owing to the lack of efficient capital markets. In addition, the amount of revenue raised would be constrained by the current flow of savings if there is a lack of existing private wealth, capital markets and foreign capital, while the privatization process would be slowed up if the state desires to maximize revenues from sales (note that the authors are not convinced that a mass give-away is necessarily a very rapid way to privatize, but in any case they argue that the maximization of the proceeds from the sale of state assets is a more important consideration than accelerating the pace of privatization). Instead of simple auctions, Bolton and Roland propose auctions in which there is a mixture of cash and non-cash bids. The latter involve various forms of debt and equity, specified promises of future payments to the state out of future earnings. Apart from helping to solve the problems outlined above, the government would be able to write off the existing enterprise debts without substantial revenue loss, since the debt write-offs would be reflected in higher bids for the state enterprises. The criticisms that have been levelled at the scheme include the following: (1) the great difficulty of evaluating competing bids and ensuring the honouring of commitments (2) the continuing role of the state and the possibility of substantial renationalization in the event of enterprise failures; (3) the corporate tax system could be used to ensure future revenue to the state; (4) the possibility of leasing as an alternative.

ALBANIA

October 1991. Albania becomes a member of the IMF.

13 September 1992. Ramiz Alia is placed under house arrest for alleged abuse of state power.

16 December 1992. Albania announces its intention to apply for membership of Nato.

Economic reform after July 1992. The IMF-inspired economic reform programme of the Democratic Party government was supposed to be introduced on 1 July 1992, but most of it was postponed because of the forthcoming 26 July local elections (in which, in fact, the Socialist Party came out on top). The main features were as follows:

1. The phasing out of the generous unemployment compensation scheme whereby 80 per cent of previous wages was received (formally due to circumstances beyond the control of workers, such as the lack of raw materials). Gramoz Pashko claimed that more than a quarter of workers were receiving these benefits (cited in *The Economist*, 4 July 1992, p. 46). The figure would be reduced to 60 per cent of former wages at first, with a further reduction after six months (*Albanian Life*, 1992, no. 53, p. 4).

2. The lek was devalued from fifty to 110 to the US dollar as a step on the path to convertibility.

3. Most prices were to be liberalized, the exceptions being basic products such as bread, cooking oil and sugar. In the interim there were to be substantial price increases, e.g. a doubling of post and telecommunications charges and of electicity tariffs (except for household users of electricity).

4. An austerity programme, including the reduction of subsidies for prices (implicit in price liberalization) and for state industry. The budget deficit in 1991 was a massive 60 per cent of GDP (Natasha Narayan, *The Independent*, 24 August 1992, p. 21).

5. Higher tariffs on imports such as colour television sets and second-hand cars. *Political developments. EEN* (1992, vol. 6, no. 25, p.9) reports that the Democratic Party became increasingly fractious following the formal setting up in November 1992 of the Democratic Alliance party by six former Democratic Party MPs, including Gramoz Pashko.

Agriculture. About 90 per cent of non-state farm land has now been privatized, with state farms destined to be privatized during 1993 (*EEN*, 14 December 1992, vol. 6, no. 25, p. 9).

Aid. EEN (1992, vol. 6, no. 25, p. 9) reports that the Italian aid programme has been extended to 1994, with up to 140 billion lira earmarked. Agricultural aid in 1993 could amount to $100 million (mostly G24).

Economic performance. In August 1992 Genc Ruli, the Minister of Finance and the Economy, forecast that 'it will take at least two years to put industry and agriculture on their feet; for all the economic mechanisms to function it will take another ten years' (*Albanian Life*, 1992, no. 53, p. 4). *EEN* (2 November 1992, vol. 6, no. 22, p. 7) reports the following: Though the economy is still dependent on foreign aid, private agriculture continues to develop slowly. Industrial production remains extremely low, but is picking up in mining and the metallurgical sector. *EEN* (14 December 1992, vol. 6, no. 25, p. 9) cites the following figures: in the first six months of 1992 overall output was 70 per cent of the 1991 level; unemployment is about 25 per cent, including half the industrial workforce; the current annual inflation rate is 200 per cent. *Euromoney* (September 1992, p. 72) forecast a fall in GNP of 16.7 per cent in 1992.

BULGARIA

The OECD (*Bulgaria: An Economic Assessment*, 1992) provides the following additional information:

1. Total subsidies as a percentage of GDP fell from 14.9 per cent in 1990 to 4.0 per cent in 1992 (p. 15).

2. For all practical purposes, prices are now free except for energy prices and other prices set by public utilities (p. 39).

3. Industrial enterprises and shops nationalized in 1947 are to be returned to their former owners, as are shops which were confiscated after 1973. The question of compensation in cases where restitution is not possible has not yet been resolved (p. 32). (By June 1992 43 per cent of the total stock of small private properties, i.e. houses, restaurants and shops, had been returned to the former owners or heirs; the figure was 65 per cent for shops and 63 per cent for restaurants: *Employment Observatory*, 1992, no. 3 pp. 1–2; in the first half of 1992 private businesses were responsible for about 42 per cent of retail sales, but only about 1 per cent of industrial output: p. 6.)

4. The 1990 decree on unemployment compensation fixed the sum at the minimum wage plus 20 per cent of the difference between the minimum wage and the average wage received during the last six months before dismissal. The maximum duration is twelve months, after which social assistance is paid (p. 35).

5. Wage bill targets were reinforced by an excess wage tax with progressive rates, ranging from 50 per cent for increases above the norm of 1 to 2 per cent to 400 per cent for overruns over 4 per cent. These rates have been doubled for 1992 (p. 67).

6. In February 1991 all quantitative import restrictions were abolished and the granting of import licences was made automatic (except for a few goods, such as military equipment). Export bans and licensing requirements were retained for twenty-one items. As temporary measures the authorities imposed a 20 to 30 per cent export tax on twenty-six goods (mostly raw materials and clothing) and a 15 per cent import surcharge on most imports. The former was eliminated in June 1991 and the latter in July 1992 (pp. 39–40). (In the first half of 1992 the EC accounted for just over 30 per cent of imports and just under 30 per cent of exports: *Employment Observatory*, 1992, no. 3, p. 5.)

April 1992. The IMF comments favourably on the results of the first year of the economic reform, particularly with respect to stabilization (*Annual Report*, 1992, p. 26). The stand-by arrangement for SDR 155 million is approved on 17 April 1992 (p. 58).

6 October 1992. Bulgaria resumes interest payments on its foreign debt

29 October 1992. A motion of no confidence in the government is passed in parliament by 120 votes to 111, alleging attempts to supply arms to Macedonia in breach of the UN embargo. Prime Minister Dimitrov has to be given first try at forming a new government since his is the largest party.

3 November 1992. Former prime minister Georgi Atanasov is given a ten-year prison sentence for the misuse of state funds and former economics minister Stoyan Ovcharov is sentenced to nine years.

20 November 1992. Dimitrov fails to form a new government.

16 December 1992. The Paris Club of Western creditor nations agree to reschedule Bulgaria's foreign debt over ten years with a six-year grace period (*IHT*, 17 December 1992, p. 11).

23 December 1992. Lyuben Berov is asked to try to form a government (an economic adviser to the president, he was nominated by the MRF). Parliament approves the new government of technocrats on 30 December.

Agriculture. Land legislation was approved in March 1992. Virginia Marsh (*FT*, 19 November 1992, p. 34) reports the following: While co-operatives have been disbanded, by the end of October 1992 only around 24 per cent of land had been redistributed, leaving much farmland unworked. Agriculture has also been adversely affected by the division of land into small units. The land law allows for restitution of up to 30 ha (74 acres) per person, but there are relatively few claims of this size. Small holdings, rarely more than 5 ha, predominated in pre-socialist Bulgaria (except in the wheat-growing Dobrudga region). In addition, where there was one owner before, there may be several descendants making claims, resulting in even smaller plots of land. The grain and sugar beet harvests may be only 7.1 million tonnes and 400,000 tonnes respectively in 1992, compared with 10.2 million tonnes and 1.6 million tonnes respectively in 1980.

Disagreement between the Union of Democratic Forces (UDF) and the ethnic Turkish Movement for Rights and Freedoms (MRF) was partly caused by differences over agricultural policy (*EEN*, 5 October 1992, vol. 6, no. 20, p. 7). While the UDF was restoring land to its pre-1944 owners, the MRF (and the Bulgarian Socialist Party) wanted land to be allocated to co-operative farm members (post-1944) according to how much labour they contributed to the co-operative (before the socialist land reforms the Turks had relatively little land per head). (Note that between the spring of 1992 and the writing of the *EEN* report 100,000 of the remaining 500,000 to 600,000 ethnic Turks had left for Turkey, almost entirely for economic reasons.)

The OECD (*Bulgaria: An Economic Assessment*, 1992, p. 32) reports amendments to the land law in 1992, including the following: restituted agricultural land can now be sold immediately; the time limit during which there is a restriction on the maximum amount of land that one individual can hold has been reduced to two years.

Economic performance. The OECD's estimates for GDP and inflation respectively are as follows (*OECD Economic Outlook*, December 1992, pp. 123–6): 1992, –10 per cent and 90 per cent; 1993, –4 per cent and 60 per cent; 1994, 0 per cent and 60 per cent.

CZECHOSLOVAKIA

The June 1992 election produced the following distribution of seats in the Czech and Slovak National Councils. The Czech National Council: Civic Democratic Party (76), Left Bloc (35), Liberal Union (16), Social Democrats (16), Christian Democrats (15), Civic Democratic Alliance (14), Movement for Democratic Self-administration Society of Moravia and Silesia (14), Republican Party (14). The Slovak National Council: Movement for a Democratic Slovakia (74), Party of the Democratic Left (29), Christian Democrats (18), Slovak National Party (15), Hungarian People's Party (14).

24 June 1992. Meciar becomes Slovak prime minister.

26 June 1992. The government of Marian Calfa resigns, but stays in office until a new one is formed. A Slovak, Calfa applied for Czech citizenship in October.

1 July 1992. A transitional federal government is formed, with five posts each for the Czechs and Slovaks. Jan Strasky becomes prime minister and the Slovak Rudolph Filkus becomes deputy premier.

16 July 1992. In the next round of the presidential election the sole candidate, Miroslav Sladek of the Republican Party, fails to be elected.

17 July 1992. Slovakia declares sovereignty. Havel announces his resignation, effective 20 July 1992.

23 July 1992. Klaus and Meciar to ask parliament to pass a 'law on the mode of extinction of the federation and settlement of property and other affairs' by 30 September 1992.

30 July 1992. The next round of the presidential election is cancelled owing to the lack of an acceptable candidate.

27 August 1992. Meciar and Klaus agree on the terms for dividing the country by 1 January 1993; they were optimistic that the 30 September 1992 deadline for the passage of federal laws would be met. The arrangements were to be as follows:

1. A customs union. Apart from the absence of tariffs between the two countries, there would be free movement of people and capital. There would be no labour or residence permits. Slovakia, unlike the Czech republic, would permit dual nationality. A division of EC quotas was agreed later.

2. A common currency would be used for some time after separation (until 30 June 1993, it was subsequently decided) and monetary policy would be co-ordinated. When separate currencies were introduced the exchange rate would be one-to-one initially and then the currencies would float (FT Survey, 11 January 1993, p. 1).

3. There would be separate budgets (the principle of 'each state on its own') and Czech subsidies would cease by the end of 1992. The basic principle for the division of assets and liabilities has been a two-thirds (Czech republic) and one-third (Slovakia) split. The division of assets has created the greatest difficulties. Moveable property has caused the least problems and the issue of compensation in other cases the greatest.

4. Foreign and defence policies would be co-ordinated. It is generally thought that the renegotiation of international agreements will prove to be more difficult for Slovakia.

5. The first round of privatization would proceed, but the second round would be split. In its programme, the government of the Slovak republic 'will adopt a privatization concept in which the basic principles will be support for the domestic entrepreneurial sector and creation of a competitive environment . . . Also envisaged are instalment forms of privatization and sales to managements and employees . . . The government will adopt principles which will prevent sell-outs of national property to foreign buyers at low prices, and undesirable concentration of ownership' (*Czechoslovak Economic Digest*, 1992, no. 4, p. 7). Consideration was also to be given to the idea of the state having 'golden shares' in enterprises (pp. 11, 13). There is need to delineate 'state participation in strategic areas', while the voucher method of privatization will only be 'a residual or supplementary method' (*Czechoslovak Economic Digest*, 1992, no. 5, pp. 11–13).

The Slovak government's programme clearly shows a more interventionist streak than that of the Czech government, including greater subsidies to and tariff protection of Slovak industry (pp. 6, 7, 10, 11). Some basic demographic statistics are provided by *The Guardian* (28 December 1992, p. 6) and *The Times* (31 December 1992, p. 10). The Czech republic has a population of 10.3 million, of which 81.3 per cent are Czechs, 13.2 per cent are Moravians and 5.5 per cent are Slovaks. Slovakia has a population of 5.3 million, of which 85.6 per cent are Slovaks, 10.8 per cent are Hungarians and 3.6 per cent are Gypsies (another source puts the shares at Slovaks 85.6 per cent, Hungarians 10.8 per cent, Czechs 1.1 per cent and 'other' 2.5 per cent: *The Telegraph*, 31 December 1992, p. 15).

Foreign capital. Slovakia accounted for only 13 per cent of an estimated $1.1 billion of foreign investment; as of 30 June 1992 there were 2,129 joint ventures in Slovakia, compared with 7,657 in the Czech republic (Clifford Stevens, *IHT*, 18 December 1992, p. 10). In 1992 direct foreign investment amounted to $1.2 billion, of which 93 per cent went to the Czech republic and only 7 per cent to Slovakia (Deutsche Bank, *Focus: Eastern Europe*, 1992, no. 65, p. 8).

1 September 1992.: The Slovak parliament approves a new constitution. The Christian Democrats vote against it. The Hungarian representatives show their disapproval by walking out (the constitution, for example, refers to 'We the Slovak people').

Alexander Dubcek has a serious road accident (he died 7 November 1992).

24 September 1992. The sole candidate in the next round of the presidential election fails to be elected.

Late September 1992. The EC postpones ratification of the association agreement.

1 October 1992. The federal parliament narrowly rejects the separation Bill. The Bill contained three procedures for dissolving the federation so as to overcome the constitutional requirement of a referendum, namely a federal parliamentary declaration, an accord between the Czech and Slovak parliaments and the secession of one of the republics. Opponents of the Bill included the left and most deputies of the Movement for a Democratic Slovakia. They favoured a new Czech-Slovak union of the two republics, with a single president and a union government co-ordinating the economy (there would be a common budget), defence, foreign affairs, social affairs and environmental issues. Klaus, however, still wanted a quick divorce. On 30 September Havel pronounced against a referendum, given the seeming desire of the Slovak people for independence and on 4 October said that the separation should be speeded up.

4 November 1992. Charter 77 is formally disbanded.

17 November 1992. Havel formally declares his candidature for the Czech presidency. Both the Czech and Slovak National Councils pass a joint resolution authorizing the split. Endorsement by the federal parliament would be sufficient to avoid a referendum.

25 November 1992. The Federal Assembly accepts the division of the country. A constitutional amendment reads 'the Czech and Slovak federative republic ceases to exist on 31 December 1992, with the successor states being the Czech and Slovak republics'.

2 December 1992. The first round of large privatization ends. It was later reported that 92.8 per cent of available shares had been taken up, with 8.54 million people involved (*FT*, 23 December 1992, p. 3).

1 January 1993. The Czech republic and Slovakia become independent countries.

Economic performance in 1992. The OECD (*OECD Economic Outlook*, December 1992, pp. 123–6) forecast a 7 per cent fall in GDP in 1992 and an inflation rate of 11 per cent. In November 1992 the unemployment rate was 2.5 per cent in the Czech republic and 10.3 per cent in Slovakia (*The Economist*, 26 December 1992, p. 43).

Unemployment in Czechoslovakia reached a peak in January 1992 and then fell (*Employment Observatory*, 1992, no. 3, p. 8); note that unemployment benefit has been limited to 3,000 crowns (around two-thirds of the average wage) and that the minimum level has been abolished (p. 13). In 1992 the EC took around 50 per cent of Czechoslovak exports (*FT Survey*, 11 January 1993, p. 4). One source provides the following forecasts for 1993 for the Czech republic and Slovakia (*IHT*, 31 December 1992, p. 2): GDP, 4 per cent and −1.9 per cent respectively; inflation, 17 per cent and 40 per cent respectively. The government of the new Czech republic forecast GDP growth of between 1 and 2 per cent in 1993, an inflation rate of between 15 and 18 per cent, an unemployment rate of around 5 per cent and a balance of payments surplus (*FT Survey*, 1 January 1993, p. 4).

(Note that in the text it was not made clear that other investors had the right to submit privatization plans besides enterprises; the final chioce was a ministerial one.)

EAST GERMANY

The Treuhandanstalt (THA)

In mid-1992 the *Treuhand-Initiative Mittelstand* was given particular attention. The *Mittelstand is a* term which has been used to refer to small and medium-sized private companies in West Germany clustered in the high-technology and service sectors. The THA initiative offers for sale by tender enterprises employing up to fifty people.

The overall situation at the end of June 1992 was as follows (Deutsche Bank, *Focus: Germany*, 1992, no. 89, pp. 2–4): 8,175 enterprises privatized; 5,950 remaining, but only 4,340 to be sold (the rest to be liquidated); of the 4,340 nearly two-thirds employ fewer than 100 people, a quarter employ 100–500, and 380 employ more than 500; proceeds amounted to DM 30.7 billion; investment pledges amounted to DM 144 million and job pledges to 1.2 million;

of the 4.1 million originally employed in THA enterprises just under 1 million remain; 1,500 management buy-outs (nearly two-thirds employ less than 100 workers) and around 150 staff buy-outs (employees acquire stakes in their companies); foreigners had purchased 412 firms, pledging DM 12 billion in investment and promising to save 111,000 jobs (Swiss companies were involved in seventy-one investment projects, UK companies in sixty-nine, French companies in fifty-three, and Austrian companies in forty-eight); the THA had also privatized 15,000 ha of arable land and 8,050 real estate units (via a real estate subsidiary); note that the privatization of retail trade and hotel/catering had been completed in 1991. The THA's financing gap was just over DM 20 billion in 1991; by the end of March 1992 THA indebtedness amounted to DM 49 billion. The THA's annual credit ceiling has been raised from DM 25 billion to DM 30 billion (in addition the Ministry of Finance is able to authorize an overrun of DM 8 billion). A financing gap of more than DM 30 billion was expected in 1992. The THA hoped to complete its operations ahead of schedule, specifically by the end of 1993.

A survey in the *IHT* (16 December 1992, p. 14) provides the following information. By the end of October 1992 more than 9,250 enterprises had been privatized, leaving around 3,200. Total investment commitments rose to DM 157.6 billion ($98.5 billion) and 1.3 million jobs were guaranteed by the new owners. The THA has developed an innovative form of corporate ownership called 'management KG' (*Kommanditgesellschaft*: partnership limited by shares). Experienced directors are placed at the head of companies owning a range of individual enterprises in order to make full use of their expertise. Finance is provided by private sector sources and backed by public sector guarantees. Two such holding companies have already been set up. David Marsh and Leslie Colitt (*FT*, 12 November 1992, p. 23) report that around 1,600 enterprises have been closed down.

Wolfgang Münchau (*The Times*, 22 December 1992, p. 19) considers that the THA 'has been a great disappointment. Industrial output in the former East Germany has plummeted. The mechanism suffered massive fraud, estimated at DM 3 billion. West German industrialists have frequently abused the Treuhand mechanism in order to close down East German competitors, even if these companies might otherwise have been viable.' In a later article (*The Times*, 12 January 1993, p. 25) he added, 'Companies have been auctioned off to the highest bidders with utter disregard for industrial consequences. Whole industries have disappeared.' The European Commission has expressed increasing concern about the implications for EC competition policy of the level of THA support for East German enterprises (*IHT*, 31 December 1992, p. 11).

Economic performance in 1993. The five institutes' autumn 1992 report provides the following forecasts for East Germany in 1993: GDP, 7.5 per cent; GNP, 7.0 per cent; inflation, 8.5 per cent (DIW, *Economic Bulletin*, 1992, vol. 29, no. 10, pp. 2, 16). The net transfer of public funds from West to East Germany was DM 46.2 billion in 1990 and DM 131.8 billion in 1991. The estimated respective figures for 1992 and 1993 are DM 163 billion (the equivalent of two-thirds of East German GNP or 5.5 per cent of West German GNP) and DM 161 billion (more than half of East German GNP or 6 per cent of West German GNP) (pp. 13–14).

Official figures for 1992 were released on 13 January 1993 (*FT*, 14 January 1993, p. 2; *IHT*, 14 January 1993, p. 11; the *Guardian*, 14 January 1993, p. 13). West German GNP grew by only 0.8 per cent (the worst performance since 1982, when output fell by more than 1 per cent, and compared with growth of 3.6 per cent in 1991); GDP increased by 1.5 per cent (compared with 3.7 per cent the year before). East German GNP increased by 6.4 per cent in 1992 and GDP by 6.1 per cent. Pan-German growth figures for 1992 show GNP growing by 1.3 per cent and GDP by 1.9 per cent. East Germany's GNP accounted for 8 per cent of the pan-German total in 1992 (compared with 6.9 per cent in 1991). (Note that forecasts for growth in 1993 became more pessimistic as 1992 wore on.) Although average wages in East Germany are now 63 per cent of West German rates, productivity is less than 40 per cent of the West German level (*FT*, 14 January 1993, p. 2).

A chronology of events

The number of racist attacks, aimed mainly at asylum-seekers, has caused growing concern. About 130 attacks were recorded in 1990 and 1,500 in 1991. In the first ten months of 1992 the police registered around 1,800 incidents of arson, assault and other violence, including 1,000 after late August, when youths besieged an immigrant hostel in Rostock (East Germany) for a week before being dispersed by the police (*IHT*, 6 November 1992, p. 5). In the first nine months of 1992 319,674 asylum-seekers were registered. Some 500,000 were expected for the whole year, compared with 193,063 in 1990 and 256,112 in 1991 (more than 60 per cent of the EC's total) (Judy Dempsey, *FT*, 9 November 1992, p. 2; 16 November 1992, p. 12). In the end, the actual number in 1992 turned out to be 438,000. Thirteen people died in attacks on foreigners in the first ten months of 1992 (*The Guardian*, 9 November 1992, p. 22) (the number went up to sixteen on 23 November, when three resident Turkish women died in an arson attack, and seventeen by the end of the year). During this period members of the armed forces were on manslaughter charges in three of these cases (in total twenty-four soldiers were accused of participating in racist incidents). Jewish memorials have also been damaged.

The German government has speeded up asylum procedures and aims to amend the liberal law (introduced as an atonement for the Hitler era, especially since Jews experienced great difficulty in attaining asylum in other countries). Article 16 of the 1949 Basic Law (constitution) states that 'persons persecuted on political grounds shall enjoy the right of asylum' (by way of comparison, the Geneva Convention defines a refugee as 'any person fleeing from well-founded fear of being persecuted for reasons of race, religion, nationality . . . '). One agreement, signed on 24 September 1992, gave DM 30 million to Romania to take back asylum-seekers (mainly Gypsies). The funds were supposed to be used for retraining and other means of support. An agreement had already been reached with Poland and on 12 November 1992 Bulgaria was induced to take back those refused asylum by DM 28 million over five years. On 6 December 1992 the main political parties agreed to present the following proposals to parliament: war refugees to stay only until fighting in their own countries ceases; Germany to be able to refuse entry to those arriving via countries adhering to the Geneva Convention on Refugees; Germany is entitled to reject automatically applications from citizens of countries deemed 'free of political persecution'.

It should be noted that there have been mass demonstrations against neo-Nazi activities, while Germany has taken a large number of refugees. Between June 1991 and early November 1992 200,000 people from the former Yugoslavia alone went to Germany, half of these after January 1992 (Judy Dempsey, *FT*, 13 November 1992, p. 3). All told, there were around 1.4 million refugees in Germany (*The Economist*, 14 November 1992, p. 50). Six million foreigners live in Germany, including 1.8 million Turks. In the first seven months of 1992 the Interior Ministry registered 1,443 criminal acts against foreigners, compared with 246 in the whole of 1990 and 2,427 in 1991 (Judy Dempsey, *FT*, 16 November 1992, p. 12, and 25 November 1992, p. 2). On 9 December 1992 the government announced that the number of anti-foreigner crimes had risen to 4,587.

15 May 1992. Honecker and five others are formally charged with a 'shoot to kill' policy.

11 July 1992. The Committee for Justice was formed as an East German protest movement. The co-founders were Gregor Gysi and Peter-Michael Diestel (of the CDU in East Germany).

29 July 1992. Honecker returns to Berlin on manslaughter charges (new figures reveal that 350–400 died trying to escape the GDR rather than 187). The next day he was charged with forty-nine accounts of manslaughter over the period 1961–89 and with misappropriation of state funds.

7 September 1992. Chancellor Kohl proposes a round table to discuss a 'solidarity pact'. The pact was to help solve the mounting economic problems and participants were to include the government, opposition parties, industry and trade unions.

14 September 1992. The Bundesbank lowers the Lombard rate from 9.75 per cent to 9.5 per cent and the discount rate from 8.75 per cent to 8.25 per cent. This was the first fall in interest rates since 1987.

15 September 1992. The THA enters the international bond market.

23 September 1992. An emergency programme is announced for East German industrial enterprises adversely affected by the collapse of East European markets. The measures included an extension of credit guarantees to barter and compensation deals until the end of 1994, cheaper credit, an increase in federal purchases, subsidies for East German companies bidding for infrastructural projects in Eastern Europe, help in switching to Western markets and the auctioning of unsold stock.

26 October 1992. Chancellor Kohl reveals that in 1995 the government has to take over a debt of at least DM 400 billion, DM 250 billion from THA and DM 150 billion in accumulated debts of the socialist regime. Debt servicing will amount to around DM 40 billion a year.

12 November 1992. The trial of Honecker and five others begins. They are charged with thirteen cases of manslaughter (rather than forty-nine). Two of the other five (former prime minister Willi Stoph and Stasi chief Erich Mielche) are then spared the trial on health grounds. Honecker's trial for manslaughter was stopped on 12 January 1993 (and for embezzlement the following day) because he was terminally ill with liver cancer. On release he flew to Chile to join his wife and daughter.

27 November 1992. The neo-Nazi Nationalist Front is banned.

10 December 1992. The German Alternative is banned.

21 December 1992. The Alliance of German Comrades is banned.

22 December 1992. The National Offensive is banned.

3 January 1993. Möllemann resigns as Economics Minister (he had personally signed a letter promoting a product manufactured by a family member).

An excellent guide to the political, social and economic aspects of reunification is to be found in Jonathan Osmond (ed.) *German Reunification: a Reference Guide and Commentary*, London: Longman (1992).

HUNGARY

8 April 1992. Under the bankruptcy law, enterprises with debts more than ninety days overdue are obliged to file for bankruptcy. Creditors then have ninety days to develop a restructuring plan and, failing agreement on such a plan, the enterprise is put up for liquidation (*OECD Economic Outlook*, December 1992, p. 129).

Mid-August 1992. Creation of an interbank foreign exchange market.

20 August 1992. A speech by Istvan Csurka, one of the six vice-presidents of the Hungarian Democratic Forum (HDF), caused deep concern. An extreme right-wing nationalist, Csurka attacked Jews, international bankers, foreigners, Gypsies, communists and liberals. He refers to 'the Paris, New York and Tel Aviv networks' and 'the Hungarian Jewish position of hegemony'. The irredentist streak in Csurka's ideas is fed by the fact that over 3.5 million ethnic Hungarians live outside the country. There are between 1.6 million and 2 million in Romania (mostly in Transylvania), 567,000–650,000 in Slovakia, 340,000–400,000 in Serbia (mostly in Vojvodina), 160,000–200,000 in Ukraine,

25,000–40,000 in Croatia and 8,500–10,000 in Slovenia (*The Independent*, 11 January 1993, p. 6). The government distanced itself, but the liberal wing of the HDF demanded that Csurka be criticized in stronger terms.

Privatization. On 28 August 1992 the government revealed a list of around 160 enterprises that it intends to keep wholly or partially in state ownership (*The Independent*, 29 August 1992, p. 17). An absolute state majority would be retained in its main oil company, telecommunications firm and airline. But the state's stake in large industrial, steel and aluminium companies would be limited to 25 per cent plus one vote. The 25 per cent ceiling applies to all but one of the large state chemical and pharmaceutical companies. The new banking law already obliges the state to reduce its ownership of each bank to a maximum 25 per cent by the start of 1997 (the 1 December 1991 banking law limited any single investor to a maximum 25 per cent in a bank, unless the investor is another bank: *The Banker*, July 1992, p. 29). A new state holding company (State Property Management) would group the state's long-term equity stakes in enterprises that are of strategic importance or that need significant restructuring before privatization. The old State Property Agency will retain responsibility for selling off other state enterprises.

Nicholas Denton (*FT Survey*, 29 October 1992, p. 33, and *FT*, 23 December 1992, p. 3) reports the following. After disposing of only a tenth of the state's commercial holdings, privatization is suffering from exhaustion. To help remedy this the Hungarian public would be encouraged to purchase, with the aid of low-interest, long-maturity loans, enterprises which cannot be floated. Foreign investors provided about 70 per cent of privatization proceeds in 1991. The new privatization law includes provision for all methods of privatization, including employee share ownership and management buy-outs: *The Banker*, July 1992, p. 30).

In December 1992 the Pick Salami Company and the Danubius Hotel and Spa Company were successfully floated. Between ten and twenty enterprises, including the national telecommunications company, were planned to be floated in 1993 (Nicholas Denton, *FT*, 23 December 1992, p. 3).

Yudit Kiss ('Privatization in Hungary – two years later', *Soviet Studies*, 1992, vol. 44, no. 6) provides the following information. By the end of April 1992 about 10–13 per cent of state assets had been privatized (pp. 1015, 1033). As much as 85 per cent of all privatization income is in hard currency. In 1991 $770 million of hard currency flowed into the country in connection with privatization, in the form of purchase price or additional capital investment in already existing companies (p. 1029). The share of foreign capital in the economy is now about 8 per cent, compared with 3 per cent in 1990; there is a heavy foreign presence in food processing, sugar, beverages, cars, printing and services (p. 1029).

Foreign investment. Anthony Robinson (*FT Survey*, 29 October 1992, pp. 31–3) reports the following. Foreign investment has amounted to more than $4.1 billion over the past three years (the total for East and Central Europe is $7 billion). Over 60 per cent has gone into industry. Between 1972 and 1989 Hungary attracted $570 million in foreign investment. In 1990 direct foreign investment was $354 million and in 1991 $1.46 billion (Hafna Lorinc, 'Foreign debt, debt management and implications for Hungary's development', *Soviet Studies*, 1992, vol. 44, no. 6, p. 1001).

Agriculture. Anthony Robinson (*FT Survey*, 29 October 1992, p. 32) provides the following information. The legal framework exists and the aim is to put nearly 80 per cent of crop land in private hands by the end of 1994. But there is little desire or ability to return to small-scale peasant farming. Ownership of most of the nearly 1,400 agricultural co-operatives will be transferred into the hands of 270,000 active co-operative members, 380,000 pensioners and 460,000 former members and former owners or their heirs. The co-operatives will lose their social obligations to local villages and many of their agro-industrial activities will be privatized. They will be replaced by a mixture of private and family farms, farming associations and new types of co-operatives based on shared ownership. Most of the 130 state farms will be privatized, although fourteen of the largest and most technically advanced will remain state-owned for research purposes.

The budget. The budget deficit in 1992 was an estimated 7.5 per cent of GDP (Deutsche Bank, *Focus: Eastern Europe*, 29 December 1992, no. 65, p. 8). The 1993 budget was approved on 2 December 1992, with a target deficit of 185 billion forints or 5.9 per cent of GDP (in line with IMF recommendations).

Economic performance. Official estimates indicate a 5 per cent decline in GDP in 1992. Official statistics, however, only cover enterprises employing more than fifty people (Anthony Robinson and Nicholas Denton, *FT Survey*, 29 October 1992, p. 32). The gross foreign debt has stabilized at a little below $23 billion, while the net debt has fallen to around $15 billion. The gross debt service ratio has fallen from 63 per cent in 1990 to 38 per cent at present. In September 1992 exports to the EC exceeded 50 per cent of the total for the first time; in the 1970s the figure was 14 per cent and in the 1980s 25 per cent. The unemployment rate is now 11.1 per cent. (Above statistics provided by Anthony Robinson, p. 33.) One source forecast an inflation rate of 25 per cent in 1992 (DIW, *Economic Bulletin*, 1992, vol. 29, no. 10, p. 3). The OECD's estimates for GDP and inflation respectively are as follows (*OECD Economic Outlook*, December 1992, pp. 123–6): 1992, −4.0 per cent and 21 per cent; 1993, 0.0 per cent and 15 per cent; 1994, 3 per cent and 9 per cent. Ian Traynor (*The Guardian*, 9 January 1993, p. 13) reports an unemployment rate of 13 per cent. The authorities predict that GDP will stabilize in 1993 and could grow by up to 3 per cent (Nicholas Denton, *FT*, 9 January 1993, p. 2).

Early September. Negotiations with the IMF were resumed.

Late September 1992. The EC ratified the association agreement (in 1991 the EC accounted for 46.7 per cent of Hungary's exports and 42.7 per cent of imports).

On 24 October 1992 the Slovak government (the Czechs wanted a delay) went ahead with the controversial plan to divert water from the Danube as part of the Gabcikovo hydro-electric power scheme. Hungary and Czechoslovakia jointly signed an agreement in 1977, but Hungary stopped work on the scheme in 1989 after a powerful campaign by environmentalists and formally withdrew from the project in May 1992. Hungary also complained that the diversion violated the international border between the two countries. On 29 October the European Commission engineered a deal whereby work would cease while the disputing parties tried to reach agreement. If no agreement was forthcoming by 15 November, the parties would submit to binding arbitration. Czechoslovakia subsequently agreed to an EC proposal to halt work by 21 November and then await the result of the discussions.

11 November 1992. On the occasion of a visit by Yeltsin, Russia and Hungary agreed to cancel out compensation claims arising from former Soviet military assets and the ensuing environmental damage. The issue of the trade debt (nearly $2 billion) owed by Russia to Hungary was not fully resolved.

POLAND

5 July 1992. During his visit to Poland President Bush donated the $200 million US share of the (unused) $1 billion stabilization fund, subject to conformity with the IMF conditions. He also said that he would ask the other contributors to do the same. On 8 July the G7 countries agreed to this in principle.

Hanna Suchochka of Democratic Union was appointed prime minister on 10 July 1992, the first woman premier in Polish history. The next day the Sejm approved a seven-party coalition (including Democratic Union, the Liberal

Democratic Congress, the Christian National Union, Farmers' Solidarity, and the Christian Democrats). The main opposition parties were the Alliance of the Democratic Left (which became the largest party in October 1992 when Democratic Union lost some of its members) and the Confederation for an Independent Poland (KPN). Suchochka was committed to constitutional reform and at the start of August the Sejm passed amendments which gave greater powers to both the government and the president. The government was able to issue policy decisions by decree. The president was able to appoint the government in the event of a deadlock, but not to dismiss it.

Suchochka was also committed to the economic reform programme and part of the rationale of the constitutional changes was to speed it up. The government adopted a tough line on strikes involving large wage claims (in industries such as coal, steel, aircraft, copper, motor cars and the railways).

18 August 1992. The Polish cabinet agreed on draft legislation to create twenty NWMFs; the registration fee for each individual to receive vouchers would not exceed 10 per cent of the average monthly wage (Deutsche Bank, *Focus: Eastern Europe*, 1992, no. 55, p. 4).

The private sector has grown by 710,000 small businesses and 50,000 corporations since the end of 1989. More than 2 million people (about 15 per cent of non-agricultural employment) have joined the private sector, which now accounts for more than half of GDP and which continues to grow rapidly (Jeffrey Sachs and David Lipton, *FT*, 16 October 1992, p. 23). In 1991 the private sector (including agriculture) accounted for 45 per cent of GDP; in 1992 the percentage was nearly 50 per cent of GNP (compared with 28 per cent in 1989) and nearly 60 per cent of employment (Deutsche Bank, *Focus: Eastern Europe*, 1992, no. 55, p. 4; no. 65, p. 4). Andrzej Kozminski ('Transition from planned to market economy: Hungary and Poland compared', *Studies in Comparative Communism*, 1992, vol. XXV, no. 4, pp. 321–2) provides

the following information. The percentage of GNP contributed by the private non-agricultural sector increased from 8 per cent in 1989 to 12 per cent in 1990 and to 20 per cent in 1991. In 1991 the private sector contributed 22.1 per cent of industrial sales, 43.9 per cent of construction and 16.3 per cent of transport. Between December 1990 and the end of 1991 employment in the private sector increased from 39.5 per cent to 44.8 per cent. *The Economist* (23 January 1993, p. 241) calculates that the private sector now produces nearly 50 per cent of GDP and employs 55–60 per cent of the workforce (compared with 46 per cent in 1990).

9 September 1992. The government reveals its proposal for an 'enterprise pact'. Workers and management in each enterprise would be given three months to produce their own restructuring and privatization programme (the choice would be from five alternative models of privatization, including sales to foreigners and worker or management buy-outs). Non-compliance would mean imposed restructuring and possible liquidation. Indebted state enterprises which agree on an adjustment programme with their creditors would earn partial debt remission from the government and the banks. The 'dividend' (a tax on the value of the assets of an enterprise) would be replaced by a tax on profits. The *popiwek* would be replaced by a consultative system of wage control involving a tripartite national negotiating commission (comprising government, management and trade unions). Profitable enterprises would be given far greater flexibility in determining wages.

28 October 1992. The last Russian combat troops leave Poland.

4 January 1993. Balcerowicz agrees to join the president's Council of Economic Advisers.

The budget. The IMF-agreed targets for the budget as a proportion of GDP were 7.5 per cent in 1992 and 5.5 per cent in 1993. September 1992 forecasts put the 1992 figure in the range 8–8.5 per cent, while the Deutsche Bank estimated 7.5–8.0 per cent (*Focus: Eastern Europe*, 29 December 1992, no. 65, p. 9). The government ran into some problems on 19 October 1992 when the Sejm rejected the proposal to keep pension increases below the rate of inflation. But the Sejm accepted a 3 per cent increase in the turnover tax and a 6 per cent import surcharge.

24 November 1992. The IMF programme had been suspended in September 1991, but on 24 November 1992 the IMF and Poland finally agreed terms for a fourteen-month stand-by loan of $660 million (expected to be approved in January 1993). The budget deficit target for 1993 was fixed at 5.1 per cent of GDP.

Foreign investment. The amount of 'invested Western capital' was $353 million in 1990 and $670 million in 1991 (Kozminski 1992: 323). On 1 January 1993 the State Foreign Investment Agency revealed that in 1992 foreign investment had exceeded $4 billion (four times the 1991 level), the figures referring to investments due to be implemented over the next few years. Italy had become the biggest single economic partner, e.g. the Fiat company (*IHT*, 2 January 1993, p. 9).

Economic performance. The OECD's estimates for GDP and inflation respectively are as follows (*OECD Economic Outlook*, December 1992, pp. 123–6): 1992, –2 per cent and 40 per cent; 1993, 2 per cent and 35 per cent; 1994, 3 per cent and 25 per cent. Industrial output rose by 13.1 per cent in September 1992 (compared with the same month of the previous year) and by 0.6 per cent over the first nine months of 1992 (Christopher Bobinski, *FT*, 20 October 1992, p. 2). *The Economist* (9 January 1993, p. 38) estimates inflation at about 45 per cent in 1992 and 38 per cent in 1993. Julian Borger (*The Guardian*, 9 January 1993, p. 13) reports estimated growth rates in 1992 of 3.5 per cent in industrial production and of between zero and 1 per cent in GDP (the article also reports the World Bank's evidence of encouraging signs of adaptation in parts of state industry). The World Bank Study, which examined seventy-five state enterprises, concluded that 'Success stories are emerging and the state sector is far from a write-off . . . good

and bad performers are emerging in all sectors'; inflation was 43 per cent in 1992 (Christopher Bobinski, *FT*, 16 January 1993, p. 2).

ROMANIA

The economy

The Deutsche Bank (*Focus: Eastern Europe*, 30 September 1992, no. 58) provides the following information.

Privatization (pp. 4–5). The private sector now accounts for 18 per cent of retail trade, compared with 1 per cent in 1990. The Private Ownership Funds were to be converted into investment funds within five years. The 340 large enterprises excluded from the privatization programme include electricity production, railways and the postal service. They account for roughly half of the value-added of all companies. The first of the thirty early privatizations was carried out in August 1992 when a textile enterprise sold 51 per cent of its shares to an Italian company.

A stand-by agreement was signed with the IMF in May for the disbursement of $440 million within ten months and for the drawing down of a further tranche of $108 million from the compensatory and contingency fund set up previously (p. 6). In August 1992 the IMF praised Romania for meeting its monetary and fiscal targets (p. 3). On 1 September 1992 a further quarter of all foodstuff subsidies in retail trade were removed. The goal was to liberalize all prices by the end of 1992 (p. 4). In November 1992 the IMF presented $75 million in the form of a grant.

The EC's *Employment Observatory* (1992, no. 3, pp. 13–14) adds the following information: At the end of September 1992 there were 16,223 foreign companies with a total capital of $503 million (p. 2). The period of entitlement to unemployment compensation has been extended from six to nine months and a new 'support allowance' has been introduced for up to a maximum of eighteen months for those no longer eligible for benefit.

30 September 1992. The US House of Representatives rejects MFN status for Romania.

Economic performance. The OECD's estimates for GDP and inflation respectively are as follows (*OECD Economic Outlook*, December 1992, pp. 123–6): 1992, –13 per cent and 200 per cent; 1993, –5 per cent and 95 per cent; 1994, –2 per cent and 50 per cent. *The Economist* (19 December 1992, p. 34) estimated inflation in 1992 at 130 per cent (compared with 265 per cent in 1991).

The elections of September and October 1992

The general election and the presidential election both took place on 27 September 1992. International observers approved the process in general, although there were a high number of invalid votes (13 per cent) and votes cast away from the place of residence (10 per cent). The first round of the presidential election gave Ion Iliescu, the candidate of the Democratic National Salvation Front (DNSF), 47.34 per cent of the vote and Emil Constantinescu, rector of Bucharest University and the candidate of the Democratic Convention, 31.24 per cent (the DC, composed of seventeen groupings, included parties such as the National Peasant Party and Civic Alliance and favoured continuing the economic reform programme). Iliescu campaigned on a platform of cautious economic reform. His support lay mainly in the rural areas (where there seemed to be the impression that landlords would otherwise take away peasant land) and among the working class (especially in the heavy industrial areas), fearful of unemployment. The second round, held on 11 October, was won convincingly by Iliescu with 61.4 per cent of the vote. He was sworn in on 30 October.

The general election involved competition for the 484 seats in parliament (the Chamber of Deputies and the Senate). The turn-out was 74 per cent and there was a 3 per cent threshold. There was no clear-cut result, but the DNSF did surprisingly well, becoming the largest single party in parliament, while the DC was very disappointed. The distribution of seats was as follows: DNSF, 166; DC, 116; National Salvation Front (NSF, led by Petre Roman), sixty-one; Romanian National Unity Party (RNUP; extreme nationalist), forty-four; Democratic Union of Hungarians in Romania (DUHR), thirty-nine; Greater Romania Party (GRP; extreme nationalist), twenty-two; Socialist Labour Party (SLP), eighteen.

Nicolae Vacaroiu (aged forty-nine), a senior civil servant in the Ministry of Finance (head of taxation), was appointed prime minister on 4 November 1992 after Theodor Stolojan declined to stay on. The cabinet mainly comprised other senior civil servants and DNSF members, with no seats for DC. Misu Negritoiu, a reform-minded independent, was put in charge of economic reform. It is not exactly certain where Vacaroiu stands on economic reform in general, but he seems to be cautious. For example, he favours spreading the liberalization of prices over a period of three years. *EEN* (1992, vol. 6, no. 23, p. 4) points out that he was dismissed from Petre Roman's cabinet in November 1990 for opposing the lifting of state subsidies and price controls. Vacaroiu has been reported as saying that 'the continuity of Romania's reforms can be achieved only at a bearable social cost' (*IHT*, 18 December 1992, p. 2) and that 'construction of a market economy is a long-term project' (Alec Russell, *The Telegraph*, 21 December 1992, p. 7).

YUGOSLAVIA

The effects of the crisis

The refugee problem. UN figures for the number of refugees within the former Yugoslavia are as follows: 1,890,723, comprising 600,172 from Croatia and 1,290,551 from Bosnia-Hercegovina (*FT*, 29 July 1992, p. 2); 1,936,500, 617,500, and 1,288,000 respectively (*The Times*, 25 August 1992, p. 9). In addition there were 445,731 refugees who had fled to other countries, such as Germany (200,000), Sweden (55,000), Austria (50,000), and Hungary (50,000) (*FT*, 13 August 1991, p. 2). The *Financial Times* (21 November 1992, p. 8) reports the following figures. More than 1.5 million Bosnians are now considered 'displaced persons' within the territory of the former Yugoslavia. Of these around 800,000 are in Bosnia-Hercegovina itself and 340,000 are in Croatia. The UN places the total number of people uprooted by the Croatian and Bosnian wars at 2.1 million. In addition more than 550,000 refugees had fled to other countries.

Atrocities. It is now clear that most atrocities have been committed by Serbs in Bosnia-Hercegovina. The scale has been large enough to be catagorized as crimes against humanity. The mass rape of Moslem women and girls (up to 20,000 according to an EC report) by Serbs became an ingredient of ethnic cleansing.

The number of casualties in Bosnia-Hercegovina. Early August 1992 report by the Bosnian government: 8,272 confirmed deaths. US Senate report on visit 7–14 August 1992: 35,000, with more than 20,000 killed in the Serbian 'ethnic cleansing' of Moslems. 11 September 1992: Sarajevo medical crisis centre estimates 10,503 killed in the whole of Bosnia-Hercegovina and 44,955 seriously wounded. Another 53,200 were classified as missing or 'liquidated'. 1 October 1992 report: since April 14,364 dead, nearly 50,000 wounded and 57,000 missing (these figures exclude Serbs); 80 per cent of the victims were civilians; 1,447 children killed and 8,500 missing. 13 November 1992: the Bosnian foreign minister estimated that 100,000 people, mostly Moslems, had been killed in Serbian attacks since spring 1992, while other Bosnian officials believed that 140,000 men alone had been killed since the fighting began (*IHT*, 14 November 1992, p. 2). The Bosnian foreign minister later put the number of dead at 200,000 and the number of homeless at 1.5 million (*The Times*, 14 January 1993, p. 14). This contrasts with a more commonly given figure for the number of dead in Bosnia of

17,000 (e.g., *FT*, 14 January 1993, p. 19).

Society and the economy. Harrowing stories and pictures of conditions within besieged cities like Sarajevo have played a major role in increasing international pressure on Serbia. The area of Bosnia-Hercegovina occupied by the Serbs is the subject of some dispute. The Serbs claimed 70 per cent. On 17 August 1992 Bosnian president Izetbegovich put the percentage of land occupied by both Serbs and Croats at 55 per cent. One estimate put Croatian-controlled territory at 25 per cent.

Euromoney (September 1992, p. 72) provides estimates of the falls in GNP in 1992: Serbia and Montenegro, 21.8 per cent; Croatia, 9.0 per cent; and Slovenia, 8.5 per cent. Laura Silber (*FT*, 10 December 1992, p. 4) reports the following figures for Slovenia: unemployment 11.5 per cent; in 1991 GDP fell by 9 per cent and industrial output by 10 per cent. In Croatia in the first half of 1992 (compared with the same period a year earlier) industrial output plunged by 28 per cent and total national output would fall by at least 20 per cent in 1992; the registered unemployment rate was nearly 20 per cent, but unofficial estimates put the figure at over 30 per cent; the inflation rate for the year to September 1992 was 727 per cent (Deutsche Bank, *Focus: Eastern Europe*, 30 November 1992, no. 62, p. 3). There is severe hyperinflation and sharply declining output in Serbia. Robert Block (*The Independent*, 4 January 1992, p. 6) reports the following official estimates. In 1992 inflation was 19,810 per cent, while GDP fell by 26 per cent (GDP in 1992 was nearly 45 per cent down on the 1989 level) (note, however, that agricultural output was relatively buoyant). In real terms the average monthly salary in Serbia is now only a tenth of what it was five years ago (Laura Silber, *FT*, 18 December 1992, p. 12), while the unemployment rate is 40 per cent (Tim Judah, *The Times*, 18 December 1992, p. 10). Roger Boyes (*The Times*, 9 January 1993, p. 11) reports that in Serbia there are 550,000 working citizens, 750,000 unemployed and 1.4 million on temporary lay-off.

The continuing story

15–17 July 1992 London conference, chaired by Lord Carrington and attended by representatives of the Moslems, Croats and Serbs (the leader of the Bosnian Serbs was Radovan Karadzic and the leader of the Bosnian Croats was Mate Boban). A ceasefire (the nineteenth arranged by the EC) was to begin in Bosnia-Hercegovina as of 6.00 p.m. on 19 July 1992 and was to last for fourteen days. The participants were to return to London on 27 July. The UN was to 'supervise' heavy weaponry and the refugees were to return to their homes. But there was a complete failure to carry out the terms of the agreement. Indeed, there was a quarrel with the UN Secretary General, Boutros Boutros Ghali, who complained of not being consulted and argued that timely monitoring of heavy weapons was not feasible with the limited resources at the disposal of the UN. The parties did reconvene on 27–9 July, but all that the talks produced was agreement to set up a 'Co-ordinating Committee' to monitor a ceasefire, the distribution of aid, the return of refugees, and the exchange of prisoners.

19 July 1992. Yugoslav prime minister Panic flies to Sarajevo to see Bosnian president Izetbegovich.

20 July 1992. The EC calls for the expulsion of (new) Yugoslavia from the UN and all other international organizations.

29–30 July 1992. Geneva meeting to discuss the refugee problem.

6 August 1992. The United States grants full diplomatic recognition to Slovenia, Croatia and Bosnia-Hercegovina.

10 August 1992. The United States, the UK and France agree to submit the following draft resolution to the UN: 'All measures necessary to facilitate, in co-ordination with the UN, the delivery of humanitarian assistance to Sarajevo, and wherever needed in other parts of Bosnia-Hercegovina'. Also demanded was unimpeded access to all camps, prisons and detention centres.

12 August 1992. President Tudjman of Croatia says he is not against the idea of UN protectorate status for Bosnia-Hercegovina.

Second week of August 1992. The new Yugoslavia recognizes Slovenia.

13 August 1992. The UN Security Council agrees the following resolutions: 'Calls upon states to take . . . all measures necessary to facilitate, in co-ordination with the UN, delivery of . . . humanitarian assistance to Sarajevo and wherever needed in other parts of Bosnia-Hercegovina'; 'Demands that unimpeded and continuous access to all camps, prisons and detention centres be granted immediately . . . and that all detainees therein receive humane treatment'; 'Reaffirms that all parties to the conflict are bound to comply with their obligations under international humanitarian law . . . and that persons . . . are individually responsible in respect of such breaches'; 'Strongly condemns any violation of international humanitarian law, including those involved in the practice of "ethnic cleansing".'

A special human rights rapporteur (investigator) was to be appointed. During the debate preceding the vote the US speaker, John Bolton, said: 'We ask the people of Serbia-Montenegro the simple question: do they wish to go down in history as citizens of the last fascist state in Europe?'

14 August 1992. The UN Human Rights Commission appoints the former Polish prime minister Tadeusz Mazowiecki as special rapporteur. In his first report published at the end of August he attached most blame for human rights violations on the Serbs. He recommended that the UN forces should be expanded to cover the whole of Bosnia-Hercegovina, and given the power to intervene to stop such violations and to gain access to detention centres. There should be an international war crimes commission.

24 August 1992. Lord (Peter) Carrington steps down as EC special envoy on Yugoslav peace talks.

26–7 August 1992. Joint EC–UN conference, held in London and jointly chaired by John

Major and Boutros Boutros Ghali. The conference did not attempt to produce an immediate end to hostilities in Bosnia-Hercegovina or a detailed blueprint to solve the whole problem. Instead four papers were endorsed, which provided a framework for an ongoing negotiating forum based on the UN in Geneva and a set of principles to guide an eventual settlement. Most blame was attached to Serbian aggression and sanctions were to be tightened up (the new federal republic of Yugoslavia continued to evade many of the sanctions, however). But there was still to be no use of force by the international community to impose a solution or lifting of the arms embargo against Bosnia-Hercegovina (the openly declared ruling out of the use of force against the Serbs in the earlier stages of the conflict and the inclusion of Bosnia in the arms embargo are the focus of criticism levelled at the West).

1. A Central Strategic Committee was set up, chaired by Lord Carrington's successor, Lord (David) Owen, and Cyrus Vance, the UN's special envoy and former US Secretary of State. They would supervise six steering committees, dealing with the rights of ethnic minorities, human rights, economic issues, the states seeking successor status to the old Yugoslavia, confidence-building measures, and humanitarian aid. The conference urged all sides 'immediately and without preconditions' to resume negotiations on the future constitutional arrangements for Bosnia-Hercegovina. A political settlement was to include 'a full and permanent cessation of hostilities'. Radovan Karadzic promised to gather Serbian heavy weapons around Sarajevo, Goradze, Bihac and Jajce, and to allow UN monitoring of them; he expected the Bosnian government to take reciprocal action (he also offered to return up to 20 per cent of the land occupied by the Serbs). The conference would ask the UN to provide observers to monitor Bosnia's borders with Serbia, Montenegro and Croatia in an attempt to stem the flow of weapons, while the military use of aircraft and helicopters by the Serbs was to be banned.

2. The principles were as follows: guarantee Bosnia's international frontiers (the 'return of territory taken by force' was called for); an end to 'ethnic cleansing' (described as 'inhuman and illegal'; refugees should be 'progressively returned' to their homes or receive compensation, and the rights of ethnic minorities were to be guaranteed); detention camps to be closed down; it was reaffirmed that 'any persons who commit or order the commission of grave breaches of the Geneva conventions are individually responsible'; and more UN personnel would help ensure the delivery of humanitarian aid.

There appeared to be a growing rift between Panic and Milosevic at the conference, the former being the more dominant and conciliatory personality. For example, Panic favours recognizing the other republics within existing borders, believes in the right of refugees to return home and supports educational rights for Albanians in Kosovo. Milosevic accepted the idea of international human rights observers in Kosovo, but ruled out political autonomy. Bosnian president Izetbegovich put forward the idea of a secular and decentralized country, but not one based on ethnic divisions (he thought that only further 'ethnic cleansing' would make this technically feasible); a second parliamentary chamber would give each of the three main communities a right of veto (on 17 August he considered the idea of a temporary UN protectorate). Despite the conference, however, hostilities continued.

30 August 1992. The Serbs claim to have lifted the siege of Gorazde.

2 September 1992. Karadzic claims that Serbian heavy weapons around Sarajevo, Bihac and Jajce come under UN monitoring. But fighting continues.

3 September 1992. Italian aid plane shot down. Aid flights are suspended and not resumed until 3 October.

4 September 1992. Panic wins a vote of no confidence in parliament, proposed by some deputies from the Socialist Party and by the Serbian Radical Party (led by the extreme nationalist Vojislav Seselj). Panic is supported by Serbian president Cosic and Montenegrin president Bulatovic. Parliament approves the London conference agreements.

6 September 1992. Vance and Owen give Bosnian Serbs until midday 12 September to place heavy weapons around the four cities under UN monitoring. Alleged compliance, but the firing continues.

The Non-aligned Nations' summit in Jakarta condemns Serbian 'ethnic cleansing'.

8 September 1992. UN aid convoy fired on at Sarajevo airport.

10 September 1992. Serbian foreign minister Vladislav Jovanovich resigns in protest at the position taken by Panic.

13 September 1992. EC agrees to support the idea of a 'no-fly zone' over Bosnia-Hercegovina, with observers based at airports.

14 September 1992. UN approves up to 6,000 more troops for humanitarian aid purposes (to join the 1,500 already there). Note that UN headquarters have been switched from Sarajevo to Zagreb.

20 September 1992. UN Security Council recommends to the General Assembly that the new Yugoslavia should be denied recognition as the legal successor to the old one. An application would be required to join the UN.

22 September 1992. The General Assembly agrees.

30 September 1992. Tudjman meets Yugoslav president Cosic; agreement reached to demilitarize the Prevlaka peninsula on the Adriatic south of Dubrovnik (the Bosnian government became increasingly concerned about a possible bilateral agreement between Bosnian Serbs and Croats). The UN peacekeeping forces persuade Croatian civilians not to march into Serb-held areas of Croatia to reclaim their homes.

6 October 1992. The UN Security Council authorizes the creation of a war crimes commission. This would conduct investigations into atrocities and report its findings and recommendations to the council.

Fall of Bosanski Brod to Serbs. The were rumours that the Croatians arranged this as a *quid pro quo* for Prevlavka.

9 October 1992. The UN Security Council declares an air exclusion zone ('no fly' zone) for military flights for combatants over Bosnia-Hercegovina. In cases of violation, urgent consideration will be given to 'further measures necessary to enforce the ban'. It seems as though the Serbs ignored the ban for a short while, but on 14 October Karadzic agreed to transfer Bosnian-Serb combat aircraft to UN-monitored airfields in the new Yugoslavia. But infringements of the ban on military flights were subsequently recorded.

The Bosnian government fears a bilateral ceasefire between the Serbs and Croats.

12 October 1992. Serbia withdraws from scheduled talks between the Yugoslav and Croatian governments on the re-establishment of economic relations and transport links and the return of Croatian refugees to Serb-held areas of Croatia.

13 October 1992. Serbia forcibly disperses a demonstration by Albanians in Pristina, the capital of Kosovo. The focus was educational reforms.

15 October 1992. Panic meets Ibrahim Rugova in Pristina. Panic promises to end discrimination against Albanians in Kosovo. It is proposed that joint working groups be set up to discuss discrimination and other violations of human rights, the media and education.

16 October 1992. President Dobrica Cosic of Yugoslavia calls for the resignation of Milosevic, for the disarming of paramilitary groups in Bosnia and for an end to sorties of fighters from Serbia into Bosnia.

18 October 1992. Cosic calls for a lifting of the siege of Sarajevo and for the demilitarization of the city.

19 October 1992. Cosic meets Bosnian president Izetbegovich amid reports that the latter had accepted decentralization along non-ethnic lines.

Serbian police seize control of the federal (Yugoslav) Interior Ministry's building, claiming that this was simply the result of a property dispute. Possible seizure of documents implicating individuals in war crimes. Note that while the police support Milosevic, Cosic claims the support of the army.

20 October 1992. Cosic willing to hold war crimes trials.

21 October 1992. Izetbegovich says that he would be prepared to accept a 'decentralized state with a high level of local autonomy. It will not be an ethnic country, but one with many regions, maybe between eight and ten.' He announces that he will step down as president of Bosnia at the end of 1992.

Fighting begins in Bosnia between Moslems and Croats. There are reports later on of ethnic cleansing undertaken by Croats against Moslems.

23 October 1992. The local UN forces persuade military representatives of the three sides in the conflict to meet to discuss the situation in Sarajevo.

25 October 1992. President Cosic announces Yugoslav elections for 20 December 1992.

28 October 1992. The Vance–Owen draft proposals for Bosnia-Hercegovina are announced. The proposals 'deemed it necessary to reject any model based on three separate, ethnic, confessionally based states'. Bosnia's sovereignty should be preserved within existing borders. These are concessions to the Moslems, but, in deference to the Serbs and Croats, 'a centralized state would not be accepted by at least two of the principal ethnic, confessional groups since it would not protect their interests in the wake of the bloody civil strife'. The functions of central and provincial government would be divided up as follows:

1. The central government would be confined to foreign affairs and foreign trade, defence (a single army would be formed under international supervision) and finance (there would be a single currency). The central government would have representatives from the four communities, namely Moslem, Croat, Serb and 'other'. Parliament would have a lower House (which would elect the prime minister)

elected by proportional representation and an upper House appointed by the provincial governments. A presidency, comprising provincial governors, would be responsible for appointing a president. The president, choosen from among the major ethnic groups on a rotating basis, would carry out largely ceremonial duties.

2. The seven to ten provinces would be responsible for education, health, the local economy, the courts and police. Provincial boundaries should take into account not only ethnic considerations but also geography and traditional economic links (each province should be a viable economic unit). Where possible each province should contain a majority ethnic group. Provinces would not be permitted to grant their own citizenship or link up with any other state.

There would be strong international involvement, especially in the enforcement of human rights. The constitution would give foreign judges a majority on both a constitutional court and a human rights court. The Geneva conference on the former Yugoslavia would appoint human rights ombudsmen and an international human rights commission with a wide remit to investigate abuses.

The Bosnian Serbs and Croats reject the proposals. Karadzic claims that they favour the Moslems. He argues that all the Serbs should be in one region, while the others could make as many regions as they wish. The Serbs and Croats had intensified the fighting prior to the publication of the proposals in order to create 'facts on the ground'.

29 October 1992. Vance and Owen visit Kosovo. They obtain agreement to resume primary education for ethnic Albanian children by 9 November, but Rugova refuses to talk direct to the Serbs.

The Serbs take Jajce (under the terms of the London conference Serbian heavy weapons were supposed to have been monitored by the UN).

30 October 1992. President Tudjman of Croatia sees no alternative to a three-way division of Bosnia-Hercegovina. He had earlier expressed the desire to regain control over the Serbian areas of Croatia from the UN Protection Force by the spring of 1993.

1 November 1992. The Serbs from Bosnia and Croatia announce the creation of the Union of Serbian States, which would have a common citizenship, use a common currency and form a joint army. The Croatian Serb leader, Goran Hadzic, saw this as laying the foundation of a four-republic federation with Serbia and Montenegro. He hoped that this could be formed by the spring of 1993.

Supposed start of a 'week of tranquillity' for the children of Bosnia-Hercegovina, organized by Unicef.

2 November 1992. There is a decisive vote of no confidence against Panic in the lower House of the parliament of the federal republic of Yugoslavia. But a majority vote is also required in the upper House, where the next day Panic manages to survive by eighteen votes to seventeen with the support of the Montenegrin representatives (who have an equal share of the forty seats in the upper House). There is speculation that Montenegro could declare independence after the 20 December 1992 election.

The Bosnian Serbs threaten for a while to withdraw from the UN peace talks unless the principle of self-determination is granted.

4 November 1992. Karadzic signs an accord allowing the stationing of UN observers on six Serb-controlled airports in Croatia and Bosnia-Hercegovina.

5 November 1992. Slovenia and the EC sign a trade and economic co-operation accord.

8 November 1992. Four die in a clash between ethnic Albanians and police in Macedonia. Note that in the spring of 1992 Greece rejected a proposal by Milosevic to divide Macedonia between Greece and the federal republic of Yugoslavia (Kerin Hope and Judy Dempsey, *FT*, 13 November 1992, p. 3).

9 November 1992. Karadzic presents a seven-point plan, including a division of Bosnia-Hercegovina on ethnic lines, a ceasefire at the current front lines (where UN troops should be deployed), a withdrawal of Croatian forces from Bosnia and the release of all civilian hostages.

10 November 1992. Military officers from all sides meeting in Sarajevo agree on a ceasefire throughout Bosnia-Hercegovina as from midnight the following day. After a short period of patchy success the ceasefire breaks down.

12 November 1992. President Cosic warns that the Yugoslav army will return to Bosnia-Hercegovina unless Croatian army units are withdrawn.

16 November 1992. The UN Security Council votes for tighter sanctions against the federal republic of Yugoslavia, with the use of force authorized. Stop and search powers were to be available along the Danube and in the Adriatic, while transit traffic would need permission from the UN sanctions committee.

20 November 1992. NATO and the WEU agree to a full naval blockade of the Adriatic.

23 November 1992. The UN reports over 100 violations of the ban on military flights.

25 November 1992. The UN decides to send twelve observers to Macedonia to assess the prospects for a peacekeeping force.

A one-day Balkan conference in Istanbul, hosted by Turkey, urges the UN to examine the possibility of deploying forces in Kosovo, Vojvodina and the Sanjak (to a large extent Moslem) region of Serbia as well as in Macedonia (only CSCE monitors had been allowed by Serbia, which was not invited to attend the conference; Montenegro was also not invited and Greece declined an invitation). The conference also recommends the setting up of militarily safe areas ('safe havens') in Bosnia-Hercegovina. A consultative council is to be set up.

29 November 1992. An agreement between the Serbs and Croats to end cross-border shelling was supposed to come into effect at midnight, with regular Croatian troops leaving Bosnia-Hercegovina.

1 December 1992. Panic announces that he will oppose Milosevic in the Serbian presidential election on 20 December. The electoral commission declared Panic ineligible on the grounds that he had not lived in Yugoslavia long enough, but was overruled by the supreme court.

The UN Human Rights Commission decides that the Bosnian Serbs are primarily responsible for the atrocities and poses the question whether 'ethnic cleansing' is a form of genocide.

2 December 1992. A conference of foreign ministers, chaired by Cyrus Vance and Lord Owen, is fixed for 16 December.

2–3 December 1992. The Islamic Conference Organization (which Albania joins) urges the use of force against Serbia and the lifting of the arms embargo on Bosnia-Hercegovina. The UN is given until 15 January 1993 to find a solution.

6 December 1992. Milan Kucan wins the Slovenian presidential election with 64 per cent of the votes. As a result of the general election the Liberal Democratic Party is the largest party in parliament, but with only twenty-two out of ninety seats a coalition government was again formed.

10 December 1992. The UN Security Council states that the renewed Serbian offensive in Bosnia-Hercegovina, particularly against Sarajevo, is a threat to 'international peace and security' (a phrase that opens the way to intervention under the UN charter). If the attacks do not cease, the UN will consider taking 'further measures'.

11 December 1992. The UN agrees to send 700 military observers to Macedonia as an act of 'preventative diplomacy' or 'preventative peacekeeping' (the first time the UN has agreed to send troops anywhere to prevent fighting breaking out). The borders with Kosovo and Albania will be monitored.

13 December 1992. Military officers from all sides agree on another ceasefire in Bosnia-Hercegovina.

16 December 1992. The US Secretary of State, Lawrence Eagleburger, names seven individuals (four Serbs, including Vojislav Seselj, the leader of the 'Chetniks' paramilitary force, and three Croats) who should be tried for war crimes. He also says that 'Leaders such as Slobodan Milosevic, the president of Serbia, Radovan Karadzic, the self-declared president of the Serbian-Bosnian republic, and General Ratko Mladic, commander of the Bosnian Serbian military forces, must eventually explain whether and how they sought to ensure, as they must under international law, that their forces complied with international law.'

17 December 1992. In an article published in *The Guardian* (17 December 1992, p. 17) Adrian Hastings claims that 'at least half of Bosnia's Serbs are opposed to Karadzic (who is not even a Bosnian . . .). Serbs include at least 10 per cent of the Bosnian Defence Force even today, and one of its two deputy C-in-Cs.' (Karadzic was born in Montenegro.)

17 December 1992. NATO gives a cautious commitment to enforce the ban on military flights should the UN adopt such a resolution. There had been 225 violations of the ban up to that point. (Note that on 18 December 1992, in a meeting of the NATO Co-operation Council, the thirty-seven NATO and former Warsaw Pact countries agreed to 'joint sessions on planning of peacekeeping missions, joint participation in peacekeeping training and consideration of possible peacekeeping exercises'. Actual peacekeeping would be in response to requests from the UN and CSCE.)

18 December 1992. The UN Security Council condemns the systematic rape carried out by Serbs.

20 December 1992. The Yugoslav elections are held (discussed below).

23 December 1992. Two threats are made: (1) the chief of staff of the Yugoslav army declares that the army is prepared to retaliate in the event of foreign intervention in Bosnia-Hercegovina; (2) Karadzic warns that, since 'countries that belong to NATO [have] already declared themselves hostile to the Serbian people', their UN contingents should be replaced by troops 'from countries which have not spoken in favour of military intervention'.

28 December 1992. Karadzic proposes that UN monitors 'be specifically allocated to each aircraft, that they have full [and unrestricted] access to these aircraft, and that in the event that these aircraft have to fly, for whatever reason, they will be allowed to travel on board'. The contents of a letter, delivered on 25 December, from US President Bush to both Milosevic and the chief of staff of the Yugoslav army are revealed. Bush warns that 'In the event of conflict in Kosovo caused by Serbian action, the United States will be prepared to employ military force against the Serbs in Kosovo and in Serbia proper.' In addition 'the United States is prepared to use military force to respond to interference with humanitarian relief deliveries in Bosnia' and 'will be prepared to use military force in defence of Unprofor'. (Unprofor is short for the UN Protection Force.)

29 December 1992. Panic is replaced as Yugoslav prime minister after votes of no confidence are passed overwhelmingly in both Houses of the Yugoslav parliament. Panic says that this is unconstitutional and vows to stay on until a new government is formed.

31 December 1992. Karadzic issues an order that the only flights to continue should be by helicopters carrying the wounded.

10 January 1993. The French foreign minister proposes that force should be used if necessary to liberate the detention camps (there has been an international outcry over conditions in Serbian-run camps, where there is evidence of rape, torture and murder). The proposal causes disarray in the French cabinet.

17 January 1993. The Yugoslav army fires on Bosnian government forces across the border, allegedly in retaliation.

The Yugoslav elections of 20 December 1992

In the Serbian presidential election Milosevic (56.32 per cent of the vote) comfortably beat the main contender, Panic (34.02 per cent). In the Serbian parliamentary election the Serbian Socialist Party (SSP) led by Milosevich (101 seats) remained the largest party in the 250-seat Serbian National Assembly, with the extreme nationalist Serbian Radical Party (SRP) led by Vojislav Seselj (seventy-four seats) making great strides to come second. The preliminary results gave the Depos opposition alliance forty-nine seats, the Democratic Union of Hungarians in Vojvodina nine seats, the Democratic Party seven seats, and Citizens of Kosovo-Metohija five seats.

Momir Bulatovic won 43 per cent of the votes in the first round of the Montenegrin presidential election, with Branko Kostic (who favours close ties with Serbia) winning 24 per cent. In the second round, held on 10 January 1993, the former was re-elected with 63.3 per cent of the votes, while the latter secured 36.7. The distribution of seats in the eighty-five-seat Montenegrin Assembly was as follows: the Democratic Party of Socialists forty-six, the People's Party fourteen, the Liberal Alliance thirteen, the Serbian Radical Party eight, and the Social Democratic Party of Reformists four.

The Albanians in Kosovo boycotted the election, as did most Moslems in the Sanjak (which straddles Serbia and Montenegro). In the words of the CSCE observers in Serbia 'the electoral process was seriously flawed'. Examples of wrongdoing included media manipulation, at least 5 per cent of (mainly young) voters excluded from the electoral register, some being given two votes (mainly married women registered under their married and maiden names), unsealed ballot boxes and lack of voting secrecy.

The Geneva conference

The first round lasted from 3 to 5 January 1993 (there was a break for the Orthodox Christmas, with the second round scheduled to begin on 10 January). This was the first occasion on which political and military representatives from all the warring factions in Bosnia-Hercegovina had direct talks. The Vance–Owen proposal to divide the country into ten largely autonomous provinces was accepted as a starting point for negotiations, but many points were contentious. For example, the ethnic criterion seemed to be dominant in drawing up the map, with each main group (Moslem, Serb and Croat) to varying degrees in the majority in three provinces. The Bosnian government were aggrieved that the results of ethnic cleansing were thus incorporated to a large extent. The three proposed Serbian provinces constituted about 43 per cent of the total area. The Serbs were concerned about the separation of Serb provinces. In the provincial government of Sarajevo the three groups would be equally represented, while the capital itself would become a demilitarized 'open city'. The nine-member presidency of the new state would be composed of three representatives from each of the main ethnic groups. The first round of talks ended without agreement, the positions of the three main groups being laid out as follows:

1. The Croats were the only group to accept all the political and military proposals (note, however, that bitter fighting broke out in parts of Bosnia between Croats and Moslems). The Croat provinces constituted about 25 per cent of the total area.

2. The Bosnian government, as indicated, had qualms about the map. But the main fear was that the high level of ethnically based provincial autonomy, coupled with a weak central government, could lead to the break-up of the country. Its minimum demands were that Bosnia-Hercegovina should be recognized as an independent sovereign state (so that no provinces could choose to join Serbia or Croatia) and that all heavy weaponry be placed under effective UN control.

3. The Serbs wanted an independent 'state within a state', with a common Serb administration, its own foreign policy and the right to self-determination. This is, of course, totally incompatible with the concept of Bosnian sovereignty. The Bosnian government feared that the Serbs would eventually hold a referendum and join 'Greater Serbia'. Indeed, the Vance–Owen proposals are clear on this issue. They say that the provinces would not have the right to forge any international relations of their own: 'the provinces shall not have any legal personality and may not enter into agreements with foreign states or international organizations'.

The negotiations resumed on 10 January 1993 despite the killing two days earlier at a Serbian check-point of a Bosnian deputy prime minister, who was travelling in a UN convoy from Sarajevo airport. Karadzic, who had the first round adjourned so that he could consult the Bosnian Serbs, returned with an eight-point programme. This included the idea of a 'composite state' made up of 'three constituent peoples as its three constituent units'. On 12 January the conference looked doomed earlier on, but in a seemingly remarkable about-turn Karadzic declared that he would accept the Vance-Owen constitutional proposals for a sovereign Bosnian state, subject to approval by the Bosnian Serb 'parliament' within seven days (the word 'seemingly' is used because of the possibility that the drama was staged-managed). Both Milosevic and Cosic were portrayed as putting pressure on Karadzic to accept. It was certainly the case that Milosevic was concerned that the Western countries would increasingly get involved – to enforce the ban on military flights in the first instance, but also the possibility of actions such as the destruction of Serb heavy weapons, the lifting of the arms embargo on the Bosnian government and the creation of safe havens (the over-stretched Serbian lines and the Islamic Conference Organization were a further consideration). Milosevic was also anxious to avoid a tightening of the economic embargo on the new Yugoslavia (the EC threatened the 'total isolation' of Yugoslavia if the proposals were rejected). The Vance-Owen proposals themselves were only slightly revised. There was a merger of two of the articles of the original ten-point constitutional framework, namely moving up article four (the recognition of three 'constituent peoples') and amalgamating it with article one (a decentralized state made up of largely self-governing provinces). The two chairmen announced to the press that 'the constitution shall recognize three constituent peoples as well as a group of others with most government functions carried out by its provinces.'

The Bosnian Serb 'parliament' voted to accept the Vance–Owen constitutional proposals on 20 January 1993, albeit still insisting in the statement issued after the meeting on the right to self-determination. There were fifty-five votes in favour, fifteen against and one absten-tion. But it is very difficult to be optimistic about the prospects of peace in Bosnia-Hercegovina. Talks were to resume, but highly contentious issues, such as the provincial borders, remained to be settled along with the military aspects. The Serbs undoubtedly see the Vance–Owen proposals as merely an imposed staging post on the way to the creation of a 'Greater Serbia'. In addition, the Moslems remain suspicious of the Croats. (On 22 January 1993 the Croat army launched on offensive across UN ceasefine lines into parts of the Serbian Krajina region of Croatia.)

BIBLIOGRAPHY

Periodicals and reports

Abecor *Country Reports* are distributed in Britain by Barclays Bank on behalf of an association of European banks. The *Vietnam Courier* is published in Hanoi. Periodicals and reports mentioned in the text are abbreviated as follows:

CDSP	*Current Digest of the Soviet Press* (since 5 February 1992 *Post-Soviet*)
EEN	*Eastern Europe Newsletter*
EIU	Economist Intelligence Unit
FEER	*Far Eastern Economic Review*
FT	*Financial Times*
IHT	*International Herald Tribune*

Books and journals

Adam, J. (1987) 'The Hungarian economic reform of the 1980s', *Soviet Studies*, vol. XXXIX, no. 4.

—— (1989a) *Economic Reforms in the Soviet Union and Eastern Europe since the 1960s*, London: Macmillan.

—— (1989b) 'Work-teams: a new phenomenon in income distribution in Hungary', *Comparative Economic Studies*, vol. XXXI, no. 1.

Adirim, I. (1989) 'A note on the current level, pattern and trends of unemployment in the USSR', *Soviet Studies*, vol. XLI, no. 3.

Aganbegyan, A. (1988a) 'The economics of *perestroika*', International Affairs (London), vol. 64, no. 2.

—— (1988b) *The Challenge: Economics of perestroika*, London: Hutchinson.

—— (1989) *Moving the Mountain: Inside the perestroika Revolution*, London: Bantam Press.

Akerlof, G., Rose, A., Yellen, J. and Hessenius, H. (1991) 'East Germany in from the cold; the economic aftermath of currency union', *Brookings Papers on Economic Activity*, no. 1.

Allison, G. and Blackwill, R. (1991) 'America's stake in the Soviet future', *Foreign Affairs*, vol. 70, no. 3.

Angelov, I. (1989) 'Framework of the Bulgarian economic reform' in Economic Commission for Europe (1989).

Arnot, B. (1988) *Controlling Soviet Labour*, London: Macmillan.

Aroio, Z. (1989) 'The enterprise in the People's Republic of Bulgaria' in *Economic Commission for Europe* (1989).

Artisien, P. (1989) *Yugoslavia to 1993*, London: EIU.

Ash, R. (1988) 'The evolution of agricultural policy', *China Quarterly*, no. 116.

Ash, T. (1992) *Agricultural Reform in Central and Eastern Europe*, Edinburgh: Heriot-Watt University: Discussion Paper in Economics no. 14.

Åslund, A. (1984) 'The Functioning of private enterprise in Poland', *Soviet Studies*, vol. XXXVI, no. 3.

—— (1985) *Private Enterprise in Eastern Europe*, London: Macmillan.

—— (1989) *Gorbachev's Struggle for Economic Reform: The Soviet Reform Process, 1985–88*, 1st edn, London: Pinter.

—— (1991a) *Gorbachev's Struggle for Economic Reform: The Soviet Reform Process, 1985–88*, 2nd edn, London: Pinter.

—— (1991b) 'Gorbachev, *perestroyka*, and economic crisis', Problems of Communism, January–April.

—— (ed.) (1992a) *The Post-Soviet Economy; Soviet and Western Perspectives*, London: Pinter.

—— (1992b) 'A critique of Soviet reform plans' in Åslund (1992a).

Åslund, A. and Sjöberg, O. (1991) *Privatization and Transition to Market Economy in Albania*, Stockholm Institute of Soviet and East European Economics: Working Paper no. 27.

Aubert, C. (1990) 'The Chinese model and the future of rural–urban development' in Wädekin (1990a).

Azicri, M. (1988) *Cuba: Politics, Economics and Society*, London: Pinter.

Babic M. and Primorac, E. (1986) 'Some causes of the

Yugoslav external debt', *Soviet Studies*, vol. XXXVIII, no. 4.

Balcerowicz, L. (1989) 'Polish economic reform, 1981–88: an overview' in Economic Commission for Europe (1989).

Batt, J. (1988) *Economic Reform and Political Change in Eastern Europe: A Comparison of the Czecho-slovak and Hungarian Experiences*, London: Macmillan.

—— (1991) *East Central Europe from Reform to Transformation*, London: Pinter (Chatham House Papers: the Royal Institute of International Affairs).

Bauer, T. (1988) 'Economic reforms within and beyond the state sector', *American Economic Review*, Papers and Proceedings (May).

Baylis, T. (1986) 'Explaining the GDR's economic strategy', *International Organisation*, vol. 40, no. 2.

Bechtold, H. and Helfer, A. (1987) 'Stagnation problems in socialist economies' in Gey *et al.* (1987).

Begg, D. (1991) 'Economic reform in Czechoslovakia: should we believe in Santa Klaus?', *Economic Policy*, no. 13 (October).

Bendekovic, J. and Teodorovic, I. (1988) 'Investment decision-making in Yugoslavia' in Saunders (1988).

Ben-Ner, A. and Neuberger, E. (1990) 'The feasibility of planned market systems: the Yugoslav visible hand and negotiated planning', *Journal of Comparative Economics*, vol. 14, no. 4.

Beresford, M. (1988) *Vietnam: Politics, Economics and Society*, London: Pinter.

—— (1990) 'Vietnam: socialist agriculture in transition', *Journal of Contemporary Asia*, vol. 20, no. 4.

—— (1992) 'Industrial reform in Vietnam' in Jeffries (1992).

Berg, A. and Sachs, J. (1992) 'Structural adjustment and international trade in Eastern Europe: the case of Poland', *Economic Policy*, no. 14.

Bergson, A. (ed.) (1953) *Soviet Economic Growth*, New York: Row Peterson.

—— (1961) *The Real National Income of Soviet Russia since 1928*, Cambridge, Mass.: Harvard University Press.

—— (1985) 'A visit to China's economic reform', *Comparative Economic Studies*, vol. XXVII, no. 2.

Berliner, J. (1976) *The Innovation Decision in Soviet Industry*, Cambridge, Mass.: MIT Press.

Bethkenhagen, J. (1987) 'The GDR's energy policy and its implications for the intensification drive', *Studies in Comparative Communism*, vol. XX, no. 1.

Biberaj, E. (1989) 'Romania' in DIW (1989).

—— (1991) 'Albania at the crossroads', *Problems of Communism* (September–October).

Bideleux, R. (1985) *Communism and Development*, London: Methuen.

Birman, I. (1978) 'From the achieved level', *Soviet Studies*. vol.XXXI, no.2.

Blanchard, O., Dornbusch, R., Krugman, P., Layard, R. and Summers, L. (1991) *Reform in Eastern Europe*, Cambridge, Mass.: MIT Press.

Blanchard, O. and Layard, R. (1990) *Economic Change in Poland*, London: Centre for Research into Communist Economies (New Series 1, July).

Blazyca, G. (1980a) 'An assessment of Polish economic development in the 1970s', *European Economic Review*, vol. 14.

—— (1980b) 'Industrial structure and the economic problems of industry in a centrally planned economy: the Polish case', *Journal of Industrial Economics* (March).

—— (1982) 'The degeneration of central planning in Poland' in J. Woodall (ed.) *Policy and Politics in Contemporary Poland: Reform and Crisis*, London: Pinter.

—— (1985) 'The Polish economy under martial law: a dissenting view', *Soviet Studies*, vol. 37, no. 3.

—— (1986) *Poland to the 1990s: Retreat or Reform?*, London: EIU (August).

—— (1987) 'The new round of economic reform in Eastern Europe', *National Westminster Review* (November).

—— (1991) *Poland's Next Five Years: the Dash for Capitalism*, London: EIU.

—— (1992) 'Poland' in Jeffries (1992).

Bleaney, M. (1988) *Do Socialist Economies Work? The Soviet and East European Experience*, Oxford: Basil Blackwell.

Blejer, M. and Szapary, G. (1990) 'The evolving role of tax policy in China', *Journal of Comparative Economics*, vol. 14, no. 3.

Borensztein, E. and Kumar, M. (1991) 'Proposals for privatization in Eastern Europe', *IMF Staff Papers*, vol. 38, no. 2.

Bornstein, M. (1988) 'Price reform in the USSR: comment on Shmelev', *Soviet Economy*, vol. 4, no. 4.

—— (1991) 'Soviet assessments of economic reforms in other socialist countries', *Soviet Economy*, vol.7, no.1.

Bova, R. (1987) 'On *perestroyka*: the role of workplace participation', *Problems of Communism*, (July–August).

Bowers, S. (1989) 'Stalinism in Albania: domestic affairs under Enver Hoxha', *East European Quarterly*, vol.XXII, no.4.

Bowles, P. and White, G. (1989) 'Contradictions in China's financial reforms: the relationship between banks and enterprises', *Cambridge Journal of Economics*, vol. 13, no. 4.

Boycko, M. (1991) 'Price decontrol: the micro-economic case for the "big bang" approach', *Oxford Review of Economic Policy*, vol. 7, no. 4.

Boyd, M. (1988) 'The performance of private and socialist agriculture in Poland: the effects of policy and organization', *Journal of Comparative Economics*, vol. 12, no. 1.

—— (1990) 'Organizational reform and agricultural performance: the case of Bulgarian agriculture, 1960–85', *Journal of Comparative Economics*, vol. 14, no. 1.

Brada, J. and King, A. (1992) 'Is there a J-curve for the economic transition from socialism to capitalism?', *Economics of Planning*, vol. 25, no. 1.

Brada, J. and Wädekin, K-E. (1988) *Socialist Agriculture in Transition: Organizational Response to Failing Performance*, Boulder: Westview Press.

Breuel, B. (1991) 'A social market economy cannot be introduced overnight', *European Affairs*, no. 6.

Brezinski, H. (1987) 'The second economy in the GDR: pragmatism is gaining ground', *Studies in Comparative Communism*, vol. XX, no. 1.

—— (1990) 'Private agriculture in the GDR: limitations of orthodox socialist agricultural policy', *Soviet Studies*, vol. 42, no. 3.

Brodzka, T. (1987) 'Stage two of the reform', *Polish Perspectives*, vol. XXX, no. 3.

Brooks, K. (1990a) 'Soviet agriculture's halting reform', *Problems of Communism*, March–April.

—— (1990b) 'Soviet agricultural policy and pricing under Gorbachev' in Gray (1990).

—— (1990c) 'Perestroika in the countryside: agricultural reform in the Gorbachev era', *Comparative Economic Studies*, vol. XXXII, no. 2.

Brooks, K., Guash, L., Braverman, A. and Csaki, C. (1991) 'Agriculture and the transition to the market', *Journal of Economic Perspectives*, vol. 5, no. 4.

Brus, W. (1982) 'The economic policy of Poland' in Höhmann *et al.* (1982).

Bryson, P. (1984) *The Consumer under Socialist Planning: the East German Case*, New York: Praeger.

Bryson, P. and Melzer, M. (1987) 'The Kombinat in GDR economic organisation' in Jeffries *et al.* (1987).

Buck, H.F. (1987) 'The GDR financial system' in Jeffries *et al.* (1987)

Buechtemann, C. and Schupp, J. (1992) 'Repercussions of reunification: patterns and trends in the socio-economic transformation of East Germany', *Industrial Relations Journal*, vol. 23, no. 2.

Butterfield, J. (1990) 'Devolution in decision-making and organizational change in Soviet agriculture', *Comparative Economic Studies*, vol. XXXII, no. 2.

Calvo, G. and Frenkel, J. (1991a) 'From centrally planned to market economy', *IMF Staff Papers*, vol. 38, no. 2.

—— (1991b) 'Credit markets, credibility, and economic transformation', *Journal of Economic Perspectives*, vol. 5, no. 4.

Cavoski, K. (1988) 'Comment' in Winiecki (1988b).

Cepl, V. (1991) 'A note on the restitution of property in post-communist Czechoslovakia', *Journal of Communist Studies*, vol. 7, no. 3.

Cerny, R. (1988) 'The restructuring of the economic mechanism in agriculture', *Czechoslovak Economic Digest*, no. 4.

Cervinka, A. (1987) 'The State Enterprise Act', *Czechoslovak Economic Digest*, no. 6.

Chamberlain, H. (1987) 'Party–management relations in Chinese industry: some political dimensions of economic reform', *China Quarterly*, no. 112 (December).

Chan, T. (1986) 'China's price reform in the 1980s', discussion paper no. 78, Department of Economics, University of Hong Kong.

Chapman, J. (1988) 'Gorbachev's wage reform', *Soviet Economy*, vol. 4, no. 4.

—— (1989) 'Income distribution and social justice in the Soviet Union', *Comparative Economic Studies*, vol. XXXI, no. 1.

Charemza, W. (1992) 'Market failure and stagflation: some aspects of privatization in Poland', *Economics of Planning*, vol. 25, no. 1.

Chelstowski, S. (1988) 'The second stage scenario', *Polish Perspectives*, vol. XXXI, no. 1.

Chen, K., Jefferson, G., and Singh, I. (1992) 'Lessons from China's economic reform', *Journal of Comparative Economics*, vol. 16, no. 2.

Cheung, S. (1986) *Will China go Capitalist?*, London: Institute of Economic Affairs (Hobart Papers).

Childs, D. (1987) *East Germany to the 1990s: Can it Resist Glasnost?*, London: EIU.

—— (1988) *The GDR: Moscow's German Ally*, 2nd edn., London: Unwin Hyman.

Childs, D. Baylis, T. and Rüschemeyer, M. (eds) (1989) *East Germany in Comparative Perspective*, London: Routledge.

Chon, Soohyun (1989) 'South Korean–Soviet trade relations: involvement in Siberian development', *Asian Survey*, vol. XXIX, no. 12.

Chung, J. (1983) 'Economic planning in North Korea' in Scalapino and Kim (1983).

—— (1986) 'Foreign trade of North Korea: performance, policy and prospects' in Scalapino and Lee (1983).

CIA (1990) *Eastern Europe: Long Road Ahead to Economic Well-being*, Washington: CIA.

CIA Analyst (1986) 'Polish agriculture: policy and prospects' in US Congress, Joint Economic Committee, Washington, DC: US Government Printing Office.

Cochrane, N. (1988) 'The private sector in East European agriculture', *Problems of Communism*, (March–April).

—— (1990a) 'Reforming agricultural prices in Eastern Europe', *Problems of Communism*, January–February.

—— (1990b) 'Reforming socialist agriculture: Bulgarian and Hungarian experience and implications for the USSR' in Wädekin (1990b).

Collier, I. and Siebert, H. (1991) 'The economic integration of post-Wall Germany', *American Economic Review*, Papers and Proceedings (May).

Collins, S. (1991) 'Policy watch: US economic policy toward the Soviet Union and Eastern Europe', *Journal of Economic Perspectives*, vol. 5, no. 4.

Comisso, D. and Marer, P. (1986) 'The economics and politics of reform in Hungary', *International Organisation*, vol. 40, no. 2.

Commission of the European Communities (1990) *European Economy: Economic Transformation in Hungary and Poland*, no. 43 (March).

Cook, E. (1984) 'Agricultural reform in Poland: background and prospects', *Soviet Studies*, vol. XXXVI, no. 3.

—— (1986a) 'Prospects for Bulgarian agriculture in the 1980s', US Congress, Joint Economic Committee, Washington, DC: Government Printing Office.

—— (1986b) 'Prospects for Polish agriculture', US Congress, Joint Economic Committee.

—— (1988) 'Prospects for Polish agriculture' in Brada and Wädekin (1988).

Cooper, J. (1991) 'Military cuts and conversion in the defence industry', *Soviet Economy*, vol. 7, no. 2

Corbett, J. and Mayer, C. (1991) 'Financial reform in Eastern Europe: progress with the wrong model', *Oxford Review of Economic Policy*, vol. 7, no. 4.

Cornelsen, D. (1987) 'The GDR economy in the eighties: economic strategy and structural adjustments', *Studies in Comparative Communism*, vol. XX, no. 1.

Costa, N. (1988) 'Albania: a nation of contradictions', *East European Quarterly*, vol. XXII, no. 2.

Crane, K. (1986) 'Foreign trade decision-making under balance of payments pressure: Poland versus Hungary', US Congress, Joint Economic Committee, Washington, DC: Government Printing Office.

Crosnier, M-A. and Lhomel, E. (1990) 'A first assessment of the Vietnamese economic reforms', CEDUCEE, Paris: paper presented to the IV World Congress for Soviet and East European Studies (Harrogate, July).

Crowther, W. (1988) *The Political Economy of Romanian Socialism*, New York: Praeger.

Cukor, E., and Kovari, G. (1991) 'Wage trends in Hungary', *International Labour Review*, vol. 130, no. 2.

Cumings, B. (1988) 'Korea', *The Guardian*, 17 June 1988, p. 14 (author of *The Origins of the Korean War*, Vols 1 and 2. Princeton, NJ: Princeton University Press).

Cummings, R. (1986) 'Agricultural performance and prospects in Czechoslovakia through the eighties', US Congress, Joint Economic Committee, Washington, DC: Government Printing Office.

Davidova, S. (1991) 'Bulgarian farm structure: from paralysis to reform', *Food Policy*, vol. 16, no. 3.

Debardeleben, J. (1985) *The Environment and Marxism–Leninism: the Soviet and East German Experience*, Boulder: Westview Press.

Deere, C., and Meurs, M. (1992) 'Markets, markets everywhere? Understanding the Cuban anomaly', *World Development*, vol. 20, no. 6.

Dellin, L. (1970) 'Bulgaria's economic reform', Problems of Communism (September–October).

Dellmo, H., Granlund, J. and Gustaffson, A. (1990) *Vietnam's Economic Reforms and their Effects on State Enterprises*, Stockholm: Swedish International Development Authority.

Dennis, M. (1988) *The German Democratic Republic: Politics, Economics and Society*, London: Pinter.

Dijmarescu, E. (1989) 'The New Economic Mechanism in Romania' in Economic Commission for Europe (1989).

Dittmer, L. (1989) 'The Tiananmen massacre', *Problems of Communism*, September–October.

DIW (1989) *GDR and Eastern Europe – a Handbook*, Aldershot: Avebury.

DIW Handbuch (1985), Hamburg: Rowohlt.

Dollar, D. (1990) 'Economic reform and allocative efficiency in China's state-owned industry', *Economic Development and Cultural Change*, vol. 39, no. 1.

Dominguez, J. (1986) 'Cuba in the 1980s', *Foreign Affairs*, vol. 65, no. 1.

Donnithorne, A. (1967) *China's Economic System*, London: Allen & Unwin.

Dyker, D. (1981) *The Process of Investment in the Soviet Union*, Cambridge: Cambridge University Press.

—— (1985) *The Future of the Soviet Planning System*, London: Croom Helm.

—— (ed.) (1987) *The Soviet Union under Gorbachev: Prospects for Reform*, Chapters 3, 'Industrial planning', and 4, 'Agriculture', London: Croom Helm.

—— (1988) 'Restructuring and radical reform: the articulation of investment demand' in Linz and Moskoff(1988).

—— (1990) *Yugoslavia: Socialism, Development and Debt*, London: Routledge.

—— (1992a) *Yugoslavia, Brighton: University of Sussex: Discussion Paper no. 04/92*.

—— (1992b) The Soviet Union, Brighton: University of Sussex: Discussion Paper no. 05/92.

East, R. (1992) *Revolutions in Eastern Europe*, London: Pinter.

Eckstein, S. (1981) 'The debourgeoisement of Cuban cities' in Horowitz (1981).

Economic Commission for Europe (1989) *Economic Reform in the European Centrally Planned Economies*, Economic Studies no. 1, New York: UN.

Economist Surveys:

—— (1985) 'Comecon', 20 April.

—— (1988) 'The Soviet Economy', 9 April.

—— (1989) 'Eastern Europe', 12 August.

—— (1989) 'Russia's anti-drink campaign', 23 December

—— (1990) '*Perestroika*', 28 April.

—— (1990) 'The new Germany', 30 June.

—— (1990) 'The Soviet Union', 20 October.

—— (1991) 'Business in Eastern Europe', 21 September.

—— (1992) 'Germany', 23 May.

Edwards, G. (1985) *GDR Society and Institutions*, London: Macmillan.

Eichengreen, B. and Uzan, M. (1992) 'The Marshall Plan: economic effects and implications for Eastern Europe and the former USSR', *Economic Policy*, no. 14.

Elliott, J. (1992) 'The future of socialism: Vietnam, the way ahead?', *Third World Quarterly*, vol. 13, no. 1.

Ellman, M. (1986) 'Economic reform in China', *International Affairs*, vol. 62, no. 3.

—— (1989a) *Socialist Planning*, 2nd edn, London: Cambridge University Press.

—— (1989b) *The USSR in the 1990s*, London: EIU.

Estrin, S. (1983) *Self-management: Economic Theory and Yugoslav Practice*, Cambridge: Cambridge University Press.

—— (1991) 'Yugoslavia: the case of self-managing market socialism', *Journal of Economic Perspectives*, vol. 5, no. 4.

Estrin, S., Moore, R. and Svejnar, J. (1988) 'Market imperfections, labour management and earnings in a developing country: theory and evidence for Yugoslavia', *Quarterly Journal of Economics*, vol. CIII, no. 3.

Estrin, S. and Takla, L. (1992) 'Reform in Yugoslavia: the retreat from self-management' in Jeffries (1992).

European Commission (1990) 'The European Community and German unification', *Bulletin of the European Committees*, Supplement 4.

European Economy; the Path of Reform in Central and Eastern Europe (1991) special edition no. 2, Brussels: Commission of the European Communities.

European Parliament: Directorate-General for Research (1990) *The Impact of German Unification on the European Community* (Working Document No. 1), Luxembourg: Office for Official Publications of the European Communities.

Faber, M. (1990) 'Mongolia: moves towards *perestroika*', Development Policy Review, vol. 8, no. 4.

Fallenbuchl, Z. (1986) 'The economic crisis in Poland and prospects for recovery' in US Congress, Joint Economic Committee, Washington, DC: US Government Printing Office.

—— (1991) 'Polish privatization policy', Comparative Economic Studies, vol. XXXIII, no. 2.

Federal Ministry for Inner-German Relations (1985) *DDR Handbuch*, Bonn.

Feiwell, G. (1968) *New Economic Patterns in Czechoslovakia*, New York: IASP.

—— (1979) 'Economic reform in Bulgaria', Osteuropa Wirtschaft, no. 2.

—— (1982) 'Economic development and planning in Bulgaria in the 1970s' in Höhmann *et al.* (1982).

Ferfila, B.(1991) 'Yugoslavia: confederation or disintegration?', *Problems of Communism*, July–August.

Fforde, A. (1987) 'Industrial development in the Democratic Republic of Vietnam', London: Birkbeck College Discussion Paper 2.

—— (1988) 'Specific aspects of the collectivization of wet-rice cultivation: Vietnamese experience' in Brada and Wädekin (1988).

Fforde, A. and de Vylder, S. (1988) *Vietnam – an Economy in Transition*, Stockholm: Swedish International Development Authority (1988).

Fforde, A. and Paine, S. (1987) *The Limits of National Liberation: Economic Management and the Re-unification of the Democratic Republic of Vietnam*, London: Croom Helm.

Fidler, S. (1988) 'Banks at odds over North Korean deal', *The Financial Times*, 19 July 1988, p.25.

—— (1990) 'Institute of International Finance report', The *Financial Times*, 17 April, p.4.

Field, R. (1984) 'Changes in Chinese industry since 1978', *China Quarterly*, December.

Figueras, M. (1991) 'Structural changes in the Cuban economy', *Latin American Perspectives*, vol. 18, no. 2.

Filatotchev, I., Buck, T. and Wright, M. (1992) 'Privatization and buy-outs in the USSR', *Soviet Studies*, vol. 44, no. 2.

Filtzer, D. (1989) 'The Soviet wage reform of 1956–1962', *Soviet Studies*, vol. XLI, no. 1.

—— (1991) 'The contradictions of the marketless market: self-financing in the Soviet industrial enterprise 1986–90', *Soviet Studies*, vol. 43, no. 6.

Financial Times (various surveys)

Bulgaria: 7 December 1984; 27 October 1988; 17 May 1991.

China: 9 December 1985; 20 August 1986; 5 September 1986; 22 September 1986; 29 September 1986; 30 September 1986; 18 December 1986; 18 December 1987; 12 December 1989; 24 April 1991; 16 June 1992.

Counter-trade: 11 February 1986; East–West Trade: 13 December 1988; 6 June 1989; 8 December 1989.

Cuba: 17 February 1989.

Czechoslovakia: 23 October 1985; 8 November 1991.

Eastern Europe: 4 February 1991.

GDR: 3 October 1989.

Germany: 29 October 1990; 10 April 1991; 28 October 1991.

Hungary: 11 September 1987; 17 September 1990; 30 October 1991.

Poland: 25 May 1989; 20 November 1990; 2 May 1991; 28 April 1992.

Privatization in Eastern Europe: 3 July 1992.

Russia: 13 May 1992.

Slovenia: 30 March 1992.

Soviet Union: 12 March 1990.

Vietnam: 14 November 1991.

World economy: 24 September 1990.

Yugoslavia: 18 June 1984; 21 December 1984; 21 June 1985; 17 December 1985; 17 June 1986; 16 December 1986; 22 December 1987; 22 June 1988; 6 December 1988; 29 June 1989; 5 December 1989; 6 July 1990; 17 December 1990; 27 June 1991.

Fischer, S. (1992) 'Stabilization and economic reform in Russia', *Brookings Papers on Economic Activity*, no. 1.

Fischer, S. and Frenkel, J. (1992) 'Macroeconomic issues of Soviet reform', *American Economic Review*, Papers and Proceedings (May).

Fischer, S. and Gelb, A. (1991) 'The process of socialist economic transformation' *Journal of Economic Perspectives*, vol. 5, no. 4.

Fitzgerald, F. (1988) 'The Sovietization of Cuba thesis revisited' in Zimbalist (1988a).

—— (1989) 'The reform of the Cuban economy, 1976–86: organizations, incentives and patterns of behaviour', *Journal of Latin American Studies*, vol. 21, part 2.

Fry, M., and Nuti, D. (1992) 'Monetary and exchange-rate policies during Eastern Europe's transition: some lessons from further east', *Oxford Review of Economic Policy*, vol. 8, no. 1.

Gagnon, V. (1987) 'Gorbachev and the collective contract brigade', *Soviet Studies*, vol. XXXIX, no. 1.

Gardner, R. (1990) 'L. V. Kantorovich: the price implications of optimal planning', *Journal of Economic Literature*, vol. XXVIII, no. 2.

Gey, P. (1987) 'The Cuban economy under the new system of management and planning: success or failure?' in Gey *et al.* (1987).

—— (1990) 'Cuba: a unique variant of Soviet-type agriculture' in Wädekin 1990a.

Gey, P., Kosta, J. and Quaisser, W. (1987) *Crisis and Reform in Socialist Economies*, London: Westview Press.

Ghai, D., Kay, C. and Peek, P. (1988) *Labour and Development in Rural Cuba*, London: Macmillan.

Gilberg, T. (1975) *Modernization in Romania since World War II*, New York: Praeger.

Gills, B. (1992) 'North Korea and the crisis of socialism: the historical ironies of national division', *Third World Quarterly*, vol.13, no.1.

Gold, T. (1989) 'Urban private business in China', *Studies in Comparative Communism*, vol. XXII, nos 2 and 3.

Goldman, M. and Goldman, M. (1988) 'Soviet and Chinese economic *reforms', Foreign Affairs*, vol. 66, no. 3

Gomulka, S. (1990) 'Reform and budgetary policies in Poland, 1989–90' in Commission of the European Communities (1990).

Gomulka, S. and Rostowski, J. (1984) 'The reformed Polish economic system 1982–3', *Soviet Studies*, vol. 36, no. 3.

Gomulka, S., Yong-Chool Ha and Cae-One Kim (eds) (1989) *Economic Reforms in the Socialist World*, London: Macmillan.

Gora, M. (1991) 'Shock therapy for the Polish labour market', *International Labour Review*, vol. 130, no. 2.

Gorbachev, M. (1987) *Perestroika: New Thinking for our Country and the World*, London: Collins; New York: Harper & Row.

Gordon, R. and Li, W. (1991) 'Chinese economic reforms, 1979–89: lessons for the future', *American Economic Review*, Papers and Proceedings (May).

Granick, D. (1975) *Enterprise Guidance in Eastern Europe*, Princeton, NJ: Princeton University Press.

—— (1990) *Chinese State Enterprises: a Regional Property Rights Analysis*, Chicago: University of Chicago Press.

—— (1991) 'Multiple labour markets in the industrial state enterprise sector', *China Quarterly*, no. 126 (June).

Gray, E. (ed.) (1990) *Soviet Agriculture: Comparative Perspectives*, Ames, Iowa: Iowa State University Press.

Gregory, P. (1989a) 'Soviet bureaucratic behaviour: khozyaistvenniki and apparatchiki', *Soviet Studies*, vol. XLI, no. 4.

—— (1989b) 'The Soviet bureaucracy and *perestroika*', Comparative Economic Studies, vol. XXXI, no. 1.

Gregory, P. and Collier, I. (1988) 'Unemployment in the Soviet Union: evidence from the Soviet interview project', *American Economic Review* (September).

Gregory, P. and Stuart, R. (1990) *Soviet Economic Structure and Performance*, 4th edn, New York: Harper & Row (2nd edn 1981 and 3rd edn 1986).

Grosfeld, I. (1990a) 'Reform economics and Western economic theory: unexploited opportunities', *Economics of Planning*, vol. 23, no. 1.

—— (1990b) 'Prospects for privatization in Poland' in Commission of the European Communities (1990).

Grosfeld, I. and Hare, P. (1991) 'Privatization in Hungary, Poland and Czechoslovakia' in European Economy (1991).

Grossman, G. (1989) 'The second economy: boon or bane of the first economy' in Gomulka *et al.* (1989).

Guardian (various surveys)

China: 13 October 1986; regional China – Jiangsu and Guangdong 16 October 1987;

Shanghai: 19 November 1987.

Hungary: 31 October 1985; 20 October 1986; 5 May 1988; 8 February 1991.

Soviet Union: 6 November 1987; 24 June 1988; 13 December 1988; 5 April 1989.

Yugoslavia: 27 October 1986;

Slovenia, 16 May 1988.

Hagelberg, G. (1981) 'Cuba's sugar policy' in Horowitz (1981).

Halliday, J. (1987) 'The economics of North and South Korea' in J. Sullivan and R. Foss (eds) *Two Koreas – One Future*, Lanham, Md: University Press of America.

Halpern, N. (1985) 'China's industrial economic reform: the question of strategy', *Asian Survey*, vol. XXV, no. 10.

Hamel, H. and Leipold, H. (1987) 'Economic reform in the GDR: causes and effects' in Jeffries *et al.* (1987).

Hanson, P. (1989a) 'The Soviet economy at the end of year IV', *Detente, no. 14*.

—— (1989b) 'Capitalism or socialism?', Detente, no. 16.

—— (1990a) 'Gorbachev's policies after four years' in T. Hasegawa and A. Pravda (eds) *Perestroika: Soviet Domestic and Foreign Policies*, London: Sage (Royal Institute of International Affairs).

—— (1990b) 'Property rights in the new phase of reforms', *Soviet Economy*, vol. 6, no. 2.

Hare, P. (1987) 'Resource allocation without prices: the Soviet economy', *The Economic Review*, vol. 5, no. 2.

—— (1990a) 'Creating market economies: Eastern Europe in the 1990s', *The Economic Review*, vol. 7, no. 5.

—— (1990b) 'From central planning to market economy: some microeconomic issues', *Economic Journal*, vol. 100, no. 401.

—— (1991) 'Eastern Europe: the transition to a market economy', *The Royal Bank of Scotland Review*, no. 169 (March).

—— (1992) 'Hungary' in Jeffries (1992).

Hare, P., Radice, H. and Swain, N. (1981) *Hungary: a Decade of Reform*, London: Allen & Unwin.

Hare, P. and Revesz, T. (1992) 'Hungary's transition to the market: the case against a "big-bang"', *Economic Policy*, no. 14.

Hars, A., Kovari, G. and Nagy, G. (1991) 'Hungary faces unemployment' *International Labour Review*, vol. 130, no. 2.

Hartford, K. (1985) 'Hungarian agriculture: a model for the socialist world?', *World Development*, vol. 13, no. 1.

—— (1987) 'Socialist countries in the world food system: the Soviet Union, Hungary and China', *Food Research Institute Studies*, vol. XX, no. 3.

Haustein, H-D. (1989) 'Role and functioning of industrial enterprises in the GDR' in Economic Commission for Europe (1989).

Hedlund, S. (1990) 'Private plots as a system stabiliser' in Wädekin (1990b).

Heinrich, H-G. (1986) *Hungary: Politics*, Economics and Society, London: Francis Pinter.

Heinrichs, W. (1988) 'Growth and the foreign balance: experience and the problem of the GDR' in Saunders (1988).

Herer, W. (1988) 'Planning the development of agriculture under the conditions of Polish economic reform' in Brada and Wädekin (1988).

Hewett, E. (1988) *Reforming the Soviet Economy: Equality versus Efficiency*, Washington, DC: Brookings Institution.

—— (1989) '*Perestroika* and the Congress of People's Deputies', *Soviet Economy*, vol. 5, no. 1.

—— (1990) 'The new Soviet plan', *Foreign Affairs*, vol. 69, no. 5

Höhmann, H-H., Nove, A. and Seidenstecher, G. (eds) (1982) *The East European Economies in the 1970s*, London: Butterworth.

Holesovsky, V. (1968) 'Financial aspects of the Czechoslovak reforms' in M. Bornstein (ed.) *Plan and Market*, New Haven: Yale University Press.

—— (1973) 'Planning and the market in the Czechoslovak reform' in M. Bornstein (ed.) *Plan and Market*, New Haven: Yale University Press.

Holzman, F. (1976) *International Trade under Communism*, New York: Basic Books.

—— (1987) *The Economics of Soviet Bloc Trade and Finance*, Boulder and London: Westview Press.

—— (1991) 'Moving towards rouble convertibility', *Comparative Economic Studies*, vol. XXXIII, no. 3.

Horowitz, I. (ed.) (1981) *Cuban Communism*, 4th

edn, New Brunswick and London: Transaction Books.

Hristov, E. (1987) 'Perestroika', Bulgaria (September–October).

Hsu, R. (1989) 'Changing conceptions of the socialist enterprise in China, 1979–88', Modern China, vol. 14, no. 4.

—— (1992) 'Industrial reform in China' in Jeffries (1992).

Hu, Teh-wei, Li, Ming and Shi, Shuzhong (1988) 'Analysis of wages and bonus payments among Tianjin urban workers', China Quarterly, no. 113.

Huang Yasheng (1990) 'Webs of interest and patterns of behaviour of Chinese local economic bureaucracies and enterprises during reforms', China Quarterly, no. 123 (September).

Hughes, G. (1991) 'Foreign exchange, prices and economic activity in Bulgaria' in European Economy.

Hughes, G. and Hare, P. (1991) 'Competitiveness and industrial restructuring in Czechoslovakia, Hungary and Poland' in European Economy.

—— (1992) 'Industrial policy and restructuring in Eastern Europe', Oxford Review of Economic Policy, vol. 8, no. 1.

Hussain, A. and Stern, N. (1991) 'Effective demand, enterprise reforms and public finance in China', Economic Policy, no. 12.

Iancu, A. (1989) 'Role and functioning of the enterprise in Romania' in Economic Commission for Europe (1989).

IMF, World Bank, OECD and EBRD (1990) The Economy of the USSR, Washington, DC: The World Bank.

Information Mongolia (1990) Compiled and edited by the Mongolian Academy of Sciences, Oxford: Pergamon Press.

Institute of International Finance (April 1990), Building Free Market Economies in Central and Eastern Europe: Challenges and Realities, Washington, DC.

International Herald Tribune (various surveys)
China: 15 September 1986; 9 July 1986.
East–West Trade: 6 June 1989.
Germany: 10 April 1991.
Hungary: 12 June 1985; 4 March 1991.
Soviet Union: 7–8 November 1985; 7 November 1988.

Ishihara, K. (1987) 'Planning and the market in China', The Developing Economies, vol. XXV, no. 4.

—— (1990) 'Inflation and economic reform in China', The Developing Economies, vol.XXVIII, no.2.

Jackson, M. (1986a) 'Recent economic performance and policy in Bulgaria' in US Congress, Joint Economic Committee, Washington, DC: Government Printing Office.

—— (1986b) 'Romania's debt crisis: its causes and consequences', US Congress, Joint Economic Committee.

—— (ed.) (1991) 'Privatization in Central Europe', Eastern European Economics, vol. 30, no. 1.

Jackson, S. (1986) 'Reform of state enterprise management in China', China Quarterly, no. 107.

Jacobsen, H-D. (1987) 'The foreign trade and payments of the GDR' in Jeffries et al. (1987).

Jahne, G. (1990) 'Socialist agriculture outside Europe: new ways in Mongolian agriculture?' in Wädekin (1990a).

Janeba, V. (1988) 'Experience gained from the comprehensive experiment', Czechoslovak Economic Digest, no. 4.

Jefferson, G. and Xu, W. (1991) 'The impact of reform on socialist enterprises in transition: structure, conduct, and performance in Chinese industry', Journal of Comparative Economics, vol. 15, no. 1.

Jeffries, I. (ed.) (1981) The Industrial Enterprise in Eastern Europe, New York: Praeger.

—— (1990) A Guide to the Socialist Economies, London: Routledge.

—— (ed.) (1992) Industrial Reform in Socialist Countries: from Restructuring to Revolution, Aldershot: Edward Elgar.

Jeffries, I. Melzer, M. (eds), and Breuning, E. (advisory ed.) (1987) The East German Economy, London: Croom Helm.

Jerome, R. (1988) 'Sources of economic growth in Hungary', East European Quarterly, vol. XXII, no. 1.

Jimenez, A. (1987) 'Worker incentives in Cuba', World Development, vol. 15, no. 1.

Joglekar, G. and Zimbalist, A. (1989) 'Dollar GDP per capita in Cuba: estimates and observations on the use of the physical indicators method', Journal of Comparative Economics, vol. 13, no. 1.

Johnson, D. (1988a) 'Economic reforms in the People's Republic of China', Economic Development and Cultural Change, vol. 36, no. 3.

—— (1988b) 'Agriculture' in A. Cracraft (ed.) The Soviet Union Today, Chicago: University of Chicago Press.

Johnson, S. and Kroll, H. (1991) 'Managerial strategies for spontaneous privatization', Soviet Economy, vol. 7, no. 4.

Jones, A. and Moskoff, W. (1989) 'New co-operatives in the USSR', Problems of Communism, November–December.

Jones, D. (1991) 'The Bulgarian labour market in transition', International Labour Review, vol. 130, no. 2.

—— (1992) 'The transformation of labor unions in Eastern Europe: the case of Bulgaria', Industrial and Labor Relations Review, vol. 45, no. 3.

Jones, D. and Meurs, M. (1991a) 'On the entry of new firms in socialist economies: evidence from Bulgaria', *Soviet Studies*, vol. 43, no. 2.

—— (1991b) 'Worker participation and worker self-management in Bulgaria', *Comparative Economic Studies*, vol. XXXIII, no. 4.

Jones, K. and Rich, D. (1988) *Opportunities for US-Cuban Trade*, Baltimore, Md.: John Hopkins University Press.

Kaczurba, J. (1988) 'The external context', *Polish Perspectives*, vol. XXXI, no. 1.

Kamath, S. (1990) 'Foreign direct investment in a centrally planned developing economy: the Chinese case', *Economic Development and Cultural Change*, vol. 39, no. 1.

Kane, P. (1988) *Famine in China (1959–61): Demographic and Social Implications*, London: Macmillan.

Kang, Myung-Kyu. (1989) 'Industrial management and reforms in North Korea' in Gomulka *et al.* (1989).

Kaplan, N. (1953) 'Capital formation and allocation' in Bergson (1953).

Karabashev, V. (1991) 'The economic reform in Bulgaria: first results and prospects for development' *Bulgarian Quarterly*, vol. 1, no. 2.

Karatnycky, A. (1992) 'The Ukrainian factor', *Foreign Affairs*, vol. 71, no. 3.

Kaser, M. (1981) 'The industrial enterprise in Bulgaria' in Jeffries (1981).

—— (1986) 'Albania under and after Enver Hoxha', US Congress, Joint Economic Committee, Washington DC: Government Printing Office.

—— (1987a) 'One economy, two systems: parallels between Soviet and Chinese reforms', *International Affairs*, vol. 63, no. 3.

—— (1987b) 'Mongolia and the Asian wave of socialist economic reform', paper presented at the conference on 'Mongolia Today', 27 November, at the SOAS, University of London.

—— (1990) 'The technology of decontrol: some macroeconomic issues', *Economic Journal*, vol. 100, no. 401.

—— (1992) 'Mongolia' in Jeffries (1992).

Kaser, M. and Allsopp, C. (1992) 'The assessment: macroeconomic transition in Eastern Europe, 1989–91', *Oxford Review of Economic Policy*, vol. 8, no. 1.

Katsenelinboigen, A. (1977) 'Coloured markets in the Soviet Union', *Soviet Studies*, vol. 29, no. 1.

Kay, C. (1988) 'Cuban economic reforms and collectivisation', *Third World Quarterly*, vol. 10, no. 3.

Kenen, P. (1991) 'Transitional arrangements for trade and payments among the CMEA countries', *IMF Staff Papers*, vol. 38, no. 2.

Keren, M. (1973) 'The New Economic System in the GDR', *Soviet Studies*, vol. XXIV, no. 4.

Kerner, A. (1988) 'Reflections on the draft bill on the state enterprise', *Czechoslovak Economic Digest*, no. 2.

Kerpel, E. and Young, D. (1988) *Hungary to 1993: Risks and Rewards of Reform*, London: EIU.

Kessides, C. *et al.* (eds) (1989) *Financial Reform in Socialist Economies*, Washington, DC: The World Bank.

Klaus, V. (1992a) 'Policy dilemmas of Eastern European reforms: notes of an insider' in A. Prindle (ed.) *Banking and Finance in Eastern Europe*, London: Woodhead-Faulkner.

—— (1992b) 'Transition: an insider's view', Problems of Communism, January–April.

Klein, W. (1987) 'The role of the GDR in Comecon: some economic aspects' in Jeffries *et al.* 1987).

Kohler, G. (1989) 'Economic and social development in the GDR' in Economic Commission for Europe (1989).

Kojima, R. (1990) 'Achievements and contradictions in China's economic reform', *The Developing Economies*, vol. XXVIII, no. 4.

Kolankiewicz, G. (1987) 'Polish trade unions "normalized"', *Problems of Communism*, November–December.

Kolankiewicz, G., and Lewis, P. (1988) *Poland: Politics*, Economics and Society, London: Pinter.

Koo, A. (1990) 'The contract responsibility system: transition from a planned to a market system', *Economic Development and Cultural Change*, vol. 35, no. 4.

Korbonski, A. (1990a) 'Soldiers and peasants: Polish agriculture after martial law' in Wädekin (1990b).

—— (1990b) 'CMEA, economic integration, and *perestroika*, 1949–1989', *Studies in Comparative Communism*, vol. XXIII, no. 1.

Kornai, J. (1986) 'The Hungarian reform process: visions, hopes and reality', *Journal of Economic Literature*, vol. XXIX (December).

—— (1990a) *The Road to a Free Economy*, New York: W.W. Norton.

—— (1990b) 'Comment' in Brookings Papers on Economic Activity, no. 1.

—— (1992a) *The Socialist System: the Political Economy of Communism*, Oxford: Oxford University Press.

—— (1992b) 'The postsocialist transition and the state: reflections in the light of Hungarian fiscal problems', *American Economic Review*, Papers and Proceedings (May).

Korzec, M. (1988) 'Contract labour, the right to work and new labour laws in the People's Republic of China', *Comparative Economic Studies*, vol. XXX, no. 2.

Kosta, J. (1987) 'The Chinese economic reform: approaches, results and prospects' in Gey *et al.* (1987).

Kostakov, V. (1988) 'Labour problems in the light of *perestroyka*', *Soviet Economy*, vol. 4 (January–March).

Kroll, H. (1988) 'The role of contracts in the Soviet economy', *Soviet Studies*, vol. XL, no. 3.

—— (1991) 'Monopoly and the transition to the market', *Soviet Economy*, vol. 7, no. 2.

Kueh, Y. (1989) 'The Maoist legacy and China's new industrialization strategy', *China Quarterly*, no. 119.

Kupka, M. (1992) 'Transformation of ownership in Czechoslovakia', *Soviet Studies*, vol. 44, no. 2.

Kurakowski, S. (1988) *Poland: Stagnation, Collapse or Growth?*, London: Centre for Research into Communist Economies.

Kushnirsky, F. (1989) 'The new role of normatives in Soviet economic planning', *Soviet Studies*, vol. XLI, no. 4.

—— (1991) 'Conversion, civilian production, and goods quality in the Soviet Union', *Comparative Economic Studies*, vol. XXXIII, no. 1.

Kwon, Y. (1989) 'An analysis of China's taxation of foreign direct investment', *The Developing Economies*, vol. XXVII, no. 3.

Kyn, O. (1970) 'The rise and fall of economic reforms in Czechoslovakia', *American Economic Review*, Papers and Proceedings.

Lampe, J. (1986) *The Bulgarian Economy in the Twentieth Century*, London: Croom Helm.

Lang, I., Csete, L. and Harnos, Z. (1988) 'The enterprisal system of an adjusting agriculture in Hungary', *European Review of Agricultural Economics*, vol. 15, nos 2–3.

Larrabee, F. (ed.) (1989) *The Two German States and European Security*, London: Macmillan.

Le Duc Thuy, Luong Xuan Quy and To Xuan Dan (1991) 'The market mechanism in the new economic management system in Vietnam' in Ronnas and Sjöberg (1991a).

Le Trang (1990) 'Renewal of industrial management policy and organisation' in Ronnas and Sjöberg (1990).

Lee, K. (1990) 'The Chinese model of the socialist enterprise: an assessment of its organization and performance', *Journal of Comparative Economics*, vol. 14, no. 3.

Lee, Kie-Young (1990) 'Economic reforms and the "open door" policy in North Korea', Hyundai Research Institute (Seoul, South Korea): paper presented to the IV World Congress of Soviet and East European Studies, Harrogate (July).

Lee, P. (1986) 'Enterprise autonomy in post-Mao China: a case study of policy-making, 1978–83', *China Quarterly*, no. 105.

Leptin, G. (1989) 'Economic relations between the two German states' in Larrabee (1989).

Leptin, G. and Melzer, M. (1978) *Economic Reform in East German Industry*, Oxford: Oxford University Press.

Lho, Kyongsoo (1989) 'Seoul–Moscow relations: looking to the 1990s', Asian Survey, vol. XXIX, no. 12.

Li Yunqi (1989) 'China's inflation: causes, effects and solutions', *Asian Survey*, vol. XXIX, no.7.

Lin, J. (1988) 'The household responsibility system in China's agricultural reform; a theoretical and empirical study', *Economic Development and Cultural Change*, vol. 36, no. 3 (Supplement).

—— (1990) 'Collectivization and China's agricultural crisis in 1959–61', *Journal of Political Economy*, vol. 98, no. 6.

—— (1992) 'Rural reforms and agricultural growth in China', *American Economic Review*, vol. 82, no. 1.

Ling, L. (1988) 'Intellectual responses to China's economic reforms', *Asian Survey*, vol. XXVIII, no. 5.

Linz, S. (1988) 'Managerial autonomy in Soviet firms', *Soviet Studies*, vol. XL, no. 2.

Linz, S. and Moskoff, W. (1988) (eds) *Reorganisation and Reform in the Soviet Union*, Armonk, NY, and London: M.E. Sharpe.

Lipton, D. and Sachs, J. (1990a) 'Creating a market in Eastern Europe: the case of Poland', *Brookings Papers on Economic Activity*, no. 1.

—— (1990b) 'Privatization in Eastern Europe: the case of Poland', *Brookings Papers on Economic Activity*, no. 2.

Lisiecki, J. (1990) 'Financial and material transfers between East and West Germany', *Soviet Studies*, vol. 42, no. 3.

Litvin, V. (1987) 'On *perestroyka*: reforming economic management', *Problems of Communism* (July–August).

Lockett, M. (1987) 'China's development strategy: the Seventh Five Year Plan and after', *Euro-Asia Business Review* (July).

Lodahl, M. (1989) 'Czechoslovakia' in DIW (1989).

Loncarevic, I. (1987) 'Prices and private agriculture in Yugoslavia', *Soviet Studies*, vol. XXXIV, no. 4.

—— (1988) 'Price policy and price formation in the Yugoslav agro-food sector' in Brada and Wädekin (1988).

Long, S. (1990) *China Against the tide*, London: EIU.

Losch, D. (1990) 'The post-war transformation of West Germany's economy: a model for the GDR?', *Intereconomics*, vol. 25, no. 2.

Lydall, H. (1989) *Yugoslavia in Crisis*, Oxford: Clarendon Press.

MacEwan, A. (1981) *Revolution and Economic Development in Cuba*, London: Macmillan.

Magas, I. (1990) 'Reforms under pressure: Hungary', *East European Quarterly*, vol. XXIV, no. 1.

Makarov, V. (1988) 'On the strategy for implementing economic reform in the USSR', *American Economic Review*, Papers and Proceedings (May).

Mao, Y. and Hare, P. (1989) 'Chinese experience in the introduction of a market mechanism into a planned economy: the role of pricing', *Journal of Economic Surveys*, vol. 3, no. 2.

Marer, P. (1986a) 'Economic reform in Hungary: from central planning to regulated market', US Congress, Joint Economic Committee, Washington DC: Government Printing Office.

—— (1986b) 'Hungary's balance of payments crisis and response, 1978–84', US Congress, Joint Economic Committee.

—— (1986c) 'Economic policies and systems in Eastern Europe and Yugoslavia: commonalities and differences', US Congress, Joint Economic Committee.

Marr, D. and White, C. (eds) (1988) *Postwar Vietnam: Dilemmas in Socialist Development*, New York: Cornell University Southeast Asia Program.

Marrese, M. (1986a) 'Hungarian agriculture: moving in the right direction', US Congress, Joint Economic Committee.

—— (1986b) 'CMEA: effective but cumbersome political economy', *International Organisation*, vol. 40, no. 2.

—— (1990) '*Perestroika* and socialist privatization: a comment', *Comparative Economic Studies*, vol. XXII, no. 3.

—— (1991) 'Progress in transforming Hungarian agriculture', *Comparative Economic Studies*, vol. XXXIII, no. 2.

Matousek, J. (1988) 'Draft law on co-operative farming', *Czechoslovak Economic Digest*, no. 1.

McCauley, M. (1983) *The German Democratic Republic since 1945*, London: Macmillan.

McConnell, C. and Brue, S. (1986) *Contemporary Labour Economics*, New York: McGraw-Hill.

McFarlane, B. (1988) *Yugoslavia: Politics, Economics and Society*, London: Pinter.

McIntyre, R. (1988a) Bulgaria: Politics, Economics and Society, London: Pinter.

—— (1988b) 'The small enterprise and agricultural initiatives in Bulgaria: institutional invention without reform', *Soviet Studies*, vol. XL, no. 4.

—— (1992) 'Innovation with an unchanging core: no path to the market in Bulgaria?', in Jeffries (1992).

McKinnon, R. (1992) 'Taxation, money, and credit in a liberalizing socialist economy', *Economics of Planning*, vol. 25, no. 1.

McMillan, J., Whalley, J. and Lijing Zhu (1989) 'The impact of China's economic reforms on agricultural productivity growth', *Journal of Political Economy*, vol. 97, no. 4.

Melzer, M. (1981) 'Combine formation and the role of the enterprise in East German industry' in Jeffries (1981).

—— (1982) 'The GDR – economic policy caught between pressure for efficiency and lack of ideas' in Höhmann *et al.* (1982).

—— (1983) 'Wandlungen im Preissystem der DDR' in G. Gütmann (ed.) Das Wirtschaftssystem der DDR, Stuttgart: Fischer-Verlag.

—— (1987a) 'The pricing system of the GDR: principles and problems' in Jeffries *et al.* (1987).

—— (1987b) 'The new planning and steering mechanisms in the GDR', *Studies in Comparative Communism*, vol. XX, no. 1.

—— (1987c) 'The perfecting of the planning and steering mechanisms' in Jeffries *et al.* (1987).

Mencinger, J. (1987) 'The crisis and the reform of the Yugoslav economic system in the eighties' in Gey *et al.* (1987).

Merkel, K. (1987) 'Agriculture' in Jeffries *et al.* (1987).

Mesa-Lago, C. (1981) 'Economics: realism and rationality' in Horowitz (1981).

—— (1989) 'Cuba's economic counter-reform (*rectificación*): causes, policies and effects', *Journal of Communist Studies*, vol. 5, no. 4.

Meurs, M. (1992) 'Popular participation and central planning in Cuban socialism: the experience of agriculture in the 1980s', *World Development*, vol. 20, no. 2.

Micklewright, J. (1992) *Income Support for the Unemployed*, LSE Welfare State Programme (London): Discussion Paper WSP/67.

Milanovic, B. (1992) 'Poland's quest for economic stabilization, 1988–91: interaction of political economy and economics', *Soviet Studies*, vol. 44, no. 3.

Milivojevic, M. (1987) 'The Mongolian People's Army', *Armed Forces*, vol. 6, no. 12.

Miller, R. (1988) 'Recent agricultural policy in Yugoslavia: a return to the private sector' in Brada and Wädekin (1988).

Mirkovic, D. (1987) 'Sociological reflections on Yugoslav participatory democracy and social ownership', *East European Quarterly*, vol. XXI, no. 3.

Miskiewicz, S. (1987) 'Social and economic rights in Eastern Europe', *Survey*, vol. 29, no. 4.

Mizsei, K. (1992) 'Privatization in Eastern Europe: a comparative study of Poland and Hungary', *Soviet Studies*, vol. 44, no. 2.

Montero, A. and Gonzalez, P. (1989) 'Cuba's external economic constraints in the 1980s: an assessment of the potential role of the United States', *Journal of Communist Studies*, vol. 5, no. 4.

Montias, J. (1991) 'The Romanian economy: a survey of current problems' in European Economy.

Mroz, B. (1991) 'Poland's economy in transition to private ownership', *Soviet Studies*, vol. 43, no. 4.

Mullineux, A. (1992a) *Banks, Privatization and Restructuring in Poland*, University of Birmingham: Discussion Paper IFGWP-92–02.

—— (1992b) *Privatization in the UK and Germany: Lessons for Central and Eastern Europe*, University of Birmingham: Discussion Paper IFGWP-92–01.

Murrell, P. (1990) *The Nature of Socialist Economies: Lessons from Eastern European Foreign Trade*, Princeton, NJ: Princeton University Press.

—— (1992) 'Evolutionary and radical approaches to economic reform', *Economics of Planning*, vol. 25, no. 1.

Myant, M. (1989) *The Czechoslovak Economy 1948–1988: the Battle for Economic Reform*, Cambridge: Cambridge University Press.

Nello, S. (1990) 'Some recent developments in EC–East European economic relations', *Journal of World Trade*, vol. 24, no. 1.

Nguyen Tuong Lai and Nguyen Thanh Bang (1991) 'A new development policy for human resources within the socio-economic strategy of Vietnam up to the year 2000' in Ronnas and Sjöberg (1991b).

Nguyen Van Huy (1990) 'Renewal of economic policies and economic management organisation in Vietnam' in Ronnas and Sjöberg (1990).

Nguyen Van Linh (1987) *Some Pressing Problems on the Distribution and Circulation of Goods*, Hanoi: Foreign Languages Publishing House.

Nordhaus, W. (1990) 'Soviet economic reform: the longest road', *Brookings Papers on Economic Activity*, no. 1.

Noti, S. (1987) 'The shifting position of Hungarian trade unions amidst social and economic reforms', *Soviet Studies*, vol. XXXIX, no. 1.

Nove, A. (1961) *The Soviet Economy*, London: Allen & Unwin.

—— (1981) 'The Soviet industrial enterprise' in Jeffries (1981).

—— (1986) *The Soviet Economic System*, 3rd edn, London: Allen & Unwin.

—— (1987) 'Soviet agriculture: light at the end of the tunnel?', *Detente*, nos 9–10.

Nuti, D. (1977) 'Large corporations and the reform of Polish industry', *Jahrbuch der Wirtschaft Osteuropas*.

—— (1981a) 'Industrial enterprises in Poland, 1973–80: economic policies and reforms' in Jeffries (1981).

—— (1981b) 'The Polish crisis: economic factors and constraints' in R. Miliband, R. and J. Savile (eds) *The Socialist Register*, London: Merlin Press.

—— (1989) 'Feasible financial innovation under market socialism' in Kessides *et al.* (1989).

—— (1990) 'Market socialism', *Russia and the World*, no. 18.

Ofer, G. (1987) 'Soviet economic growth: 1928–1985', *Journal of Economic Literature*, vol. XXV (December).

Oxenstierna, S. (1992) 'Trends in employment and unemployment' in Åslund (1992a).

Pak, Ky-Hyuk (1983) 'Agricultural policy and development in North Korea' in Scalapino and Kim (1983).

Panova, G. (1988) 'Recent developments in Soviet banking', *National Westminster Bank Quarterly Review* (August).

Panusheff, E. and Smatrakelev, G. (1990) 'Bulgaria towards Europe: taking the challenge', *National Westminster Bank Quarterly Review*, November.

Parsons, J. (1986) 'Credit contracts in the GDR: decentralised investment decisions in a planned economy', *Economics of Planning*, vol. 20, no. 1.

Pashko, G. (1991) 'The Albanian economy at the beginning of the 1990s' in Sjöberg and Wyzan (1991).

Pearson, M. (1991) 'The erosion of controls over foreign capital in China', *Modern China*, vol. 17, no. 1.

Perez-Lopez, J. (1986) 'Cuba's economy in the 1980s', *Problems of Communism*, vol. XXXV, no. 5.

—— (1989) 'Sugar and structural change in the Cuban economy', *World Development*, vol. 17, no. 10.

—— (1990) 'Rectification at three: impact on the Cuban economy', *Studies in Comparative International Development*, vol. 25, no. 3.

—— (1991) 'Bringing the Cuban economy into focus: conceptual and empirical challenges', *Latin American Research Review*, vol. 26, no. 3.

—— (1992) 'The Cuban economy: rectification in a changing world', *Cambridge Journal of Economics*, vol. 16, no. 1.

Perkins, D. (1988) 'Reforming China's economic system', *Journal of Economic Literature*, vol. XXVI, no. 2.

Phan Van Tiem (1991) 'Finance and capital mobilization policies in the socio-economic strategy 1991–2000' in Ronnas and Sjöberg (1991a).

Phillips, D. (1986) 'Special Economic Zones in China's modernisation: changing policies and changing fortunes', *National Westminster Review* (February).

Pike, D. (1987) *Vietnam and the Soviet Union*, Boulder and London: Westview Press.

Pingali, P. and Vo-Tong Xuan (1992) 'Decollectivization and rice productivity growth', *Economic Development and Cultural Change*, vol. 40, no. 4.

Pishev, O. (1991) 'The Bulgarian economy: transition or turmoil' in Sjöberg and Wyzan (1991).

Plokker, K. (1990) 'The development of individual and co-operative labour activity in the Soviet Union', *Soviet Studies*, vol. 42, no. 3.

Porter, G. (1990) 'The politics of "renovation" in Vietnam', *Problems of Communism*, May–June.

Portes, R. (1990) 'Introduction' in Commission of the European Communities (1990).

Post, K. (1988) 'The working class in North Viet Nam and the launching of the building of socialism', *Journal of Asian and African Studies*, vol. XXIII, nos 1–2.

Pouliquen, A. (1989) 'The structural modernization of Polish private agriculture: the turning point in the 1980s', *Comparative Economic Studies*, vol. XXXI, no. 2.

Poznanski, K. (1992) 'Privatization of the Polish economy: problems of transition', *Soviet Studies*, vol. 44, no. 4.

Prasnikar, J. and Pregl, Z. (1991) 'Economic development in Yugoslavia in 1990 and prospects for the future', *American Economic Review*, Papers and Proceedings, May.

Prescott, L. (1986) 'Farming policy in Albania', *Albanian Life*, no. 2 (no. 35 in the series).

Primorac, E. and Babic, M. (1989) 'Systematic changes and unemployment growth in Yugoslavia, 1965–84', *Slavic Review*, vol. 48, no. 2.

Prout, C. (1985) *Market Socialism in Yugoslavia*, London: Oxford University Press.

Prybyla, J. (1985) 'The Chinese economy: adjustment of the system or systemic reform?', *Asian Survey*, vol. XXV, no. 5.

—— (1986) 'China's economic experiment: from Mao to market', *Problems of Communism*, vol. XXXV, no. 1.

—— (1987) 'On some questions concerning price reform in the People's Republic of China', Working Paper 9–87–16, Pennsylvania State University.

Pryor, F. (1991) 'Third World decollectivization: Guyana, Nicaragua and Vietnam', *Problems of Communism*, vol. XL, no. 3 (May-June).

Purcell, S. (1990) 'Cuba's cloudy future', *Foreign Affairs*, vol. 69, no. 3.

—— (1992) 'Collapsing Cuba', *Foreign Affairs*, vol. 71, no. 1.

Putterman, L. (1988) 'Group farming and work incentives in collective-era China', *Modern China*, vol. 14, no. 4.

Quaisser, W. (1986) 'Agricultural price policy and peasant agriculture in Poland', *Soviet Studies*, vol. XXXVIII, no. 4.

—— (1987) 'The new agricultural reform in China: from the people's communes to peasant agriculture' in Gey *et al.* (1987).

Rabkin, R. (1990) 'Implications of the Gorbachev era for Cuban socialism', *Studies in Comparative Communism*, vol. XXIII, no. 1.

Radell, W. (1991) 'The Cuban sugar export dependency question: premises and controversy', *World Development*, vol. 19, no. 7.

Radice, H. (1981) 'The state enterprise in Hungary' in Jeffries (1981).

Richman, B. (1969) *Industrial Society in Communist China*, New York: Random House.

Riskin, C. (1987) *The Political Economy of Chinese Development* since 1949, London: Oxford University Press.

Roca, S. (1981) 'Cuban economic policy in the 1970s: the trodden paths' in Horowitz (1981).

Rodriguez, J. (1987) 'Agricultural policy and development in Cuba', *World Development*, vol. 15, no. 1

—— (1988) 'Cubanology and the provision of basic needs in the Cuban revolution' in Zimbalist (1988a).

Rohlicek, R. (1987) 'Fundamental principles of the restructuring of the economic mechanism', *Czechoslovak Economic Digest*, no. 7.

Rollo, J. *et al.* (1990) *The New Eastern Europe: Western Responses*, London: Royal Institute of International Affairs (Chatham House Papers).

Ronnas, P. (1989) 'Turning the Romanian peasant into a new socialist man: an assessment of rural development policy in Romania', *Soviet Studies*, vol. XLI, no. 4.

—— (1990) *The Economic Legacy of Ceausescu*, Stockholm Institute of Soviet and East European Economies, Working Paper no. 11.

—— (1991a) 'The economic legacy of Ceausescu' in Sjöberg and Wyzan (1991).

Ronnas, P. and Sjöberg, Ö. (eds) (1990) *Doi Moi: Economic Reforms and Development Policies in Vietnam*, Stockholm: Swedish International Development Authority.

—— (1991a) 'Economic reform in Vietnam: dismantling the centrally planned economy' *Journal of Communist Studies*, vol. 7, no. 1.

—— (1991b)(eds) Socio-economic Development in Vietnam: the Agenda for the 1990s, Stockholm: Swedish International Development Authority.

Rosati, D. (1992) 'The CMEA demise, trade restructuring, and trade destruction in Central and Eastern Europe', *Oxford Review of Economic Policy*, vol. 8, no. 1.

Rostowski, J. (1989) 'The decay of socialism and the growth of private enterprise in Poland', *Soviet Studies*, vol. XLI, no. 2.

Roucek, L. (1988) 'Private enterprise in Soviet political debates', *Soviet Studies*, vol. XL, no. 1.

Roy, D. (1990) 'Real product and income in China, Cuba, North Korea and Vietnam', *Development Policy Review*, vol. 8, no. 1.

Rubin, M. (1990) 'Self-interest and the Kosygin reforms', *Journal of Comparative Economics*, vol. 14, no. 3.

Rybczynski, T. (1991) 'The sequencing of reform', *Oxford Review of Economic Policy*, vol. 7, no. 4.

Rychetnik, L. (1981) 'The industrial enterprise in Czechoslovakia' in Jeffries (1981).

—— (1992) 'Industrial reform in Czechoslovakia' in Jeffries (1992).

Sachs, J. (1992) 'The economic transformation of Eastern Europe: the case of Poland', *Economic of Planning*, vol. 25, no. 1.

Sachs, J. and Lipton, D. (1990) 'Poland's economic reform', *Foreign Affairs*, vol. 69, no. 3.

Sacks, S. (1983) *Self-management and Efficiency: Large Corporations in Yugoslavia*, London: Allen & Unwin.

Sanders, A. (1987) *Mongolia: Politics*, Economics and Society, London: Pinter.

Sandström, P., and Sjöberg, Ö. (1991) 'Albanian economic perfomance: stagnation in the 1980s', *Soviet Studies*, vol. 43, no. 5.

Santana, S. (1988) 'Some thoughts on vital statistics and health status in Cuba' in Zimbalist (1988a).

Saunders, C. (ed.) (1988) *Macroeconomic Management and the Enterprise in East and West*, London: Macmillan.

Scalapino, R., and Kim, Jun-Yop (eds) (1983) *North Korea Today: Strategic and Domestic Issues*, Berkeley, Cal.: Institute of Asian Studies, University of California.

Scalapino, R., and Lee, H. (eds) (1986) *North Korea in a Regional and Global Context*, Berkeley, Cal.: Institute of East Asian Studies, University of California.

Schäuble, W. (1988) 'Relations between the two states in Germany: problems and prospects', *International Affairs*, vol. 64, no. 2.

Schimmerling, H. (1991) 'Agricultural development in Czechoslovakia: prospects after the 1989 revolution', *Food Policy*, vol. 16, no. 3.

Schinke, E. (1988) 'The reform of agricultural prices in the GDR' in Brada and Wädekin (1988).

—— (1990) 'New forms of farm organisation in the GDR as compared to the USSR and East European states' in Wädekin (1990b).

Schnytzer, A. (1982) *Stalinist Economic Strategy in Practice: the Case of Albania*, London: Oxford University Press.

—— (1992) 'Albania: the purge of Stalinist economic ideology' in Jeffries (1992).

Schram, S. (1988) 'China after the 13th Congress', *China Quarterly*, no. 114.

Schroeder, G. (1982) 'Soviet economic reform decrees: more steps on the treadmill', US Congress, Joint Economic Committee, Washington, DC: Government Printing Office.

—— (1986) *The System versus Progress: Soviet Economic Problems*, London: Centre for Research into Communist Economies.

—— (1988a) 'Organisations and hierarchies: the perennial search for solutions' in Linz and Moskoff (1988).

—— (1988b) 'Property rights issues in economic reforms in socialist countries', *Studies in Comparative Communism*, vol. XXI, no. 2.

—— (1992) 'The Soviet industrial enterprise in the 1980s' in Jeffries (1992).

Schüller, A. (1988) *Does Market Socialism Work?*, London: The Centre for Research into Communist Economies.

Schwartz, G. (1991) 'Privatization: possible lessons from the Hungarian case', *World Development*, vol. 19, no. 12.

Scott, N. (1992) 'The implications of the transition for foreign trade and investment', *Oxford Review of Economic Policy*, vol. 8, no. 1.

Sedivy, Z. (1989) 'Economic policy aims in Czechoslovakia and their implementation' in Economic Commission for Europe (1989).

Severin, B. (1990) 'The March 1986 agricultural decree in perspective' in Wädekin (1990b).

Shafir, M. (1985) *Romania: Politics, Economics and Society*, London: Pinter.

Shambaugh, D. (1989) 'The forth and fifth plenary sessions of the 13th CCP Central Committee', *China Quarterly*, no. 120.

Shcherbakov, V. (1987) 'The wholesale restructuring of wages', Problems of Economics, vol. XXX, no. 6.

—— (1991) 'Remuneration of labour in the USSR: problems and prospects', *International Labour Review*, vol. 130, no. 2.

Shen Xiaofang (1990) 'A decade of direct foreign investment in China', Problems of Communism, March–April.

Shleifer, A. and Vishny, R. (1991) 'Reversing the Soviet economic collapse', *Brookings Papers on Economic Activity*, no. 2.

Sicular, T. (1988a) 'Plan and market in China's agricultural commerce', *Journal of Political Economy*, vol. 96, no. 2.

—— (1988b) 'Grain pricing: a key link in Chinese economic policy', *Modern China*, vol. 14, no. 4.

—— (1988c) 'Agricultural planning and pricing in the post-Mao period', *China Quarterly*, no. 116.

Siebert, H. (1991a) *German Unification: the Economics of Transition*, Kiel Institute of World Economics Working Paper no. 468.

—— (1991b) 'German unification: the economics of transition', *Economic Policy*, no. 13 (October).

Sirc, L. (1979) *The Yugoslav Economy under Self-management*, London: Macmillan.

—— (1981) 'The industrial enterprise in Yugoslavia' in Jeffries (1981).

Sjöberg, Ö. (1989) *The Agrarian Sector in Albania during the 1980s: a Changing Regional Focus*, Economic Research Institute of the Stockholm School of Economics: Research Report no. 4.

—— (1990) *The Albanian Economy in the 1980s: the Nature of a Low-performing System*, Economic Research Institute of the Stockholm School of Economics: Working Paper no. 10.

—— (1991a) 'The Albanian economy in the 1980s: coping with a centralised system' in Sjöberg and Wyzan (1991).

—— (1991b) *Rural Change and Development in Albania*, Boulder: Westview Press.

Sjöberg, Ö. and Wyzan, M. (eds) (1991) *Economic Change in the Balkan States: Albania, Bulgaria, Romania and Yugoslavia*, London: Pinter.

Skinner, G. (1985) 'Rural marketing in China: repression and revival', *China Quarterly*, no.103.

Slider, D. (1987) 'The brigade system in Soviet industry: an effort to restructure the labour force', *Soviet Studies*, vol. XXXIX, no. 3.

—— (1991) 'Embattled entrepreneurs: Soviet co-operatives in an unreformed society', *Soviet Studies*, vol. 43, no. 5.

Smith, A. (1980) 'Romanian economic reforms' in Nato (1980) *Economic Reforms in Eastern Europe and Prospects for the 1980s*, London: Pergamon Press.

—— (1981) 'The Romanian industrial enterprise' in Jeffries (1981).

—— (1983) *The Planned Economies of Eastern Europe*, London: Croom Helm.

—— (1992) 'The Romanian enterprise' in Jeffries (1992).

Solinger, D. (1989a) 'Urban reform and relational contracting in post-Mao China: an interpretation of the transition from plan to market', *Comparative Communism*, vol. XXII, nos 2 and 3.

—— (1989b) 'Capitalist measures with Chinese characteristics', *Problems of Communism*, vol. XXXVIII, January–February.

Spigler, I (1973) *Economic Reform in Rumanian Industry*, Princeton, NJ: Princeton University Press.

Spoor, M. (1987) 'Finance in a socialist transition: the case of the Democratic Republic of Vietnam (1955–1964)' *Journal of Contemporary Asia*, vol. 17, no. 3.

—— (1988a) 'Reforming state finance in post-1975 Vietnam', *Journal of Development Studies*, vol. 24, no. 4.

—— (1988b) 'State finance in the Socialist Republic of Vietnam', in Marr and White (1988).

Stahnke, A. (1987) '*Kombinate* as the key structural element in the GDR intensification', *Studies in Comparative Communism*, vol. XX., no. 1.

Staller, G. (1968) 'Czechoslovakia: the new model of planning and management', *American Economic Review*, no. 2.

Standing, G. (1991) 'Wages and work motivation in the Soviet labour market: why a "BIP" not a "TIP" is required', *International Labour Review*, vol. 130, no. 2.

Stavis, B. (1989) 'The political economy of inflation in China', *Studies in Comparative Communism*, vol. XXII, nos 2 and 3.

Strassburger, J. (1985) in DDR *Handbuch*.

Suh, Sang-Chul (1983) 'North Korean industrial policy and trade' in Scalapino and Kim (1983).

Summers, M. (1992) 'Privatization by coupon in Czechoslovakia', *Economic Affairs*, vol. 12, no. 3.

Swain, N. (1987) 'Hungarian agriculture in the early 1980s: retrenchment followed by reform', *Soviet Studies*, vol. XXXIX, no. 1.

Swaine, M. (1990) 'China faces the 1990s: a system in crisis', *Problems of Communism*, May–June.

Szamuely, L. (1989) 'Ideological features yet to be overcome in Soviet-type economies' in Gomulka *et al.* (1989).

Sziraczki, G. (1990) 'Unemployment policy and labour market in transition: from labour shortage to unemployment', *Soviet Studies*, vol. 42, no. 4.

Taga, L. (1989) 'The Soviet firm in the "large-scale experiment"', *Comparative Economic Studies*, vol. XXXI, no. 2.

Tam, On-Kit (1988) 'Rural finance in China', *China Quarterly*, no. 113.

Tedstrom, J. (1987) 'On perestroyka: analysing the basic provisions, *Problems of Communism* (July–August).

Teichova, A. (1988) *The Czechoslovak Economy 1918–80*, London: Routledge.

Teodorescu, A. (1991) 'The future of a failure: the Romanian economy' in Sjöberg and Wyzan (1991).

Thalheim, K. (1981) *Die wirtschaftliche Entwicklung der beiden Staaten in Deutschland*, Opladen: Leske Verlag & Budrich GmbH.

—— (1986) *Stagnation or Change in Communist Economies*, London: Centre for Research into Communist Economies.

The Times (1986) Survey on China, 10 October.

The Times Guide to Eastern Europe (1990) Edited by Keith Sword, London: Times Books.

Tomes, I. (1991) 'Social reform: a cornerstone in Czechoslovakia's new economic structure', *International Labour Review*, vol. 130, no. 2.

Tran Duc Nguyen (1991) 'Vietnam's socio-economic development to the year 2000: approaches and objectives' in Ronnas and Sjöberg (1991a).

Tran Ngoc Vinh (1990) 'Renewal of financial and monetary policies, and the circulation of material and goods at home and foreign trade' in Ronnas and Sjöberg (1990).

Trehub, A. (1987) 'Social and economic rights in the Soviet Union', *Survey*, vol. 29, no. 4.

Treml, V. (1989) 'The most recent input–output table: a milestone in Soviet statistics', *Soviet Economy*, vol. 5, no. 4.

Tröder, M. (1987) 'The 1981–5 Order of Planning' in Jeffries *et al.* (1987).

Tsantis, A. and Pepper, R. (1979) *Romania: the Industrialization of an Agrarian Economy under Socialist Planning*, Washington, DC: World Bank.

Turgeon, L. (1990) Review of A. Zimbalist (1987) Cuba's Socialist Economy: Toward the 1990s, Boulder: Rienner (figures quoted on p. 16 of Zimbalist), *Journal of Comparative Economics*, vol. 14, no. 1.

Turits, R. (1987) 'Trade, debt and the Cuban economy', *World Development*, vol. 15, no. 1.

Turnock, D. (1986) *The Romanian Economy in the Twentieth Century*, London: Croom Helm.

Ungar, E. (1987–88) 'The struggle over the Chinese community in Vietnam, 1946–86', *Pacific Affairs*, vol. 60, no. 4.

United Nations Economic Commission for Europe (1992) *Economic Survey of Europe in 1991–1992*, New York: United Nations.

US Congress, Joint Economic Committee (1977) *East European Economies Post-Helsinki*, Washington, DC: US Government Printing Office.

—— (1979) *Soviet Economy in a Time of Change*, Washington, DC.

—— (1982) *Soviet Economy in the 1980s: Problems and Prospects*, Washington, DC.

—— (1986) *East European Economies: Slow Growth in the 1980s*, vol. 3: Country Studies on Eastern Europe and Yugoslavia, Washington, DC.

Uvalic, M. (1991a) 'Property reforms in Yugoslavia', *Nomisma*, no. 3.

—— (1991b) 'How different is Yugoslavia?' in *European Economy*.

Vacic, A. (1989) in Economic Commission for Europe (1989).

Valenta, F. (1989) 'Framework of economic reform in Czechoslovakia' in Economic Commission for Europe (1989).

Van Arkadie, B. (1991) 'Comment' in Ronnas and Sjöberg (1991a).

Van Brabant, J. (1988) 'Planned economies in the GATT framework: the Soviet case', *Soviet Economy*, vol. 4 (Jan-March).

—— (1989) *Economic Integration in Eastern Europe*, London: Harvester Wheatsheaf.

—— (1990) 'Reforming a socialist developing country – the case of Vietnam', *Economics of Planning*, vol. 23, no. 3.

—— (1991) 'Renewal of co-operation and economic transition in Eastern Europe', *Studies in Comparative Communism*, vol. XXIV, no. 2.

Van Ree, E. (1989) 'The limits of Juche: North Korea's dependence on Soviet industrial aid, 1953–76', *Journal of Communist Studies*, vol. 5, no. 1.

Vankai, T. (1986) 'Hungarian agricultural performance and prospects during the eighties', US Congress, Joint Economic Committee.

Vetrovsky, J. and Hrinda, V. (1988) 'Direct relations: clearing operations in the national currencies of Czechoslovakia and the Soviet Union', *Czechoslovak Economic Digest*, no. 4.

Vincentz, V. (1991) *Privatization in Eastern Germany: Principles and Practice*, Munich Eastern Europe Institute Working Paper, no. 146.

Vo Nhan Tri (1988) 'Party politics and economic performance: the Second and Third Year Plans examined' in Marr and White (1988).

Von Beyme, K. and Zimmerman, H. (1984) *Policy-making in the German Democratic Republic*, Aldershot: Gower.

Von Czege, A. (1987) 'Hungary's New Economic Mechanism: upheaval or continuity' in Gey *et al.* (1987).

Voracek, J. (1988) in *Economic Bulletin for Europe*, vol. 40, no. 4.

Vortmann, H. (1985) in *DIW Handbuch*.

Voszka, E. (1989) 'Role and functioning of the enterprise in post-reform Hungary' in Economic Commission for Europe (1989).

Wädekin, K-E. (1982) Agrarian Policies in Communist Europe, Totowa, NJ: Rowman & Allanheld (1989).

—— (1988) 'Soviet agriculture: a brighter prospect' in P. Wiles (ed.) The *Soviet Economy on the Brink of Reform*, London: Unwin Hyman.

—— (ed.) (1990a) *Communist Agriculture: Farming in the Far East and Cuba*, London: Routledge.

—— (1990b) *Communist Agriculture: Farming in the Soviet Union and Eastern Europe*, London: Routledge.

—— (1990c) 'Private agriculture in socialist countries: implications for the USSR' in Gray (1990).

Walder, A. (1989) 'Factory and manager in an era of reform', *China Quarterly*, no. 118.

Wall, D. (1991) 'Special economic zones and industrialisation in China', Discussion Paper no. 01/91, International Economics Research Centre at the University of Sussex.

Wallace, W. and Clarke, R. (1986) *Comecon, Trade and the West*, London: Pinter.

Wang Jun (1989) 'The export-oriented strategy of

China's coastal areas: evaluation and prospects', University of Leicester, Department of Economics, Discussion Paper no. 116 (September).

Wang Zhonghui (1990) 'Private enterprise in China: an overview', *Journal of Communist Studies*, vol. 6, no. 3.

Wanless, P. (1980) 'Economic reform in Poland 1973–9', *Soviet Studies*, vol. XXII, no. 1.

Wanniski, J. (1992) 'The future of Russian capitalism', *Foreign Affairs*, vol. 71, no. 2.

Watson, A. (1988) 'The reform of agricultural marketing in China', *China Quarterly*, no. 113.

Wegren, S. (1992) 'Private farming and agrarian reform in Russia', *Problems of Communism*, May–June.

Werner, J. (1988) 'The problem of the district in Vietnam's development policy' in Marr and White (1988).

White, C. (1985) 'Agricultural planning, pricing policy and co-operatives in Vietnam', *World Development*, vol. 13, no. 1.

White, G. (1987a) 'Cuban planning in the Mid-1980s: centralisation, decentralisation and participation', *World Development*, vol. 15, no. 1.

—— (1987b) 'The politics of economic reform in Chinese industry: the introduction of the labour contract system', *China Quarterly*, no. 111.

—— (1988) 'State and market in China's labour reform', *Journal of Development Studies*, vol. 24, no. 4.

White, G., and Bowles, P. (1988) 'China's banking reforms: aims, methods and problems', *National Westminster Bank Quarterly Review (November)*.

Wiedemann, P. (1980) 'The origins and development of agro-industrial development in Bulgaria', in R. Francisco, B. Laird, and R. Laird (eds) (1980) *Agricultural Policies in the USSR and Eastern Europe*, Boulder: Westview Press.

Winiecki, J. (1988a) *The Distorted World of Soviet-type Economies*, London: Croom Helm.

—— (1988b) *Gorbachev's Way Out?*, London: CRCE.

—— (1989) 'CPEs' structural change and world market performance', *Soviet Studies*, vol. XLI, no. 3.

Wong, C. (1986) 'The economics of shortage and the problems of reform in Chinese industry', *Journal of Comparative Economics*, vol. 10, no. 4.

—— (1988) 'Interpreting rural industrial growth in post-Mao China', *Modern China*, vol. 14, no. 1.

—— (1989) 'Between plan and market: the role of the local sector in post-Mao reforms in China' in Gomulka *et al.* (1989).

—— (1991) 'Central–local relations in an era of fiscal decline', *China Quarterly*, no. 128 (December).

Wong, E. (1987) 'Recent developments in China's Special Economic Zones: problems and prognosis', *The Developing Economies*, vol. XXV, no. 1.

Wood, A. (1989) 'Deceleration of inflation with acceleration of price reform: Vietnam's remarkable recent experience', *Cambridge Journal of Economics*, vol. 13, no. 4.

World Bank (1984) *China: Socialist Economic Development*, vols 1 and 2, Washington, DC.

—— (1988) Report in Polish Perspectives, vol. XXXI, no. 1.

Wu, J. and Reynolds, B. (1988) 'Choosing a strategy for China's economic reform', *American Economic Review*, Papers and Proceedings (May).

Wyzan, M. (1989) 'The small enterprise and agricultural initiative in Bulgaria: a comment on Robert J. McIntyre', *Soviet Studies*, vol. XLI, no. 4.

—— (1990a) 'Bulgarian agriculture: sweeping reform, mediocre performance' in Wädekin (1990b).

—— (1990b) 'The Bulgarian experience with centrally planned agriculture: lessons for Soviet reformers' in Gray (1990).

—— (1990c) *The Bulgarian Economy in the Immediate Post-Zhivkov Era: a Western Perspective*, Stockholm Institute of Soviet and East European Economics: Working Paper no. 7.

—— (1991) 'The Bulgarian economy in the immediate post-Zhivkov era' in Sjöberg and Wyzan (1991).

Yoon, Suk Bum (1986) 'Macroeconomic interaction between domestic and foreign sectors in the North Korean economy: a schematic interpretation' in Scalapino and Lee (1986).

Zhu Ling (1990) 'The transformation of the operating mechanism in Chinese agriculture', *Journal of Development Studies*, vol. 26, no. 2.

Zimbalist, A. (1987) 'Cuba's socialist economy toward the 1990s', *World Development*, vol. 15, no. 1.

—— (ed.) (1988a) Cuban Political Economy, Boulder and London: Westview Press.

—— (1988b) 'Cuba's statistical and price systems: interpretation and reliability', *Latin American Perspectives*, vol. 15, no. 2.

—— (1988c) 'Cuba's external economy: reflections on export dependence, Soviet aid and foreign debt', *Comparative Economic Studies*, vol. XXX, no. 2.

—— (1989) 'Incentives and planning in Cuba', *Latin American Research Review*, vol. XXIV, no. 1.

—— (1992a) 'Industrial reform and the Cuban economy' in Jeffries (1992).

—— (1992b) 'Teetering on the brink: Cuba's current economic and political crisis', *Journal of Latin American Studies*, vol. 24, no. 2.

Zimbalist, A., and Eckstein, S. (1987) 'Patterns of Cuban development: the first twenty-five years', *World Development*, vol. 15, no. 1.

Zimbalist, A., Sherman, H., and Brown, S. (1989) *Comparing Economic Systems: a Political–Economic Approach*, 2nd edn, New York: Harcourt Brace Jovanovich.

GLOSSARY

agrarno-promishlen komplex (APK) Agro-industrial complex in socialist Bulgaria. Normally a horizontal integration of co-operative farms, state farms and their servicing centres.

Basic Organization of Associated Labour (BOAL) A legal and economic unit in Yugoslavia. The smallest unit producing a marketed or marketable product.

'big bang' The rapid, comprehensive transformation of a centrally planned economy into a market economy. Sometimes the term is used interchangeably with 'shock' therapy, but it may be more useful to think of 'shock' treatment as a series of austerity measures dealing with severe macroeconomic disequilibrium (see below).

bilateral trade The balancing of trade between two countries over a period of time. Characterizes trade between command economies.

centrala 'Central' in socialist Romania, usually the result of country-wide, horizontal integration of one large enterprise with smaller ones.

Charter 77 A Czechoslovak civil and human rights group founded in 1977. It led to the setting up of Civic Forum in November 1989.

Chuch'e The North Korean policy of 'self-reliance'.

Civic Forum See *Charter 77*.

civil society Widespread activities by individuals who voluntarily associate together in various forms outside the control of the state. Life outside the state. The self-organization of individuals in society.

Comecon (CMEA) Council of Mutual Economic Assistance. Set up in 1949, there were eventually ten full members: the Soviet Union, Bulgaria, Czechoslovakia, Hungary, Poland, Romania, the GDR, Mongolia, Cuba and Vietnam. Wound up in 1991.

Cominform The Communist Information Bureau was set up in September 1947 to promote international communism and Soviet control over the movement. It was dissolved in 1956. Its predecessor was the Comintern (1919–43).

Commonwealth of Independent States (CIS) The successor to the Soviet Union, set up towards the end of 1991.

Commune ('people's commune') Key institution during the Chinese Great Leap Forward.

Comprehensive (Complex) Programme A 1971 Comecon programme for the further extension and improvement of co-operation and development of socialist integration to the year 2000.

control figures Initial, tentative output targets passed down by the State Planning Commission.

convertibility Holzman (1991: 6) defines 'resident' or 'internal' convertibility to mean that a country's citizens and enterprises are free to purchase foreign currency for use in either current account (to purchase goods and services) or capital account (e.g. to invest abroad) transactions. Internal convertibility has been adopted by some of the countries studied in this book. But there are sometimes restrictions even on the purchase of foreign currency for current account transactions and controls relating to capital account transactions are the rule.

Full convertibility Implies the unconstrained freedom of any enterprise or person to buy or sell a nation's currency for foreign currencies at the existing exchange rate.

counter-plans Designed as an inducement to managers of socialist enterprises to adopt more demanding targets than those set out in the five year plan.

CSCE Conference on Security and Co-operation in Europe.

Cultural Revolution Officially covered the period 1966–76 in China, but the more extreme elements were ended by 1969.

danwei The workplace in China. Not only a production unit, but historically represents an important provider of housing and the chief provider of welfare services.

destatization (destatification) (razgosudarstvleniye)
A broader concept than privatization. In the initial
stages joint stock companies may be formed,
whose shares could be held by state holding
companies. It can involve, for example, leasing,
employee ownership and co-operative ownership.

doi moi 'Renovation' (Vietnam).

Durzhavenski Stopanski Obedineniya (DSO) State
Economic Organization. The basic production unit
in socialist Bulgaria, comprising horizontally
integrated enterprises.

EBRD European Bank for Reconstruction and
Development. An organization set up in 1990
mainly to promote the private sector in Eastern
Europe.

EC The European Community.

Economic Community Gorbachev's failed attempt at
setting up a mechanism in the Soviet Union to
co-ordinate economic policy among sovereign
republics.

economic levers Prices, taxes, interest rates and so
on, used to steer the economy indirectly.

edinonachalie The principle of one-man responsibility and control, applying to the management of the
Soviet enterprise by the director.

emerging (or new) democracies (emerging market
economies or transitional economies) The
post-communist regimes.

ethnic cleansing Ethnically mixed areas are
'cleansed' by forcibly driving out other ethnic
groups (see Yugoslavia).

extensive growth Growth of the economy achieved
mainly through increasing inputs.

GATT General Agreement on Tariffs and Trade.

GDP and GNP (see Net Material Product) Gross
Domestic Product (GDP) is a measure of the goods
and services produced annually within the
geographical area of a country, while Gross
National Product (GNP) is a measure of the
national income accruing to residents of a country.
The difference between the two is net (inflows
minus outflows) of income from factor services,
e.g. wages and salaries earned by residents
working abroad and profits earned by foreign
companies.

GEMU German economic and monetary union.

glasnost Openness. Freedom of speech.

glavki Chief administrations. Bodies linking
ministries and enterprises in the traditional Soviet
economic system.

GLF Great Leap Forward in China 1958–60.

goods inconvertibility If one command economy has
a trade surplus with another, it cannot be
automatically converted into a claim on particular
goods in the latter country, because of the lack of
direct and free exchange between ultimate
purchaser and supplier. This claim can only be met
by negotiations and provisions in central plans.

Gosbank The Soviet State Bank.

Gosplan The Soviet State Planning Commission.

Gospriomka The Soviet State Quality Commission.

Gossnab The Soviet State Committee for
Material–Technical Supply.

goszakazy State orders in the Soviet Union.

Grand Bargain Large-scale Western aid in return for
a programme to adopt political democracy, a
market economy and macroeconomic stabilization
measures.

guidance planning In China, the use of suggested
rather than mandatory plan targets; the state
encourages compliance by means of economic
levers.

hard goods Those commodities particularly sought
after in Comecon, because the internal price
system undervalued them and they could be sold
and purchased on the world market for hard
(convertible) currencies (e.g. foodstuffs, fuels and
raw materials).

higher-level co-operative In Vietnamese agriculture
this differs from the 'lower-level co-operative' in
that labour is the sole source of remuneration.

higher-type agricultural co-operative A transitional
institution in socialist Albania towards a full state
farm, differing from the traditional co-operative in
ways such as the fact that it received state
budgetary grants instead of repayable long-term
loans.

Household Responsibility System (HRS) The
household is now the basic production unit in
Chinese agriculture. After meeting sales quotas,
tax obligations and payments for collective
services, the household is able to make its own
output and input decisions.

Hural Mongolian parliament, with the Great and
Little Hurals (or councils).

IMF International Monetary Fund. Set up in 1944 to
provide short-term finance for countries with
temporary balance of payments problems. But
today provides credits and technical advice in
return for implementing anti-inflationary and
pro-market policies.

initial (primary) stage of socialism The stage in
China that started in the 1950s and which could
last beyond the mid-twenty-first century. A process
of gradually moving towards a modern industrial
economy.

intensive growth Output increases largely accounted
for by increases in the efficiency of input use,
especially by means of an improvement in the
application of modern science and technology.

Intensivierung Intensification in the GDR. Approximately equivalent to 'intensive growth'.

internal convertibility See *convertibility*.

'iron rice bowl' Literally, everyone eats from the same pot regardless of work effort. Chinese workers are assured of a job and a wage.

Junta Central de Planificación (Juceplan) Cuban Central Planning Board.

khozraschyot Economic accounting. On this basis the Soviet industrial enterprise is a financially separate and accountable unit for the purpose of efficiently implementing the *tekhpromfinplan*.

'know-how' fund Aid in the form of technical advice for setting up a market economy, e.g. the UK fund.

kolkhoz The Soviet collective farm.

Kombinat The GDR combine. A horizontal and vertical amalgamation of enterprises under the unified control of a director-general.

link A small Soviet agricultural group that is given responsibility for a piece of land or livestock, allocated inputs and set broad output targets. The group is paid according to results, but is not set work assignments.

London Club Western creditor banks.

lower-level co-operative (production collective) A farm in Vietnam where individual income depends on both labour and contributed land and means of production.

macroeconomic disequilibrium See *'big bang'*, *'shock' therapy* and *macroeconomic stabilization*.

macroeconomic stabilization Anti-inflationary measures involving tight fiscal, monetary and incomes policies, e.g. expenditure cuts, high interest rates, price liberalization (including the reduction of subsidies on basic products) and wage inflation taxes. A cure for macroeconomic disequilibrium.

market socialism A market economy in which social ownership predominates.

marketization Progress towards introducing a market economy.

Marshall Plan The US programme to aid the post-Second World War recovery of Europe. Launched in April 1948.

material balances The basic planning technique used in command economies, involving the drawing up of the major sources of supply and demand for a particular commodity with the aim of attaining a rough balance.

Materials allocation The administrative distribution of raw materials, intermediate goods, and capital goods.

MOFERT The Chinese Ministry of Foreign Economic Relations and Trade.

monetary overhang Unplanned accumulation of cash and savings accounts ('forced savings') because of the lack of desired goods and services. Ellman (1989a: 244) defines the term as the excess of purchasing power over the total supply of goods and services at effective prices.

monobank The 'one bank' arrangement in the traditional Soviet economic system, with no separation of the central bank from independent commercial banks.

'moral economy' stage During the Cuban development of 1966–70 emphasis was placed on moral incentives and collective interests rather than on individual material incentives.

naryad Soviet allocation certificate for non-labour inputs.

National Salvation Front Took over the reins of government after the fall of the Ceausescu regime in Romania.

NEP The New Economic Policy in the Soviet Union (1921–28), characterized by considerable concessions to private enterprise and the restoration in large part of the market mechanism.

Net Material Product (NMP) The Soviet 'material product system' differs from the 'system of national accounts' recommended by the United Nations and used in the West in that it excludes so-called 'non-productive' services. These include (with some variation) defence, general administration, education, finance and credit, and transport and communications serving households. 'NMP produced' minus exports plus imports, measured in domestic prices, and minus losses due to abandoned construction and accidental damage, gives 'NMP utilized'. As a very rough approximation, the Soviet definition gives a figure about 20 per cent less than its Western counterpart.

Neues Ökonomisches System (NES) The GDR's New Economic System 1963–70 was a period that saw the greatest use of indirect steering of the economy by means of mainly monetary instruments.

New Economic Mechanism (NEM) Introduced in Hungary on 1 January 1968. The term was also used in Bulgaria throughout the 1970s, but any resemblance to the Hungarian system was in name only.

new economic zones Resettlement plan in Vietnam to move mainly northern people to zones in central and south Vietnam.

nomenklatura A system whereby the communist party makes all the important appointments, including those in the economy.

normative net output Required as opposed to actual wage costs, social insurance, and profit. A sort of 'shadow price' that can be used to determine the entire NNO for the enterprise by multiplying it by the actual output.

Noul Mecanism Economico-Financiar Socialist Romania's New Economic and Financial Mechanism, introduced at the start on 1979.

Nov Sistem na Rukovodstvo Socialist Bulgaria's New System of Management.

NPK Socialist Bulgaria's 'scientific–productive complex', incorporating scientific institutes.

obedineniye The Soviet association, a mainly horizontal amalgamation of enterprises.

OECD Organization for Economic Co-operation and Development. The OECD replaced the OEEC (Organization for European Economic Co-operation), founded in 1948, in 1961. In March 1990 the OECD created the Centre for Co-operation with European Economies in Transition.

'open door' policy Introduced in China in 1978 to open the economy to foreign trade, capital, technology and know-how.

Ordnungspolitik Government policy which merely provides a framework for the operation of market forces, i.e. creating the right environment for the private sector to flourish in the form of a basic infrastructure, a sound currency and a competitive environment.

PAK Socialist Bulgaria's 'industro-agrarian complex', a vertical merger of farms with industrial enterprises processing and selling agricultural products.

Paris Club Western creditor governments.

perestroika The Soviet term for the restructuring of the whole of economic and social life. All-round economic and social reforms associated with Mikhail Gorbachev.

Phare Poland, Hungary, Aid for Reconstruction of the Economy. Technical assistance programme for Hungary and Poland of July 1989. Other countries were subsequently included: July 1990 Bulgaria, Czechoslovakia, and Yugoslavia; January 1991 Romania; July 1991 the EC decides to incorporate Albania. Estonia, Latvia and Lithuania were also included in 1991. The EC co-ordinates G24 aid.

Plan tekniko-industrial financiar Socialist Albania's technical–industrial–financial plan for the industrial enterprise.

Planungsordnung The GDR's Order of Planning.

polny khozraschyot 'Full economic accounting'. All expenditure incurred by the Soviet enterprise, including investment, had to be covered from revenue earned or credits borrowed.

predpriyatiye The Soviet enterprise.

Preisausgleich 'Price equalization'. The mechanism by which exports and imports in a command economy are involved in a sort of price equalization with world and domestic prices respectively.

prestavba Socialist Czechoslovakia's term for *perestroika*.

Prinzip der Einzelleitung Principle of individual management in the GDR. The equivalent of *edinonachalie*.

privatization Usually refers to the transformation of state into private ownership. 'Major' or 'large' privatization applies to large enterprises, while 'minor' or 'small' applies to small enterprises such as shops and restaurants.

prodrazvyorstka Compulsory requisitioning of agricultural products used during the Soviet War Communism period, 1918–21.

property rights Van Brabant (in Ronnas and Sjöberg 1991: 220): 'A property right is a socially recognized and legally enforceable right to select users of scarce goods. The crucial element is Roman law, i.e. the right of use, employment of the fruits, and disposal of the object of ownership (*ius utendi, fruendi et abutendi*).'

raspilenie sredstv 'Scattering' (excessive spread) of investment resources in command economies. Construction projects whose completion times are excessive relative both to the plan and to those taken in market economies.

ratchet effect ('base-year approach'; 'planning from the achieved level') This period's achievement by the socialist enterprise is the starting point for next period's plan.

rectification campaign The period 1966–70 in Cuba, when emphasis was placed on moral incentives and collective (group) interests rather than on individual material incentives.

regulated market economy Gorbachev's proposal for a mixed (in terms of ownership) market economy regulated by the state.

resident convertibility See convertibility.

restitution Physical (natural) restitution refers to the return of property to former owners or their heirs. Financial compensation or coupons exchangeable for shares in enterprises to be privatized may be available if this is not possible or desired.

samofinansirovanie Soviet 'self-financing'. Both operating costs and capital expenditure had to be covered out of revenue earned by the enterprise; investment was normally to be financed out of retained profit or from credits that had to be repaid.

samookupaemost This concept entails at least a minimum rate of return on Soviet investment, whatever the source of finance.

samoupravleniye Soviet 'self-management'. The workforce takes a more active part in enterprise plan formulation and in the election of management.

second economy The non-regulated sector, including both legal and illegal activity.

Sejm Polish parliament.

self-management Self-management of the 'socially owned' Yugoslav industrial enterprise by the workers via an elected workers' council.

'sequencing' or 'sequential' ('staged') programming The transition from a centrally planned to a market economy, involving various sequences or orders of reforms.

shinechiel Mongolian *perestroika*; renewal.

'shock' therapy (treatment) Severe austerity measures involving strict fiscal, monetary and incomes policies to combat a high degree of macroeconomic disequilibrium in the form of open and/or repressed inflation. See *'big bang'*.

shturmovshchina The Soviet term for 'storming'. A mad rush by enterprises to fulfil the plan towards the end of the planning period.

Sistema de Dirección de la Economia The Cuban System of Economic Management and Planning.

social market economy A market economy with the government intervening in forms such as the provision of a comprehensive social security safety net.

'socialism or death' Fidel Castro's response to and rejection of the Eastern European path to democracy and the market after 1989.

soft budget constraint State financial support in the form of subsidies, price increases or tax reductions is forthcoming to cover any losses made by enterprises.

soft goods The reverse of *hard goods* (see above). Includes examples such as low quality, obsolete machinery and equipment.

Solidarity Polish trade union and political organization.

sovkhoz The Soviet state farm. Literally, 'Soviet economic unit'.

Special Economic Zones (SEZs) An important feature of China's 'open door' policy. Direct foreign investment is attracted by special concessions such as low tariff and tax rates.

stabilization fund Here refers to Western aid in the form of a hard currency fund to support the convertibility of a formerly inconvertible currency.

state orders See *goszakazy*.

stavka Basic wage rate set for a particular branch of Soviet industry.

storming See *shturmovshchina*.

structural (commodity) bilateralism The balancing of trade in *'hard'* and *'soft'* goods separately.

subsidy-based bureaucratic centralism model The Vietnamese term for the traditional Soviet-type economic system with a soft budget constraint.

supply-side recession An economic recession (low level of economic activity) due not to a lack of demand but to the disruption of supply links (lack of inputs) as the old command system disintegrates and a new market system has not yet been set up.

'systematization' ('systemization') (sistematizare) Ceausescu's programme to destroy many Romanian villages and create 'agro-industrial centres' instead.

taut planning Implies pressure to sqeeze maximum output from given resources.

tekhpromfinplan The technical–industrial–financial plan to be fulfilled by the enterprise in the traditional Soviet economic system.

Tiananmen The bloody suppression by the army of Chinese students demonstrating in favour of democracy in Tiananmen Square (Beijing) on 4 June 1989.

togrog The Mongolian currency unit. Equals 100 mongo.

tolkachi Soviet 'pushers', unofficial supply agents.

transferable rouble A unit of account used in transacting intra-Comecon trade.

Treuhandanstalt A trust body dealing with privatization, restructuring, liquidation and credit guarantees in East Germany.

trudoden The Soviet agricultural 'work day'. Not literally a calendar day, but each particular piece of work is valued at so many 'work days'.

turnover tax Essentially the difference between the wholesale and retail price. Typically the tax is price-determined, that is, the residual resulting from attempts to equate supply and demand.

Union of Sovereign States (USS) See *Union Treaty*.

Union Treaty Gorbachev's failed attempt to form a *Union of Sovereign States* to succeed the Soviet Union.

uskorenie The Soviet term for 'acceleration' of growth achieved by means such as increasing investment.

valovaya produktsiya The Soviet term for gross output. Measures the value of finished output plus net change in the value of goods in the process of production.

valuta Foreign currency.

'velvet revolution' The relatively peaceful process of change to political democracy and the market in Czechoslovakia after November 1989.

Vervollkommnung 'Perfecting' of planning, management and economic accounting in the GDR.

vstrechnye plany Soviet term for counter-plans. See *counter-plans*.

vyrobni hospodarska jednotka (VHJ) Socialist Czechoslovakia's industrial association.

War Communism The period 1918–21 in the Soviet Union, characterized by extreme nationalization and an attempt at a form of moneyless administration.

wielkie organizacje gospodarcze Polish 'large economic organizations'.

zastoi The Soviet term for 'stagnation'. Refers to the stagnation of the Brezhnev era.

zayavka The Soviet indent (request) for non-labour inputs.

'zero option' Castro's programme of severe austerity measures for coping with post-1989 disrupted Comecon trade links and rapidly diminishing Soviet aid.

zjednoczenie 'Association' of enterprises in socialist Poland.

zrzeszenie 'Amalgamation' of enterprises in socialist Poland.

zveno The Soviet term for link. See *link*.

INDEX